Adult Development and Aging

Sixth Edition

John C. Cavanaugh
Pennsylvania State System of Higher Education

Fredda Blanchard-Fields
Georgia Institute of Technology

WADSWORTH
CENGAGE Learning

Australia • Brazil • Japan • Korea • Mexico • Singapore • Spain • United Kingdom • United States

WADSWORTH
CENGAGE Learning

***Adult Development and Aging*, Sixth Edition**
John C. Cavanaugh and Fredda
Blanchard-Fields

Editor: Jaime Perkins

Assistant Editor: Page Leeds

Editorial Assistant: Philip Hovanessian

Media Editor: Mary Noel

Marketing Manager: Kim Russell

Marketing Assistant: Molly Felz

Marketing Communications Manager:
Talia Wise

Senior Content Project Manager: Pat Waldo

Creative Director: Rob Hugel

Art Director: Vernon Boes

Print Buyer: Paula Vang

Rights Acquisitions Account Manager,
Text: Margaret Chamberlain-Gaston

Rights Acquisitions Account Manager,
Image: Don Schlotman

Production Service: Niranjana Harikrishnan,
Integra

Text Designer: Lisa Delgado

Photo Researcher: Tim Herzog/Bill Smith
Group

Copy Editor: Linda Ireland

Illustrator: Integra

Cover Designer: Denise Davidson

Cover Image: Westend61/Getty Images

Compositor: Integra

For product information and technology assistance, contact us at
Cengage Learning Customer & Sales Support, 1-800-354-9706.
For permission to use material from this text or product,
submit all requests online at **www.cengage.com/permissions.**
Further permissions questions can be e-mailed to
permissionrequest@cengage.com.

Library of Congress Control Number: 2009925570

ISBN-13: 978-0-495-60344-3

ISBN-10: 0-495-60344-9

Wadsworth
20 Davis Drive
Belmont, CA 94002-3098
USA

Cengage Learning is a leading provider of customized learning solutions with office locations around the globe, including Singapore, the United Kingdom, Australia, Mexico, Brazil, and Japan. Locate your local office at: **www.cengage.com/global.**

Cengage Learning products are represented in Canada by Nelson Education, Ltd.

To learn more about Wadsworth, visit **www.cengage.com/Wadsworth.**

Purchase any of our products at your local college store or at our preferred online store **www.ichapters.com**

Printed in the United States of America
2 3 4 5 6 7 13 12 11

To Chris and Dorothy

Brief Contents

Contents

Chapter 3

Chapter 4

Chapter 5

Chapter 6

Preface

The 21st century is certainly one of major change. The issues confronting society are the reason that having a solid grounding in research and theory about adult development and aging is essential even for understanding news events. The health care debate of 2009 brought many issues to the fore, including Medicare, end-of-life issues, and longevity. Other news stories about genetic breakthroughs, stem cell research, new brain-imaging techniques for studying cognition, and the latest breakthrough in treating dementia were reported quite frequently. To understand why these issues are so critical, one must understand aging in a broader context. That is why *Adult Development and Aging* is now in its sixth edition.

The first few decades of this century will witness a fundamental change in the face of the population—literally. Along with many countries in the industrialized world, the United States will experience an explosive growth in the older adult population due to the aging of the baby-boom generation. Additionally, the proportion of older adults who are African American, Latino, Asian American, and Native American will increase rapidly. To deal with these changes, new approaches will need to be created through the combined efforts of people in many occupations—academics, gerontologists, social workers, health care professionals, financial experts, marketing professionals, teachers, factory workers, technologists, government workers, human service providers, and nutritionists, to mention just a few. Every reader of this book, regardless of his or her area of expertise, will need to understand older adults in order to master the art of living.

This sixth edition of *Adult Development and Aging* continues to provide in-depth coverage of the major issues in the psychology of adult development and aging. The sixth edition adds numerous topics and provides expanded coverage of many of the ones discussed in earlier editions.

Major New Features

The sixth edition represents a thorough revision from the fifth edition, with a new chapter discussing neuroscience and aging. Among the most important changes are:

- New discussions on the link between brain and behavior.
- New discussions of global aging and the economics of aging.
- New discussions of microgenetic research and the meta-analytic technqiue.
- Revised discussions of osteoporosis, arthritis, theories of aging, and new information about dietary sodium and treatment for chronic obstructive pulmonary disease.
- New How Do We Know? features in Chapters 2, 3, 4, 10, 11, and 13.
- New or revised Current Controversies features in Chapters 2, 3, 5, 10, 11, 13, and 14.
- New discussion of aging in place, home modification, congregate housing, assisted living, special care units, and the Green House concept of small home nursing homes.
- New discussion on ecology of aging and community-based living options, including discussions of assisted living.
- New discussion of gender differences in depression and mortality, and inclusion of a life-span view of alcohol abuse.

- New Discovering Development features on caring for aging parents and on successful aging.
- A new combined chapter on attention and memory that integrates these two areas of research into a more general information processing framework. Links are also made to the earlier chapter on neuroscience and aging.
- New subsection on making end-of-life intentions known.
- New discussion of the four-component model of grief, and the dual process model of coping with grief.
- New section on Social Security and Medicare.
- New discussions on nutrition and exercise.

Writing Style

Although *Adult Development and Aging* covers complex issues and difficult topics, we use clear, concise, and understandable language. We examined all terms to ensure that their use was essential; otherwise, they were eliminated.

The text is aimed at upper-division undergraduate students. Although it will be helpful if students have completed an introductory psychology or life-span human development course, the text does not assume this background.

Instructional Aids

The many pedagogical aids in the fifth edition have been retained and enhanced in the sixth edition.

- *Learning Aids in the Chapter Text.* Each chapter begins with a chapter outline. At the start of each new section, learning objectives are presented. These objectives are keyed to each primary subsection that follows, and they direct the students' attention to the main points to be discussed. At the conclusion of each major section are concept checks, one for each primary subsection, which help students spot-check their learning. Key terms are defined in context; the term itself is printed in boldface, with the sentence containing the term's definition in italic.
- *End-of-Chapter Learning Aids.* At the end of each chapter are summaries, organized by major sections and primary subsection heads. This approach helps students match the chapter outline with the summary. Numerous review questions, also organized around major sections and primary subsections, are provided to assist students in identifying major points. Integrative questions are included as a way for students to link concepts across sections within and across chapters. Key terms with definitions are listed. Suggestions for additional readings from both the scientific and popular literatures are provided, with estimates of difficulty level based on undergraduates' evaluations. Key websites are included with brief descriptions of the content of each site.
- *Boxes.* Three types of boxes are included. Those entitled *How Do We Know?* draw attention to specific research studies that were discussed briefly in the main body of the text. Details about the study's design, participants, and outcomes are presented as a way for students to connect the information about these issues in Chapter 1 with specific research throughout the text. *Current Controversies* boxes raise controversial and provocative issues about topics discussed in the chapter. These boxes get students to think about the implications of research or policy issues and may be used effectively as points of departure for class discussions. *Discovering Development* boxes give students a way to see developmental principles and concepts in the "real world" as well as some suggestions on how to find others. These boxes provide a starting point for applied projects in either individual or group settings, and help students understand how development is shaped by the interaction of biological, psychological, sociocultural, and life-cycle forces.

Instructor's Manual with Test Bank ISBN-10: 0495603457 | ISBN-13: 9780495603450

The sixth edition of *Adult Development and Aging* is accompanied by an instructor's manual with test bank. Each chapter begins with a lecture outline that highlights the main points of the chapter. Additionally, supplemental information is included, as are suggested activities and discussion topics. A list of suggested videos is also provided. Included in the manual are numerous test items, which are also available in electronic format.

PowerLecture with Examview
ISBN-10: 0495829838 |
ISBN-13: 97804950829836

The fastest, easiest way to build powerful, customized media-rich lectures, PowerLecture provides a collection of book-specific PowerPoint lectures by Neil Davis, University of West Florida, and class tools to enhance the educational experience. Featuring automatic grading, ExamView® allows you to create, deliver, and customize tests and study guides (both print and online) in minutes.

Acknowledgments

As usual, it takes many people to produce a textbook; such is the case with the sixth edition. The editorial group at Wadsworth is excellent.

We also want to thank the reviewers of the sixth edition, who provided extremely helpful and insightful commentary that improved the book: Lisa M. Renzi, University of Georgia; Michael Trent, Triton College; Terry Webster, University of California, Irvine; and Ronaele Whittington, University of Hawaii. We would also like to thank Tarra Jefferson, Marisa Arroyo, Guy von Wiegand, and Daniel Pierce for their valuable work on the literature search and references. We would also like to thank Audrey Duarte for her invaluable comments on the Neuroscience chapter.

Finally, to a group too often overlooked—the sales representatives. Without you none of this would have any payoff. You are an extension of us and the whole Wadsworth editorial and production team. What a great group of hard working folks you are!

Thanks to you all. Live long and prosper!

John C. Cavanaugh
Fredda Blanchard-Fields

About the Authors

John C. Cavanaugh is Chancellor of the Pennsylvania State System of Higher Education. Previously, he was President of the University of West Florida. A researcher and teacher of adult development and aging for more three decades, he has published nearly 80 articles and chapters and authored, co-authored, or co-edited 15 books on aging, information technology, and higher education policy. He is a Past President of Division 20 (Adult Development and Aging) of the American Psychological Association (APA) and is a Fellow of APA (Divisions 1, 2, 3, and 20) and the Gerontological Society of America, and a Charter Fellow of the Association for Psychological Science. He has held numerous leadership positions in these associations, including Chair of the Committee on Aging for APA. He has served on numerous state and national committees for aging-related and higher education organizations. John is a devoted fan of *Star Trek* and a serious traveler, backpacker, cook, and chocoholic.

Fredda Blanchard-Fields, Ph.D., is Professor and Chair of the School of Psychology at Georgia Institute of Technology. She received her undergraduate degree from the University of California, Los Angeles, and her Ph.D. in developmental psychology from Wayne State University in 1983. She is a Fellow of the APA (Divisions 1, 3, and 20), the Gerontological Society of America, and the American Psychological Society. She is currently the editor of *Psychology and Aging.* She also has served on numerous national committees, including the executive committee of Division 20 (adult development and aging) of the APA and on the editorial boards of *Psychology and Aging, Journal of Gerontology: Psychological Sciences,* and the *Journal of Adult Development.* Finally, she has served as the chair of the National Institutes of Health grant review study section for social psychology, emotion, and personality research. Her program of research examines adaptive developmental changes in adulthood in various areas of social cognition and emotion. She has numerous publications in the general area of social cognition, emotion, and aging, including everyday problem solving, emotion regulation, and social judgments from adolescence through older adulthood. She has co-edited two books, including *Perspectives on Cognitive Change in Adulthood and Aging* and *Social Cognition and Aging.* Her research on everyday problem solving, emotion regulation, and aging is currently funded by grants from the National Institute on Aging.

1

Studying Adult Development and Aging

Dara Torres of United States celebrates winning the silver medal in the women's 4 × 100-meter medley relay final during the swimming competitions in the National Aquatics Center at the Beijing 2008 Olympics in Beijing.

In this July 29, 2008 file photo, Republican presidential candidate, Sen. John McCain, R-Ariz., speaks during a town hall meeting at the Reed High School in Sparks, Nevada.

IN 2008, TWO U.S. CITIZENS MADE HISTORY BECAUSE OF THEIR AGE. AT THE OLYMPIC GAMES IN Beijing, swimmer Dara Torres, at age 41, the oldest woman ever to compete in that sport at this level, redefined people's beliefs about world-class athletes and mothers (her daughter was aged two at the time). She won three silver medals, missing a gold by .01 second. Competing in her fifth Olympic Games, Torres clearly demonstrated that a combination of great genes and a highly rigorous training regimen enabled her to compete in a sport in which most world-class women swimmers' careers are over by the time they are in their mid-twenties.

At the same time, Senator John McCain became, at age 72, the oldest person to be nominated for a first term as president by a major political party. Senator McCain had a long, distinguished career as an officer in the U.S. Navy, was a prisoner of war for 5 years during the Vietnam conflict, and went on to be elected to Congress from Arizona. By his own admission, McCain was in better health than many other people of his age at the time of his campaign. When questioned about his age, he pointed out his 96-year-old mother, who accompanied him on many of his campaign trips. His (and his mother's) energy and stamina demonstrated that chronological age alone is a very poor index of people's capabilities.

Dara Torres and John McCain are great examples of how middle-aged and older adults are being looked at differently today. They showed that adults are capable of doing things thought unimaginable or inappropriate just a few years ago. They also illustrate how the normal changes people experience as they age vary across individuals and why we need to rethink common stereotypes about age.

In this chapter, we examine a seemingly simple question: Who are older people? We will see that the answer is more complicated than you might think. We also consider the ways in which gerontologists study adults and how adults develop.

1.1 Perspectives on Adult Development and Aging

LEARNING OBJECTIVES
* What is gerontology? How does ageism relate to stereotypes of aging?
* What is the life-span perspective?
* What are the characteristics of the older adult population?
* How are they likely to change?

Roberto's great-grandmother Maria is 89 years old. Maria tells Roberto that when she was a young girl in El Paso, there were very few older women in either her family or the neighborhood. Roberto knows there are many older people, mostly women, in his own neighborhood, and wonders when and why this changed over her lifetime.

Before you read any more, take a minute and think about your own grandparents or great-grandparents. How would you and other people describe them? Do you want to be like them when you are their age?

We are all headed toward old age. How do you want to be thought of and treated when you get there? Do you look forward to becoming old, or are you afraid about what may lie ahead? Most of us want to enjoy a long life like Maria's but don't think much about growing old in our daily lives.

Reading this book will give you the basic facts about growing older. You will learn how to organize these facts by putting them into two contexts, the biopsychosocial framework and the life-span approach). By the time you are finished, you should have a new, different way of thinking about aging.

You already enjoy a major advantage compared with Maria. She and other people her age did not have the opportunity as young students to learn much about what is typical and what is not typical about aging. Until the last few decades, very little information was available about old age, which people generally thought to be characterized only by decline. *Over the past 50 years, though, the science of* **gerontology,** *which is the study of aging from maturity through old age, has flourished.* As you can imagine from reading the vignette about Dara Torres and John McCain, and as you will see

throughout this book, aging reflects the individual differences you have come to expect across people as they change over time. Still, many myths about old people persist. *These myths of aging lead to negative stereotypes of older people, which may result in* **ageism,** *a form of discrimination against older adults based on their age.* Ageism has its foundations in myths and beliefs people take for granted (Terry, 2008). It may be as blatant as believing that all old people are senile and are incapable of making decisions about their lives. It may occur when people are impatient with older adults in a grocery store checkout line. Or it may be as subtle as dismissing an older person's physical complaints with the question "What do you expect for someone your age?" As you will learn by doing the activities in the Discovering Development feature, such stereotypes surround us.

This book rebuts these erroneous ideas, but it does not replace them with idealized views of adulthood and old age. Rather, it paints an accurate picture of what it means to grow old today, recognizing that development across adulthood brings growth and opportunities as well as loss and decline. To begin, we consider the life-span perspective, which helps place adult development and aging into the context of the whole human experience. Afterward, we consider the fundamental developmental forces, controversies, and models that form the foundation for studying adult development and aging. In particular, we examine the biological, psychological, sociocultural, and life-cycle forces, and the nature–nurture and continuity–discontinuity controversies. We consider some basic definitions of age, and you will see that it can be viewed in many different ways. Finally, by examining various research methods we show how the information presented in this book was obtained.

The Life-Span Perspective

Imagine trying to understand, without knowing anything about his or her life, what your best friend is like. We cannot understand adults' experiences without appreciating what came before in childhood and adolescence. Placing adulthood in this broader context is what the life-span perspective is

We are surrounded by misconceptions of older adults. We have all seen cartoons making jokes about older adults whose memories are poor or whose physical abilities have declined. Most damaging are the ideas portrayed in the media that older adults are incapable of leading productive lives and making a difference. For example, many greeting cards portray older people as having little memory, no teeth, and no desire for sex. As a way to discover something about development, try to find several examples of myths or stereotypes about aging. Look at those greeting cards, cartoons, advertisements, and articles in popular magazines, television shows, and music. Gather as many as you can, and then check them against the research on the topic discussed in this text. By the end of the course, see how many myths and stereotypes you can show to be wrong.

all about. The **life-span perspective** divides human development into two phases: an early phase (childhood and adolescence) and a later phase (young adulthood, middle age, and old age). The early phase is characterized by rapid age-related increases in people's size and abilities. During the later phase, changes in size are slow, but abilities continue to develop as people continue adapting to the environment (Baltes, Lindenberger, & Staudinger, 2006).

Viewed from the life-span perspective, adult development and aging are complex phenomena that cannot be understood within the scope of a single disciplinary approach. Understanding how adults change requires input from a wide variety of perspectives. Moreover, aging is a lifelong process, meaning that human development never stops.

One of the most important perspectives on life-span development is that of Paul Baltes (1987; Baltes et al., 2006), who identified four key features of the life-span perspective:

- *Multidirectionality:* Development involves both growth and decline; as people grow in one area, they may lose in another and at different rates. For example, people's vocabulary ability tends to increase throughout life, but reaction time tends to slow down.
- *Plasticity:* One's capacity is not predetermined or set in concrete. Many skills can be trained or improved with practice, even in late life. There are limits to the degree of potential improvement, however, as described in later chapters.

- *Historical context:* Each of us develops within a particular set of circumstances determined by the historical time in which we are born and the culture in which we grow up. Maria's experiences were shaped by living in the 20th century in a Chicano neighborhood in southwest Texas.
- *Multiple causation:* How people develop results from a wide variety of forces, which we consider later in this chapter. You will see that development is shaped by biological, psychological, sociocultural, and life-cycle forces.

The life-span perspective emphasizes that human development takes a lifetime to complete. It sets the stage for understanding the many influences we experience and points out that no one part of life is any more or less important than another.

Basing their theories on these principles, Baltes et al. (2006) argue that life-span development consists of the dynamic interactions among growth, maintenance, and loss regulation. In their view, four factors are critical:

- As people grow older, they show an age-related reduction in the amount and quality of biologically based resources.
- There is an age-related increase in the amount and quality of culture needed to generate continuously

higher growth. Usually this results in a net slowing of growth as people age.

- People show an age-related decline in the efficiency with which they use cultural resources.
- There is a lack of cultural, "old-age friendly" support structures.

Taken together, these four factors create the need to shift more and more resources to maintain function and deal with biologically related losses as we grow old, leaving fewer resources to be devoted to continued growth. As we see throughout this book, this shift in resources has profound implications for experiencing aging and for pointing out ways to age successfully.

The Demographics of Aging

Take a look around at the people you see in your everyday life in your hometown. There have never been as many older adults as there are now, especially people over age 85. Why? Most important, health care improved during the 20th century, and many fewer women died during childbirth. Let's take a closer look.

Population Trends in the United States. Look closely at the age distributions in the U.S. population for 2000 and projections for 2025, 2050, and 2100. These show that the population is aging (see Figures 1.1, 1.2, 1.3, and 1.4). In 2000, there were many more people between their mid-30s and 40s than any other age group. Projections for 2025 (when nearly all the baby boomers have reached age 65) show that the distribution will have changed dramatically; the baby boomers' aging makes the graph look much more rectangular. By 2050, the shape of the distribution will be more like a beehive, as more people continue to live into their 80s, 90s, and 100s. The biggest change by the year 2100 will be in the number of older men.

The coming dramatic change in the number of older adults has already had profound effects on everyone's lives. Through the first few decades of the 21st century, older adults will be a major economic

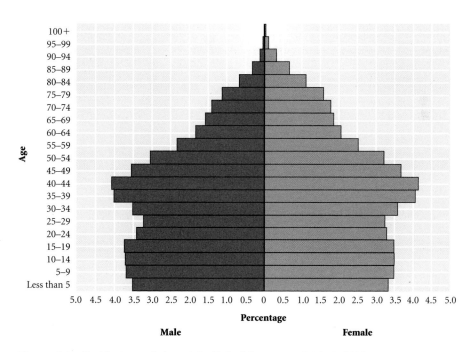

Figure 1.1 Resident population of the United States as of July 1, 2000.

Source: National Projections Program, Population Division, U.S. Census Bureau, Washington, D.C. 20233.

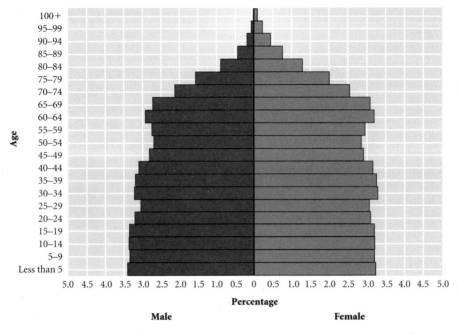

Figure 1.2 Projected resident population of the United States as of July 1, 2025.

Source: National Projections Program, Population Division, U.S. Census Bureau, Washington, D.C. 20233.

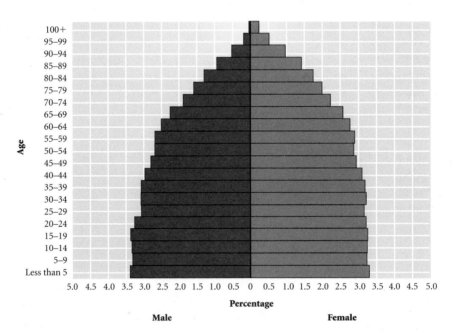

Figure 1.3 Projected resident population of the United States as of July 1, 2050.

Source: National Projections Program, Population Division, U.S. Census Bureau, Washington, D.C. 20233.

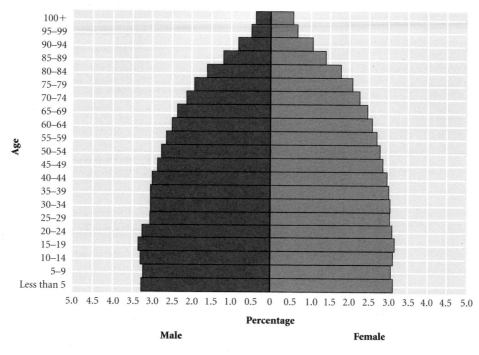

Figure 1.4 Projected resident population of the United States as of July 1, 2100.

Source: National Projections Program, Population Division, U.S. Census Bureau, Washington, D.C. 20233.

and political force. There is fear that they will drain the Social Security and other pension systems, make health care increasingly unaffordable, and force other human services to choose between serving older adults and serving other age groups. The costs will be borne by smaller groups of taxpayers in younger generations.

The strain on health and social services will be exacerbated because the most rapidly growing segment of the U.S. population is people over age 85. In fact, the number of such people will increase nearly 500% between 2000 and 2050, compared to about a 50% increase in the number of 20 to 29 year olds during the same period (U.S. Census Bureau, 2008a). As we discuss in Chapter 4, people over age 85 generally need more assistance with daily living than do people under age 85.

Diversity of Older Adults in the United States. Just like people your age, older adults are not all alike. The number of older adults among ethnic minority groups is increasing faster than among European

Americans. For example, the number of Native American elderly has increased 65% in recent decades; Asian and Pacific Islander elderly have quadrupled; older adults are the fastest-growing segment of the African American population; and the number of Latino American elderly is also increasing rapidly (U.S. Census Bureau, 2008a). Projections for the future diversity of the U.S. population are shown in Figure 1.5. You should note the very large increases in the number of Asian, Native, and Latino American older adults relative to European and African American older adults.

Future older adults will be better educated. At present a little more than half of the people over age 65 have only a high school diploma or some college, and about 18% have a bachelor's degree or higher. By 2030 it is estimated that 85% will have a high school diploma and 75% will have a college degree (U.S. Census Bureau, 2008a). These dramatic changes will be due mainly to better educational opportunities for more students and greater need for formal schooling (especially college) to find a

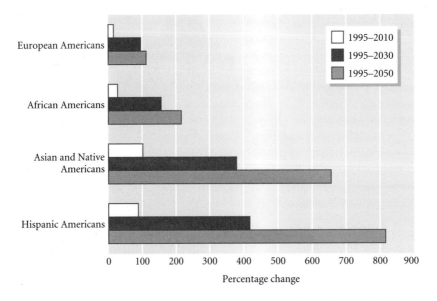

Figure 1.5 Projected growth of minority populations of older adults in the United States, 1995–2050.

Source: Data from the U.S. Census Bureau.

good job. Also, better-educated people tend to live longer, mostly because they have higher incomes, which give them better access to good health care and a chance to follow healthier lifestyles. We examine these issues in more detail in Chapter 4.

You probably know some older adults who are fiercely independent, who view the challenges of aging as something you face mainly alone or with help from professionals. You also probably know others who view themselves as part of a larger unit, typically family, and see the same challenges as something one faces with other family members as a group. In more formal terms, the first group of people represents individualism, and the second group reflects collectivism (Ajrouch, 2008).

As the number of ethnic minority older adults continues to increase, an important emerging issue will be the differences in these perspectives. This matters because the ways in which intervention is done differs a great deal. For those who emphasize individualism, the emphasis and approach is very much focused on only the person in question. In contrast, intervention with those who fit the collectivism approach needs to include the broader family or even friendship network. As the United States

becomes more diverse, these views, which reflect different cultures globally, will increasingly need to be taken into account by all organizations.

Johnson Lund/Sam Diephuis/Jupiter Images

This Latina older woman represents the changing face of older adults in the U.S.

Population Trends Around the World. How much do you know about global aging? Before you continue, test your knowledge by taking the 20 Questions about Global Aging quiz on page 11.

The population trends in the United States are not unique. As you can see in Figures 1.6 and 1.7, the number of older adults will increase dramatically in nearly all areas of the world over the next several decades. Overall, the "oldest" area of the world will continue to be Europe. The "youngest" area will continue to be Africa, where overall poor access to health care and a high incidence of AIDS significantly shorten lives (U.S. Census Bureau, 2008a).

Economically powerful countries around the world such as Japan are trying to cope with increased numbers of older adults that strain the country's resources. Indeed, the rate of growth of older adults in Japan is the highest in the industrialized world, due to a declining birth rate; by 2025 there will be twice as many adults over age 65 as there will be children (Ministry of Internal Affairs and Communications, 2005). The economic impact will be substantial for Japan, and in general the aging of the world's population will have significant effects on the world economy (Krueger & Ludwig, 2007). For example, pension and health care costs will increase dramatically, and there will be fewer workers to bear the burden in many industrialized countries. Canada leads the industrialized world in the rate of increase in the older adult population: between 2000 and 2030, it will increase by 126%.

But that's nothing compared to the explosive increase in the population of older adults that faces developing countries (Kinsella & Velkoff, 2001). For example, Singapore will see a 372% increase in older adults by 2050, with Malaysia (277%), Colombia (258%), and Costa Rica (250%) all seeing rises of more than 250%.

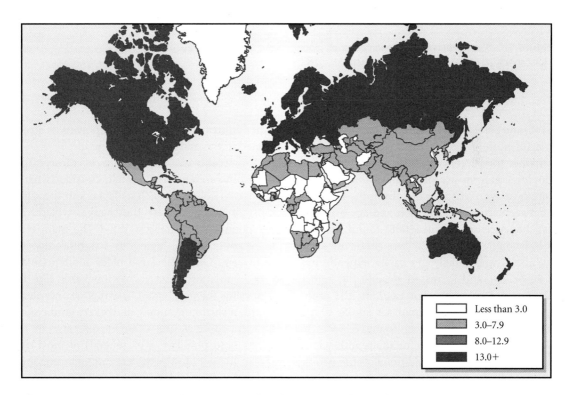

Figure 1.6 Percentage of people in countries globally aged 65 and over, 2000.

Source: U.S. Census Bureau, 2000a.

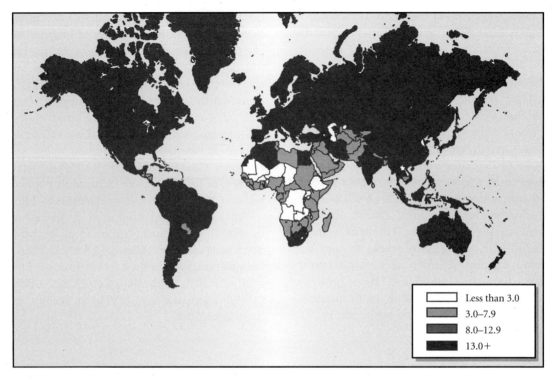

Figure 1.7 Percentage of people in countries globally aged 65 and over, 2030.

Source: U.S. Census Bureau, 2000a.

Economic conditions in different countries have a powerful effect on aging. One way to see this is to ask whether the parents of adults in households in developing countries are alive. Given that the parents are over age 50 (if they are alive), the relationship between economic situation and age becomes clearer. Banerjee and Duflo (2008) found that the odds of having a living parent was about the same for all adults whose daily per capita expenditures were $4 or less, and increased steadily the higher the daily expenditure got. For example, the probability of having a living parent for adults whose daily expenditures were between $6 and $10 was 36 percentage points higher than for adults with a daily expenditure of $1 or $2. Additionally, for people living in India, Indonesia, or Vietnam, the odds that people over age 50 with daily expenditures of $1 or $2 will die in the next 5–7 years is at least three times greater than it is for people whose daily

expenditures are $6–10. Clearly, poverty is strongly related to the odds of living a long life.

The worldwide implications of these population shifts are enormous. First, consider what will happen in countries such as Japan and throughout most of Europe, where the changes will result in net population decreases. Why? The main reason these countries are "aging" is a significantly lower birth rate. Once the large older-adult population dies, population decreases are inevitable. For them, it presents the problem of how their economies will handle a shrinking supply of workers (and consumers). In contrast, the dramatic increase in older adults (and population in general) of most of the rest of the world presents the multiple problems of caring for more older adults in health care systems that are already inadequate and strained, as well as trying to absorb more workers in fragile economies (Kinsella & Velkoff, 2001).

G L O B A L
A G I N G   Q U I Z

A Test of Your Knowledge of Global Aging for the 21st Century

1. *True or false?* In the year 2000, children under the age of 15 still outnumbered elderly people (aged 65 and over) in almost all nations of the world.

2. Which of the world's developing regions has the highest aggregate percentage of elderly?
   a. Africa
   b. Latin America
   c. The Caribbean
   d. Asia (excluding Japan)

3. *True or false?* More than half of the world's elderly today live in the industrialized nations of Europe, North America, and Japan.

4. *True or false?* Current demographic projections suggest that 35% of all people in the United States will be at least 65 years of age by the year 2050.

5. *True or false?* The number of the world's "oldest old" (people aged 80 and over) is growing more rapidly than that of the elderly as a whole.

6. More than one third of the world's oldest old live in which three countries?
   a. Germany, the United States, and the United Kingdom
   b. India, China, and the United States
   c. Japan, China, and Brazil
   d. Russia, India, and Indonesia

7. Japan has the highest life expectancy at birth among the major countries of the world. How many years can the average Japanese baby born in 2000 expect to live?
   a. 70 years
   b. 75 years
   c. 81 years
   d. 85 years

8. *True or false?* Today in some countries life expectancy at birth is less than 40 years.

9. What are the leading killers of elderly women in Europe and North America?
   a. Cancers
   b. Circulatory diseases
   c. Respiratory diseases
   d. Accidents

10. There are more older widows than widowers in virtually all countries because
    a. Women live longer than men
    b. Women typically marry men older than themselves
    c. Men are more likely than women to remarry after divorce or the death of a spouse
    d. All of the above

11. In developed countries, recent declines in labor force participation rates of older (55 and over) workers are due almost entirely to changing work patterns of
    a. Men
    b. Women
    c. Men and women

12. What proportion of the world's countries has a public old-age security program?
    a. All
    b. Three fourths
    c. One half
    d. One fourth

Answers

1. **True.** Although the world's population is aging, children still outnumber the elderly in all major nations except six: Bulgaria, Germany, Greece, Italy, Japan, and Spain.

2. **c.** The Caribbean, with 7.2% of all people aged 65 or older. Corresponding figures for other regions are: Asia (excluding Japan), 5.5%; Latin America, 5.3%; and Africa, 3.1%.

3. **False.** Although industrialized nations have higher percentages of elderly people than do most developing countries, 59% of the world's elderly now live in the developing countries of Africa, Asia, Latin America, the Caribbean, and Oceania.

4. **False.** Although the United States will age rapidly when the baby boomers (people born between 1946 and 1964) begin to reach age 65 after the year 2010, the percentage of population aged 65 and over in the year 2050 is projected to be slightly above 20% (compared with about 13% today).

5. **True.** The oldest old are the fastest-growing component of many national populations. The world's growth rate for the oldest-old population from 1999 to 2000 was 3.5%, whereas that of the world's older-adult population as a whole was 2.3% (compared with 1.3% for the total, or all ages, population).

6. **b.** India has roughly 6.2 million people aged 80 and over, China has 11.5 million, and the United States 9.2 million. Taken together, these people constitute nearly 38% of the world's oldest old.

7. **c.** 81 years, up from about 52 in 1947.

8. **True.** In some African countries (e.g., Malawi, Swaziland, Zambia, and Zimbabwe) where the HIV/AIDS epidemic is particularly devastating, average life expectancy at birth may be as much as 25 years lower than it otherwise would be in the absence of HIV/AIDS.

9. **b.** Circulatory diseases (especially heart disease and stroke) typically are the leading cause of death as reported by the World Health Organization. In Canada in 1995, for example, 44% of all deaths occurring to women at age 65 or above were attributed to circulatory disease. The percentage was virtually the same for elderly men.

10. **d.** All of the above.

11. **a.** From the late 1960s until very recently, labor force participation rates of older men in developed countries were declining virtually everywhere, whereas those for women were often holding steady or increasing. But because older men work in much greater numbers than do older women, increases in female participation were more than offset by falling male participation.

12. **b.** Of the 227 countries/areas of the world with populations of at least 5,000, 167 (74%) reported having some form of an old-age/disability/survivors program circa 1999.

Source: Adapted from U.S. Census Bureau, 2001.

1.2 Issues in Studying Adult Development and Aging

LEARNING OBJECTIVES

- What four main forces shape development?
- What are normative age-graded influences, normative history-graded influences, and nonnormative influences?
- How do culture and ethnicity influence aging?
- What is the meaning of age?
- What are the nature–nurture, stability–change, continuity–discontinuity, and the "universal versus context-specific development" controversies?

Levar Johnson smiled broadly as he held his newborn granddaughter for the first time. So many thoughts rushed into his mind. He could only imagine the kinds of things Devonna would experience growing up. He hoped that she would have a good neighborhood in which to play and explore her world. He hoped that she inherited the family genes for good health. He wondered how Devonna's life growing up as an African American in the United States would be different from his experiences.

Like many grandparents, Levar wonders what the future holds for his granddaughter. The questions he considers are interesting in their own right, but they are important for another reason: They get to the heart of general issues of human development that have intrigued philosophers and scientists for centuries. You have probably wondered about many similar issues. How do some people manage to remain thin, whereas other people seem to gain weight merely by looking at food? Why do some people remain very active and mentally well into later life? How does growing up in a Spanish-speaking culture affect one's views of family caregiving? Answering these questions requires us to consider the various forces that shape us as we mature. Developmentalists place special emphasis on four forces: biological,

psychological, sociocultural, and life cycle. These forces direct our development much as an artist's hands direct the course of a painting or sculpture.

Following from the forces that shape adult development and aging are questions such as: What is the relative importance of genetics and environment on people's behavior? Do people change gradually, or do they change more abruptly? Do all people change in the same way? These questions reflect controversies that historically underlie the study of human development (Lerner, 2001): the nature–nurture controversy, the change–stability controversy, the continuity–discontinuity controversy, and the "universal versus context-specific development" controversy.

Having a firm grasp on the forces and controversies of development is important because it provides a context for understanding why researchers and theorists believe certain things about aging or why some topics have been researched a great deal and others have been hardly studied at all. For example, someone who believes that a decline in intellectual ability is an innate and inevitable part of aging is unlikely to search for intervention techniques to raise performance. Similarly, someone who believes that personality characteristics change across adulthood would be likely to search for life transitions.

The Forces of Development

Gray hair, remembering, activity levels—Why do adults differ so much on these and other things? This question requires us to understand the basic forces that shape us. Developmentalists typically consider four interactive forces (shown in Figure 1.8):

- **Biological forces** *include all genetic and health-related factors that affect development.* Examples of biological forces include menopause, facial wrinkling, and changes in the major organ systems.
- **Psychological forces** *include all internal perceptual, cognitive, emotional, and personality factors that affect development.* Collectively, psychological forces provide the characteristics we notice about people that make them individuals.
- **Sociocultural forces** *include interpersonal, societal, cultural, and ethnic factors that affect development.* Sociocultural forces provide the overall contexts in which we develop.

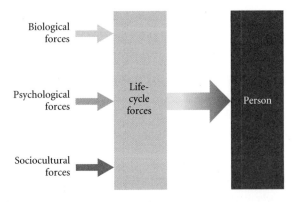

Figure 1.8 Each person is the product of the interaction of biological, psychological, sociocultural, and life-cycle forces.

- **Life-cycle forces** reflect differences in how the same event or combination of biological, psychological, and sociocultural forces affects people at different points in their lives. Life-cycle forces provide the context for the developmental differences of interest in adult development and aging.

One useful way to organize the biological, psychological, and sociocultural forces on human development is with the **biopsychosocial framework.** Together with life-cycle forces, the biopsychosocial framework provides a complete overview of the shapers of human development. Each of us is a product of a unique combination of these forces. Even identical twins growing up in the same family eventually have their own unique friends, partners, occupations, and so on. To see why all these forces are important, imagine that we want to know how people feel about forgetting. We would need to consider several biological factors, such as whether the forgetting was caused by an underlying disease. We would want to know about such psychological factors as what the person's memory ability has been throughout his or her life and about his or her beliefs about what happens to memory with increasing age. We would need to know about sociocultural factors, such as the influence of social stereotypes about forgetting. Finally, we would need to know about the age of the person when a forgetting experience occurs. Focusing on only one (or even two or three) of the forces would provide an incomplete view of how the person feels. The biopsychosocial framework, along with life-cycle forces, will provide a way to understand all the developmental outcomes you will encounter in this text.

Interrelations among the Forces: Developmental Influences

All the forces we have discussed combine to create people's developmental experiences. One way to consider these combinations is to consider the degree to which they are common or unique to people of specific ages. An important concept in this approach is cohort. *A* **cohort** *is a group of people born at the same point or specific time span in historical time.* So everyone born in 1985 would be the 1985 cohort; similarly, those born between 1946 and 1964 represent the baby-boom cohort. Based on this approach, Baltes (1987; Baltes et al., 2006) identifies three sets of influences that interact to produce developmental change over the life span: normative age-graded influences, normative history-graded influences, and nonnormative influences.

Normative age-graded influences *are experiences caused by biological, psychological, and sociocultural forces that occur to most people of a particular age.* Some of these, such as puberty, menarche, and menopause, are biological. These normative biological events usually indicate a major change in a person's life; for example, menopause is an indicator that a woman can no longer bear children without medical intervention. Normative psychological events include focusing on certain concerns at different points in adulthood, such as a middle-aged person's concern with socializing the younger generation. Other normative age-graded influences involve sociocultural forces, such as the time when first marriage occurs and the age at which someone retires. Normative age-graded influences typically correspond to major time-marker events, which are often ritualized. For example, many younger adults formally celebrate turning 21 as the official transition to adulthood, getting married typically is surrounded with much celebration, and retirement often begins with a party celebrating the end of employment. These events provide the most convenient way to judge where we are on our social clock.

Normative history-graded influences *are events that most people in a specific culture experience at the* *same time.* These events may be biological (such as epidemics), psychological (such as particular stereotypes), or sociocultural (such as changing attitudes toward sexuality). Normative history-graded influences often give a generation its unique identity, such as the baby-boom generation (people born roughly between 1946 and 1964), generation X (people born roughly between 1965 and 1975), and the millennial generation (sometimes called the Echo Boomers or generation Y, born between 1979 and 1994). These influences can have a profound effect. For example, the attacks on the World Trade Center on September 11, 2001, fundamentally changed attitudes about safety and security that had been held for decades.

Nonnormative influences *are random or rare events that may be important for a specific individual but are not experienced by most people.* These may be favorable events, such as winning the lottery or an election, or unfavorable ones, such as an accident or layoff. The unpredictability of these events makes them unique. Such events can turn one's life upside down overnight.

Life-cycle forces are especially key in understanding the importance of normative age-graded, normative history-graded, and nonnormative influences. For example, history-graded influences may produce generational differences and conflict; parents' experiences as young adults in the 1960s and 1970s (before AIDS, instant messaging, and global terrorism) may have little to do with the complex issues faced by today's young adults. In turn, these interactions have important implications for understanding differences that appear to be age related. That is, differences may be explained in terms of different life experiences (normative history-graded influences) rather than as an integral part of aging itself (normative age-graded influences). We will return to this issue when we discuss age, cohort, and time-of-measurement effects in research on adult development and aging.

Culture and Ethnicity

Culture and ethnicity jointly provide status, social settings, living conditions, and personal experiences for people of all ages, and they influence and are influenced by biological, psychological, and life-cycle developmental forces. Culture can be defined as shared basic value orientations, norms,

beliefs, and customary habits and ways of living. Culture provides the basic worldview of a society in that it gives it the basic explanations about the meanings and goals of everyday life (Luborsky & McMullen, 1999). Culture is such a powerful influence because it connects to biological forces through family lineage, which is sometimes the way in which members of a particular culture are defined. Psychologically, culture shapes people's core beliefs; in some cases this can result in ethnocentrism, or the belief that one's own culture is superior to others. Being socialized as a child within a culture usually has a more profound effect on a person than when one adopts a culture later in life, resulting in significant life-cycle timing effects. Culture is extremely important in gerontology because how people define basic concepts such as *person, age,* and *life course* varies a great deal across cultures.

Members of the !Kung tribe experience development in ways very different from the ways most Americans do.

Equally important is the concept of ethnicity, which is an individual and collective sense of identity based on historical and cultural group membership and related behaviors and beliefs (Luborsky & McMullen, 1999). Compared with culture, ethnic group identities have both solid and fluid properties, reflecting the fact that there are both unchanging and situation-specific aspects to ethnic identity (Luborsky & Rubinstein, 1997). An example of these properties is that the terms referring to an ethnic group can change over time; for example, the terms *colored people, Negroes, black Americans,* and *African Americans* have all been used to describe Americans of African ancestry. Ethnic identity is first influenced by biology through one's parents. However, how one incorporates ethnic identity depends on numerous psychological factors as well as age.

Both culture and ethnicity are key dimensions along which adults vary. However, we know very little about how culture or ethnicity affects how people experience old age. Throughout the rest of this book, we explore areas in which culture and ethnicity have been studied systematically. Unfortunately, most research focuses only on European Americans. Given the demographic trends discussed earlier, this focus must change so we can understand the experience of growing older in the United States in the next few decades.

The Meaning of Age

When you are asked the question "How old are you?" what crosses your mind? Is it the number of years since the day of your birth? Is it how old you feel at that time? Is it defined more in terms of where you are biologically, psychologically, or socially than in terms of calendar time? You may not have thought about it, but age is not a simple construct (and in the case of people such as the !Kung, it has no meaning at all).

Likewise, aging is not a single process. Rather, it consists of at least three distinct processes: primary, secondary, and tertiary aging (Birren & Cunningham, 1985). **Primary aging** *is normal, disease-free development during adulthood.* Changes in biological, psychological, sociocultural, or life-cycle processes in primary aging are an inevitable part of the developmental process; examples include menopause, decline in reaction time, and the loss of family and friends. Most of the information in this book represents primary aging. **Secondary aging** *is developmental changes that are related to disease, lifestyle, and other environmentally induced changes that are not inevitable (e.g., pollution).* The progressive loss of intellectual abilities in Alzheimer's disease and related forms of dementia are examples of secondary aging. Finally, **tertiary aging** *is the rapid losses that occur shortly before death.* An example of tertiary aging is a phenomenon known as terminal drop, in which intellectual abilities show a marked decline in the last few years before death.

Everyone does not grow old in the same way. Whereas most people tend to show usual patterns of aging that reflect the typical, or normative, changes with age, other people show highly successful aging in which few signs of change occur. For example, although most people tend to get chronic diseases as they get older, some people never do. What makes people who age successfully different? At this point, we do not know for sure. It may be a unique combination of genetics, optimal environment, flexibility in dealing with life situations, a strong sense of personal control, and maybe a bit of luck. For our present discussion, the main point to keep in mind is that everyone's experience of growing old is somewhat different. Although many people develop arthritis, how each person learns to cope is unique.

When most of us think about age, we usually think of how long we have been around since our birth; this way of defining age is known as chronological age. *Chronological age* is a shorthand way to index time and organize events and data by using a commonly understood standard: calendar time. Chronological age is not the only shorthand index variable used in adult development and aging. Gender, ethnicity, and socioeconomic status are others. No index variable itself actually causes behavior. In the case of gender, for example, it is not whether a person is male or female per se that determines how long he or she will live on average but rather the underlying forces, such as hormonal effects, that are the true causes. This point is often forgotten when age is the index variable, perhaps because it is so familiar to us and so widely used. However, age (or time) does not directly cause things to happen, either. Iron left out in the rain will rust, but rust is not caused simply by time. Rather, rust is a time-dependent process involving oxidation in which time is a measure of the rate at which rust is created. Similarly, human behavior is affected by experiences that occur with the passage of time, not by time itself. What we study in adult development and aging is the result of time- or age-dependent processes, not the result of age itself.

Describing a person's age turns out to be quite complicated. Here's why. *Perceived age* refers to the age you think of yourself as. The saying "You're only as old as you feel" captures perceived age. Where people are, relative to the maximum number of years they could possibly live, is their biological age. *Biological age* is assessed by measuring the functioning of the various vital, or life-limiting, organ systems, such as the cardiovascular system.

Psychological age refers to the functional level of the psychological abilities people use to adapt to changing environmental demands. These abilities include memory, intelligence, feelings, motivation, and other skills that foster and maintain self-esteem and personal control.

Finally, *sociocultural age* refers to the specific set of roles individuals adopt in relation to other members of the society and culture to which they belong. Sociocultural age is judged on the basis of many behaviors and habits, such as style of dress, customs, language, and interpersonal style. Sociocultural age is especially important in understanding many of the family and work roles we adopt. When to get married, have children, make career moves, retire, and so on often are influenced by what we think our sociocultural age is. Such decisions also play a role in determining our self-esteem and other aspects of personality. Many of the most damaging stereotypes about aging (e.g., that older people should not have sex) are based on faulty assumptions about sociocultural age.

In sum, a person's age turns out to be quite complex. Think about yourself. You probably have days

when even though the calendar says you're a certain age, your exploits the day before resulted in your feeling much younger at the time and much older the next morning. How "old" anyone is can change from one moment to the next.

Core Issues in Development

Is it your genes or experiences that determine how intelligent you are? If a young adult woman is outgoing, does this mean she will be outgoing in late life? If people change, is it more gradual or sporadic? Is aging the same around the world? These and similar questions have occupied some of the greatest Western philosophers in history: Plato, Aristotle, René Descartes, John Locke, and Ludwig Wittgenstein, among many others. Four main issues occupy most of the discussion: nature versus nurture, stability versus change, continuity versus discontinuity, and universal versus context-specific development. Because each of these issues cuts across the topics we discuss in this book, let's consider each briefly.

The Nature–Nurture Issue.   Think for a minute about a particular characteristic that you and several people in your family have, such as intelligence, good looks, or a friendly, outgoing personality.

Why is this trait so prevalent? Is it because you inherited the trait from your parents? Or is it because of where and how you and your parents were brought up? *Answers to these questions illustrate different positions on the* **nature–nurture issue**, *which involves the degree to which genetic or hereditary influences (nature) and experiential or environmental influences (nurture) determine the kind of person you are.* Scientists once hoped to answer these questions by identifying either heredity or environment as *the* cause of a particular aspect of development. The goal was to be able to say, for example, that intelligence was due to heredity or that personality was due to experience. Today, however, we know that virtually no features of life-span development are due exclusively to either heredity or environment. Instead, development is always shaped by both: Nature and nurture are mutually interactive influences.

Does Personality in Young Adulthood Determine Personality in Old Age?

Lest you think the controversies underlying adult development and aging do not reflect ongoing debate, consider the case of personality in adulthood. Perhaps no other topic in gerontology has resulted in such heated debates as whether people's basic personality remains the same throughout adulthood or undergoes fundamental change. As we explore in detail in Chapter 9, numerous theories have been developed just to account for the data on this one topic.

Consider yourself and other adults you know. Is the person labeled "class clown" in high school likely to be as much of a fun-loving person 10, 20, or 30 years later? Will the shy person who would never ask anyone to dance be as withdrawn? Or will these people be hardly recognizable at their various class reunions? Probably in your experience you've encountered both outcomes; that is, some people seem to remain the same year after year, whereas some people seem to undergo tremendous change. Why is that?

For one thing, it depends on how specific you get in looking at aspects of a person's personality. In the case of a very specific trait, such as shyness, you will probably see overall stability across adulthood. But if you look at a more global aspect such as the degree to which a person is concerned with the next generation, then you are more likely to find change.

What does this mean? Certainly, it means you have to be very careful in making general statements about stability or change. It also means you have to be quite specific about what you are interested in measuring and at what level of complexity. We will encounter many more examples of both stability and change throughout the book that reflect both these needs.

For example, it is known that some forms of Alzheimer's disease are genetically linked. However, whether one actually gets Alzheimer's disease, and possibly even how the disease progresses, may be influenced by the environment. Specifically, an environmental trigger may be needed for the disease to occur. Moreover, some evidence indicates that providing a supportive environment for people with Alzheimer's disease improves their performance on cognitive tasks, at least for a while (Camp, 2001).

So in order to understand a newborn's future we must simultaneously consider his or her inborn, hereditary characteristics and the environment. Both factors must be considered together to yield an adequate account of why we behave the way we do. To explain a person's behavior and discover where to focus intervention, we must look at the unique interaction for that person between nature and nurture.

The Stability–Change Issue. Ask yourself the following question: Are you pretty much the same as you were 10 years ago, or are you different? How so? Depending on what aspects of yourself you considered, you may have concluded that you are pretty much the same (perhaps in terms of learning style) or that you are different (perhaps in some physical feature such as weight). The **stability–change issue** *concerns the degree to which people remain the same over time,* as discussed in the Current Controversies feature. Stability at some basic level is essential for us (and others) to recognize that one is the same individual as time goes on. But we also like to believe that our characteristics are not set in concrete, that we can change ourselves if we so desire. (Imagine not being able to do anything to rid yourself of some character defect.)

Although there is little controversy about whether children change in some ways from birth through age 18, there is much controversy about whether adults do as well. Much of the controversy over stability and change across adulthood stems from how specific characteristics are defined and measured. How much we remain the same and how much we change, then, turns out to be a difficult issue to resolve in an objective way. For many gerontologists, whether stability or change is the rule depends on what personal aspect is being considered and what theoretical perspective one is adopting.

The Continuity–Discontinuity Controversy. The third major issue in developmental psychology is a derivative of the stability–change controversy. The **continuity–discontinuity controversy** *concerns whether a particular developmental phenomenon represents a smooth progression over time (continuity) or a series of abrupt shifts (discontinuity).* Continuity approaches usually focus on the amount of a characteristic a person has, whereas discontinuity approaches usually focus on the kinds of characteristics a person has. Of course, on a day-to-day basis, behaviors often look nearly identical, or continuous. But when viewed over the course of many months or years, the same behaviors may have changed dramatically, reflecting discontinuous change. Throughout this book, you will find examples of developmental changes that appear to be more on the continuities side and ones that appear to be more on the discontinuities side.

An example of continuity is discussed in Chapter 6: reaction time. As people grow older, the speed with which they can respond slows down. But in Chapters 8 you will read about an example of discontinuity: How people approach problems, especially ones with complex and ambiguous features, undergoes fundamental shifts from young adulthood through middle age.

Within the discontinuity view lies the issue of how adaptable people are in situations as they age. Baltes and colleagues (1998; Baltes et al., 1999) use the term *plasticity* to describe this in relation to people's capacity. **Plasticity** *refers to the belief that capacity is not fixed, but can be learned or improved with practice.* For example, people can learn ways to help themselves remember information, which in turn may help them deal with declining short-term memory ability with age. Although plasticity can be demonstrated in many arenas, there are limits to the degree of potential improvement, as we will see in later chapters.

The Universal versus Context-Specific Development Controversy. The **universal versus context-specific development controversy** *concerns whether there is just one path of development or several.* Consider the !Kung tribe, who live in the Kalahari Desert of Botswana in southwest Africa (Lee, Hitchcock, & Biesele, 2002). If you were to ask an older !Kung "How old are you?" you would quickly learn that the question has no meaning. !Kung also do not keep track of the number of years they have been alive, the number of children they have, or how often they move. !Kung mothers can describe in detail each of their children's births, but they leave it to others to figure out how many children this adds up to. To the !Kung, age per se is unimportant; when asked to describe people who are "younger" or "older," they give the names of specific people. Social roles among the !Kung also do not differ by age; for example, women in their 20s and 60s all tend gardens, draw water from wells, and take care of children.

Life among !Kung adults contrasts sharply with life among adults in the United States, where age matters a great deal and social roles differ accordingly. Can one theory explain development in both groups? Maybe. Some theorists argue that such differences are more apparent than real and that development worldwide reflects one basic process for everyone. According to this view, differences in development are simply variations on a fundamental developmental process, much as Hershey, Nestlé, Lindt, and Godiva chocolates are all products of the same basic manufacturing process.

The opposing view is that differences between people may not be just variations on a theme. Advocates of this view argue that adult development and aging are inextricably intertwined with the context in which they occur. A person's development is a product of complex interactions with the environment, and these interactions are not fundamentally the same in all environments. Each environment has its own set of unique procedures that shape development, just as the "recipes" for chocolates, computers, and pens have little in common.

The view adopted in this book is that adult development and aging must be understood within the contexts in which they occur. In some cases, this means that contexts are sufficiently similar that general trends can be identified. In others, such as the !Kung and U.S. societies, these differences prevent many general statements. In Levar's case with his granddaughter, it may be a blend of the two.

Concept Checks

1. What are some examples of the biological, psychological, sociocultural, and life-cycle forces of development?
2. What are the major issues in each of the controversies underlying adult development and aging?
3. What are the three distinct processes of aging?

1.3 Research Methods

LEARNING OBJECTIVES

- What approaches do scientists use to measure behavior in adult development and aging research?
- What are the general designs for doing research?
- What specific designs are unique to adult development and aging research?
- What ethical procedures must researchers follow?

eah and Sarah are both 75 years old and are in fairly good health. They believe their memory is not as good as it once was, so they both use various memory aids: Leah tries to think of images in her mind to remember her grocery list, whereas Sarah writes them down. Leah and Sarah got into a discussion recently about which technique works better.

You might be asking yourself why you need to know about research methods when you could just Google the topic and find out all sorts of things about it. Here's why—there is good research and bad research and everything else in between. The only way to tell the difference is by knowing what makes good research that results in trustworthy information.

Just as in any profession, gerontology has certain tools of the trade that are used to ensure good research. That's what we will be considering in this section—the tools that gerontologists have used for decades in discovering the secrets of adult development and aging.

This section is so important that if you have trouble understanding the information after reading it a few times, ask your instructor.

So suppose Leah and Sarah know that you're taking a course in adult development and aging, and they ask you to settle the matter. You know research could show whose approach is better under what circumstances, but how? Gerontologists must make several key decisions as they prepare to study any topic. They need to decide how to measure the topic of interest, they must design the study, they must choose a way to study development, and they must respect the rights of the people who will participate in the study.

What makes the study of adult development and aging different from other areas of social science is the need to consider multiple influences on behavior. Explanations of development entail consideration of all the forces we considered earlier. This makes research on adult development and aging more difficult, if for no other reason than it involves examining more variables.

Measurement in Adult Development and Aging Research

Researchers typically begin by deciding how to measure the topic of interest. For example, the first step toward resolving Leah and Sarah's discussion about remembering grocery items would be to decide how to measure remembering. Gerontologists usually use one of three approaches: observing systematically, using tasks to sample behavior, and asking people for self-reports. In addition, researchers need to be concerned with how representative the participants in the study are of the larger group of people in question.

Regardless of the kind of method chosen, researchers must show it is both reliable and valid. *The* **reliability** *of a measure is the extent to which it provides* *a consistent index of the behavior or topic of interest.* A measure of memory is reliable to the extent that it gives a consistent estimate of performance each time you administer it. All measures used in gerontological research must be shown to be reliable, or they cannot be used. *The* **validity** *of a measure is the extent to which it measures what researchers think it measures.* For example, a measure of memory is valid only if it can be shown to actually measure memory (and not vocabulary ability, for example). Validity often is established by showing that the measure in question is closely related to another measure known to be valid. Because it is possible to have a measure that is reliable but not valid (a ruler is a reliable measure of length but not a valid measure of memory), researchers must ensure that measures are both reliable and valid.

Systematic Observation. *As the name implies,* **systematic observation** *involves watching people and carefully recording what they say or do.* Two forms of systematic observation are common. In naturalistic observation, people are observed as they behave spontaneously in some real-life situation. For example, Leah and Sarah could be observed in the grocery store purchasing their items as a way to test how well they remember.

Structured observations differ from naturalistic observations in that the researcher creates a setting that is particularly likely to elicit the behavior of interest. Structured observations are especially useful for studying behaviors that are difficult to observe naturally. For example, how people react to emergencies is hard to study naturally because emergencies generally are rare and unpredictable events. A researcher could stage an emergency and watch how people react. However, whether the behaviors observed in staged situations are the same as would happen naturally often is hard to determine, making it difficult to generalize from staged settings to the real world.

Sampling Behavior with Tasks. When investigators can't observe a behavior directly, another popular alternative is to create tasks that are thought to sample the behavior of interest. For example, one way to test older adults' memory is to give them a grocery list to learn and remember. Likewise, police training includes putting the candidate in a building in which targets pop up that may be either criminals or innocent bystanders. This approach is popular with gerontological researchers because it is so convenient. The main question with this approach is its validity: Does the task provide a realistic sample of the behavior of interest? For example, asking people to learn grocery lists would have good validity to the extent it matched the kinds of lists they actually use.

Self-Reports. The last approach, self-reports, is a special case of using tasks to sample people's behavior. **Self-reports** *are simply people's answers to questions about the topic of interest.* When questions are posed in written form, the verbal report is a questionnaire; when they are posed verbally, it is an interview. Either way, questions are created that probe different aspects of the topic of interest. For example, if you think imagery and lists are common ways people use to remember grocery items, you could devise a questionnaire and survey several people to find out.

Although self-reports are very convenient and provide information on the topic of interest, they are not always good measures of people's behavior, because they are inaccurate. Why? People may not remember accurately what they did in the past, or they may report what they think the researcher wants to hear.

Representative Sampling. Researchers usually are interested in broad groups of people called populations. Examples of populations are all students taking a course on adult development and aging or all Asian American widows. Almost all studies include only a sample of people, which is a subset of the population. Researchers must be careful to ensure that their sample is truly representative of the population of interest. An unrepresentative sample can result in invalid research. For example, what would you think of a study of middle-aged parents if you learned that the sample consisted entirely of two-parent households? You would, quite correctly, decide that this sample is not representative of all middle-aged parents and question whether its results apply to single middle-aged parents.

As you read on, you'll soon discover that most of the research we consider in this text has been conducted on middle-class, well-educated European Americans. Are these samples representative of all people in the United States? In the world? Sometimes, but not always. Be careful not to assume that findings from this group apply to people of other groups. In addition, some developmental issues have not been studied in all ethnic groups and cultures. For example, the U.S. government does not always report statistics for all ethnic groups. To change this, some U.S. government agencies, such as the National Institutes of Health, now require samples to be representative. Thus in the future we may gain a broader understanding of aging.

General Designs for Research

Having selected the way we want to measure the topic of interest, researchers must embed this measure in a research design that yields useful, relevant results. Gerontologists rely on primary designs in planning their work: experimental studies, correlational studies, and case studies. The specific design chosen for research depends in large part on the questions the researchers are trying to address.

Experimental Design. To find out whether Leah's or Sarah's approach to remembering works better, we could gather groups of older adults and try the following. We could randomly assign the participants into three groups: those who are taught to use imagery, those who are taught to use lists, and those who are not taught to use anything. After giving all the groups time to learn the new technique (where appropriate), we could test each group on a new grocery list to see who does better.

What we have done is an example of an **experiment,** which involves manipulating a key factor that the researcher believes is responsible for a particular behavior and randomly assigning participants to the experimental and control groups. In our case, the key variable being manipulated (termed the **independent variable**) is the instructions for how to study. In a study of memory, a typical behavior that is observed (termed the **dependent variable**) is the amount of information actually remembered.

More generally, in an experiment the researcher is most interested in identifying differences between groups of people. One group, the experimental group, receives the manipulation; another group, the control group, does not. This sets up a situation in which the level of the key variable of interest differs across groups. In addition, the investigator exerts precise control over all important aspects of the study, including the variable of interest, the setting, and the participants. Because the key variable is systematically manipulated in an experiment, researchers can infer cause-and-effect relations about that variable. In our example, we can conclude that type of instruction (how people study) causes better or worse performance on a memory test. Discovering such cause-and-effect relations is important if we are to understand the underlying processes of adult development and aging.

Finally, we must note that age cannot be an independent variable, because we cannot manipulate it. Consequently, we cannot conduct true experiments to examine the effects of age on a particular person's behavior. At best, we can find age-related effects of an independent variable on dependent variables.

Correlational Design. *In a* **correlational study,** *investigators examine relations between variables as they exist naturally in the world.* In the simplest correlational study, a researcher measures two variables, and then sees how they are related. Suppose we wanted to know whether the amount of time spent studying a grocery list such as one that Sarah might create was related to how many items people remember at the store. To find out, the researcher would measure two things for each person in the study: the length of study time and the number of items purchased correctly.

The results of a correlational study usually are measured by computing a correlation coefficient, abbreviated r. Correlations can range from -1.0 to 1.0, reflecting three different types of relations between study time and number of groceries remembered.

- When $r = 0$, the two variables are unrelated: Study time has no relation to remembering groceries.
- When $r > 0$, the variables are positively related: As study time increases (or decreases), the number

of grocery items remembered also increases (or decreases).

- When $r < 0$, the variables are inversely related: When study time increases (or decreases), the number of groceries remembered decreases (or increases).

Correlational studies do not give definitive information about cause-and-effect relations; for example, the correlation between study time and the number of groceries remembered does not mean that one variable caused the other, regardless of how large the relation was. However, correlational studies do provide important information about the strength of the relation between variables, which is reflected in the absolute value of the correlation coefficient. Moreover, because developmental researchers are interested in how variables are related to factors that are very difficult, if not impossible, to manipulate, correlational techniques are used a great deal. In fact, most developmental research is correlational at some level because age cannot be manipulated within an individual. This means we can describe a great many developmental phenomena, but we cannot explain very many of them.

Case Studies. Sometimes researchers cannot obtain measures directly from people and are able only to watch them carefully. *In certain situations, researchers may be able to study a single individual in great detail in a* **case study.** This technique is especially useful when researchers want to investigate very rare phenomena, such as uncommon diseases or people with extremely high ability. Identifying new diseases, for example, begins with a case study of one individual who has a pattern of symptoms that is different from any known syndrome. Case studies are also very valuable for opening new areas of study, which can be followed by larger studies using other methods (e.g., experiments). However, their primary limitation is figuring out whether the information gleaned from one individual holds for others as well.

Designs for Studying Development

Once the general design is chosen, most gerontologists must decide how to measure possible changes or age differences that emerge as people develop. For example, if we want to know how people continue (or fail) to use imagery or lists in remembering grocery items as they get older, we will want to use a design that is particularly sensitive to developmental differences. Such designs are based on three key variables: age, cohort, and time of measurement. Once we have considered these, we will examine the specific designs for studying development.

Age, Cohort, and Time of Measurement. Every study of adult development and aging is built on the combination of three building blocks: age, cohort, and time of measurement (Cavanaugh & Whitbourne, 2003).

Age effects *reflect differences caused by underlying processes, such as biological, psychological, or sociocultural changes.* Although usually represented in research by chronological age, age effects are inherent changes within the person and are not caused by the passage of time per se.

Cohort effects *are differences caused by experiences and circumstances unique to the generation to which one belongs.* In general, cohort effects correspond to the normative history-graded influences discussed earlier. However, defining a cohort may not be easy. Cohorts can be specific, as in all people born in one particular year, or general, such as the baby-boom cohort. As described earlier, each generation is exposed to different sets of historical and personal events (such as World War II, home computers, or opportunities to attend college). Later in this section we consider evidence of how profound cohort effects can be.

Time-of-measurement effects reflect differences stemming from sociocultural, environmental, historical, or other events at the time the data are obtained from the participants. For example, data about wage increases given in a particular year may be influenced by the economic conditions of that year. If the economy is in a serious recession, pay increases probably would be small. In contrast, if the economy is booming, pay increases could be large. Clearly, whether a study is conducted during a recession or a boom affects what is learned about pay changes. In short, the point in time in which a researcher decides to do research could lead him or her to different conclusions about the phenomenon being studied.

Table 1.1

Three Basic Building Blocks of Developmental Research

	Time of Measurement			
Cohort	2000	2010	2020	2030
1950	50	60	70	80
1960	40	50	60	70
1970	30	40	50	60
1980	20	30	40	50

Cohort is represented by the years in the first column, time of measurement by the years across the top, and age by the values in the cells.

The three building-block variables (age, cohort, and time of measurement) can be represented in a single chart, such as the one shown in Table 1.1. Cohort is represented by the years in the first column, time of measurement is represented by the years across the top, and age is represented by the numbers in the individual cells. Note that age is computed by subtracting the cohort year from the time of measurement.

In conducting adult development and aging research, investigators have attempted to identify and separate the three effects. This has not been easy, because all three influences are interrelated. If one is interested in studying 40-year-olds, one must necessarily select the cohort that was born 40 years ago. In this case age and cohort are *confounded,* because one cannot know whether the behaviors observed occur because the participants are 40 years old or because of the specific life experiences they have had as a result of being born in a particular historical period. *In general,* **confounding** *is any situation in which one cannot determine which of two or more effects is responsible for the behaviors being observed.* Confounding of the three effects we are considering here is the most serious problem in adult development and aging research.

What distinguishes developmental researchers from their colleagues in other areas of psychology is a fundamental interest in understanding how people change. Developmental researchers must look at the ways in which people differ across time. Doing so

necessarily requires that they understand the distinction between age change and age difference. An age change occurs in an individual's behavior over time. Leah's or Sarah's memory at age 75 may not be as good as it was at age 40. To discover an age change one must examine the same person (in this case, Leah or Sarah) at more than one point in time. An age difference is obtained when at least two different people of different ages are compared. Leah and Sarah may not remember as many grocery items as another person of age 40. Even though we may be able to document substantial age differences, we cannot assume they imply an age change. We do not know whether Leah or Sarah has changed since she was 40, and of course we do not know whether the 40-year-old will be any different at age 75. In some cases age differences reflect age changes, and in some cases they do not.

If what we really want to understand in developmental research is age change (what happens as people grow older), we should design our research with this goal in mind. Moreover, different research questions necessitate different research designs. We next consider the most common ways in which researchers gather data about age differences and age changes: cross-sectional, longitudinal, time lag, and sequential designs.

Cross-Sectional Designs. *In a* cross-sectional study, developmental differences are identified by testing people of different ages at the same time. Any single column in Table 1.2 represents a cross-sectional design. Cross-sectional designs allow researchers to examine age differences but not age change.

Cross-sectional research has several weaknesses. Because people are tested at only one point in their development, we learn nothing about the continuity of development. Consequently, we cannot tell whether someone who remembers grocery items well at age 50 (in 2000) is still able to do so at age 80 (in 2030), because the person would be tested at age 50 or 80, but not both. Cross-sectional studies also are affected by cohort effects, meaning that differences between age groups (cohorts) may result as easily from environmental events as from developmental processes. Why? Cross-sectional studies assume that when the older participants were younger, they resembled the people in the younger

Table 1.2

Cross-Sectional Design

Cohort	Time of Measurement			
	2000	2010	2020	2030
1950	**50**	60	70	80
1960	**40**	50	60	70
1970	**30**	40	50	60
1980	**20**	30	40	50

Cohort is represented by the years in the first column, time of measurement by the years across the top, and age by the values in the cells.

age groups in the study. This isn't always true, of course, which makes it difficult to know why age differences are found in a cross-sectional study. In short, age and cohort effects are confounded in cross-sectional research.

Despite the confounding of age and cohort and the limitation of being able to identify only age differences, cross-sectional designs dominate the research literature in gerontology. Why? The reason is a pragmatic one: Because all the measurements are obtained at one time, cross-sectional research can be conducted more quickly and inexpensively than research using other designs. In addition, one particular variation of cross-sectional designs is used the most: the extreme age groups design.

Suppose you want to investigate whether people's ability to remember items at the grocery store differs with age. Your first impulse may be to gather a group of younger adults and compare their performance with that of a group of older adults. Typically, such studies compare samples obtained in convenient ways; younger adults usually are college students, and older adults often are volunteers from senior centers or church groups.

Although the extreme age groups design is very common (most of the studies cited in this book used this design), it has several problems (Hertzog & Dixon, 1996). Three concerns are key. First, the samples are not representative, so we must be very careful not to read too much into the results; findings from studies on extreme age groups may not generalize to people other than ones like those who

participated. Second, age should be treated as a continuous variable, not as a category ("young" and "old"). Viewing age as a continuous variable allows researchers to gain a better understanding of how age relates to any observed age differences. Finally, extreme age group designs assume the measures used mean the same thing across both age groups. Measures may tap somewhat different constructs, so the reliability and validity of each measure should be checked in each age group.

Despite the problems with cross-sectional designs in general and with extreme age groups designs in particular, they can provide useful information if used carefully. Most importantly, they can point out issues that may provide fruitful avenues for subsequent longitudinal or sequential studies, in which case we can uncover information about age changes.

Longitudinal Designs. *In a* **longitudinal study,** *the same individuals are observed or tested repeatedly at different points in their lives.* As the name implies, a longitudinal study involves a lengthwise account of development and is the most direct way to watch growth occur. A longitudinal design is represented by any horizontal row in Table 1.3. A major advantage of longitudinal designs is that age changes are identified because we are studying the same people over time.

Usually the repeated testing of longitudinal studies extends over years, but not always. *In a* **microgenetic study,** *a special type of longitudinal design, participants are tested repeatedly over a*

Table 1.3

Longitudinal Design

Cohort	Time of Measurement			
	2000	2010	2020	2030
1950	50	60	70	80
1960	**40**	**50**	**60**	**70**
1970	30	40	50	60
1980	20	30	40	50

Cohort is represented by the years in the first column, time of measurement by the years across the top, and age by the values in the cells.

span of days or weeks, typically with the aim of observing change directly as it occurs. For example, researchers might test children every week, starting when they are 12 months old and continuing until 18 months. Microgenetic studies are particularly useful when investigators have hypotheses about a specific period when developmental change should occur (Flynn, Pine, & Lewis, 2006). In this case, researchers arrange to test individuals frequently before, during, and after this period, hoping to see change as it happens (e.g., Opfer & Siegler, 2004).

Microgenetic studies are particularly useful in tracking change as a result of intervention. For example, older adults could be given a series of measures of memory ability and interviewed about their use of memory strategies. A series of training sessions about how to improve memory could be introduced including additional memory tests and interviews, followed by a posttest to find out how well the participants learned the skills they were trained. The microgenetic method would look in detail at the performance of those who learned and improved after training compared to those who did not and search for differences in either the pattern of performance in the memory tests or in the details in the interviews for reasons why some people improved whereas others did not. This would provide a vivid portrait of change over the period of the intervention.

If age changes are found in longitudinal studies, can we say why they occurred? Because only one cohort is studied, cohort effects are eliminated as an explanation of change. However, the other two potential explanations, age and time of measurement, are confounded. For example, suppose we wanted to follow the 1980 cohort over time. If we wanted to test these individuals when they were 20 years old, we would have to do so in 2000. Consequently, any changes we identify could result from changes in underlying processes or factors related to the time we choose to conduct our measurement. For instance, if we conducted a longitudinal study of salary growth, the amount of salary change in any comparison could stem from real change in the skills and worth of the person to the company or from the economic conditions of the times. In a longitudinal study we cannot tell which of these factors is more important.

Longitudinal studies have three additional potential problems. First, if the research measure requires some type of performance by the participants, we may have the problem of practice effects. Practice effects result from the fact that performance may improve over time simply because people are tested over and over again with the same measures. Second, we may have a problem with participant dropout because it is difficult to keep a group of research participants intact over the course of a longitudinal study. Participants may move, lose interest, or die. Participant dropout can result in two different outcomes. We can end up with positive selective survival if the participants at the end of the study tend to be the ones who were initially higher on some variable (e.g. the surviving participants are the ones who were the most healthy at the beginning of the study). In contrast, we could have negative selective survival if the participants at the conclusion of the study were initially lower on an important variable (e.g. the surviving participants may have been those who initially less healthy).

The third problem with longitudinal designs is that our ability to apply the results to other groups is limited. The difficulty is that only one cohort is followed. Whether the pattern of results that is observed in one cohort can be generalized to another cohort is questionable. Thus researchers using longitudinal designs run the risk of uncovering a developmental process that is unique to that cohort.

Because longitudinal designs necessarily take more time and usually are expensive, they have not been used very often. However, researchers now recognize that we badly need to follow individuals over time to further our understanding of the aging process. Thus, longitudinal studies are becoming more common.

Sequential Designs. Thus far, we have considered two developmental designs, each of which has problems involving the confounding of two effects. These

Table 1.4

Sequential Design

Cohort	Time of Measurement			
	2000	2010	2020	2030
1950	50	60	70	80
1960	**40**	**50**	**60**	70
1970	30	**40**	**50**	**60**
1980	20	30	40	50

Cohort is represented by the years in the first column, time of measurement by the years across the top, and age by the values in the cells.

effects are age and cohort in cross-sectional designs, and age and time of measurement in longitudinal designs. These confounds create difficulties in interpreting behavioral differences between and within individuals, as illustrated in the How Do We Know? feature. Some of these interpretive dilemmas can be alleviated by using more complex designs called sequential designs, which are shown in Table 1.4. Keep in mind, though, that sequential designs do not cure the confounding problems in the three basic designs.

Sequential designs *represent different combinations of cross-sectional or longitudinal studies.* In the table, a cross-sequential design consists of two or more cross-sectional studies conducted at two or more times of measurement. These multiple cross-sectional designs include the same age ranges; however, the participants are different in each wave of testing. For example, we might compare performances on intelligence tests for people between ages 20 and 50 in 1980 and then repeat the study in 1990 with a different group of people aged 30 to 60.

Table 1.4 also depicts the longitudinal sequential design. A longitudinal sequential design consists of two or more longitudinal designs that represent two or more cohorts. Each longitudinal design in the sequence begins with the same age range and follows people for the same length of time. For example, we may want to begin a longitudinal study of intellectual development with a group of 50-year-olds in

1980, using the 1930 cohort. We would then follow this cohort for a period of years. In 1990 we would begin a second longitudinal study on 50-year-olds, using the 1940 cohort, and follow them for the same length of time as we follow the first cohort. This design helps clarify whether the longitudinal effects found in a single longitudinal study are cohort-specific or are more general findings.

Although sequential designs are powerful and provide by far the richest source of information about developmental issues, few researchers use them, because they are costly. Trying to follow many people over long periods of time, generating new samples, and conducting complex data analyses are expensive and time consuming. Clearly, this type of commitment to one project is not possible for most researchers.

Integrating Findings from Different Studies

Several times in the past few pages, we've emphasized the value of using different methods to study the same phenomenon. The advantage of this approach is that conclusions are most convincing when the results are the same regardless of method.

In reality, though, findings are often inconsistent. Suppose, for example, many researchers find that people often share personal information with friends (e.g., MySpace or Facebook), some researchers find that people share occasionally with friends, and a few researchers find that people never share with friends. What results should we believe? What should we conclude? **Meta-analysis** *allows researchers to synthesize the results of many studies to estimate relations between variables* (Becker, 2003). In conducting a meta-analysis, investigators find all studies published on a topic over a substantial period of time (e.g., 10 to 20 years), and then record and analyze the results and important methodological variables.

Thus, meta-analysis is a particularly powerful tool because it allows scientists to determine whether a finding generalizes across many studies that used different methods. In addition, meta-analysis can reveal the impact of those different methods on results.

Conflicts between Cross-Sectional and Longitudinal Data

Who was the investigator and what was the aim of the study? In the 1950s, little information was available concerning longitudinal changes in adults' intellectual abilities. What there was showed a developmental pattern of relative stability or slight decline, quite different from the picture of substantial across-the-board decline obtained in cross-sectional studies. To provide a more thorough picture of intellectual change, K. Warner Schaie began the Seattle Longitudinal Study in 1956.

How did the investigator measure the topic of interest? Schaie used standardized tests of primary mental abilities to assess a wide range of abilities such as logical reasoning and spatial ability.

Who were the participants in the study? Over the course of the study, more than 5,000 individuals have been tested at eight testing cycles (1956, 1963, 1970, 1977, 1984, 1991, 1998, and 2005). The participants were representative of the upper 75% of the socioeconomic spectrum and were recruited through a very large health maintenance organization in Seattle. Extensions of the study include longitudinal data on second-generation family members and on the grandchildren of some of the original participants.

What was the design of the study? To provide a thorough view of intellectual change over time, Schaie invented a new type of research design—the sequential design. Participants were tested every 7 years. Like most longitudinal studies, Schaie's sequential study encountered selectivity effects—that is, people who return over the years for retesting tend to do better initially than those who fail to return (in other words, those who don't perform well initially tend to drop out of the study). However, an advantage of Schaie's sequential design is that by bringing in new groups of participants, he was able to estimate the importance of selection effects, a major improvement over previous research.

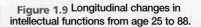

Figure 1.9 Longitudinal changes in intellectual functions from age 25 to 88.

Source: From "Intellectual Development Across Adulthood" by K. Warner Schaie and Faika A. K. Zanjani, in *Handbook of Adult Development and Learning,* ed. by C. Hoare, p. 102. Copyright © 2006 by Oxford University Press.

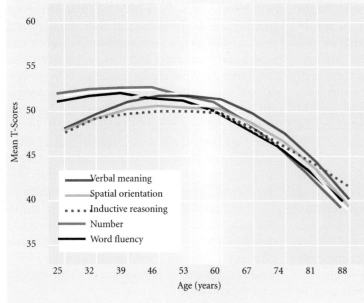

Were there ethical concerns with the study? The most serious issue in any study in which participants are followed over time is confidentiality. Because people's names must be retained for future contact, the researchers were very careful about keeping personal information secure.

What were the results? Among the many important findings from the study are differential changes in abilities over time and cohort effects. As you can see in Figure 1.9, scores on tests of primary mental abilities improve gradually until the late 30s or early 40s. Small declines begin in the 50s, increase as people age into their 60s, and become increasingly large in the 70s (Schaie & Zanjani, 2006).

Cohort differences were also found. Figure 1.10 shows that on some skills, such as inductive reasoning ability, but not others, more recently born younger and middle-aged cohorts performed better than cohorts born earlier. An example of the latter is that older cohorts outperformed younger ones on number skills (Schaie & Zanjani, 2006). These cohort effects probably reflect differences in educational experiences; younger groups' education emphasized figuring things out on one's own, whereas older groups' education emphasized rote learning. Additionally, older groups did not have calculators or computers, so they had to do mathematical problems by hand.

Schaie uncovered many individual differences as well; some people showed developmental patterns closely approximating the overall trends, but others showed unusual patterns. For example, some individuals showed steady declines in most abilities beginning in their 40s and 50s, others showed declines in some abilities but not others, but some people showed little change in most abilities over a 14-year period. Such individual variation in developmental patterns means that average trends, like those depicted in the figures, must be interpreted cautiously; they reflect group averages and do not represent the patterns shown by each person in the group.

Another key finding is that how intellectual abilities are organized in people does not change over time (Schaie et al., 1998). This finding is important because it means that the tests, which presuppose a particular organizational structure of intellectual abilities, can be used across different ages. Additionally, Schaie (1994) identified several variables that appear to reduce the risk of cognitive decline in old age:

- Absence of cardiovascular and other chronic diseases
- Living in favorable environmental conditions (such as good housing)

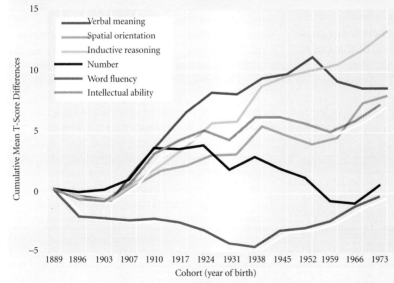

15

Cumulative Mean T-Score Differences

— Verbal meaning
— Spatial orientation
— Inductive reasoning
— Number
— Word fluency
— Intellectual ability

10

5

0

−5

1889 1896 1903 1907 1910 1917 1924 1931 1938 1945 1952 1959 1966 1973

Cohort (year of birth)

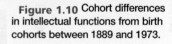

Figure 1.10 Cohort differences in intellectual functions from birth cohorts between 1889 and 1973.

Source: From "Intellectual Development Across Adulthood" by K. Warner Schaie and Faika A. K. Zanjani, in *Handbook of Adult Development and Learning*, ed. by C. Hoare, p. 106. Copyright © 2006 by Oxford University Press.

- Remaining cognitively active through reading and lifelong learning
- Having a flexible personality style in middle age
- Being married to a person with high cognitive status
- Being satisfied with one's life achievements in middle age

What did the investigator conclude? Three points are clear. First, intellectual development during adulthood is marked by a gradual leveling off of gains, followed by a period of relative stability, and then a time of gradual decline in most abilities. Second, these trends vary from one cohort to another. Third, individual patterns of change vary considerably from person to person.

Overall, Schaie's findings indicate that intellectual development in adulthood is influenced by a wide variety of health, environmental, personality, and relationship factors. By attending to these influences throughout adulthood, we can at least stack the deck in favor of maintaining good intellectual functioning in late life.

What converging evidence would strengthen these conclusions? Although Schaie's study is one of the most comprehensive ever conducted, it is limited. Studying people who live in different locations around the world would provide evidence as to whether the results are limited geographically. Additional cross-cultural evidence comparing people with different economic backgrounds and differing access to health care would also provide insight into the effects of these variables on intellectual development.

Conducting Research Ethically

Choosing a good research design involves more than just selecting a particular method. Researchers must determine whether the methods they plan on using are ethical. That is, when designing a research study, investigators must do so in a way that does not violate the rights of people who participate. To verify that every research project has these protections, local panels of experts and community representatives review proposed studies before any data are collected. Only with the approval of this panel can scientists begin their study. If the review panel objects to some aspects of the proposed study, the researcher must revise those aspects and present them anew for the panel's approval. Likewise, each time a component of a study is changed, the review panel must be informed and give its approval.

To guide review panels, professional organizations (e.g., the American Psychological Association) and government agencies (e.g., the National Institutes of Health) have codes of conduct that specify the rights of research participants and procedures to protect these participants. The following essential guidelines are included in all of these codes:

- *Minimize risks to research participants.* Use methods that have the least potential for causing harm or stress for research participants. During the research, monitor the procedures to be sure to avoid any unforeseen stress or harm.

- *Describe the research to potential participants so they can determine whether they wish to participate.* Prospective participants must be told the purpose of the project, what they will be asked to do, whether there are any risks or potential harm, any benefits they may receive, that they are free to discontinue participation at any time without penalty, that they are entitled to a complete debriefing at the end of the project, and any other relevant information the review panel deems appropriate. After the study has been explained, participants sign a document that says they understand what they will do in the study. Special caution must be exercised in obtaining consent for the participation of children and adolescents, as well as people who have conditions that affect intellectual functioning (e.g., Alzheimer's disease, severe head injury). In these cases, consent from a parent, legal guardian, or other responsible person, in addition to the agreement of the person him- or herself, is necessary for participation.

- *Avoid deception; if participants must be deceived, provide a thorough explanation of the true nature of the experiment as soon as possible.* Providing complete information about a study in advance sometimes biases or distorts a person's responses.

Consequently, investigators may provide participants with partial information about the study or even mislead them about its true purpose. As soon as it is feasible—typically just after the experiment—any false information that was given to research participants must be corrected, and the reasons for the deception must be provided.

- *Results should be anonymous or confidential.* Research results should be anonymous, which means that people's data cannot be linked to their name. When anonymity is not possible, research results should be confidential, which means the identity of participants is known only to the investigator conducting the study.

The requirement for informed consent is very important. If prospective participants cannot complete the informed consent procedure themselves, perhaps because they are incapacitated or because they have a condition, such as Alzheimer's disease, that causes intellectual impairment, special cautions must be taken. The American Geriatrics Society (2007), among other professional organizations, published guidelines outlining some of these protections. For example, when the participant cannot understand the consent process, someone else (usually a family member) must complete it. In addition, the researcher must describe the procedures to the participant and still obtain the participant's assent. However, this process is task specific; some

cognitively impaired people, particularly early in the disease process, can respond appropriately to certain types of consent. And researchers can obtain advance consent for future participation when the cognitive impairment is more severe. In all cases, though, researchers must take extra precautions to be sensitive to these individuals; for example, if it becomes apparent that the participant does not like the procedures, the researcher must stop collecting data from that individual.

These ethical principles provide important protections for participants and investigators alike. By treating research participants with respect, investigators are in a better position to make important discoveries about adult development and aging.

Concept Checks

1. What are the three major approaches to measuring a behavior or topic of interest?
2. What are the key differences among experimental, correlational, and case study designs?
3. What three basic effects are examined in all developmental research?
4. What are the advantages and disadvantages of cross-sectional, longitudinal, and sequential designs?
5. What are the limitations of the extreme age groups design?
6. What steps do researchers need to take before conducting a study involving human participants?

Creating sound social policy requires good information. Elected officials and others who create policy rely on research findings to provide the basis for policy. In terms of social policies affecting older adults, the data obtained through the use of the research designs discussed earlier are critical.

For example, research such as Schaie's research on intellectual development described in the How Do We Know? feature had a major impact on the elimination of nearly all mandatory retirement rules in the 1980s. Research on worker satisfaction and post-retirement lifestyles influenced decisions in corporations such as McDonald's and Wal-Mart to hire older adults, who are highly reliable employees.

In each of the remaining chapters we will be highlighting a particular social policy and how it relates to research. By making these ties, you will be able to understand better how research findings can be applied to address social issues.

Summary

1.1 Perspectives on Adult Development and Aging

What is gerontology? How does ageism relate to stereotypes of aging?

- Gerontology is the study of aging from maturity through old age, as well as the study of older adults as a special group.
- Myths of aging lead to negative stereotypes of older people, which can result in ageism, a form of discrimination against older people simply because of their age.

What is the life-span perspective?

- The life-span perspective divides human development into two phases: an early phase (childhood and adolescence) and a later phase (young adulthood, middle age, and old age).
- There are four key features of the life-span perspective: multidirectionality, plasticity, historical context, and multiple causation.

What are the characteristics of the older adult population?

- The number of older adults in the United States and other industrialized countries is increasing rapidly because of better health care, including declines in mortality during childbirth. The large numbers of older adults have important implications for human services.
- The number of older Latino, Asian American, and Native American adults will increase much faster between now and 2050 than will the number of European American and African American older adults.
- Whether older adults reflect individualism or collectivism has implications for interventions.
- The increase in numbers of older adults is most rapid in developing countries.

1.2 Issues in Studying Adult Development and Aging

What four main forces shape development?

- Development is shaped by four forces. Biological forces include all genetic and health-related factors. Psychological forces include all internal perceptual, cognitive, emotional, and personality factors. Sociocultural forces include interpersonal, societal, cultural, and ethnic factors. Life-cycle forces reflect differences in how the same event or combination of biological, psychological, and sociocultural forces affects people at different points in their lives.

What are normative age-graded influences, normative history-graded influences, and nonnormative influences?

- Normative age-graded influences are life experiences that are highly related to chronological age. Normative history-graded influences are events that most people in a specific culture experience at the same time. Nonnormative influences are events that may be important for a specific individual but are not experienced by most people.

How do culture and ethnicity influence aging?

- Culture and ethnicity jointly provide status, social settings, living conditions, and personal experiences for people of all ages. Culture can be defined as shared basic value orientations, norms, beliefs, and customary habits and ways of living, and it provides the basic worldview of a society. Ethnicity is an individual and collective sense of identity based on historical and cultural group membership and related behaviors and beliefs.

What is the meaning of age?

- Three types of aging are distinguished. Primary aging is normal, disease-free development during adulthood. Secondary aging is developmental changes that are related to disease. Tertiary aging is the rapid losses that occur shortly before death.

- Chronological age is a poor descriptor of time-dependent processes and serves only as a shorthand for the passage of calendar time. Time-dependent processes do not actually cause behavior.

- Perceived age is the age you think of yourself as being.

- Better definitions of age include biological age (where a person is relative to the maximum number of years he or she could live), psychological age (where a person is in terms of the abilities people use to adapt to changing environmental demands), and sociocultural age (where a person is in terms of the specific set of roles adopted in relation to other members of the society and culture).

What are the nature–nurture, stability–change, continuity–discontinuity, and the "universal versus context-specific development" issues?

- The nature–nurture issue concerns the extent to which inborn, hereditary characteristics (nature) and experiential, or environmental, influences (nurture) determine who we are. The focus on nature and nurture must be on how they interact.

- The stability–change issue concerns the degree to which people remain the same over time.

- The continuity–discontinuity issue concerns competing views of how to describe change: as a smooth progression over time (continuity) or as a series of abrupt shifts (discontinuity).

- The issue of universal versus context-specific development concerns whether there is only one pathway of development or several. This issue becomes especially important in interpreting cultural and ethnic group differences.

1.3 Research Methods

What approaches do scientists use to measure behavior in adult development and aging research?

- Measures used in research must be reliable (measure things consistently) and valid (measure what they are supposed to measure).

- Systematic observation involves watching people and carefully recording what they say or do. Two forms are common: naturalistic observation (observing people behaving spontaneously in a real-world setting) and structured observations (creating a setting that will elicit the behavior of interest).

- If behaviors are hard to observe directly, researchers often create tasks that sample the behavior of interest.

- Self-reports involve people's answers to questions presented in a questionnaire or interview about a topic of interest.

- Most research on adults has focused on middle-class, well-educated European Americans. This creates serious problems for understanding the development experiences of other groups of people.

What are the general designs for doing research?

- Experiments consist of manipulating one or more independent variables, measuring one or more dependent variables, and randomly assigning participants to the experimental and control groups. Experiments provide information about cause and effect.

- Correlational designs address relations between variables; they do not provide information about cause and effect but do provide information about the strength of the relation between the variables.

- Case studies are systematic investigations of individual people that provide detailed descriptions of people's behavior in everyday situations.

What specific designs are unique to adult development and aging research?

- Age effects reflect underlying biological, psychological, and sociocultural changes. Cohort effects are differences caused by experiences and circumstances unique to the generation to which one belongs. Time-of-measurement effects reflect influences of the specific historical time when one is obtaining information. Developmental research designs represent various combinations of age, cohort, and time-of-measurement effects. Confounding is any situation in which one cannot determine which of two or more effects is responsible for the behaviors being observed.

- Cross-sectional designs examine multiple cohorts and age groups at a single point in time. They can identify only age differences and confound age and cohort. The use of extreme age groups (young and older adults) is problematic in that the samples may not be representative, age should be treated as a continuous variable, and the measures may not be equivalent across age groups.

- Longitudinal designs examine one cohort over two or more times of measurement. They can identify age change but have several problems, including practice effects, dropout, and selective survival. Longitudinal designs confound age and time of measurement. Microgenetic studies are short-term longitudinal designs that measure behaviors very closely over relatively brief periods of time.

- Sequential designs involve more than one cross-sectional (cross-sequential) or longitudinal (longitudinal sequential) design. Although they are complex and expensive, they are important because they help disentangle age, cohort, and time-of-measurement effects.

- Meta-analyses examine the consistency of findings across many research studies.

What ethical procedures must researchers follow?

- Investigators must obtain informed consent from their participants before conducting research.

Review Questions

1.1 Perspectives on Adult Development and Aging

- What are the premises of the life-span perspective?
- How are population demographics changing around the world, and what difference does it make?

1.2 Issues in Studying Adult Development and Aging

- What are the four basic forces in human development?
- What are the major characteristics of normative age-graded, normative history-graded, and nonnormative influences?
- How do nature and nurture interact?
- What are culture and ethnicity?
- In what ways can age be defined? What are the advantages and disadvantages of each definition?
- What is the stability–change issue?
- What is the continuity–discontinuity issue? What kinds of theories derive from each view?
- What is the universal versus context-specific development issue, and how does it relate to sociocultural forces?

1.3 Research Methods

- What are the reliability and validity of a measure?
- What are the three main approaches scientists use to measure behavior in adult development

and aging research? What are the strengths and weaknesses of each?

- How do we know whether a sample is representative?
- What is an experiment? What information does it provide?
- What is a correlational design? What information does it provide?
- What is a case study? What information does it provide?
- What are age, cohort, and time-of-measurement effects? How and why are they important for developmental research?
- What is a cross-sectional design? What are its advantages and disadvantages?
- What is a longitudinal design? What are its advantages and disadvantages?
- What differences are there between cross-sectional and longitudinal designs in terms of uncovering age differences and age changes?
- What are sequential designs? What different types are there? What are their advantages and disadvantages?
- What are the limitations of the extreme age groups design?
- What steps must researchers take to protect the rights of participants?

Integrating Concepts in Development

- Analyze each of the four major controversies in development in terms of the four developmental forces. What real-world examples can you think of that are examples of each combination of controversy and force?
- Using yourself as an example, figure out your age using chronological, perceived, biological, psychological, and sociocultural definitions. How do they differ? Why?
- Using the Leah and Sarah vignette as an example, design cross-sectional, longitudinal, and sequential studies of two different styles of caring for people with Alzheimer's disease. What will you learn from each of the studies?

Key Terms

age effects One of the three fundamental effects examined in developmental research, along with cohort and time-of-measurement effects, which reflects the influence of time-dependent processes on development.

ageism The untrue assumption that chronological age is the main determinant of human characteristics and that one age is better than another.

biological forces One of four basic forces of development that includes all genetic and health-related factors.

biopsychosocial framework Way of organizing the biological, psychological, and sociocultural forces on human development.

case study An intensive investigation of individual people.

cohort A group of people born at the same point or specific time span in historical time.

cohort effects One of the three basic influences examined in developmental research, along with age and time-of-measurement effects, which reflects differences caused by experiences and circumstances unique to the historical time in which one lives.

confounding Any situation in which one cannot determine which of two or more effects is responsible for the behaviors being observed.

continuity–discontinuity controversy The debate over whether a particular developmental phenomenon represents smooth progression over time (continuity) or a series of abrupt shifts (discontinuity).

correlational study An investigation in which the strength of association between variables is examined.

cross-sectional study A developmental research design in which people of different ages and cohorts are observed at one time of measurement to obtain information about age differences.

dependent variable Behaviors or outcomes measured in an experiment.

experiment A study in which participants are randomly assigned to experimental and control groups and in which an independent variable is manipulated to observe its effects on a dependent variable so that cause-and-effect relations can be established.

gerontology The study of aging from maturity through old age.

independent variable The variable manipulated in an experiment.

life-cycle forces One of the four basic forces of development that reflects differences in how the same event or combination of biological, psychological, and sociocultural forces affects people at different points in their lives.

life-span perspective A view of the human life span that divides it into two phases: childhood/adolescence and young/middle/late adulthood.

longitudinal study A developmental research design that measures one cohort over two or more times of measurement to examine age changes.

meta-analysis A technique that allows researchers to synthesize the results of many studies to estimate relations between variables.

microgenetic study A special type of longitudinal design in which participants are tested repeatedly over a span of days or weeks, typically with the aim of observing change directly as it occurs.

nature–nurture controversy A debate over the relative influence of genetics and the environment on development.

nonnormative influences Random events that are important to an individual but do not happen to most people.

normative age-graded influences Experiences caused by biological, psychological, and sociocultural forces that are closely related to a person's age.

normative history-graded influences Events experienced by most people in a culture at the same time.

plasticity The belief that capacity is not fixed, but can be learned or improved with practice.

primary aging The normal, disease-free development during adulthood.

psychological forces One of the four basic forces of development that includes all internal perceptual, cognitive, emotional, and personality factors.

reliability The ability of a measure to produce the same value when used repeatedly to measure the identical phenomenon over time.

secondary aging Developmental changes that are related to disease, lifestyle, and other environmental changes that are not inevitable.

self-reports People's answers to questions about a topic of interest.

sequential designs Types of developmental research designs involving combinations of cross-sectional and longitudinal designs.

sociocultural forces One of the four basic forces of development that includes interpersonal, societal, cultural, and ethnic factors.

stability–change controversy A debate over the degree to which people remain the same over time as opposed to being different.

systematic observation A type of measurement involving watching people and carefully recording what they say or do.

tertiary aging Rapid losses occurring shortly before death.

time-of-measurement effects One of the three fundamental effects examined in developmental research, along with age and cohort effects, which result from the time at which the data are collected.

universal versus context-specific development controversy A debate over whether there is a single pathway of development, or several.

validity The degree to which an instrument measures what it is supposed to measure.

Resources

www.cengage.com/psychology/cavanaugh

Visit the companion website, where you will find tutorial quizzes, glossary, flashcards, and more. You can also access the following websites from the companion website.

Statistical information about older adults on a variety of topics is collected annually by the U.S. government. In addition, several reports are available on such things as demographic projections and health. One good source is the Administration on Aging.

AARP is the largest group of people dedicated to shaping and enriching the experience of aging for all. The organization produces numerous reports and engages in much advocacy work on behalf of midlife and older adults.

One of the best sites on the Web for starting a search for information about any aspect of aging is the Division of Adult Development and Aging

(Division 20) of the American Psychological Association. The division maintains links to many other aging-related sites.

Readings

Baltes, P. B. (1987). Theoretical propositions of life-span developmental psychology: On the dynamics between growth and decline. *Developmental Psychology, 23,* 611–626. One of the great classics, a discussion of basic concepts underlying a life-span perspective; medium difficulty.

Berg, B. L. (2008). *Qualitative research methods for the social sciences* (4th ed.). Boston: Allyn & Bacon. A more detailed discussion of observational, case study, and other nonexperimental research methods; easy to moderate difficulty.

Cavanaugh, J. C., & Whitbourne, S. K. (1999). Research methods. In J. C. Cavanaugh & S. K. Whitbourne (Eds.), *Gerontology: An interdisciplinary perspective* (pp. 33–64). New York: Oxford University Press. A more detailed discussion of general research issues; moderate difficulty.

Malley, G. (2007). *The declaration.* New York: Bloomsbury Publishing. A novel about a society in which the drug Longevity has eradicated aging, explores the issues of overpopulation and the ethics of immortality; easy reading.

McLoyd, V. C. (2004). Linking race and ethnicity to culture: Steps along the road from inference to hypothesis testing. *Human Development, 47,* 185–191. A thorough discussion of the complexities and dynamics of culture from a theoretical perspective; moderate difficulty.

2

Neuroscience as a Basis for Adult Development and Aging

AS DEPICTED IN THE PHOTOGRAPH, YOU SEE AND HEAR MORE AND MORE ADVERTISEMENTS AND literature touting the importance of "brain fitness." In the grocery store and on television, marketers and self-help solicitors are encouraging people to eat the right "brain foods" filled with antioxidants. They make promises that doing this will dampen the effect of

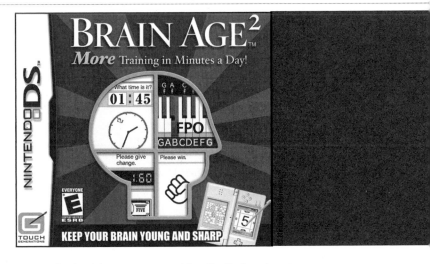

free radicals (which can cause damage to the brain) as we grow older. Similarly, advertisements promote exercising your brain through mental aerobics such as playing chess, reading the newspaper, and attending plays. There is an entire cottage industry of online and computerized brain-training games aimed at delaying the onset of cognitive decline. The lion's share of this media explosion is focused on the aging brain and how to prolong its vitality. This relatively recent phenomenon has coincided with the rapid surge of research in neuroscience or the study of the brain—in particular, plasticity of the aging brain. Evidence that the brain can change for the better as we grow older sends an intriguing message to our aging population. However, the danger in this, as in any relatively new field, is the tendency for the media to reach well beyond the scope of our scientific understanding of the brain.

In this chapter we explore the status of our understanding of the aging brain by examining contemporary theories and recent empirical findings of neuroscience and aging while at the same time outlining future challenges that need to be addressed. First we briefly review the various neuroscience approaches to studying the brain coupled with advances in technology that account for much of the rise in research in this area. Next we focus on cognitive neuroscience and aging including age-related change in brain structure, neurochemical properties, and brain function. Two contemporary areas of research are explored including culture, the brain, and aging as well as neural plasticity in later adulthood. Finally, we explore more recent developments in the area of social neuroscience and aging—in particular, intriguing findings that reveal the neurological underpinnings of enhanced emotional processing in older adulthood as compared to declines in cognitive processing such as the ability to control information in the conscious mind.

2.1 The Neuroscience Approach

LEARNING OBJECTIVES

- How do the basic developmental forces benefit from the neuroscience approach?
- What is the major focus of the neuropsychological approach to neuroscience?
- Describe the difference between the correlational approach and the activation imaging approach to studying neuroscience.
- What is the difference between MRI and fMRI scanning?

At age 70, Margaret was diagnosed as having a tumor in her right motor cortex. She was treated with radiation therapy. Surgery could have left her paralyzed on the left side. With the aid of image-guided surgery, the tumor was found to be more accurately located in the front of the motor cortex. The tumor was removed and Margaret recovered comfortably.

An advanced technology involving a magnetic resonance imaging (MRI) scan was conducted on Margaret. This allowed areas of the brain associated with specific functions to be identified and the level of activity in these areas to be monitored. The scan produced an image showing the anatomical location of interest and the degree to which it was activated. In this case it was used to show more accurately the outline of a tumor and the critical areas of the cerebral cortex, especially those areas involved in controlling movement, sensation, speech, or vision. In addition to the clinical implications of MRI scanning, we are interested in how such tools advance our understanding of how the brain changes as we grow older. Do the changes reflect decline, stability, or perhaps improvement and compensation? Is there plasticity in the aging brain? These are important questions that researchers in the field of contemporary neuroscience and aging are exploring.

The 21st century has been described as the century of the brain. This is partly a function of numerous recent technological advances, such as the development of magnetic resonance imaging (MRI) that was used in Margaret's surgery. This procedure and others have facilitated the study of brain structure and functions using noninvasive methods. Because of these advances we can now more systematically examine the links between brain function and behavior in living beings. Of particular importance to the graying of America, neuroscientific approaches are being widely applied to research questions that deal with both cognitive and social-emotional aging. Although the greater part of neuroscience and aging research has focused on cognitive functioning alone in older adults, recently researchers have used these techniques to investigate processing preferences for emotional compared to neutral information in older adults (see Mather, Canli, English et al., 2004). Similarly, research in the emerging field of social cognitive neuroscience has shown associations between brain structures and a variety of social cognitive tasks such as person perception, stereotypes, and theory of mind (Amodio & Frith, 2006; Ochsner & Lieberman, 2001). One of the challenges for adult development theories will be to incorporate these models and techniques into our conceptual understanding of the aging process. We will introduce the neuroscience approach in this chapter and refer back to this approach when we tackle the specific areas of cognition, social cognition, and emotion.

A neuroscientific approach to the study of aging has specific advantages. For example, one particularly beneficial outcome of this approach to research is that the neuroscience approach has taken intervention research to new pinnacles. Interventions that are important in enhancing the quality of life of older adults can now be evaluated not only by observing behavioral change but also at the neurological level (e.g., Colcombe, Erickson, Raz et al., 2003). In particular, the neuroscience approach offers a new level of analysis to understanding cognitive and social-emotional functioning. For example, neuroscience research demonstrates that areas of the brain related to visual processing decline with age. This provides a neurobiological link for behavioral studies that show decline in visual functioning in older age is linked to declines in cognitive performance (Baltes & Lindenberger, 1997).

Implications of the Developmental Forces

The neuroscience approach offers a new level of analysis relating to the life-span thread that runs throughout this book, that is, behavior and development are multiply determined. At the simplest level, age is not the best predictor of behavior. As we learned earlier, age is related to specific psychological, social, and biological phenomena that are associated with age-related change. Behavior across the life span is determined by multiple forces, some of which are age-related, such as biological changes, differing opportunity structures in society, and changes in motivational orientations and emotional functioning. From the perspective of neuroscience and aging, researchers now acknowledge that cognitive, social, and emotional change in older adulthood is influenced at multiple levels of analysis including both structural changes in brain volume and density and functional changes of brain areas. We must consider these biological changes in concert with behavior levels of analysis, including performance on cognitive tasks and social variables such as the positive and negative effects of stereotyping on cognition. As indicated, more complete investigation of these multiple forces on development has become more tractable for the biological level of analysis as new technologies and research methods, such as brain imaging, have evolved.

Advances in understanding the dynamic and interactive process of these levels of analysis will be best exemplified when we talk about plasticity of the brain later in this chapter. Instead of simply looking at changes at the behavioral level, we can more directly observe the influence of environmental interventions on the structure and activation of the brain itself. This can have important implications for our understanding of irreversible and reversible changes in the brain and the possibility for behavioral changes that can occur throughout the life span. We have more converging evidence on the degree to which social interventions, biological interventions, and psychological interventions influence positive change and negative change as we grow older.

Neuroscience Tools

Magnetic resonance imaging (MRI) is a noninvasive technique that employs a powerful magnet (the MRI scanner) and radio waves to produce images of the brain. Whereas an MRI focuses on the structure of the brain, functional magnetic resonance imaging (fMRI) focuses on the function of the brain. The MRI scanner has the ability to monitor the blood flow to different regions of

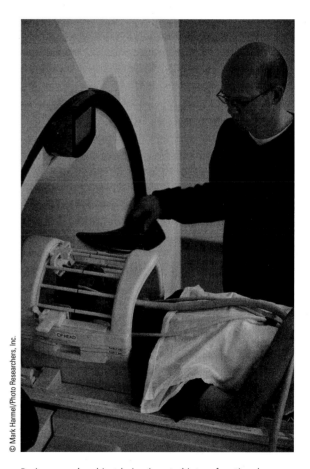

© Mark Harmel/Photo Researchers, Inc.

Brain research subject being inserted into a functional magnetic resonance imaging machine (fMRI). Special glasses are being worn to measure visual stimulation. Functional magnetic resonance imaging (fMRI) is used to visualize brain function, by visualizing changes in chemical composition of brain areas or changes in the flow of fluids that occur over timespans of seconds to minutes. The fMRI model is a Siemens Trio 3T MR Scanner.

the brain as the participants in a particular study respond to specific stimuli such as an image of a face, words, or sounds. The difference between the MRI and the fMRI is that the more conventional MRI provides static snapshots of specific brain structures, whereas the fMRI monitors activities in the brain that are time-locked to behavioral performance.

These techniques and others offer new opportunities to test models of cognitive aging. Neuroscience has become increasingly more relevant to cognitive aging research as the focus has expanded beyond studying pathologies of the aging brain, such as Alzheimer's or Parkinson's disease, toward investigating normal and healthy aging. In addition, neuroscientific data are more informative for models of cognitive aging and usher in increased progress in the field by testing established theories using cutting-edge methods. Furthermore, examination of the structure and function of the brain has become even more informative for cognitive aging research as the focus has shifted from describing brain activation patterns toward explaining them. However, it is easy to be seduced by these novel and available methods of neuroscientific investigation. The field of neuroscience and aging must be careful to base empirical studies on a solid theoretical foundation. The field of cognitive aging is a good example of an area that has profited from major advances in neuroimaging techniques, which have revealed findings that enhance our understanding of normal and pathological aging, yet require theoretical explanations (see Cabeza, 2004; Hedden & Gabrieli, 2004; Kramer, Fabiani, & Colcombe, 2006).

Neuroscience Perspectives

Researchers take three general methodological perspectives in tackling the neuroscience of aging: the neuropsychological, the correlational, and the activation imaging approach (see Cabeza, 2004). *The* **neuropsychological approach** *compares brain functioning of healthy older adults with adults displaying various pathological disorders in the brain.* In this approach researchers are interested in whether patients of any age with damage in specific regions of the brain show similar cognitive deficits to those shown by healthy older adults. If this is the case, then researchers can conclude that decline in cognitive functioning as we grow older may be related to unfavorable changes in the same specific regions of the brain observed in the brain-damaged patients. This type of comparison is typically made between healthy older adults and patients showing frontal lobe damage. For example, patients with brain damage in the frontal lobe display lower levels of dopamine (an important brain transmitter substance), which results in a decrease in speed of processing (resembling what is observed in healthy older adults). Another important objective of research using this approach is to isolate the neural or brain mechanisms that are associated with both normal and pathological decline in cognitive functions. These findings stimulate theoretical development by identifying influential factors that warrant theoretical explanation as to how and why these factors may cause cognitive decline as we age.

The **correlational approach** *attempts to link measures of cognitive performance to measures of brain structure or functioning.* For example, a researcher may be interested in the correlation between cognitive behavior, such as the ability to control the contents of the conscious mind using working memory, and neural structural measures, such as the volume of the brain (Raz, 2000). This example focuses on the role of brain structure in explaining cognitive decline (see Raz, 2000). Instead of direct measures of brain structure or functioning, some researchers investigate the correlation between behavioral tests that are associated with the function of specific brain regions (e.g., frontal lobe tests). However, this latter approach is more speculative in that there can be much uncertainty as to whether the tests accurately reflect anatomical and functional authenticity of the specific brain region under investigation.

Finally, *the* **activation imaging approach** *attempts to directly link functional brain activity with cognitive behavioral data.* This approach allows the in vivo investigation of changes in brain

What Do People Believe about Brain Fitness?

With all the hype about keeping your brain fit, what do people believe you have to do to accomplish this? To find out, ask some people of different ages these questions: What happens to the brain as we grow older? What do you think causes these changes? What do you think you can do to make sure that the brain stays fit as you grow older? Compile the results from your interviews and compare them with what you discover in this chapter. To what extent do people's beliefs correspond to the scientific evidence? In which areas are they completely off base?

function as they affect cognitive performance in older adults. For example, studies using this approach have found that younger adults' brains show unilateral activation (i.e., activation in only one hemisphere of the brain) when they perform specific cognitive tasks whereas older adults' brains tend to show increased activation in both brain hemispheres when performing the same tasks (see Cabeza, 2002). As we will discuss later, this differential activation in younger and older adult brains may provide neurological evidence that older adults undergo **compensatory** *changes that allow them to adapt to the inevitable decline of specific areas of the brain.*

Overall, these neuroscientific approaches to studying cognitive aging promote theoretical development in the field of adulthood in several ways. First, theories can be further tested using these approaches. For instance, the idea that we can selectively direct our attention to specific characteristics of our environment can be further validated by examining how age-related changes in performance are associated with both functional and structural brain variables. In other words, we can explain how the brain influences performance. This also could be investigated in the maturing brains of adolescents and children. Second, research methods that focus on the age-related changes in the architecture and functioning of the brain can help to explain why certain cognitive functions, such as well-practiced tasks, vocabulary, and wisdom, can be preserved

into old age while other functions, such as processing speed, decline rapidly as people age.

Neuroscientific methods, however, have limitations (Cabeza, 2004). For instance, documenting activities in different brain regions does not necessarily imply that different psychological processes are involved (e.g., sensory motor functioning, vision, and hearing may be similar cognitive processes but may engage different regions of the brain). Nevertheless, advances in the field of neuroscience have had a major impact on our understanding of cognitive aging because they have revealed new findings that psychological theories have to account for and be consistent with.

Before we explore some of the scientific research on age-related changes in the brain, complete the Discovering Development exercise. Compare your findings with the evidence described in the text that follows. What similarities and differences are revealed?

Concept Checks

1. How might developmental forces interact in the context of understanding brain changes as we grow older?
2. What is the basic premise of the neuropsychological approach to neuroscience?
3. What are the limitations of the correlational approach to neuroscience?
4. What is the major advantage of the activation imaging approach?

2.2 Neuroscience and Cognitive Aging

LEARNING OBJECTIVES
* What are the basic structural changes in the brain as we age?
* What cognitive functions are associated with volume shrinkage in the aging brain?
* How do decreases in the dopaminergic system relate to changes in cognitive functioning as we grow older?
* What happens to brain activation as we age?
* What are the cultural implications of neuroimaging?
* How does bilateral activation serve a functional role in older adults' cognitive functioning?
* What are the major differences between the HAROLD and STAC models of brain activation and aging?

Samuel is 73 and he is worried about contracting Alzheimer's disease. He remembers that his father became disoriented at this age and had trouble remembering things that he was just told. How can Samuel find out if his brain is aging normally or pathologically? Psychological tests are somewhat, but not completely, predictive of disease. This is a dilemma older adults are facing in our society today.

A major thrust of adult development and aging research has focused on cognitive aging, both normal and pathological. The development of classic theories of cognitive aging has been primarily based on behavioral data (see Chapter 6; Salthouse, 1996; Schaie, 1996). More recently the availability of neuroscientific methods such as those described earlier has stimulated research that allows us to study cognitive processes—and changes in these processes—in the living brain using noninvasive brain imaging techniques, such as the magnetic resonance imaging (MRI) and functional magnetic resonance imaging (fMRI) techniques discussed earlier. For example, Stephen Rao and his colleagues found a means to identify Alzheimer's disease as much as 10–15 years before memory problems and other symptoms occured (Leveroni, Seidenbert, Mayer, Mead, Binder, &

Rao, 2000). By focusing on the brain's ability to recognize famous faces, they discovered that images of famous faces activate those areas of the brain that are first assaulted by Alzheimer's disease. They suggested that a lack of activity in these regions may signal the onset of the disease. This is exactly the type of information in which Samuel would be interested. In order to make these types of discoveries, we must first have a strong knowledge base of how the brain ages normally. Let's examine what the field of neuroscience and aging has contributed to our knowledge of the aging brain.

Structure of the Brain

It will be useful at this point to provide a brief overview of the anatomy of the human brain (see Figure 2.1). Neuroanatomy is fundamental to the discipline of neuroscience, and we will refer to a number of brain regions that exhibit age-related changes in both structure and function. The cerebral cortex is the area to which neuroscience has dedicated most of its effort. In this area, there are two major hemispheres, right and left, which are linked via a thick bundle of axons called the corpus callosum.

Each region of the brain has distinguishing features. For example, in most people, language processing is associated primarily with the left hemisphere, whereas recognizing nonspeech sounds, emotions, and faces is associated with the right hemisphere. As we shall see in the following sections, the frontal cortex is a focal area for research. This area is intimately involved in *higher-order* **executive functions** such as *the ability to make and carry out plans, switch between tasks, and maintain attention and focus*. In addition, there is the cerebellar cortex which contains the **cerebellum**. Details regarding the functional aspects of the various regions of the brain will be discussed more fully with respect to age-related change.

Age-Related Changes in the Structure of the Brain. The majority of studies examining structural changes

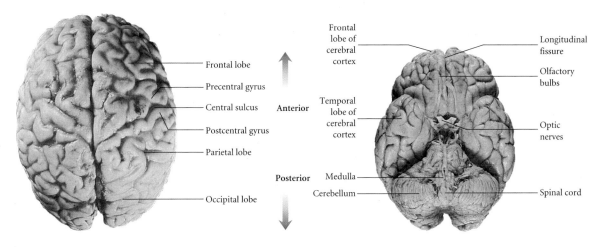

Figure 2.1   The human brain.

Source: From James W. Kalat, Biological Psychology, 10E, Figure 1.1, Pg 2. © 2009 Wadsworth, a part of Cengage Learning, Inc. Reproduced by permission. Courtesy of Dr. Dana Copeland.

in the brain as we grow older have applied a correlational approach by employing postmortem analyses of young and older adult brains or by using cross-sectional and longitudinal designs to examine age differences in the brain using structural MRI techniques. In these studies, different regions of the brain are examined in terms of thinning and shrinkage in volume and density. Other structural deficiencies can also be detected such as the declining health of the white matter of the brain, or white matter hyperintensities (WMH). WMH is determined by the observation of high signal intensity or a bright spotty appearance which indicates brain pathologies such as myelin loss or neural atrophy (Nordahl, Ranganath, Yonelinas, DeCarli, Fletcher, & Jagust, 2006).

Overall, postmortem and neuroimaging studies demonstrate that considerable shrinkage occurs in the aging brain. However, this shrinkage is selective (Raz & Rodrigue, 2006). For example, *the prefrontal cortex,* the **hippocampus** (*which is associated with memory*), and the cerebellum show profound shrinkage (Raz & Rodrigue, 2006). The sensory cortices, such as the visual cortex, show relatively little shrinkage.

The white matter area also shows deterioration with increasing age. A *neuroimaging method* called **diffusion tensor imaging (DTI)** *assesses the rate and direction that water diffuses through the white matter.* This results in an index of density or structural health of the white matter (Park & Reuter-Lorenz, 2008). By using DTI, studies examining WMH have demonstrated that such disruptions of white matter integrity may represent a mechanism for prefrontal cortex dysfunction in older adults (Nordahl et al., 2006). As we will see later, this has important implications for cognitive functioning in older adulthood. Of particular importance is the fact that WMH are linked to cerebrovascular disease (e.g., hypertension), which is preventable and can be treated through medication and changes in lifestyle. The critical issue is that it is possible that some of the age-related cognitive decline we observe can be treated or even prevented (Nordahl et al., 2006).

An important question to ask in order to understand the impact of these deteriorating structural changes in the aging brain is how they relate to cognitive functioning. With increasing age, many facets of information processing become less efficient, including speed of processing, executive function, and declarative long-term memory. Memory and executive function have received a preponderance of attention in the cognitive neuroscience and aging literature. Executive functioning includes processes such as inhibitory control or the ability to control the contents of the conscious mind using working memory. Executive function failures in older adults include erroneous selection of irrelevant information to process in working memory, the inability to divert attention away from irrelevant information to the task in question, and attentional dysregulation such as inefficiency in switching tasks among others (Park & Reuter-Lorenz, 2008). For example, when older adults are reading an article that is filled with information that is true and false, even if they are told which information is false, they still have a difficult time factoring out the false information in their understanding of the article.

Some evidence suggests that volume shrinkage in the brain is linked to poor cognitive performance on such tasks. For example, WMH in nondemented, healthy older adults have been linked to lower cognitive test scores and decreased executive functioning (de Groot, de Leeuw, Oudkert, van Gijn, Hofman, Jolles, & Breteler, 2002; Madden, Whiting, Huettel, White, MacFall, & Provenzale, 2004). Poor performance on executive functioning tasks has also been linked with decreased volume of the prefrontal cortex (Raz & Rodrigue, 2006). Studies also have shown that observed reductions in cortical volume in the hippocampal regions are related to memory decline (Rosen, Prull, Gabrieli, Stoub, O'Hara et al., 2003). It should be noted, however, that studies of the role of frontal volume as a predictor of cognitive function have yielded some inconsistent findings. Whereas some studies have found prefrontal volume to be linked to working memory performance (holding and manipulating information in consciousness); Salat, Kaye, & Janowsky, 2002), others have not (Gunning-Dixon & Raz, 2003). Nevertheless, overall, the majority of evidence suggests that age-related change in frontal regions of the brain correlates with executive dysfunction and memory decline (Buckner, 2004).

Similar to the point made earlier regarding WMH, Buckner (2004) points out that age-related decline in vascular functioning may affect white matter structures that underlie the areas important to executive functioning. Finally, decline in other areas of cognitive performance has been differentially linked to specific brain regions. Acquiring new skills has been linked to volumes of the striatum, prefrontal cortex, and cerebellum; spatial memory has been linked to hippocampal volume (Raz & Rodrigue, 2006).

The neuropsychological approach also has shed light on the link between structural changes in the aging brain and cognitive functioning. A proliferation of research has examined specific areas in the temporal lobe (medial-temporal) and its influence on memory by examining patients with Alzheimer's disease. For example, brain atrophy, cellular pathology, and cell loss are observed in this region of the brain in Alzheimer's patients, who also show profound memory impairment (Buckner, 2004). As Buckner points out, this has raised challenges to aging research by asking the question about whether Alzheimer's disease is reflective of an acceleration of normal aging processes as opposed to a disease process. Indeed, research on nondemented older adults has found similar correlations between medial-temporal lobe atrophy and poor memory performance (Rodrigue & Raz, 2004), although again this conclusion is not straightforward, as other studies have not found such an association (Van Petten, 2004).

In a recent review, Raz and Rodrigue (2006) pointed out that much of the conflicting findings in this area could be a result of the sample composition, whether cross-sectional differences or longitudinal changes are being examined, whether different subregions are under investigation, and whether different cognitive tests are used. One way to handle some of these concerns is to provide converging evidence from both cross-sectional and longitudinal studies of brain structure changes. For example, Raz and Rodrigue (2006) point to converging evidence between these two approaches that suggests age-related increases in white matter lesions. In addition, the prefrontal cortex, hippocampus, and cerebellum appear to be aging-sensitive. With respect to linkages between brain structure and cognitive performance, longitudinal studies indicate a stronger relationship. By examining individual differences in change, longitudinal studies converge with cross-sectional studies showing that increases in WMH are associated with reduced performance on executive functioning tasks (Cook, Leuchter, Morgan, Dunkin, Witte, David et al., 2004).

Age-Related Changes in Neurochemical Properties

Advances have also been made in techniques measuring neurochemical changes in the aging brain, particularly in studies examining the role of brain dopamine (DA), a neurotransmitter substance that sends messages throughout the brain, in performance on various cognitive tasks (Bäckman, Nybert, Lindenberger, Li, & Farde, 2006). First, it is important to note that the **dopaminergic system** *is associated with higher-level cognitive functioning like inhibiting thoughts, attention, and planning* (Park & Reuter-Lorenz, 2008). In other words, high dopamine levels are linked to cognitive processing that is effortful and deliberate, but not to the processes that are more automatic and less effortful. To investigate dopamine, the majority of studies have used postmortem analyses, neuropsychological patient studies, and simulated modeling and the imaging of dopamine activity. Bäckman et al. (2006) have drawn several conclusions regarding this research. For example, there is increasingly clear evidence that effective functioning of the dopaminergic system declines in normal aging.

Researchers have found that declines in the dopaminergic system are related to declines in episodic memory and speed tasks (Bäckman, Ginovart, Dixon, Robins, Wahlin, Wahlin, Halldin, & Farde, 2000), age-related deficits in working memory (Erixon-Linddroth, Farde, Robins, Wahlin, Sovago, Halldin, & Bäckman, 2005), as well as declines in memory (Yang, Chiu, Chen, Chen, Yeh, & Lee,

2003). As we shall see in Chapter 6, these are cognitive tasks that are effortful and not automatic. Less age differences are observed in more automatic tasks like familiarity of information. Overall, the brief review of studies using molecular methods to examine dopamine changes with increasing age suggest that dopaminergic receptors play a role in cognitive aging. These studies expand our understanding of the neurochemical processes affected by increasing age that influence structural and cognitive changes.

Age-Related Changes in Brain Activity

We have just reviewed the literature addressing structural and neurochemical changes in the brain as we grow older and how deteriorative structural changes relate to decreases in cognitive functioning. We now explore other brain-related factors that might explain age differences in cognitive functioning: age-related changes in brain activity. **Functional imaging** (e.g., fMRI) *examines how changes in brain activity occur in correspondence to changes in task demands and the type of cognitive functioning under investigation.* In other words, we are interested in examining the functional consequences of age-related deterioration in specific brain structures. A second aim of these types of studies is to identify patterns of how the brain recruits different regions for activation in older adults that may occur in service of compensation when tasks pose a distinct difficulty. In other words, do older adults in comparison to younger adults recruit different regions of the brain in order to perform cognitive tasks more effectively? This could reveal, on the one hand, neurological underpinnings of the cognitive decline observed in older adults. On the other hand, perhaps these changes reflect adaptive accommodations that the brain makes in order to assist older adults to adjust to the neurological impairment that occurs with increasing age. This would allow them to function adaptively in everyday life.

Functional Consequences of Brain Deterioration

The major theoretical approach reviewed above focuses on age-related changes in brain function and is typically labeled the frontal lobe theory of aging (Buckner, 2004; Raz, 2000; West, 1996). This theoretical approach suggests that the many age-related declines in cognitive functioning are a function of insults to the frontal lobes, both structurally and neurochemically. Functional neuroimaging examines the neural substrates of cognitive decline. The typical finding that corroborates this approach is reduced activation in older as compared to younger adults in prefrontal and medial-temporal areas supporting cognitive functioning, such as memory (Grady, McIntosh, Horwitz, Maisog, Ungerleider et al., 1995; Logan, Sanders, Snyder, Morris, & Buckner, 2002). Interestingly, some studies also have shown a marked increase in prefrontal activity during cognitive tasks, specifically memory, in older adults as compared to younger adults (Cabeza, Anderson, Locantorre, & McIntosh, 2002; Grady, Bernstein, Siegenthaler, & Beig, 2002; Gutchess et al., 2005). However, we will come back to this point later.

An example of the first finding is a fairly recent study that demonstrated age-related differences in activation of the anterior cingulate cortex during a verbal working memory task (Otsuka, Osaka, Morishita, Kondo, & Osaka, 2006). As indicated earlier, working memory is linked to executive functioning and involves temporary storage and processing of information which supports higher-order cognitive functioning. In particular, it serves an attentional role by controlling attentional resources for performance on cognitive tasks. *The **anterior cingulate cortex** is affiliated with the prefrontal cortex and is also involved in executive control* (Bunge, Klineberg, Jacobsen, & Gabrieli, 2000). The overall finding is that reduced working memory performance is related to decreased activation of the anterior cingulate cortex in older adults as compared to younger adults (Otsuka et al., 2006). Other research further supports this finding, suggesting that reduced brain activation

or **under-recruitment** of the prefrontal cortex occurs during intentional cognitive processing (Buckner, 2004).

Furthermore, Buckner (2004) points out that reduced frontal recruitment in aging is context-dependent. For example, research has demonstrated that older adults show reduced activation or recruitment of the appropriate frontal regions associated with intentional memory. At the same time older adults recruit these regions almost to the same degree as younger adults when support is offered during a memory encoding task (Logan, Sanders, Snyder, Morris, & Buckner, 2002). The researchers have concluded that this may be a matter of decreased flexibility on the part of older adults to produce effective retrieval strategies. However, other studies have shown that younger and older adults display comparable frontal activity or recruitment, for example, when examining memory retrieval (Schacter et al., 1996). As we will see later in this chapter, an increase in frontal recruitment may serve adaptive functioning purposes in older adults.

Culture, Neuroimaging, and Aging

Before we examine adaptive functioning and changes in the brain, we will look at another important area that is receiving growing attention: the interplay between culture and neurobiological aging as it affects the mind. Denise Park has spearheaded this approach by asking questions such as where we are likely to find neurocultural differences in the aging brain. She became particularly interested in the ventral visual cortex, which is the perceptual region of the brain. This is a highly specialized region that shows little shrinkage with age. Interestingly, some areas of age-related changes in perceptual processing do not show cultural differences, whereas other areas do (Goh, Chee, Tan, Venkatraman, Hebrank et al., 2007). For example, older adults from Western cultures showed significantly greater object-processing adaptation in the **lateral occipital complex,** which is involved in visual processing, than did older East Asians, who showed almost no adaptation (Goh et al., 2007). This finding provides neuroimaging evidence for

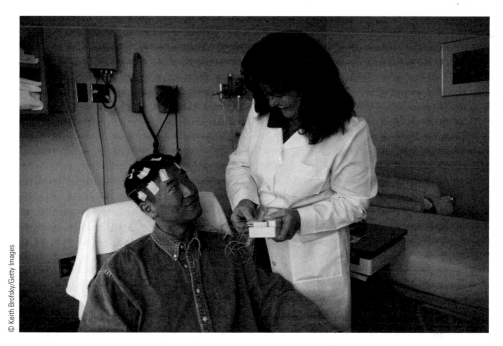

© Keith Brofsky/Getty Images

Monitoring Epilepsy

cultural biases in perceptual processing of objects. Overall, however, age-related change seems to have a more profound effect on changes in brain functioning than culture.

Compensation and Prefrontal Bilaterality

One of the most significant findings in the cognitive aging neuroscience literature is the observed discontinuity of neural activation patterns when comparing younger and older adults' brain activity during the performance of cognitive tasks. As indicated earlier, it is not simply that older adults show reduced activation in regions associated with a particular cognitive task. Initial studies focusing on verbal working memory and long-term memory presented evidence for focal, unilateral activity in the left prefrontal region in younger adults and **bilateral activation** (*i.e., in both the left and right prefrontal areas*) in older adults when performing the same tasks (Buckner, 2004; Cabeza, 2002; Reuter-Lorenz, 2002). These findings ushered in a flurry of discussion as to what this means for the

aging brain. Is the older brain working harder to compensate for deterioration in these focal regions related to the cognitive task, or is its inefficient operation of inhibitory mechanisms rendering the activation as interference to optimal functioning (Park & Reuter-Lorenz, 2008)?

In a recent review of this literature, Park and Reuter-Lorenz (2008) noted that there is now a growing body of evidence indicating that this bilateral activation in older adults may serve a functional and supportive role in their cognitive functioning. Findings include the association between bilateral activation in older adults and higher performance (not found in younger adults) (Cabeza et al., 2002; Reuter-Lorenz et al., 2001; Rypma & D'Esposito, 2001) in a number of tasks including category learning tasks, visual field tasks, and various memory tasks. Figure 2.2 shows that there is more frontal bilateral activity in older adults during working memory tasks than in younger adults (Park & Reuter-Lorenz, 2008). On the left side of the figure, you can see that there is left lateralized frontal engagement in younger adults, whereas older adults further engage the right frontal areas.

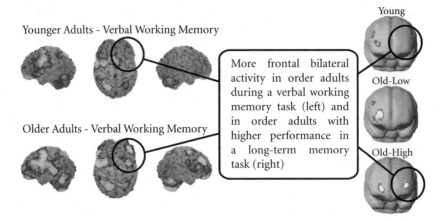

Figure 2.2 Frontal bilaterality is increased with age.

Source: Park, D. C., & Reuter-Lorenz, P. (2008). The Adaptive Brain: Aging and Neurocognitive Scaffolding. Copyright 2009, Reprinted with permission from the Annual Review of Psychology, Volume 60, www.annualreviews.org

The right side demonstrates that younger adults and low-performing older adults show right lateralized activation during a long-term memory task. Interestingly, high-performing older adults show bilateral frontal engagement. It may be that high-functioning older adults are more adept at compensating for normative deterioration in the brain by utilizing other areas of the brain. Whether or not this is an accurate conclusion is still being debated in the literature. We will examine this in the Current Controversies section.

More recently, Park and Reuter-Lorenz (2008) have proposed the STAC (*scaffolding theory of cognitive aging*) model. They maintain that one needs to push the envelope regarding the compensatory role of bilateral activation and **over-recruitment.** In other words, one must ask what aspects of cognitive function the compensation serves. For example, there is growing evidence that the increase in frontal activity in older adults may be a response to the decreased efficiency of neural processing related to the perceptual areas of the brain (Park & Reuter-Lorenz, 2008). Interesting findings also have emerged when examining the **default network** of the brain. *This refers to regions of the brain that are most active at rest,* for example, when an individual lies quietly in the magnetic imaging machine and is not directly engaged in a cognitive task (Raichle et al., 2001). When an individual

begins a demanding cognitive task, this default network is suppressed. A number of researchers have found that older adults display less suppression of this default network than younger adults do (Grady et al., 2006) and that this is related to lower cognitive performance (Persson et al., 2007). Thus, this failure to shift from a resting state to a more active state to engage in cognitive processing may be another reason for increased frontal activity in older adults (Reuter-Lorenz & Cappell, 2008; Reuter-Lorenz & Lustig, 2005).

The STAC model (Park & Reuter-Lorenz, 2008) suggests that the reason older adults continue to perform at high levels despite neuronal deterioration is because of compensatory scaffolding. This is the recruitment of additional circuitry to bolster functional decline. A difference between this model and others is that compensation is not simply a neural response to brain insults as we grow older, but the brain's response to challenge in general. Thus, you may see this occurring when younger adults are learning a new task. Learning moves from effortful processing to overlearning. The neurological shift is from a broader dispersed network (the scaffold) to a more focal and optimal circuit of neural regions. However, what Park and Reuter-Lorenz point out is that the initial scaffolding remains available as a secondary circuitry that can be counted on when performance is challenged. This is what older adults

A number of studies have shown evidence for increased frontal bilaterality and decreased hippocampal activity in older adults across numerous tasks including attention, working memory, and long-term memory (Cabeza et al., 2004), suggesting the global nature of this phenomenon. In sum, additional age-related neural activation (especially in prefrontal areas) may be functional and adaptive for optimal performance. Researchers now suggest that these activation patterns may reflect an adaptive brain that functionally reorganizes (Park & Reuter-Lorenz, 2008).

A number of models have been used to attempt to explain these findings, including the HAROLD model by Cabeza (2002), the CRUNCH model developed by Reuter-Lorenz and her colleagues (Reuter-Lorenz, 2002; Reuter-Lorenz & Mikels, 2006), and most recently the STAC model (Park & Reuter-Lorenz, 2008). Again, these models make the assumption that the primary reason for greater activation in different brain regions as well as bilaterality is the need for the recruitment of additional brain regions in order to successfully execute cognitive functions.

As indicated, numerous studies have documented the fact that younger adults show unilateral brain activation when performing various cognitive tasks. In contrast, older adults' brains tend to show increased activation in both brain hemispheres. This finding has led to various theoretical developments including the formation of the HAROLD (*hemispheric asymmetry reduction in older adults*) model (Cabeza, 2002). The HAROLD model elegantly explains the empirical findings of reduced lateralization in prefrontal lobe activity in older adults. It suggests that the function of the reduced lateralization is compensatory in nature, that is, additional neural units are being recruited to increase attentional resources, processing speed, or inhibitory control.

According to the CRUNCH (*compensation-related utilization of neural circuits hypothesis*) model developed by Reuter-Lorenz and her colleagues (Reuter-Lorenz, 2002; Reuter-Lorenz & Mikels, 2006), the aging brain adapts to neurological decline by recruiting additional neural circuits (in comparison to younger adults) to perform tasks adequately. This model incorporates bilaterality of activation, but suggests this is not the only form of compensation. Two main mechanisms are suggested that the older brain uses to perform tasks: "more of the same" and "supplementary processes." When task demands are increased, more activation can be found in the same brain region relative to easier tasks. This effect can be found in younger as well as older adults. In older adults, neural efficiency declines, and therefore additional neuronal circuits are recruited earlier than in younger adults. **Supplementary processes** are taking place *when different brain regions are activated to compensate for lacking processing resources.* Reduced lateralization is one way of recruiting additional resources. In addition, however, compared to younger adults' brains, older adult brains also show overactivation in different brain regions, suggesting that compensation can take different forms in the aging brain.

These findings have stimulated scientific debates on the mechanisms and functional adaptiveness of reduced lateralization. Whereas Cabeza and Reuter-Lorenz and colleagues interpret their findings in the light of a compensational framework, other researchers have challenged this interpretation by suggesting that the over-recruitment of neurons is not necessarily specific to the areas that control the identified cognitive processes (see Kramer et al., 2006; Logan, Sanders, Snyder, Morris, & Buckner, 2002). If researchers cannot link the over-recruitment to specific processes to improve cognitive functioning, then a compensation interpretation is in question. This highlights the fact that to date theoretical work and empirical data in the field of neurocognitive science are still in the early stages of development. Therefore, definitive conclusions about the adaptiveness and functionality of the observed patterns of increased brain activation cannot be drawn at this point in time.

may be doing. However, scaffolded networks are less efficient than the honed, focal ones. For older adults, the focal networks become less efficient, and therefore they engage in the scaffolded circuits which may be less efficient and associated with poorer performance. The trade-off is that without the scaffolding, performance would be even worse because older adults would have to rely on the more focal areas. The elegance of this model is that older adults' performance can be understood in terms of factors that impact decline and those that impact compensation. As Park and Reuter-Lorenz argue, this integrative approach embraces a lifelong potential for plasticity and the ability to adapt to age-related changes.

In sum, neuroscientific methods have demonstrated that cognitive functioning can be understood at new levels. Advances in methods allow us to adequately test conditions under which age-related structural change is associated with decline, compensation, or even improvement in functioning. Rather than using general biological deterioration as the default explanation for cognitive changes, we can now identify specific biological mechanisms reflected in different structures of and activation patterns in the brain. In addition to identifying regions of the brain that decline, these techniques have also allowed us to differentiate preserved areas of the brain, such as the **amygdala** (*which is involved in emotional processing*) from areas that are more prone to decay, such as specific areas in the prefrontal cortex. These respective areas relate to preserved emotional processing on the one hand, and decline in other more higher-order executive cognitive processes on the other. These areas will be explored in a later section on social-emotional neuroscience and aging.

Concept Checks

1. What age-related changes occur in the structure of the brain? What cognitive functions are they related to?
2. How are age-related changes in the dopaminergic system related to cognitive aging?
3. What support is there for the argument that bilateral activation serves an adaptive role for older adults in their cognitive functioning?
4. How does the STAC model improve upon the CRUNCH and HAROLD models of brain activation change and aging?
5. What are the cultural differences in brain activation?

2.3 Neural Plasticity and the Aging Brain

LEARNING OBJECTIVES
- How do animal models contribute to our understanding of neural plasticity and aging?
- What evidence is there for neural plasticity in aging humans?
- How does aerobic exercise influence cognitive aging?

Marisa has been playing incessantly with her latest Nintendo Wii video game. Her grandmother, Leticia, became captivated by her granddaughter's gaming and asked her granddaughter to teach her how to do it. Marisa was delighted and helped her grandmother learn the game. After months of practice, Leticia noted that she seemed stronger in her normal physical activities and her perceptual skills seemed to improve. In addition, she and her granddaughter Marisa had more in common than ever before.

As discussed previously, models explaining age-related changes in brain functions as a form of compensation embrace the notion that there is plasticity in both behavior and at the level of changes in the brain across the adult life span. **Plasticity** *involves the interaction between the brain and the environment and is mostly used to describe the effects of experience on the structure and functions of the neural system.* This is certainly evidenced by Leticia's observations of the positive changes that took place after she started playing the Wii video game.

Plasticity is a multifaceted concept that applies across the life span. For example, as illustrated in the previous section, it can refer to the ability to compensate for declining performance from a behavioral perspective or to the reorganization of neural circuitry as a form of compensation from a neuroscience perspective. Many attempts have been made to assess the potential for plasticity in cognitive functioning by focusing on the potential to improve cognitive performance following training (a good example would be Leticia's practice on the video game).

One of the more prominent behavioral findings in the literature can be found in P. Baltes and collegues' attempts to examine the range of plasticity in older adult cognitive performance (e.g., Baltes & Kliegl, 1992; Willis, Bliezner, & Baltes, 1982). They found that whereas older adults are able to improve cognitive ability in memory tasks through tailored strategy training beyond the level of untrained younger adults, this is highly task-specific, and the ability-level gains are very narrow in focus.

More recently from a behavioral perspective, research has suggested that basic cognitive processes affected by aging can be improved through training and transfer to multiple levels of functioning as long as the basic functions are shared across tasks (e.g., Dahlin, Neely, Larsson, Backman, & Nyberg, 2008). From a neural plasticity perspective, more recent work on animal models of plasticity have revealed compelling evidence that demonstrates the effects of experience on various aspects of brain functioning in adulthood and aging (see Jessberger & Gage, 2008). Interesting

research shows that **neural stem cells** (*which give rise to new neurons*) persist in the adult brain and can generate new neurons throughout the life span (Gage, 2000; Jessberger & Gage, 2008). This has shed doubt on the long-standing belief that neurogenesis (i.e., the development of new neurons) dwindles away at the end of embryonic development, and gives new life to debunking the old myth that you cannot teach an old dog new tricks.

Moreover, this more recent research has added a whole new level of understanding to what happens to individuals as they grow older. For example, even though aging is associated with a striking decrease in the number of new neurons, this may be altered even at advanced ages. When older mice were exposed to enriched environments, they performed much better on spatial memory tasks than mice in more deprived environments (Kempermann et al., 2002). This was demonstrated by changes in the structure of the brain. Figure 2.3 illustrates that younger mice showed a high number of neural stem cells (depicted in the sprouting black illustrations on the left of panel A). For older mice, there was a drop in the amount of hippocampal neurogenesis, as seen in the middle of panel A. However, with enriched experience, this was somewhat reversed (see the third part

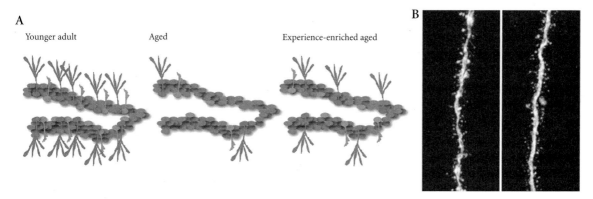

Figure 2.3 Stem-cell associated structural and functional plasticity in the aging hippocampus.

Source: Jessberger, S., & Gage, F.H. (2008). Stem-Cell Associated Structural and Functional Plasticity in the Aging Hippocampus. *Psychology and Aging, 23,* 684–691. Copyright (c) 2008, American Psychological Association. Reproduced by permission.

Playground area for Hamster and mouse. Made out of paper tubes, gift box package and cartons.

© Maximilian Weinzer/Alamy

of panel A). Panel B shows that the number of dendrites in young (on the left) and older (on the right) mice does not differ. This suggests that the speed of neuronal maturation is not substantially affected in older rodents.

Similarly, physical exercise in elderly mice enhanced the number of newly generated neurons about fivefold (van Praag et al., 2005), and this was also associated with improved performance. The most compelling finding from this study is that the exercise started very late in the life of the mice. Thus, even in advanced stages of aging, the brain retains its capacity to react to external stimuli that are related to improved cognitive performance. Furthermore, **environmental enrichment** periods were short and yet sufficient to enhance both the generation of new neurons and behavioral performance in aged mice (Jessberger & Gage, 2008). Of course, these leaps and bounds found in aging mice may not be comparable to the leaps and bounds of younger mice, as indicated by the Baltes et al. research discussed above, but this new research certainly sheds a more optimistic note to the concept of aging.

Evidence of these types of effects in human brains is growing. For example, new learning has been linked to structural changes in the brain.

Draganski and colleagues (2004) demonstrated positive structural changes in the brain in individuals who were novices at juggling to begin with in comparison to learning the skill after a period of three months. Similarly, evidence indicates that hippocampal volume increased in medical students after extensive studying for an exam (Draganski, Gaser, Kempermann, Kuhn, Winkler, Buchel et al., 2006).

These types of findings extend to older adults as well, although limited in nature. For example, positive biochemical changes, such as increased creatine and choline signals in the hippocampus, in healthy older adults were observed after five weeks of training using **method of loci** mnemonic strategies to improve memory (Valenzuela, Jones, Wen, Rae, Graham, Shnier, & Sachdev, 2003). Mnemonics strategies involve using personally relevant cues to help one remember information. In a study using positron emission tomography (PET) scans, Nyberg and colleagues (2003) further investigated brain activation, comparing younger and older adults, after the method of loci training. They found that younger adult brains' showed increased metabolic activity in the left dorsolateral prefrontal cortex when applying the method of loci, but this activity was not observed in older age groups. However, both younger and older adults who showed a benefit from the method displayed increased left occipito-parietal activity. Another group of unimproved older adults showed no increase in activity of either brain areas. Similar to what we discussed earlier, they concluded that, at a neural level, although neural plasticity is present across the adult life span, there are age-related reductions in this plasticity and the potential for functional improvement.

Certainly, studies on neural plasticity in humans are limited. However, with advancements in histological and molecular techniques for examining human postmortem samples, along with in vivo noninvasive methods such as MRI, fMRI, PET, and others, future research may be able to close the apparent gap between animal and human research in the context of adulthood and aging neural plasticity. Some of the most compelling work so far has moved

Aerobic Fitness and Hippocampal
Volume in Older Adults

Who were the investigators, and what were the aims of the studies? Behavioral studies suggest that aerobic fitness training improves cognitive functioning in older adults and improves brain health in aging laboratory animals. In particular, research suggests that aerobic fitness may provide a means to improve brain health in aging humans. Erickson and his colleagues (2009) investigated whether older adults with higher levels of aerobic fitness showed greater brain volume, more specifically in the hippocampus (which is important for memory and learning) in comparison to older individuals with lower fitness levels.

How did the investigators measure the topic of interest? Aerobic fitness was measured in terms of cardiorespiratory fitness. This was assessed by maximal graded exercise testing on a motorized treadmill while the participant's respiration, heart rate, and blood pressure were continuously monitored by a cardiologist and nurse. In order to get a behavioral measure of hippocampal integrity, a spatial memory task was administered. Finally, magnetic resonance imaging (MRI) was used to analyze hippocampal volume.

Who were the participants in the studies? Participants were 165 older adults (109 female; 56 male) between the ages of 59 and 81 years. All participants were screened for dementia to obtain a sample of mentally healthy older adults. It is important in this kind of study to screen participants to make sure they do not have previous head trauma, head or neck surgery, or other neurological conditions.

What was the design of the studies? This study used a correlational approach by examining the degree to which aerobic fitness was correlated with hippocampal volume density and the degree to which aerobic fitness was correlated with spatial memory. In addition, the researchers were interested in a more complex relationship: Does higher hippocampal volume account for the relationship between aerobic fitness and good performance on a spatial memory task?

Were there ethical concerns with the study? Participants in the study were provided with informed consent and also received a physician's clearance to engage in the maximal graded aerobic exercise test. They were also closely monitored throughout the study by a physician. Thus, there were no ethical concerns.

What were the results? Results showed that higher aerobic fitness levels were associated with the preservation of hippocampal volume. Higher aerobic fitness levels were also associated with better performance on the spatial memory task. Furthermore, larger hippocampal volume was the most important predictor of better spatial memory functions.

What did the investigators conclude? Erickson and his colleagues concluded that higher levels of aerobic fitness are associated with the preservation of hippocampal volume (an important brain structure for learning and memory) in older adults. This, in turn, translates into better memory functioning. They warn, however, that clinical trials are needed to determine whether exercise fitness improvements can reliably treat or reverse hippocampal decay.

beyond an examination of training to improve cognitive skills to an examination of the influence of aerobic exercise. Dramatic findings regarding the influence of exercise on cognitive functioning in older adulthood are described in detail in the How Do We Know? feature.

1. What effect does environmental enrichment have on aging rodents?

2. Does environmental enrichment affect neural plasticity in aging humans?

3. What are the benefits of aerobic exercise on the developing brain?

2.4 Neuroscience and Socio-Emotional Aging

LEARNING OBJECTIVES

- Are there differences in the brain for cognitive versus socio-emotional functioning?
- What is the neural circuitry responsible for enhanced memory for emotional information?
- What are the neural underpinnings of the positivity effect found in older adults?

During a family squabble, Shelby chooses to focus her attention on reducing the impact of the negative quarreling and on the positive side of things. In doing so, her composure is much better than that of her adult children Michael and Robin and her grandchild Bella. Shelby celebrates the fact that she can remain so calm in these situations compared to the rest of her family.

The finding that an older adult, like Shelby, can better regulate her emotions is very much corroborated in the socio-emotional literature on aging. What is equally impressive is that there is growing evidence of documenting such age differences from a neuroscience perspective. The emerging field of social neuroscience has taken advantage of advancements in technologies to investigate the neural underpinnings of social cognitive and emotional processing.

In the mainstream literature, for example, Lieberman, Gaunt, Gilbert, and Trope (2002) have outlined a social cognitive neuroscience approach to attributional inferences, or how people make causal judgments about why social situations occur. They have identified a social judgment process that involves a relatively automatic system in which we read cues in the environment quickly and easily without deliberation in making social judgments. For example, if someone is staggering down the hallway, we may automatically assume the person is intoxicated without taking into consideration many other factors that might be involved. In other words, we automatically put the person into a pre-existing social category. We base this judgment on easily activated, well-practiced categories of information, and we do this most prominently when the situation is ambiguous. Because of the ambiguity in a situation, we are more likely to interpret it automatically based on our past experiences and current goals instead of focusing on the current characteristics of the information (Lieberman et al., 2002). Of interest to this chapter is that these researchers have presented compelling evidence for the existence of this system in neuroanatomy. Areas such as the lateral temporal cortex, amygdala, and **basal ganglia** are often associated with automatic social cognition (Adolphs, 1999; Knutson, Adams, Fong, & Hommer, 2001).

These researchers also have identified another system that is a more deliberative form of social cognitive judgments, employing symbolic logic and reflective awareness. The neural basis of this system appears to reside in the prefrontal cortex, anterior cingulate, and hippocampus (Goel & Dolan, 2000; Lieberman et al., 2002). Interestingly, the amygdala and the basal ganglia are areas that show less deterioration in the aging brain, whereas the prefrontal cortex shows more severe deterioration. Furthermore, the basal ganglia and, more specifically, the amygdalae are linked to emotional processing, which appears to be relatively spared in the aging adult. Researchers suggest that whereas we observe decline in cognitive functioning in older adults, we do not observe the same in the experience of emotions. Older adults maintain emotional experience as well as processing emotional information well into older adulthood. Thus, the area of emotional processing has witnessed a proliferation in both theoretical conceptualizations and corresponding empirical work. We will examine this further in later chapters. For the purposes of this chapter, the neural underpinnings of socio-emotional processing with increasing age will be the focus.

Emotional Processing and the Brain

Given the differences between cognitive and emotional aging, a number of questions have served to guide contemporary research in the area of emotional processing. Such questions include: what declines, what is preserved, and what improves? In addition, it is important to identify the conditions under which we observe decline, preservation, and improvement. The neuroscience approach takes this a step further by identifying the specific biological mechanism reflected in the structure and activation patterns of the brain associated with, for example, preserved emotional processing.

As we saw in the cognitive neuroscience section, neuroimaging allows us to identify brain regions of activation that underlie successful information processing, for example, activation of the **prefrontal cortex (PFC)** during encoding relates to better memory. Much behavioral work indicates that if information has emotional significance, we will more likely remember it than information that is more neutral in nature. A number of researchers have been interested in uncovering the neural circuitry that is most responsible for this enhanced memory for emotional information (e.g., Kensinger & Corkin, 2004).

Kensinger and colleagues (Kensinger, 2006; Kensinger & Corkin, 2004) propose two distinct cognitive and neural processes that contribute to emotional memory enhancement. Processing of negative high-arousal information for memory is relatively automatic in nature and is linked to activation of the amygdala as it interacts with the hippocampus to support memory performance. For memory processing of negative low-arousal stimuli, more activation of the prefrontal cortex–hippocampus network is necessary. This area is associated with **controlled self-generated encoding processes** (Kensinger & Corkin, 2004). Kensinger

(2006) argues that emotional enhancement in memory for detail is a result of more engagement in emotion-specific processes that are linked to these distinct neural processes. Thus, when one accurately remembers negative high-arousal items, this corresponds to increased activation of the amygdala and orbitofrontal cortex. Other studies support this in that if the amygdala is damaged, individuals do not attend to arousing stimuli. How do structural and functional changes in the brain affect these processes?

Aging and Emotional Processing

Similar to the behavioral research on younger adults above, there is growing research indicating that older adults also detect emotional information (e.g., in visual search tasks; Leclerc & Kensinger, 2008) and remember emotional information (e.g., remembering emotional words; Kensinger, 2008) better than nonemotional information. However, despite this emotional enhancement effect on information processing, evidence suggests that younger and older adults process positive and negative information differently. An abundance of research has examined a **positivity effect** in older adults (e.g., Carstensen, Isaacowitz, & Charles, 1999).

© Jose Luis Pelaez Inc./Getty Images

Portrait of senior adult African American woman smiling.

This research has shown that *older adults are more motivated to derive emotional meaning from life and to maintain positive affect*. Given these goals, older adults are more likely than younger adults to attend to the emotional meaning of information or to how information makes them feel (Carstensen & Mikels, 2005). In fact, studies show that younger adults have a tendency to attend to and remember more negative information relative to positive information, while older adults display a tendency to attend to and remember more positive information relative to negative information (e.g., Mather & Carstensen, 2005).

Neurological Recruitment Underlying the Positivity Effect in Memory

We begin this section by examining what we know about the emotional memory network and the degree to which corresponding brain structures decline or are preserved with increasing age. Interestingly, the regions implicated in emotional processing such as the **ventromedial prefrontal cortex (VMPFC)** undergo relatively modest structural changes with aging, and the amygdala is relatively structurally preserved with aging (Raz, 1996). In contrast, other regions of the prefrontal cortex (PFC) undergo a more rapid and earlier pace of decline, such as the dorsolateral regions of the PFC (Raz, 1996). Even more importantly, it is necessary to examine the function (i.e., activation) of emotion processing regions of the brain across the adult life span.

LaBar and Cabeza (2006) describe a core emotional memory network that consists of the amygdala, hippocampus, and lateral orbitofrontal cortex. Activation in these areas relate to the successful encoding of emotional information in general. Again, these regions are well preserved in emotional memory as one grows older. Indeed, for both younger and older adults, activation of the amygdala and lateral orbitofrontal cortex corresponds to memory performance for both positive and negative items (Kensinger & Schacter, 2008). There are also areas in the brain beyond this emotional core that are more valence-dependent. For example, for both younger and older adults, the occipito-temporal regions (more specifically the fusiform gyrus) are more likely to be recruited during successful encoding of negative information, whereas anterior prefrontal regions are activated during successful encoding of positive information (Mickley & Kensinger, 2008).

Neuroimaging studies reveal differential age-related activation of neural substrates that might help us understand the neurological mechanisms underlying the positivity effect. For example, older adults show activation of the medial prefrontal cortex and regions of the cingulate gyrus when responding to positive stimuli whereas younger adults do not (Kensinger & Schacter, 2008). Similarly, compared to the young, older adults show greater amygdala activation for positive pictures than for negative ones (Mather et al., 2004). Such findings indicate that it may not be overall decline in functioning of the amygdala that causes age-related responding to emotional stimuli, but rather a shift in the type of emotional stimuli to which the amygdala is most responsive (Leclerc & Kensinger, 2008).

Finally, another intriguing possibility raised in the literature is that the positivity effect may arise from changes in controlled emotional processing or emotion regulation (Leclerc & Kensinger, 2008; Mather & Knight, 2005). It is proposed that the positivity effect should be seen only when an individual has a high degree of cognitive control resources. If these resources are limited, this reduces the ability to regulate responses to emotional information. Accordingly, older adults who are low in resources show no positivity effect (Mather & Knight, 2005).

Research conducted in different domains of emotional processing also has demonstrated age-related differences in brain activation. For example, fMRI studies have found age differences in brain activation when viewing faces with negative emotional expressions (e.g., Anderson, Christoff, Panitz, De Rosa, & Gabrieli, 2003). Younger adults show increased activity in the amygdala when viewing negative emotional expressions, whereas activity in the amygdala is reduced in older adults when viewing these faces. Interestingly over-recruitment of areas such as the anterior cingulate gyrus is increased in older adults when viewing these faces (Gunning-Dixon et al., 2003). This is quite reminiscent of the compensation models discussed in the context of cognitive aging and neuroscience perspectives.

Overall, findings in this line of research have revealed that the core emotional memory network is preserved with aging. Age-related differences are most evident in the successful encoding of positive information as opposed to processes contributing to the memory for negative information. Thus, the structural preservation with increasing age of various regions in the cortex may subserve the preservation of emotional processing.

Concept Checks

1. How does emotional processing differ from cognitive processing in older adulthood?
2. How does the neural circuitry operate when younger and older adults process emotional information?
3. How do age-related changes in brain structure account for the positivity effect found in older adults?

On the one hand, the dismal thought that the human brain gradually loses tissue from age 30 onward and the projected rapid growth of an aging population present society with numerous public policy issues regarding the staggering costs of geriatric care. On the other hand, the good news is that advanced research in neuroscience tells us that this is an oversimplification of what happens to the aging brain. Of importance to policymakers is to realize that researchers are identifying ways in which such cerebral deterioration can be reduced or even reversed. In addition, researchers have identified areas of the brain that are relatively preserved and may even show growth. Thus, it is important for policymakers to obtain a more complete picture of aging.

Research in neuroscience and aging is extremely important, not only for health care policies, but also for the psychological and physiological well-being of the aging adult. The mission of the National Institute on Aging has focused much of its efforts onto biomarkers of healthy aging, demanding more interdisciplinary work in this area. Whereas behavioral research alone has been sufficient to move our understanding of aging forward, it is critical to incorporate all levels of understanding, including the neurological/biological aspects, in future work. A good example is the compelling findings regarding aerobic exercise and aging. The use-it-or-lose-it model of aging has reached new heights. We are not only talking about weight loss with respect to aerobics, but now we are talking about extending the vitality of older adulthood. Finally, evidence showing that emotional brain functions may improve with age provides a platform from which new interventions might be developed to draw on strategies of emotional control to better cope with any declines in functioning.

Summary

2.1 The Neuroscience Approach

How do the basic developmental forces benefit from the neuroscience approach?

- The neuroscience approach adds to the converging evidence on how interventions at the social, biological, and psychological level influence positive and negative change as we grow older.

What is the major focus of the neuropsychological approach to neuroscience?

- The neuropsychological approach compares brain-related psychological functioning of healthy older adults with adults displaying pathological disorders in the brain.

Describe the difference between the correlational approach and the activation imaging approach to studying neuroscience.

- The correlational approach links measures of behavioral performance to measures of neural structure or functioning.
- The activation imaging approach directly links functional brain activity with behavioral data.

What is the difference between MRI and fMRI scanning?

- MRI is a noninvasive technique producing images of the brain's structure.
- fMRI focuses more on the functioning of the brain.

2.2 Neuroscience and Cognitive Aging

What are the basic structural changes in the brain as we age?

- There is considerable shrinkage that occurs in the aging brain, but it is selective and differential.
- The white matter of the brain shows deterioration with increasing age.

What cognitive functions are associated with volume shrinkage in the aging brain?

- Volume shrinkage in the brain is linked to poor cognitive performance such as executive functioning, which has been associated with decreased volume of the prefrontal cortex.
- Comparisons of structural changes in Alzheimer's patients with those of healthy aging adults have revealed that deterioration of the medial-temporal area influences memory performance.

How do decreases in the dopaminergic system relate to changes in cognitive functioning as we grow older?

- Using a neuropsychological approach, studies find that the overall efficacy of the dopaminergic system declines in normal aging.
- Dopaminergic receptors are related to higher-order cognitive functioning such as the regulation of attention.

What happens to brain activation as we age?

- Frontal lobe theory suggests that many age-related declines in cognitive functioning are a function of insults to the frontal lobes.
- Cognitive decline is associated with reduced activation of neurons in prefrontal and medial-temporal areas supporting memory and other cognitive functions.
- Brain activation reveals under-recruitment of the prefrontal cortex during performance on cognitive tasks.

What are the cultural implications of neuroimaging?

- Neuroimaging evidence suggests that there are cultural biases in perceptual processing. However, age-related change has a more profound effect on changes in the brain than culture.

How does bilateral activation serve a functional role in older adults' cognitive functioning?

- The neural patterns of younger and older adults differ significantly. Whereas younger adults' brain activity is localized in one hemisphere of the brain, older adults' brain activity appears in both hemispheres or more than one location.
- Bilateral activation in older adults may serve a supportive role in their cognitive functioning.

What are the major differences between the HAROLD and STAC models of brain activation and aging?

- The HAROLD model suggests that the bilateral activation found in older adults is compensatory in that additional neural units are recruited to increase resources.
- The STAC model suggests that the reason older adults perform at high levels despite neuronal deterioration is because of compensatory scaffolding or the recruitment of additional circuitry to bolster functional decline. However, this model further states that compensation is the brain's response to challenge in general.

2.3 Neural Plasticity and the Aging Brain

How do animal models contribute to our understanding of neural plasticity and aging?

- Even though aging is associated with a striking decrease in the number of new neurons, this may be altered even at advanced ages.
- Even in advanced stages of aging, the brain retains its capacity to react to external stimuli that are related to improved cognitive performance.

What evidence is there for neural plasticity in aging humans?

- Positive biochemical changes in healthy older adults were observed after five weeks of training using method of loci mnemonic strategies to improve memory.
- Although neural plasticity is present across the adult life span, there are age-related reductions in this plasticity and the potential for functional improvement.

How does aerobic exercise influence cognitive aging?

- Higher levels of aerobic fitness are associated with the preservation of the hippocampus (involved in learning and memory) in older adults.

2.4 Neuroscience and Socio-Emotional Aging

Are there differences in the brain for cognitive versus socio-emotional functioning?

- Areas such as the temporal cortex, amygdalae, and basal ganglia are associated with automatic social cognitive processes and emotional processing. This area seems to be relatively spared with aging.
- The neural basis of a more deliberative social cognition is in the prefrontal cortex, anterior cingulate, and hippocampus. These areas show the most deterioration with aging.

What is the neural circuitry responsible for enhanced memory for emotional information?

- There are two distinct neural processes that contribute to emotional memory: the amygdalae, which is linked to the processing of negative high-arousal information, and the prefrontal cortex–hippocampus network, which is implicated for memory processing.
- Increased activation in these areas corresponds to remembering negative high- versus low-arousal information.

What are the neural underpinnings of the positivity effect found in older adults?

- The brain areas associated with emotional processing undergo relatively modest structural changes with aging. This is described as the core emotional memory network.
- Neuroimaging studies reveal that when older adults are presented with positive information, different areas of the brain are activated in comparison to younger adults (e.g., the medial prefrontal cortex and regions of the cingulated gyrus).
- Changes in the positivity effect may also arise from better emotion regulation.

Review Questions

2.1 The Neuroscience Approach

- Describe the three neuroscience methodological perspectives used to study the aging brain. What are their strengths and limitations?
- What are the major differences between MRI and fMRI scanning techniques?
- How does the neuroscience level of examination contribute to our understanding of adult development and aging?

2.2 Neuroscience and Cognitive Aging

- Describe the basic structural changes in the aging brain.
- What changes are observed in cognitive functions that are associated with volume shrinkage in the brain?
- What happens to dopamine functioning in the aging brain?
- What are the differences in brain activation during cognitive tasks for younger and older adults?
- How does bilateral activation serve an adaptive function for older adults?
- Describe the HAROLD, CRUNCH, and STAC models of brain activation and aging.

2.3 Neural Plasticity and the Aging Brain

- What can animal models tell us about neural plasticity in the aging brain?
- Does aerobic fitness improve cognition as we grow older?

2.4 Neuroscience and Socio-Emotional Aging

- How does the brain operate differently for cognitive versus socio-emotional processing?
- What are the brain structures underlying the enhancement of emotional information in memory?
- What is the positivity effect? What is the neuroscience evidence for this phenomenon?

Integrating Concepts in Development

- Which of the theories of bilateral activation in older adults' brains makes the most sense to you? Why?
- What would you say about the stereotypes of aging now that you understand the plasticity of brain functioning?
- What does the work on brain plasticity imply for exercising the mind and body?
- How does the research on neuroscience and cognition compare to the behavioral research on cognition and aging in Chapter 6?
- How does the research on neuroscience and socio-emotional functioning compare to the behavioral research discussed in Chapter 8?

Key Terms

activation imaging approach Attempts to directly link functional brain activity with cognitive behavioral data.

Alzheimer's disease A disease commonly found in the elderly that is characterized by a decline in memory and a progressive destruction of brain cells.

amygdala The region of the brain, located in the medial-temporal lobe, believed to play a key role in emotion.

anterior cingulate Located in the front part of the cingulated cortex, this region of the brain plays a role in autonomic functions, cognitive functions, and emotion.

basal ganglia A group of nuclei interconnected with the cerebral cortex. They are associated with motor control, cognition, and emotions.

bilateral activation Involves activation of a specific brain structure in both lateral hemispheres of the brain.

cerebellum The part of the brain that is associated with motor functioning and balance equilibrium.

compensatory Involves the use of a behavior or function to aid in performance that has been otherwise compromised.

controlled self-generated encoding When individuals elaborate on information by relating it to themselves and rehearse the information in this way.

correlational approach Attempts to link measures of cognitive performance to measures of brain structure or functioning.

default network The regions of the brain that are most active at rest.

diffusion tensor imaging The measurement of the diffusion of water molecules in tissue in order to study connections of neural pathways in the brain.

dopaminergic system Involves dopamine neurotransmission. Dopamaine is a neurotransmitter and is critically implicated in multiple cognitive functions.

environmental enrichment In animal studies, involves raising animals in large groups filled with changing arrangements of toys/objects.

executive functions Include the ability to make and carry out plans, switch between tasks, and maintain attention and focus.

functional imaging (e.g., fMRI) Examines how changes in brain activity occur in correspondence to changes in task demands and the type of cognitive functioning under investigation.

hippocampus Located in the medial-temporal lobe, this part of the brain plays a major role in memory and learning.

lateral occipital complex A highly specialized neural site involved in processing the face, place, and object areas.

method of loci A memory technique for remembering things by linking them to places.

neostriatum Receives input from the cerebral cortex and other brain areas and provides output to the basal nuclei.

neural stem cells Those that give life to new neurons throughout the life span.

neuropsychological approach Compares brain functioning of healthy older adults with adults displaying various pathological disorders in the brain.

over-recruitment Occurs when additional neurons fire and shore up declining brain structures that are inefficient.

Parkinson's disease A brain disease caused by an extreme drop in the neurotransmitter dopamine.

plasticity Involves the interaction between the brain and the environment and is mostly used to describe the effects of experience on the structure and functions of the neural system.

positivity effect When an individual remembers more positive information relative to negative information.

prefrontal cortex (PFC) Part of the frontal lobe that is involved in executive functioning.

selective allocation of attention When something in the environment captures one's attention and the individual allocates more resources in the attention to that item.

supplementary processes When different brain regions are activated to compensate for lacking processing resources.

under-recruitment Occurs when neuronal firing is limited when the brain is activated.

ventromedial prefrontal cortex (VMPFC) Part of the prefrontal cortex, this may be involved in decision making and processing risk.

white matter hyperintensities (WMH) Abnormalities in the brain often found in older adults; correlated with cognitive decline.

working memory performance Holding and manipulating information in consciousness.

Resources

www.cengage.com/psychology/cavanaugh

Visit the companion website, where you will find tutorial quizzes, glossary, flashcards, and more. You can also access the following websites from the companion website.

The National Institute on Aging (NIA) publishes informative brochures on neuroimaging and brain plasticity as well as a focus on social neuroscience and cognitive neuroscience and aging. These are all based on scientific findings.

Center for Cognitive and Social Neuroscience at the University of Chicago is a leading resource for information on events, resources, and brain and behavior research. Their website provides a wide variety of information and resources and summaries of legislative and advocacy activities.

The Society for Neuroscience is another good source of the latest research on neuroscience and aging and brain facts.

Readings

Baltes, P. B., Reuter-Lorenz, P., and Rosler, F. (2006). *Lifespan Development and the Brain: The Perspective of Biocultural Co-Constructivism*. New York: Cambridge University Press. A comprehensive collection of chapters on plasticity of numerous areas of the brain. Moderate to difficult reading.

Cabeza, R., Nyberg, L., and Park, D. (2005). *Cognitive Neuroscience of Aging: Linking Cognitive and Cerebral Aging*. U.S.: Oxford University Press. A compilation of chapters on cognitive neuroscience and aging. Moderate reading.

3

Physical Changes

Although most Olympic athletes in events such as swimming are young adults like Michael Phelps, middle-aged adults like Dara Torres can achieve world class performance through a combination of good genes and a very healthy life style.

THE SUMMER OLYMPICS HELD IN BEIJING IN 2008 WERE SPECIAL FOR MANY reasons. Among the most important were accomplishments and milestones in swimming. Michael Phelps set the record for most gold medals won in a single Olympics (8) and overall (14). At age 23, he had reached the highest level of performance for a male swimmer. Phelps epitomizes the fact that most world-class amateur and professional athletes reach their peak in their twenties. Then there are people who rewrite our beliefs about athletic performance. At the same competition, Dara Torres was competing in her fifth Olympics. As we noted in Chapter 1, she became, at age 41, the oldest swimmer ever to win an Olympic medal (she won three silver medals), and one of only a few who have won medals in five different Olympic games. Middle-aged adults everywhere were thrilled that someone who traditionally would have been written off as too old defeated women less than half her age.

What's ahead for Michael Phelps and Dara Torres? Although we can't predict how many and which events they will win over the coming years, or how long they will continue to compete, it is clear that our beliefs about physical performance are undergoing change. To be sure, athletic success is a combination of years of intense practice and excellent genes. But before Beijing, no one would have thought that a middle-aged woman could compete at that level.

Phelps and Torres represent the best. What about the rest of us? In this chapter, we will discover how physical abilities typically change across adulthood. What makes Phelps and Torres (and other world-class amateur and professional athletes) different is that because they stay in great physical condition, the normative changes tend to happen more slowly.

3.1 Why Do We Age? Biological Theories of Aging

LEARNING OBJECTIVES
- How do rate-of-living theories explain aging?
- What are the major hypotheses in cellular theories of aging?
- How do programmed-cell-death theories propose that we age?
- How do the basic developmental forces interact in biological and physiological aging?

Before he started selling his Lean Mean Grilling Machine, George Foreman was a champion boxer. In fact, he became, at age 44, the oldest boxer ever to win the heavyweight championship. Foreman's success in the boxing ring came after a 10-year period when he did not fight and despite the belief that his career was finished.

Why is it that some people, like George Foreman and Dara Torres, manage to stay competitive in their sports into middle age and others of us experience significant physical decline? For that matter, why do we age at all? After all, some creatures, such as lobsters, do not age as humans do. (As far as scientists can tell, lobsters never show measurable signs of aging, such as changes in metabolism or declines in strength or health.) Scientists and philosophers have pondered the question of why people grow old and die for millennia. Their answers have spurred researchers to create a collection of theories based on basic biological and physiological processes. The search has included many hypotheses, such as metabolic rates and brain sizes, that haven't proved accurate. But as scientists continue unlocking the keys to our genetic code, hope is rising that we may eventually have an answer. To date, though, none of the more than 300 existing theories provides a complete explanation of all the normative changes humans experience (Vintildea & Miguel, 2007).

Before we explore some of the partial explanations from scientific research, complete the Discovering Development exercise. Compare your results of this exercise with some of the theories described next. What similarities and differences did you uncover?

Rate-of-Living Theories

One theory of aging that makes apparent common sense postulates that organisms have only so much energy to expend in a lifetime. (Couch potatoes might like this theory, and may use it as a reason why they are not physically active.) If we examine the metabolic rate of certain animals and look for correlations with their life spans, we find some support for this idea. For example, insects' life spans can be increased by not allowing them to fly, and some mammals live longer when they are induced to hibernate (Cristofalo et al., 1999).

Additionally, there are some data showing that the number of calories animals and people eat is related to longevity. Reducing caloric intake in rodents and rhesus monkeys lowers the risk of premature death, slows down a wide range of normative age-related changes, and in some cases results in longer life spans than do normal diets (Hayflick, 1996; Roth et al., 1995). On the human front, Okinawans, who consume only 60% of the calories in a normal Japanese diet, have 40 times as many centenarians (people who are at least 100 years old) per capita as there are in the rest of Japan. Moreover, the Okinawan incidence of cardiovascular disease, diabetes, and cancer is half that in the rest of Japan (Monczunski, 1991).

But does metabolism relate directly to longevity across species? Apparently not (de Magalhães, Costa, & Church, 2007). Although the age at which a mammal becomes mature is related to longevity, a detailed review of data from many species does not support the view that metabolism is related to length of life. So saving your energy won't directly result in living longer.

Cellular Theories

A second family of ideas points to causes of aging at the cellular level. One notion focuses on the number of times cells can divide, which presumably limits the life span of a complex organism. Cells grown in laboratory culture dishes undergo only a fixed number of divisions before dying, with the number of possible divisions dropping depending on the age of the donor organism; this phenomenon is called the Hayflick limit, after its discoverer, Leonard Hayflick (Hayflick, 1996). For example, cells from human fetal tissue are capable of 40 to 60 divisions; cells from a human adult are capable of only about 20. What causes cells to limit their number of divisions? *Evidence suggests that the tips of the chromosomes, called* **telomeres,** *play a major role in aging by adjusting the cell's response to stress and growth stimulation based on cell divisions and DNA damage* (Aubert & Lansdorp, 2008). Healthy, normal telomeres help regulate the cell division and reproduction process. An enzyme called *telomerase* is needed in DNA replication to fully reproduce the telomeres when cells divide. But telomerase normally is not present in somatic cells, so with each replication the telomeres become shorter. Eventually, the chromosomes become unstable and cannot replicate because the telomeres become too short (Saretzki & Zglinicki, 2002). Some researchers believe that in some cases cancer cells proliferate so quickly because telomeres are not able to regulate cell growth and reproduction (Londoño-Vallejo, 2008). Current thinking is that one effective cancer treatment may involve targeting telomerase (Harley, 2008). Research also shows that exercise may slow the rate at which telomeres shorten, which may help slow the aging process itself (Cherkas et al., 2008).

A second cellular theory is based on a process called **cross-linking,** *in which certain proteins in human cells interact randomly and produce molecules that are linked in such a way as to make the body stiffer* (Cavanaugh, 1999c). The proteins in question, which make up roughly one third of the protein in the body, are called collagen. Collagen in soft body tissue acts much like reinforcing rods in concrete. The more cross-links there are, the stiffer the tissue. For example, leather tanning involves using chemicals that create many cross-links to make the leather stiff enough for use in shoes and other products. As we age, the number of cross-links increases. This process may explain why muscles, such as the heart, and arteries become stiffer with age. However, few scientific data demonstrate that cross-linking impedes metabolic processes or causes the formation of faulty molecules that would constitute a fundamental cause of aging (Hayflick, 1998). Thus, even though cross-linking occurs, it probably is not an adequate explanation of aging.

A third type of cellular theory proposes that aging is caused by unstable molecules called **free radicals,** *which are highly reactive chemicals produced randomly in normal metabolism* (Cristofalo et al., 1999). When these free radicals interact with nearby molecules, problems may result. For example, free radicals may cause cell damage by changing the oxygen levels in cells (Lu & Finkel, 2008). The most important evidence that free radicals may be involved in aging comes from research with substances that prevent the development of free radicals in the first place. These substances, called antioxidants, prevent oxygen from combining with susceptible molecules to form free radicals. Common antioxidants include vitamins A, C, and E, and coenzyme Q. A growing body of evidence shows that ingesting antioxidants postpones the appearance of age-related diseases such as cancer, cardiovascular disease, and immune system dysfunction (Lu & Finkel, 2008), but there is no direct evidence yet that taking antioxidants actually increases the life span, although research is ongoing (Miwa, Beckman, & Muller, 2008). Nevertheless, it can't hurt to include foods high in antioxidants, such as apples, berries, and red beans (Jacka & Berk, 2007).

Programmed-Cell-Death Theories

What if aging were programmed into our genetic code? This possibility seems more likely as the explosion of knowledge about human genetics continues to unlock the secrets of our genetic code. Even when cell death appears random, researchers believe that such losses may be part of a master genetic program that underlies the aging process (Pankow & Solotoroff, 2007). Programmed cell death appears to be a function of physiological processes, the innate ability of cells to self-destruct, and the ability of dying cells to trigger key processes in other cells. At present, we do not know how this self-destruct program is activated, nor do we understand how it works. Nevertheless, there is increasing evidence that many diseases associated with aging (such as Alzheimer's disease) have genetic aspects.

It is possible that the other explanations we have considered in this section and the changes we examine throughout this text are the result of a genetic program. For example, there is evidence that osteoporosis (Riancho, Zarrabeitia, & Macías, 2008), changes in brain cells (Martin, 1998), Alzheimer's disease (Wolfson, 2008), certain types of memory (Johansson et al., 1999), and well-being

(Weiss, Bates, & Luciano, 2008) have key genetic underpinnings. As genetics research continues, it is likely that we will have some exciting answers to the question, Why do we age?

Implications of the Developmental Forces

Although scientists do not yet have one unified theory of biological and physiological aging, the picture is becoming clearer. We know that there are genetic components, that the body's chemistry lab sometimes produces incorrect products, and that errors occur in the operation and replication of DNA (Vintildea & Miguel, 2007). From the perspective of the basic developmental forces, the biological theories provide ways to describe the biological forces. As we examine specific body systems in this chapter and health-related processes in Chapter 4, we will begin to integrate the biological forces with the psychological, sociocultural, and life-cycle forces. In those discussions, notice how changes in body systems and diseases are influenced by these other factors.

The implication of this dynamic, interactive process is that the diagnosis and treatment of health-related concerns must also include many perspectives. It is not enough to have your physical functioning checked to establish whether you are healthy. Rather, you need not only a typical bodily physical but also a checkup of psychological and sociocultural functioning. Finally, the results of all these examinations must be placed in the context of the overall life span. Although scientists do not yet have a unified theory of biological and physiological aging and are not likely to in the near future (Vintildea & Miguel, 2007), such a theory would have to account for a wide array of changes relating not only to biological forces but to other forces as well. Perhaps then we'll discover why George Foreman was still successful in the boxing ring and Dara Torres was winning in the pool when most of their peers were watching them on television.

Or we just might discover how to reverse or stop aging. The business of "antiaging medicine," products designed to stop or prevent aging, is booming. Although most researchers who specialize in studying the fundamental mechanisms of aging largely dismiss such efforts, not all do (Juengst et al., 2003). Healthy behaviors that delay the effects of aging are legitimate activities that have a research foundation; whether they should be called "antiaging" is another matter (Palmore, 2007). Exercise has been shown to delay many aspects of aging; cosmetic surgery aimed at making someone look younger does not, and is likely more related to aging stereotypes than healthy lifestyles.

There are three general research-based approaches to the work aimed at slowing or reversing aging. First, the goal is to delay the chronic illnesses of old age. Second, there is research aimed at slowing the fundamental processes of aging so that the average life span is increased to over 110 years (from roughly 78 now). Third, some researchers seek to arrest or even reverse aging, perhaps by removing the damage inevitably caused by metabolic processes.

Research separating healthy behaviors from age denials is key (Palmore, 2007). Legitimate research sponsored by such agencies as the National Institutes of Health gets confused with counterfeit antiaging interventions. If the legitimate research unlocks the secrets of aging, then a serious public discussion is needed to prepare society for the implications of a possible significant lengthening of the life span.

Concept Checks

1. What is the basic premise of all rate-of-living theories?
2. What are the major types of cell theories? What are their similarities and differences?
3. What mechanism is thought to underlie programmed cell death?
4. How might the four developmental forces interact in the context of biological and physiological aging?

3.2 Appearance and Mobility

LEARNING OBJECTIVES

- How do our skin, hair, and voices change with age?
- What happens to our body build with age?
- What age-related changes occur in our ability to move around?

By all accounts, Kristina is extremely successful. She was a famous model in her late teens and 20s, and by the time she was 36 she had learned enough about the business to start her own multinational modeling agency. The other day Kristina was very upset when she looked in the mirror and saw a wrinkle. "Oh no," she exclaimed, "I can't be getting wrinkles! What am I going to do?"

Kristina's experience isn't unique. We all see the outward signs of aging first in the mirror: gray hair, wrinkled skin, and an expanding waistline or hips. These changes occur gradually and at different rates; some of us experience all the changes in young adulthood, whereas others don't have them until late middle or old age. How we perceive the person staring back at us in the mirror says a great deal about how we feel about aging; positive feelings about the signs of aging are related to positive self-esteem.

How easily we move our changing bodies in the physical environment is also a major component of adaptation and well-being in adulthood. If we cannot get around, we must depend on others, which lowers our self-esteem and sense of competence. Having a body that moves effectively also lets us enjoy physical activities such as walking, swimming, and skiing.

Changes in Skin, Hair, and Voice

When we, like Kristina, see the first visible signs of aging, it makes no difference that these changes are universal and inevitable. Nor does it matter that our wrinkles are caused by a combination of changes in the structure of the skin and its connective and supportive tissue and the cumulative effects of exposure to sunlight. As normal as the loss of hair pigmentation is, we may still want to hide the gray (Aldwin & Gilmer, 2004). What matters on that day is that we have seen our first wrinkle and gray hair.

Changes in the Skin. Why does our skin wrinkle? Wrinkling is actually a complex, four-step process (Gilchrest, 1995). First, the outer layer of skin becomes thinner through cell loss, causing the skin to become more fragile. Second, the collagen fibers that make up the connective tissue

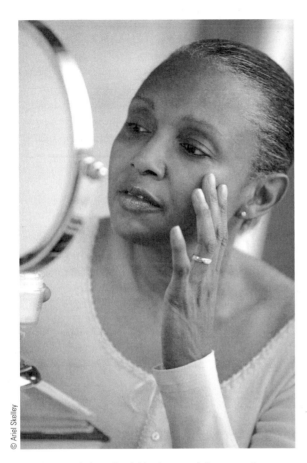

© Ariel Skelley

Getting gray hair and wrinkles is part of the normative aging process.

smoking, may slow the development of wrinkles. The message is clear: Young adults who are dedicated sun-worshippers or are smokers eventually pay a high price.

Older adults' skin is naturally thinner and drier, giving it a leathery texture, making it less effective at regulating heat or cold, and making it more susceptible to cuts, bruises, and blisters. To counteract these problems, people should use skin moisturizers, vitamin E, and facial massages (Mayo Clinic, 2007a; Ramirez & Schneider, 2003). The coloring of light-skinned people undergoes additional changes with age. The number of pigment-containing cells in the outer layer decreases, and those that remain have less pigment, resulting in lighter skin. In addition, age spots (areas of dark pigmentation that look like freckles) and moles (pigmented outgrowths) appear more often. Some of the blood vessels in the skin may become dilated and create small, irregular red lines. Varicose veins may appear as knotty, bluish irregularities in blood vessels, especially on the legs (Aldwin & Gilmer, 2004; Gilchrest, 1995).

Changes in the Hair. Gradual thinning and graying of the hair of both men and women occur inevitably with age, although there are large individual differences in the rate of these changes. Hair loss is caused by destruction of the germ centers that produce the hair follicles, whereas graying results from a cessation of pigment production. Men usually do not lose facial hair as they age; you probably have seen many balding men with thick, bushy beards. In addition, men often develop bushy eyebrows and hair growth inside the ears. In contrast, women often develop patches of hair on the face, especially on the chin (Aldwin & Gilmer, 2004). This hair growth is related to the hormonal changes of the climacteric, discussed later in this chapter.

Changes in the Voice. The next time you're in a crowd of people of different ages, close your eyes and listen to the way they sound. You probably will be fairly accurate in guessing how old the speakers are just from the quality of the voices you hear. Younger adults' voices tend to be full and resonant, whereas

lose much of their flexibility, making the skin less able to regain its shape after a pinch. Third, elastin fibers in the middle layer of skin lose their ability to keep the skin stretched out, resulting in sagging. Finally, the underlying layer of fat, which helps provide padding to smooth out the contours, diminishes.

It may surprise you to know that how quickly your face ages is largely under your control. Two major environmental causes of wrinkles are exposure to ultraviolet rays from the sun, which breaks down the skin's connective tissue, and smoking, which restricts the flow of blood to the skin around the lips (Mayo Clinic, 2007a). Using sunscreens and sunblocks properly and limiting your exposure to sunlight, as well as quitting older adults' voices tend to be thinner or weaker. Age-related changes in one's voice include lowering of pitch, increased breathlessness and trembling, slower and less precise pronunciation, and decreased volume. A longitudinal study of Japanese adults revealed that women have more changes in their fundamental frequency, and shimmer and glottal noise is characteristic of older voices (Kasuya et al., 2008). Some researchers report that these changes are due to changes in the larynx (voice box), the respiratory system, and the muscles controlling speech. However, other researchers contend that these changes result from poor health and are not part of normal aging.

Changes in Body Build

If you have been around the same older people, such as your grandparents, for many years, you undoubtedly have noticed that the way their bodies look changed over time. Two changes are especially visible: a decrease in height and fluctuations in weight. Height remains fairly stable until the 50s, but between the mid-50s and mid-70s men lose about 1 inch and women lose about 2 inches (de Groot et al., 1996). This height loss usually is caused by compression of the spine from loss of bone strength, changes in the discs between the vertebrae in the spine, and changes in posture (Gerhart, 1995). We consider some specific aspects of changes in bone structure a bit later.

Weight gain in middle age followed by weight loss in later life is common. Typically, people gain weight between their 20s and their mid-50s but lose weight throughout old age. In part, the weight gain is caused by changes in body metabolism, which tends to slow down, and reduced levels of exercise, which in turn reduces the number of calories needed daily. Unfortunately, many people do not adjust their food intake to match these changes. The result is often tighter-fitting clothes. For men, this weight gain tends to be around the abdomen, creating middle-aged bulge. For women, this weight gain tends to be around the hips, giving women the familiar "pear-shaped" figure. By late life, though, the body loses both muscle and bone, which weigh more than fat, in addition to some fat, resulting in weight loss (Yang, Bishai, & Harman, 2008). Research on the relationships among body weight, health, and survival shows that older adults who have normal body weight at age 65 have longer life expectancy and lower rates of disability than 65-year-olds in other weight categories (Yang et al., 2008). Keeping your weight in the normal range for your height, then, may help you live longer.

Changes in Mobility

Being able to get around on one's own is an important part of remaining independent. As you will see, we all experience some normative changes that can affect our ability to remain mobile, but most of these changes do not inevitably result in serious limitations.

Muscles and Balance. Although the amount of muscle tissue in our bodies declines with age, this loss is hardly noticeable in terms of strength and endurance; even at age 70 the loss is no more than 20%. After that, however, the rate of change increases. By age 80 the loss in strength is up to 40%, and it appears to be more severe in the legs than in the arms and hands. However, some people retain their strength well into old age (Booth et al., 1994; Skelton et al., 1994). Research evidence suggests that muscle endurance also diminishes with age but at a slower rate. Men and women show no differences in the rate of muscle change (Spirduso & MacRae, 1990).

This loss of muscle strength is especially important in the lower body (El Haber et al., 2008). As lower body strength declines, the likelihood of balance problems and falls increases, as do problems with walking. Exercise may help delay these changes.

Bones. You have probably seen commercials and advertisements aimed mostly at women for products that help maintain bone mass. If you surmise that such products reflect a serious and real health concern, you are correct. Normal aging is accompanied by the loss of bone tissue throughout the body.

Bone loss begins in the late 30s, accelerates in the 50s (particularly in women), and slows by the 70s (National Institute of Arthritis and Musculoskeletal and Skin Diseases, 2005). The gender difference in bone loss is important. Once the process begins, women lose bone mass approximately twice as fast as men. The difference results from two factors. First, women have less bone mass than men in young adulthood, meaning that they start out with less ability to withstand bone loss before it causes problems. Second, the depletion of estrogen after menopause speeds up bone loss.

What happens to aging bones? The process involves a loss of bone mass inside the bone, which makes bones more hollow. In addition, bones tend to become porous. The changes result from body weight, genetics, and lifestyle factors such as smoking, alcohol use, and diet (Aldwin & Gilmer, 2004). All these bone changes cause an age-related increase in the likelihood of fractures, because hollow, porous bones are easier to break. Furthermore, broken bones in older people present more serious problems than in younger adults, because they are more likely to be clean fractures that are difficult to heal. Bones of younger adults fracture in such a way that there are many cracks and splinters to aid in healing. This is analogous to the difference between breaking a young, green tree branch (which is harder to do) and snapping an old, dry twig.

Women are especially susceptible to severe bone degeneration, a disease called **osteoporosis,** *in which the loss of bone mass and increased porosity create bones that resemble laced honeycombs.* You can see the result in Figure 3.1. Eventually, people with osteoporosis tend to develop a distinct curvature in their spines, as shown in Figure 3.2.

Osteoporosis is the leading cause of broken bones in older women (National Institute of Arthritis and Musculoskeletal and Skin Diseases, 2008a). Although it is most common in older adults, osteoporosis can occur in people in their 50s.

Osteoporosis is more common in women than men, largely because women have less bone mass in general, because some girls and women do not consume enough dietary calcium to build strong bones when they are younger (i.e., build bone mass), and because the decrease in estrogen following menopause greatly accelerates bone loss (National Institute of Arthritis and Musculoskeletal and Skin Diseases, 2008a). According to a national study of 48,000 postmenopausal women in the United States, low bone mass occurs in 65% of Asian American, 59% of Native American, 56% of Latina, 51% of European, and 38%

Osteoporotic bone tissue

Normal bone tissue

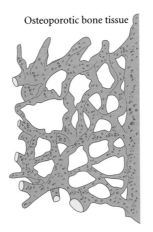 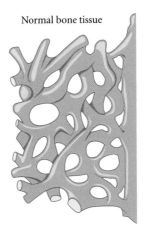

Figure 3.1   Osteoporotic and normal bone structures. Notice how much mass the osteoporotic bone has lost.

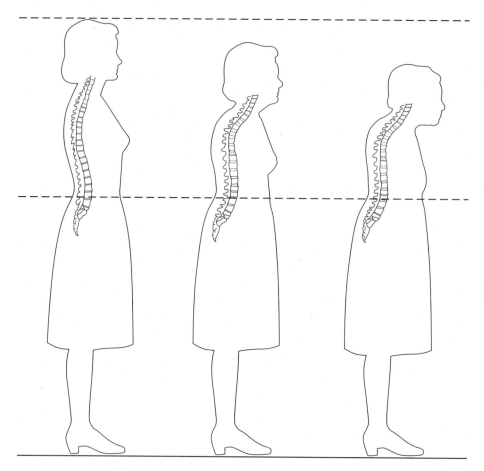

Figure 3.2 Changes in the curvature of the spine as a result of osteoporosis. These changes create the stooping posture common to older people with advanced osteoporosis.

Source: Reprinted with permission from Ebersole, P., & Hess, P., *Toward Healthy Aging* (5e, p. 395). Copyright © 1998 Mosby St. Louis: with permission from Elsevier.

of African American women. Additional evidence form bone scans indicates that 65% of women over age 60 and nearly all women over age 90 are affected; in total, over 20 million American women have osteoporosis and millions more are at risk.

Osteoporosis is caused in part by having low bone mass at skeletal maturity (the point at which your bones reach peak development), deficiencies in calcium and vitamin D, estrogen depletion, and lack of weight-bearing exercise that builds up bone mass. Other risk factors include smoking, high-protein diets, and excessive intake of alcohol, caffeine, and sodium. Women who are being treated for asthma, cancer, rheumatoid arthritis, thyroid problems, or epilepsy are also at increased risk because the medications used can lead to the loss of bone mass.

The National Institutes of Health (Bennett, 2003) recommends getting enough vitamin D and dietary calcium as ways to prevent osteoporosis. There is evidence that calcium supplements after menopause may slow the rate of bone loss and delay the onset of osteoporosis, but benefits appear to be greater when the supplements are provided before menopause (Bennett, 2003; National Institutes of

Health, 2008). People should consume foods (such as milk or broccoli) that are high in calcium and should also take calcium supplements if necessary. Recommended calcium intake for men and women of various ages are shown in Table 3.1. Data clearly show that metabolizing vitamin D directly affects rates of osteoporosis; however, whether supplementary dietary vitamin D retards bone loss is less certain (National Institute of Arthritis and Musculoskeletal and Skin Diseases, 2008b).

In terms of medication interventions, biophosphonates are the most commonly used and are highly effective (Kennel, 2007). Fosamax, Actonel, and Boniva are three common examples of this family of medications. Biophosphonates slow the bone breakdown process by helping to maintain bone density during menopause. Research indicates that using biophosphonates for up to five years appears relatively safe if followed by stopping the medication (called a "drug holiday"); there is evidence for protective effects lasting up to five years more.

Table 3.1

Recommended Calcium Intakes

Age	Amount of Calcium
Infants	
Birth–6 months	210 mg
6 months–1 year	270 mg
Children/Young Adults	
1–3 years	500 mg
4–8 years	800 mg
9–18 years	1,300 mg
Adult Women & Men	
19–50 years	1,000 mg
50 +	1,200 mg
Pregnant or Lactating	
18 years or younger	1,300 mg
19–50 years	1,000 mg

Sources: National Academy of Sciences, 1997; http://www.niams.nih.gov/Health_Info/Bone/Bone_Health/Nutrition/default.asp (revised November 2005).

Lowering the risk of osteoporosis involves dietary, medication, and activity approaches (National Institutes of Health, 2008). Some evidence also supports the view that taking supplemental magnesium, zinc, vitamin K, and special forms of fluoride may be effective. Estrogen replacement is effective in preventing women's bone loss after menopause but is controversial because of potential side effects (as discussed later). There is also evidence that regular weight-bearing exercise (e.g., weight lifting, jogging, or other exercise that forces you to work against gravity) is beneficial.

Joints. Many middle-aged and older adults complain of aching joints. They have good reason. Beginning in the 20s, the protective cartilage in joints shows signs of deterioration, such as thinning and becoming cracked and frayed. Two types of arthritis can result: osteoarthritis and rheumatoid arthritis. These diseases are illustrated in Figure 3.3.

Over time the bones underneath the cartilage become damaged, which can result in **osteoarthritis,** *a disease marked by gradual onset and progression of pain and disability, with minor signs of inflammation* (National Institute of Arthritis and Musculoskeletal and Skin Diseases, 2006). The disease usually becomes noticeable in late middle age or early old age, and it is especially common in people whose joints are subjected to routine overuse and abuse, such as athletes and manual laborers. Thus osteoarthritis is a wear-and-tear disease. Pain typically is worse when the joint is used, but skin redness, heat, and swelling are minimal or absent. Osteoarthritis usually affects the hands, spine, hips, and knees, sparing the wrists, elbows, shoulders, and ankles. Effective management approaches consist mainly of certain steroids and anti-inflammatory drugs, rest, nonstressful exercises that focus on range of motion, diet, and a variety of homeopathic remedies.

A second form of arthritis is **rheumatoid arthritis,** *a more destructive disease of the joints that also develops slowly and typically affects different joints and causes other types of pain than osteoarthritis* (Mayo Clinic, 2008a). Most often, a pattern of morning stiffness and aching develops in the fingers, wrists, and ankles on both sides of

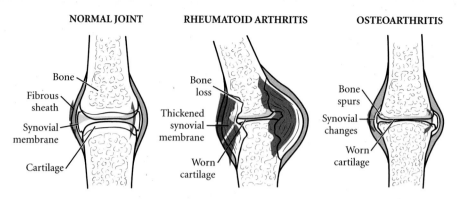

NORMAL JOINT   **RHEUMATOID ARTHRITIS**   **OSTEOARTHRITIS**

Figure 3.3   Rheumatoid arthritis versus osteoarthritis. Osteoarthritis, the most common form of arthritis, involves the wearing away of the cartilage that caps the bones in your joints. With rheumatoid arthritis, the synovial membrane that protects and lubricates joints becomes inflamed, causing pain and swelling. Joint erosion may follow.

the body. Joints appear swollen. The typical therapy for rheumatoid arthritis consists of aspirin or other nonsteroidal anti-inflammatory drugs, such as Advil or Aleve. Newer treatments include disease-modifying anti-rheumatic drugs (DMARDs) (such as hydroxycholorquine and methotrexate) that limit the damage occurring in the joints, and TNF-alpha inhibitors that act as an anti-inflammatory agent and have been shown to stop the disease's progression in some patients. Rest and passive range-of-motion exercises are also helpful. Contrary to popular belief, rheumatoid arthritis is not contagious, hereditary, or self-induced by any known diet, habit, job, or exposure. Interestingly, the symptoms often come and go in repeating patterns (National Institute of Arthritis and Musculoskeletal and Skin Diseases, 2004). Although apparently not directly inherited, family history of rheumatoid arthritis plays a role because researchers think that you can inherit a predisposition for the disease (Mayo Clinic, 2008a).

Surgical interventions for arthritis have advanced significantly (Mayo Clinic, 2008a). For example, *arthroplasty,* or the total replacement of joints damaged by arthritis, continues to improve as new materials help artificial joints last longer. When joints become inflamed, surgeons may be able to remove the affected tissue. Or in some cases cartilage may be transplanted into a damaged joint. These latter two approaches help patients avoid full joint replacement, generally viewed as the method of last resort.

Comparisons among osteoporosis, osteoarthritis, and rheumatoid arthritis can be seen in Table 3.2.

Psychological Implications

The appearance of wrinkles, gray hair, fat, and the like can have major effects on a person's self-concept (Aldwin & Gilmer, 2004) and reflect ageism in society (Clarke & Griffin, 2008). Middle-aged adults may still think of themselves as productive members of society and rebel against being made invisible (Clarke & Griffin, 2008). Because U.S. society places high value on looking young, middle-aged and older adults, especially women, may be regarded as inferior on a number of dimensions, including intellectual ability. Consequently, women report engaging in "beauty work" (dyeing their hair, cosmetic surgery, and the like) in order to remain visible in society. In contrast, middle-aged men with some gray hair often are considered distinguished, more experienced, and more knowledgeable than their younger counterparts.

Table 3.2

Similarities and Differences Among Osteoporosis, Osteoarthritis, and Rheumatoid Arthritis

	Osteoporosis	Osteoarthritis	Rheumatoid Arthritis
Risk Factors			
Age-related	X	X	
Menopause	X		
Family history	X	X	X
Use of certain medications such as glucocorticoids or seizure medications	X		
Calcium deficiency or inadequate vitamin D	X		
Inactivity	X		
Overuse of joints		X	
Smoking	X		
Excessive alcohol	X		
Anorexia nervosa	X		
Excessive weight		X	
Physical Effects			
Affects entire skeleton	X		
Affects joints		X	X
Is an autoimmune disease			X
Bony spurs		X	X
Enlarged or malformed joints	X	X	
Height loss	X		

Sources: National Institute of Arthritis and Musculoskeletal and Skin Diseases (2006), http://www.niams.nih.gov/Health_Info/Bone/Osteoporosis/Conditions_Behaviors/osteoporosis_arthritis.asp.

Given the social stereotypes we examined in Chapter 1, many women (and increasingly, some men) use any available means to compensate for these changes. Some age-related changes in facial appearance can be disguised with cosmetics. Hair dyes can restore color. Surgical procedures such as face-lifts can tighten sagging and wrinkled skin. But even plastic surgery only delays the inevitable; at some point everyone takes on a distinctly old appearance.

Losses in strength and endurance in old age have much the same psychological effects as changes in appearance (Aldwin & Gilmer, 2004). In particular, these changes tell the person that he or she is not as capable of adapting effectively to the environment. Loss of muscle coordination (which may lead to walking more slowly, for example) may not be inevitable, but it can prove embarrassing and stressful. Exercise and resistance training can improve muscle strength, even up to age 90, and may also reduce the odds of getting dementia (Andel et al., 2008). Interestingly, the rate of improvement does not seem to differ with age; older adults get stronger at the same rate as younger adults.

The changes in the joints, especially in arthritis, have profound psychological effects (Aldwin & Gilmer, 2004). These changes can severely limit movement, thereby reducing independence and the ability to complete normal daily routines. Moreover, joint pain is very difficult to ignore or disguise, unlike changes in appearance. Consequently, the person who can use cosmetics to hide changes in appearance cannot use the same approach to deal with constant pain in the joints. Older adults use a wide range of adaptive behaviors to cope (Gignac et al., 2000). For example, participation in an exercise program appears to have some benefit. Older adults who suffer bone fractures face several other consequences in addition to discomfort. For example, a hip fracture may force hospitalization or even a stay in a nursing home. For all fractures, the recovery period is much longer than for a younger adult. In addition, older people who witness friends or relatives struggling during rehabilitation may reduce their own activities as a precaution.

Concept Checks

1. What changes occur with age in skin, hair, and voice?
2. What changes occur with age in muscles, bones, and joints?
3. What are the major psychological consequences of changes in appearance and mobility?

3.3 Sensory Systems

LEARNING OBJECTIVES

- What age-related changes happen in vision?
- How does hearing change as people age?
- What age-related changes occur in people's senses of touch and balance?
- What happens to taste and smell with increasing age?

Bertha has attended Sunday services in her local AME (African Methodist Episcopal) church for 82 years. Over the past few years, though, she has experienced greater difficulty in keeping her balance as she walks down the steps from her row house to the sidewalk. Bertha is noticing that her balance problems occur even when she is walking on level ground. Bertha is concerned that she will have to stop attending her beloved church because she is afraid of falling and breaking a bone.

You have probably seen people like Bertha walking slowly and tentatively along the sidewalk. Why do older people have these problems more often? If you said it is because the sensory system directly related to maintaining balance, the vestibular system, and muscle strength decline with age, you would only be partly correct. It turns out that keeping one's balance is a complex process in which we integrate input from several sources, such as vision and touch, as well as bones and joints. In this section we examine the changes that occur in our sensory systems. These changes challenge our ability to interact with the world and communicate with others.

Vision

Have you ever watched middle-aged people try to read something that is right in front of them? If they do not already wear glasses or contact lenses, they typically move the material farther away so that they can see it clearly. This change in vision is one of the first noticeable signs of aging, along with the wrinkles and gray hair we considered earlier. Because we rely extensively on sight in almost every aspect of our waking life, its normative, age-related changes have profound and pervasive effects on people's everyday lives, especially feelings of sadness and loss of enjoyment of life (Mojon-Azzi, Sousa-Poza, & Mojon, 2008).

How does eyesight change with age? The major changes are best understood by grouping them into two classes: changes in the structures of the eye, which begin in the 40s, and changes in the retina, which begin in the 50s (Mojon-Azzi et al., 2008).

Structural Changes in the Eye. Two major kinds of age-related structural changes occur in the eye. One is a decrease in the amount of light that passes through the eye, resulting in the need for more light to do tasks such as reading. As you might suspect, this change is one reason why older adults do not see as well in the dark, which may account in part for their reluctance to go places at night. One possible logical response to the need for more light would be to increase illumination levels in general. However, this solution does not work in all situations because we also become increasingly sensitive to glare (Aldwin & Gilmer, 2004). In addition, our ability to adjust to changes in illumination, called adaptation, declines. Going from outside into a darkened movie theater involves dark adaptation; going back outside involves light adaptation. Research indicates that the time it takes for both types of adaptation increases with age (Charman, 2008). These changes are especially important for older drivers, who have more difficulty seeing after confronting the headlights of an oncoming car.

The other key structural changes involve the lens (Charman, 2008). As we grow older, the lens becomes more yellow, causing poorer color discrimination in the green–blue–violet end of the spectrum. Also, the lens's ability to adjust and focus declines as the muscles around it stiffen. *This is what causes difficulty in seeing close objects clearly (called* **presbyopia**), *necessitating either longer arms or corrective lenses.* To complicate matters further, the time our eyes need to change focus from near to far (or vice versa) increases. This also poses a major problem in driving. Because drivers are constantly changing their focus from the instrument panel to other autos and signs on the highway, older drivers may miss important information because of their slower refocusing time.

Besides these normative structural changes, some people experience diseases caused by abnormal structural changes. *First, opaque spots called* **cataracts** *may develop on the lens, which limits the amount of light transmitted.* Cataracts often are treated by surgical removal and use of corrective lenses. *Second, the fluid in the eye may not drain properly, causing very high pressure; this condition, called* **glaucoma,** *can cause internal damage and loss of vision.* Glaucoma, a fairly common disease in middle and late adulthood, is usually treated with eye drops.

Retinal Changes. The second major family of changes in vision result from changes in the retina. The retina lines approximately two thirds of the interior of the eye. The specialized receptor cells in vision, the rods and the cones, are contained in the retina. They are most densely packed toward the rear and especially at the focal point of vision, a region called the macula. At the center of the macula is the fovea, where incoming light is focused for maximum acuity, as when you are reading. With increasing age the probability of degeneration of the macula increases (Kupfer, 1995). Macular degeneration involves the progressive and irreversible destruction of receptors from any of a number of causes. This disease results in the loss of the ability to see details; for example, reading is extremely difficult, and television often is reduced to a blur. Roughly 1 in 5 people over age 75, especially smokers and European American women, have macular degeneration, making it the leading cause of functional blindness in older adults.

A second age-related retinal disease is a by-product of diabetes, a chronic disease described in detail in Chapter 4. Diabetes is accompanied by accelerated aging of the arteries, with blindness being one of the more serious side effects. Diabetic retinopathy, as this condition is called, can involve fluid retention in the macula, detachment of the retina, hemorrhage, and aneurysms (Kupfer, 1995). Because it takes many years to develop, diabetic retinopathy is more common among people who developed diabetes early in life.

The combined effects of the structural changes in the eye create two other types of changes. First, the ability to see detail and to discriminate different visual patterns, called acuity, declines steadily between ages 20 and 60, with a more rapid decline thereafter. Loss of acuity is especially noticeable at low light levels (Charman, 2008).

Older drivers may miss information due to changes in vision.

Psychological Effects of Visual Changes. Clearly, age-related changes in vision affect every aspect of older adults' daily lives and their well-being (Mojon-Azzi et al., 2008). Research indicates that there can be as much as a sixfold decline in visual ability in everyday situations, depending on the skill needed (Schneider, 1996). Imagine the problems people experience performing tasks that most young adults take for granted, such as reading a book, watching television, reading grocery labels, or driving a car. Fortunately, some of the universal changes, such as presbyopia, can be corrected easily through glasses or contacts. Surgery to correct cataracts is now routine. The diseased lens is removed and an artificial one is inserted in an outpatient procedure that usually lasts about 30 minutes, with little discomfort. Patients usually resume their normal activities in less than a week and report much improved daily lives.

If you want to provide environmental support for older adults, taking their vision changes into account, you need to think through your intervention strategies carefully. For example, simply making the environment brighter may not be the answer. For increased illumination to be beneficial, surrounding surfaces must not increase glare. Using flat latex paint rather than glossy enamel and avoiding highly polished floors are two ways to make environments "older adult–friendly." There should be high contrast between the background and operational information on dials and controls, such as on stoves and radios. Older adults may also have trouble seeing some fine facial details which may lead them to decrease their social contacts for fear of not recognizing someone.

Among people who have experienced substantial vision loss, it appears that conscientiousness predicts how they handle their vision loss. People high in conscientiousness perceive vision loss as a challenge to be overcome. As a result, they are more willing to invest the time and energy necessary to complete tasks and to learn alternative strategies (Casten et al., 1999). Visual problems also increase vulnerability to falls because the person may be unable to see hazards in his or her path or to judge distance very well. Thus, part of Bertha's concern about falling may be caused by changes in her ability to tell where the next step is or to see hazards along the sidewalk.

Hearing

Experiencing hearing loss is one of the most well-known normative changes with age (Aldwin & Gilmer, 2004). A visit to any housing complex for older adults will easily verify this point; you will quickly notice that television sets and radios are turned up fairly loud in most of the apartments. Yet you don't have to be old to experience significant hearing problems. When he began to find it difficult to hear what was being said to him, President Bill Clinton obtained two hearing aids. He was 51 years old at the time, and he attributed his hearing loss to too many high school bands and rock concerts when he was young. His situation is far from unique. Loud noise is the enemy of hearing at any age. You probably have seen people who work in noisy environments wearing protective gear on their ears so that they are not exposed to loud noise over extended periods of time.

But you can do serious damage to your hearing with short exposure too; in 1988, San Francisco punk rock bassist Kathy Peck was performing with her all-female punk band "The Contractions" at the Oakland Coliseum and played so loudly that she had ringing in her ears for 3 days and suffered permanent hearing loss. As a result, she founded Hearing Education and Awareness for Rockers (HEAR; http://www.hearnet.com) shortly thereafter to educate musicians about the need to protect their ears (Noonan, 2005). You don't need to be at a concert to damage your hearing, either. Using headphones or earbuds, especially at high volume, can cause the same serious damage and should be avoided. It is especially easy to cause hearing loss with headphones or earbuds if you wear them while exercising; the increased blood flow to the ear during exercise makes hearing receptors more vulnerable to damage. Hearing loss from this and other sources of loud noise is on the increase in younger adults, meaning that hearing loss is likely to increase among older adults in the future (Agrawal, Platz, & Niparko, 2008).

The cumulative effects of noise and normative age-related changes create the most common age-related hearing problem: reduced sensitivity to high-pitched tones, called **presbycusis,** *which occurs earlier and more severely than the loss of sensitivity to low-pitched tones* (Agrawal et al., 2008). Research indicates that by the late 70s, roughly half of older adults have presbycusis. Men typically have greater loss than women, but this may be because of differential exposure to noisy environments. Hearing loss usually is gradual at first but accelerates during the 40s, a pattern shown clearly in Figure 3.4.

Presbycusis results from four types of changes in the inner ear (Gulya, 1995): sensory, consisting of

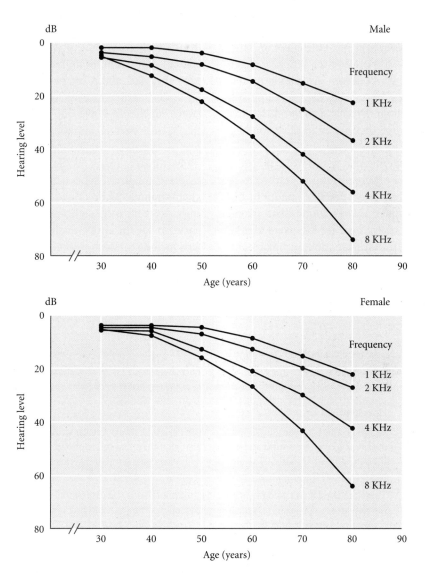

Figure 3.4 Gender differences in hearing loss. Notice that the changes in men are greater.

Source: J. M. Ordy, K. R. Brizzee, T. Beavers, & P. Medart. Age differences in the functional and structural organization of the auditory system in man. In J. M. Ordy & K. R. Brizzee (Eds.), *Sensory systems and communication in the elderly.* Copyright © Lippincott, Williams & Wilkins, 1979.

atrophy and degeneration of receptor cells; neural, consisting of a loss of neurons in the auditory pathway in the brain; metabolic, consisting of a diminished supply of nutrients to the cells in the receptor area; and mechanical, consisting of atrophy and stiffening of the vibrating structures in the receptor area. Knowing the cause of a person's presbycusis is important, because the different causes have different implications for other aspects of hearing (Whitbourne, 1996a). Sensory presbycusis has little effect on other hearing abilities. Neural presbycusis seriously affects the ability to understand speech. Metabolic presbycusis produces severe loss of sensitivity to all pitches. Finally, mechanical presbycusis also produces loss across all pitches, but the loss is greatest for high pitches.

Because hearing plays a major role in social communication, its progressive loss could have an equally important effect on people's quality of life. Dalton and colleagues (2003) found that people with moderate to severe hearing loss were significantly more likely to have functional impairments with tasks in daily life (e.g., shopping). In addition, they were more likely to have decreased cognitive functioning. Clearly, significant hearing impairment can result in decreased quality of life.

Loss of hearing in later life can also cause numerous adverse emotional reactions, such as loss of independence, social isolation, irritation, paranoia, and depression. Much research indicates hearing loss per se does not cause social maladjustment or emotional disturbance. However, friends and relatives of an older person with hearing loss often attribute emotional changes to hearing loss, which strains the quality of interpersonal relationships (Whitbourne, 1996a). Thus, hearing loss may not directly affect older adults' self-concept or emotions, but it may negatively affect how they feel about interpersonal communication. By understanding hearing loss problems and ways to overcome them, people who have no hearing loss can play a large part in minimizing the effects of hearing loss on the older people in their lives.

Fortunately, many people with hearing loss can be helped through two types of amplification systems and cochlear implants, described in Table 3.3. Analog hearing aids are the most common and least expensive, but they provide the lowest-quality sound. Digital hearing aids include microchips that can be programmed for different hearing situations. Cochlear implants do not amplify sound; rather, a microphone transmits sound to a receiver, which stimulates auditory nerve fibers directly. Although technology continues to improve,

Table 3.3

Helping People with Hearing Loss

Type of Device	How It Works
Analog hearing aid	Although there are various styles, the basic design is always the same. A mold is placed in the outer ear to pick up sound and send it through a tube to a microphone. The microphone sends the sound to an amplifier. The amplifier enhances the sound and sends it to the receiver. The receiver sends the amplified sound to the ear.
Digital hearing aid	These are similar to analog hearing aids, but digital aids use directional microphones to control the flow of sound. Compression technology allows the sound to be increased or decreased as it rises and falls naturally in the room. Microchips allow hearing aids to be programmed for different hearing situations. This technology also uses multiple channels to deliver sound with varying amplification characteristics.
Cochlear implant	The main difference between hearing aids and cochlear implants is that implants do not make the sound louder. Rather, the implant is a series of components. A microphone, usually mounted behind the ear on the scalp, picks up sound. The sound is digitized by microchips and turned into coded signals, which are broadcast via FM radio signals to electrodes that have been inserted into the inner ear during surgery. The electrodes stimulate the auditory nerve fibers directly.

none of these devices can duplicate your original equipment, so be kind to your ears.

Somesthesia and Balance

Imagine that you are locked in an embrace with a lover right now. Think about how good it feels when you are caressed lovingly, the tingly sensations you get. You can thank your somesthetic system for that; without it, you probably wouldn't bother. Remember Bertha, the older woman worried about falling? To maintain balance and avoid falls, your somesthetic system integrates a great deal of information about your body position.

Somesthesia. As you've probably discovered, a lover's touch feels different on various parts of your body. That's because the distribution of touch receptors is not consistent throughout the body; the greatest concentrations are in the lips, tongue, and fingertips. Although it takes more pressure with age to feel a touch on the smooth (nonhairy) skin on the hand such as the fingertips (Stevens, 1992), touch sensitivity in the hair-covered parts of the body is maintained into later life (Whitbourne, 1996a).

Older adults often report that they have more trouble regulating body temperature so that they feel comfortable. However, the research evidence to support this perception is conflicting. Some data suggest that the threshold for warmth increases somewhat (Whitbourne, 1996a). These data appear to conflict with lowered cold tolerance by older adults, which should create a much larger change in threshold. The discrepancy may be caused by different age effects between temperature sensitivity and temperature regulation, but we do not know for certain (Whitbourne, 1996a).

Sensations from the skin, internal organs, and joints serve critical functions. They keep us in contact with our environment, help us avoid falling, help us communicate, keep us safe, and factor into our perception of pain. In terms of self-esteem, how well our body is functioning tells us something about how well we are doing. Losing bodily sensations can have major implications; loss of sexual sensitivity and changes in the ability to regulate one's body temperature affect the quality of life. How a person views these changes is critical for maintaining self-esteem. We can help by providing supportive environments that lead to successful compensatory behaviors. Despite years of research, we do not understand how or even whether our ability to perceive these sensations changes with age. Part of the problem has to do with how such sensations, including pain, are measured and how individual differences in tolerance affects people's reports.

Balance. Bertha, the older woman we met in the vignette, as well as anyone riding a bicycle, is concerned about losing balance and falling. Bertha (and each of us) gets information about balance from the vestibular system, housed deep in the inner ear. The vestibular system is designed to respond to the forces of gravity as they act on the head and then to provide this information to the parts of the brain that initiate the appropriate movements so that we can maintain balance.

Dizziness (the vague feeling of being unsteady, floating, and light-headed) and vertigo (the sensation that one or one's surroundings are spinning) are common experiences for older adults. Although age-related structural changes in the vestibular system account for some of the problems, they do not entirely account for increases in dizziness and vertigo. Also, it takes older adults longer to integrate all the other sensory information coming to the brain to control posture (Aldwin & Gilmer, 2004). And dizziness can be a side effect of certain medications and physical illnesses.

Because of these changes, the likelihood of falling increases with age, especially after age 70 (Vereeck et al., 2008). Falls may be life-threatening events for older adults, especially for those with osteoporosis, because of the increased risk of broken bones. Environmental hazards such as loose rugs and slippery floors are more likely to be a factor for healthy, community-dwelling older adults, whereas disease is more likely to play a role in institutionalized people. Increases in body sway, the natural movement of the body to maintain balance, occur with increasing age. Connections between the degree of body sway and likelihood of falling have been shown, with people who fall often having more body sway (El Haber et al., 2008).

Preventing Falls through Tai Chi

Who were the investigators, and what were the aims of the studies? Helping older adults improve their balance is an important way to help lower the risk of falling. Tai chi, an ancient Chinese martial art, enhances body awareness. Previous research had shown that tai chi is an effective approach to improving balance, but whether it could be used with typical community-dwelling older adults was unknown. Li et al. (2008) examined whether using tai chi to improve balance could be implemented in a community-based senior center.

How did the investigators measure the topic of interest? Each Tai Chi—Moving for Better Movement class began with warm-up exercises, followed by teaching and practicing the 8-form variation of tai chi for 45 minutes, and ended with a 5-minute cooldown period. Program effectiveness was measured as the change in physical performance and quality of life as indexed by the functional reach test, the up-and-go test, time to rise from a chair, the 50-foot speed walk, and a 12-item physical and mental health scale. Frequency of falls was monitored monthly using a falls calendar in which participants marked when falls occurred. Long-term maintenance of the program was measured as the degree to which participants continued during the 12 weeks after the formal program ended.

Who were the participants in the study? Participants were 140 community-dwelling adults in Oregon who were over age 60, in good health, physically mobile, and did not show any mental deficits. The study was conducted in senior centers.

What was the design of the studies? The researchers used a pretest-posttest design to measure change. Participants took the one-hour tai chi classes twice per week for 12 weeks.

Were there ethical concerns with the study? Participants in the study were provided with informed consent and were closely monitored throughout the study, so there were no ethical concerns.

What were the results? Results showed that participants improved on all measures during the course of the program. No loss of improvement was observed in the 12 weeks following the end of the formal program.

What did the investigators conclude? Li and colleagues concluded that tai chi represents an effective intervention to improve older adults' movement to lower the risk of falling. It was easily adapted in senior centers, making it a low-cost, high-payoff intervention. Because tai chi is a low-impact martial art, it is easily adapted for use by older adults.

Because fear of falling has a real basis, it is important that concerns not be taken lightly. Older adults can be taught to pay greater attention to other cues, such as somesthetic ones. During times of dizziness or vertigo, people can learn to attend to the position of lower body limbs to better use this feedback in adjusting posture (Hu & Woollacott, 1994a, 1994b). People can also be trained to prevent falls through tai chi (Li et al., 2008), described in detail in the How Do We Know? feature.

Taste and Smell

Taste. There is an expression "too old to cut the mustard," which dates back to when people made mustard at home by grinding mustard seed and adding just the right amount of vinegar ("cutting the mustard") to balance the taste. If too much vinegar was added, the concoction tasted terrible, so the balance was critical. Many families found that older members tended to add too much vinegar.

Despite the everyday belief that taste ability changes with age, we do not have much data documenting what actually happens. We do know that the ability to detect different tastes declines gradually and that these declines vary a great deal from flavor to flavor and person to person and the amount of experience one has with particular substances (Bitnes et al., 2007). Whatever age differences we observe are not caused by a decline in the sheer number of taste buds; unlike other neural cells, the number of taste cells does not change appreciably across the life span (Whitbourne, 1996a).

Despite the lack of evidence of large declines in the ability to taste, there is little question that older adults complain more about boring food and are at risk for malnutrition as a result (Henkin, 2008). The explanation may be that changes in the enjoyment of food are caused by psychosocial issues (such as personal adjustment), changes in smell (which we consider next), or disease. For instance, we are much more likely to eat a balanced diet and to enjoy our food when we do not eat alone and when we get a whiff of the enticing aromas from the kitchen.

Smell. "Stop and smell the roses." "Ooh! What's that perfume you're wearing?" "Yuck! What's that smell?" There is a great deal of truth in the saying "The nose knows." Smell is a major part of our everyday lives. How something smells can alert us that dinner is cooking, warn of a gas leak or a fire, let us know that we are clean, or be sexually arousing. Many of our social interactions involve smell (or the lack of it). We spend billions of dollars making our bodies smell appealing to others. It is easy to see that any age-related change in sense of smell would have far-reaching consequences.

Researchers agree that the ability to detect odors remains fairly intact until the 60s, when it begins to decline, but there are wide variations across people and types of odors (Aldwin & Gilmer, 2004). These variations could have important practical implications. A large survey conducted by the National Geographic Society indicated that older adults were not as able to identify particular odors as younger people. One of the odors tested was the substance added to natural gas that enables people to detect leaks—not being able to identify it is a potentially fatal problem.

Abnormal changes in the ability to smell are turning out to be important in the differential diagnosis of probable Alzheimer's disease, resulting in the development of several quick tests such as the Pocket Smell Test (Steffens & Potter, 2008). According to several studies, people with Alzheimer's disease can identify only 60% of the odors identified by age-matched control participants; in more advanced stages of the disease, this further declined to only 40% compared with controls. These changes give clinicians another indicator for diagnosing suspected cases of Alzheimer's disease.

The major psychological consequences of changes in smell concern eating, safety, and pleasurable experiences. Odors play an important role in enjoying food and protecting us from harm. Socially, decreases in our ability to detect unpleasant odors may lead to embarrassing situations in which we are unaware that we have body odors or need to brush our teeth. Social interactions could suffer as a result of these problems. Smells also play a key role in remembering life experiences from the past. Who can forget the smell of cookies baking in Grandma's oven? Loss of odor cues may mean that our sense of the past suffers as well.

Concept Checks

1. What major structural changes in the eye occur with age? What functional effects do these changes have?
2. How does hearing change with age?
3. With age, what changes occur in somesthesia and balance?
4. How do the abilities to taste and smell change with age?

3.4 Vital Functions

LEARNING OBJECTIVES

- What age-related changes occur in the cardiovascular system? What types of cardiovascular disease are common in adult development and aging? What are the psychological effects of age-related changes in the cardiovascular system?

- What structural and functional changes occur with age in the respiratory system? What are the most common types of respiratory diseases in older adults? What are the psychological effects of age-related changes in the respiratory system?

Steve is an active 73-year-old man who walks and plays golf regularly. He smoked earlier in his life, but he quit years ago. He also watches his diet to control fat intake. Steve recently experienced some chest pains and sweating but dismissed it as simply age-related. After all, he thinks, I take care of myself. However, Steve's wife, Grace, is concerned he may have a more serious problem.

Two of the systems that are essential to life are the cardiovascular system and the respiratory system; that's why they are called vital functions. Each undergoes important normative changes with age that can affect the quality of life. In this section, we'll find out whether Grace has reason to worry about Steve's symptoms. We'll also discover why figuring out the pattern of age-related changes in the respiratory system is very difficult (here's a tip—it has to do with biological-psychological-environmental interactions). Overall, the age-related changes in the cardiovascular and respiratory systems are excellent examples of how the forces of development interact. On the biological front, we know that some cardiovascular and respiratory diseases have important genetic links. Psychologically, certain personality traits have been linked with increased risk of disease. Socioculturally, some cardiovascular and respiratory diseases are clearly tied to lifestyle. The impact of both cardiovascular and respiratory diseases also differs as a function of age. Let's explore in more detail how these various forces come together.

Cardiovascular System

Tune into your pulse. The beating of your heart is the work of an amazing organ. In an average lifetime, the heart beats more than 3 billion times, pumping the equivalent of more than 900 million gallons of blood. Two important age-related structural changes in the heart are the accumulation of fat deposits and the stiffening of the heart muscle caused by tissue changes. By the late 40s and early 50s, the fat deposits in the lining around the heart may form a continuous sheet. Meanwhile, healthy muscle tissue is being replaced by connective tissue, which causes a thickening and stiffening of the heart muscle and valves. These changes reduce the amount of muscle tissue available to contract the heart. The net effect is that the remaining muscle must work harder. To top it off, the amount of blood that the heart can pump declines from roughly 5 liters per minute at age 20 to about 3.5 liters per minute at age 70 (National Institute on Aging, 2008).

The most important change in the circulatory system involves the stiffening (hardening) of the walls of the arteries. These changes are caused by calcification of the arterial walls and by replacement of elastic fibers with less elastic ones.

The combination of changes in the heart and the circulatory system results in a significant decrease in a person's ability to cope with physical exertion, especially aerobic exercise. By age 65, the average adult has experienced a 60 to 70% decline in the aerobic capacity since young adulthood. However, if you stay in good shape throughout adulthood, the decline is much less (National Institute on Aging, 2008). This decline is one reason why older adults who are not in good shape are more likely to have heart attacks while performing moderately exerting tasks such as shoveling snow. The changes that occur with aging in the heart related to exercise are shown in Figure 3.5.

Cardiovascular Diseases. In the United States, someone dies from cardiovascular disease every 33 seconds (American Heart Association, 2004). It is the leading cause of death in all ethnic groups in the United States and in many other countries. The prevalence of cardiovascular disease increases dramatically with age, with the rates for men higher until age 75, when the rates for women are higher. Rates of cardiovascular disease have been declining in the United States among men since the 1980s (American Heart Association, 2007). These declines may be deceiving, though, because key risk factors are actually increasing; for example, over 66% of adults are classified as overweight, and rates of diabetes are going up.

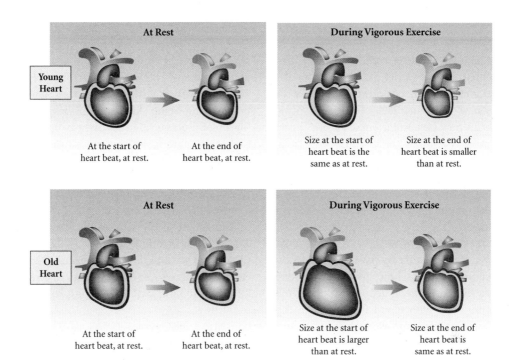

At Rest — Young Heart

At the start of heart beat, at rest.

At the end of heart beat, at rest.

During Vigorous Exercise — Young Heart

Size at the start of heart beat is the same as at rest.

Size at the end of heart beat is smaller than at rest.

At Rest — Old Heart

At the start of heart beat, at rest.

At the end of heart beat, at rest.

During Vigorous Exercise — Old Heart

Size at the start of heart beat is larger than at rest.

Size at the end of heart beat is same as at rest.

Figure 3.5 The Heart: Young and Old.

Source: National Institute on Aging (2008). *Aging hearts and arteries: A scientific quest.* Retreived September 3, 2008, from http://www.nia.nih.gov/HealthInformation/Publications/AgingHeartsandArteries/default.htm. Design by Levine and Associates, Washington, DC.

There are important ethnic and gender differences in cardiovascular disease. Why? Ethnic differences may be caused by differential genetic predisposition, quality of and access to health care, diet, weight, and stress (American Heart Association, 2008a). Although many people believe that gender differences can be traced to hormonal protection in premenopausal women caused by estrogen, the elimination of the gender gap by age 75 is not caused mostly by the lack of estrogen in postmenopausal women. Rather, the difference has more to do with the leveling off of death rates in men (Avis, 1999). However, menopause is associated with lower levels of HDL ("good") cholesterol and higher levels of LDL ("bad") cholesterol (Brown et al., 1993), so the full role of estrogen in cardiovascular disease has yet to be uncovered.

Several types of cardiovascular disease are noteworthy. **Congestive heart failure** *occurs when cardiac output and the ability of the heart to contract severely decline, making the heart enlarge, pressure in the veins increase, and the body swell.* Congestive heart failure is the most common cause of hospitalization for people over age 65. **Angina pectoris** *occurs when the oxygen supply to the heart muscle becomes insufficient, resulting in chest pain.* Angina may feel like chest pressure, a burning pain, or a squeezing that radiates from the chest to the back, neck, and arms (Mayo Clinic, 2007b). In most cases the pain is induced by physical exertion and is relieved within 5 to 10 minutes by rest. The most common treatment of angina is nitroglycerine, although in some cases coronary arteries may need to be cleared through surgical procedures or replaced through coronary bypass surgery.

Heart attack, called **myocardial infarction (MI)**, *occurs when blood supply to the heart is severely reduced or cut off.* Mortality after a heart attack is much higher for older adults (Centers for Disease Control and Prevention, 2008a). The initial symptoms of an MI are identical to those of angina but typically are more severe and prolonged; there may also be nausea, vomiting, severe weakness, and sweating, which Steve experienced in the vignette. Thus, Grace is right to be concerned about Steve's symptoms. In as many as 25% of patients, however, chest pain may be absent. These "silent" heart attacks are more common in older adults, especially those with diabetes (Centers for Disease Control and Prevention, 2008b). Treating heart attack victims of all ages includes careful evaluation and a prescribed rehabilitation program consisting of lifestyle changes in diet and exercise.

Atherosclerosis *is an age-related disease caused by the buildup of fat deposits on and the calcification of the arterial walls* (Mayo Clinic, 2008b). Much like sandbars in a river or mineral deposits in pipes, the fat deposits interfere with blood flow through the arteries. These deposits begin very early in life and continue throughout the life span. Some amount of fat deposit inevitably occurs and is considered a normal part of aging. However, excess deposits may develop from poor nutrition, smoking, and other aspects of an unhealthy lifestyle.

When severe atherosclerosis occurs in blood vessels that supply the brain, neurons may not receive proper nourishment, causing them to malfunction or die, a condition called cerebrovascular disease. *When the blood flow to a portion of the brain is completely cut off, a* **cerebrovascular accident (CVA),** *or stroke, results.* Estimates are that every 53 seconds someone in the United States has a CVA, making stroke one of the most common forms of cardiovascular disease (Centers for Disease Control and Prevention, 2008b). Causes of CVAs include clots that block blood flow in an artery or the actual breaking of a blood vessel, which creates a cerebral hemorrhage. The severity of a CVA and likelihood of recovery depend on the specific area of the brain involved, the extent of disruption in blood flow, and the duration of the disruption. Consequently, a CVA may affect such a small area that it goes almost unnoticed, or it may be so severe as to cause death. Two common problems following a CVA are *aphasia* (problems with speech) and *hemiplegia* (paralysis on one side of the body).

The risk of a CVA increases with age; in fact, CVAs are among the leading causes of death and chronic disorders among older adults in the United States (Centers for Disease Control and Prevention, 2008a). In addition to age, other risk factors include being male, being African American, and having high blood pressure, heart disease, or diabetes. The higher risk among African Americans appears to be caused by a greater prevalence of hypertension in this population compounded by poorer quality and access to health care in general (Centers for Disease Control and Prevention, 2008c).

Treatment of CVA has advanced significantly. The most important advance is use of the clot-dissolving drug tissue plasminogen activator (tPA) to treat CVAs (American Heart Association, 2008b). Currently, tPA is the only approved treatment for CVAs caused by blood clots, which constitute 80% of all CVAs. Not every patient should receive tPA treatment, and tPA is effective only if given promptly, which is vitally important. So if you or a person you know thinks they are experiencing a CVA, get medical attention immediately, because tPA therapy must be started within 3 hours after the onset of a stroke to be most effective. Recovery from CVA depends on the severity of the stroke, area and extent of the brain affected, and patient age.

Besides blood clots, high blood pressure plays a major role in CVAs. (Do you know what yours is?) Blood pressure consists of measuring two types of pressure: the pressure during the heart's contraction phase when it is pumping blood through the body, called the systolic pressure, and the pressure during the heart's relaxation phase between beats, called the diastolic pressure. The systolic pressure is always given first. On average, a blood pressure of 120 over 80 mm Hg (millimeters of mercury, the scale on which the pressure is measured) is considered optimal for adults. As we grow older, blood pressure tends to increase normally, mostly because of structural changes in the cardiovascular system. *When blood pressure increases become severe, defined as 140 mm Hg or more systolic pressure (the top number in a blood pressure reading) or 90 mm Hg or more diastolic pressure (the lower number in the reading), the disease* **hypertension**

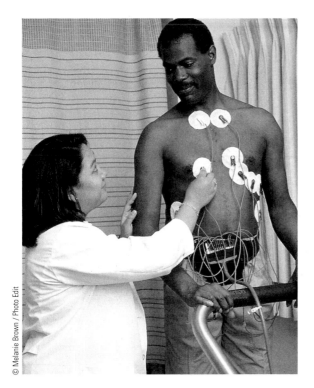

© Melanie Brown / Photo Edit

African American men are at especially high risk for hypertension.

results (American Heart Association, 2008c). Roughly 30% of the population age 20 and older has some degree of hypertension. This rate is roughly the same for European Americans and Mexican Americans, but jumps to about 42% among African Americans (Centers for Disease Control and Prevention, 2008c). This difference may be caused by a genetic mutation affecting enzymes that help control blood pressure and by environmental factors related to stress, poor access to health care, and poverty.

Hypertension is a disease you ignore at the risk of greatly increasing your chances of dying. Older adults with hypertension have three times the risk of dying from cardiovascular disease, and it has important negative effects on cognitive abilities and a host of other organs including kidney function (American Heart Association, 2008c; Centers for Disease Control and Prevention, 2008a). Because hypertension is a disease with no clear symptoms, most people with undiagnosed hypertension are not aware they have a problem. Regular blood pressure

monitoring is the only sure way to find out whether you have hypertension. It could save your life.

What causes this silent killer? Two primary causes are stress and dietary sodium. Stress comes from many sources besides the more obvious ones that quickly come to mind (e.g., job). For example, Espino and Maldonado (1990) report that the rate of hypertension was higher among Mexican Americans who were more acculturated into the American lifestyle. In fact, degree of acculturation was a better predictor of hypertension than were socioeconomic variables such as income. They speculate that with acculturation come higher levels of stress and the adoption of a less healthful diet that puts such people at risk. Similarly, Cooper and colleagues (1999) showed that people of African descent around the world differ significantly in their rates of hypertension: Societies in which racism is a major social problem (especially the United States and the United Kingdom) have the highest rates.

Eating sodium in one's diet is essential for life because the body needs a certain amount each day to regulate blood pressure and blood volume properly (McGee, 2007). Too much sodium can have several very bad health effects: In addition to hypertension, it can cause congestive heart failure and kidney disease (McGee, 2007). Sodium occurs naturally in many foods, such as raw celery, many cheeses, and scallops. It is also present in nearly all processed foods, often in high concentrations; for example, one serving of typical saltine crackers contains 1,100 milligrams, pretzels have 1,650, and a hot dog about 1,100. When you consider that the American Heart Association (2008d) recommends that adults should not consume more than 2,300 milligrams per day (about a teaspoon), it is clear that getting too much sodium is easy to do.

Another chronic cardiovascular condition that is discussed less often is *hypotension,* or low blood pressure. Symptoms of hypotension include dizziness or light-headedness that is caused most commonly when you stand up quickly after lying down or sitting, or sometimes after eating (Weinrauch, 2007). Hypotension often is related to anemia and is more common in older adults. Although hypotension per se is not a dangerous condition, the resulting dizziness can increase the likelihood of fainting and falls, which may result in more serious injury.

Respiratory System

You probably don't pay much attention to your breathing unless you're gasping for breath after exercise—or you're an older adult. Older adults tend to notice their breathing a great deal more. Why? With increasing age, the rib cage and the air passageways become stiffer, making it harder to breathe. The lungs change in appearance over time, going gradually from their youthful pinkish color to a dreary gray, caused mainly by breathing in carbon particles (from air pollution). The maximum amount of air we can take into the lungs in a single breath begins to decline in the 20s, decreasing by 40% by age 85. And the rate at which we can exchange oxygen for carbon dioxide drops significantly as the membranes of the air sacs in the lungs deteriorate (Pride, 2005).

One of the difficulties in understanding age-related changes in the respiratory system is that it is hard to know how much of the change is caused specifically by normative developmental factors and how much is caused by environmental factors. For example, it is difficult to determine how much age-related change in respiratory function is due to air pollution.

Respiratory Diseases. *The most common and incapacitating respiratory disorder in older adults is* **chronic obstructive pulmonary disease (COPD),** *a family of diseases that includes chronic bronchitis and emphysema.* By 2005, COPD was the fourth leading cause of death in the United States, with rates higher in women than in men. Smoking is the most important cause of COPD, but secondhand smoke, air pollution, and industrial dusts and chemicals can also cause it (American Lung Association, 2008).

Emphysema *is the most serious type of COPD and is characterized by the destruction of the membranes around the air sacs in the lungs* (American Lung Association, 2008). This irreversible destruction creates holes in the lung, drastically reducing the ability to exchange oxygen and carbon dioxide. To make matters worse, the bronchial tubes collapse prematurely when the person exhales, thereby preventing the lungs from emptying completely.

Emphysema is a very debilitating disease. In its later stages, even the smallest physical exertion causes a struggle for air. People with emphysema may have such poorly oxygenated blood that they become confused and disoriented. About 95% of the cases of emphysema are self-induced by smoking; the remaining cases are caused by a genetic deficiency of a protein known as an a_1-antitrypsin (American Lung Association, 2008). This protein, a natural "lung protector," is made by the liver; when it is missing, emphysema is inevitable. Although some drugs are available to help ease breathing, lung transplantation remains a treatment of last resort for people with emphysema, especially in the genetic form of the disease.

Chronic bronchitis can occur at any age, but it is more common in people over age 45, especially among people who are exposed to high concentrations of dust, irritating fumes, and air pollution. Treatment usually consists of medication (called bronchodilators) to open bronchial passages and a change of work environment. Similarly, asthma is another very common respiratory disease that is increasing in prevalence. Treatment for asthma also involves the use of bronchodilators.

Overall, treatment for COPD needs to begin as soon as a problem is diagnosed. That may involve stopping smoking (the best treatment available for smokers). In other cases, supplemental oxygen or using glucocorticosteroid medications may provide some relief. The thing to remember, though, is that the damage caused by COPD is irreversible.

Concept Check

1. What are the major age-related changes in the cardiovascular system?
2. What are the major age-related changes in the respiratory system?

3.5 The Reproductive System

LEARNING OBJECTIVES

- What reproductive changes occur in women?
- What reproductive changes occur in men?
- What are the psychological effects of reproductive changes?

*H*elen woke up in the middle of the night drenched in sweat. She'd been feeling fine when she went to bed after her 48th birthday party, so she wasn't sure what was the matter. She thought she was too young to experience menopause. Helen wonders what other things she'll experience.

As you probably surmised, Helen has begun going through "the change," a time of life that many women look forward to and just as many see as the beginning of old age. *It is a time during which a major biological process, called the* **climacteric,** *occurs during which a woman will pass from her reproductive to nonreproductive years. In Helen's case, she is entering the perimenopausal phase, which leads into* **menopause,** *the point at which her ovaries will stop releasing eggs.* For women, the climacteric is the defining physiological event in middle age. Men do not endure such sweeping biological changes but experience several gradual changes instead. Beyond the physiological effects, these changes have important psychological implications because many people think midlife is a key time for redefining ourselves. Let's see how the experience differs for women and men.

Female Reproductive System

As Helen is beginning to experience, the major reproductive change in women during adulthood is the loss of the natural ability to bear children. Called *perimenopause,* this transition begins in the 40s, as menstrual cycles become irregular and some women experience things such as night sweats, and is generally complete by age 50 to 55 (National Women's Health Information Center, 2008a). This time of transition is called *menopause,* and how long it lasts varies considerably (Mayo Clinic, 2002a). The gradual loss and eventual end of monthly periods is accompanied by decreases in estrogen and progesterone levels, changes in the reproductive organs, and changes in sexual functioning (National Women's Health Information Center, 2008a).

A variety of physical and psychological symptoms may accompany perimenopause and menopause with decreases in hormonal levels (National Women's Health Information Center, 2008b): hot flashes, night sweats, headaches, sleep problems, mood changes, more urinary infections, pain during sex, difficulty concentrating, vaginal dryness, less interest in sex, and an increase in body fat around the waist. Many women report no symptoms at all, but most women experience at least some, and there are large ethnic and cultural group differences in how they are expressed (Banger, 2003). For example, women in the Mayan culture of Mexico and Central America welcome menopause and its changes as a natural phenomenon and do not attach any stigma to aging (Mahady et al., 2008). In the United States, Latinas and African Americans, especially working-class women, tend to view menopause more positively whereas European American women describe it more negatively (Dillaway et al., 2008).

Cultural differences are exemplified in Lock's (1991) classic study of Japanese women. Fewer than 13% of Japanese women whose menstrual periods were becoming irregular reported having hot flashes during the previous 2 weeks, compared with nearly half of Western women. In fact, fewer than 20% of Japanese women in the study had ever had a hot flash, compared with nearly 65% of Western women. However, Japanese women reported more headaches, shoulder stiffness, ringing in the ears, and dizziness than Western women. Why? The answer seems to be the power of sociocultural forces. In Japan, society considers "menopausal syndrome" to be a modern affliction of women with too much time on their hands. With this official attitude, it is hard to know whether Japanese women actually experience menopause differently or may simply be reluctant to describe their true experience.

Similar findings were reported by Fu, Anderson, and Courtney (2003), who compared Taiwanese and Australian women. Significant differences were found in their attitudes toward menopause, menopausal symptoms, and physical vitality. These results clearly indicate that sociocultural factors are critical in understanding women's experience during menopause.

One way to address the symptoms associated with the climacteric is hormone replacement therapy. Many physicians point out that having women take hormones after menopause may also provide some protection against cardiovascular disease, as described earlier in this chapter. Although there

CURRENT CONTROVERSIES

Hormone Replacement Therapy

There is probably no medical topic more controversial than hormone replacement therapy (HRT). For many years, women have had the choice of taking medications to replace the female hormones that are not produced naturally by the body after menopause. HRT may involve taking estrogen alone, or in combination with progesterone (or progestin in its synthetic form). Until about 2003, it was thought that HRT was beneficial for most women, and results from several studies were positive. But results from the Women's Health Initiative research in the United States and the Million Women Study in the United Kingdom indicated that for some types of HRT there were several potentially very serious side effects. Consequently, physicians are now far more cautious in recommending HRT.

The Women's Health Initiative (WHI), begun in the United States in 1991, was a very large study (National Heart, Lung, and Blood Institute, 2003). The postmenopausal hormone therapy clinical trial had two parts. The first involved 16,608 postmenopausal women with a uterus who took either estrogen plus progestin therapy or a placebo. The second involved 10,739 women who had a hysterectomy and were taking estrogen alone or a placebo. The estrogen plus progestin trial used 0.625 milligram of estrogens taken daily plus 2.5 milligrams of medroxyprogesterone acetate taken daily (Prempro). This

combination was chosen because it is the mostly commonly prescribed form of the combined hormone therapy in the United States, and, in several observational studies, it had appeared to benefit women's health. The women in the WHI estrogen plus progestin study were aged 50 to 79 when they enrolled in the study between 1993 and 1998. The health of study participants was carefully monitored by an independent panel called the Data and Safety Monitoring Board (DSMB). The study was stopped in July 2002 because investigators discovered a significant increased risk for breast cancer and that overall the risks outnumbered the benefits. However, in addition to the increased risk of breast cancer, heart attack, stroke, and blood clots, HRT resulted in fewer hip fractures and lower rates of colorectal cancer.

The Million Women Study began in 1996 and included 1 in 4 women over age 50 in the United Kingdom, the largest study of its kind ever conducted. Like the Women's Health Initiative, the study examined how HRT (both estrogen/progestin combinations and estrogen alone) affects breast cancer, cardiovascular disease, and other aspects of women's health.

Results from these large-scale studies are confusing (Shapiro, 2007). An overview of the results based on what type of HRT women were taking is presented in Table 3.4.

A newer approach to HRT involves a class of compounds called *selective estrogen receptor modulators (SERMs)*, which can be considered "designer estrogens," each of which has its own way of acting and so must be evaluated individually (Shelly et al., 2008). SERMs have the protective properties of estrogen on bone tissue and the cardiovascular system and seem to block some estrogen effects on breast tissue. However, there is some evidence that they may stimulate growth of uterine cells, slightly increasing the risk of uterine cancer, or may cause hot flashes. In essence, they have the advantages of traditional HRT with fewer negative side effects. Two SERMs that have been approved for use in preventing breast cancer and are being intensively studied are tamoxifen and raloxifene, with others in development (National Cancer Institute, 2007).

In sum, women have difficult choices to make when deciding whether to use HRT to combat certain symptoms related to menopause and to protect themselves against other diseases. To date, research evidence about the long-term risks of HRT is clear in the case of the most common estrogen-progesterone combination. The best course of action is to consult closely with one's physician to weight the benefits and risks.

Table 3.4

Benefits and Risks of HRT Therapy

	Women with a Uterus Estrogen + Progestin	Women Without a Uterus* Estrogen Only
BENEFITS		
Relieves hot flashes/night sweats	Yes	Yes
Relieves vaginal dryness	Yes	Yes
Reduces risk of bone fractures	Yes	Yes
Improves cholesterol levels	Yes	Yes
Reduces risk of colon cancer	Yes	Don't know
RISKS		
Increases risk of stroke	Yes	Yes
Increases risk of serious blood clots	Yes	Yes
Increases risk of heart attack	Yes	No
Increases risk of breast cancer	Yes	Possibly
Increases risk of dementia, when begun by women age 65 and older	Yes	Yes
Unpleasant side effects, such as bloating and tender breasts	Yes	Yes
Pill form can raise level of triglycerides (a type of fat in the blood)	Yes	Yes

*Women who have had a hysterectomy and have had their uterus removed.

Source: National Institute on Aging (2006); http://www.niapublications.org/tipsheets/hormones.asp.

is evidence that estrogen and progesterone influence the brain mechanisms that underlie learning and memory, the value of hormone replacement therapy as a treatment or deterrent for cognitive impairment remains largely unknown (Dohanich, 2003). For these reasons, as discussed in the Current Controversies feature, probably no other area of medical research has resulted in more contradictory data about the potentially serious side effects (or lack thereof) than has work on hormone replacement therapy.

Women's genital organs undergo progressive change after menopause (Aldwin & Gilmer, 2004).

The vaginal walls shrink and become thinner, the size of the vagina decreases, vaginal lubrication is reduced and delayed, and the external genitalia shrink somewhat. These changes have important effects on sexual activity, such as an increased possibility of painful intercourse and a longer time and more stimulation needed to reach orgasm. Failure to achieve orgasm is more common in midlife and beyond than in a woman's younger years. However, maintaining an active sex life throughout adulthood lowers the degree to which problems are encountered. Despite these changes, there is no physiological reason not to continue having an active and enjoyable sex life from middle age through late life. The vaginal dryness that occurs, for example, can be countered by using personal lubricants, such as *K-Y* or *Astroglide*.

Whether women continue to have an active sex life has a lot more to do with the availability of a suitable partner than a woman's desire for sexual relations. This is especially true for older women. The AARP *Modern Maturity* sexuality study (AARP, 1999a) and the *Sex in America* study (Jacoby, 2005) found that older married women were far more likely to have an active sex life than unmarried women. The primary reason for the decline in women's sexual activity with age is the lack of a willing or appropriate partner, not a lack of physical ability or desire (AARP, 1999a; Jacoby, 2005).

Male Reproductive System

Unlike women, men do not have a physiological (and cultural) event to mark reproductive changes, although there is a gradual decline in testosterone levels (Seidman, 2003). Men do not experience a complete loss of the ability to father children, as this varies widely from individual to individual, but men do experience a normative decline in the quantity of sperm (Knowles, 2006). However, even at age 80 a man is still half as fertile as he was at age 25 and is quite capable of fathering a child.

With increasing age the prostate gland enlarges, becomes stiffer, and may obstruct the urinary tract. Prostate cancer becomes a real threat during middle age; annual screenings are extremely important for men over age 50 (American Cancer Society, 2008a). Testosterone levels stay about the same or decrease only slightly in most men (Knowles, 2006). However, some men who experience an abnormally rapid decline in testosterone production during their late 60s report symptoms similar to those experienced by some menopausal women, such as hot flashes, chills, rapid heart rate, and nervousness (Ebersole et al., 2004).

Men experience some physiological changes in sexual performance. By old age, men report less perceived demand to ejaculate, a need for longer time and more stimulation to achieve erection and orgasm, and a much longer resolution phase during which erection is impossible (Saxon & Etten,

1994). Older men also report more frequent failures to achieve orgasm and loss of erection during intercourse (AARP, 1999a; Jacoby, 2005). However, the advent of Viagra and other medications to treat erectile dysfunction has provided older men with easy-to-use medical treatments and the possibility of an active sex life well into later life.

As with women, as long as men enjoy sex and have a willing partner, sexual activity is a lifelong option. Also as with women, the most important ingredient of sexual intimacy for men is a strong relationship with a partner (AARP, 1999a; Jacoby, 2005). For example, married men in early middle age tend to have intercourse four to eight times per month. The loss of an available partner is a significant reason frequency of intercourse drops on average by two and three times per month in men over age 50 and 60, respectively (Araujo, Mohr, & McKinlay, 2004).

Psychological Implications

Older adults say that engaging in sexual behavior is an important aspect of human relationships throughout adulthood (AARP, 1999a; Jacoby, 2005). Healthy adults at any age are capable of having and enjoying sexual relationships. Moreover, the desire to do so normally does not diminish. Unfortunately, one of the myths in our society is that older adults cannot and should not be sexual. Many young adults find it difficult to think about their grandparents in this way.

Such stereotyping has important consequences. What do you think to yourself when we see an older couple being publicly affectionate? Can you envision your grandparents enjoying an active sex life? Many people feel that such behavior is cute. But observers tend not to refer to their own or their peers' relationships in this way. Many nursing homes and other institutions actively dissuade their residents from having sexual relationships and may even refuse to allow married couples to share the same room. Adult children may believe their widowed parent does not have the right to establish a new sexual relationship. The message we are sending is that sexual activity is fine for the young but not for the old. The major reason why older women do not engage in sexual relations is the lack of a socially sanctioned partner. It is not that they have lost interest; rather, they believe they are simply not permitted to express their sexuality any longer.

Concept Check
1. What physical symptoms accompany age-related changes in women's reproductive system?
2. What are the major changes in men's reproductive system?
3. How does sexual activity change with age?

3.6 The Nervous System

LEARNING OBJECTIVES

- How do we measure changes in the brain?
- What major changes occur in neurons? How does the ability of neurons to communicate with each other change with age? What are the psychological effects of changes in the brain?
- What major changes occur in the autonomic nervous system?

Jorge is an active 83-year-old former factory worker who lives with his wife, Olivia, in a crowded apartment in Los Angeles. Over the past few years, Jorge has had increasing difficulty handling the heat of southern California summers. Olivia has noticed that Jorge takes more naps during the day and sleeps poorly at night. Jorge and Olivia wonder whether there is something wrong with him.

Our brains are the most complex structures yet discovered in the universe. Everything that makes us individuals is housed in the brain, and we are only now beginning to unlock its mysteries. The major challenge is that observing age-related changes in the brain is difficult. Usually we must rely on indirect evidence such as memory problems. However, advances in brain-imaging techniques are making it easier to watch ongoing brain activity in people of different ages.

In this section, we consider the age-related changes that occur in the central nervous system (the brain and spinal cord) and the autonomic nervous system (nerves in the rest of the body). Understanding normative changes in the central nervous system sets the stage for understanding diseases such as Alzheimer's disease, discussed in Chapter 4, as well as many of the cognitive changes discussed in Chapters 2, 6, 7, and 8. Jorge's experiences are related to changes in the autonomic nervous system; we'll discover whether Jorge's problems are normative.

Studying Brain–Behavior Relations: Imaging Techniques

If we could peek inside a living, working brain, what would we find? The answer to this question turns out to be one of the most exciting avenues of research on brain development. Investigators can now use computer-enhanced images to assist in diagnosing disease and even to study the thinking brain. As described in Table 3.5, researchers use three main imaging techniques to do this: computed

Table 3.5

Brain-Imaging Techniques

Type of Imaging	Description
Computed tomography (CT)	Images created by passing highly focused X-rays in various directions through the patient, with computers creating a three-dimensional image.
Magnetic resonance imaging (MRI)	Images produced by reorienting the body's molecules with large and very powerful magnets; detectors pick up radio frequencies that are shot through the body section under study. Can be used to study some physiological processes.
Positron emission tomography (PET)	Images created by injecting a radioactive isotope and passing positrons (subatomic particles) through the body from various directions, detecting them, and analyzing them. Very useful technique for studying brain activity, typically by examining glucose metabolism.

tomography (CT) scans, magnetic resonance imaging (MRI), and positron emission tomography (PET). CT and MRI are widely used not only in research but also in diagnosing brain diseases such as tumors and strokes. All three have provided fascinating insights into brain functioning.

Future insights into brain aging will come from neuroscience research using imagery techniques that examine relations with specific findings from molecular biological and genetic studies.

Central Nervous System

If you ask older adults to describe their experience of changes in their central nervous system, it's likely that they will be hard pressed to do so. This is because the age-related changes in the brain that we will consider begin very subtly; they are often difficult to notice in the beginning and to document because they are microscopic and are hard to tie to specific behaviors. *Changes in the brain occur mainly at the level of individual brain cells, called* **neurons.** Much of what we have learned about age-related brain changes has come from highly sophisticated computer-enhanced imaging techniques and from careful research in neuroscience (described in Chapter 2). In this discussion we consider primarily changes that are currently viewed as normative. Abnormal brain aging, such as that which occurs in Alzheimer's disease, is considered in more detail in Chapter 4.

As you can see in Figure 3.6, neurons have several parts that play specialized roles in receiving, conducting, and transmitting information. At the left end of the neuron in the figure are the *dendrites,* which pick up the chemical signals coming in from other nearby neurons much as TV antennae pick up signals from nearby stations. The signal is brought into the *cell body,* where it is converted into an electrochemical impulse and sent down the *axon* to the terminal branches. The *terminal branches,* shown at the right end of the drawing, act like transmitter stations. Chemicals called *neurotransmitters* are released at the terminal branches and carry the information signal to the next neuron's dendrites. The neurotransmitters are necessary for communication between neurons because neurons do not physically touch one another. The gap between the terminal branches of one neuron and the dendrites of another, across which neurotransmitters travel, is called the synapse.

We are born with roughly 1 trillion neurons of different sizes and shapes, which constitute all the neurons we will ever have. The good news is that neurons can grow in size and complexity

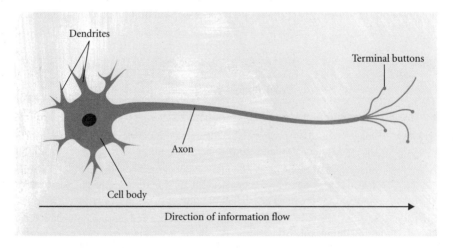

Figure 3.6 Diagram of a typical neuron.

across the life span; the bad news is that, like heart muscle cells, neurons cannot regenerate (Green & Ostrander, 2008). Once a neuron dies, it is lost forever. But we will also see that there is a line of exciting research that indicates the brain may be able to resist negative changes and provide alternative ways to process information.

Individual neurons undergo a wide variety of normative age-related changes. In most people, these changes produce little noticeable difference in behavior until very old age. However, when the changes are widespread and occur more rapidly, disease typically is present. One problem in differentiating between normal and abnormal brain aging is that many of the same changes underlie both; for example, the defining characteristics of brain changes in Alzheimer's disease also are normative. So in order to differentiate normative and abnormal brain aging, repeated assessment using sophisticated brain-imaging techniques is usually necessary (Carlson et al., 2008).

A second problem is that although we have documented many neuronal changes, we understand the implications of only a few. Tying specific brain changes to specific behaviors is very difficult. However, significant advances have been made using sophisticated brain-imaging techniques.

Structural Changes in Neurons. How does the structure of neurons change with age? The most important change in the cell body and axon involves changes in the fibers contained there. *Sometimes, for reasons we do not understand, neurons in certain parts of the brain develop* **neurofibrillary tangles,** *in which fibers in the axon become twisted together to form paired helical, or spiral, filaments* (Green & Ostrander, 2008). Large concentrations of neurofibrillary tangles are associated with behavioral abnormalities and are one defining structural brain change characteristic of Alzheimer's disease (Wippold, 2008). However, researchers do not yet understand what causes neurofibrillary tangles or why the rate of change differs across people. To complicate matters even more, some degree of neurofibrillary tangling occurs normally as we age. This is an example of why it is sometimes difficult to tell the difference between normal and abnormal aging.

Changes in the dendrites are complex. As some neurons deteriorate and die, there is a compensatory lengthening and increase in the number of dendrites of the remaining neurons (Matus, 2005). There is ample evidence, though, that the organization of the brain's circuitry is constantly changing as a result of experience (Kolb et al., 2003; Matus, 2005). *This capability of the brain to adapt its functional and structural organization to current requirements is called* **plasticity** (Matus, 2005; Röder & Rösler, 2003).

One promising line of research shows that exercise may be an effective way to enhance brain health and plasticity (Churchill et al., 2002; Cotman & Berchtold, 2002). Voluntary exercise increases levels of brain-derived neurotrophic factor (BDNF) and other brain growth factors, which play a major role in supporting the survival and growth of neurons (Cotman & Berchtold, 2002; Lu, 2003). In addition, these compounds help make synapses work more efficiently and effectively, and foster the creation of alternative pathways to process information. All these effects help keep brain function intact, thereby possibly slowing the rate of change.

The new connections between the dendrites may make up for the loss of neurons, but only to a point. Eventually, the loss of neurons outpaces the ability of remaining neurons to make connections. The rate of this shift may be a difference between normal and abnormal aging, but additional research on this issue is necessary.

Damaged and dying neurons sometimes collect around a core of protein and produce **amyloid plaques.** Brain-imaging techniques show that amyloid plaques can develop in various parts of the brain (Nordberg, 2008). Although the number of neuritic plaques increases with age, large numbers of them are not observed in normal brain aging until late in life. Until then, high concentrations of neuritic plaques are considered characteristic of abnormal aging; for example, they are also indicative of Alzheimer's disease (Nordberg, 2008).

The normative loss and growth pattern in neurons may provide insight into abnormal brain aging. It could be that abnormal brain aging occurs when losses greatly outnumber gains before very old age. This is clearly the case in conditions such as Alzheimer's disease and related disorders, in which there is massive progressive loss of neurons in many areas of the brain.

Changes in Communication between Neurons. Because neurons do not physically touch one another, they must communicate by releasing neurotransmitters into the synapse. Are there age-related changes in neurotransmitters? Yes, and the changes help us understand why some older adults experience certain kinds of problems and diseases. Changes in the level of neurotransmitters affect the efficiency of information transmission between neurons. Age-related changes occur along several neurotransmitter pathways, which are groups of neurons that use the same neurotransmitter (Whitbourne, 1996a).

One pathway in the brain that is responsible for controlling motor movements uses the neurotransmitter dopamine. *As we age, the level of dopamine decreases; if this decline is extreme due to the loss of dopamine-producing neurons, we develop* **Parkinson's disease** (National Institute of Neurological Disorders and Stroke, 2008). Parkinson's disease is characterized by four key sets of symptoms: tremors of the hands, arms, and legs, which decrease when one is performing voluntary tasks; rigidity or stiffness in the arms, legs, and trunk; difficulty keeping one's balance; and a shuffling walking style

Jamie McCarthy/WireImage for The Michael J Fox Foundation/Getty Images

Parkinson's disease has become better known because it has struck famous people, such as Michael J. Fox.

(National Institute of Neurological Disorders and Stroke, 2008). Many famous people, including former boxer Muhammad Ali and actor Michael J. Fox, have Parkinson's disease.

Recent evidence indicates that Parkinson's disease may be induced by frequent use of MDMA, more commonly known as "ecstasy" (Kuniyoshi & Jankovic, 2003). The drug's effects on the dopamine system appear to trigger the symptoms of the disease.

Although there is no cure, medications or surgery can alleviate the symptoms of Parkinson's disease, and researchers have discovered a gene they believe is responsible for a form of Parkinson's that may result in future innovative treatments. One drug, L-dopa, is converted into the neurotransmitter dopamine, which helps restore the normal balance of the neurotransmitter (National Institute of Neurological Disorders and Stroke, 2008). Drugs that mimic dopamine's role in the brain also allow patients to regain some of their lost muscle control.

Additionally, two catechol-O-methyltransferase (COMT) inhibitors (e.g., entacapone and talcapone) are approved for use with L-dopa in the United States (National Institute of Neurological Disorders and Stroke, 2008). COMT inhibitors block a key enzyme responsible for breaking down L-dopa before it reaches the brain, making L-dopa more effective. Surgical interventions include "brain pacemakers," which consist of a wire surgically implanted deep within the brain and connected to a pulse generator, similar to a cardiac pacemaker, implanted near the collarbone. Whenever a tremor begins, a patient can activate the device by passing a handheld magnet over the generator. Other surgical interventions include destroying certain parts of the brain that are overactive in Parkinson's disease (National Institute of Neurological Disorders and Stroke, 2008).

Recently, much attention has been focused on transplanting fetal tissue containing dopamine neuron precursors as a potential treatment for Parkinson's disease; this approach has shown some promise (Svendsen, 2008). Because stem cells are the parent cells of all tissues in the body, researchers believe that one day they may be able to direct the cells to become dopamine-producing neurons that could provide a treatment, but not a cure (Svendsen, 2008).

Despite the range of therapies available to ease the disease's debilitating symptoms, however, treatments now on the market can neither replace the faulty nerve cells that cause the disease nor stop Parkinson's from progressing.

Age-related declines in other neurotransmitters are well documented. For example, the age-related declines in the neurotransmitter acetylcholine are linked with both normative memory problems in old age and several diseases (Katz & Peters, in press). Research interest in acetylcholine is spurred by its link to both Alzheimer's disease and Huntington's disease. For example, levels are reduced by as much as 90% in Alzheimer's disease (Giacobini, 2003). Much of the search for drugs to alleviate the symptoms of Alzheimer's focuses on this and other enzymes related to acetylcholine.

In a thorough review of the clinical evidence concerning compounds that are thought to affect the brain mechanisms underlying memory, McDaniel, Maier, and Einstein (2002) conclude that very little evidence supports the idea that there may be "brain-specific" nutrients that enhance memory. They point out that early positive results in animal research do not always translate into human benefits, and that the complex brain processes involved in cognitive functioning make it difficult to isolate individual compounds that are effective. Dodge and colleagues (2008) concluded that the use of compounds such as *Ginkgo biloba* may help prevent mild cognitive decline, but only when participants adhered to the scheduled dosage. But because the experimental group also had more strokes, they concluded that the results were too tentative to draw any firm conclusions.

Autonomic Nervous System

Do you feel hot or cold right now? Do your palms sweat when you get nervous? These and other regulation functions in your body are controlled by the autonomic nervous system. Fortunately, few changes occur in the autonomic nervous system as we age, but two changes do tend to get people's attention: body temperature control and sleep. Jorge, whom we met in the vignette, is experiencing both of these changes.

Regulating Body Temperature. Every year, newscasts around the world report that during cold or hot spells more older adults die than people in other age groups. Why does this happen? We considered evidence earlier in this chapter that cold and warm temperature thresholds may change little. If older people can feel cold and warm stimuli placed against them about as well as people of other age groups, what accounts for these deaths?

It turns out that older adults have difficulty telling that their core body temperature is low (Van Someren, 2007). In other words, older people are much less likely to notice that they are cold. To make matters worse, older adults also have slower vasoconstrictor response, which is the ability to raise core body temperature when the body's peripheral temperature drops (DeGroot & Kenney, 2007; Van Someren, 2007). Similarly, older adults have trouble responding to high heat, because they do not sweat as much (Kenney & Munce, 2003). Even when they are hot, older adults are less likely to drink water, because they have lower thirst sensitivity (Phillips et al., 1991).

Taken together, the difficulties older adults have in regulating body temperature in extreme cold and heat are the primary reason why older adults are much more susceptible to hypothermia (body temperature below 95°F over a long period) and hyperthermia (body temperature above 98.6°F that cannot be relieved by sweating) (Kenney & Munce, 2003). This is why social service agencies are especially mindful of older adults during major weather events.

Sleep and Aging. How did you sleep last night? If you are older, chances are that you had some trouble. In fact, sleep complaints and problems are common in older adults (Wolkove et al., 2007a). These complaints most often concern difficulty in falling asleep, frequent or prolonged awakenings during the night, early morning awakenings, and a feeling of not sleeping very well. Effects of poor sleep are experienced the next day; moodiness, poorer performance on tasks involving sustained concentration, fatigue, and lack of motivation are some of the telltale signs.

Nearly every aspect of sleep undergoes age-related changes (Wolkove et al., 2007a). It takes older adults longer to fall asleep, they are awake more at night, they are more easily awakened, and they experience major shifts in their sleep–wake cycles, called circadian rhythms. Across adulthood, circadian rhythms move from a two-phase pattern of sleep (awake during the day and asleep at night for most people) to a multiphase rhythm reminiscent of that of infants (daytime napping and shorter sleep cycles at night). These changes are related to the changes in regulating core body temperature discussed earlier. Other major causes of sleep disturbance include *sleep apnea* (stopping breathing for 5 to 10 seconds), periodic leg jerks, heartburn, frequent need to urinate, poor physical health, and depression.

Older adults try lots of things to help themselves, such as taking daytime naps, without success (Wolkove et al., 2007b). As a result, many older adults are prescribed sleeping pills or hypnotic sedatives. But these medications must be used with great caution with older adults, and often do not help alleviate the problem in any case. Among the most effective treatments of sleep problems are increasing physical exercise, reducing caffeine intake, avoiding daytime naps, and making sure that the sleeping environment is as quiet and dark as possible (Passarella & Duong, 2008; Wolkove et al., 2007b).

As we now know, Jorge's difficulty with heat and sleep reflect normative changes that occur with age. Olivia should be informed of these changes and encouraged to make sure Jorge drinks plenty of water and adopts good sleep habits.

Psychological Implications

Probably the worst stereotype about aging is that older adults "get senile." Older adults may even consider an insignificant memory lapse as evidence of impending senility, even though memory lapses normally occur throughout life (see Chapter 6). But the term *senility* has no valid medical or psychological meaning, and its continued use simply perpetuates the myth that drastic mental decline is a product of normal aging (Qualls, 1999; Woodruff-Pak & Papka, 1999). It is not. The diseases involving loss of memory, emotional response, and bodily functions are dementias, which are discussed in Chapter 4. Dementia is not a part of normal aging; roughly 6 to 8% of people over age 65 have dementia, with the risk doubling about every 5 years (see Chapter 4). People who develop dementia may show severe and progressive impairments of memory, judgment, comprehension, and motor functions. It is often the fear of developing dementia that makes people interpret the slightest mental or physical mistake as symptomatic.

Nevertheless, several aspects of psychological functioning are affected by normal brain aging, which may, in turn, affect adults' adaptation to the environment (Whitbourne, 1996a). For example, age-related declines in recent memory may be caused by neuronal losses. These changes make it more difficult for older adults to complete daily routines that demand remembering information over time, and older adults become less efficient at learning new facts and skills. In contrast, continued dendritic growth may be one reason why there is little evidence of age-related changes in experience-based problem solving, reasoning, and judgment until late in life (Schaie & Zanjani, 2006).

Concept Checks

1. What structural changes occur in the neurons?
2. What changes occur with age in neurotransmitters?
3. What changes occur with age in the autonomic nervous system?
4. What is the most damaging stereotype about the psychological effects of brain aging?

SOCIAL POLICY IMPLICATIONS

As we have noted, the normative changes that occur in the brain with age have potentially profound effects, particularly when these changes result in disease. Consequently, considerable resources are put into research on the causes and outcomes of such structural brain changes. In the United States, major research support is provided by the National Institutes of Health. For example, the national Institute on Aging provides research emphases in neuroscience and neuropsychology of aging and provides support for research and training to further the understanding of the aging process in the structure and functioning of the nervous system. These topics include basic neuroscience to understand the underlying brain mechanisms, sleep and biological rhythms, sensory processes, motor functioning, the brain processes underlying cognition, and the various types of dementias.

This research is very important as it provides the basis for understanding future trends in health care. For example, by understanding how the changes that occur normally in the brain sometimes result in disease or other behavioral problems, policymakers have better data with which to predict future health care needs. With the leading edge of the baby-boom generation now eligible for Social Security, such data are key in creating budgets at the state and federal levels so that the health care needs of these people are met. Thus, it is important that the federal government continue to fund research on basic brain processes; indeed, the NIH's budget has increased steadily over the past decade in response in part to the need to understand brain–behavior relations.

A question that is both crucial and as yet unaddressed in the United States is whether the brain-imaging diagnostic techniques we considered earlier should be available to everyone regardless of cost and whether the individual has health insurance. The rationing of certain medical interventions and diagnostic tools is a very difficult issue, one that will likely be debated for years to come.

Summary

3.1 Why Do We Age? Biological Theories of Aging

How do rate-of-living theories explain aging?
- Rate-of-living theories are based on the idea that people are born with a limited amount of energy that can be expended at some rate unique to the individual.
- Metabolic processes such as eating fewer calories or reducing stress may be related to living longer.
- The body's declining ability to adapt to stress with age may also be a partial cause of aging.

What are the major hypotheses in cellular theories of aging?
- Cellular theories suggest that there may be a limit on how often cells may divide before dying (called the Hayflick limit), which may partially explain aging. The shortening of telomeres may be the major factor.
- A second group of cellular theories relate to a process called cross-linking that results when certain proteins interact randomly and produce molecules that make the body stiffer. Cross-links interfere with metabolism.
- A third type of cellular theory proposes that free radicals, which are highly reactive chemicals produced randomly during normal cell

metabolism, cause cell damage. There is some evidence that ingesting antioxidants may postpone the appearance of some age-related diseases.

How do programmed-cell-death theories propose that we age?

- Theories about programmed cell death are based on genetic hypotheses about aging. Specifically, there appears to be a genetic program that is triggered by physiological processes, the innate ability to self-destruct, and the ability of dying cells to trigger key processes in other cells.

How do the basic developmental forces interact in biological and physiological aging?

- Although biological theories are the foundation of biological forces, the full picture of how and why we age cannot be understood without considering the other three forces (psychological, sociocultural, and life cycle).

3.2 Appearance and Mobility

How do our skin, hair, and voice change with age?

- Normative changes with age in appearance or presentation include wrinkles, gray hair, and thinner and weaker voice.

What happens to our body build with age?

- Normative changes include decrease in height and increase in weight in midlife, followed by weight loss in late life.

What age-related changes occur in our ability to move around?

- The amount of muscle decreases with age, but strength and endurance change only slightly.
- Loss of bone mass is normative; in severe cases, though, the disease osteoporosis may result, in which bones become brittle and honeycombed.
- Osteoarthritis and rheumatoid arthritis are two diseases that impair a person's ability to get around and function in the environment.

What are the psychological implications of age-related changes in appearance and mobility?

- Cultural stereotypes have an enormous influence on the personal acceptance of age-related changes in appearance.

- Loss of strength and endurance, and changes in the joints, have important psychological consequences, especially regarding self-esteem.

3.3 Sensory Systems

What age-related changes happen in vision?

- Several age-related changes occur in the structure of the eye, including decreases in the amount of light passing through the eye and in the ability to adjust to changes in illumination, yellowing of the lens, and changes in the ability to adjust and focus (presbyopia). In some cases these changes result in various diseases, such as cataracts and glaucoma.
- Other changes occur in the retina, including degeneration of the macula. Diabetes also causes retinal degeneration.
- The psychological consequences of visual changes include difficulties in getting around. Compensation strategies must take several factors into account; for example, the need for more illumination must be weighed against increased susceptibility to glare.

How does hearing change as people age?

- Age-related declines in the ability to hear high-pitched tones (presbycusis) are normative.
- Exposure to noise speeds up and exacerbates hearing loss.
- Psychologically, hearing losses can reduce the ability to have satisfactory communication with others.

What age-related changes occur in people's senses of touch and balance?

- Changes in sensitivity to touch, temperature, and pain are complex and not understood; age-related trends are unclear in most cases.
- Dizziness and vertigo are common in older adults and increase with age, as do falls. Changes in balance may result in greater caution in older adults when walking.

What happens to taste and smell with increasing age?

- Age-related changes in taste are minimal. Many older adults complain about boring food; however, these complaints appear to be largely unrelated to changes in taste ability.
- The ability to detect odors declines rapidly after age 60 in most people. Changes in smell are

primarily responsible for reported changes in food preference and enjoyment.

3.4 Vital Functions

What age-related changes occur in the cardiovascular system?

- Some fat deposits in and around the heart and inside arteries are a normal part of aging. Heart muscle gradually is replaced with stiffer connective tissue. The most important change in the circulatory system is the stiffening (hardening) of the walls of the arteries.

- Overall, men have a higher rate of cardiovascular disease than women. Several diseases increase in frequency with age: congestive heart failure, angina pectoris, myocardial infarction, atherosclerosis (severe buildup of fat inside and the calcification of the arterial walls), cerebrovascular disease (cardiovascular disease in the brain), and hypertension (high blood pressure).

What structural and functional changes occur with age in the respiratory system?

- The amount of air we can take into our lungs and our ability to exchange oxygen and carbon dioxide decrease with age. Declines in the maximum amount of air we can take in also occur.

- Chronic obstructive pulmonary disease (COPD), such as emphysema, increases with age. Emphysema is the most common form of age-related COPD; although most cases are caused by smoking, a few are caused by secondhand smoke, air pollution, or genetic factors. Chronic bronchitis also becomes more prevalent with age.

3.5 The Reproductive System

What reproductive changes occur in women?

- The transition from childbearing years to the cessation of ovulation is called the climacteric; menopause is the point at which the ovaries stop releasing eggs. A variety of physical and psychological symptoms accompany menopause (e.g., hot flashes), including several in the genital organs; however, women in some cultures report different experiences.

- Hormone replacement therapy remains controversial because of conflicting results about its long-term effects.

- No changes occur in the desire to have sex; however, the availability of a suitable partner for women is a major barrier.

What reproductive changes occur in men?

- In men, sperm production declines gradually with age. Changes in the prostate gland occur and should be monitored through yearly examinations.

- Some changes in sexual performance, such as increased time to erection and ejaculation and increased refractory period, are typical.

What are the psychological implications of age-related changes in the reproductive system?

- Healthy adults of any age are capable of engaging in sexual activity, and the desire to do so does not diminish with age. However, societal stereotyping creates barriers to free expression of such feelings.

3.6 The Nervous System

How do we measure changes in the brain?

- Three types of brain imaging are used in research: computed tomography (CT), magnetic resonance imaging (MRI), and positron emission tomography (PET). Each provides important information about brain structures. CT and MRI scans are used most often in routine diagnosis of brain diseases. PET scans also provide information on brain metabolism.

What major changes occur in neurons? How does the ability of neurons to communicate with each other change with age?

- Neurons are the basic cells in the brain. Some neurons develop neurofibrillary tangles, new fibers produced in the axon that are twisted. Large numbers of these are associated with Alzheimer's disease. Some neurons lose dendrites with age, whereas others gain dendrites. Damaged or dying neurons sometimes become surrounded by protein and form amyloid plaques. Large numbers of plaques are associated with Alzheimer's disease.

- Several neurotransmitter levels decrease with age, including those of dopamine, acetylcholine, and serotonin. Some diseases, such as Parkinson's, Alzheimer's, and Huntington's, are related to changes in neurotransmitter levels.

What major changes occur in the autonomic nervous system?

- Regulating body temperature becomes increasingly problematic with age. Older adults have difficulty telling when their core body temperature drops, and their vasoconstrictor response diminishes. When they become very hot, older adults are less likely to drink water.
- Sleep patterns and circadian rhythms change with age. Older adults are more likely to compensate by taking daytime naps, which exacerbates the problem. Effective treatments include exercising, reducing caffeine, avoiding daytime naps, and making the sleep environment as quiet and dark as possible.

What are the psychological implications of changes in the brain?

- The term *senility* no longer has medical meaning, nor do all (or even most) older adults become "senile." However, many people remain concerned about this issue. Brain changes underlie many behavioral changes, including memory.

Review Questions

3.1 Why Do We Age? Biological Theories of Aging

- What biological theories have been proposed to explain aging? What are their similarities and differences?
- Why do some people argue that diets high in antioxidants can prolong life?
- What are some of the sociocultural forces that operate on the biological theories? What are some examples of these forces?

3.2 Appearance and Mobility

- What age-related changes occur in appearance?
- How does body build change with age?
- How do muscle and bone tissue change with age?

3.3 Sensory Systems

- What age-related changes occur in vision? What are the psychological effects of these changes?
- What age-related changes occur in hearing? What are the psychological effects of these changes?
- What age-related changes occur in somesthesia and balance?
- What age-related changes occur in taste and smell?

3.4 Vital Functions

- What changes occur with age in the cardiovascular system? What gender differences have been noted? Which cardiovascular diseases increase in frequency with age?
- What changes occur with age in the respiratory system? How are respiratory diseases related to age?

3.5 The Reproductive System

- What age-related changes occur in women's and men's reproductive ability?
- How does interest in sexual activity change with age? What constraints operate on men and women?

3.6 The Nervous System

- What structural changes occur with age in the neuron? How are these changes related to diseases such as Alzheimer's?
- What changes occur with age in neurotransmitters?
- What types of brain-imaging techniques are used, and what structures and processes do they measure?
- What changes occur in people's ability to regulate body temperature?
- How does sleep change with age?

Integrating Concepts in Development

- How do the various biological theories of aging match with the major age-related changes in body systems? Which theories do the best job? Why?
- Given what you now know about normative changes in appearance, what would you say about

the stereotypes of aging you identified in the Discovering Development exercise you did in Chapter 1?

- Why do you think the rates of death from cardiovascular disease are so much higher in industrialized countries than elsewhere?

- How might the age-related changes in the respiratory system be linked with societal policies on the environment?

- What changes in memory and intelligence would you expect based on the changes in the nervous system that occur with aging? (Check your answer against the descriptions of these changes in Chapters 6, 7, and 8.)

Key Terms

amyloid plaques A normative change in the brain involving amyloid protein collecting on dying or dead neurons. A large number of amyloid plaques is a defining characteristic of Alzheimer's disease.

angina pectoris A painful condition caused by temporary constriction of blood flow to the heart.

atherosclerosis A process by which fat is deposited on the walls of arteries.

cataracts Opaque spots on the lens of the eye.

cerebrovascular accident (CVA) An interruption of the blood flow in the brain.

chronic obstructive pulmonary disease (COPD) A family of age-related lung diseases that block the passage of air and cause abnormalities inside the lungs.

climacteric The transition during which a woman's reproductive capacity ends and ovulation stops.

congestive heart failure A condition occurring when cardiac output and the ability of the heart to contract severely decline, making the heart enlarge, increasing pressure to the veins, and making the body swell.

cross-linking Random interaction between proteins that produce molecules that make the body stiffer.

emphysema Severe lung disease that greatly reduces the ability to exchange carbon dioxide for oxygen.

free radicals Deleterious and short-lived chemicals that cause changes in cells that are thought to result in aging.

glaucoma A condition in the eye caused by abnormal drainage of fluid.

hypertension A disease in which one's blood pressure is too high.

menopause The cessation of the release of eggs by the ovaries.

myocardial infarction (MI) A heart attack.

neurofibrillary tangles A normative age-related change in the brain involving the production of new fibers in the neuron. A large number of neurofibrillary tangles is a defining characteristic of Alzheimer's disease.

neurons The basic cells in the brain.

osteoarthritis A form of arthritis marked by gradual onset and progression of pain and swelling, caused primarily by overuse of a joint.

osteoporosis A degenerative bone disease more common in women in which bone tissue deteriorates severely to produce honeycomb-like bone tissue.

Parkinson's disease A brain disease caused by an extreme drop in the neurotransmitter dopamine.

plasticity The capability of the brain to adapt its functional and structural organization to current requirements.

presbycusis A normative age-related loss of the ability to hear high-pitched tones.

presbyopia The normative age-related loss of the ability to focus on nearby objects, usually resulting in the need for glasses.

rheumatoid arthritis A destructive form of arthritis involving more swelling and more joints than osteoarthritis.

telomeres Tips of the chromosomes that shorten with each replication.

Resources

www.cengage.com/psychology/cavanaugh

Visit the companion website, where you will find tutorial quizzes, glossary, flashcards, and more. You can also access the following websites from the companion website.

Lighthouse International is a leading resource worldwide for information on visual impairment and intervention. Their website provides a wide variety of information and resources and summaries of legislative and advocacy activities.

The American Heart Association provides a wide range of information, including risk assessments, on its website. Information includes preventive measures, diet recommendations, and basic information about cardiovascular and circulatory diseases. In addition, you can access the American Stroke Association site.

The National Institute on Aging (NIA) publishes several informative brochures and reports about many aspects of physical aging, such as menopause, cardiovascular disease, and sensory changes. All the information is based on scientific research.

Readings

Cozolino, L. (2008). *The healthy aging brain: Sustaining attachment, achieving wisdom.* New York: Norton. A good overview of brain development through late life; easy to moderate reading.

Jaff, N. (2008). *Menopause: The complete guide* (rev. ed.). New York: Penguin Group. A good overview of the various changes that occur during menopause; easy reading.

Kirkwood, T. B. L. (1999). *The time of our lives: The science of human aging.* New York: Oxford University Press. A very readable account of the biological and physical changes that occur with age; easy reading.

4

Longevity, Health, and Functioning

"WHEN YOU GET REAL OLD, HONEY," SAID ELIZABETH (BESSIE) DELANY, "YOU LAY IT ALL ON the table. There's an old saying: Only little children and old folks tell the truth." And tell the truth she did. Along with her sister Sarah (Sadie), Bessie Delany told the story of more than 100 years of living through segregation, discrimination, the civil rights movement, and the women's movement. Imagine the stories they could tell: They were born more than a decade before the first airplane flew, and they lived to see men walk on the moon. Each of them rose to professional prominence, Bessie as the second African American woman to be licensed as a dentist in New York, Sadie as the first African American to teach domestic science on the high school level in New York City public schools. They never married. Their story became two best-selling books and a highly successful Broadway play.

Sadie and Bessie Delany were blessed with very long, full lives. Sadie died in 1999 at age 109, and Bessie died in 1995 at age 104. They certainly had excellent genes, but there's more to living a long and healthy life than that. We'll discover in this chapter that longevity depends on a complex set of variables. Sadie and Bessie's good health meant that they enjoyed good quality of life and avoided chronic disease. Compared with most older adults, they had little experience with medications, a potential source of problems for many older people. That Sadie and Bessie were independent and lived that way puts them in the majority of older adults who are not disabled.

Will you live to be 100 years old? If you are lucky enough to experience the right confluence of genetics, psychological characteristics, and socioeconomic factors and avoid key events at particular points in your life, you just might. Whether your life will be a big hit remains to be seen.

4.1 How Long Will We Live?

LEARNING OBJECTIVES
- What is the average and the maximum longevity for humans?
- What genetic and environmental factors influence longevity?
- What ethnic factors influence average longevity?
- What factors create gender differences in average longevity?

Susie is a 51-year-old Chinese American living in San Francisco. Susie's mother (age 76), father (age 77), and grandmother (age 103), who are all in excellent health, live with her and her husband. Susie knows that several of her other relatives have lived long lives but wonders whether this has any bearing on her own life expectancy.

As we saw in Chapter 1, many more people are living to old age today than ever before. Like Susie, people today have already seen far more older

Did you ever speculate about how long you might live? Are you curious? If you'd like a preview of several of the key influences on how long we live, try completing the questions at http://www.livingto100.com. Take notes about why you think each question is being asked. Once you're finished, submit your form. Take time to read about each of the topics, then read more about them in the text. Will you live to be 100? Only time will tell.

adults than their great-great-grandparents did. The tremendous increase in the number of older adults has focused renewed interest in how long you might live. Susie's question about her own longevity exemplifies this interest. Knowing how long we are likely to live is important not only for us but also for government agencies, service programs, the business world, and insurance companies. Why? The length of life has an enormous impact on just about every aspect of life, from decisions about government health care programs (how much money to allocate to health care programs to pay for much higher costs to care for more chronically ill people) to retirement policy (debates over the age at which people may collect maximum retirement benefits) to life insurance premiums (longer lives on average mean cheaper rates for young adults). Longer lives have forced change in all these areas and will continue to do so for the next several decades.

Life expectancy can be examined from the perspective of the basic developmental forces, because how long we live depends on complex interactions among biological, psychological, socioeconomic, and life-cycle forces. For example, some people, like Susie, have many relatives who live to very old age, whereas others have relatives who die young. Tendencies toward long lives (or short ones, for that matter) tend to run in families. As you will see, our "long-life genes" play a major role in governing how long we are likely to live.

But the world in which we live can affect how long we live, too. Environmental factors such as disease and toxic chemicals modify our genetic heritage and shorten our lifetime, sometimes drastically. By the same token, environmental factors such as access to high-quality medical care can sometimes offset genetic defects that would have caused early death, thereby increasing our longevity. In short, no single developmental force can account for the length of life. Let's begin by exploring the concept of longevity. To get started, complete the exercise in the Discovering Development feature and see how long you might live. When you have finished, continue reading to discover the research base behind the numbers.

Average and Maximum Longevity

How long you live, called longevity, is jointly determined by genetic and environmental factors. Researchers distinguish between two different types of longevity: average longevity and maximum longevity. **Average longevity** is commonly called average life expectancy and refers to the age at which half of the individuals who are born in a particular year will have died. Average longevity is affected by both genetic and environmental factors.

Average longevity can be computed for people at any age. The most common method is to compute average longevity at birth, which is the projected age at which half of the people born in a certain year will have died. This computation takes into account people who die at any age, from infancy onward. Thus an average longevity of 78 years at birth means that 78 years after a group of people are born, half of them will still be alive. When average longevity is computed at other points in the life span, the calculation is based on all the people who are alive at that age; people who died earlier are not included. For example, computing the average longevity for people currently 65 years old would provide a predicted age at which half of those people will have died. People who were born into the same birth cohort but who died before age 65 are not counted. Eliminating those who die at early ages from the computation of average longevity at a specific age makes projected average longevity at age 65 longer than it was at birth. In the United States, females currently aged 65 can expect to live about 20 more years; men about 16 more years.

For people in the United States, average longevity has been increasing steadily since 1900; recent estimates for longevity at birth and at age 65 are presented in Figure 4.1. Note in the figure that the most rapid increases in average longevity at birth occurred in the first half of the 20th century. These increases in average longevity were caused mostly by declines in infant mortality rates, brought about by eliminating diseases such as smallpox and polio and through better health care. The decrease in the number of women who died during childbirth was especially important in raising average life expectancies for women, both at birth and at age 65. Advances in medical technology and improvements in health care mean that more people survive to old age, thereby increasing average longevity in the general population.

Maximum longevity *is the oldest age to which any individual of a species lives.* Although the biblical character Methuselah is said to have lived to the ripe old age of 969 years, modern scientists are more conservative in their estimates of a human's maximum longevity. Even if we were able to eliminate all diseases, most researchers estimate the limit to be somewhere around 120 years because key body

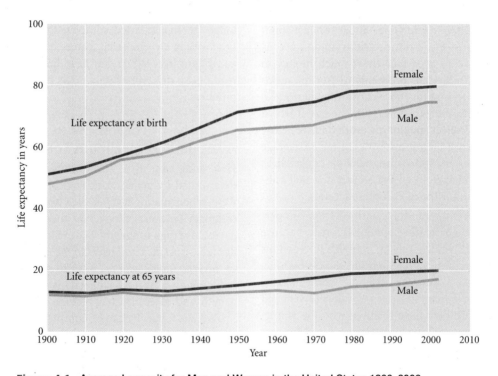

Figure 4.1 Average Longevity for Men and Women in the United States 1900–2003.

Source: Data from Centers for Disease Control and Prevention, National Center for Health Statistics, National Vital Statistics System (2008).

systems such as the cardiovascular system have limits on how long they can last (Hayflick, 1998). Genetic theories also place the human limit around 120 years (Barja, 2008).

Whether this estimate of maximum longevity will change as new technologies produce better artificial organs and health care remains to be seen. An important issue is whether extending the life span indefinitely would be a good idea. Because maximum longevity of different animal species varies widely (Barja, 2008), scientists have tried to understand these differences by considering important biological functions such as metabolic rate or brain size (Hayflick, 1996). But no one has figured out how to predict longevity. For example, why the giant tortoises of the Galapagos Islands typically live longer than we do remains a mystery.

Increasingly, researchers are differentiating between **active life expectancy** and **dependent life expectancy;** *the difference is between living to a healthy old age (active life expectancy) and simply living a long time (dependent life expectancy).* Said another way, it is the difference between adding years to life and adding life to years. One's active life expectancy ends at the point when one loses independence or must rely on others for most activities of daily living (e.g., cooking meals, bathing). The remaining years of one's life constitute living in a dependent state. How many active and dependent years one has in late life depends a great deal on the interaction of genetic and environmental factors, to which we now turn.

Genetic and Environmental Factors in Average Longevity

Let's return to Susie, who wonders whether she can expect to live a long life. What influences how long we will live on average? Our average longevity is influenced most by genetic, environmental, ethnic, and gender factors. Clearly, these factors interact; being from an ethnic minority group or being poor, for example, often means that one has a higher risk of exposure to a harmful environment and less access to high-quality health care. But it is important to examine each of these factors and see how they influence our longevity. Let's begin with genetic and environmental factors.

Genetic Factors. Living a long life has a clear, but probably complex, genetic link (Kirkwood, 2008). We have known for a long time that a good way to increase one's chances of a long life is to come from a family with a history of long-lived individuals. For example, if your mother lives to at least age 80, roughly 4 years are added to your average longevity (Woodruff-Pak, 1988). Alexander Graham Bell (the same guy who received the credit for inventing the telephone) was one of the first people to demonstrate systematically the benefits of coming from a long-lived family. Bell considered 8,797 of William Hyde's descendants and found that children of parents who had lived beyond 80 survived about 20 years longer than children whose parents had both died before they were 60. Thus Susie's long-lived family sets the stage for Susie to enjoy a long life herself.

One exciting line of contemporary research, the Human Genome Project, completed in 2003, has mapped all our genes. This research and its spinoffs in microbiology and behavior genetics are continuing to produce some astounding results in terms of genetic linkages to disease and aging (you can track these through the main website of the Project, http://www.ornl.gov/sci/techresources/Human_Genome/research/spinoffs.shtml). Based on this gene mapping work, attempts are being made to treat diseases by improving the way that medications work and even by implanting "corrected" genes into people in the hopes that the good genes will reproduce and eventually wipe out the defective genes (Kanehisa et al., 2008). Payoffs from such research are helping us understand how increasing numbers of people are living to 100 or older. For example, research on people over age 100 (centenarians) in Italy showed a connection between genetics and ability to cope with disease (Franceschi et al., 2008). The oldest-old, such as Susie's grandmother, are hardy because they have a high threshold for disease and show slower rates of disease progression than their peers who develop chronic diseases at younger ages and die earlier.

Coming from a family with many long-lived members increases your chances of having a long life yourself.

Environmental Factors. Although genes are a major determinant of longevity, environmental factors also affect the life span, often in combination with genes (Perls & Terry, 2003). Some environmental factors are more obvious; diseases, toxins, lifestyle, and social class are among the most important. Diseases, such as cardiovascular disease and Alzheimer's disease, and lifestyle issues, such as smoking and exercise, receive a great deal of attention from researchers. Environmental toxins, encountered mainly as air and water pollution, are a continuing problem. For example, toxins in fish, bacteria and cancer-causing chemicals in drinking water, and airborne pollutants are major agents in shortening longevity.

The impact of social class on longevity results from the reduced access to goods and services, especially medical care, that characterizes most ethnic minority groups, the poor, and many older adults (National Center for Health Statistics, 2008a). Most of these people have little or no health insurance, and many cannot afford the cost of a more healthful lifestyle. For example, air pollution, poor drinking water, and lead poisoning from old water pipes are serious problems in large urban areas, but many people simply cannot afford to move. How environmental factors influence average life expectancy changes over time. For example, acquired immunodeficiency syndrome (AIDS) has had a devastating effect on life expectancy in Africa, where in some countries (e.g., Botswana, Namibia, South Africa, Zimbabwe) average longevity may be reduced by as much as 30 years from otherwise expected levels (Kinsella & Phillips, 2005). In contrast, negative effects of cardiovascular diseases on average longevity are lessening as the rates of those diseases decline in many developed countries (National Center for Health Statistics, 2008a).

The sad part about most environmental factors is that we are responsible for most of them. Denying adequate health care to everyone, continuing to pollute our environment, and failing to address the underlying causes of poverty have undeniable consequences: They needlessly shorten lives and dramatically increase the cost of health care.

Ethnic Differences in Average Longevity

People in different ethnic groups do not have the same average longevity at birth. For example, African Americans' average longevity at birth is roughly 6.5 years lower for men and about 5 years lower for women than it is for European Americans (National Center for Health Statistics, 2008a). Why do such large differences exist? The most important reasons are the substantial differences in most environmental variables between European Americans and other ethnic groups.

In the United States, these differences can be dramatic. For example, although African Americans' average life expectancy at birth is about 6 years less for men and about 4 years less for women than it is for European Americans, by age 65 this gap has narrowed to about 2 and 1.5 years, respectively, for men and women. By age 85, African Americans tend to outlive European Americans. Why the shift over time? Perhaps because of their lower access to good-quality health care in general, those African Americans who live to age 85 tend to be in better health on average than their European American counterparts. But this is just a guess. Latinos have higher average life expectancies than European Americans at all ages despite having, on average, less access to health care (National Center for Health Statistics, 2008a).

Gender Differences in Average Longevity

A visit to a senior center or to a nursing home can easily lead to the question "Where are all the very old men?" Women's average longevity is about 5 years more than men's at birth (in 2004), narrowing to roughly 1 year by age 85 (Arias, 2006; National Center for Health Statistics, 2008a). These differences are fairly typical of most industrialized countries but not of developing countries. Indeed, the female advantage in average longevity in the United States became apparent only in the early 20th century (Hayflick, 1996). Why? Until then, so many women died in childbirth that their average

longevity as a group was reduced to that of men. Death in childbirth still partially explains the lack of a female advantage in developing countries today; however, part of the difference in some countries also results from infanticide of baby girls. In industrialized countries, socioeconomic factors such as access to health care, work and educational opportunities, and athletics also help account for the emergence of the female advantage (Hayflick, 1998).

Many ideas have been offered to explain the significant advantage women have over men in average longevity in industrialized countries (Hayflick, 1996). Overall, men's rates of dying from the top 15 causes of death are significantly higher than women's at nearly every age, and men are also more susceptible to infectious diseases. These differences have led some to speculate that perhaps it is not just a gender-related biological difference at work in longevity, but a more complex interaction of lifestyle, much greater susceptibility in men of contracting certain fatal diseases, and genetics (Hayflick, 1996).

Other researchers disagree; they argue that there are potential biological explanations. These include the fact that women have two X chromosomes, compared with one in men; men have a higher metabolic rate; women have a higher brain-to-body weight ratio; and women have lower testosterone levels. However, none of these explanations has sufficient scientific support to explain why most women in industrialized countries can expect, on average, to outlive most men (Hayflick, 1996).

Despite their longer average longevity, women do not have all the advantages. Interestingly, older men who survive beyond age 90 are the hardiest segment of their birth cohort in terms of performance on cognitive tests (Perls & Terry, 2003). Between ages 65 and 89, women score higher on cognitive tests; beyond age 90, men do much better.

International Differences in Average Longevity

Countries around the world differ dramatically in how long their populations live on average. As you can see in Figure 4.2, the current range extends

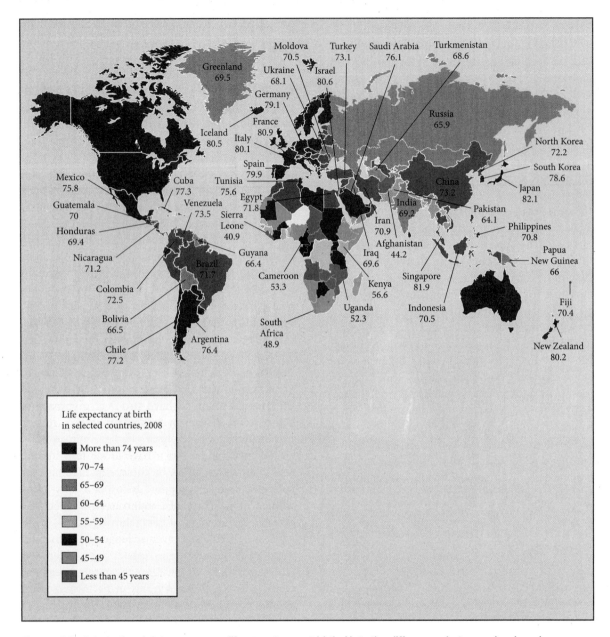

Figure 4.2 International data on average life expectancy at birth. Note the differences between developed and developing countries.

Source: http://www.census.gov/ipc/www/idb/tables.html.

from 38 years in Sierra Leone in Africa to 80 years in Japan. Such a wide divergence in life expectancy reflects vast discrepancies in genetic, sociocultural and economic conditions, health care, disease, and the like across industrialized and developing nations.

1. What are some of the main reasons that average longevity increased during the 20th century?

2. What evidence is there that genetics influences average longevity? What are the key environmental influences on average longevity?

3. What are some of the reasons for ethnic differences in average longevity?

4. What explanations have been offered to account for women's longer average longevity?

4.2 Health and Illness

LEARNING OBJECTIVES

- *What are the key issues in defining health and illness?*
- *How is the quality of life assessed?*
- *What normative age-related changes occur in the immune system?*
- *What are the developmental trends in chronic and acute diseases?*
- *What are the key issues in stress across adulthood?*

Rosa is a 72-year-old immigrant from Mexico living in a small apartment in a large city in the southwestern United States. For most of her life she has been very healthy, but lately she has noticed it is getting harder to get up every morning. In addition, when she gets a cold she takes longer to recover than when she was younger. Rosa wonders whether these problems are typical or whether she is experiencing something unusual.

Each of us has had periods of health and of illness. Most people are like Rosa—healthy for nearly all our lives. In this section, we will tackle the difficult issue of defining health and illness. We will consider quality of life, an increasingly important notion as medical technology keeps people alive longer. We will see how the differences between acute and chronic disease become more important with age. Because our immune system plays such a central role in health and illness, we will examine key age-related changes in it. Finally, we will consider how stress can affect our health.

Defining Health and Illness

What does the term *health* mean to you? The total lack of disease? Complete physical, mental, and social well-being? Actually, scientists cannot agree on a comprehensive definition, largely because the term has been used in so many different contexts (Davies, 2007). Many people now include biological, psychological, sociocultural, spiritual, and environmental components; as Davies (2007) puts it, health is an ongoing outcome from the processes of a life lived well.

The World Health Organization defines **health** *as a state of complete physical, mental, and social well-being, and not merely the absence of disease or infirmity* (World Health Organization, 2007). **Illness** *is the presence of a physical or mental disease or impairment.*

Think for a moment about your health. How would you rate it? Although this question looks simple, how people answer it turns out to be predictive of illness and mortality (Idler & Benyamini, 1997). Why? There are several possibilities (Wolinsky & Tierney, 1998). One is that self-rated health captures more aspects of health than other measures. A second possibility is that poor self-rated health reflects respondents' belief that they are on a downward trajectory in functioning. A third is that people's self-ratings affect their health-related behaviors, which in turn affect health outcomes. Finally, self-rated health may actually represent an assessment of people's internal and external resources that are available to support health. Research data support all these ideas; a review of more than 30 years of research showed that self-ratings of health are very predictive of future health outcomes (Blazer, 2008).

Self-ratings also tend to be fairly stable over time. Wolinsky and colleagues (2008) followed 998 African Americans aged 49 to 65 for four years, and found that 55% had the same self-rating over time (25% improved and 20% declined). Overall, men rated their health worse than women did. Among the oldest-old, self-rated health is a powerful predictor of mortality across cultures; for example, a two-year study in China showed that self-rated health still predicted mortality even after socioeconomic status and health conditions had been accounted for (Chen & Wu, 2008).

However, self-ratings of health do reflect differences in socioeconomic background in terms of how healthy people say they are. For example, indigenous

Australians rate their health as significantly poorer than nonindigenous Australians, mainly due to differences in economic variables (e.g., access to health care) (Booth & Carroll, 2008).

Overall, given the strong relation between self-rated health and actual health-related outcomes, including one's own mortality, it should come as no surprise that researchers often include such measures in their studies of older adults. Such measures provide a good proxy (or stand-in) variable for health, avoiding a time-consuming (and possibly costly) assessment of health. This approach works most of the time; as we proceed, times when it doesn't will be noted.

Quality of Life

We'll bet if you asked most people what they want out of life, they would say something about a good quality of life. But what does that mean? Precise definitions are hard to find. Sometimes people find it easier to say what quality of life is not: being dependent on a respirator while in a permanent vegetative state is one common example. Researchers, though, like to be more specific. They tend to look at several specific aspects of quality of life: health-related quality of life and non-health-related quality of life. Health-related quality of life includes all of the aspects of life that are affected by changes in one's health status. Non-health-related quality of life refers to things in the environment, such as entertainment, economic resources, arts, and so on that can affect our overall experience and enjoyment in life.

Most research on quality of life has focused on two areas: quality of life in the context of specific diseases or conditions and quality of life relating to end-of-life issues. We briefly lay out the issues here and return to them as we discuss specific situations in this chapter and in Chapters 5 (interventions that increase quality of life) and 13 (end-of-life issues).

In many respects, quality of life is a subjective judgment that can be understood in the context of broader models of adult development and aging. One such model describes ways in which people select domains of relative strength, optimize their use of these strengths, and compensate for age-related changes (Baltes et al., 2006). In addition, one must also consider not only the physical health aspects but also mental health in assessing quality of life (Kaplan et al., 2004). From this perspective, quality of life is a successful use of the selection, optimization, and compensation model (SOC) to manage one's life, resulting in successful aging. Applying this approach to research in health care, quality of life refers to people's perceptions of their position in life in context of their culture (Karim et al., 2008).

In general, research on health-related quality of life addresses a critical question (Lawton et al., 1999): To what extent does distress from illness or side effects associated with treatment reduce the person's wish to live? Lawton and colleagues (1999) show that the answer to this question depends a great deal on a person's *valuation of life,* the degree to which a person is attached to his or her present life. How much one enjoys life, has hope about the future, and finds meaning in everyday events, for example, has a great deal of impact on how long that person would like to live.

Narrowing the focus of the quality-of-life concept as it relates to specific conditions brings us to the domains of physical impairment or disability and of dementia. Quality of life in the former context includes issues of environmental design that improve people's functioning and well-being, such as handicapped accessible bathrooms and facilities (Lawton, 1999). We examine environmental influences in Chapter 5. Quality of life is more difficult to assess in people with dementia, although new assessment instruments have been developed (Karim et al., 2008). For example, the quality of life of residents in Alzheimer's treatment centers is complex (Hubbard et al., 2003). We consider this issue in more detail in Chapter 10 when we focus on Alzheimer's disease.

Changes in the Immune System

Every day, our bodies are threatened by invaders: bacterial, viral, and parasitic infections (as well as their toxic by-products) and abnormal cells such as precancerous and tumor cells. Fortunately

How much a person enjoys everyday tasks, such as working the daily crossword puzzle, affects how that person may want to live.

© iStockphoto.com/nano

for us, we have a highly advanced defense system against foreign invaders: the immune system. The National Cancer Institute provides a Web-based overview of how our immune system works; check it out at http://www.cancer.gov/cancertopics/understandingcancer/immunesystem.

Much about how our immune system works remains unknown. For instance, one great mystery is how the immune system learns to differentiate your own cells from invaders. Researchers think the mechanism involves recognizing certain substances, called *antigens,* on the surface of invading bacteria and cells that have been taken over by viruses. Regardless of how this actually happens, once the immune system has learned to recognize the invader, it creates a defense against that invader.

How does this defense system work? It's an amazing process that is based essentially on only three major types of cells that form a network of interacting parts (Sompayrac, 2008): cell-mediated immunity (consisting of cells originating in the thymus gland, or *T-lymphocytes*), humoral immunity based on antibodies (*B-lymphocytes*), and nonspecific immunity (*monocytes* and *polymorphonuclear neutrophil leukocytes*). The primary job of the T- and B-lymphocytes is to defend against malignant (cancerous) cells, viral infection, fungal infection, and

some bacteria. Natural killer (NK) cells are another, special type of lymphocytes that monitor our bodies to prevent tumor growth and are our primary defense against cancer, although how this happens is not fully understood (Sompayrac, 2008). NK cells also help fight viral infections and parasites. In addition, there are five major types of specialized antibodies called immunoglobulins (IgA, IgD, IgE, IgG, and IgM). For example, IgM includes the "first responders" in the immune system, IgE is involved in allergies and asthma, and IgG (also called g-globulin) helps fight hepatitis.

How does aging affect the immune system? Researchers are only beginning to understand this process, and there are large gaps in the literature (Sompayrac, 2008). Moreover, the immune system is sensitive to a wide variety of lifestyle and environmental factors, such as diet, stress, exercise, and disease, making it very difficult to isolate changes caused by aging alone (Aldwin & Gilmer, 2004; Burns & Leventhal, 2000).

Changes in health with age provide insights into immune functioning. Older adults are more susceptible to certain infections and have a much higher risk of cancer (both of which are discussed in more detail later in this chapter), so most researchers believe that the immune system changes with age. Indeed, NK cells and several other aspects of the immune system decrease in effectiveness with age (Srinivasan et al., 2005). For one thing, older adults' immune systems take longer to build up defenses against specific diseases, even after an immunization injection. This is probably caused by the changing balance in T-lymphocytes and may partially explain why older adults need to be immunized earlier against specific diseases such as influenza. Similarly, B-lymphocytes decrease in functioning. Research examining the administration of substances such as growth hormones to older adults to stimulate lymphocyte functioning indicates that some specific lymphocyte functioning returns to normal with treatment, and can regenerate the thymus gland, both of which are important in treating individuals with HIV (Chidgey, 2008). This process for T- and B-lymphocytes is described in Figure 4.3.

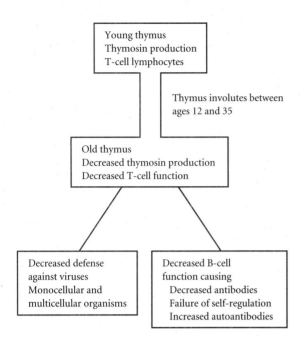

Figure 4.3 Process of aging of the immune system.

Source: Reprinted with permission from Ebersole, P., & Hess, P., *Toward Healthy Aging* (5e, p. 41) Copyright © 1998 Mosby St. Louis: with permission from Elsevier.

The changes in immune system function have important implications (Aldwin & Gilmer, 2004; Srinivasan et al., 2005). Older adults become more prone to serious consequences from illnesses that are easily defeated by younger adults. In addition, various forms of leukemia, which are cancers of the immune cells, increase with age, along with other forms of cancer. *Finally, the immune system can begin attacking the body itself in a process called* **autoimmunity.** Autoimmunity results from an imbalance of B- and T-lymphocytes, giving rise to autoantibodies, and is responsible for several disorders, such as rheumatoid arthritis (Melikterminas, Ranganath, & Furst, 2008; Yung & Julius, 2008).

A growing body of evidence is pointing to key connections between our immune system and our psychological state. Over 20 years of research shows how our psychological state, or a characteristic such as our attitude, creates neurological, hormonal, and behavioral responses that directly change the immune system and make us more likely to become ill (Irwin, 2008). **Psychoneuroimmunology** *is the study of the relations between psychological, neurological, and immunological systems that raise or lower our susceptibility to and ability to recover from disease.* The focus of much of this research has been on identifying the psychological triggers that start the process and result in cancer. Two general types of investigations have been conducted (Irwin, 2008): predicting which healthy older adults are likely to eventually get cancer and predicting those who will live longer after being diagnosed with cancer. So far, findings are mixed. Some results show that having a positive attitude and a good social support system predict longer life for middle-aged patients with cancer but not for older ones (Schulz et al., 1996). To make matters more complicated, some evidence suggests that the effects of social support are more important for women than for men. Interestingly, factors such as depression have not yet been shown to have strong effects (Cohen & Herbert, 1996).

AIDS and Older Adults. An increasing number of older adults have AIDS; the Centers for Disease Control and Prevention (2008e) estimate that in the United States roughly 15,000 people over age 65 have AIDS. These statistics include people who contracted the human immunodeficiency virus (HIV) during middle age and survived to later life and people who contracted the disease as older adults. Unfortunately, because of the social stereotype that older adults are not sexually active, many physicians do not test older patients; however, as HIV/AIDS rates increase among older adults, the importance of testing is being emphasized (Longo et al., 2008).

Although older men are at higher risk for AIDS, older women also are at significant risk. For men, the most common risk factor is homosexual or bisexual behavior. In contrast, AIDS usually is transmitted to older women through heterosexual contact with infected partners. Older adults may be more susceptible to HIV infection because of the changes in the immune system discussed earlier. For women, the thinning of the vaginal wall with age makes it more likely that it will tear, making it easier for the HIV to enter the bloodstream. Older adults may believe that condom use is no longer necessary, which also raises the risk (Tangredi et al., 2008). Once they are infected, the progression from

HIV-positive status to AIDS is more rapid among older adults. Once they are diagnosed with AIDS, older adults' remaining life span is significantly shorter than it is for newly diagnosed young adults and mortality rates are higher (Emlet & Farkas, 2002). However, age is not a significant predictor of who will use services from a human service agency (Emlet & Farkas, 2002).

Clearly, older adults need to be educated about their risk for HIV and AIDS, and about the continued need for condom use (Tangredi et al., 2008). Few media stories about the problem focus on older adults, who thus may mistakenly believe they have nothing to worry about. They are less likely to raise the issue with a physician, less likely to be tested, and, if diagnosed, less likely to seek support groups. In short, we need to change the stereotypes about older adults and sexuality and focus on health and prevention.

Chronic and Acute Diseases

Rosa, the immigrant from Mexico, is typical of older adults: She is beginning to experience some recurring health difficulties and finding out that she does not recover as quickly from even minor afflictions. You probably have had several encounters with illnesses that come on quickly, may range from mild to very severe, last a few days, and then go away. Illnesses such as influenza and strep throat are examples. You also may have experienced conditions that come on more slowly, last much longer, and have long-term consequences. Kidney disease, diabetes, and arthritis are examples. Your experiences reflect the difference between acute and chronic diseases.

Acute diseases *are conditions that develop over a short period of time and cause a rapid change in health.* We are all familiar with acute diseases, such as colds, influenza, and food poisoning. Most acute diseases are cured with medications (such as antibiotics for bacterial infections) or allowed to run their course (the case with most viral infections). *In contrast,* **chronic diseases** *are conditions that last a longer period of time (at least 3 months) and may be accompanied by residual functional impairment*

that necessitates long-term management. Chronic diseases include arthritis and diabetes mellitus.

What do you think happens to the incidence of acute and chronic diseases as people age? If you say that the rates of acute diseases go down whereas the rates of chronic diseases go up, you are correct. Contrary to what many people believe, older adults have fewer colds, for example, than younger adults. However, when they do get an acute disease, older adults tend to get sicker; recovery takes longer and death from acute disease occurs more often (National Center for Health Statistics, 2008b). Thus, although they get fewer acute infections, older people may actually spend more days feeling sick than their younger (and, based on frequency of occurrence, "sicker") counterparts.

This is probably why many people mistakenly believe that the rates of acute disease increase with age. Because they have more problems fighting acute infections, older adults are more at risk from dying of an acute condition. For example, the rate of respiratory infection is about the same for younger and older adults, but people over age 65 account for roughly 90% of deaths from pneumonia and influenza. For these reasons, health professionals strongly recommend that older adults be vaccinated against pneumonia and influenza; these shots reduce the risk of pneumonia by about two thirds and influenza by half (Centers for Disease Control and Prevention, 2008f).

Until the 1990s, chronic disease was simply viewed as a part of aging. With the publication in 1991 of the historic document *Healthy People 2000: National Health Promotion and Disease Prevention* (U.S. Department of Health and Human Services, 1991), the view shifted dramatically to one of prevention and wellness. As we see a bit later in this chapter, advances in managing chronic conditions have been made.

The Role of Stress

You know what it feels like to be stressed. Whether it's from the upcoming exam in this course, the traffic jam you sat in on your way home yesterday, or the demands your children place on you, stress seems to be everywhere. There is plenty of scientific evidence that over the long term, stress is very bad for your health. But despite thousands of scientific studies, scientists still cannot agree on a formal definition of *stress*. To some, it involves specific physiological responses (Gewirtz et al., 2002). To others, stress results from people's evaluation of events in the context of the various resources they have (Cohen et al., 1995; Lazarus & Folkman, 1984). This approach emphasizes that stress is defined by the person and that no two people experience the same event in exactly the same way. To still others, stress is a property of specific events, such as the death of a partner (McLeod, 1996). In this approach, events vary in how stressful they are, but everyone who experiences a particular event comes under the same level of stress.

Because the first and second views are the most widely used approaches for studying stress and the ways in which people deal with it, we examine them in more detail. For the first view, we focus on the roles played by the nervous system responses and the endocrine system's hormones. For the second, we focus on Richard Lazarus and Susan Folkman's framework as the best-researched representative of the view that whether a person feels stressed depends on how he or she evaluates the situation at hand.

Stress as a Physiological State. There is widespread agreement that people differ in their physiological responses to stress (Aldwin & Gilmer, 2004). Prolonged exposure to stress results in damaging influences from the sympathetic nervous system (which controls such things as heart rate, respiration, perspiration, blood flow, muscle strength, and mental activity); these bad effects include temporary increases in risk of cardiovascular disease (Black & Garbutt, 2000), impaired immune system function (Black & Garbutt, 2000), and some forms of cancer (Aldwin & Gilmer, 2004).

Taylor and colleagues (2000) have reported an interesting gender difference in physiological responses to stress. Men overwhelmingly choose to wait alone before a stressful procedure, whereas women want to be with other people. Taylor and

colleagues believe that this difference may be due to the role that the hormone oxytocin plays in women and not in men. Oxytocin is the hormone important in reproductive activities, such as breast feeding, and for establishing strong bonds with one's children (Campbell, 2008). The researchers speculate that when stressed, men opt for a "flight or fight" approach whereas women opt for a "tend and befriend" approach.

The Stress and Coping Paradigm. Suppose you are stuck in a traffic jam. Depending on whether you are late for an appointment or have plenty of time on your hands, you will probably feel very different about your situation. The **stress and coping paradigm** *views stress not as an environmental stimulus or as a response but as the interaction of a thinking person and an event* (Lazarus, 1984; Lazarus et al., 1985; Lazarus & Folkman, 1984). How we interpret an event such as being stuck in traffic is what matters, not the event itself or what we do in response to it. Put more formally, stress is "a particular relationship between the person and the environment that is appraised by the person as taxing or exceeding his or her resources and endangering his or her well-being" (Lazarus & Folkman, 1984, p. 19). Note that this definition states that stress is a transactional process between a person and the environment, that it takes into account personal resources, that the person's appraisal of the situation is key, and that unless the situation is considered to be threatening, challenging, or harmful, stress does not result. A diagram of the transactional model is shown in Figure 4.4.

What exactly does this definition mean? Think about our traffic jam example. The transactional model of stress says that each time you are in a traffic jam you make a separate judgment as to whether it is stressful depending on the resources you have and your interpretation of them. The resources a person has include such things as the cumulative experience of dealing with similar situations (traffic jams) before, knowledge or access to information about the event, the ability to get help if necessary, and the time needed to engage in any actions necessary to address the situation. Clearly, these resources vary a great deal from person to person and reflect the

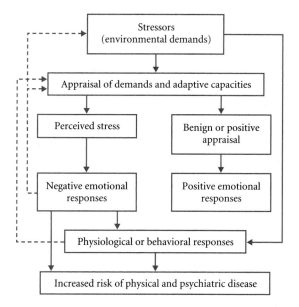

Figure 4.4 An example of a transactional model of stress.

Source: From *Measuring Stress: A Guide For Health And Social Scientists,* edited by Sheldon Cohen, Kessler & Gordon. Copyright © 1995 by Oxford University Press, Inc. Used with permission from Oxford University Press, Inc.

influence of biological (e.g., genetic), psychological (e.g., personality), sociocultural (e.g., ethnicity), and life-cycle (e.g., life-stage) forces. These differences in resources are extremely important in understanding why some people have little trouble dealing with very difficult events (e.g., a severe illness) whereas other people seem to have trouble with seemingly routine events (e.g., calming a crying child). Recognizing these differences, let's begin a closer look at the stress and coping paradigm with the concept of appraisal.

Appraisal. Lazarus and Folkman (1984) describe three types of appraisals of stress. **Primary appraisal** *categorizes events into three groups based on the significance they have for our well-being: irrelevant, benign or positive, and stressful.* Irrelevant events are ones that have no bearing on us personally; hearing about a typhoon nowhere near land in the South Pacific while sitting in your living room in Boston is an example. Benign or positive events are ones that have good effects, such as a long-anticipated pay increase. Finally, stressful events are ones, such

as an upcoming operation or test, that are appraised as harmful, threatening, or challenging.

Primary appraisals act as a filter for events we experience. Specifically, any event that is appraised as either irrelevant or as benign or positive is not stressful. In a real sense, we decide which events are potentially stressful and which ones are not. This is an important point for two reasons. First, it means we can effectively sort out the events that may be problems and those that are not, allowing us to concentrate on dealing with life's difficulties more effectively. Second, it means that we could be wrong about our reading of an event. A situation that may appear at first blush to be irrelevant, for example, may actually be very important, or a situation deemed stressful initially may turn out not to be. Such mistakes in primary appraisal could set the stage for real (or imagined) crises later on.

If a person believes that an event is stressful, a second set of decisions, called secondary appraisal, is made. **Secondary appraisal** *evaluates our perceived ability to cope with harm, threat, or challenge.* Secondary appraisal is the equivalent of asking three questions: "What can I do?" "How likely is it that I can use one of my options successfully?" and "Will this option reduce my stress?" How we answer these questions sets the stage for addressing them effectively. For example, if you believe there is something you can do in a situation that will make a difference, then your perceived stress may be reduced and you may be able to deal with the event successfully. In contrast, if you believe there is little that you can do to address the situation successfully or reduce your feelings of stress, then you may feel powerless and ineffective, even if others around you believe there are steps you could take.

What matters in secondary appraisals (and all other decisions in this framework) is what you think is true, not what others think. After you make a decision about an event and reach a preliminary conclusion about what you should do about it (if anything), the situation continues to play itself out. As the event continues to unfold, you begin to get an idea as to whether your primary (and secondary, if necessary) appraisal was accurate. If it was, then you would probably stick with your original evaluation.

However, sometimes you learn additional information or experience another situation that indicates you should reappraise the original event. **Reappraisal** *involves making a new primary or secondary appraisal resulting from changes in the situation.* For example, you may initially dismiss an accusation that your partner is cheating on you (i.e., make a primary appraisal that the event is irrelevant), but after being shown pictures of your partner in a romantic situation with another person, you reappraise the event as stressful. Reappraisal can either increase stress (if your partner had initially denied the encounter) or lower stress (if you discovered that the photographs were fakes).

The three types of appraisals demonstrate that determining whether an event is stressful is a dynamic process. Initial decisions about events may be upheld over time, or they may change in light of new information or personal experience. Thus different events may be appraised in the same way, and the same event may be appraised differently at any two points in time. This dynamic process helps explain why people react the way they do over the life span. For example, as our physiological abilities change with increasing age, we may have fewer physical resources to handle particular events. As a result, events that were appraised as not stressful in young adulthood may be appraised as stressful in late life.

Coping. During the secondary appraisal of an event labeled stressful in primary appraisal, we may believe there is something we can do to deal with the event effectively. *Collectively, these attempts to deal with stressful events are called* **coping.** Lazarus and Folkman (1984) view coping more formally as a complex, evolving process of dealing with stress that is learned. Much like appraisals, coping is seen as a dynamic, evolving process that is fine-tuned over time. Our first attempt might fail, but if we try again in a slightly different way we may succeed. Coping is learned, not automatic. That is why we often do not cope very well with stressful situations we are facing for the first time (such as the end of our first love relationship). The saying "practice makes perfect" applies to coping, too. Also, coping takes time and effort. Finally, coping entails only managing the situation; we need not overcome or control it. Indeed, many stressful events cannot be fixed or undone; many times the best we can do is to learn to live with the situation. It is in this sense that we may cope with the death of a spouse.

The ways in which people cope can be classified in several different ways. At a general level we can distinguish between problem-focused coping and emotion-focused coping. *Problem-focused coping* involves attempts to tackle the problem head-on. Taking medication to treat a disease and spending more time studying for an examination are examples of problem-focused coping with the stress of illness or failing a prior test. In general, problem-focused coping entails doing something directly about the problem at hand. *Emotion-focused coping* involves dealing with one's feelings about the stressful event. Allowing oneself to express anger or frustration over becoming ill or failing an exam is an example of this approach. The goal here is not necessarily to eliminate the problem, although this may happen. Rather, the purpose may be to help oneself deal with situations that are difficult or impossible to tackle head-on. Several other behaviors can also be viewed in the context of coping. Many people believe that their relationship with God is an important aspect of coping (Kinney et al., 2003). Psychoanalytic researchers point to Freud's notion of defense mechanisms as behaviors that may be used to reduce stress. In short, people use many different types of behaviors when they feel stressed.

How well we cope depends on several factors. For example, healthy, energetic people are better able to cope with an infection than frail, sick people. Psychologically, a positive attitude about oneself and one's abilities is also important. Good problem-solving skills put one at an advantage by creating several options with which to manage the stress. Social skills and social support are important in helping one solicit suggestions and assistance from others. Finally, financial resources are important; having the money to pay a mechanic to fix your car allows you to avoid the frustration of trying to do it yourself.

Religiosity and spirituality are important aspects of a person's lifestyle that must be considered in holistic approaches to health and wellness.

Aging and the Stress and Coping Paradigm. Two important age-related differences in the stress and coping paradigm are the sources of stress and coping strategies. Age-related differences have been described for the kinds of things people report as everyday stresses (Aldwin et al., 1996; Moos et al., 2006). Younger adults experience more stress in the areas of finance, work, home maintenance, personal life, family, and friends than do older adults. These differences probably exist because young adults are likely to be parents of small children and are likely to be employed; parenting and work roles are less salient to retired older adults. The stresses reported frequently by older adults may be more age related than role related. That is, environmental stress may be caused by a decreased ability to get around rather than by a specific role.

There is some evidence that the old-old report having fewer stressors in the past week than any other age group (Aldwin et al., 1996). Why this is so is unclear. Maybe in late life people begin to narrow their focus and thus have fewer areas of life that could produce stress. Or, as you will see in Chapter 10, the old-old may adopt a more philosophical outlook on life and not let things bother them as much. Age differences in coping strategies across the life span are striking and consistent (Martin et al., 2008). One key difference is that adults over age 80 are less likely to use active coping strategies and are more likely to use past experience in coping as a guide. Active coping styles are related to better health outcomes. Another important finding is that approaches to coping tend to be consistent across different domains, meaning that people tend to deal with stress related to family and health issues in roughly the same ways.

When combined with the earlier discussion that chronic stress has serious negative effects on health, the importance of age changes in coping styles becomes clearer. Two strategies become apparent: reducing stress or using more active coping. One way to interpret these findings is to focus on "management strategies" (Aldwin et al., 1996). As people age, some older adults become better at managing their lives so as to avoid problems in the first place, so they don't need to cope with stress. And coping resources are better predictors of well-being in older adults than in younger and middle-aged adults (Hamarat et al., 2001; Martin et al., 2008). But becoming better at managing life does not mean that older adults are willing to give up meaningful roles when they encounter stressful events.

We explore the relation between age and stress in more detail in the How Do We Know? feature. Cairney and Krause (2008) use data from a large Canadian study to show that the experience of negative life events matters in the lives of older adults.

Effects of Stress on Health. How does stress affect us? If the stress is short, such as being stuck in a traffic jam for an hour when we're already late in an otherwise relaxed day, the answer is that it probably will have little effect other than on our temper. But if the stress is continuous, or chronic, then the picture changes dramatically. Chronic stress has several potentially serious effects (Davis et al., 2000; Kemeny, 2003), including pervasive negative effects on the immune system that causes increased susceptibility to viral infections, increased risk of atherosclerosis and hypertension, and impaired memory and cognition (Webster-Marketon & Glaser, 2008). In women, chronic stress can also inhibit menstruation, and women react to a wider range of outside stressors than do men.

Research indicates that different types of appraisals that are interpreted as stressful create different

HOW DO WE KNOW?

Negative Life Events and Mastery

Who were the investigators, and what was the aim of the study? How older adults cope with the effects of stressful events related to personal mastery (whether people feel in control of things in their life) is important in understanding how people manage their lives. John Cairney and Neal Krause (2008) decided to see if exposure to life events affects age-related decline in feelings of mastery.

How did the investigators measure the topic of interest? To get a broad assessment of the key variables, Cairney and Krause used several self-report measures. *Mastery* was measured by a seven-item self-report questionnaire that is widely used in this type of research (a sample item is "You have little control over the things that happen to you."). *Recent life events* were measured by the number of negative life events that the respondent or someone close to the respondent had experienced in the previous 12 months. *Physician contact* was measured by asking the respondent how many times he or she had seen or talked with a family physician or general practitioner in the past 12 months. *Physical health concerns* were measured by asking respondents about 21 chronic health conditions, and by asking about limitations in daily activities. *Social support* was measured by asking whether respondents had someone (a) to confide in, (b) to count on, (c) who could give them advice, and (d) who made them feel loved. *Socioeconomic measures* included the highest education level the respondent had obtained and a five-level measure of income adequacy.

Who were the participants in the study? The sample was drawn from the longitudinal biennial National Population Health Survey (NPHS) conducted by Statistics Canada. This telephone survey consists of a national probability sample of Canadian residents across all 10 provinces every two years beginning in 1994 (Wave 1). For Wave 1, of the 18,342 possible respondents aged 12 and over, 17,626 participated (96.1%); 16,291 were over age 18. After eliminating cases with missing data, the final sample consisted of 15,410 respondents. Wave 4 (in 2000) included the same set of measures as Wave 1 for mastery, allowing a comparison over time. Of the respondents who completed Wave 1, 840 died and 5,049 could not be relocated, declined to participate, or provided incomplete data in Wave 4. This left 9,521 respondents for this longitudinal study.

What was the design of the study? Cairney and Krause used a longitudinal design with two times of measurement: 1994 and 2000.

Were there ethical concerns in the study? Because people had the right not to participate, there were no ethical concerns with the study.

What were the results? Because of the problems inherent in longitudinal designs (see Chapter 1), Cairney and Krause checked for systematic differences in participants in the Wave 1 and Wave 4 data. They found that men, those from higher income groups, those with only a high school education, older adults, and those with more physical disabilities or health problems were more likely to have died by Wave 4. Single individuals, those with lower income adequacy, with more physical disability, and with higher levels of social support were more likely to drop out by Wave 4.

An analysis of the effects of stress on perceived mastery was done by comparing outcomes at ages 25, 45, and 65. This analysis showed that at each time of measurement for people in all three age groups, exposure to more negative life events was associated with decline in mastery, with this outcome being strongest with the age 65 group. Looking at the data longitudinally, the effects of more negative life events over time was greatest for the group that was age 65 in Wave 1.

What did the investigators conclude? These findings show that experiencing negative life events is a major source of age-related declines in feelings of personal mastery. In turn, loss of personal mastery may explain why older adults are more vulnerable to the negative effects of stress.

physiological outcomes (Kemeny, 2003; Webster-Marketon & Glaser, 2008). This means that different types of stress are associated with different emotions, which trigger different neural pathways. This may mean that how the body reacts to stress depends on the appraisal process; the reaction to different types of stress is not the same. In turn, this implies that changing people's appraisal may also be a way to lower stress.

Additional research shows that the effects of coping strategies on physiological outcomes and health depend on whether they have affected a person's sense of well-being (Aldwin & Yancura, 2004). To the extent that they do, the effects can be more negative. Coping strategies clearly affect the progress of disease, probably through the person's compliance to medical regimens. Most important, as noted earlier, the ability to deal with the hormones produced by stress declines due to age changes in immune functioning (Webster-Marketon & Glaser, 2008). So coping may be a key; given the higher prevalence of chronic diseases in older adults, how well one copes may have important effects on the quality of life (Aldwin & Gilmer, 2004).

Concept Checks

1. How do researchers define *health*? What problems do these definitions have?
2. How is *quality of life* defined?
3. What are the major age-related changes in immune system functioning?
4. What are the differences between chronic and acute diseases?
5. What is the stress and coping paradigm? What are the key age-related changes that occur?

4.3 Common Chronic Conditions and Their Management

LEARNING OBJECTIVES
- *What are the most important issues in chronic disease?*
- *What are some common chronic conditions across adulthood?*
- *How can people manage chronic conditions?*

Moses is a 75-year-old African American man who worked as a lawyer all his life. Recently, he was diagnosed as having prostate cancer. Moses has heard about several treatment options, such as surgery and radiation therapy, and he is concerned about potential side effects, such as impotence. Moses wonders what he should do.

Every day, millions of older adults get up in the morning and face another day of dealing with chronic diseases such as diabetes and arthritis. Although medical advances are made every year, true cures for these conditions probably are not imminent. We considered some chronic diseases in Chapter 3 in the context of discussing age-related changes in major body systems; arthritis and cardiovascular disease were among them. In this section, we will consider other chronic conditions, such as diabetes and cancer. We will see that Moses's concern about how to deal with his prostate cancer is one facing many men. As Moses will discover, in many situations there is no clear-cut "right" way to proceed. We will also examine some ways to help alleviate the effects of some chronic conditions and consider some ways in which we may be able to prevent such diseases or at least reduce our chances of getting them.

General Issues in Chronic Conditions

Having a chronic disease does not mean that one becomes incapacitated. Even though the type and severity of chronic conditions vary across people, most older adults manage to figure out how to accomplish the necessary tasks of daily living despite having a chronic condition.

Although most people manage to accomplish the necessary tasks of daily living, they may experience limitations in functioning. Chronic conditions can make life unpleasant and in some cases can increase susceptibility to other diseases. Understanding chronic conditions requires understanding how the four developmental forces interact. We saw in Chapter 3 that researchers are beginning to understand genetic connections with such chronic conditions as cardiovascular disease and cancer. Other biological aspects include the changes in physical systems with age, including the immune system, that can set the stage for chronic conditions. Psychological aspects key to chronic disease include the coping skills people bring to bear on their conditions; we consider some of these later in this chapter. Sociocultural factors include the lack of adequate health care, which creates barriers to treatment. The ethnic group differences in some chronic conditions, such as hypertension, are also important to keep in mind. Finally, life-cycle factors help us understand why reactions to the same chronic condition vary with the age of onset. Moreover, some conditions, such as rheumatoid arthritis, can occur at any point in adulthood, whereas others, such as prostate cancer, tend to occur most after midlife. As the number of older adults increases rapidly, so will the extent of chronic conditions as health problems. This will necessitate a fundamental change in health care, reflecting a shift from an acute care focus to one that focuses much more on managing chronic conditions. Let's consider some of the most common chronic conditions.

Common Chronic Conditions

What are the most common chronic conditions experienced by older adults? Arthritis and various forms of cardiovascular disease are the most prevalent (National Center for Health Statistics, 2008b). Four others are also extremely important: diabetes, cancer, incontinence, and stress.

Arthritis. We saw in Chapter 3 that osteoarthritis and rheumatoid arthritis afflict many adults. It is estimated that everyone over age 60 shows some physical evidence of one form of arthritis, with most of them reporting pain (National Institute of Arthritis and Musculoskeletal and Skin Diseases, 2008a, 2008b). Because it is so common, most people assume that arthritis is simply a part of normal aging and further assume they must simply learn to live with it. Consequently, many people fail to seek appropriate therapy.

Rheumatoid arthritis is not strictly an age-related condition; in fact, many young and middle-aged adults have symptoms. The cause of rheumatoid arthritis remains unknown. In contrast,

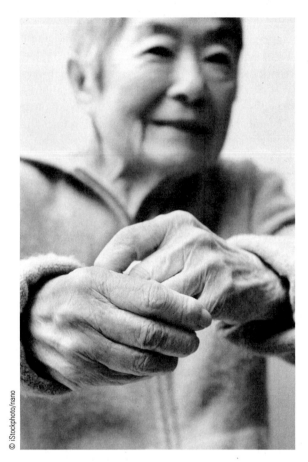

© iStockphoto/nano

Arthritis is a painful and debilitating disease that decreases the quality of life.

osteoarthritis is age related, with symptoms usually not beginning until later in life. Genetic and environmental factors (such as overuse) have been identified. As you would imagine, the primary problem facing people with arthritis is pain. Strangely, the pain often is variable; people have both good days and bad days. In most cases, people with arthritis structure their days around these variations, doing more when they can. However, reducing physical activity has a paradoxical effect. Movement stimulates the secretion of synovial fluid, which lubricates the surfaces between and increases blood flow to the joints. Movement also keeps muscles toned and limber. All are important in keeping joints flexible; refraining from movement ultimately makes the joints hurt worse. Lack of movement over long periods of time can eventually result in the joints "freezing" in place, a condition called contracture that may require physical therapy to address. Thus people with arthritis must be encouraged to keep moving, because the pain accompanying the arthritis is usually less than the pain that results from the effects of contracture.

There are several ways to treat arthritis (MedlinePlus, 2008). Several types of medication help alleviate the pain of arthritis. Exercise is essential for maintaining healthy joints and should include range-of-motion, strength training, and low-impact aerobics. Other prevention approaches include taking glucosamine and chondroitin, and eating a diet rich in antioxidants and omega-3 fatty acids (found in cold-water fish such as salmon as well as some nuts, such as walnuts). The pain of arthritis can be managed in most people by taking over-the-counter medications, such as acetaminophen or aspirin, or one of several prescription drugs, such as nonsteroidal anti-inflammatory drugs (NSAIDs), cyclo-oxygenase-2 (COX-2) inhibitors (particularly helpful for people who cannot take NSAIDs due to stomach problems), corticosteroids, disease-modifying anti-rheumatic drugs (DMARDs, which help over the long term), and a new class of DMARDs called tumor necrosis factor (TNF) blockers. All these drugs have potentially serious side effects, so they should be taken only under the supervision of a physician; for example, the Food and Drug Administration has warned about fungal infections as a side effect of TNF blockers (Food and Drug Administration, 2008).

Diabetes Mellitus. *The disease* **diabetes mellitus** *occurs when the pancreas produces insufficient insulin.* The primary characteristic of diabetes mellitus is above-normal sugar (glucose) in the blood and urine caused by problems in metabolizing carbohydrates. People with diabetes mellitus can go into a coma if the level of sugar gets too high, and they may lapse into unconsciousness if it gets too low.

There are two general types of diabetes. Type I diabetes usually develops earlier in life and requires the use of insulin, hence it is sometimes called *insulin-dependent diabetes.* Type II diabetes typically develops in adulthood and is often effectively managed through diet. There are three groups of older adults with diabetes: those who developed diabetes as children, adolescents, or young adults; those who developed diabetes in late middle age and also typically developed cardiovascular problems; and those who develop diabetes in late life and usually show mild problems. This last group includes the majority of older adults with diabetes mellitus. In adults, diabetes mellitus often is associated with obesity. The symptoms of diabetes seen in younger people (excessive thirst, increased appetite and urination, fatigue, weakness, weight loss, and impaired wound healing) may be far less prominent or absent in older adults. As a result, diabetes mellitus in older adults often is diagnosed during other medical procedures, such as eye examinations or hospitalizations for other conditions.

Overall, diabetes is more common among older adults, members of minority groups, and women; for example, African Americans and Latinos born in 2000 have a 2 in 5 risk for diabetes over their lifetimes, more than twice the rate for European Americans (Office of Minority Health and Health Disparities, 2008). The chronic effects of increased glucose levels may result in complications. The most common long-term effects include nerve damage, diabetic retinopathy (discussed in Chapter 3), kidney disorders, cerebrovascular accidents (CVAs), cognitive dysfunction, damage to the coronary arteries, skin problems, and poor circulation in the arms and legs, which may lead to gangrene. Diabetes also increases the chance of developing atherosclerosis and coronary heart disease.

Although it cannot be cured, diabetes can be managed effectively through a low-carbohydrate and low-calorie diet; exercise; proper care of skin, gums, teeth, and feet; and medication (insulin). For older adults, it is important to address potential memory difficulties with the daily testing and management regimens. Education about diabetes mellitus is included in Medicare coverage, making it easier for older adults to learn how to manage the condition.

Cancer. Cancer is the second leading cause of death in the United States, behind cardiovascular disease. Every year, nearly 1.5 million new cases of cancer are diagnosed, and more than 565,000 diagnosed persons die (American Cancer Society, 2008b). Over the life span, nearly one in every two American men and one in three American women will develop cancer (American Cancer Society, 2008b). There is evidence that cancer is present in many people whose cause of death is officially listed as some other disease, such as pneumonia, so that the true incidence rate may be underestimated.

Many current deaths caused by cancer are preventable. Some forms of cancer, such as lung and colorectal cancer, are caused in large part by unhealthy lifestyles. The American Cancer Society (2008c) estimates that cancers caused by smoking alone account for about 1 in every 5 deaths in the United States each year. Most skin cancers can be prevented by limiting exposure to the sun's ultraviolet rays. Clearly, changes in lifestyle would have a major impact on cancer rates. The risk of getting cancer increases markedly with age (American Cancer Society, 2008b). Figure 4.5 depicts the incidence rates for cancer as a function of age. As can be seen, the largest number of cases occurs in the

age group 80 to 84. Notice that after age 40 the incidence rate increases sharply.

The incidence and mortality rates of some common forms of cancer in men and women are shown in Figure 4.6. Notice that prostate cancer is the most common form of cancer in men and breast cancer is the most common form in women in all ethnic groups (American Cancer Society, 2008b). Gender differences are apparent in some forms of cancer; for example, lung cancers are more common in men (American Cancer Society, 2008b). Ethnic differences are apparent in cancer rates, as depicted in Figure 4.7.

Death rates from various forms of cancer differ: Lung cancer kills more than three times as many men as prostate cancer and considerably more women than breast cancer (in women). Five-year survival rates for these cancers also differ dramatically. Whereas only 15% of patients with lung cancer are still living 5 years after diagnosis, an average of 86% of female patients with breast cancer and 97% of patients with prostate cancer are (American Cancer Society, 2008b).

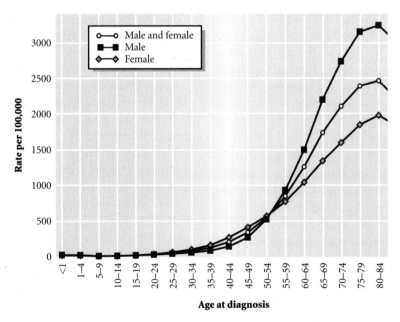

Figure 4.5 Cancer incidence crude rates, nine registries, 1973–2000.

Source: National Cancer Institute. http://canques.seer.cancer.gov/cgi-bin/

Estimated New Cases*		Estimated Deaths	
Male	**Female**	**Male**	**Female**
Prostate	Breast	Lung & bronchus	Lung & bronchus
186,320 (25%)	182,460 (26%)	90,810 (31%)	71,030 (26%)
Lung & bronchus	Lung & bronchus	Prostate	Breast
114,690 (15%)	100,330 (14%)	28,660 (10%)	40,480 (15%)
Colon & rectum	Colon & rectum	Colon & rectum	Colon & rectum
77,250 (10%)	71,560 (10%)	24,260 (8%)	25,700 (9%)
Urinary bladder	Uterine corpus	Pancreas	Pancreas
51,230 (7%)	40,100 (6%)	17,500 (6%)	16,790 (6%)
Non-Hodgkin lymphoma	Non-Hodgkin lymphoma	Liver & intrahepatic bile duct	Ovary
35,450 (5%)	30,670 (4%)	12,570 (4%)	15,520 (6%)
Melanoma of the skin	Thyroid	Leukemia	Non-Hodgkin lymphoma
34,950 (5%)	28,410 (4%)	12,460 (4%)	9,730 (3%)
Kidney & renal pelvis	Melanoma of the skin	Esophagus	Leukemia
33,130 (4 %)	27,530 (4%)	11,250 (4%)	9,250 (3%)
Oral cavity & pharynx	Ovary	Urinary bladder	Uterine corpus
25,310 (3%)	21,650 (3%)	9,950 (3%)	7,470 (3%)
Leukemia	Kidney & renal pelvis	Non-Hodgkin lymphoma	Liver & intrahepatic bile duct
25,180 (3%)	21,260 (3%)	9,790 (3%)	5,840 (2%)
Pancreas	Leukemia	Kidney & renal pelvis	Brain & other nervous system
18,770 (3%)	19,090 (3%)	8,100 (3%)	5,650 (2%)
All sites	All sites	All sites	All sites
745,180 (100%)	692,000 (100%)	294,120 (100%)	271,530 (100%)

*Excludes basal and squamous cell skin cancers and in situ carcinoma except urinary bladder.

©2008, American Cancer Society, Inc., Surveillance Research

Figure 4.6 Leading Sites of New Cancer Cases and Deaths–2008 Estimates.

Source: American Cancer Society. Cancer Facts and Figures 2008. Atlanta: American Cancer Society.

Why older people have a much higher incidence of cancer is not understood fully. Part of the reason is the cumulative effect of poor health habits over a long period of time, such as cigarette smoking and poor diet. In addition, the cumulative effects of exposure to pollutants and cancer-causing chemicals are partly to blame. As noted earlier in this chapter, some researchers believe that normative age-related changes in the immune system, resulting in a decreased ability to inhibit the growth of tumors, may also be responsible. Research in molecular biology and microbiology is increasingly pointing to genetic links, likely in combination with environmental factors (Wallace, 2006). The National Cancer Institute initiated the Cancer Genome Anatomy Program (CGAP, http://cgap.nci.nih.gov/) to develop a comprehensive list of all genes responsible for cancer. For example, two breast cancer susceptibility genes that have been identified are *BRCA1* on chromosome 17 and *BRCA2* on chromosome 13. When a woman carries a mutation in either *BRCA1* or *BRCA2,* she is at a greater risk of being diagnosed with breast or ovarian cancer at some point. Similarly, a potential susceptibility locus for prostate cancer has been identified on chromosome 1, called *HPC1,* which may account for about 1 in 500 cases of prostate cancer.

Although genetic screening tests for breast and prostate cancer for the general population are not yet warranted, such tests may one day be routine. Genetics also is providing much of the exciting new research on possible treatments by giving investigators new ways to fight the disease. Age-related tissue changes have been associated with the development of tumors, some of which become cancerous; some of these may be genetically linked as well. The discovery that the presence of telomerase causes cells to grow rapidly and without limits on the number

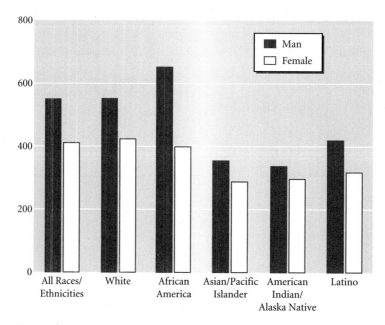

Figure 4.7 Cancer incidence rates by race and ethnicity, all types of cancer.

Source: Ries, L.A.G., Melbert, D., Krapcho, M., Stinchcomb, D.G., Howlader, N., Horner, M.J., Mariotto, A., Miller, B.A., Feuer, E.J., Alterkruse, S.F., Lewis, D.R., Clegg, L., Eisner, M.P., Reichman, M., & Edwards, B.K. (eds). *SEER Cancer Statistics Review,* 1975–2005, National Cancer Institute. Bethesda, MD, http://seer.cancer.gov/csr/1975_2005/, based on November 2007 SEER data submission, posted to the SEER website, 2008.

of divisions they can undergo provides additional insights into how cancer develops (Londoño-Vallejo, 2008; see Chapter 3). What remains to be seen is how these genetic events interact with environmental factors, such as viruses or pollutants. Understanding this interaction process, predicted by the basic developmental forces, could explain why there are great differences among individuals in when and how cancer develops.

The most effective way to address the problem of cancer is through increased use of screening techniques and preventive lifestyle changes. The American Cancer Society (2008) strongly recommends these steps for people of all ages, but older adults need to be especially aware of what to do. Table 4.1 shows guidelines for the early detection of some common forms of cancer.

As Moses is learning, one of the biggest controversies in cancer prevention concerns screening and treatment for prostate cancer. The Current Controversies feature summarizes the issues: lack of data about the causes and the course of the disease and disagreement over treatment approaches. This controversy mirrors similar debates over the treatment of breast cancer, contrasting the relative merits of radical mastectomy (removal of the breast and some surrounding tissue) with lumpectomy (removal of the cancerous tumor only) and how chemotherapy, radiation, and drugs such as tamoxifen fit into the overall treatment approach.

In general, cancer treatment involves several major approaches that are typically used in combination (National Cancer Institute, 2008): surgery, chemotherapy, radiation, and others (e.g., biological therapy, gene therapy, bone marrow transplant). In addition, numerous alternative therapies, such as herbal approaches, exist. Continued advances in genetic research probably will result in genetically

Table 4.1

Summary of American Cancer Society (ACS) Recommendations for Early Cancer Detection

Site	Recommendation
Cancer-related checkup	A cancer-related checkup is recommended every 3 years for people aged 20–40 and every year for people age 40 and older. This exam should include health counseling and, depending on a person's age, might include examinations for cancers of the thyroid, oral cavity, skin, lymph nodes, testes, and ovaries, as well as for some nonmalignant diseases.
Breast	Women 40 and older should have an annual mammogram and an annual clinical breast exam (CBE) performed by a health care professional and should perform monthly breast self-examination. The CBE should be conducted close to the scheduled mammogram. Women ages 20 to 39 should have a CBE performed by a health care professional every 3 years and should perform monthly breast self-examination.
Colon and rectum	Men and women aged 50 or older should follow one of the examination schedules below: A fecal occult blood test every year and a flexible sigmoidoscopy every 5 years.* A colonoscopy every 10 years.* A double-contrast barium enema every 5 to 10 years.* A CT colonography (virtual colonoscopy) every 5 years.
Prostate	The ACS recommends that both the prostate-specific antigen blood test and the rectal examination be offered annually, beginning at age 50, to men who have a life expectancy of at least 10 years and to younger men who are at high risk. Men in high-risk groups, such as those with a strong familial predisposition (i.e., two or more affected first-degree relatives) and African Americans, may begin at a younger age (i.e., 45 years).
Uterus	**Cervix:** All women who are or have been sexually active or who are 18 and older should have an annual Pap test and pelvic examination. After three or more consecutive satisfactory examinations with normal findings, the Pap test may be performed less frequently. Discuss the matter with your physician. **Endometrium:** Women at high risk for cancer of the uterus should have a sample of endometrial tissue examined when menopause begins.

A digital rectal exam should be done at the same time as sigmoidoscopy, colonoscopy, or double-contrast barium enema. People who are at moderate or high risk for colorectal cancer should talk with a doctor about a different testing schedule. Adapted from the American Cancer Society (2008d).

engineered medications designed to attack cancer cells. As with any health care decision, people with cancer need to become as educated as possible about the options.

Incontinence. *For many people, the loss of the ability to control the elimination of urine and feces on an occasional or consistent basis, called* **incontinence**, *is a source of great concern and embarrassment.* As you can imagine, incontinence can result in social isolation and lower quality of life if no steps are taken to address the problem.

Urinary incontinence, the most common form, increases with age and varies across ethnic groups as a function of gender (Tennstedt et al., 2008). Among community-dwelling older adults, roughly 20% of women and 10% of men have urinary incontinence. But rates are much higher if the person has dementia and is living in the community (about 35%) or if the person is living in a nursing home (roughly 70%). European American women report a higher rate of urinary incontinence than either African American or Latina women; rates for men do not vary across ethnic groups.

Urinary incontinence occurs for five major reasons (Department of Urology, Cornell University, 2008). *Stress incontinence* happens when pressure in the abdomen exceeds the ability to resist urinary

Roughly the size of a walnut and weighing about an ounce, the prostate gland is an unlikely candidate to create a major medical controversy. The prostate is located in front of the rectum and below the bladder and wraps around the urethra (the tube carrying urine out through the penis). Its primary function is to produce fluid for semen, the liquid that transports sperm. In half of all men over age 60, the prostate tends to enlarge, which may produce such symptoms as difficulty in urinating and frequent nighttime urination.

Enlargement of the prostate can happen for three main reasons: prostatitis (an inflammation of the prostate that is usually caused by an infection), benign prostatic hyperplasia (BPH), and prostate cancer. BPH is a noncancerous enlargement of the prostate that affects the innermost part of the prostate first. This often results in urination problems as the prostate gradually squeezes the urethra, but it does not affect sexual functioning. Prostate cancer often begins on the outer portion of the prostate, which seldom causes symptoms in the early stages. Each year, more than 200,000 men in the United States are diagnosed with prostate cancer; 35,000 die. For reasons we do not yet understand, African American men such as Moses have a 40% higher chance of getting prostate cancer. In addition, a genetic link is clear: A man whose brother has prostate cancer is four times more likely to get prostate cancer than a man with no brothers having the disease.

Part of the controversy surrounding prostate cancer relates to whether early detection reduces mortality from the disease. The American Cancer Society (2008e), the National Comprehensive Cancer Network (NCCN, 2007), and other groups have conducted aggressive campaigns to encourage men over age 50 (age 40–45 in high-risk groups) to undergo two diagnostic tests annually: the digital rectal examination (DRE, in which a physician examines the prostate by touch) and the prostate-specific antigen (PSA) blood test. In sharp contrast to clear evidence that early detection of breast cancer in women reduces mortality by at least 30% among older women, no similar statistics exist for prostate cancer. This lack of data led the U.S. Preventive Services Task Force, the Canadian Task Force on the Periodic Health Examination, and others to recommend abandoning routine prostate cancer screening because of the cost and the uncertain benefits associated with it.

The American Cancer Society and the National Comprehensive Cancer Network jointly created a guide to prostate cancer screening and treatment to help men negotiate the confusing state of affairs (Version VI, completed in 2007, is available at http://www.nccn.org/patients/patient_gls/_english/pdf/NCCN%20Prostate%20Guidelines.pdf). Although not a replacement for physician input, the screening and treatment charts and decision tools can be very useful in sorting through the various options.

The sharp division among medical experts highlights the relation between carefully conducted research and public health policy. At present, there has been no systematic comparison of various treatment options (which include surgery, radiation, hormones, and drugs), nor do we fully understand the natural course of prostate cancer in terms of which types of tumors spread to other organs and which ones do not (American Cancer Society & National Comprehensive Cancer Network, 2007). Given that some of the side effects of surgery include urinary incontinence and impotence, and that some of the other therapies may produce other unpleasant effects, there is debate on whether the disease should be treated at all in most patients (American Cancer Society & National Comprehensive Cancer Network, 2007).

At present, men who experience prostate-related symptoms are left to decide for themselves what to do. Many men opt for immediate treatment and learn how to live with the subsequent side effects. Support groups for men with prostate cancer are becoming more common, and many encourage the patient's partner to participate. The controversy surrounding early screening and detection of prostate cancer is unlikely to subside soon because the necessary research concerning effective treatment and survival will take years to conduct. Until then, if you or someone you know is over 50 or is in a high-risk group, the decision still must be made. Talk at length with a physician who is up-to-date on the topic and educate yourself about the alternatives.

flow. This may occur when a person coughs, sneezes, or lifts a heavy object. *Urge incontinence* usually is caused by a central nervous system problem after a CVA or urinary tract infection. People feel the urge to urinate but cannot get to a toilet quickly enough. *Overflow incontinence* results from improper contraction of the kidneys, causing the bladder to become overdistended. Certain drugs, tumors, and prostate enlargement are common causes of overflow incontinence. *Functional or environmental incontinence* occurs when the urinary tract is intact but because of physical disability or cognitive impairment the person is unaware of the need to urinate. *Iatrogenic incontinence* usually is caused by medication side effects. Changing the dosage often solves the problem.

Most types of incontinence can be alleviated with interventions. Among the most effective are behavioral interventions, which include diet changes, relearning to recognize the need to toilet, and pelvic floor muscle training for stress incontinence (Zahariou, Karamouti, & Papaioannou, 2008). Certain medications and surgical intervention may be needed in some cases. Numerous products such as protective undergarments and padding also are available to help absorb leaks. All these options help alleviate the psychological and social effects of incontinence and help people live better lives (Burgio et al., 2001).

Managing Pain

One of the most unpleasant aspects of many chronic diseases is pain. Pain is disruptive, saps energy, negatively affects quality of life, and can lead to an ever-intensifying cycle of pain, anxiety, and anguish.

Pain is also one of the most common complaints of older adults, and does not necessarily reflect the same things as pain in younger adults; for older adults it not only is an indication that something is wrong, but also can be responsible for depression, sleep disorders, decreased social interaction, impaired mobility, and increased health care costs (Karp et al., 2008).

Unfortunately, many myths exist about pain in older adults, such as that older adults should simply accept the physical pain they experience as part of growing older. Failure to understand the real nature of pain in older adults can lead to a failure to relieve it.

How do people manage pain? Perhaps the most important step is to understand that pain is not a necessary part of treatment, people can control their pain, no one approach is likely to be sufficient, and asking for pain relief is to be expected. There are two general pain management techniques: pharmacological and nonpharmacological (Karmol, 2008). These approaches often are used together for maximum pain relief. Pharmacological approaches to pain management include nonnarcotic and narcotic medications. Nonnarcotic medications are best for mild to moderate pain, whereas narcotic medications are best for severe pain. Nonnarcotic medications include NSAIDs, such as ibuprofen and acetaminophen. However, these drugs must be used with caution because they may cause toxic side effects in older adults. Narcotic drugs that work well in older adults include morphine and codeine; other commonly used drugs, such as meperidine and pentazocine, should be avoided because of age-related changes in metabolism. Patients taking any of these medications must be monitored very closely. Nonpharmacological pain control includes a variety of approaches, all of which are effective with some people; the trick is to keep trying until the best approach is found. Common techniques include the following:

- Deep and superficial stimulation of the skin through therapeutic touch, massage, vibration, heat, cold, and various ointments
- Electrical stimulation over the pain site or to the spine
- Acupuncture and acupressure
- Biofeedback, in which a person learns to control and change the body processes responsible for the pain
- Distraction techniques such as soft music that draw a person's attention away from the pain
- Relaxation, meditation, and imagery approaches that rid the mind of tension and anxiety
- Hypnosis, either self-induced or induced by another person

Like other treatments, nonpharmacological interventions have both advantages and disadvantages. The best approach is to try various techniques until the best relief is obtained.

The most important point is that pain is not a necessary part of growing old or having a disease. Pain relief is an important part of recovery and should be included in any treatment regimen for adults of all ages.

Concept Checks

1. What are the most important things to consider in chronic diseases?
2. What are some of the most common chronic conditions in older adults?
3. How is pain managed?

4.4 Pharmacology and Medication Adherence

LEARNING OBJECTIVES

- *What are the developmental trends in using medication?*
- *How does aging affect the way the medications work?*
- *What are the consequences of medication interactions?*
- *What are the important medication adherence issues?*

Lucy is an 80-year-old woman who has several chronic health problems. As a result, she takes 12 medications every day. She must follow the regimen very carefully; some of her medications must be taken with food, some on an empty stomach, and some at bedtime. Lucy's daughter is concerned that Lucy may experience serious problems if she fails to take her medications properly.

One of the most important health issues for older adults is the use of both prescription and over-the-counter medications. In fact, older adults take more medications on average than any other age group, roughly half of all drugs prescribed in the United States (Shea, 2006). When over-the-counter drugs are included, this translates into about six or seven medications per older adult; Lucy takes more than the average. Like Lucy, most people take these drugs to relieve pain or related problems resulting from chronic conditions.

Patterns of Medication Use

The explosion of new prescription and over-the-counter medications over the past few decades has created many options for physicians in treating disease, especially chronic conditions. Although advances in medication are highly desirable, there are hidden dangers for older adults. Until the late 1990s, clinical trials of new medications were not required to include older adults. Thus, for most of the medications on the market, it is unclear whether they are as effective for older adults as they are for younger or middle-aged adults. In addition, because of normative changes in metabolism with age, the effective dosage of medications may change as people get older, which can mean a greater risk of overdose or the need to increase the dose in order to get the desired effect.

When one considers that many of these newer, often more effective medications are very expensive, the ability of many older adults to afford the best medication treatments is questionable. The prescription drug insurance most older Americans have through Medicare leaves significant gaps for most; this means that many still cannot afford them because the deductibles and co-payments are too high for their fixed incomes. Additionally, figuring out which option is best can be quite complex, serving as a further barrier. (You can get much more information from the official Medicare prescription drug coverage website: http://www.medicare.gov/pdphome.asp.)

As even more medications are developed and approved, the use of multiple medications will continue and likely increase. When used appropriately, medications can improve people's lives; when used inappropriately, they can cause harm. Understanding how medications work and how these processes change with age is extremely important.

Developmental Changes in How Medications Work

When Lucy takes her medications every day, what happens? Understanding how medications work involves knowing the developmental changes in absorption, distribution, metabolism, and excretion of medications (Hacker, Messer, & Bachmann, 2009).

Absorption is the time needed for one of Lucy's medications to enter the bloodstream. For drugs taken orally, a key factor is the time it takes for the medication to go from the stomach to the small intestine, where maximum absorption occurs. This transfer may take longer than expected in older adults, resulting in too little or too much absorption, depending on the drug. For example, if a drug takes longer to transfer from the stomach to the small intestine in older adults, too little of the drug may be left to be effective. However, once in the small intestine, absorption does not appear to differ among older, middle-aged, or younger adults (Hacker et al., 2009).

Once in the bloodstream, the medication is *distributed throughout the body*. How well distribution occurs depends on the adequacy of the cardiovascular system. Maximal effectiveness of a drug depends on the balance between the portions of the drug that bind with plasma protein and the portions that remain free. As we grow older, more portions of the drug remain free; this means that toxic levels of a drug can build up more easily in older adults. Similarly, drugs that are soluble in water or fat tissue can also build up more easily in older adults because of age-related decreases in total body water or

possible increases in fat tissue. The effective dosage of a drug depends critically on the amount of free drug in the body; thus, whether the person is young or old, thin or obese, is very important to keep in mind (Hacker et al., 2009).

Getting rid of medications in the bloodstream is partly the job of the liver, a process called drug *metabolism*. There is much evidence that this process is slower in older adults, meaning that drugs stay in the body longer as people grow older (Cusack, 1995). Slower drug metabolism can also create the potential for toxicity if the medication schedule does not take this into account. Sometimes drugs are decomposed into other compounds to help eliminate them. Drug *excretion* occurs mainly through the kidneys in urine, although some elimination occurs through feces, sweat, and saliva. Changes in kidney function with age, related to lower total body water content, are common. This means that drugs often are not excreted as quickly by older adults, again setting the stage for possible toxic effects (Hacker et al., 2009).

What do these changes mean? Most important, the dosage of a drug needed to get the desired effect may be different for older adults than for middle-aged or younger adults. In many cases, physicians recommend using one third to one half the usual adult dosage when the difference between the effective dosages and toxic dosages is small or there is a high rate of side effects (Hacker et al., 2009). In addition, because of age-related physiological changes, several drugs are not recommended for use by older adults. In general, a dosage strategy of "start low and go slow" is best.

Medication Side Effects and Interactions

Because of their high rate of medication use, older adults also have the highest risk of adverse drug effects (Kane et al., 1994). In part, these problems result from physiological changes that occur with age in how drugs are absorbed into the body, how long they remain, and how well they work. For example, changes in the stomach may slow down the rate at which drugs enter the body, meaning that achieving the effective level of the drug in the body may take longer. Changes in liver and kidney functioning affect how rapidly the drug is removed and excreted from the body, meaning that levels of the drug may remain high for longer periods of time.

As we have seen, age-related increases in the frequency of chronic conditions means that older adults are likely to have more than one medical problem for which they take medications. In this regard, Lucy is fairly typical. *Treating multiple conditions results in* **polypharmacy,** *the use of multiple medications.* Polypharmacy is potentially dangerous because many drugs do not interact well; the action of some drugs is enhanced in combination with others, whereas other drugs may not work at all in combination. Drug interactions may create secondary medical problems that in turn need to be treated, and the primary condition may not be treated as effectively. Moreover, drug interactions can produce symptoms that appear to be caused by other diseases; in some cases they may cause confusion and memory loss that mimics Alzheimer's disease. Professionals and family members need to monitor the situation closely (Arnold, 2008).

Lucy's daughter is correct in worrying about her mother taking her medications as prescribed. Analyzing a person's medication regimen, including both prescription and over-the-counter medications, and asking the patient or caregiver to describe how they are taken is important in diagnosing health problems. Given the high level of medication use among older adults, what can be done to minimize drug interaction effects? Physicians play a key role, but other health care professionals also must be alert because older adults typically go to more than one physician. Accurate medication histories including all types of medicines are essential. Inappropriate use of drugs, such as antipsychotics to control behavior, must also be monitored.

Adherence to Medication Regimens

The likelihood of adverse drug reactions increases as the number of medications increases. Taking more drugs also means that keeping track of each becomes more difficult. Imagine having to keep track of six different medications, each of which has a different schedule, as presented in Table 4.2.

Medication adherence (taking medications correctly) becomes less likely the more drugs people take and the more complicated the regimens are. Combined with sensory, physical, and cognitive changes in older adults, medication adherence is a significant problem in this age group (Bosworth, Oddone, & Weinberger, 2005; Shea, 2006). The oldest old are especially at risk; the most common problem is that they simply forget to take the medication. (We consider ways to help people remember to take their medications in Chapter 7.) Yet adherence is crucial to treatment success. Christensen

Table 4.2

Example of a Drug Regimen

	Morning	Dinner	Bedtime
Large yellow pill	Take 1 each day with food		
Small blue pill	Take 1 every other day		
Small white pill	Take 2 per day for two days, then 1 per day; repeat		
Round pink tablet		Take 1 every other day	
Oval white pill			Take 2 each night with plenty of water
Small yellow pill			Take one per week

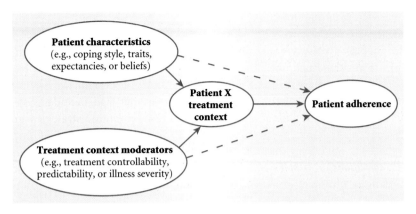

Figure 4.8 Conceptual representation of the patient-by-treatment-context interactive framework. The dashed lines reflect the fact that research generally does not find that patient characteristics or contextual features have a significant effect on adherence.

and Johnson (2002) present an interactive model that describes the context of patient adherence. This model is shown in Figure 4.8.

The best approach, of course, is to keep the number of medications to a minimum (Shea, 2006). If the use of drugs is determined to be essential, then periodic reevaluations should be conducted and the medication discontinued when possible. In addition, the lowest effective dosage should be used. In general, medication use by older adults should get the same careful consideration as by any other age group.

Concept Checks

1. How many medications does the average older adult take?
2. What changes occur with age in the ways in which medications work?
3. What side effect and drug interaction concerns do older adults face?

4.5 Functional Health and Disability

LEARNING OBJECTIVES

- *What factors are important to include in a model of disability in late life?*
- *What is functional health?*
- *What causes functional limitations and disability in older adults?*

Brian is a 68-year-old former welder who retired 3 years ago. He and his wife, Dorothy, had planned to travel in their RV and see the country. But Brian's arthritis has been getting worse lately, and he is having increasing difficulty getting around and doing basic daily tasks. Brian and Dorothy wonder what the future holds for them.

Brian and Dorothy are not alone. Many couples plan to travel or to do other activities after they retire, only to find health issues complicating the situation. As the focus on health has shifted over the past several decades to chronic disease, researchers have increasingly focused on how well people can function in their daily lives. In this section, we examine how functional health is determined and how disability occurs.

A Model of Disability in Late Life

As we saw earlier in this chapter, one defining characteristic of a chronic condition is that it lasts a long time. This means that for most adults, the time between the onset of a chronic condition and death is long, measured in years and even decades. Chronic diseases typically involve some level of discomfort, and physical limitations are common, everyday issues for most people, as they are for Brian. Over the course of the disease, these problems usually increase, resulting in more efforts by patients and health care workers to try to slow the progress of the disease. In many cases, these efforts allow people to resume such activities as daily walks and shopping and to feel optimistic about the future (Verbrugge, 1994). This is especially true for the oldest old (Fauth, Zarit, & Malmberg, 2008).

In the context of chronic conditions, **disability** *is the effects of chronic conditions on people's ability to engage in activities that are necessary, expected, and personally desired in their society* (Verbrugge, 1994). When people are disabled as a result of a chronic condition, they have difficulty doing daily tasks, such as household chores, personal care, job duties, active recreation, socializing with friends and family, and errands. One of the most important research efforts related to health and aging is seeking to understand how disability results from chronic conditions and what might be done to help prevent it. It is important to understand the changing context of disability in the United States. As Fries (2003) points out, considerable data document an overall declining rate of disability since the early 1980s of roughly 2% per year. When compared to the overall decline in mortality of 1% per year over the same period, these changes create what is called the compression of morbidity.

Compression of morbidity *refers to the situation in which the average age when one becomes disabled for the first time is postponed, causing the time between the onset of disability and death to be compressed into a shorter period of time.* This implies that older adults in the United States are becoming disabled later in life, but are disabled a shorter time before dying than in past generations.

Verbrugge and Jette (1994) proposed an excellent and comprehensive model of disability resulting from chronic conditions that has greatly influenced research, which is shown in Figure 4.9. The model consists of four main parts. The main pathway is an adaptation of frameworks proposed by the World Health Organization (1980) and the U.S. Academy of Science's Institute of Medicine (Pope & Tarlov, 1991), both of which were based on work by sociologist Saad Nagi (1965, 1991). This pathway emphasizes the relations between

pathology (the chronic conditions a person has), impairments of organ systems (such as muscular degeneration), functional limitations in the ability to perform activities (such as restrictions in one's mobility), and disability.

The model also includes risk factors and two types of intervention strategies: environmental and health care (*extraindividual factors*) and behavioral and personality (*intraindividual factors*). Risk factors are long-standing behaviors or conditions that increase one's chances of functional limitation or disability. Examples of risk factors include low socioeconomic status, chronic health conditions, and health-related behaviors such as smoking. Extraindividual factors include interventions such as surgery, medication, social support services (e.g., Meals on Wheels), and physical environmental supports (e.g., wheelchair ramps). The presence of these factors often helps people maintain their independence and may make the difference between living at home and living in a long-term care facility. Intraindividual factors include such things as beginning an exercise program, keeping a positive outlook, and taking advantage of transportation programs to increase mobility.

Femia, Zarit, and Johansson (2001) and Fauth and colleagues (2008) validated Verbrugge and Jette's (1994) model in research on older adults over age 79 in Sweden. Among the most important results were the mediating role of psychosocial factors such as mastery, depression, and loneliness on risk factors for disability; for example, higher feelings of mastery resulted in lower levels of disability.

Both extraindividual and intraindividual interventions are aimed at reducing the restrictions and difficulties resulting from chronic conditions. Unfortunately, sometimes they do not work as intended and may even create problems of their own. For example, a prescribed medication may produce negative side effects that, instead of alleviating the condition, create a new problem. Or social service agencies may have inflexible policies about when a particular program is available, which may make it difficult for a person who needs the program to participate in it. Such situations are called *exacerbators*, because they make the situation worse than it was

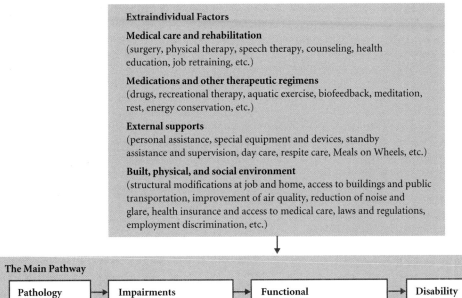

Extraindividual Factors

Medical care and rehabilitation
(surgery, physical therapy, speech therapy, counseling, health education, job retraining, etc.)

Medications and other therapeutic regimens
(drugs, recreational therapy, aquatic exercise, biofeedback, meditation, rest, energy conservation, etc.)

External supports
(personal assistance, special equipment and devices, standby assistance and supervision, day care, respite care, Meals on Wheels, etc.)

Built, physical, and social environment
(structural modifications at job and home, access to buildings and public transportation, improvement of air quality, reduction of noise and glare, health insurance and access to medical care, laws and regulations, employment discrimination, etc.)

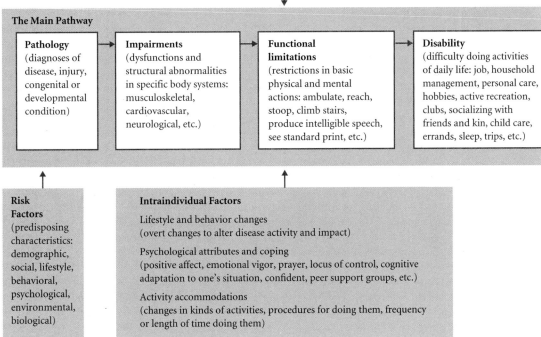

The Main Pathway

Pathology
(diagnoses of disease, injury, congenital or developmental condition)

Impairments
(dysfunctions and structural abnormalities in specific body systems: musculoskeletal, cardiovascular, neurological, etc.)

Functional limitations
(restrictions in basic physical and mental actions: ambulate, reach, stoop, climb stairs, produce intelligible speech, see standard print, etc.)

Disability
(difficulty doing activities of daily life: job, household management, personal care, hobbies, active recreation, clubs, socializing with friends and kin, child care, errands, sleep, trips, etc.)

Risk Factors
(predisposing characteristics: demographic, social, lifestyle, behavioral, psychological, environmental, biological)

Intraindividual Factors

Lifestyle and behavior changes
(overt changes to alter disease activity and impact)

Psychological attributes and coping
(positive affect, emotional vigor, prayer, locus of control, cognitive adaptation to one's situation, confident, peer support groups, etc.)

Activity accommodations
(changes in kinds of activities, procedures for doing them, frequency or length of time doing them)

Figure 4.9 A model of the disablement process.

Source: Verbrugge, L.M., & Jette, A.M. (1994). The disablement process. *Social Science and Medicine, 38,* 4. Reprinted with permission.

originally. Although they may be unintended, the results of exacerbators can be serious and necessitate additional forms of intervention.

One of the most important aspects of Verbrugge and Jette's (1994) model is the emphasis on the fit between the person and the environment. When a person's needs are met by the environment, the person's quality of life and adaptation are optimal. We take a close look at this principle in Chapter 5 when we examine theoretical models of person–environment fit in detail. In addition to person–environment theories, Putnam (2002) points out that disability models can be understood within other social theories of aging frameworks. Research not only focuses on rehabilitation, but also on the role of the workplace, community, social networks, and cultural attitudes and beliefs in shaping the life experiences of people with disabilities (Fougeyrollas & Beauregard, 2001).

Determining Functional Health Status

How can we determine where a person is along Verbrugge and Jette's continuum? The answer to this question describes a person's functional health status, that is, how well the person is functioning in daily life. In making these assessments, it is essential to differentiate the tasks a person reports he or she can do, tasks a person can demonstrate in a laboratory or clinic that simulates the same tasks at home, and tasks the person actually does at home (Glass, 1998). To determine functional health status accurately, we must ensure that the assessment tool used measures a person's true functional level.

In many cases, assessing functional health status is done for a very practical reason: to identify older adults who need help with everyday tasks. **Frail older adults** *are those who have physical disabilities, are very ill, and may have cognitive or psychological disorders and need assistance with everyday tasks.* They constitute a minority of older adults, but the size of this group increases a great deal with age.

Frail older adults are people whose competence is declining. However, they do not have one specific problem that differentiates them from their active, healthy counterparts; rather, they tend to have several (Rockwood et al., 2004). To identify the areas in which people experience limited functioning, researchers have developed observational and self-report techniques to measure how well people can accomplish daily tasks.

Everyday competence assessment consists of examining how well people can complete activities of daily living and instrumental activities of daily living (Johnson et al., 2004; Sternberg & Grigorenko, 2004). **Activities of daily living (ADLs)** *include basic self-care tasks such as eating, bathing, toileting, walking, or dressing.* A person can be considered frail if

he or she needs help with one or more of these tasks. **Instrumental activities of daily living (IADLs)** *are actions that entail some intellectual competence and planning.* Which activities constitute IADLs varies widely across cultures. For example, for most adults in Western culture, IADLs would include shopping for personal items, paying bills, making telephone calls, taking medications appropriately, and keeping appointments. In other cultures, IADLs might include caring for animal herds, making bread, threshing grain, and tending crops.

The number of older adults who need assistance with ADLs and IADLs increases with age (AgingStats.gov, 2008b). As you can see in Figure 4.10, about 26% of older adults enrolled in Medicare need assistance with at least one ADL, about 12% need help with at least one IADL, and about 4% are sufficiently impaired that they live in an assisted living or nursing home facility. As you can see in Figure 4.11, the percentage of people needing assistance increases with age, from 8.2% of people aged 65–69 to 30% of those over age 80 (Steinmetz, 2006). The percentage of people needing assistance also varies across ethnic groups, with European Americans over age 65 having the lowest rate (15%), African Americans having the highest rate (25%), and Asian Americans (19%) and Latino Americans (21%) in between (Administration on Aging, 2001). Rates for Native Americans were not reported.

In addition to basic assistance with ADLs and IADLs, frail older adults have other needs. Research shows that these individuals are also more prone to depression and anxiety disorders (Solano, 2001). Although frailty becomes more likely with increasing age, especially during the last year of life, there are many ways to provide a supportive environment for frail older adults. We take a closer look at some of them in Chapter 5.

What Causes Functional Limitations and Disability in Older Adults?

As you were reading about the Verbrugge and Jette (1994) model, you may have been thinking about Brian's situation and those of other adults you know. If you and your classmates created a list of all the conditions you believe cause functional limitations

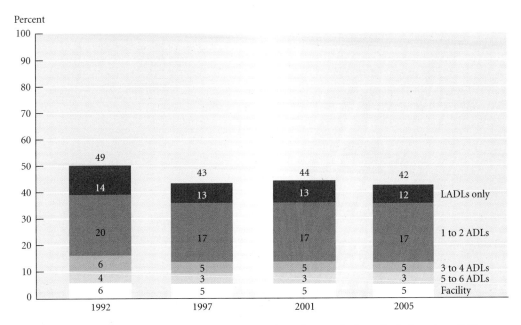

Figure 4.10 Percentage of Medicare enrollees age 65 and over who have limitations in activities of daily living (ADLs) or instrumental activities of daily living (IADLs), or who are in a facility, selected years 1992–2005.

Source: http://www.census.gov/ipc/www/idb/tables.html.

and disabilities in older adults, the list undoubtedly would be long. (Try it and see for yourself.) Indeed, over the years researchers have discovered the same thing and have reported numerous conditions that cause these problems (Boult et al., 1994). But by strategically combining a large representative sample of conditions with sophisticated statistical analyses, this list can be shortened greatly. If these steps are taken, what conditions best predict future problems in functioning?

One answer to this question comes from a classic study by Boult and colleagues (1994), which was designed to identify chronic medical conditions that result in severe functional limitations. They studied nearly 7,000 noninstitutionalized people over age 70 living in the United States at two points in time (1984 and 1988). At each point in time they classified people as being functionally intact, functionally limited because of their inability to perform at least one of seven target activities, or deceased.

An important aspect of this investigation was that the researchers took exercise habits and demo-graphic, socioeconomic, and psychosocial factors into account. Although the study was not designed as a direct test of the Verbrugge and Jette (1994) model, all these factors are considered important in it. Boult and associates (1994) reported that two chronic conditions were strong predictors of functional limitations: cerebrovascular disease and arthritis. In addition, the findings suggested that coronary artery disease may also be a predictor, but the statistical evidence for this was weaker. The authors concluded that focusing attention on identifying these conditions as early as possible may reduce the incidence of severe functional limitations in older adults. Because Brian has arthritis, it is a good bet that he will experience greater disability in the future. In addition to specific chronic diseases, several additional predictive factors for subsequent disability have been identified.

In another classic longitudinal study over three decades, Strawbridge and colleagues (1998) found that smoking, heavy drinking, physical inactivity, depression, social isolation, and fair or poor

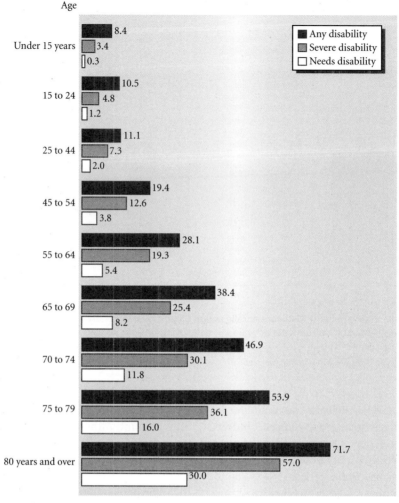

Age

Under 15 years
8.4
3.4
0.3

15 to 24
10.5
4.8
1.2

25 to 44
11.1
7.3
2.0

45 to 54
19.4
12.6
3.8

55 to 64
28.1
19.3
5.4

65 to 69
38.4
25.4
8.2

70 to 74
46.9
30.1
11.8

75 to 79
53.9
36.1
16.0

80 years and over
71.7
57.0
30.0

- Any disability
- Severe disability
- Needs disability

Note: Children under 6 years old were not asked about activities of daily living.

Figure 4.11 Prevalence of disability and the need for assistance by age, 2002 (percentage).

perceived health also predicted who would become disabled in some way.

How Important Are Socioeconomic Factors? Once we have identified the specific conditions that are highly predictive of future functional limitations, an important question is whether the appropriate intervention and prevention programs should be targeted at particular groups of people. That is, would people who are well educated and have high incomes have the

same rate of key chronic conditions as people in lower socioeconomic groups? If not, then people with different socioeconomic backgrounds have different needs.

One of the best large-scale studies of this question was conducted by Reed and colleagues (1995), who tackled this question by comparing roughly 2,000 residents of Marin County, California, over age 65 with the total U.S. population in the same age group. The researchers chose Marin County because it is among the most affluent in California and because it could be viewed as a healthy community environment. Their findings came as a surprise. As expected, residents of Marin County lived on average longer than the typical American. However, despite their privileged status, the Marin County residents had the same prevalence of disease and disability as the U.S. population at large. The implications of these findings, if further research substantiates them, are sobering. Because of their greater average longevity, people from affluent communities can expect to spend a longer period of their later lives living with disabilities and in need of medical care (Reed et al., 1995); they will have longer dependent life expectancy. This is especially true for women, because of their greater average longevity. Chronic conditions do not appear to be postponed in affluent people; indeed, such people may simply live with disabilities for a longer period of time.

Do Gender and Ethnicity Matter? Throughout this and previous chapters, we have encountered important differences between men and women and between various ethnic groups. Thus we might expect such differences in the area of disability. This is particularly the case when it comes to cross-cultural comparisons involving developing countries that focus on adults' abilities to perform routine tasks, an important component in the model of health we examined earlier in this section.

In one of the few studies in this area, Rahman and colleagues (1994) compared representative samples of men and women in the United States, Jamaica, Malaysia, and Bangladesh. In making their comparisons, Rahman and colleagues made corrections for gender differences in mortality and socioeconomic differences. Two of their findings are noteworthy. First, women's self-reported health was worse in all the countries studied. Second, self-reported health problems were much more prevalent in the developing countries than in the United States. Rahman et al.'s (1994) findings indicate that gender makes a difference in health and that the differences between men and women hold up across selected cultures. Although access to health care and lifestyle factors are likely explanations, it is too early to know for certain how these factors create the observed differences.

Of additional concern to researchers is whether ethnic groups differ from each other. In a large study of more than 5,100 older African American and European American men and women, Johnson and Wolinsky (1994) used the concepts of pathology, functional limitation, and disability to predict people's perceived health. Several of their findings are important. First, they discovered that the components of some scales used to measure such things as ability to care for oneself had different measurement properties for each group (e.g., African American men versus women, European American men versus women, African Americans versus European Americans). This means that the scales may be measuring different things in different groups, making it very difficult to generalize findings from one group to another. However, some scales (e.g., lower body disabilities) were equally valid across ethnic groups. Second, Johnson and Wolinsky found several gender differences, especially in the European American group. For both ethnic groups, women's perceived health status was predicted by both the ability to perform several basic functions (e.g., personal care) and disability involving body mobility, whereas men's perceived health status was predicted mainly by ability to perform basic functions. In the European American group, ability to perform complex daily tasks, such as managing money, was more predictive of men's than of women's perceived health status.

Rahman et al.'s (1994) cross-cultural findings and Johnson and Wolinsky's (1994) results point to important gender, ethnic, and cultural differences in health, as well as differences in which specific aspects of chronic conditions, functional limitations, and disabilities predict what people perceive their health status to be. Such differences must be taken into account in designing intervention programs; a one-size-fits-all approach will not be equally successful across these different groups of people.

Concept Checks

1. What factors should be included in a model of adults' disability?

2. How is functional health determined? What are the major issues in ADLs and IADLs?

3. What are the primary causes of disability in older adults?

SOCIAL POLICY IMPLICATIONS

Two demographic trends will create the potential for significant worldwide change over the next few decades. First, increasing longevity in developed countries will result in more older adults. Second, the size of various generations will either exacerbate or lessen this problem. That is, the large baby-boom generation, combined with increased longevity, will make the issue of more older adults acute; the lower birth rate of the subsequent generation will lessen the pressures. Consequently, for the next few decades there will be increased emphasis on social policies that directly benefit older adults, and they are likely to demand such policies. While they have the numbers, and the concomitant political power, such policies are likely to be adopted, perhaps to the detriment of younger generations. The shift became apparent during the U.S. presidential election in 2000, in which issues pertaining directly to older adults, such as the Social Security program,

were debated for the first time. Similar discussions occurred during the 2004 election.

However, as the baby boomers age and die, two things will occur. First, there will be a tremendous transfer of wealth to a smaller generation, with the likely outcome of concentrating the wealth in fewer hands. Second, policies generally favorable to older adults may get changed as the next large generation (the baby boomers' grandchildren) enters middle age. These shifts in policy could have major implications for everything from housing (e.g., more state and federal support for subsidized housing for older adults) to health care (e.g., substantially more expenditures for older adults' health care). If the policies change to reflect the demographic needs of the day, then such policies could need to be undone in the future, which is often politically difficult to accomplish. Close attention to all these issues is necessary for the best policies to be enacted.

Summary

4.1 How Long Will We Live?

What is the average and maximum longevity for humans?

- Average longevity is the age at which half of the people born in a particular year will have died. Maximum longevity is the longest time a member of a species lives. Active longevity is the time during which people are independent. Dependent life expectancy is the time during which people rely on others for daily life tasks.

- Average longevity increased dramatically in the first half of the 20th century, but maximum longevity remains at about 120 years. This increase resulted mainly from the elimination of many diseases and a reduction in deaths during childbirth.

What genetic and environmental factors influence longevity?

- Having long- or short-lived parents is a good predictor of your own longevity.

- Living in a polluted environment can dramatically shorten longevity; being in a committed relationship lengthens it. Environmental effects must be considered in combination.

What ethnic factors influence average longevity?

- Different ethnic groups in the United States have different average longevity. However, these differences result primarily from differences in nutrition, health care, stress, and financial status. In late life, people in some ethnic minority groups live longer than European Americans.

What factors create gender differences in average longevity?

- Women tend to live longer than men, partly because men are more susceptible to disease and environmental influences. Numerous hypotheses have been offered for this difference, but none have been supported strongly.

4.2 Health and Illness

What are the key issues in defining health and illness?

- Health is the absence of acute and chronic physical or mental disease and impairments. Illness is the presence of a physical or mental disease or impairment.
- Self-rated health is a good predictor of illness and mortality. However, gender and cultural differences have been found.

How is the quality of life assessed?

- Quality of life is a multidimensional concept encompassing biological, psychological, and sociocultural domains at any point in the life cycle.
- In the context of health, people's valuation of life is a major factor in quality of life.

What normative age-related changes occur in the immune system?

- The immune system is composed of three major types of cells that form a network of interacting parts: cell-mediated immunity (consisting of thymus-derived, or T-lymphocytes), humoral immunity (B-lymphocytes), and nonspecific immunity (monocytes and polymorphonuclear neutrophil leukocytes). Natural killer (NK) cells are also important components.
- The total number of lymphocytes and NK cells does not change with age, but how well they function does.
- The immune system can begin attacking itself, a condition called autoimmunity.
- Psychoneuroimmunology is the study of the relations between psychological, neurological, and immunological systems that raise or lower our susceptibility to and ability to recover from disease.
- HIV and AIDS are growing problems among older adults.

What are the developmental trends in chronic and acute diseases?

- Acute diseases are conditions that develop over a short period of time and cause a rapid change in health. Chronic diseases are conditions that last a longer period of time (at least 3 months) and may be accompanied by residual functional impairment that necessitates long-term management.
- The incidence of acute disease drops with age, but the effects of acute disease worsen. The incidence of chronic disease increases with age.

What are the key issues in stress across adulthood?

- The stress and coping paradigm views stress not as an environmental stimulus or as a response but as the interaction of a thinking person and an event.
- Primary appraisal categorizes events into three groups based on the significance they have for our well-being: irrelevant, benign or positive, and stressful. Secondary appraisal assesses our ability to cope with harm, threat, or challenge. Reappraisal involves making a new primary or secondary appraisal resulting from changes in the situation.
- Attempts to deal with stressful events are called coping. Problem-focused coping and emotion-focused coping are two major categories. People also use religion as a source of coping.
- There are developmental declines in the number of stressors and in the kinds of coping strategies people use.
- Stress has several negative consequences for health.

4.3 Common Chronic Conditions and Their Management

What are the most important issues in chronic disease?

- Chronic conditions are the interaction of biological, psychological, sociocultural, and life-cycle forces.

What are some common chronic conditions across adulthood?

- Arthritis is the most common chronic condition. Arthritis and osteoporosis can cause mild to severe impairment.
- Cardiovascular and cerebrovascular diseases can create chronic conditions after stroke.

- Diabetes mellitus occurs when the pancreas produces insufficient insulin. Although it cannot be cured, it can be managed effectively. However, some serious problems, such as diabetic retinopathy, can result.

- Many forms of cancer are caused by lifestyle choices, but genetics also plays an important role. The risk of getting cancer increases markedly with age. Prostate and breast cancer involve difficult treatment choices.

- For many people, the inability to control the elimination of urine and feces on an occasional or consistent basis, called incontinence, is a source of great concern and embarrassment. Effective treatments are available.

How can people manage chronic conditions?

- Effective pain management occurs through pharmacological and nonpharmacological approaches. Pain is not a normal outcome of aging and is not to be dismissed.

4.4 Pharmacology and Medication Adherence

What are the developmental trends in using medication?

- Older adults use nearly half of all prescription and over-the-counter drugs. The average older adult takes six or seven medications per day.

How does aging affect the way that medications work?

- The speed with which medications move from the stomach to the small intestine may slow with age. However, once drugs are in the small intestine, absorption rates are the same across adulthood.

- The distribution of medications in the bloodstream changes with age.

- The speed of drug metabolism in the liver slows with age.

- The rate at which drugs are excreted from the body slows with age.

What are the consequences of medication interactions?

- Older adults are more prone to harmful medication side effects.

- Polypharmacy is a serious problem in older adults and may result in serious drug interactions.

What are the important medication adherence issues?

- Polypharmacy leads to lower rates of correct adherence to medication regimens.

4.5 Functional Health and Disability

What factors are important to include in a model of disability in late life?

- Disability is the effects of chronic conditions on people's ability to engage in activities in daily life.

- A model of disability includes pathology, impairments, functional limitations, risk factors, extraindividual factors, and intraindividual factors. This model includes all four main developmental forces.

What is functional health?

- Frail older adults are those who have physical disabilities, are very ill, and may have cognitive or psychological disorders and who need assistance with everyday tasks.

- Activities of daily living (ADLs) include basic self-care tasks such as eating, bathing, toileting, walking, and dressing.

- Instrumental activities of daily living (IADLs) are actions that entail some intellectual competence and planning.

- Rates of problems with ADLs and IADLs increase dramatically with age.

What causes functional limitations and disability in older adults?

- The chronic conditions that best predict future disability are arthritis and cerebrovascular disease. Other predictors include smoking, heavy drinking, physical inactivity, depression, social isolation, and fair or poor perceived health.

- Being wealthy helps increase average longevity but does not protect one from developing chronic conditions, meaning that such people may experience longer periods of disability late in life.

- Women's health generally is poorer across cultures, especially in developing countries.

- Ethnic group differences are also important. The validity of measures of functioning sometimes differs across ethnicity and gender.

Review Questions

4.1 How Long Will We Live?

- What is the difference between average longevity and maximum longevity?
- What genetic and environmental factors influence average longevity?
- What ethnic and gender differences have been found?

4.2 Health and Illness

- How are the definitions of health and illness linked?
- How is the quality of life defined generally and in relation to health?
- What are the major age-related changes in the immune system? How do they affect health and illness?
- What is the difference between acute and chronic diseases? How do the rates of each change with age?
- How does the stress and coping paradigm explain the experience of stress? What age-related changes occur in the process?

4.3 Common Chronic Conditions and Their Management

- What are the general issues to consider in managing chronic disease?
- What are some common chronic diseases experienced by older adults?
- How is pain managed?

4.4 Pharmacology and Medication Adherence

- What is the typical pattern of medication use in older adults?
- What changes occur with age that influence how well medications work?
- What are the major risks for side effects and drug interactions?

- How can adherence to medication regimens be improved?

4.5 Functional Health and Disability

- What are the key components in a model of disability in older adults?
- What are ADLs and IADLs? How does the number of people needing assistance change with age?
- What conditions result in disability most often?
- How do socioeconomic status, ethnicity, and gender affect health and disability?

Integrating Concepts in Development

- What physiological changes described in Chapter 2 are important in understanding health?
- Based on information in Chapters 2 and 3, how might a primary prevention program be designed to prevent cardiovascular disease? (Compare your answer with the intervention types described in Chapter 5.)
- How do the ethnic differences in average longevity and in health relate to the diversity issues we examined in Chapter 1?

Key Terms

active life expectancy The age to which one can expect to live independently.

activities of daily living (ADLs) Basic self-care tasks such as eating, bathing, toileting, walking, and dressing.

acute diseases Conditions that develop over a short period of time and cause a rapid change in health.

autoimmunity The process by which the immune system begins attacking the body.

average longevity The length of time it takes for half of all people born in a certain year to die.

chronic diseases Conditions that last a longer period of time (at least 3 months) and may be accompanied by residual functional impairment that necessitates long-term management.

compression of morbidity The situation in which the average age when one becomes disabled for the first time is postponed, causing the time between the onset of disability and death to be compressed into a shorter period of time.

coping In the stress and coping paradigm, any attempt to deal with stress.

dependent life expectancy The age to which one can expect to live with assistance.

diabetes mellitus A disease that occurs when the pancreas produces insufficient insulin.

disability The effects of chronic conditions on people's ability to engage in activities that are necessary, expected, and personally desired in their society.

frail older adults Older adults who have physical disabilities, are very ill, and may have cognitive or psychological disorders and need assistance with everyday tasks.

health The absence of acute and chronic physical or mental disease and impairments.

illness The presence of a physical or mental disease or impairment.

incontinence The loss of the ability to control the elimination of urine and feces on an occasional or consistent basis.

instrumental activities of daily living (IADLs) Actions that entail some intellectual competence and planning.

maximum longevity The maximum length of time an organism can live, roughly 120 years for humans.

polypharmacy The use of multiple medications.

primary appraisal First step in the stress and coping paradigm in which events are categorized into three groups based on the significance they have for our well-being: irrelevant, benign or positive, and stressful.

psychoneuroimmunology The study of the relations between psychological, neurological, and immunological systems that raise or lower our susceptibility to and ability to recover from disease.

reappraisal In the stress and coping paradigm, this step involves making a new primary or secondary appraisal resulting from changes in the situation.

secondary appraisal In the stress and coping paradigm, an assessment of our perceived ability to cope with harm, threat, or challenge.

stress and coping paradigm A model that views stress not as an environmental stimulus or as a response but as the interaction of a thinking person and an event.

Resources

www.cengage.com/psychology/cavanaugh

Visit the companion website, where you will find tutorial quizzes, glossary, flashcards, and more. You can also access the following websites from the companion website.

The American Cancer Society maintains an excellent site that has a range of information for laypeople and professionals. Especially useful are their reports and treatment and prevention guidelines.

The National Center for Chronic Disease Prevention and Health Promotion has a very informative website concerning all aspects of chronic disease. This center is part of the Centers for Disease Control and Prevention.

RxList provides an online index to medications that includes information about how the drugs are used, usual dosage, side effects, and other useful data. Also included in the website is a discussion list for commonly prescribed medications. Although this site is not a replacement for physicians or pharmacists, it can be used to gather information about medications.

Readings

Numerous well-written pamphlets on topics related to cancer prevention, assessment, and treatment can be obtained from your local chapter of the American Cancer Society. These pamphlets are easy to read yet provide up-to-date information on technical topics.

Hazzard, W. R., Ouslander, J. G., & Halter, J. B. (2009). *Hazzard's geriatric medicine and gerontology.* New York: McGraw-Hill. Moderately difficult overview of geriatric medicine.

Institute of Medicine. (2008). *Retooling for an aging America: Building the health care workforce.* Washington, D.C.: National Academies Press. Easy to moderately difficult overview of the career opportunities and need to respond to an aging population.

Levine, R. (2008). *Aging with attitude: Growing older with dignity and vitality.* Westport, CT: Greenwood Publishing Group. Easy-to-read summary of research on aging and the steps you can take to stay healthy.

5

Where People Live: Person–Environment Interactions

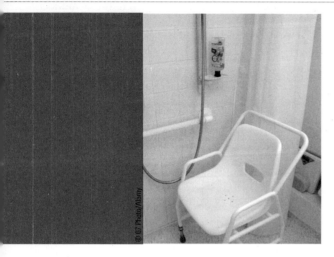

YOU ENCOUNTER THEM EVERY DAY—
DEVICES SUCH AS GRIP BARS IN BATH-
ROOMS, WIDER DOORWAYS, RAMPS
leading to building entrances. You may even
take them for granted. But these environmental
modifications may mean the difference between
living independently and living somewhere else.
Supportive environments for adults, especially
older adults with significant physical or cognitive
impairment, are a relatively recent phenomenon.
Research on how people deal with the settings
in which they reside has revolutionized the way
we design houses and care facilities. The rapidly
increasing need for alternatives to nursing homes
has resulted in the creation of a wide range of options for families. All of this started with
the simple observation that behavior is a function of the environment in which it occurs in
interaction with the individual's personal characteristics.

In this chapter, we explore how differences in the interaction between personal characteristics
and the living environment can have profound effects on our behavior and our feelings about
ourselves. Several theoretical frameworks are described that can help us understand how to
interpret person–environment interactions in a developmental context. Next, we consider the
ecology of aging, and discover how people can age in place, along with the support systems that
underpin that goal. We consider the role of adult day care and several different housing options
that help people stay in the community as much as possible. Because some people need more
intensive support, we take a close look at nursing homes. Even though we must sometimes
consider the person separately from the environment, keep in mind throughout the chapter that
in the end it is the interaction of the two that we want to understand.

5.1 Describing Person–Environment Interactions

LEARNING OBJECTIVES
- What is the competence and environmental press model?
- What is the congruence model?
- What are the major aspects of stress and coping theory relating to person–environment interactions?
- What are the common themes in the theories of person–environment interactions?

Hank has lived in the same poor neighborhood all of his 75 years. He has been living alone for the past several months, ever since his wife, Marilyn, had a stroke and was placed in a nursing home. Hank's oldest daughter has been concerned about her father and has been pressing him to move in with her. Hank is reluctant: He likes knowing his neighbors, shopping in familiar stores, and being able to do what he wants. And he wonders how well he could adapt to living in a new neighborhood after all these years. He realizes it might be easier for him to cope if he lived with his daughter, but it's a tough decision.

To appreciate the roles different environments play in our lives, we need a framework for interpreting how people interact with them. Theories of person–environment interactions help us understand how people view their environments and how these views may change as people age. These views have been described since the 1930s and have had significant impact on the study of adults (Pynoos, in press). We consider four that have affected views of adult development and aging: competence and environmental press, congruence, stress and coping, and everyday competence.

All these theories can be traced to a common beginning. Many years ago Kurt Lewin (1936) conceptualized person–environment interactions in the equation: $B = f(P, E)$. *This relationship defining* **person–environment interactions** *means that behavior (B) is a function of both the person (P) and the environment (E).* More recent theorists have taken Lewin's equation and described the components in the equation in more detail. Specifically, their speculations concern the characteristics of people and environments that combine to form behavior.

Most of these models emphasize the importance of people's perceptions of their environments. That is, although objective aspects of environments (e.g., crime, housing quality) are important, personal choice plays a major role. For example, many people deliberately choose to live in New York or Atlanta, even though crime rates in those cities are higher than in Selma or Walla Walla. The importance of personal perception in environments is similar to the role of personal perception in social cognition and in concepts such as personal control (see Chapter 9). As you will see, these ideas, especially the notion of personal control, have been included in many approaches to understanding person–environment interactions.

Competence and Environmental Press

Understanding psychosocial aging requires attention to individuals' needs rather than treating all older adults alike. One way of doing this is to focus on the relation between the person and the environment (Wahl, 2001). The competence–environmental press approach is a good example of a theory that

incorporates elements of the biopsychosocial model into the person–environment relation (Lawton & Nahemow, 1973; Moore et al., 2003; Nahemow, 2000; Wahl, 2001).

Competence *is defined as the upper limit of a person's ability to function in five domains: physical health, sensory-perceptual skills, motor skills, cognitive skills, and ego strength.* These domains are viewed as underlying all other abilities and reflect the biological and psychological forces. **Environmental press** *refers to the physical, interpersonal, or social demands that environments put on people.* Physical demands might include having to walk up three flights of stairs to your apartment. Interpersonal demands include having to adjust your behavior patterns to different types of people. Social demands include dealing with laws or customs that place certain expectations on people. These aspects of the theory reflect biological, psychological, and social forces. Both competence and environmental press change as people move through the life span; what you are capable of doing as a 5-year-old differs from what you are capable of doing as a 25-, 45-, 65-, or 85-year-old. Similarly, the demands put on you by the environment change as you age. Thus, the competence–environmental press framework reflects life-cycle factors as well.

The competence and environmental press model, depicted in Figure 5.1, shows how the two are related. Low to high competence is represented on the vertical axis, and weak to strong environmental press is represented on the horizontal axis. Points in the figure represent various combinations of the two. Most important, the shaded areas show that adaptive behavior and positive affect can result from many different combinations of competence and environmental press levels. **Adaptation level** *is the area where press level is average for a particular level of competence; this is where behavior and affect are normal. Slight increases in press tend to improve performance; this area on the figure is labeled the* **zone of maximum performance potential.** *Slight decreases in press create the* **zone of maximum comfort,** *in which people are able to live happily without worrying about environmental demands.* Combinations of competence and environmental

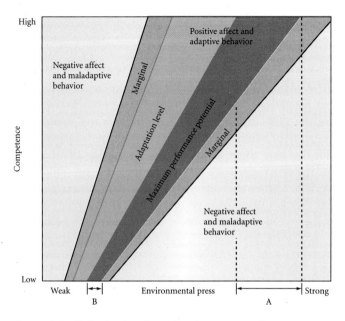

Figure 5.1 Behavioral and emotional outcomes of person–environment interactions based on the competence and environmental press model. This figure indicates that a person of high competence will show maximum performance over a larger range of environmental conditions than will a person with lower levels of competence. The range of optimal environments occurs at a higher level of environmental press (A) for the person with the most competence than it does for the person with the lowest level of competence (B).

Source: Lawton, M. P. & L. Nahemow. Ecology of the Aging Process. In C. Eisdorfer & M. P. Lawton (Eds.), *The Psychology of Adult Development and Aging*, p. 661. Copyright © 1973 Reprinted with permission from the American Psychological Association.

press that fall within either of these two zones result in adaptive behavior and positive emotion, which translate into a high quality of life.

As one moves away from these areas, behavior becomes increasingly maladaptive and affect becomes negative. Notice that these outcomes, too, can result from several different combinations, and for different reasons. For example, too many environmental demands on a person with low competence and too few demands on a person with high competence both result in maladaptive behaviors and negative emotion.

What does this mean with regard to late life? Is aging merely an equation relating certain variables? The important thing to realize about the competence–environmental press model is that each

person has the potential of being happily adapted to some living situations, but not to all. Whether people are functioning well depends on whether what they are able to do fits what the environment forces them to do. When their abilities match the demands, people adapt; when there is a mismatch, they don't. In this view, aging is more than an equation, as the best fit must be determined on an individual basis.

How do people deal with changes in their particular combinations of environmental press (such as adjusting to a new living situation) and competence (perhaps due to illness)? People respond in two basic ways (Lawton, 1989; Nahemow, 2000). *When people choose new behaviors to meet new desires or needs, they exhibit* **proactivity** *and exert control over their lives. In contrast, when people allow the* *situation to dictate the options they have, they demonstrate* **docility** *and have little control.* Lawton (1989) argues that proactivity is more likely to occur in people with relatively high competence, and docility in people with relatively low competence.

The model has considerable research support. For example, the model accounts for why people choose the activities they do (Lawton, 1982), how well people adhere to medication regimens (LeRoux & Fisher, 2006), how people adapt to changing housing needs over time (Iwarsson, 2005; Nygren et al., 2007) and the need to exert some degree of control over their lives (Langer & Rodin, 1976). It helps us understand how well people adapt to various care situations, such as adult day care (Moore, 2005). In short, there is considerable merit to the view that aging is a complex interaction between a person's competence level and environmental press, mediated by choice. This model can be applied in many different settings.

As an example of Lawton and Nahemow's model, consider Rick. Rick works in a store in an area of Omaha, Nebraska, where the crime rate is moderately high, representing a moderate level of environmental press. Because he is very good at self-defense, he has high competence; thus he manages to cope. Because the Omaha police chief wants to lower the crime rate in that area, he increases patrols, thereby lowering the press level. If Rick maintains his high competence, maladaptive behavior may result because he has more competence than is optimal for the new environment. But if instead of the police a street gang moved in, he would have to increase his competence and be more prepared to maintain his adaptation level. Other changes in the environment (such as arson threats) or in his competence (such as a broken arm) would create other combinations.

Before leaving Lawton and Nahemow's model, we need to note an important implication for aging. The less competent the person is, the greater the impact of environmental factors. To the extent that people experience declines in health, sensory processes, motor skills, cognitive skills, or ego strength, they are less able to cope with environmental demands. For example, personal competence predicts how well older adults adapt after being discharged from a hospital (Lichtenberg et al., 2000). Thus, for older adults to maintain good adaptational levels, changes to lower environmental press or raise competence are needed. This point is made clearer in the Discovering Development feature. Take some time to complete it.

Because most older adults prefer to live at home, examining issues of competence and environmental press in that context is very important (Gitlin, 2003). Given the importance of creating residential alternatives and offering them to older adults with physical limitations, it is critical that we understand how the environment affects people's day-to-day functioning in the home. For example, the changing balance between competence and environmental press is a major factor in older adults' decisions to relocate (Sergeant & Ekerdt, 2008). Additionally, the competence and environmental press model has been the basis for interventions with people who have severe cognitive impairments, such as those of Alzheimer's disease (Smyer & Qualls, 1999). To manage severe cognitive impairment effectively, caregivers must identify the right level of environmental support based on the patient's level of competence. For example, people with mild cognitive impairment may be able to live independently, but as the impairment increases additional levels of support are needed. The model has provided the basis for designing special care units for people with Alzheimer's disease. In these units, special environmental supports, such as color-coded room doors, help people with dementia identify where they belong.

The Congruence Model

Another way to consider how people and environments interact is to look for the best fit for a specific person in a particular environment. This is what Kahana (1982) focuses on in her congruence model. Kahana includes the ideas of competence and environmental press but applies them differently. In Kahana's view people vary in their needs, and environments differ in their ability to satisfy them. *According to the* **congruence model,** *people with particular needs search for the environments that meet them best.* To the extent that a match exists, the person feels content and satisfied; when a mismatch occurs, stress and discomfort result.

Congruence between the person and the environment is especially important when personal or environmental options are limited. Limitations can occur for three reasons: Environmental characteristics are restricted, as when public transportation is unavailable for going shopping; a person's freedom is limited, as when he or she must always eat at the same time every day; and one believes that one has limited freedom, as when one thinks that there is no way to get around despite a reliable bus system. By these criteria, Hank fits well with his current environment because he has ready access to all his basic necessities. Restricted environments are exemplified most clearly by long-term care facilities such as nursing homes and hospitals. Limits on individual freedom can result from age-related declines in competence. Self-perceptions of limited freedom reflect the belief that one's life is controlled by external forces, in the ways described in Chapter 9.

When applied specifically to the older adult, Kahana's congruence model shows that several points should be considered in optimizing the person–environment fit (Kahana & Kahana, 1983).

One must consider not only the kind of situation, such as whether the person is in a single-family, congregate, or institutional living arrangement, but also personal factors. Personal factors are very important, because people vary in their needs. Some of us value autonomy and independence highly, for example, whereas others place less importance on them. When designing programs and interventions for adults, we must be careful to take these individual differences into account. Otherwise, we may unintentionally increase the discrepancy between the person and the environment, resulting in increases in stress for the people we intended to help.

Kahana's model is especially useful in health care settings such as nursing homes and hospitals. Indeed, most of the research that has examined issues such as autonomy has been done in these settings (Harnett & Greaney, 2008). This makes sense when you realize that in these settings difficult decisions are most often made that involve trade-offs between personal freedom and institutional requirements, and how these decisions interface with personal values

(Mars et al., 2008). Research shows that as many as 80% of dependent behaviors demonstrated by nursing home residents were the result of residents being compliant with instructions from staff, not because they were actually dependent (Zarit et al., 1999). Residents also are fully aware that they are not performing behaviors they are competent to perform (Wahl, 1991). The importance of person–environment fit also lies in its ability to account for differences in competence between adults that cannot be attributed to problems with cognition or related abilities (Schaie & Willis, 1999).

What would happen if there were better congruence between residents' abilities and the nursing home environment? Could residents' self-efficacy be improved? If so, what would happen to their health?

Through a series of now classic studies, Langer decided to find out. She believed that the important factor in residents' well-being is the degree to which they perceive that they are in control of their lives (Langer, 1985). To demonstrate her point, she conducted an ingenious experiment that is now one of the classic studies in gerontology. One group of nursing home residents was told that staff members were there to care for them and to make decisions for them about their daily lives. In contrast, a second group of residents was encouraged to make their own decisions about meals, recreational activities, and so forth. The second group showed greater well-being and higher activity levels than the first group (Langer & Rodin, 1976). These differences were still seen 18 months later; in fact, the second group also seemed to have lower mortality rates (Rodin & Langer, 1977).

Based on her findings, Langer became convinced that making residents feel competent and in control were key factors in promoting positive person–environment interactions in nursing homes. Langer (1985) points to several aspects of the nursing home environment that fail in this regard. First, the decision to place a person in a nursing home often is made by people other than the person involved. Staff members may communicate their belief that the resident is incapable of making decisions or may treat him or her like a child rather than like an adult who is moving to a new home.

Second, the label "nursing home resident" may have strong negative connotations. This is especially true if as a younger adult the person had negative ideas about why people go to nursing homes. A long history of social psychological research shows that the person may begin to internalize these stereotypical beliefs, even if they are unwarranted (Kelley, 1967). Other labels such as "patient" may have similar effects.

Third, what staff consider to be simply the demonstration of tender loving care may reinforce the belief in one's incompetence. That is, in helping people perform basic tasks such as getting dressed, we run the risk of increasing their level of incompetence and dependence on others. Again, providing assistance where none is needed may be a way in which the staff communicates its belief that the resident cannot fend for himself or herself at all.

The physical aspects of the environment may also reinforce the belief of no control. To the extent that the environment is unfamiliar or is difficult to negotiate, people living in it may feel incompetent. Mastering the environment increases feelings of control, but if this process is not allowed or is made too easy, the outcome may be negative.

Finally, Langer (1985) argues that routine is also detrimental to well-being. If the environment is too predictable, there is little for people to think about; in Langer's terms, we become mindless. In this state, we are typically not aware of what we do; we behave as if we were on automatic pilot. If nursing home environments promote mindlessness, then residents behave automatically and have difficulty remembering what happened even a short time before. When this occurs, the staff may view the person as incompetent. But because we all engage in mindless activity (e.g., performing a series of complex but automatic functions while driving) about which we have no recollection (one often cannot recall anything about driving the last several miles), we cannot justify considering this same mindlessness as indicative of incompetence in older adults.

Other researchers have replicated Langer's basic findings in nursing homes (Schulz & Hanusa, 1979) and retirement communities (Slivinske & Fitch,

1987). Buschmann and Hollinger (1994) found that providing affective social support through touching is an effective substitute for residents' inability to control their environment. Whether the benefits of increased control last over the long run is still an open issue. Whether we should treat nursing home residents with respect is not.

Stress and Coping Framework

As you know from your own experience, sometimes your interaction with the environment is stressful. Schooler (1982) has applied Lazarus and Folkman's cognitive theory of stress and coping, described in Chapter 4, to the understanding of the older person's interaction with the environment. The basic premise of Lazarus's theory is that people evaluate situations to assess their potential threat value. Situations can be evaluated as harmful, beneficial, or irrelevant. When situations are viewed as harmful or threatening, people also establish the range of coping responses that they have at their disposal for avoiding the harmful situation. This process results in a coping response. Outcomes of coping may be positive or negative depending on many contextual factors.

Schooler (1982) argues that this perspective is especially helpful in understanding older adults like Hank because of their greater vulnerability to social and physical hazards. To test his ideas, Schooler evaluated retest data on a sample of 521 people drawn from a national sample of 4,000 older adults living in long-term care facilities. In particular, he examined the impact of three potential stressors (environmental change, residential mobility, and major life events) on health or morale. He also examined the buffering, or protective, effects of social support systems and ecological factors on the relationships between the stressors and outcomes. Consistent with the theory, Schooler showed that the presence of social support systems affected the likelihood that particular situations would be defined as threatening. For example, living alone is more likely to be viewed as stressful when one has little social support than when one has many friends who live nearby.

Schooler's initial work provides an important theoretical addition because it deals with the relation between everyday environmental stressors and the adaptive response of community-dwelling individuals. His ideas have been extended to other contexts. For example, when certified nurse aides (CNAs) working in nursing homes were provided with training and empowered as a way to deal with environmental stressors, the result was better care for residents, better cooperation between CNAs and nurses, and reduced turnover (Yeatts & Cready, 2008). Caregivers of persons with dementia also show resilience when they have effective ways of dealing with environmental stressors (Gaugler, Kane, & Newcomer, 2007).

Common Theoretical Themes and Everyday Competence

The three theories we have considered have much in common. Most important, all agree that the focus must be on the interaction between the person and the environment, not on one or the other. Another important common theme is that no one environment meets everyone's needs. Rather, a range of potential environments may be optimal.

Several researchers have built on these ideas and focused on people's everyday competence (Diehl, 1998; Diehl et al., 2005). **Everyday competence** *is a person's potential ability to perform a wide range of activities considered essential for independent living; it is not the person's actual ability to perform the tasks.* Everyday competence also involves a person's physical, psychological, and social functioning, which interact in complex ways to create the person's day-to-day behavior (Diehl, 1998; Diehl et al., 2005). Within each of these domains, a person's behavior involves many elements. For example, an older person's competence in the psychological domain includes cognitive problem-solving abilities, beliefs about personal control and self-efficacy, and styles of coping (Diehl et al., 2005).

Although everyday competence is most often considered in the context of activities of daily living (ADLs) and instrumental activities of daily living (IADLs; see Chapter 4), it can also be

© Leland Bobbè / CORBIS

Older adults' ability to perform typical daily activities is essential for assessing everyday competence.

considered more broadly as described here. The reason is that a behavior must not be viewed in isolation; behavior is expressed in a particular environmental context. In particular, researchers and clinicians need to be sensitive to cultural and contextual differences in everyday competence across different environments (Diehl, 1998; Diehl et al., 2005).

Using these ideas, Willis (1991, 1996a; Allaire & Willis, 2006; Schaie & Willis, 1999) developed a model of everyday competence that incorporates all the key ideas discussed earlier. Willis distinguishes between antecedents, components, mechanisms, and outcomes of everyday competence. Antecedents include both individual (e.g., health, cognition) and sociocultural (e.g., cultural stereotypes, social policy, health care policy) factors. These influence the intraindividual and contextual components, the particular domains and contexts of competence. Which components are most important or exert the most influence depends on the overall conditions under which the person lives. These elements of the model reflect the basic ideas in both the competence and environmental press model and the person–environment model we

considered earlier. The mechanisms involve factors that moderate the way in which competence is actually expressed; for example, whether one believes that he or she is in control of the situation influences how competent the person turns out to be. Finally, the model proposes that the primary outcomes of everyday competence are psychological and physical well-being, which are two of the major components of successful aging.

Understanding the complexities of everyday competence is important as a basis for considering whether people, especially some older adults, are capable of making certain decisions for themselves. This issue often arises in terms of competence to make key health care and other decisions, a topic we consider in more detail later in this chapter. Willis's model also points out that the health outcomes of one episode of everyday competence are the antecedents of the next, illustrating how future competence is related to current competence. Finally, decline in older adults' ability to handle everyday problems predicts mortality, indicating that everyday competence may be a reasonable indicator of health status (Allaire & Willis, 2006).

All of this research supports the idea that older adults can age in place to the extent that their everyday competence permits. Aging in place requires that whatever necessary services and supports an older adult needs in order to live in the community be provided or made available. This approach has been adopted by governments (e.g., Australia; Bigby, 2008), and is the goal for much of the smart technology available for homes (Coughlin & Pope, 2008). We will consider aging in place in more detail in the next section.

Concept Checks

1. What do the terms *competence, environmental press,* and *adaptation level* mean?
2. What are the basic components of the congruence model?
3. What are the main aspects of Schooler's stress and coping theory?
4. How can everyday competence be modeled?

5.2 The Ecology of Aging

LEARNING OBJECTIVES

- What is aging in place?
- How do people decide the best option?
- How can a home be modified to provide a supportive environment?
- What options and services are provided in adult day care?
- What is congregate housing?
- What are the characteristics of assisted living?

Mark was diagnosed as having vascular dementia about six months ago. Because he now has difficulty in remembering to turn off his gas stove, his daughter and son-in-law think that it may be best for him to move into an assisted living facility. They have had Mark evaluated by his physician, who indicates that she thinks it is a good idea for safety reasons, especially because Mark's family lives several hundred miles away.

Most people go through young adulthood, middle age, and into later life performing routine daily tasks without much thought. As we grow older, though, the normative changes that occur often result in more challenges in dealing with environments that were once not a problem at all. Even our homes, formerly a comfortable supportive place, can present difficult challenges; for example, the walk up the stairs to a bedroom may become an equivalent of climbing a mountain.

Mark is typical of a growing number of older adults in the United States and other countries—he is experiencing a significant decline in functioning, lives alone, and his adult child and family live in another city some distance away. As a result, he, like many other older adults, needs a different living situation. He does not need full-time nursing care at this point, but does need a more supportive environment.

Changes in functional status and how these changes are helped or hurt by the environments in which we live are an important aspect of the experience of growing older for many people. *These changes are studied in a field called the* **ecology of aging** *or environmental psychology, which seeks to understand the dynamic relations between older adults and the environments they inhabit* (Scheidt & Schwarz, in press). It is important to understand how even seemingly small changes in a person's environment can result in major changes in behavior, changes that can make the difference between a person being able to live independently or needing a more supportive situation.

In this section, we will consider options for older adults that help them maintain as much independence as possible. First, we will consider the concept of aging in place. Then we will consider three approaches to helping people live in the community as long as possible: home modification, and two living situations that provide various levels of support—congregate housing and assisted living.

Aging in Place

Imagine you are an older adult who has difficulty cooking meals and getting around. If you had a choice of where you wanted to live, where would it be? Maybe some of your family members are urging you to move to a place where your meals are provided and you can be driven where you need to go, while others are urging you to stay in your own place even though there will be challenges. What do you do?

Based on the competence–environmental press model described earlier, older adults have options (Scheidt & Schwarz, in press). As the environment in which one lives becomes more restrictive, many older adults engage in selection and compensation to cope. They may select a different place to live. Or they may adapt their behaviors in order to compensate for their limitations, such as using microwaveable prepared foods instead of cooking meals from scratch. Using a cane or other device to assist in walking is another example of compensation.

The idea of aging in place reflects a balancing of environmental press and competence through selection and compensation. Being able to maintain one's independence in the community is often important for people, especially in terms of their self-esteem and ability to continue engaging in meaningful ways with friends, family, and others. This is very important psychologically (Rowles,

Oswald, & Hunter, 2004). Older adults who age in place form strong emotional and cognitive bonds with their residences that help transform a "house" into a "home." Having a "home" provides a strong source of self-identity.

Throughout adulthood, people adapt to changes in the places where they live, sometimes even having to sever connections with past settings (Rowles & Watkins, 2003). Making a change in where one lives, and having to psychologically disconnect with a place where one may have lived for many decades, can be difficult and traumatic. There is no question that people develop attachments to place, deriving a major portion of their identity from it and feeling that they own it.

Rowles (2006) discusses the process of how a place becomes a home. Because of the psychological connections, the sense that one is "at home" becomes a major concern in relocation, especially if the relocation involves giving up one's home. Later in this chapter, we will consider how a nursing home might become a home, but for now the important idea is that a key factor is a sense of belonging.

Feeling that one is "at home" is a major aspect of aging in place. Providing an older adult a place to call one's own that supports the development of the psychological attachments necessary to convert the place to a home is the basis (Scheidt & Schwarz, in press). Aging in place provides a way for older adults to continue finding aspects of self-identity in where they live, and to take advantage of support systems that are established and familiar.

The growing understanding of the importance of aging in place has resulted in a rethinking of certain housing options that provide a way for frail older adults to stay in their communities. Such options are important for frail older adults who are poor and cannot afford more expensive formal assisted living or nursing home facilities (discussed later). One alternative is cluster housing, which combines the aging in place philosophy with supportive services (Golant, 2008).

Golant (2008) describes several types of affordable cluster housing care. A key feature is that services are provided to the residents by staff hired by the owner or by a service provider under contract. These services might range from having a service case manager only to actually providing information, caregiving assistance (e.g., meals, housekeeping), transportation, or health care. The aging in place philosophy in these settings emphasizes individual choice on the part of residents in terms of what services to use.

Although cluster housing and other approaches to aging in place make sense as lower-cost alternatives to nursing homes that help keep people in their communities, funding is often difficult. Unlike nursing homes, cluster housing developments are not covered by Medicaid or other insurance. Finding solutions to the funding issue will be an important aspect for keeping costs down yet providing supporting environments for older adults who need support. For many, making modifications to their existing housing represents a more cost-effective option, and provides a research-based way to remain in a familiar environment. We will consider this approach later in this section.

Deciding on the Best Option

One of the most difficult decisions individuals and families have to make is where an older member should live. Such decisions are never easy, and can be quite wrenching. Figuring out the optimal "fit" where the individual's competence and the environmental press are in the best balance rests on the ability of all concerned to be objective about the individual's competence and on the ability of the lived-in environment to provide the level of support necessary. It requires a degree of honesty in communication with oneself and one's family that is sometimes challenging.

There are several key decision points in addressing the issue of the optimal environment. First, it must be determined whether the individual has significant cognitive or physical impairment requiring intervention. If so, then a determination of the severity of the impairment is needed. Next, an assessment of the ability of family members or friends to provide support or care must be made. Once that information is understood, a series of decisions can be made about the best way to provide the necessary environmental supports to create the optimal "fit." Assuming that all information points to the need for some sort of intervention, the next critical decision is deciding whether there is an option for providing that intervention in the current home situation or whether other options need to be pursued. Later, we will consider several living options for individuals needing support ranging from minor modifications of one's present home to skilled care nursing homes.

Throughout this process, the individual in question needs to be an integral part of the decision making to the extent possible. This is especially important when the outcome is likely to be a placement that involves moving from the person's current residence. The degree to which the person actually understands the options, why the options are being pursued, and the long-term meaning of the decision being considered is an integral part of the person's right to determine his or her own life outcome (a point considered in more detail later).

Individuals and families facing these decisions should at least consult with the person's physician after a thorough diagnostic evaluation. Additionally, objective information about available options can be obtained from local senior centers, offices on aging, and other nonprofit service providers.

Home Modification

The discussion of the competence–environmental press model earlier provided two options for people who experience difficulties dealing with the tasks of daily life. On the one hand, people can increase their competency in order to develop better or new skills for handling the tasks. For example, to remember better where you put your car keys, you can learn a new memory strategy. On the other hand, people can also modify the environment to make the task easier. For example, you can put a hook for the car keys next to the door you exit so that you see them on your way out.

These two options represent applications of theory to real-world settings that also apply to helping people deal with the challenges they face in handling tasks of daily living in their homes. When it comes

to these kinds of issues, the most frequent solution involves modifying one's home (i.e., changing the environment) in order to create a new optimal balance or better "fit" between competence and environmental press (Scheidt & Schwarz, 2009).

Many strategies are available for modifying one's home to help a person accommodate to changing competencies. Minor structural changes, such as installing assistive devices like hand rails in bathrooms and door handles that are easier to grip, are common strategies. In other cases, more extensive modifications may be needed to make a home fully accessible, such as widening doorways, lowering countertops, and constructing wheelchair ramps.

Although minor alterations can often be done at low cost, more extensive modifications needed by people with more extensive limitations may be unaffordable for low-income individuals. Even though the cost of such interventions is significantly lower than placement in nursing homes or even assisted living, funding is lacking. As a result, many older adults with functional impairments experience a mismatch between their competency and their environment (Wahl, Fänge, Oswald, Gitlin, & Iwarsson, in press).

Research indicates that home modifications that are done to address difficulties with accomplishing activities of daily living (ADLs) typically reduce disability-related outcomes (Wahl et al., in press). Whether these modifications also help older adults who are prone to falling remains inconclusive.

Adult Day Care

In some cases, older adults need more support than is possible with just home modification, but still do not need it on a full-time basis. For them, one possible option may be adult day care. **Adult day care** *is designed to provide support, companionship, and certain services during the day.* This situation arises most often when the primary caregiver is employed or has other obligations and is unavailable during the day.

The primary goal of adult day care is to delay placement into a more formal care setting. It achieves this goal by providing alternative care that enhances the client's self-esteem and encourages socialization. Three general types of adult day care are available (National Adult Day Services Association, 2008). The first provides only social activities, meals, and recreation, with only minimal health services. The second type is adult day health care that provides more intensive health and therapy intervention and social services for people who have more serious medical problems or who require more intensive nursing care for a specific medical condition. The third provides specialized care to particular populations, such as people with dementia or developmental disabilities. Adult day care centers can be independent or sponsored by a profit (22%) or nonprofit (78%) organization. They may provide transportation to and from the center. Depending on the services received, Medicaid or other insurance may cover some of the expenses (Medicare does not). Because some states do not license adult day care centers, careful screening of a particular center is advised.

About 35% of adult day care clients live with an adult child, and 20% with a spouse or partner. The average age of clients is 72, with about two-thirds being women (National Adult Day Services Association, 2008). Family members who choose adult day care (and can afford it) typically do so because they need occasional assistance with caregiving, have safety concerns about the care recipient when the caregiver is not around, take increasing amounts of time off from work for caregiving, are experiencing problems in their relationship with the care recipient, or the care recipient could benefit from more contact with other older adults (MetLife, 2006).

For people with cognitive impairment, changes in routine can result in confusion or disruptive behavior. It is especially important for them, as it is for all older adults who may become adult day care clients, to inform them of this choice. A good strategy is to engage in a few trials to find out how well the person acclimates to the different surroundings and activities.

Research demonstrates that adult day care is a viable and important option for caregivers. They are interested in the kinds of programs that meet the needs of their loved ones, and are generally satisfied with the services provided (Madeo, Feld, & Spencer, 2008). Family members clearly seek what is best for their loved one in searching for and helping make the transition to adult day care centers (Bull & McShane, 2008). Evidence is clear that, compared with keeping relatives with cognitive impairment at home, good adult day care programs can reduce problematic

Adult day care centers provide a way for adult child and spousal caregivers to continue being employed and provide care to their loved one.

behaviors and lower the need for psychotropic medication in clients, and result in lower reports of caregiving burden among caregivers (Mosello et al., 2008). However, a key factor in the success of day care programs is having culturally appropriate programs in interventions, as demonstrated in a study of Korean clients who benefitted most when programs took their background into account (Park, 2008).

Congregate Housing

Congregate housing includes a range of living options. The most common form is an apartment complex of older adults that provides a level of support, such as shared meals. Congregate housing is often the least expensive form of supported living for older adults, as the cost is typically subsidized by various government agencies and nonprofit organizations. Because of its affordability, it is an especially important option for low-income older adults who need some support to remain out of a nursing home. However, there is a shortage of congregate housing in the United States.

Traditional congregate housing differs from assisted living in terms of the level of services provided. Although many traditional congregate housing complexes do not include individual kitchens and provide shared meals, the level of medical assistance, for example, is lower than in assisted living. Congregate housing facilities do not provide 24-hour medical services on site. However, newer congregate housing complexes are including higher levels of other service, so the distinction with assisted living is being blurred.

The service coordination that is provided in congregate living accomplishes several things: interface with housing officials, individual service plans for residents, coordination of shared activities (e.g., cleaning common spaces), and mediation of resident conflicts. Most congregate housing complexes require that residents be capable of independent living and not require continual medical care, be medically stable, know where they are and oriented to time (e.g., know today's date and other key time-related information), show no evidence of disruptive behavior, be able to make independent decisions, and be able to follow any specific service plan developed for them. If at some point a resident no longer meets one of the criteria, he or she is usually required to move out.

The decision to move into congregate housing is usually done in conjunction with one's family, and is typically a response to a significant decline in functioning or other health-related problem (Sergeant & Ekerdt, 2008). Families are generally satisfied with the outcomes following the move (Williams et al., 2008).

Assisted Living

Given that maintaining a sense of place, a home, is very important to older adults, it should not come as a surprise that they would prefer living options that help foster that desire. That is how the option of assisted living came into being (Scheidt & Schwarz, in press). **Assisted living facilities** *are housing options for older adults that provide a supportive living arrangement for people who need assistance with personal care (such as bathing or taking medications) but who are not so impaired physically or cognitively that they need 24-hour care.*

An ideal assisted living situation has three essential attributes (Scheidt & Schwarz, in press). First, the physical environment where a person lives is designed to be as much like a single-family house as possible. That way, the setting has a residential appearance, a small scale, and personal privacy that includes at a minimum a private room and a full bath that is not shared with other residents unless the resident explicitly wishes. The public spaces in the facility are designed to provide indoor and outdoor access, which enhances a resident's autonomy and independence.

Second, the philosophy of care at an ideal assisted living facility emphasizes personal control, choice, dignity, and autonomy, and promotes a preferred lifestyle that residents and their families consider to be a "normal," good quality of life. This philosophy is implemented by understanding residents' personal preferences and priorities, and allowing residents to exert control over their lives, their schedules, and their private dwellings.

Third, ideal assisted living facilities should be able to meet residents' routine services and special needs. "Essential elements in service capacity include offering or arranging: competent initial assessments of needs and preferences; individualized service planning; kind, capable, and responsive personal care 24 hours a day, 7 days a week; 3 meals a day; housekeeping; identification of changes in residents' physical functioning and condition; arrangements for specialized assessments and interventions; and responses to emergency situations. The provider must also offer or arrange routine nursing service, including mediations management, but 'nursing services' should not be construed as services that can only be performed by a registered or licensed nurse" (Kane & Brown-Wilson, 2001, p. 3).

Despite the fact that assisted living facilities have existed for more than 20 years, there are serious gaps (Scheidt & Schwarz, in press). For example, no national consensus or federal guidelines exist to govern the characteristics of the people who can and should be served in these facilities, the services that can be provided, or the minimum staffing standards. The different combinations of housing and service arrangements that today are called assisted living "make simple generalizations about either their physical settings or their care environments particularly challenging—and inevitably contribute to consumer confusion" (Golant, 2008, p. 7).

Despite the problems with precisely defining assisted living facilities, the number of them continues to grow. Between 1998 and 2000, the number of licensed assisted living residence units grew 33%, slowed to 13% between 2000 and 2002, slowed even more to 3% between 2002 and 2004, but increased to 6% between 2004 and 2007. By 2007 there were 947,585 units in 38,373 licensed facilities (Mollica, 2008). One important reason for this growth is the fact that assisted living offers a more cost-effective approach than nursing homes for those older adults who cannot live independently but who do not need the level of nursing care provided in a nursing home.

Residents in assisted living facilities are in independent apartments or similar units. The services that are provided vary, but usually include moni-

toring and management of health care, assistance with activities of daily living, housekeeping and laundry, reminders or assistance with medication, recreation and entertainment activities, transportation, and security (U.S. Department of Health and Human Services, 2005). Before choosing an assisted living facility, you should check several things:

- Think ahead. What will the resident's future needs be and how will the facility meet those needs?
- Is the facility close to family and friends? Are there any shopping centers or other businesses nearby (within walking distance)?
- Do admission and retention policies exclude people with severe cognitive impairments or severe physical disabilities?
- Does the facility provide a written statement of the philosophy of care?
- Visit each facility more than once, sometimes unannounced.
- Visit at meal times, sample the food, and observe the quality of mealtime and the service.
- Observe interactions among residents and staff.
- Check to see if the facility offers social, recreational, and spiritual activities.
- Talk to residents.
- Learn what types of training staff receive and how frequently they receive training.
- Review state licensing reports.

Residents generally pay the costs of assisted living facilities, which averaged about $35,000 per year in 2008. Medicare does not pay for either living costs or any of the services that are provided. In some cases, Medicaid may pay for services depending on the situation. Given that assisted living is usually less expensive than nursing homes, the lack of broad financial support for these programs means that the cost of care is not as low as it could be.

Research on assisted living has increased as more assisted living options have appeared. Despite knowledge gaps, the findings support the importance of the central attributes of assisted living for frail elderly (Polivka & Salmon, 2008; Zimmerman et al., 2005). Future assisted living facilities will have to be able to serve residents who, because they will be more frail, will have more service needs. Assisted living facilities will have to be based on more adaptive and flexible designs in order to serve older adults with a broad range of care demands.

One of the main future challenges will be the blurring of congregate (independent) living, assisted living, and nursing homes into hybrids of these arrangements (Scheidt & Schwarz, in press). The hope is that more stringent regulations will follow the blending of these forms of housing, and that services will not destroy the special characteristics of assisted living. Another future challenge will be the cost of assisted living, which could put it out of the reach of many American elderly. Finally, the future role of the government in providing funds for affordable shelter and care will continue to be limited. Therefore experts predict that families will assume the largest financial burden of providing long-term care funds for their loved ones (Golant, 2008).

Concept Checks

1. How does one age in place?
2. What process do people go through to make the best living arrangement decision?
3. What modifications are typically done in a person's current home to provide a more supportive environment?
4. What services are provided in adult day care?
5. What is congregate housing?
6. What are the characteristics of assisted living facilities?

5.3 Living in Nursing Homes

LEARNING OBJECTIVES
- What are the major types of nursing homes?
- Who is most likely to live in nursing homes?
- What are the key characteristics of nursing homes?
- What are special care units?
- How can a nursing home be a home?
- How should people communicate with nursing home residents?
- How is decision-making capacity assessed?
- What are some new directions for nursing homes?

The last place Maria thought she would end up was a bed in one of the local nursing homes. "That's a place where old people go to die," she used to say. "It's not gonna be for me." But here she is. Maria, 84 and living alone, fell and broke her hip. She needs to stay for a few weeks while she recovers. She hates the food; "tasteless goo," she calls it. Her roommate, Arnetta, calls the place a "jail." Arnetta, 79 and essentially blind, has Alzheimer's disease.

Maria and Arnetta may be the kind of people you think of when you conjure up images of nursing homes. To be sure, you will probably find some people like them there. But for each Maria or Arnetta, there are many more who come to terms with their situation and struggle to make sense of their lives. Nursing homes are indeed places where people who have very serious health problems go, and for many it is their final address. Yet if you visit a nursing home, you will find many inspiring people with interesting stories to tell.

Misconceptions about nursing homes are common. Contrary to what some people believe, only about 5% of older adults live in nursing homes on any given day. As you can see in Figure 5.2, the percentage of older adults enrolled in Medicare who live in a long-term care facility at any given point in time increases from 1% in those aged 65–74 to about 17% of adults over age 85 (AgingStats.gov, 2008); however, over their lifetime, about 50% of people who live past age 85 will spend at least some time in a long-term care facility (National Academy on an Aging Society, 2003). Thus, over the adult life span, the number of people who spend time in a nursing home is rather large.

However, the rate of nursing home residence for people over age 65 has been declining slightly since the mid-1980s (AgingStats.gov, 2008). This decline is most likely due to the large increase in the number of assisted living facilities, a housing option discussed earlier (AgingStats.gov, 2008).

Long-term care settings are very different environments from those we have considered so far. The residents of such facilities differ in many respects from their community-dwelling counterparts. Likewise, the environment itself is very different from neighborhood and community contexts. But because many

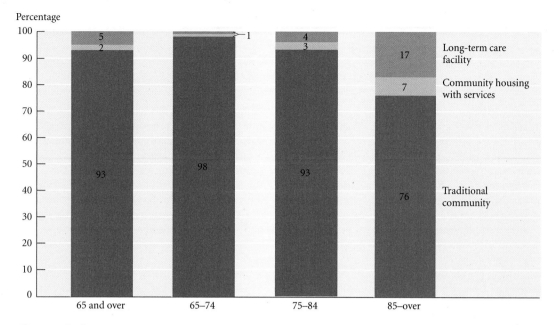

Percentage

Figure 5.2 Percentage of Medicare enrollees age 65 and over residing in selected residential settings by age, 2005.

Source: Centers for Medicare and Medicaid Services, Medicare Current Beneficiary Survey.

aspects of the environment in these facilities are controlled, they offer a unique opportunity to examine person–environment interactions in more detail.

In this section we examine types of long-term care settings, the typical resident, the psychosocial environment in the facilities, and residents' ability to make decisions for themselves.

Types of Nursing Homes

Nursing homes house the largest number of older residents of long-term care facilities. They are governed by state and federal regulations that establish minimum standards of care. Two levels of care in nursing homes are defined in U.S. federal regulations (Ebersole et al., 2004). Skilled nursing care consists of 24-hour care including skilled medical and other health services, usually from nurses. Intermediate care is also 24-hour care including nursing supervision, but at a less intense level. In actual practice, the major differences between the two are the types and numbers of health care workers on the staff. Perhaps

for this reason, the distinction between skilled and intermediate care often is blurred.

The cost of nursing home care is very high. With the aging of the baby-boom generation, how this cost will be met is an issue confronting millions of families. As noted in the Current Controversies feature, funding for nursing homes will be an increasingly important political issue in the coming decades.

Who Is Likely to Live in Nursing Homes?

Who is the typical resident of a nursing home? She is over age 85, European American, recently admitted to a hospital, lives in a retirement home rather than being a homeowner, is congitively impaired, has problems with IADLs, is probably widowed or divorced, and has no siblings or children living nearby (Davis & Lapane, 2004). Maria and Arnetta, whom we met in the vignette, reflect these characteristics. Major risk factors are summarized in Table

The current system of financing long-term care in the United States is in very serious trouble. The average cost of a private room is close to $80,000 per year (New York Life, 2007) and is by far the leading catastrophic health care expense. The Centers for Medicare and Medicaid Services (2007) estimates that between 2008 and 2017 national expenditures for nursing home care will rise from about $137 billion to $218 billion. Contrary to popular belief, Medicare does not cover nursing home care but does have limited nursing home and home care benefits for people who need skilled nursing services and who meet other criteria. Private insurance plans pay only around 7% of the costs nationally. About 25% of the expense is paid for directly by nursing home residents. When residents become impoverished (a definition that varies widely from state to state), they become dependent on Medicaid, which pays the bulk of the total. (In 2005, the total Medicaid expenditures for skilled nursing home care were roughly $59 billion, or 45.4% of the total national expenditure.) Given these expenses and the lack of insurance coverage, how will we be able to finance the long-term health care system?

Several options have been proposed (Feder, Komisar, & Friedland, 2007). Four main strategies are possible:

- A strategy that promotes long-term care insurance that keeps public financing as a safety net. This approach would spread the risk without expanding the demands on federal or state budgets and on taxpayers to pay fully for long-term care. Still, a public safety net would be essential.
- A strategy to expand the public safety net for people with low to moderate incomes, with people from higher-income brackets expected to provide for themselves through private financing. This approach targets the people with the greatest need and the fewest resources.
- A strategy to establish public catastrophic long-term care insurance and support complementary private insurance to fill the gap along with the public safety net. This approach would spread the risk and the burden on a greater number of people, reducing the cost of private insurance, but still pricing it beyond the means of many older adults.
- A strategy to establish universal public long-term care insurance that would be supplemented with private financing and a public safety net. This approach spreads the burden over the greatest number of people, thereby addressing the problem of affordability of private insurance.

Despite the wide range of options, many of them place the burden on individuals to come up with ways of financing their own care. Given the cost, and the fact that millions of Americans do not have access to health insurance, large subsidies from the government will still be needed for long-term care regardless of what the private sector does.

Given that government subsidies for long-term care will be needed for the foreseeable future, the question becomes how to finance them. Under the current Medicaid system, older adults are not protected from becoming impoverished, and in essence are required to have few assets in order to qualify. With the aging of the baby-boom generation, many more people will spend their assets, causing Medicaid costs to skyrocket. If we want to continue the program in its current form, additional revenues will be needed, either in the form of taxes or dramatic spending reductions in other areas of public budgets.

The questions facing us are whether we want to continue forcing older adults to become totally impoverished when they need long-term care, whether we want the government to continue subsidy programs, whether we should do more to encourage those who can afford it to have long-term care insurance, and whether we would be willing to pay higher taxes for better coverage. How we answer these questions will have a profound impact on the status of long-term care over the next few decades.

Table 5.1

Characteristics of People Most Likely to Be Placed in a Nursing Home

Over age 85

Female

Recently admitted to a hospital

Lives in retirement housing rather than being a homeowner

Unmarried or lives alone

Has no children or siblings nearby

Has some cognitive impairment

Has one or more problems with instrumental activities of daily living

Source: Summarized from Davis and Lapane (2004).

5.1. Figure 5.3 shows the average age, gender, and race breakdown of the typical nursing home in the United States. Note that the characteristics of the typical nursing home resident are not similar to the population at large, as discussed in Chapter 1. For example, men are underrepresented in nursing homes, as are ethnic minorities. The reasons for the lower rate among minorities are not entirely clear; for example, despite more availability of nursing homes for African Americans, they remain less likely to use them (Akamigbo & Wolinsky, 2007). Higher rates of poverty may explain why minorities who live in nursing homes tend to be more impaired than European American residents, in that residents of color delay placement as long as possible (Davis & Lapane, 2004).

What are the health issues and functional impairments of typical nursing home residents? For the most part, the average nursing home resident has significant mental and physical problems. This is borne out by the fact that the main reason for placing almost 80% of nursing home residents is significant health problems (AgingStats.gov, 2008). Estimates are that nearly 80% of residents have mobility problems, and more than one third have

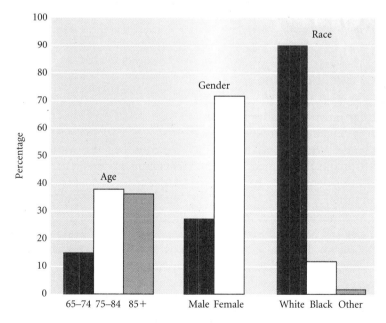

Figure 5.3 Demographic characteristics of nursing home residents over age 65.

Source: Kail/Cavanaugh, Human Development: A Life-Span View, 5e (2010), 0495600377 © 2010 (Wadsworth).

mobility, eating, and incontinence problems. In addition, the rates of mental health and cognitive impairment problems are high, with between 30 and 50% of residents showing signs of clinical depression, for example.

As you may have surmised from the high level of impairment among nursing home residents, frail older people and their relatives do not see nursing homes as an option until other avenues have been explored. This may account for the numbers of truly impaired people who live in nursing homes; the kinds and number of problems make life outside the nursing home very difficult for them and their families and beyond the level of assistance provided by assisted living facilities. For these reasons, the decision to place a family member in a nursing home is a very difficult one (Caron, Ducharme, & Griffith, 2006), and often is made quickly in reaction to a crisis, such as a person's impending discharge from a hospital or other health emergency. The decision tends to be made by partners or adult children, a finding that generalizes across ethnic groups such as European Americans and Mexican Americans, especially when there is evidence of cognitive impairment (Almendarez, 2008; Caron et al., 2006).

Characteristics of Nursing Homes

Nursing homes vary a great deal in the amount and quality of care they provide. One useful way of evaluating them is by applying the competence–environmental press model. When applied to nursing homes, the goal is to find the optimal level of environmental support for people who have relatively low levels of competence.

Selecting a nursing home should be done carefully. The Centers for Medicare and Medicaid Services of the U.S. Department of Health and Human Services provides a detailed *Nursing Home Quality Initiative* website that is a guide for choosing a nursing home based on several key quality factors. Among the most important things to consider are quality of life for residents (e.g., whether residents are well groomed, the food is tasty, and rooms contain comfortable furniture); quality of care (whether staff respond quickly to calls, whether staff and family

are involved in care decisions); safety (whether there are enough staff, whether hallways are free of clutter); and other issues (whether there are outdoor areas for residents to use). These aspects of nursing homes reflect those dimensions considered by states in their inspections and licensing process.

Individuals and families should also keep several other things in mind:

- Skilled nursing care is usually available only for a short time following hospitalization, whereas custodial care may be an option for a much longer period. If a facility offers both types, it may or may not be possible to shift level of care without relocating to another room.

- Nursing homes that only take Medicaid residents may offer longer term but less intensive care levels. Nursing homes that do not accept Medicaid may force the resident to leave when Medicare or private funds run out.

- Ensure that the facility and its administrator are fully licensed, and that a full array of staff training is available on such topics as recognizing abuse and neglect, how to deal with difficult residents, and how to investigate and report your complaints.

- Ensure that the resident's care plan is put together by a team of professionals, and that residents have choices, can exert some control over their routines and care, and will have appropriate assistance with ADLs and IADLs.

- Ask questions about staff educational levels (including continuing education) and turnover.

Based on the various theories of person–environment interaction discussed earlier in this chapter, the best nursing homes use what researchers recommend—a "person-centered planning" approach to nursing home policies (Reese, 2001), especially when working with people who have cognitive impairment (Lawlor & York, 2007). This approach is based on promoting residents' well-being through increasing their perceived level of personal control and treating them with respect. Taking this approach means such things as residents getting to decorate their own rooms, choosing what they want to eat from a buffet, and deciding whether they want to take a shower or a bath. Person-centered planning focuses on the individual, and does not use a one-size-fits-all approach. Most important, this approach involves a team who knows and cares about the individual who work together with the person to create the best supportive environment possible.

Such policies are grounded in classic research showing that residents who have higher perceived personal control show significant improvement in well-being and activity level, and actually live longer (Langer & Rodin, 1976; Rodin & Langer, 1977). Nursing homes that use the person-centered planning approach also note major decreases in the need for certain medications (e.g., sleep and anti-anxiety drugs) and soft restraints, as well as substantial declines in the number of residents who are incontinent (Reese, 2001). Feelings of self-efficacy are crucial to doing well and have a profound impact on nursing home residents' functional abilities (Johnson et al., 1998; Reese, 2001).

Although the person-centered planning approach has been around for years, many nursing homes still rely on a traditional approach of rules, routines, and requirements (Robinson & Gallagher, 2008). Perhaps the best way to begin changing the culture from one in which residents are expected to be passive to one that includes them in their own care is to focus on activities related to dining. Choosing what one eats, being able to socialize with one's friends, and interacting with staff while enjoying a meal is one way to create the level of personal involvement and trust necessary to implement a person-centered approach.

Today, person-centered care is considered a best practice in nursing homes (Dellefield, 2008). Including nursing home residents in the planning of their own care represents a major shift in culture, and is an example of the application of research to practice.

Special Care Units

Most residents of nursing homes have cognitive impairment, and the majority of those individuals have dementia. Providing a supportive environment for people with moderate to severe dementia requires certain specialized design and intervention features. This need has resulted in the development of special care units in many nursing homes.

Well-designed special care units for people with dementia provide a supportive and therapeutic set of programs that help the person function at the highest level possible. Optimally, staff who work in special care units receive special training in working with persons with dementia. The best units have physical design elements that take functional limitations into account; for example, the hallways of some facilities are designed in such a way that if residents wander, they merely follow the interior halls or exterior path in a circle so that they do not leave the building or the complex, and the decorating is done in a way to minimize confusion. Most facilities have residents with cognitive impairment wear wrist or ankle bands that trigger alarms if they wander beyond a certain point or exit the facility, another safe way to provide opportunities for residents to move about freely but safely. The best facilities also permit residents to bring a few personal items as reminders of their past in order to provide a more homelike environment. They also provide a private dining area in a family-like setting in order to minimize possible negative interactions between residents with dementia and residents without cognitive impairment.

Selecting the right special care unit for a person with dementia must be done carefully (Paris, 2008). As noted in the competence–environmental press model, as competence declines the environment must provide more support in order for behavior to be optimized. So the special care unit must have the right level of environmental support at the placement, as well as the availability of additional levels of support when the person's competence level continues to decline. Memory aids should be built into the unit, such as color-coded halls. Staffing levels and training are key, as is the range of intervention programs and activities available. Such programs should be research based, such as ones based on the Montessori techniques discussed in Chapter 10.

The research-based staff training required at the best special care units includes several aspects of caring for older adults with moderate to severe cognitive impairment:

- Appropriate and effective communication techniques (as discussed later in this section)
- Behavioral management techniques to address aggressive or agitated behavior (a common symptom in dementia)
- Appropriate techniques for assisting with personal health and hygiene that protect residents' dignity
- Appropriate methods for dealing with incontinence
- Appropriate techniques for handling sexuality in persons with dementia
- Effective techniques for controlling wandering (in addition to physical design aspects of the facility)
- Appropriate ways of supervising or assisting with eating
- Appropriate techniques and interventions to address memory failure and disorientation
- Appropriate techniques for assisting with mobility (e.g., walking, using a wheelchair)

Training in these areas will not guarantee high-quality care, but it will increase the likelihood of it.

Research indicates that upon admission residents of special care units are younger and are more behaviorally impaired than general nursing home residents when both exist in the same facility (e.g., Gruneir et al., 2008a; Nobili et al., 2008). Residents of special care units tend to have lower hospitalization rates and use of physical restraints (Nobili et al., 2008) and a higher rate of use of antipsychotic medication (Gruneir et al., 2008a). The increased quality of care residents of special care units receive is more the result of a difference in philosophy of care between nursing homes with and without special care units than it is due to the special care unit itself (Gruneir et al., 2008b). Given that the use of physical restraints is associated with higher morbidity (Reid, 2008), it may be that nursing homes that include special care units also have different approaches for dealing with problem behaviors that help avoid the use of physical restraints.

Can a Nursing Home Be a Home?

One key aspect of nursing homes has been largely overlooked: To what extent do residents consider a nursing home to be home? This gets to the heart of what makes people feel that the place in which they live is more than just a dwelling. On the surface, it appears that nursing homes are full of barriers to this

© Jeff Greenberg / Photo Edit

Nursing home residents benefit from social activities and interaction with other residents and staff.

feeling. After all, they may have regulations about the extent to which residents may bring their own furnishings and other personal effects with them, and residents are in an environment that has plenty of structural reminders that this is not a house in suburbia. Not having one's own refrigerator, for example, means that one can no longer invite friends over for a home-cooked meal (Shield, 1988).

Can nursing home residents move beyond these barriers and reminders and achieve a sense of home? Apparently so, but with some very important qualifications. Groger (1995) proposed that a nursing home can, indeed, be perceived as a home. She interviewed 20 older African American adults, 10 who lived in nursing homes and 10 who were home care clients. Groger's analysis of her interviews revealed that nursing home residents can indeed feel at home. The circumstances that foster this feeling include having the time to think about and participate in the placement decision, even if only minimally; having prior knowledge of, and positive experience with, a specific facility; defining home predominantly in terms of family and social relationships rather than in terms of place, objects, or total autonomy; and being able to establish some kind of continuity between home and nursing home either through activities or through similarities in living arrangements.

Groger (1995) also reports that getting nursing home residents to reminisce about home may actually facilitate adjustment. Some residents concluded only after long and detailed reflection on their prior home that the nursing home was now home. In addition, it may be easier for nursing home residents to feel at home on some days than others and from one situation to another, depending on the events or stimuli at the time.

Helping nursing home residents feel at home is an important issue that must be explored in more detail. Perhaps having people think about what constitutes a home, before and after placement, may make the transition from community to the facility easier to face. For those who need the care provided in a nursing home, anything that can be done to ease the transition would be a major benefit. Assessing the degree to which residents feel at home is possible (Molony, McDonald, & Palmisano-Mills, 2008).

At a general level, nursing home residents' satisfaction relates to several key variables: facility factors, staff factors, and resident factors, as shown in Figure 5.4 (Chou et al., 2003). Research indicates that staff satisfaction plays a crucial role in nursing home residents' satisfaction. In contrast, providing more care does not (Chou et al., 2003). In addition, when residents have a voice in determining the

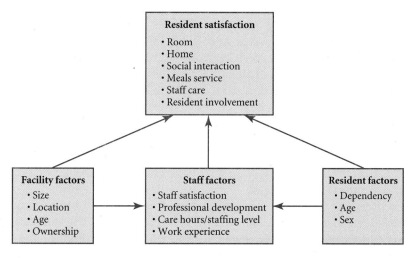

Figure 5.4 Major factors influencing resident satisfaction in nursing homes.

Source: Chou, S-C., Boldy, D. P., & Lee, A. H. (2003). Factors influencing residents' satisfaction in residential aged care. *The Gerontologist* 43, 459–472, p. 460. Copyright © Reprinted with permission from the Gerontological Society of America.

quality of care, their satisfaction improves (Boldy & Grenade, 2001). As we will see next, how people communicate with residents is also key.

Communicating with Residents

Have you ever been to a nursing home? If so, one of the things you may have found difficult is talking with the residents, especially when interacting with residents who are cognitively impaired. Unfortunately, this uneasiness often results in people relying on stereotypes of older adults in general and nursing home residents in particular in speaking to them, which results in inappropriate communication styles.

The communication style most people adopt is one in which younger adults overaccommodate their speech based on their stereotyped expectations of dependence and incompetence. This style is described as a general "communication predicament" of older adults (Ryan et al., 1986). Such speech conveys a sense of declining abilities, loss of control, and helplessness, which, if continued, may cause older adults to lose self-esteem and withdraw from social interactions. As time goes on, older adults who are talked to in this way may even begin behaving in ways that reinforce the stereotypes.

Inappropriate speech to older adults that is based on stereotypes of incompetence and dependence is called **patronizing speech.** Patronizing speech is slower speech marked by exaggerated intonation, higher pitch, increased volume, repetitions, tag and closed-end questions, and simplification of vocabulary and grammar. Speaking in this way can be conceptualized as "secondary baby talk," which is baby talk inappropriately used with adults (Ryan et al., 1993). *Secondary baby talk, also called* **infantilization or elderspeak,** *also involves the unwarranted use of a person's first name, terms of endearment, simplified expressions, short imperatives, an assumption that the recipient has no memory, and cajoling as a way to demand compliance* (Whitbourne et al., 1995).

Whitbourne and colleagues (1995) showed that infantilizing speech is viewed extremely negatively

by some older adults. They found that community-dwelling older adults rated infantilizing speech especially negatively and were particularly resentful of its intonation aspects as indicative of a lack of respect. Nursing home residents were less harsh in their judgments, giving support to the idea that being exposed to infantilizing speech lowers one's awareness of its demeaning qualities. Whitbourne and colleagues also found no evidence that infantilizing speech is high in nurturance, as some previous authors had suggested.

Similarly, Harwood and colleagues (1997) demonstrated that adults to whom patronizing speech is directed are more likely to be blamed for accidents, especially when the target is an older adult. Residents with dementia tend to be more resistive to care when they are the targets of elderspeak (Williams et al., 2008).

How should people talk to older adults, especially those living in nursing homes? Ryan and her colleagues (1995) propose the communication enhancement model as a framework for appropriate exchange. This model is based on a health promotion model, which seeks opportunities for health care providers to optimize outcomes for older adults through more appropriate and effective communication. As you can see from Figure 5.5, this model emphasizes that communication with older adults must be based on recognizing individualized cues, modifying communication to suit individual needs and situations, appropriately assessing health and social problems, and empowering both older adults and health care providers.

What happens when residents respond in different ways to a staff member's patronizing speech? Ryan and colleagues (2000) examined what happened when nursing home residents responded passively, assertively, or humorously to a nurse's patronizing speech, which was then either maintained or changed to reflect more respect for the resident. Details of the study are provided in the How Do We Know? feature.

The interchanges were rated by nursing home residents, staff, and community-residing older adults. Patronizing speech was rated negatively by everyone (but less so by the nursing home

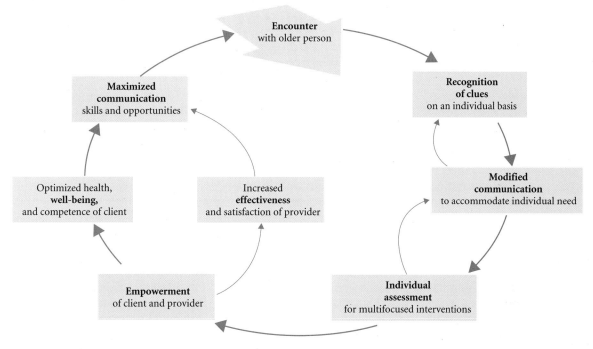

Multiple environmental influences

Figure 5.5 The communication enhancement model. Note that this model is dynamic in that there are opportunities to modify communication interactions and to have the outcomes of one interaction serve as input for another.

Source: E. B. Ryan, S. D. Meredith, M. J. MacLean, and J. B. Orange, 1995. Changing the way we talk with elders: Promoting health using the Communication Enhancement Model. *International Journal of Aging and Human Development* 41, 89–107. Reproduced by permission.

residents). The nurse who continued to speak patronizingly when the resident responded assertively was rated most negatively, but residents were the most reluctant to endorse the assertive way of responding. Humorous responses were rated in between, perhaps being a safer alternative for residents to use to express opposition to a request yet still maintain an appearance of cooperation. Taken together, these results show the degree to which patronizing speech is disliked by community-dwelling older adults but accepted as expected by nursing home residents.

Ryan and colleagues' model and research can be readily applied to interactions with older adults from different ethnic groups and with older adults who have cognitive impairments. For example, an analysis of intergenerational communication comparing Western and Eastern cultures showed complex cultural variability, including the occurrence of less positive perceptions of conversations in some cases from respondents in Korea, Japan, China, Hong Kong, and the Philippines than in some Western countries (Williams et al., 1997).

In general, an approach to communication based on the model promotes mental, social, and physical well-being among older adults and counters the fostering of dependence that follows from the traditional medical model discussed earlier. When patronizing speech occurs in nursing homes, active steps should be taken to ensure that the appropriate steps are taken to eliminate it (Dobbs et al., 2008). Most important, this research reminds us that we must speak to all older adults in a way that conveys the respect they deserve.

So what should you do as a visitor? The first time most people visit a nursing home, they are

H O W   D O
W E   K N O W ?

How Do People Respond to Patronizing Speech?

Who were the investigators, and what was the aim of the study? Older adults who live in nursing homes face many difficulties with the way people talk to (or about) them. The concept of patronizing speech, discussed in the text, captures the essence of the problem. Ryan and colleagues (2000) decided to see how different groups of people (nursing home residents, staff, and community-residing older adults) respond when a nurse talks in a patronizing way to a resident, who then responds.

How did the investigators measure the topic of interest? A written description of the context of an interaction between a nurse and a resident of a fictitious Canadian nursing home was followed by an audiotape of a conversation in which the nurse reminded the resident that it was time to go to a craft activity. Respondents then answered a questionnaire based on the kind of response the resident gave to the nurse. Respondents rated the nurse and the resident separately on a list of 12 adjectives rating her competence ("From this conversation, I would say the nurse [resident] is [competent, respectful, likeable, and helpful]"), manner ("From this conversation, I would say the nurse [resident] is trying to be [polite, cooperative, in control]"),

and similar ratings for control adjectives and appropriateness adjectives.

Who were the participants in the study? In Study 1, participants were 48 nursing home residents with no known cognitive impairment and 48 staff members. In Study 2, participants were 49 nursing home residents with no known cognitive impairment, 48 staff, and 48 community-residing older adults. Staff members were about 40 years younger than residents in both studies and about 33 years younger than the community residents in Study 2.

What was the design of the study? For the major project in Study 2, the design examined three groups (nursing home residents, staff, and community-residing older adults), three response styles by the resident (passive, assertive, and humorous), and two further styles by the nurse (continuing to patronize or shift to accommodating). The conversation scripts had three different responses from the resident to the nurse's patronizing statement ("Did we forget again, sweetie? It's time for crafts!"). In one, the resident gave a passive response to the request ("I know it's time to go. I'd rather not, but if you insist, I'll go"). In a second, the resident gave an assertive response ("I've already planned to watch my

favorite TV program, so I won't have time to go today"). The third version had a humorous response ("I think I'll just pass today. I've made more crafts in my lifetime than an overachieving Girl Guide group at Christmas"). In addition, there were two different versions of what the nurse said next: either continuing to be patronizing ("Now, now, I just know we'll have a nice time. It's important that we get out of our room for awhile, dear. You just have to give it a try!") or shifting to an accommodating style ("I can see that you are not eager today. But it is important for you to get out of your room for awhile. Mrs. Brown, please consider joining us").

Were there ethical concerns with the study? All participants were volunteers. Nursing home residents were screened for cognitive impairments. Because all participants were given the opportunity to withdraw and were given informed consent, there were no ethical concerns.

What were the results? The nurse who shifted to an accommodating style was rated more positively, and respondents could clearly describe the differences between the nurse's responses. However, nursing home residents were much more tolerant of patronizing speech. Patronizing speech was rated more negatively when the resident responded assertively, perhaps because the patronizing speaker appeared less appropriate in contrast. Interestingly, the assertive response did not elicit higher competency ratings.

What did the investigators conclude? The findings are consistent with previous data showing that patronizing speech is not viewed positively. However, this study marked the first time that this rating was obtained as a direct result of a speaker shifting styles. The tolerance of patronizing speech by nursing home residents and the failure to rate assertive responses as reflecting higher competence is troubling and shows the degree to which a culture of dependency pervades many nursing homes.

ill-prepared to talk to family members who are frail, have trouble remembering, and cannot get around very well. The hardest part is trying to figure out what to say in order to avoid patronizing speech. However, visiting residents of nursing homes is a way to maintain social contacts and provide a meaningful activity. Even if the person you are visiting is frail or has a sensory impairment or some other type of disability, visits can be uplifting. As noted earlier in the chapter, high-quality social contacts help older adults maintain their life satisfaction. Here are several suggestions for making visits more pleasant (Papalia & Olds, 1995; adapted from Davis, 1985):

- Concentrate on the older adult's expertise and wisdom, as discussed in Chapter 14, by asking for advice on a life problem that he or she knows a lot about, such as dealing with friends, cooking, or crafts.

- Allow the older person to exert control over the visit: where to go (even inside the facility), what to wear, what to eat (if choices are possible).

- Listen attentively, even if the older person is repetitive. Avoid being judgmental, be sympathetic to complaints, and acknowledge feelings.

- Talk about things the person likes to remember, such as raising children, military service, growing up, work, courtship, and so on.

- Do a joint activity, such as putting a jigsaw puzzle together, arranging a photograph album, or doing arts and crafts.

- Record your visit on audiotape or videotape. This is valuable for creating a family history that you will be able to keep. The activity may facilitate a life review as well as provide an opportunity for the older person to leave something of value for future generations by describing important personal events and philosophies.

- Bring children when you visit, if possible. Grandchildren are especially important, as most older adults are very happy to include them in conversations. Such visits also give children the opportunity to see their grandparents and learn about the diversity of older adults.

- Stimulate as many senses as possible. Wearing bright clothes, singing songs, reading books, and sharing foods (as long as they have been checked with the staff) help keep residents involved with their environment. Above all, though, hold the resident's hands. There's nothing like a friendly touch.

Always remember that your visits may be the only way that the residents have of maintaining social contacts with friends and family. By following these guidelines, you will be able to avoid difficulties and make your visits more pleasurable.

Decision-Making Capacity and Individual Choices

Providing high-quality care for nursing home residents means putting into practice the various competence-enhancing interventions we have considered relating to personal control and communication. Doing so means that residents participate in making decisions about their care. But how can we make sure that residents understand what they are being asked to decide, especially when a majority of them have cognitive impairment?

The need to address this question became apparent in 1991 with the enactment of the Patient Self-Determination Act (PSDA). This law mandated that all facilities receiving Medicare and Medicaid funds comply with five requirements regarding advance care planning, referred to as advance directives (Emanuel, 2008): providing written information to people at the time of their admission about their right to make medical treatment decisions and to formulate advance directives (i.e., decisions about life-sustaining treatments and who can make medical decisions for them if they are incapacitated), maintaining written policies and procedures regarding advance directives, documenting the completion of advance directives in the person's medical chart, complying with state law regarding the implementation of advance directives, and providing staff and community education about advance directives.

The PSDA mandates work well with most people. However, assessing a person's capacity to make medical decisions is a tremendous challenge for medical ethics (American Geriatrics Society Ethics Committee, 1996). In theory, advance directives enable people to choose the type of medical treatment they prefer in advance of a medical crisis. However, numerous studies show that the theory does not hold up well in practice: Most people, especially older adults, see such planning as a family process. They engage in informal advance care planning, preferring to allow family members to make decisions for them when the need arises and to give them leeway in interpreting advance directives even when they exist (Allen & Shuster, 2002). Thus it is unlikely that a person being admitted to a nursing home will have completed a formal advance directive. Because placement in a nursing home is already stressful and likely to occur in the context of a medical crisis, the new resident is unlikely to understand the information presented as mandated by the PSDA. To make matters worse, if new residents are cognitively impaired, they may be unable to act in their own behalf in communicating end-of-life wishes and understanding the consequences of their choices (Allen et al., 2003). Research clearly

shows that even people with undocumented mild cognitive impairment do not understand the information presented to them under PSDA guidelines (Frank et al., 1999) even though over 80% of people in one study could understand simple treatment preferences (Allen et al., 2003). This raises important ethical questions concerning whether physicians can trust any advance directive signed by such individuals after they move to a nursing home (Kapp, 2008).

Assessing a nursing home resident's ability to make medical treatment decisions can be conceptualized as a problem involving the fit between the original intent of the law and the resident's cognitive capacity (Smyer & Allen-Burge, 1999). Several researchers have tackled the problem of how to assess decision-making capacity with varying results. Most important, a careful assessment of the resident's capacity to understand treatment and intervention options is necessary (Kapp, 2008).

Still, many problems remain. No uniform approach to determining residents' cognitive competence exists, although progress is being made through the establishment of guidelines (American Bar Association/American Psychological Association, 2005, 2006, 2008). One barrier to a common approach is that each state sets the criteria needed to demonstrate cognitive competence (which is usually approached from the opposite side—what it takes to establish incompetence). To complicate matters further, research also shows lack of agreement between what nursing home residents want and what their families think they would want, which also varies with ethnicity (Allen-Burge & Haley, 1997; Smyer & Allen-Burge, 1999). Resolving the problem will involve using the various approaches we have considered for determining person–environment interactions, combined with strong clinical assessment (see Chapter 10), in the context of specific treatment goals and maintaining quality of life. Clearly, creating an optimal solution takes an interdisciplinary team of professionals, residents, and family members working together.

One solution may be to assess key members of the family (who serve as proxies in completing the forms) as to their beliefs as well as careful observation of the resident's capacity by the staff (Allen et al., 2003). Health care staff also need to sit down with family members and talk with them directly about treatment options.

New Directions for Nursing Homes

Nursing homes are not static entities. New ways of approaching care continue to be developed. Three of the more interesting new developments are the Eden Alternative, the Green House Project, and the Pioneer Network.

The Eden Alternative. Imagine an approach to caring for frail older adults that starts from the premise that skilled care environments are habitats for people rather than facilities for the frail. Such an environment has the potential to address issues such as boredom, loneliness, and helplessness. The Eden Alternative (http://www.edenalt.org) takes this approach.

Founded by Dr. William and Judy Thomas, the Eden Alternative approaches care from the perspective of protecting the dignity of each person. It is based on the following 10 principles:

1. The three plagues of loneliness, helplessness, and boredom account for the bulk of suffering among our elders.

2. An elder-centered community commits to creating a human habitat where life revolves around close and continuing contact with plants, animals, and children. It is these relationships that provide the young and old alike with a pathway to a life worth living.

3. Loving companionship is the antidote to loneliness. Elders deserve easy access to human and animal companionship.

4. An elder-centered community creates opportunity to give as well as receive care. This is the antidote to helplessness.

5. An elder-centered community imbues daily life with variety and spontaneity by creating an environment in which unexpected and unpredictable interactions and happenings can take place. This is the antidote to boredom.

6. Meaningless activity corrodes the human spirit. The opportunity to do things that we find meaningful is essential to human health.

7. Medical treatment should be the servant of genuine human caring, never its master.

8. An elder-centered community honors its elders by de-emphasizing top-down bureaucratic authority, seeking instead to place the maximum possible decision-making authority into the hands of the elders or into the hands of those closest to them.

9. Creating an elder-centered community is a never-ending process. Human growth must never be separated from human life.

10. Wise leadership is the lifeblood of any struggle against the three plagues. For it, there can be no substitute.

Arguably, the Eden Alternative helped launch a culture change in nursing homes that has improved residents' quality of life (Rahman & Schnelle, 2008). The main outcomes of this movement are resident-directed care and staff empowerment. Research indicates that the cultural changes resulting from the Eden Alternative are associated with less feelings of boredom and helplessness (Bergman-Evans, 2004).

Green House Project. The Green House concept is grounded in the Eden Alternative. It is a radical departure from the concept that skilled nursing care is best provided in large residential facilities. In contrast, a Green House aims at providing older adults who need skilled nursing care a small, homelike environment that shifts the focus from a large facility to a more homelike setting. Only 6–10 residents live there, in a dwelling that blends architecturally with houses in the neighborhood, making it much more homelike (Rabig et al., 2006).

The Green House concept emphasizes the importance of encouraging residents to participate in their care through helping with daily tasks such as cooking and gardening, assisted by specially trained staff (Johnson & Rhodes, 2007). By emphasizing participation in one's own care to the extent possible, personal dignity is maintained, and quality of life improved (Kane et al., 2007). As a result, the Green House concept is spreading across the United States as a viable alternative to large nursing homes.

The Pioneer Network. The Pioneer Network (http://www.pioneernetwork.net) is also dedicated to changing the way older adults are treated in society, particularly in care facilities. The Pioneer Network focuses on changing the culture of aging in America irrespective of where older adults live. Like the Eden Alternative, this approach focuses on respecting older adults and providing maximally supportive environments for them. Their values are also similar in spirit:

- Know each person.
- Each person can and does make a difference.
- Relationship is the fundamental building block of a transformed culture.
- Respond to spirit, as well as mind and body.
- Risk taking is a normal part of life.
- Put the person before the task.
- All elders are entitled to self-determination wherever they live.
- Community is the antidote to institutionalization.
- Do unto others as you would have them do unto you.
- Promote the growth and development of all.
- Shape and use the potential of the environment in all its aspects: physical, organizational, and psychosocial/spiritual.

- Practice self-examination, searching for new creativity and opportunities for doing better.
- Recognize that culture change and transformation are not destinations but a journey, always a work in progress.

The Pioneer Network advocates for a major emphasis on making nursing homes more like a home, and works in cooperation with the Centers for Medicare and Medicaid Services to work for revisions in nursing home regulations (Pioneer Network, 2008). This work is aimed at creating a new culture of aging.

What the Eden Alternative, the Green House concept, and the Pioneer Network have in common is a commitment to viewing older adults as worthwhile members of society regardless of their physical limitations. Treating all people with dignity is an important aspect in maintaining a person's quality of life. Everyone deserves that.

Concept Checks

1. What are the types of nursing homes?
2. Who is most likely to be a nursing home resident?
3. What are the characteristics of nursing homes?
4. What are special care units?
5. Under what conditions can a nursing home be a home for its residents?
6. What is the communication enhancement model?
7. What are the issues concerning decision-making capacity in nursing home residents?
8. What are some new directions for nursing homes?

One recurring theme in this chapter is the problem of financing health care interventions in later life for people in the United States. The Current Controversies feature raises several key points about the costs of nursing homes in the United States and the lack of ways to finance those costs. With the aging of the baby-boom generation, it is possible that the coming wave of older adults will be unable to afford the level and quality of care they expect to receive.

This is not the way it is in other countries. For example, U.S. health care expenditures as a percentage of its gross domestic product are nearly 5 times greater than they are in Singapore, but Singapore's health care is more effective as measured by the World Health Organization in terms of health attainment of the average resident, affordability, and responsiveness (Murray & Evans, 2003). As such, mere expenditures are not a good indicator of quality.

International funding models for long-term care reflect a wide variety of approaches, including social insurance, universal coverage through public services, financial need based systems, and hybrid approaches. Similarly, there is an equally wide array of ways for limiting expenses. Many countries provide services from in-home through skilled nursing care, and some have formal evaluation procedures to determine the best approach to care for each individual.

What is clear is that there is an array of successful models of providing long-term care to older adults that range from those completely supported by taxes to those that combine public and private contributions. The key is that each has advantages (and disadvantages) that could inform discussions in the United States. It is equally clear that the current U.S. model is not sustainable financially, and that without serious attention there will be major difficulties faced by the coming generation of aging baby boomers.

Summary

5.1 Describing Person–Environment Interactions

What is the competence–environmental press model?

- Competence is the upper limit on one's capacity to function.

- Environmental press reflects the demands placed on a person.

- Lawton and Nahemow's model establishes points of balance between the two, called adaptation levels. One implication of the model is that the less competent a person is, the more impact the environment has.

- People can show proactivity (doing something to exert control over their lives) or docility (letting the situation determine their lives).

What is the congruence model?

- Kahana's congruence model proposes that people search for environments that best meet their needs. Congruence between the person and the environment is especially important when either personal or environmental options are limited.

- The congruence model helps focus on individual differences and on understanding adaptation in nursing homes and other long-term care facilities. Giving people a sense of control over some aspect of their lives is key to successful adaptation.

What are the major aspects of stress and coping theory relating to person–environment interaction?

- Schooler applied Lazarus's model of stress and coping to person–environment interactions. Schooler claims that older adults' adaptation depends on their perception of environmental stress and their attempts to cope. Social systems and institutions may buffer the effects of stress.

What are the common themes in the theories of person–environment interactions?

- All theories agree that the focus must be on interactions between the person and the environment. No single environment meets everyone's needs.

- Everyday competence is a person's potential ability to perform a wide range of activities considered essential for independent living.

- Everyday competence forms the basis for deciding whether people are capable of making decisions for themselves.

5.2 The Ecology of Aging: Community Options

What is aging in place?

- Aging in place reflects the balance of environmental press and competence through selection and compensation.

- Throughout adulthood people compensate for change; aging in place represents a continuation of that process.

- Aging in place has resulted in a rethinking of housing options for older adults.

How do people decide the best option?

- The best placement options are based on whether a person has cognitive or physical impairment, the ability of family or friends to provide support, and whether intervention, if needed, can be provided in the current residence or a move is necessary.

How can a home be modified to provide a supportive environment?

- Modifying a home can be a simple process (such as adding hand rails in a bathroom) or extensive (such as modifying doorways and entrances for wheelchair access).

What options are provided in adult day care?

- Adult day care provides support, companionship, and certain types of services. Programs include social, health care, and specialized services.

- Introduction of adult day care needs to be done carefully with persons who have cognitive impairment.

What is congregate housing?

- Congregate housing includes a range of options, which provide social support and meals, but not ongoing medical care.

What are the characteristics of assisted living?

- Assisted living provides options for adults who need a supportive living environment, assistance with activities of daily living, and a modest level of medical care.

- The philosophy of care emphasizes personal control, choice, and dignity.

- Research shows that assisted living is especially helpful for frail older adults.

5.3 Living in Nursing Homes

- At any given time, only about 5% of older adults are in nursing homes. Such facilities are excellent examples of the importance of person–environment fit.

What are the major types of nursing homes?

- A distinction within nursing homes is between skilled nursing care and intermediate care.

- Costs of nursing home care are very high, and only certain types of insurance cover part of the costs.

Who is likely to live in nursing homes?

- The typical resident is female, European American, very old, financially disadvantaged, widowed/divorced or living alone, has no children or family nearby, and has significant problems with activities of daily living.

- Placement in nursing homes is seen as a last resort and is often based on the lack of other alternatives, lack of other caregivers, or policies governing the level of functioning needed to remain in one's present housing. It often occurs quickly in the context of a medical crisis.

What are the key characteristics of nursing homes?

- Selection of nursing homes must be done carefully and take the person's health conditions and financial situation into account.
- Person-centered planning is the best approach.

What are special care units?

- Special care units provide a supportive environment for people with specific problems such as dementia.
- Residents of special care units tend to be younger and more impaired than the rest of the nursing home residents.

Can a nursing home be a home?

- Residents of nursing homes can come to the conclusion that this can be home. Home is more than simply a place to live: Coming to the feeling that one is at home sometimes entails reflection on what one's previous home was like and recognizing that a nursing home can have some of the same characteristics.

How should people communicate with nursing home residents?

- Inappropriate speech to older adults is based on stereotypes of dependence and lack of abilities. Patronizing and infantilizing speech are examples of demeaning speech, which are rated very negatively by older adults. The communication enhancement model has been proposed as a framework for appropriate exchange. This model is based on a health promotion model that seeks opportunities for health care providers to optimize outcomes for older adults through more appropriate and effective communication.

How is decision-making capacity assessed?

- The Patient Self-Determination Act (PSDA) requires people to complete advance directives when admitted to a health care facility. A major ethical issue concerns how to communicate this information to people with cognitive impairment in nursing homes.

What are some new directions for nursing homes?

- The Eden Alternative, the Green House concept, and the Pioneer Network have a commitment to viewing older adults as worthwhile members of society regardless of their physical limitations.

Review Questions

5.1 Describing Person–Environment Interactions

- What are person–environment interactions?
- Describe Lawton and Nahemow's theory of environmental press. In their theory, what is adaptation level?
- Describe Kahana's congruence model. In what settings is this model especially appropriate?
- Describe the application of the stress and coping model to person–environment interactions. What kinds of things buffer stress?
- What are the common themes expressed by the various theories of person–environment interactions?
- What are the key components of everyday competence?

5.2 The Ecology of Aging: Community Options

- What is aging in place?
- What factors should people use to make decisions about the most supportive environment in which to live?
- How can homes be modified to support older adults?
- What services are provided at adult day care centers?
- What is congregate housing?
- What services are provided at assisted living facilities?

5.3 Living in Nursing Homes

- How many older adults live in long-term care facilities at any given time?
- What types of nursing homes are there?

- Who is most likely to live in a nursing home? Why?
- How have the characteristics of nursing homes been studied?
- Why do special care units often reflect better placement for people with significant physical or cognitive impairment?
- How does a resident of a nursing home come to view it as a home?
- What are the characteristics of inappropriate speech aimed at older adults? What is an alternative approach?
- How does the Patient Self-Determination Act relate to residents' decision-making capacity?
- What do the Eden Alternative, the Green House concept, and the Pioneer Network have in common?

Integrating Concepts in Development

- What do the demographics about the aging of the population imply about the need for long-term care through the first few decades of the 21st century?
- How do the theories of person–environment interaction include the basic developmental forces?
- How might a better financing arrangement for alternative living environments be designed?

Key Terms

adaptation level In Lawton and Nahemow's model, the point at which competence and environmental press are in balance.

adult day care Designed to provide support, companionship, and certain services during the day.

assisted living facilities Housing options for older adults that provide a supportive living arrangement for people who need assistance with personal care (such as bathing or taking medications) but who are not so impaired physically or cognitively that they need 24-hour care.

competence In Lawton and Nahemow's model, the theoretical upper limit of a person's ability to function.

congruence model In Kahana's model, the notion that people need to find the environment in which they fit and that meets their needs the best.

docility When people allow the situation to dictate the options they have and exert little control.

ecology of aging Also called environmental psychology, a field of study that seeks to understand the dynamic relations between older adults and the environments they inhabit.

environmental press In Lawton and Nahemow's model, the demands put on a person by the environment.

everyday competence A person's potential ability to perform a wide range of activities considered essential for independent living.

infantilization or elderspeak Also called secondary baby talk, a type of speech that involves the unwarranted use of a person's first name, terms of endearment, simplified expressions, short imperatives, an assumption that the recipient has no memory, and cajoling as a means of demanding compliance.

patronizing speech Inappropriate speech to older adults that is based on stereotypes of incompetence and dependence.

person–environment interactions The interface between people and the world in which they live that forms the basis for development, meaning that behavior is a function of both the person and the environment.

proactivity When people choose new behaviors to meet new desires or needs and exert control over their lives.

zone of maximum comfort In competence–environmental press theory, area in which slight decreases in environmental press occur.

zone of maximum performance potential In competence–environmental press theory, area in which increases in press tend to improve performance.

Resources

www.cengage.com/psychology/cavanaugh

Visit the companion website, where you will find tutorial quizzes, glossary, flashcards, and more. You can also access the following websites from the companion website.

The Centers for Medicare and Medicaid Services home page includes links to several important sites, including information about Medicare and an outstanding guide to selecting a nursing home. This site provides several very helpful guides in various formats.

The Eden Alternative, the Green House Project, and the Pioneer Network are dedicated to changing the culture concerning older adults. They have developed informative websites about their values, mission, and resources.

Eldercare.gov provides information about services available to older adults in communities in the United States.

Readings

Bornstein, R. F., & Languirand, M. A. (2009). *When someone you love needs nursing home, assisted living, or in-home care.* New York: Newmarket Press. Guide for family members to help them navigate through the eldercare system. Easy to read.

Kidder, T. (1994). *Old friends.* Boston: Houghton. Mifflin. A moving story of two older men adjusting to life in a nursing home. Easy reading.

Schor, J. (2008). *The nursing home guide: A doctor reveals what you need to know about long-term care.* New York: Penguin Group. A guide to nursing homes by a physician expert in geriatric medicine. Easy to read.

6

Attention and Memory

JERRY LUCAS IS KNOWN FOR MANY THINGS, INCLUDING BEING A TOP BASKETBALL PLAYER IN COLLEGE AT

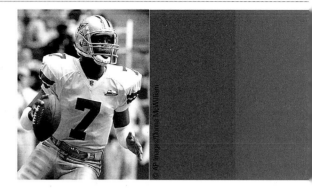

Ohio State University and in the pros (New York Knicks), a telecommunications professional, and of interest here, a world's leading authority in memory training which has earned him the name Dr. Memory. In fact he is touted as having written more material on memory training than anyone else. He has an intense dedication to having a positive impact on education. As Dr. Memory, what can he do? In front of millions of people on television he has memorized the names of up to 700 people in a television audience and an entire 100-page magazine.

What is particularly relevant to this chapter is that he has developed a business based on his "Lucas Learning System" techniques. These techniques are teachable and transferable to everyone, including the elderly. He touts that people can discover "Learning That Lasts." This spells much optimism to the growing elderly segment of our population.

As we shall see, memory training takes on considerable importance in this chapter because memory is such a pervasive aspect of our daily lives that we take it for granted. From remembering where we keep our toothbrush to tying our shoes to timing soft-boiled eggs, memory is always with us. Moreover, it gives us a sense of identity. Imagine how frightening it would be to wake up and have no memory whatsoever—no recollection of your name, address, parents, or anything else.

Perhaps that is why we put so much value on maintaining a good memory in old age and why memory training such as that espoused by Lucas becomes so important. Society uses memory as the yardstick by which to judge whether a person's mind is intact. Older adults are stereotyped as people whose memory is on the decline, people for whom forgetting is not to be taken lightly. Many people think that forgetting to buy a loaf of bread when one is 25 is all right, but forgetting it when one is 65 is cause for concern ("Do I have Alzheimer's disease?"). We will see that this belief is wrong. In fact, older adults are quite adept at using strategies in their everyday life contexts to remember what they need to know.

In this chapter, we will explore cognition by focusing on both memory and attention, as they go hand in hand. In general, we will be examining how people process information from the world around them and make sense out of it. Stage theories charting information processing from lower-level processes like sensation to higher-order processing such as reasoning were once popular in memory, attention, and aging research. The goal was to try to identify where the bottleneck existed to account for the fact that older adults perform more poorly than young adults. However, cognition is a highly dynamic thing; lower-order processes such as attention help create and influence higher-order thought, and higher-order thought helps determine where we focus our attention. We need to notice things in order to build our knowledge, but what we know shapes what we notice. Thus, current research emphasizes changes in the qualitatively different nature in how we process information and quantitative differences in the amount of processing that occurs as we grow older. This paints a much more optimistic picture of cognitive change in the latter half of the adult life span.

Along the same lines, the study of how cognition changes as we grow older has moved from a general normative approach (e.g., overall, memory declines with age) to considering how cognition changes in light of specific domains of cognition. Whether or not we observe age-related decline in cognitive processes such as memory and attention depends upon the type of task being administered or the nature of the context in which memory is operating. Some tasks show large impairment on the part of older adults like memorizing long lists of words, whereas others show no decline or even improvement in older adulthood like remembering information that is emotionally charged or personally relevant. Thus, important questions revolve around explaining why we see such variability. In other words, we need to identify when and under what conditions age-related changes in a cognitive function are likely to be challenging for older adults.

This question brings us back to a life-span perspective. In examining laboratory research on changes in attention or memory processes that may show decline, we need to consider how this translates into the everyday cognitive functioning of older adults. In other words, what are the practical implications of changes in cognitive functioning in older adulthood? We use memory not only as an end product, but also as a means to an end. For example, we use memory when we summarize the most recent episode of our favorite soap opera, tell other people about ourselves, or reminisce about our high school days. In these situations we are using memory, but the point is not just how much we remember. More often, the idea is to facilitate social exchange, to allow other people to get to know us, or to give ourselves a shared past with others. We will return to this idea when we examine cognition in context later in the chapter.

In this chapter, we will first see how people pay attention to things, and what paying attention consists of. Next we will address some intriguing questions about memory and adult development and aging. Are there differences in the ways in which adults of different ages use memory? How would these differences affect performance on traditional memory tests? What should our criteria be for good versus poor memory? These questions are something to think about as we explore what has been discovered about aging and memory.

We will attempt to answer the questions posed by looking at memory from different vantage points. First, we will see what happens to various memory processes. Second, we will focus specifically on how we keep information stored in memory and how we get it back out. An important aspect here will be how adults use different types of strategies to help themselves remember. Third, we will look at several factors that affect memory as we grow older. Fourth, we will look at memory for discourse and see how people vary in the kinds of information they remember (e.g., prose passages and television plots). Fifth, we will consider several ways in which adults remember things in everyday contexts and the differences between these settings and the laboratory research setting. Sixth, we will examine how we use memory as a yardstick by which we judge our competence. In particular, we will consider the processes by which we evaluate our memory. Seventh, we will see how we can intervene to improve memory. Finally, we will discuss clinical issues regarding memory. Chapter 7 continues with the examination of higher-order processes such as intelligence and problem solving.

Throughout this chapter, we will be considering results from experiments in which people made responses on computers. Although there is substantial evidence for age differences in some of the ways young and older adults process information, part of the difference may be due to cohort effects. Specifically, older adults in general are much less used to working on computers than are younger adults, making the task relatively unfamiliar to older adults. Consequently, they may not perform up to their maximum. Whether this experiential difference accounts for much or only a small amount of the age differences researchers have uncovered remains to be seen; however, given that the research is cross-sectional, meaning that age and cohort effects are confounded, this explanation remains a possibility.

6.1 Overview of Information Processing

LEARNING OBJECTIVES
- What are the primary aspects of the information-processing model?
- What are the areas where we observe differential age changes in attention and memory?

Trey strolled into a Lamborghini dealership and convinced the salesperson to let him take a Countach for a spin around the block. When he climbed behind the wheel of the most expensive sports car, his excitement almost got the better of him. But as he started it up and eased into first gear, he was filled with utter terror. He suddenly realized that he must pay complete attention to what he was doing. After all, he wouldn't want to have an accident. Now he was faced with the need to filter out everything—people's conversations, the radio, and the sound of the wind whipping through his hair.

How can Trey filter everything out? More importantly, what abilities can he use to avoid an accident? If something happened on the road, how quickly could he respond? Would these abilities be any different in a younger adult than in an older adult? And, by the way, did you know that a Lamborghini Countach is a sports car before you read this? If so,

how did you access this knowledge? If not, how did you incorporate this new knowledge?

How do we learn, remember, and think about things? Psychologists do not know for sure. About the best they can do is create models or analogues of how they believe our cognitive processes work. In this section, we will consider the most popular model: the information-processing model.

Information-Processing Model

The **information-processing approach** *uses a computer metaphor to explain how people process stimuli.* Just as with a computer, information enters the system (people's brains) and is transformed, coded, and stored in various ways. Information enters storage temporarily, as in a computer's buffer, until it is sometimes stored more permanently, as on a computer disk. At a later time, information can be retrieved in response to some cue, such as a command to retrieve a file. Let's see how this works more formally.

The **information-processing model** is based on three assumptions (Neisser, 1976): (1) People are active participants in the process; (2) both quantitative (how much information is remembered) and qualitative (what kinds of information are remembered) aspects of performance can be examined;

and (3) information is processed through a series of processes. First, incoming information is transformed based on such things as what a person already knows about it. The more one knows, the more easily the information is incorporated. Second, researchers look for age differences in both how much information is processed and what types of information are remembered best under various conditions. Finally, researchers in adult development and aging focus on several specific aspects of information processing: early aspects, which include a very brief sensory memory and attention; and active processing, which transfers information into a longer term store (e.g., long-term memory).

Using the information-processing model poses three fundamental questions for adult development and aging: (1) Which areas of information processing show evidence of age differences (e.g., early stages of processing such as attention, working memory, long-term memory)? (2) How can we explain variability when we find age differences in information processing? (3) What are the practical implications of age-related changes in information processing?

In this chapter, we first focus on early aspects of processing, that is, attention. Then we consider different domains of memory performance and how attentional systems influence memory. In doing so, we differentiate between short-term memory and working memory; processes involved in long-term memory, including implicit and explicit memory; and episodic and semantic memory. Next, we address the reasons for age differences in these processes. Finally, we discuss the exciting new work on interventions to improve memory functioning similar to those described in Chapter 2. By the end of this chapter, we will have a relatively complete picture of how we have acquired, processed, stored, and will remember the information in this chapter.

Attentional and Perceptual Processing

All memories start as sensory stimuli—a song heard, a person seen, a hand felt. We need to experience these things for only a small fraction of a second

in order to process the information. This ability is due to the earliest step in information processing, sensory memory, where new, incoming information is first registered. **Sensory memory** takes in very large amounts of information very rapidly. It does not appear to have the limits that other processes do when attentional focus is applied. It is more like *a very brief and almost identical representation of the stimuli that exists in the observable environment*. The representation exists in your mind in the absence of the stimuli itself.

However, unless we pay attention to sensory information, the representation will be lost very quickly. For example, try drawing either side of a U.S. penny in detail. (Those who are not from the United States can try drawing a common coin in their own country.) Most of us find this task difficult despite seeing the coins every day. Much detailed information about pennies has passed through our sensory memory repeatedly, but because we failed to pay attention, it was never processed to a longer lasting store. Age differences are not typically found in sensory memory (Poon & Fozard, 1980; Smith, 1975); however, they do begin to appear when attentional processes are applied to sensory memory.

As Joan McDowd and Raymond Shaw (2000) have maintained, attention and perceptual processing are best conceived from a functional perspective. Attention, for example, is composed of separable dimensions serving different functions. McDowd and Shaw note that the complex tasks we engage in when processing information usually require more than one attentional function. For example, in the case of Trey, he must selectively attend to or focus on the road and its obstacles while at the same time filtering out distracting information. In addition, attentional processes are influenced by the capacity to direct and sustain attention and the speed with which information is processed.

Concept Checks

1. What are the three assumptions underlying the information-processing approach?
2. What is the pattern of age differences in sensory memory?

6.2 Attentional Control

LEARNING OBJECTIVES

- What is processing speed? What age differences are found?
- What are the processing resources that underlie information processing?
- What is inhibition loss? When are age differences found?
- What are attentional resources? Under what conditions are age differences observed?
- How do automatic and effortful processes differ? In what situations are age differences present?

Chloe was gazing out the window during her history class. The teacher sternly told her to "Pay attention!" As the teacher came to the question-and-answer period of class, she immediately called on Chloe. Of course, Chloe did not know the answer. "I expect you to pay better attention to class!" was the teacher's next remark.

All of us probably have had similar experiences. Someone asks us a question and we continue to stare off into space. We are driving along a long, boring stretch of interstate highway and suddenly realize we have gone 20 miles with no awareness at all of anything that we saw along the way. The examples are quite varied, but the outcome is the same: Somehow we come to realize that lots of information was available to us that we never processed. In short, we simply did not pay attention. Let us look at the role attention plays in theories of cognitive aging.

Researchers typically look at how we regulate or control attention. Broadly defined, attentional control is linked to frontal lobe processes discussed in Chapter 2 and involves working memory, inhibitory control, and task switching (Luszcz & Lane, 2008). These components are typically treated as cognitive primitives or foundations of cognitive processing that undergo change as we grow older. In fact, leading theories of cognitive aging involve these processes.

Speed of Processing

Speed of processing reflects the outcomes of sensory memory and attention, in that researchers are examining relatively early aspects of information processing. In fact, some of the ways in which speed is measured, such as how fast you can react to a stimulus, are indices of sensory memory functioning. Thus, **speed of processing** can be viewed to some extent as a reflection of *how quickly and efficiently these early steps in information processing are completed.*

Researchers previously adopted the notion that a decline in speed of processing explains age-related changes in cognitive functioning (e.g., Cerella, 1990). This theory has fallen out of favor because research shows that whether or not you observe slowing depends on what the task is. This is because all components of mental processing do not slow equivalently. Instead of cognitive decline being reduced to one basic change, slowing (Salthouse, Atkins, & Berish, 2003), an alternative perspective suggests that age-related slowing is specific to particular levels of processing (e.g., response selection) and that the level in which slowing affects processing may vary from one task to another (Allen, Madden, & Slane, 1995; Antsey, Hofer, & Luszez, 2003; MacDonald et al., 2003; Zimprich & Martin, 2002).

Processing Resources

Another alternative theoretical explanation for age-related changes in cognitive functioning focuses on why older adults have more problems performing more difficult tasks, or tasks on which they have little practice, simultaneously? Many theorists and researchers believe that with increasing age comes a decline in the amount of available **processing resources,** *the amount of attention one has to apply to a particular situation.* The idea of declining processing resources is appealing, because it would account for poorer performance not only on attention but also on a host of other areas (Salthouse, 1991, 1996).

On the surface the notion of age-related decrements in processing resources offers a concise explanation of a wide range of age-related performance differences. But there is a nagging problem about the processing resource construct: It has never been clearly defined (McDowd & Shaw, 2000; Neumann,

1996; Salthouse, 1991) and is too broad. In fact, although Salthouse (1996) was able to show that some kind of processing resource notion is a parsimonious explanation, the strong version of the resource decline idea that marks much current research has little empirical support. Thus, there have been a number of alternative ways of examining a processing resource hypothesis. Two prominent alternative approaches are inhibitory loss and attentional resources.

Inhibitory Loss

One popular hypothesis is that older adults have reduced processing resources due to greater difficulty inhibiting the processing of irrelevant information (Hasher & Zacks, 1988; Persad, Abeles, Zacks, & Denburg, 2002). That is, older adults have more task-irrelevant thoughts during processing and have trouble keeping them out of their minds. This difference could explain why older people tend to have trouble with switching and dividing their attention.

The inhibition idea has considerable support (Kane, Hasher, Stoltzfus, Zacks, & Connelly, 1994; Persad et al., 2002). For example, McDowd, Filion, and Oseas-Kreger (1991) showed that when relevant and irrelevant information were both presented in the same modality (e.g., visually), older adults could not focus more attention on the relevant stimuli. That is, older adults distributed their attention more equally between the two types of information than younger adults. However, when relevant information was presented in one modality (say, visually) and irrelevant information in another (auditorily), older and younger adults both showed similar patterns of attention allocation. Thus, older adults apparently have more trouble selectively attending to relevant information when it and the irrelevant information are both presented in the same modality. One practical implication of this concerns driving, where lots of both relevant and irrelevant information occurs visually. Given these research findings, we would expect that older adults would have more difficulty in this situation, which could result in accidents. We will check our prediction a bit later in this chapter.

Additional research shows that the problem with inhibition is not universal across all aspects of stimuli (Connelly & Hasher, 1993; Gamboz, Russo, & Fox, 2002; Lustig, Hasher, & Toney, 2006). Adults were presented with letter pairs. They were required to name the target letter that always appeared in red and ignore the distracter letter that always appeared in green. The letter pairs were also presented in one of four locations. Young adults demonstrated appropriate inhibition, because their response time was slowed down when a previous target in red (e.g., the letter K) became a distracter in green on a subsequent trial. Older adults did not. Such age-related inhibitory deficits, however, may be limited to an item's identity. When inhibition was assessed by examining location (i.e., the target stimulus appeared in the same location as the to-be-suppressed distracter on an earlier trial), there were no age differences. Moreover, attempts to get older adults to inhibit processing of key aspects of a distracter by increasing the time the target and distracter were displayed did not appear to work (Kane et al., 1994). Such data provide support for Hasher and Zacks' (1988) inhibition hypothesis, but mean that inhibitory deficits are probably localized to specific aspects of stimuli.

Finally, it is interesting to note that there are strategies to compensate for older adults' difficulties with inhibiting irrelevant information. You simply ask older adults to close their eyes or avert their gaze away from irrelevant information. Using this strategy, older adults were just as good as young adults in attending to auditory stimuli (Einsten, Earles, & Collins, 2002). More currently, researchers are asking whether there is a beneficial effect of the distraction incurred in one task on the performance of a subsequent task. In other words, is there a positive consequence of distraction that older adults are utilizing?

In a recent study by Kim, Hasher, and Zacks (2007) older and younger adults were instructed to ignore distraction when reading passages with interspersed distracting words. Some of the distracters actually served as solutions to a subsequent set of verbal problems. Older adults showed significant activation and processing of the distraction information (in other words, they could not "control" their attention so as not to process this information), whereas younger adults did not. Most interestingly, the age-related reductions in attentional control over information that was not initially relevant led to superior problem-solving performances for older adults in comparison to younger adults.

Once again, we embrace a life-span perspective: Adult developmental changes in cognitive functioning are characterized by both gains and losses. It is important to consider inhibitory loss in both ways. Under certain conditions it can be a hindrance, and in others it can be helpful. It all depends upon the situation (Healey, Campbell, & Hasher, 2008).

Attentional Resources

Another way of looking at processing resource issues is through the lens of attention. In particular, **divided attention** addresses the question of how much information can be processed at any given time. Craik (1977) wrote that one of the clearest findings in cognitive aging research is the fact that older adults are more penalized when they must divide their attention between sources of information and/or responding. This type of task looks at *how well people perform multiple tasks simultaneously.* For example, paying attention to a lecture in class while simultaneously taking notes requires us to monitor two things (lecture content and what we are writing) simultaneously.

Life is full of situations in which we need to do at least two things at once. Two common examples are listening to a lecture while writing in a notebook and driving a car while conversing with a passenger. Each of these situations requires monitoring what is going on in at least two different domains. How well we are able to perform these multiple simultaneous tasks depends on how much attentional capacity we have available for each. To the extent that any one task requires a great deal of our capacity, our ability to do other things may be impaired.

Older adults report that dividing attention among most combinations of activities becomes more difficult with increasing age and, compared to young adults, rate most combinations of activities as more difficult (Tun & Wingfield, 1995). However, ratings of one's ability to perform various types of activities vary a great deal across tasks. Keeping track of novel information in combinations of tasks is perceived as more difficult than activities involving routine tasks or speech processing. These findings reflect the importance of self-evaluations on how well people think they can (or did) perform, which may have important implications for performance.

Self-reports about the difficulty of divided-attention activities are consistent with other findings that older adults perform tasks requiring divided attention more poorly than younger adults do (McDowd & Shaw, 2000; Verhaeghen, Steitz, Sliwinski, & Cerella, 2003). Experimental research on divided attention is a good example of how conclusions about age differences can change in the face of new evidence. At one time, researchers were convinced that age-related decrements in divided attention were inevitable (Craik, 1977). But Somberg and Salthouse's research in 1982 changed all that. By equalizing the amount of attention allocated on two tasks, Somberg and Salthouse were able to eliminate age differences on the divided-attention task. Other researchers have corroborated

Dividing one's attention between driving and talking on the phone may be done better by young adults but may also not be safe for them to do.

At the beginning of this section we encountered several examples of divided-attention tasks. You are very familiar with one of them—writing notes while listening to a lecture. An interesting developmental question is whether the ability to take good notes differs with age. One way to find out informally is to compare the notes taken in the same class by younger adult and older adult students. If there are no older adults in your class, there may be some in other courses. Ask them if you can compare their notes with those of someone much younger. What predictions would you make based on the research evidence you have read thus far? What role would practice play in these differences? Whose notes are actually better? Why do you think this is?

Somberg and Salthouse's findings (e.g., Wickens, Braune, & Stokes, 1987). Researchers have had to go back to the laboratory to try and account for these new data.

Subsequent studies have clarified things. It turns out that age differences are found on some divided-attention tasks and not others (Fernandes & Moscovitch, 2003; Whiting, 2003). Part of the explanation involves task complexity and practice. When the divided-attention tasks are relatively easy, age differences are typically absent. However, when the tasks become more complicated, then we observe age differences (Kramer & Larish, 1996; Salthouse, Fristoe, Lineweaver, & Coon, 1995). In other words, adults of all ages can perform multiple easy tasks simultaneously, but older adults do not do as well as younger adults when they must perform multiple difficult tasks at the same time.

Age differences on divided-attention tasks can be minimized if older adults are given extensive practice in performing the tasks, thereby reducing the demands on attention (Kramer, Larish, & Strayer, 1995; Tsang & Shaner, 1998). For example, when very large numbers of practice trials (from roughly 500 to over 11,000) are provided, age differences may disappear; with fewer practice trials (less than 300), age differences are often still found (Kramer et al., 1995; Kramer, Larish, Weber, & Bardell, 1999; Rogers, Bertus, & Gilbert, 1994). These results imply that older adults may be able to learn through experience how to divide their attention effectively between tasks. Check out this idea by completing the Discovering Development feature.

So, you may ask, when do older adults have difficulty performing multiple tasks simultaneously? You may have observed older adults having difficulty trying to remember something as they are walking down a staircase, or trying to simply walk and talk at the same time. Li and colleagues (Li et al., 2001) found that older adults prioritize walking and maintaining balance at the expense of memory. In other words, older adults focused on the task that was most important to them, walking and balancing to prevent falls. Younger adults, on the other hand, optimized their memory performance and ignored walking and balancing. Similarly, Kemper et al. (2003) found that both younger and older adults were able to simultaneously walk and talk, but that they accomplished this by using different strategies. Younger adults reduced their sentence length and grammar complexity, while older adults reduced their rate of speech.

In sum, divided-attention ability per se does not differ with age. Rather, older adults are at a disadvantage when they must perform two or more complex tasks simultaneously (McDowd & Shaw, 2000; Verhaeghen et al., 2003). Moreover, age differences on divided-attention tasks may actually reflect the fact that each task involves different component processes that are separately affected by aging (Fernandes & Moscovitz, 2003; Salthouse et al., 1995). This is exemplified in how older adults compensate by using strategies to focus on the task of most importance to them.

Integration: Attention and Cognitive Change in Older Adulthood

Finally, related constructs that must be considered when studying attentional capacity as a pool of resources available to support information-processing activity are automatic and effortful processing. In other words, a key assumption to information processing is that some processing occurs automatically whereas other processing requires effort. Researchers who study aging and cognition investigate both automatic processing and effortful processing, and then often look at differences in performance across the two categories.

Automatic processing places minimal demands on attentional capacity. Some automatic processes appear to be "prewired" in the sense that they require no attentional capacity and do not benefit from practice; others are learned through experience and practice (Smith & Earles, 1996). In either case, *information that is processed automatically gets into the system largely without us being aware of it.* For example, those who have been driving a car for many years are usually unaware of how hard they are pressing the accelerator pedal to make the car go forward from a stop. We will see that performance that is automatic in nature does not produce significant age differences in processing information.

In contrast, **effortful processing** *requires all of the available attentional capacity. Most of the tasks involving deliberate memory,* such as learning the words on a list, require effortful processing. In these cases, we are typically aware of what we are doing. For example, when we are first learning how to drive a car with a clutch, we are very aware of the

information we are processing (e.g., how much to let up on the clutch versus how hard to press the accelerator pedal). It is with effortful processing that age differences tend to emerge.

Finally, when considering attentional resources, it is extremely important to ask the question: Is it a fixed capacity that decreases with age? Researchers have observed decline in older adults' performance on laboratory tasks assessing memory, for example. However, a different picture may emerge when we consider that the functional capacity or resources necessary in specific task contexts can be modifiable depending upon the relevance and accessibility of knowledge and expertise related to the cognitive processes required (Hertzog, 2008). For example, two-process models have emerged that are similar to the automatic-effortful distinction discussed above. Under conditions where the task requirement is to simply have a familiarity with the information, there are no age differences. However, when there is effortful and deliberate processing involved to recollect the information, age differences emerge. Again, theories of cognitive aging are moving away from one-process views of cognitive functioning using standardized tests. These may underestimate older adults' competencies. Instead, the question now asked is: When and under what circumstances will we observe age-related change in cognitive functioning, and when is that change problematic? (Hertzog, 2008).

Concept Checks

1. Under what conditions do age differences disappear in inhibition tasks?
2. What are processing resources?
3. What are automatic processes?
4. Are attentional resources a fixed capacity that declines with age?

6.3 Memory Processes

LEARNING OBJECTIVES
• What is working memory? What age differences have been found in working memory?

- How does implicit and explicit memory differ across age?
- How does episodic and semantic memory performance differ across age?
- What age differences have been found in the autobiographical aspects of episodic memory?

Susan is a 75-year-old widow who feels that she does not remember recent events, such as whether she took her medicine, as well as she used to. She also occasionally forgets to turn off the gas on her stove and sometimes does not recognize her friend's voice on the phone. However, she has no trouble remembering things from her 20s. Susan wonders if this is normal or whether she should be worried.

Memory researchers have long focused on three general steps in memory processing as potential sources of age differences: encoding, storage, and retrieval (Smith, 1996). **Encoding** *is the process of getting information into the memory system.* **Storage** *involves the manner in which information is represented and kept in memory. Getting information back out of memory is termed* **retrieval.** Because there is no evidence for age differences in how information is organized in storage, most research has examined encoding and retrieval as sources of age differences (Light, 1996; Zacks, Hasher, & Li, 2000).

As discussed earlier, researchers have looked to research on speed of processing and impaired inhibition as providing insights into why age differences in memory occur. We will also add the process of working memory to this list. These mechanisms involve information that is being actively processed at any point in time, and they are aspects of memory showing clear age differences. More recently, researchers have examined contextual features and social-emotional contextual factors that could account for age-related differences in memory. We will see that these approaches offer alternative explanations for changes in memory as we grow older.

Our focus in this section will be on two main components of memory: short-term memory, including both short-term capacity and working memory, and multiple processes of long-term memory. The multiple processes of long-term memory are what Susan is most worried about. As we shall

see, it is very common to have memory problems that involve remembering more recent episodes and events as opposed to more remote memories from the past.

Working Memory

In this section we are interested in how information is kept in one's mind for additional processing into long-term memory or is being held temporarily during retrieval. How this happens involves working memory.

Originally, this type of immediate memory process was conceptualized as passive short-term storage or short-term memory. The idea is that individuals have a limited capacity for remembering information (about seven chunks of information, Miller, 1956). The question is whether older adults maintain this capacity. A typical short-term memory task measures the longest span of digits an individual can recall immediately after presentation. Studies have typically reported small or no age differences on these simple and passive span measures (Zacks et al., 2000).

However, some researchers have found evidence that, depending on the stimuli presented, older adults perform more poorly on simple span tasks than younger adults (Zacks et al., 2000). This age difference in span, though, can be accounted for by other more active information-processing variables involved in short-term memory (Verhaeghen et al., 1993). One such variable is working memory, an age-sensitive factor that affects long-term memory processing, for example, encoding information into long-term memory (Zacks et al., 2000). **Working memory** *is the active processes and structures involved in holding information in mind and simultaneously using that information, sometimes in conjunction with incoming information, to solve a problem, make a decision, or learn new information* (Zacks et al., 2000). Researchers typically consider it an umbrella term for many similar short-term holding and computational processes relating to a wide range of cognitive skills and knowledge domains (Zacks et al., 2000). This places working memory right in the thick of things—it plays an active, critical, and central role in encoding, storage, and retrieval.

Recall that sensory memory has a very large capacity to deal with incoming information. In contrast, researchers generally agree that working memory has a relatively small capacity. This capacity limitation of working memory operates like a juggler who can only keep a small number of items in the air simultaneously. Because working memory deals with information being processed right at this moment, it also acts as a kind of mental scratchpad. This means that unless we take direct action to keep the information active, the page we are using will get used up quickly and tossed away. For this reason, we need to have some way to keep information in working memory.

Most evidence indicates that there is greater age-related decline in working memory relative to passive short-term memory described earlier (Bopp & Verhaeghen, 2005; Zacks et al., 2000), although the extent of the decline is still in doubt. Researchers find that when the information load is increased (e.g., the number of tasks to be performed increases), older adults' lower storage capacity results in impaired working memory performance more so than for younger adults (Chen, Hale, & Myerson, 2003; McCabe & Hartman, 2003). This finding is consistent with the notion that the ability to allocate capacity in working memory to more than one task declines with age.

Salthouse and colleagues (1996; Verhaeghen & Salthouse, 1997) believe that working memory is the key to understanding age differences in memory. They argue that the loss of some of the ability to hold items in working memory may limit older adults' overall cognitive functioning. For example, many researchers propose working memory as the basis for understanding reasoning (Brigman & Cherry, 2002; Salthouse et al., 2003) and memory (Park et al., 2002). This idea is based on the extremely important role that working memory is believed to play in information processing. For example, working memory is where all the action is during processing: It is where information obtains meaning

Activities such as spinning involve retrieving elaborate memory representation for each aspect of the activity as well as accurately monitoring what one is doing.

and is transformed for longer storage. As a result, age differences here would have profound implications for just about all aspects of memory. The idea is that if information becomes degraded or is only partially integrated into one's knowledge base, it will be very difficult to remember it.

However, some evidence suggests that age differences in working memory are not universal. For example, working memory appears to depend on the type of information being used and may even vary across different tasks (Hale, Myerson, Rhee, Weiss, & Abrams, 1996; Logie, 1995). Such differences complicate matters. Chen, Hale, and Myerson (2003) find that age-related decline in spatial working memory is much greater than that in verbal working memory, although there is decline in both types of working memory. In other words, age differences were more pronounced in tasks that asked the individual to remember locations than in those where they were asked to remember digits.

Recent research has examined what causes working memory deficits in older adults. Oberauer and colleagues (2003) found that older adults have no trouble initially accessing multiple pieces of information at one time. The source of the problem is that they have difficulty juggling all of the elements once they are accessed. Interestingly, West and colleagues (2002) found that time of day affected the strength of age differences observed in working memory. Typically alertness is higher in the morning for older adults and in the evening for younger adults. When working memory was tested in the evening, the age differences were much stronger.

Overall, the evidence for age-related decline in working memory is not entirely clear; however, there is compelling evidence for how age differences in working memory relate to performance on more complex cognitive tasks. Yet, a great deal more needs to be done. Differential magnitude of decline in different domains of working memory suggest that it may not be a matter of overall general decline, but much more specified in certain areas and not others. There is little doubt at this point of the importance of working memory as a critical concept for understanding age-related differences in memory performance. For example, researchers have begun to show that working memory may be key to understanding the age differences in recall performance, especially in situations in which few cues for remembering exist (Park et al., 2002).

Implicit versus Explicit Memory

In addition to short-term and working memory, we can further divide memory systems into **explicit memory** *(sometimes called declarative), which is intentional and conscious remembering of information that is learned and remembered at a specific point in time,* and **implicit memory** *(sometimes called procedural memory), which involves retrieval of information without conscious or intentional recollection.* This distinction is important because research during the last 20 years shows that aging impacts these two forms of memory very differently. Overall, implicit memory shows much smaller age differences than explicit memory (Mitchell & Bruss, 2003). The distinction between the explicit and the implicit memory system is important and needs to be taken into account when evaluating the degree to which performance on a particular task involves intentional (explicit) or nonintentional (implicit) memory retrieval (Old & Naveh-Benjamin, 2008).

Implicit Memory. Implicit memory is a facilitation or change in task performance that is attributable to having been exposed to information at some earlier point in time, but which does not involve active, explicit memory. A good example of implicit memory is a language task such as stem completion. In a stem completion task, you would be required to complete a word stem with the first word that comes to mind (for instance, *con___*). Previously, you may have been shown a list of words that contained a valid completion of the stem (such as *contact*). If you have seen valid completions of the stems, you are more likely to use them later to complete the stems than you are to make up a different one (such as *contest*). This facilitation is called priming (Zacks et al., 2000). The memory aspect of the task is that you remember the stem completion you were shown; the implicit part is remembering it without being told to do so.

Research on implicit memory focused on demonstrating that it was a separate process from explicit memory. For example, whereas explicit memory performance is affected by having people think about the meaning of the items, implicit memory is not, and people with amnesia show severe problems on explicit memory tests but often perform similarly to normal people on implicit memory tests (Schacter, 2000; Yu & Yang, 2003). These findings suggest that implicit memory may be an exception to the general finding of age-related decline in long-term memory for new information (Lazzara, Yonelinas, & Ober, 2002; Mitchell & Bruce, 2003).

However, there are some qualifications to this conclusion. Age differences on implicit memory tests either are not there or are notably smaller than age effects on more explicit memory tasks (Fleischman & Gabrieli, 1998). When age differences do appear, they are almost always in favor of younger adults, though the age difference is smaller than for explicit memory tests (LaVoie & Light, 1994). In addition, some differences exist among various types of implicit memory tests. The most important distinction has been between perceptually based and conceptually based tests (Mitchell & Bruss, 2003; Roediger & McDermott, 1993). Perceptually based implicit memory tasks rely on processing the physical features of a stimulus; an example would be to process whether a word appears in lowercase or uppercase letters. Conceptually based implicit memory tasks rely on the semantic meaning of the items, such as whether the word is a verb. Depending on what people are asked to process (i.e., physical features or semantic meaning), performance on the tests differ (Toth, 2000).

The difference between the types of tests has important implications for age differences (Mitchell & Bruss, 2003). Results from several studies reveal a mixed pattern of age differences in implicit memory; some studies find no differences on conceptual tasks and find age differences on perceptual tasks (Lazzara et al., 2002), whereas others find the reverse pattern (e.g., Dennis, Howard, & Howard, 2003). Furthermore, others find that older adults show greater conceptual priming whereas younger adults do not (Multhaup, Hasher, & Zacks, 1998).

However, overall evidence suggests equal age effects in the two types of priming (Fleischman & Gabrieli, 1998; Lazzara et al., 2002).

What accounts for the sparing of implicit memory with age? Recent research in cognitive neuroscience (see Chapter 2) suggests that there is differential age-related deterioration in the brain underlying more explicit forms of memory (e.g., frontal-striatal system) as opposed to those underlying implicit memory (e.g., cerebral neocortex) (Lazzara et al., 2002; Prull et al., 2000; Tulving & Schacter, 1990). Behaviorally oriented researchers also point out that when age-related decline is evident in implicit memory tasks, it is probably because the tasks are contaminated with some explicit memory demands (McCarley et al., 2004; Mitchell & Bruss, 2003).

Long-Term Memory

When most people think about memory, they think about having to remember something over time, whether a few minutes or many days. Everyday life is full of examples—remembering routines, performing on an exam, summarizing a book or movie, and remembering an appointment. These types of situations constitute what memory researchers call long-term memory (Zacks et al., 2000). **Long-term memory** *refers to the ability to remember rather extensive amounts of information from a few seconds to a few hours to decades.* Memory researchers have created a wide variety of tasks requiring individuals to remember all sorts of information for varying lengths of time. Over a century of research has indicated that long-term memory represents a relatively large-capacity store in which information can be kept for long periods. More recently, mounting research in cognitive neuroscience suggests that long-term memory is not a unitary construct, but consists of distinct multiple systems (see Chapter 2) that are functionally different and are served by different brain structures.

Let us focus first on the more deliberate and effortful systems of explicit long-term memory. Two important types of long-term memory are semantic and episodic memory. **Semantic memory** *concerns learning and remembering the meaning of* *words and concepts that are not tied to specific occurrences of events in time.* Examples of semantic memory include knowing the definitions of words in order to complete crossword puzzles, being able to translate this paragraph from English into French, and understanding what the instructor is saying in a lecture. The distinction between episodic and semantic memory is important. **Episodic memory** *is the general class of memory having to do with the conscious recollection of information from a specific event or point in time.* Examples of episodic memory include learning the material in this course so that you will be able to reproduce it on an examination in the future, remembering what you did on your summer vacation last year, and memorizing a speech for a play.

Like implicit versus explicit memory, episodic and semantic memory appear to be impacted differently by aging (Rönnlund, Nyberg, Bäckman, & Nilsson, 2005; Spaniol Madden, & Voss, 2006). For example, episodic memory stays fairly stable until around 55–60 years of age and then shows a precipitous decline beginning around age 65. In contrast, semantic memory increases from 35–55 years of age and then levels off. Although semantic memory starts to decline at age 65, the decline is much less substantial than for episodic memory (Rönnlund et al., 2005).

Semantic Memory. As indicated previously, semantic memory is relatively spared with age in the absence of a disease state. Evidence suggests that there are no deficits in semantic memory processes such as language comprehension, the structure of knowledge, and the activation of general knowledge (Light, 1996; Nyberg et al., 2003). Semantic memory retrieval typically does not tax working memory, and thus older adults can draw upon experience in word meanings and/or general world knowledge. In addition, whereas retrieval of episodic memories is based on cues to the original experience, semantic memories are retrieved conceptually as part of our world knowledge. However, research also shows that although information in semantic memory is retained in older adults, sometimes it is hard to access if it is not exercised on a regular basis (Hertzog et al., 2003). The fact that semantic memory emphasizes the retrieval of general knowledge is coextensive with a major component of intelligence, acquired knowledge, which is discussed later in Chapter 7. As we shall see, intelligence as acquired knowledge remains stable throughout most of older adulthood.

The major area in which age-related decline in semantic memory can be observed is in its accessibility. This is illustrated in word-finding deficits. Older adults typically have more trouble retrieving a target word when presented with a definition of the word, and they tend to encounter more "tip-of-the-tongue" experiences (Fraas et al., 2002; James & Burke, 2000; MacKay & Abrams, 1996). A tip-of-the-tongue (TOT) experience is when you try to retrieve a name or word and you feel you know the word, but it is not quite accessible. For example, you are at a party and you see someone very familiar; you "know" that person's name, but you simply cannot retrieve it. Another aspect of this TOT experience is

© Robin Nelson/PhotoEdit

Older adults have a difficult time remembering even familiar information.

that you can retrieve partial information such as the number of syllables in that person's name, the initial sounds or letters, and where to stress each syllable (stress pattern). Older adults not only experience more TOT's, but also report less partial information about the target, both in the laboratory and in everyday life (MacKay & Abrams, 1996). Such TOT problems indicate that even highly familiar information can become more difficult to retrieve as we grow older.

Episodic Memory. Because episodic memory includes so many of the day-to-day activities we adults perform, it has been the focus of more research than any other single topic in memory development (Lovden et al., 2004; Wingfield & Kahana, 2002; Zacks et al., 2000). Typically, researchers study episodic memory by having people learn information, such as a list of words, and then asking them to recall or recognize the items. In a **recall** test, *people are asked to remember information without hints or cues.* Everyday examples of recall include telling everything that you can remember about a movie or taking an essay exam. **Recognition,** on the other hand, *involves selecting previously learned information from among several items.* Everyday examples of recognition include taking multiple-choice tests and picking out the names of your high school friends from a complete list of your classmates.

Memory researchers use several techniques to study the variables that influence episodic memory performance. For example, they may vary the way that the information to be learned is presented (e.g., in organized groups, with cues, or randomly); the speed at which it is presented; the familiarity of the material; and the conditions for remembering the items (e.g., giving recall cues or making a recognition test easy or hard).

The results from hundreds of studies point to several conclusions. Overall, older adults perform worse than younger adults on tests of episodic memory recall in that they omit more information, include more intrusions, and repeat more previously recalled items (Allen et al., 2002; Lovden et al., 2004; Nyberg et al., 2003; Zacks et al., 2000). These age differences are large; for example, more

than 80% of a sample of adults in their 20s will do better than adults in their 70s (Verhaeghen & Salthouse, 1997). These differences are not reliably lowered either by providing slower presentation or by giving cues or reminders during recall. On recognition tests, older adults do fare better in that differences between older and younger adults are reduced. However, in comparison with young adults, older adults are more likely to accept never-represented items as having occurred on the test especially if they share a conceptual meaning or perceptual resemblance to the previously presented items (Palfai et al., 2003; Verhaeghen et al., 2000; Zacks et al., 2000).

Older adults also tend to be less efficient at spontaneously using internal study strategies, such as using imagery or putting items into categories in one's mind to organize information during study. When older adults are instructed to use internal organizational strategies such as categorization, however, they not only can do so but also show significant improvement in performance. However, these improvements are not sufficient, in general, to substantially reduce age differences in recall performance (Kahana & Wingfield, 2000; Larsson et al., 2003; Taconnat & Insingrini, 2004; Verhaeghen et al., 1993). These findings suggest that older adults are not as successful in situations requiring them to devise an efficient way to acquire disorganized information, especially when they will be expected to recall it later.

Age differences between older and younger adults can be reduced in several ways. First, allowing older adults to practice or to perform a similar task before learning a new list improves performance. Knowing what one is expected to do usually makes it easier to perform well. Interestingly, better memory performance after practice parallels similar improvements following practice on tests of skills related to fluid intelligence (discussed in Chapter 7). Second, using material that is more familiar to older adults also improves their performance. For example, older adults do not remember words such as *byte* or *Walkman* as well as words such as *jitterbug* or *bobbysox*. Third, older adults may use compensatory strategies to help themselves remember, which we will examine later in this chapter. Their beliefs about memory also create an influence on their ability to remember.

What, then, can we conclude about episodic memory? Older adults are apparently disadvantaged when left on their own to face relatively rapid-paced, disorganized information. However, memory performance appears to be somewhat flexible and can be manipulated, with improvements coming from a variety of sources. Later we will consider some attempts to explain why age differences occur and several ways in which memory problems can be corrected, but first we will examine an episodic memory process that is relatively spared with age: autobiographical memory.

Autobiographical Memory. Information that needs to be kept for a very long time (from a few hours to many years) includes facts learned earlier, the meaning of words, past life experiences, and the like. Very little research has been conducted on age differences in such long-term memory for a variety of reasons. For one thing, designing an adequate test of very long-term memory so that we know how to interpret performance is difficult. For example, we often cannot know whether an incident that someone recalls from the past is what actually happened, because we cannot verify the facts. Additionally, if a person does not remember a fact from years past, it may be due either to an inability to retrieve the information or to a failure to have learned the information in the first place. This latter issue is especially important when older and younger adults are compared; we must make certain that both groups had the opportunity and learned the information. Some ingenious researchers, though, have managed to circumvent these problems and have studied a particular aspect of very long-term episodic memory: autobiographical memory.

Autobiographical memory *involves remembering information and events from our own life.* These recollections provide each of us with a personal history and help define who we are. As important as autobiographical memory is, though, very few studies have looked at how well people remember things over the course of their lives.

Autobiographical memory is primarily a form of episodic memory, although it can also involve semantic memory. The episodic component of autobiographical memory is the conscious recollection of temporal and spatial events from one's past. The semantic component consists of knowledge and facts of one's past (e.g., personal characteristics, knowledge that an event occurred) without having to remember exactly when things occurred and in what order. The episodic details of autobiographical memory are more difficult for older adults, whereas the semantic aspects are much more easily remembered (Barsalou, 1998; Levine, 2004). Accordingly, older adults have been shown to be worse than younger adults in reporting vivid recollections of their past (Levine et al., 2002). However, older adults' general memories of real-life events have been shown to contain more personal thoughts and feelings and have been rated more interesting than those of younger adults (Hashtroudi et al., 1990; Levine et al., 2002).

In some areas we can assess the accuracy of very long-term memory. Being able to verify what individuals remember accompanied by some record of true events is extremely important in evaluating our ability to remember over long periods of time. Only in cases where records have been kept for many years is this usually possible. Coleman, Casey, and Dwyer (1991) examined records that were available from the Harvard Longitudinal Studies of Child Health and Development on individuals from birth to age 50. Detailed information was collected over the years on such things as which childhood diseases the participants had, whether they smoked cigarettes, and what kinds and how much food they ate. At age 50, participants completed a lengthy questionnaire about these issues, and their responses were compared with similar reports made 10 and 20 years earlier, as well as with the official records. Coleman and colleagues found amazing accuracy for information such as whether a person had ever been a smoker or had a particular disease such as chicken pox. In fact, half of the memories elicited at age 50 were more accurate than the memories for the same information elicited 10 years earlier at age 40! However, information about amounts of food consumed or about individual episodes was not remembered very well. Apparently, these events tend to get blended together and are not stored as separate incidents.

Memory for faces from the past can be maintained for long periods of time, as people have experienced at high school reunions as far back as 50 years.

What distinguishes events that are memorable from those that are not? What makes a moment we will remember the rest of our lives? Many people think that highly traumatic events are ones that are indelibly etched in our memories. If so, then people who survived Nazi concentration camps should have vivid memories of their experiences. Wagenaar and Groeneweg (1990) examined the testimony of 78 survivors of Camp Erika, a Nazi concentration camp in The Netherlands during World War II. Dutch police initially interviewed the survivors about their experiences between 1943 and 1948. In 1984, during a war crimes trial for an accused Nazi collaborator, these witnesses gave sworn depositions about their experiences at Camp Erika.

The camp survivors' recollections were a mix of accurate and inaccurate information. In many cases memory was quite good; even 40 years later about half of the survivors remembered the exact date of their arrival at the camp and their entire identification number. They were able to recall the general conditions of the camp, overall treatment, and the like. However, they also had forgotten many important details, including in some cases their own brutal treatment. Wagenaar and Groeneweg point out that these forgotten details mean that even extreme trauma is no guarantee that an event will be remembered. Perhaps forgetting the horrors of being brutalized is even a type of self-protection.

Events do not always have to be personally traumatic to be highly memorable, though. Some historical events that have considerable personal relevance, very unusual or novel events, and other events that are highly emotional are also remembered very well. Such memories are called flashbulb memories because they are so vivid that it seems as if we have a photograph of the event (Fitzgerald, 1999; Rubin, 1996). Although many events tend to be of major historical significance, such as the assassinations of John F. Kennedy and Martin Luther King, Jr., or the September 11, 2001, terrorist attack, flashbulb memories may also involve personal autobiographical events (Rubin, 1996). Such events tend to impress into memory the circumstances in which the person first heard the news about the event; memories of the circumstances include information about the place, other people present at the time, what activities were occurring, the source of the information, and even associated smells (Cohen, Conway, & Maylor, 1994; Maylor et al., 2002).

An interesting phenomenon arises when you examine vivid autobiographical events across individuals' life spans. In particular, the age at which a memory is established becomes quite important. As Susan found in the vignette, and as can be seen in Figure 6.1, for both younger and older adults, vivid memories experienced earlier in life (between 10 and 30 years of age) are reported more often than those occurring during middle adulthood (between 30 and 50 years of age; Fitzgerald, 1999; Rubin & Schulkind, 1997; Willander & Larsson, 2006). In addition, on a factual memory test of Academy Award winners, news stories, and teams that played in the World Series, those events that occurred earlier rather than later in life were remembered better (Rubin, Rahhal, & Poon, 1998). Bernsten and Rubin (2002) found that for older adults, the bump in memory was most evident for happiest memories. In contrast, very sad memories showed a decline in recall. It may be that this earlier period of life has importance in defining oneself and thus helps to organize personal memories, but that emotionally negative events are not included as importance is determined (Bernsten & Rubin, 2002; Bluck, 2003; Conway & Holmes, 2004; Pasupathi & Carstensen, 2003).

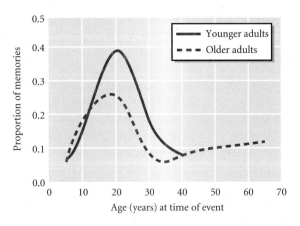

Figure 6.1 The distribution of flashbulb memories produced by younger and older adults.

Source: Reprinted from Social cognitions in aging, T. M. Hess & Blanchard-Fields, Fitzgerald, J. M., *Autobiographical Memory and Social Cognition: Development of the Remembered Self in Adulthood,* p. 161, Copyright © 1999, with permission from Elsevier.

Concept Checks

1. Why is working memory important in understanding age differences in performance?

2. What major differences are there between older and younger adults' working memory?

3. What are the age-related differences between implicit and explicit memory?

4. What accounts for the fact that implicit memory is spared with aging?

5. How do age differences in episodic and semantic memory compare?

6. What differences have been observed between older and younger adults in aspects of autobiographical memory?

6.4 Factors Affecting Age Differences in Memory

LEARNING OBJECTIVES

- What evidence is there for age differences in encoding?
- What age differences have been observed in retrieval?
- What are the relative contributions of encoding and retrieval in explaining age differences in performance? How does a neuroscience perspective help us understand these contributions?
- How does automatic retrieval affect age differences in memory?
- What age differences have been observed in processing misinformation as true?

Cynthia is an elderly woman sitting on a jury for the first time. The crime is a burglary. An eyewitness speculates about whether the defendant had a crowbar given that someone told him that there was a crowbar at the crime scene. The judge announces to the jury to disregard that statement. It is from an unreliable source. Back in deliberation, Cynthia has trouble remembering if evidence of a crowbar in the hands of the defendant was to be disregarded or to be believed.

We have seen that older and younger adults differ in how well they perform on some memory tasks. Why do these age differences exist? Is it that older adults are poorer at getting information into and out of memory? Given these age differences, how can we explain the fact that older adults' memory can operate just fine in an everyday context? Is it related to how efficiently they manipulate information in working memory? Or does it involve the source of the information, as is the case with Cynthia?

Age Differences in Encoding versus Retrieval

For many years, researchers examining age differences in memory performance have tried to implicate either encoding or retrieval as the source of memory processing. However, such attempts have met with mixed results (Zacks et al., 2000). As we will see, however, more recent work based on brain metabolism, automaticity in retrieval, and the social context of memory raises some interesting questions about the source of memory changes. But before moving to those subjects, we will examine the evidence for the relative contribution of encoding and retrieval to memory performance in older adults.

Encoding. Results from years of research suggest an age-related decrement in encoding processes (Craik & Byrd, 1982; Koutstaal, 2003; Smith, 1996; Zacks et al., 2000). An example of an encoding process that affects memory is elaborative rehearsal. *Elaborative* **rehearsal** *involves making connections between incoming information and information already known.* For example, a person presented with the word *emu* and told that this is a bird that does not fly may try to think of other flightless birds. With some thought, *ostrich* may come to mind. Linking *emu* and *ostrich* would be an example of this type of rehearsal.

Research in support of an age-related decrement in elaborative rehearsal finds that older adults have more difficulty making such connections than younger adults do (Light, 1996; Smith, 1996). Interestingly, however, once these connections have been made, older and younger adults maintain them equivalently (which supports the conclusion that whereas encoding differences exist, storage differences do not). In other words, older adults would be slower than younger adults at making the emu-ostrich connection, but once it was made, both groups would remember it just as well.

This example of the encoding process involves intentional learning of information. However, what happens when information is learned and there are no expectations of testing this memory later on (e.g., when a person witnesses a crime)? This latter type of memory processing is sometimes called incidental learning. For example, a study compared incidental and intentional learning of names in younger and older adults (Troyer, Häfliger, Cadieux, & Craik, 2006). Their instructions for encoding the names varied from stating the first letter of the name to defining the name to simply trying to remember the name for a later test. Younger adults tended to outperform older adults for intentionally learned names, but older adults did as well as younger adults whenever they encoded the information incidentally (e.g., remembering the first letter or defining the name).

Why do these age differences in intentional versus incidental encoding occur? Anderson and colleagues (1998) conclude that attentional resources are consumed to a greater extent during intentional encoding. If you were asked to study some materials that you would be tested on while at the same time you had to tune out a conversation going on in the same room, you would place a lot of effort into using strategies to effectively focus on the information to be studied. However, while you were studying the materials, if you were told that the conversation in the room was about you, you would probably extend more effort to listening to the conversation. You would perform better on the test in the first case than in the second case. Attentional control would be necessary while you encoded the information to succeed on the test. Thus, the distracting conversation would not hurt you when you were able to focus your attention more exclusively on the test.

One important aspect of attentional control and expending attentional resources in the example above is that when we are confronted with large amounts of information that we need to remember, we tend to use *various techniques, called* **strategies** *that make the task easier and increase the efficiency of storage.* We will examine strategy differences in the elderly next.

Use of Strategies during Encoding. A critical issue is whether older adults behave strategically when studying information to be remembered. Two effective strategies for learning new information are to organize it and to establish links to help you remember the information. For example, consider a student's efforts to learn the information in college courses. Learning the necessary facts of chemistry, psychology, literature, and so forth is much easier if separate notebooks are kept for each class. Imagine the potential for confusion if all of the class notes were simply mixed together. Keeping them separate is an example of an organizational strategy.

It may be that older adults do not spontaneously use such effective encoding strategies in comparison to younger adults (Hertzog, Dunlosky, & Robinson, 2007). For example, older adults are less likely to take advantage of similarities in meaning among words (such as the link between *river* and *lake*) presented randomly in a list as a way to organize the items. Because the number of items remembered from such a list is highly related to the use of organization, younger adults outperform older adults on such tasks. However, the available evidence suggests that the spontaneous production of effective strategies is not a sufficient account of age differences in memory performance (Hertzog & Hultsch, 2000; Hertzog et al., 2007; Light, 1996).

Hertzog, McGuire, and Lineweaver (1998) found that only 35% of older adults compared to 49% of younger adults used optimal strategies for encoding (e.g., placing related items into meaningful categories); however, as Figure 6.2 shows, there were large age differences in recall irrespective of strategy methods used. They also found that strategy production had a very modest effect on age differences in recall. In support of this finding, Dunlosky and Hertzog (1998) found that large age differences in recall remained even when older adults were instructed to use effective strategies. However, as Hertzog and Hultsch (2000) have pointed out, producing a strategy does not necessarily imply that the strategy was used effectively. We need more research to differentiate the quality of implementation of strategies as opposed to their production. Current thinking suggests that this is an important avenue for future research in order to better understand adaptive behavior in learning new information (Hertzog & Hultsch, 2000). We will explore this more when we discuss remediation of memory deficits later.

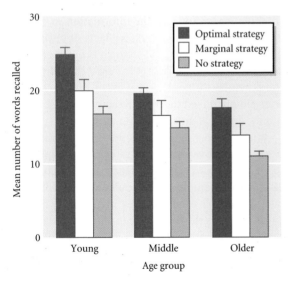

Figure 6.2 **Mean recall for young, middle-aged, and older adults as a function of strategy groups.**

Source: "Aging, Attributions, perceived control, and Strategy Use in a Free Recall Task", by C. Hertzog, C.L. McGuire, & T.T. Lineweaver, 1998. In *Aging, Neuropsychology, and Cognition, Vol. 5*, pp.95, 85–106.

Retrieval. Age-related differences on explicit memory tasks are affected by the degree to which a task employs retrieval cues. It has been long known that age differences are more pronounced on free-recall tests which provide no cues to individuals (Old & Naveh-Benjamin, 2008; Spencer & Raz, 1995). However, for recognition tests, the original target to be learned is presented as a cue. Accordingly, fewer age differences are found (Spencer & Raz, 1995). In addition, older adults show greater frequency of tip-of-the-tongue states and feeling-of-knowing (feeling you know something yet you are not sure what it is) after failure to retrieve information (Burke et al., 1988; MacKay & Abrams, 1996; Maylor, 1990). This is probably due to a temporary inaccessibility. In fact, older adults are as likely as younger adults to recognize the material they cannot recall when in the TOT state.

Craik (1986) suggests that age differences in memory where there are limited cues (e.g., free recall) may be a function of limited self-initiated operations in older adults. This idea suggests that older adults have difficulties in performing tasks that do not have a high level of environmental support. For example, when you are recognizing a previous piece of information, the fact that the target is in front of you creates a high level of environmental support. However, a free-recall task demands that you access that information with limited help and cues from the environment.

Based on the evidence so far, we find that memory functioning in the aging adult is influenced by deficits in both encoding and retrieval (Zacks et al., 2000). However, there are other factors that may qualify this conclusion, suggesting that the picture is a more complicated. In order to explore this, we need to consider whether the cognitive process is automatic or deliberate as well as implicit or explicit. But first let's revisit cognitive neuroscience evidence for encoding and retrieval processing.

Cognitive Neuroscience Revisited. Cognitive neuroscience (discussed in Chapter 2) also presents evidence suggesting age differences in encoding and retrieval. Using PET scans, Grady and her research team (1995) found that both younger and older age groups showed similar patterns of increased blood flow in specific areas of the brain during recognition, but differed significantly during encoding. Compared with older adults, younger adults showed significantly greater increases in blood flow to the left prefrontal and temporal areas of the brain. (Recall that this is called lateralization to a specific hemisphere or asymmetry.) Grady and colleagues interpreted these differences as evidence that age-related memory differences may be due to older adults' failure to encode information adequately. Inadequate encoding could result in information not getting into memory at all, or not being as elaborately encoded, making retrieval more difficult at best. Furthermore, fMRI studies have found that age-related reductions in frontal-lobe activation are associated with reduced ability in encoding words in memory (Stebbins et al., 2002). In addition, the hippocampal region has been related to current memory functioning as well as predicting the rate of further memory decline over time (Prull et al., 2000).

Cabeza and colleagues (Cabeza, 2002; Cabeza et al., 2003), however, found that prefrontal activity during memory performance is less lateralized (activity found more equally in both brain hemispheres instead of localized in one hemisphere) in older adults than in younger adults. Lateralization (found in young adults) leads to more effective processing of information. It may be, though, that those older adults who show strong bilateralization (i.e., activity in both hemispheres) when processing information also show enhanced cognitive performance relative to older adults who show less bilateralization and less lateralization. The additional activity across many brain regions that occurs when older adults process information may enhance performance on the specific task investigated.

In sum, the research on encoding and retrieval processes is important for three reasons. First, it emphasizes that age-related decrements in memory are complex; they are not due to changes in a single process. Second, intervention or training programs must consider both encoding and retrieval. Training people to use encoding strategies without also training them how to use retrieval strategies will not work. To the extent that only partial information is encoded, retrieval strategies need to focus on helping people find whatever aspects are available. Third, theories of how memory changes with age

must take individual differences into account, especially differential rates of change in component processes and lateralization. Overall, finding the sources of memory decline demonstrates the importance of considering multiple levels of influence.

Theories of memory development must consider those components of processes that change and those that do not. However, not all aspects of retrieval are effortful and do not necessarily demand resources that overburden older adults' processing. We next examine a relatively recent area of research that centers on automatic retrieval processes that tend to be equivalent for older and younger adults.

The Emerging Role of Automatic Retrieval

Larry Jacoby and his colleagues (Hay & Jacoby, 1999; Jacoby, 1991; Yonelinas, 2002) found that memory situations involve both automatic and deliberate retrieval processes. They used a clever procedure called the "process-dissociation paradigm" to separate out the different contributions of each of these two types of processes in a memory task. To illustrate, Jacoby and colleagues conducted a series of studies examining the "false-fame" effect (Dywan & Jacoby, 1990; Jennings & Jacoby, 1993). In a typical study, older and younger adults were asked to first read a list of nonfamous names. Then they were given a new list consisting of three types of names: names from the first list, additional new nonfamous names, and moderately famous names. Participants were asked to indicate which of the names presented were famous. They were also told that the names on the original list were nonfamous. If they were to recognize any names from that list, they should exclude them from further consideration.

The false-fame effect results when a previously observed nonfamous name (on the original list) is mistakenly identified as a famous name at testing. What happens is this: Studying the original nonfamous names increases their familiarity, so when people see this name again *and* they do not consciously recollect that it was on the original list, they will produce the false-fame effect, in other words, mistake familiarity for fame. Dywan and Jacoby (1990) found that older adults produced a larger false-fame effect than young adults did. In a subsequent study, Jennings and Jacoby (1993) added another condition: Adults were told that the names from the original list were actually obscure famous names, so if one looked familiar at testing, it would be appropriate to label it as famous whether or not they consciously recollected it. The first experiment assessed how conscious recollection affects memory, and the second study assessed how familiarity affects memory.

Overall, the assessment of conscious recollection was lower for older adults than for younger adults, but the assessment for automatic retrieval (in this case familiarity testing) in the second study did not differ across age groups. Thus, although conscious recollection is impaired as suggested earlier in this chapter; automatic retrieval of familiar information is spared. Jacoby and colleagues suggest that difficulties in recollection on the part of older adults are largely a function of an inability during retrieval to access the details of an episode and may account for situations where older adults display memory problems. This idea relates back to our distinction between implicit and explicit memory as well as episodic and semantic memory. Both implicit and semantic memory tasks do not require such detailed conscious recollection of information; therefore, researchers have not seen poor performance on the part of older adults in these areas.

Misinformation and Memory

The fact that older adults exhibit the false-fame effect to a greater degree than younger adults suggests that although familiarity is intact, conscious recollection is not, thus allowing familiarity to misinform the older adult's performance. Two other recent areas of research have further explored older adults' susceptibility to misinformation due to memory deficits: source memory and false memory.

Source Memory. One perspective on the false-fame effect is to consider it a function of deficient source monitoring. **Source memory** *refers to the ability to remember the source of a familiar event as well as the ability to determine if an event was imagined or actually experienced* (Mitchell & Johnson, 2000; Schacter et al., 1998). For example, it is important

Accurate memory for events becomes particularly important when older adults serve on juries.

for an older adult to be able to discriminate whether she actually remembered to take her medication or only thought to do it. The ability to discriminate between these two events necessitates that one is able to retrieve information about the context in which the event in question originally occurred. By reconstructing the original event accurately, the older adult will remember whether she actually took the medication or not.

Research on age differences in source memory reveals that older adults are less accurate at a number of source-memory tasks (Mitchell et al., 2003; Schacter et al., 1997; Simons, Dodson, Bell, & Schacter, 2004). For example, in one study (Simons et al., 2004), younger and older adults heard sentences that were read by one of four speakers (male or female). At the same time they viewed the written sentences and photos of the speakers. In a later surprise test, they were asked to distinguish between old and new sentences. Although there were no age differences in distinguishing between the old and new sentences, older adults were less able to identify the speakers of the presented sentences. The conclusion was that older adults have most difficulty in remembering the source (voices and faces) associated with the sentences.

We can relate this type of finding back to the role retrieval cues play in older adults' memory functioning. In a recent review, Old and Naveh-Benjamin

(2008) suggest that contextual details can serve as retrieval cues and that without access to them older adults may have more difficulty in remembering events. Furthermore, episodic memory is more highly dependent upon contextual information, which could explain why older adults have difficulties with that kind of task.

There are cases, however, where older adults do not show source-memory problems. For example, older adults showed poor performance at detecting whether a male or female made an earlier statement, but they performed as well as younger adults when the task was more emotional in nature, such as whether a speaker was evil or good (Rahhal et al., 2002). This relates to the idea that older adults perform a cognitive task better when it involves more emotionally salient material. We will explore this later in Chapter 8.

False Memory. Another line of research that examines misinformation effects in older adults is false memory. **False memory** *is when one remembers items or events that did not occur.* Here the focus is on memory errors. False memory is typically studied by presenting participants with a list of words that are all associated with a specific word that was not presented. So, for example, the experimenter presents the words *nurse, hospital, patient,* and *surgery* for the participant to study. At recall, she adds words such as *doctor* that did not appear on the original list, yet are semantically related to the list of words. People tend to falsely recall and incorrectly recognize such a target word (e.g., *doctor*) and feel very confident about it (Roediger & McDermott, 2000). Older adults tend to show an even greater degree of false memories under such conditions (Benjamin, 2001; Jacoby & Rhodes, 2006; Karpel et al., 2001).

Once again, an explanation for this effect is that older adults have more difficulty in correctly identifying information as false because they have trouble linking content information to its context (Dehon & Bredart, 2004; Smith, Lozito, & Bayen, 2005). In fact, when older adults are warned in advance to examine the origin of the information presented, the false-memory effect is reduced (i.e., educating them about the phenomenon reduces the false-memory effect) (Dehon & Bredart, 2004; McCabe

& Smith, 2002). Furthermore, a cognitive neuroscience approach to this kind of misinformation effect shows that older adults with lower frontal lobe functioning are particularly susceptible to false memories (Roediger & Geraci, 2007).

Both false memory and source memory have been investigated together in the context of falsely identifying a familiar but innocent bystander in a criminal lineup. For example, in a typical study, older and younger adults are shown photographs of perpetrators and then a series of mug shots of innocent bystanders. A week later, in a lineup containing both the bystanders and perpetrators, older adults were worse at picking out the perpetrator. This deficit was related to older adults' difficulties in remembering the context in which they observed the photographs (Memon et al., 2003). Interestingly, this inaccuracy during the lineup was not evident for older adults if they observed older instead of younger faces (Perfect & Harris, 2003). Other ways to help older adults suppress the false-memory effect is to make the new information more distinctive (Dodson & Schacter, 2002).

From a practical, everyday perspective, the misinformation effects in older adults we've reviewed, including the false-fame effect, source-memory deficits, and false memories, could render older adults more susceptible to deception, as in consumer scams. In fact, Larry Jacoby (1999) suggests that the elderly are targets for fraudulent practices because of misinformation effects and aging. For example, Jacoby (1999) describes a typical scam perpetrated by con artists who telephone seniors to talk with them and surreptitiously gather as much personal information on them as possible. In a later callback, the con artist asks questions based on the previously gathered personal information and determines whether the older adult fails to remember the previous conversation. If so, the memory deficit is exploited with a false claim: "We received a check from you for $1,200 but it should have only been $950. Please send us another check for $950 and we will send the original check back to you." Of course, no check was sent earlier. Jacoby calls this the "I-told-you" claim. The controversial issue is how do we explain this memory deficit? Is it a false memory, faulty source monitoring, or

How Do We Explain False Memories?

Larry Jacoby (1999) asks the question: What causes the effect in the "I-told-you" claim? Does the claim create a false memory? From this perspective, exposure to misleading questions about an event can result in a permanent loss from memory of details of the actual experience (Loftus, 1975). In other words, the experience is overwritten by the misleading information. A "blocking" account suggests that exposure to misinformation impairs accessibility to the correct information, but does not overwrite it (Ayers & Reder, 1998). A source-memory account suggests that memory of the

original experience coexists with the misleading information; however, confusion arises as to the source of the information (Lindsay & Johnson, 1989).

Jacoby (1999) suggests that it is improbable that the false "I-told-you" claim is a function of memory alterations such as those suggested above. He maintains that it is probably a function of bias or guessing. In other words, a false claim might occur only if people are unable to remember the original experience itself, and then resort to guessing. Acceptance of the false claim might rely on a person's forgetting the original experience (the initial

phone call) and willingness to guess that the claim is valid. Thus, it may be that apparent memory impairment producing misinformation effects is due to forgetting and guessing rather than to real changes in the memory itself. Jacoby (1999) has conducted a number of studies demonstrating this last alternative. He calls this phenomenon the accessibility bias that influences guessing (in this case, that the older adult did send the $1,200 check) and proposes that it is a basis of responding (sending the con artist a check for $950) independent of remembering.

faulty accessibility? This is discussed in the Current Controversies feature.

The importance of this area of research is in its implications for helping older adults form a counterattack for deceptions. For example, older adults can be trained to counter deception by refusing to respond unless they are certain that they can recollect what happened (Jacoby, 1999). Another strategy is to generate an alternative response to the first response that comes to mind, such as asking the con artist to return the earlier check before sending a new one (Jacoby, 1999).

Concept Checks

1. What are the relative age differences in encoding and retrieval?

2. What age differences have been found in the use of memory strategies?

3. How has recent evidence from brain scans affected our understanding of the relative importance of encoding and retrieval?

4. How do age differences compare in automatic versus deliberate retrieval?

5. How does processing of misinformation differ in older and younger adults?

6.5 Memory for Discourse

LEARNING OBJECTIVES

- What age differences are observed in text-based levels of memory for discourse?
- What age differences are observed for situation models of discourse memory?
- What social factors and characteristics of individuals influence memory for discourse?

An elderly woman, Dorothy, loves the movies. In fact, her adult children go to her for advice on good movies to see. She is able to recount in elaborative strokes what the movie was all about, what the moral of the story was, and how it relates to life in general. At the same time, she can never remember the specific details such as the type of car the heroine drove or the names of the actors and actresses. But her children love her recounting of the movies and are not dismayed by her lack of detail.

Typically, memory for structured materials that relate to prior knowledge is better than memory for information that is unfamiliar or is unstructured (Johnson, 2003; Zacks et al., 2000). The question is whether there are age differences in memory for structured information that relates to prior knowledge? This is most evident in memory for text or discourse.

Adults of all ages spend a great deal of time reading books, magazines, and newspapers, and watching television programs and movies, like Dorothy. Collectively, such material is termed discourse. Indeed, how well adults remember prose, or text passages, is one of the fastest-growing areas in memory research. In part, this rapid growth reflects the realization that prose (e.g., a newspaper story) is something people need to remember in everyday life; word lists typically are not.

In this section, we mainly focus on adults' ability to remember information they have read. We examine the types of situations and conditions that put older adults at a disadvantage in remembering text and when older adults are at an advantage in remembering text. In order to do this, we look at researchers who have examined memory in terms of the different levels of linguistic structure in text. At a basic level, specific propositions or each of the basic ideas are represented in a text. In addition, propositions can be central to the story or relatively less important to the integrity of the story. For example, in a story about a burglary, the fact that the neighbor stole the woman's purse is central to the story, and the fact that the purse was purple is less important. These propositions are considered text-based levels for processing (i.e., central or main ideas versus less important details).

A higher level of text representation is called a **situation model.** Unlike the propositions, which are text-based, at this level individuals use their world knowledge to construct a more global understanding of what the text is about (Wingfield & Stine-Morrow, 2000; Zwaan & Radvansky, 1998). For example, comprehension of the story about the burglary involves elaborating upon the story with several kinds of knowledge relevant to the situation, for example, damage done by the break-in, anger felt from this violation, and loss of priceless mementos. Let's now look at age differences in remembering text at each of these two levels.

Text-Based Levels

Most of the work conducted in aging and discourse processing has examined memory at text-based levels. Because texts are constructed with information at these different hierarchical levels of importance, a key question is whether there are age differences in memory for these different levels. Answering this question amounts to looking for age differences between memory for main ideas and memory for details. The literature on this issue is large and complex (Johnson, 2003; Wingfield & Stine-Morrow, 2000). In general, the data indicate two important points. First, when text is clearly organized, with emphasis on structure and the main ideas, older adults are similar to younger adults in recalling more main ideas than less important details.

However, in addition to these competencies in text processing, older adults exhibit observed deficits under specific conditions. Studies show that older adults are adversely affected by rapid presentation, highly unpredictable or unorganized material, and material that is dense in propositions (Hartley, Stojack, Mushaney, Annon, & Lee, 1994; Stine, Wingfield, & Lindfield, 1995). Older adults may be at a disadvantage when presented with text at speeds geared to younger adults. Indeed, when the speed-of-presentation variable is removed and participants can pace themselves, age differences are eliminated (Wingfield & Lindfield, 1995; Stine-Morrow et al., 2001). In addition, the more predictable and meaningful the text, the better the older adults perform

© Jeff Greenber /PhotoEdit

Older and younger adults remember the gist of information from text, but younger adults tend to remember more low-level details.

even at rapid rates (Gordon-Salant & Fitzgibbons, 1997; Wingfield, 1996). Finally, high verbal ability reduces age differences in overall recall during rapid presentation (Wingfield & Stine-Morrow, 2000). Another area of difficulty for older adults appears when the text becomes propositionally dense (an increase in the number of propositions) and less familiar. In this case older adults have more difficulty than younger adults do in identifying or inhibiting less important details (Hartley, 1993; Wingfield & Stine, 2000).

An important aspect of text variables is that they may interact with personal characteristics of the reader to create differences in memory for discourse. An example of this interaction involves situations in which people hold opinions or have knowledge about a topic and are then presented additional written information. In terms of people's ability to remember this new information, does it

matter whether the new information agrees or disagrees with what people already know?

To answer this question, Rice and Okun (1994) tested older adults' memory for accurate information about osteoarthritis that either contradicted their previously held false beliefs or affirmed their previously held accurate beliefs. All of the participants reported having osteoarthritis for at least 2 years. Rice and Okun found that older adults recall and recognize information that contradicts their previously held beliefs less accurately than they recall and recognize information that affirms their initial beliefs. These findings point out that individuals who educate older adults must be careful to identify misconceptions that they may bring into the situation. However, Rice and Okun also found that if the disconfirming material was stated explicitly, older adults were better at remembering the information later. Thus, explicitly stating that certain information is often misunderstood, and then stating the correct information, may help older adults remember the accurate information.

Situation Models

Sometime in your educational career you probably had to read a rather lengthy novel for a literature class. Providing you opted for the book rather than the video or Cliff Notes version, you probably were surprised at how much different your recollections of the story were compared with those of your classmates. Many of these differences are due to how individuals construct their situation model of the text. Situation models of the text include other features besides text-based information such as characters' emotional states, goals, and personality characteristics as well as spatial relationships among the people, objects, and events described (Morrow, Stine-Morrow, Leirer, Andrassy, & Kahn, 1997; Zwaan & Radvansky, 1998). In addition, the reader's characteristics influence the situation model, such as personal biases, the social context in which you are recalling a text, and personal motivations for remembering certain bits of information while forgetting others.

The Influence of Social Context on Memory Performance

Who were the investigators and what was the aim of the study? How do younger and older adults adapt their story-retellings to two different types of listeners: a young child and an adult experimenter? One hypothesis is that the child as listener is more relevant to the social roles of aging. Therefore, in this social context older adults should recall information better compared to older adults in the experimenter-as-listener context. Cynthia Adams and colleagues (2002) tested this hypothesis to see whether this happens.

How did the investigators measure the topic of interest? Adams and colleagues assessed story recall performance by asking women to learn one of two stories with the goal of retelling the story from memory either to an experimenter or to a young child.

Who were the participants in the study? A sample of 48 older women and 47 younger women participated.

What was the design of the study? Adams and colleagues studied story recall using a cross-sectional research design with the two listener conditions described above.

Were there ethical concerns with the study? There were no concerns in this study; the topics were not controversial nor were they likely to cause strongly negative feelings.

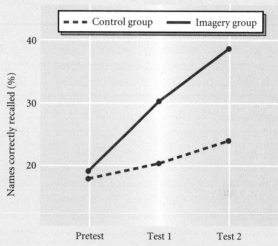

Figure 6.3 Mean number of propositions recalled as a function of age group and type of listener.

Source: Cynthia Adams, Malcolm C. Smith, Monisha Pasupathi, and Loretta Vitolo, Social context effects on story recall in older and younger women: Does the listener make a difference? *The Journals of Gerontology Series B: Psychological Sciences and Social Sciences* 57, P28–P40, Copyright © 2002, Reprinted with permission from the Gerontological Society of America.

What were the results? As illustrated in Figure 6.3, Adams and colleagues found that when the child was the listener, older but not younger story-retellers recalled more text-based content. In addition, both older and younger story-retellers generated more elaborations upon the text. Finally, both older and younger story-retellers tended to reduce the complexity of the more complicated stories. In all, older story-retellers were better able to adapt the complexity of the retellings of the stories to the needs of the listener.

What did the investigators conclude? An important implication of Adams and colleagues' findings is that it is important to consider the social and collaborative interaction between people and their contexts in memory-aging research to gain a more complete picture of memory changes as we grow older.

Overall, both younger and older adults construct and update situation models similarly (Dijkstra et al., 2004; Radvansky et al., 2003; Zacks et al., 2000). For example, Morrow and colleagues (1997) had older and younger adults memorize a map of a building in which there were several rooms with different objects in each of the rooms. They then read a narrative about a character who was moving from one room to another. The situation model consisted of a spatial organization centered on the main character and her location. When they interrupted the participants' reading of the narratives and asked them whether certain objects were near or far from the main character's current location, both younger and older adults gave answers that were more accurate and faster when the object was close to the main character. However, older adults took longer to memorize the maps and were slower overall in their reading times. Morrow and colleagues (1997) concluded that although older and younger adults use qualitatively similar strategies to update their situation models, the updating process is more effortful for older adults.

How adults decide to retell a story is also important. Adams, Labouvie-Vief, Hobart, and Dorosz (1990) presented fables and nonfables to younger and older adults and examined their story recall styles. They found that older adults used a more integrative or interpretive style for nonfable passages, whereas younger adults used a more literal or text-based style. Age differences were not found for the fable passages. These findings mean that younger adults may spontaneously shift their recall style depending on the type of passage, whereas older adults may use a more consistently integrative style regardless of passage type.

Another variable that affects performance is amount of prior knowledge or expertise. Miller (2003) compared time allocated to texts related to cooking versus general information in younger and older adults who either had high or low knowledge about cooking. High-knowledge individuals, whether they were younger or older, showed greater recall for the cooking texts. In other words, the benefits of knowledge were equal for both younger and older adults.

Finally, another variable affecting both higher and lower levels of text is the social context of remembering. Retelling information more typically occurs in a social context in everyday life. After we see a movie we retell its contents to our friends. Or we recount a story we have just read to a friend over the telephone. An interesting question posed by Cynthia Adams and colleagues (2002) is whether some contexts are more optimal for remembering for older adults than are others. In essence she finds that the social context matters and older adults' retelling of stories varies depending upon who the listener is. We examine this finding in more detail in the How Do We Know feature.

The study by Adams and colleagues is a prime example of why we cannot study memory in a social and everyday vacuum. We must consider the multiple layers of context that influence memory functioning in older adults in everyday life. Being old does not necessarily mean that one cannot remember, especially if the situation provides an optimal opportunity to do so. This is where we turn our attention to next.

Concept Checks

1. How do age differences vary as a function of text-based and situation model levels of discourse processing?
2. How does the organization of text influence memory?
3. How do social factors influence memory for discourse?

6.6 Memory in Context

LEARNING OBJECTIVES

- What age differences are there in prospective memory?
- What are some factors that help preserve memory as we grow older?

Tyler, an elderly man of 80, has been exercising his memory abilities since he reached his 60th birthday. He has made sure to read voraciously, has done his crossword puzzles religiously, and has kept up on current events. At a recent family gathering, it was quite evident that such behavior paid off. In a game of *trivial pursuit, he was the ultimate winner. However, when his grandson told him nonstop about a car he wanted to buy, Tyler later had trouble recalling all of the details.*

As noted at the beginning of this chapter, memory is so integral to our everyday life that we take it for granted. In the case of Tyler, using his memory of previously studied knowledge was extremely important in participating in family games. However, he still had trouble remembering the details of recently learned information. This difference in memory ability has been the focus of a proliferation of research on age differences in memory in context or how memory operates in everyday life (Hertzog & Dunlosky, 1996; Park & Brown, 2001). This research is extremely important for three reasons. First, it may shed some light on the generalizability of findings based on laboratory tasks such as word-list recall. Second, new or alternative variables that affect performance could be uncovered, for example, factors that enhance memory functioning in older adults could be identified. Third, research on everyday memory may force us to reconceptualize memory itself.

Prospective Memory

One area that has received increasing attention is prospective memory. **Prospective memory** *involves remembering to perform a planned action in the future* (Henry et al., 2004; Zacks et al., 2000), such as remembering to take medication. The study of prospective memory is a good illustration of how performance on everyday memory tests stacks up to performance on traditional laboratory tests.

For example, prospective memory has been examined in a naturalistic context such as remembering to take medication. Findings are somewhat counterintuitive: Older adults with rheumatoid arthritis were better at remembering to take their medications than middle-aged patients (ages 34–54) (Park, Hertzog, Leventhal, Morrell, Leventhal, Birchmore, Martin, & Bennett, 1999). In fact, despite strong evidence for age-related cognitive decline in the older adults on traditional psychometric measures, older adults had the cognitive ability to manage medications. What about the middle-aged adults? It

turned out that a busy lifestyle in middle age was the major determinant of who was at risk for forgetting to take medications. As Park et al. suggest, physicians should not assume that older adults do not have the cognitive capacity to manage medications. In fact, very busy middle-aged adults appear to be more at risk for managing medications improperly.

The success of prospective memory in naturalistic settings motivated researchers to more systematically examine the phenomenon in laboratory studies. In doing so, Einstein and McDaniel (1990) introduced a distinction between event-based and time-based prospective memory tasks. In event-based tasks, an action is to be performed when a certain external event happens, such as giving a certain person a message. A time-based task involves performing an action after a fixed amount of time, such as pressing a key every 8 minutes, or at a fixed point in time, such as remembering an appointment at 1:00 P.M. Researchers found that time-based tasks showed more age differences as long as people used self-generated strategies to remember, as these tend to decline with age; the cues in event-based tasks helped reduce age differences (Bastin & Meulemans, 2002; Einstein et al., 2000; McDaniel et al., 2003; Reese & Cherry, 2002).

It also may be that whether age differences are evident depends on the difficulty of the task. If the task is complex and places high cognitive demands on people, older adults do not perform as well as younger adults when self-initiated retrieval is required (West & Craik, 2001; West et al., 2003; Zeintl, Kliegel, & Hofer, 2007). These findings imply that, like remembering events from the past, prospective memory involves a complex interaction of aspects of information processing. It involves multiple processes ranging from controlled monitoring of the environment to being able to retrieve the intended action (McDaniel & Einstein, 2007). It also accounts for success in naturalistic settings: Older adults compensate for complexity by using and generating external cues like notes to themselves. Thus, whether there are age differences in prospective memory is a complex issue. It appears to depend on the type of task, the cues used, and what is being measured.

Factors That Preserve Memory

As indicated by the Adams research placing memory in a social context, in many situations, older adults perform quite well at memory tasks. In addition, a number of cognitive reserve factors, such as IQ, educational level, occupation, and activity levels, may enhance cognitive functioning as we grow older (Scarmeas & Stern, 2003; Valenzuela & Sachdev, 2006). **Cognitive reserve** involves *factors that lessen cognitive decline in that they provide flexibility in responding and adapting to changes in the environment* (Buckner, 2004). Let's investigate some of these conditions.

Exercising Memory. One approach to cognitive reserve is to view memory as a mental muscle. By applying this approach, older adults should benefit from repetitive practice, which involves using specific memory exercises. Exercising memory on one type of task strengthens it, setting the stage for better memory in a variety of other tasks (Colcombe & Kramer, 2003). For example, practicing how to organize a grocery list over and over will help one learn to organize other kinds of lists as well. Similarly, both physical and mental activity may serve as a protective factor against memory decline in later life. In fact, reduction in activity has been correlated with decline in cognitive performance (Mackinnon et al., 2003). Fitness training also has increased cognitive performance in older adults regardless of the training method or the older adults' personal characteristics (Colcombe & Kramer, 2003). Recall that we examined this phenomenon in Chapter 2 by showing that physical exercise has effects at a biological level on the structure and functioning of the brain.

Multilingualism and Cognitive Functioning. In a recent study, Kavé and colleagues (2008) explored whether the number of languages a person speaks positively influences the cognitive state of older adults. In fact, older adults from 75 to 95 years of age who spoke four languages or more showed the best cognitive state. This suggests that multilingualism might be a protective factor for maintaining our cognitive state as we age. Interestingly, it did not matter whether the individuals had high or low education—speaking many languages had the same protective effect. The authors suggest that knowledge of many languages might reflect an innate flexibility in using brain structures, thus serving a proxy role for brain reserve.

Semantic Memory in Service of Episodic Memory. Given that semantic memory is relatively unimpaired as we grow older (as discussed earlier), it may have an enhancement effect on episodic memory for older adults. Accordingly, Verhaeghen and colleagues (1993) found that many studies have shown that the ability to group to-be-remembered episodic information into previously learned semantic categories reduces age differences on such memory tasks. Similarly, a number of studies have shown that older adults perform better when they can use previously learned semantic information to support episodic knowledge (Naveh-Benjamin, Craik, Gues, & Kreuger, 2005). For example, older adults are better at memory for related as opposed to unrelated word pairs (Naveh-Benjamin, 2000).

Negative Stereotypes and Memory Performance. A number of studies have demonstrated factors that can negatively influence memory performance in older adults. As a result, the elimination of such factors could enhance memory functioning in older adults. A primary example under investigation is negative stereotypes of aging. Briefly, older adults may not perform at optimal levels because they are aware of and threatened by the typical belief that aging hampers memory ability (Levy, 1996; Hess, Auman, Colcombe, & Rahhal, 2003). We will further explore this psychosocial factor influencing cognition in Chapter 8. At this point, be aware that a wealth of factors have been positively and negatively associated with older adults' memory functioning beyond cognitive mechanisms such as working memory, speed of processing, and encoding and retrieval abilities. In the next section, we explore two more factors in depth: self-evaluations of memory and memory training.

Concept Checks

1. Why is task complexity important in prospective memory?

2. What factors help preserve memory? What factors hamper memory?

6.7 Self-Evaluations of Memory Abilities

LEARNING OBJECTIVES

- What are the major types of memory self-evaluations?
- What age differences have been found in metamemory?
- How do younger and older adults compare on memory monitoring tasks? How is task experience important?

Eugene has just reached his 70th birthday. However, he is greatly concerned. He has believed since he was very young that this is the age when memory really goes downhill. He has a great fear of losing his memory completely. He has taken to asking people to repeat things to him over and over for fear he will forget them. It has taken a toll on his self-concept. He doesn't feel that he has control over his life the way he used to.

How good is your memory? Are you absent-minded? Or are you like the proverbial elephant who never forgets anything? Like most people, you probably tend to be your own harshest critic when it comes to evaluating your memory performance. We analyze, scrutinize, nitpick, and castigate ourselves for the times we forget; we rarely praise ourselves for all the things we do remember, and we continue to be on guard for more memory slips. The self-evaluations we make about memory may affect our daily life in ways that traditionally were unrecognized. This is exactly what is happening to Eugene. His negative evaluations of his memory ability are creating much undue stress in his life.

The self-evaluations we make about memory are complex (Cavanaugh, 1996; Hertzog & Hultsch, 2000). They are based not only on memory and performance per se but also on how we view ourselves in general, our theories about how memory works, what we remember from past evaluations, and our attributions and judgments of our effectiveness.

Aspects of Memory Self-Evaluations

Researchers of memory self-evaluation have focused primarily on two types of awareness about memory.

The first type involves *knowledge about how memory works and what we believe to be true about it; this type of self-evaluation is referred to as* **metamemory.** For instance, we may know that recall is typically harder than recognition, that memory strategies are often helpful, and that working memory is not limitless. We may also believe that memory declines with age, that appointments are easier to remember than names, and that anxiety impairs performance. Metamemory is most often assessed with questionnaires that ask about these various facts and beliefs.

The second *type of self-evaluation, called* **memory monitoring,** *refers to the awareness of what we are doing with our memory right now.* We can be aware of the process of remembering in many ways. At times we know how we are studying, how we are searching for some particular fact, or how we are keeping track of time for an appointment. At other times we ask ourselves questions while doing a memory task. For example, when faced with having to remember an important appointment later in the day, we may consciously ask ourselves whether the steps we have taken (e.g., writing a note) are sufficient.

Age Differences in Metamemory

Researchers have explored age differences in metamemory mainly by using questionnaires (see Berry, 1999; Hertzog & Hultsch, 2000 for reviews). Many questionnaires have been developed over the years. Some of them, such as the Metamemory in Adulthood questionnaire (Dixon, Hultsch, & Hertzog, 1988) and the Cognitive Failures Questionnaire (Gilewski, Zelinski, & Schaie, 1990), tap several different areas of knowledge about memory, including knowledge about strategies, tasks, change with age, and capacity. Other questionnaires, such as the Memory Self-Efficacy Questionnaire (Berry, West, & Dennehey, 1989) and the Memory Controllability Inventory (Cavanaugh & Baskind, 1996; Lachman, Bandura, Weaver, & Elliott, 1995), assess specific aspects of memory beliefs.

The pattern of age differences in metamemory is interesting. Older adults seem to know less than younger adults about the internal workings of memory and its capacity, view memory as less stable, expect that memory will deteriorate with age, and perceive that they have less control over memory (Blatt-Eisengart & Lachman, 2004; Hertzog & Hultsch, 1995; Lane & Zelinksi, 2003; Lineweaver & Hertzog, 1998; McDonald-Miszczak, Ryan & Kwong See, 1998; Soderberg & Lachman, 1999). The belief in inevitable decline with age is potentially damaging. For example, the belief that memory inevitably declines may negatively influence the performance of older adults, as indicated in the studies of negative stereotypes, and may also discourage people from strategy training because they may think that it is useless and that there is little point in exerting effort to try and remember something that does not come to mind immediately (Cavanaugh, 1996).

Interestingly, the belief in inevitable decline does not apply equally to all aspects of memory. Older adults view memory for names as declining more rapidly than memory for things that happened long ago (Lineweaver & Hertzog, 1998). Similarly, adults report that different kinds of information pose different likelihoods of being troublesome. For example, remembering names is universally problematic, but especially for older adults (Cohen, 1993; Leirer, Morrow, Sheikh, & Pariante, 1990). In contrast, remembering to pay bills, meet appointments, and take medications appears to remain unchanged with age (Cohen, 1993).

The Role of Memory Self-Efficacy

Belief in one's ability to accomplish things is a pervasive theme in literature, religion, psychotherapy, and many other diverse arenas (Berry, 1999; Cavanaugh & Green, 1990). *As it applies to memory, belief in oneself is referred to as* **memory self-efficacy;** it is the belief that one will be able to perform a specific task. This is an important construct in understanding how memory changes with age (Berry, 1999; Cavanaugh, 1996). Memory self-efficacy is an important type of memory belief that is distinct from general knowledge about memory because, for example, one may know a great deal about how memory works but still believe that one's ability to perform in a specific situation is poor.

Memory self-efficacy has emerged as one of the key aspects of metamemory due to its importance in accounting for performance in several different types of situations, as well as helping to explain how people make performance predictions in the absence of direct experience with tasks (a topic considered in the next section) (Berry, 1999; Cavanaugh, 1996). Welch and West (1995) propose that memory self-efficacy is also a key to understanding a broader array of phenomena, such as mastering the environment. Briefly, they propose that some older adults hold the assumption that memory inevitably declines with age and have experienced some age-related decreases in performance themselves. As people experience tasks or situations across adulthood that they complete successfully, their memory self-efficacy should remain strong; those who experience failure should show decrements in memory self-efficacy. These experiences should influence subsequent behavior; people who experience success may be more likely to seek out more challenging cognitive environments, whereas people experiencing failure may seek less cognitively demanding environments.

Overall, studies show that older adults with lower memory self-efficacy perform worse on memory tasks (Berry, 1999; Blatt-Eisengart & Lachman, 2004; Valentijn, Hill, Van Hooren et al., 2006; Zelinski & Gilewski, 2004). Yet older adults with low memory self-efficacy compensate for poor memory performance by using people for assistance and using compensatory strategies to aid in their memory performance (de Frias et al., 2003).

Age Differences in Memory Monitoring

Memory monitoring involves knowing what you are doing mentally right now. The most popular way researchers study memory monitoring is by having people predict how well they will do on a memory task. One variation of this technique requires that people predict how well they will do before they get a chance to see the task. For example, participants are asked to predict how many words they think they can remember from a 20-item list before they see the list. The second variation requires people to make performance predictions after they have seen the task. This time, they see the list first, and are then asked to predict how many words they will remember.

Predictions without Experience. Estimating our performance without having a chance to see what we are up against is hard. For example, guessing how well we will do on the first exam in a course is tough if we do not know anything about the exam style of the instructor. How well we think we will do depends on lots of test-related variables: item difficulty, fact versus concept questions, and the like.

When older adults are put in the position of having to estimate performance without seeing the task, past research suggests that they tend to overestimate how well they will do (Bruce et al., 1982). For example, older adults typically predict that they will be able to remember more items than they actually can. Younger adults tend to be more accurate. However, more recent research suggests that this finding depends upon the level of recall (Connor, Dunlosky, & Hertzog, 1997). In other words, older adults who had low levels of recall were the ones who were more overconfident in their predictions. Unfortunately, not all older adults use monitoring strategies spontaneously (Dunlosky & Connor, 1997). However, they can be trained to do so, as we shall see in a later section.

Predictions after Experience. A much different picture of age differences emerges when participants have a chance to see the task before making a performance prediction. One way this is done is by asking people to rate their confidence that they will be able to remember each item on a list of words that will be learned. Results from several studies using this approach suggest strongly that older adults are just as accurate in predicting their recall and recognition performances as younger adults (Conner et al., 1997; Devolder, Brigham, & Pressley, 1990; Hertzog et al., 1994). The usual finding is that, regardless of age, adults overestimate performance on recall tasks but underestimate performance on recognition tasks.

Comparing Prediction Types. Based on the research we have reviewed, older adults are at a disadvantage when asked to predict performance if they are given no information about the task. But when this information is forthcoming—either from direct experience, from instructions pertaining to important things to think about, or from a request for predictions on familiar everyday tasks—older adults do as well as younger adults. However, these studies do not address a very important question: What happens if people are given multiple trials with a task and are asked to predict performance on each trial?

Hertzog, Dixon, and Hultsch (1990) found that older and younger adults adjust their predictions across trials on a list-learning task. On the first trial, performance predictions tend to be inaccurate, and predictions are influenced by scores on memory questionnaires. On subsequent trials, though, predictions are more heavily influenced by actual performance on the preceding trial. Going one step further, Bieman-Copland and Charness (1994) had younger and older adults make predictions over trials on list-learning tasks in which they were given letter, rhyme, or meaning cues. Age differences were found in the ways younger and older adults adjusted their predictions from Trial 1 to Trial 2. Whereas younger adults raised or lowered their predictions across cue types based on their previous performance, older adults based their changed predictions on global differences between their previous prediction and performance.

These results indicate that the presence or absence of age differences on the first trial of a task, determined by whether people have experience in advance of doing the task, may be due to factors different from those responsible for age differences in how people change predictions over trials. Metamemory may be more important in understanding how people formulate initial predictions; analyzing one's previous performance may be more important for subsequent predictions. The good news is that evidence suggests that in older adulthood, the ability to monitor multiple aspects of memory functioning is relatively spared (Hertzog & Hultsch, 2000; Hertzog et al., 2002).

1. What is metamemory?

2. What is the difference between memory knowledge and memory self-efficacy?

3. What age differences are found in memory monitoring when predictions are made without any experience with the task?

6.8 Memory Training

LEARNING OBJECTIVES

- What are the major ways that memory skills are trained? How effective are these methods?
- What are the key individual difference variables in memory training?

After retirement, Alison and Charlie noticed that they were having trouble remembering things more so than they used to. They were worried that given their advanced age there was nothing they could do about it. However, one night they saw an advertisement on television suggesting that we have control over our memory fitness. As fate would have it, the next day there was a flyer posted in their condominium recreation room for a memory training class to help older adults overcome memory failures. They immediately signed up.

Imagine that you have problems remembering where you left your keys. Or suppose that someone you love has gone through a comprehensive diagnostic process like that advocated in the previous section, and a memory problem was discovered. Is there anything that can be done to help people remember? In most cases, the answer is yes. Fortunately for Alison and Charlie they learned of this. Researchers have developed different types of memory training programs, many of which are effective even for persons with severe memory impairments (Camp, 1998; West, 1995). In this section we examine some of the attempts at remediating memory problems and some of the individual differences that affect the success of these programs.

Training Memory Skills

The notion that memory can be improved through acquiring skills and practicing them is very old,

dating back to prehistory (Yates, 1966). For example, the story in *The Iliad* was told for generations through the use of mnemonic strategies before it was finally written down. Books that teach readers how to improve their own memory have also been around for a very long time (Grey, 1756). Interestingly, the old how-to books taught techniques that are virtually identical with those advocated in more contemporary books such as those generated by Jerry Lucas (Green, 1999; Lorayne & Lucas, 1996).

Training people how to remember information more effectively can be aimed not only at people with identifiable disorders, but also at people whose memory performance has declined as a result of normal, age-related changes (Camp, 1998; West, 1995). As you may have realized in our earlier discussion about memory strategies, most of them share several things in common. First, they require paying attention to the incoming information. Second, they rely on already stored information to facilitate making new connections with the new material. Finally, the best strategies are those that, in the process of encoding, provide the basis for future retrieval cues. In short, the very best memory strategies are the ones that practically guarantee that the appropriate cue will be available to access the stored information when it must be retrieved (West, 1995).

Memory aids or strategies can be organized into meaningful groups. Among the most useful of these classifications is Camp and colleagues' (1993) E-I-E-I-O framework. The E-I-E-I-O framework combines two types of memory, explicit memory and implicit memory, with two types of memory aids, external aids and internal aids. Explicit memory involves the conscious and intentional recollection of information; remembering this definition on an exam is one example. Implicit memory involves effortless and unconscious recollection of information; knowing that stop signs are red octagons is usually not something that people need to exert effort to remember when they see one on the road. **External aids** *are memory aids that rely on environmental resources, such as notebooks or calendars.* **Internal aids** *are memory aids that rely on mental processes, such as imagery.* The Aha! or O!

Table 6.1		
The E-I-E-I-O Framework		
	External	**Internal**
Explicit	Appointment book Grocery list	Mental imagery Rote rehearsal
Implicit	Color-coded maps Sandpaper letters	Spaced retrieval Conditioning

experience in the framework is the one that comes with suddenly remembering something. As you can see in Table 6.1, the E-I-E-I-O framework helps organize how different types of memory can be combined with different types of memory aids to provide a broad range of intervention options to help people remember.

We can use Camp and colleagues' approach to examine research on external and internal memory aids. In addition, we will briefly review two alternatives, memory exercises and medications.

External Memory Aids. External memory aids are objects such as diaries, address books, calendars, notepads, microcomputers, and other devices commonly used to support memory in everyday situations such as taking notes during a visit to the physician (McGuire & Codding, 1998). Some external aids involve actually using some external device to store information (e.g., computers and date books), whereas others involve the use of external aids to cue action (e.g., setting a book out so you won't forget it).

In general, explicit-external interventions are the most frequently used, probably because they are easy to use and widely available (Cavanaugh, Grady, & Perlmutter, 1983). For example, virtually everyone owns an address book, and small notepads are sold in hundreds of stores. These explicit-external interventions have potential value for improving older adults' cognitive performance in real-world settings. In a simulation of juror behavior, older adults who took notes when viewing a complex trial provided more detailed and cohesive accounts of the crime (Fitzgerald, 2000). The problem of remembering one's medication schedule is

best solved with an explicit-external intervention: a pillbox that is divided into compartments corresponding to days of the week and different times of the day. Research shows that this type of pillbox is the easiest to load and results in the fewest errors (Park, Morrell, Frieske, Blackburn, & Birchmore, 1991; Park, Morrell, & Shifrin, 1999). Along these same lines, Morrow, Hier, Menard, and Leirer (1998) trained older adults with external aids such as icons representing time of day and the number of pills to take. This also helps older adults remember their medication. Memory interventions like this can help older adults maintain their independence. Nursing homes also use explicit-external interventions, such as bulletin boards with the date and weather conditions, to help residents keep in touch with current events.

Advocating the use of external aids in memory rehabilitation is becoming increasingly popular. Camp (1998) recommends external aids in working with Alzheimer's patients. For example, caregivers may label their kitchen cabinets to make it easier for the person with Alzheimer's disease to remember what is in them. Harris (1984a) suggests that for external cues to be most effective, they should (1) be given close to the time that action is required, (2) be active rather than passive, (3) be specific to the particular action, (4) be portable, (5) fit a wide range of situations, (6) store many cues for long periods, (7) be easy to use, and (8) not require a pen or pencil.

Countering this trend toward greater use of external strategies, West (1995) cautions that over-reliance on external aids can be a problem. She argues that memory is much like a muscle, which needs to be exercised in order to stay in shape, an approach we will consider a bit later.

External-implicit combinations, more widely used with children, nevertheless have applicability with older adults in some situations. For example, many nursing homes use different color schemes to designate different wings or sections of the building. Because people process the color-coded aspects of the building automatically, the implicit nature of this external cue makes it ideal for people who may otherwise have difficulty learning and remembering new information.

Internal Memory Aids. Looking at Camp and colleagues' examples of internal memory aids may trigger some personal experiences. For example, most people use rote rehearsal in preparing for an examination (repeating Camp—E-I-E-I-O over and over), or use mental imagery in remembering the location of their car in a parking lot (we're parked near the giraffe on the light post). Most research on memory training concerns improving people's use of these and other internal strategies that supply meaning and help organize incoming information (Backman & Larson, 1992; Willis, 1996). Classic examples of formal internal strategies include the method of loci (remembering items by mentally placing them in locations in a familiar environment), mental retracing (thinking about all the places you may have left your keys), turning letters into numbers, and forming acronyms out of initial letters (such as NASA from National Aeronautic and Space Administration).

Most memory improvement courses train people to become proficient at using one of these internal strategies. For example, Yesavage (1983) trained older adults to use images to help themselves remember people's names. As shown in Figure 6.4, this training was effective. Interestingly, certain personality traits may be associated with who benefits most from training. Gratzinger, Sheikh, Friedman, and Yesavage (1990) found that people who scored high on openness to experience (a dimension of personality) performed better with imagery than other people. In particular, the fantasy subfactor of the openness dimension (i.e., the tendency to engage in internal fantasizing) was related to greater improvement as a result of imagery training. It may be that people who find it easy to fantasize may be better at coming up with the imagery that help them remember people's names.

More recent research has also shown that training on internal strategies improves memory significantly. For example Dunlosky and colleagues (2003) trained older adults either to use standard strategies such as imagery or to use imagery strategies along with skills to accurately monitor and control their learning. Both groups outperformed a control group that received no training. Most important,

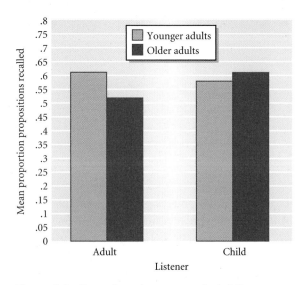

Figure 6.4 Proportion of names recalled at three points in the study. Pretest occurred in the first session before any training. Test 1 was after imagery training (in the imagery group) and after attitude training (in the control group). Test 2 was after both groups had received training in the face-name mnemonic.

Source: "Imagery Pretraining and Memory Training in the Elderly," by J. A. Yesavage, 1983, *Gerontology, 29,* 271–275. Copyright 1983 by S. Karger. Reprinted with permission.

older adults who were also trained to rely on monitoring their learning performed substantially better than those adults who were just trained on standard imagery strategies. Clearly, more research needs to be conducted to understand why adults stop using internal memory strategies that are effective in improving recall and how long they maintain the effects of training after the sessions are over.

The internal strategies we have examined so far fall into the explicit-internal category in Camp and colleagues' system. However, as noted earlier, explicit strategies require effortful processing and are more taxing on the elderly. Thus, explicit memory intervention would most likely boost memory performance for those elderly who are least likely to suffer failures or for young adults (Rybash, 1996). In fact, healthy older adults are less willing to use effortful internal strategies. In addition, older adults with dementia are unlikely to benefit from these types of strategies (Camp, 1998). Thus, Camp

© Lara Hartley

A cookbook can be an effective and helpful memory aid, no matter how often one has made black bean soup.

argues that older adults would benefit more from preserved implicit memory abilities.

One implicit-internal memory aid that has proven quite powerful is based on a technique called spaced retrieval. Camp and colleagues (Camp, 1998; Bourgeois et al., 2003) relate that even people with Alzheimer's disease can learn new things with this technique. The researchers were able to teach people with Alzheimer's disease the names of the staff who worked with them even though they had no idea of when or where they acquired this information.

Memory Drugs. Although considerable research has focused on the underlying neurological mechanisms in memory, little definitive information is available that can be easily translated into treatment approaches, though this is not for lack of trying. For example, we still are not sure which neurotransmitters are primarily involved with memory. Many attempts at enhancing memory through the use of drugs that affect neurotransmitters (e.g., acetylcholine) have been made, but so far have produced only modest, short-term improvements with no long-term changes. Much of the work aimed at improving specific types of memory also has been disappointing (Lombardi & Weingartner, 1995). This kind of research is especially important for people with Alzheimer's disease and related disorders.

Combining Strategies. Which memory strategy is best clearly depends on the situation. For example, remembering names probably demands an internal strategy, whereas remembering appointments can most easily be helped by external strategies. For optimal improvement, the best approach is to tailor specific strategies to specific situations.

This is exactly what McEvoy and Moon (1988) did. They designed a comprehensive multiple-strategy training program for improving older adults' memory in everyday situations. To remember names, older adults were taught an internal strategy emphasizing the need to associate new names with already known information. In contrast, use of external aids with information on how to review them was used for remembering appointments such as occasional physician visits. McEvoy and Moon found that after training, participants had fewer complaints about their memory for names and faces, appointments, routine tasks, and spatial orientation.

McEvoy and Moon's study points out the importance of tailoring an intervention to fit the problem. What works best for one kind of information may not help us remember another. Moreover, their work also emphasizes the need for broad-based comprehensive intervention programs. Training people to remember only one kind of information is not helpful when their daily lives are filled with far more complicated demands.

Individual Difference Variables in Memory Training

As we have seen throughout this chapter, adults are a very heterogeneous group when it comes to memory performance. Research reviewed earlier has shown that verbal ability, prior knowledge, and familiarity influence how well one performs on memory tasks. Herrmann (1993) argued that individual difference variables should be considered when designing memory training programs. Moreover, training may be more effective when changes in emotional status (Herrmann, 1993) and feelings of self-efficacy (Berry, 1999; West et al., 2003; West & Yassuda, 2004) are major goals of the program. Research finds that the benefits of memory training depend on the specific needs of the client (Bendiksen & Bendiksen, 1996; de Frias et al., 2003). For example, older adults who are highly verbal have benefited most from a training program emphasizing ways to connect incoming information with information they already know.

An approach to memory training that includes both training on specific strategies with such relevant factors as relaxation (Stigsdotter, Neely, & Backman, 1993a, 1993b, 1995) and social support (Flynn & Storandt, 1990) has typically resulted in performance gains. However, whether the gains due to the combined approach are greater than those following traditional strategy training is unclear (Stigsdotter, Neely, & Backman, 1993a, 1993b,

1995). Moreover, although providing memory strategies improves performance for adults of all ages, surprisingly little research has been done to identify how broadly the effects of training generalize across tasks and individuals.

To examine these issues, Stigsdotter, Neely, and Backman (1995) compared performance in a control group and a group given composite training involving encoding operations, attentional functions, and relaxation. The training task involved learning a list of concrete words, and generalization of the strategy was tested on tasks involving recall of objects, recall of participant-performed tasks, and recall of abstract words. People who were trained on the combined strategy still outperformed the control group 6 months after training, but only generalized their strategy to the recall-of-objects task.

Additionally, age, education level, and level of general cognitive functioning did not predict performance after training; only performance on the pretraining task predicted future performance. These findings indicate that performance gains remain several months after strategy training on a specific task, but that people tend not to use the strategy in other situations very much.

In sum, the memory training literature is emerging as an important area for addressing questions about how memory performance differs with age. Although much more work on the issues of generalization and individual differences in the effectiveness of training remains to be done, the available research demonstrates that training may need to include not only a memory technique, but also memory-related components such as self-efficacy, relaxation, and so forth. Also remaining to be answered are the questions of how to predict who will benefit from memory training and why people differ in the degree to which they benefit from training.

Concept Checks

1. What is the E-I-E-I-O framework, and how does it help organize memory training?

2. What effect does combining approaches, such as memory training with relaxation, have on performance in memory training?

6.9 Clinical Issues and Memory Testing

LEARNING OBJECTIVES

- What is the difference between normal and abnormal memory aging?
- What is the connection between memory and mental health?
- How is memory affected by nutrition and drugs?

Latarra's children are concerned. Latarra is 80 and is becoming more and more forgetful. With the scare of Alzheimer's disease so salient in our society, they are concerned that their mother is its next victim. What should they do? A friend tells them that memory decline is normal with aging. But to ease their concerns they make an appointment for a clinical screening for their mother. This could reassure them that it is only normal aging causing her forgetfulness, and not Alzheimer's disease.

To this point we have been trying to understand the changes that occur in normal memory with aging. But what about situations where people have serious memory problems that interfere with their daily lives? How do we tell the difference between normal and abnormal memory changes? These are but two of the issues that clinicians face. Latarra's children are facing this critical issue. Like Latarra's children, clinicians are often confronted with relatives of clients who complain of serious memory difficulties. Clinicians must somehow differentiate the individuals who have no real reason to be concerned from those with some sort of disease. What criteria should be used to make this distinction? What diagnostic tests would be appropriate to evaluate adults of various ages?

Unfortunately, there are no easy answers to these questions. First, as we have seen, the exact nature of normative changes in memory with aging is not yet understood completely. This means that we have few standards by which to compare people who may have problems. Second, there are few comprehensive batteries of memory tests that are specifically designed to tap a wide variety of memory functions (Mayes, 1995). Too often clinicians are left with hit-or-miss approaches and have little choice but to piece together their own assessment battery (Edelstein & Kalish, 1999).

Fortunately, the situation is changing. Since the mid-1980s researchers and clinicians have begun to work closely to devise better assessments (Mayes, 1995). This collaboration is producing results that will help address the key questions in memory assessment: Has something gone wrong with memory? Is the loss normal? What is the prognosis? What can be done to help the client compensate or recover?

In this section we consider some of the efforts being made to bridge the gap between laboratory and clinic. We begin with a brief look at the distinction between normal and abnormal memory changes. Because abnormal memory changes could be the result of a psychological or physical condition, we consider links between memory and mental health. After that, we discuss how memory is affected by nutrition and drugs.

Normal versus Abnormal Memory Aging

Many normative changes take place in memory as people grow old, such as those in working memory and secondary memory. Still, many aspects of memory functioning do not change, such as the ability to remember the gist of a story. Increasingly forgetting names or what one needs at the supermarket, though annoying, appears to be part of aging. However, some people experience far greater changes, such as forgetting where they live or their spouse's name. Where is the line dividing normative memory changes from abnormal ones?

From a functional perspective, one way to distinguish normal and abnormal changes is to ask whether the changes disrupt a person's ability to perform daily living tasks. The normative changes we have encountered in this chapter usually do not interfere with a person's ability to function in everyday life. When problems appear, however, it would be appropriate to find out what is the matter. For example, a person who repeatedly forgets to turn off the stove or forgets how to get home is clearly experiencing changes that affect personal safety and interfere with his or her daily life. Such changes should be brought to the attention of a physician or psychologist.

As indicated in Chapter 2, recent advances in neuroscience, especially the study of brain–behavior relations, has led to an explosion in our knowledge of specific diseases and brain changes that can create abnormal memory performance. For example, researchers can test for specific problems in visual and verbal memory through neuroimaging by examining glucose metabolism with PET scans and fMRIs (Prull et al., 2000). Such brain-imaging techniques also allow researchers to find tumors, strokes, and other types of damage or disease that could account for poorer-than-expected memory performance. Certain changes in brain wave patterns in the medial-temporal lobe of the brain are indicative of decrements during encoding and retrieval of verbal information (Gabrieli, Brewer, Desmond, & Glover, 1997; Tulving, Markowitsch, Kapur, Habib, & Houlse, 1994). Finally, significantly poorer-than-normal performance on neuropsychological tests of memory are also useful in establishing that the memory changes observed are indeed abnormal (Prull et al., 2000).

Some diseases, especially the dementias, are marked by massive changes in memory. For example, Alzheimer's disease involves the progressive destruction of memory beginning with recent memory and eventually including the most personal—self-identity. Wernicke-Korsakoff syndrome involves major loss of recent memory and sometimes a total inability to form new memories after a certain point in time.

The most important point to keep in mind is that telling the difference between normal and abnormal memory aging, and in turn between memory and other cognitive problems, is often very difficult (Fisher, Plassman, Heeringa, & Langa, 2008; Prull et al., 2000). There is no magic number of times someone must forget something before getting concerned. Because serious memory problems can also be due to underlying mental or physical health problems, these must be thoroughly checked out in conjunction with obtaining a complete memory assessment.

Memory and Mental Health

Several psychological disorders involve distorted thought processes, which sometimes result in serious memory problems. The two disorders that have been the main focus of research are depression (Lockwood et al., 2002; Watts, 1995) and the dementias (Brandt & Rich, 1995); but other disorders, such as amnesia following a head injury or brain disease, are also important (O'Connor, Verfaellie, & Cermak, 1995). Depression is characterized by feelings of helplessness and hopelessness (American Psychiatric Association, 1994). Dementia, such as Alzheimer's disease, involves substantial declines in cognitive performance that may be irreversible and untreatable (Mattson, 2004). Much of the research on clinical memory testing is on differentiating the changes in memory due to depression from those involved in Alzheimer's disease.

Serious depression impairs memory (Backman, Small, & Wahlin, 2000; Gotlib, Roberts, & Gilboa, 1996; Luszcz & Lane, 2008). For example, severely depressed people show a decreased ability to learn and recall new information (Lockwood et al., 2000, 2002); a tendency to leave out important information (McAllister, 1981); a decreased ability to organize (Backman & Forwell, 1994); less effective memory strategies (de Frias et al., 2003); an increased sensitivity to sad memories (Kelley, 1986); and decreased psychomotor speed (La Rue, Swan, & Carmelli, 1995).

An interesting finding emerges from the literature when age-related differences in the effects of depression on memory are considered. Two studies have found that the negative effects of depression on memory are greater in young and middle-aged adults than in older adults (Burt, Zembar, & Niederehe, 1995; Kindermann & Brown, 1997). This suggests that the effect of depression on memory may decrease gradually as we grow older, and even more so in very old age (Backman, Hassing, Forsell, & Viitanen, 1996). It may be that once normative age differences in episodic memory are eliminated statistically, few differences between depressed and nondepressed elderly remain. Thus, at this point the memory impairments that accompany severe depression appear to be equivalent across adulthood.

However, much more research needs to be done before we have a clear picture. Additionally, we need to know more about the possible effects of mild and moderate levels of depression.

Alzheimer's disease is characterized by severe and pervasive memory impairment that is progressive and irreversible (Mattson, 2004; Spaan et al., 2003). The memory decrements in Alzheimer's disease involve the entire memory system, from sensory to long-term to remote memory. The changes that occur early in Alzheimer's disease are very similar to those that occur in depression. However, because depression is treatable and Alzheimer's disease is not, clinicians must differentiate the two. This differentiation is the underlying reason for the major effort to develop sensitive and comprehensive batteries of memory tests (Rentz et al., 2004).

Memory, Nutrition, and Drugs

Researchers and clinicians often overlook nutrition as a cause of memory failures in later life (Perlmutter et al., 1987). Unfortunately, we know very little about how particular nutrient deficiencies relate to specific aspects of memory. In a recent study of widely marketed and purported memory enhancers, more solid findings were limited to studies with animals. For example, phosphatidylserine (PS) attenuated neuronal deterioration effects of aging and restored normal memory on a variety of tasks in rodents (McDaniel et al., 2002). Preliminary findings with humans are limited. In fact, studies have failed to show this relationship for older adults with probable Alzheimer's disease. However, for older adults with moderate cognitive impairment, PS did show modest increases in memory.

Likewise, many drugs have been associated with memory problems. The most widely known of these are alcohol and caffeine, which if abused over a long period are associated with severe memory loss (Ryan et al., 2002; Schinka et al., 2003). Less well known are the effects of prescription and over-the-counter medications. For example, sedatives and tranquilizers have been found to impair memory performance (Block, DeVoe, Stanley, Stanley, & Pomara, 1985).

These data indicate that it is important to consider older adults' diets and medications when assessing their memory performance. What may appear to be serious decrements in functioning may, in fact, be induced by poor nutrition or specific medications. Too often, researchers and clinicians fail to inquire about eating habits and the medications people take. Adequate assessment is essential to avoid diagnostic errors.

Concept Checks

1. From a functional perspective, how does one tell the difference between normal and abnormal memory aging?
2. How does severe depression affect memory?
3. How do alcohol and nutrients affect memory?

SOCIAL POLICY IMPLICATIONS

With the graying of America we will see more and more older adults with memory-related problems. Thus, one important implication of this demographic trend is to meet the needs of this growing issue. The number of funded outreach memory and aging centers is growing in the United States (e.g., the center partnered by Auburn University and East Alabama Medical Center, and those at the University of California and in San Francisco). Such centers attract individuals with any level of memory impairment. These outreach programs to local communities provide educational and referral opportunities along with skill development and training and resource development. The centers are important because they can bridge the gap between research, education, and patient care. Many of these centers are interdisciplinary in nature and thus have the benefit of collaborations with researchers in aging, neurologists, neuropsychologists, nurses, and pharmacists. They serve as catalysts to facilitate interactions among local networks of researchers and other more applied centers such as chapters of the Alzheimer's Disease Association to enhance education and information dissemination. Thus, the implications of memory and aging research are becoming more important in our society. With the aging of the baby boomers, the social implications of understanding the memory competencies of our newest older generation have only begun to become apparent.

Summary

6.1 Overview of Information Processing

What are the primary aspects of the information-processing model?

- The information-processing model assumes an active participant, both quantitative and qualitative aspects of performance, and processing of information through a series of systems.

What are the areas where we observe differential age changes in attention and memory?

- Sensory memory is the first level of processing incoming information from the environment. Sensory memory has a large capacity, but information only lasts there a very short time.

6.2 Attentional Control

What is processing speed? What age differences are found?

- An important issue in the literature is whether processing speed represents a general phenomenon that affects all mental processing.

- Alternatively, evidence shows that age-related slowing is specific to particular levels of processing and specific tasks.

What are the processing resources that underlie information processing??

- Some researchers claim that older adults have fewer processing resources than younger adults do. However, this conclusion is suspect because processing resources is ill defined.

What is inhibition loss? When are age differences found?

- Older adults have more difficulty filtering out or inhibiting irrelevant information than younger adults do, but this may also have a beneficial effect.

What are attentional resources? Under what conditions are age differences observed?

- Divided attention assesses attentional resources and involves doing more than one task that demands attention. Age differences in divided attention depend on the degree of task complexity and practice.

How do automatic and effortful processes differ? In what situations are age differences present?

- Automatic processing places minimal demands on attentional capacity whereas effortful processing requires all of the available attentional capacity. There are relatively no age differences in the former and pronounced age differences in the latter.

6.3 Memory Processes

What is working memory? What age differences have been found in working memory?

- Working memory refers to the processes and structures involved in holding information in mind and simultaneously using that information, sometimes in conjunction with incoming information, to solve a problem, make a decision, or learn. Information is kept active through rehearsal.

- In general, working memory capacity and rehearsal decline with age, although the extent of the decline is still in doubt. There is some evidence that age differences in working memory are not universal.

How does implicit and explicit memory differ across age?

- Implicit memory is the facilitation or change in task performance that is attributable to having been exposed to information at some earlier point in time, but which does not involve active, explicit memory.

- Older adults are generally better at implicit memory tasks than explicit memory tasks.

How does episodic and semantic memory performance differ across age?

- In episodic memory, age-related decrements are typically found on recall tests but not on recognition tests. Older adults tend not to use memory strategies spontaneously as often or as well as younger adults.

- Semantic memory concerns learning and remembering the meaning of words and concepts that are not tied to specific occurrences of events in time. Fewer age differences are found in semantic memory.

What age differences have been found in the autobiographical aspects of episodic memory?

- Some aspects of autobiographical memory remain intact for many years whereas other aspects do not. Verification of autobiographical memories is often difficult.

- Older adults have fewer flashbulb memories and their impact is restricted to particular points in the life span.

6.4 Factors Affecting Age Differences in Memory

What evidence is there for age differences in encoding?

- Age-related decrements in encoding may be due to decrements in rehearsal in working memory and being slower at making connections with incoming information. Older adults do not spontaneously organize incoming information as well as younger adults, but they can use organizational helps when told to do so. However, the benefits of this approach are short-lived.

- Although older adults tend not to use optimal encoding strategies, this does not account for poor memory performance.

What age differences have been observed in retrieval?

- Age differences are greater for tip-of-the-tongue memory failures. Age differences are greater on recall than on recognition tests. Older adults benefit more than younger adults from retrieval cues, but age differences in performance are not eliminated.

What are the relative contributions of encoding and retrieval in explaining age differences in performance? How does a neuroscience perspective help us understand these contributions?

- Changes in memory with age are due to both encoding and retrieval problems. Research involving brain-imaging studies of blood flow in the brain shows substantially less brain activity and less lateralization in older adults compared with younger adults during encoding.

How does automatic retrieval affect age differences in memory?

- Although conscious recollection shows decline with age, nonconscious, automatic retrieval of information does not reveal decline.

What age differences have been observed in processing misinformation as true?

- The ability to remember the source of a familiar event or whether the event was imagined or experienced declines with age.

- Older adults are more susceptible to false memories in that they remember items or events that did not occur under specific conditions of plausibility.

6.5 Memory for Discourse

What age differences are observed in text-based levels of memory for discourse?

- Age differences are more pronounced for text-based levels of discourse such as lower-level detailed information.

- Age differences in performance are influenced by the use of effective reading strategies, how a story is retold, and prior knowledge. Older adults are especially likely to put pieces of prior knowledge in their recall of newly learned text.

- Higher presentation speeds may put older adults at a disadvantage; age differences are reduced when self-pacing is used. Age differences in recall tend to increase as the length of reading time is increased. Age-related slowing in cognitive processing explains much of this difference.

- Age differences are usually not found for the major organizational elements of text, but performance is related to verbal ability. With well-organized text, which emphasizes the structure and main ideas, age differences are typically not found. Older adults may be more interested in learning general points than in learning the details. Prior beliefs also make it difficult to learn and remember elements of text.

What age differences are observed for situation models of discourse memory?

- Age differences are less pronounced at higher levels of text, such as the situation, which can involve emotional information, goals, and personality characteristics of main characters.

- The characteristics of the reader, such as personal biases and personal motivations, influence the situation model level of discourse.

What social factors and characteristics of individuals influence memory for discourse?

- Social context matters, and older adults' retelling of stories varies depending upon who the listener is.

6.6 Memory in Context

What age differences are there in prospective memory?

- Age differences are less likely on event-based prospective memory tasks than on time-based prospective memory tasks. How accurately prospective memory tasks are performed depends on the time of day. Processing speed may help explain these age differences.

What are some factors that help preserve memory as we grow older?

- Exercise, education, multilingualism, and use of semantic memory are all factors that can enhance memory in older adults and delay cognitive decline.

6.7 Self-Evaluations of Memory Abilities

What are the major types of memory self-evaluations?

- There are two general categories of memory self-evaluations. Metamemory refers to knowledge about how memory works and what one believes to be true about it. Memory monitoring refers to the awareness of what we are doing with our memory right now.

What age differences have been found in metamemory?

- Metamemory is typically assessed with questionnaires. Older adults seem to know less than younger adults about the workings of memory and its capacity, view memory as less stable, believe that their memory will decline with age, and feel that they have little control over these changes. However, the belief in inevitable decline does not apply equally to all aspects of memory.

- How metamemory is organized may differ across adulthood. Memory self-efficacy is the belief in how well one will perform in a specific situation and is an important construct in understanding how people make judgments about performance before they have experience with a task.

How do younger and older adults compare on memory monitoring tasks? How is task experience important?

- Older adults often overestimate how well they will do when making predictions without knowledge of or experience with the task. With task knowledge or experience, age differences are usually absent. These changes in patterns of prediction appear to be due to individuals being able to use performance on earlier trials to adjust their predictions in subsequent trials.

6.8 Memory Training

What are the major ways that memory skills are trained? How effective are these methods?

- The E-I-E-I-O framework, based on explicit-implicit aspects of memory and external-internal types of strategies, is a useful way to organize memory training.

- Older adults can learn new internal memory strategies but, like all adults, will usually abandon them over time.

- External-explicit strategies (such as lists and calendars) are common, but internal-implicit strategies are effective even with persons who have Alzheimer's disease.

- Practicing remembering things helps to improve memory. Use of memory enhancing drugs does not work over the long run. Combining types of strategies may represent the best approach.

What are the key individual difference variables in memory training?

- Memory training may be more effective when individual difference factors, such as emotional issues, are taken into account. Combining memory strategy training with relaxation training, for example, has been shown to be effective. However, older adults appear not to generalize the strategies across a range of different tasks.

6.9 Clinical Issues and Memory Testing

What is the difference between normal and abnormal memory aging?

- Whether memory changes affect daily functioning is one way to separate normal from abnormal aging. Brain-imaging techniques allow localization of problems with more precision.

- Some diseases are marked by severe memory impairments. However, in many cases, telling the difference between normal changes and those associated with disease or other abnormal events is difficult.

What is the connection between memory and mental health?

- Dementia (such as Alzheimer's disease) and severe depression both involve memory impairment. In depression, negative belief systems may underlie these memory problems. Researchers and clinicians must learn to differentiate the various types of mental health problems.

How is memory affected by nutrition and drugs?

- Drugs such as alcohol and caffeine, and some prescription and over-the-counter medications, have deleterious effects on memory.

Review Questions

6.1 Overview of Information Processing

- What is working memory? What is inhibition loss? What age differences have been found? What role do these processes play in understanding age differences in memory?
- What is episodic memory? What is semantic memory? How are they tested? What patterns of age differences have been found? What happens to the use of memory strategies with age?
- What is implicit memory? How does implicit memory differ with age?
- What is autobiographical memory and how does it differ with age?

6.2 Attentional Control

- How do processing speed and processing resources affect older adults' information processing?
- In what way do older adults have difficulty filtering out information?
- How do automatic and effortful processing contribute to age differences in information processing?
- Why are attentional resources important to our understanding of age differences in memory?

6.3 Memory Processes

- What are working memory processes and how do they differ with increasing age?
- What are the age differences in implicit and explicit memory?
- Why are there age differences in episodic but not semantic memory?
- Why do some aspects of autobiographical memory remain intact whereas others do not with increasing age?

6.4 Factors Affecting Age Differences in Memory

- What age differences have been found in encoding processes?
- What age differences have been found in retrieval processes?
- What are the relative contributions of encoding and retrieval in understanding age differences in memory?
- What is the emerging role of automatic retrieval in understanding age differences in memory?
- How do source memory and false memories change with age?

6.5 Memory for Discourse

- What age differences have been uncovered related to text-based memory?
- What age differences are evident for situational information?
- How do the patterns of age differences for discourse and list learning compare?
- What text variables are most important?

6.6 Memory in Context

- What types of prospective memory have been distinguished? What age differences are there in prospective memory?
- What are factors preventing decline in memory functioning? How do they work?

6.7 Self-Evaluations of Memory Abilities

- What major types of self-evaluations have been described?
- What age differences are there in memory knowledge and in beliefs about memory?
- What age differences have been found in making predictions about performance? What factors influence people's predictions?

6.8 Memory Training

- What is the E-I-E-I-O framework? How does it help organize memory training programs?

- How much do older adults benefit from each of the major types of memory training programs?
- What kinds of memory interventions work over time?

6.9 Clinical Issues and Memory Testing

- What criteria are used to determine the difference between normal and abnormal changes in a person's memory?
- What are the major mental health conditions that involve significant memory problems?
- What effects do nutrition and drugs have on memory?

Integrating Concepts in Development

- Based on material in Chapter 2 on cognitive neuroscience and the material in this chapter, what are the major factors involved in understanding age-related differences in memory?
- What aspects of neurological functioning would be important to consider in designing memory training programs?
- How would you design an informational brochure for older adults to maximize their ability to remember it?

Key Terms

autobiographical memory Remembering information and events from your own life.

automatic processesing Processes that are fast, reliable, and insensitive to increased cognitive demands.

cognitive reserve Factors that provide flexibility in responding and adapting to changes in the environment.

divided attention The ability to pay attention and successfully perform more than one task at a time.

effortful processing It requires all of the available attentional capacity when processing information.

encoding The process of getting information into the memory system.

episodic memory The general class of memory having to do with the conscious recollection of information from a specific event or point in time.

explicit memory The conscious and intentional recollection of information.

external aids Memory aids that rely on environmental resources.

false memory When one remembers items or events that did not occur.

implicit memory The effortless and unconscious recollection of information.

information-processing approach The study of how people take in stimuli from their environment and transform them into memories; the approach is based on a computer metaphor.

internal aids Memory aids that rely on mental processes.

long-term memory The aspects of memory involved in remembering rather extensive amounts of information over relatively long periods of time.

memory monitoring The awareness of what we are doing in memory right now.

memory self-efficacy The belief in one's ability to perform a specific memory task.

metamemory Memory about how memory works and what one believes to be true about it.

processing resources The amount of attention one has to apply to a particular situation.

prospective memory Process involving remembering to remember something in the future.

recall Process of remembering information without the help of hints or cues.

recognition Process of remembering information by selecting previously learned information from among several items.

rehearsal Process by which information is held in working memory, either by repeating items over and over or by making meaningful connections between the information in working memory and information already known.

retrieval The process of getting information back out of memory.

semantic memory Learning and remembering the meaning of words and concepts that are not tied to specific occurrences of events in time.

sensory memory The earliest step in information processing where new, incoming information is first registered.

situation model When individuals use their world knowledge to construct a more global understanding of what a text is about.

source memory The ability to remember the source of a familiar event as well as the ability to determine if an event was imagined or actually experienced.

speed of processing How quickly and efficiently the early steps in information processing are completed.

storage The manner in which information is represented and kept in memory.

strategies Various techniques that make learning or remembering easier and that increase the efficiency of storage.

working memory Refers to the processes and structures involved in holding information in mind and simultaneously using that information, sometimes in conjunction with incoming information, to solve a problem, make a decision, or learn new information.

Resources

www.cengage.com/psychology/cavanaugh
Visit the companion website, where you will find tutorial quizzes, glossary, flashcards, and more.

Readings

Blanchard-Fields, F., & Hess, T. M. (Eds.). (1996). Perspectives on cognitive changes in adulthood and aging. New York: McGraw Hill. The best basic overview of age-related cognitive changes. Easy to moderate difficulty.

Craik, F. I. M., & Salthouse, T. A. (Eds.). (2000). The handbook of aging and cognition. Hillsdale, NJ: Erlbaum. One of the best overviews of memory and cognition in one volume. Moderate to difficult reading.

Park, D. C., & Hall Gutchess, A. (2009). Cognitive aging and everyday life. In D. C. Park & N. Schwarz (Eds.), *Aging and cognition: A student primer* (pp. 217–232). Philadelphia: Psychology Press. A broad discussion of many different aspects of cognitive aging. Moderate difficulty.

7

Intelligence

The Dalai Lama is the spiritual leader of the Tibetan people, was the recipient of the 1989 Nobel Peace Prize, and is recognized as a leader in Buddhist philosophy, human rights, and global environmental problems. He has reached this stature as a simple Buddhist monk, in which he claims he is "no more, no less." To the world, the Dalai Lama is recognized for his wisdom. A sample of this wisdom is in his plea for "a new way of thinking . . . for responsible living and acting. If we maintain obsolete values and beliefs, a fragmented consciousness and a self-centered spirit, we will continue to hold to outdated goals and behaviors. Such an attitude by a large number of people would block the entire transition to an interdependent yet peaceful and cooperative global society." He also states that as a Buddhist monk, he tries to develop compassion within, not simply as religious practice, but at a human level. To facilitate this he "sometimes finds it helpful to imagine himself standing as a single individual on one side, facing a huge gathering of all other human beings on the other side. Then he asks himself, 'Whose interests are more important?' To him it is quite clear that however important he feels he is, he is just one individual while others are infinite in number and importance."

The Dalai Lama drives home the point that wisdom has long been associated with age. Surprisingly, psychologists have only recently become interested in wisdom, perhaps because they have been busy studying a related topic—intelligence. Another reason for not researching wisdom was the widespread belief that it would be a waste of time. At one time researchers and theorists were convinced that all intellectual abilities inevitably declined as people aged, because of biological deterioration. For instance, Wechsler (1958) wrote that "nearly all studies have shown that most human abilities decline progressively after reaching a peak somewhere between ages 18 and 25" (p. 135).

In the decades since Wechsler stated this pessimistic view, many things have changed. Researchers have discovered that intellectual development is an extremely complex process. We cannot give a simple yes or no answer to the question "Does intelligence decline with age?" And we continue to move farther away, rather than closer to, a simple answer. Controversy is now quite common. The controversy was accelerated in the 1970s. Considering methodological comparisons between cross-sectional and longitudinal studies, Baltes and Schaie (1974) concluded that "general intellectual decline is largely a myth" (p. 35). Botwinick (1977) countered that "decline in intellectual ability is clearly a part of the aging picture" (p. 580).

Who is right? Where do we stand now? Does intelligence decline, or is that a myth? Does wisdom come with age? Answering these questions will be our goal in this chapter. Such widely divergent conclusions about age-related changes in intelligence reflect different sets of assumptions about the nature of intelligence, which are then translated into different theoretical and methodological approaches. We will examine three avenues of research on intelligence and age: the psychometric approach, the life-span approach, and the cognitive-structural approaches. Along the way we look at some attempts to modify intellectual abilities through training programs. But first we need to consider what intelligence is.

7.1 Defining Intelligence

LEARNING OBJECTIVES

- How do people define intelligence in everyday life?
- What are the major components of the life-span approach?
- What are the major research approaches for studying intelligence?

After Toni graduated from high school she decided to start her own pet-sitting business. She started small, but ultimately cornered the market in her city. She lives a comfortable and wealthy lifestyle. After high school Stacey went to college and majored in math. She pursued her doctorate and now lives a comfortable and modest lifestyle as a university professor. In comparing Toni and Stacey on intellectual ability, who would come out on top?

In terms of intelligence, the distinction between Toni and Stacey's success points to an important question to ask: What do we mean by intelligence? Is it being able to learn new things very quickly? Is it knowing a great deal of information? Is it the ability to adapt to new situations or to create new things or ideas? Or is it the ability to make the most of what we have and to enjoy life? Intelligence is all these abilities and more, as we can see in the different pathways Toni and Stacey took. It is all in the sense that people who stand out on these dimensions are often considered smart, or intelligent. It is more than just these abilities because intelligence also involves the qualitative aspects of thinking style, or how one approaches and conceptualizes problems.

Intelligence in Everyday Life

Some intriguing work by Sternberg and his colleagues points out that intelligence involves more than just a particular fixed set of characteristics (Berg & Sternberg, 1992; Sternberg et al., 1981). They compiled a list of behaviors that laypeople at a train station, supermarket, or college library reported to be distinctly characteristic of exceptionally intelligent, academically intelligent, everyday intelligent, or unintelligent people. This list of behaviors was then given to experts in the field of intelligence and to a new set of laypeople, who were asked to rate either how distinctively characteristic each behavior was of an ideally intelligent, academically intelligent, or everyday intelligent individual or how important each behavior was in defining these types of intelligent individuals. Ratings were analyzed separately for the experts and the laypeople.

Sternberg and his colleagues found extremely high agreement between experts and laypeople on ratings of the importance of particular behaviors in defining intelligence. The two groups agreed that intelligence consisted of three major clusters of related abilities: problem-solving ability, verbal ability, and social competence. Problem-solving ability consists of behaviors such as reasoning logically, identifying connections among ideas, seeing all aspects of a problem, and making good decisions. Verbal ability includes such things as speaking articulately, reading with high comprehension, and having a good vocabulary. Social competence includes behaviors such as accepting others for what they are, admitting mistakes, displaying

Vocabulary ability, essential in solving crossword puzzles, is one example of an intellectual ability that shows improvement or stability across adulthood.

interest in the world at large, and being on time for appointments.

Berg and Sternberg (1992) also wanted to know how these conceptions of intelligence differed across the adult life span. To find out, people aged 22 to 85 were asked to rate 55 behaviors that they viewed as characteristic of exceptionally intelligent 30-, 50-, or 70-year-olds. Behaviors such as motivation, intellectual effort, and reading were said to be important indicators of intelligence for people of all ages. But other behaviors were specific to particular points in the life span. For example, for a 30-year-old planning for the future and being open-minded were listed most often. The intelligent 50- and 70-year-olds were described as acting responsibly, adjusting to life situations, being verbally fluent, and displaying wisdom.

The Big Picture: A Life-Span View

One thing is clear about the ways people view intelligence—everyone considers it a complex construct. In the big picture, then, intelligence consists of many different types of skills. *Theories of intelligence, therefore, are* **multidimensional;** *that is, they specify many domains of intellectual abilities.* Although people disagree on the number of dimensions, they do agree that no single generic type of intelligence is responsible for all the different kinds of mental activities we perform.

Baltes and colleagues (Baltes, 1993; Baltes et al., 1999) take a broad view of intellectual development. The life-span concepts discussed in Chapter 1 including multidirectionality, plasticity, and interindividual variability play an important role in this conceptualization of intellectual change. Overall, this perspective asserts that some intellectual decline may be seen with age but that stability and growth in mental functioning also can be seen across adulthood. It emphasizes the role of intelligence in human adaptation and daily activity.

The first concept, **multidirectionality,** *refers to the distinct patterns of change in abilities over the life span, with these patterns differing for different abilities.* For example, developmental functions for specific abilities differ, meaning that the directional change in intelligence depends on the skills in question. As you will see later on, everyday knowledge accumulates over time and thus increases with age. However, basic cognitive mechanisms show more declines, especially into older age.

The term **plasticity** *refers to the range of functioning within an individual and the conditions under which a person's abilities can be modified within a specific age range.* Plasticity implies that what may appear to be declines in some skills may in part represent a lack of practice in using them. Current studies examining brain plasticity and behavior find that experience alters the brain across the life span (see Chapter 2). For example, Patty Reuter-Lorenz (2002; Reuter-Lorenz & Mikels, 2006) found that older and young adults show different activation patterns in the brain when they perform cognitive tasks. Furthermore, older adults seem to activate areas in the brain that compensate for decline in their performance, resulting in optimal performance. In other words, older adults may activate new areas in the brain to compensate for decline in other areas. Finally, the research on training cognitive abilities described later in this chapter also supports this view in that older adults who show decline in cognitive functioning can be trained to perform at a higher level.

The last concept, **interindividual variability,** *acknowledges that adults differ in the direction of their intellectual development* (MacDonald, Hultsch, & Dixon, 2003; Schaie, 2008). Schaie's sequential research indicates that within a given cohort or generation some people show longitudinal decline in specific abilities, whereas some people show stability of functioning in those same abilities. Finally, others show increments in performance in those same abilities (Schaie, 2008). Consequently, a curve representing typical or average changes with age may not really represent how the various individuals in a group function.

Using these four concepts of multidimensionality, plasticity, multidirectionality, and interindividual variability, Baltes and his colleagues proposed the dual-component model of intellectual functioning. Two interrelated types of developmental processes are postulated. The first component,

termed the mechanics of intelligence, concerns the neurophysiological architecture of the mind (Baltes et al., 1999; Li et al., 2004). Cognitive abilities include basic forms of thinking associated with information processing and problem solving such as reasoning, spatial orientation, or perceptual speed. Intellectual change in this first component is greatest during childhood and adolescence, as we acquire the requisite skills to handle complex cognitive tasks, such as those encountered in school. The second component, pragmatic intelligence, concerns acquired bodies of knowledge available from and embedded within culture. In other words, it includes everyday cognitive performance and human adaptation. Such abilities include verbal knowledge, wisdom, and practical problem solving. Pragmatic intellectual growth dominates adulthood.

These different trajectories of development are illustrated in Figure 7.1. As the figure suggests, different weightings of the forces of intelligence lead to specific predictions regarding the developmental pathway they take across the adult life span. If biological-genetic forces are considered to govern the mechanics more, a downward trajectory appears with age. However, if the pragmatics of intelligence is considered to be governed more by environmental-cultural factors, an upward trajectory is maintained across the adult life span.

This broad view of intellectual development in adulthood provides the background for asking more specific questions about particular aspects of intelligence. As we will see, three primary research approaches have emerged.

Research Approaches to Intelligence

Sternberg's work points out that many different skills are involved in intelligence, depending on one's point of view. Interestingly, the behaviors listed by Sternberg's participants fit nicely with the more formal attempts at defining intelligence that we will encounter in this chapter. Researchers have studied these skills from many different perspectives, depending on their theoretical orientation. For example, some investigators approach these skills from a factor analysis approach and study them as

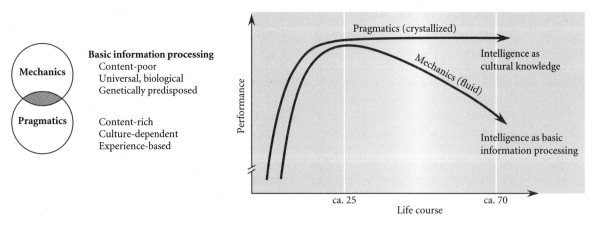

Figure 7.1 Life-span conceptualization of fluid mechanics and crystallized pragmatics of intelligence.

Source: Reprinted with permission from Baltes, P. B., Staudinger, U. M., & Lindenberger, U. (1999). Lifespan psychology: Theory and application to intellectual functioning. *Annual Review of Psychology* 50, 487. Copyright © 1999 by Annual Reviews. www.annualreviews.org

separate pieces that can be added together to form intelligence. Others take a more holistic view and think of intelligence as a way or mode of thinking. These various theoretical orientations result in very different means of studying intelligence.

Some investigators, such as Schaie and Horn, have concentrated on measuring intelligence as performance on standardized tests; this view represents the **psychometric approach.** For example, the problem-solving and verbal abilities in Sternberg and co-workers' study would be assessed by tests specifically designed to assess these skills. These tests focus on getting correct answers and tend to give less emphasis on the thought processes used to arrive at them. Other researchers, such as Salthouse and Craik, focus on information-processing mechanisms reviewed in Chapter 6. This approach aims at a detailed analysis of aging-associated changes in components of cognitive mechanisms and their interactions. Finally, a number of researchers have focused their efforts on reconceptualizing the meaning and measurement of intelligence by taking a cognitive-structural approach. *In the* **cognitive-structural approach** *researchers have been more concerned with the ways in which people conceptualize and solve problems than with scores on tests.* Such approaches to intelligence emphasize developmental changes in the modes and

styles of thinking. These include a search for post-formal operations (e.g., Labouvie-Vief, 1992; Sinnott, 1996), the assessment of wisdom (e.g., Baltes et al., 1995; Baltes & Kunzmann, 2003; Mickler & Staudinger, 2008), and studies of practical intelligence (e.g., Allaire & Marsiske, 2002; Bosworth & Ayotte, 2009; Marsiske & Willis, 1995). The age differences Sternberg found in which abilities their respondents believed were important correspond to the qualitative changes discussed by these theorists.

In this chapter, we will consider these theories and the research they stimulated. We will discover that each approach has its merits and that whether age-related changes in intelligence are found depends on how intelligence is defined and measured. But before you continue, complete the exercise in the Discovering Development feature. The information you uncover will be useful as you read the rest of the chapter.

Concept Checks

1. What three clusters of ability did Sternberg and colleagues identify in their study of people's everyday conceptualizations of intelligence?

2. What are the four major aspects of intelligence emphasized by the life-span approach?

3. What are the three major approaches for researching intelligence?

How Do People Show Intelligence?

Earlier in this section, we encountered Sternberg and colleagues' research on people's implicit theories of intelligence. However, that study only examined broad categories of behavior that could be considered intelligent. Moreover, it was not conducted in such a way as to permit comparisons with research-based approaches to intelligence.

You and your classmates could address these shortcomings in the following way. Ask adults of different ages what they think constitutes intelligent behavior, much the same as Sternberg and colleagues did. However, be careful to make sure people are specific about the abilities they nominate. In addition, ask them about what makes adults' thinking different from adolescents' thinking and

whether they believe there might be different stages of adults' thinking. Again, try to get your respondents to be as specific as possible.

Collate all the data from the class. Look for common themes in specific abilities, as well as in the qualitative aspects of thinking. As you read the rest of the chapter, see to what extent your data parallels that from more formal investigations.

7.2 Developmental Trends in Psychometric Intelligence

LEARNING OBJECTIVES

- What are primary mental abilities? How do they change across adulthood?
- What are secondary mental abilities? What are the developmental trends for fluid and crystallized intelligence?
- What are the primary moderators of intellectual change?
- How successful are attempts at training primary mental abilities?

Linda and Jerry have recently retired. They are delighted with the prospect of engaging in activities they did not have time for in the past because of work and child-rearing responsibilities. They have both enrolled in courses at the local community college, to pursue their mutual interests in English literature. After the first day of class, they both revealed that they were worried about being able to keep up with the younger students and wondered if they were smart enough. They both shrugged their shoulders and realized they would find out soon enough.

Many older adults like Linda and Jerry who are returning to a learning environment worry that they may not be "smart enough" to keep up with 18- or 19-year-olds. Are these fears realistic? Extensive evidence taking a psychometric approach describes how intellectual performance changes through the latter half of the life span.

One way to psychometrically measure intelligence is to focus on individuals' performances on various tests of intellectual abilities and on how these performances are interrelated. This approach to intelligence has a long history; the ancient Chinese and Greeks used this method to select people for certain jobs, such as master horseman (Doyle, 1974; DuBois, 1968). It also served as the basis for Binet's (1903) pioneering work in developing standardized intelligence tests, as well as many modern theories of intelligence.

Because of this long history of research in psychometric intelligence, we probably know more about this area than any other area in cognitive aging except for episodic memory. Yet this still has provided no sense of closure as to how intelligence changes with age. There is substantial agreement on descriptions of change in different intellectual abilities (as we will discuss later) and agreement on the methodological issues that need to be addressed when studying intellectual change. However, there is little convergence on the proper interpretation of the data. For example, what does it mean that changes in intellectual abilities are related to increasing age? Remember in Chapter 1 we noted that age does not cause change. That age is related to intellectual abilities is not the same thing as "aging" per se. As we shall see, age-graded intellectual change is also related to important variables such as health, activity level, and educational achievements. It is in these areas that much of the controversy is still brewing.

The Measurement of Intelligence

Because the psychometric approach focuses on the interrelationships among intellectual abilities, the major goal is to describe the ways in which these relationships are organized (Sternberg, 1985). This organization of interrelated intellectual abilities is termed the structure of intelligence. The most common way to describe the structure of intelligence is to picture it as a hierarchy (Cunningham, 1987).

Each higher level of this hierarchy represents an attempt to organize components of the level below in a smaller number of groups. The lowest level consists of individual test questions—the specific items that people answer on an intelligence test. These items can be organized into tests at the second level. *The third level,* **primary mental abilities,** *reflects interrelationships among performances on intelligence tests.* The interrelationships uncovered among the primary mental abilities produce the secondary mental abilities at the fourth level. Third-order mental abilities in turn represent interrelationships among the secondary mental abilities. Finally, general intelligence at the top refers to the interrelationships among the third-order abilities.

Keep in mind that each time we move up the hierarchy we are moving away from people's actual performance. Each level above the first represents a theoretical description of how things fit together. Thus there are no tests of primary abilities per se; primary abilities represent theoretical relationships among tests, which in turn represent theoretical relationships among actual performance.

So exactly how do researchers construct this theoretical hierarchy? The structure of intelligence is uncovered through sophisticated statistical detective work using factor analysis. First, researchers obtain people's performances on many types of problems. Second, the results are examined to determine whether performance on one type of problem, such as filling in missing letters in a word, predicts performance on another type of problem, such as unscrambling letters to form a word. *If the performance on one test is highly related to the performance on another, the abilities measured by the two tests are interrelated and are called a* **factor.**

Most psychometric theorists believe that intelligence consists of several factors. However, we should note that although factor analysis is a sophisticated statistical technique, it is not an exact technique. Thus estimates of the exact number of factors vary from a few to over 100. Most researchers and theorists believe the number to be relatively small. We will examine two types of factors: primary and secondary mental abilities.

Primary Mental Abilities. Early in the 20th century researchers discovered the existence of several independent intellectual abilities, each indicated by different combinations of intelligence tests (Thurstone, 1938). The abilities identified in this way led to the proposition that intelligence is composed of several independent abilities, labeled primary mental abilities. Thurstone initially examined seven primary mental abilities: number, word fluency, verbal meaning, associative memory, reasoning, spatial orientation, and perceptual speed. Over the years this list has been refined and expanded, resulting in a current list of 25 primary mental abilities that have been documented across many studies (Ekstrom et al., 1979). Because it is difficult to measure all 25 primary abilities in the same study, researchers following in Thurstone's tradition concentrate on measuring only a subset. Typically, this subset originally consisted of the following five primary mental abilities:

- *Numerical facility,* or the basic skills underlying one's mathematical reasoning
- *Word fluency,* or how easily one can produce verbal descriptions of things
- *Verbal meaning,* or one's vocabulary ability
- *Inductive reasoning,* or one's ability to extrapolate from particular facts to general concepts
- *Spatial orientation,* or one's ability to reason in the three-dimensional world in which we live

Two other important information-processing abilities, perceptual speed and verbal memory, were incorporated into the battery of measures in subsequent work (Schaie, 1994, 1996):

- *Perceptual speed* is one's ability to rapidly and accurately find visual details and make comparisons.
- *Verbal memory* refers to the ability to store and recall meaningful language units. Note that tests for this ability typically include word fluency. In these analyses, word fluency is eliminated as a separate ability.

Next we consider how these abilities fare with age.

Age-Related Changes in Primary Abilities

One of the most important research projects on adult intellectual development is the longitudinal study being conducted by K. Warner Schaie and his colleagues in Seattle, Washington, which began in 1956 as Schaie's dissertation (Schaie, 1996, 2005). This study has not only uncovered most of what we know about how primary mental abilities change across adulthood, but it also has been the basis for creating new research methodologies such as the sequential designs discussed in Chapter 1. Over the course of the study, more than 5,000 people have been tested over eight testing cycles (1956, 1963, 1970, 1977, 1984, 1991, 1998, 2005). All the participants were recruited through a very large health maintenance organization in Seattle that is representative of the upper 75% of the socioeconomic spectrum. Like most longitudinal studies, though, Schaie's project has encountered selectivity effects; that is, people who return over the years for retesting tend to do better than those who fail to return. However, an

Cognitive abilities are assessed across the life span using standardized tests.

advantage of Schaie's sequential design is that by bringing in new groups of participants, he has been able to estimate the importance of selection effects, a major improvement over previous research.

Schaie (1996, 2005) proposes a hierarchical relationship in intellectual abilities. Information-processing abilities such as perceptual speed and verbal memory are considered the most basic and are tied to neuropsychological functioning (Li et al., 2004; Salthouse, 1991). Mental abilities such as reasoning and numbering are products of acquired information. Finally, all mental abilities underlie all meaningful activities of a person's daily life (Schaie & Willis, 1998; Willis, 1996a). Thus the developmental trends uncovered in the Seattle Longitudinal Study provide important insights into the course of intellectual changes that ultimately affect people's work and daily living routines.

Schaie (2005) summarizes the findings as follows. Analysis of the data collected through the sixth time of measurement shows that people tend to improve on the primary abilities tested until their late 30s or early 40s. Scores then tend to stabilize until people reach their mid-50s or early 60s. But by their late 60s, people tend to show consistent declines in each testing. Although some people begin to show declines in their mid-50s, these decrements tend to be small until the mid-70s. Considering the modest improvements that most people make between young adulthood and middle age, scores are significantly lower than they were in young adulthood (roughly age 25) only by the mid-70s. These changes are depicted in Figure 7.2.

Do the general trends observed reflect global or specific changes in intelligence? That is, to what extent do people decline on all the primary abilities tested or only some of them? As you can see in Figure 7.3, even though by age 60 nearly everyone shows decline on one ability, very few people show decline on four or five abilities (Schaie, 1996). Even by age 88, only an extremely small number of people had declined significantly on all five abilities.

What happens when we consider both pragmatic types of abilities and mechanic types of abilities related to Baltes's two-component theory of intelligence? Abilities that are typical of mechanics such as reasoning, verbal memory, spatial orientation, and perceptual speed typically show a pattern of decline during adulthood, with some acceleration in very old age. These abilities show a steady pattern of decline. However, more pragmatic abilities, such as verbal meaning or ability and numerical ability, tend to remain stable or even increase up to the 60s and 70s. There are little or no age decrements before the age of 74. They start to show decline only in very old age. It appears that most of the loss occurs in highly challenging, complex, and stressful situations that require activating cognitive reserves (Baltes et al., 2006).

These patterns may reflect a strategy of optimization of cognitive functioning in late life by selectively maintaining some abilities and not others (Baltes et al., 2006). Even so, the evidence is clear that significant decrements in both types of intellectual abilities occur by the time people are in their 80s. In addition, although the distinction between pragmatic and mechanic types of abilities still exists into very old age (over 80), they both show precipitous decline, just at different levels of functioning (Ghisletta & Lindenberger, 2003; Lindenberger & Baltes, 1997; Lindenberger & Reischies, 1999).

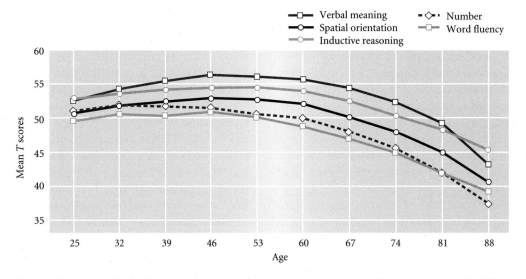

Figure 7.2 Longitudinal estimates of age changes on observed measures of five primary mental abilities.

Source: Schaie, K. W. (1994). The course of adult intellectual development. *American Psychologist* 49, 304–313. Copyright © 1994 Reprinted with permission from the American Psychological Association.

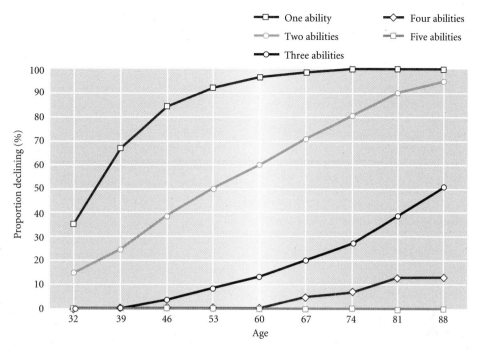

Figure 7.3 Cumulative proportion by age of individuals who show significant decline on one or more primary mental abilities.

Source: Schaie, K. W. (1989). The hazards of cognitive aging. *The Gerontologist 29*, 490. Reprinted with permission.

Secondary Mental Abilities

Because so many primary mental abilities have been identified, some researchers think it may be easier to understand intellectual development by looking at interrelationships among them. *Careful consideration of the relationships among the primary mental abilities has resulted in the identification of* **secondary mental abilities,** *which are broad-ranging skills, each composed of several primary abilities* (Horn, 1982; Horn & Hofer, 1992). At present, at least six secondary abilities have been found. Each of these is described in Table 7.1. Most of the developmental research and discussion of these abilities has been focused on two: fluid intelligence and crystallized intelligence.

Fluid and Crystallized Intelligence. Crystallized and fluid intelligence include many of the basic abilities that we associate with intelligence, such as verbal comprehension, reasoning, integration, and concept formation (Horn, 1982; Horn & Hofer, 1992). Interestingly, they are associated with age differently, are influenced by different underlying variables, and are measured in different ways.

Fluid intelligence *consists of the abilities that make you a flexible and adaptive thinker, that allow you to draw inferences, and that enable you to understand the relations among concepts independent of acquired knowledge and experience.* It reflects the abilities you need to understand and respond to any situation, but especially new ones: inductive reasoning, integration, abstract thinking, and the like (Horn, 1982). Here is an example of a question that taps fluid abilities: "What letter comes next in the series *d f i m r x e* ——?"[1]

Other typical ways of testing fluid intelligence include mazes, puzzles, and relations among shapes.

---

[1] The next letter is *m*. The rule is to increase the difference between adjacent letters in the series by one each time. Thus, *f* is two letters away from *d*, *i* is three letters away from *f*, and so on.

Table 7.1

Descriptions of Major Second-Order Mental Abilities

Crystallized intelligence (Gc)

This form of intelligence is indicated by a very large number of performances indicating breadth of knowledge and experience, sophistication, comprehension of communications, judgment, understanding of conventions, and reasonable thinking. The factor that provides evidence of Gc is defined by primary abilities such as verbal comprehension, concept formation, logical reasoning, and general reasoning. Tests used to measure the ability include vocabulary (What is a word near in meaning to *temerity*?), esoteric analogies (Socrates is to Aristotle as Sophocles is to _____?), remote associations (What word is associated with *bathtub, prizefighting,* and *wedding*?), and judgment (Determine why a foreman is not getting the best results from workers). As measured, the factor is a fallible representation of the extent to which a person has incorporated, through the systematic influences of acculturation, the knowledge and sophistication that constitutes the intelligence of a culture.

Fluid intelligence (Gf)

The broad set of abilities of this intelligence includes those of seeing relationships between stimulus patterns, drawing inferences from relationships, and comprehending implications. The primary abilities that best represent the factor, as identified in completed research, include induction, figural flexibility, integration, and, cooperatively with Gc, logical reasoning and general reasoning. Tasks that measure the factor include letter series (What letter comes next in the series *d f i m r x e*?), matrices (Discern the relationships between elements of 3-by-3 matrices), and topology (From among a set of figures in which circles, squares, and triangles overlap in different ways, select a figure that will enable one to put a dot within a circle and a square but outside a triangle). The factor is a fallible representation of such fundamental features of mature human intelligence as reasoning, abstracting, and problem solving. In Gf these features are not imparted through the systematic influences of acculturation but instead are obtained through learning that is unique to an individual or is in other ways not organized by the culture.

Visual organization (Gv)

This dimension is indicated by primary mental abilities such as visualization, spatial orientation, speed of closure, and flexibility of closure, measured by tests such as gestalt closure (Identify a figure in which parts have been omitted), form board (Show how cutout parts fit together to depict a particular figure), and embedded figures (Find a geometric figure within a set of intersecting lines). To distinguish this factor from Gf, it is important that relationships between visual patterns be clearly manifest so performances reflect primarily fluency in perception of these patterns, not reasoning in inferring the process.

Auditory organization (Ga)

This factor has been identified on the basis of several studies in which primary mental abilities of temporal tracking, auditory cognition of relations, and speech perception under distraction of distortion were first defined among other primary abilities and then found to indicate a broad dimension at the second order. Tasks that measure Ga include repeated tones (Identify the first occurrence of a tone when it occurs several times), tonal series (Indicate which tone comes next in an orderly series of tones), and cafeteria noise (Identify a word amid a din of surrounding noise). Like Gv, this ability is best indicated when the relationships among stimuli are not such that one needs to reason for understanding but instead are such that one can fluently perceive patterns among the stimuli.

Short-term acquisition and retrieval

This ability comprises processes of becoming aware and processes of retaining information long enough to do something with it. Almost all tasks that involve short-term memory have variance in this factor. Span memory, associative memory, and meaningful memory are primary abilities that define the factor, but measures of primary and secondary memory can also be used to indicate the dimension.

Long-term storage and retrieval

Formerly this dimension was regarded as a broad factor among fluency tasks, such as those of the primary abilities called associational fluency, expressional fluency, and object flexibility. In recent work, however, these performances have been found to align with others indicating facility in storing information and retrieving information that was acquired in the distant past. It seems, therefore, that the dimension mainly represents processes for forming encoding associations for long-term storage and using these associations, or forming new ones, at the time of retrieval. These associations are not so much correct as they are possible and useful; to associate *teakettle* with *mother* is not to arrive at a truth so much as it is to regard both concepts as sharing common attributes (e.g., warmth).

Source: Horn, J. L. (1982). The aging of human abilities. In B. B. Wolman (Ed.), *Handbook of Developmental Psychology* (pp. 847–870). Englewood Cliffs, NJ: Prentice Hall. Reprinted with permission.

Such tests are usually timed, and higher scores are associated with faster solutions.

Crystallized intelligence *is the knowledge that you have acquired through life experience and education in a particular culture.* Crystallized intelligence includes your breadth of knowledge, comprehension of communication, judgment, and sophistication with information (Horn, 1982). Your ability to remember historical facts, definitions of words, knowledge of literature, and sports trivia information are some examples. Many popular television game shows (such as "Jeopardy" and "Wheel of Fortune") are based on tests of contestants' crystallized intelligence. However, even though crystallized intelligence involves cultural knowledge, it is based partly on the quality of a person's underlying fluid intelligence (Horn, 1982; Horn & Hofer, 1992). For example, the breadth of your vocabulary depends

to some extent on how quickly you can make connections between new words you read and information already known, which is a component of fluid intelligence.

Any standardized intelligence test taps abilities underlying both fluid and crystallized intelligence. No single test of either ability exists, because each represents a cluster of underlying primary abilities. As a general rule, tests that minimize the role of acquired, cultural knowledge involve mainly fluid intelligence; those that maximize the role of such knowledge involve mainly crystallized intelligence.

Developmentally, fluid and crystallized intelligence follow two very different paths, similar to the individual primary abilities characterized by the pragmatics and mechanics of intelligence. This pattern is depicted in Figure 7.4. Notice that fluid intelligence declines significantly throughout adulthood,

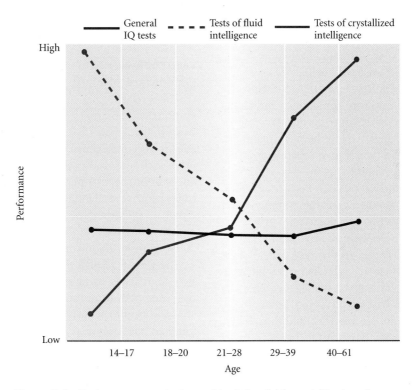

Figure 7.4 Performances on tests used to define fluid, crystallized, and general intelligence, as a function of age.

Source: Horn, J. L. (1970). Organization of data on life-span development of human abilities. In L. R. Goulet & P. B. Baltes (Eds.), *Life-span Development Psychology: Research and Theory* (p. 463). Copyright © 1970 by Academic Press, reproduced by permission of the publisher.

whereas crystallized intelligence improves. Although we do not fully understand why fluid intelligence declines, it may be related to underlying changes in the brain from the accumulated effects of disease, injury, and aging or from lack of practice (Horn & Hofer, 1992). In contrast, the increase in crystallized intelligence (at least until late life) indicates that people continue adding knowledge every day.

What do these different developmental trends imply? First, they indicate that although learning continues across adulthood, it becomes more difficult the older one gets. Consider what happens when Michele, age 17, and Marion, age 70, try to learn a second language. Although Marion's verbal skills in her native language (a component of crystallized intelligence) are probably better than Michele's verbal skills, Michele's probable superiority in the fluid abilities necessary to learn another language will usually make it easier for her to do so.

Second, these developmental trends point out once again that intellectual development varies a great deal from one set of skills to another. Beyond the differences in overall trends, individual differences in fluid and crystallized intelligence also exist. Whereas individual differences in fluid intelligence remain relatively uniform over time, individual differences in crystallized intelligence increase or remain stable with age, largely because maintaining one's crystallized intelligence depends on being in situations that require one to use it (Finkel et al., 2003; Horn & Hofer, 1992). For example, few adults get much practice in solving complex letter series tasks such as the one described earlier. But because people can improve their vocabulary skills by reading, and because people vary considerably in how much they read, differences are likely to emerge. In short, crystallized intelligence provides a rich knowledge base to draw on when material is somewhat familiar, whereas fluid intelligence provides the power to deal with learning in novel situations.

Moderators of Intellectual Change

Based on the research we have considered thus far, two different developmental trends emerge: We see gains in experience-based processes but losses in information-processing abilities. The continued growth in some areas is viewed as a product of lifelong learning. The losses are viewed as an inevitable result of the decline of physiological processes with age.

A number of researchers, though, emphasize individual differences in the rate of change in intellectual aging (Arbuckle et al., 1998; Baltes et al., 2006; MacDonald et al., 2004; Schaie, 1996; Wilson et al., 2002). These researchers do not deny that some adults show intellectual decline. Based on large individual differences in intellectual performance over time, they simply suggest that these decrements may not happen to everyone to the same extent. They argue that many reasons besides age explain performance differences. In this section, we will explore some of the social and physiological factors that have been proposed as modifiers of intellectual development. These include cohort differences, educational level, social variables, personality, health and lifestyle, and relevancy and appropriateness of tasks.

Cohort Differences. Do the differences in intellectual performance obtained in some situations reflect true age-related change or mainly cohort, or generational, differences? This question gets right to the heart of the debate over interpreting developmental research on intelligence. On the one hand, dozens of cross-sectional studies document significant differences in intellectual performance with age. On the other hand, several longitudinal investigations show either no decrement or even an increase in performance (Hertzog, Dixon et al., 2003; Schaie, 2005, 2008; Zelinski, Kennison, Watts, & Lewis, 2009).

The way to resolve the discrepancy between the two approaches involves comparing data collected over long periods of time from several samples and analyzed simultaneously in both cross-sectional and longitudinal designs as we discussed in Chapter 1. When this has been done, the results indicate that part of the apparent decline with age in performance on intelligence tests is due to generational differences rather than age differences (Schaie, 1996, 2005).

Marked generational changes in levels of performance on tests of primary abilities have been

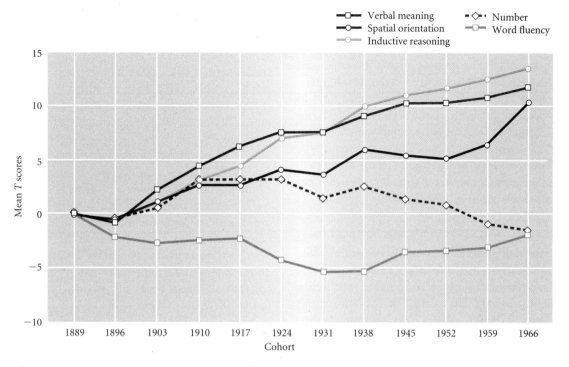

Figure 7.5 Cohort gradients showing cumulative cohort differences on five primary mental abilities for cohorts born from 1889 to 1966.

Source: Schaie, K. W. (1994). The course of adult intellectual development. American Psychologist, 49, 304–313. Copyright (c) 1994, American Psychological Society. Reprinted with Permission.

noted in the Seattle Longitudinal Study (Schaie, 1996, 2005). As you can see in Figure 7.5, more recent cohorts generally score better than earlier cohorts on verbal meaning, spatial orientation, and inductive reasoning. These trends reflect better educational opportunities (e.g., in the past, compulsory education varied widely by state, in contrast to today), better lifestyles, better nutrition, and improved health care. Note that cohort differences on number ability show gradual declines over the middle 20th century and that word fluency is gradually increasing after showing declines earlier in the 20th century.

The complex pattern of cohort differences indicates that interpreting data from cross-sectional studies is difficult. Recall from Chapter 1 that cross-sectional studies confound age and cohort; because there are both age- and cohort-related changes in intellectual abilities, drawing any meaningful conclusions is nearly impossible. Schaie (1996, 2005) argues that the trends indicate a leveling off of cohort differences, which may come to a halt in the early part of the 21st century. This conclusion is supported by a study of 531 adult parent–offspring pairs that indicated that generational (cohort) improvements were becoming smaller for more recently born pairs (Schaie et al., 1992).

What about one's generation affects rate of intellectual change? The importance of education for intellectual development during adulthood may partially account for cohort differences. People who are more highly educated tend to adopt lifestyles that foster the maintenance of cognitive abilities. Highly educated older adults are also the exception in their generation; opportunities to go to college were not as prevalent 50 years ago as they are now.

Thus one source of the cohort effect may be differences in the type and amount of education.

The evidence points to the maintenance of intellectual abilities in well-educated adults at least into old age (Schaie, 1990, 1996, 2005). As better-educated cohorts grow old, education may also provide an explanation of why cohort differences on many measures are not increasing at the same rates as they did in the 20th century (Schaie, 2008). In sum, cohort differences provide important evidence about changes in intellectual abilities in adulthood. However, we must be careful not to read too much into these trends and to recognize that they may not be sustained into the 21st century.

Information Processing. A number of researchers suggest that general processing constraints that occur with aging may help identify mechanisms that underlie decline in mechanic and fluid intelligence abilities with age (Baltes et al., 2006; Salthouse, 1997; Zimprich & Martin, 2002, 2009). For example, evidence suggests that perceptual speed accounts for the lion's share of age-related decline in both fluid and crystallized mental abilities. Similarly, working memory decline with increasing age accounts for poor performance on the part of older adults when the tasks involve coordinating both new incoming information and stored information such as those found in the fluid and/or mechanic component of intelligence (Mayr & Kliegl, 2003; Salthouse, 1991). Finally, evidence suggests that the inability to inhibit actions and thoughts or to avoid interference typically found in older adults may also account for efficient functioning in fluid and/or mechanic abilities (Brainerd, 1995; Stoltzfus et al., 1996).

Overall, processing rate, working memory, and ability to inhibit tend to show decline during later adulthood and old age and are linked to physiological decline. However, studies in this area are still inconclusive in that it is difficult to make a clear-cut distinction between these three information-processing mechanisms. For example, proneness to interference when performing a task is highly correlated with perceptual speed (Hasher et al., 2002; Lustig et al., 2009; Salthouse & Meinz, 1995). As indicated earlier, it may be the case that future developments in cognitive neuroscience are likely to shed more light on the determinants of mental abilities involved in intellectual functioning (Baltes et al., 2006; Gazzaniga, 1995; Reuter-Lorenz, 2002).

Social and Lifestyle Variables. Numerous social demographic variables have been identified as important correlates of intellectual functioning. Think for a minute about the kind of job you currently have or would like to get. What kinds of intellectual skills does it demand? What similarities or differences are there between your chosen job (e.g., school counselor) and a different one (say, accountant)? An interesting line of research concerns how the differences in cognitive skills needed in different occupations makes a difference in intellectual development (Bosma et al., 2003; Schooler et al., 1999). To the extent that a job requires you to use certain cognitive abilities a great deal, you may be less likely to show declines in them as you age.

Support for this hypothesis comes from a study that examined both psychometric intelligence and practical intelligence as defined by Sternberg, discussed earlier. Practical intelligence, in this case in bank managers, is tacit knowledge (generic knowledge about a particular area) and expertise (Colonia-Willner, 1998). As expected, age was associated with decreases in psychometric test performance. However, decline was not found in more practical intelligence areas such as tacit knowledge and managerial skills.

Support for this hypothesis also comes from a longitudinal study showing that as adults grow

More and more women are employed in demanding occupations.

older, the level of complexity of their occupation continues to affect the level of their intellectual functioning as it did when they were 20 to 30 years younger (Schooler et al., 1999). This finding held for both men and women. It appears that occupations that require complex thought and independent judgment raise the level of people's intellectual functioning, whereas occupations that do not require such complex processes decrease their level of intellectual functioning. Interestingly, the positive effect of job complexity is greater for older than for younger workers (Schooler & Caplan, 2009; Schooler et al., 1999).

Other social demographic variables implicated in slower rates of intellectual decline include a higher education and socioeconomic status (Cagney & Lauderdale, 2002; Turrell et al., 2002; Schaie, 2008), exposure to stimulating environments, the utilization of cultural and educational resources throughout adulthood (Schaie, 2008), and strong social engagement (Zunzunegui et al., 2003). For example, recent work examining social engagement suggests that loneliness is associated with more rapid cognitive decline (Tilvis et al., 2004; Wilson, Krueger et al., 2007). Social engagement has also been studied in dementia patients yielding similar results. High levels of social activity have been associated with a reduced risk in developing dementia (Fabrigoule et al., 1995; Wang et al., 2002; Wilson, Kreuger et al., 2007). Overall, there is growing evidence that higher levels of social interaction and engagement are related to reduced risk of cognitive decline and dementia in old age.

Finally, although some researchers suggest that a cognitively engaging lifestyle is a predictor of intellectual functioning (Arbuckle et al., 1998), it is still a matter of considerable debate (Hertzog et al., 2009). We examine this debate in the Current Controversies feature.

Personality. Several aspects of personality have been proposed as important for understanding intellectual change. Similar to research we examined in Chapter 6 on memory, one of these aspects concerns self-efficacy (Lachman et al., 1995). High initial levels of fluid abilities and a high sense of internal control led to positive changes in people's perceptions of their abilities; low initial levels led to decreases in perceptions of ability and behavior (Lachman et al., 1995; Lachman & Andreoletti, 2006). A related personality aspect concerns people's perceptions of changes in their intellectual performance (Schaie et al., 1994; Schaie, 1996). By comparing people's perceptions to actual test performance, Schaie and colleagues classified people as realists (people who accurately estimated changes in performance), optimists (people who overestimated positive change), and pessimists (people who overestimate negative change). Most people were classified as realists, although women were more likely than men to be pessimists on spatial abilities, and older people were more likely than younger people to be pessimists on verbal meaning and inductive reasoning.

Neuroticism and chronic psychological distress have been implicated in rapid cognitive decline (Wilson, Arnold et al., 2006; Wilson, Bennett et al., 2005). This makes sense given that neuroticism is strongly associated with frequency of negative emotions. Negative emotions and psychological distress go hand-in-hand. Furthermore, neurobiological research suggests that chronic psychological distress may cause deteriorative changes in the limbic system of the brain that helps regulate emotion and cognition (Dwivedi et al., 2003; Webster et al., 2002). These deteriorative changes could cause cognitive impairment. However, this area is still in its infancy and further research is needed.

On a more positive note, positive beliefs and attitudes also have important indirect effects on cognitive enrichment. This indirect effect is reflected in the influence of these beliefs and attitudes on desirable behaviors such as exercise and mental stimulation that are known to be associated with enrichment effects on intelligence (Hertzog et al., 2009). For example, research indicates that people who have flexible attitudes at midlife tend to experience less decline in intellectual competence than people who are more rigid in middle age (Lachman, 2004; Schaie, 1996; Willis & Boron, 2008). Similarly, motor-cognitive flexibility in one's 60s is highly predictive of numerical and verbal abilities in late life (O'Hanlon, 1993).

Health. One of the most difficult problems in any study of aging is the separation of normal processes from abnormal ones. So far our discussion of

CURRENT CONTROVERSIES

Problems in Detecting Lifestyle Effects on Intellectual Functioning

In an interesting debate in the literature, researchers from two major longitudinal studies on intellectual change in older adulthood (the Victoria Longitudinal Study and Canadian War Veterans Study) found conflicting results regarding the effects of an active lifestyle on intellectual functioning. On the one hand, Pushkar, Etezadi, Andres, Arbuckle, Schwartzman, and Chaikelson (1999) claim that they show evidence that engaged lifestyles have significant but small causal effects on verbal performance across the adult life span. In other words, an engaging and intellectually active adult lifestyle is associated with a more complex social environment in which intellectual abilities can flourish.

However, Hertzog, Hultsch, and Dixon (1999) did not find this relationship in their study. They argue that the verdict is still out, given conflicting findings in the literature and underdeveloped methods of assessing engaging lifestyles. Current research has weighed in on this debate suggesting that those studies that find cognitive enrichment effects do not find them on all cognitive measures (Hertzog et al., 2009). Some astounding findings suggest that mentally stimulating activities during adulthood are associated with a reduced incidence of mild cognitive impairment and dementia later on in adulthood (Wilson, Scherr et al., 2007). It is also important to unravel the causal direction of these effects. Does activity facilitate

cognitive functioning, or are those individuals with high cognitive functioning the ones who engage in an active lifestyle (Mackinnon et al., 2003)? Finally, none of these research teams would discourage older adults from actively engaging in intellectual activities and social lives such as crossword puzzles, reading, and adult education. Instead, Hertzog and colleagues (1999, 2009) argue that the current research suggests that mentally stimulating and cognitive enrichment activities have the effect of delaying the onset of cognitive decline, not preventing it. The positive aspect of this is that it thereby reduces the proportion of old age spent in a cognitively disabled state (Hertzog et al., 2009).

---

intellectual development has ignored this distinction; we have been concerned only with normal changes. However, not everyone is healthy, experiencing only normal cognitive aging. Moreover, disease is a hit-or-miss proposition, affecting some people primarily physically, as in arthritis, and others primarily cognitively, as in the early stages of dementia. Thus we need to consider how specific aspects of health influence intellectual ability.

The most obvious relationship between health and intelligence concerns the functioning of the brain itself. We noted in Chapter 3 that several normative changes in brain structure with age affect functioning. Disorders such as Alzheimer's disease and head injuries may damage the brain

and interfere with its functioning. In some cases these problems get worse as the individual ages. Obviously, the more extensive the damage, the more significant the impairment of intellectual ability.

The connection between disease and intelligence has been established fairly well in general (Rosnick et al., 2004) and in cardiovascular disease in particular (Spiro & Brady, 2008). Vascular diseases are linked to a pattern of cognitive impairment that is typically observed in "normal" cognitive aging. Some researchers suggest that the effects of age on intelligence and cognition are related at least in part to vascular disease that selectively affects the prefrontal brain (Spiro & Brady, 2008; Waldstein et al., 2005). Findings concerning hypertension are complex. Whereas severe hypertension has been associated with earlier-than-usual declines, mild hypertension may actually have positive effects on intellectual functioning (Sands & Meredith, 1992).

Finally, other research indicates that health-related factors are related to very specific types of intellectual functioning. For example, in a longitudinal study the absence of an *APOE* genotype (associated with Alzheimer's disease discussed in Chapter 3) and self-reported sensory functioning were associated with spatial functioning whereas reports of current health symptoms, depression, and anxiety were associated with perceptual speed (Christensen et al., 1999; Christensen et al., 2001; Hofer et al., 2002). Similarly, Ulman Lindenberger and Paul Baltes (Baltes & Lindenberger, 1997; Lindenberg et al., 2001) found that visual and auditory acuity (measures of sensory functioning) were related to fluid intelligence, which may explain why we see age-related decline in these intellectual abilities. In fact, they suggest sensory functioning is a better predictor of intellectual ability than variables such as educational level or occupational success. Given these findings, it appears that a variety of variables, including health, sensory functioning, lifestyle, and education, predict the variability in individual trajectories of intellectual change in adulthood (Christensen et al., 1999).

Relevancy and Appropriateness of Tasks. All the psychometric tests used today trace their origin to Binet's (1903) original attempt to measure academic performance. Some researchers argue that the academic settings and skills that led to the development of these tests may not be equally important or relevant to adults. Consequently, they argue that we need new tests based on the problems adults typically face.

To build new tests requires understanding what types of skills adults use in everyday situations. Given that a major concern of older adults is to maintain independent living, Willis and colleagues have been conducting a program of research examining the relationship between mental abilities and older adults' competence in everyday situations (Diehl et al., 1995; Willis & Schaie, 1993). They drew on the seven domains of daily living outlined by the Instrumental Activities of Daily Living (IADL) scale (Fillenbaum, 1985). These include taking medications, managing finances, shopping for necessities, using the telephone, managing transportation, preparing meals, and housekeeping. The responses provide a very different starting point for developing tasks for an intelligence test than trying to figure out how to measure classroom learning potential.

Willis and colleagues (Allaire & Marsiske, 2002; Diehl, 1998; Marsiske & Willis, 1995, 1998) examined the relationships among seven primary mental abilities, measured by traditional tests, and eight categories of everyday tasks, measured by the ETS Basic Skills Test. The categories of everyday tasks included

There is a qualitative difference in the cognitive functioning of healthy versus unhealthy older adults.

Typical IQ testing doesn't necessarily tap into everyday decision making such as the decision to buy a new product.

There has been a recent surge in older adults attending classes in continuing education.

understanding labels on medical or household articles, reading street maps, understanding charts or schedules, comprehending paragraphs, filling out forms, reading newspaper and phone directory ads, understanding technical documents, and comprehending news text. Three scores on the skills test were calculated; two scores reflected different levels of comprehension and information processing (literal and inference), and the third was the total score. Correlations between the scores for primary abilities and basic skills were very high for the older adults, indicating that the two tests were measuring similar things.

When Willis and colleagues examined their data to see which of the primary abilities best predicted each of the eight categories of everyday tasks, some interesting findings emerged. They had expected their measures of crystallized intelligence to be the best predictors, on the basis that these everyday skills reflect cultural knowledge and should not decline with age. Much to their surprise, the measures of fluid intelligence, especially figural relations, were the best predictors most of the time. Moreover, older adults did not always perform as well as the younger adults on the everyday skills test. In fact, the younger adults obtained near-perfect scores, whereas the older adults were significantly below

ceiling, on average. Finally, a longitudinal analysis indicated that crystallized and fluid measures of intelligence predicted everyday functioning 7 years from the first time of measurement.

The Willis study is important for two reasons. First, it shows that traditional tests of primary mental abilities may predict performance on everyday tasks. For supporters of the psychometric approach, these data show that a total rejection of traditional tests on the ground that they are inadequate may be unwarranted. Second, the findings also show that tests consisting of what appear to be more relevant tasks may tap some of the same components of intelligence that the traditional tests are thought to measure. This suggests that we might develop new tests that consist of familiar tasks but those skills still tap the components of intelligence identified in psychometric research. Later we will return to this point when we discuss everyday problem solving.

The issue of task relevancy is still far from being settled, however. As we will see, many researchers and theorists argue quite strongly that only by abandoning a purely psychometric approach and moving to a focus on everyday uses of intelligence will we advance our understanding of intellectual aging. As with most controversies, there is something to be said for both sides.

Modifying Primary Abilities

As you have seen, older adults do not perform as well on tests of some primary abilities as younger adults, even after taking the moderators of performance into account (Schaie, 1995). In considering these results, investigators began asking whether there was a way to slow down or even reverse the declines. As we saw earlier, there has been a surge of studies examining the effects of lifestyle, health, and personality on intelligence. Now we will pursue this issue further, asking a number of relevant questions regarding training. Are the age-related differences that remain after cohort and other effects are removed permanent? Or might these differences be reduced or even eliminated if older adults were given appropriate training? Can we modify adults' intelligence? This again addresses the important issue of plasticity in intellectual functioning, one of the life-span tenets discussed in Chapter 1.

Attempts to answer these questions have appeared with increasing frequency since the mid-1970s. Several types of tasks have been examined, ranging from tests of skills underlying primary mental abilities (Willis & Schaie, 1999) to the information-processing skills necessary to drive a car (Myers et al., 2000). Of these, perhaps the most interesting and important research area is the attempt to modify primary abilities that show early and substantial declines.

Primary abilities that are known to begin to decline relatively early in adulthood—such as inductive reasoning, spatial orientation, memory abilities, and figural abilities—have been examined most closely in intervention research (Willis & Schaie, 1999). In a prototypical study, performance on a fluid ability is measured on the training task (e.g., inductive reasoning) and on a new transfer task that participants had not seen during training (e.g., a different measure of inductive reasoning). Training is given to three groups. Members of the first group are told to give themselves self-directional statements and feedback. The second group combines these with additional statements that are designed to help them cope with anxiety and to emphasize self-approval and success. Members of the third group receive unspecific training; they simply practice taking the test with no instructions or feedback. Typical findings demonstrate that inductive reasoning can be increased through training (Baltes et al., 2006; Willis, 1996b; Willis & Schaie, 1999). There is also evidence for transfer of the training effects, because the performance of the trained groups was also better on the new measure of fluid skill.

In addition to primary mental abilities, significant training effects have been found for other areas of cognitive functioning including memory, problem solving, and perceptual speed (Ball et al., 2002; Kliegl et al., 1990; Larsson et al., 2003).

Project ADEPT and Project ACTIVE. A much more comprehensive training study, involving a series of short longitudinal studies, was Pennsylvania State University's Adult Development and Enrichment Project (ADEPT) (Baltes & Willis, 1982). The training studies conducted as part of ADEPT included two levels of intervention in addition to a no-training control group. All groups were equivalent at the outset.

The first level of intervention involved minimal direct training and had test familiarity as its goal. Participants were given the same tests on several occasions to familiarize them with test taking, so that the researchers could learn about the effects of repeated testing alone.

The second type of training involved interventions tailored specifically for each of the primary abilities tested. Each training package was based on a thorough task analysis of the thinking processes involved in each ability. The resulting training programs varied a little in specific details, but in general they focused on teaching the relational rules associated with each test problem, over five sessions. Training on figural relations, for instance, involved practice with paper-and-pencil tests, oral feedback by the experimenter, group discussion, and review of the kinds of problems involving figural-relations ability.

Overall, the ability-specific training resulted in improvements in primary abilities. But the ability to maintain and to transfer the training effects varied. Evidence for long-term and broad transfer effects were strongest for figural relations. Training effects were found for inductive reasoning and attention/memory, but these effects did not transfer as well to new tasks.

These findings from the training studies are impressive when we consider their implications. The size of Baltes and Willis's improvements in fluid abilities were equivalent to the average 21-year longitudinal decline in these abilities reported by Schaie (1983). The implication of this comparison is that the decline in primary abilities can be slowed or even reversed by proper intervention strategies. The results are even more exciting given that the training packages in ADEPT were fairly short: an average of five 1-hour sessions. Although the reversal of age-related declines in all primary abilities and the duration of the effects of training remain to be seen, clearly we need to revise our view of pervasive, universal decline in primary abilities.

Other Attempts to Train Fluid Abilities. Willis has extended the findings from Project ADEPT in studies accessing the Seattle Longitudinal Study (Willis, 1990; Willis & Schaie, 1992, 1999) and in a newer project, ACTIVE, which involves fluid ability training among the elderly. The first approach involves the participants in Schaie's longitudinal study in Seattle. In one study (Schaie & Willis, 1986), participants were assigned to one of two groups based on their performance over a 14-year period (1970 to 1984). One group showed significant decline on either spatial ability or reasoning ability, and the other group remained stable on these measures. Schaie and Willis then provided a 5-hour training session on spatial ability and a similar session on reasoning ability for those who had declined. To examine the effects of training as a function of amount of decline, training was also provided to the individuals who had remained stable.

Schaie and Willis found that the cognitive training techniques could reverse declines that had been reliably documented over the 14-year period. However, the effects of cognitive training were largely ability specific. That is, gains were largest when the training matched the ability being tested; only modest gains were found in abilities that were not trained.

Most exciting, the improvements for both spatial and reasoning abilities essentially returned to their earlier levels of functioning in people who had

declined. In addition, the training procedures even enhanced the performance of many older people who had remained stable. This finding demonstrates that training is effective not only in raising the performance of decliners but also in improving functioning in nondecliners beyond their initial levels (Willis, 1990).

The ACTIVE project findings show that cognitive training interventions improved mental abilities and daily functioning in older independent living adults (Ball et al., 2002). Recent findings also indicate that older adults have a production deficiency in that they do not spontaneously use effective cognitive strategies. Strategy-training groups increased older adults' cognitive skills and improved reasoning ability (Saczynski et al., 2002). In another research lab, Dunlosky and colleagues (2003) found that strategy training was not enough. When older adults learned how to regulate their studying through self-testing, this improved cognitive performance above and beyond training for strategies alone.

Considered together, the results from Projects ADEPT and ACTIVE, and the data from Schaie and Willis's research, allow us to conclude that declines in fluid abilities may be reversible. But how long do the improvements last?

Long-Term Effects of Training. Getting older adults to do better on skills underlying fluid intelligence is impressive. Having those benefits last over time would be even better, because it would provide a powerful argument in favor of providing intervention programs to more people.

Willis and Nesselroade (1990) report results from a 7-year follow-up to the original ADEPT study. Participants were initially trained in 1979 and received booster training sessions in 1981 and 1986. Significant training effects were found at each point, indicating that people continue to benefit from cognitive intervention as they move from young-old to old-old age. Even people in their late 70s and early 80s continued to perform at levels better than they had 7 years earlier prior to training. In fact, 64% of the training group's performance was above their pretraining baseline, compared with only 33% of the control group. As indicated earlier, the ACTIVE project findings show that cognitive training interventions improved mental abilities in older adults. In addition, the lasting effects of this training were detected as much as 2 years later (Ball et al., 2002).

Similarly positive results were reported by Willis and colleagues (2006), who showed that the effects of training after 5 years were not only substantial, but most impressive for people who had shown declines in the skills trained over the previous 14 years. In addition, older adults who were in the training group showed milder decline in their instrumental activities of daily living. All of these training effects relate to the neurological plasticity discussed in Chapter 2. For example, evidence suggests that there is plasticity in the striatum in older adults which is proposed to be involved in updating operations (O'Reilly & Frank, 2006).

What can we conclude from these findings? First, there is strong evidence that in the normal course of development no one is too old to benefit from training and that training slows down the rates of decline for those fluid abilities examined. However, unless people are somehow reminded of the training through booster sessions, gains demonstrated during training may well be lost. Second, transfer is limited to similar tests of the same ability. Third, there are exceptions to the specificity of training. When training involves executive functioning and working memory, the effects generalize to many different tasks (Basak et al., 2008; Dahlin et al., 2008). Also, training teaches people to be aware and use strategies that apply to many learning situations (Dunlosky et al., 2007). Finally, training gains are durable and last up to several years (Ball et al., 2002).

Overall, these studies suggest cognitive plasticity in fluid skills persists well into old age and can be activated in intervention techniques. However, the question still remains, Do these training gains apply to related abilities in everyday functioning (Baltes et al., 1999)? In addition, what is the scope of plasticity during adulthood? Are there limits? This question is addressed in studies designed to uncover age differences in the upper limits of mental abilities (Baltes & Kliegl, 1992; Brehmer, Li et al., 2007; Lindenberger & Baltes, 1995). In these studies, training of a mental ability continues until younger and older adults reach their maximum level of performance. Two findings are important. First, both younger and older adults improve their performance. Second, performance at maximum levels indicates that sizable age differences still remain. Younger adults outperform older adults. In other words, not a single older adult reached the performance level of younger adults. This is a good reminder that genuine age decline does occur. But it is also important to remember that relative to the older adult himself or herself, there is always room for improvement.

Concept Checks

1. What primary mental abilities have been studied most?
2. How do the developmental trajectories of fluid and crystallized intelligence differ?
3. What are the main moderators of intellectual change, and what influences do they have?
4. How effective are programs aimed at training primary mental abilities?

7.3 Qualitative Differences in Adults' Thinking

LEARNING OBJECTIVES

- What are the main points in Piaget's theory of cognitive development?
- What evidence is there for continued cognitive development beyond formal operations?
- What is the role of both emotion and cognition in cognitive maturity?

Eddie, a student at a local university, thought the test he had just taken in his math course was unfair because the instructors simply marked the answers to complex problems right or wrong. He complained that he deserved partial credit for knowing how to set up the problem and being able to figure out some of the steps.

Although Eddie did not know it, his argument parallels one in the intelligence literature—the debate on whether we should pay attention mainly to whether an answer is right or wrong or to how the person reasons the problem through. The psychometric approach we considered earlier does not focus on the thinking processes that underlie intelligence; rather, psychometrics concentrates on interrelationships among answers to test questions. In contrast, cognitive-structural approaches focus on the ways in which people think; whether a particular answer is right or wrong is not very important.

We will consider two theories that represent cognitive-structural approaches. First, we will examine Piaget's theory as a foundation for this approach. Second, we will explore the discussions concerning possible extensions of it, post-formal theory. Both these approaches postulate that intellectual changes are mainly qualitative, even though they differ on many points.

Piaget's Theory

According to Piaget (1970, 1980), intellectual development is adaptation through activity. We create the very ways in which our knowledge is organized and, ultimately, how we think. Piaget believed that the development of intelligence stems from the emergence of increasingly complex cognitive structures. He organized his ideas into a theory of cognitive development that changed the way psychologists conceptualize intellectual development.

Basic Concepts. For Piaget, thought is governed by the principles of adaptation and organization. Adaptation is the process of adjusting thinking to the environment. Just as animals living in a forest feed differently from the way animals living in a desert feed, how we think changes from one developmental context to another. Adaptation occurs through organization, which is how the organism is put together. Each component part has its own specialized function, which is coordinated into the whole. In Piaget's theory, the organization of thought is reflected in cognitive structures that change over the life span. Cognitive structures determine how we think. It is the change in cognitive structures, the change in the fundamental ways in which we think, that Piaget tried to describe.

What processes underlie intellectual adaptation? Piaget defined two: assimilation and accommodation. **Assimilation** *is the use of currently available knowledge to make sense out of incoming information.* It is the application of cognitive structures to the world of experience that makes the world understandable. For example, a child who only knows the word *dog* may use it for every animal she encounters. So, when the child sees a cat and calls it a dog, she is using available knowledge, the word *dog,* to make sense out of the world—in this case the cat that is walking across the living room. The process of assimilation sometimes leads to considerable distortion of incoming information, because we may have to force-fit it into our knowledge base. This is apparent in our tendency to forget information about a person that violates a stereotype.

Accommodation *involves changing one's thought to make it a better approximation of the world of experience.* The child in our example who thought that cats were dogs eventually learns that cats are cats. When this happens, she has accommodated her knowledge to incorporate a new category of animal.

The processes of assimilation and accommodation serve to link the structure of thought to observable behavior. Piaget believed that most changes during development involved cognitive structures. His research led him to conclude that there were four structures (i.e., four stages) in the development of mature thought: sensorimotor, preoperational, concrete operational, and formal operational. We will consider the major characteristics of each stage briefly. Because we are most interested in Piaget's description of adult thought, we will emphasize it.

Sensorimotor Period. In this first stage of cognitive development, intelligence is seen in infants' actions. Babies and infants gain knowledge by using their sensory and motor skills, beginning with basic reflexes (sucking and grasping) and eventually moving to purposeful, planned sequences of behavior (such as looking for a hidden toy). The most important thing that infants learn during the sensorimotor period is that objects continue to exist even when they are out of sight; this ability is called object permanence.

Preoperational Period. Young children's thinking is best described as egocentric. This means that young children believe all people and all inanimate objects experience the world just as they do. For example, young children believe dolls feel pain. Although young children can sometimes reason through situations, their thinking is not based on logic. For example, a young child may believe his father's shaving causes the tap water to be turned on, because the two events always happen together.

Concrete Operational Period. Logical reasoning emerges in the concrete operational period. Children become capable of classifying objects into groups, such as fruits or vegetables, based on a logical principle; mentally reversing a series of events; realizing that when changes occur in one perceptual dimension and they are compensated for in another, no net change occurs (termed conservation); and understanding the concept of transitivity (for instance, if A > B and B > C, then A > C). However, children are still unable to deal with abstract concepts such as love; for example, to children love is a set of concrete actions and not an ill-defined abstract concept.

Formal Operational Period. For Piaget, the acquisition of formal operational thought during adolescence marks the end of cognitive development. Because he argues that formal operational thinking characterizes adult thought, we will consider this level in some detail. Several theorists have commented on the characteristics of formal operational thought (Basseches, 1984; Kramer, 1989; Labouvie-Vief, 1980, 1981, 1984; Sinnott, 1984). We will use these commentaries to focus on four aspects of formal operational thought: (1) It takes a hypothesis-testing approach (termed hypothetico-deductive) to problem solving; (2) thinking is done in one framework at a time; (3) the goal is to arrive at one correct solution; and (4) it is unconstrained by reality.

Piaget describes the essence of formal operational thought as a way of conceiving abstract concepts and thinking about them in a very systematic, step-by-step way. Formal operational thought is governed by a generalized logical structure that provides solutions to problems that people have never seen and may never encounter. Hypothetico-deductive thought is similar to using the scientific method, in that it involves forming a hypothesis and testing it until it is either confirmed or rejected. Just as scientists are very systematic in testing experimental hypotheses, formal operational thinking allows people to approach problem solving in a logical, methodical way.

Consider the situation when your car breaks down. When you take it for repairs, the mechanic forms hypotheses about what may be wrong, based on a description of the trouble. The mechanic then begins to test each hypothesis systematically. For example, the compression of each cylinder may be checked, one cylinder at a time. This ability to hold other factors constant while testing a particular component is one of the hallmarks of formal operational thought. By isolating potential causes of the problem, the mechanic very efficiently arrives at a correct solution.

When we use hypothetico-deductive thought, we do so to arrive at one unambiguous solution to the problem (Kramer & Woodruff, 1986; Labouvie-Vief, 1980, 1984, 1992). Formal operational thought is aimed at resolving ambiguity; one and only one answer is the goal. When more than one solution occurs, there is a feeling of uneasiness, and people begin a search for clarification. This situation can be observed in high school classes when students press their teacher to identify the right theory (from among several equally good ones) or the right way to view a social issue (such as abortion). Moreover, when people arrive at an answer, they are quite certain about it, because it was arrived at through the use of logic. When answers are checked, the same logic and assumptions are typically used, which sometimes means that the same mistake is made several times in a row. For example, a person may repeat a simple subtraction error time after time when trying to figure out why his or her checkbook failed to balance.

Formal operational thinking knows no constraints (Labouvie-Vief, 1984; Piaget, 1970, 1980). It can be applied just as easily to real or to imaginary situations. It is not bound by the limits of reality

Many adults are reluctant to draw conclusions based on limited information when multiple perspectives are involved.

(Labouvie-Vief, 1980). Whether one can implement a solution is irrelevant; what matters is that one can think about it. This is how people arrive at solutions to disarmament, for example, such as getting rid of all nuclear warheads tomorrow. To the formal operational thinker, that this solution is logistically impossible is no excuse. The lack of reality constraints is not all bad, however. Reasoning from a "Why not?" perspective may lead to the discovery of completely new ways to approach a problem or even to the invention of new solutions.

One serious problem for Piaget's theory is that many adults apparently do not attain formal operations. Several studies report that only 60 to 75% of American adolescents can solve any formal operational problems (Neimark, 1975), and some researchers estimate that no more than 30% of adults ever complete the transition to the highest levels of formal operational thought (Kuhn, 1992). Piaget (1972) himself admitted that formal operations were probably not universal but, rather, tended to appear only in those areas in which individuals were highly trained or specialized. This has inspired a number of researchers to look beyond formal operations in determining pathways of adult cognitive development.

Going Beyond Piaget: Post-Formal Thought

Consider the following problem (Adams et al., 1988):

> John is known to be a heavy drinker, especially when he goes to parties. Mary, John's wife, warns him that if he gets drunk one more time, she will leave him and take the children. Tonight John is out late at an office party. John comes home drunk. Does Mary leave John? How certain are you of your answer? (p. 13)

When this and similar problems are presented to people of different ages, interesting differences emerge. Formal operational adolescents' responses clearly showed the ambiguity of the situation but also clearly reflected the need to search for the right answer. The ambiguity was considered a problem rather than an acceptable state of affairs. This is evident in the following answer (Adams et al., 1988):

> It's a good chance that she would leave him because she warns him that she will leave him and take the children, but warning isn't an absolute thing. . . . And, I'd be absolutely sure that, well let's see . . . I'm trying to go all the way. I'm trying to think of putting everything

[together] so I can be absolutely certain of an answer. . . . It's hard to be absolutely certain. "If he gets drunk, then she'll leave and take the children." I want to say yes "cause everything"s in that favor, in that direction, but I don't know how I can conclude that she does leave John. (pp. 17–18)

When adults were given the same problem, they handled it differently, for the most part. Their responses showed a combination of logic, emotion, and tolerance for ambiguity, as can be seen in the following example (Adams et al., 1988):

There was no right or wrong answer. You could get logically to both answers [yes or no]. . . . It depends on the steps they take to their answer. If they base it on what they feel, what they know, and they have certain steps to get an answer, it can be logical. (p. 41)

Based on a strict interpretation of formal operational thought, the adults who made responses like the second example showed little evidence of formal operational thinking. Thus it could be argued that Adams and colleagues' research supports the data described earlier that point to declines in formal operational thought across adulthood. But not everyone agrees that the research examining formal operational thinking across adulthood points to loss. Rather than concluding that differences in performance reflect declines in ability, the results are seen as indicative of another, qualitatively different, style of thinking. This latter interpretation implies that Piaget's theory may need modification. Specifically, some researchers have proposed that these performance differences on Piagetian tasks reflect cognitive development beyond formal operations.

Developmental Progressions in Adult Thought. By the 1970s, it was clear that Piaget's contention that formal operations was the end point of cognitive development had serious problems. One of the first to formally propose an alternative model was Riegel (1973, 1976), who argued that formal operations was quite limited in its applicability. By the mid-1980s many other authors agreed (Basseches, 1984; Cavanaugh et al., 1985; Commons et al., 1982; Labouvie-Vief, 1980, 1992; Sinnott, 1984).

Riegel and other writers point out that Piaget is concerned with describing logical, hypothetico-deductive thinking in his stage of formal operations but that this is not the only kind of thinking that adults do. In addition, they argue that Piaget's stage of formal operations is primarily limited to explaining how people arrive at one correct solution. How adults discover or generate new problems and how they sometimes appear to accept several possible solutions are not explained. Finally, that adults often limit their thinking in response to social or other realistic constraints appears to conflict with the unconstrained generation of ideas characteristic of formal operations.

For these reasons some researchers have proposed that cognitive growth continues beyond formal operations (Commons et al., 1984; Commons et al., 1989; Sinnott, 1996). **Post-formal thought,** *as it is called, is characterized by a recognition that truth (the correct answer) varies from situation to situation, that solutions must be realistic to be reasonable, that ambiguity and contradiction are the rule rather than the exception, and that emotion and subjective factors usually play a role in thinking.*

In one of the first investigations of cognitive growth beyond adolescence, Perry (1970) traced the development of thinking across the undergraduate years. He found that adolescents relied heavily on the expertise of authorities to determine what was right and wrong. At this point thinking is tightly bound by the rules of logic, and the only legitimate conclusions are those that are logically derived. For Perry, the continued development of thinking involves the development of increased cognitive flexibility. The first step in the process is a shift toward relativism. Relativism in thought entails realizing that more than one explanation of a set of facts could be right, depending on one's point of view. Although relativism frees the individual from the constraints of a single framework, it also leads to skepticism. Because one can never be sure if one is right or wrong, the skeptic may not try to develop knowledge further, which may lead to feeling confused or adrift. Perry points out that the price of freeing oneself from the influence of authority is the loss of the certainty that came from relying on logic for all the answers.

To develop beyond skepticism, Perry showed, adults develop commitments to particular viewpoints. In Perry's later stages, adults recognize that they are their own source of authority, that they must make a commitment to a position, and that others may hold different positions to which they will be equally committed. In other words, mature thinkers can understand many perspectives on an issue, choose one, and still allow others the right to hold differing viewpoints. Thinking in this mature way is different from thinking in formal operational terms.

Reflective Judgment. Perry's landmark research opened the door to documenting systematic changes in thinking beyond formal operations. One of the best approaches to emerge is King and Kitchener's (1994) refined descriptions of the development of reasoning in young adults. *On the basis of nearly two decades of research, they mapped the development of* **reflective judgment,** *which involves how people reason through dilemmas involving current affairs, religion, science, and the like.* On the basis of well-designed longitudinal studies of young adults, they identified a systematic progression of thinking, which is described in Table 7.2.

The first three stages in the model represent prereflective thought. People at this stage do not acknowledge, and may not even perceive, that knowledge is uncertain. Consequently, they do not understand that some problems exist for which there is not a clear and absolutely correct answer. Stages 4 and 5 represent quasi-reflective thinking, as people recognize that some problems contain an element of uncertainty. However, although people at this level use evidence, they are not adept at how to use evidence to draw a conclusion. Stages 6 and 7 represent true reflective judgment. People at this level realize that knowledge must be constructed, that claims about knowledge must be evaluated within the context in which they were generated, and that conclusions, though based on data, are open to reevaluation.

More recent research has found that reflective judgment increases over 10 years in a sample of 24- to 50-year-olds (Pirttilae-Backman & Kajanne,

2001). In addition, education, profession, exposure to diversity, and an exploratory orientation were related to this developmental trend.

How does a person move from prereflective judgment to reflective judgment? Is the progression gradual? Does it involve qualitative shifts? Kitchener and Fischer (1990) argue that the progression involves both, depending on which aspect of development one emphasizes. Their view is based on the distinction between optimal level and skill acquisition aspects of development. *The* **optimal level of development** *is the highest level of information-processing capacity of which a person is capable.* The optimal level increases with age and is marked by relatively abrupt changes ("growth spurts") followed by periods of relative stability. Each spurt represents the emergence of a new developmental level ("stage") of thinking; the period of stability reflects the time needed by the individual to become proficient at using the newly acquired skills. **Skill acquisition** *describes the gradual, and somewhat haphazard, process by which people learn new abilities.* People progress through many small steps in acquiring skills before they are ready for the next growth spurt.

The optimal level provides an indication of the highest stage a person has achieved in cognitive development but probably does not indicate the level he or she will use most of the time (King & Kitchener, 1994). Why? Mostly, it is because the environment does not provide the supports necessary for high-level performance, especially for issues concerning knowledge. Consequently, people will, if pushed and if provided the necessary supports, demonstrate a level of thinking and performance far higher than they typically show on a daily basis. This discrepancy may provide an explanation of why fewer people are found at each successively more complex level of thinking who consistently use it.

Absolutist, Relativistic, and Dialectical Thinking. A growth in reflective judgment is not the only aspect of post-formal thought that researchers have examined. For example, Kramer, Kahlbaugh, and Goldston (1992) identified three distinct styles of thinking: absolutist, relativistic, and dialectical. Absolutist thinking involves firmly believing that there is only

Table 7.2

Description of the Stages of Reflective Judgment

Stage 1

View of knowledge Knowledge is assumed to exist absolutely and concretely. It can be obtained with absolute certainty through direct observation.

Concept of justification Beliefs need no justification because there is assumed to be an absolute correspondence between what is believed and what is true. There are no alternatives.

Stage 2

View of knowledge Knowledge is absolutely certain, or certain but not immediately available. Knowledge can be obtained via direct observation or via authorities.

Concept of justification Beliefs are justified via authority, such as a teacher or a parent, or are unexamined and unjustified. Most issues are assumed to have a right answer, so there is little or no conflict in making decisions about disputed issues.

Stage 3

View of knowledge Knowledge is assumed to be absolutely certain or temporarily uncertain. In areas of temporary uncertainty, we can know only via intuition and bias until absolute knowledge is obtained.

Concept of justification In areas in which answers exist, beliefs are justified via authorities. In areas in which answers do not exist, because there is no rational way to justify beliefs, they are justified arationally or intuitively.

Stage 4

View of knowledge Knowledge is uncertain and idiosyncratic because situational variables (e.g., incorrect reporting of data, data lost over time) dictate that we cannot know with certainty. Therefore we can only know our own beliefs about the world.

Concept of justification Beliefs often are justified by reference to evidence but still are based on idiosyncratic reasons, such as choosing evidence that fits an established belief.

Stage 5

View of knowledge Knowledge is contextual and subjective. Because what is known is known via perceptual filters, we cannot know directly. We may know only interpretations of the material world.

Concept of justification Beliefs are justified within a particular context via the rules of inquiry for that context. Justifications are assumed to be context-specific or are balanced against each other, delaying conclusions.

Stage 6

View of knowledge Knowledge is personally constructed via evaluations of evidence, opinions of others, and so forth across contexts. Thus we may know only interpretations of the material world.

Concept of justification Beliefs are justified by comparing evidence and opinion on different sides of an issue or across contexts and by constructing solutions that are evaluated by personal criteria, such as one's personal values or the pragmatic need for action.

Stage 7

View of knowledge Knowledge is constructed via the process of reasonable inquiry into generalizable conjectures about the material world of solutions for the problem at hand, such as what is most probable based on the current evidence or how far it is along the continuum of how things seem to be.

Concept of justification Beliefs are justified probabilistically via evidence and argument or as the most complete or compelling understanding of an issue.

Source: King, P. M., & Kitchener, K. S. (1994). *Developing Reflective Judgment: Understanding and Promoting Intellectual Growth and Critical Thinking in Adolescents and Adults.* Copyright © 1994. Reprinted with permission from Jossey-Bass, Inc., a subsidiary of John Wiley & Sons, Inc.

one correct solution to problems and that personal experience provides truth. Adolescents and young adults typically think this way. Relativistic thinking involves realizing that there are many sides to any issue and that the right answer depends on the circumstances. Young and early middle-aged adults often think relativistically. One potential danger here is that relativistic thinking can lead to cynicism or an "I'll do my thing, and you do yours" approach to life. Because relativistic thinkers reason things out on a case-by-case basis, based on the situation, they are not likely to be strongly committed to any one position. The final step, dialectical thinking, clears up this problem. Dialectical thinkers see the merits in the different viewpoints but can synthesize them into a workable solution. This synthesis often produces strong commitment and a definite plan of action.

Notice that there is considerable agreement between the first two styles in Kramer's model and the progression described in the reflective judgment model. Both talk about moving from an "I'm right, because I've experienced it" position to an "I'm not so sure, because your experience is different from mine" position. Both also provide insight into how young adults are likely to approach life problems. The absolutist, relativistic, and dialectical framework has been adopted widely in the study of post-formal thought. However, assessments of older adults seem to show an increase in dualistic reasoning (Hood & Deopere, 2002), although less dualistic thinking and more relativistic thinking were related to higher levels of education. Sinnott (1994a, 1994c) applied this framework to understanding how adults learn and how they should be taught. In this regard, teachers need to recognize that relativistic thought marks the point at which learning processes become inherently social.

Integrating Emotion and Logic. A theme in descriptions of the first set of qualitative changes in post-formal thinking is a movement from "I'm right, because I've experienced it" to an "I'm not so sure who's right, because your experience is different than mine" position. These differences in thinking provide insights into how thinking styles have major implications for dealing with life problems. For example, couples who can understand and synthesize each other's point of view are much more likely to resolve conflicts; couples not able to do so are more likely to feel resentful, drift apart, or even break up (Kramer, 1989). How can people avoid conflicts and become more able to deal with life problems?

Labouvie-Vief (1992, 1997, 2003, 2004) proposes that the answer lies in adults' gaining the ability to integrate emotion with logic in their thinking. She sees the main goal of adult thought as effectiveness in handling everyday life, rather than as the generation of all possible solutions. To her, adults make choices not so much on logical grounds but on pragmatic, emotional, and social grounds. Mature thinkers realize that thinking is a social phenomenon that demands making compromises and tolerating ambiguity and contradiction.

Consider the evidence that despite the possibility of pregnancy or of contracting AIDS or other sexually transmitted diseases, adolescents still tend not to use contraceptives when they have sexual relations. Why? Labouvie-Vief would argue that sexuality is too emotionally charged for adolescents to deal with intellectually. But is this a reasonable interpretation?

It may be. In a very provocative study, Blanchard-Fields (1986) asked high school students, college students, and middle-aged adults to resolve three fictitious dilemmas. One dilemma had low emotional involvement: conflicting accounts of a war between two fictitious countries, North and South Livia, each written by a supporter of one country. The other two dilemmas had high emotional involvement: a visit to the grandparents in which the parents and their adolescent son disagreed about going (the son did not want to go), and a pregnancy dilemma in which a man and a woman had to resolve their unintentional pregnancy (the man was antiabortion, the woman was pro-choice).

Results are shown in Figure 7.6. Two important findings emerged. First, there were clear developmental trends in reasoning level, with the middle-aged adults scoring highest. Second, the high school and college students were equivalent on the fictitious war dilemma, but the high school students scored significantly lower on the grandparents and the pregnancy

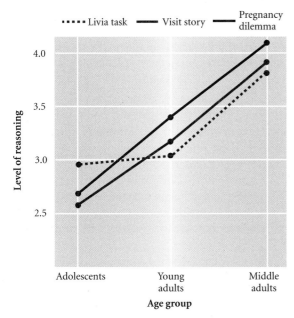

Figure 7.6 Level of reasoning as a function of age group and socioemotional task.

Source: Blanchard-Fields, F. (1986). Reasoning on social dilemmas varying in emotional saliency: An adult developmental study. *Psychology and Aging* 1, 325–333. Copyright © 1986 Reprinted with permission from the American Psychological Association.

dilemmas. These findings suggest that high school students tend to think at a lower developmental level when confronted with problems that are especially emotionally salient to them. Although more evidence is certainly needed, Blanchard-Fields's findings provide support for the idea that emotion and logic are brought together in adulthood.

Whether the findings from research examining relativistic or other forms of post-formal thought document qualitative cognitive growth has been a topic of debate. Overall, Cavanaugh and Stafford (1989) point out that because the roles of experience and education are not understood and because the measures of post-formal thought vary considerably from study to study, firm conclusions on the nature of adult cognitive development may be premature.

Gender Issues and Post-Formal Thought. The evidence of differences between adolescents' and adults' thinking is clearly substantial. However, the research that

has produced this evidence is typically grounded in the assumption that men and women think in essentially similar ways. Is this a reasonable assumption?

Some researchers do not think so; they argue that men and women use different thinking styles. Within this critique, researchers argue that the styles of thinking that we have discussed so far reflect a male bias and do not describe how women know the world. The most prominent of these critiques was Belenky, Clinchy, Goldberger, and Tarule's (1986) identification of five ways of knowing in women: silent, received, subjective, procedural, and constructed. *Silent knowing* reflects the passive acceptance of others' knowledge and one's own incompetence. *Received knowing* involves accepting from authorities ideas that are concrete, absolute, and dualistic (i.e., representing dichotomies such as good versus bad, with no gray areas). *Subjective knowing* involves using personal and private intuitions as the major source of understanding and authority. *Procedural knowing* involves adopting the dominant viewpoint and using a systematic and deliberate process of analysis in two ways. One way of accomplishing procedural knowing is using impersonal strategies based on the criteria of justice and fairness to establish what is "right." The second way is using interdependence and caring as the basis for establishing truth. Finally, *constructed knowing* includes being articulate about the self, reflecting one's own personal point of view, while tolerating contradiction and ambiguity.

These descriptions are certainly reminiscent of the styles of thinking considered earlier. For example, relativistic thinking has much in common with constructed knowing. Moreover, Belenky et al.'s description has an implicit developmental progression, in that each way of knowing appears to reflect a higher level of complexity. Thus important questions are whether the proposed women's ways of knowing indeed reflect a developmental progression, are indeed more typical of women, and are related to other descriptions of post-formal thinking.

Orr and Luszcz (1994) decided to address these issues by assessing the ways of knowing and

In numerous settings, individuals must clearly articulate their points of view while at the same time acknowledging the point of view of others.

relativistic thinking in a sample of male and female undergraduate and graduate students. They found that education, but not age, predicted relativistic thinking but not constructed knowing. Women used subjective knowing more than men, but men used procedural knowing more than women. No gender differences were observed for either constructed knowing or relativistic thinking, but the degree to which traditional notions of femininity was endorsed was positively related to both. Finally, procedural knowing decreased whereas constructed knowing increased with increasing evidence of relativistic thinking. Overall, these results point to minimal differences between men's and women's thinking; Belenky et al.'s (1986) ways of knowing do not appear unique to women. However, the ways of knowing do seem to reflect a developmental progression of increasingly complex thought. Still, differences do exist between constructed knowing and relativistic thinking that need to be pursued in additional studies.

The possibility of stages of cognitive development beyond formal operations is intriguing and has focused our attention on the existence of different styles of thinking across adulthood. It has certainly presented a counter to the stereotype of inevitable decline. The evidence supporting a separate stage of cognitive development beyond formal operations is growing, and its applicability has extended to solving practical problems, which we will explore a little later in this chapter. At this point, though, the existence of different styles of thinking in adulthood may help us understand why people sometimes have difficulty understanding each other.

Concept Checks

1. What are the four stages of cognitive development and their respective characteristics in Piaget's theory?
2. What are the major styles of thinking that have been identified beyond formal operations?
3. What role does emotion play in post-formal thinking?

7.4 Everyday Reasoning and Problem Solving

LEARNING OBJECTIVES

- What are the characteristics of older adults' decision making?
- What are optimally exercised abilities and unexercised abilities? What age differences have been found in practical problem solving?
- What is encapsulation, and how does it relate to expertise? What is the role of experience in expertise?
- What is wisdom, and how does it relate to age and life experience?

Kim is a 75-year-old grandmother visiting her 14-year-old grandson. When he asks her to help with his algebra homework, she declines, stating that she just does not have enough schooling to understand it. However, when he has trouble communicating with his parents, Kim can give him excellent advice on how to understand things from both their perspective and his. He ends up getting what he wanted and is delighted to know that he can always go to his grandma for advice.

So far, our consideration of intellectual abilities has included examinations of how people's performance on standardized tests and their modes of thinking differ with age. But what we have not considered in detail yet is how people actually use their intellectual abilities and demonstrate characteristics we associate with intelligent people: solving problems, making decisions, gaining expertise, and becoming wise. This contrast in intellectual abilities is illustrated in Kim's lack of algebraic skills, yet wisdom in her interpersonal skills and the conduct of life. What we have discovered in this chapter to this point is that people's crystallized intelligence, reflecting life experience, continues to grow (or at least not decline) until later in life, and that one hallmark of adults' thinking is the integration of emotion and logic. One might expect, then, that the ability to make decisions and solve real-life problems would not decline until late adulthood, that expertise would increase, and that wisdom would be related to age. Are these expectations correct? Let's find out.

As we have discussed, there are many age-related declines in basic cognitive and sensory mechanisms (Chapter 6 and earlier in this chapter). We have also learned that there are age-related increases in experience and the pragmatics of knowledge (illustrated by wisdom and expertise, discussed later). Given these two perspectives on aging, an important distinction must be made. Although there are distinct age-related declines in the structure and processes of cognitive functioning, it is also important to consider the functional architecture of everyday behavior that is cognitively demanding. Thus, even though older adults may experience decline in memory, for example, they may have appropriate skills and knowledge adequate for tasks in their daily lives. In other words, we cannot necessarily take information we learn in laboratory experiments on cognitive and intellectual aging and easily apply it to everyday life. Let's explore this distinction first in the area of everyday decision making.

Decision Making

A cursory look at the decision making literature initially suggests that older adults demonstrate less effective decision making when the decision-making situation is novel and unfamiliar to them (Chasseigne et al., 1997; Finucane et al., 2002; Mutter & Pliske, 1994; Sanfey & Hastie, 2000). For example, older adults have difficulty in deciding how water temperature is determined from numerous gauges on a cellar boiler (Chasseigne et al., 1997). Older adults also have difficulty making decisions when under time pressure (Johnson, 1990). When decision making involves a high degree of working memory capacity (e.g., a lot of information must be held in memory simultaneously in order to make quick decisions), older adults do not perform as well (Peters et al., 2007; Sanfey & Hastie, 2000). However, everyday decision making does not necessarily reflect the firm time constraints and cognitive demands that are studied in the above research. Let's examine other types of situations.

A number of different types of everyday decision-making situations have been examined across the adult life span. These range from assessing automobiles for future purchase (Johnson, 1990; Lambert-Pandraud, Laurent, & Lapersonne, 2005) and treatment decisions for breast cancer (Meyer et al., 1994; Meyer et al., 2007), to retirement and financial planning (Hershey, Jacobs-Lawson et al., 2003; Walsh & Hershey, 1993). Findings are quite comparable. Younger adults are much quicker at coming to a decision. Older adults search for less information in order to arrive at a decision, require less information to arrive at a decision, and rely on easily accessible information (Mata, Schooler, & Rieskamp, 2007; Reed, Mikels, & Simon, 2008). However, the important point here is that despite these age-related characteristics, the literature suggests no age differences in the quality of the decisions made in such everyday contexts (Chen & Sun, 2003).

When decision making taps into relevant experience or knowledge, older adults tend to be just as effective in making decisions as younger adults or even better at it. For example, experience tends to make older adults less susceptible to irrational biases in their decision making in comparison to younger adults (Tentori et al., 2001). It may be that when decisions are personally relevant it bolsters older adults' attentional focus on important cues resulting in efficient decisions (Hess et al., 2005; Meyer et al., 2007).

These findings suggest some interesting directions for future research. Is it that older adults try to conserve diminishing resources when making decisions, and thus search for less information? Are there cohort differences in the belief in powerful others or trusting authority (therefore less need for deliberation)? For example, older cohorts are socialized to believe in the ultimate word of the physician and not question his or her opinion. Or do older adults draw on a rich and elaborate knowledge system that makes them somewhat "experts" in particular areas of decision making? In this case, experts do not exhaustively search for information given their sophisticated knowledge base. All these possible explanations need to be explored to yield a better understanding of everyday decision making in older adults.

An area that has received considerable attention is the role emotion plays in age differences in decision making. Negative emotions such as anger and fear can be evoked when making a decision. For example, health-related decisions are particularly loathsome because they can involve threat, are high in personal relevance, and are of high importance to the individual (Lockenhoff & Carstensen, 2007). In support of the idea that older adults are motivated to reduce the experience of negativity and enhance the experience of positivity (Carstensen & Mikels, 2005), research shows that older adults focused more on positive information when making a health decision (Lockenhoff & Carstensen, 2007). Interestingly Kim and colleagues (2008) found that older adults focused more on positive information than younger adults did when making a decision only when they were asked to explicitly evaluate their options before making a choice. If not asked to do so, there were no age differences in decision making.

Furthermore, these researchers asked participants how satisfied they were with their decision. For the older adult group that was asked to evaluate their options, their focus on the positive and their satisfaction with their decision remained high over two weeks. In other words, older adults' high level of satisfaction with their decisions increased and persisted over two weeks by simply asking them to spend a few minutes evaluating their options. This did not happen for younger adults. Kim et al. (2008) comment on how advertisements or interventions that have a positive impact on one age group may have a completely different impact on another.

Problem Solving

One of the most important ways in which people use their intellectual abilities is to solve problems. Think for a minute about everyday life and the number of problem-solving situations one encounters in school, on the job, in relationships, driving a car, and so forth. Each of these settings requires one to analyze complex situations quickly, to apply knowledge, and to create solutions, sometimes in a matter of seconds.

Some people tend to be better at dealing with certain problems than with others. Why is that? One possible explanation has to do with the kinds of abilities we use regularly versus the abilities we use only occasionally. Nancy Denney proposed a more formal version of this explanation, which we will consider next.

Denney's Model of Unexercised and Optimally Exercised Abilities. Denney (1984) postulates that intellectual abilities relating to problem solving follow two types of developmental functions. One of these functions represents unexercised, or unpracticed, ability, and the other represents optimally trained, or optimally exercised, ability. **Unexercised ability** *is the ability a normal, healthy adult would exhibit without practice or training.* Fluid intelligence is thought to be an example of untrained ability, because, by definition, it does not depend on experience and is unlikely to be formally trained (Horn & Hofer, 1992). **Optimally exercised ability** *is the ability a normal, healthy adult*

The quality of older adults' decisions in making major purchases does not appear to differ significantly from that of younger adults.

© Spencer Grant / PhotoEdit

would demonstrate under the best conditions of training or practice. Crystallized intelligence is an example of optimally exercised ability, because the component skills (such as vocabulary ability) are used daily.

Denney argues that the overall developmental course of both abilities is the same: They tend to increase until late adolescence or early adulthood and slowly decline thereafter. At all age levels there is a difference in favor of optimally exercised ability, although this difference is less in early childhood and old age. As the developmental trends move away from the hypothetical ideal, Denney argues, the gains seen in training programs will increase. As we noted earlier in our discussion of attempts to train fluid intelligence, it appears that this increase occurs.

Practical Problem Solving. Denney's model spurred considerable interest in how people solve practical problems. Based on the model, adults should perform better on practical problems than on abstract ones like those typically used on standardized intelligence tests. Tests of practical problem solving would use situations such as the following (Denney et al., 1982): "Let's say that a middle-aged woman is frying chicken in her home when, all of a sudden, a grease fire breaks out on top of the stove. Flames begin to shoot up. What should she do?" (p. 116).

Findings from studies examining how well adults solve problems like this are mixed (Cornelius, 1990; Denney, 1990). Although most researchers find better performance on practical problems, how this performance differs with age is unclear. Some investigators (e.g., Denney & Pearce, 1989) find that performance peaks during midlife and decreases after that, as predicted by Denney's model. Other researchers (e.g., Cornelius & Caspi, 1987) find continued improvement at least until around age 70.

Performance on practical problems clearly increases from early adulthood to middle age. Differences among studies occur in the age at which maximal performance is attained and in the direction and degree of change beyond midlife. However, some important differences among these studies could explain the differences in findings. One key difference is that several different measures are used in assessing practical problem-solving ability.

Marsiske and Willis (1995) addressed this issue by using three separate measures of practical problem solving and seeing if they converged on a single set of abilities. Their results were enlightening. Each measure proved reliable and apparently valid, but they were not strongly interrelated and their relation to age also varied. Thus competence in solving practical problems is a multidimensional construct, much like intelligence itself, calling into question whether a global construct of practical problem solving exists at all.

One way to assess practical problem solving in more focused terms is to create measures with clearly identifiable dimensions that relate to specific types of problems. This is what Diehl, Willis, and Schaie (1995) did by creating the Observed Tasks of Daily Living (OTDL) measure. The OTDL consists of three dimensions, which reflect three specific problems in everyday life: food preparation, medication intake, and telephone use. Each of these dimensions also reflects important aspects of assessing whether people can live independently, a topic we explored in Chapter 5. Diehl et al. showed that performance on the OTDL is directly influenced by age, fluid intelligence, and crystallized intelligence and indirectly by perceptual speed, memory, and several aspects of health. These results provide important links between practical problem solving and basic elements of psychometric intelligence and information processing. However, more recent study findings indicate that basic measures of inductive reasoning, domain-specific knowledge, memory, and working memory were related to everyday assessments of each of these abilities (Allaire & Marsiske, 1999, 2002; Thornton & Dumke, 2005). Allaire and Marsiske (1999, 2002) conclude that everyday problems reflecting well-structured challenges from activities of daily living show a strong relationship to traditional psychometric abilities.

The search for relations between psychometric intelligence and practical problem-solving abilities is only one way to examine the broader linkages with intellectual functioning. It focuses on the degree to which everyday problem solving is a manifestation of underlying intellectual abilities (Berg, 2008). However, recall that post-formal thinking is grounded in the ways in which people conceptualize situations.

Indeed, much of the research that led to the discovery of post-formal thought involved presenting adults with lifelike problems; Blanchard-Fields's (1986) study that we considered earlier is an excellent example. This approach enlarges the scope of what we consider everyday problem solving to include not just cognitive abilities, but also social, motivational, and cultural factors influencing how we solve problems (Berg, 2008).

For example, solving practical problems also involves the role of emotionality. Remember that one of the key aspects of post-formal thinking is the integration of emotion and logic. Blanchard-Fields, Jahnke, and Camp (1995) took this as a starting point and carefully manipulated the emotionality of problems. As described in more detail in the How Do We Know? feature, they found important age differences in problem-solving styles that were highly dependent on whether the problem situation was emotionally salient.

Another important factor that influences the way we solve everyday problems is the context in which the problem occurs. Do we use the same strategies when solving a family conflict between two siblings as we do when solving a conflict over the leading role in a project at work? The answer is no. Interestingly, however, age differences reveal that younger adults are more likely to use a similar strategy across problem-solving contexts: self-action in order to fix the problem. Older adults, on the other hand, are more likely to vary their strategy given the problem-solving context. For example, in interpersonal conflict problems (e.g., family conflict) they use more emotion-regulating strategies (i.e., managing their emotions) whereas in more instrumental situations (e.g., dealing with defective merchandise) they use self-action strategies (return the product) (Blanchard-Fields et al., 1997). Blanchard-Fields et al. (1997) argue that as we grow older and accumulate more everyday experience, we become more sensitive to the problem context and use strategies accordingly.

There are also individual differences in the way the same problem situation is interpreted. In other words, how individuals represent problems differs and could vary across the life span as developmental life goals change (Berg et al., 1998). Berg and colleagues (Berg et al., 1998; Strough et al., 1996) find that there are age differences in how individuals define their own everyday problems. Overall, middle-aged older adults defined problems more in terms of interpersonal goals (e.g., getting along with a person or spending more time with an individual), whereas adolescents and young adults focused more on competence goals (e.g., losing weight or studying for an exam). Furthermore, problem-solving strategies fit the problem definitions. For example, older adults defined problems more in terms of interpersonal concerns and subsequently reported strategies such as regulating others or including others, whereas competence goals resulted in strategies that involved more self-action. Along these lines Artistico, Cervone, and Pezzuti (2003) found that older adults were more confident and generated more effective solutions to problems that were typical of the life stage of older adults. Finally, Blanchard-Fields, Mienaltowski, and Seay (2007) found that older adults were rated as more effective in their everyday problem-solving strategy use than younger adults across all types of problem situations.

What can we conclude from the research on practical problem solving? First, practical problem-solving abilities are multidimensional and may not even interrelate strongly with each other. Second, the developmental functions of these abilities are complex and may differ somewhat across abilities. Third, the relations between practical problem-solving abilities and psychometric intelligence are equally complex. Finally, the close connection between solving practical problems and emotion and motivation may prove fruitful in furthering our understanding of individual differences in abilities. In short, solving practical problems offers an excellent way to discover how all the topics we have considered in this chapter come together to produce behavior in everyday life.

Expertise

On many basic information-processing tasks, younger adults clearly outperform older adults. Yet many people in their 60s and some in their 70s hold jobs that demand complex decision making, abstract reasoning, and memory for a lot of information. How do they do it?

The Role of Emotionality in Solving Real-Life Problems

Who were the investigators and what was the aim of the study? Fredda Blanchard-Fields, Heather Jahnke, and Cameron Camp (1995) were interested in the link between practical problem solving and post-formal thinking. This is especially true when problems that have an emotional aspect are examined. As they point out, most of the research on practical problem solving uses problems that have little emotional content in them. This may stack the deck against older adults, because of the connection between higher emotional intensity and demonstrating dialectical thinking (Kramer, 1990) and because they make more relativistic causal attributions in problem situations that are high in emotional salience (Blanchard-Fields & Norris, 1994). Age differences in problem-solving styles tend to be absent on problems low in emotional salience; however, on problems high in emotional salience, older adults showed more awareness of when to avoid or passively accept a situation within interpersonal, emotional domains, whereas younger adults tended to use a cognitive-analytic approach to all problems (Blanchard-Fields & Camp, 1990). What would happen if the emotional salience of problems were carefully manipulated? Would it influence

people's preferred mode of problem solving?

How did the investigators measure the topic of interest? Participants were given a total of 15 problem situations, with five rated in each of three categories as high (such as caring for an ill or aging parent), medium (such as moving to a new town), or low (such as returning defective merchandise) in emotional salience. Each solution was rated as reflecting one of four problem-solving styles: problem-focused action, involving overt behaviors that deal directly with the problem; cognitive problem analysis, involving cognitive efforts to solve the problem by thinking it through; passive-dependent behavior, involving attempts to withdraw from the situation in some way; and avoidant thinking and denial, involving attempts to manage the meaning of the problem.

Who were the participants in this study? Blanchard-Fields et al. studied 70 adolescents (aged 14 to 17), 69 young adults (aged 25 to 35), 74 middle-aged adults (aged 45 to 55), and 74 older adults (aged 65 to 75).

What was the design of the study? The study was a cross-sectional examination of age differences in adults' problem-solving strategies.

Were there ethical concerns with the study? Because the

study used volunteers and received parental permission for adolescents and the tasks contained no questions about sensitive topics, there were no ethical concerns.

What were the results? Results showed that emotional salience has a clear effect on the problem-solving approaches people of different ages adopt. No age differences were found in relation to problem-focused strategies; they were found in all age groups with all types of problems. However, these strategies decreased as the emotional salience of the problem increased. In fact, passive-dependent and cognitive-analysis strategies increased with greater emotional salience of the problems. Younger adults preferred cognitive-analysis strategies in comparison with any other age group, which fits with their tendency to adopt formal operational or absolutist thinking. Although all age groups adopted avoidant-denial strategies as their second most preferred choice, older adults were especially likely to adopt this approach. Similarly, older adults used passive-dependent strategies more than younger adults in situations with high emotional saliency.

The tendencies of younger adults to use cognitive-analysis strategies and for older adults

The most popular answer is that older adults compensate for poorer performance through their expertise. That is, through years of experience and practice, adults build up a wealth of knowledge about alternative ways to solve problems or make decisions that enables them to bypass steps needed by younger adults (Ericsson & Charness, 1994). In a way, this represents "the triumph of knowledge over reasoning" (Bosman & Charness, 1996); experience and age can defeat skill and youth. In research terms, older people are sometimes able to compensate for declines in some basic intellectual abilities (e.g., the information-processing skills underlying fluid abilities).

Figuring out exactly what expertise is turns out to be difficult. Charness and Bosman (1990) point out that experts are identified at times because they use novel approaches to solve difficult problems, because they have extensive knowledge about a particular topic, or because they are highly practiced. For example, expert physicians diagnose diseases differently from novice physicians (Patel & Groen, 1986), chess masters quickly evaluate very complex board positions (Charness & Bosman, 1990), and typists look ahead to help avoid mistakes (see Chapter 5).

What research has been conducted on age differences in expertise? Within a specified domain, expert performance tends to hold up as we grow older, with only slight declines in older age groups (Charness & Bosman, 1990; Kramer & Willis, 2002; Morrow et al., 2001). The important issue here is whether this increase in expertise makes up for losses in fluid intelligence. The results are encouraging in that acquired knowledge (i.e., expertise) helps the aging adult compensate for losses in other skills

such as those strongly related to fluid intelligence (Bosman & Charness, 1996; Dixon & Bäckman, 1995; Kramer & Willis, 2002; Masunaga & Horn, 2001; Morrow et al., 2003). In other words, older adults may be compensating for underlying decline by relying more on their experience.

Notice that the different developmental trajectories for expertise and basic information-processing abilities apparently mean the two are not strongly related. How can this be? Rybash, Hoyer, and Roodin (1986) proposed a process called encapsulation as the answer. *The term* **encapsulation** *refers to the idea that the processes of thinking (such as attention, memory, and logical reasoning) become connected to the products of thinking (such as knowledge about world history).* This process of encapsulation allows expertise to compensate for decrements in underlying processing ability, perhaps by making thinking in the particular domain more efficient.

Encapsulation reflects the fact that in adulthood knowledge becomes more and more specialized based on experience, which in turn reflects a lesser role of age-related neurological development and social demands for increased specialization of knowledge and expertise (Hoyer & Rybash, 1994). The emergence of encapsulated knowledge, unique to adulthood, becomes increasingly complex and resistant to change. Because it is experientially based, the development of cognition in adulthood is directed toward mastery and adaptive competency in specific domains, making it quite different from cognitive development during childhood, which is more genetically driven and uniform across content domains (Hoyer & Rybash, 1994). Knowledge encapsulation also implies that the notion of a general slowing of processing underlying cognitive

This is but one example of older adults imparting advice and compassion to younger generations.

changes in later life may be wrong. Research examining processing in different domains indicates that speed of processing differs across knowledge domains (Clancy & Hoyer, 1994). These findings indicate that the efficiency of the underlying mechanics (e.g., neural pathways), procedures, or computations required to carry out cognitive tasks depends on the amount of experientially acquired knowledge a person has in that domain.

Knowledge encapsulation has important implications for studying intellectual development in adulthood. Encapsulated knowledge cannot be decomposed to study its constituent parts, meaning that mechanistic approaches (such as the one used in the psychometric research we examined earlier in this chapter) or ones predicating across-the-board declines are inappropriate. Rather, approaches that take a more holistic view and that stress developing formal models of computational processes with a specific domain in particular contexts are more appropriate (Hoyer & Rybash, 1994).

In the next section, we will also see how the role of experience in cognitive development is changing the way we conceptualize wisdom. As we will see,

wisdom is more closely associated with having certain types of experiences than it is with age per se.

Wisdom

We began this chapter with a description of the wisdom of the Dalai Lama. Similarly, a number of folktales recount the wisdom of older characters. For example, caught in a no-win situation with his son-in-law, an old alchemist comes up with an insightful and clever solution on how to turn base elements (dirt) into gold. Chinen (1989) points out that folktales highlight several aspects of wisdom: It involves practical knowledge, it is given altruistically, it involves psychological insights, and it is based on life experience.

A growing body of research has been examining these aspects of wisdom. Baltes and colleagues (Baltes & Kunzmann, 2003; Baltes & Staudinger, 2000) conclude that implicit conceptions of wisdom are widely shared within a culture and include exceptional levels of functioning; a dynamic balance between intellect, emotion, and motivation; a high degree of personal and interpersonal competence; and good intentions. Drawing from this cultural-historical and philosophical analysis of wisdom, psychologists have attempted to operationalize wisdom in order to study it scientifically. Studies examining wisdom cross-culturally find that Westerners tend to define it using cognitive dimensions (e.g., experienced and knowledgeable), whereas people from Eastern cultures tend to define wisdom by stressing affective dimensions (e.g., emotional empathy, emotional regulation) (Takahashi & Bordia, 2000; Takahashi & Overton, 2002).

One of the best-known programs of research on wisdom and aging is the Berlin Wisdom Paradigm (Baltes & Kunzmann, 2003; Baltes & Staudinger, 2000). In this line of research, wisdom is conceptualized as an expert system dealing with the meaning and conduct of life (Baltes & Smith, 1990; Staudinger & Baltes, 1994). Similarly, Sternberg's (1998, 2004) research on wisdom defines it as the application of tacit knowledge and values toward the achievement of the common good.

To define wisdom as expertise, Baltes and colleagues specified the content of wisdom in terms of the fundamental pragmatics of life. This includes knowledge and judgment about the human condition and ways to plan, manage, and understand a good life. Based on years of research using in-depth think-aloud interviews with young, middle-aged, and older adults about normal and unusual problems that people face, Baltes and Staudinger (2000) studied the nature of wisdom and how it relates to age and other psychosocial factors. In order to study wisdom scientifically, Baltes and Staudinger used their general framework to develop five specific criteria for determining whether a person demonstrates wisdom. These are described in Table 7.3.

One important issue with Baltes and Staudinger's approach to wisdom is whether it has a psychological

Table 7.3

Five Criteria for Wisdom-Related Performance

Basic Criteria

Factual knowledge	To what extent does this performance show general (*conditio humana*) and specific (e.g., life events, variations, institutions) knowledge about life matters and demonstrate scope and depth in the coverage of issues?
Procedural knowledge	To what extent does this performance consider strategies of decision making (e.g., cost-benefit analysis), self-regulation, life interpretation, life planning (e.g., means-ends analysis), and advice giving (e.g., timing, withholding)?

Metalevel Criteria

Life-span contextualism	To what extent does this performance consider the past, current, and possible future contexts of life and the many circumstances (e.g., culturally graded, age-graded, idiosyncratic) in which a life is embedded and how they relate to each other?
Value relativism	To what extent does this performance consider variations in values and life priorities and the importance of viewing each person within his or her own framework of values and life goals, despite a small set of universal values such as the orientation toward the well-being of oneself and others?
Awareness and management of uncertainty	To what extent does this performance consider the inherent uncertainty of life (in terms of interpreting the past, predicting the future, managing the present) and effective strategies for dealing with uncertainty (e.g., backup solutions, optimizing gain-loss ratio)?

Source: Staudinger, U. M. (1999) Older and wiser? Integrating results on the relationship between age and wisdom-related performance. *International Journal of Behavioral Development* 23. Copyright © 1999 Reprinted with permission from Sage Publications.

bias. That is, the framework and criteria may not capture the "true" essence of wisdom, if one were to examine the characteristics of what people in everyday life define as wise behavior. To examine this possibility, Baltes, Staudinger, Maercker, and Smith (1995) compared people who were nominated as wise to groups of clinical psychologists and highly educated older and younger groups. Their results indicated that the wise nominees performed as well on the five criteria of wisdom as did the clinical psychologists, who in other studies had outperformed other groups. The wisdom nominees also scored extremely well in tasks involving life management and on the criterion of recognizing that the "right thing to do" varies across people. Based on these findings, Baltes et al. concluded that their framework and criteria are not biased in such a way as to differentially favor psychologists.

Two important aspects of wisdom have been demonstrated fairly clearly. First, wisdom is not the same thing as creativity; wisdom is the growth of expertise and insight, whereas creativity is the generation of a new solution to a problem (Simonton, 1990).

Second, the relationship between age and wisdom is complex. Certainly, wisdom has long been characterized as the province of older adults. For example, studies of people's implicit theories of wisdom, in which people are asked to nominate the wisest person they know, indicate that people of all ages tend to nominate someone who is older than they are (Denney et al., 1995). However, when the criteria for wisdom discussed earlier are applied to people's knowledge and actions, a different picture emerges. The typical way in which wisdom is assessed is to have adults respond to hypothetical life-planning problems, such as whether to accept a promotion or whether to retire (Staudinger & Baltes, 1996). The problems were presented as dilemmas facing fictitious people, and participants had to reason out a solution. For example, one study had people respond to life-planning problems such as this: A 15-year-old girl wants to get married right away. What should she consider and do? Answers were then analyzed in terms of the degree to which they reflect the five wisdom-related criteria listed earlier. High and low wisdom-related responses are shown in Table 7.4.

Contrary to our stereotypes about wisdom and aging, in a number of studies using this method, Baltes and colleagues (Baltes & Staudinger, 2000;

Table 7.4

Illustration of a Wisdom-Related Task with Examples of Extreme Responses

A 15-year-old girl wants to get married right away.
What should she consider and do?

Low wisdom-related score:

"A 15-year-old girl wants to get married? No, no way, marrying at age 15 would be utterly wrong. One has to tell the girl that marriage is not possible." (After further probing) "It would be irresponsible to support such an idea. No, this is just a crazy idea."

High wisdom-related score:

"Well, on the surface, this seems like an easy problem. On average, marriage for 15-year-old girls is not a good thing. But there are situations where the average case does not fit. Perhaps in this instance, special life circumstances are involved, such that the girl has a terminal illness. Or the girl has just lost her parents. And also, this girl may live in another culture or historical period. Perhaps she was raised with a value system different from ours. In addition, one has to think about adequate ways of talking with the girl and to consider her emotional state."

Source: Baltes, P. B. & Staudinger, U. M. (2000). Wisdom: A metaheuristic (pragmatic) to orchestrate mind and virtue toward excellence. *American Psychologist* 55, 136. Copyright © 2000, Reprinted with permission from the American Psychological Association.

Smith & Baltes, 1990; Staudinger, 1999) found no association between age and wise answers. Instead, they found evidence of wisdom in adults of all ages. The key variable appears to be having extensive life experience with the type of problem given, not just life experience in general. Thus, given the right circumstances, a 35-year-old and a 75-year-old could give equally wise solutions to a life problem.

Research based on cognitive developmental changes in adulthood such as those discussed earlier concerning post-formal thinking has uncovered other aspects in the growth of wisdom. Several investigators point out that a wise person is one who is can integrate thinking, feeling, and acting into a coherent approach to a problem (Labouvie-Vief, 1990; Orwoll and Perlmutter, 1990). This research implies that empathy or compassion is an important characteristic of wise people, due to their ability to overcome automatic responses to show concern for core human experiences and values (Pascual-Leone, 2000). Thus, wise people can see through situations and get to the heart of the matter, rather than be caught in the superficial aspects of the situation.

So what specific factors help one become wise? Baltes and Staudinger (2000) identify three factors: (1) general personal characteristics, such as mental ability; (2) specific expertise conditions, such as mentoring or practice; and (3) facilitative life contexts, such as education or leadership experience. First, the most important personal characteristics related to wisdom were cognitive style (evaluation of issues, moving beyond existing rules, and tolerance for ambiguity) and creativity (Staudinger et al., 1997). Second, people with expertise in the form of professional clinical psychology showed higher levels of wisdom-related performance than other groups (Smith et al., 1994; Staudinger et al., 1992). Finally, social intelligence, social collaboration, and cooperative conflict management facilitate wisdom-related performance, and older adults profited more from this collaboration than the young ones did (Kunzmann & Baltes, 2003; Staudinger & Baltes, 1996; Staudinger & Pasupathi, 2003).

Other researchers point to additional criteria. For example, Labouvie-Vief (1990) argues that the integration of affect and cognition that occurs during adulthood results in the ability to act wisely. Personal growth across adulthood, reflecting Erikson's concepts of generativity and integrity, helps foster the process as well. All these factors take time. Thus, although growing old is no guarantee that wisdom will develop, it provides one with the time that, if used well, will provide a supportive context for it.

The picture of wisdom that is emerging appears to support the opening tale. Just as the old alchemist's response was based on his own specific experience with trying to make gold, so too our own wisdom comes from becoming experts at dealing with particular kinds of problems.

Concept Checks

1. What differentiates an older decision maker from a younger one?
2. What do optimally exercised abilities and unexercised abilities mean?
3. How does the process of encapsulation occur?
4. What are the five criteria of determining whether someone is wise according to Baltes and colleagues?

SOCIAL POLICY IMPLICATIONS

In the section on training, evidence suggests that a cognitively enriched lifestyle can positively influence intellectual change as we grow older. This suggests that there is promise in developing long-term cognitive enrichment programs to reduce morbidity and dependence in older adults. For example, it may be the case that we can defer the need for assited living, improve well-being, and reduce health care costs. Projects aimed at training intellectual abilities in older adult populations thus have important public policy implications in terms of funding priorities and reducing the burden on public funding for disabilities in senior citizens. The long-term goals of projects such as ACTIVE is to reduce public health problems associated with the increasing need for more formal care and hospitalization along with the loss of independence in the growing number of American senior citizens.

Richard M. Suzman, Ph.D., Associate Director for the Behavioral and Social Research Program at the National Institute on Aging (NIA), says,

The trial (*ACTIVE trials*) was highly successful in showing that we can, at least in the laboratory, improve certain thinking and reasoning abilities in older people. The findings here were powerful and very specific. Although they did not appear to make any real change in the actual, daily activities of the participants, I think we can build on these results to see how training ultimately might be applied to tasks that older people do everyday, such as using medication or handling finances. This intervention research, aimed at helping healthy older people maintain cognitive status as they age, is an increasingly high priority of the NIH/National Institute on Aging.

Summary

7.1 Defining Intelligence

How do people define intelligence in everyday life?

- Experts and laypeople agree that intelligence consists of problem-solving ability, verbal ability, and social competence. Motivation, exertion of effort, and reading are important behaviors for people of all ages; however, some age-related behaviors are also apparent.

What are the major components of the life-span approach?

- The life-span view emphasizes that there is some intellectual decline with age, primarily in the mechanics, but there is also stability and growth, primarily in the pragmatics. Four points are central. Plasticity concerns the range within which one's abilities are modifiable. Multidimensionality concerns the many abilities that underlie intelligence. Multidirectionality concerns the many possible ways individuals may develop. Interindividual variability acknowledges that people differ from each other.

What are the major research approaches for studying intelligence?

- Three main approaches are used to study intelligence. The psychometric approach focuses on performance on standardized tests. The cognitive-structural approach emphasizes the quality and style of thought. The information-processing approach emphasis basic cognitive mechanisms.

7.2 Developmental Trends in Psychometric Intelligence

What are primary mental abilities and how do they change across adulthood?

- Primary abilities comprise the several independent abilities that form factors on standardized intelligence tests. Five have been studied most: number, word fluency, verbal meaning, inductive reasoning, and spatial orientation.

- Primary mental abilities show normative declines with age that may affect performance in everyday life after around age 60, although declines tend to be small until the mid-70s. However, within-individual differences show that very few people decline equally in all areas.

What are secondary mental abilities? What are the developmental trends for fluid and crystallized intelligence?

- Fluid intelligence involves innate abilities that make people flexible and adaptive thinkers and that underlie the acquisition of knowledge and experience. Fluid intelligence normally declines with age. Crystallized intelligence is knowledge acquired through life experience and education. Crystallized intelligence does not normally decline with age until very late life. As age increases, individual differences remain stable with fluid intelligence but increase with crystallized intelligence.

What are the primary moderators of intellectual change?

- Age-related declines in fluid abilities have been shown to be moderated by cohort, education, social variables, personality, health, lifestyle, and task familiarity. Cohort effects and familiarity have been studied most. Cohort differences are complex and depend on the specific ability. Age differences in performance on familiar tasks are similar to those on standardized tests. Although taking both into account reduces age differences, they are not eliminated.

How successful are attempts at training primary mental abilities?

- Several studies show that fluid intelligence abilities improve after direct training and after anxiety reduction. Improvements in performance match or exceed individuals' level of decline. Training effects appear to last for several years regardless of the nature of the training, but generalization of training to new tasks is rare.

7.3 Qualitative Differences in Adults' Thinking

What are the main points in Piaget's theory of cognitive development?

- Key concepts in Piaget's theory include adaptation to the environment, organization of thought, and the structure of thought. The processes of thought are assimilation (using previously learned knowledge to make sense of incoming information) and accommodation (making the knowledge base conform to the environment). According to Piaget, thought develops through four stages: sensorimotor, preoperations, concrete operations, and formal operations.

What evidence is there for continued cognitive development beyond formal operations?

- Considerable evidence shows that the style of thinking changes across adulthood. The development of reflective judgment in young adulthood occurs as a result of seven stages. Other research has identified a progression from absolutist thinking to relativistic thinking to dialectical thinking. A key characteristic of post-formal thought is the integration of emotion and logic. Much of this research is based on people's solutions to real-world problems. Although there have been suggestions that women's ways of knowing differ from men's, research evidence does not provide strong support for this view.

7.4 Everyday Reasoning and Problem Solving

What are the characteristics of older adults' decision making?

- Older adults make decisions in a qualitatively different way from younger adults. They tend to search for less information, require less information, and rely on preexisting knowledge structures in making everyday decisions. Older adults perform more poorly when asked to create or invent new decision rules, in unfamiliar situations, and when the decision task requires high cognitive load.

What age differences are found in practical problem solving?

- In Denney's model, both unexercised and optimally exercised abilities increase through early adulthood and slowly decline thereafter. Performance on practical problem solving increases through middle age. Research indicates that sound measures of practical problem solving can be constructed, but these measures do not tend to relate to each other, indicating that problem solving is multidimensional. The emotional salience of problems is an important feature that influences problem-solving style with older adults performing better when problems involve interpersonal and emotional features.

What is the role of experience in expertise and problem solving?

- Older adults can often compensate for declines in some abilities by becoming experts, which allows them to anticipate what is going to be required on a task. Knowledge encapsulation occurs with age, in which the processes of thinking become connected with the products of thinking. Encapsulated knowledge cannot be decomposed and studied component by component.

What is wisdom and how does it relate to age and life experience?

- Wisdom involves four general characteristics: it deals with important matters of life; it consists of superior knowledge, judgment, and advice; it is knowledge of exceptional depth; and it is well intentioned. Five specific behavioral criteria are used to judge wisdom: expertise, broad abilities, understanding how life problems change, fitting the response with the problem, and realizing that life problems are often ambiguous. Wisdom also entails integrating thought and emotion to show empathy or compassion. Wisdom may be more strongly related to experience than to age.

Review Questions

7.1 Defining Intelligence

- How do laypeople and researchers define intelligence?
- What are the two main ways that intelligence has been studied? Define each.

7.2 Developmental Trends in Psychometric Intelligence

- What are primary mental abilities? Which ones have been studied most? How do they change with age?
- Define fluid and crystallized intelligence. How does each change with age?
- What factors moderate age changes in fluid intelligence? What role does cohort play? What role do health and lifestyle play?
- What benefits do older people get from intervention programs aimed at improving fluid abilities? What training approaches have been used? How well do trained skills generalize?
- Are there any limitations on the extent to which older adults can improve their cognitive performance?

7.3 Qualitative Differences in Adults' Thinking

- What are the key concepts in Piaget's theory?
- What stages of cognitive development did Piaget identify? Do adults use formal operations?
- What is reflective judgment? What are the stages in its development? What are absolutist, relativistic, and dialectical thinking?
- How do emotion and logic become integrated?
- What evidence is there for gender differences in post-formal thinking?

7.4 Everyday Reasoning and Problem Solving

- How do older adults differ from younger adults in everyday decision making?
- What are unexercised and optimally exercised abilities? How do their developmental paths differ from each other?

- What are the developmental trends in solving practical problems? How does emotional salience of problems influence problem-solving style?
- What is an expert? How is expertise related to age?
- What is knowledge encapsulation?
- What criteria are used to define wisdom? How is wisdom related to age?

Integrating Concepts in Development

- How are the primary and secondary mental abilities related to the aspects of information processing considered in Chapters 6 and 7?
- What do you think an integrated theory linking post-formal thinking, practical problem solving, expertise, and wisdom would look like?
- What aspects of secondary mental abilities do you think would be most closely linked to expertise? Why?
- How does effective social cognitive functioning considered in Chapter 9 relate to wisdom-related behaviors?

Key Terms

accommodation Changing one's thought to better approximate the world of experience.

assimilation Using currently available knowledge to make sense out of incoming information.

cognitive-structural approach An approach to intelligence that emphasizes the ways in which people conceptualize problems and focuses on modes or styles of thinking.

crystallized intelligence Knowledge acquired through life experience and education in a particular culture.

encapsulation The idea that the processes of thinking become connected to the products of thinking.

factor The interrelations among performances on similar tests of psychometric intelligence.

fluid intelligence Abilities that make one a flexible and adaptive thinker, that allow one to draw inferences, and that allow one to understand the relations among concepts independent of acquired knowledge and experience.

interindividual variability An acknowledgment that adults differ in the direction of their intellectual development.

multidimensional The notion that intelligence consists of many dimensions.

multidirectionality The distinct patterns of change in abilities over the life span, with these patterns being different for different abilities.

optimal level of development In the reflective judgment framework, the highest level of information-processing capacity that a person is capable of.

optimally exercised ability The ability a normal, healthy adult would demonstrate under the best conditions of training or practice.

plasticity The range of functioning within an individual and the conditions under which a person's abilities can be modified within a specific age range.

post-formal thought Thinking characterized by a recognition that truth varies across situations, that solutions must be realistic to be reasonable, that ambiguity and contradiction are the rule rather than the exception, and that emotion and subjective factors play a role in thinking.

primary mental abilities Independent abilities within psychometric intelligence based on different combinations of standardized intelligence tests.

psychometric approach An approach to intelligence involving defining it as performance on standardized tests.

reflective judgment Thinking that involves how people reason through dilemmas involving current affairs, religion, science, and the like.

secondary mental abilities Broad-ranging skills composed of several primary mental abilities.

skill acquisition In the reflective judgment framework, the gradual, and somewhat haphazard, process by which people learn new abilities.

unexercised ability The ability a normal, healthy adult would exhibit without practice or training.

Resources

You may wish to view current research on the Berlin Wisdom Paradigm and the ACTIVE project on the sites for these individual websites.

Readings

King, P. M., & Kitchener, K. S. (1994). *Developing reflective judgment: Understanding and promoting intellectual growth and critical thinking in adolescents and adults.* San Francisco: Jossey-Bass. The most thorough description of the reflective judgment framework, including excellent discussions on the longitudinal data on which it is based. Easy reading.

Labouvie-Vief, G. (1994). *Psyche and Eros: Mind and gender in the life course.* New York: Cambridge University Press. A thorough examination of the adult developmental pathway to the reintegration of emotion and logic. It draws from multiple areas including psychological research, mythology, religion, and literature. Moderate reading.

Schaie, K. W. (2005). *Developmental influences on adult intelligence: The Seattle Longitudinal Study.* New York: Oxford University Press. The most up-to-date review of the Seattle Longitudinal Study in a single volume. A must-read not only for the information about psychometric intelligence but also for the information on research methodology. Moderately difficult reading.

Sinnott, J. D. (Ed.). (1994). *Interdisciplinary handbook of adult lifespan learning.* Westport, CT: Greenwood Press. An excellent eclectic collection of chapters on various topics pertaining to intellectual development in adulthood. Easy to moderately difficult reading.

Sternberg, R. J. (Ed.). (1990). *Wisdom: Its nature, origins, and development* (pp. 279–313). Cambridge, UK: Cambridge University Press. One of the few collections of articles on wisdom that provides a broad survey of the topic. Moderately difficult reading.

Sternberg, R. J. (2003). *Wisdom, intelligence, and creativity synthesized.* New York: Cambridge University Press. This book represents a critical review and summary of current views of human intelligence. Moderately difficult reading.

8

Social Cognition

WHEN A PROMINENT
DEMOCRAT MARRIES A
PROMINENT REPUBLICAN, AS
occurred when the top consultants to
the competing presidential candidates
of 1992 tied the knot, people try to
make sense of it. Many thought the
marriage of Mary Matalin (Bush's
political director) and James Carville
(Clinton's campaign strategist) was
doomed because they were political

© Will Hart/Photo Edit

"opposites." In contrast, the newlyweds saw their passion for politics as a core similarity.

The public speculation about the Matalin-Carville relationship illustrates how people
try to make sense of other people's behavior. As we will see, this is the essence of social cognitive
functioning. In this chapter, we will consider how the social context is involved
in our cognitive processes. We will take a closer look at how our basic cognitive abilities influence our
social cognitive processing. We will examine how our past experiences and beliefs influence our social
judgment processes such as how people make impressions
and explain behavior (causal attributions). Finally we will examine four aspects of social
cognition: the role of motivational and emotion as processing goals, how stereotypes
affect how we judge older adults' behavior, how much personal control people feel they have, and
how cognition is affected when we are communicating to others in a social context.

But first we need to highlight the importance of social-contextual aspects of cognition.
As discussed in Chapter 6, traditional cognitive aging research has focused on the basic
architecture of human information processing and how it is tied to physiological decline.
In pursuit of this goal, painstaking efforts have been made to try to create tasks and
stimuli that are not familiar to the participants in the study and devoid of social implications. Although
these traditional approaches to cognition and aging are important to identify
basic cognitive processes and how they change over time, they do not tell us how social knowledge
(e.g., beliefs about aging), social goals (e.g., what is important for "me" to remember in this task), and
emotion affect cognition.

A new wave of social cognition research has raised some important issues for aging research such as
how our life experiences and emotions, as well as changes in our pragmatic knowledge, social expertise,
and values, influence how we think and remember. To address these issues, we must consider both the
basic cognitive architecture of the aging adult (identified in Chapter 6) and the functional architecture of

everyday cognition in a social context (discussed in Chapter 7). Even if certain basic cognitive mechanisms decline (such as episodic memory recall or speed of processing), older adults still have the social knowledge and skills that allow them to function effectively. In fact, by taking into consideration social and emotional factors, researchers find that older adults' cognitive functioning often remains intact and may even improve across the life span (Blanchard-Fields, Horhota, & Mienaltowski, 2008; Carstensen & Mikels, 2005; Hess, 2005). This approach reinforces the perspective of this textbook that views effective development as a lifelong adaptive process.

8.1 Social Judgment Processes

LEARNING OBJECTIVES
- What is the negativity bias in impression formation, and how does it influence older adults' thinking?
- Are there age differences in accessibility of social information?
- How does processing context influence social judgments?
- To what extent do processing capacity limitations influence social judgments in older adults?

Alexandra and Klaus were taking care of their grandchildren for the weekend. They took them to the zoo for an outing. When they passed the gift shop, the children would not stop whining that they wanted a present. This frustrated Alexandra and Klaus, and they both tried to come up with an explanation for this distressing behavior. At first, they were worried because it seemed that the behavior of their grandchildren indicated that they were, in essence, selfish children. But on further reflection, they considered other factors. The parents always bought the children a gift at the zoo, and so the children naturally expected it to happen again. The grandparents felt better about the situation after considering the parents' role in it, and bought the gifts for the children.

In this situation, Alexandra and Klaus were making important social judgments. They carefully analyzed the situation to try and understand their grandchildren's behavior by focusing on all the factors involved in it. Alexandra and Klaus show how we can correct our initial assessments of others if we take the time to reflect about all of the extenuating circumstances. But what would have happened

if they had not had the time to think about it, and instead had had multiple distractions such as dealing with the emotional outbursts of their grandchildren as well as their own emotional reactions? Their judgments also could have been influenced by some very strong beliefs about how children should behave in a social situation such as this one. We will consider the influence of both of these factors on making social judgments: the role that is played by cognitive capacity, or by having enough time and making the effort to reflect on a situation, and social knowledge and beliefs. However, first let us explore the age differences in making social judgments.

Many laboratory studies have examined abstract cognitive skills and how they change as we get older (see Chapter 6). Like the everyday cognition research discussed in Chapter 7, an important question in social cognition research is: to what extent do the findings from the lab translate into understanding behavior in everyday contexts as people grow older? The social cognition perspective provides a way of examining how basic cognitive abilities operate in social situations. The basic goal of the social cognition approach is to understand how people make sense of themselves, others, and events in everyday life (Fiske, 1993).

Impression Formation

In an intriguing set of studies, Hess and colleagues (Hess, 2006; Hess, Germain, Rosenberg, Leclerc, & Hodges, 2005; Hess, Osowski, & Leclerc, 2005) examined age differences in social judgments by examining **impression formation,** *or the way people form and revise first impressions.* They examined how people use diagnostic trait information in making initial impressions of an individual and how this varies with age. To study this, one group of adults was first presented with positive information about a person, such as evidence of honesty. They were then presented with negative information, including incidents of dishonest behavior. Another group of adults was presented the information in reverse: first they were given a negative portrayal (dishonesty) and then were given incidents of positive behavior (e.g., honest behavior).

As you can see from Figure 8.1, Hess and Pullen (1994) found that all study participants modified their impressions. When new negative information was presented after the initial positive portrayal of the target, older adults were willing to modify their impression of the target from positive to negative. However, they were less willing to modify their first impression when the negative portrayal was followed by positive information. Younger adults did not show this pattern. Instead, they were more concerned with making sure the new information was consistent with their initial impression. To do so, they modified their impressions to correspond with the new information regardless of whether it was positive or negative.

Hess and Pullen suggest that older adults may rely more on life experiences and social rules of behavior when making their interpretations, whereas younger adults may be more concerned with situational consistency of the new information

presented. They also suggest that given older adults' experience in life, *older adults let their initial impressions stand because negative information was more striking to them and thus affected them more strongly. This is called a* **negativity bias.** This bias corresponds well with other studies demonstrating that older adults pay attention to and seek out emotional information more than do younger people (Carstensen, 1995; Carstensen et al., 2003). We will discuss this further later in the chapter. This bias suggests that decline in cognitive functioning limits the ability of older adults to override the impact of their initial impressions.

Further evidence shows that the social judgments older adults make appear to be more sensitive to the *diagnosticity* of the information that is available (Hess, 2006). For example, if young adults receive new information about a person that contradicts their original impression, they are likely to adjust that initial impression. However, older adults are more selective in the information they choose to use in forming their judgments. They focus more on details that are most relevant to making those judgments and change their initial impression only if the new information is *diagnostic,* in other words, relevant and informative (Hess et al., 1999; Hess et al., 2005). It appears that for older adults to invest information-processing resources in making a judgment, they need to be invested in the social situation in which the judgment is made.

In some situations older adults may be at a disadvantage when processing social information. For example, researchers have found that although younger and older adults can process social information similarly, older adults are at a disadvantage when the social context is cognitively demanding (Mutter, 2000; Ybarra & Park, 2002). A cognitively demanding situation would be similar to Alexandra and Klaus's situation where they were trying to understand their grandchildren's behavior under conditions of time pressure and multiple distractions. Studies find that, indeed, when older adults take their time to make a social judgment, they process information similarly to younger adults and take into consideration all of the relevant information. However, when given a time limit, they have

Older adults tend to hold onto first impressions longer when meeting new people.

Positive initial portrayal of target

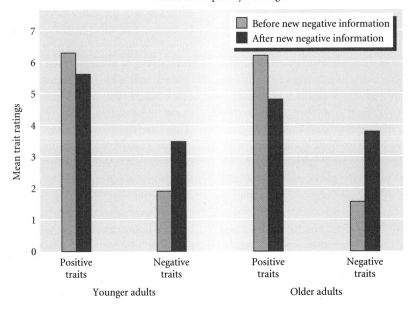

Negative initial portrayal of target

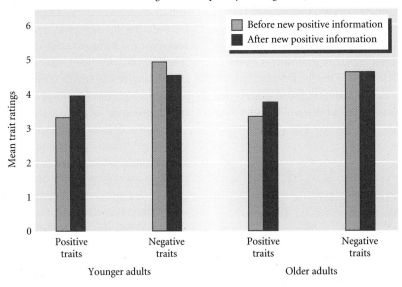

Figure 8.1 **Mean Trait Ratings Before and After Presentation of New Negative or Positive Information.**

Source: A modified graph of the Hess, T. M., & Pullen, S. M. (1994). Adult age differences in impression change processes. *Psychology and Aging* 9, p. 239. Copyright © 1994 Reprinted with permission from the American Psychological Association.

difficulty remembering the information they need to make their social judgments (Ybarra & Park, 2002).

In the next section, we examine processes involved in accessing knowledge used to make social judgments.

Knowledge Accessibility and Social Judgments

When we are faced with new situations, we draw on our previous experiences stored in memory, in other words, our **social knowledge.** The content of those experiences and knowledge and how easily we can retrieve it will affect what types of social judgments we make and how we behave in social situations. If you are attending your first day of class, for example, in order to act appropriately you draw on social knowledge that tells you "how to behave in a classroom." This process includes having available stored representations of the social world or memories of past events, how to apply those memories to various situations, and easy access to the memories.

We draw on implicit theories of personality (our personal theories of how personality works) to make judgments, for example, about how a professor should act in a classroom. If the professor's behavior is inconsistent with our implicit theory of how he or she should act, this will affect the impression we form of the professor. If a professor dresses in shorts and makes casual references to the party he attended last night, this may violate our implicit theory that professors are reserved and work all the time. Research supports this in that implicit personality theories we have about people, in general, influence the impressions we form about specific individuals (Epstein et al., 1992; Skowronski & Carlston, 1989).

However, availability of social information in memory does not necessarily imply easy access to that information. The degree to which information in memory is easily accessible will determine the extent to which that information will guide social judgments and/or behavior. Easy access to information will be influenced by a number of variables. First, accessibility depends on the strength of the information stored in memory. For example, if you have extensive past experience retrieving and applying a particular construct, such as a personality trait (aggressive), you will have a highly accessible social knowledge structure representing features of this particular personality trait (e.g., dominant in social situations, highly competitive, and so on). Thus you would judge a person as "aggressive" by interpreting dominant behaviors as clearly diagnostic of aggressiveness. The personality trait construct would not be easily accessible for other people who do not have experience with aggressive people so that the trait of aggressiveness may not have been retrieved very often. These people would be likely to interpret the behavior very differently (Bargh, 1997; Higgins et al., 1977). For example, they may see the dominant or aggressive person as an expert in the area.

Age differences in the accessibility of social knowledge influence social judgments. First, as you saw in the case of impression formation, older adults rely on easily accessible social knowledge structures such as the initial impression made about an individual. Second, *age differences in knowledge accessibility also depend on the extent to which people rely on* **source judgments,** *in other words, when they try to determine the source of a particular piece of information.* For example, suppose you and a friend were introduced to two new people last week. Jane is an athlete and Sereatha is a bookworm. Sereatha revealed to you that she loves to play tennis. Today, your friend asks you whether it was Jane or Sereatha that loves to play tennis. This is a source judgment.

Mather and colleagues (Mather et al., 1999; Mather & Johnson, 2003) have found that when making source judgments, older adults rely more on easily accessible knowledge than do younger adults. In the example of meeting Jane and Sereatha, older adults would be more likely to erroneously remember that Jane loves to play tennis, as they would rely on an easily accessible stereotype that the athlete is more likely to love tennis than the bookworm.

Finally, older adults make more social judgment biases because they have trouble distinguishing between information that is true and information that is false (Chen, 2002; Chen & Blanchard-Fields, 2000). In studies by Chen and colleagues, older adults were instructed to disregard false information (printed in red) and pay attention to true information (printed in black) when reading criminal reports. However, the older adults had difficulty in doing so, and thus the false information (e.g., information that exacerbated the nature of the crime) biased their judgments about how dangerous the criminal was and affected their determination of the criminal's prison sentence.

A Processing Capacity Explanation for Age Differences in Social Judgments

Based on the research discussed so far, it appears that processing resource limitations play an important role in understanding how older adults process and access social information. In fact, social cognitive researchers use information-processing models to describe how individuals make social judgments (e.g., Gilbert & Malone, 1995). For example, Gilbert and his colleagues have shown that the ability to make unbiased social judgments depends on the cognitive demand accompanying those judgments. In other words, we all make snap judgments, but then we reconsider and evaluate possible extenuating circumstances to revise those initial judgments. This takes processing resources, and if we are busy thinking about something else we may not be able to revise our initial judgments.

As we will consider in more depth in the section on causal attributions later, Blanchard-Fields and colleagues (Blanchard-Fields, 1999; Blanchard-Fields & Beatty, 2005) have found that older adults consistently hold to their initial judgments or conclusions of why negative events occur more often than do younger adults. They appear not to adjust their initial judgments by considering other factors, as Alexandra and Klaus were able to do when they revised their interpretation of their grandchildren's behavior.

Because older adults typically exhibit lower levels of cognitive processing resources (see Salthouse, 1996, and Chapter 6), it is possible that this decline in resource capacity might impact social judgment processes. In the case of impression formation, older adults may have limited cognitive resources to process detailed information presented after the initial impression is formed. Use of such information overworks processing resources. Similarly, source judgments and

selectively attending only to true information also places demands on one's cognitive resources.

If indeed processing resource capacity is the major factor explaining social judgment biases, then it should affect all types of situations that older people encounter. However, it also may be that the extent to which social information is accessible operates independently of a processing resource limitation to influence social judgments. We will now examine the implications of this by considering how social knowledge and beliefs and motivation affect these types of social judgment biases. Before we can entertain the notion that knowledge influences social cognitive processing, we must first explore how social knowledge and beliefs develop and change as we grow older.

Concept Checks

1. How is impression formation affected by processing resource capacity?
2. How does knowledge accessibility influence age-related differences in social judgments?

8.2 Social Knowledge Structures and Beliefs

LEARNING OBJECTIVES
- What are social knowledge structures?
- What are social beliefs, and how do they change with age?

Anna is going on her first date since the death of her husband one year ago. She is 62 years of age and was married for 30 years, so she is extremely nervous about what to do and how to act. When her date, Eric, picks her up, he announces that he has made reservations at a nice Italian restaurant, and that afterward they will go to a late movie. Although Anna is nervous, she makes it through the date with few problems. To her delight, how she needs to act and what she should do seem to come flooding back to her without an ounce of effort.

Similar to our knowledge of how a professor should act, on her date Anna experienced the easy accessibility of a well-learned social script or social knowledge on how to behave on a date. Social cognitive research has paid considerable attention to how social knowledge structures and social beliefs guide behavior. What are social knowledge structures and social beliefs? They are defined in terms of how we represent and interpret the behavior of others in a social situation (Fiske, 1993). They come in many different forms. For example, we have scripted knowledge structures regarding everyday activities such as what people should do when they are going to the doctor's office or a restaurant. We have been socialized to adhere to and believe in social rules, or how to behave in specific social situations, such as how a husband should act toward his wife.

Understanding Age Differences in Social Beliefs

Two interesting developmental questions arise with respect to social knowledge structures. First, does the content of our social knowledge and beliefs change as we grow older? And second, how do our knowledge structures and beliefs affect our social judgments, memory, problem solving, and more?

There are many types of belief systems, which differ in content across age groups and also influence behavior. Understanding age differences in social belief systems has three important aspects (Blanchard-Fields & Hertzog, 2000). First, we must examine the specific content of social beliefs (i.e., the particular beliefs and knowledge individuals hold about rules, norms, and patterns of social behavior). Second, we must consider the strength of these beliefs to know under what conditions they may influence behavior. And, third, we need to know the likelihood that these beliefs will be automatically activated when a person is confronted with a situation in which these beliefs are being violated or questioned. If these three aspects of the belief system are understood, it will be possible to explain when and why age differences occur in social judgments.

In other words, older adults may hold different beliefs than other age groups (e.g., different rules for appropriate social behavior during Anna's situation of dating). Not only that, but how strongly individuals hold these beliefs may vary as a function of how

particular generations were socialized. For example, although younger and older generations may both believe that people should not live together before marriage, the oldest generation may be more adamant and rigid about this belief. However, evidence of age differences in the content of social beliefs does not provide a sufficient basis for understanding age differences in how and when such beliefs will be activated and how they will influence behavior.

Social cognition researchers argue that there are individual differences in the strength of social representations of rules, beliefs, and attitudes that are linked to specific situations (Mischel & Shoda, 1995). Such representations can be both cognitive (how we conceptualize the situation) and emotional (how we react to the situation). When encountering a specific situation, the individual's belief system predictably triggers an emotional reaction and related goals tied to the content of that situation. This in turn drives social judgments. Let's take the rule "You should never live with a romantic partner before you are married." If you were socialized from childhood on to believe in this rule, then you would negatively evaluate anyone violating it. For example, if you were told that Allen was putting pressure on Joan to live with him before they were married, and they subsequently broke up, you might have a negative emotional response and blame Allen for the breakup of the relationship because he was lobbying for cohabitation.

In a study exploring social beliefs, age differences were found in the types of social rules evoked in different types of situations (Blanchard-Fields, 1996, 1999). For example, in a situation where a husband chooses to work long hours instead of spending more time with his wife and family, the social rule "Marriage is more important than a career" tended to increase with age. As can be seen in Figure 8.2, this was particularly evident from age 24 to age 65. Figure 8.2 also shows that the social rule "The marriage was already in trouble" has an inverted U-shaped relationship. In other words, adults around ages 35 to 55 years as compared to 24- to 35-year-olds and those over 65 years produced this social rule the most.

These findings may relate to how the oldest generation was socialized with respect to the "important social rules" of marriage. Your grandmother's

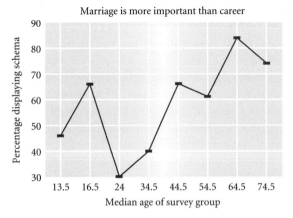

Marriage is more important than career

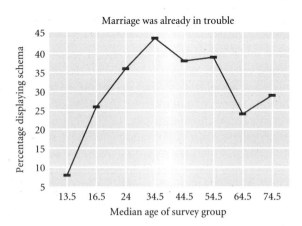

Marriage was already in trouble

Figure 8.2 Age differences in social rules in relationships.

generation was probably socialized very differently from your generation as to what is appropriate behavior on the part of husbands and wives. Thus these findings may reflect such cohort differences. Alternatively, viewing marriage as more important than one's career may relate to the particular life stage and life circumstances different age groups confront. During mid-career/mid-family stages, making a living and proving oneself in a career may take precedence (Schaie, 1977–1978). In contrast, during the retirement/empty nest phase, the importance of a marital relationship may reemerge. In contrast, the middle-aged group may not have relied on social rules to guide their thinking about the problem situation and focused more on the marital conflict itself. This could possibly reflect a by-product of the 1960s focus on communication of feelings. These are only a few examples of sociocultural experiential factors that may influence different social beliefs.

For a situation involving a youthful couple who eloped despite the objections of their parents, the social rules "Parents should have talked to, not provoked, the young couple" and "They were too young" also displayed an inverted U-shaped relationship with age. In other words, middle-aged individuals endorsed these rules, whereas younger and older age groups did not. In contrast, the social rule "You can't stop true love" displayed a U-shaped relationship with age. In other words, younger and older age groups endorsed this rule whereas

individuals in middle adulthood did not. It may be the case that in middle adulthood, between the ages 30 and 45, people are not focusing on issues of "Love conquers all." This makes sense given that they are in the stage of life where the pragmatic aspects of building a career are important. They also emphasized the pragmatics of age (e.g., being too young) as an important factor in marriage decisions.

One possible explanation for the preceding findings was that cohort effects or generational differences (discussed in Chapter 1) influenced whether or not strong family social rules would be activated. For example, older women adopted the social rule "Marriage is more important than career" considerably more than did men of their same generation and more than did women and men of younger generations. That older women more strongly endorsed this social rule in comparison to the other age groups is a good example of how emotionally laden values are evoked from these situations. An interesting question is whether these age differences in social schematic beliefs influence social judgments. We will explore that next in our section on causal attributions.

Concept Checks

1. How do social beliefs differ with age?
2. What are the possible explanations for age differences in social beliefs?

8.3 Social Judgments and Causal Attributions

LEARNING OBJECTIVES
- What are causal attributions?
- What is the correspondence bias?
- How does the nature of our causal attributions change with age?
- What alternative explanations are there for the dispositional bias found in older adults?

Erin is cleaning up after her son, who spilled his dinner all over the table and floor. At the same time, she is listening on the cordless phone to her coworker, Brittany, describing how anxious she was when she gave the marketing presentation in front of their new clients that day. Brittany is also describing how the boss had told her the company depended on this presentation to obtain a contract from the new clients. After the phone call, Erin reflected on Brittany's situation. She decided Brittany is an anxious person and should work on reducing her anxiety in these types of situations.

Erin was interested in what caused her coworker Brittany's anxiety when presenting information at work. Was it something about Brittany, such as being an anxious person? Or was it due to some other reason, such as luck or chance? Or was it due to the pressure placed on Brittany by her boss? Answers to these questions provide insights into particular types of social judgments people make to explain their behavior, which are referred to as *causal attributions.* **Causal attributions** *can be behavioral explanations that reside within the actor, such as "Brittany is an anxious person." This is called a* **dispositional attribution.** *Or the explanation can reside outside the actor, such as "Brittany is succumbing to pressures from her boss." This is called a* **situational attribution.** In this case, Erin made a dispositional attribution about Brittany. In this section, we explore whether there are age differences in the tendency to rely more on dispositional or situational attributions or on a combination of both when making causal attributions.

Historically, the study of attributions and aging has been confined to studying attributional judgments made about the aging population, usually involving competence in memory or cognition. We will discuss these issues when we examine research on stereotypes and attributions about older adults' mental competence. In that case, attributions about older persons' successes and failures are compared to similar successes and failures of younger adults. Such attributions go hand-in-hand with the stereotyping of older adults. However, more recently the focus in attribution and aging research has turned to the examination of changes in the nature of attributional processes, per se, from an adult developmental context. Thus the question can be asked whether findings typically found in social psychological attribution theory and research hold true beyond the college years (Blanchard-Fields et al., 2008).

Attributional Biases

For many years, we have known that college students typically produce informational distortions when making causal attributions about problem solving (e.g., Gilbert & Malone, 1995). *This is typically called* **correspondence bias.** In this case, youth rely more on dispositional information in explaining behavior and ignore compelling situational information such as extenuating circumstances. For example, suppose you tried to approach your psychology professor yesterday. She did not even acknowledge that you were there but just kept walking with her face buried in a manuscript. You might decide that because your professor ignored your question, she is arrogant (a dispositional attribution). At the same time, you may have ignored important situational information, such as that she has recently been overwhelmed by upcoming deadlines. Thus you did not consider all the pertinent information to make a more accurate judgment. This type of finding has been primarily documented with college youths. However, it may be the case that the life experience accumulated by middle-aged and older adults causes them to reach different conclusions and that they consider equally both types of information in explaining why things happen the way they do.

In a series of creative investigations, Blanchard-Fields (1994, 1996; Blanchard-Fields & Beatty, 2005; Blanchard-Fields & Horhota, 2005; Blanchard-Fields et al., 2007; Blanchard-Fields & Norris, 1994; Blanchard-Fields et al., 1998; Blanchard-Fields et al., 1999) studied the differences in causal attributions across the adult life span. In a number of studies, Blanchard-Fields presented participants with different situations having positive or negative outcomes and asked them to decide whether something about the main character in the story (dispositional attributions), the situation (situational attributions), or a combination of both (interactive attributions) was responsible for the event. For example, the vignettes represented situations such as that described earlier where Allen was pressuring Joan to live with him before marriage, Joan protested but Allen continued to pressure her, and the relationship ended up falling apart.

When the target events were ambiguous as to what was the specific cause of the outcome, as with Allen and Joan, all adults tended to make interactive attributions, but older adults did so at a higher rate. However, as can be seen from Figure 8.3, older adults paradoxically also blamed the main character more

(dispositional attributions) than younger groups, especially in negative relationship situations.

In another study, Blanchard-Fields and Norris (1994) examined the connection between cognitive level similar to post-formal reasoning discussed in Chapter 7 (e.g., the ability to consider multiple perspectives and to synthesize them into a workable solution) and attributions. They found that middle-aged adults scored higher on dialectical attributional reasoning (considering multiple explanations such as dispositional and situational factors and how these factors can be incorporated into a workable explanation of behavior) than adolescents, young adults, or older adults. And, again, older adults made stronger dispositional attributions.

Blanchard-Fields and Norris took a sociocultural perspective in explaining why older adults were more predisposed to making dispositional attributions and engaged in less dialectical reasoning in negative relationship situations. First, note that the correspondence bias in older adults only occurred in negative relationship situations. In this case, older adults appeared to apply specific social rules about relationships in making their attributional judgments, apparently because of their stage in life and the cohort in which they were socialized (such as the rule "Marriage comes before career"). In these situations, strong beliefs about how one should act in relationship situations appeared to be violated for the older adults, particularly older women. Therefore, these women made snap judgments about the main character who violated their strong beliefs and did not feel it was necessary to engage in conscious, deliberate analyses. They *knew* the character was wrong, as in the husband who chose to work long hours and not spend time with his family.

The interesting question arises, however, as to whether these attributional biases in older adults are truly due to activated belief systems that strongly impact their judgments or whether the older adults are deficient in conducting a causal analysis. This deficiency could take the form of limited cognitive resources that might prevent them from processing all details of the situation (e.g., extenuating situational circumstances). The vignette involving

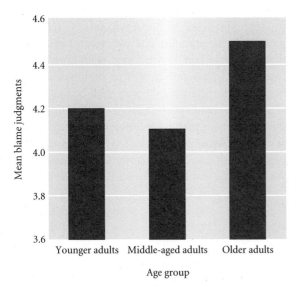

Figure 8.3 Dispositional attributions as a function of age.

Who was the investigator and what was the aim of the study? Yiwei Chen and Fredda Blanchard-Fields (1997) tested the idea that processing resource limitations accounted for the dispositional bias typically observed in older adults. Does older adults' limited resource capacity prevent them from adjusting initial dispositional biases? In addition, would older adults engage in an adjustment procedure if they were given more time, which would reduce cognitive processing demands? Alternatively, do strong social beliefs and social rules better explain older adults' dispositional biases?

How did the investigators measure the topic of interest? Chen and Blanchard-Fields presented 12 social dilemmas to participants. Within each situation a character violated a social rule about what is appropriate social behavior in the specific type of situation. On a computer screen, participants had to rate the degree to which the character was to blame for the situation either immediately following the story or 30 seconds later.

Who were the participants in the study? Chen and Blanchard-Fields selected a random sample of older adults and younger adults from the U.S. Southeast. Given that the younger adults were college students and the older adults were from the community, the sample was not representative of the population at large.

Were there ethical concerns with the study? Because the study used volunteers who performed the computerized task and there were no questions about sensitive topics, there were no ethical concerns.

What were the results? As you can see from Figure 8.4, older adults made higher dispositional ratings than younger adults did in the immediate-rating condition only. Older adults made lower dispositional attribution ratings (i.e., adjusted more) when they were forced to take more time to think about the situations than in the immediate-rating condition.

The age differences in immediate versus delayed conditions defined processing limitations in terms of time constraints. Given more time, older adults will adjust their attributions. However, we can only infer this, because the manipulation of processing constraints was not directly

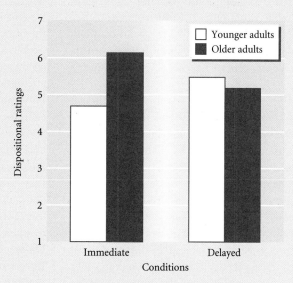

Figure 8.4 Dispositional ratings as a function of age group and rating condition.

Source: Chen, Y., & Blanchard-Fields, F. (1997). Age differences in stages of attributional processing. *Psychology and Aging* 12, p. 698. Copyright © 1997 Reprinted with permission from the American Psychological Association.

(Continued)

compared within participants. Also, adjustment does not always work in the same way. For example, younger adults had a slight tendency to increase their dispositional attributions given more time.

However, Chen and Blanchard-Fields also asked participants to complete brief written essays explaining their attributional judgments. The content of their statements was used to identify each individual's social rules regarding appropriate behaviors in the social situations portrayed in the vignettes. They found that older adults made more evaluative rule statements about the main character in the immediate-rating condition (e.g., "You shouldn't take friendship for granted"). In addition, high dispositional attributional ratings were correlated with such evaluative rule statements about the main character. Finally, the degree to which a participant produced evaluative rule statements about the main character accounted for the relationship between age and dispositional ratings about the main character in the immediate-rating condition.

What did the investigators conclude? Chen and Blanchard-Fields provide evidence against a resource limitation explanation for older adults' dispositional bias and provide evidence that the degree to which an individual endorses social rules determines when a dispositional bias will be made. In this case, older adults had more social rules violated in these vignettes and thus displayed a dispositional bias more than did younger adults.

Erin shows how, on the one hand, we can rely on our experience as older adults to guide us through uncomfortable situations; however, on the other hand, a reduction in our capacity does not allow us to consider all the relevant information, in this case, to make an accurate judgment about Brittany's behavior.

Remember, earlier we questioned whether a processing resource hypothesis was the best explanation of social judgment biases. Again, this is particularly important because in Blanchard-Fields's attribution studies, the dispositional bias was only found for older adults when they were presented with negative relationship situations. This issue was addressed in a study by Chen and Blanchard-Fields (1997), reviewed in the How Do We Know? feature. Finally, Klaczynski and Robinson (2000) have found that everyday reasoning biases in older adults occur not because of declining cognitive ability, but because older adults are more likely than younger adults to base their judgments on their own beliefs.

These findings indicate that the explanations people create to account for behavior vary depending on the type of situation (e.g., relationship or achievement situations), the age of the person, and whether strong social beliefs have been violated by a person in the situation. What is also emerging is the importance of the sociocultural context in which people are socialized, as this appears to create different social rules that are then used to make causal attributions. Additional research supports this idea. For example, Blanchard-Fields and colleagues (2007) examined causal attributions in Chinese younger and older adults in comparison to American younger and older adults. Interestingly they found that older Americans showed a greater correspondence bias than younger Americans. However, both younger and older Chinese performed similarly and showed less correspondence bias. Older Americans may focus their attributions on the individual due to a lifelong experience of an individualistic orientation. In order to adjust this initial judgment, the contextual information must be made salient to them in a socially meaningful manner. Support for this idea comes from studies showing that when there is a plausible motivation for the target's behavior, older adults can correct their judgments to be less biased than in a standard attitude attribution paradigm (Blanchard-Fields & Horhota, 2005).

For older Americans to correct their attributions, the constraint needs to provide a meaningful reason why a person would contradict his or her own beliefs. For Chinese older adults, the meaningful nature of the situation does not need to be emphasized because to them situational influences and constraints represent a naturally occurring manner in which to approach any judgment situation and they have a lifelong experience of a collectivist orientation. More research is needed to shed additional light on how these age differences are created and under what circumstances they appear.

8.4 Motivation and Social Processing Goals

LEARNING OBJECTIVES

- How do goals influence the way we process information, and how does this change with age?
- How do emotions influence the way we process information, and how does this change with age?
- How does a need for closure influence the way we process information, and how does it change with age?

Tracy and Eric are visiting their children and all their grandchildren on Cape Cod. They all are having a good time until their son, Eddie, brings up the hot topic of the upcoming presidential election. The debate between family members as to whom they should vote for becomes heated. Tracy and Eric are very concerned about the negative feelings generated in the debate and try to encourage everyone to change the topic. However, the brothers and sisters are more interested in settling the issue now.

Tracy and Eric cannot handle the negative energy and retire to bed early.

Why did Tracy and Eric focus on the emotional side of the problem (the increase in negative feelings), whereas the siblings focused on the more instrumental side of the problem (e.g., whom to vote for)? The different foci of Tracy and Eric in contrast to the children resulted in very different problem-solving strategies. Much like the research on social rules and social judgments, there is a growing area of research that suggests that change in the relative importance of social goals and motivation across the life span profoundly influences how we interpret and use social information or direct attention and effort to certain aspects of the problem situation (Hess, 2006). The idea is that goals change with age as a function of experience and time left in the life span. This can influence the degree to which we observe age differences in social cognitive functioning, such as the desire to focus on preserving ones' resources or eliminating negative affect in problem situations. Let's explore these further.

Personal Goals

Personal goals play a major role in creating direction in our lives. They consist of underlying motivations for our behavior and how we perceive our own ever-changing environment. Across the life span, personal goals change to match our needs, with young adults striving mainly for achievement, like completing a college degree or starting a career, and middle-aged and older adults seeking a balance between functioning independently and sharing their lives with others (e.g., children, spouses, etc.).

Selective optimization with compensation (SOC) is an important theoretical model which suggests that development occurs as we continuously update our personal goals to match our appraisal of available resources to obtain those goals (Baltes & Baltes, 1990). We choose manageable goals based upon our interests as well as physical and cognitive strengths and limitations.

As we grow older our limitations become more salient and require us to reevaluate our interests. Therefore, in older adulthood, research suggests that interests shift toward physical health and socio-emotional domains (Carstensen & Mikels, 2005; Rowe & Kahn, 1998).

This shift in priorities means that goals for the same event may be perceived differently by older and younger adults. A clear example of this shift in goal selection can be seen in research that examines how younger and older adults prioritize how they would like to perform in a dual-task situation. Younger and older adults were asked to memorize a list of words while simultaneously maintaining their balance as they navigated through an obstacle course (Li, Lindenberger, Freund, & Baltes, 2001). Although age differences in performing two tasks at the same time were more costly for the memory task than for the walking task, older adults chose to forgo aids that would improve their memory (e.g., a list) and instead chose to use aids designed to optimize walking performance (e.g., a handrail). When deciding which was more important to them, memory performance versus balance, older adults displayed a preference for their physical safety even if it meant that they would perform badly on a cognitive test. From this example, we see that life-span shifts in personal goals can be both helpful and harmful.

Goal selection requires that we thoughtfully choose where we should invest our resources. For example, in the lab younger adults are primarily motivated to achieve maximum performance on any cognitive task presented to them. Older adults take a different perspective. They prefer to maintain steady performance by optimizing their current resources rather than risking loss with an unknown strategy (Ebner, Freund, & Baltes, 2006). Thus, although older adults are less willing than younger adults to invest energy into improving their cognitive performance, their strategy choice is more optimal for them because they are more interested in retaining their autonomy by maintaining abilities at their current level. Although this does not directly translate into cognitive gains, it does help older adults optimize their cognitive performance in those domains

that they prioritize in their lives (Riediger, Freund, & Baltes, 2005). Although we cannot compensate for all of the resource limitations that come with advancing age, we can invest those resources we have into those goals that maximize an independent lifestyle and a positive sense of well-being.

Along these lines, recent work by Carstensen and her colleagues suggests that the pursuit of emotionally gratifying situations becomes a primary motivation that can substantially influence cognition in the latter half of the life span (Carstensen & Mikels, 2005). We therefore turn next to the impact of emotional processing goals on cognition.

Emotion as a Processing Goal

We will examine the idea of socio-emotional selectivity with aging in Chapter 10. For the purposes of this chapter you need to know that this theory maintains that emotional goals become increasingly important and salient as we grow older (Carstensen, 1995; Carsetensen et al., 2003). It is primarily a motivational model, which posits that the degree to which an individual construes time as limited or expansive leads to the ranking of emotional goals as high or knowledge-seeking goals as high in priority, respectively. Thus, given limited time left in the life span, older adults may be more motivated to emphasize emotional goals and aspects of life. We will examine this motivational factor in the context of maintaining and choosing intimate relationships in Chapter 10. However, it also can be applied in the context of social information processing.

A growing number of studies suggest that *older adults avoid negative information and focus more on positive information when making decisions and judgments and when remembering events* (Carstensen et al., 2000; Carstensen, Mikels, & Mather, 2006; Charles et al., 2003; Mather & Carstensen, 2003). *This phenomenon has received much attention in the literature and is called a* **positivity effect**. For example, older adults remember more positive images than negative ones, whereas younger adults remember both positive and negative images equally well (Charles et al., 2003). When examining what types of stimuli younger and older adults initially attend to, Mather and Carstensen (2003) found that older adults allocate less attention to negative stimuli (e.g., angry faces) than younger adults do. Older adults also remember more positive information when recalling their own autobiographical information (Kennedy, Mather, & Carstensen, 2004) and remember the positive aspects of their decisions more so than the negative ones (Mather, Knight, & McCaffrey, 2005).

An alternative perspective proposes that focusing on negative information is adaptive because it signals danger and vulnerability and thus is important for survival. This emphasis on negativity has been found in both the social and cognitive neuroscience literature for well over a decade (e.g., Lane & Nadel, 2000; Rozin & Royzman, 2001). Within the social cognitive aging literature, some studies demonstrate that older adults spend more time viewing negative stimuli (Charles et al., 2003) and display a negativity effect (Thomas & Hasher, 2006; Wood & Kisley, 2006). With respect to memory, Grühn and colleagues (2005) found no evidence for a positivity effect, and instead, found evidence for reduced negativity effect in older adults when remembering a list of words with negative, positive, and neutral valence. When incidentally encoding pictures, both younger and older adults recalled the central element more than the peripheral elements only for negative scenes. However, when instructed to attend to this difference, only younger adults overcame this encoding bias, whereas older adults could not overcome the memory trade-off (Kensinger, Piguet, Krendl, & Corkin, 2005).

Emotional goals appear to help older adults in that they can create a supportive context for their cognitive functioning. Remember we discussed the fact that older adults create more false memories than younger adults do in Chapter 6. Research on the interface between emotions and cognition suggest that the distinctiveness of emotions helps older adults to reduce the number of false memories produced (Kensinger & Corkin, 2004; May, Rahhal, Berry, & Leighton, 2005). However, it is important to also recognize that there are times when emotions may impede information processing. For example, situations that are highly arousing and require a great amount of executive control processing (discussed in Chapter 6) may lead older adults to be poorer at remembering and processing information (Kensinger & Corkin, 2004; Mather & Knight, 2005; Wurm, Labouvie-Vief, Aycock, Rebucal, & Koch, 2004). In addition, a focus on only positive information can interfere with decision making by leading older adults to miss out on important negative information necessary for making a quality decision (Löckenhoff & Carstensen, 2004).

Cognitive Style as a Processing Goal

Another type of motivational goal that can influence our thinking comes from our **cognitive style,** *or how we approach solving problems.* Examples include a need for closure and the inability to tolerate ambiguous situations. People with a high need for closure prefer order and predictability, are uncomfortable with ambiguity, are closed-minded, and prefer quick and decisive answers (Kruglanski et al., 1997; Neuberg et al., 1997). Empirical research on this construct has resulted in the development of well-validated questionnaires such as the Need for Closure scale (Webster & Kruglanski, 1994) and the Personal Need for Structure scale (Thompson et al., 1992).

The question is whether cognitive resources or need for closure are implicated in biased judgments. As we discussed earlier, situations that require substantial cognitive resources (i.e., require a lot of effort in cognitive processing such as processing information under time pressure) result in an increase in inaccuracies and biases in how we represent social information (Kruglanski & Webster, 1996). However, biased judgments can also be caused by motivational differences such as an increase in need for closure. In fact, research using need for closure instruments suggests that high need for closure and/or structure is related to attributional biases, the tendency to make stereotyped judgments, the formation of spontaneous trait inferences, and the tendency to assimilate judgments to primed constructs (Schaller et al., 1995).

It may also be the case that limited cognitive resources and motivational differences are both age-related and influence social judgments in interaction with each other. Hess and colleagues (Hess, Follett, & McGee, 1998) argue that changes in resources with aging (as in the declines we observed in working memory in Chapter 6) may lead to an increase in a need for closure with age. This can lead to biases in the way in which older adults process social information. In a recent study Hess, Waters, and Bolstad (2000) found that a high need for closure did not influence susceptibility to emotional priming influences on neutral stimuli of young and middle-aged adults. However, priming effects increased with higher need for structure in older adults. In other words, older adults with a high need for closure could not inhibit the affects of an emotional prime (e.g., a subliminally presented negative word) on their subsequent behavior (e.g., whether they liked or disliked an abstract figure). Because of age-related changes in personal resources (social and cognitive), motivational factors such as coming to quick and decisive answers to conserve resources become important to the aging adult.

Concept Checks

1. What is SOC and how does it influence processing goals?
2. What is the positivity effect?
3. What is need for closure, and how does it influence social judgments?

8.5 Stereotypes and Aging

LEARNING OBJECTIVES
- How does the content of stereotypes about aging differ across adulthood?
- How do younger and older adults perceive the competence of the elderly?
- How do negative stereotypes about aging unconsciously guide our behavior?

Mark, a 70-year-old man, was getting ready to go home from a poker game at his friend's house. However, he could not find his keys. Down the street, Guy, a 20-year-old college student, was ready to go home from a party at his friend's house, and he also could not find his keys. Each of their respective friends at the two social events had very different perceptions of Mark and Guy. Mark's friends started to worry whether Mark was becoming senile, speculating that it might be all downhill from now on. They wondered whether this was serious enough to call the doctor. However, Guy's friends attributed Guy's forgetfulness to being busy, under a lot of stress, and nervous about his upcoming date.

What accounts for these very different explanations of losing one's keys for Mark and Guy? An explanation for the attributions Mark's friends made involves the negative stereotype of aging that older adults are slow-thinking and incompetent. Negative stereotypes of aging are extremely pervasive throughout our culture. Just peruse your local greeting card store and you will find humorous birthday cards capitalizing on our negative expectations about aging. For example, jokes run amuck about the older adult who keeps losing his or her memory. For a notorious example, see the cartoon depicting the grandchildren reveling in their grandfather's loss of memory so they can obtain extra allowance. This captures all our negative stereotypes about memory and aging.

Fortunately, positive expectations about aging coexist with the negative ones (Hummert, 1999; Kite & Wagner, 2002). On the one hand, older adults are seen as grouchy, forgetful, and losing physical stamina and sexual abilities. Yet, on the other hand, older adults are seen as wise, generous, and responsible. The important question researchers ask is what effect stereotypes have on our social judgments and our behavior toward others, such as those in Mark's situation.

Content of Stereotypes

Stereotypes *are a special type of social knowledge structure or social belief. They represent socially shared beliefs about characteristics and behaviors of a particular social group.* We all have stereotypes of groups of individuals and beliefs about how they will act in certain situations, such as "Older adults will be more rigid in their point of view" or "Older adults will talk on and on about their past." These beliefs affect how we interpret new information (Cuddy & Fiske, 2002). In other words, we use them to help us process information when we are engaged in social interactions. Just as with the literature on impression formation discussed earlier, we use our stereotypes to size up people when we first meet them. It helps us understand why they behave the way they do and guides us in our behavior toward other people. Remember that stereotypes are not inherently negative in their effect. However, too often they are applied in ways that underestimate the potential of the person we are observing. This will become more evident as we explore age-related stereotypes.

Much research has examined adult developmental changes in the content and structure of stereotypes (e.g., Hummert, 1999; Kite & Wagner, 2002). From a developmental perspective we would ask if there are changes in the nature and strength of our stereotypes, as we grow older. However, as you can see in Table 8.1, Hummert (1999) has found that older and younger adults hold quite similar age stereotypes. Such stereotypes include clusters of cognitive, personality, and general physical traits. When asked to generate and sort a list of traits associated with the category *older person,* young, middle-aged, and older adults shared the same categories of aging, including golden-ager, John Wayne conservative, perfect grandparent, shrew/curmudgeon, recluse, despondent,

www.CartoonStock.com

"GRANDPA'S AT THAT WONDERFUL AGE WHEN HE CAN'T REMEMBER IF HE ALREADY GAVE ME MY ALLOWANCE."

Many cartoons and greeting cards depict our fear of memory loss as we grow older.

and severely impaired (Hummert, 1999). Note from Table 8.1 that there are as many positive stereotypes for older adults as there are negative stereotypes. Recent research also shows that African Americans have similar stereotypes (Adams & Hummert, 2004). Overall, the consensus seems to be growing that adults of all ages have access to multiple stereotypes of older adults (Cuddy & Fiske, 2002; Kite & Wagner, 2002; Matheson et al., 2000).

Table 8.1

Traits Associated with Stereotypes of Older Adults

Stereotype	Traits
Negative	
Severely impaired	Slow-thinking, incompetent, feeble, inarticulate, incoherent, senile
Despondent	Depressed, sad, hopeless, afraid, neglected, lonely
Shrew or curmudgeon	Complaining, ill-tempered, demanding, stubborn, bitter, prejudiced
Recluse	Quiet, timid, naïve
Positive	
Golden-ager	Active, capable, sociable, independent, happy, interesting
Perfect grandparent	Patriotic, conservative, determined, proud, religious, nostalgic
John Wayne conservative	Loving, supportive, understanding, wise, generous, kind

Source: Reprinted from Hummert, M. L., A social cognitive perspective on age stereotypes. In Hess, T. M., & Blanchard-Fields, F. (Eds.) *Social Cognition and Aging.* San Diego: Academic Press, p. 179, Copyright © 1999, with permission from Elsevier.

Yet there are also age differences in how we perceive older adults. The consensus on stereotype categories across age groups just depicted is accompanied by developmental changes in the complexity of age stereotype beliefs. For example, Heckhausen, Dixon, and Baltes (1989) have shown that older adults identify a greater number of desirable and undesirable traits that characterize people as they develop across the life span. They also found that older adults perceive a greater potential for change in these characteristics in older age. Other studies have shown that older adults identify more categories that fit under the superordinate category "older adult" than do younger and middle-aged adults (Brewer & Lui, 1984; Heckhausen et al., 1989; Hummert et al., 1994). For example, as can be seen in Table 8.1, "golden-ager" only came up as a category for "older adults" when elderly people were included in the study (Hummert et al., 1994). Overall, these findings suggest that as we grow older, our ideas and age stereotypes become more elaborate and rich as we integrate our life experiences into our beliefs about aging (Baltes et al., 1999b; O'Brien & Hummert, 2006).

Are there age differences in how negatively or positively one views older adults? One recent study showed that older adults have a more positive view of aging in comparison to younger adults (Wentura & Brandstädter, 2003). However, an experimental study that more directly examined when stereotypes are activated suggested that younger adults' perceptions of older adults may be changing. For example, both younger and older adults displayed a positive bias toward older adults (Chasteen et al.; Park, 2002). In other words, when presented with the concept of "old," they did not show any signs of ageism.

Age Stereotypes and Perceived Competence

Stereotypes are not simply reflected in our perceptions of what we think are representative personality traits or characteristics of older adults. We also make appraisals or attributions of older adults' competence when we observe them perform tasks, and we assess whether we can count on them to perform important tasks. No area is more susceptible to negative stereotyped attributions of aging than memory competence. As you may recall from Chapter 6, people of all ages believe that memory decreases with age and that we have less and less control over current and future memory functioning as we grow older (e.g., Lineweaver & Hertzog, 1998).

The interesting question is, how does this strong belief in age-related loss of memory affect our attributions (explanations) about older adults' competencies? In an elegant series of studies, Joan Erber (Erber & Prager, 1999) found an age-based double standard in judging the competence of old versus young adults. The **age-based double standard** is operating when an individual attributes an older person's failure in memory as more serious than a memory failure observed in a young adult. So, for example, if an older adult cannot find her keys, this is seen as a much more serious memory problem (e.g., possibly attributed to senility) than if a younger adult cannot find her keys. This is most evident when younger people are judging the memory failure. In contrast, when older people observe the memory failure, they tend to judge both young and old targets of the story more equally. In fact, most of the time older adults are more lenient toward memory failures in older adults. However, in other types of competence judgments, older adults also display the age-based double standard. For example, when assessing the *cause* of a memory failure, both younger and older people felt that the failure was due to greater mental difficulty in the case of an older adult, whereas for younger adults participants attributed it to a lack of effort or attention (Erber et al., 1990).

The preceding tasks involve global attributions of memory failures in younger and older adults. However, what happens when you are asked to decide if an older adult should get a job or perform a task that demands memory capabilities? In several studies Erber and colleagues presented younger and older participants with an audiotaped interview of people applying for various volunteer positions, such as in a museum (Erber & Prager, 1997; Erber & Szuchman, 2002). The applicant was either old or young, and either forgetful or not forgetful. They found that despite the age-based double standard in judging older adults' memory failures found in earlier studies, people (both young and old) had more confidence in and would assign tasks or jobs to nonforgetful people irrespective of their age.

What accounts for this apparent discrepancy in findings? Maybe, when forming an impression about someone's capability, people take other factors into consideration. For example, traits could come into play, such as how responsible the person is. Remember that stereotypes about older adults included many positive ones, including being responsible. In fact, in another study young adults were asked whom they would choose to be a neighbor they could rely on. Despite forgetfulness ratings, they consistently chose older neighbors over younger ones (Erber et al., 1993). They also judged older neighbors to be more responsible, reliable, dependable, and helpful than younger ones. Thus, being able to access these positive traits may have compensated for older neighbors' forgetfulness. In a more recent follow-up study, younger and older adults rated both younger and older targets similarly on negative traits such as forgetfulness; however, only the older targets were rated higher on desirable traits such as responsibility (Erber & Szuchman, 2002).

What can we conclude from the trait studies of stereotypes and the attribution studies of stereotypes? First, when more individualized information (e.g., providing an audiotaped interview of the person) is provided and the individual is considered in a social setting (e.g., a volunteer position interview, a neighborly interaction), people consider more than just negative trait-based stereotypes in making social judgments. As in the neighborly interaction, we consider additional and more positive trait information such as reliable or dependable. The volunteer position may be perceived as a context in which older adults would be effective regardless of their memory competence. In fact, research is drawing on these findings to identify what types of social

environments will most facilitate older adults' social competence. We will examine this later.

Activation of Stereotypes

From the preceding review of research we know that stereotypes of older adults exist in the form of personality traits and perceptions of competence. They also influence our judgments about how capable older adults will be in memory-demanding situations. However, it is not enough to know that the stereotypes exist; we need to know under what conditions they are activated, and if activated, how they affect our behavior and social judgments. For example, why do negative stereotypes of older adults tend to influence our behaviors (e.g., talking down to older adults as if they were children) and attitudes (Hummert, 1999)? Considerable work focuses on stereotype activation as a relatively unconscious and automatic process that guides our behavior and social judgments (Bargh, 1997; Kunda & Spencer, 2003).

Social psychologists suggest that the reason stereotypes are automatically activated is that they become overlearned and thus are spontaneously activated when we encounter a member or members of a stereotyped group, such as African Americans (Greenwald et al., 1998; Kunda et al., 2002; Wheeler & Petty, 2001). *The activation of strong stereotypes, called* **implicit stereotyping,** *is not only automatic but also unconscious.* Thus it is more likely that they will influence our behavior without our being aware of it. The effects of such implicit stereotyping are illustrated in a clever study conducted by John Bargh and colleagues (Bargh et al., 1996). They demonstrated that if you subliminally (outside of conscious awareness) prime young people with the image of an elderly person, the young people's actual behavior is influenced in an age-related manner. In this case, the implicitly primed young adults walked down the hall more slowly after the experiment than did young adults who were not primed with the elderly image. This is a powerful demonstration of how our unconscious stereotypes of aging can guide our behavior.

Measuring implicit aging stereotyping is a challenge because by definition it is inaccessible. However, recent research using a clever technique called the Age Attitude IAT (Implicit Attitudes Test; Hummert et al., 2002) has overcome this challenge. In this test, individuals categorize photographs of faces by indicating as fast as they can whether the photo is a younger or older person. They are asked to press a button with their right hand to indicate young and with their left hand to indicate old. Then they categorize other photographs as pleasant or unpleasant with the right hand indicating pleasant and the left hand indicating unpleasant. Next is the two-part test of implicit aging stereotypes. Part one consists of a combination of the young-old and pleasant-unpleasant categorization task using the same hands as just indicated. In this test, the right hand is associated with both young and pleasant, whereas the left hand is associated with both old and unpleasant. The second part reverses the hands for young-old. Now the right hand is associated with old and the left hand is associated with young. The right hand is still associated with pleasant, and the left hand with unpleasant. The logic is this: If you have a negative stereotype regarding aging, you will be much slower in your response during the second test. In other words, it becomes difficult to use your right hand to indicate old because it is also associated with pleasant. This difficulty slows your response down.

Using this methodology Hummert and colleagues (2002) found that people of all ages were faster to respond to young-pleasant and old-unpleasant trials than to old-pleasant and young-unpleasant trials. Furthermore, all individuals had implicit age attitudes that strongly favored the young over the old. If you would like to experiment with this test, it is on the Internet. See the reference at the end of this chapter for the Book Companion Website, where you will find the URL for this test. These experiments and others (Levy, 2003) demonstrate that the activation of our negative stereotypes about aging affects our behavior without us being aware of it.

Implicit stereotyping is illustrated in many different domains of our behavior toward others as well. For example, in many situations nursing staff or younger adults in general are trying to instruct or communicate with older adults, as seen in the photo. Much evidence suggests that younger people engage in patronizing talk toward older adults in these situations (Hummert, 1999; Kemper, 2001). **Patronizing talk** *is when you slow your speech, use childlike vocabulary, dramatically articulate your words, speak with a demeaning emotional tone (e.g., overbearing or overly familiar), and engage in superficial conversation.* It is very similar to the way adults engage in baby talk to very young children. Research shows that negative age stereotypes are a primary cause for this behavior (Hummert et al., 1998; Kemper et al., 1998). Patronizing talk can cause social alienation and damaging effects on older adults' self-esteem (Hummert, 1999). Interestingly, when people who are likely to engage in patronizing talk to older adults evaluate it in others, they themselves describe it as disrespectful and demeaning (Ryan et al., 1994).

Why is this so? Again, implicit stereotyping may be the answer. When communicating to others, we try to accommodate to our audience so they will understand what we are trying to say. In this case, when communicating to an older adult, negative stereotypes of older adults as less competent, less able to hear, and having poorer memories may be activated and unconsciously and inadvertently result in an inaccurate assessment of how to accommodate our speech (Hummert, 1999; Ryan et al., 1994).

However, changing our speech to accommodate older adults can also have beneficial effects (Gould et al., 2002; Kemper, 2001; McGuire et al., 2000). If you adjust your speech when talking to older adults by using repetitions, including more elaborations, and speaking with less complexity, older adults are shown to have less comprehension failures (Kemper, 2001). The trick is to avoid high pitch, very slow speaking rates, and exaggerated tone. These latter characteristics are what older adults see as insulting and result in disenfranchising older adults from full participation in a conversational interaction.

Nursing home staff must be careful not to communicate with older adult residents as if they are childlike.

about academic ability. In turn, you may perform more poorly on a task associated with that stereotype irrespective of high competence in academic settings.

In a seminal study, African Americans at Stanford University were divided into two groups. Both groups scored very high on their SAT verbal scores. However, one group was told that they were going to take a test that was highly diagnostic of their verbal ability. The other group did not receive this very evaluative instruction. When scores were compared on verbal tests for both groups, despite the fact that all individuals were highly verbal, the group that received the diagnostic instructions performed more poorly. Caucasians in the diagnostic evaluation group did not differ from Caucasians in the nondiagnostic group. However, they did outperform African Americans in the diagnostic condition. Importantly, there were no differences between African Americans and Caucasians in the nondiagnostic group. Why? Steele argues that the performance of African Americans in the diagnostic condition suffered because they felt threatened by the negative stereotype that African Americans perform poorly on academic ability tests. This same type of effect was found when women were told that a test evaluated their mathematical competency. In this case, women are the stigmatized group because of negative stereotypes suggesting that women are less capable at math than men.

Recently, substantial attention has focused on understanding the harmful effects of negative aging stereotypes on memory performance in older adults (Andreoletti & Lachman, 2004; Chasteen, Bhattacharyya, Horhota, Tam, & Hasher, 2005; Hess, Auman, Colcombe, & Rahhal, 2003; Levy, 1996; Rahall et al., 2001; Stein, Blanchard-Fields, & Hertzog, 2002). In other words, do older adults belong to a stigmatized group that is vulnerable to stereotype threat? Some researchers have suggested that negative stereotypes do adversely affect older adults' cognitive functioning and may contribute to our perception of age-related decline in cognitive functioning (see Chapter 6). The initial studies examining this possibility used techniques similar to our discussion of stereotype activation: assessing implicit stereotyping.

Stereotype Threat

Another important question to ask is whether implicit negative stereotypes of aging influence the cognitive functioning of older adults. This possibility is raised in the context of widely cited social psychological research on stereotype threat. Claude Steele and colleagues have conducted a number of studies suggesting that stigmatized groups such as African Americans and women are vulnerable to stereotype threat (Spencer et al., 1999; Steele, 1997; Steele & Aronson, 1995). **Stereotype threat** *is an evoked fear of being judged in accordance with a negative stereotype about a group to which you belong.* For example, if you are a member of a stigmatized group such as African Americans, you are vulnerable to cues in your environment that activate stereotype threat

CURRENT CONTROVERSIES

Are Stereotypes of Aging Associated with Lower Cognitive Performance?

A major controversial issue in the cognitive aging literature is whether living in a society that equates old age with memory decline, senility, and dependency produces what Langer (1989) calls a "premature cognitive commitment" early in life. As children we acquire ideas of what it means to be old, usually negative, and these stereotypes guide and influence our behavior later in life. Thus, the question is the degree to which negative societal beliefs, attitudes, and expectations determine the cognitive decline we observe in older adults.

When Levy and Langer (1994) compared memory performance and attitudes on aging of Chinese older adults, hearing American older adults, and deaf American older adults, they found that the Chinese older adults outperformed both groups of American older adults on several memory tasks. In addition, the deaf American older adults outperformed their hearing American counterparts. Attitudes on aging held by the different cultures were related to memory performance (Chinese had more positive attitudes, whereas Americans had more negative attitudes). The

conclusion drawn is that negative stereotypes in American culture accounted for this difference.

However, the results are not definitive, because this is a correlational study. In other words, does enhanced memory performance lead to more positive attitudes, or do positive attitudes lead to enhanced memory performance? Are there educational differences between the two cultural groups? Are the memory tests really the same given that they had to be translated into Chinese?

To further test this notion, Levy (1996) subliminally primed younger and older adults with negative stereotypes of an older adult (e.g., the word *senile*) or positive stereotypes (e.g., the word *wise*). She found that when older adults were primed with negative aging stereotypes, their performance was worse on memory tests than that of older adults primed with positive stereotypes. To further bolster this stereotype effect, Stein, Blanchard-Fields, and Hertzog (2002) tried to replicate this finding. Importantly they did find that negative stereotypes adversely affected older adults' memory, but only for those individuals who were unaware

of the subliminal presentation of negative stereotypes. This emphasizes how powerful unconscious activation of stereotypes can be in influencing our behavior.

It is intriguing and intuitive to believe that a self-fulfilling prophecy operates with respect to older adults' memory performance. If society portrays older adults as declining in cognitive capacity and you are socialized to believe so at a very young age, then it makes sense that this will influence your memory performance as an older adult. However, as we observed in Chapter 6, there are other processes related to physiological decline (e.g., speed of processing) that substantially account for declines in memory performance. All in all, negative stereotypes of aging exist. They may indeed have an effect on cognitive performance, although they may not account for all of it. Thus, although you may not be able to eliminate decline in performance, interventions in improving your attitudes and outlook on aging do have the potential to improve the quality of performance relative to your own level of functioning.

Becca Levy (1996) conducted the initial study in this area, and it caused some controversy. Let us examine this initial research in the Current Controversies feature. What do you think?

More recently additional studies have confirmed the damaging effects of negative aging stereotypes on memory (Hess, Hinson, & Statham, 2004; Levy & Leifheit-Limson, 2009). For example, Rahhal,

Hasher, and Colcombe (2001) examined the effect of experimental instructions on older adults' memory performance. If older adults were told they were about to take a memory test, they performed more poorly than younger adults. However, when they were told the task emphasized learning about new information, older adults performed as well as younger adults. Hess, Auman, Colcombe, and Rahhal (2003) also found support for the influence of stereotype threat on older adults' memory. Younger and older adults read two newspaper-styled reports that discussed either research findings indicating that older adults' memory is worse than that of younger adults, or positive research findings indicating memory loss in older adulthood is not inevitable and can be controlled to some extent. The researchers found support for the influence of stereotype threat; older adults who read the negative report performed more poorly on memory tasks than did older adults who read the positive report. Interestingly, this manipulation had no effect on younger adults. This suggests that self-relevance is important in understanding the effect of aging stereotypes. Younger adults were not affected because the stereotypes did not relate to their self-identity (Levy, 2003).

An important point about the Hess et al. (2003) study needs to be noted. The negative effect of stereotype threat on older adults was most evident in those older adults who put a lot of investment in memory competence. Older adults who did not worry about this were not as adversely affected by the negative stereotypes of an aging mind. As Zebrowitz (2003) suggests, maybe older adults can defend against negative aging stereotypes through inoculation, that is, by not identifying with the category "elderly." Instead, they can embrace the positive aspects of themselves and apply strategies to compensate for any decline, thus fending off the self-fulfilling prophecy of "incompetent behavior" as dictated by the negative aging stereotypes. Finally, education may act as a buffer to the influence of stereotypes. Older adults with high education were not affected by stereotypes on a memory task, whereas individuals with lower amounts of education were affected by stereotype manipulations (Andreoletti & Lachman, 2004).

There is also evidence that middle-aged adults are susceptible to negative age stereotypes (O'Brien & Hummert, 2006). Middle-aged adults who identified with older adulthood showed poorer memory performance if they were told that their performance would be compared with other older adults. Middle-aged adults with more youthful identities did not show differences in memory performance regardless of whether they were told they would be compared to younger or older individuals.

Although the lion's share of the research in this area has focused on the detrimental effects of stereotypes, some evidence also exists for the beneficial effects of positive stereotypes on older adults' cognitive performance (Hess et al., 2004; Levy, 2003; Stein et al., 2002).

The influence of stereotypes on performance is not restricted only to memory. In a recent study, Levy and Leifheit-Limson (2009) found that subliminally inducing physical negative aging stereotypes had a harmful effect on older adults' balance performance. In contrast, presenting older adults with positive physical aging stereotypes resulted in better balance performance. Levy and colleagues (2000) found that older adults exposed to negative aging stereotypes showed a heightened cardiovascular response to a stressful situation compared to older adults exposed to positive aging stereotypes. Levy argues that negative aging stereotypes can be viewed as direct stressors. Positive aging stereotypes, in contrast, could potentially have the ability to reduce cardiovascular stress. Finally, Levy, Slade, and Kasl (2002) found in a longitudinal study that older adults who maintained positive perceptions of themselves as aging individuals tended to be healthier over time than those who held a negative self-perception of aging. Thus it is important to recognize the role of positive stereotypes on older adults. Remember, however, that this is correlational data. It does not tell us whether positive stereotypes cause people to be healthy across their adult life span. Nevertheless, overall, the findings discussed here demonstrate how pervasive and powerful stereotypes can be on our behavior.

8.6 Personal Control

LEARNING OBJECTIVES

- What is the multidimensionality of personal control?
- How do assimilation and accommodation influence behavior?
- What is primary and secondary control?
- What is the primacy of primary control over secondary control?

*D*aniel did not perform as well as he thought he was going to on his psychology exam. He now had the unhappy task of trying to determine why he did poorly. Was it his fault? Was the exam too picky? To add insult to injury, Daniel needed to pick his grades up to maintain his scholarship grant. He decided the exam was too picky. This helped Daniel motivate himself to study for his next exams.

How Daniel answered such questions sheds light on how we tend to explain, or attribute, our behavior, as in the earlier discussion of causal attributions. Among the most important ways in which we analyze the cause of events is in terms of who or what is in control in a specific situation. **Personal control** *is the degree to which one believes that one's performance in a situation depends on something that one personally does.* A high sense of personal control implies a belief that performance is up to you, whereas a low sense of personal control implies that your performance is under the influence of forces other than your own.

Personal control has become an extremely important idea in a wide variety of settings because of the way in which it guides behavior and relates to well-being (Baltes & Baltes, 1990; Brändstadter, 1997; Lachman, 2006; Rowe & Kahn, 1997; Schulz et al., 2003). For example, it is thought to play a role in memory performance (see Chapter 6),

in intelligence (see Chapter 7), in depression (see Chapter 4), and in adjustment to and survival in institutions (see Chapter 5).

Multidimensionality of Personal Control

The general consensus about personal control is that it is multidimensional (Lachman, Rosnick, & Röcke, 2009; Soederberg, Miller, & Lachman, 1999a). Specifically, one's sense of control depends on which domain, such as intelligence or health, is being assessed. As can be seen from Figure 8.5, Grob, Little, and Wanner (1999) found an increase for perceived control for social (harmony within a close relationship) and personal (personal appearance) issues up to early middle age (e.g., middle 30s), and thereafter there was a general decline into old age. However, perceived control over societal issues (e.g., a natural environmental problem such as the demise of forests from pollution) was low across the adult life span, with a slight decrease in older adulthood.

More recently Lachman and colleagues (2009) also found interesting changes in control beliefs depending upon the domain being examined. For example, they found no changes in a sense of control over one's health up to the early 70s. However, when

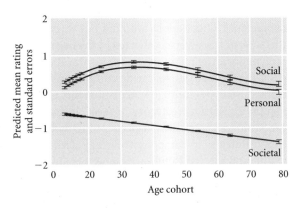

Figure 8.5 Developmental trajectories of the four control-related judgments across three life domains.

Source: Grob, A., Little, T. D., & Wanner, B. (1999). Control judgments across the lifespan. *International Journal of Behavioral Development* 23, p. 844. Copyright © 1999 Reprinted with permission from Sage Publications.

older adults transition from the early 70s to the mid-70s and 80s, their sense of control over their health declines. This makes sense given that the oldest old experience accumulated losses in their reserved capacity to function. Similarly, it is only the oldest old that show a decline in control over their well-being. Finally, these researchers found that maintaining a sense of control throughout adulthood is linked to better quality of social relationships, better health, and higher cognitive functioning. They suggest that sense of control may operate as a protective factor for one's well-being in the face of declining health and other losses associated with the oldest old.

In an academic context such as college, attributions of control are particularly important in determining the causes of success and failure in school. It would be interesting to explore the notion of control in regard to class performance among older and younger students. The exercise in the Discovering Development feature helps to examine this question.

Control Strategies

The research just reviewed primarily examined control-related beliefs such as the belief that control is in one's own hands or in the hands of others. However, a number of theoretical approaches and empirical work have examined control-related strategies. For example, Brandtstädter (1999) proposes that the preservation and stabilization of a positive view of the self and personal development in later life involve three interdependent processes. *First, people engage in* **assimilative activities** *that prevent or alleviate losses in domains that are personally relevant for self-esteem and identity.* For example, people may use memory aids more if having a good memory is an important aspect of self-esteem and identity. *Second, people make* **accommodations** *and readjust their goals and aspirations as a way to lessen or neutralize the effects of negative self-evaluations in key domains.* For instance, if a person notices that the time it takes to walk a mile at a brisk pace has increased, then the target time can be increased to help lessen the impact of feelings of failure. *Third, people use* **immunizing mechanisms** *that alter the effects of self-discrepant evidence.* In this case, a person who

is confronted with evidence that his or her memory performance has declined can look for alternative explanations or simply deny the evidence.

Taking a similar approach, Heckhausen and Schulz (1999; Schulz et al., 2003) view control as a motivational system that regulates human behavior over the life span, in other words, individuals' abilities to control important outcomes. These researchers define control-related strategies in terms of primary control and secondary control. *Much like Brandtstädter's assimilative activities,* **primary control** *involves bringing the environment into line with one's desires and goals.* Action is directed toward changing the external world. *Much like Brandtstädter's accommodative activities,* **secondary control** *involves bringing oneself in line with the environment.* It typically involves cognitive activities directed at the self. *So, for example, if you lost your job, and thus your income,* **primary control strategies** *would entail an active search for another job (changing the environment so you once again have a steady income).* **Secondary control strategies** *could involve appraising the situation in terms of how you really did not enjoy that particular job.*

An important part of this theoretical perspective is that primary control has functional primacy over secondary control. In other words, primary control lets people shape their environment to fit their goals and developmental potential. Thus primary control has more adaptive value to the individual. The major function of secondary control is to minimize losses or expand levels of primary control.

Heckhausen and Schulz (1999) believe this has important implications for aging. They find that in childhood much development is directed at expanding the child's primary control potential, and they predict stability in primary control striving through most of adult life. However, as we enter old age, the maintenance of primary control increasingly depends on secondary control processes. This is due to threats to primary control as a function of biological decline that occurs as we grow older. Thus secondary control will increase with age. Research shows that secondary control does indeed increase with age (Grob et al., 1999; Heckhausen & Schulz, 1999).

How Much Control Do You Have over Your Cognitive Functioning?

As you progress through college, you are concerned with your grade-point average, how much you will learn relative to your profession of choice, and your performance on exams. The more control you perceive that you have over the situation, the more confident you feel. There are two types of control attributions you can make. You can make an "entity" attribution about your performance in school. This means you attribute control to your innate ability to perform. Or you can hold a "skill" perspective. You now attribute control over your performance in terms of how much effort you exert, such as how much you study for an exam.

Are there age differences in these control beliefs? To find out, talk to students at your university ranging from first-year students to seniors and also ranging in age. There are a lot of older students coming back to school, for example. Find out what they believe is the major cause of the successes and failures in school. Bring your results to class and pool them. See if there are college-level differences and/or age differences in perceptions of control over academic performance. Compare your findings to age differences reported in the text.

A particularly important question is how control strategies and beliefs affect emotional well-being. A growing number of studies suggest that control beliefs are important contributors to both positive and negative well-being. For example, if someone perceives he or she has control over desirable outcomes, this control is associated with high emotional well-being (Kunzmann et al., 2002). However, how adaptive control beliefs relate to well-being varies with life stage. For young and middle-aged adults, a strong sense of control relates to how we compensate for failure, for example, "We can overcome this momentary failure." Older adults focus a sense of control on how to master everyday demands (Lang & Heckhausen, 2001). Finally, for all age groups, planning for the future enhances one's sense of perceived control, and this in turn relates to high life satisfaction (Lachman et al., 2009).

Some Criticisms Regarding Primary Control

The notion of increases in accommodative strategies (Brandtstädter, 1999) and secondary strategies (Heckhausen & Schulz, 1999) in older age is not without its criticisms. For example, Carstensen and Freund (1994) question whether losses people experience, though real, actually threaten the self. In addition, these authors argue that age-related changes in goals could also be the result of natural movement through the life cycle, not simply of coping with blocked goals.

Criticisms also can be launched against these approaches to control by considering the globalization of so many aspects of our functioning. From a sociocultural perspective (e.g., cross-cultural research), there is much criticism regarding a bias toward Western cultures in the development of theories such as primary and secondary control, and in particular, the primacy of primary control over secondary control. In a fascinating rebuttal of the Heckhausen and Schulz theory, Stephen J. Gould (1999) suggests that in collectivist societies such as those found in Asia, the emphasis is not on individualistic strategies such as those found in primary control. Instead, the goal is to establish interdependence with others, to be connected to them and bound to a larger social institution. He cites studies that show that throughout adulthood, Asian cultures exceed Western cultures in levels of secondary control and emotion-focused coping (Gould, 1999; Seginer et al., 1993).

Thus one's sense of personal control is a complex, multidimensional aspect of personality. Consequently, general normative age-related trends might not be found. Rather, changes in personal control may well depend on one's experiences in different domains and the culture one grows up in, and may differ widely from one domain to another.

Concept Checks

1. What control strategies are related to preserving a positive perspective?
2. How do control beliefs and strategies affect older adults' emotional well-being?

8.7 Social Situations and Social Competence

LEARNING OBJECTIVES
- What is the social facilitation of cognitive functioning?
- What is collaborative cognition, and does it facilitate memory in older adults?
- How does the social context influence memory performance in older adults?

B randon and Stephanie's granddaughter asked them what happened when they first met. Stephanie recalled that they met at a social gathering for World War II soldiers but couldn't remember the name of the person who introduced them. She could only describe him as tall and dark-haired. However, this cued Brandon; he remembered the man's name was Tucker. This back-and-forth remembering continued until, to their own amazement, they had successfully reconstructed the whole gathering. Their granddaughter was delighted and complimented them on their good memories.

When we typically think about the memories of older adults, we don't usually think of these kinds of successes. Brandon and Stephanie's reliance on each other to remember a past event shows how

our social cognitive processes serve adaptive functions. In fact, there is a growing interest in how the social context can compensate for memory loss and facilitate memory performance. In this section, we will examine two approaches to this issue: collaborative cognition and facilitative social contexts.

Similar to practical intelligence, wisdom, and everyday problem solving discussed in Chapter 7, the social cognition perspective offers us an enriched understanding of social competence in older adulthood. We are interested in how changes in social cognitive functioning both reflect the changing life contexts of the individual and affect adaptation to these changing contexts. In the previous sections, we have primarily focused on how developmental changes in representations of self or other (such as social beliefs and self-beliefs) influence social cognitive processes such as making attributional judgments. In this section we focus on social cognition as it relates to the dynamic interplay between self, others, and context. For example, a less researched, but extremely important, domain of social cognition and aging is how the particular types of social settings in which we communicate with others influence our cognitive processing. This relates to a different aspect of social cognition and

Older adults tend to use compensatory strategies for failing memories by jointly remembering events.

aging research: the social facilitation of cognitive functioning.

Collaborative Cognition

There has been a recent focus in the social cognition and aging literature to examine cognition in social contexts, that is, how cognition works when we are interacting with others. This can be seen in work on the benefits and costs of collaborative cognition on cognitive performance (e.g., memory and problem solving) (Dixon, 1999; Meegan & Berg, 2002). **Collaborative cognition** *occurs when two or more people work together to solve a cognitive task.*

Current research shows that collaborative cognition enhances older adults' performance on a variety of memory and problem-solving tasks (Meegan & Berg, 2002; Strough & Margrett, 2002), thus serving a very important adaptive function for older adults. Following the old saying "Two heads are better than one," researchers are interested in examining how this type of collaborative context could mitigate deficits in memory that we typically see when assessing older adults in the laboratory (see Chapter 6). Research shows that older adults can collaborate on story recall as well as problem-solving performance and that their performance is better than the average performance of older adults in individual settings (Dixon, 1999; Dixon & Gould, 1998; Gould et al., 2002). In other words, cognitive performance improves with a collaborative context. On a recall task, by using a cognitive style together that minimizes working memory demands, older married couples performed just as well as younger couples. It is rare that you find older adults' cognitive performance equal to that of younger adults.

Another way to look at the benefits of collaborative cognition is to examine how groups accomplish what they want to accomplish. What kinds of processes do older adults use to effectively remember an event as Brandon and Stephanie did? How do older adults divide up the cognitive work when they cooperate on a task? Older married couples produced more statements resulting from a shared discussion (Gould et al., 1994). Unacquainted older adult pairs produced more sociability or support statements. Sociability statements were about agreeing with the partner's recall or comparing the story with events in their own lives. Thus older married couples know each other well and get right down to business. Older unacquainted couples are more concerned with being sociable to the other member of the dyad. Older married couples were experienced enough with one another to bypass the sociability concern and concentrate on better strategies to improve their performance. Overall, findings indicate that well-acquainted older couples demonstrate an expertise to develop an adaptive pattern of recalling information, which includes both social support issues and strategic efforts.

There is also growing evidence of the positive outcomes of collaboration when older adults tackle everyday problem-solving tasks such as errand running and planning a vacation (Berg et al., 2003; Margrett & Marsiske, 2002; Strough et al., 2003). Interestingly, older adults prefer to collaborate in their problem solving when they perceive deficiencies in their own functioning but prefer to work alone when they feel competent in the area (Strough et al., 2002). Collaborators of all ages report that the benefits include optimizing the decision, enhancing the relationship, and compensating for individual weaknesses (Berg et al., 2003). However, collaboration is not without its costs, such as selfishness, withholding of one's honest opinion, and not meeting the other partner's needs.

Social Context of Memory

Another approach to identifying conditions under which social facilitation of cognition in older adults occurs is in examining contextual variables that influence memory performance. For example, Cynthia Adams argues that memory performance is influenced when the task approximates a real-world learning and social memory experience (Adams et al., 2002). In this case, what happens to memory performance when the assessment situation approximates the kinds of memory demands that naturally occur in a real-life situation?

For example, a typical and relevant cognitive task for older adults is to transmit sociocultural information to younger generations (Adams et al., 1994). In this context, the older adult would be motivated to communicate effectively. A storytelling situation is a good example. This kind of context is very different from the traditional laboratory context, in which the demand is to reproduce as much of the content of a text as possible. Adams et al. (2002) found that when they placed older adults in a storytelling situation in which they were asked to learn and retell a story from memory to a young child, their retellings of the story contained more detail and were more fluent than those of younger adults. Perhaps this superior performance stems from increased motivation in a social context where their concerns were directed at producing an interesting and coherent story for the child. This is a demonstration of how the social-communicative context or experience can enhance what is most salient to the individual. Again, this finding illustrates the importance of taking into consideration the social context of a task situation when examining change in cognitive functioning as we grow older.

Concept Checks

1. What is collaborative cognition?
2. What is a social-communicative context?

SOCIAL POLICY IMPLICATIONS

The research on social cognition and aging further accentuates why it is important to consider social factors to explain cognitive functioning in older adulthood. Factors such as the social context in which we communicate, the emotions we are feeling, and the strength of our beliefs and values drive our decisions and social judgments in important ways. Thus it is important not to limit explanations of changes in thinking and decision making to cognitive processing variables. Important social factors influence how and when an individual will attend to specific information and when this information will influence social cognitive functioning. These factors include those we have discussed earlier: motivational goals, cognitive style, attitudes, and values, among others. By not considering these factors, we run the risk of underestimating the competence of older adults. By considering these factors we can explore the conditions under which older adults flourish and the conditions where we need to focus aid and attention. This has important policy implications with respect to how we treat older adults in the workforce, establishing health policies, and enhancing the treatment of our older adult population. We can be very optimistic about the future promise of research on aging and social cognition for identifying and probing such important social components of information processing. In sum, by looking at cognition in a social context, we get a more complete picture of how cognition operates in an everyday social environment.

Summary

8.1 Social Judgment Processes

What is the negativity bias in impression formation, and how does it influence older adults' thinking?

- When forming an initial impression, older adults rely heavily on preexisting social structures.
- Older adults weigh negative information more heavily in their social judgments than do younger adults.
- Older adults use less detailed information in forming impressions than do younger adults.

Are there age differences in accessibility of social information?

- Social knowledge structures must be available to guide behavior.
- Social information must be easily accessible to guide behavior.
- Accessibility depends on the strength of the information stored in memory.
- How the situation is framed influences what types of social knowledge will be accessed.

How does processing context influence social judgments?

- Age-related changes in processing capacity influence social judgments.
- Stages of processing suggest we make initial snap judgments and later correct or adjust them based on more reflective thinking.

To what extent do processing capacity limitations influence social judgments in older adults?

- Older adults tend to make more snap judgments because of processing resource limitations.

8.2 Social Knowledge Structures and Beliefs

What are social knowledge structures?

- To understand age differences in social beliefs, we must first examine content differences.
- Second, we must assess the strength of the beliefs.
- Third, we need to know the likelihood that beliefs will affect behavior.

What are social beliefs, and how do they change with age?

- Age differences in social beliefs can be attributed to generational differences and life-stage differences.

8.3 Social Judgments and Causal Attributions

How do causal attributions and the correspondence bias change with age?

- Older adults display a dispositional bias when confronted with negative relationship situations.
- Older adults display more interactive attributions in negative relationship situations.

What alternative explanations are there for the dispositional bias found in older adults?

- The dispositional bias on the part of older adults can be attributed to both processing resource limitations and differences in social knowledge that influence their attributional judgments.
- Older adults display a higher level of social expertise than younger adults do when forming impressions.

8.4 Motivation and Social Processing Goals

How do goals influence the way we process information, and how does this change with age?

- Life-span shifts in goal orientation show that interests shift toward physical health and socio-emotional domains increase with age.

How do emotions influence the way we process information, and how does this change with age?

- Older adults tend to focus their processing on positive emotional information more than negative information.

How does a need for closure influence the way we process information, and how does it change with age?

- Need for closure is a need for a quick and decisive answer with little tolerance for ambiguity.
- Older adults' social judgment biases are predicted by the degree to which they need quick and decisive closure. This is not so for younger age groups.

8.5 Stereotypes and Aging

How does the content of stereotypes about aging differ across adulthood?

- The content of stereotypes varies by age: older adults include more positive stereotypes along with negative ones.

How do younger and older adults perceive the competence of the elderly?

- An age-based double standard operates when judging older adults' failures in memory.
- Younger adults rate older adults as more responsible despite their memory failures.

How do negative stereotypes about aging unconsciously guide our behavior?

- Automatically activated negative stereotypes about aging guide behavior beyond the individual's awareness.
- Implicit stereotyping influences the way we patronize older adults in our communications.

What are the ways the positive and negative aging stereotypes influence older adults' behavior?

- Stereotypic beliefs have a negative impact on the cognitive performance of older adults.
- Stereotypic beliefs influence older adults' health and physical behavior.

8.6 Personal Control

What is personal control, and what age differences exist in this area?

- Personal control is the degree to which one believes that performance depends on something one does.
- Age differences in the degree of personal control depend on the domain being studied. Some evidence suggests that people develop several strategies concerning personal control to protect a positive self-image.

What is the multidimensionality of personal control?

- Older adults perceive less control over specific domains of functioning such as intellectual changes with aging.
- Perceived control over health remains stable until it declines in very old age.
- Older adults perceive less control over social issues and personal appearance.

How do assimilation and accommodation influence behavior?

- Assimilative strategies prevent losses important to self-esteem.
- Accommodative strategies readjust goals.
- Immunizing mechanisms alter the effects of self-discrepant information.

What is primary and secondary control?

- Primary control helps change the environment to match one's goals.
- Secondary control reappraises the environment in light of one's decline in functioning.

What is the primacy of primary control over secondary control?

- Primary control has functional primacy over secondary control.
- Cross-cultural perspectives challenge the notion of primacy of primary control.

8.7 Social Situations and Social Competence

What is the social facilitation of cognitive functioning?

- Particular types of social settings in which we communicate with others influence our cognitive processing.

What is collaborative cognition, and does it facilitate memory in older adults?

- Collaborating with others in recollection helps facilitate memory in older adults.
- Collaborating with others enhances problem solving in older adults

How does the social context influence memory performance in older adults?

- The social context can serve a facilitative function in older adults' memory performance.

Review Questions

8.1 Social Judgment Processes

- What are the stages in attributional processing?
- What is the negativity bias, and what are the age differences in its impact?
- Describe the age differences in the extent to which trait information is used in forming an impression.
- How does processing capacity affect social cognitive processing?
- What influences the accessibility of social information?
- What is the status of processing resource limitations as an explanation for social judgment biases?

8.2 Social Knowledge Structures and Beliefs

- What three important factors need to be considered to understand implicit social beliefs?
- Describe evidence for age differences in the content of social beliefs.

8.3 Social Judgments and Causal Attributions

- What are causal attributions?
- What is a correspondence bias?
- Are there age differences in the correspondence bias? If so, under what conditions?
- What accounts for the age differences in the correspondence bias?

8.4 Motivation and Social Processing Goals

- How do personal goals influence behavior?
- To what extent are there age differences in emotion as a processing goal in social cognitive functioning?
- What is need for closure?
- How does need for closure influence the processing of social information?
- Are there age differences in the degree to which need for closure influences social information processing?

8.5 Stereotypes and Aging

- What are stereotypes?
- How is the content of stereotypes similar across age groups?
- How does the content of stereotypes differ across age groups?
- What is the age-based double standard of perceived competence in younger and older adults?
- What do older and younger adults perceive as the cause of memory failure in older individuals?
- How does perceived competence influence the way tasks are assigned to older and younger targets?
- What other factors besides competence are taken into consideration when judging older adults' future performance?
- What evidence supports the notion that stereotypes can be automatically activated out of conscious awareness?
- What is implicit stereotyping?
- Under what conditions are stereotypes activated?
- How do negative stereotypes of aging influence young adults' behavior?

8.6 Personal Control

- What evidence is there of age differences in personal control beliefs?
- In what domains do older adults exhibit low perceived control, and in what domains do they exhibit higher levels of perceived control?
- How are assimilative and accommodative strategies adaptive in older adults' functioning?
- Why is primary control viewed as having more functional primacy than secondary control?
- What cross-cultural evidence challenges the notion of primary control as functionally more important?
- How does personal control influence older adults' emotional well-being?

8.7 Social Situations and Social Competence

- What is collaborative cognition?
- What evidence suggests that collaborative cognition compensates for memory failures in older adults?
- How does collaborative cognition facilitate problem-solving behavior?
- How do marital relationships influence collaborative cognition?
- How does a storytelling context influence age differences in memory for stories?
- What does it mean to say that the social context facilitates cognitive performance?

Integrating Concepts in Development

- To what degree are declines in processing resource capacity discussed in Chapter 6 as ubiquitous in their effects on social cognitive processes?
- What relations can be found among dispositional traits, personal concerns, and life narratives?
- How does emotion as a processing goal relate to socio-emotional selectivity theory in Chapter 10?
- How does social cognition relate to post-formal thought (Chapter 7)?
- How does personal control relate to concepts such as memory self-efficacy discussed in Chapter 6?

Key Terms

accommodations Readjustments of goals and aspirations as a way to lessen or neutralize the effects of negative self-evaluations in key domains.

age-based double standard When an individual attributes an older person's failure in memory as more serious than a memory failure observed in a young adult.

assimilative activities Exercises that prevent or alleviate losses in domains that are personally relevant for self-esteem and identity.

causal attributions Explanations people construct to explain their behavior, which can be situational, dispositional, or interactive.

cognitive style A traitlike pattern of behavior one uses when approaching a problem-solving situation.

collaborative cognition Cognitive performance that results from the interaction of two or more individuals.

control strategies Behavior patterns used to obtain a sense of control over how an outcome or desired goal will be achieved.

correspondence bias Relying more on dispositional information in explaining behavior and ignoring compelling situational information such as extenuating circumstances.

dispositional attribution An explanation for someone's behavior that resides within the actor.

immunizing mechanisms Control strategies that alter the effects of self-discrepant evidence.

implicit stereotyping Stereotyped beliefs that affect your judgments of individuals without your being aware of it (i.e., the process is unconscious).

impression formation The way in which people combine the components of another person's personality and come up with an integrated perception of the person.

negativity bias Weighing negative information more heavily than positive information in a social judgment.

patronizing talk Using superficial conversation, slowed speech, simple vocabulary, carefully articulated words, and a demeaning emotional tone.

personal control The belief that what one does has an influence on the outcome of an event.

positivity effect The tendency to attend to and process positive information over negative information.

primary control The act of bringing the environment into line with one's own desires and goals, similar to Brandstädter's assimilative activities.

secondary control The act of bringing oneself in line with the environment, similar to Brandstädter's accomodative activities.

situational attribution An explanation for someone's behavior that is external to the actor.

social knowledge A cognitive structure that represents one's general knowledge about a given social concept or domain.

source judgments Process of accessing knowledge wherein one attempts to determine where one obtained a particular piece of information.

stereotypes Beliefs about characteristics, attributes, and behaviors of members of certain groups.

stereotype threat An evoked fear of being judged in accordance with a negative stereotype about a group to which an individual belongs.

Resources

Readings

Baltes, P. B., & Staudinger, U. (1996). *Interactive minds*. Cambridge, UK: Cambridge University Press. A collection of chapters focusing on the area of collaborative cognition. Moderate to difficult reading.

Hess, T. M., & Blanchard-Fields, F. (1999). *Social cognition and aging*. San Diego: Academic Press. An excellent collection of chapters discussing all aspects of social cognition covered in this chapter. Moderate to difficult reading.

Kunda, Z. (1999). *Social cognition: Making sense of people*. Cambridge, MA: MIT Press. A comprehensive book covering all aspects of social cognition research. Easy to moderate reading.

9

Personality

Levels of Analysis and Personality Research

AP Images

MAYA ANGELOU MAINTAINS THAT "THERE IS NO AGONY LIKE BEARING AN UNTOLD STORY INSIDE OF YOU." True to her conviction, she has spent a lifetime writing her story in numerous books, poems, and other literary works. She describes an incredible developmental path of oppression, hatred, and hurt that is ultimately transformed into self-awareness, understanding, and compassion. For example, in her later years she realized that in confronting the atrocities of the world, if she accepts the fact of evil, she must accept the fact of good, providing her with as little fear as possible for the anticipation of death. Another example involves integrating spirituality into her self-perception. She was asked how spirituality fits into a way of life. She answered, "There is something more, the spirit, or the soul. I think that that quality encourages our courtesy, and care, and our minds. And mercy, and identity."

Maya Angelou's writings reflect some of the key issues involved in personality development that we will examine in this chapter. First, we will consider whether personality changes or remains stable across adulthood. We will examine this from a trait perspective as well as personal concerns that change across the life cycle. This will lead us to the study of individuals' life narratives, as well as changes in identity and self.

One of the oldest debates in psychology concerns whether personality development continues across the life span. From the earliest days, prominent people argued both sides. William James and Sigmund Freud, for example, believed that personality was set by the time adulthood rolled around. Indeed, Freud thought that development was essentially complete in childhood. In contrast, Carl Jung asserted the viewpoint that personality was continually shaped throughout our lives. Aspects of personality come and go as people's experiences and life issues change.

Although we still have two main theoretical camps, one arguing for stability and the other for change, there is a movement in the field to try and reconcile these differences. Although the data can be viewed as contradictory, results often depend on which specific measures researchers use and the aspect of personality that is investigated.

Why is the area of personality controversial? The answer lies in the paradoxical beliefs we hold about personality itself. At one level we all believe people have complex personalities that remain relatively constant over time. A person with a stable personality is easier to deal with across different situations; when a person behaves in ways that violate our expectations, we act surprised. Imagine the chaos that would result if every week or so everyone woke up with a brand new personality: The once easygoing husband is now a real tyrant, trusted friends are now completely unpredictable, and our patterns of social interaction are in a shambles. Clearly, to survive in day-to-day life we must rely on consistency of personality.

Still, we like to believe that we can change undesirable aspects of our personalities. Imagine what it would be like, for example, if we could never overcome shyness; if anxiety were a lifelong, incurable curse; or if our idiosyncratic tendencies that cause others to tear their hair out could not be eliminated. The assumption of the modifiability of personality is very strong indeed. The existence of psychotherapy is a formal verification of that assumption.

Levels of Analysis and Personality Research

The debate over the degree to which personality in adulthood remains stable or changes is one that has generated numerous studies and theoretical perspectives. Consequently, sorting out the various approaches helps us understand what aspects of personality the various researchers are describing. Drawing on the work of several theorists and researchers, McAdams (1999) describes three parallel levels of personality structure and function. Each level contains a wide range of personality constructs. McAdams refers to the levels with rather generic names: dispositional traits, personal concerns, and life narrative.

Dispositional traits *consist of aspects of personality that are consistent across different contexts and can be compared across a group along a continuum representing high and low degrees of the characteristic.* Dispositional traits are the level of personality most people think of first, and they include commonly used descriptors such as *shy, talkative, authoritarian,* and the like. **Personal concerns** *consist of things that are important to people, their goals, and their major concerns in life.* Personal concerns are usually described in motivational, developmental, or strategic terms; they reflect the stage of life a person is in at the time. **Life narrative** *consists of the aspects of personality that pull everything together, those integrative aspects that give a person an identity or sense of self.* The creation of an identity is the goal of this level.

In a recent reformulation of McAdams's model of personality, Karen Hooker (Hooker, 2002; Hooker & McAdams, 2003) has added three processes that act in tandem with the three structural components of personality proposed by McAdams. These social cognitive processes give personality its dynamic character. In other words, it is more likely that you will see a change in personality when you are examining the dynamic nature of the processes.

For example, acting along with dispositional traits are *state processes:* transient, short-term changes in emotion, mood, hunger, anxiety, and so on. *Personal concerns* act in tandem with self-regulatory processes, which include such processes as primary and secondary control (discussed in Chapter 8). Finally, life narratives act jointly with *cognitive processes* of recounting life narratives or self-narrating, such as the natural interaction that occurs between a storyteller and listener. These processes are central in organizing life stories.

Finally, as one moves from examining dispositional traits to personal concerns to life narrative (and their corresponding processes), it becomes more likely that observable change will take place (McAdams, 1999). In a sense, the level of dispositional traits can be viewed as the "raw stuff" of personality, whereas each successive level must be constructed to a greater extent. In the following sections, we will use McAdams's levels to organize our discussion of personality in adulthood. Let's begin with the "raw stuff" and see how dispositional traits are structured in adulthood.

9.1 Dispositional Traits across Adulthood

- What is the five-factor model of dispositional traits?
- What evidence is there for long-term stability in dispositional traits?
- What criticisms have been leveled at the five-factor model?
- What can we conclude from theory and research on dispositional traits?

Would your classmates' personalities remain the same at your college reunion?

Abby was attending her high school reunion. She hadn't seen her friend Michelle in 20 years. Abby remembered that in high school Michelle was always surrounded by a group of people. She always walked up to people and initiated conversations, was at ease with strangers, was pleasant, and was often described as the "life of the party." Abby wondered if Michelle would be the same outgoing person she was in high school.

Most of us will eventually attend a high school reunion. It is amusing, so it is said, to see how our classmates have changed over the years. In addition to noticing gray or missing hair and a few wrinkles, we should pay attention to personality characteristics. The questions that arose for Abby are similar to the ones we generate ourselves. For example, will Katy be the same outgoing person she was as captain of the cheerleaders? Will Ted still be as concerned about social issues at 48 as he was at 18? To learn as much about our friends as possible, we could make careful observations of our classmates' personalities over the course of several reunions. Then, at the gathering marking 60 years since graduation, we could examine the trends we observed. Did our classmates' personalities change substantially? Or did they remain essentially the same as they were 60 years earlier?

How we think these questions will be answered provides clues to our personal biases concerning personality stability or change across adulthood. As we will see, biases about continuity and discontinuity are more obvious in personality research than in any other area of adult development.

In addition to considering the old debate of whether Michelle's personality characteristics will have remained stable or have changed, Abby's description of Michelle suggests that Michelle is an outgoing, or extroverted, person. How did Abby arrive at this judgment? She probably combined several aspects of Michelle's behavior into a concept that describes her rather concisely. What we have done is to use the notion of a personality trait. Extending this same reasoning to many areas of behavior is the basis for trait theories of personality. More formally, people's characteristic behaviors can be understood through attributes that reflect underlying dispositional traits, which are relatively enduring aspects of personality. We use the basic tenets of trait theory when we describe ourselves and others with such terms as *calm, aggressive, independent, friendly,* and so on.

Three assumptions are made about traits (Costa & McCrae, 1998). First, traits are based on comparisons of individuals, because there are no absolute quantitative standards for concepts such as friendliness. Second, the qualities or behaviors making up a particular trait must be distinctive enough to avoid confusion. Imagine the chaos if friendliness and aggressiveness had many behaviors in common yet had some that were vastly different! Finally, the traits attributed to a specific person are assumed to be stable characteristics. We normally assume that people who are friendly in several situations are going to be friendly the next time we see them. These three assumptions are all captured in the definition of a trait: A trait is any distinguishable, relatively enduring way in which one individual differs from others (Guilford, 1959, p. 6). Based on this definition, trait theories assume that little change in personality will

Photo credit: © Steven Rubin / The Image Works

occur across adulthood. The primary interest here is when trait stability peaks and when traits stop changing.

Most trait theories have several guiding principles in common. An important one for our present discussion concerns the structure of traits. Structure concerns the way in which traits are organized within the individual. This organization is usually inferred from the pattern of related and unrelated traits and is generally expressed in terms of dimensions. Personality structures can be examined over time to see whether they change with age.

The Case for Stability: The Five-Factor Model

Although many different trait theories of personality have been proposed over the years, few have been concerned with or have been based on adults of different ages. A major exception to this is the five-factor model proposed by Costa and McCrae (1994; McCrae, 2002). Their model is strongly grounded in cross-sectional, longitudinal, and sequential research. *The **five-factor model** consists of five independent dimensions of personality: neuroticism, extraversion, openness to experience, agreeableness, and conscientiousness.*

The first three dimensions of Costa and McCrae's model—neuroticism, extraversion, and openness to experience—have been the ones most heavily researched. Each of these dimensions is represented by six facets that reflect the main characteristics associated with it. The remaining two dimensions were added to the original three in the late 1980s to account for more data and to bring the theory closer to other trait theories. In the following sections we will consider each of the five dimensions briefly.

Neuroticism. The six facets of neuroticism are anxiety, hostility, self-consciousness, depression, impulsiveness, and vulnerability. Anxiety and hostility form underlying traits for two fundamental emotions: fear and anger. Although we all experience these emotions at times, the frequency and intensity with which they are felt vary from one person to another. People who are high in trait anxiety are nervous, high-strung, tense, worried, and pessimistic. Besides being prone to anger, hostile people are irritable and tend to be hard to get along with.

The traits of self-consciousness and depression relate to the emotions shame and sorrow. Being high in self-consciousness is associated with being sensitive to criticism and teasing and to feelings of inferiority. Trait depression involves feelings of sadness, hopelessness, loneliness, guilt, and low self-worth.

The final two facets of neuroticism—impulsiveness and vulnerability—are most often manifested as behaviors rather than as emotions. Impulsiveness is the tendency to give in to temptation and desires because of a lack of willpower and self-control. Consequently, impulsive people often do things in excess, such as overeating and overspending, and they are more likely to smoke, gamble, and use drugs. Vulnerability involves a lowered ability to deal effectively with stress. Vulnerable people tend to panic in a crisis or emergency and tend to be highly dependent on others for help.

Costa and McCrae (1998) note that, in general, people high in neuroticism tend to be high in each of the traits involved. High neuroticism typically results in violent and negative emotions that interfere with people's ability to handle problems or to get along with other people. We can see how this cluster of traits would operate. A person gets anxious and embarrassed in a social situation such as a class reunion, the frustration in dealing with others makes the person hostile, which may lead to excessive drinking at the party, which may result in subsequent depression for making a fool of oneself, and so on.

Extraversion. The six facets of extraversion can be grouped into three interpersonal traits (warmth, gregariousness, and assertiveness) and three temperamental traits (activity, excitement seeking, and positive emotions). Warmth, or attachment, is a friendly, compassionate, intimately involved style of interacting with other people. Warmth and gregariousness (a desire to be with other people) make up what is sometimes called sociability. Gregarious people thrive on crowds; the more social interaction, the better. Assertive people make natural leaders, take charge easily, make up their own minds, and readily express their thoughts and feelings.

Temperamentally, extraverts like to keep busy; they are the people who seem to have endless energy, talk fast, and want to be on the go. They prefer to be in stimulating, exciting environments and will often go searching for a challenging situation. This active, exciting lifestyle is evident in the extravert's positive emotion; these people are walking examples of zest, delight, and fun.

An interesting aspect of extraversion is that this dimension relates well to occupational interests and values. People high in extraversion tend to have people-oriented jobs, such as social work, business administration, and sales. They value humanitarian goals and a person-oriented use of power. People low in extraversion tend to prefer task-oriented jobs, such as architecture or accounting.

Openness to Experience. The six facets of openness to experience represent six different areas. In the area of fantasy, openness means having a vivid imagination and active dream life. In aesthetics, openness is seen in the appreciation of art and beauty, sensitivity to pure experience for its own sake. Openness to action entails a willingness to try something new, whether it be a new kind of cuisine, a new movie, or a new travel destination. People who are open to ideas and values are curious and value knowledge for the sake of knowing. Open people also tend to be open-minded in their values, often admitting that what may be right for one person may not be right for everyone. This outlook is a direct outgrowth of open individuals' willingness to think of different possibilities and their tendency to empathize with others in different circumstances. Open people also experience their own feelings strongly and see them as a major source of meaning in life.

Not surprisingly, openness to experience is also related to occupational choice. Open people are likely to be found in occupations that place a high value on thinking theoretically or philosophically and less emphasis on economic values. They are typically intelligent and tend to subject themselves to stressful situations. Occupations such as psychologist or minister, for example, appeal to open people.

Agreeableness. The easiest way to understand the agreeableness dimension is to consider the traits that characterize antagonism. Antagonistic people tend to set themselves against others; they are skeptical, mistrustful, callous, unsympathetic, stubborn, and rude; and they have a defective sense of attachment. Antagonism may be manifested in ways other than overt hostility. For example, some antagonistic people are skillful manipulators or aggressive go-getters with little patience.

Scoring high on agreeableness, the opposite of antagonism, may not always be adaptive either, however. These people may tend to be overly dependent and self-effacing, traits that often prove annoying to others.

Conscientiousness. Scoring high on conscientiousness indicates that one is hardworking, ambitious, energetic, scrupulous, and persevering. Such people have a strong desire to make something of themselves. People at the opposite end of this scale tend to be negligent, lazy, disorganized, late, aimless, and not persistent.

What Is the Evidence for Trait Stability or Change? Costa and McCrae have investigated whether the traits that make up their model remain stable across adulthood (e.g., Costa & McCrae, 1988, 1997; McCrae & Costa, 1994). In fact, they suggest personality traits stop changing by age 30 and appear to be "set in plaster" (McCrae & Costa, 1994, p. 21). The data from the Costa, McCrae, and colleagues' studies came from the Baltimore Longitudinal Study of Aging for the 114 men who took the Guilford-Zimmerman Temperament Survey (GZTS) on three occasions, with each of the two follow-up testings about 6 years apart. What Costa and colleagues found was surprising. Even over a 12-year period, the 10 traits measured by the GZTS remained highly stable; the correlations ranged from .68 to .85. In much of personality research we might expect to find this degree of stability over a week or two, but to see it over 12 years is noteworthy.

We would normally be skeptical of such consistency over a long period. But similar findings were obtained in other studies. In a longitudinal study of 60-, 80-, and 100-year-olds, Martin and colleagues (2003) found that there were no significant changes across overall personality patterns.

However, some interesting changes did occur in the very old. There was an increase in suspiciousness and sensitivity. This could be explained by increased wariness of victimization in older adulthood. Stability was also observed in past longitudinal data conducted over an 8-year span by Siegler, George, and Okun (1979) at Duke University, a 30-year span by Leon, Gillum, Gillum, and Gouze (1979) in Minnesota, and in other longitudinal studies (Schaie & Willis, 1995; Schmitz-Scherzer & Thomae, 1983). Even more amazing was the finding that personality ratings by spouses of each other showed no systematic changes over a 6-year period (Costa & McCrae, 1988). Thus, according to this evidence it appears that individuals change very little in self-reported personality traits over periods of up to 30 years long and over the age range of 20 to 90 years of age.

However, there is growing evidence that both stability and change can be found in personality trait development across the adult life span (Allemand, Zimprich, & Hendriks, 2008; Caspi, Roberts, & Shiner, 2005; Mathias, Allemand, Zimprich, & Martin, 2008). These findings came about because of recent advances in statistical techniques. Researchers find that the way people differ in their personality becomes more pronounced with older age (Allemand et al., 2008). Furthermore, other studies (Donnellan & Lucas, 2008) find that extraversion and openness decrease with age whereas agreeableness increases with age. Middle-aged adults are the most conscientious. Finally, neuroticism slightly decreases or is absent with increasing age. Such changes are found in studies that examine larger populations across a larger age range (e.g., 16 to mid-80s) and across greater geographical regions (e.g., United States and Great Britain).

Clearly, lots of things change in people's lives over 30 years. They marry, divorce, have children, change jobs, face stressful situations, move, and maybe even retire. Social networks and friendships come and go. Society changes, and economic ups and downs have important effects. Personal changes in appearance and health occur. People read books, see dozens of movies, and watch thousands of hours of television. There are other approaches that examine underlying personality dispositions that also detect change across the adult life span.

Additional Studies of Dispositional Traits

Despite the impressive collection of research findings for personality stability using the five-factor model, as we can see from the previous discussion there is growing evidence for personality change. Ursula Staudinger and colleagues have a perspective that reconciles these differences (Staudinger & Kunzman, 2005; Staudinger & Kessler, 2008). They suggest that personality takes on two forms: adjustment and growth. Adjustment involves developmental changes in terms of their adaptive value and functionality such as funcitoning effectively within society and how personality contributes to everyday life running smoothly. Personality growth refers to ideal end states such as increased self-transcendence, wisdom, and integrity. Examples of this will be discussed later on including Eirkson's theory and Loevinger's theory. Both of these types of personality dimensions interact in that growth cannot occur without adjustment. However, Staudinger argues that while growth in terms of ideal end states does not necessarily occur in everyone, as it is less easily acquired, strategies for adjustment develop across the latter half of the life span. We can take this framework and interpret stability and change in the Big Five personality factors.

First, the most current consensus of change in the Big Five with increasing age is the absence of neuroticism and the presence of agreeableness and conscientiousness. These traits are associated with personality adjustment. This pattern of traits is related to becoming emotionally less volatile and more attuned to social demands and social roles (Staudinger & Kunzmann, 2005). These characteristics prepare adults to tackle developmental tasks and adult roles. In fact, they allow older adults to maintain and regain levels of well-being in the face of loss, threats, and challenges in life.

Studies also show a decrease in openness to new experiences with increasing age (e.g., Helson & Kwan, 2000; Roberts et al., 2006; Srivastava et al.,

2003). Staudinger argues that openness to experience is related to personal maturity in that it is highly correlated with ego development, wisdom, and emotional complexity. Evidence suggests that these three aspects of personality (ego level, wisdom, and emotional complexity) do not increase with age and may show decline (Dörner & Staudinger, 2005; Labouvie-Vief & Medler, 2002). Staudinger concludes that personal growth in adulthood appears to be rare rather than normative.

In sum, there appears to be increases in adjustment aspects of personality with increasing age and it could be normative. However, indicators of personality growth tend to show stability or decline. It is not that personality growth cannot occur in older age; it may simply take very special circumstances and environmental push to occur. It is important to keep in mind that personality-related adjustment continues to grow as we face ever-changing developmental challenges and tasks to accomplish such as establishing a career, marriage, and family.

Other studies support Staudinger's model of personality and illustrate how our techniques for assessing personality have changed. For example, Srivastava, John, Gosling, and Potter (2003) conducted a large Internet study examining the Big Five traits of more than 130,000 people ranging in age from 21 to 60 years. This study is a testament to how changes in our technology allow more in-depth analyses of larger samples of individuals. Not only has technology changed our techniques for assessment (using the Internet), but it also has changed our techniques for recruitment. For example, to attract a broad and diverse sample, these researchers used two types of web pages. One was a guide to personality instructing individuals on the fundamental dimensions of personality, and the second was a page headed "Find your *Star Wars* Twin" that included feedback about the characters from *Star Wars* with whom the participant was most similar. Needless to say they had no trouble obtaining a large sample of participants. They found that none of the Big Five personality traits remained stable after age 30. Supporting the research discussed earlier, conscientiousness showed the most change in early adulthood, a time when adults are advancing in the workforce and forming intimate relationships. Agreeableness showed the largest changes in middle adulthood, when adults are typically caring for their children. The researchers concluded, as well, that it is important to link personality and environmental changes to one another.

Finally, it is important to consider not only age changes in personality traits such as neuroticism but also cohort differences. Twenge (2000) conducted an analysis across many longitudinal studies and found that Americans have shown higher levels of anxiety and neuroticism during recent decades. In other words, she found a cohort difference that may influence future observations of changes in neuroticism across adulthood. The average American child in the 1980s reported more anxiety than children in the 1950s. Perhaps increases in divorce rate could account for these findings. Twenge concludes that broad social trends may have an important impact on personality development, particularly in childhood, that may have interesting effects on what we observe in adulthood.

Finally, we need to briefly consider two other longitudinal studies of dispositional traits that move beyond the Big Five factors.

The Berkeley Studies. Researchers in Berkeley, California, conducted one of the largest longitudinal studies on personality development. In this investigation, the parents of participants being studied in research on intellectual development were followed for roughly 30 years between ages 40 and 70 (Maas, 1985; Maas & Kuypers, 1974; Mussen, 1985). From the enormous amount of data gathered over the years, researchers were able to categorize men and women into subgroups based on their lifestyles (for instance, whether mothers were employed) and personality type. Based on the longitudinal follow-up data, gender differences were identified in terms of the best predictors of life satisfaction in old age. The data suggest that lifestyle during young adulthood is the better predictor of life satisfaction in old age for women but that personality is the better predictor for men (Mussen, 1985).

Additional analyses of the Berkeley data provide other insights into personality development. For example, the transition to parenthood in young adulthood and family and work-related transitions (e.g., retirement) in later adulthood showed much more variability than stability. Again, the sociocultural context was important in determining under what conditions we see change and when we do not. These results also do not necessarily support the notion that personality becomes rigid in old age (Field & Millsap, 1991; Labouvie-Vief et al., 2000).

Women's Personality Development during Adulthood. Several longitudinal studies of women's personality development have adopted a process approach in which they examine the interplay between social context and personality development (Helson & Moane, 1987; Helson et al., 1995; Roberts et al., 2002; Stewart et al., 2001). Helson and her colleagues followed the lives of women who chose a typcally feminine social clock (get married, have children, etc.) and examined how they adapted to the roles of wife and mother. This adaptation process was typically accompanied by a withdrawal from social life, the suppression of impulse and spontaneity, a negative self-image, and decreased feelings of competence. Of the women who adhered to the social clock, 20% were divorced between the ages of 28 and 35. However, of these divorced women, those who also had careers by the age of 28 were less respectful of norms and more rebellious toward what they experienced. Note that these women were not lower on femininity or on well-being; they were simply more independent and self-assertive than those who followed the social clock (Helson & Moane, 1987). Follow-ups showed that these independent women remained so and showed greater confidence, initiative, and forcefulness than women who did not. In fact, women were better adjusted at age 52 than at age 21. They became less impulsive, more considerate of others, more organized, more complex, and better able to adapt to various settings (Roberts et al., 2002; Stewart et al., 2001). Overall Helson and her colleagues show that women's personality change was systematic in both early and middle adulthood, yet changes were evident in the context of specific changes in social roles and transitions in social contexts (Labouvie-Vief et al., 2000; Van Manen & Whitbourne, 1997).

Middle-aged women are becoming more active and visible in our society.

Critiques of the Five-Factor Model

In a major review of the literature, Block (1995) raises several concerns with the Costa and McCrae approach. Most of Block's criticisms are based on perceived methodological problems, such as the way the dimensions were identified statistically and the way the questionnaire assessment was developed and used. This critique is based on the view that the statistical and empirical grounds on which the five-factor model is built are shaky. For example, Block argues that using laypeople to specify personality descriptors, the approach used to create the terms used in the five-factor model, is fraught with risk, chiefly due to the lack of any compelling scientific data to support such labeling. Thus Block argues that the wide acceptance of the five-factor model is premature and that considerably more research needs to be done. Block also argues in favor of personality research that takes into consideration the sociocultural context in which personality development occurs and the variability that occurs across the life course (Labouvie-Vief & Diehl, 1999; Labouvie-Vief et al., 2000). As we can see from the preceding studies, current research has followed suit with this criticism.

Finally, McAdams (1996, 1999) has raised additional limitations of the five-factor model. He points out that any model of dispositional traits says nothing about the core or essential aspects of human nature. In contrast, theorists we will consider later, such as Erikson and Loevinger, do discuss such core aspects, which cannot be translated into the language of dispositional traits. Second, dispositional traits rarely provide enough information about people so that accurate predictions can be made about how they will behave in a particular situation. Third, the assessment of dispositional traits generally fails to provide compelling explanations of why people behave the way they do. Fourth, dispositional traits are seen as independent of the context in which the individual operates. In other words, similar to Block's objections, the five-factor model approach ignores the sociocultural context of human development. Fifth, the assessment of dispositional traits reduces a person to a set of scores on a series of linear continua anchored by terms that are assumed to be both meaningful and opposite. Sixth, the assessment of dispositional traits through questionnaires assumes that the respondent is able to take an objective, evaluative stance regarding his or her personal characteristics. McAdams's criticisms nevertheless reflect the view that assessing dispositional traits has its place in personality research; his point is simply that dispositional traits should not be viewed as reflecting one's entire personality.

As we might expect, the critiques themselves are controversial. For example, Costa and McCrae (1995, 1998) and Goldberg and Saucier (1995) point to flaws in Block's argument, such as his overlooking of research favorable to the five-factor model. Arguments about the place for assessing dispositional traits within the study of personality reflect the biases of the authors. The controversy surrounding Costa and McCrae's basic claim that dispositional traits typically remain stable in adulthood will continue, and it is likely to result in more, and even better, research.

In fact, one of the most recent and exciting approaches to this controversy is to take an intraindividual perspective (Mroczek & Spiro, 2003). Mroczek and colleagues challenge the conclusions drawn from the typical longitudinal studies on stability and change in personality by examining personality across the adult life span at the level of the individual. We describe this challenge in more detail in the Current Controversies feature.

Conclusions about Dispositional Traits

What can we conclude from the research on the development of personality traits across adulthood? From both conceptual and empirical perspectives it seems that the idea that personality traits stop changing at age 30 does not have uniform support. On the one hand, we have a definition of traits that requires stability. Costa and McCrae, among others, argue strongly for this position; they report that there is little evidence (and perhaps possibility) of change. On the other hand, Staudinger's perspective, the Berkeley group, and Helson and colleagues argue for both change and stability. They say that at least some traits change, opening the door to personality development in adulthood. One partial resolution can be found if we consider how the research was done. Clearly, the overwhelming evidence supports the view that personality traits remain stable throughout adulthood when data are averaged across many different kinds of people. However, if we ask about specific aspects of personality in very specific kinds of people, we are more likely to find some evidence of both change and stability.

The recent critiques of the five-factor model have created a climate in which more careful scrutiny of research on dispositional traits is likely to occur. More sophisticated statistical techniques are now being applied, and more attention is being paid to individual differences in change as we saw in the Current Controversies feature. Helson and colleagues (2002) suggest that we need to consider personality as consistent yet adaptive to changing biological and environmental contexts. These approaches to personality help address many of the criticisms.

In addition, the idea that trait stability may not be fixed at age 30 invites the question as to whether periods beyond age 30 may be associated with greater trait stability (Roberts & Del Vecchio, 2000). In fact, Roberts and Del Vecchio find that trait stability peaks in middle age when identity certainty (achieving a strong sense of identity, ability to choose environments that fit well with one's identity, and the ability to assimilate more experience into one's identity) is more likely to be achieved (Stewart et al., 2001). Future research needs to examine the extent to which many factors

The controversy continues today as to whether personality remains stable across the life span or whether it changes. Given that personality traits have been shown to be important predictors of mental and physical health as well as psychological well-being, potential changes in personality can have important implications for gains and declines in such life outcomes. However, as this chapter indicates, there is no clear evidence for one position or the other. An important aspect to consider in this controversy is the level of analysis in which stability and change is determined. Typically, stability and change are examined through mean level comparisons over time. In other words, does an age group's mean level on a particular personality trait such as extraversion remain stable from one point in time to another (say 10 years apart) or does it change?

Mroczek and Spiro (2003) suggest that examining change in mean levels of a personality trait does not adequately address stability and change at the level of the individual. In other words, a group mean hides the extent to which individual people change. In their recent work, they examine the extent to which each person in their longitudinal study changes or remains the same over time. This allowed them to ask the questions "Do some people remain stable whereas others change?" and, if there are people who change, "Do some people change more than others?" They examined individual patterns of change for 1,366 men over a 6-year period. They ascertained personality change and stability by examining each individual's change pattern, called an individual growth curve. They then grouped each individual into categories of no change in the personality trait, increases in the personality trait, and decreases in the personality trait. Preliminary findings indicate that over a 6-year period, a large proportion of older men remained stable with respect to extraversion, whereas a smaller but substantial proportion of men changed. In addition, among those who changed, an equal number of men increased and decreased in extraversion. The researchers found similar results for neuroticism. These findings indicate important individual differences in the extent to which men change.

This approach allows a more detailed answer to questions of stability and change. When we rely on the major longitudinal approaches such as McCrae and Costa's (1994), we see that at the group level there is primarily stability. However, when we examine individuals' growth curves, we see a more complete picture of personality development. Whereas a large proportion of individuals may remain stable, there is a substantial group of individuals whose personality traits either increase or decrease over time. Perhaps we can see a resolution to this debate in the future as more intraindividual studies on personality development emerge.

that may be linked to increased stability, such as a stable environment or identity integration, account for age and trait stability (Roberts & Del Vecchio, 2000; Roberts et al., 2002).

Another important issue for future research is the role of life experiences. If a person experiences few events that induce him or her to change, then change is unlikely. In this view a person will be at 60 very much the same as he or she is at 30, all other factors being held constant. As we will see later, this idea has been incorporated formally into other theories of personality. On the basis of dispositional traits, then, we should have little difficulty knowing our high school classmates many years later.

1. What are the five dimensions of the five-factor model?

2. What criticisms are aimed at the five-factor model?

3. What were the main findings from more current research on changes in dispositional traits?

4. Are dispositional traits stable over time?

9.2 Personal Concerns and Qualitative Stages in Adulthood

LEARNING OBJECTIVES

- What are personal concerns?
- What are the main elements of Jung's theory?
- What are the stages in Erikson's theory? What types of clarifications and extensions of it have been offered? What research evidence is there to support his stages?
- What are the stages in Loevinger's theory? What evidence is there to support her stages?
- What are the main points and problems with theories based on life transitions?
- How is midlife best described?
- What can we conclude about personal concerns?

Andy showed all the signs. He divorced his wife of nearly 20 years to enter into a relationship with a woman 15 years younger, sold his ordinary-looking mid-size sedan for a red sports car, and began working out regularly at the health club after years of being a couch potato. Andy claims he hasn't felt this good in years; he is happy to be making this change in middle age. All of Andy's friends agree: This is a clear case of midlife crisis. Or is it?

Many people believe strongly that middle age brings with it a normative crisis called the midlife crisis. There would appear to be lots of evidence to support this view, based on case studies like Andy's. But is everything as it seems? We'll find out in this section. First we consider the evidence that people's priorities and personal concerns change throughout adulthood, requiring adults to reassess themselves from time to time. This alternative position to the five-factor model discussed earlier claims that change is the rule during adulthood.

What does it mean to know another person well? McAdams (1999) believes that to know another

Getting to know a person crosses generations.

person well takes more than just knowing where he or she falls on the dimensions of dispositional traits. Rather, it also means knowing what issues are important to a person, what the person wants, how the person goes about getting what he or she wants, what the person's plans for the future are, how the person interacts with others who provide key personal relationships, and so forth. In short, we need to know something about a person's personal concerns. Personal concerns reflect what people want during particular times of their lives and within specific domains; they are the strategies, plans, and defenses people use to get what they want and to avoid getting what they don't want.

What's Different about Personal Concerns?

Recently, many researchers have begun analyzing personality in ways that are explicitly contextual, in contrast to work on dispositional traits, which ignores context. This recent work emphasizes the importance of sociocultural influences on development that shape people's wants and behaviors (Hooker, 2002). For example, Thorne (Thorne & Klohnen, 1993) showed that when people talk about themselves, they go well beyond speaking in dispositional trait terms. Rather, people provide more narrative descriptions that rely heavily on their life circumstances, that is, the sociocultural experiences they have had that shape their lives. Moreover, people are highly likely to describe developmentally linked concerns that change over time. Cantor (1990; Cantor & Harlow, 1994) highlighted this aspect of self-descriptions in differentiating between "having" traits and "doing" everyday behaviors that address the strivings, tasks, and goals that are important in everyday life. This latter aspect of personality emphasizes the importance of understanding culturally mandated, developmentally linked "life tasks" that reflect these changing concerns.

Although relatively little research has been conducted on the personal concerns level of personality, a few things are clear (Hooker & McAdams, 2003; McAdams, 1999). Personality constructs at this level are not reducible to traits. Rather, such constructs need to be viewed as conscious descriptions of what a person is trying to accomplish during a given period of life and what goals and goal-based concerns the person has. As Cantor (1990) notes, these constructs speak directly to the question of what people actually do in life. Moreover, we would expect that considerable change would be seen at this level of personality, given the importance of sociocultural influences and the changing nature of life tasks as people mature. Accompanying these goals and motivations that define personal concerns are the self-regulation processes implemented to effect change in personal concerns. For example, the transition from primary control to secondary control or from assimilative to accommodative coping discussed in Chapter 8 enable people to recalibrate their goals and personal concerns in later life. This process serves the important function of maintaining satisfaction and meaningfulness in life (Hooker & McAdams, 2003).

In contrast to the limited empirical data on the development of personal concerns, the theoretical base is arguably the richest. For the better part of a century, the notion that people's personality changes throughout the life span has been described in numerous ways, typically in theories that postulate qualitative stages that reflect the central concern of that period of life. In this section, we will consider several of these theories and evaluate the available evidence for each. Let's begin with Carl Jung's theory—the theory that got people thinking about personality change in midlife.

Jung's Theory

Jung represents a turning point in the history of psychoanalytic thought. Initially allied with Freud, he soon severed the tie and developed his own ideas, which have elements of both Freudian theory and humanistic psychology. He was one of the very first theorists to believe in personality development in adulthood; this marked a major break with Freudian thought, which argued that personality development ended in adolescence.

Jung's theory emphasizes that each aspect of a person's personality must be in balance with all the others. This means that each part of the personality will be expressed in some way, whether through normal means or through neurotic symptoms or in dreams. Jung asserts that the parts of the personality are organized in such a way as to produce two basic orientations of the ego. One of these orientations is concerned with the external world; Jung labels it extraversion. The opposite orientation, toward the inner world of subjective experiences, is labeled introversion. To be psychologically healthy, both of these orientations must be present, and they must be balanced. Individuals must be able to deal with the external world effectively and also be able to evaluate their inner feelings and values. When people emphasize one orientation over another, they are classified as extraverts or introverts.

Jung advocates two important age-related trends in personality development. The first relates to the introversion–extraversion distinction. Young adults are more extraverted than older adults, perhaps because of younger people's needs to find a mate, have a career, and so forth. With increasing age, however, the need for balance creates a need to focus inward and explore personal feelings about aging and mortality. Thus, Jung argued that with age comes an increase in introversion.

The second age-related trend in Jung's theory involves the feminine and masculine aspects of our personalities. Each of us, according to Jung, has elements of both masculinity and femininity. In young adulthood, however, most of us express only one of them while usually working hard to suppress the other. In other words, young adults most often act in accordance with gender-role stereotypes appropriate

Solitude becomes more precious as one grows older.

to their culture. As they grow older, people begin to let out the suppressed parts of their personality. This means that men begin to behave in ways that earlier in life they would have considered feminine, and women behave in ways that they formerly would have thought masculine. These changes achieve a better balance that allows men and women to deal more effectively with their individual needs rather than being driven by socially defined stereotypes. This balance, however, does not mean a reversal of sex roles. On the contrary, it represents the expression of aspects of ourselves that have been there all along but that we have simply not allowed to show. We will return to this issue at the end of the chapter when we consider gender-role development.

More recently, Jung's ideas that self and personality are organized by symbols and stories and the notion that we transcend the dualities of femininity–masculinity, conscious–unconscious, among others, have become active areas of research (Labouvie-Vief & Diehl, 1999; McAdams, 1995). However, as Labouvie-Vief and colleagues (Labouvie-Vief & Diehl, 1999; Labouvie-Vief & Medler, 2002) point out, most empirical evidence suggests that these reorganizations proposed by Jung are more indicative of advanced or exceptional development (Labouvie-Vief et al., 1995).

Jung stretched traditional psychoanalytic theory to new limits by postulating continued development across adulthood. Other theorists took Jung's lead and argued not only that personality development occurred in adulthood but also that it did so in an orderly, sequential fashion. We will consider the sequences developed by two theorists, Erik Erikson and Jane Loevinger.

Erikson's Stages of Psychosocial Development

The best-known life-span theorist is Erik Erikson (1982), who called attention to cultural mechanisms involved in personality development. According to him, personality is determined by the interaction between an inner maturational plan and external societal demands. He proposes that the life cycle has eight stages of development, summarized in Table 9.1. Erikson believed the sequence of stages is biologically fixed.

Each stage in Erikson's theory is marked by a struggle between two opposing tendencies, both of which are experienced by the person. The names of the stages reflect the issues that form the struggles. The struggles are resolved through an interactive process involving both the inner psychological and the outer social influences. Successful resolutions establish the basic areas of psychosocial strength; unsuccessful resolutions impair ego development in a particular area and adversely affect the resolution of future struggles. Thus each stage in Erikson's theory represents a kind of crisis.

The sequence of stages in Erikson's theory is based on the **epigenetic principle,** *which means that each psychosocial strength has its own special time of ascendancy, or period of particular importance.* The eight stages represent the order of this ascendancy. Because the stages extend across the whole life span, it takes a lifetime to acquire all of the psychosocial strengths. Moreover, Erikson realizes that present and future behavior must have its roots in the past, because later stages build on the foundation laid in previous ones.

Erikson argues that the basic aspect of a healthy personality is a sense of trust toward oneself and others. Thus the first stage in his theory involves trust versus mistrust, representing the conflict that

Table 9.1

Summary of Erikson's Theory of Psychosocial Development, with Important
Relationships and Psychosocial Strengths Acquired at Each Stage

Stage	Psychosocial Crisis	Significant Relations	Basic Strengths
1. Infancy	Basic trust versus basic mistrust	Maternal person	Hope
2. Early childhood	Autonomy versus shame and doubt	Paternal people	Will
3. Play age	Initiative versus guilt	Basic family	Purpose
4. School age	Industry versus inferiority	"Neighborhood," school	Competence
5. Adolescence	Identity versus identity confusion	Peer groups and outgroups; models of leadership	Love
6. Young adulthood	Intimacy versus isolation	Partners in friendship, sex competition, cooperation	Love
7. Adulthood	Generativity versus stagnation	Divided labor and shared household	Care
8. Old age	Integrity versus despair	Humankind, "my kind"	Wisdom

Source: From The Life Cycle Completed: A Review by Erik H. Erikson. Copyright © 1982 by Rikan Enterprises, Ltd. Used by permission of W. W. Norton & Company, Inc.

an infant faces in developing trust in a world it knows little about. With trust come feelings of security and comfort.

The second stage, autonomy versus shame and doubt, reflects children's budding understanding that they are in charge of their own actions. This understanding changes them from totally reactive beings to ones who can act on the world intentionally. Their autonomy is threatened, however, by their inclinations to avoid responsibility for their actions and to go back to the security of the first stage.

In the third stage the conflict is initiative versus guilt. Once children realize they can act on the world and are somebody, they begin to discover who they are. They take advantage of wider experience to explore the environment on their own, to ask many questions about the world, and to imagine possibilities about themselves.

The fourth stage is marked by children's increasing interests in interacting with peers, their need for acceptance, and their need to develop competencies. Erikson views these needs as representing industry versus inferiority, which is manifested behaviorally in children's desire to accomplish tasks by working hard. Failure to succeed in developing self-perceived competencies results in feelings of inferiority.

During adolescence, Erikson believes, we deal with the issue of identity versus identity confusion. The choice we make—that is, the identity we form—is not so much who we are but, rather, whom we can become. The struggle in adolescence is choosing from among a multitude of possible selves the one we will become. Identity confusion results when we are torn over the possibilities. The struggle involves trying to balance our need to choose a possible self and the desire to try out many possible selves.

During young adulthood the major developmental task, achieving intimacy versus isolation, involves establishing a fully intimate relationship with another. Erikson (1968) argues that intimacy means the sharing of all aspects of oneself without fearing the loss of identity. If intimacy is not achieved, isolation results. One way to assist the development of intimacy is to choose a mate who represents the ideal of all one's past experiences. The psychosocial strength that emerges from the intimacy–isolation struggle is love.

With the advent of middle age the focus shifts from intimacy to concern for the next generation, expressed as generativity versus stagnation. The struggle occurs between a sense of generativity (the feeling that people must maintain and perpetuate society) and a sense of stagnation (the feeling of self-absorption). Generativity is seen in such things as parenthood; teaching, like the man in the photograph; or providing goods and services for the benefit of society. If the challenge of generativity is accepted, the development of trust in the next generation is facilitated, and the psychosocial strength of care is obtained.

In old age individuals must resolve the struggle between ego integrity and despair. This last stage begins with a growing awareness of the nearness of the end of life, but it is actually completed by only a small number of people (Erikson, 1982). The task is to examine and evaluate one's life and accomplishments in order to try and make sense of one's life. This process often involves reminiscing with others and actively seeking reassurance that one has accomplished something in life. People who have progressed successfully through earlier stages of life face old age enthusiastically and feel their life has been full. Those who feel a sense of meaninglessness do not anxiously anticipate old age, and they experience despair. The psychosocial strength achieved from a successful resolution of this struggle is wisdom. Integrity is not the only issue facing older adults; Erikson points out that they have many opportunities for generativity as well. Older people often play an active role as grandparents, for example, and many maintain part-time jobs.

Clarifications and Expansions of Erikson's Theory. Erikson's theory has had a major impact on thinking about life-span development. However, some aspects of his theory are unclear, poorly defined, or unspecified. Traditionally, these problems have led critics to dismiss the theory as untestable and incomplete. The situation is changing, however. Other theorists have tried to address these problems by identifying common themes, specifying underlying mental processes, and reinterpreting and integrating the theory with other ideas. These ideas are leading researchers to reassess the usefulness of Erikson's theory as a guide for research on adult personality development.

Logan (1986) points out that Erikson's theory can be considered as a cycle that repeats: from basic trust to identity and from identity to integrity. In this approach the developmental progression is trust → achievement → wholeness. Throughout life we first establish that we can trust other people and ourselves. Initially, trust involves learning about ourselves and others, represented by the first two stages (trust versus mistrust and autonomy versus shame and doubt). The recapitulation of this idea in the second cycle is seen in our struggle to find a person with whom we can form a very close relationship yet not lose our own sense of self (intimacy versus isolation). In addition, Logan shows how achievement—our need to accomplish and to be recognized for it—is a theme throughout Erikson's theory. During childhood this idea is reflected in the two stages initiative versus guilt and industry versus inferiority, whereas in adulthood it is represented by generativity versus stagnation. Finally, Logan points out that the issue of understanding ourselves as worthwhile and whole is first encountered during adolescence (identity versus identity confusion) and is re-experienced during old age (integrity versus despair). Logan's analysis emphasizes that psychosocial development, although complicated on the surface, may actually reflect only a small number of issues. Moreover, he points out that we do not come to a single resolution of these issues of trust, achievement, and wholeness. Rather, they are issues that we struggle with our entire lives.

Slater (2003) has expanded on Logan's reasoning, suggesting that the central crisis of generativity versus stagnation includes struggles between pride and embarrassment, responsibility and ambivalence, career productivity and inadequacy, as well as parenthood and self-absorption. Each of these conflicts provides further knowledge about generativity as the intersection of society and the human life cycle.

Some critics argue that Erikson's stage of generativity is much too broad to capture the essence of adulthood. For example, Kotre (1984, 1999) contends that adults experience many opportunities to express generativity that are not equivalent and do not lead to a general state. Rather, he sees generativity more as a set of impulses felt at different times in different settings, such as at work or in grandparenting. More formally, Kotre describes five types of generativity: biological and parental generativity, which concerns

Many men, like the man in the photograph, report that priorities change during middle age.

raising children; technical generativity, which relates to the passing of specific skills from one generation to another; cultural generativity, which refers to being a mentor (as discussed in more detail in Chapter 12); agentic generativity, which refers to the desire to be or to do something that transcends death; and communal generativity, which represents a person's participation in a mutual, interpersonal reality. Only rarely, Kotre contends, is there a continuous state of generativity in adulthood. He asserts that the struggles identified by Erikson are not fought constantly; rather, they probably come and go. We will examine this idea in more detail in the next section.

Finally, Hamachek (1990) provided behavioral and attitudinal descriptors of Erikson's last three stages. These descriptors are meant to create a series of continua of possibilities for individual development. This reflects the fact that few people have an exclusive orientation to either intimacy or isolation, for example, but more commonly show some combination of the two. These behavioral and attitudinal descriptors provide a framework for researchers who need to operationalize Erikson's concepts.

Research on Generativity. Perhaps the central period in adulthood from an Eriksonian perspective is the stage of generativity versus stagnation. One of the best empirically based efforts to describe generativity is McAdams's model (McAdams, 2001; McAdams et al., 1998) shown in Figure 9.1. This multidimensional model shows how generativity results from the complex interconnections among societal and inner forces. The tension between creating a product or outcome that outlives oneself and selflessly bestowing one's efforts as a gift to the next generation (reflecting a concern for what is good for society) results in a concern for the next generation and a belief in the goodness of the human enterprise. The positive resolution of this conflict finds middle-aged adults developing a generative commitment, which produces generative actions. A person derives personal meaning from being generative by constructing a life story or narration, which helps create the person's identity (Whitbourne, 1996c, 1999).

The components of McAdams's model relate differently to personality traits. For example, generative *concern* is a general personality tendency of interest in caring for younger individuals, and generative *action* is the actual behaviors that promote the well-being of the next generation. Generative concern relates to life satisfaction and overall happiness, whereas generative action does not (de St. Aubin & McAdams, 1995; McAdams et al., 1998; McAdams,

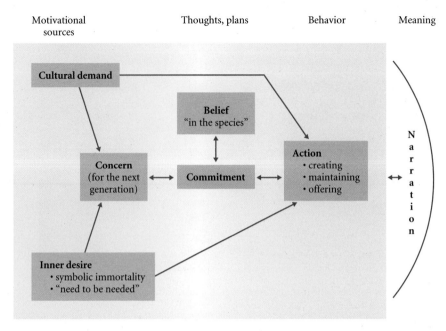

Motivational sources   Thoughts, plans   Behavior   Meaning

Figure 9.1   McAdams's model of generativity.

Source: McAdams, D. P., Hart, H. M., & Maruna, S. (1998). The anatomy of generativity. In D. P. McAdams & E. de St. Aubin (Eds.), *Generativity and Adult Development: How and Why We Care for the Next Generation* (p. 7). Copyright © 1998 Adapted by permission from the American Psychological Association.

2001). New grandparents may derive much satisfaction from their grandchildren and are greatly concerned with their well-being but have little desire to engage in the daily hassles of caring for them on a regular basis. These results have led to the creation of positive and negative generativity indices that reliably identify differences between generative and nongenerative individuals (Himsel et al., 1997).

Although they can be expressed by adults of all ages, certain types of generativity are more common at some ages than others. For example, middle-aged and older adults show a greater preoccupation with generativity themes than do younger adults in their accounts of personally meaningful life experiences (Norman et al., 2002; Zucker et al., 2002). Middle-aged adults make more generative commitments (e.g., "save enough money for my daughter to go to medical school"), reflecting a major difference in the inner and outer worlds of middle-aged and older adults as opposed to younger adults (McAdams et al., 1993).

Similar research focusing specifically on middle-aged women yields comparable results. Peterson and Klohnen (1995) examined generativity from the viewpoint of personality characteristics, work productivity, parental involvement, health concerns, and political interests in separate samples of Mills College and Radcliffe College alumnae who were in their early to mid-40s. They found that women who exhibit high generativity tend to have prosocial personality traits, are personally invested in being a parent, express generative attitudes at work, and exhibit caring behaviors toward others outside their immediate families (Peterson & Klohnen, 1995), as well as show high well-being in their role as a spouse (MacDermid et al., 1996).

These data demonstrate that the personal concerns of middle-aged adults are fundamentally different from those of younger adults. In fact, generativity may be a stronger predictor of emotional well-being in midlife adults (Ackerman et al., 2000; Keyes & Ryff, 1998). For example, among women and men generativity was associated with positive emotion and satisfaction with life and work. Finally, these concerns are not consistently or uniformly related to dispositional traits. Considered together, these findings provide considerable support for Erikson's contention that the central concerns for adults change with age. However, the data also indicate that generativity is much more complex than Erikson originally proposed and may not diminish in late life.

Loevinger's Theory

Loevinger (1976, 1998) saw a need to extend the groundwork laid by Erikson both theoretically and empirically. For her, the ego is the chief organizer: the integrator of our morals, values, goals, and thought processes. Because this integration performed by the ego is so complex and is influenced by personal experiences, it is the primary source of individual differences at all ages beyond infancy. **Ego development,** *which results from dynamic interaction between the person and the environment, consists of fundamental changes in the ways in which thoughts, values, morals, and goals are organized.* Transitions from one stage to another depend on both internal biological changes and external social changes to which the person must adapt.

Although Loevinger proposes eight stages of ego development, beginning in infancy, we will focus on the six that are observed in adults (see Table 9.2). An important aspect of her theory is that most people never go through all of them; indeed, the last level is achieved by only a handful of individuals. Cross-sectional and longitudinal evidence suggests these stages are age related (Cook-Greuter, 1989; Loevinger, 1997, 1998; Redmore & Loevinger, 1979). At each stage Loevinger identifies four areas that she considers important to the developmental progression: character development (reflecting a person's standards and goals); interpersonal style (representing the person's pattern of relations with others); conscious preoccupations (reflecting the most important things on the person's mind); and cognitive style (reflecting the characteristic way in which the person thinks). As we consider the ego levels important for adults, we will examine them in terms of these four areas.

A few adults operate at the *conformist level.* Character development at this stage is marked by absolute conformity to social rules. If these rules are broken, feelings of shame and guilt result. Interpersonally, conformists need to belong and show a superficial niceness. Of central importance is appearance and social acceptability. Conformists see the world only in terms of external tangibles, such as how one looks and if one behaves according to group standards. Thinking is dominated by stereotypes and clichés and is relatively simplistic.

Most adults in American society operate at the *conscientious-conformist level.* At this stage character development is marked by a differentiation of norms and goals; in other words, people learn to separate what they want for themselves from what

---

Table 9.2

Summary of Loevinger's Stages of Ego Development in Adulthood

Stage	Description
Conformist	Obedience to external social rules
Conscientious-conformist	Separation of norms and goals; realization that acts affect others
Conscientious	Beginning of self-evaluated standards
Individualistic	Recognition that the process of acting is more important than the outcome
Autonomous	Respect for each person's individuality, tolerance for ambiguity
Integrated	Resolution of inner conflicts

social norms may dictate. People deal with others by recognizing that they have an impact on them and on the group as a whole. People at this level begin to be concerned with issues of personal adjustment and coping with problems; they need reasons for actions and recognize that life presents many opportunities from which they may choose. They are still concerned with group standards, and the desire for personal adjustment is sometimes suppressed if it conflicts with the needs of the group.

The next level is marked by a cognitive style in which individuals begin to understand the true complexity of the world. *People at this* **conscientious stage** *focus on understanding the role that the self plays; character development involves self-evaluated standards, self-critical thinking, self-determined ideals, and self-set goals.* This level represents a shift away from letting other people or society set their goals and standards for them. Intensity, responsibility, and mutual sharing characterize interpersonal relations. People evaluate behavior using internalized standards developed over the years. They come to realize that they control their own future. Although more complex, conscientious people still think in terms of polarities, such as love versus lust or inner life versus outer appearance. But they recognize responsibility and obligation in addition to rights and privileges.

Loevinger postulates that the individualistic level builds on the previous (conscientious) level. A major acquisition at the *individualistic level* is a respect for individuality. Immature dependency is seen as an emotional problem, rather than as something to be expected. Concern for broad social problems and differentiating one's inner life from one's outer life become the main preoccupations. People begin to differentiate process (the way things are done) from outcome (the answer); for example, people realize that sometimes the solution to a problem is right but the way of getting there involves hurting someone. The dominant trait of the individualistic person is an increased tolerance for oneself and others. Key conflicts are recognized as complex problems: dependence as constraining versus dependence as emotionally rewarding, and morality and responsibility versus achievement for

oneself. The way of resolving these conflicts, however, usually involves projecting the cause onto the environment rather than acknowledging their internal sources.

At Loevinger's *autonomous level* comes a high tolerance for ambiguity with conflicting needs both within oneself and others. Autonomous individuals' interpersonal style is characterized by a respect for each person's independence but also by an understanding that people are interdependent. The preoccupations at this level are vividly conveyed feelings, self-fulfillment, and understanding of the self in a social context. Autonomous people have the courage to acknowledge and face conflict head-on rather than projecting it onto the environment. They see reality as complex and multifaceted and no longer view it in the polarities of the conscientious stage. Autonomous individuals recognize that problems can be viewed in multiple ways and are comfortable with the fact that other people's viewpoints may differ from their own. They recognize the need for others' self-sufficiency and take a broad view of life.

The final level in Loevinger's theory is termed the *integrated stage*. Inner conflicts are not only faced but also reconciled and laid to rest. Goals that are recognized to be unattainable are renounced. People at the integrated level cherish an individuality that comes from a consolidated sense of identity. They are very much like Maslow's (1968) self-actualized person; that is, they are at peace with themselves and have realized their maximum potential. They recognize that they could have chosen other paths in life but are content with and make the most out of the one that they picked. Such people are always open to further growth-enhancing opportunities and make the most out of integrating new experiences into their lives.

Loevinger has spent decades developing the Sentence Completion Test, which provides a measure of ego development. The measure consists of sentence fragments (similar to "When I think of myself, I _____") that respondents complete. Responses are then scored in terms of the ego developmental level they represent. Although it is a difficult instrument to learn how to use, the Sentence Completion Test has very good reliability.

Being committed to broad social concerns is the essence of Loevinger's individualist phase of ego development.

Trained coders have high rates of agreement in rating responses, often over 90% of the time.

Loevinger's theory is having an increasing impact on adult developmental research. One of its advantages is that because of the Sentence Completion Test it is more empirically based than Erikson's theory, so that researchers can document the stages more precisely. Loevinger's theory is the major framework for research examining relationships between cognitive development and ego development (King et al., 1989). For example, Blanchard-Fields and Norris (1994) found ego level was the best predictor of social judgments from adolescents, and from young, middle-aged, and older adults, about negative outcomes in personal relationship situations. Likewise, Labouvie-Vief, Hakim-Larson, and Hobart (1987) reported that ego level was a strong predictor of the coping strategies used across the life span from childhood to old age. Both studies documented age-related increases in ego level that were associated with higher levels of social reasoning or with more mature coping styles.

Theories Based on Life Transitions

Jung's belief in a midlife crisis, Erikson's belief that personality development proceeds in stages, and Loevinger's notion that cognitive and ego development are mutually interactive laid the foundation for other theorists' efforts. For many laypeople, the idea that adults go through an orderly sequence of stages that includes both crises and stability reflects their own experience. This is probably why books such as Sheehy's *Passages* (1976), *Pathfinders* (1981), *New Passages* (1995), and *Understanding Men's Passages* (1998) are met with instant acceptance, or why Levinson's (Levinson et al., 1978) and Vaillant's works (Vaillant, 1977; Vaillant & Vaillant, 1990) have been applied to everything from basic personality development to understanding how men's occupational careers change. A universal assumption of these theories is that people go through predictable age-related crises. Some life transition theories (e.g., Levinson's) also propose that these crises are followed by periods of relative stability. The overall view is that adulthood consists of a series of alternating periods of stability and change.

Compared with the theories we have considered to this point, however, theories based on life transitions are built on shakier ground. For example, some are based on small, highly selective samples (such as men who attended Harvard) or surveys completed by readers of particular magazines. This is in contrast, for example, to the large databases used to test the five-factor model and Loevinger's theory. These theories are associated with psychometrically sound measures and are well researched. Thus the research methods used in studies of life transitions may not be valid.

An important question about life transition theories is the extent to which they are real and actually occur to everyone. Life transition theories typically present stages as if everyone universally experiences them. Moreover, many have specific ages tied to specific stages (such as age-30 or age-50 transitions). As we know from cognitive developmental research reviewed in Chapter 7, however, this is a very tenuous assumption. Individual variation is the rule, not the exception. What actually happens may be a combination of expectations and socialization. For example, Dunn and Merriam (1995) examined data from a large, diverse national sample and found that less than 20% of people in their early 30s experienced the age-30 transition (which encompasses the midlife crisis) that forms a cornerstone of Levinson and colleagues' (1978) theory. The experience of a midlife crisis, discussed next, is an excellent case in point.

In Search of the Midlife Crisis. One of the most important ideas in theories that consider the importance of life transitions (subsequent to periods of stability) is that middle-aged adults experience a personal crisis that results in major changes in how they view themselves. During a midlife crisis, people are supposed to take a good hard look at themselves and, they hope, attain a much better understanding of who they are. Difficult issues such as one's own mortality and inevitable aging are supposed to be faced. Behavioral changes are supposed to occur;

Middle-aged women struggle to reconcile physical aging and self-development.

we even have stereotypic images of the middle-aged male, like Andy, running off with a much younger female as a result of his midlife crisis. In support of this notion, Levinson and his colleagues (1978; Levinson & Levinson, 1996) write that middle-aged men in his study reported intense internal struggles that were much like depression.

However, far more research fails to document the existence and more importantly the universality of a particularly difficult time in midlife. In fact, those who do experience a crisis may be suffering from general problems of psychopathology (Labouvie-Vief & Diehl, 1999; Rosenberg et al., 1999). Baruch (1984) summarizes a series of retrospective interview studies of American women between the ages of 35 and 55. The results showed that women in their 20s were more likely to be uncertain and dissatisfied than were women at midlife. Middle-aged women only rarely mentioned normative developmental milestones such as marriage, childbirth, or menopause as major turning points in their lives. Rather, unexpected events such as divorce and job transfers were more likely to cause crises. Studies extending Levinson's theory to women have not found strong evidence of a traumatic midlife crisis either (Harris et al., 1986; Reinke et al., 1985; Roberts & Newton, 1987).

The midlife crisis was also missing in data obtained as part of the Berkeley studies of personality traits. Most middle-aged men said that their careers were satisfying (Clausen, 1981), and both men and women appeared more self-confident, insightful, introspective, open, and better equipped to handle stressful situations (Haan, 1985; Haan et al., 1986). Even direct attempts to find the midlife crisis failed. In two studies, Costa and McCrae (1978) could identify only a handful of men who fit the profile, and even then the crisis came anytime between ages 30 and 60. A replication and extension of this work, conducted by Farrell and colleagues (Farrell et al., 1993; Rosenberg, 1991; Rosenberg et al., 1992, 1999), confirmed the initial results.

Researchers point out that the idea of a midlife crisis became widely accepted as fact because of the mass media (McCrae & Costa, 1990; Sterns & Huyck, 2001). People take it for granted that they will go through a period of intense psychological turmoil in their 40s. The problem is that there is little hard scientific evidence of it. The data suggest that midlife is no more or no less traumatic for most people than any other period in life. Perhaps the most convincing support for this conclusion comes from research conducted by Farrell and Rosenberg (Rosenberg et al., 1999). These investigators initially set out to prove the existence of a midlife crisis, because they were firm believers in it. After extensive testing and interviewing, however, they emerged as nonbelievers.

However, Labouvie-Vief and Diehl (1999) offer some good evidence for a reorganization of self and values across the adult life span. They suggest that the major dynamic driving such changes may not be age dependent but may follow general cognitive changes. As discussed in Chapter 8, individuals around middle adulthood show the most complex understanding of self, emotions, and motivations. Cognitive complexity also is shown to be the strongest predictor of higher levels of complexity in general. Thus a midlife crisis may be the result of general gains in cognitive complexity from early to middle adulthood (Labouvie-Vief & Diehl, 1999).

Abigail Stewart (1996) found that those well-educated women who reported regrets for adopting a traditional feminine role in life (i.e., they wished they had pursued an education or a career) and subsequently made adjustments in midlife were better off than those who did not make adjustments or had no role regrets at all. *Stewart suggests that rather than a midlife crisis, such an adjustment may be more appropriately considered a **midlife correction,** reevaluating one's roles and dreams and making the necessary corrections.*

Perhaps the best way to view midlife is as a time of both gains and losses (Lachman et al., 1994; Lachman, 2001). That is, the changes people perceive in midlife can be viewed as representing both gains and losses. Competence, ability to handle stress, sense of personal control, purpose in life, and social responsibility are all at their peak, whereas physical abilities, women's ability to bear children, and physical appearance are examples of changes many view as negative. This gain–loss view emphasizes two things. First, the exact timing of change

is not fixed but occurs over an extended period of time. Second, change can be both positive and negative at the same time. Thus, rather than seeing midlife as a time of crisis, one may want to view it as a period during which several aspects of one's life acquire new meanings.

Finally, we cannot overlook examining midlife crises from a cross-cultural perspective. Menon and Shweder (1998; Menon, 2001; Sterns & Huyck, 2001) suggest that midlife crisis is a cultural invention. They present anthropological evidence suggesting that the concept of midlife itself is limited to adults studied in the United States. In other cultures, for example, transitions and crises are linked to role relations such as marriage and relocation into the spouse's family. Major transitions are defined by children's marriages and mothers-in-law moving into the older adult role of observer (Kakar, 1998; Menon, 2001). Again, this is a good reminder that the cultural context plays an important role in adult development.

Conclusions about Personal Concerns

The theories and research evidence we have considered show that substantive change in adults' personal concerns definitely occurs as people age. This conclusion is in sharp contrast to the stability observed in dispositional traits but does support McAdams's (1999) contention that this middle level of personality should show some change. What is also clear, however, is that a tight connection between such change and specific ages is not supported by the bulk of the data. Rather, change appears to occur in wide windows of time depending on many factors, including one's sociocultural context. For example, parents report that their children helped them integrate previous stages of development, enhanced cognitive functioning, and afforded them a fresh perspective on life (Dillon, 2002). Thus interactions with one's children can also be considered an important sociocultural influence on adult development. Finally, more research is needed in this area, especially investigations that provide longitudinal evidence of change within individuals.

1. What do we mean by the term *personal concerns*?

2. What happens in midlife, according to Jung?

3. What are Erikson's eight stages?

4. What are the main points in Loevinger's theory?

5. What is the principal problem with theories based on life transitions?

6. Do personal concerns change across adulthood?

9.3 Life Narratives, Identity, and the Self

LEARNING OBJECTIVES
- What are the main aspects of McAdams's life-story model?
- What are the main points of Whitbourne's identity theory?
- How does self-concept come to take adult form? What is its development during adulthood?
- What are possible selves? Do they show differences during adulthood?
- What role does religion play in adult life?
- How does gender-role identity develop in adulthood?
- What conclusions can be drawn from research using life narratives?

*A*ntje is a 19-year-old sophomore at a community college. She expects her study of early childhood education to be difficult but rewarding. She figures that along the way she will meet a great guy, whom she will marry soon after graduation. They will have two children before she turns 30. Antje sees herself getting a good job teaching preschool children and someday owning her own day care center.

Who are you? What kind of person are you trying to become? These are the kinds of questions Antje is trying to answer. Answering these questions requires concepts of personality that go beyond dispositional traits and personal concerns. The aspects of personality we have discussed thus far are important, but they lack a sense of integration, unity, coherence, and overall purpose (McAdams, 1999, 2001). For example, understanding a person's goals (from the level of personal concerns) does not reveal who a person is trying to be, or what kind of person the person is trying to create. What is lacking in other levels of analysis is a sense of the person's identity or sense of self.

In contrast to Erikson's (1982) proposition that identity formation is the central task of adolescence, many researchers are now coming to understand the important ways in which identity and the creation of the self continue to develop throughout adulthood (e.g., Labouvie-Vief et al., 1995; Whitbourne & Connolly, 1999). This emerging field of how adults continue constructing identity and the self relies on life narratives, or the internalized and evolving story that integrates a person's reconstructed past, perceived present, and anticipated future into a coherent and vitalizing life myth (McAdams, 1994, 2001). Careful analysis of people's life narratives provides insight into their identity.

In this section, we will consider two evolving theories of identity. Dan McAdams is concerned with understanding how people see themselves and how they fit into the adult world. Susan Krauss Whitbourne investigated people's own conceptions of the life course and how they differ from age norms and the expectations for society as a whole. To round out our understanding of identity and the self, we will also examine related constructs. Before beginning, though, take time to complete the exercise in the Discovering Development feature. It will give you a sense of what a life narrative is and how it might be used to gain insight into identity and the sense of self.

McAdams's Life-Story Model

McAdams (1994, 1999, 2001) argues that a person's sense of identity cannot be understood using the language of dispositional traits or personal concerns. It is not just a collection of traits, nor is it a collection of plans, strategies, or goals. Instead, it is based on a story of how the person came into being, where the person has been, where he or she is going, and who he or she will become, much like Antje's story. McAdams argues that people create a life story that is an internalized narrative with a beginning, a middle, and an anticipated ending. The life story is created and revised throughout adulthood

From the time you were a child, people have posed this question to you. In childhood, you probably answered by indicating some specific career, such as firefighter or teacher. But now that you are an adult, the question takes on new meaning. Rather than simply a matter of picking a profession, the question goes much deeper to the kinds of values and the essence of the person you would like to become.

Take a few minutes and think about who you would like to be in another decade or two (or maybe even 50 years hence). What things will matter to you? What will you be doing? What experiences will you have had? What lies ahead?

This exercise can give you a sense of the way in which researchers try to understand people's sense of identity and self through the use of personal narrative. You could even keep what you have written, and check it when the appropriate number of years have elapsed.

---

as people change and the changing environment places different demands on them.

McAdams's (2001) research indicates that people in Western society begin forming their life story in late adolescence and early adulthood, but it has its roots in the development of one's earliest attachments in infancy. As in Erikson's theory, adolescence marks the full initiation into forming an identity, and thus, a coherent life story begins. In early adulthood it is continued and refined, and from midlife and beyond it is refashioned in the wake of major and minor life changes. Generativity marks the attempt to create an appealing story "ending" that will generate new beginnings for future generations.

Paramount in these life stories is the changing personal identity reflected in the emotions conveyed in the story (from tragedy to optimism or through comic and romantic descriptions). In addition, motivations change and are reflected in the person repeatedly trying to attain his or her goals over time. The two most common goal themes are agency (reflecting power, achievement, and autonomy) and communion (reflecting love, intimacy, and a sense of belonging). Finally, stories indicate one's beliefs and values, or the ideology, a person uses to set the context for his or her actions.

Every life story contains episodes that provide insight into perceived change and continuity in life. People prove to themselves and others that they have either changed or remained the same by pointing to specific events that support the appropriate claim. The main characters in people's lives represent idealizations of the self, such as "the dutiful mother" or "the reliable worker." Integrating these various aspects of the self is a major challenge of midlife and later adulthood. Finally, all life stories need an ending through which the self can leave a legacy that creates new beginnings. Life stories in middle-aged and older adults have a clear quality of "giving birth to" a new generation, a notion essentially identical to generativity.

One of the more popular methods for examining the development of life stories is through autobiographical memory (Bluck & Habermas, 2000; Thorne, 2000). When people tell their life stories to others, the stories are a joint product of the speaker and the audience (Pasupathi, 2001). Pasupathi finds that the responses of the audience affect how the teller remembers his or her experiences. This is a good example of conversational remembering, much like collaborative cognition discussed in Chapter 8.

Overall, McAdams (1994, 2001) believes that the model for change in identity over time is a process of fashioning and refashioning one's life story. This process appears to be strongly influenced by culture. At times, the reformulation may be at a conscious level, such as when people make explicit decisions about changing careers. At other times, the revision process is unconscious and implicit, growing out of everyday activities. The goal is to create a life story that is coherent, credible, open to new possibilities, richly differentiated, reconciling of opposite aspects of oneself, and integrated within one's sociocultural context (McAdams, 1994, 1999, 2001).

Whitbourne's Identity Theory

A second and related approach to understanding identity formation in adulthood is Whitbourne's (1987, 1996c) idea that people build their own conceptions of how their lives should proceed. *The result of this process is the* **life-span construct,** *the person's unified sense of the past, present, and future.*

There are many influences on the development of a life-span construct: identity, values, and social context are a few. Together, they shape the life-span construct and the ways in which it is manifested. The life-span construct has two structural components, which in turn are the ways in which it is manifested. The first of these components is the scenario, which consists of expectations about the future. The scenario translates aspects of our identity that are particularly important at a specific point into a plan for the future. The scenario is strongly influenced by age norms that define key transition points; for example, graduating from college is a transition that is normally associated with the early 20s. In short, a scenario is a game plan for how we want our lives to go.

Kim, a typical college sophomore, may have the following scenario: She expects that her course of study in nursing will be difficult but that she will finish on time. She hopes to meet a nice guy along the way whom she will marry shortly after graduation. She imagines she will get a good job at a major medical center that will offer her opportunities for advancement. She and her husband will probably have a child, but she expects to keep working. Because she feels she will want to advance, she assumes that at some point she will earn a master's degree. In the more distant future she hopes to be a department head and to be well respected for her administrative skills.

Tagging certain expected events with a particular age or time by which we expect to complete them creates a social clock (see Chapter 1). Kim will use her scenario to evaluate her progress toward her goals. With each major transition she will check how she is doing against where her scenario says she should be. If she has achieved her goals earlier than she expected, she will be proud of being ahead of the game. If things work out more slowly than she planned, she may chastise herself for being slow. If she begins to criticize herself a great deal, she may end up changing her scenario altogether; for example, if she does not get a good job and makes no progress, she may change her scenario to one that says she should stay home with her child.

As Kim starts moving into the positions laid out in her scenario, she begins to create the second component of her life-span construct, her life story. The life story is a personal narrative history that organizes past events into a coherent sequence. The life story gives events personal meaning and a sense of continuity; it becomes our autobiography. Because the life story is what we tell others when they ask about our past, it eventually becomes somewhat over-rehearsed and stylized. An interesting aspect of the life story, and autobiographical memory in general, is that distortions will occur with time and retelling (Fitzgerald, 1999; Pasupathi, 2001). In life stories, distortions allow the person to feel that he or she was on time, rather than off time, in terms of past events in the scenario. In this way, people feel better about their plans and goals and are less likely to feel a sense of failure.

Whitbourne (1986) conducted a fascinating cross-sectional study of 94 adults ranging in age from 24 to 61. They came from all walks of life and represented a wide range of occupations and life situations. Using data from very detailed interviews, Whitbourne was able to identify what she believes is the process of adult identity development based on equilibrium between identity and experience.

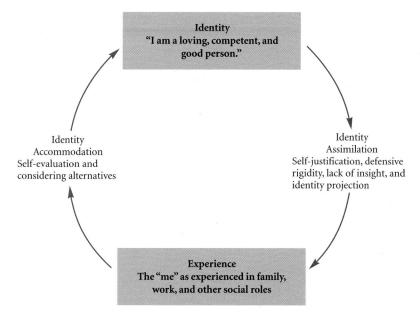

Figure 9.2 Whitbourne's model of adult identity processes.

Source: Whitbourne, S. K. (1986). The psychological construction of the life span. In J. E. Birren & K. W. Schaie (Eds.), *Handbook of the Psychology of Aging* (pp. 594–619). New York: Van Nostrand Reinhold. All rights reserved. Reproduced by permission of the author.

Her model is presented in Figure 9.2. As the figure shows, there is continuous feedback between identity and experience; this explains why we may evaluate ourselves positively at one point in time, yet appear defensive and self-protective at another.

As you can see, the processes of equilibrium are based on Piaget's concepts of assimilation and accommodation (see Chapter 7). Whitbourne has explicitly attempted to integrate concepts from cognitive development with identity development to understand how identity is formed and revised across adulthood. The assimilation process involves using already existing aspects of identity to handle present situations. Over-reliance on assimilation makes the person resistant to change. Accommodation, in contrast, reflects the willingness of the individual to let the situation determine what he or she will do. This often occurs when the person does not have a well-developed identity around a certain issue.

Not surprisingly, Whitbourne (1986) found that the vast majority of adults listed family as the most important aspect of their lives. Clearly, adults'

identity as loving constitutes the major part of the answer to the question "Who am I?" Consequently, a major theme in adults' identity development is trying to refine their belief that "I am a loving person." Much of this development is in acquiring and refining deep, emotional relationships.

A second major source of identity for Whitbourne's participants was work. In this case, the key seemed to be keeping work interesting. As long as individuals had an interesting occupation that enabled them to become personally invested, their work identity was more central to their overall personal identity. This is a topic we will pursue in Chapter 12.

Although Whitbourne found evidence of life transitions, overall she found scant evidence that these transitions occurred in a stagelike fashion or were tied to specific ages. Rather, she found that people tended to go through transitions when they felt they needed to and to do so on their own time line. More recently, Whitbourne (1996a) has developed the Identity and Experiences Scale–General to measure identity processes in adults. Her model has been expanded to incorporate how people adapt more generally to middle age and the aging process (Whitbourne, 1996b; Whitbourne & Connolly, 1999). This scale assesses an individual's use of assimilation and accommodation in forming identity in a general sense, and is based on her earlier work (Whitbourne, 1986).

In a recent study, Sneed and Whitbourne (2003) did find that identity assimilation and identity accommodation change with age. Whereas identity assimilation was higher in older adulthood, identity accommodation was higher in younger adulthood. Furthermore, identity assimilation in older adulthood was associated with maintaining and enhancing positive self-regard through the minimization of negativity. In contrast, a changing identity (e.g., through accommodation) in older adulthood was associated more with poor psychological health. The ability to integrate age-related changes into one's identity and maintain a positive view of oneself is crucial to aging successfully (Holahan, 2003; Sneed & Whitbourne, 2003). This suggests that people may make behavioral adjustments to promote healthy adaptation to the aging process (see Chapter 3).

Self-Concept

As we have seen, an important aspect of identity in adulthood is how one integrates various aspects of the self. Self-perceptions and how they differ with age have been examined in a wide variety of studies and are related to many behaviors. Changes in self-perceptions are often manifested in changed beliefs, concerns, and expectations. **Self-concept** *is the organized, coherent, integrated pattern of self-perceptions.* It includes the notions of self-esteem and self-image.

Kegan (1982) attempted to integrate the development of self-concept and cognitive development. He postulated six stages of the development of self, corresponding to stages of cognitive development described in Chapter 7. Kegan's first three stages—which he calls incorporative, impulsive, and imperial—correspond to Piaget's sensorimotor, preoperational, and concrete operational stages (see Chapter 7). During this time, he believes children

move from knowing themselves on the basis of reflexes to knowing themselves through needs and interests. At the beginning of formal operational thought during early adolescence (see Chapter 7), he argues, a sense of interpersonal mutuality begins to develop; he terms this period the interpersonal stage. By late adolescence or young adulthood, people move to a mature sense of identity based on taking control of their own life and developing an ideology; Kegan calls this period the institutional stage. Finally, with the acquisition of post-formal thought (see Chapter 7) comes an understanding that the self is a very complex system that takes into account other people; Kegan terms this period the interindividual stage. Kegan's (1982) work emphasizes the fact that personality development does not occur in a vacuum. Rather, we must not forget that the person is a complex integrated whole. Consequently, an understanding of the development of self-concept or any other aspect of personality is enhanced by an understanding of how it relates to other dimensions of development.

This point was clearly demonstrated by Labouvie-Vief and colleagues (1995). Working within a cognitive-developmental framework, they documented age differences in self-representation in people ranging in age from 11 to 85 years. Specifically, they found that mature adults move from representations of the self in young adulthood that are relatively poorly differentiated from others or from social conventions and expectations, to representations in middle age that are highly differentiated, to representations in old age that are less differentiated. An important finding was that the degree of differentiation in self-representation was related to the level of cognitive development, providing support for Kegan's position. Along similar lines, lacking a coherent sense of self has been shown to have cumulative negative effects across the adult life span, with its most pronounced effect in older age (Diehl et al., 2001).

In one of the few longitudinal studies of self-concept, Mortimer, Finch, and Kumka (1982) followed a group of men for 14 years, beginning when the participants were college freshmen. They found that self-image consisted of four dimensions: well-being, interpersonal qualities, activity,

Employees who remain above average in their competency report fewer job problems and higher marital and life satisfaction.

and unconventionality. Well-being included self-perceptions concerning happiness, lack of tension, and confidence. Interpersonal qualities referred to self-perceptions concerning sociability, interest in others, openness, and warmth. The activity component consisted of self-perceptions of strength, competence, success, and activity. The unconventionality dimension indicated that men saw themselves as impulsive, unconventional, and dreamy. Clearly, what Mortimer and colleagues found concerning self-image is very closely related to Costa and McCrae's model of personality, described earlier in this chapter.

Over the 14-year period the men in the Mortimer study showed little change as a group. The structure of self-concept remained stable. Some fluctuation at the level of self-image was noted, though. Both well-being and competence declined during college but rebounded after graduation. Self-perceptions of unconventionality declined after college. Sociability showed a steady decline across the entire study.

At the intraindividual level, the data indicated that self-perceptions of confidence were related to life events. The course of a man's career, his satisfaction with career and marriage, his relationship with

his parents, and his overall life satisfaction followed patterns that could be predicted by competence. For example, employees like the man in the photo—whose competence scores remained above the group average—reported fewer job problems and higher marital and life satisfaction than men whose competence scores were below the group average.

Interestingly, a man's degree of confidence as a college senior influenced his later evaluation of life events, and it may have even set the stage for a self-fulfilling prophecy. Mortimer and colleagues suggest that these men may actively seek and create experiences that fit their personality structure. Similarly, this hypothesis is supported by longitudinal research on gifted women, whose high self-confidence in early adulthood becomes manifested as a high life satisfaction during their 60s (Sears & Barbee, 1978).

The results from the Mortimer, Finch, and Kumka (1982) study are strikingly similar to the data from the Berkeley studies described earlier in this chapter. Recall that data from these studies also support the idea that life events are important influences on personality development. In the present case, life events clearly influence one's self-concept. We will consider in the next section how adults explain why certain things or certain events happen to them.

Possible Selves

Another important aspect of self-concept and creating a scenario about ourselves is the ability to project ourselves into the future and to speculate about what we might be like (Markus & Nurius, 1986). How do we do this? *Projecting ourselves into the future involves creating* **possible selves** *that represent what we could become, what we would like to become, and what we are afraid of becoming.* What we could or would like to become often reflects personal goals; we may see ourselves as leaders, as rich and famous, or as in shape. What we are afraid of becoming may show up in our fear of being undervalued, overweight, or lonely. Our possible selves are very powerful motivators; indeed, much of our behavior can be viewed as efforts to approach or avoid these various possible selves and to protect the current view of self (Markus & Nurius, 1986).

The topic of possible selves offers a way to understand how both stability and change operate in adults' personality. On the one hand, possible selves tend to remain stable for at least some period of time and are measurable with psychometrically sound scales (Hooker, 1999; Ryff, 1991). On the other hand, possible selves may change in response to efforts at personal growth (Cross & Markus, 1991; Frazier et al., 2000; Hooker, 1991), which would be expected from ego development theory. In particular, possible selves facilitate adaptation to new roles across the life span. For example, a full-time mother who pictures herself as an executive once her child goes to school may begin to take evening courses to acquire new skills. Possible selves thus offer a way to bridge the experience of the current self and our imagined future self.

Researchers have begun studying age differences in the construction of possible selves (Cross & Markus, 1991; Frazier et al., 2000; Frazier et al., 2002; Hooker, 1999; Morfei et al., 2001). In a set of similar studies conducted by Cross and Markus (1991) and Hooker and colleagues (Frazier et al., 2000; Hooker, 1999; Hooker et al., 1996; Morfei et al., 2001), people across the adult life span were asked to describe their hoped-for and feared possible selves. Responses are grouped into categories (such as family, personal, material, relationships, occupation). Several interesting age differences emerged. In terms of hoped-for selves, young adults listed as most important family concerns (Cross & Markus, 1991) (for instance, marrying the right person), whereas Hooker et al. (1996) also found getting started in an occupation was important in this age group. In contrast, middle adults listed family concerns last; their main issues were personal concerns (such as being a more loving and caring person) (Cross & Markus, 1991). By ages 40 to 59, Cross and Markus found that family issues again became most common (such as being a parent who can "let go" of his or her children). Hooker and Kaus (1994) also found that reaching and maintaining satisfactory performance in one's occupational career and accepting and adjusting to the physiological changes of middle age were also important to this age group. Both sets of studies found that for the two younger groups, being overweight and, for women, becoming wrinkled and unattractive when old were commonly mentioned as feared possible selves. For the middle-aged and older adult groups, fear of having Alzheimer's disease or being unable to care for oneself was a frequent response.

For adults over 60, researchers found that personal issues were most prominent (e.g., being able to be active and healthy for another decade at least) (Cross & Markus, 1991; Smith & Freund, 2002). Similarly Hooker and colleagues (Frazier et al., 2000; Frazier et al., 2002; Morfei et al., 2001) found that continuity in possible selves was much more prevalent than change in later life especially in independence, physical, and lifestyle areas. However, they also found that change did occur in older age. The greatest amount of change occurred in the health domain; it became the most important domain for hoped-for and feared possible selves. The health domain is the most sensitive and central to the self in the context of aging (Frazier et al., 2000).

Overall, adolescents and young adults are far more likely to have multiple possible selves and to believe more strongly that they can actually become the hoped-for self and successfully avoid the feared possible self. By old age, though, both the number of possible selves and strength of belief have

Like Linus in the Peanuts cartoon, young and middle-aged adults see themselves as improving with age.

PEANUTS reprinted by permission of United Feature Syndicate, Inc.

decreased. Older adults are more likely to believe that neither the hoped-for nor the feared possible self is under their personal control. These findings may reflect differences with age in personal motivation, beliefs in personal control, and the need to explore new options.

Other researchers have examined possible selves in a different way by asking adults to describe their present, past, future, and ideal self (Keyes & Ryff, 1999; Ryff, 1991). Instead of examining categories of possible selves, this approach focuses on people's perceptions of change over time. The data indicate that young and middle-aged adults see themselves as improving with age (like Linus in the cartoon) and expecting to continue getting better in the future. In contrast, older adults see themselves as having remained stable over time, but they foresee decline in their future. These findings may indicate that the older adults have internalized negative stereotypes about aging, especially because they are well educated and currently healthy (see Chapter 8).

This general look at the issues that most influence possible selves indicates that the most important ones differ with age. But how are these issues reflected in aspects of personal well-being? Do the age differences in possible selves depend on whether one is projecting into the future or into the past? Such questions require a more complex approach.

This is exactly the approach taken by Ryff (1991). In a fascinating series of studies, she adopted the notion of possible selves as a way to redefine the meaning of well-being in adulthood and showed how adults' views of themselves are different at various points in adulthood. Examining the responses of hundreds of adults, Ryff (1989, 1991) identified six dimensions of psychological well-being for adults and discovered many important age and gender differences in well-being based on these components:

Self-acceptance: having a positive view of oneself; acknowledging and accepting the multiple parts of oneself; and feeling positive about one's past

Positive relation with others: having warm, satisfying relationships with people; being concerned with their welfare; being empathic, affectionate, and intimate with them; and understanding the reciprocity of relationships

Autonomy: being independent and determining one's own life; being able to resist social pressures to think or behave in a particular way; evaluating one's life by internal standards

Environmental mastery: being able to manipulate, control, and effectively use resources and opportunities

Purpose in life: having goals in life and a sense of direction in one's life; feeling that one's present and past life has meaning; having a reason for living

Personal growth: feeling a need for continued personal improvement; seeing oneself as getting better and being open to new experiences; growing in self-knowledge and personal effectiveness

Religious practice in all forms is evident throughout the latter half of the life span.

How do these aspects of well-being change in adulthood? The How Do We Know? feature has one answer.

Taken together, the research on possible selves opens up new and exciting avenues for personality research. Possible selves research offers a way to examine the importance of personal perception in determining motivation to achieve and change, as well as a way to study personality systematically with sound research methods. For example, it enables us to examine the creation of scenarios and life stories systematically. Because it provides an interesting bridge between different approaches to personality theory, it will likely be the focus of much research in the future.

Religiosity and Spiritual Support

For many adults, the relationship they have with a god or divine being is a key aspect of their identity. In addition, when faced with the daily problems of living, older adults use their religious faith more than anything else, including family or friends, as a coping mechanism (Krause, 2003; McFadden, 1996). When asked to describe their most frequent ways of dealing with problems in life, nearly half of the people surveyed in one study listed coping

strategies associated with religion (Koenig et al., 1988). Of these, the most frequently used were placing trust in God, praying, and getting strength and help from God. These strategies can also be used to augment other ways of coping. Spouses caring for partners with Alzheimer's disease also report using religion as a primary coping mechanism (Ishler et al., 1998).

As a key factor in understanding how older adults cope, researchers are increasingly focusing on **spiritual support,** *which includes seeking pastoral care, participating in organized and nonorganized religious activities, and expressing faith in a God who cares for people.* McFadden (1996) points out that even when under high levels of stress, people such as the Buddhist monks in the photograph who rely on spiritual support report better personal well-being. Krause (1995, 2003) reports that feelings of self-worth are lowest for those older adults with very little religious commitment, a finding supported by cross-cultural research with Muslims, Hindus, and Sikhs (Mehta, 1997). Van Ness and Stanislav (2003) find that high religious attendance was associated with lower cognitive dysfunction in older adults. However, Pargament and colleagues (1995) also note the importance of individual differences in the effectiveness of spiritual support,

Views of Life: Well-Being and Aging

Who was the investigator, and what was the aim of the study? How people see themselves is an important part of their sense of well-being. However, previous research on well-being in late life has been conducted without theoretical guidance (Ryff, 1989). Consequently, many researchers approached well-being from the perspective of loss; that is, researchers assumed that well-being, like physical prowess, was something that declined as people age. Carol Ryff (1989; Keyes & Ryff, 1998) disagreed with this loss perspective and set out to demonstrate her point. She thought that well-being is a more complex issue and that it can improve in late life.

How did the investigator measure the topic of interest? In preliminary studies, Ryff administered numerous self-report scales that measured many aspects of personality and well-being. Her method in this investigation represented a new approach, one aimed at describing the complex developmental patterns she wanted to uncover. This new approach drew from life-span developmental theories (such as those presented in this text), clinical theories of personal growth adapted from successful techniques in psychotherapy, and various definitions of mental health, yielding the most complete description yet

of well-being in adulthood. On the basis of her research and thinking, Ryff (1989, 1991) developed a new measure of well-being that reflects the six-dimension model discussed earlier. This new measure allowed her to obtain people's ratings of how they view themselves right now, what they were like in the past, what they think they might be like in the future, and what they would most like to be like.

Who were the participants in this study? A total of 308 young, middle-aged, and older men and women participated. The middle-aged and older adults were contacted through community and civic organizations. All participants were relatively well educated.

What was the design of the study? Ryff used a cross-sectional design that compared young adult, middle-aged, and older adult groups.

Were there ethical concerns with this study? There were no serious concerns; each participant was informed about the purpose of the study, and participation was voluntary.

What were the results? The most important discovery from Ryff's research is that young, middle-aged, and older adults have very different views of themselves, depending on whether they are describing their present, past, future, or ideal self-perceptions. The left graph

in Figure 9.3 shows that young and middle-aged adults are much more accepting of their ideal and future selves than they are of their present and past selves. For older adults, differences are much smaller. The right graph shows a similar pattern for autonomy, the feelings of being independent and determining one's own life.

Perhaps the most interesting findings of Ryff's research concern the difference between people's ideal vision of themselves and what they thought they were really like. If you carefully look at the graphs, you will notice that the differences between the "ideal self" ratings and the "present self" ratings diminish with age. When combined with similar findings in other aspects of well-being, this implies that older adults see themselves as closer to really being the person they wanted to become than does any other age. Ryff's data fit well with Erikson's (1982) idea of integrity. As people achieve integrity, they view their past less critically and become content with how they have lived their lives.

What did the investigator conclude? As Ryff (1991; Keyes & Ryff, 1999) notes, only by including all of these self-ratings will we understand people's sense of personal progress or decline over time from their goal of ideal functioning. Clearly, people judge themselves by many standards, and these differ with age.

(Continued)

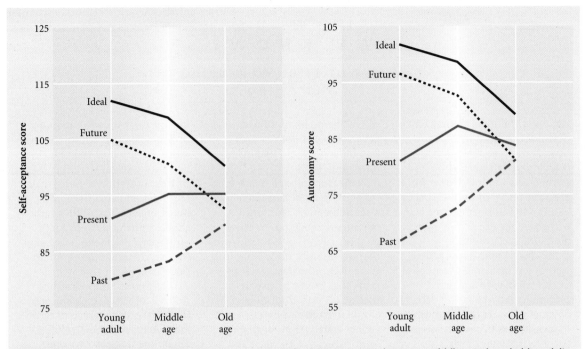

Figure 9.3 Age differences in self-acceptance scores and autonomy scores in young, middle-aged, and older adults.

Source: Ryff, C. D. (1991). Possible selves in adulthood and old age: A tale of shifting horizons. *Psychology and Aging* 6, 286–295. Copyright © 1991 Adapted with permission from the American Psychological Association.

because some people are helped more than others, some problems are more amenable to religious coping, and certain types of religious coping may be more effective than others. Importantly, however, religious involvement seems to continue throughout the very last months of life in older adulthood (Idler et al., 2001).

Reliance on religion in times of stress appears especially important for many African Americans, who as a group are intensely involved in religious activities (Krause, 2002, 2003; Levin et al., 1994). Churches offer considerable social support for the African American community as well as serving an important function for the advocacy of social justice (Roberts, 1980). For example, Dr. Martin Luther King, Jr., a Baptist minister, led the civil rights movement in the 1950s and 1960s, and contemporary congregations champion equal rights. The role of the church in African Americans' lives

is central; indeed, one of the key predictors of life satisfaction among African Americans is regular church attendance (Coke, 1992; Krause, 2002).

Within the African American community, religion is especially important to many women. The greater importance of the church in the lives of older African American women is supported by results from four national surveys of African American adults (Levin et al., 1994). The women participants reported that they are more active in church groups and attend services more frequently than do African American men or either European American men or women. However, the gender differences diminish in people over age 70; among the participants, religion became equally important for older African American men. Religion and spiritual support also serve as more important resources for many African American caregivers than for European American caregivers (Picot et al., 1997).

Many older persons of Mexican heritage adopt a different approach. Research indicates that they use *la fé de la gente* ("the faith of the people") as a coping strategy (Villa & Jaime, 1993). The notion of *fé* incorporates varying degrees of faith, spirituality, hope, cultural values, and beliefs. *Fé* does not necessarily imply that people identify with a specific religious community. Rather, they identify with a cultural value or ideology.

Among many Native Americans, the spiritual elders are the wisdom-keepers, the repositories of the sacred ways and natural world philosophies that extend indefinitely back in time (Wall & Arden, 1990). The wisdom-keepers also share dreams and visions, perform healing ceremonies, and may make apocalyptic prophecies. The place of the wisdom-keepers in the tribe is much more central than that of religious leaders in Western society.

Service providers would be well advised to keep in mind the self-reported importance of religion in the lives of many older adults when designing interventions to help them adapt to life stressors. For example, older adults may be more willing to talk with their minister about a personal problem than they would be to talk with a psychotherapist. When they seek help from a professional, that person is more often their family physician. When working with people of Mexican heritage, providers need to realize that a major source of distress for this group is lack of familial interaction and support. Overall, many churches offer a wide range of programs to assist poor or homebound older adults in the community. Such programs may be more palatable to recipients than programs based in social service agencies. To be successful, service providers should try to understand life as their clients see it.

Gender-Role Identity

People's beliefs about the appropriate characteristics for men and women reflect shared cultural beliefs and stereotypes of "masculinity" and "femininity" (Best & Williams, 1993; Huyck, 1999; Sinnott & Shifren, 2001). Across a wide age range in U.S. society, women are traditionally described as weaker, with lower self-esteem, less active, more concerned with affiliation, and more nurturing and deferential. Men are regarded as stronger, more active, and higher in autonomy, risk taking, achievement, and aggression (Huyck, 1999; Robinson et al., 2002). Collectively, such descriptions help form one's gender-role identity.

In addition, some gender stereotypes are also sensitive to age (Gutmann, 1994). Old men are seen as less stereotypically masculine or warrior-like than are younger men and more as powerful elderly men striving for peace. Old women are noted for their greater assertiveness and control than are younger women; stereotypes include matriarchs overseeing extended families and dangerous witches who use power malevolently. Some cultures view older adults as genderless, having lost the need for differentiated gender-role identity after they concluded their child-rearing duties (Gailey, 1987).

As we know, the five-factor model makes a strong case for the stability of personality traits through adulthood. In contrast, we have seen that people's priorities and personal concerns change during adulthood. Does stability or change describe what happens to the gender-role identity of the man and woman in the photograph?

Beginning with Jung (1933), several researchers and theorists argue for a "crossover effect" of

What happens to the gender identity of the man and the woman in the photograph as they age?

gender identity during middle age. As we noted earlier, Jung (1933) proposed that in adolescence women initially suppress their masculine aspects and men initially suppress their feminine aspects. Each discovers these suppressed aspects and develops them in midlife, with the goal of achieving a balance between one's masculine and feminine characteristics. For example, during midlife women may place increased emphasis on achievement and accomplishment, and men may place more emphasis on familial and nurturant concerns (Parker & Aldwin, 1997).

Overall, the data on actual changes in people's gender-role identity are mixed. Some studies find a tendency for middle-aged and older adults to endorse similar self-descriptions concerning gender-role identity. For example, data from the Berkeley studies document a move toward greater similarity between older men and older women. Haan (1985; Haan et al., 1986) and Livson (1981) found that both men and women described themselves as more nurturant, intimate, and tender with increasing age, trends that are related to generativity. Gutmann (1987), Sinnott (1986), and Turner (1982) reported similar findings. Huyck (1996) finds evidence of **androgyny,** *or acceptance of the most adaptive aspects of both the traditional masculine and feminine roles,* in midlife. Other studies show decreasing endorsement of traditional feminine traits in both men and women, but stable endorsements of masculine traits (Parker & Aldwin, 1997). Collectively, the data indicate that men and women are most different in their gender-role identities in late adolescence and young adulthood but become increasingly similar in midlife and old age (Huyck, 1999).

Longitudinal data on individual gender-role development are largely lacking. What evidence is available suggests that a majority (54%) of people remain in the same gender-role category over a 10-year period (Hyde et al., 1991). However, this still means that a substantial number of people change. As Hyde and coworkers (1991) note, however, we currently have no way of predicting who will change and who will not.

Increasing similarity in self-descriptions does not guarantee increased similarity in the way men and women behave. For example, older men often indicate a greater willingness to develop close relationships, but few actually have the skills to do so (Turner, 1982). Thus the change may be more internal than behavioral (Parker & Aldwin, 1997; Troll & Bengtson, 1982). Moreover, much of the change may be due to the failing health of elderly men. Because older wives tend to be healthier than their husbands, the balance of power may of necessity shift to wives, and men may be forced to accept a more dependent role.

Does gender-role identity converge with increasing age? It is still debatable. The lack of consistent behavioral evidence and the statistically small differences in some of the self-assessment data lead some authors to argue that no changes in personality occur (e.g., McCrae & Costa, 1994). In contrast, others see the convergence in self-assessments as evidence that older men and women transcend stereotypes to become essentially gender free (Sinnott, 1986; Sinnott & Shifren, 2001). Still others view any change in self-assessment, no matter how small, as at least personally relevant (Gutmann, 1987).

It will be interesting to see whether the trend toward similarity continues over the next few generations. Changes in how younger men and women view themselves as a result of women's new roles in society may shift the trend downward in age or may make it disappear altogether. As noted in Chapter 1, gender is one way that societies stratify themselves. Whether changes in self-report have any bearing on true behavioral change is something that only time will tell.

Conclusions about Narratives, Identity, and the Self

We have seen that to fully understand a person, we must consider how the individual integrates his or her life into a coherent structure. The life-narrative approach provides a way to learn how people accomplish this integration. The theoretical frameworks developed by McAdams and by Whitbourne offer excellent avenues for research.

One of the most promising new areas of inquiry, possible selves, is already providing major insights into how people construct future elements of their life stories.

When combined with the data from the dispositional trait and personal concerns literatures, research findings on identity and the self provide the capstone knowledge needed to understand what people are like. The complexity of personality is clear from this discussion; perhaps that is why it takes a lifetime to complete.

Concept Checks

1. What is a life story as defined in McAdams's theory?
2. What connection is there between Whitbourne's theory of identity and Piaget's theory of cognitive development?
3. What are possible selves?
4. How does religiosity factor into identity?
5. How does gender-role identity develop in adulthood?
6. Does the sense of identity and self change in adulthood?

SOCIAL POLICY IMPLICATIONS

As we have seen, personality change has important implications for promoting emotional well-being in older adulthood. In fact, some studies suggest that health and an emotionally stable personality are extremely important factors for life satisfaction among the very old (e.g., Hilleras et al., 2001). Thus, it is not simply health and financial security that contribute to the quality of life in older age, but a compilation of factors including a healthy personality and outlook on life.

The fact is life events (such as widowhood, retirement, relocation into a nursing home) influence our personality, both positively and negatively, thus accounting for malleability in personality functioning in older adulthood. Research on personality and aging helps debunk popular beliefs suggesting that with increasing age we become more hypochondriac or rigid in our attitudes and opinions. In contrast, psychological maturation appears to be a lifelong process.

Summary

9.1 Dispositional Traits across Adulthood

What is the five-factor model of dispositional traits?

- The five-factor model posits five dimensions of personality: neuroticism, extraversion, openness to experience, agreeableness, and conscientiousness. Each of these dimensions has several descriptors.
- Several longitudinal studies indicate that personality traits show long-term stability.

What evidence is there for long-term stability in dispositional traits?

- Studies find evidence for change in Big Five factors such as neuroticism, agreeableness, conscientiousness, and extraversion. These are related to two dimensions of personality: adjustment and growth.
- Evidence from the Berkeley studies shows that lifestyle is a better predictor of life satisfaction for women, but personality is a better predictor for men.
- Both stability and change characterize personality development in advanced old age.

- Women's personality change is systematic in early and middle adulthood and is a function of changes in social roles and social contexts.

What criticisms have been leveled at the five-factor model?

- Several criticisms of the five-factor model have been made: The research may have methodological problems; dispositional traits do not describe the core aspects of human nature and do not provide good predictors of behavior; and dispositional traits do not consider the contextual aspects of development.
- An intraindividual perspective challenges stability by examining personality at the level of the individual.

What conclusions can we draw about dispositional traits?

- The bulk of the evidence suggests that dispositional traits are relatively stable across adulthood, but there may be a few exceptions. Criticisms of the research point to the need for better statistical analyses and a determination of the role of life experiences.
- Stability in personality traits may be more evident later in the life span.

9.2 Personal Concerns and Qualitative Stages in Adulthood

What's different about personal concerns?

- Personal concerns take into account a person's developmental context and distinguish between "having" traits and "doing" everyday behaviors. Personal concerns entail descriptions of what people are trying to accomplish and the goals they create.

What are the main elements of Jung's theory?

- Jung emphasized various dimensions of personality (masculinity–femininity; extraversion–introversion). Jung argues that people move toward integrating these dimensions as they age, with midlife being an especially important period.

What are the stages in Erikson's theory?

- The sequence of Erikson's stages is trust versus mistrust, autonomy versus shame and doubt, initiative versus guilt, industry versus inferiority, identity versus identity confusion, intimacy versus isolation, generativity versus stagnation, and ego integrity versus despair. Erikson's theory can be seen as a trust-achievement-wholeness cycle repeating twice, although the exact transition mechanisms have not been clearly defined.
- Generativity has received more attention than other adult stages. Research indicates that generative concern and generative action can be found in all age groups of adults, but they are particularly apparent among middle-aged adults.

What are the stages in Loevinger's theory?

- Loevinger proposed eight stages of ego development, six of which can occur in adulthood: conformist, conscientious-conformist, conscientious, individualistic, autonomous, and integrated. Most adults are at the conscientious-conformist level. Linkages to cognitive development are apparent.

What are the main points and problems with theories based on life transitions?

- In general, life transition theories postulate periods of transition that alternate with periods of stability. These theories tend to overestimate the commonality of age-linked transitions.

- Research evidence suggests that crises tied to age 30 or the midlife crisis do not occur for most people. However, most middle-aged people do point to both gains and losses, which could be viewed as change.
- A midlife correction may better characterize this transition for women.

What can we conclude about personal concerns?

- Theory and research both provide support for change in the personal concerns people report at various times in adulthood.

9.3 Life Narratives, Identity, and the Self

What are the main aspects of McAdams's life-story model?

- McAdams argues that people create a life story that is an internalized narrative with a beginning, middle, and anticipated ending. An adult reformulates that life story throughout adulthood. The life story reflects emotions, motivations, beliefs, values, and goals to set the context for his or her behavior.

What are the main points of Whitbourne's identity theory?

- Whitbourne believes that people have a life-span construct: a unified sense of their past, present, and future. The components of the life-span construct are the scenario (expectations of the future) and the life story (a personal narrative history). She integrates the concepts of assimilation and accommodation from Piaget's theory to explain how people's identity changes over time. Family and work are two major sources of identity.

What is self-concept and how does it develop in adulthood?

- Self-concept is the organized, coherent, integrated pattern of self-perception. The events people experience help shape their self-concept. Self-presentation across adulthood is related to cognitive-developmental level. Self-concept tends to stay stable at the group mean level.

What are possible selves and how do they show differences during adulthood?

- People create possible selves by projecting themselves into the future and thinking about what they would like to become, what they could become, and what they are afraid of becoming.

- Age differences in these projections depend on the dimension examined. In hoped-for selves, young adults and middle-aged adults report family issues as most important, whereas 25- to 39-year-olds and older adults consider personal issues to be most important. However, all groups include physical aspects as part of their most feared possible selves.

- Although younger and middle-aged adults view themselves as improving, older adults view themselves as declining. The standards by which people judge themselves change over time.

- Ryff has identified six aspects to well-being; self acceptance, positive relations with others, autonomy, environmental mastery, purpose in life, and personal growth. Older adults view their past more positively than younger or middle-aged adults, and they see themselves as closer to their ideal selves.

What role does religiosity and spiritual support play in adult life?

- Older adults use religion and spiritual support more often than any other strategy to help them cope with problems in life. This provides a strong influence on identity. This is especially true for African American women, who are more active in their church groups and attend services more frequently. Other ethnic groups also gain important aspects of identity from religion.

How does gender-role identity develop in adulthood?

- There is some evidence that gender-role identity converges in middle age, to the extent that men and women are more likely to endorse similar self-descriptions. However, these similar descriptions do not necessarily translate into similar behavior.

What conclusions can we draw about narratives, identity, and the self?

- The life-narrative approach provides a way to learn how people integrate the various aspects of their personality. Possible selves, religiosity, and gender-role identity are important areas in need of additional research.

Review Questions

9.1 Dispositional Traits across Adulthood

- What is a dispositional trait?

- Describe Costa and McCrae's five-factor model of personality. What are the descriptors in each dimension? How do these dimensions change across adulthood?

- What evidence is there in other longitudinal research for change in personality traits in adulthood? Under what conditions is there stability or change?

- What are the specific criticisms that have been raised concerning the five-factor model?

- What does most of the evidence say about the stability of dispositional traits across adulthood?

9.2 Personal Concerns and Qualitative Stages in Adulthood

- What is meant by a personal concern? How does it differ from a dispositional trait?

- Describe Jung's theory. What important developmental changes did he describe?

- Describe Erikson's eight stages of psychosocial development. What cycles have been identified? How has his theory been clarified and expanded? What types of generativity have been proposed? What evidence is there for generativity? What modifications to Erikson's theory has this research suggested?

- Describe Loevinger's theory of ego development, with particular emphasis on the stages seen in adults.

- What are the major assumptions of theories based on life transitions? What evidence is there that a midlife crisis really exists? How can midlife be viewed from a gain–loss perspective?

- Overall, what evidence is there for change in personal concerns across adulthood?

9.3 Life Narratives, Identity, and the Self

- What are the basic tenets of McAdams's life-story theory? What are the seven elements of a life story?
- What is Whitbourne's life-span construct? How does it relate to a scenario and a life story? How did Whitbourne incorporate Piagetian concepts into her theory of identity?
- What is self-concept? What shapes it?
- What are possible selves? What developmental trends have been found in possible selves?
- How are religiosity and spiritual support important aspects of identity in older adults?
- How does gender-role identity develop across adulthood?

Integrating Concepts in Development

- What relations can be found among dispositional traits, personal concerns, and life narratives?
- How does personality development reflect the four basic forces of development discussed in Chapter 1?
- How does cognitive development relate to personality change?
- How does personality change relate to stages in occupational transition?

Key Terms

androgyny Gender role reflecting the acceptance of the most adaptive aspects of both the traditional masculine and feminine roles.

conscientious stage According to Loevinger's theory, a point at which one focuses on understanding the role that the self plays. Character development involves self-evaluated standards, self-critical thinking, self-determined ideals, and self-set goals.

dispositional trait A relatively stable, enduring aspect of personality.

ego development The fundamental changes in the ways in which our thoughts, values, morals, and goals are organized. Transitions from one stage to another depend on both internal biological changes and external social changes to which the person must adapt.

epigenetic principle In Erikson's theory, the notion that development is guided by an underlying plan in which certain issues have their own particular times of importance.

five-factor model A model of dispositional traits with the dimensions of neuroticism, extraversion, openness to experience, agreeableness–antagonism, and conscientiousness–undirectedness.

life narrative The aspects of personality that pull everything together, those integrative aspects that give a person an identity or sense of self.

life-span construct In Whitbourne's theory of identity, the way in which people build a view of who they are.

midlife correction Reevaluating one's roles and dreams and making the necessary corrections.

personal concerns Things that are important to people, their goals, and their major concerns in life.

possible selves Aspects of the self-concept involving oneself in the future in both positive and negative ways.

self-concept The organized, coherent, integrated pattern of self-perceptions.

spiritual support Includes seeking pastoral care, participating in organized and nonorganized religious activities, and expressing faith in a God who cares for people as a key factor in understanding how older adults cope.

Resources

www.cengage.com/psychology/cavanaugh

Visit the Book Companion Website where you will find tutorial quizzes, flashcards, and web links for every chapter, a final exam, and more!

Readings

Erikson, E. H. (1982). *The life cycle completed: Review.* New York: Norton. Erikson's own summary of his theory that highlights adulthood. Moderately difficult reading.

Funder, D. C., Parke, R. D., Tomlinson-Keasey, C., & Widaman, K. (Eds.). (1993). *Studying lives through time: Personality and development.* Washington, DC: American Psychological Association. Moderate reading.

Labouvie-Vief, G. (1994). *Psyche and Eros: Mind and gender in the life course.* New York: Cambridge University Press. An interesting perspective on changes in gender identity in later adulthood. Moderately difficult reading.

Lachman, M. (Ed.). (2001). *Handbook of midlife development.* New York: Wiley. An excellent compilation of psychological issues in midlife. Moderately difficult reading.

McAdams, D. P. (1993). *The stories we live by: Personal myths and the making of the self.* New York: Morrow. Fascinating reading that lays the groundwork for McAdams's theory of life narratives. Easy to moderate reading.

McAdams, D. P. (1999). Personal narratives and the life story. In L. Pervin & O. John (Eds.), *Handbook of personality: Theory and research* (2nd ed., pp. 478–500). New York: Guilford Press. A more explicit formulation of McAdams's theory of life narratives. Moderate reading.

Pervin, L. A. (1996). *The science of personality.* New York: Wiley. General overviews of personality research and theories in adulthood. Moderate reading.

Whitbourne, S. K. (1996). *The aging individual: Physical and psychological perspectives.* New York: Springer. The general overview of Whitbourne's theory of identity from a cognitive perspective. Interesting reading that is easy to moderately difficult.

Clinical Assessment, Mental Health, and Mental Disorders

Former President of the United States, Ronald Reagan, died from Alzheimer's disease.

Baroness and Former Prime Minister of the United kingdom Margaret Thatcher developed Alzheimer's disease in later life.

ALTHOUGH THE INCIDENCE OF MANY DISEASES OFTEN VARIES ACROSS SOCIOECONOMIC CLASS, DEMENTIA

does not. It does not care whether you are rich and famous or not. As evidence, Rosa Parks, Ronald Reagan, and Margaret Thatcher are only three major historical figures to have been diagnosed with dementia. As the person who started the modern civil rights movement by refusing to give up her seat on a bus in Montgomery, Alabama, in 1955, Rosa Parks (1913–2005) became a major national figure and her action launched the career of Rev. Martin Luther King, Jr. For the rest of her life she championed the cause of equal rights.

Ronald Reagan (1911–2004) was the oldest man ever elected as president of the United States, winning election to his first term at age 69 and to his second term at age 73. He served as the 40th president from 1981 to 1989. As a well-known actor and two-term governor of California, Reagan had broad experience in the limelight. Enormously popular during his tenure, Reagan presided over the United States at a time of major global change. He is still remembered and respected by millions of people for his actions during his presidency. Shortly after he left office, however, Reagan began to experience serious memory difficulties along with other serious problems. Eventually he was diagnosed with Alzheimer's disease, and his condition slowly deteriorated as the disease progressed.

Margaret Thatcher (born 1925) was the first woman to serve as Prime Minister of Great Britain, holding that office from 1979 to 1990. A political conservative who was closely aligned with President Reagan, Prime Minister Thatcher was well known for instituting many economic changes in Britain, and for her staunchly anticommunist stance. She built strong relations with the United States, particularly on issues related to the Soviet Union, which ultimately dissolved. Lady Thatcher's cognitive problems were revealed by her daughter in 2008.

In this chapter, we consider situations such as those of Rosa Parks, Ronald Reagan, and Margaret Thatcher in which the aging process goes wrong. Such problems happen to families every day across all demographic categories, as is clear when famous people such as President Reagan are diagnosed with Alzheimer's disease. Certainly, Alzheimer's disease is not part of normal aging, nor are the other problems we consider.

This chapter is about the people who do not make it through adulthood to old age in the usual way. A minority of adults develop mental health difficulties that cause them problems in their daily lives and sometimes rob them of their dignity. We consider how mental health is defined and how these problems are assessed and treated. We focus on several specific problems, including depression, delirium, dementia, anxiety disorders, psychotic disorders, and substance abuse. As we consider different types of mental disorders, we note how each is diagnosed, what is known about causes, and what effective treatments are available.

Rosa Parks, the black seamstress who pioneered the struggle for civil rights in America in the 1950s by refusing to give up her seat on a bus to a white man, smiles during a ceremony, held to present her with the Congressional Gold Medal, developed Alzheimer's disease late in her life.

10.1 Mental Health and the Adult Life Course

LEARNING OBJECTIVES
- How are mental health and psychopathology defined?
- What are the key dimensions used for categorizing psychopathology?
- Why are ethnicity and aging important variables to consider in understanding mental health?

*J*anet lives alone in a small apartment. Lately, some of her neighbors have noticed that Janet doesn't come to church services as regularly as she used to. Janet's friend Betty noticed that Janet cries a lot when she's asked whether anything is wrong, and sometimes she seems very confused. Betty also notes that several of Janet's friends have died recently but still wonders whether something more serious is wrong with her.

Situations like Janet's are common. Like Betty, we could think that Janet is simply trying to deal with the loss of friends and is simply experiencing grief. But there may be something more serious the matter; Janet's confusion may be out of the ordinary. Janet's situation points out the difficulty in knowing exactly where mental health ends and mental illness or mental disorder begins. What distinguishes the study of mental disorders, or psychopathology, in adulthood and aging is not so much the content of the behavior as its context, that is, whether it interferes with daily functioning. To understand psychopathology as it is manifested in adults of different ages, we must see how it fits into the life-span developmental perspective outlined in Chapter 1.

Defining Mental Health and Psychopathology

The difference between mental health and mental disorder has never been clearly stated (Qualls, 1999). Most scholars avoid the issue entirely or try simply to say what mental health or psychopathology is not. How to tell the difference between normal or abnormal behavior is hard to define precisely, because expectations and standards for behavior change over time, over situations, and across age groups (Zarit & Zarit, 2006). Thus what is considered mental health depends on the circumstances under consideration. Researchers and practitioners still refer to Birren and Renner's (1980) argument that mentally healthy people have the following characteristics: a positive attitude toward self, an accurate perception of reality, a mastery of the environment, autonomy, personality balance, and growth and self-actualization.

One could argue that to the extent these characteristics are absent, mental disorder or psychopathology becomes more likely. In that case, we would consider behaviors that are harmful to oneself or others, lower one's well-being, and are perceived as distressing, disrupting, abnormal, or maladaptive. Although this approach is used frequently with younger or middle-aged adults, it presents problems when applied to older adults

(Zarit & Zarit, 2006). Some behaviors that would be considered abnormal under this definition may actually be adaptive under some circumstances for many older people (such as isolation, passivity, or aggressiveness). Consequently, an approach to defining abnormal behavior that emphasizes considering behaviors in isolation and from the perspective of younger or middle-aged adults is inadequate for defining abnormal behaviors in older adults. For example, because of physical, financial, social, health, or other reasons, some older adults do not have the opportunity to master their environment. Depression or hostility may be an appropriate and justified response to such limitations. Moreover, such responses may help them deal with their situation more effectively and adaptively. Figure 10.1 compares some common forms of mental disorder as a function of age.

The important point in differentiating normal from abnormal behavior (or mental health from psychopathology) is that behaviors must be interpreted in context. In other words, we must consider what else is happening and how the behavior fits the situation in addition to such factors as age and other personal characteristics.

A Multidimensional Life-Span Approach to Psychopathology

Suppose two people, one young and one old, came into your clinic, each complaining about a lack of sleep, changes in appetite, a lack of energy, and feeling down. What would you say to them?

If you evaluate them in identical ways, you might be headed for trouble. Just as we have seen in other chapters that older and younger adults may think differently or view themselves differently, the meaning of their symptoms and complaints may also differ, even though they appear to be the same. This point is not always incorporated into views of psychopathology. For example, some approaches assume that the same underlying cause is responsible for abnormal or maladaptive behavior regardless of age and that the symptoms of the mental disease are fairly constant across age. Although such

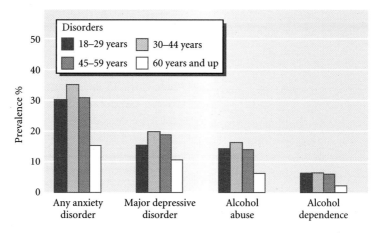

Figure 10.1 Lifetime prevalence of age-of-onset distribution of DSM-IV Disorders in the National Comorbidity Survey Replication.

Source: Kessler, Ronald C., Berglund, Patricia, Demler, Olga, Jin, Robert, Merakangas, Kathleen, & Walters, Ellen. (2005). *Arch Gen Psychiatry*, 62, 593–602. Copyright © 2005 by American Medical Association. All rights reserved.

models often are used in clinical diagnosis, they are inadequate for understanding psychopathology in old age. Viewing adults' behavior from a life-span developmental forces perspective makes a big difference in how we approach psychopathology. Let's see why.

Biological Forces. Various chronic diseases, functional limitations, and other ailments can change behavior. Because health problems increase with age (see Chapters 3 and 4), we must be more sensitive to them when dealing with older adults. In addition, genetic factors often underlie important problems in old age. For example, the evidence is growing that Alzheimer's disease has a genetic component.

Physical problems may provide clues about underlying psychological difficulties; for example, marked changes in appetite may be a symptom of depression. Moreover, some physical problems may present themselves as psychological ones. For example, extreme irritability can be caused by thyroid problems, and memory loss can result from certain vitamin deficiencies. In any case, physical health

and genetic factors are very important dimensions to take into account in diagnosing psychopathology in adults and should be among the first avenues explored.

Psychological Forces. Psychological forces across adulthood are key for understanding psychopathology. As we saw in Chapters 6, 7, and 8, several important changes in attention, memory, and intellectual performance must be considered carefully in interpreting behavior. Normative changes with age in these abilities can mimic certain mental disorders; likewise, these changes can make it more difficult to tell when an older adult has a given type of psychopathology.

In addition, the nature of a person's relationships with other people, especially family members and friends, is a key dimension in understanding how psychopathology is manifested in adults of different ages. Important developmental differences occur in the interpersonal realm; for example, younger adults are more likely to be expanding their network of friends, whereas older adults are more likely to be experiencing losses. Chapter 11 summarizes developmental changes in key relationships that may influence adults' interpretation of symptoms.

Sociocultural Forces. The social norms and cultural factors we all experience also play a key role in helping define psychopathology. They influence people's behaviors and affect our interpretation of them. For example, an older woman who lives alone in a high-crime area may be highly suspicious of other people. To label her behavior "paranoid" may be inappropriate because her well-being may depend on maintaining a certain level of suspicion of others' motives toward her. Because customs differ across cultures, behaviors that may be normative in one culture may be viewed as indicating problems in another. In short, we must ask whether the behavior we see is appropriate for a person in a particular setting.

Life-Cycle Factors. How one behaves at any point in adulthood is strongly affected by one's past experiences and the issues one is facing. These life-cycle factors must be taken into account in evaluating adults' behaviors. For example, a middle-aged woman who wants to go back to school may not have an adjustment disorder; she may simply want to develop a new aspect of herself. Some might interpret her behavior as an inability to cope with her current life situation when that is not the case at all; rather, she has a rational evaluation of her life and realizes, for example, that she needs a degree to advance in her profession. Likewise, an older man who provides vague answers to personal questions may not be resistant; he may simply be reflecting his generation's reluctance to disclose one's inner self to a stranger. Most important, the meaning of particular symptoms may change with age. For example, problems with early morning awakenings may indicate depression in a young adult but may simply be a result of normal aging in an older adult (see Chapter 3).

Ethnicity, Aging, and Mental Health

As you saw first in Chapter 1 and elsewhere in the text, sociocultural influences are a major and often overlooked factor in understanding people's behavior and developmental history. Mental health is no exception; in fact, sociocultural influences must be considered in assessing people's behavior to understand its meaning more adequately and in designing effective ways to treat their problems (Jang, Borenstein, Chiriboga, & Mortimer, 2005). For example, by the time most minorities reach old age in the United States, they have experienced a lifetime of inadequate health care, greater exposure to environmental risks, and the stress of prejudice and discrimination (see Chapters 3 and 4). Many personally experienced discrimination—and, in the case of Japanese Americans, even internment camps—that affect their trust of the health care system (Haley et al., 1998). Let's look more closely at the key issues.

In neither the general nor the ethnic populations do most people have mental disorders (Qualls & Layton, 2009; Zarit & Zarit, 2006). Still, very little is known about the nature and extent of the difficulties people face in ethnic populations, especially for groups other than African Americans. Neither positive mental health nor psychopathology has been adequately defined in any group, and no current approach takes social context into account in such a way as to be sensitive to contextual differences in ethnic communities. For example, although many explanations of deviant and antisocial behavior are grounded in the oppressive life conditions that characterize many ethnic communities, the conceptualization of positive mental health for older ethnic groups does not take into account the lifetime accumulation of such effects (Jackson et al., 1995) nor the effects of a lifetime of inadequate access to health care (Miranda, McGuire, Williams, & Wang, 2008). However, such sensitivity to conditions does not preclude finding commonalities across ethnic groups; indeed, identifying such commonalities would be an excellent place to start.

What little data we have suggest both similarities and differences in the incidence of specific types of psychopathology across different ethnic groups. Most epidemiological studies of the prevalence and incidence of mental disorders in young adults show little difference across ethnic groups (Jackson et al., 1995). However, a much more complex picture emerges when older adults are studied (Stanford & DuBois, 1992). For example, among Hispanic older adults, men show higher rates than women of alcohol abuse, whereas women have higher rates than men of phobia and panic disorders. Native American men also have high rates of alcohol abuse. Rates of depression are lower among older African Americans than they are for other ethnic groups (Moulton, 1997).

The complicated relations among age, ethnicity, and risk of developing a mental disorder merely emphasize the importance of including age and ethnicity in studies of psychopathology. Clearly, a life-course perspective that includes ethnicity would be the best approach. But even if such a framework were adopted, we would still be faced with another problem: appropriate assessment of functioning.

People have different ways of describing how they feel. Such differences are amplified by ethnic and cultural differences in what one is supposed to reveal to strangers about one's inner self. Placed in a context of important differences in social stressors, physical health, and age, assessing mental health in older ethnic adults is a daunting task. Currently, there is disagreement in the literature over some key issues. For example, do ethnicity and social class change the relation between chronic stressors and mental health? To what extent do social support, religiosity, and the family support system buffer people against stress differently across ethnic groups? Answers to these questions are difficult, and the few studies that address them provide inconclusive results (Jackson et al., 1995; Yancura & Aldwin, 2010).

What can be done to determine the ways in which ethnicity influences mental health? Jackson et al. (1995) argue that researchers should adopt an ethnic research matrix that takes as its defining elements ethnicity, national origin, racial group membership, gender, social and economic statuses, age, acculturation, coping reactions, and mental health outcomes (e.g., psychopathology, positive adjustment). Only by adopting this comprehensive approach can we understand what, how, and when aspects of race, ethnicity, age, and the life course influence mental health.

Concept Checks

1. How is *psychopathology* defined?
2. What biological factors are important to consider in psychopathology?
3. What is known about the role of ethnicity and aging in mental health?

10.2 Developmental Issues in Assessment and Therapy

LEARNING OBJECTIVES
- What key areas are included in a multidimensional approach to assessment?
- What factors influence the assessment of adults?
- How are mental health issues assessed?
- What are some major considerations for therapy across adulthood?

Juan is a 76-year-old World War II veteran who lives in California. Over the past year, his wife, Rocio, has noticed that Juan's memory isn't quite as sharp as it used to be; Juan also has less energy, stays home more, and does not show as much interest in playing dominos, a game at which he excels. Rocio wonders what might be wrong with Juan.

Many adults can relate to Rocio because they are concerned about someone they know. Whether the person is 25 or 85, it is important to be able to determine whether memory problems, energy loss, social withdrawal, or other areas of concern really indicate an underlying problem. As you might suspect, health care professionals should not use identical approaches to assess and treat adults of widely different ages. In this section, we consider how assessment methods and therapies must take developmental differences into account.

Areas of Multidimensional Assessment

What does it mean to assess someone? Assessment makes it possible to describe the behavior or other characteristics of people in meaningful ways (Stoner, O'Riley, & Edelstein, 2009). Assessment is a formal process of measuring, understanding, and predicting behavior. It involves gathering medical, psychological, and sociocultural information about people through various means, such as interviews, observation, tests, and clinical examinations.

As we noted in Chapter 1, two central aspects of any assessment approach are reliability and validity. Without these psychometric properties, we cannot rely on the assessment method to provide good information. In addition, any assessment method must be of practical use in determining the nature of the problem and choosing the appropriate treatment.

A multidimensional assessment approach is most effective (Stoner et al., 2009; Zarit & Zarit, 2006). Multidimensional assessment often is done by a team of professionals; for example, a physician may examine the medication regimen; a psychologist,

A thorough assessment of physical health is an essential part of a comprehensive mental health assessment.

the cognitive functioning; a nurse, the daily living skills; and a social worker, the economic and environmental resources. Let's consider Juan's situation as an example.

A thorough assessment of Juan's physical health is essential, as it is for adults of all ages, especially for older adults. Many physical conditions can create (or hide) mental health problems, so it is important to identify any underlying issues. Laboratory tests can also be ordered that can provide additional clues to the presence or even the cause of the problem.

Establishing Juan's cognitive ability is also key. Complaints of cognitive problems increase across adulthood, so it is important to determine the extent to which abnormal changes in older people are discriminated from normative change. Adults of all ages can be given intelligence tests, neuropsychological examinations, and mental status examinations. **Mental status exams** *are especially useful as quick screening measures of mental competence that are used to screen for cognitive impairment;* one commonly used instrument, the Mini Mental Status Exam (MMSE), is shown in Table 10.1. If Juan's score on these brief measures indicated potential problems, more complete follow-up assessments would be used. It is important to remember that scales such as the MMSE are only used for general screening and not for final diagnosis.

Psychological functioning typically is assessed through interviews, observation, and tests or questionnaires. Usually a clinician begins with an interview of Juan and brief screening instruments and follows up, if necessary, with more thorough personality inventories, tests, or more detailed interviews.

How well Juan functions in his daily life is also assessed carefully. Usually this entails determining whether he has difficulty with activities of daily living and instrumental activities of daily living (see Chapter 4). Also assessed is the person's decision-making capacity; each state has legal standards guiding the competency assessment.

Social factors in Juan's life such as social support constitute the final area of assessment. Rook,

Table 10.1

A Sampling of Questions from the Mini Mental Status Exam

Cognitive Area	Activity
Orientation to time	"What is the date?"
Registration stop	"Listen carefully. I am going to say three words. You say them back after I say them. Ready? Here they are ... APPLE [pause], PENNY [pause], TABLE [pause]. Now repeat those words back to me." [Repeat up to 5 times, but score only the first trial.]
Naming	"What is this?" [Point to a pencil or pen.]
Reading stimulus form	"Please read this and do what it says." [Show examinee the words on the form.]
	CLOSE YOUR EYES

Source: Reproduced by special permission of the Publisher, Psychological Assessment Resources, Inc., 16204 North Florida Avenue, Lutz, Florida 33549, from the Mini Mental Status Examination, by Marshal Folstein and Susan Folstein. Copyright 1975, 1998, 2001 by Mini Mental LLC, Inc. Published 2001 by Psychological Assessment Resources, Inc. Further reproduction is prohibited without permission of PAR, Inc. The MMSE can be purchased from PAR, Inc., by calling (813) 968-3003.

Mavandadi, Sorkin, and Zettel (2007) describe three dimensions of social functioning: ties with one's social network, the content of interactions with members of the social network, and the number and quality of interactions with network members. Addressing all areas of Juan's physical, cognitive, psychological, and social functioning will help determine whether Rocio has reason to be concerned. Most important, social functioning and social networking provide a major resource for health and well-being.

Factors Influencing Assessment

Health care professionals' preconceived ideas about the people they assess may have negative effects on the assessment process (Stoner et al., 2009). Two areas of concern are biases (negative or positive) and environmental conditions (where the assessment occurs, sensory or mobility problems, and health of the client).

Many types of bias have been documented as affecting the assessment process (Stoner et al., 2009). Negative biases about people are widespread and include racial, ethnic, and age stereotypes. For example, clinicians may hold negative biases against younger adults of ethnic minorities and more readily "diagnose" problems that do not truly exist. Likewise, because of ageism, older adults may be "diagnosed" with untreatable problems such as Alzheimer's disease rather than treatable problems such as depression (see Chapter 1). In contrast, positive biases about certain people also work against accurate assessment. For example, a belief that women do not abuse alcohol may result in a misdiagnosis; beliefs that older adults are "cute" may mitigate against accurate assessment of abilities. Clearly, the best defense against bias is for clinicians to be fully educated about their prospective clients.

The environmental conditions in which the assessment occurs can also work against accurate outcomes. Clinicians do not always have the option of selecting an ideal environment; rather, assessments sometimes occur in hallways, with a bedridden patient, or in a noisy emergency room. People with sensory or motor difficulties must be accommodated with alternative assessment formats. The patient's physical health may also complicate assessment; in many cases with older adults, it can also create a negative bias in that mental health issues may be overlooked when a health problem is discovered (Qualls & Benight, 2007).

Taken together, clinical assessment is an excellent example of how the forces of development come together. Only when all four forces are considered can mental health problems be assessed accurately.

Assessment Methods

How are adults assessed? In terms of cognitive, psychological, and social assessments, there are six primary methods (Edelstein & Kalish, 1999): interview, self-report, report by others, psychophysiological assessment, direct observation, and performance-based assessment.

Clinical interviews are the most widely used assessment method (Stoner et al., 2009). They are useful because they provide both direct information in response to the questions and nonverbal information such as emotions. Interviews can be used to obtain historical information, determine appropriate follow-up procedures, build rapport with the client, obtain the client's informed consent to participate in the assessment, and evaluate the effects of treatment. All these tasks are important with adults of all ages. When interviewing older adults, though, it is important to use somewhat shorter sessions, learn something about the social history of the cohort, and be aware of sensory deficits and cognitive and medical conditions that may interfere with the interview.

As described in Chapter 1, self-report instruments include a wide array of measures in which the client responds to surveys and questionnaires. Many commonly used assessment measures are presented in a self-report format. As noted in Chapter 1, a major concern is the reliability and validity of these measures with older adults.

Family members and friends are an important source of information. In some cases, such as Alzheimer's disease, discrepancies between the client's and others' description of the problem can be diagnostic. Such sources also are valuable if the client is unlikely or unable to tell the whole story. Such information can be obtained through interviews or self-report.

Psychophysiological assessment examines the relation between physical and psychological functioning. One common psychophysiological measure is the electroencephalogram (EEG), which measures brain wave activity. Other measures include heart rate, muscle activity, and skin temperature. Such measures provide a way to measure the body's reaction to certain stimuli, especially when the client gets anxious or fearful in response to them.

In some cases it is possible to observe the client through systematic or naturalistic observation (see Chapter 1). Direct observation is especially useful when the problem involves specific behaviors, as in eating disorders. A variety of techniques exist for structuring observations, and they can be used in a wide array of settings, from homes to nursing homes.

Finally, performance-based assessment involves giving clients a specific task to perform. This approach underlies much cognitive and neuropsychological assessment. For example, a person's memory is assessed by giving him or her a list of items to remember and then testing retention. Some neuropsychological tests involve drawing or copying pictures.

Developmental Issues in Therapy

Assuming that Juan is assessed properly and is found to have a mental disorder, what next? How can he be helped? Therapy for mental disorders generally involves two approaches (Qualls & Layton, 2009): medical treatment and psychotherapy. Medical treatment most often involves the use of various medications, which are based on the underlying physiological causes of the disorders. Psychotherapy usually involves talking to a clinician or participating in a group. In either case, it is essential to take into account developmental differences in people as they age.

As we saw in Chapter 3, the ways in which medications work change with age. The effective dosage of a specific medication may be very different for younger, middle-aged, and older adults. In some cases, medications that work in one age group do not work for others.

In terms of psychotherapy, adults of different ages deal with different major developmental issues as they grow older (Zarit & Zarit, 2006). As we saw in Chapter 9, various hypotheses suggest that as adults age, different life issues become central. For example, according to Erikson (1982) young adults deal with forming intimate relationships with others, middle-aged adults grapple with passing on their experience to younger generations, and older adults struggle with the meaning of their lives. Such issues often are the major issue when people enter therapy. Thus to make sense of their problems clinicians must be sensitive to the primary developmental issues facing people of different ages.

Another major issue in psychotherapy is establishing whether a particular therapeutic approach is effective, based on research and clinical evidence. Major professional associations provide guidelines in their respective fields; for example, the American Medical Association provides evidence-based approaches to medical therapy (American Medical Association, 2009), and the American Psychological Association has developed a set of criteria for evidence-based psychotherapy (American Psychological Association, 2005). The therapeutic approaches that meet the standard for adult therapy appear to be effective for a wide range of ages and are generally the therapies of choice. As we consider specific disorders, we will focus on evidence-based approaches to therapy.

Concept Checks

1. What are the major areas of thorough clinical assessment?
2. What factors must be considered in conducting clinical assessment?
3. What are the major clinical assessment techniques?
4. What developmental factors must be considered in therapy?

10.3 The Big Three: Depression, Delirium, and Dementia

LEARNING OBJECTIVES

- What are the most common characteristics of people with depression? How is depression diagnosed? What causes depression? What is the relation between suicide and age? How is depression treated?
- What is delirium? How is it assessed and treated?
- What is dementia? What are the major symptoms of Alzheimer's disease? How is it diagnosed? What causes it? What intervention options are there?

What are some other major forms of dementia? What do family members caring for patients with dementia experience?

Ling has lived in the same neighborhood in New York for all of her 74 years. Her son, who visits her every week, has started noticing that Ling's memory problems have gotten much worse, her freezer is empty, and her refrigerator has lots of moldy food. When he investigated further, he found that her bank accounts were in disarray. Ling's son wonders what could be wrong with her.

Ling's behaviors certainly do not appear to be typical of older adults. Unfortunately, Ling is not alone in experiencing difficulties; many older adults have similar problems. In this section, we consider three of the most common difficulties: depression, delirium, and dementia. As we will see, both depression and delirium are treatable; the most common form of dementia, Alzheimer's disease, is not. The three conditions are connected by overlapping symptoms and the possibility that they may coexist. Let's consider each in detail.

Depression

Most people feel down or sad from time to time, perhaps in reaction to a problem at work or in one's relationships. But does this mean that most people are depressed? How is depression diagnosed? Are there age-related differences in the symptoms examined in diagnosis? How is depression treated?

First of all, let's dispense with a myth. Contrary to the popular belief that most older adults are depressed, the rate of severe depression *declines* from young adulthood to old age for healthy people (Gatz, 2000; NIMH, 2008), a fact that also holds cross-culturally (Chou & Chi, 2005). Rates for depression tend to be higher in Latino older adults than for other groups of older adults (Centers for Disease Control and Prevention and National Association of Chronic Disease Directors, 2008). In the United States, less than 5% of older adults living in the community show signs of depression, but the percentage rises to over 13% among those who require home health care (NIMH, 2008). Young adults are at the most risk. If we consider people's reports of symptoms of depression, a different picture emerges. In this case, the highest rates occur in younger adults and people over age 75, with middle-aged adults having a lower rate (Rothermund & Brandtstäter, 2003). Importantly, there is also evidence of a cohort effect, with more recent-born cohorts showing higher rates of depression.

Finally, depression commonly accompanies other chronic conditions. For example, research indicates that 33% of people with diabetes also show symptoms of depression, as do 42% of people with cancer and 45% of people who have had a recent heart attack (National Academy on an Aging Society, 2000b). For those people who do experience depression, let's examine its diagnosis and treatment.

General Symptoms and Characteristics of People with Depression. *The most prominent feature of clinical depression is* **dysphoria,** *that is, feeling down or blue.* There are important developmental differences in how this feature is expressed (Gatz, 2000). Older adults may not label their down feelings as depression but rather as pessimism or helplessness (Zarit & Zarit, 2006). Indeed, a large community study of more than 6,500 adults revealed that older adults were much less likely to endorse statements relating to dysphoria (Gallo et al., 1994). In addition, older adults are more likely to show signs of apathy, subdued self-deprecation, expressionlessness, and changes in arousal than are younger people (Zarit & Zarit, 2006). It is common for depressed older adults to withdraw, not speak to anyone, confine themselves to bed, and not take care of bodily functions. Younger adults may engage in some of these behaviors but do so to a much lesser extent. Thoughts about suicide are common, and may reflect a shutdown of a person's basic survival instinct.

The second major component of clinical depression is the accompanying physical symptoms. These include insomnia, changes in appetite, diffuse pain, troubled breathing, headaches, fatigue, and sensory loss (Zarit & Zarit, 2006). The presence of these physical symptoms in older adults must be evaluated carefully. As noted in Chapter 3, some sleep disturbances may reflect normative changes that are unrelated to depression; however, certain types of sleep disturbance, such as regular early morning awakening, are related to depression, even in older adults (Krahn, 2005). Alternatively, the physical symptoms may reflect an underlying physical disease that is manifested as depression. Indeed, many older adults admitted to the hospital with depressive symptoms turn out to have previously undiagnosed medical problems that are uncovered only after thorough examinations and evaluations (Mulley, 2008). A list of some of the most common diseases that are often accompanied by depression can be seen in Table 10.2.

Table 10.2
Physical Illnesses That Cause Depression in Older Adults

Coronary artery disease
  Hypertension, myocardial infarction, coronary artery bypass surgery, congestive heart failure

Neurological disorders
  Cerebrovascular accidents, Alzheimer's disease, Parkinson's disease, amyotrophic lateral sclerosis, multiple sclerosis, Binswanger's disease

Metabolic disturbances
  Diabetes mellitus, hypothyroidism or hyperthyroidism, hypercortisolism, hyperparathyroidism, Addison's disease, autoimmune thyroiditis

Cancer
  Pancreatic, breast, lung, colonic, and ovarian carcinoma; lymphoma; and undetected cerebral metastasis

Other conditions
  Chronic obstructive pulmonary disease, rheumatoid arthritis, deafness, chronic pain, sexual dysfunction, renal dialysis, chronic constipation

Source: Sunderland, T., Lawlor, B. A., Molchan, S. E., & Martinez, R. A. (1988). Depressive syndromes in the elderly: Special concerns. *Psychopharmacology Bulletin, 24,* 567–576.

The third primary characteristic is that the symptoms must last at least 2 weeks. This criterion is used to rule out the transient symptoms that are common to all adults, especially after a negative experience such as receiving a rejection letter from a potential employer or getting a speeding ticket.

Fourth, other causes for the observed symptoms must be ruled out (Mulley, 2008). For example, other health problems, neurological disorders, medications, metabolic conditions, alcoholism, or other forms of psychopathology can cause depressive symptoms. These causes influence appropriate treatment decisions.

Finally, the clinician must determine how the person's symptoms are affecting his or her daily life. Is the ability to interact with other people impaired? Can he or she carry out domestic responsibilities? What about effects on work or school? Is the person taking any medication? Clinical depression involves significant impairment in daily living.

Although the primary risk factors for depression do not change with age, some important personal characteristics do. Being female, unmarried, widowed, or recently bereaved; experiencing stressful life events; and lacking an adequate social support network are more common among older adults with depression than younger adults (Zarit & Zarit, 2006). Subgroups of older adults who are at greater risk include those with chronic illnesses (of whom up to half may have major depression), nursing home residents, and family caregivers (who commonly report feeling depressed; DeFries & Andresen, 2009).

Rates of clinical depression vary across ethnic groups, although correct diagnosis is frequently a problem with minorities due to inadequate access to care (Alegría et al., 2008). Older people of ethnic minorities who are not highly acculturated in the United States tend to show higher rates of depression; this is especially true for Chinese Americans and Mexican Americans (Lam et al., 1997). Immigrants who live alone are also at higher risk for depression (Wilmoth & Chen, 2003). Latinos have a higher rate of depression overall, with some estimates indicating that up to one fourth of older Latinos have depression or related disorder, possibly caused by poor health in general. Latinos who speak primarily Spanish or are foreign-born are especially likely to show depression (Mercado-Crespo et al., 2008). Older African Americans have lower rates of depression than European Americans (Moulton, 1997). Clearly, the pattern of ethnic differences indicates that the reasons for them are complex and not well understood.

Gender and Depressive Symptoms. Women tend to be diagnosed as being depressed more often than are men (Barry et al., 2008). A longitudinal study over 6 years showed that this is due in part to women being more susceptible than men to depression (Barry et al., 2008). Additionally, the symptoms of dysphoria and feelings of guilt or self-blame are present in classic clinical depression but appear to be absent in a version of depression experienced by

© Eastcott / Momatiuk / The Image Works

Contrary to myth, the rate of depression actually declines with age.

older women called the *depletion syndrome of the elderly* (Kasl-Godley et al., 1999).

Gender differences in mortality related to depression have been reported. In men but not in women, minor depression is associated with significantly higher mortality; major depression is associated with higher mortality in both genders (Anstey & Luszcz, 2002; Penninx et al., 1999). Some evidence also indicates that men who were taking antidepressants were also more likely to die (Ryan et al., 2008). Why these consistent gender differences are observed are unknown.

Assessment Scales. Numerous scales are used to assess depression, but because most were developed on younger and middle-aged adults, they are most appropriate for these age groups. The most important difficulty in using these scales with older adults is that they all include several items assessing physical symptoms. For example, the Beck Depression Inventory (Beck, 1967) contains items that focus on feelings and physical symptoms. Although the presence of such symptoms usually is indicative of depression in younger adults, as we noted earlier such symptoms may not be related to depression at all in older adults. Scales such as the Geriatric Depression Scale (Yesavage et al., 1983) aimed specifically at older adults have also been developed. Physical symptoms are omitted, and the response format is easier for older adults to follow. This approach reduces the age-related symptom bias and scale response problems with other self-report scales measuring depressive symptoms. A third screening inventory, the Center for Epidemiologic Studies-Depression Scale (CES-D; Radloff, 1977) is frequently used in research.

An important point to keep in mind about these scales is that the diagnosis of depression should never be made on the basis of a test score alone. As we have seen, the symptoms observed in clinical depression could be indicative of other problems, and symptom patterns are very complex. Moreover, there is some evidence of gender bias; in one study, both the Geriatric Depression Scale and the Beck Depression Inventory were more accurate in diagnosing depression in older women than in older men (Allen-Burge et al., 1994). Only by assessing many aspects of physical and psychological functioning can a clinician make an accurate assessment.

Causes of Depression. Several biological and psychosocial theories about the causes of depression have been proposed (Langlieb & DePaulo, 2008). Both theories are related to two types of situations: sudden severe loss and long-term, high-level stress.

Biological theories focus most on genetic predisposition and changes in neurotransmitters. The genetic evidence is based on several studies that show higher rates of depression in relatives of depressed people than would be expected given base rates in the population. This genetic link is stronger in early-onset depression than it is in depression that has its onset in late life (Kasl-Godley et al., 1999).

There is substantial research evidence that severe depression is linked to imbalance in neurotransmitters such as low levels of serotonin. Low levels of serotonin are a likely result from high levels of stress experienced over a long period. The usual signs of low serotonin levels include waking up in the early morning (often around 4:00 A.M.), difficulty in concentrating and paying attention, feeling tired and listless, losing interest in activities such as sex or visiting friends, and racing of the mind with strong feelings of guilt and of reliving bad past experiences and creating negative thoughts. These effects of low serotonin are very similar to those that characterize depression, which is why researchers believe that one possible cause is low serotonin. Low levels of another neurotransmitter, norepinephrine, which regulates arousal and alertness, may be responsible for the feelings of fatigue associated with depression. These neurochemical links are the basis for the medications developed to treat depression that we will consider a bit later.

The most common theme of psychosocial theories of depression is loss (Langlieb & DePaulo, 2008). Bereavement or other ways of losing a relationship is the type of loss that has received the most attention, but the loss of anything considered personally important could also be a trigger. Moreover, these losses may be real and irrevocable, threatened and potential, or imaginary and fantasized. The likelihood that these losses will occur varies with age. Middle-aged adults are more likely to experience the loss of physical attractiveness, for example, whereas older adults are more likely to experience the loss of a loved one.

Behavioral and cognitive-behavioral theories of depression adopt a different approach. The behavioral approach argues that people with depression engage in fewer pleasant activities and receive less pleasure from them than do nondepressed people (Zarit & Zarit, 2006). This link between behaviors and mood is the basis for various therapeutic interventions. The cognitive-behavioral approach emphasizes internal belief systems and focuses on how people interpret uncontrollable events (Beck, 1967). The idea underlying this approach is that experiencing unpredictable and uncontrollable events instills a feeling of helplessness, which results in depression. In addition, perceiving the cause of negative events as some inherent aspect of the self that is permanent and pervasive also plays an important role in causing feelings of helplessness and hopelessness. In short, according to the cognitive-behavioral approach, people who are depressed believe that they are personally responsible for their plight, that things are unlikely to get better, and that their whole life is a shambles.

An alternative psychosocial explanation argues that whether a person experiences depression depends on a balance among biological dispositions, stress, and protective factors (Gatz, 2000). Developmentally, biological factors become more important with age, whereas stress factors diminish. Protective factors, such as psychological coping skills, also improve, which may account in part for the decreased incidence of depression in later life.

Treatment of Depression. As we have seen, depression is a complex problem that can result from a wide variety of causes. However, an extremely crucial point is that all forms of depression benefit from some form of therapy and that they are quite effective (Zarit & Zarit, 2006). Treatment of depression falls roughly into two categories: medical treatments and psychotherapy.

Medical treatments are typically used in cases of severe depression and involve mainly medication, but in some cases of long-term severe depression,

these treatments include electroconvulsive therapy. For less severe forms of depression, and usually in conjunction with medication for severe depression, there are various forms of psychotherapy. A summary of the various treatment options is presented in Table 10.3.

Three families of medications are used to combat severe depression. Each has potentially serious side effects (for a summary, see the Mayo Clinic's website on side effects of antidepressant medications at http://www.mayoclinic.com/health/antidepressants/MH00062). One type of first-line medications used to treat depression is selective serotonin reuptake inhibitors (SSRIs; Mulley, 2008). SSRIs have the lowest overall rate of side effects of all antidepressants. SSRIs work by boosting the level of serotonin, a neurotransmitter involved in regulating moods that was discussed earlier. One of the SSRIs, Prozac, became controversial because it was linked in a small number of cases with the serious side effect of high levels of agitation. Drugs such as fluoxetine HCl (Prozac) make people "not sad," which is different from making people happy. Other SSRIs include paroxetine (Paxil), sertraline (Zoloft), citalopram (Celexa), and escitalopram (Lexapro). Other types of first-line medications are serotonin and norepinephrine reuptake inhibitors (SNRIs), norepinephrine and dopamine reuptake inhibitors (NDRIs), combined reuptake inhibitors and receptor blockers, and tetracyclic antidepressants.

If the first-line medications do not work, the next most popular medications are the tricyclic antidepressants. Although these are effective in at least 70% of cases, they are most effective with younger and middle-aged people. The main problem with tricyclic antidepressants in older adults is that these people are more likely to have other medical conditions or to be taking other medications that preclude their use. For example, people who are taking antihypertensive medications or who have any of a number of metabolic problems should not take the tricyclic antidepressants. Moreover, the risk of side effects beyond dry mouth, some of which can be severe, is much greater in older adults, although some of the newer tricyclics have significantly lower risk. Because tricyclic antidepressants must be taken

Table 10.3

Summary of Depression Treatment Options

Antidepressant medications	Several options, including selective serotonin uptake inhibitors (SSRIs), tricyclics, MAO inhibitors, and others that have been shown to be effective in clinical trials research.	Adequate dosages, plasma levels, and treatment duration are essential to minimize response. Response may take 6–12 weeks, somewhat longer than in younger patients. Side effects may limit use.
Augmentation of antidepressants with lithium, thyroid medications, carbamazepine	Patients nonresponsive to several weeks of treatment with standard antidepressant medications may respond rapidly after these medications are added. Evidence is based on case series and reports.	May be useful in patients who are not responding or only partially responding to standard antidepressant medications. Constitutes acceptable clinical practice.
Electroconvulsive therapy	Clearly effective in severe depression, depression with melancholia, and depression with delusions, and when antidepressants are not fully effective. Sometimes combined with antidepressants.	In medication-resistant patients, acute response rate is approximately 50%. Relapse rate is high, necessitating attention to maintenance antidepressant treatment. Effects are more favorable with increasing age.
Psychotherapy	More effective treatment than waiting list, no treatment, or placebo; equivalent to antidepressant medications in geriatric outpatient populations generally, with major or minor depression. About half of studies are group interventions. Therapy orientations were cognitive, interpersonal, reminiscence, psychodynamic, and eclectic.	Studies have been in older outpatients who were not significantly suicidal and for whom hospitalization was not indicated. There is no evidence of efficacy in severe depression. Distribution of responses may be different from the response to medication.
Combined antidepressant medication and psychotherapy	Effective in outpatients using manual-based therapies; the relative contributions of each component are not well understood.	Combined therapy has not been adequately studied in older adults.

Source: U.S. Public Health Service (1993).

for roughly a week before the person feels relief, compliance with the therapy sometimes is difficult.

If none of these medications are effective, a third group of drugs that relieve depression is the monoamine oxidase (MAO) inhibitors, so named because they inhibit MAO, a substance that interferes with the transmission of signals between neurons. MAO inhibitors generally are less effective than the tricyclics and can produce deadly side effects. Specifically, they interact with foods that

contain tyramine or dopamine—mainly cheddar cheese but also others, such as wine and chicken liver—to create dangerously and sometimes fatally high blood pressure. MAO inhibitors are used with extreme caution, usually only after SSRIs and HCAs have proved ineffective.

If periods of depression alternate with periods of mania or extremely high levels of activity, a diagnosis of bipolar disorder is made (American Psychiatric Association, 1994). Bipolar disorder is characterized by unpredictable, often explosive mood swings as the person cycles between extreme depression and extreme activity. The drug therapy of choice for bipolar disorder is lithium (Buffum & Buffum, 1998). Lithium is very effective in controlling the mood swings, although researchers do not completely understand why it works. The use of lithium must be monitored very closely because the difference between an effective dosage and a toxic dosage is very small. Because lithium is a salt, it raises blood pressure, making it dangerous for people who have hypertension or kidney disease. The effective dosage for lithium decreases with age; physicians unaware of this change run the risk of inducing an overdose, especially in older adults (Buffum & Buffum, 1998). Compliance is also a problem, because no improvement is seen for 4 to 10 days after the initial dose and because many people with bipolar disorder do not like having their moods controlled by medication.

Electroconvulsive therapy (ECT) is an effective treatment for severe depression, especially in people whose depression has lasted a long time, who are suicidal, who have serious physical problems caused by their depression, and who do not respond to medications. Unlike antidepressant medications, ECT has immediate effects. Usually only a few treatments are needed, in contrast to long-term maintenance schedules for drugs. But ECT may have some side effects that affect cognitive functioning (Gardner & O'Connor, 2008). Memory of the ECT treatment itself is lost. Memory of other recent events is temporarily disrupted, but it usually returns within a week or two.

Psychotherapy is a treatment approach based on the idea that talking to a therapist about one's problems can help. Often psychotherapy can be very effective by itself in treating depression. In cases of severe depression, psychotherapy may be combined with drug therapy or ECT. Two general approaches seem to work best for depression: **behavior therapy,** *which focuses on attempts to alter current behavior without necessarily addressing underlying causes,* and **cognitive therapy,** *which attempts to alter the ways people think.*

The fundamental idea in behavior therapy is that depressed people receive too few rewards or reinforcements from their environment (Lewinsohn, 1975). Thus the goal of behavior therapy is to get them to increase the good things that happen to them. Often this can be accomplished by having people increase their activities; if they do more, the likelihood is that more good things will happen. In addition, behavior therapy seeks to get people to decrease the number of negative thoughts they have because depressed people tend to look at the world pessimistically. They get little pleasure out of activities that nondepressed people enjoy a great deal: seeing a funny movie, playing a friendly game of volleyball, or being with a lover.

To get activity levels up and negative thoughts down, behavior therapists usually assign tasks that force clients to practice the principles they are learning during the therapy sessions. This may involve going out more to meet people, joining new clubs, or just learning how to enjoy life. Family members are instructed to ignore negative statements made by the depressed person and to reward positive self-statements with attention, praise, or even money.

Cognitive therapy for depression is based on the idea that depression results from maladaptive beliefs or cognitions about oneself. From this perspective, a depressed person views the self as inadequate and unworthy, the world as insensitive and ungratifying, and the future as bleak and unpromising (Beck et al., 1979). In cognitive therapy the person is taught how to recognize these thoughts, which have become so automatic and ingrained that other perspectives are not seen. Once this awareness has been achieved, the person learns how to evaluate the self, world, and future more realistically. These goals may be accomplished through homework assignments similar to those used in behavior therapy. These often involve reattributing the causes of events, examining the evidence before drawing conclusions, listing the pros and cons of maintaining an idea, and examining the consequences of that idea. Finally, people are taught to change the basic beliefs that are responsible for their negative thoughts. For example, people who believe that they have been failures all their lives or that they are unlovable are taught how to use their newfound knowledge to achieve more realistic appraisals of themselves.

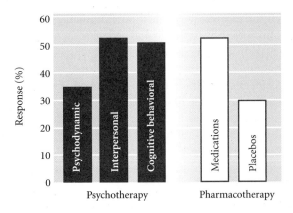

Figure 10.2 Percentage of patients responding to psychotherapy versus medications and pill placebo.

Source: Hollon, Thase, & Markowitz (2002).

Which therapy works best? Hollon, Thase, and Markowitz (2002) examined this question in a thorough review of the research. Their conclusions, shown in Figure 10.2, were that no one approach works for everyone. Rather, it appears that there are several options available. Medications have the most research support, although cognitive-behavioral therapy has considerable evidence behind it as well. Most important, though, is that treatment may need to be continuous, as the relapse rate is high for all treatments if they are not ongoing.

Delirium

A **delirium** *is characterized by a disturbance of consciousness and a change in cognition that develop over a short period of time* (American Psychiatric Association, 1994). The changes in cognition can include difficulties with attention, memory, orientation, and language. Delirium can also affect perception, the sleep–wake cycle, personality, and mood. Although the onset of delirium usually is rapid, its course can vary a great deal over the course of a day, with cognitive symptoms in older adults generally more severe than in younger or middle-aged adults (Leentjens et al., 2008).

Delirium can be caused by any of a number of medical conditions (such as stroke, cardiovascular disease, metabolic condition), medication side effects, substance intoxication or withdrawal, exposure to toxins, or any combination of factors (Leentjens et al., 2008; Zarit & Zarit, 2006). Because they take more medications on average than other age groups, older adults are particularly susceptible to delirium. In the general community, the rate of delirium in people over age 55 is low (between 0.4% and 1.1%), but among people who are ill the rate is much higher, with as many as 50% of postoperative patients experiencing delirium (Qualls, 1999).

Assessment and treatment of delirium focus on the physiological causes. In general, the most important aspect of diagnosis is differentiating delirium from depression and dementia. The key features of each are shown in Table 10.4. The severity of delirium is related to the level of underlying physiological problem. In many cases, delirium is accompanied by severe misinterpretations of the environment and confusion, which is best alleviated by having one reliable family member or friend provide reassurance to the patient (Leentjens et al., 2008).

If the cause of the delirium can be identified and addressed, most cases of delirium can be cured. In some cases, however, delirium can be fatal or result in permanent brain damage (Leentjens et al., 2008).

Dementia

Probably no other condition associated with aging is more feared than the family of disorders known as dementia. In dementia one can literally lose one's mind, being reduced from a complex, thinking, feeling human being to a confused, vegetative victim unable even to recognize one's spouse and children. Dementias serious enough to impair independent functioning affect over 5 million Americans, with the incidence increasing with age, rising from extremely low rates in the 50s to about half of the people aged 85 and older (National Institute on Aging, 2007a). Estimates are that unless a cure or prevention is found, the number of people with dementia will increase by 50% by 2030 to nearly 8 million and could triple by 2050 to over 16 million (Alzheimer's Association, 2008a).

Table 10.4

Comparison of Characteristics of Depression, Delirium, and Dementia

Clinical Feature	Delirium	Dementia	Depression
Onset	Acute or subacute, depends on cause, often at twilight or in darkness	Chronic, generally insidious, depends on cause	Coincides with major life changes, often abrupt
Course	Short diurnal fluctuations in symptoms, worse at night, in darkness, and on awakening	Long, no diurnal effects, symptoms progressive yet stable over time	Diurnal effects, typically worse in the morning, situational fluctuations, but less than with delirium
Progression	Abrupt	Slow but uneven	Variable, rapid, or slow but even
Duration	Hours to less than 1 month, seldom longer	Months to years	At least 6 weeks, can be several months to years
Awareness	Reduced	Clear	Clear
Alertness	Fluctuates, lethargic or hypervigilant	Generally normal	Normal
Attention	Impaired, fluctuates	Generally normal	Minimal impairment, but is easily distracted
Orientation	Generally impaired, severity varies	Generally normal	Selective disorientation
Memory	Recent and immediate impaired	Recent and remote impaired	Selective or patchy impairment, islands of intact memory
Thinking	Disorganized, distorted, fragmented, incoherent speech, either slow or accelerated	Difficulty with abstraction, thoughts impoverished, judgment impaired, words difficult to find	Intact but with themes of hopelessness, helplessness, or self-deprecation
Perception	Distorted, illusions, delusions, and hallucinations, difficulty distinguishing between reality and misperceptions	Misperceptions usually absent	Intact, delusions and hallucinations absent except in severe cases
Psychomotor behavior	Variable, hypokinetic, hyperkinetic, and mixed	Normal, may have apraxia	Variable, psychomotor retardation or agitation
Sleep–wake cycle	Disturbed, cycle reversed	Fragmented	Disturbed, usually early morning awakening
Associated features	Variable affective changes, symptoms of autonomic hyperarousal, exaggeration of personality type, associated with acute physical illness	Affect tends to be superficial, inappropriate, and labile, attempts to conceal deficits in intellect, personality changes, aphasia, agnosia may be present, lacks insight	Affect depressed, dysphoric mood, exaggerated and detailed complaints, preoccupied with personal thoughts, insight present, verbal elaboration
Assessment	Distracted from task, numerous errors	Failing highlighted by family, frequent "near miss" answers, struggles with test, great effort to find an appropriate reply, frequent requests for feedback on performance	Failings highlighted by individual, often answers "don't know," little effort, often gives up, indifferent toward test, does not care or attempt to find answer

Source: Foreman, M. D., Fletcher, K., Mion, L. C., et al. (1996). Assessing cognitive function. *Geriatric Nursing, 17,* 228. Reprinted with permission from Elsevier.

Although there is a real basis for fearing dementia, most older adults are not demented. For many people, the fear of dementia is the most serious problem, leading them to consider every lapse of memory a symptom. It is hard to know how many older adults have unstated fears about no longer being able to remember things in the same ways they did when they were younger. But as noted in Chapter 6, memory abilities show some normative changes with age. Consequently, what many people believe are signs that they are becoming demented are actually quite normal.

The Family of Dementias. **Dementia** *is not a specific disease but rather a family of diseases that are characterized by cognitive and behavioral deficits involving some form of permanent damage to the brain.* About a dozen forms of dementia have been identified. Dementia involves severe cognitive and behavioral decline and is not caused by a rapid onset of a toxic substance or by infection (American Psychiatric Association, 2000). If delirium is present, dementia cannot be diagnosed.

We focus on several types of dementias that are irreversible and degenerative. The most common and widely known of these is Alzheimer's disease, but others are important as well: vascular dementia, Parkinson's disease, Huntington's disease, alcoholic dementia, and AIDS dementia complex.

Alzheimer's Disease. **Alzheimer's disease** *is the most common form of progressive, degenerative, and fatal dementia, accounting for perhaps as many as 70% of all cases of dementia* (Alzheimer's Association, 2008a). New knowledge about Alzheimer's disease is discovered all the time, so it is important to monitor the research literature. However, because it is such a terrible disease, news of potential breakthroughs too often do not pan out.

Alzheimer's disease has several characteristics that we will consider, both in terms of specific changes in the brain and behavioral symptoms.

Neurological Changes in Alzheimer's Disease The changes in the brain that characterize Alzheimer's disease are microscopic. Although great progress has been made in diagnosing the disease, it is still the case that definitive diagnosis of the disease can be done only at autopsy (Feldman et al., 2008). These progressive changes eventually cause so much brain destruction that the person dies. The microscopic changes that define Alzheimer's disease are rapid cell death, neurofibrillary tangles, and neuritic plaques. Several changes in neurotransmitter levels also are observed. Rapid cell death occurs most in the hippocampus (a structure in the brain most closely involved in memory), the cortex (the outer layer of the brain in which our higher-level cognitive abilities reside), and the basal forebrain (the lower portion of the front of the brain). This cell death occurs at a rate much greater than normal.

Neurofibrillary tangles (see Chapter 3) are accumulations of pairs of filaments in the neuron that become wrapped around each other; when examined under a microscope, these paired filaments look like intertwined spirals. Neurofibrillary tangles occur in several areas of the brain, and the number of tangles is directly related to the severity of symptoms, specifically the severity of memory impairment (Guillozet et al., 2003).

Neuritic or amyloid plaques (see Chapter 3) are spherical structures consisting of a core of **beta-amyloid,** *a protein, surrounded by degenerated fragments of dying or dead neurons.* The plaques are found in various parts of the brain, with the amount of beta-amyloid moderately related to the severity of the disease (Guillozet et al., 2003). Degeneration of neurons in some areas of the brain results in the formation of vacuoles, or spaces that become filled with fluid and granular material. Considerable recent research has focused on beta-amyloid as a major factor in Alzheimer's disease, both in terms of the cause and possible avenues for treatment. For example, there is some evidence that abnormal levels of copper, zinc, and iron may cause beta-amyloid deposits (Finefrock, Bush, & Doraiswamy, 2003).

Although the structural changes occurring in the brains of people with Alzheimer's disease are substantial, we must use caution in assuming that they represent qualitative differences from normal aging. They may not. As we saw in Chapter 3, all

Alzheimer's disease is a degenerative brain disorder that is, at present, incurable.

the changes seen in Alzheimer's disease, including the structural and neurotransmitter changes, are also found in normal older adults. To be sure, the changes in Alzheimer's disease are much greater. But the important point is that Alzheimer's disease may be merely an exaggeration of normal aging and not something qualitatively different from it.

Recent research has also implicated certain neurochemicals as other possible causes of Alzheimer's disease. For example, increased levels of plasma homocysteine have been associated with the level of cognitive impairment observed in Alzheimer's disease (Blasko et al., 2008; Bleich et al., 2003). Screening for these increased levels may improve diagnostic accuracy, and these levels are directly addressed by medication with memantine (discussed later).

Symptoms and Diagnosis The major symptoms of Alzheimer's disease are gradual changes in cognitive functioning: declines in memory beginning with loss of recent memory and progressing to loss of remote memory, learning, attention, and judgment; disorientation in time and space; difficulties in word finding and communication; declines in

personal hygiene and self-care skills; inappropriate social behavior; and changes in personality (American Psychiatric Association, 2000).

These symptoms tend to be vague in the beginning, and they mimic other psychological problems such as depression or stress reactions. For example, an executive may not be managing as well as she once did and may be missing deadlines more often. Slowly, the symptoms get worse. This executive, who once could easily handle millions of dollars, can no longer add two small numbers. A homemaker cannot set the table. A person who was previously outgoing is now quiet and withdrawn; a gentle person is now hostile and aggressive. Emotional problems become increasingly apparent, including depression, paranoia, and agitation. Wandering becomes a serious problem, especially because the person may have no idea where he or she is or how to get home, thus posing a genuine safety concern.

As the disease progresses, the patient becomes incontinent and more and more dependent on others for care, eventually becoming completely incapable of even such simple tasks as dressing and eating. *In general, the symptoms associated with Alzheimer's disease are worse in the evening than in the morning, a phenomenon that caregivers call* **sundowning.**

The rate of deterioration in Alzheimer's disease varies widely from one patient to the next, although progression usually is faster when onset occurs earlier in life (Wilson et al., 2000). However, we can identify a series of stages that the patient goes through (Reisberg et al., 1982). Many diseases cause problems similar to those observed in the early stages of Alzheimer's disease. In fact, fewer than 10% of those who show mild cognitive impairment go on to develop more serious cognitive impairment within several years of the clinical evaluation (Reisberg et al., 1985).

Although a definitive diagnosis of Alzheimer's disease depends on an autopsy, the number and severity of neurological and behavioral changes allow clinicians to make increasingly accurate early diagnoses (Feldman et al., 2008). For an earlier diagnosis to be accurate, however, it must be comprehensive and broad. Figure 10.3 provides an overview of the process that should be used to differentiate Alzheimer's disease from other conditions. Note that a great deal of the diagnostic effort goes into ruling out other possible causes for the observed cognitive deficits: All possible treatable causes for the symptoms must be eliminated before a diagnosis of Alzheimer's disease can be made. Unfortunately, many clinicians do not conduct such thorough diagnoses; general practice physicians miss nearly half the cases of dementia (Boise et al., 1999).

As noted in Figure 10.3, the clinical diagnosis of Alzheimer's disease consists of carefully noting the history of the symptoms, documenting the cognitive impairments, conducting a general physical exam and neurological exam, performing laboratory tests to rule out other diseases, obtaining a psychiatric evaluation, performing neuropsychological tests, and assessing functional abilities. To rule out physical illness, it is critical to conduct a thorough medical examination prior to any psychological or other follow-up tests. Recent evidence suggests that the measurement of p-tau proteins may provide a good biological marker of Alzheimer's disease (Hampel, Goernitz, & Buerger, 2003). More important, measures of p-tau proteins can differentiate between Alzheimer's disease, other forms of dementia, and depression. In addition, brain-imaging techniques, such as magnetic resonance imaging (MRI) and spiral computed tomography (spiral CT) scans, are often used to rule out other diseases.

As research findings provide ways to improve the accuracy of diagnosis of Alzheimer's disease, home testing kits are becoming available. The Early Alert Alzheimer's Home Screening Test (AHST), costing roughly $20, is one example (Higuera et al., 2008; Kier & Molinari, 2003). The AHST is based on the Smell Identification Test (SIT), which in turn is based on some research evidence that individuals with Alzheimer's disease have trouble identifying certain smells. Unfortunately, so do individuals with several other disorders, such as vascular dementia, human immunodeficiency virus (HIV) infection, and multiple sclerosis, making it very difficult to conclude that olfactory dysfunction is uniquely related to Alzheimer's disease. Moreover, the general public, untrained in Alzheimer's disease diagnosis, may not understand the difference between a screening test (the AHST) and a diagnostic test. In short, although the concept of a home test for Alzheimer's disease may have merit, a much more accurate test is necessary, coupled with better education in its use.

Searching for a Cause We do not know for certain what causes Alzheimer's disease. There are many hypotheses, as described in Table 10.5. At present, the main focus of research is on a genetic link (McQueen & Blacker, 2008; Wilmot et al., 2008). The strong possibility that at least some forms of Alzheimer's disease are inherited is a major concern of patients' families. The research evidence to date indicates that genetic factors may be a powerful determinant of Alzheimer's disease, and possible markers on chromosomes have been found (McQueen & Blacker, 2008; Wilmot et al., 2008). Genetic research has identified links to both early onset and late onset of Alzheimer's disease. Other research has investigated other possible causes, such as beta-amyloid, as noted earlier.

Several sites on various chromosomes have been tentatively identified as being involved in the

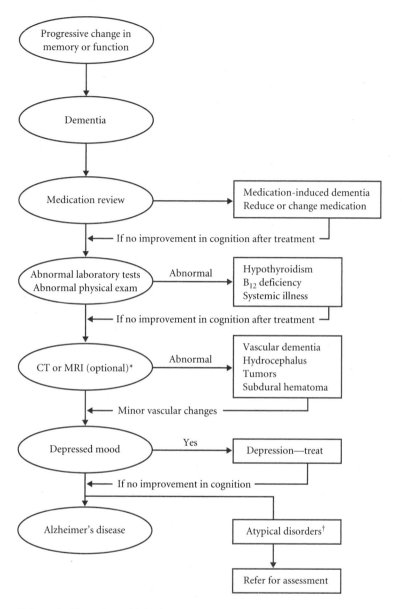

*It is required in patients with focal signs, rapid progression, and headache.
†This category contains rare dementias (e.g., frontotemporal degenerations, Jakob–Creutzfeldt disease, Parkinson's disease, and other movement disorders that present with dementias) that should be considered when unusual clinical features are present or a rapidly progressive course is noted.

Figure 10.3 Differential diagnosis and Alzheimer's disease algorithm.

Source: Alzheimer's Association online document. http://www.alz.org/medical/rtalgrthm.htm
Developed and endorsed by the TriAD Advisory Board. Copyright 1996 Pfizer Inc. and Esai Inc.
with special thanks to J. L. Cummings. Algorithm reprinted from TriAD, *Three for the Management of Alzheimer's Disease,* with permission.

Table 10.5

Hypotheses of the Cause of Alzheimer's Disease

Factors	Action or Hypothesis	Results	Progress
Neurotransmitters			
Acetylcholine	Acetylcholine levels drop by about 90%.	Decline in memory.	Drug therapies aimed at postsynaptic receptor sites: vitamin E and Deprenyl being tested in clinical trials.
Serotonin, somatostatin, noradrenaline	Levels lower than normal.	Sensory disturbance, aggressive behavior, neuron death.	
Phospholipids	Shape and action of the receptors may play role.	Abnormalities transmit garbled messages from one neuron to another because of dysfunction or blockage of relay points.	
Beta-amyloid	Forms insoluble plaque.	Possible neuron death.	Studies link the disruption of K^1 and Ca^{11} levels; link between cholinergic neuron death and beta-amyloids.
Tau	Neurofibrillary tangles.	Twisted paired helical filaments destabilize the microtubule structure.	
Genes			
1, 14, 19 (Apo E4)	Protein and amyloid become insoluble, leading to deposition of plaque.	Linked to late onset of Alzheimer's; increases deposits of beta-amyloid.	How tau and beta-amyloids react to APP.
	Tau protein allows structure of microtubules to become undone, causing tangles.	Directly regulates apolipoprotein (Apo E4) and quickly binds with beta-amyloid.	
21	Neurons with short dendrites; carries code for mutated amyloid precursor protein (APP) familial Alzheimer's disease.	Early Alzheimer's.	Supports theory that beta-amyloids play a role in Alzheimer's disease; also gene found in Down's syndrome.
Metabolism			
Glucose and O_2 molecules	Altered glucose metabolism.	Dramatic decline in glucose and oxygen as neurons degenerate and die or neuron degeneration causes glucose decline.	Neurons having problems with metabolism react abnormally to another neurotransmitter, glutamate.

(Continued)

Factors	Action or Hypothesis	Results	Progress
Metabolism			
Calcium	A rise in Ca^{11} level inside the cell.	Series of cascades of biochemical events, allowing a rise in calcium channels admit in excess Ca^{11}.	
	Levels rise because of energy-level crisis in neurons.	A defect in structure leads to an increase in storage or pumping calcium out.	
		Chronically high levels of neurotransmitter glutamate disrupts metabolism, causing an influx of Ca^{11}.	
	Hormone glucocorticoid.	Neuron death and dysfunction caused in hippocampus.	
Environment			
Aluminum	Trace metal in brain.	Turns up in more than normal amounts in many brain autopsies of patients with Alzheimer's.	Nothing confirmed.
Zinc	Too little or too much.	Found on brain autopsy of patients with Alzheimer's.	
Food-borne poisons	Food toxins.	Causes soluble beta-amyloid of the cerebral spinal fluid to clump together, similar to plaque of patients with Alzheimer's; may cause neurologic damage and enhance the action of neurotransmitters glutamate.	
Viruses	A virus or other infection.		

Source: National Institute on Aging (1995).

transmission of Alzheimer's disease, including chromosomes 12, 14, 19, and 21. The most promising work has noted links between the genetic markers and the production of amyloid protein, the major component of neuritic plaques (McQueen & Blacker, 2008). Much of this research focuses on apolipoprotein E4 (apo E4), associated with chromosome 19, which may play a central role in creating neuritic plaques. Interestingly, another version, apo E2, seems to have the reverse effect: It decreases the risk of Alzheimer's disease (Bathum et al., 2006). Despite the relation between apo E4 and neuritic plaques, researchers have yet to establish strong relations between apolipoprotein E and general cognitive functioning (Bathum et al., 2006). However, researchers have established a link between the cystatin C gene (CST3) and late-onset Alzheimer's disease (Finckh et al., 2000).

Researchers can already identify genetic markers responsible for certain forms of early-onset

Genetic Tests for Dementia: Difficult Choices

When scientists discovered that they could determine whether someone was carrying the gene for Huntington's disease, they created the opportunity for people to know something about their future. Huntington's disease is a genetic, fatal, degenerative disease that typically manifests itself in adults between 30 and 45 (Sharon, Ersan, & Sharon, 2007). Dementia is part of the disease; other symptoms include uncontrollable, jerking movement of the limbs, torso, and face. Individuals who have one parent with the disease run a 50–50 chance of having it themselves and, if they have children, of passing it on to them.

The ability to determine in advance who would develop or escape the disease offers a difficult choice for potentially affected individuals and families, allowing them to plan more practically about having children, choosing jobs, obtaining insurance, organizing finances, and pursuing social and leisure interests. This difficult choice involves possibly learning that they have a fatal disease.

Deciding to undergo this kind of test is not easy. This is not due to the test, which involves a genetic analysis of blood samples taken from the person being tested and from six or so family members. The difficulty lies in the fact that a positive result on

the test means a high probability of developing the disease, and, if one has children, a 50% chance of passing it to them. The test is 99% accurate.

For some young adults who are at risk for Huntington's disease, taking the test removes the uncertainty in their lives (Duncan et al., 2007, 2008). People who took the test described both harms and benefits. The harms included knowledge of future illness, witnessing distress among and negative effects on family relationships and friendships, effects upon employment and school, experiencing regret, feeling guilty, and having to confront difficult issues (e.g., the inevitability of one's own illness). The benefits included knowledge of gene-negative status, witnessing relief in parents and family members, feeling able to plan for the future, positive effects on family relationships and friendships, feeling empowered, and experiencing a sense of clarity about what is important in life.

Whether people decide to take predictive genetic tests is a personal issue that should be respected. In addition to the clinical information and options, supportive counseling before and after testing is a critical aspect that must be available. The Huntington's Disease Program at the University of Virginia suggests that those thinking

about taking the test and those close to them consider several questions (University of Virginia Huntington's Disease Program, 2003):

- What does it mean for you to be at risk for HD?
- How has it affected your life and your plans for the future?
- Would this be different if you knew whether you are going to develop HD?
- How will it make you feel if you are told you have inherited the gene for HD?
- What will it mean for you if you have not inherited the gene for HD?
- How will the results of the test affect other members of your family?
- How have you coped with difficult times in the past?
- Have there been stressful or difficult times in your life?
- Are there people in your life who will help you cope?
- Who will you tell about your decision to have predictive testing?
- Who will accompany you when you receive the results of the test?
- Would you want some time off from work after you receive the results?
- Are you thinking about having children?
- Would you like more information about the options available for testing a pregnancy for HD?

Alzheimer's disease, and they have developed a test to see whether people have the inheritance pattern (McQueen & Blacker, 2008; Steinbart et al., 2001). Although research shows no significant negative consequences to people when they know that they have the marker for Alzheimer's disease (Marteau et al., 2005), difficult choices may remain. For example, individuals who know they have the genes responsible for the disease may be faced with difficult decisions about having children and how to live out their lives. Genetic counseling programs, which currently focus mostly on diseases of childhood, would need to be expanded to help individuals face decisions about diseases occurring later in life. Even if a specific gene is identified for each type of Alzheimer's disease, many questions about the cause of Alzheimer's disease will remain. Why does it take so long for the genetic defect to appear? What mechanism starts it? Why is there so much variation when it appears? Answers to these questions will help us understand how Alzheimer's disease develops.

Tests can be developed to detect genes that transmit diseases. Such a test already exists for Huntington's disease. As discussed in the Current Controversies feature, however, taking the test is not an easy decision, even when there is a high risk of passing the disease on to one's children.

Intervention Strategies Alzheimer's disease is incurable. However, much research has been done to find ways to alleviate the cognitive deficits and behavioral problems that characterize the disease.

Much of the recent research has focused on various drugs that could improve memory, although no medication currently available can reverse or cure dementia (Voisin et al., 2005). These drugs include a wide variety of compounds aimed at improving cerebral blood flow or levels of various neurotransmitters. Some drugs, such as tacrine (Cognex), donepezil (Aricept), galantamine (Razadyne), and rivastigmineta (Exelon) have been approved by the U.S. Food and Drug Administration (FDA) for the treatment of Alzheimer's disease. All these drugs have been reported to improve cognitive functioning, although these successes often have been achieved with carefully selected patients on carefully selected tests, and none of the drugs has shown reliable improvements in a wide variety of patients (Mayo Clinic, 2007c). Still, they offer options for treating the cognitive impairments in mild to moderate Alzheimer's disease.

Other medical interventions address some of the hypothesized causes. This work represents a different approach—attacking some of the hypothesized causes of Alzheimer's disease rather than the symptoms. For example, researchers are experimenting with some drugs that address the acetylcholine declines and inhibit the formation of beta-amyloid plaques (Giacobini, 2003). Similarly, nonsteroidal anti-inflammatory drugs (NSAIDs, see Chapter 4) such as ibuprofen have been shown to reduce the risk of Alzheimer's disease and slow disease progression, among other effects in animals (Yan et al., 2003). Drugs that treat the toxic effects of excess copper and zinc may be a promising new avenue for reducing the effects of beta-amyloid (Finefrock et al., 2003). Statins, the most commonly used cholesterol fighting drugs, significantly lower the levels of beta-amyloid in research on animals (Stuve et al.,

2003). Giving agents to people so that they can produce antibodies to beta-amyloid significantly slows the rate of decline in cognitive functioning (Hock et al., 2003).

Another line of research is investigating the effects of memantine (Namenda), a medication that addresses increased levels of plasma homocysteine. Evidence from clinical trials research indicates that memantine is effective in treating mild to severe Alzheimer's disease with few side effects (Bakchine & Loft, 2008). Such results provide hope that a new generation of medical interventions for Alzheimer's disease is in the offing.

Improving behavioral problems manifested by people with Alzheimer's disease is also possible (Howard et al., 2007). Donepezil is effective in reducing agitation, and drugs that are used primarily in younger patients to treat schizophrenia, such as thioridazine and haloperidol, are effective in alleviating the severe psychiatric symptoms that develop during the course of Alzheimer's disease. Similarly, antidepressants are effective in alleviating the depressive symptoms that typically accompany the early stages of the disease, and sedatives may be effective for sleep disturbances. However, these medications should be used with caution, because dosage levels for older adults may be far lower than those for younger patients, and side effects may be much more serious.

Caring for Patients with Dementia at Home
Watching a loved one struggle with Alzheimer's diesease can be both heartrending and uplifting for family members (O'Dell, 2007). Watching a spouse, parent, or sibling go from being an independent, mature adult to not remembering the names of family members is extremely difficult. But the unconditional love shown by family caregivers and the opportunity for family members to develop closer relationships can be quite positive. In this section, we consider some of the key issues regarding caregiving for persons with dementia; we consider caregiving more generally in Chapter 11.

Most people with dementia (as well as other impairments) are cared for by their family members at home (MetLife Mature Market Institute and National Alliance for Caregiving, 2006). Over 23 million households provide an average of 21 hours per week in unpaid care for relatives; this is estimated to be worth well over $300 billion annually. About 60% of caregivers are over age 50 and are working, mostly full time. Roughly 60% of caregivers are women, a number that has been declining due to greater participation of men in providing care for older relatives. Caregivers tend to be of moderate financial means, with many being poor.

One useful way to conceptualize family caregiving is as an unexpected career (Aneshensel et al., 1995). The caregiving career begins with the onset of the illness and moves through a number of separate steps. Note that the process does not end with the placement of the affected family member in a nursing home, or even with that person's death. Rather, Aneshensel et al. (1995) point out that the career continues through the bereavement and social readjustment period, at which point one may continue with life. Note that the kind of caregiving changes, from the comprehensive caregiving, which covers all aspects of the process, to sustained caregiving in the home, to foreshortened caregiving in the nursing home, to withdrawal from caregiving.

Much research has documented that caregivers are at risk for depression (Eisdorfer et al., 2003). It is important that caregivers who show depressive symptoms receive appropriate treatment for it. One effective intervention is family therapy combined with an integrated computer-telephone system that allows family members who cannot physically attend therapy sessions to participate by phone (Eisdorfer et al., 2003). This intervention proved especially effective for Cuban Americans in the study.

Because the majority of people with dementia have Alzheimer's disease, most of the research focuses on caregivers of these patients. However, the discussion in this chapter applies to caregivers of all patients with dementia. Let's consider some behavioral intervention strategies that work.

Effective Behavioral Strategies Many actions can be taken to improve the lives of people with dementia. Key steps to be taken once a diagnosis is made include obtaining accurate information about the disease, involving the patient as much as possible in decisions, identifying the primary caregiver, reassessing the patient's living situation, setting realistic goals, making realistic financial plans, identifying a source of regular medical care, maximizing the patient's opportunity to function at his or her optimal level, making realistic demands of the patient, and using outside services as needed. The goal of these early steps is to build a broad support network of relatives, medical personnel, and service providers that may be needed later. The new responsibilities of family members require changes in daily routines; people adjust to these roles at different rates.

When they find themselves caring for a person with Alzheimer's disease, caregivers must rethink many behaviors and situations that they otherwise take for granted. Dressing, bathing, and grooming become more difficult or even aversive to the affected person. Use of Velcro fasteners, joining the person during a bath or shower, and other such changes may be necessary. Nutritional needs must be monitored, because people with dementia may forget they have just eaten or may forget to eat. Medications must be used with caution. Changes in personality and sexual behavior must be viewed as part of the disease. Sleeplessness can be addressed by establishing consistent bedtimes, giving warm milk or tryptophan before bedtime, and limiting caffeine intake. Wandering is especially troublesome because it is difficult to control; making sure that the affected person has an identification bracelet with the nature of the problem on it and making the house accident-proof are two preventive steps. In severe cases of wandering it may be necessary to use restraints under the direction of a health care professional. Incontinence, which usually occurs late in the disease, is a troubling and embarrassing issue for the person with dementia; use of special undergarments or medications to treat the problem are two options. Incontinence is not necessarily related to Alzheimer's disease; for example, stress

© Photograph courtesy of Stanley-Senior Technologies manufacturer of the WanderGuard® departure alert system. WanderGuard is a registered trademark of Stanley Logistics, Inc.

The WanderGuard device on the woman's wrist keeps people like her with dementia from wandering away and potentially getting lost or injured.

incontinence, which is fairly common among older women, is unrelated to dementia.

Many caregivers need to be taught how to accomplish these tasks. In general, interventions to assist caregivers rarely result in large effects, although such programs typically produce focused improvements in such things as psychological distress (Schulz et al., 2002). Burgio and colleagues (2003) showed that such skills training is effective for European American and African American caregivers, and reduces the number of problem behaviors the caregivers must face from care recipients. Similarly, European American and Latino caregivers both reported significant reductions in depressive symptoms, increased use of adaptive coping, and decreased use of negative coping strategies after training and practice in the use of specific cognitive and behavioral skills

(Gallagher-Thompson et al., 2003). Additionally, home intervention strategies can result in caregivers having more time to themselves and a decrease in the amount of assistance they need from external sources (Nichols et al., 2008).

One of the most difficult issues caregivers face concerns taking things away from the affected person and restricting activity. For example, in many cases the person experiences problems handling finances. It is not uncommon for them to spend hundreds or even thousands of dollars on strange items, to leave the checkbook unbalanced and bills unpaid, and to lose money. Although they can be given some money to keep, someone else must handle the day-to-day accounts. That transition may be traumatic, and the caregiver may be accused of trying to steal money.

Traveling alone is another sticky issue. Families of people with dementia often do not recognize their loved one's deteriorating condition until a calamity occurs during travel. Families should limit solo excursions to places within walking distance; all other trips should be made with at least one family member along. Related to this, driving is often a contentious issue, especially if the person does not recognize his or her limitations. Once it is clear that the patient cannot drive, the family must take whatever steps are necessary. In some cases this entails simply taking the car keys, but in others it becomes necessary to disable the car. Suggesting that the patient could be chauffeured is another alternative. In any case, caregivers may be subjected to various sorts of accusations related to these issues.

How can family members and health care professionals deal with the behavioral and cognitive problems experienced by people with Alzheimer's disease? One successful approach for dealing with difficult behavior is a technique called differential reinforcement of incompatible behavior (DRI) (Burgio et al., 1995; Fisher et al., 2008). In DRI, caregivers reduce the incidence of difficult behavior by rewarding the person with Alzheimer's disease for engaging in appropriate behaviors that cannot be done at the same time as the problem behaviors. For example, a person who throws food during dinner could be rewarded for sitting quietly and eating.

One major advantage of DRI for caregivers is that the technique can be used in the home, and provides a good way to deal with troublesome behaviors (Fisher et al., 2008). Most important, the DRI technique is easily learned, has no side effects, and can be as effective as or more effective than medical treatments (Burgio, 1996).

Numerous effective behavioral and educational interventions have also been developed to address the memory problems in early and middle-stage dementia. *One behavioral intervention involves using an implicit-internal memory intervention called spaced retrieval.* Adapted by Camp and colleagues (Camp, 2001), spaced retrieval involves teaching persons with Alzheimer's disease to remember new information by gradually increasing the time between retrieval attempts. This easy, almost magical technique has been used to teach names of staff members and other information; it holds considerable potential for broad application. Research shows that combining spaced retrieval with additional memory encoding aids helps even more (Kinsella et al., 2007).

In designing interventions for persons with Alzheimer's disease, the guiding principle should be optimizing the person's functioning. Regardless of the level of impairment, attempts should be made to help the person cope as well as possible with the symptoms. The key is helping all persons maintain their dignity as human beings. This can be achieved in some very creative ways, such as adapting the principles of Montessori methods of education to bring older adults with Alzheimer's disease together with preschool children so that they can perform tasks together (Camp et al., 1997; Malone & Camp, 2007). One example of this approach is discussed in the How Do We Know? feature.

Taking care of a person with dementia is usually very stressful for families. As you can imagine, family members who are caring for a parent with dementia while also holding down a job and raising children puts incredible demands on time. Two options available to provide some relief for caregivers are respite care and adult day care.

Respite care is designed to allow family members to get away from the caregiving situation for a time. It

HOW DO WE KNOW?

Training Persons with Dementia to Be Group Activity Leaders

Who were the investigators, and what was the aim of the study? Dementia is marked by progressive and severe cognitive decline. But despite these losses, can people with dementia be trained to be group leaders? Most people might think the answer is "no," but Cameron Camp and Michael Skrajner (2005) decided to find out by using a training technique based on the Montessori method.

How did the investigators measure the topic of interest? The Montessori method is based on self-paced learning and developmentally appropriate activities. As Camp and Skrajner point out, many techniques used in rehabilitation (e.g., task breakdown, guided repetition, moving from simple to complex and concrete to abstract) and in intervention programs with people who have dementia (e.g., use of external cues and implicit memory) are consistent with the Montessori method.

For this study, a program was developed to train group leaders for Memory Bingo (see Camp, 1999a and 1999b, for details about this game). Group leaders had to learn which cards to pick for the game, where the answers were located on the card, where to "discard" the used (but not the winning) cards, and where to put the winning cards. Success in the program was measured by research staff raters, who made ratings of the type and quality of engagement in the task shown by the group leader.

Who were the participants in the study? Camp and Skrajner tested four people who had been diagnosed as probably having dementia who were also residents of a special care unit of a nursing home.

What was the design of the study? The study used a longitudinal design so that Camp and Skrajner could track participants' performance over several weeks.

Were there ethical concerns with the study? Having persons with dementia as research participants raises important issues with informed consent. Because of their serious cognitive impairments, these individuals may not fully understand the procedures. Thus, family members such as a spouse or adult child caregiver are also asked to give informed consent. Additionally, researchers must pay careful attention to participants' emotions; if participants become agitated or frustrated, the training or testing session must be stopped. Camp and Skrajner took all these precautions.

What were the results? Results showed that at least partial adherence to the established game protocols was achieved at a very high rate. Indeed, staff assistance was not required at all for most of the game sessions for any leader. All of the leaders said that they enjoyed their role, and one recruited another resident to become a leader in the next phase of the project.

What did the investigators conclude? It appears that persons with dementia can be taught to be group activity leaders through a procedure based on the Montessori method. This is important as it provides a way for such individuals to become more engaged in an activity and to be more productive.

Although more work is needed to continue refining the technique, applications of the Montessori method offer a promising intervention approach for people with cognitive impairments.

---

can consist of in-home care provided by professionals or temporary placement in a residential facility. In-home care typically is used to allow caregivers to do errands or to have a few hours free, whereas temporary residential placement is usually reserved for a more extended respite, such as a weekend. Research documents that using respite care is a help to caregivers (Roberto & Jarrott, 2008; Zarit & Femia, 2008).

Adult day care provides placement and programing for frail older adults during the day. The goal of adult day care is to delay institutionalization, enhance self-esteem, and encourage socialization (ElderCare.gov, 2005). Adult day care typically provides more intensive intervention than respite care. This option is used most often by adult children who are employed. In general, adult day care is an effective approach for caregivers (Roberto & Jarrott, 2008).

The demand for respite and adult day care far exceeds their availability, making them limited options. An additional problem is that many insurance programs do not pay for these services, making them too expensive for caregivers with limited finances. Clearly, with the increase in numbers of people who have dementia, ways to provide support for assistance to family caregivers must be found.

Other Forms of Dementia. As we have noted, dementia is a family of different diseases. We consider several of them briefly.

Vascular Dementia Until it was discovered that Alzheimer's disease was not rare, most physicians and researchers believed that most cases of dementia resulted from cerebral arteriosclerosis and its consequent restriction of oxygen to the brain. As described in Chapter 3, arteriosclerosis is a family of diseases that, if untreated, may result in heart attacks or strokes. For the present discussion it is the stroke, or cerebrovascular accident (CVA), that concerns us. CVAs (see Chapter 3) result from a disruption of the blood flow, called an infarct, which may be caused by a blockage or hemorrhage.

A large CVA may produce severe cognitive decline, but this loss is almost always limited to specific abilities. This pattern is different from the classic, global deterioration seen in dementia. Numerous small cerebral vascular accidents can result in a disease termed vascular dementia. Vascular dementia may have a sudden onset after a CVA, and its progression is described as stepwise. This is in contrast to the slow onset and gradual progression of Alzheimer's disease. The symptom pattern in vascular dementia is highly variable, especially early in the disease. Again, this is in contrast to the similar cluster of cognitive problems shown by Alzheimer's disease patients. Most people who have vascular dementia have a history of cerebrovascular disease, and typical symptoms include hypertension, specific and extensive alterations on an MRI, and differential impairment on neuropsychological tests (a pattern of scores showing some functions intact and others significantly below average) that assess the ability to establish or maintain a mental set (i.e., the ability to keep focused on a particular task or situation) and visual imagery, with relatively higher scores on tests of delayed recognition memory (Cosentino et al., 2004). Individuals' specific symptom patterns may vary a great deal, depending on which specific areas of the brain are damaged. In some cases, vascular dementia has a much faster course than Alzheimer's disease, resulting in death an average of 2 to 3 years after onset; in others, the disease may progress much more slowly with idiosyncratic symptom patterns.

Parkinson's Disease Parkinson's disease is known primarily for its characteristic motor symptoms: very slow walking, difficulty getting into and out of chairs, and a slow hand tremor. These problems are caused by a deterioration of neurons in the midbrain that produce the neurotransmitter dopamine. Former boxing champion Muhammad Ali and actor Michael J. Fox are some of the more famous individuals who have Parkinson's disease. Parkinson's disease occurs in about 1 in 100 people over age 60, the average age of diagnosis, with less than 10% of cases occurring in people under age 40 (National Parkinson's Foundation, 2007).

Symptoms are treated effectively with several medications (Parkinson's Disease Foundation, 2005); the most popular are levodopa, which raises the functional level of dopamine in the brain; Sinemet® (a combination of levodopa and carbidopa), which gets more levodopa to the brain;

Heavyweight boxing champion Muhammad Ali, along with many other famous people, has Parkinson's disease.

and Stalevo® (a combination of Sinemet® and entacapone), which extends the effective dosage time of Sinemet®. Recent research indicates that a device called a neurostimulator, which acts like a brain pacemaker by regulating brain activity when implanted deep inside the brain, may prove effective in significantly reducing the tremors, shaking, rigidity, stiffness, and walking problems when medications fail (National Institute of Neurological Disorders and Stroke, 2007). For reasons we do not yet understand, roughly 30% to 50% of the time Parkinson's disease also involves severe cognitive impairment and eventually dementia (Schapira & Olanow, 2004).

Huntington's Disease As noted earlier in the discussion of genetic testing, Huntington's disease is an autosomal dominant disorder that usually begins between ages 30 and 45 (Sharon et al., 2007). The disease generally manifests itself through involuntary flicking movements of the arms and legs; the inability to sustain a motor act such as sticking out one's tongue; prominent psychiatric disturbances

such as hallucinations, paranoia, and depression; and clear personality changes, such as swings from apathy to manic behavior.

Cognitive impairments typically do not appear until late in the disease. The onset of these symptoms is very gradual. The course of Huntington's disease is progressive; patients ultimately lose the ability to care for themselves physically and mentally. Walking becomes impossible, swallowing is difficult, and cognitive loss becomes profound. Changes in the brain thought to underlie the behavioral losses include degeneration of the caudate nucleus and the small-cell population, as well as substantial decreases in the neurotransmitters g-aminobutyric acid (GABA) and substance P. As noted earlier, a test is available to determine whether someone has the marker for the Huntington's disease gene.

Alcohol-Related Dementia Chronic alcohol abuse or dependence may result in cognitive decline, ranging from limited forms of amnesia or mild cognitive impairment to dementia (Kapaki, 2006).

The causes of these memory problems include deficiency of nutritional factors (such as B-complex vitamins) that cause Wernicke-Koraskoff's syndrome, and/or other problems such as cerebrovascular disease. However, progressive cognitive impairment can occur in the absence of syndromes such as Wernicke-Korsakoff's, and has been attributed to the direct toxic effect of ethanol on the brain.

One key symptom of alcohol-related dementia is confabulation, in which the person makes up what sounds to be very believable, but completely fictitious, stories that cover the gaps in memory. Other symptoms include personality changes (e.g., frustration, anger, suspicion, and jealousy), loss of problem-solving skills, communication problems (e.g., word-finding difficulty), and disorientation to time and place. Early in the course of the disease, the memory problems may be reduced or reversed if the person stops drinking alcohol, eats a well-balanced diet, and is given vitamin replacements (especially thiamine and vitamin B1). Thiamine, which limits some of the toxic effects of alcohol, is an important supplement for heavy drinkers.

AIDS Dementia Complex AIDS dementia complex (ADC), or HIV-associated encephalopathy, occurs primarily in persons with more advanced HIV infection (National Institute of Neurological Disorders and Stroke, 2008b). The virus does not appear to directly invade nerve cells, but it jeopardizes their health and function. The resulting inflammation may damage the brain and spinal cord and cause symptoms such as confusion and forgetfulness, behavioral changes (e.g., apathy, loss of spontaneity, depression, social withdrawal, and personality changes), severe headaches, progressive weakness, loss of sensation in the arms and legs, and stroke. Cognitive motor impairment or damage to the peripheral nerves is also common. Research has shown that the HIV infection can significantly alter the size of certain brain structures involved in learning and information processing. Symptoms include encephalitis (inflammation of the brain), behavioral changes, and a gradual decline in cognitive function, including trouble with concentration, memory, and attention. Persons with ADC also show progressive slowing of motor function and loss of dexterity and coordination. When left untreated, ADC can be fatal. In the terminal phase of ADC, patients are bedridden, stare vacantly, and have minimal social and cognitive interaction. Because HIV infection is largely preventable, ADC can be reduced through the practice of safe sex.

Concept Checks

1. How does depression in older adults differ from depression in younger adults? How do these differences affect treatment?

2. What are the characteristics of delirium?

3. What are the underlying causes and changes in Alzheimer's disease? What can be done to help patients?

10.4 Other Mental Disorders and Concerns

LEARNING OBJECTIVES

- What are the symptoms of anxiety disorders? How are they treated?
- What are the characteristics of people with psychotic disorders?
- What are the major issues involved with substance abuse?

Daisy forces herself to do her daily routine. She is shaky all the time because she just doesn't feel safe. Her neighborhood is deteriorating, and she is afraid of what the teenagers will do to her. She imagines all sorts of horrible things that they could do to her. Her worst fear is that no one would know. Her heart races when she thinks about it. She rarely goes out now, and she has convinced her son to bring her groceries and other supplies.

Daisy's feelings indicate that people have difficulties for many reasons. She is clearly afraid, which could reflect a realistic assessment of her neighborhood. But her feelings also make her heart race, which is unusual. In this section, we examine three disorders that are receiving increased attention: anxiety disorders, psychotic disorders, and substance abuse.

Anxiety Disorders

Imagine that you are about to give a speech before an audience of 500 people. In the last few minutes before your address, you begin to feel nervous, your heart starts to pound, and your palms get sweaty. (You now have something in common with Daisy's reactions.) These feelings, common even to veteran speakers, are similar to those experienced by people with anxiety disorders: a group of conditions that are based on fear or uneasiness.

Anxiety disorders include problems such as feelings of severe anxiety for no apparent reason, phobias with regard to specific things or places, and obsessive–compulsive disorders, in which thoughts or actions are repeatedly performed (Beck & Averill, 2004; Mohlman et al., 2004). Although anxiety disorders occur in adults of all ages, they are particularly common in older adults due to loss of health, relocation stress, isolation, fear of losing independence, and many other reasons. Anxiety disorders are diagnosed in approximately 17% of older men and 21% of older women (Fitzwater, 2008). The reasons for this gender difference are unknown.

Symptoms and Diagnosis of Anxiety Disorders. Common to all the anxiety disorders are physical changes that interfere with social functioning, personal relationships, or work. These physical changes include dry mouth, sweating, dizziness, upset stomach, diarrhea, insomnia, hyperventilation, chest pain, choking, frequent urination, headaches, and a sensation of a lump in the throat (Beck & Averill, 2004). These symptoms occur in adults of all ages, but they are particularly common in older adults because of loss of health, relocation stress, isolation, fear of losing control over their lives, or guilt resulting from feelings of hostility toward family and friends.

An important issue concerning anxiety disorders in older adults is that anxiety may be an appropriate response to the situation. For example, helplessness anxiety such as Daisy is experiencing is generated by a potential or actual loss of control or mastery (Verwoerdt, 1981). In addition, a series of severe negative life experiences may result in a person's reaching the breaking point and appearing highly anxious. Many older adults who show symptoms of anxiety disorder have underlying health problems that may be responsible for the symptoms. In all cases the anxious behavior should be investigated first as an appropriate response that may not warrant medical intervention. The important point is to evaluate the older adult's behavior in context.

These issues make it difficult to diagnose anxiety disorders, especially in older adults (Beck & Averill, 2004; Fitzwater, 2008; Mohlman et al., 2004). The problem is that there usually is nothing specific that a person can point to as the specific trigger or cause. In addition, anxiety in older adults often accompanies an underlying physical disorder or illness. These secondary causes of anxiety must be disentangled from the anxiety symptoms so that each may be dealt with appropriately. In short, the trick is to distinguish between the "worried" and the well. Wetherell, Le Roux, and Gatz (2003) report that the key features of late-life anxiety disorder are distress and impairment, frequency and uncontrollability of worry, muscle tension, and sleep disturbance.

Treating Anxiety Disorders. Anxiety disorders can be treated with medication and psychotherapy (Beck & Averill, 2004). The most commonly used medications are benzodiazepine (e.g., Valium and Librium), SSRIs (Paxil, among others), buspirone, and beta-blockers. Though moderately effective, these drugs must be monitored very carefully in older adults because the amount needed to treat the disorder is very low and the potential for side effects is great. For older adults, the clear treatment of choice is psychotherapy, especially relaxation therapy (Beck & Averill, 2004). Although benzodiazepines are effective with adults of all ages, they must be used very carefully with older adults.

Effective dosage levels are lower in older adults, and the potential for side effects is much greater. Most important, these drugs can cause decreased cognitive functioning, which may be mistaken for early dementia. In general, the benzodiazepines may cause drowsiness, loss of coordination, headaches, and lower energy levels. Moreover, because of the potential for addiction, the long-term use of these drugs should be avoided.

In most cases the treatment of choice for anxiety disorders is psychotherapy. A broad range of approaches is effective with adults of all ages (Niederehe & Schneider, 1998). These include relaxation training, substituting rational for irrational thoughts, and gradual exposure to images or real situations that generate anxiety. Relaxation therapy is especially effective, is easily learned, and presents a technique that is useful in many situations (e.g., falling asleep at night). The advantage of these psychotherapeutic techniques is that they usually involve only a few sessions, have high rates of success, and offer clients procedures that they can take with them.

Psychotic Disorders

Some forms of psychopathology, called psychoses, involve losing touch with reality and the disintegration of personality. Two behaviors that occur in these disorders are delusions, which are belief systems not based on reality, and hallucinations, which are distortions in perception.

Although the development of psychotic disorders is rare across adulthood, the number of new cases declines with age (Jeste et al., 1995). The behaviors present in psychotic disorders are commonly manifested as secondary problems in other disorders, especially in dementia (Rabins, 1992). Indeed, psychotic symptoms are an important aspect of the diagnosis of some of these other disorders and can be managed in the same way.

Schizophrenia. Schizophrenia is characterized by the severe impairment of thought processes, including the content and style of thinking, distorted perceptions, loss of touch with reality, a distorted sense of self, and abnormal motor behavior (American Psychiatric Association, 1994). People with schizophrenia may show these abnormal behaviors in several ways: loose associations (such as saying that they have a secret meeting with the president of the United States in the local bowling alley), hearing voices that tell them what to do, believing that they can read other people's minds, believing that their body is changing into something else, or sometimes having bizarre delusions (e.g., that they are Jesus or that they are being spied on). In addition, schizophrenic people tend to show very little or highly inappropriate emotionality (laughing hysterically at the news of a major tragedy, for instance). They are often confused about their own identity, have difficulty working toward a goal, and tend to withdraw from social contact.

The second hallmark symptom of schizophrenia is delusions, or well-formed beliefs not based in reality. Most often, these delusions involve persecution ("People are out to get me"). The distinction between paranoid disorders and schizophrenia is fuzzy; indeed, one type of schizophrenia is called paranoid-type schizophrenia. In general, hallucinations, loose associations, and absent or inappropriate emotions do not occur in paranoid disorders (American Psychiatric Association, 1994).

The beliefs underlying delusions can result in anger, resentment, or even violent acts. Because people with psychoses are extremely suspicious and rarely seek help on their own, such people tend to come to the attention of authorities after having repeated run-ins with the police or neighbors, starting legal proceedings against others on mysterious grounds, or registering complaints about fictitious or distorted events.

The onset of schizophrenia occurs most often between ages 16 and 30, and much less often after age 40 (Clare & Giblin, 2008). The symptoms of schizophrenia also differ by age; for example, older adults show less thought disorder and less flattening of their emotions than do younger adults (Clare & Giblin, 2008). Some researchers disagree, however, maintaining that there are few differences with age in the numbers of people who experience schizophrenic symptoms and no differences in the nature of the symptoms. In any case, there is agreement that new cases of schizophrenia are rare in late life.

Psychotherapy has been shown to be as effective with older adults as with younger adults.

Longitudinal research indicates that the natural course of schizophrenia is improvement over the adult life span (Smyer & Qualls, 1999). Studies show that the first 10 years of the disorder are marked by cycles of remission and worsening, but symptoms generally lessen in more than half of people with schizophrenia in later life. This may be caused by a rebalancing of the neurotransmitters dopamine and acetylcholine, which are heavily weighted toward dopamine in younger adults with schizophrenia. Additional rebalancing of other neurotransmitters may also play a role.

Treating Schizophrenia. Traditionally, treatment of schizophrenia has emphasized medication. Drug therapy consists of antipsychotics, medications that are believed to work on the dopamine system (see Chapter 2). Some of the more commonly used antipsychotics are haloperidol (Haldol), chlorpromazine HCl (Thorazine), and thioridazine HCl (Mellaril). These medications must be used with extreme caution in adults of all ages because of the risk of serious toxic side effects, especially the loss of motor control. Despite these risks, antipsychotics often are used in nursing homes and other institutions as tranquilizing agents to control difficult patients.

In general, people with schizophrenia are difficult to treat with psychotherapy. The severe thought disturbances characteristic of schizophrenia make it difficult for therapists to work with such clients. Because of their extreme suspiciousness, paranoid people may be reluctant to cooperate in psychotherapy. However, there is evidence that a comprehensive and integrated social rehabilitation program combined with health care management intervention can be effective (Pratt, Bartels, Mueser, & Forester, 2008). The goals of therapy for such people tend to be adaptive rather than curative, helping these people adapt to daily living.

Substance Abuse

Although you might think that substance abuse is primarily a problem of adolescents and young adults, it's not—older adults also have the problem (National Institute on Alcohol Abuse and Alcoholism, 2008). Because of the differences in the types of substances abused by younger and older adults (younger adults are more likely to abuse illegal drugs than are older adults), alcohol provides the best common basis for comparison.

What constitutes alcoholism? Alcoholism, also known as alcohol dependence, is a disease that includes alcohol craving and continued drinking despite repeated alcohol-related problems, such as losing

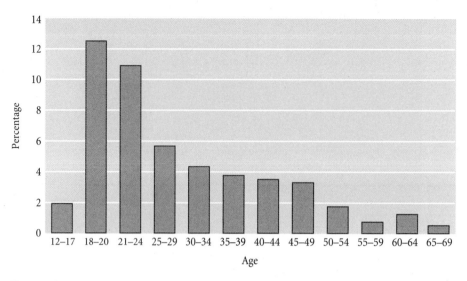

Figure 10.4 Prevalence of past-year DSM-IV alcohol dependence by age in the United States.

Source: NIAAA 2001–2002 National Epidemiological Survey on Alcohol and Related Conditions (NESARC) data (18–60+ years of age) and Substance Abuse and Mental Administration (SAMHSA) 2003 National Survey on Drug Use and Health (NSDUH) (12–17 years of age).

a job or getting into trouble with the law. Alcoholism includes four symptoms: craving, impaired control, physical dependence, and tolerance.

As you can see in Figure 10.4, the prevalence of alcohol dependency drops significantly with age (National Institute on Alcohol Abuse and Alcoholism, 2008). However, when data are examined more closely, there are gender and ethnic group differences in alcohol abuse. For example, the percentages of men who abuse alcohol ranges from about 2 times (ages 18–29) to 6 times (ages 65 and over) higher than those for women. Native Americans have the highest rate of abuse, followed by European Americans, Latinos, African Americans, and Asian Americans (Grant et al., 2004). Two patterns of onset are evident with older people with alcohol dependency: early-onset in young adulthood or middle-age lifelong problem drinking, and late-onset problem drinking (Smyer & Qualls, 1999). Left untreated, alcohol dependency does not improve over time.

Taking a life-span view of alcohol dependence provides insights into important differences in drinking patterns and outcomes (National Institute on Alcohol

Abuse and Alcoholism, 2008). For example, young adults are more likely to binge drink, and consequently are more likely to experience problems such as alcohol poisoning, drunk-driving offenses, and assaults. The earlier drinking begins, especially if it starts in adolescence, the more likely that brain damage occurs and alcohol dependence develops. Young adult drinkers are less likely to feel the effects of alcohol, such as getting sleepy or losing motor coordination, which may result in their drinking more at one time ("binging"). However, young adults' cognitive performance is more impaired. Taken together, these effects create a very dangerous situation—they do not feel the effects as easily, so tend to underestimate the degree to which they are impaired, and are worse at performing complex tasks such as driving, providing an explanation of why drunk driving is more prevalent among young adults.

Middle age is when the effects of continued alcohol dependence that began in young adulthood become evident. Diseases of the liver, pancreas, and various types of cancer and cardiovascular disease may occur. In part due to these health problems, middle-aged adults are the most likely group to seek treatment for their problem.

Drinking among older adults presents a more complicated picture. Even older adults who drink only modest amounts may experience dangerous interactions with medications they may be taking. Additionally, they metabolize alcohol much more slowly, meaning that it remains in the bloodstream longer. As a result, older adults are at higher risk for abusing alcohol if they simply continue habits of drinking from earlier points in their lives, even if their consumption when they were younger was only moderate. Diagnosing alcohol dependence in older women can be especially difficult given the higher likelihood that they live alone.

Treatment for substance abuse in all age groups focuses on three goals (Smyer & Qualls, 1999): stabilization and reduction of substance consumption, treatment of coexisting problems, and arrangement of appropriate social interventions.

Which treatment approach works best depends on the age of the person in question (National Institute on Alcohol Abuse and Alcoholism, 2008). Younger adults tend to respond best to short-term programs tailored specifically to them; traditional programs such as Alcoholics Anonymous are less effective. On college campuses, these programs tend to target high-risk groups (e.g., fraternities, sororities, athletes) and focus on DUI prevention. Middle-aged adults respond to a variety of approaches, but individual differences are quite large, meaning that it may be necessary to try several different treatments. Older adults often respond better to education programs rather than direct confrontation to reduce their denial of their problem and to make sure they understand the age-related changes in alcohol metabolism.

Addressing other problems, such as depression and anxiety, may be effective in helping people use substances more appropriately. Training in self-management techniques to improve coping skills can also help, especially in cases of substance abuse involving pain medications (Dupree & Schonfeld, 1996). Although adults of all age groups can respond to treatment, success rates often are low, and older adults take longer to withdraw from substances than younger adults (Lisansky, Gomberg, & Zucker, 1999). Take the time to complete the Discovering Development feature. Finding out the treatment options in your area may enable you to help a friend; the lack of certain types of treatment options may also surprise you.

SOCIAL POLICY IMPLICATIONS

As we have seen, Alzheimer's disease is a devastating condition, not only to patients, but to those who care for them as well. To the extent we can design effective interventions for caregivers so that they acquire the necessary skills to provide quality care, society would benefit by delaying placement into nursing homes, keeping the costs of care as low as possible, and improving the quality of life.

To achieve these societal benefits, though, we must have solid research evidence that intervention programs work. Pillemer, Suitor, and Wethington (2003) point out that intervention programs need to be firmly based on a close link between theory and research. What is the evidence to date? Schulz and colleagues (2002) took a close look. They found that intervention programs for caregivers were socially effective, in that participants rated them as beneficial, helpful, or valuable. But policymakers look for something more: clinical significance. To date, the evidence on this front is that intervention programs can reduce depressive symptoms, and to a lesser degree anxiety, anger, and hostility. The most impressive clinical effects have been demonstrated for delaying institutionalization. However, quality of life for caregivers tends not to improve in clinically significant ways.

From a social policy perspective, what these results mean is that caregiver intervention programs are better at addressing specific, focused outcomes, such as the number and severity of depressive symptoms or when a patient is admitted to a nursing home, than they are at improving general quality of life. Thus policymakers are more likely to support, through direct appropriation and research funding, programs in these areas. Indeed, the White House Conference on Aging in 2005 had several such recommendations for future policy actions because targeted intervention efforts have the potential to have far-reaching effects for promoting the mental health of caregivers and reducing the costs of care.

Summary

10.1 Mental Health and the Adult Life Course

How are mental health and psychopathology defined?

- Definitions of mental health must reflect appropriate age-related criteria.

- Behaviors must be interpreted in context. Mentally healthy people have positive attitudes, accurate perceptions, environmental mastery, autonomy, personality balance, and personal growth.

What key areas are included in a multidimensional approach to assessment?

- Considering key biological, psychological, sociocultural, and life-cycle factors is essential for accurate diagnosis of mental disorders.

- Diagnostic criteria must reflect age differences in symptomatology.

Why are ethnicity and aging important variables to consider in understanding mental health?

- Little research has been done to examine ethnic differences in the definition of mental health and psychopathology in older adults.

- There is some evidence of different incidence rates across groups.

10.2 Developmental Issues in Assessment and Therapy

What are the key dimensions used for categorizing psychopathology?

- Accurate assessment depends on measuring functioning across a spectrum of areas, including medical, psychological, and social.

What factors influence the assessment of adults?

- Negative and positive biases can influence the accuracy of assessment.
- The environmental conditions under which the assessment is made can influence its accuracy.

How are mental health issues assessed?

- Six assessment techniques are used most: interview, self-report, report by others, psychophysiological assessment, direct observation, and performance-based assessment.

What are some major considerations for therapy across adulthood?

- The two main approaches are medical therapy (usually involving drugs) and psychotherapy.
- With psychotherapy, clinicians must be sensitive to changes in the primary developmental issues faced by adults of different ages.
- Clear criteria have been established for determining "well established" and "probably efficacious" psychotherapies.

10.3 The Big Three: Depression, Delirium, and Dementia

What are the most common characteristics of people with depression? How is depression diagnosed? What causes depression? What is the relation between suicide and age? How is depression treated?

- Depression is the most common mental disorder in adults, but it declines in frequency with age. Gender and ethnic differences in rates have been noted.

- Common features of depression include dysphoria, apathy, self-deprecation, expressionlessness, changes in arousal, withdrawal, and several physical symptoms. In addition, the problems must last at least 2 weeks, not be caused by another disease, and negatively affect daily living. Clear age differences exist in the reporting of symptoms. Some assessment scales are not sensitive to age differences in symptoms.
- Possible biological causes of severe depression are neurotransmitter imbalance, abnormal brain functioning, or physical illness. Loss is the main psychosocial cause of depression. Internal belief systems also are important.
- Three families of drugs (SSRIs, HCAs, and MAO inhibitors), electroconvulsive therapy, and various forms of psychotherapy are all used to treat depression. Older adults benefit most from behavior and cognitive therapies.

What is delirium? How is it assessed and treated?

- Delirium is characterized by a disturbance of consciousness and a change in cognition that develop over a short period of time.
- Delirium can be caused by a number of medical conditions, medication side effects, substance intoxication or withdrawal, exposure to toxins, or any combination of factors. Older adults are especially susceptible to delirium.
- Most cases of delirium are cured, but some may be fatal.

What is dementia? What are the major symptoms of Alzheimer's disease? How is it diagnosed? What causes it? What intervention options are there? What are some other major forms of dementia? What do family members caring for patients with dementia experience?

- Dementia is a family of disorders. Most older adults do not have dementia, but rates increase significantly with age.
- Alzheimer's disease is a progressive, fatal disease that is diagnosed at autopsy through neurological changes that include neurofibrillary tangles and neuritic plaques.

- Major symptoms of Alzheimer's disease include gradual and eventually pervasive memory loss, emotional changes, and eventual loss of motor functions.

- Diagnosis of Alzheimer's disease consists of ruling out all other possible causes of the symptoms. This involves thorough physical, neurological, and neuropsychological exams.

- Current research suggests that Alzheimer's disease may be genetic, perhaps with an autosomal dominant inheritance pattern, although other hypotheses have been proposed.

- Although no cure for Alzheimer's disease is available, interventions to relieve symptoms are advisable and possible, including various drug and behavioral interventions. Dealing with declining functioning is especially difficult. Respite and adult day care are two options for caregivers.

- Vascular dementia is caused by several small strokes. Changes in behavior depend on where in the brain the strokes occur.

- Characteristic symptoms of Parkinson's disease include tremor and problems with walking. Treatment is done with drugs. Some people with Parkinson's disease develop dementia.

- Huntington's disease is a genetic disorder that usually begins in middle age with motor and behavioral problems.

- Alcoholic dementia (Wernicke-Korsakoff syndrome) is caused by a thiamine deficiency.

- AIDS dementia complex results from a by-product of HIV. Symptoms include a range of cognitive and motor impairments.

10.4 Other Mental Disorders and Concerns

What are the symptoms of anxiety disorders? How are they treated?

- Anxiety disorders include panic, phobia, and obsessive–compulsive problems. Symptoms include a variety of physical changes that interfere with normal functioning. Context is important in understanding symptoms. Both drugs and psychotherapy are used to treat anxiety disorders.

What are the characteristics of people with psychotic disorders?

- Psychotic disorders involve personality disintegration and loss of touch with reality. One major form is schizophrenia; hallucinations and delusions are the primary symptoms.

- Schizophrenia is a severe thought disorder with an onset usually before age 45, but it can begin in late life. People with early-onset schizophrenia often improve over time as neurotransmitters become more balanced. Treatment usually consists of drugs; psychotherapy alone is not often effective.

What are the major issues involved with substance abuse?

- With the exception of alcohol, the substances most likely to be abused vary with age; younger adults are more likely to abuse illicit substances, whereas older adults are more likely to abuse prescription and over-the-counter medications.

- Alcohol dependency declines with age from its highest rates in young adulthood. Older adults take longer to withdraw, but similar therapies are effective in all age groups.

Review Questions

10.1 Mental Health and the Adult Life Course

- How do definitions of mental health vary with age?
- What are the implications of adopting a multidimensional model for interpreting and diagnosing mental disorders?
- Why are ethnicity and gender important considerations in understanding mental health?

10.2 Developmental Issues in Assessment and Therapy

- What is multidimensional assessment? How is it done?
- What major factors affect the accuracy of clinical assessment?
- How do the developmental forces influence assessment?
- What are the main developmental issues clinicians must consider in selecting therapy?

10.3 The Big Three: Depression, Delirium, and Dementia

- How does the rate of depression vary with age, gender, and ethnicity?
- What symptoms are associated with depression? How do they vary with age?
- What biological causes of depression have been proposed? How are they related to therapy?
- How is loss associated with depression?
- What treatments for depression have been developed? How well do they work with older adults?
- What is delirium? What causes it? Why are older adults more susceptible?
- What is Alzheimer's disease? How is it diagnosed?
- What causes Alzheimer's disease? What interventions are available?
- What other types of dementia have been identified? What are their characteristics?

10.4 Other Mental Disorders and Concerns

- What symptoms are associated with anxiety disorders? How are anxiety disorders treated?
- What are psychoses? What are their major symptoms? What treatments are most effective for schizophrenia?
- What developmental differences have been noted regarding substance abuse? How is alcohol dependency defined?

Integrating Concepts in Development

1. Why is it so difficult to diagnose mental disorders in older adults? What concepts from Chapters 3 and 4 provide major reasons?
2. Why do you think people with Alzheimer's disease might experience hallucinations and delusions?
3. Why is there a connection between depression and dementia?
4. What would studying people with Alzheimer's disease tell us about normal memory changes with age?

Key Terms

Alzheimer's disease An irreversible form of dementia characterized by progressive declines in cognitive and bodily functions, eventually resulting in death; it accounts for about 70% of all cases of dementia.

behavior therapy A type of psychotherapy that focuses on and attempts to alter current behavior. Underlying causes of the problem may not be addressed.

beta-amyloid A type of protein involved in the formation of neuritic plaques both in normal aging and in Alzheimer's disease.

cognitive therapy A type of psychotherapy aimed at altering the way people think as a cure for some forms of psychopathology, especially depression.

delirium A disorder characterized by a disturbance of consciousness and a change in cognition that develop over a short period of time.

dementia A family of diseases characterized by cognitive decline. Alzheimer's disease is the most common form.

dysphoria Feeling down or blue, marked by extreme sadness; the major symptom of depression.

mental status exam A short screening test that assesses mental competence, usually used as a brief indicator of dementia or other serious cognitive impairment.

spaced retrieval A behavioral, implicit-internal memory intervention used in early- and middle-stage dementia.

sundowning The phenomenon in which people with Alzheimer's disease show an increase in symptoms later in the day.

vascular dementia A form of dementia caused by a series of small strokes.

Resources

www.cengage.com/psychology/cavanaugh

Visit the companion website, where you will find tutorial quizzes, glossary, flashcards, and more. You can also access the following websites from the companion website.

The Alzheimer's Association website has a wide range of information on the disease, including current research information, tips for caregivers, and links to local chapters.

The National Institute on Alcohol Abuse and Alcoholism website provides many useful summaries, data, and links to other good websites.

The National Institute of Mental Health has several useful sites regarding mental health in adults, and the National Institute on Aging has good sites specific to older adults. Both have helpful links to other organizations.

Readings

Mace, N. L., & Rabins, P. V. (2006). *The 36-hour day: A family guide to caring for people with Alzheimer's disease, other dementias, and memory loss in later life* (4th ed.). Baltimore: Johns Hopkins University Press. Still the best guidebook to caregiving for people with various forms of memory impairment. Easy reading.

Thompson, T. (1996). *The beast: A journey through depression.* New York: Penguin. A moving firsthand account of living with depression. Easy reading.

Whitehouse, P. J., & George, D. (2008). *The myth of Alzheimer's: What you aren't being told about today's most dreaded diagnosis.* New York: St. Martin's Press. Co-authored by one of the world's leading experts on Alzheimer's disease, this book challenges traditional views. Easy reading.

Zarit, S. H., & Zarit, J. M. (2006). *Mental disorders in older adults* (2nd ed.). New York: Guilford. A comprehensive overview of mental health issues in older adults. Easy to moderate difficulty.

11

Relationships

BARACK AND MICHELLE OBAMA
ARE, BY NEARLY EVERY MEASURE,
A VERY SUCCESSFUL COUPLE.

Elected president at age 47, Barack Obama
was supported by his wife, Michelle, who herself was a very successful professional. Their
relationship provides them the grounding
necessary to support each other. Neither of
them could have achieved what they did
without the help of many friends.

Barack's and Michelle's experiences
reflect some of the key aspects of
relationships we examine in this chapter.
First, we consider friendships and love
relationships and how they change across
adulthood. Because love relationships usually involve a couple, we will explore how two people
find each other and marry and how marriages develop. We also consider singlehood, divorce,
remarriage, and widowhood. Finally, we take up some of the important roles associated with personal
relationships, including parenting, family roles, and grandparenting.

© Ron Sachs-Pool / Getty Images

11.1 Relationship Types and Issues

LEARNING OBJECTIVES
- What role do friends play across adulthood?
- What characterizes love relationships? How do they vary across cultures?
- What are abusive relationships? What characterizes elder abuse, neglect, and exploitation?

Jamal and Kahlid have known each other all their lives. They grew up together in New York, attended the same schools, and even married sisters. Their business careers took them in different directions, but they and their families always got together on major holidays. Now as older men, they feel a special bond; many of their other friends have died.

Jamal and Kahlid remind us that some of the most important people in our lives are our friends. They are often the people to whom we are closest, and are there when we need someone to lean on. Sometimes friendships turn into something more. Love blossoms, and relationships become more intimate and intense. In this section, we examine friendships and love relationships in adulthood and see why and how they are central to our lives.

Friendships

What is an adult friend? Someone who is there when you need to share? Someone not afraid to tell you the truth? Someone to have fun with? Friends, of course, are all of these and more. Researchers define friendship as a mutual relationship in which those involved influence one another's behaviors and beliefs, and define friendship quality as the satisfaction derived from the relationship (Flynn, 2007).

Friends are a source of support throughout adulthood (Arnett, 2007). Friendships are pre-dominantly based on feelings and are grounded in reciprocity and choice. Friendships are different from love relationships in that they are less emo-tionally intense and involve less sexual energy or contact (Rose & Zand, 2000). Having good friendships helps boost self-esteem (Bagwell et al., 2005). Friendships also help us become socialized into new roles throughout adulthood.

Friendship in Adulthood. From a developmental perspective, adult friendships can be viewed as having identifiable stages (Levinger, 1980, 1983): Acquaintanceship, Buildup, Continuation, Deterioration, and Ending. This ABCDE model describes not only the stages of friendships but also the processes by which they change. For example, whether a friendship will develop from Acquaintanceship to Buildup depends on where the individuals fall on several dimensions, such as the basis of the attraction, what each person knows about the other, how good the communication is between the partners, the perceived importance of the friendship, and so on. Although many friendships reach the Deterioration stage, whether a friendship ultimately ends depends heavily on the availability of alternative relationships. If new potential friends appear, old friendships may end; if not, they may continue even though they may no longer be considered important by either person.

Longitudinal research shows how friendships change across adulthood, sometimes in ways that are predictable and sometimes not. For example, as you probably have experienced, life transitions (e.g., going away to college, getting married) usually result in fewer friends and less contact with the friends you keep (Flynn, 2007). People tend to have more friends and acquaintances during young adulthood than at any subsequent period (Sherman, de Vries, & Lansford, 2000). Friendships are important throughout adulthood, in part because a person's life satisfaction is strongly related to the quantity and quality of contacts with friends. College students who have strong friendship networks adjust better to stressful life events (Brissette, Scheier, & Carver, 2002) and have better self-esteem (Bagwell et al., 2005).

The importance of maintaining contacts with friends cuts across ethnic lines as well. Additionally, people who have friendships that cross ethnic groups have more positive attitudes toward people with different backgrounds (Aberson, Shoemaker, & Tomolillo, 2004). Thus, regardless of one's background, friendships play a major role in determining how much we enjoy life.

The quality of late-life friendships is particularly important (Rawlins, 2004). Having at least one very close friend or confidant provides a buffer against the losses of roles and status that accompany old age, such as retirement or the death of a loved one, and can increase people's happiness and self-esteem (Rawlins, 2004; Sherman, de Vries, & Lansford, 2000). Patterns of friendship among older adults tend to mirror those in young adulthood (Rawlins, 2004). That is, older women have more numerous and more intimate friendships than older men do. As noted previously, these differences help explain why women are in a better position to deal with the stresses of life. Men's friendships, like women's, evolve over time and become important sources of support in late life (Adams & Ueno, 2006).

Researchers have uncovered three broad themes that underlie adult friendships (de Vries, 1996):

- The most frequently mentioned dimension represents the *affective* or emotional basis of friendship. This dimension refers to self-disclosure and expressions of intimacy, appreciation, affection, and support, all of which are based on trust, loyalty, and commitment.
- A second theme reflects the *shared or communal* nature of friendship, in which friends participate in or support activities of mutual interest.
- The third dimension represents *sociability and compatibility;* our friends keep us entertained and are sources of amusement, fun, and recreation.

These three dimensions are found in friendships among adults of all ages (de Vries, 1996). They characterize both traditional (e.g., face-to-face) and new forms (e.g., online) of friendships (Ridings & Gefen, 2004).

In the case of online friendships, trust develops on the basis of four sources: (1) reputation, whether grounded in an anonymous avatar or screen name or in the person's actual offline identity; (2) performance, or what users do online, due to the scope for enhanced performance in online communication, especially in simulated environments; (3) precommitment, through personal self-disclosure, which in turn encourages a "leap of faith" and reciprocal self-disclosure; and (4) situational factors, especially the premium placed on intimacy and the relationship in contemporary societies (Henderson & Gilding, 2004). Online environments are more conducive to people who are lonely, providing an opportunity to meet others in an initially more anonymous interaction in which social interaction and intimacy levels can be carefully controlled (Morahan-Martin & Schumacher, 2003). This relative anonymity provides a supportive context for the subsequent development of friendships online.

Perceptions of friendship vary. What it takes for one person to call someone a "friend" may not be what it takes for another. Surprisingly little research has examined the role of people's definitions of friendship, especially in comparing definitions across cultures. Adams and colleagues' (2000) study comparing older adults' definitions of friendship in Greensboro, North Carolina, and Vancouver, British Columbia, Canada, is one of the best. They found that psychological and sociocultural forces result in marked differences in how people define friendship. In Vancouver, people based their definitions mostly on the affective (feeling) and cognitive processes of friendship (what they think about relationships), whereas in Greensboro people relied more on behavioral, relational quality (what they actually do for others) and being like themselves (solidarity and homogeneity) aspects. Life-cycle forces also played a role, in that middle-aged and young–old participants in both cities were less likely than middle–old and old–old participants to use relational quality and solidarity and homogeneity as part of their definitions. So although people around the world all have friendships, how they define them differs.

One special type of friendship exists with one's siblings. Although little research has focused on the development and maintenance of sibling friendships across adulthood, we know that sibling relationships play an important role in young adulthood (Schulte, 2006) and that the importance of these relationships varies with age. As you can see in Figure 11.1, women place more importance on sibling ties across adulthood than do men; however, for both the strength of these ties is greatest in

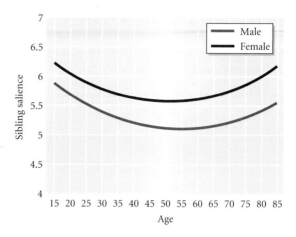

Figure 11.1 Strength of sibling ties across adulthood.

Source: From Schmeeckle, M., Giarusso, R., & Wang, Q. (1998, November). *When being a brother or sister is important to one's identity: Life stage and gender differences.* Paper presented at the annual meeting of the Gerontological Society, Philadelphia.

adolescence and late life (Schmeeckle, Giarusso, & Wang, 1998).

Developmental Aspects of Friendships and Socio e-motional Selectivity. Why are friends so important to older adults? Some researchers believe that one reason may be older adults' concerns about becoming burdens to their families (Roberto & Scott, 1986). As a result, they help their friends foster independence. This reciprocity is a crucial aspect of friendship in later life because it allows the paying back of indebtedness over time. Also important is that friends are fun for people of all ages (Cavanaugh, 1999b).

Older adults tend to have fewer relationships with people in general and to develop fewer new relationships than people do in midlife and particularly in young adulthood (Carstensen, Isaacowitz, & Charles, 1999). For many years, researchers tended to view this phenomenon as merely a reflection of the loss of relationships in late life through death and other means. However, Carstensen and colleagues (Carstensen et al., 1999; Carstensen, Mikels, & Mather, 2006) have shown that the changes in social behavior seen in late life reflect a much more complicated and important process. They propose a life-span theory of **socioemotional selectivity**, *which argues that social contact is motivated by a variety of goals, including information seeking, self-concept, and emotional regulation.*

Each of these goals is differentially salient at different points of the adult life span and results in very different social behaviors. For example, when information seeking is the goal, such as when a person is exploring the world, trying to figure out how he or she fits, what others are like, and so forth, meeting many new people is an essential part of the process. However, when emotional regulation is the goal, people tend to become highly selective in their choice of social partners and nearly always prefer people who are familiar to them.

Carstensen and colleagues (Carstensen et al., 1999, 2006) believe that information seeking is the predominant goal for young adults, that emotional regulation is the major goal for older people, and that both goals are in balance in midlife. Their research supports this view; people become increasingly selective in whom they choose to have contact with. Additionally, Magai (2008) summarizes several approaches to emotional development across adulthood and concludes that people orient more toward emotional aspects of life and personal relationships as they grow older and that emotional expression and experience become more complex and nuanced. Carstensen's theory provides a more complete explanation of why older adults tend not to replace, to any great extent, the relationships they lose: Older adults are more selective and have fewer opportunities to make new friends, especially in view of the emotional bonds involved in friendships.

With time, older adults begin to lose members of their friendship network, usually through death. Rook (2000) proposes that older adults compensate for this loss through three strategies: forming new ties, redefining the need for friends, or developing alternative nonsocial activities. Although not always successful, these strategies reflect the need to address an important loss in people's lives.

Men's, Women's, and Cross-Sex Friendships. Men's and women's friendships tend to differ in adulthood, reflecting continuity in the learned behaviors from childhood (Fehr, 1996; Sherman et al., 2000). Women tend to base their friendships on more intimate and emotional sharing and use friendship as a means to confide in others. For women, getting together with friends often takes the form of getting together to discuss personal matters. Confiding in others is a basis of women's friendships. In contrast, men tend to base friendships on shared activities or interests. They are more likely to go bowling or fishing or to talk sports with their friends. For men, confiding in others is inconsistent with the need to compete; this may be one reason men are reluctant to do so (Cutrona, 1996). Rather, competition often is a part of men's friendships, as evidenced in basketball games with friends. However, the competition usually is set up so that the social interaction is the most important element, not who wins or loses (Rawlins, 1992). Men's friendships usually are less intimate than women's, no matter how one defines intimacy (Fehr, 1996).

Women tend to have more close relationships than do men. Although you may think this puts women at an advantage, research shows that this is not always the case. Sometimes friends can get on people's nerves or make high demands. When these things happen, women tend to be less happy even when they have lots of friends (Antonucci, Akiyama, & Lansford, 1998).

Why are women's friendships typically more intimate than men's? Compared to men, women have much more experience with such intimate sharing from early childhood, and they are more comfortable with vulnerability. Social pressure on men to be brave and strong may actually inhibit their ability to form close friendships (Rawlins, 1992).

What about friendships between men and women? These friendships have a beneficial effect, especially for men (Piquet, 2007). Cross-sex friendships tend to help men have lower levels of dating anxiety and to have higher capacity for intimacy. Interestingly, such benefits are not found clearly for women. These patterns hold across ethnic groups, too. But cross-sex friendships also can prove troublesome due to misperceptions. For example, some research shows that men tend to overperceive and women tend to underperceive their friends' sexual interest in them (Koenig, Kirkpatrick, & Ketelaar, 2007). Maintaining cross-sex friendships once individuals enter into exclusive dating relationships, marriage, or committed relationships is very difficult, and often results in one partner feeling jealous (Williams, 2005).

Love Relationships

Love is one of those things everybody feels but nobody can define completely. (Test yourself: Can you explain fully what you mean when you look at someone special and say, "I love you"?) One way researchers have tried to understand love is to think about what components are essential. In an interesting series of studies, Sternberg (2006) found that love has three basic components: (1) *passion*, an intense physiological desire for someone; (2) *intimacy*, the feeling that one can share all one's thoughts and actions with another; and (3) *commitment*, the willingness to stay with a person through good and bad times. Ideally, a true love relationship has all three components; when couples have equivalent amounts of love and types of love, they tend to be happier. As we will see next, the balance among these components often shifts as time passes.

Love through Adulthood. The different combinations of love can be used to understand how relationships develop (Sternberg, 2006). Research shows that the development of romantic relationships is a complex process influenced by relationships in childhood and adolescence (Collins & van Dulmen, 2006). Early in a romantic relationship, passion is usually high, but intimacy and commitment tend to be low. This is infatuation: an intense, physically based relationship in which the two people have a high risk of misunderstanding and jealousy.

But infatuation is short-lived. Whereas even the smallest touch is enough to drive each partner into wild, lustful ecstasy in the beginning, with time it takes more and more effort to get the same level of feeling. As passion fades, either a relationship acquires emotional intimacy or it is likely to end. Trust, honesty, openness, and acceptance must be a part of any strong relationship; when they are present, romantic love develops.

Although it may not be the stuff of romance novels, this pattern is a good thing. Research shows that people who select a partner for a more permanent relationship (e.g., marriage) during the height of infatuation are likely to support the idea that "love is blind," and those couples are more likely to divorce (Hansen, 2006). But if the couple gives it more time and works at their relationship, they may become committed to each other. By spending much of their time together, making decisions together, caring for each other, sharing possessions, and developing ways to settle conflicts, they up the chances that the relationship will last. Such couples usually show outward signs of commitment, such as wearing a lover's ring, having children together, or simply sharing the mundane details of daily life, from making toast at breakfast to before-bed rituals.

Lemieux and Hale (2002) demonstrated that these developmental trends hold in romantically involved couples between 17 and 75 years of age. As the length of the relationship increases, intimacy and passion decrease, but commitment increases.

Falling in Love. Everybody wants to be loved by somebody, but actually having it happen is fraught with difficulties. In his book, The Prophet, Kahlil Gibran points out that love is two-sided: Just as it can give you great ecstasy, so can it cause you great pain. Yet most of us are willing to take the risk.

As you may have experienced, taking the risk is fun (at times) and difficult (at other times). Making a connection can be ritualized, as when people use pickup lines in a bar, or it can happen almost by accident, as when two people literally run into each other in a crowded corridor. The question that confronts us is "How do people fall in love?" Do birds of a feather flock together? Or do opposites attract?

The best explanation of the process is the theory of assortative mating, *which states that people find partners based on their similarity to each other.* Assortative mating occurs along many dimensions, including religious beliefs, physical traits, age, socioeconomic status, intelligence, and political ideology, among others (Sher, 1996). Such nonrandom mating occurs most often in Western societies, which allow people to have more control over their own dating and pairing behaviors. Common activities are one basis for identifying potential mates.

Does commonality tend to result in happier relationships? The research findings are mixed. Jenkins (2007) found that couples higher in marital satisfaction were similar in terms of their openness to experience, but not on other aspects of personality. However, a study of 12,000 Dutch couples showed that healthy people tended to be in relationships with other healthy people, and that unhealthy people tended to be in relationships with unhealthy people; these results may have been due to couples' similar levels of education, which were related to shared circumstances (Monden, 2007).

People meet people in all sorts of places. Does where people meet influence the likelihood that they will "click" on particular dimensions and will form a couple? Kalmijn and Flap (2001) found that it did. Using data from more than 1,500 couples, they found that meeting at school was most likely to result in the most forms of homogamy, *or the degree to which people share similar values and interests.* Although meeting through other methods (being from the same neighborhood or through family networks) could promote homogamy, the odds were that these methods did not promote most forms of homogamy other than religious. Not surprisingly, the pool of available people to meet is strongly shaped by the opportunities available, which in turn constrain the type of people one is likely to meet.

The advent of online dating provides a way for adults who have social or dating anxiety to still meet people (Stevens & Morris, 2007). Emerging research indicates that virtual dating sites offer both problems and possibilities. On the one hand, researchers note that the content of member profiles may be suspect (Small, 2004). On the other hand, many couples have met and formed committed relationships mediated through online sites (Mazzarella, 2007).

Once people have met someone compatible, what happens next? Some researchers believe that couples progress in stages. According to Murstein's (1987) classic theory, people apply three filters, representing discrete stages, when they meet someone:

- *Stimulus:* Do the person's physical appearance, social class, and manners match your own?
- *Values:* Do the person's values regarding sex, religion, politics, and so on match your own?
- *Role:* Do the person's ideas about the relationship, communication style, gender roles, and so on match your own?

If the answer to all three filters is "yes," then you are likely to form a couple.

It also turns out that whether a couple find each other physically attractive is more important in love relationships than most people realize. Research shows that women tend to choose a more masculine looking man as a person with whom to have an exciting short-term relationship but tend to select more feminine looking men as better options for being their husband or as the type of man their parents would want them to date (Kruger, 2006). These findings support a study of nearly 2,000 Spanish respondents showing that physical attractiveness was important in sporadic relationships, but it also influences the way in which people fall in love and is linked to feelings and thoughts associated with love (intimacy, passion, commitment) and to satisfaction with the relationship (Sangrador & Yela, 2000).

How do these couple forming behaviors compare cross-culturally? A few studies have examined the factors that attract people to each other in different cultures. In one now-classic study, Buss and a large team of researchers (1990) identified the effects of

Physical attraction is a major component in the development of love relationships.

culture and gender on heterosexual mate preferences in 37 cultures worldwide. Men and women in each culture displayed unique orderings of their preferences concerning the ideal characteristics of a mate. When all of the orderings and preferences were compared, two main dimensions emerged.

In the first main dimension, the characteristics of a desirable mate changed because of cultural values—that is, whether the respondents' country has more traditional values or Western-industrial values. In traditional cultures, men place a high value on a woman's chastity, desire for home and children, and being a good cook and housekeeper; women place a high value on a man's ambition and industry, being a good financial prospect, and holding favorable social status. China, India, Iran, and Nigeria represent the traditional end of this dimension. In contrast, people in Western-industrial cultures value these qualities to a much lesser extent. The Netherlands, Great Britain, Finland, and Sweden represent this end of the dimension; people in these countries place more value on Western ideals.

The second main dimension reflects the relative importance of education, intelligence, and social refinement, as opposed to a pleasing disposition, in choosing a mate. People in Spain, Colombia, and Greece, for example, highly value education, intelligence, and social refinement; in contrast, people in Indonesia place a greater emphasis on having a pleasing disposition. Note that this dimension emphasizes the same traits for both men and women.

Chastity proved to be the characteristic showing the most variability across cultures, being highly desired in some cultures but mattering little in others. Interestingly, in their respective search for mates, men around the world value physical attractiveness in women, whereas women around the world look for men capable of being good providers. But men and women around the world agree that love and mutual attraction are most important, and nearly all cultures rate dependability, emotional stability, kindness, and understanding as important factors. Attraction, it seems, has some characteristics that transcend culture.

Overall, Buss and his colleagues concluded that mate selection is a complex process no matter where you live. However, each culture has a describable set of high-priority traits that men and women look for in the perfect mate. The study also shows that socialization within a culture plays a key role in being attractive to the opposite sex; characteristics that are highly desirable in one culture may not be so desirable in another.

In the How Do We Know? feature, Schmitt and his team of colleagues (2004) had 17,804 participants from 62 cultural regions complete the Relationship Questionnaire (RQ), a self-report measure of adult romantic attachment. They showed that secure romantic attachment was the norm in nearly 80% of cultures and that preoccupied romantic attachment was particularly common in East Asian cultures. In general, what these large multicultural studies show is that there are global patterns in mate selection and romantic relationships. The romantic attachment profiles of individual nations were correlated with sociocultural indicators in ways that supported evolutionary theories of romantic attachment and basic human mating strategies.

The power of culture in shaping mate selection choices must not be underestimated. For example, despite decades of sociopolitical change in China (the socialist transformation in the 1950s, the Cultural Revolution in the 1960s, and the economic reforms in the 1990s), research indicates that the same status hierarchy norms govern mating patterns in urban China (Xu, Ji, & Tung, 2000). Clearly, cultural norms are sometimes very resistant to change. Arranged marriages are a major way some cultures ensure an appropriate match on key dimensions. For example, loyalty of the individual to the family is a very important value in India; consequently, many marriages are carefully arranged to avoid selecting inappropriate mates. Data show that this approach appears to work; among urban professionals polled in one study, 81% said their marriages had been arranged, and 94% of them rated their marriage as "very successful" (Lakshmanan, 1997). Similarly, Islamic societies use matchmaking as a way to preserve family consistency and

Patterns and Universals of Romantic
Attachment Around the World

Who were the investigators and what was the aim of the study? One's attachment style may have a major influence on how one forms romantic relationships. In order to test this hypothesis, David Schmitt assembled a large international team of researchers.

How did the investigators measure the topic of interest? Great care was taken to ensure equivalent translation of the survey across the 62 cultural regions included. The survey was a two-dimension four-category measure of adult romantic attachment (the Relationship Questionnaire) that measured models of self and others relative to each other: secure romantic attachment (high scores indicate positive models of self and others), dismissing romantic attachment (high scores indicate a positive model of self and a negative model of others), preoccupied romantic attachment (high scores indicate a negative model of self and a positive model of others), and fearful romantic attachment (high scores indicate negative models of self and others). An overall score of model of self is computed by adding together the secure and dismissing scores and subtracting the combination of preoccupied and fearful

scores. The overall model of others score is computed by adding together the secure and preoccupied scores and subtracting the combination of dismissing and fearful scores.

Additionally, there were measures of self-esteem, personality traits, and sociocultural correlates of romantic attachment (e.g., fertility rate, national profiles of individualism versus collectivism).

Who were the participants in the study? A total of 17,804 people (7,432 men and 10,372 women) from 62 cultural regions around the world took part in the study. Such large and diverse samples are unusual in developmental research.

What was the design of the study? Data for this cross-sectional, nonexperimental study were gathered by research teams in each country. The principal researchers asked the research collaborators to administer a nine-page survey to the participants that took 20 minutes to complete.

Were there ethical concerns with the study? Because the study involved volunteers, there were no ethical concerns. However, ensuring that all participants' rights were protected was a challenge

because of the number of countries and cultures involved.

What were the results? The researchers first demonstrated that the model of self and others measures were valid across cultural regions, which provided general support for the independence of measures (i.e., they measure different things). Specific analyses showed that 79% of the cultural groups studied demonstrated secure romantic attachments, but that North American cultures tended to be dismissive and East Asian cultures tended to be high on preoccupied romantic attachment. These patterns are shown in Figure 11.2. Note that all the cultural regions except East Asia showed the pattern of model of self scores higher than model of others scores.

What have the investigators concluded? Overall, Schmitt and colleagues concluded that although the same attachment pattern holds across most cultures, no one pattern holds across all of them. East Asian cultures in particular tend to fit a pattern in which people report that others do not get as emotionally close as the respondent would like, and that respondents find it difficult to trust others or to depend on them.

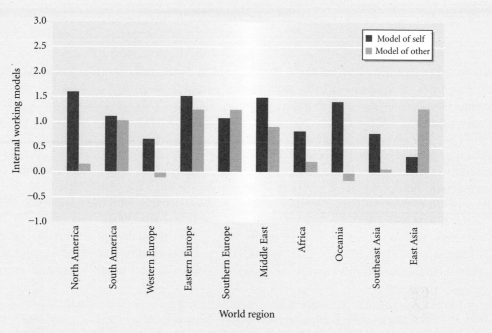

FIGURE 11.2 In research across 10 global regions, note that only in East Asian cultures were the "model of others" scores higher than the "model of self" scores.

Source: Data from Schmitt et al. (2004).

continuity, and to ensure that couples follow the prohibition on premarital relationships between men and women (Adler, 2001). Matchmaking in these societies occurs through both family connections and personal advertisements in newspapers.

Violence in Relationships

Up to this point, we have been considering relationships that are healthy and positive. Sadly, this is not always the case. *Sometimes relationships become violent; one person becomes aggressive toward the partner, creating an* abusive relationship. Such relationships have received increasing attention since the early 1980s, when the U.S. criminal justice system ruled that, under some circumstances, abusive relationships can be used as an explanation for one's behavior (Walker, 1984). *For example,* battered woman syndrome *occurs when a woman believes that she cannot leave the abusive situation and may even go so far as to kill her abuser.*

Many college students report experiencing abuse in a dating relationship; one study found 7% reported physical abuse and 36% reported emotional abuse from their partner (Knox, Custis, & Zusman, 2000). Although overall national rates of sexual assault have been declining since the early 1990s, acquaintance rape or date rape is experienced by roughly 1 in 4 college women (Rape, Abuse, and Incest National Network, 2005). Overall, the Family Violence Prevention Fund (2008) points out that between roughly 1 million and 3 million women in the United States are the victims of partner abuse each year; worldwide, at least one in every three women has been beaten, forced to have sexual relations, or otherwise abused during her lifetime. The Feminist Majority Foundation (2008) reports other key findings. Roughly 40% to 50% of women who experience physical abuse are injured during an attack. Women who are separated or divorced from their partners are most vulnerable to physical abuse. Latina women are least likely to be physically abused in all age groups.

Based on considerable research on abusive partners, O'Leary (1993) argues that there is a continuum of aggressive behaviors toward a partner, which progresses as follows: verbally aggressive behaviors, physically aggressive behaviors, severe physically aggressive behaviors, and murder (see Figure 11.3). The causes of the abuse also vary with the type of abusive behavior being expressed. Although anger and hostility in the perpetrator are associated with various forms of physical abuse, the exact nature of this relationship remains elusive (Norlander & Eckhardt, 2005).

Women are not as violent as men in heterosexual relationships (e.g., Johnson, 2001), and this distinction holds across various types of offenders

(Graham-Kevan & Archer, 2003). Within this context, however, a study of New Zealand inmates revealed that both men and women showed similar patterns of violent attitudes and histories including being more hostile, holding traditional gendered beliefs, and lacking communication and anger management skills (Robertson & Murachver, 2007). Research on violence in gay and lesbian relationships reveals similar findings. Patterns of violence among gay and lesbian couples are roughly equivalent to those shown by heterosexual couples, and reasons for abuse include alcohol abuse and dissatisfaction with the relationship (Fisher-Borne, 2007; Roberts, 2007).

Culture is also an important contextual factor in understanding partner abuse. In particular, violence against women worldwide reflects cultural

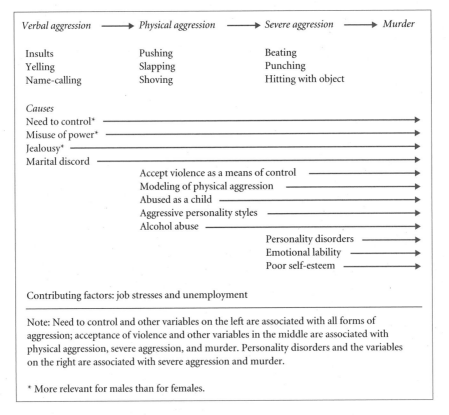

FIGURE 11.3 Continuum of progressive behaviors in abusive relationships.

Source: O'Leary, K. D. (1993). Through a psychological lens: Personality traits, personality disorders, and levels of violence. In R. J. Gelles & D. R. Loseke (Eds.), *Current controversies on family violence* (pp. 7–30). Copyright © 1993 by Sage Publications. Reprinted by permission of the publisher.

traditions, beliefs, and values of patriarchal societies, and can be seen in such acts as commonplace violent practices against women, including sexual slavery, female genital cutting, intimate partner violence, and honor killing (Parrot & Cummings, 2006). For example, cultures that emphasize honor and portray females as passive, nurturing supporters of men's activities and that emphasize loyalty and sacrifice for the family may contribute to tolerating abuse.

International data indicate that rates of abuse are higher in cultures that emphasize female purity, male status, and family honor. For example, a common cause of women's murders in Arab countries is brothers or other male relatives killing the victim because the woman violated the family's honor (Kulwicki, 2002). Intimate partner violence is prevalent in China (43% lifetime risk in one study), with strong associations with male patriarchal values and conflict resolutions (Xu et al., 2005).

Alarmed at the seriousness of abuse, many communities have established shelters for battered women and their children and programs that treat abusive men. However, the legal system in many localities is still not set up to deal with domestic violence; women in some locations cannot sue their husbands for assault, and restraining orders all too often offer little real protection from additional violence. Much remains to be done to protect women and their children from the fear and the reality of continued abuse.

Elder Abuse, Neglect, and Exploitation. Although elder abuse, neglect, and exploitation is difficult to define precisely, several different categories are commonly used (National Center on Elder Abuse, 2007a):

- *Physical abuse:* the use of physical force that may result in bodily injury, physical pain, or impairment

- *Sexual abuse:* nonconsensual sexual contact of any kind

- *Emotional or psychological abuse:* infliction of anguish, pain, or distress

- *Financial or material exploitation:* the illegal or improper use of an older adult's funds, property, or assets

- *Abandonment:* the desertion of an older adult by an individual who had physical custody or otherwise had assumed responsibility for providing care for the older adult

- *Neglect:* refusal or failure to fulfill any part of a person's obligation or duties to an older adult

- *Self-neglect:* the behaviors of an older person that threaten his or her own health or safety, excluding those conscious and voluntary decisions by a mentally competent and healthy adult

The most pressing need for cross-national research on elder abuse, neglect, or exploitation involves a common definition of such adversities against the elderly that is reflective of the values within a country (Kosberg et al., 2002). Part of the problem in agreeing on a common definition of elder abuse, neglect, or exploitation is that perceptions differ across national and ethnic groups. These ethnic differences may result in conflicts between social service workers, who may be using one set of definitions, and clients, who may be using another, in deciding who should receive protective services. Perhaps the only firm conclusion that can be drawn is that the perception of elder abuse, neglect, or exploitation is relativistic and depends on characteristics of both the perceiver and the victim (Childs et al., 2000). Despite these differences, when abuse, neglect, or exploitation occurs, it tends to reflect similar patterns across cultures; for example, researchers have documented similar types of elder abuse in China and in Western countries (Yan et al., 2002).

Researchers estimate that 1 in 4 vulnerable older adults are at risk for some type of abuse, neglect, or exploitation (Cooper, Selwood, & Livingston, 2008). Unfortunately, only a small proportion of these cases are actually reported to authorities. The most commonly reported forms are neglect (roughly 60%), physical abuse (16%), and financial or material exploitation (12%).

Risk Factors and Causes of Elder Abuse, Neglect, or Exploitation. Why elder abuse, neglect, or exploitatoin occurs is a matter of debate (National Center on Elder Abuse, 2007b). Several explanations have been offered that reflect this, but it is important to remember that elder abuse, neglect, or exploitation probably results from a combination of factors.

Because many abuse, neglect, or exploitation victims are spouses or partners, some cases reflect domestic violence that has been going on for a long time. Spouses or partners who have a history of being abusive tend to remain that way in late life.

A second major cause relates to an inability of the abuser to deal with personal problems in his or her life. This is especially true of adult children who are dependent on their victims for housing or financial assistance, and who have drug/alcohol, mental health, or other problems. Additionally, the stress of taking care of a spouse/partner or parent can overwhelm some caregivers, who resort to abuse, neglect, or exploitation.

In terms of exploitation, certain individuals take advantage of older adults who have diminished cognitive capacity. Unscrupulous businesspeople (e.g., repair companies, telemarketers), some adult children, and some spouses take advantage of cognitively disadvantaged older adults to con them out of their money through various schemes.

Clearly, elder abuse, neglect, or exploitation is an important social problem that has had insufficient attention from researchers and policymakers. Increased educational efforts, better reporting and investigation, more options for placement of victims, and better mental health treatment for victims are all needed for the problem to be adequately addressed (Wilber & McNeilly, 2001). If you suspect that an older adult is a victim of elder abuse, neglect, or exploitation, the best thing to do is to contact your local adult protective services office and report it.

Concept Checks

1. What are the key characteristics of adults' friendships?
2. How do people fall in love around the world?
3. What are the characteristics of elder abuse, neglect, or exploitation?

11.2 Lifestyles and Love Relationships

LEARNING OBJECTIVES

- What are the challenges and advantages of being single?
- Why do people cohabit?
- What are gay male and lesbian relationships like?

- What is marriage like across adulthood?
- Why do people divorce and remarry?
- What are the experiences of widows and widowers?

Bobbie and Jack were high school sweethearts who married a few years after World War II. Despite many trials in their relationship, they have remained firmly committed to each other for over 60 years. Not only are they still in love, but they are best friends. In looking back, they note that once their children moved away they grew closer again. Bobbie and Jack wonder whether this is typical.

Bobbie and Jack show us that forging relationships is only part of the picture in understanding how adults live their lives with other people. For most, one relationship becomes special and results in commitment, typically through marriage. Putting relationships in context is the goal of this section as we explore the major lifestyles of adults. First, we consider people who never get married. Next, we look at those who cohabit and those who are in same-sex relationships. We also consider those who get married and those who divorce and remarry. Finally, we discuss people who are widowed.

Singlehood

When Susan graduated from college with a degree in accounting, she took a job at a consulting firm. For the first several years in her job, she spent more time traveling than she did at home. During this time, she had a series of love relationships, but none resulted in commitment even though she had marriage as a goal. By the time she was in her mid-30s, Susan had decided that she no longer wanted to get married. "I'm now a partner in my firm, I enjoy traveling, and I'm pretty flexible in terms of moving if something better comes along," she stated to her friend Michele. "But I do miss being with someone to share my day or to just hang around with."

During early adulthood, most men and women are single, like Susan, defined as not living with an intimate partner. Estimates are that approximately 80% of men and 70% of women between ages 20 and 24 are unmarried, with increasing numbers deciding to stay that way (U.S. Census Bureau, 2008a).

What's it like to be single in the United States? It's tougher than you might think. DePaulo (2006) points out numerous stereotypes and biases against single people. Her research found that young adults characterized married people as caring, kind, and giving about 50% of the time compared with only 2% for single people. And single people also receive less compensation at work than married people do, even when age and experience are equivalent. She also found that rental agents preferred married couples 60% of the time (Morris, Sinclair, & DePaulo, 2007).

Many women and men remain single as young adults to focus on establishing their careers rather than marriage or relationships, which most do later. Others report that they simply have not met "the right person" or prefer singlehood (Lamanna & Riedmann, 2003). However, the pressure to marry is especially strong for women; frequent questions such as "Any good prospects yet?" may leave women feeling conspicuous or left out as many of their friends marry. Research indicates that single women have unresolved or unrecognized ambivalences about being single (Lewis & Moon, 1997). Such feelings result from being aware of the advantages and disadvantages of being single and ambivalence about the reasons they are single.

Men tend to remain single longer in young adulthood because they tend to marry at a later age than women (U.S. Census Bureau, 2008a). Fewer men than women remain unmarried throughout adulthood, largely because men find partners more easily as they select from a larger age range of unmarried women. Because men also tend to "marry down" in social status, women with higher levels of education are overrepresented among unmarried adults compared with men with similar levels of education.

Ethnic differences in singlehood reflect both differences in age at marriage and social factors. For example, nearly twice as many African Americans are single during young adulthood as European Americans, and more are choosing to stay that way (U.S. Census Bureau, 2008a). The most important reasons for this are the shortage of marriageable African American men and poor economic opportunities (Benokraitis, 2008). Professional African

American women show no significant differences from partnered African American women in well-being (Williams, 2006). Singlehood is also increasing among Latinos, in part because the average age of Latinos in the United States is lower than other ethnic groups, and in part due to poor economic opportunities for many Latinos (Lamanna & Riedmann, 2003). However, Latino men expect to marry (even if they do not) because it indicates achievement.

An important distinction is between adults who are temporarily single (i.e., those who are single only until they find a suitable marriage partner) and those who choose to remain single. Results from an in-depth interview study with never-married women in their 30s revealed three distinct groups: some suffer with acute distress about being single and long to be married with children; others describe experiencing the emotional continuum of desiring to be married and desiring to remain single; and others say that they are quite happy with a healthy self-image and high quality of life (Cole, 2000).

For most singles, the decision to never marry is a gradual one. This transition is represented by a change in self-attributed status that occurs over time and is associated with a cultural timetable for marriage. It marks the experience of "becoming single" that occurs when an individual identifies more with singlehood than with marriage (Davies, 2003). Still, a key question is, what marks the decision to remain single? For some, it is reaching a milestone birthday (e.g., 40) and still being single, although the particular age that reflects this varies a great deal (Davies, 2000). For many middle-aged single women, purchasing a house marks the decision: "I always thought you got married, you bought a house. Well, I bought a house and I'm not married. . . . I've laid down roots. . . . You're sort of saying, 'Okay, this is it.' And it makes you feel more settled" (Davies, 2000, p. 12).

For most middle-aged single women, though, the transition to permanent singlehood is a gradual one they drift into by circumstance rather than a lifestyle they choose, such as having to care for parents or other family members instead of attending to

Most women under age 25 are single, with increasing numbers of them deciding to stay that way throughout adulthood.

personal goals related to marriage, family, education, or career (Connidis, 2001). By the time they reach age 40, never-married women have defined family as their family of origin and friendships, and are content with their lives (McDill, Hall, & Turell, 2006).

Cohabitation

Being unmarried does not necessarily mean living alone. *People in committed, intimate, sexual relationships but who are not married may decide that living together, or* cohabitation, *provides a way to share daily life.* Cohabitation is becoming an increasingly popular lifestyle choice in the United States as well as in Canada, Europe, Australia, and elsewhere. As you can see in Figure 11.4, cohabitation in the United States has increased 10-fold over the past three decades from 523,000 in 1970 to 5.5 million in 2000, the most recent year extensive data were collected (U.S. Census Bureau, 2003). The age of people who cohabit has also changed. In 1970, the majority of cohabiting couples were adults over age 45; by 2000, the majority were adults between 25 and 44. This age change is related to a combination of increasing age of first marriage and the increased divorce rate since 1970.

Couples cohabit for three main reasons (Benokraitis, 2008). Some couples engage in *part-time or limited cohabitation,* which is usually based on convenience, sharing expenses, and sexual accessibility. There is typically no long-term commitment, and marriage is not usually a goal. Research shows that for most

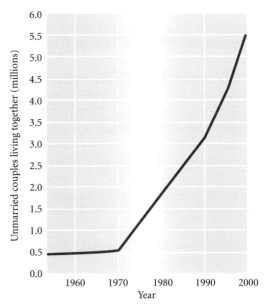

FIGURE 11.4 There has been a rapid growth in cohabitation in the United States since 1970. Does it prepare couples for marriage? Read the text to find out.

Source: From U.S. Census Bureau (2003).

American young adult couples, cohabitation is a step toward marriage (King & Scott, 2005). In this *premarital cohabitation,* the couple is actually engaging in a trial marriage. If marriage does not follow, the couple usually separates. Both part-time and premarital cohabitation are the most popular forms among young adults. Finally, some couples use cohabitation as a *substitute marriage,* which is a long-term commitment between two people without a legal marriage. Research indicates that this form is especially popular with older couples who may lose financial benefits (e.g., survivor's benefits from deceased spouses) if they remarry (King & Scott, 2005).

The picture is quite different in most European, South American, and Caribbean countries where cohabitation is a common alternative to marriage for young adults. For example, cohabitation is extremely common in The Netherlands, Norway, and Sweden, where this lifestyle is part of the culture; 99% of married couples in Sweden lived together before they married and nearly one in four couples are not legally married. Couples living together there are just as devoted to each other as are married couples, and they believe that such relationships are grounded in love and commitment to each other (Kaslow, Hansson, & Lundblad, 1994). Decisions to marry in these countries are typically made to legalize the relationship after children are born, in contrast to Americans, who marry to confirm their love and commitment to each other.

Cohabitation rates are lower in Africa and Asia. For example, in China, cohabitation is largely limited to rural villages where couples below the legal age for marriage live together (Neft & Levine, 1997).

Interestingly, having cohabitated does not seem to make American or Canadian marriages any better; in fact, it may do more harm than good, resulting in marriages that are less happy and with a higher risk of divorce (Hall & Zhao, 1995). Other research indicates that transitioning to marriage from cohabitation does not lessen depression, and concern about getting approval from friends increases distress for cohabitors who marry (Marcussen, 2001). Young adults whose parents divorced are more likely to cohabit, but this effect weakens between the late teens and early thirties (Cunningham & Thornton, 2007).

Are there differences between couples who cohabit and couples who marry right away? Longitudinal studies find few differences in couples' behavior after living together for many years regardless of whether they married without cohabiting, cohabited and then married, or simply cohabited (Stafford, Kline, & Rankin, 2004). No differences are reported in relationships between parents and adult children of married versus cohabiting couples (Daatland, 2007). Additionally, many countries extend the same rights and benefits to cohabiting couples as they do to married couples, and have done so for many years. For instance, Argentina provides pension rights to cohabiting partners, Canada extends insurance benefits, and Australia has laws governing the disposition of property when cohabiting couples sever their relationship (Neft & Levine, 1997).

Gay and Lesbian Couples

Less is known about the developmental course of gay and lesbian relationships than heterosexual relationships, largely because they were almost never the focus of research. To date, gay and lesbian relationships have been studied most often in comparison to married heterosexual couples. What is it like to be in a gay or lesbian relationship?

Like heterosexuals, gay and lesbian couples must deal with issues related to effective communication, power, and household responsibilities. For the most part, the relationships of gay and lesbian couples have many similarities to those of heterosexual couples (Kurdek, 2004). Most gay and lesbian couples are in dual-worker relationships, much like the majority of married heterosexual couples, and are likely to share household chores. In general, the same factors predict long-term success of couples regardless of sexual orientation (Mackey, Diemer, & O'Brien, 2004).

Gender differences are more important than differences in sexual orientation (Huston & Schwartz, 1995). Gay men, like heterosexual men, tend to separate love and sex and have more short-term relationships (Missildine et al., 2005); both lesbian and heterosexual women are more likely to connect sex and emotional intimacy in fewer, longer lasting relationships. Lesbians tend to make a commitment and cohabit faster than heterosexual couples (Ganiron, 2007). Men in any type of relationship tend to want more power if they earn more money. Women in any type of relationship are likely to be more egalitarian and to view money as a way to maintain independence from one's partner.

Gay and lesbian couples often report less support from family members than do either married or cohabiting couples (Benokraitis, 2008). The more that one's family holds traditional ethnic or religious values, the less likely it is that the family will provide support. At a societal level, marriage or civil unions between same-sex couples remains highly controversial in the United States, with several states passing constitutional amendments or statutes defining marriage as between a man and a woman. The lack of legal recognition for gay and lesbian relationships in the United States also means that certain rights and privileges are not granted. For example, it is difficult for gay and lesbian partners to inherit property from their partners in the absence of a will, and sometimes they are denied visitation rights when their partner is hospitalized. Although the legal status of gay and lesbian couples is changing in some countries (most notably in Scandinavia), few countries provide them with the same legal rights as married couples.

Very little research has been conducted on long-term gay and lesbian partnerships. Based on the available data, it appears that long-term relationships between gay and lesbian partners do not differ in quality from long-term heterosexual marriages (Connidis, 2001; O'Brien & Goldberg, 2000). As is true for heterosexual married couples, relationship satisfaction is better when partners communicate well and are basically happy themselves. Some researchers argue that occupying two stigmatizing statuses—being gay or lesbian *and* being old—may make aging especially challenging for these couples (Grossman, 1997). For example, age-related declines in health may force individuals to disclose their sexual orientation much more publicly.

Marriage

Most adults want their love relationships to result in marriage. However, U.S. residents are in less of a hurry to achieve this goal; the median age at first marriage for adults in the United States has been rising for several decades. As you can see in Figure 11.5, between 1970 and 2006, the median age

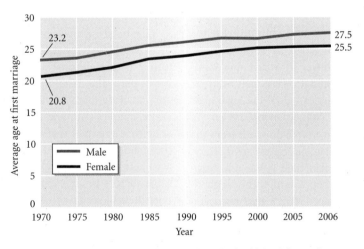

FIGURE 11.5 Median age at first marriage in the United States has increased more for women than for men since 1970.

Source: From U.S. Census Bureau, Current Population Survey, March and Annual Social and Economic Supplements, 2006 and earlier.

for first marriage rose nearly 4 years for both men and women, from roughly 23 to 27.5 for men, and from roughly 21 to 25.5 for women (U.S. Census Bureau, 2008b). This trend is not bad; women under age 20 at the time they are first married are three times more likely to end up divorced than women who first marry in their 20s, and six times more likely to end up divorced than first-time wives in their 30s (U.S. Census Bureau, 2008a). Let's explore age and other factors that keep marriages going strong over time.

Being married has benefits besides providing companionship. For example, being married encourages healthy behaviors for couples of all ages (Schone & Weinick, 1998), and married people tend to have greater average longevity (U.S. Census Bureau, 2008a).

Factors Influencing Marital Success. Why do some marriages succeed? Answer the questions in Table 11.1 and you may get some good ideas. Take time to think about your responses and why you answered the way you did. Your responses are the result of many factors, including the socialization you had about marriage. As we explore the research data about marital satisfaction, think about these and other widely held beliefs about marriage.

Although marriages, like other relationships, differ from one another, some important predictors of future success can be identified. One key factor in enduring marriages is the relative maturity of the two partners at the time they are married. In general, the younger the partners are, the lower the odds that the marriage will last, especially when the people are in their teens or early 20s (U.S. Bureau of the Census, 2008). In part, the age issue relates to Erikson's (1982) belief that intimacy cannot be achieved until after one's identity is established (see Chapter 9). Other reasons that increase or decrease the likelihood that a marriage will last include financial security and pregnancy at the time of the marriage.

A second important predictor of successful marriage is homogamy, or the similarity of values and interests a couple shares. As we saw in relation to choosing a mate, the extent to which the partners share similar values, goals, attitudes, socioeconomic status, and ethnic background increases the likelihood that their relationship will succeed.

A third factor in predicting marital success is a feeling that the relationship is equal. *According to exchange theory, marriage is based on each partner contributing something to the relationship that the other would be hard-pressed to provide.* Satisfying and happy marriages result when both partners perceive that there is a fair exchange, or equity, in all the dimensions of the relationship. Problems achieving such equity can arise because of the competing demands of work and family (see Chapter 12).

The Developmental Course of Marital Satisfaction. Few sights are happier than a couple on their wedding day; newlyweds are at the peak of marital bliss. The beliefs people bring into a marriage (which you identified in Table 11.1 in the quiz you took) influence how satisfied they will be as the marriage develops. As you might suspect, a couple's feelings change over time. Like any relationship, marriage has its peaks and valleys.

Much research has been conducted on marital satisfaction across adulthood. Research shows that for most couples overall marital satisfaction is highest at the beginning of the marriage, falls until the children begin leaving home, and rises again in later life, and that this pattern holds for both married and never-married cohabiting couples (see Figure 11.6; Hansen, Moum, & Shapiro, 2007). However, for some couples, satisfaction never rebounds and remains low; in essence, they have become emotionally divorced.

Overall, marital satisfaction ebbs and flows over time. The pattern of a particular marriage over the years is determined by the nature of the dependence of each spouse on the other. When dependence is mutual and about equal, the marriage is strong and close. When the dependence of one partner is much higher than that of the other, however, the marriage is likely to be characterized by stress and conflict. Changes in individual lives over adulthood shift the balance of dependence from one partner to the other; for example, one partner may go back to school, become ill, or lose status. Learning how to deal with these changes is the secret to long and happy marriages.

Table 11.1

Beliefs about Marriage

Why do some marriages succeed? Answer the following questions and you may get some good ideas.

1. A husband's marital satisfaction is usually lower if his wife is employed full time than if she is a full-time homemaker.

True   False

2. Marriages that last many years almost always have a higher level of satisfaction than marriages that last only a few years.

True   False

3. In most marriages, having a child improves marital satisfaction for both spouses.

True   False

4. The best single predictor of marital satisfaction is the quality of the couple's sex life.

True   False

5. Overall, married women are physically healthier than married men.

True   False

6. African American women are happier in marriage than African American men.

True   False

7. Marital satisfaction for a wife is usually lower if she is employed full time than if she is a full-time homemaker.

True   False

8. "If my spouse loves me, he/she should instinctively know what I want and need to make me happy."

True   False

9. In a marriage in which the wife is employed full time, the husband usually shares equally in the housekeeping tasks.

True   False

10. "No matter how I behave, my spouse should love me because he/she is my spouse."

True   False

11. Anglo husbands spend more time on household work than do Latino husbands.

True   False

12. Husbands usually make more lifestyle adjustments in marriage than do wives.

True   False

13. "I can change my spouse by pointing out his/her inadequacies and bad habits."

True   False

14. The more a spouse discloses positive and negative information to his/her partner, the greater the marital satisfaction of both partners.

True   False

15. For most couples, maintaining romantic love is the key to marital happiness over the life span.

True   False

All the items are false. The more "True" responses you gave, the greater your belief in stereotypes about marriage.

Source: From Benokraitis (1999, p. 235).

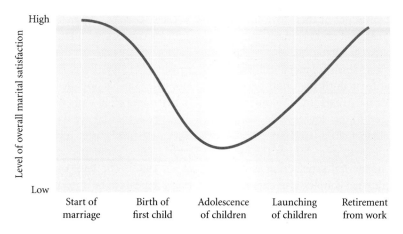

FIGURE 11.6 Marital satisfaction is highest early on and in later life, dropping during the childraising years.

Source: Kail, R., & Cavanaugh, J.C. (2010). *Human development: A life-span view* (5th ed., p. 412). Belmont, CA: Wadsworth.

The fact that marital satisfaction has a general downward trend but varies widely across couples led Karney and Bradbury (1995) to propose a *vulnerability–stress–adaptation model of marriage.* This model sees marital quality as a dynamic process resulting from the couple's ability to handle stressful events in the context of their particular vulnerabilities and resources. For example, as a couple's ability to adapt to stressful situations gets better over time, the quality of the marriage probably will improve.

The Early Years Marriages are most intense in their early days. When husbands and wives share many activities and are open to new experiences together, bliss results (Olson & McCubbin, 1983). Discussing financial matters honestly is a key to bliss, as many newly married couples experience their first marital stresses around money issues (Parkman, 2007). When there is marital conflict, the intensity of the early phase may create considerable unhappiness (Faulkner, Davey, & Davey, 2005).

Early in a marriage, the couple must learn to adjust to the different perceptions and expectations each person has for the other. Many wives tend to be more concerned than their husbands with keeping close ties with their friends. Research indicates that men and women both recognize and admit when problems occur in their marriage (Moynehan & Adams, 2007). The couple must also learn to handle confrontation. Indeed, learning effective strategies for resolving conflict is an essential component of a strong marriage, as these strategies provide ways for couples to discuss their problems maturely.

Early in a marriage, couples tend to have global adoration for their spouse regarding the spouse's qualities (Neff & Karney, 2005). For wives, but not for husbands, more accurate specific perceptions of what their spouses are really like were associated with more supportive behaviors, feelings of control in the marriage, and a decreased risk of divorce. Thus, for women, love grounded in accurate perceptions of a spouse's qualities appears to be stronger than love that is "blind" to a spouse's true qualities.

As couples settle into a routine, marital satisfaction tends to decline (Lamanna & Riedmann, 2003). Researchers have shown for many years that the primary reason for this drop for most couples is the birth of children (Carstensen et al., 1996). But it's not just a matter of having a child. The temperament of the child matters, with fussier babies creating more marital problems (Greving, 2007; Meijer & van den Wittenboer, 2007). Parenthood also means having substantially less time to devote to the marriage. Most couples are ecstatic over having their first child, a tangible product of their love for each other. But soon the reality of child care sets in, with 2:00 A.M. feedings, diaper changing, and the like, not to mention the long-term financial obligations that will continue at least until the child becomes an adult. Both African American and European American couples report an increase in conflict after the birth of their first child (Crohan, 1996).

However, using the birth of a child as the explanation of the drop in marital satisfaction is much too simplistic, as child-free couples also experience a decline in marital satisfaction (Hansen et al., 2007). It appears that a decline in overall marital satisfaction over time is a common developmental phenomenon, even for couples who choose to remain childless (Clements & Markman, 1996). Additionally, couples without children due to infertility face the stress associated with the inability to have children, which exacerbates existing stresses in the relationship and can lower marital satisfaction (Spector, 2004). Longitudinal research indicates that disillusionment, as demonstrated by a decline in feeling in love, in demonstrations of affection, and in the feeling that one's spouse is responsive, as well as an increase in feelings of ambivalence, is a key predictor of marital dissatisfaction (Huston et al., 2001).

Marriage at Midlife For most couples marital satisfaction improves after the children leave, a state called the empty nest. Midlife brings both challenges and opportunities for marriages (Karasu & Karasu, 2005). Some use the launching of children to rediscover each other, and marital satisfaction rebounds.

For some middle-aged couples, however, marital satisfaction continues to be low. *They may have grown apart but continue to live together, a situation sometimes referred to as* married singles (Lamanna & Riedmann, 2003). In essence, they have become emotionally divorced and live more as housemates than as a married couple; for these couples, spending more time together is not a welcome change. Research shows that marital dissatisfaction in midlife is a process that develops over a long period of time and is not spontaneous (Rokach, Cohen, & Dreman, 2004).

Older Couples Marital satisfaction is fairly high in older couples, who tend to describe their partner in more positive terms than do middle-aged married partners (Henry, Berg, Smith, & Florsheim, 2007). However, satisfaction in long-term marriages—that is, marriages of 40 years or more—is a complex issue. In general, marital satisfaction among older couples increases shortly after retirement but then decreases with health problems and advancing age (Miller et al., 1997). The level of satisfaction in these marriages appears to be unrelated to the amount of past or present sexual interest or sexual activity, but it is positively related to the degree of social engagement such as interaction with friends (Bennett, 2005). In keeping with the married-singles concept, many older couples have simply developed detached, contented styles (Connidis, 2001; Lamanna & Riedmann, 2003).

Older married couples show several specific characteristics (O'Rourke & Cappeliez, 2005). Many older couples show a selective memory regarding the occurrence of negative events and perceptions of their partner. Older couples have a reduced potential for marital conflict and greater potential for pleasure, are more likely to be similar in terms of mental and physical health, and show fewer gender differences in sources of pleasure. In short, most older married couples have developed adaptive ways to avoid conflict and have grown more alike. In general, marital satisfaction among older couples remains high until health problems begin to interfere with the relationship (Connidis, 2001).

Being married in late life has several benefits. A study of 9,333 European Americans, African Americans, and Latino Americans showed that marriage helps people deal better with chronic illness, functional problems, and disabilities (Pienta, Hayward, & Jenkins, 2000). The division of household chores becomes more egalitarian after the husband retires than it was when the husband was employed, irrespective of whether the wife was working outside the home (Kulik, 2001a, 2001b).

Keeping Marriages Happy. Although no two marriages are exactly the same, couples must be flexible and adaptable. Couples who have been happily married for many years show an ability to roll with the punches and to adapt to changing circumstances in the relationship. For example, a serious problem of one spouse may not be detrimental to the relationship and may even make the bond stronger. Likewise, couples' expectations about marriage change over time, gradually becoming more congruent (Weishaus & Field, 1988), with intimacy and spousal support being key factors (Patrick, Sells, Giordano, & Tollerud, 2007). In contrast, the physical illness of one spouse almost invariably affects marital quality negatively, even after other factors such as work stress, education, and income are considered (Wickrama et al., 1997).

How well couples communicate their thoughts, actions, and feelings to each other largely determines the level of conflict couples experience and, by extension, how happy they are likely to be over the long term (Notarius, 1996; Patrick et al., 2007). Increasing demands from work and family put enormous pressures on a marriage (Rogers & Amato, 1997). It appears that key factors underlying marital satisfaction do not differ between European American and African American couples (Hairston, 2001). It takes a great deal of love, humor, and perseverance to stay happily married a long time. But it *can* be done, providing couples work at these seven key things (Donatelle & Davis, 1997; Enright, Gassin, & Wu, 1992; Knapp & Taylor, 1994):

- Make time for your relationship.
- Express your love to your spouse.
- Be there in times of need.
- Communicate constructively and positively about problems in the relationship.
- Be interested in your spouse's life.
- Confide in your spouse.
- Forgive minor offenses, and try to understand major ones.

In sum, people who have been happily married for a long time act much like Bobbie and Jack, a couple married more than 60 years, who point to open and honest communication with each other, a desire to support each other no matter what, and an undying commitment to each other. Their advice to couples on how to help ensure their own golden anniversary? "Never go to sleep angry at your partner." Excellent advice.

Caring for a Partner. When couples pledge their love to each other "in sickness and in health," most envision the sickness part to be no worse than an illness lasting a few weeks. That may be the case for many couples, but for some the illness they experience severely tests their pledge.

Francine and Ron are one such couple. After 42 years of mainly good times together, Ron was diagnosed as having Alzheimer's disease. When first contacted by staff at the local chapter of a caregiver support organization, Francine had been caring for Ron for 6 years. "At times it's very hard, especially when he looks at me and doesn't have any idea who I am. Imagine, after all these years, not to recognize me. But I love him, and I know that he would do the same for me. But, to be perfectly honest, we're not the same couple we once were. We're just not as close; I guess we really can't be."

© Masterfile (Royalty-Free Div.)

Taking care of a spouse is one way that many couples demonstrate the love they have for each other.

Francine and Ron are typical of couples in which one partner cares for the other. Caring for a chronically ill partner presents different challenges than caring for a chronically ill parent. The partner caregiver assumes the new role after decades of shared responsibilities. Often without warning, the division of labor that had worked for years must be readjusted. Such change inevitably puts stress on the relationship (Cavanaugh & Kinney, 1994). This is especially true in cases involving Alzheimer's disease or other dementias because of the cognitive and behavioral consequences of the disease, but it is also the case in diseases such as AIDS. Caregiving challenges are felt by partner caregivers in any type of long-term, committed relationship.

Studies of spousal caregivers of persons with Alzheimer's disease show that marital satisfaction is much lower than for healthy couples (Cavanaugh & Kinney, 1994; Kinney et al., 1993). Spousal caregivers report a loss of companionship and intimacy over the course of caregiving, but also more rewards than adult child caregivers (Raschick & Ingersoll-Dayton, 2004). Marital satisfaction is also an important predictor of spousal caregivers' reports of depressive symptoms; the better the perceived quality of the marriage, the fewer symptoms caregivers report (Kinney et al., 1993), a finding that holds across European American and African American spousal caregivers (Parker, 2008). Sadly, caring for a partner often leads the caregiver to question the meaningfulness of life (Wells & Kendig, 1997).

Most partner caregivers are forced to respond to an environmental challenge that they did not choose—their partner's illness. They adopt the caregiver role out of necessity. Once they adopt the role, caregivers assess their ability to carry out the duties required. Although evidence about the mediating role of caregivers' appraisal of stressors is unclear, interventions that help improve the functional level of the ill partner generally improve the caregiving partner's situation (Van Den Wijngaart, Vernooij-Dassen, & Felling, 2007). However, spousal caregivers do not always remember their major hassles accurately over time; in one study, caregivers remembered only about two thirds of their major hassles after a one-month delay (Cavanaugh &

Kinney, 1998). This finding points out that health care professionals should not rely exclusively on partner caregivers' reports about the caregiving situation in making diagnostic judgments.

The importance of feeling competent as a partner caregiver fits with the docility component of the competence–environmental press model presented earlier in this chapter. Caregivers attempt to balance their perceived competence with the environmental demands of caregiving. Perceived competence allows them to be proactive rather than merely reactive (and docile), which gives them a better chance to optimize their situation.

Even in the best of committed relationships, providing full-time care for a partner is both very stressful and rewarding in terms of the marital relationship (Baek, 2005). Coping with a wife, for example, who may not remember her husband's name, who may act strangely, and who has a chronic and fatal disease presents serious challenges even to the happiest of couples. Yet even in that situation, the caregiving husband may experience no change in marital happiness despite the changes in his wife due to the disease.

Divorce and Remarriage

Despite what couples pledge on their wedding day, many marriages do not last until death parts them; instead, marriages are dissolved through divorce. But even though divorce is stressful and difficult, thousands of people each year also choose to try marriage again. Most enter their second (or third or fourth) marriage with renewed expectations of success. Are these new dreams realistic? As we'll see, it depends on many things; among the most important is whether children are involved.

Divorce. Most couples enter marriage with the idea that their relationship will be permanent. Unfortunately, fewer and fewer couples experience this permanence. Rather than growing together, couples grow apart.

Who Gets Divorced and Why? Divorce in the United States is common, and the divorce rate is substantially higher than it is in many other

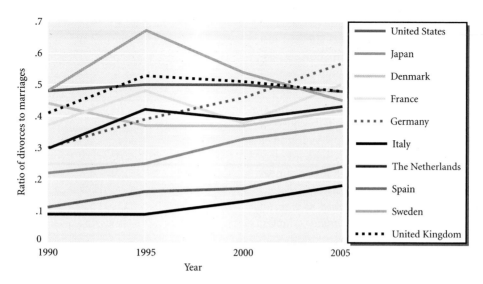

FIGURE 11.7 The United States has one of the highest divorce rates in the world.

Source: U.S. Bureau of Labor Statistics, updated and revised from "Families and Work in Transition in 12 Countries, 1980–2001," *Monthly Labor Review,* September 2003, with unpublished data. http://www.census.gov/compendia/statab/tables/08s1302.xls.

countries around the world; as you can see in Figure 11.7, couples have roughly a 50–50 chance of remaining married for life (U.S. Census Bureau, 2008a). In contrast, the ratio of divorces to marriages in Japan, Italy, and Spain are substantially lower (U.S. Census Bureau, 2008a), as are rates in Africa and Asia (United Nations, 2005). However, divorce rates in nearly every developed country have increased over the past several decades (United Nations, 2005).

One factor consistently related to divorce rates in the United States is ethnicity. Of those marriages ending in divorce, African American and Asian American couples tended to be married longer at the time of divorce than European American couples (U.S. Census Bureau, 2008a). Ethnically mixed marriages are at greater risk of divorce than ethnically homogenous ones (U.S. Census Bureau, 2008a).

Men and women tend to agree on the reasons for divorce (Amato & Previti, 2003). Infidelity is the most commonly reported cause, followed by incompatibility, drinking or drug use, and growing apart. People's specific reasons for divorcing vary with gender, social class, and life course variables.

Former husbands and wives are more likely to blame their ex-spouses than themselves for the problems that led to the divorce. Former husbands and wives claim, however, that women are more likely to have initiated the divorce.

Why people divorce has been the focus of much research. Much of the attention has been on the notion that how couples handle conflict is the key to success or failure. Although conflict management is important, it has become clear that there is more to it than that (Fincham, 2003).

Gottman and Levenson (2000) developed two models that predicted divorce early (within the first 7 years of marriage) and later (when the first child reaches age 14) with 93% accuracy over the 14-year period of their study. Negative emotions displayed during conflict between the couple predicted early divorce, but not later divorce. In general, this reflects a pattern of wife-demand–husband-withdraw (Christensen, 1990) in which, during conflict, the wife places a demand on her husband, who then withdraws either emotionally or physically. In contrast, the lack of positive emotions in a discussion of events-of-the-day and during conflict predicted later divorce, but not early divorce. An example would be a wife talking excitedly about a project she had just been given at work and her husband showing disinterest. Such "unrequited" interest and excitement in discussions likely carries over to the rest of the relationship.

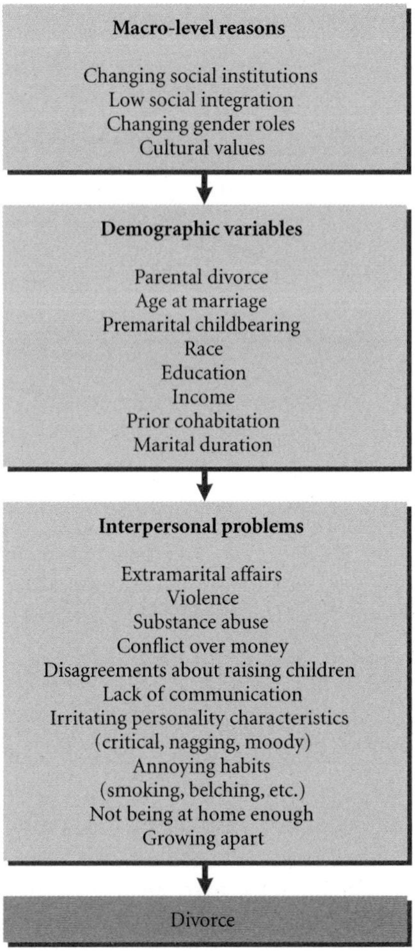

Gottman's research is important because it clearly shows that how couples show emotion is critical to marital success. Couples who divorce earlier typically do so because of high levels of negative feelings such as contempt, criticism, defensiveness, and stonewalling experienced as a result of intense marital conflict. But for many couples, such intense conflict is generally absent. Although this makes it easier to stay in a marriage longer, the absence of positive emotions eventually takes its toll and results in later divorce. For a marriage to last, people need to be told that they are loved and that what they do and feel really matters to their partner.

But we must be cautious about applying Gottman's model to all married couples. Kim, Capaldi, and Crosby (2007) reported that in lower-income high-risk couples, the variables Gottman says predict early divorce did not for that sample. However, Coan and Gottman (2007) point out that the sample differences among the various studies mean that, as noted in Chapter 1, conclusions about the predictive model must be drawn carefully.

Why people divorce is certainly complex. As shown in Figure 11.8, macro-level social issues, demographic variables, and interpersonal problems all factor into the decision to divorce (Lamanna & Riedmann, 2003). The high divorce rate in the United States and the reasons typically cited for getting divorced have sparked a controversial approach to keeping couples together, termed *covenant marriage*, which makes divorce much harder to obtain. Other proposals, such as the Healthy Marriage Initiative supported by the Heritage Foundation, raise similar issues. Will they work? That remains to be seen.

Now that some states in the United States as well as some countries worldwide recognize marriage or civil unions between same-sex couples, it is inevitable that some of them will ultimately divorce.

FIGURE 11.8 Many factors on different levels enter into the decision to divorce.

Source: From Bonokraitis, N. (2002). *Marriages and families: Changes, choices, and constraints* (4th ed., p. 401). Reprinted with permission of Pearson Education, Inc., Upper Saddle River, New Jersey.

However, as discussed in the Current Controversies feature, divorce between same sex-couples poses numerous legal challenges.

Effects of Divorce on the Couple Although the changes in attitudes toward divorce have eased the social trauma associated with it, divorce still takes a high toll on the psyche of the couple. Both partners in a failed marriage feel deeply disappointed, misunderstood, and rejected (Brodie, 1999). Unlike the

Same-Sex Divorce Presents Challenges

Imagine you are a family court judge confronted with the following case. Two professional women, married for three years, are asking for a divorce. One member of the former couple expected that she would split the property and share custody of their 4-year-old child. Her ex wanted sole custody and the ability to move out of the state. Both claims for custody were based on the same premise—the child should be with its mother.

As marriage and civil unions between same-sex couples become more common, the fact of same-sex divorce also confronts the legal system. The traditional bias of family courts to give custody preference to the mother becomes more complicated in the breakup of a lesbian couple. It is

also complex when dealing with the divorce of a gay male couple.

Same-sex divorce is an emerging area of domestic law. Because the rights of gay and lesbian couples vary in the United States from state to state and between states and the federal government, divorce presents a more complex set of issues for same-sex couples. Under the 1996 Defense of Marriage Act, states are not required to recognize a same-sex marriage that occurred in another state. For example, when heterosexual couples divorce, alimony payments are tax-deductible expenses. But because the Internal Revenue Service does not recognize the legality of same-sex marriages, such is not the case for gays or lesbians who make such payments to former partners.

Similarly, retirement plans that are more easily divided when heterosexual couples divorce must be cashed out, with significant tax penalties, when the divorce involves a same-sex couple. And if a state does not recognize same-sex marriage, it is likely that it will not grant a divorce; the couple might have to move back to the state in which they were married in order to divorce.

Clearly, the controversy surrounding same-sex marriage will continue to create issues related to same-sex divorce. In the meantime, same-sex couples whose relationships did not work out will continue to be confronted with a host of challenges on top of the stress and trauma associated with divorce in heterosexual couples.

situation when one's spouse dies, divorce often means that the person's ex-spouse is present to provide a reminder of the failure. As a result, divorced people are typically unhappy in general, at least for a while. Indeed, divorced people of all ages are less likely than married, never-married, and widowed people to say that they are "very happy" with their lives (Kurdek, 1991b; Lee, Seccombe, & Shehan, 1991). The effects of a divorce can even be traced to generations not yet born due to long-term negative consequences on education and parent–child relations in future generations (Amato & Cheadle, 2005).

Divorced people sometimes find the transition very difficult; researchers refer to these problems as "divorce hangover" (Walther, 1991).

Divorce hangover reflects divorced partners' inability to let go, develop new friendships, or reorient themselves as single parents. Indeed, ex-spouses who are preoccupied with thoughts of their former partners, and who have high feelings of hostility toward them, have significantly poorer emotional well-being than ex-spouses who are not preoccupied or who have feelings of friendship toward their former partners (Masheter, 1997). Forgiving the ex-spouse is also important for eventual adjustment postdivorce (Rye et al., 2004). Both low preoccupation and forgiveness may be indicators that ex-spouses are able to move on with their lives.

Divorce in middle age or late life has some special characteristics. If women initiate the divorce, they report self-focused growth and optimism; if they did not initiate the divorce, they tend to ruminate and feel vulnerable (Sakraida, 2005). However, in both cases they report changes in their social networks. Middle-aged and elderly women are at a significant disadvantage for remarriage—an especially traumatic situation for women who obtained much of their identity from their roles as wife and mother. Support groups help people adjust; for men this works best in large groups and for women it works best when the group provides emotional support (Oygard & Hardeng, 2001).

We must not overlook the financial problems faced by middle-aged divorced women (Gallagher, 1996; Kurz, 1995). These problems are especially keen for the middle-aged divorcee who may have spent years as a homemaker and has few marketable job skills. For her, divorce presents an especially difficult financial hardship, which is intensified if she has children in college and the father provides little support (Lamanna & Riedmann, 2003).

Remarriage. The trauma of divorce does not deter people from beginning new relationships, which often lead to another marriage. Typically, men and women both wait about 3.5 years before they remarry (U.S. Census Bureau, 2008a). However, remarriage rates vary somewhat across ethnic groups. African Americans remarry a bit more slowly than other ethnic groups (U.S. Census Bureau, 2008a).

Research indicates that there are few differences between first marriages and remarriages (Coleman & Ganong, 1990). Except for African Americans, second marriages have about a 25% higher risk of dissolution than first marriages, and the divorce rate for remarriages involving stepchildren is about three times higher than the rate for first marriages (Lamanna & Riedmann, 2003; U.S. Census Bureau, 2008a).

Although women are more likely to initiate a divorce, they are less likely to remarry (Buckle, Gallup, & Rodd, 1996) unless they are poor (Schmiege, Richards, & Zvonkovic, 2001). However, women in general tend to benefit more from remarriage than do men, particularly if they have children (Ozawa & Yoon, 2002). Although many people believe that divorced individuals should wait before remarrying to avoid the so-called "rebound effect," there is no evidence that those who remarry sooner have less success in remarriage than those who wait longer (Wolfinger, 2007).

Remarriage options for older adults after either divorce or the death of a spouse are often more constrained. In some cases, widows may lose financial benefits from pensions or other retirement plans if they remarry. This problem exists for widows across cultures; for example, in Namibia widows are constrained in their options and typically must depend on others (Thomas, 2008). Adult children may voice strong opposition to their parent remarrying, which can put sufficient pressure on the parent that they remain single. Some older adults might also believe it is inappropriate for them to remarry after a long marriage because it may be perceived as disrespectful. Still, some older adults remarry, and work through these and other issues, such as who will inherit the estate.

Adapting to new relationships in remarriage is stressful. For example, partners may have unresolved issues from the previous marriage that may interfere with satisfaction with the new marriage (Faber, 2004). The effects of remarriage on children is positive, at least for young adult children who report a positive effect on their own intimate relationships as an effect of their parent(s) remarrying happily (Yu & Adler-Baeder, 2007).

Widowhood

Alma still feels the loss of her husband, Chuck. "There are lots of times when I feel him around. We were together for so long that you take it for granted that your husband is just there. And there are times when I just don't want to go on without him. But I suppose I'll get through it."

Traditional marriage vows proclaim that the union will last "'til death do us part." Like Alma and Chuck, virtually all older married couples will see their marriages end because one partner dies. For most people, the death of a partner follows a period of caregiving (Martin-Matthews, 1999) and is one of the most traumatic events they will ever experience (Miller, Smerglia, & Bouchet, 2004). Although widowhood may occur at any age, it is much more likely to occur in old age—and to women (Martin-Matthews, 1999). More than half of all women over age 65 are widows, but only 15% of men the same age are widowers. The reasons for this discrepancy are related to biological and social forces. As we will see in Chapter 4, women have longer life expectancies. Also, women typically marry men older than themselves. Consequently, the average married woman can expect to live 10 to 12 years as a widow.

The impact of widowhood goes well beyond the ending of a long-term partnership (Martin-Matthews, 1999; Miller et al., 2004). Widowed people may be left alone by family and friends who do not know how to deal with a bereaved person. As a result, widows and widowers may lose not only a partner but also those friends and family who feel uncomfortable including a single person rather than a couple in social functions (Felber, 2000). Because women tend to have more friends than men and keep stronger family ties, widows typically get more help than widowers from siblings and friends (Barrett & Lynch, 1999; Martin-Matthews, 2000). But feelings of loss do not dissipate quickly, as the case of Alma shows clearly. As we will see in Chapter 16, feeling sad on important dates is a common experience, even many years after a loved one has died.

Men and women react differently to widowhood. In general, those who were most dependent on their partners during the marriage report the highest increase in self-esteem in widowhood because they have learned to do the tasks formerly done by their partners (Carr, 2004). Widowers are at higher risk of dying themselves soon after their partner, either by suicide or natural causes (Osgood, 1992), and are at higher risk for depression (Lee et al., 2001). Some people believe that the loss of a wife presents a more serious problem for a man than the loss of a husband for a woman. Perhaps this is because a wife is often a man's only close friend and confidant, or because men are usually unprepared to live out their lives alone (Martin-Matthews, 1999). Older men are often ill equipped to handle such routine and necessary tasks as cooking, shopping, and keeping house, and they become emotionally isolated from family members.

Although both widows and widowers suffer financial loss, widows often suffer more because survivor's benefits are usually only half of their husband's pensions (Felber, 2000; Martin-Matthews, 1999). For many women, widowhood results in difficult financial circumstances, particularly regarding medical expenses (McGarry & Schoeni, 2005).

An important factor to keep in mind about gender differences in widowhood is that men are usually older than women when they are widowed. To some extent, the difficulties reported by widowers may be partly due to this age difference. Regardless of age, men have a clear advantage over women in the opportunity to form new heterosexual relationships, as there are fewer social restrictions on relationships between older men and younger women (Matthews, 1996). However, older widowers are actually less likely to form new, close friendships than are widows. Perhaps this is simply a continuation of men's lifelong tendency to have few close friendships.

For many reasons, including the need for companionship and financial security, some widowed people cohabit or remarry (de Jong Gierveld, 2004). Widowers are about five times more likely than widows to remarry (Lee, Willetts, & Seccombe, 1998). However, remarriage after being widowed is still less likely than after divorce (Connidis, 2001). This is probably because there are objective limitations (decreased mobility, poorer health, poorer finances), absence of incentives common to younger ages (desire for children), and social pressures to protect one's estate (Talbott, 1998).

Concept Checks

1. What are the two most difficult issues for single people?
2. What are the major reasons that people cohabit?
3. What characterizes gay and lesbian couples?
4. How does marital satisfaction change across the length of the marriage?
5. What are the main reasons people get divorced and remarried?
6. What do widows and widowers experience?

11.3 Family Dynamics and the Life Course

LEARNING OBJECTIVES
- What is it like to be a parent? What are the key issues across ethnic groups? What forms of parenting are there?
- How do middle-aged adults interact with their children? How do they deal with the possibility of providing care to aging parents?
- How do grandparents interact with their grandchildren? What key issues are involved?

Susan is a 42-year-old married woman with two preadolescent children. She is an only child. Her mother, Esther, is a 67-year-old widow and has been showing signs of dementia. Esther has little money, and Susan's family is barely making ends meet. Susan knows that her mother cannot live alone much longer, and she feels that she should have her move in with their family. Susan feels that she has an obligation to provide care but also feels torn between her mother and her family and job. Susan wonders what to do.

Increasingly, families are facing the dilemma confronting Susan. As more people live long lives, the need for families to deal with health problems in their older members is on the rise. Most people understand the issues involved with raising children, but few of us are socialized for parental care.

In this section, we examine several issues relating to family dynamics. First we examine the parental role, how this varies across ethnic groups, and different forms of parenting. Important issues confront middle-aged couples: adult children moving out (and sometimes moving back) and the prospect of caring for aging parents like Susan is doing. We conclude with a discussion of grandparenthood.

The Parental Role

Today, couples have fewer children and have their first child later than in the past. The average age at the time of the birth of a woman's first child in the United States is about 25. This average age has been increasing steadily since 1970 due to two major trends: Many women postpone children in order to establish careers, and the teen birth rate dropped dramatically between the early 1990s and 2005 (but increased in 2006).

Older mothers are more at ease being parents, spend more time with their babies, and are more affectionate, sensitive, and supportive to them (Berlin, Brady-Smith, & Brooks-Gunn, 2002). The age of the father also makes a difference in how fathers interact with their children. Compared to men who become fathers in their 20s, men who become fathers in their 30s are generally more invested in their paternal role and spend up to three times as much time caring for their preschool children as younger fathers do (Cooney et al., 1993). However, men who become fathers in their 30s are also more likely to feel ambivalent and resentful about time lost to their careers (Cooney et al., 1993).

Parenting skills do not come naturally; they must be acquired. Having a child changes all aspects of couples' lives. As we have seen, children place a great deal of stress on a relationship. Both motherhood and fatherhood require major commitment and cooperation. Parenting is full of rewards, but it also takes a great deal of work. Caring for young children is demanding. It may create disagreements over division of labor, especially if both parents are employed outside the home. Even when mothers are employed outside the home (and more than 70% of women with children under age 18 are), they still perform most of the childrearing tasks. Even when men take employment leave, although they are more likely to share tasks, they still do not spend more time on them than fathers who do not take leave (Seward, Yeatts, Amin, & DeWitt, 2006).

In general, parents manage to deal with the many challenges of childrearing reasonably well. They learn how to compromise when necessary, and when to apply firm but fair discipline. Given the choice, most parents do not regret their decision to have children.

Ethnic Diversity and Parenting. Ethnic background matters in terms of family structure and the parent–child relationship. African American husbands are more likely than their European American counterparts to help with household chores, and they help more with child care (Penha-Lopes, 1995). But African American wives still do more of the traditional household chores such as cooking and cleaning. In low-income families, African American parents may buffer their children from involvement with drugs and other problems due to their more conservative views about illegal substance abuse (Paschal, Lewis, & Sly, 2007). Overall, most African American parents provide a cohesive, loving environment that often exists within a context of strong religious beliefs (Anderson, 2007), pride in cultural heritage, self-respect, and cooperation with the family (Brissett-Chapman & Issacs-Shockley, 1997).

As a result of several generations of oppression, many Native American parents have lost the cultural parenting skills that were traditionally part of Native culture where children were valued, women were considered sacred and honored, and men cared for and provided for their families (Witko, 2006). Thus, a strong sense of tribalism is a major factor in Native American families. This helps promote strong ties to parents, siblings, and grandparents (Garrod & Larimore, 1997). Native American children are viewed as very important family members, and tribal members spend great amounts of time passing cultural values to them, such as cooperation, sharing, personal integrity, generosity, harmony with nature, and spirituality, values very different from European American ones that emphasize competitiveness and individuality (Stauss, 1995). Many Native American parents worry that their children will lose their values if they are overexposed to European American values, such as during college.

Latino families are less likely than either European American or Asian American families to be two-parent families, largely due to higher rates of cohabitation, cultural values, and out-of-wedlock births (del Pinal & Singer, 1997). Among two-parent families, Mexican American mothers and fathers both tend to adopt similar authoritative behaviors in dealing with their preschool children, but mothers use these behaviors more frequently (Gamble, Ramakumar, & Diaz, 2007). Two key values among Latino families are familism and the extended family. Familism *refers to the idea that the well-being of the family takes precedence over the concerns of individual family members.* This value is a defining characteristic of

Family ties are very important in many cultures, with some placing more emphasis on the family than on individuals.

Latino families; for example, Brazilian and Mexican families consider familism a cultural strength (Carlo, Koller, Raffaelli, & de Guzman, 2007; Lucero-Liu, 2007). The extended family is also very strong among Latino families, which serves as the venue for a wide range of exchanges of goods and services, such as child care and financial support.

Like Latinos, Asian Americans value familism (Meyer, 2007) and place an even higher value on extended family. Other key values include obtaining good grades in school, maintaining discipline, being concerned about what others think, and conformity. Children are encouraged to mature at an early age, and sibling rivalry and aggressive behavior are not tolerated (Lamanna & Riedmann, 2003). Men have higher status in most Asian American families (Yu, 1995). Among recent immigrants, though, women are expanding their role by working outside the home. Research shows that Chinese American parents experience less marital stress during the transition to parenthood than European American couples, perhaps because of the clearer traditional cultural division of tasks between husbands and wives (Burns, 2005).

Raising multiethnic children presents challenges not experienced by parents of same-race children. For example, parents of biracial children may face prejudice toward themselves and their children by members of both races (Chan & Smith, 1995). These parents also worry that their children may be rejected by members of both racial communities.

Perhaps that is why parents of multiracial children tend to provide more economic and cultural resources to their children than do parents of single-race children (Cheng & Powell, 2007).

In multiethnic families, you might think that the parent from a minority group would take primary responsibility for guiding that aspect of the child's ethnic identity. A study of children of European mothers and Maori fathers in New Zealand, though, showed that the mothers played a major role in establishing the child's Maori identity (Kukutai, 2007). Similarly, European American mothers of biracial children whose fathers are African American tend to raise them as African American in terms of public ethnic identity (O'Donoghue, 2005).

As is clear, ethnic groups vary a great deal in how they approach the issue of parenting and what values are most important. Considered together, there is no one parenting standard that applies equally to all groups.

Single Parents. Although the overall number of single-parent households in the United States has remained at about 9% since 1994, the proportion of births to unmarried mothers is at an all-time high at roughly 37% (National Center for Health Statistics, 2007b). The number of single parents, most of whom are women, continues to be high in some ethnic groups. Roughly 70% of births to African American mothers, 48% of births to Latina mothers, and 25% of births to European American mothers are to unmarried women (U.S. Census Bureau, 2008a). Among the causes are high divorce rates, the decision to keep children born outside marriage, different fertility rates across ethnic groups, and the desire of many single adults to have or adopt children. Being a single parent raises important questions. Ethnic group differences are due in part to different rates at which women marry to legitimate a pregnancy (African American women do this the least) and higher rates of cohabitation among some groups (e.g., Latinos; Raley, 1999).

Two main questions arise concerning single parents: How are children affected when only one adult is responsible for child care? and How do single parents meet their own needs for emotional support and intimacy?

Many divorced single parents report complex feelings such as frustration, failure, guilt, and a need to be overindulgent (Lamanna & Riedmann, 2003). Loneliness can be especially difficult to deal with (Anderson et al., 2004). Separation anxiety is a common and strong feeling among military parents who are about to be deployed (Roper, 2007). Feelings of guilt may lead to attempts to make up for the child's lack of a father or mother. Some single parents make the mistake of trying to be peers to their children, using inconsistent discipline, or, if they are the noncustodial parent, of spoiling their children with lots of monetary or material goods.

Single parents, regardless of gender, face considerable obstacles. Financially, they are usually much less well-off than their married counterparts. Having only one source of income puts additional pressure on single parents to provide all of the necessities. Integrating the roles of work and parenthood are difficult enough for two people; for the single parent, the hardships are compounded. Financially, single mothers are hardest hit, mainly because women typically are paid less than men, and because single mothers may not be able to afford the level of child care necessary to provide the work schedule flexibility they may need for higher-paying jobs.

One particular concern for many divorced single parents is dating. Several common questions asked by single parents involve dating: "How do I become available again?" "How will my children react?" "How do I cope with my own sexual needs?" Research indicates that repartnering happens fairly quickly (Anderson et al., 2004), with half having had some dating experience even prior to the divorce filing. At one-year post filing, typically parents have dated two new partners. Among recent filers, younger parents, those with greater time since separation, and those in households containing other (nonromantic) adults are significantly more likely to have dated. There are typically no differences in dating by ethnic group, but African American parents report significantly longer times since separation.

Alternative Forms of Parenting. Not all parents raise their own biological children. In fact, roughly one third of North American couples become stepparents, foster parents, or adoptive parents sometime during their lives.

To be sure, the parenting issues we have discussed thus far are just as important in these situations as when people raise their own biological children. In general, there are few differences among parents who have their own biological children and those who become parents in some other way (Ceballo et al., 2004). However, some special problems arise for the latter group as well.

A big issue for foster parents, adoptive parents, and stepparents is how strongly the child will bond with them. Although infants less than 1 year old will probably bond well, children who are old enough to have formed attachments with their biological parents may have competing loyalties. For example, some stepchildren remain strongly attached to the noncustodial parent and actively resist attempts to integrate them into the new family ("My real mother wouldn't make me do that"), or they may exhibit behavioral problems. As a result, the dynamics in blended families can be complex (Ganong & Coleman, 2004). Stepparents must often deal with continued visitation by the noncustodial parent, which may exacerbate any difficulties. These problems are a major reason second marriages are at high risk for dissolution, as discussed later in this chapter. And they are a major reason why behavioral and emotional problems are more common among stepchildren (Crohn, 2006).

Still, many stepparents and stepchildren ultimately develop good relationships with each other. Stepparents must be sensitive to the relationship between the stepchild and his or her biological, noncustodial parent. Allowing stepchildren to develop the relationship with the stepparent at their own pace also helps. What style of stepparenting ultimately develops is influenced by the expectations of the stepparent, stepchild, spouse, and non-residential parent, but there are several styles that result in positive outcomes (Crohn, 2006).

Adoptive parents also contend with attachment to birth parents, but in different ways. Even if they don't remember them, adopted children may wish to locate and meet their birth parents. Wanting to know one's origins is understandable, but such searches can strain the relationships between these children and their adoptive parents, who may interpret these actions as a form of rejection (Rosenberg, 1992).

Families with children adopted from another culture face unique issues in terms of how to establish and maintain connection with the child's culture of origin. For mothers of transracially adopted Chinese and Korean children, becoming connected to the appropriate Asian American community is an important way to accomplish this (Johnston et al., 2007). Research in The Netherlands found that children adopted from Columbia, Sri Lanka, and Korea into Dutch homes struggled with looking different, and many expressed desires to be white (Juffer, 2006).

Foster parents tend to have the most tenuous relationship with their children because the bond can be broken for any of a number of reasons having nothing to do with the quality of the care being provided. For example, a court may award custody back to the birth parents, or another couple may legally adopt the child. Dealing with attachment is difficult; foster parents want to provide secure homes, but they may not have the children long enough to establish continuity. Furthermore, because many children in foster care have been unable to form attachments at all, they are less likely to form ones that will inevitably be broken. Thus, foster parents must be willing to tolerate considerable ambiguity in the relationship and have few expectations about the future.

Finally, many gay men and lesbian women also want to be parents. Some have biological children themselves, whereas others are increasingly choosing adoption or foster parenting (Braun, 2007). Although they often experience resistance to their having children, gay men and lesbian women make good parents. Research indicates that children reared by gay or lesbian parents do not experience any more problems than children reared by heterosexual parents and are as psychologically healthy as children of heterosexual parents (Braun, 2007). Substantial evidence exists that children raised by gay or lesbian parents do not develop sexual identity or any other problems any more than children raised by heterosexual parents (Macatee, 2007). Children of gay and lesbian parents also are no more likely than children of heterosexual parents to identify as gay, lesbian, bisexual, transgendered, or questioning.

The evidence is clear that children raised by gay or lesbian parents suffer no adverse consequences compared to children raised by heterosexual parents. Children of gay or lesbian couples and heterosexual couples are equally adjusted behaviorally, show equivalent cognitive development, and have similar behaviors in school. Indeed, one study found that the only difference between such couples was that lesbian couples exhibited more awareness of parenting skills than did heterosexual couples (Flaks et al., 1995).

Some evidence shows that children raised by gay or lesbian parents may even have some advantages over children raised by heterosexual parents (Macatee, 2007). Children of gay or lesbian parents might be better adjusted than adult children of heterosexual parents in that the adult children of gay and lesbian parents exhibit lower levels of homophobia and lower fear of negative evaluation than do the adult children of heterosexual parents. Gay men are often especially concerned about being good and nurturing fathers, and they try hard to raise their children with nonsexist, egalitarian attitudes (Flaks et al., 1995).

These data will not make the controversy go away, as much of it is based on long-held beliefs and prejudices. Admittedly, the data comparing children raised by different types of parents are inadequate; for example, there is very little information about children raised by lesbian women. Only when societal attitudes toward gay men and lesbians become more accepting will there be greater acceptance of their right to be parents like anyone else.

People like Susan in this section's opening vignette connect generations. Family ties across the generations provide the context for socialization and for continuity in the family's identity. At the center agewise are members of the middle-aged generation, like Susan, who serve as the links

between their aging parents and their own maturing children (Hareven, 2001). *Middle-aged mothers (more than fathers) tend to take on this role of* kinkeeper, *the person who gathers family members together for celebrations and keeps them in touch with each other.*

Think about the major issues confronting a typical middle-aged couple: maintaining a good marriage, parenting responsibilities, children who are becoming adults themselves, job pressures, and concern about aging parents, just to name a few. Middle-aged adults truly have quite a lot to deal with every day in balancing their responsibilities to their children and their aging parents (Riley & Bowen, 2005). *Indeed, middle-aged adults are sometimes referred to as the* sandwich generation; *they are caught between the* competing *demands of two generations (their parents and their children).* Being in the sandwich generation means different things for women and men. When middle-aged women assess how well they are dealing with the midlife transition, their most pressing issues relate more to their adolescent children than to their aging parents; for middle-aged men, it is the other way around (Riley & Bowen, 2005).

In this section, we first examine the dynamics of middle-aged parents and their maturing children and discover whether Susan's feelings are typical. Next, we consider the issues facing middle-aged adults and their aging parents. Later, we consider what happens when people become grandparents.

Midlife Issues: Adult Children and Parental Caregiving

Being a parent has a rather strange side when you think about it. After creating children out of love, parents spend considerable time, effort, and money preparing them to become independent and leave. For most parents, the leaving (and sometimes returning) occurs during midlife.

Adult Children: Becoming Friends and the Empty Nest. Sometime during middle age, most parents experience two positive developments with regard to their children. Suddenly their children see them in a new light, and the children leave home.

After the strain of raising adolescents, parents generally appreciate the transformation that occurs when their children head into young adulthood. In general, parent-child relationships improve when children become young adults (Troll & Fingerman, 1996). The difference can be dramatic, as in the case of Deb, a middle-aged mother. "When Sacha was 15, she acted as if I was the dumbest person on the planet. But now that she's 21, she acts as if I got smart all of a sudden. I like being around her. She's a great kid, and we're really becoming friends."

A key factor in making this transition as smoothly as possible is the extent to which parents foster and approve of their children's attempts at being independent. Most parents are like Esther, the mother in the earlier vignette, and manage the transition to an empty nest successfully; many mothers, in particular, use this as a time for growth (Owen, 2005). That's not to say that parents are heartless. When children leave home, emotional bonds are disrupted. Parents feel the change, although differently; women who define themselves more in their role as a mother tend to report more distress and negative mood (Hobdy, 2000). But only about 25% of mothers and fathers report being very sad and unhappy when the last child leaves home (Lewis & Lin, 1996).

Still, parents provide considerable financial help (such as paying college tuition) when possible. Most help in other ways, ranging from the mundane (such as making the washer and dryer available to their college-age children) to the extraordinary (providing the down payment for their child's house). Adult children and their parents generally believe that they have strong, positive relationships and that they can count on each other for help when necessary (Connidis, 2001).

When Children Come Back. Parents' satisfaction with the empty nest is sometimes short-lived. Roughly half of young adults in the United States return to their parents' home at least once after moving out (Osgood et al., 2005). There is evidence that these young adults, called "boomerang kids" (Mitchell, 2006), reflect a less permanent, more mobile contemporary society.

Why do children move back? Those that do typically arrive back home about the time they enter the workplace; the increased cost of living on one's own when saddled with college debt is a major factor. Several demographic and psychological factors influence the decision. Men are more likely to move back than women, as are children who had low college GPAs, low sense of autonomy, and an expectation that their parents would provide a large portion of their income following graduation (Osgood et al., 2005; Mitchell, 2006; Steen & Peterson, 2000). Adult children whose parents were verbally or physically abusive are unlikely to move back, as are those who are married.

The trend for young adults to move back home in the United States differs from the trend in some southern European countries (e.g., Italy), where the trend is for young adults to stay at home until they marry or obtain a full-time job (L' Abate, 2006). At earlier points in history, young women sometimes returned home to care for sick parents. However, the current trend is very much different, and is a reflection of changing social norms and the economics of becoming an adult more than an altruistic desire to care for one's parents.

Caring for Aging Parents. Most middle-aged adults have parents who are in reasonably good health. For a growing number of people, however, being a middle-aged child of aging parents involves providing some level of care. The job of caring for older parents usually falls to a daughter or a daughter-in-law (Stephens & Franks, 1999). Even after ruling out all other demographic characteristics of adult child caregivers and their care recipients, daughters are more than three times as likely to provide care as sons (Stephens et al., 2001). This gender difference is also found in other cultures. For example, in Japan, even though the oldest son is responsible for parental care, it is his wife who actually does the day-to-day caregiving (Morioka, 1998).

In some situations, older parents must move in with one of their children. Such moves usually occur after decades of both generations living independently. This history of independent living sets the stage for adjustment difficulties following the move; both lifestyles must be accommodated.

Most of the time, adult children provide care for their mothers, who may in turn have provided care for their husbands before they died. In other situations, adult daughters must try to manage care from a distance. As we will see later, irrespective of the location of care, women are under considerable stress from the pressures of caregiving.

Caring for one's parent presents a dilemma, especially for women (Baek, 2005; Stephens et al., 2001). *Most adult children feel a sense of responsibility, termed* filial obligation, *to care for their parent if necessary.* For example, adult child caregivers sometimes express the feeling that they "owe it to Mom or Dad" to care for them; after all, their parent provided for them for many years, and now the shoe is on the other foot (Gans, 2007). Adult children often provide care when needed to their parents in all Western and non-Western cultures studied (Hareven & Adams, 1996). Viewed globally, all but a small percentage of care to older adults is provided by adult children and other family members (Hareven & Adams, 1996; Moen, 2001). Worldwide, caregiving situations tend to be better when the economic impact on the caregiving family is minimal; for example, rural China supports the view that when middle-aged children care for aging parents, it is the financial impact on the caregivers that matters most (Zhan, 2006). Filial obligation also knows no borders; in an Australian study, middle-aged adults were found to be caring for parents in numerous other countries in Europe, the Middle East Asia, and New Zealand (Baldassar, Baldock, & Wilding, 2007).

Susan's experience embodies the notion of the "sandwich generation" noted earlier. Her need to balance caring for her daughter and for her mother can create conflict, both within herself and between the individuals involved (Neal & Hammer, 2006). Being pulled in different directions can put considerable stress on the caregiver, a topic we consider in the next section. But the rewards of caregiving are also great, and relationships can be strengthened as a result.

Roughly 44 million Americans provide care for older parents, in-laws, grandparents, and other older loved ones (AGS Foundation for Health in Aging, 2007). The typical caregiver is a 46-year-old woman who is employed outside the home and who provides more than 20 hours per week of unpaid caregiving. These family caregivers spend on average up to about $4,000 per year in support of their loved one (Gibson & Houser, 2007).

Caring for an older parent is often not easy. It usually doesn't happen by choice; each party would just as soon live independently. The potential for conflict over daily routines and lifestyles can be high. Indeed, one major source of conflict between middle-aged daughters and their older mothers is differences in perceived need for care, with middle-aged daughters believing that their mothers need care more than the mothers believe they do (Fingerman, 1996). The balance between independence and connection can be a difficult one (McGraw & Walker, 2004); among Japanese immigrants one course of conflict is between older mothers, who give unsolicited advice, and their caregiving daughters (Usita & Du Bois, 2005).

Caregiving Stresses and Rewards. Caregiving is a major source of both stresses and rewards. On the stress side, adult children and other family caregivers are especially vulnerable from two main sources (Pearlin et al., 1990):

- Adult children may have trouble coping with declines in their parents' functioning, especially those involving cognitive abilities and problematic behavior, and with the work overload, burnout, and loss of the previous relationship with a parent.
- When the caregiving situation is perceived as confining, or seriously infringes on the adult child's other responsibilities (spouse, parent, employee, etc.), the situation is likely to be perceived negatively, which may lead to family or job conflicts, economic problems, loss of self-identity, and decreased competence.

When caring for an aging parent, even the most devoted adult child caregiver feels depressed, resentful, angry, and guilty at times (Cavanaugh, 1999; Stephens et al., 2001). Many middle-aged caregivers are hard-pressed financially, as they may still be paying child care or college tuition expenses, perhaps trying to save adequately for their own retirement, and having to work more than one job to do it. Financial pressures are especially serious for those caring for parents with chronic conditions, such as Alzheimer's disease, that require services that are not covered adequately by medical insurance, even if the older parent has supplemental coverage. In some cases, adult children may even need to quit their jobs to provide care if adequate alternatives, such as adult day care, are unavailable or unaffordable.

The stresses of caring for one's parent are especially difficult for women. In terms of its timing in the life course, caring for a parent is typically something that coincides with women's peak employment years of 35–64. Longitudinal research clearly shows that employment status has no effect on women's decisions to become caregivers (many have little choice), but it has been the case for many years that becoming a caregiver makes it likely that women will reduce employment hours or stop working (Pavalko & Artis, 1997). When you consider that most women caring for parents are also mothers, wives, and employees, it should come as no surprise that stress from these other roles exacerbates the effects of stress due to caregiving (Baek, 2005; Stephens et al., 2001).

On the plus side, caring for an aging parent also has rewards. Caring for aging parents can bring parents and their adult children closer together, and provide a way for adult children to feel that they are giving back to their parents (Miller, Shoemaker, Willyard, & Addison, 2008). Cross-cultural research examining Taiwanese (Lee, 2007) and Chinese (Zhan, 2006) caregivers confirms that adults caring for aging parents can find the experience rewarding.

Ethnic differences among U.S. groups in adult children's experiences of caregiving reflect cultural norms. Compared to European Americans, Latino American family members are likely to be caring for people who are at higher risk of chronic disease and are more disabled (Aranda & Knight, 1997). A focused study of Mexican American caregivers showed that, given time and a supportive context from service providers, they come to accept services from social service agencies within their cultural norm of providing family care themselves (Crist, Garcia-Smith, & Phillips, 2006). African Americans prefer family caregiving to other options (e.g., placement in a long-term care facility) more strongly than European Americans do; European Americans are more open to having nonfamily members (such as professional paid caregivers) provide care (Foley, Tung, & Mutran, 2002). Latino American and African American caregivers, compared to European Americans, are more likely to be an adult child, friend, or other relative; report lower levels of caregiver stress, burden, and depression; believe more strongly in filial obligation; and are more likely to use prayer, faith, or religion as a coping strategy (Connell & Gibson, 1997). Such differences show that the relation between caregiving and stress is mediated by beliefs in family cohesiveness versus individual independence, as well as one's socialization. And caregivers also report experiencing rewards (Stephens & Franks, 1999).

From the parent's perspective, things aren't always rosy either. Independence and autonomy are important traditional values in some ethnic groups, and their loss is not taken lightly. Older adults in these groups are more likely to express the desire to pay a professional for assistance rather than ask a family member for help; they may find it demeaning to live with their children (Hamon & Blieszner, 1990). Most move in only as a last resort. As many as two thirds of older adults who receive help with daily activities feel negatively about the help they receive (Newsom, 1999).

Determining whether older parents are satisfied with the help their children provide is a complex issue (Newsom, 1999). Based on a critical review of the research, Newsom (1999) proposes a model of how certain aspects of care can produce negative perceptions of care directly or by affecting the interactions between caregiver and care recipient (see Figure 11.9). The important thing to conclude from the model is that even under the best circumstances, there is no guarantee that the help adult children provide their parents will be well received. Misunderstandings can occur, and the frustration caregivers feel can be translated directly into negative interactions.

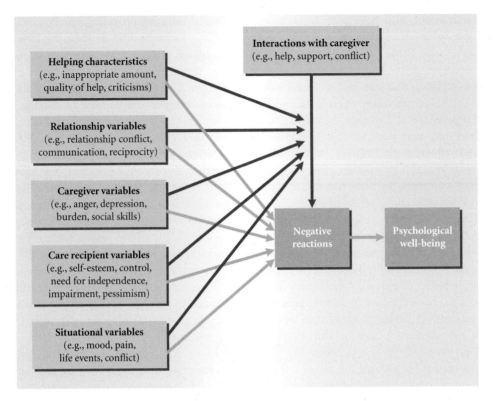

FIGURE 11.9 Whether a care recipient perceives care to be good depends on interactions with the caregiver and whether those interactions are perceived negatively.

Source: From Newsom, J. T. (1999). Another side to caregiving: Negative reactions to being helped. *Current Directions in Psychological Science, 8,* 185. Reprinted by permission of Blackwell Publishing, Ltd.

In sum, taking care of one's aging parents is a difficult task. Despite the numerous challenges and risks of negative psychological and financial outcomes, many caregivers nevertheless experience positive outcomes. Use the Discovering Development feature to learn more about supports in your community for people caring for their aging parents.

Grandparenthood

Becoming a grandparent takes some help. Being a parent yourself, of course, is a prerequisite. But it is your children's decisions and actions that determine whether you will experience the transition to grandparenthood, making this role different from most others we experience throughout life. Most people become grandparents in their 40s and 50s, though

some are older or perhaps as young as their late 20s or early 30s. In most cases, grandparents are quite likely to still be employed and to have living parents themselves. Thus, although being a grandparent may be an exciting time, it is often only one part of their busy lives.

How Do Grandparents Interact with Grandchildren? Keisha, an 8-year-old girl, smiled brightly when asked to describe her grandparents. "Nana Mary gives me chocolate ice cream, and that's my favorite! Poppy Bill sometimes takes care of me when Momma and Daddy go out, and plays ball with me." Kyle, a 14-year-old, had a different view. "My grandparents generally tell me stories of what life was like back when they were young."

As Keisha's and Kyle's experiences show, grandparents have many different ways of interacting

As we have seen, caring for aging parents can be both very stressful and uplifting. On the stress side, adult child caregivers can experience significant health effects from long-term stress. Stress may also be a factor in elder abuse, neglect, or exploitation. Thus, doing what is necessary to help deal with the stressful aspects is key.

Communities typically have several sources of help for adult children who are caring for their aging parents. Find out what is available in your area. Check with local social service agencies, organizations dedicated to serving older adults, hospitals, colleges and universities, and churches. You may be quite surprised to learn of the many options and

opportunities there are for adults to get assistance. These may range from workshops and classes to support groups to formal and informal outings.

Make a list of the programs you discover, and discuss them in class. If possible, talk with some people who run the programs and with people who take advantage of them to learn from their experiences.

---

with their grandchildren. Categorizing these styles has been attempted over the years (e.g., Neugarten & Weinstein, 1964), but none has been overly successful because grandparents use different styles with different grandchildren and styles change as grandparents and grandchildren age (Stephens & Clark, 1996).

An alternative approach involves considering the many functions grandparents serve, which can be understood as reflecting different levels of the social and personal dimensions (Cherlin & Furstenberg, 1986). The social dimension includes societal needs and expectations of what grandparents are to do, such as passing on family history to grandchildren. The personal dimension includes the personal satisfaction and individual needs that are fulfilled by being a grandparent. Many grandparents pass on skills, as well as religious, social, and vocational values (social dimension) through storytelling and advice, and they may feel great pride and satisfaction (personal dimension) from working with grandchildren on joint projects.

Grandchildren give grandparents a great deal in return. For example, grandchildren keep grandparents in touch with youth and the latest trends. Sharing the excitement of surfing the Web in school

may be one way in which grandchildren keep grandparents on the technological forefront.

Being a Grandparent Is Meaningful. Does being a grandparent matter to people? You bet it does, at least to the vast majority of grandparents. In her groundbreaking research, Kivnick (1982, 1985) identified five dimensions of meaning that grandparents often assign to their roles. However, additional research shows that grandparents can derive multiple meanings (Hayslip, Henderson, & Shore, 2003). For some, grandparenting is the most important thing in their lives, termed centrality. For others, meaning comes from being seen as wise (valued elder), from spoiling grandchildren (indulgence), from recalling the relationship they had with their own grandparents (reinvolvement with personal past), or from taking pride in the fact that they will be followed by not one but two generations (immortality through clan).

Most grandparents derive several different meanings, regardless of the style of their relationship with the grandchildren (Alley, 2004). Similar findings are reported when overall satisfaction with being a grandparent is examined; no matter what their style is, grandparents find their role meaningful (Hayslip et al., 2003). These findings have resulted in viewing grandparenthood as an aspect of generativity from which most grandparents derive a great deal of satisfaction (Thiele & Whelan, 2006, 2008).

Grandchildren also highly value their relationships with grandparents, even when they are young adults (Alley, 2004). Grandparents are valued as role models, and for their personalities, the activities they share, and the attention they show to grandchildren. Grandchildren also note that when their grandparents are frail, helping their grandparents is a way for them to act on their altruistic beliefs (Kennedy, 1991). Young adult grandchildren (ages 21–29) derive both stress and rewards from caring for grandparents, much the same way that middle-aged adults do when they care for their aging parents (Fruhauf, 2007).

Ethnic Differences. How grandparents and grandchildren interact varies in different ethnic groups. For example, African American grandmothers under age 40 report feeling pressured to provide care for grandchildren they were not eager to have; in contrast, those over age 60 tend to feel that they are fulfilling an important role (Kivett, 1991). African American grandparents tend to be more involved in teaching their grandchildren and more willing to take a grandparent education course than are European American grandparents (Watson & Koblinsky, 1997). African American grandparents also play an important role in religious education of their grandchildren (King et al., 2006). African American grandfathers tend to perceive grandparenthood as a central role to a greater degree than European American grandfathers (Kivett, 1991). And Latino American grandparents are more likely to participate in childrearing due to a cultural core value of family (Burnette, 1999).

Grandparenting style also varies with ethnicity, which may sometimes create tension within families. Kornhaber (1985) relates the case of an 18-month-old girl who had one pair of Latino grandparents and one pair of Nordic grandparents. Her Latino grandparents tickled her, frolicked with her, and doted over her. Her Nordic grandparents loved her just as much but tended to just let her be. Her Latina mother thought that the Nordic grandparents were "cold and hard," and her Nordic father accused the Latino grandparents of "driving him crazy" with their displays of affection. The child, though, was flexible enough to adapt to both styles.

Native American grandparents appear to have some interactive styles different from those of other groups (Weibel-Orlando, 1990). Fictive grandparenting is a style that allows adults to fill in for missing or deceased biological grandparents, functionally creating the role of surrogate grandparent. These adults provide a connection to the older generation that otherwise would be absent for these children. In the cultural conservator style,

© Catherine Karnow / CORBIS

How grandparents and grandchildren interact varies across culture.

grandparents request that their grandchildren be allowed to live with them to ensure that the grandchildren learn the native ways. These grandparents provide grandchildren with a way to connect with their cultural heritage, and they are likely to provide a great deal of care for their grandchildren (Mutchler, Baker, & Lee, 2007). In general, Native American grandmothers take a more active role in these styles than do grandfathers.

Asian American grandparents, particularly if they are immigrants, serve as a primary source of traditional culture for their grandchildren (Yoon, 2005). When these grandparents become heavily involved in caring for their grandchildren, they especially want and need services that are culturally and linguistically appropriate. Grandparents caring for grandchildren is a topic to which we now turn.

When Grandparents Care for Grandchildren. Grandparenthood today is tougher than it used to be. Families are more mobile, which means that grandparents are more often separated from their grandchildren by geographical distance. Grandparents are more likely to have independent lives apart from their children and grandchildren. What being a grandparent entails in the 21st century is more ambiguous than it once was (Fuller-Thompson, Hayslip, & Patrick, 2005).

Perhaps the biggest change for grandparents is the increasing number who serve as custodial parents for their grandchildren (Waldrop & Weber, 2001). Estimates are that about 5.7 million U.S. grandparents have grandchildren living with them, and 2.5 million of these grandparents provide basic needs (food, shelter, clothing) for one or more of their grandchildren (U.S. Census Bureau, 2007). These situations result most often when parents are addicted, incarcerated, or unable to raise their children for some other reason (Cox, 2000; Hayslip & Goldberg-Glen, 2000), or because of discipline or behavior problems exhibited by the grandchild (Giarusso et al., 2000). Lack of legal recognition due to the grandparents' lack of legal guardianship also poses problems and challenges, for example, in dealing with schools and obtaining records. Typically, social service workers must assist grandparents in navigating the many unresponsive policies and systems in order to provide the best assistance to their grandchildren possible (Cox, 2007). Clearly, public policy changes are needed to address these issues (Smith et al., 2000).

Raising grandchildren is not easy. Financial stress, cramped living space, and social isolation are only some of the issues facing custodial grandmothers (Bullock, 2004). Rates of problem behavior, hyperactivity, and learning problems in the grandchildren are high and negatively affect the grandparent–grandchild relationship (Hayslip et al., 1998). The grandchildren's routines, activities, and school-related issues also cause stress (Musil & Standing, 2005). Native American custodial grandparents report more symptoms of depression than European American custodial grandparents, especially those who have lower household income and spend less time with their grandchild (Litiecq, Bailey, & Kurtz, 2008). All of these stresses are also reported cross-culturally; for example, full-time custodial grandmothers in Kenya reported higher levels of stress than part-time caregivers (Oburu & Palmérus, 2005).

Even custodial grandparents raising grandchildren without these problems report more stress and role disruption than noncustodial grandparents (Emick & Hayslip, 1999). And custodial grandmothers who are employed report that they arrive late, miss work, must leave work suddenly, or leave early to tend to the grandchild's needs (Pruchno, 1999). But most custodial grandparents consider their situation better for their grandchild than any other alternative and report surprisingly few negative effects on their marriages.

Great-Grandparenthood. As we have seen, grandparenting is an important and enjoyable role for many adults. With increasing numbers of people, especially women, living to very old age, more people are experiencing great-grandparenthood. Age at first marriage and age at parenthood also play a critical role; people who reach these milestones at relatively younger ages are more likely to become great-grandparents. Most current great-grandparents are women who married relatively young and had children and grandchildren who also married and had children relatively early in adulthood.

Although surprisingly little research has been conducted on great-grandparents, their investment in their roles as parents, grandparents, and great-grandparents forms a single family identity (Drew & Silverstein, 2005). That is, great-grandparents see a true continuity of the family through the passing on of the genes. However, their sources of satisfaction and meaning apparently differ from those of grandparents (Doka & Mertz, 1988; Wentkowski, 1985). Compared to grandparents, great-grandparents are much more similar as a group in what they derive from the role, largely because they are less involved with the children than grandparents are. Three aspects of great-grandparenthood appear to be most important (Doka & Mertz, 1988).

First, being a great-grandparent provides a sense of personal and family renewal—important components for achieving integrity. Their grandchildren have produced new life, renewing their own excitement for life and reaffirming the continuance of their lineage. Seeing their families stretch across four generations may also provide psychological support, through feelings of symbolic immortality, to help them face death. They take pride and comfort in knowing that their families will live many years beyond their own lifetime.

Second, great-grandchildren provide new diversions in great-grandparents' lives. There are now new people with whom they can share their experiences. Young children can learn from a person they perceive as "really old" (Mietkiewicz & Venditti, 2004).

Third, becoming a great-grandparent is a major milestone, a mark of longevity that most people never achieve. The sense that one has lived long enough to see the fourth generation is perceived very positively.

As you might expect, people with at least one living grandparent and great-grandparent interact more with their grandparent, who is also perceived as more influential (Roberto & Skoglund, 1996). Unfortunately, some great-grandparents must assume the role of primary caregiver to their great-grandchildren, a role that few great-grandparents are prepared for (Bengtson, Mills, & Parrott, 1995; Burton, 1992). As more people live longer, it will be interesting to see whether the role of great-grandparents changes and becomes more prominent.

Concept Checks

1. What are the key aspects in the parental role and how do they differ across ethnic groups?

2. What happens to parent–child relationships as children and parents age? What are the key considerations in taking care of aging parents?

3. What are the major styles and meaning of grandparenthood?

SOCIAL POLICY IMPLICATIONS

Elder abuse and neglect is a major, underreported global problem. To help protect vulnerable older adults, the U.S. Congress has been working on the Elder Justice Act since 2007. Introduced by Senator Orrin Hatch and former Representative Rahm Emanuel (who now serves as President Obama's Chief of Staff), the bill amends the Social Security Act to create an Elder Justice Program under Title XX (Block Grants to States for Social Services).

In brief, the bill would direct the Secretary of the Department of Health and Human Services to provide grants to states for them to develop forensic expertise to improve the ability of health care and other professionals to gather evidence of elder abuse, neglect, and exploitation. Additional grants would be provided for training of staff in long-term care facilities that would improve residents' health and safety, and to perform investigations of alleged abuse, neglect, or exploitation more thoroughly. Adult Protective Services departments in states would be required to provide more complete data and better training for staff. Ombudspersons and owners or operators of long-term care facilities would be required to report suspected cases. Plans for better enforcement of laws, prevention, and treatment of victims would also be required.

If adopted, this bill would greatly strengthen the reporting, investigation, and prosecution of elder abuse, neglect, and exploitation, as well as provide better protection for victims. Such improvements are essential, especially for victims who have diminished cognitive capacity.

Summary

11.1 Relationship Types and Issues

What role do friends play across adulthood?

- People tend to have more friendships during young adulthood than during any other period. Friendships in old age are especially important for maintaining life satisfaction.

- Men tend to have fewer close friends and base them on shared activities. Women tend to have more close friends and base them on emotional sharing. Cross-gender friendships tend to be difficult.

What characterizes love relationships? How do they vary across culture?

- Passion, intimacy, and commitment are the key components of love.

- The theory that does the best job explaining the process of forming love relationships is the theory of assortative mating.

- Selecting a mate works best when there are shared values, goals, and interests. There are cross-cultural differences in which specific aspects of these are most important.

What are abusive relationships? What characterizes elder abuse, neglect, or exploitation?

- Levels of aggressive behavior range from verbal aggression to physical aggression to murdering one's partner. People remain in abusive relationships for many reasons, including low self-esteem and the belief that they cannot leave.

- Abuse, neglect, or exploitation of older adults is an increasing problem. Most perpetrators are spouses/partners or adult children. The causes are complex.

11.2 Lifestyles and Love Relationships

What are the challenges of being single?

- Most adults in their 20s are single. People remain single for many reasons; gender differences exist. Ethnic differences reflect differences in age at marriage and social factors.

- Singles recognize the pluses and minuses in the lifestyle. There are health and longevity consequences from remaining single for men but not for women.

Why do people cohabit?

- Cohabitation is on the increase globally.

- Three primary reasons for cohabiting are convenience (e.g., to share expenses), trial marriage, or substitute marriage.

What are gay and lesbian relationships like?

- Gay and lesbian couples are similar to married heterosexual couples in terms of relationship issues. Lesbian couples tend to be more egalitarian.

What is marriage like across adulthood?

- The most important factors in creating stable marriages are maturity, similarity (called homogamy), and conflict resolution skills. Exchange theory is an important explanation of how people contribute to their relationships.

- For couples with children, marital satisfaction tends to decline until the children leave home, although individual differences are apparent, especially in long-term marriages.

- Most long-term marriages tend to be happy, and partners in them express fewer negative emotions.

- Caring for a spouse presents challenges. How well it works depends on the quality of the marriage. Most caregiving spouses provide care based on love.

Why do couples divorce and remarry?

- Currently, half of all new marriages end in divorce. Reasons for divorce include a lack of the qualities that make a strong marriage. Also, societal attitudes against divorce have eased, and expectations about marriage have increased.

- Recovery from divorce is different for men and women. Men tend to have a tougher time in the short run. Women clearly have a harder time in the long run, often for financial reasons. Difficulties between divorced partners usually involve visitation and child support.

- Most divorced couples remarry. Second marriages are especially vulnerable to stress if stepchildren are involved. Remarriage in later life tends to be very happy, but may be resisted by adult children.

What are the experiences of widows and widowers?

- Widowhood is more common among women because they tend to marry men older than they are. Widowed men typically are older.

- Reactions to widowhood depend on the quality of the marriage. Men generally have problems in social relationships and in household tasks; women tend to have more financial problems.

11.3 Family Dynamics and the Life Course

What is it like to be a parent? What are the key issues across ethnic groups? What forms of parenting are there?

- Most couples choose to have children, although for many different reasons. The timing of parenthood determines in part how involved parents are in their families as opposed to their careers.

- Instilling cultural values in children is important for parents. In some cultures, familism changes the unit of analysis from the individual to the family.

- Single parents face many problems, especially if they are women and are divorced. The main problem is reduced financial resources. A major issue for adoptive parents, foster parents, and stepparents is how strongly the child will bond with them. Each of these relationships has some special characteristics. Gay and lesbian parents also face numerous obstacles, but they usually are good parents.

How do middle-aged adults get along with their children? How do they deal with the possibility of providing care to aging parents?

- Most parents do not report severe negative emotions when their children leave. Difficulties emerge to the extent that children were a major source of a parent's identity. However, parents typically report distress if adult children move back.

- Middle-aged women often assume the role of kinkeeper to the family. Middle-aged parents may be squeezed by competing demands of their children, who want to gain independence, and their parents, who want to maintain independence; therefore, they are often called the sandwich generation.

- Most caregiving by adult children is done by daughters and daughters-in-law. Filial obligation, the sense of responsibility to care for older parents, is a major factor.

- Caring for aging parents can be highly stressful. Symptoms of depression, anxiety, and other problems are widespread. Financial pressures also are felt by most. Parents often have a difficult time in accepting the care. However, many caregivers also report feeling rewarded or uplifted for their efforts.

How do grandparents interact with their grandchildren? What key issues are involved?

- Being a grandparent is a very meaningful role. Individual differences in interactive style are large.

- Ethnic differences in grandparenting are evident. Ethnic groups with strong family ties differ in style from groups who value individuality.

- Grandparents are increasingly being put in the position of raising their grandchildren. Reasons include incarceration and substance abuse by the parents.

- Great-grandparenthood is a role enjoyed by more people and reflects a sense of family renewal.

Review Questions

11.1 Relationship Types and Issues

- How does the number and importance of friendships vary across adulthood?

- What gender differences are there in the number and type of friends?

- What are the components of love?

- What characteristics make the best matches between adults? How do these characteristics differ across cultures?

- What is elder abuse, neglect, or exploitation? Why is it underreported?

11.2 Lifestyles and Love Relationships

- How do adults who never marry deal with the need to have relationships?

- What are the relationship characteristics of gay and lesbian couples?

- What are the most important factors in creating stable marriages?

- What developmental trends are occurring in marital satisfaction? How do these trends relate to having children?

- What factors are responsible for the success of long-term marriages?

- What are the major reasons people get divorced? How are these reasons related to societal expectations about marriage and attitudes about divorce?

- What characteristics about remarriage make it similar to and different from first marriage? How does satisfaction in remarriage vary as a function of age?

- What are the characteristics of widowed people? How do men and women differ in their experience of widowhood?

11.3 Family Dynamics and the Life Course

- What ethnic differences are there in parenting? What is familism and how does it relate to parenting?

- What are the important issues in being an adoptive parent, foster parent, or stepparent? What special challenges are there for gay and lesbian parents?

- What impact does children leaving home have on parents? Why do adult children return?

- What are the important issues facing middle-aged adults who care for their parents?

- How do grandparents and grandchildren relate? How do these relationships change with the age of the grandchild?

- What ethnic differences have been noted in grandparenting?

- What are the important issues and meanings of being a great-grandparent?

Integrating Concepts in Development

- What components would a theory of adult relationships need to have?
- What are some examples of each of the four developmental forces as they influence adult relationships?
- What role do the changes in sexual functioning discussed in Chapter 3 have on love relationships?
- What key public policy issues are involved in the different types of adult relationships?

Key Terms

abusive relationship A relationship in which one partner displays aggressive behavior toward the other partner.

assortative mating A theory that states that people find partners based on their similarity to each other.

battered woman syndrome A situation in which a woman believes that she cannot leave an abusive relationship and in which she may even go so far as to kill her abuser.

cohabitation Living with another person as part of a committed, intimate, sexual relationship.

exchange theory A theory of relationships based on the idea that each partner contributes something to the relationship that the other would be hard-pressed to provide.

familism Refers to the idea that the well-being of the family takes precedence over the concerns of individual family members.

filial obligation The feeling that, as an adult child, one must care for one's parents.

homogamy The notion that similar interests and values are important in forming strong, lasting interpersonal relationships.

kinkeeper The person who gathers family members together for celebrations and keeps them in touch with each other.

married singles Married couples who have grown apart but continue to live together.

sandwich generation Middle-aged adults caught between the competing demands of two generations: their parents and their children.

socioemotional selectivity A theory of relationships that argues that social contact is motivated by a variety of goals, including information seeking, self-concept, and emotional regulation.

Resources

www.cengage.com/psychology/cavanaugh

Visit the companion website, where you will find tutorial quizzes, glossary, flashcards, and more. You can also access the following websites from the companion website.

Research findings and professional materials about all aspects of families can be obtained through the National Council on Family Relations.

The Family Violence Prevention Fund (FVPF) is a national nonprofit organization that focuses on domestic violence education, prevention, and public policy reform. The National Center on Elder Abuse provides focused information on older adult victims.

Grandparents Raising Grandchildren at the USA.gov website provides much information for assistance.

The Family Caregiver Alliance provides a wealth of information about medical, policy, and resource issues concerning caregiving. It is intended for people caring for older adults.

Readings

American Bar Association. (2009). *You and your aging parents.* New York: Random House. An excellent reference for information on legal, financial, and health care matters. Easy reading.

Connidis, I. A. (2009). *Family ties and aging.* Thousand Oaks, CA: Sage Publications. A good summary of how families relate across adulthood. Moderately difficult reading.

Gottman, J. M., Gottmann, J. S., & Declaire, J. (2007). *Ten lessons to transform your marriage.* New York: Random House. A practical guide from leading researchers on the factors that create successful marriages. Easy to moderate reading.

12

Work, Leisure, and Retirement

STROM THURMOND (1902–2003) WAS THE LONGEST-SERVING U.S. SENATOR. HIS TERM EXTENDED from 1954 to 2003 when he retired at the ripe old age of 100. He ended up completing 48 years in office. Was he too old to serve? Praises from his colleagues and his continuing accomplishments suggest not. For example, he was the senior member of the Judiciary Committee; he chaired the Senate Armed Services Committee and was the senior member of the Veterans Affairs Committees. After being dogged by questions about his age, Thurmond said that his opponents should stop digging at his age, and start talking about the issues. When asked about retirement, he laughed, and said he'd have to think about that.

Strom Thurmond's tenure as U.S. senator at such an advanced age reflects some of the key issues we will examine in this chapter, especially in the section on retirement. First, we will examine how people choose occupations and how they develop in their occupations. However, there are obstacles to occupational development. Thus, next we will explore such obstacles including discrimination and bias issues. Given the current fluctuations in occupational status, we will explore how individuals make transitions within their occupation as well as to other occupations. Finally, we will answer two important questions. How do people spend time when they are not working? And what happens to them after they retire?

As will become clear, research addressing these questions about work has focused primarily on middle-class European American men; far less is known about women or about other ethnic groups. Although more research on women and on other ethnic groups is being conducted, we must be careful in applying existing research and theory to these other groups until data have been compiled.

12.1 Occupational Choice and Development

LEARNING OBJECTIVES

- How do people view work? How do occupational priorities vary with age?
- How do people choose their occupations?
- What factors influence occupational development?

- What expectations do people have about occupations?
- What role do mentors play in occupational development?
- What factors influence job satisfaction? What causes alienation and burnout?

Christiane, a 28-year-old senior, a communications major, wonders about careers. Should she enter the broadcast field as a behind-the-scenes producer, or would she be better suited as a public relations spokesperson? She thinks that her outgoing personality is a factor she should consider. Should she become a broadcast producer?

Choosing one's work is serious business. Like Christiane, we try to select a field in which we are trained, and that is appealing. Work also colors much of what else we do in life. You may be taking this course as part of your preparation for work. People make friends at work and schedule personal activities around work schedules. Parents may choose child-care centers on the basis of their proximity to their place of employment. In this section, we will explore what work means to adults. We will also examine issues pertaining to occupational selection, as well as examine occupational development. Finally, we will see how satisfaction with one's job changes during adulthood.

The Meaning of Work

In the 1960s, the phrase "different strokes for different folks" was used to get across the point that people's motives and needs differ. Thus, work has different meanings for different people. Studs Terkel, the author of the fascinating book *Working* (1974), writes that work is "a search for daily meaning as well as daily bread, for recognition as well as cash, for astonishment rather than torpor; in short, for a sort of life rather than a Monday through Friday sort of dying" (p. xiii). Kahil Gibran (1923), in his mystical book *The Prophet*, put it this way: "Work is love made visible."

For some of us, work is a source of prestige, social recognition, and a sense of worth. For others, the excitement of creativity and the opportunity to give something of themselves make work meaningful. But for most, the main purpose of work is to earn a living. This is not to imply, of course, that money is the only reward in a job; friendships, the chance to exercise power, and feeling useful are also important. The meaning most of us derive from working includes both the money that can be exchanged for life's necessities (and maybe a few luxuries, too) and the possibility of personal growth. These **occupational priorities**, *or what people want from their*

employment, reflect the culture and the times in which people live.

Occupational priorities change over time because cultural values change. An excellent example of these influences is the longitudinal study conducted by American Telephone and Telegraph (AT&T), begun in the mid-1950s (Howard & Bray, 1988). Look carefully at the graph in Figure 12.1. Three key things are depicted. First, the vertical axis represents the rating of the importance of work in employees' lives. The horizontal axis reflects two things: length of time in the study at AT&T (which gives an idea of the length of employment), and relative age (in general, the less time in the study, the younger the employee).

Notice how the importance of work changed dramatically over time. The longer employees were in the study, the more differentiated the various levels of managers became in terms of the importance of work. Underlying these changes are key differences in motivation for upward mobility, leadership, and desire for emotional support, depending on the age of the managers. For higher management levels, participants who had been in the AT&T study briefly had expectations of rewards from work that were much lower than those who had been in the study 10 years or more; they did not see most of their major rewards or life satisfaction coming from work. Interestingly, the picture was reversed for lower-level managers; those who had been in the study longer gave a lower rating of the importance of work.

The findings at AT&T are not unique. Other research has also documented that younger workers in upper management are less interested in materialism, power seeking, upward mobility, and competition; instead, they consistently emphasize individual freedom, personal growth, and cooperation (Jones, 1980; Yankelovich, 1981). In fact, a recent study suggests that negative costs are associated with goals for financial success. People with stronger financial goals tended to have lower overall life satisfaction (although this was mainly for people with low income levels) and lower satisfaction with family life irrespective of income level (Nickerson et al., 2003).

Regardless of what occupational priorities people have, they view their occupation as a key element in their sense of identity (Whitbourne, 1996). This

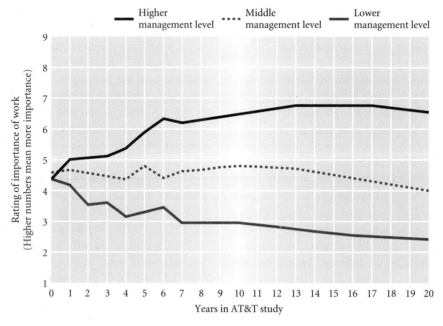

Figure 12.1 Changes in the relative importance of work at different levels of management in the AT&T study.

Source: Howard, A., & Bray, D.W. (1990, August). *Career motivation in mid-life managers.* Paper presented at the meeting of the American Psychological Association, Montreal.

feeling can be readily observed when people introduce themselves socially: "Hi, I'm Kevin. I'm an accountant. What do you do?'" Occupation affects your life in a whole host of ways, often influencing where you live, what friends you make, and even what clothes you wear. In short, the impact of work cuts across all aspects of life. Work, then, is a major social role and influence on adult life. Occupation is an important anchor that complements the other major role of adulthood—love relationships.

The Changing Nature of Work

The traditional view of work assumes that one's job consists of a certain set of tasks that need to be performed or a work-survival-status-life paradigm (Cascio, 1995). But this view is rapidly becoming outmoded. Global competition means that workers in the United States are competing for jobs with workers in the same industries in France, Russia,

Taiwan, China, Poland, Argentina, and the rest of the world (Avolio & Sosik, 1999).

The globalization of work has also resulted in massive changes in both the number and type of jobs available to U.S. workers and in the skills these jobs require (Avolio & Sosik, 1999; Gephart, 2002). For example, between 1987 and 1994 more than 7 million permanent layoffs were announced in the United States (Cascio, 1995). At that time, these layoffs were not due to companies losing money; indeed, 81% of the companies that downsized during this period were profitable during that year. Rather, layoffs occurred mostly because of competition, productivity, relocation of operations, mergers and acquisitions, infusion of new technology, or plant obsolescence. Even though many laid-off workers found new jobs, the new positions invariably involve drastic pay cuts, resulting in downward mobility. Of course, we have a whole new perspective arising with the recent economic recession. Researchers should be able to examine factors that "disappear" as a function of the economic downturn and its effect on psychological resiliency and well-being.

What do these types of changes mean? In short, a fundamental redefinition of the nature of work has occurred. Whereas traditional organizational careers consisted of meeting the needs of the organization, now the emphasis is on occupational flexibility and learning (Eby, Butts, & Lockwood, 2003; Hall & Mirvis, 1995; Sullivan, 1999). Organizations must respond rapidly to market conditions that change quickly. Managers must use flexible styles of leadership depending on the situation, with an emphasis on being able to bring out employees' creativity and best efforts. Workers must assume more autonomy and decision-making authority, must have a variety of technical skills, and must be proactive and open to experience (Eby et al., 2003). There is an increasing need for training and development in order to maintain workers' competencies and fulfillment. Furthermore, employees are requiring that their talents and abilities have added value for both organizations and themselves (Liebold & Voepel, 2006). Everyone must learn continually to stay current with the latest technology and newest skills.

In the past two decades, dramatic growth in the need for occupational flexibility is observed in an increase in telework or telecommuting, that is, working remotely, outside of the typical office environment (Bailey & Kurland, 2002; Harpaz, 2002). Overall, telework has resulted in improved productivity, organizational loyalty, and job satisfaction (Bailey et al., 2002). However, there are disadvantages such as a sense of isolation and a lack of separation between work and home, among others (Harpaz, 2002). More research is needed as to why such employees work away from the office.

As the nature of work has changed, so has the nature of the workforce. The median age of the workforce has steadily increased and is expected to reach 41.40 years by the year 2012 (Toossi, 2004). We are witnessing the "graying of the workforce." The "older worker" in the labor market is considered to be aged 50 or 55 and above. In organizations the threshold is at 40 or 45, where "old" refers to obsolete knowledge, skills, and attitudes (Kooij, De Lange, Jansen, & Dikkers, 2008). Persons aged 55 and over are expected to comprise 60% of the projected increase in the labor force in general (U.S. Census Bureau, 2004). Now that we have entered the 21st century, the aging workforce and the increasingly complex, technologically based workplace are here to stay. We must change the way we think about organizations, attend to the needs of older workers, and reassess our basic conceptions of what a job entails.

Occupational Choice

As indicated earlier, work life serves as a major source of identity, provides us with an official position, and influences lifestyle and social interactions; therefore, choosing an occupation is a serious matter. Although most people think occupational choice is largely the province of young adults, much of what we will consider also holds true for middle-aged and older workers who are seeking to change occupations either voluntarily or because they lost their jobs. As you will see later, more adults are changing occupations than ever before and have to rethink the kinds of jobs they want to hold. Moreover, as the downsizing trend in corporations and the economic recession continue, many adults may be forced to look for new employment in different fields.

From a developmental perspective, the decisions people make about occupations may change over time. As people face different life issues or achieve new insights about themselves, they may well decide that their best bet would be to change occupations. In addition, occupational choices may reflect personal or social clocks (see Chapter 1); individuals of different ages may feel different degrees of pressure to make a certain occupational choice. Regardless of age, personality and interests are important factors in deciding on an occupation. Let's turn our attention to one of the theories explaining how and why people choose the occupations they do.

Holland's Theory of Occupational Choice. Although we tend to think of occupational choice as something done during adolescence or young adulthood, recent theories and research have increasingly adopted a life course perspective (Sterns & Gray, 1999). However, the main theoretical frameworks for occupational choice have taken a trait-factor approach, which focuses on aspects of one's personality (see Chapter 9).

Holland (1985, 1987, 1996) developed a theory based on the intuitively appealing idea that people choose occupations to optimize the fit between their individual traits—such as personality, intelligence, skills, and abilities—and their occupational interests. He categorizes occupations in two ways: by the interpersonal settings in which people must function and by their associated lifestyle. He identifies six work environments in which individuals can express their vocational personalities; they are summarized in Table 12.1. Each one is best suited to a specific set of occupations, as indicated in the right-hand column of the table. Remember that these are merely prototypes. Most people do not match any one personality type exactly. Instead, their work-related personalities are a blend of the six.

Holland's theory exists at the level of interest, not at the level of performance requirements per se. He predicts that people will choose the occupation that has the greatest similarity to their personality type. By doing this, they optimize their ability to express themselves, apply their skills, and take on new roles. Having a good match between personality and occupation maximizes occupational satisfaction. This model is useful in describing the career preferences of African, Asian, European, Native, and Mexican American adults; it is also useful for both males and females (Barrick, Mount, & Gupta, 2003; Day, Rounds, & Swaney, 1998). Research also shows that when people have jobs that match their personality type, in the short run they are more productive workers, and in the long run they have more stable career paths (Holland, 1996). Similarly, in a study of 171 African American nursing personnel, Day and Bedeian (1995) found that personality traits significantly predicted job performance and how long employees remain with the same organization.

Table 12.1

General Occupational Themes in Holland's Theory

Theme	Description	Careers
Realistic	Individuals enjoy physical labor and working with their hands, and they like to solve concrete problems.	Mechanic, truck driver, construction worker
Investigative	Individuals are task-oriented and enjoy thinking about abstract relations.	Scientist, technical writer
Social	Individuals are skilled verbally and interpersonally, and they enjoy solving problems using these skills.	Teacher, counselor, social worker
Conventional	Individuals have verbal and quantitative skills that they like to apply to structured, well-defined tasks assigned to them by others.	Bank teller, payroll clerk, traffic manager
Enterprising	Individuals enjoy using their verbal skills inpositions of power, status, and leadership.	Business executive, television producer, real estate agent
Artistic	Individuals enjoy expressing themselves through unstructured tasks.	Poet, musician, actor

Source: Holland (1996).

Holland's theory does not mean that personality completely determines what occupation one chooses. The connection is that people who act or feel a certain way typically choose certain occupations. Most of us would rather do something that we like to do than something we are forced to do. Thus, unless we have little choice because of financial or other constraints, we typically choose occupations on that basis. When mismatches occur, people usually adapt by changing jobs, changing interests, or adapting the job to provide a better match.

Although the relations between personality and occupational choice are important, we must also recognize the limits of the theory as it relates to adults' occupational choices. If we simply consider the gender distribution of Holland's personality types, adult men and women are represented differently (Costa, McCrae, & Holland, 1984). Regardless of age, women are more likely than men to have social, artistic, and conventional personality types. In part, gender differences reflect different experiences in growing up (e.g., hearing that girls grow up to be nurses whereas boys grow up to be firefighters), differences in personality (e.g., gender-role identity), and differences in socialization (e.g., women being expected to be more outgoing and people-oriented than men). However, if we look within a specific occupational type, women and men are very similar to each other, and closely correspond to the interests Holland describes (Betz, Harmon, & Borgen, 1996).

We know very little about how Holland's types vary in different ethnic groups, mostly because such groups have not been included in the studies investigating the links between personality and occupation. However, more recent research using a different methodology has found that the relation between interests and ability with occupational choice is lowest for African Americans and highest for Mexican Americans (Tracey & Hopkins, 2001). Finally, Holland's theory ignores the context in which occupational decisions are made. For example, he overlooks the fact that many people have little choice in the kind of job they can get, because of external factors such as family, financial pressures, or ethnicity.

Holland's theory also ignores evidence the dynamic quality of the match between personality type and occupation—in other words, how it changes during adulthood (Adler & Aranya, 1984; Jepsen & Dickson, 2003). Holland takes a static view of both personality and occupations, but it must be recognized that what occupation we choose is not dictated solely by what we are like. Equally important is the dynamic interplay between us and the sociocultural context we find ourselves in—just as one would suspect, given the biopsychosocial model presented in Chapter 1. Occupational selection is a complex developmental process involving interactions among personal, ethnic, gender, and economic factors.

Occupational Development

For most of us, getting a job is not enough; we would also like to move up the ladder. Promotion is a measure of how well one is doing in one's career. How quickly occupational advancement occurs (or does not) may lead to such labels as "fast-tracker" or "dead-ender" (Kanter, 1976). Barack Obama, shown here being inaugurated as the president at age 47, is an example of a fast-tracker. People who want to advance learn quickly how long to stay at one level and how to seize opportunities as they occur; others soon learn the frustration of remaining in the same job, with no chance for promotion.

How a person advances in a career seems to depend on professional socialization, which includes several factors besides those that are important in choosing an occupation. Among these are expectations, support from co-workers, priorities, and job satisfaction. Before we consider these aspects, we will look at a general scheme of occupational development.

Super's Theory Over four decades, Super (1957, 1980) developed a theory of occupational development based on self-concept. He proposed a progression through five distinct stages during adulthood, resulting from changes in individuals' self-concept and adaptation to an occupational role: implementation, establishment, maintenance, deceleration, and retirement. *People are located along a continuum of*

Barack Obama is shown being inaugurated as U.S. President at age 48.

vocational maturity *through their working years; the more congruent their occupational behaviors are with what is expected of them at different ages, the more vocationally mature they are.*

Implementation → Establishment → Maintenance → Deceleration → Retirement

The initial two phases of Super's theory, crystallization (identity development as a source of career ideas) and specification (focusing on and training in specific lines of work), occur primarily during adolescence, and the first adulthood phase has its origins then as well. Each of the stages in adulthood has distinctive characteristics:

- The *implementation* stage begins in late adolescence or the early 20s, when people take a series of temporary jobs to learn firsthand about work roles and to try out some possible career choices.

- The *establishment* stage begins with selecting a specific occupation during young adulthood. It continues as the person advances up the career ladder in the same occupation.

- The *maintenance* stage is a transition phase during middle age; as workers maximize their efficiency, they begin to reduce the amount of time they spend fulfilling work roles.

- The *deceleration* stage begins as workers begin planning in earnest for their upcoming retirement and separating themselves from their work.

- The *retirement* stage begins when people stop working full time.

In Super's framework, people's occupations evolve in response to changes in their self-concept (Salomone, 1996). Consequently, this is a developmental process that reflects and explains important life changes (Jepsen & Dickson, 2003). This process sheds a developmental light on Holland's ideas. Investigative and enterprising people are likely to come from more affluent families, in which the parents tend not to have investigative or enterprising occupations. Interestingly, initial occupational goals were not as important for social types as for the other two; social types appeared more flexible in eventual occupational choice.

However, a shortcoming of Super's theory is that the progression assumes that once people choose an occupation, they stay in it for the rest of their working lives. Although this may have been true for some employees in the past, it is not the case for most North American workers today (Cascio, 1995). The downsizing of public and private organizations since the late 1980s has all but eliminated the notion of lifetime job security with a particular employer. It remains to be seen whether new developmental stages will be found to underlie the new occupational reality.

Occupational Expectations. People have expectations regarding what they want to become and when they hope to get there. Levinson and his colleagues (1978) built these expectations into their theory of adult male development, which was later extended to women (Levinson & Levinson, 1996). Based on findings from the original longitudinal study begun in the 1940s on men attending an elite private college, Levinson and his colleagues (1978) found considerable similarity among the participants in terms of major life tasks during adulthood. Forming a dream, with one's career playing a prominent role, is one of the young adult's chief tasks.

Throughout adulthood, people continue to refine and update their occupational expectations. This usually involves trying to achieve the dream, monitoring progress toward it, and changing or even abandoning it as necessary. For some, modifying the dream comes as a result of realizing that interests have changed or that the dream was not a good fit. In other cases, failure leads to changing the dream—for example, dropping a business major because one is failing economics courses. Other causes are age, racial, or sexual discrimination, lack of opportunity, obsolescence of skills, and changing interests. In some cases, one's initial occupational choice may simply have been unrealistic. For example, nearly half of all young adults would like to become professionals (such as lawyers or physicians), but only one person in seven actually makes it (Cosby, 1974). Some goal modification is essential from time to time, but it usually surprises us to realize we could have been wrong about what seemed to be a logical choice in the past. As Marie, a 38-year-old advertising manager, put it, "I really thought I wanted to be a pilot; the travel sounded really interesting. But it just wasn't what I expected."

Perhaps the rudest jolt for most of us first comes during the transition from school to the real world. **Reality shock,** *or the realization that the real world does not work like it says in the book, sets in, and things never seem to happen the way we expect.* Reality shock befalls everyone, from the young worker to the accountant who learns that the financial forecast that took days to prepare may simply end up in a file cabinet (or, worse yet, in the wastebasket) (Van Maanen & Schein, 1977). The visionary aspects of the dream may not disappear altogether, but a good dose of reality goes a long way toward bringing a person down to earth. Such feedback comes to play an increasingly important role in a person's occupational development and self-concept. For example, the woman who thought that she would receive the same rewards as her male counterparts for comparable work is likely to become increasingly angry and disillusioned when her successes result in smaller raises and fewer promotions.

The Role of Mentors. Imagine how hard it would be to figure out everything you needed to know in a new job with no support from the people around you. Entering an occupation involves more than the relatively short formal training a person receives. Indeed, much of the most critical information is not taught in training seminars. Instead, most people are shown the ropes by co-workers. In many cases, an older, more experienced person makes a specific effort to do this, taking on the role of a mentor. Although mentors by no means provide the only source of guidance in the workplace, they have been studied fairly closely.

A **mentor** *is part teacher, part sponsor, part model, and part counselor* (Heimann & Pittinger, 1996). The mentor helps a young worker avoid trouble ("Beware of what you say around Bentley"). He or she also provides invaluable information about the unwritten rules that govern day-to-day activities in the workplace (not working too fast on the assembly line, wearing the right clothes, and so on) (Leibold & Voelpel, 2006; Levinson & Levinson, 1996). As part of the relationship, a mentor makes sure that his or her protégé is noticed and receives credit for good work from supervisors. Thus, occupational success often depends on the quality of the mentor–protégé relationship. The mentor fulfills two main functions: improving the protégé's chances for advancement and promoting his or her psychological and social well-being (Eby & McManus, 2002; Kram, 1980, 1985; Linnehan, 2001; Noe, 1987).

Playing the role of a mentor is also a developmental phase in one's occupation. Helping a younger employee learn the job fulfills aspects of Erikson's (1982) phase of generativity. In particular, the mentor is making sure that there is some continuity in the field by passing on the accumulated knowledge and experience he or she has gained by being in it for a while. This function of the mentor is part of middle-aged adults' attempts at ensuring the continuity of society and accomplishing or producing something worthwhile (Erikson, 1982). In this sense, mentoring is clearly an example of intergenerational exchange in the workplace.

The mentor–protégé relationship develops over time. Based on her in-depth study, Kram (1985) proposes a four-stage sequence. The first stage, initiation, constitutes the 6- to 12-month period during which the protégé selects a mentor and they begin to develop their relationship. The second stage, cultivation, lasts from 2 to 5 years and is the most active phase of the mentoring relationship. This is the period when the mentor provides considerable occupational assistance and serves as a confidant. The third stage, separation, is the most difficult. It begins when the protégé receives a promotion, often to the level of the mentor. The protégé must emerge from the protection of the mentor to demonstrate his or her own competence. Both parties experience feelings of loneliness and separation. The final period is redefinition. In this period the protégé and mentor reestablish their relationship but with a new set of rules based more on friendship between peers. Research supports this description of the developmental process, as well as the benefits of having a mentor (Allen et al., 2004; Chao, 1997; Lankau & Scandura, 2002; Raabe & Beehr, 2003; Seibert, 1999).

Some authors suggest that women have a greater need for a mentor than men do because they receive less socialization in the skills necessary to do well in the workplace (Busch, 1985). Women with mentors also have higher expectations about career advancement opportunities (Baugh, Lankau, & Scandura, 1996). However, women seem to have a more difficult time finding adequate mentors; some evidence suggests that only one-third of professional women find mentors as young adults (Kittrell, 1998) and have more difficulty in establishing mentoring relationships with male colleagues (Welle & Heilman, 2007). One reason is that there are few female role models, such as the one shown in the photo, who could serve a mentoring function, especially in upper-level management. This is unfortunate, especially in view of evidence that women who have female mentors are significantly more productive than women with male mentors (Goldstein, 1979). Although many young women report that they would feel comfortable with a male mentor (Olian et al., 1988), researchers note that male

© Steve Raymer / CORBIS

Mentor–mentee relationships cut across all ages.

mentor–female protégé relationships may involve conflict and tension resulting from possible sexual overtones, even when there has been no overtly sexual behavior on anyone's part (Kram, 1985; Welle & Heilman, 2007). Finally, male and female mentors differ in their approach. Whereas male mentors provide more career mentoring, female mentors provide more psychosocial mentoring (Allen & Ebby, 2004).

Job Satisfaction

What does it mean to be satisfied with one's job or occupation? In a general sense, **job satisfaction** *is the positive feeling that results from an appraisal of one's work.* In general, job satisfaction tends to increase gradually with age (Bernal, Snyder, & McDaniel, 1998; Sterns, Marsh, & McDaniel, 1994). The increased satisfaction has been linked to several factors.

First, self-selection factors suggest that people who truly like their jobs may tend to stay in them, whereas people who do not may tend to leave. To the extent that this is the case, age differences in job satisfaction may simply reflect the fact that with sufficient time, many people eventually find a job in which they are reasonably happy. Furthermore, people who are willing to experience their emotions and negative feelings as well as work them through experience higher job satisfaction (Bond & Bunce, 2003; Thorsen et al., 2003). This also could be related to older adults' propensity toward positivity as discussed in Chapter 8.

Second, the relationship between worker age and job satisfaction is complex. Satisfaction does not increase in all areas and job types with age. Older workers are more satisfied with the intrinsic personal aspects of their jobs than they are with the extrinsic aspects, such as pay (Morrow & McElroy, 1987). White-collar professionals show an increase in job satisfaction, whereas those in blue-collar positions do not (Sterns et al., 1994).

Third, increases in job satisfaction may not be due to age alone but, rather, to the degree to which there is a good fit between the worker and the job (Holland, 1985). Older workers have had more time to find a job that they like or may have resigned themselves to the fact that things are unlikely to improve, resulting in a better congruence between worker desires and job attributes (White & Spector, 1987). Older workers also may have revised their expectations over the years to better reflect the actual state of affairs.

Fourth, as workers get older, they make work less of a focus in their lives partly because they have achieved occupational success (Bray & Howard, 1983). Consequently, it takes less to keep them satisfied.

Fifth, the type of job and the degree of family responsibilities at different career stages may influence the relationship between age and job satisfaction (Engle, Miguel, Steelman, & McDaniel, 1994). This suggests that the accumulation of experience, changing context, and the stage of one's career development may contribute to the increase in job satisfaction.

Finally, job satisfaction may be cyclical. That is, it may show periodic fluctuations that are not related to age per se but, rather, to changes that people intentionally make in their occupations (Shirom & Mazeh, 1988). The idea is that job satisfaction increases over time because people change jobs or responsibilities on a regular basis, thereby keeping their occupation interesting and challenging. This provocative idea of periodicity in job satisfaction is explored further in the How Do We Know? feature.

Alienation and Burnout. No job is perfect. There is always something about it that is not as good as it could be; perhaps the hours are not optimal, the pay is lower than one would like, or the boss does not have a pleasant personality. For most workers, these negatives are merely annoyances. But for others, such as air traffic controllers, they create extremely stressful situations that result in deeply rooted unhappiness with work: alienation and burnout.

When workers feel that what they are doing is meaningless and that their efforts are devalued, or when they do not see the connection between what they do and the final product, a sense of **alienation** *is likely to result.* Studs Terkel (1974) interviewed

H O W   D O
W E   K N O W ?

Periodicity and Job Satisfaction

Who were the investigators and what was the aim of the study? Why does job satisfaction tend to increase with age? One hypothesis is that job satisfaction has a complex relationship to the length of time one has been in a job, and not to age per se. Satisfaction might be high in the beginning of a job, stabilize or drop during the middle phase, and rise again later. Each time a person changes jobs, the cycle might repeat. Arie Shirom and Tsevi Mazeh (1988) decided to test this hypothesis and see whether this cycle happens.

How did the investigators measure the topic of interest? Shirom and Mazeh administered questionnaires containing items measuring teachers' satisfaction with salary, working hours, social status, contacts with pupils, autonomy, opportunities for professional growth, and opportunities for carrying out educational goals.

Who were the participants in the study? A representative sample of 900 Israeli junior high school teachers with varying seniority participated.

What was the design of the study? Shirom and Mazeh studied the cyclical nature of job satisfaction using a cross-sectional research design. By using sophisticated data analysis techniques, they were able to identify year-to-year changes in job satisfaction.

Were there ethical concerns with the study? There were no concerns in this study; the topics were not controversial nor were they likely to cause strongly negative feelings.

What were the results? Shirom and Mazeh found that teachers' job satisfaction followed systematic five-year cycles that were strongly related to seniority but unrelated to age. That is, the cycles begin when the person starts a job, and the level of satisfaction is then linked to how long the person has been on the job. Because the age at which people start new teaching jobs can vary a great deal, Shirom and Mazeh were able to show that the cycles had nothing to do with how old the teachers were; all ages showed the same basic pattern.

Most interesting, Shirom and Mazeh noted that a major work-related change, a sabbatical leave, or a change in school assignment seemed to occur approximately every five years. They concluded that such changes reinitiated the cycle with high job satisfaction. When tracked over long periods, the cycle appears to show a steady increase in overall job satisfaction. This long-term gradual increase in job satisfaction is consistent with the general finding of gradual increases in job satisfaction with age, even though the fundamental cyclic nature of job satisfaction is unrelated to age.

What did the investigators conclude? An important implication of Shirom and Mazeh's data is that change may be necessary for long-term job satisfaction. Although the teaching profession has change built into it (such as sabbatical leaves), many occupations do not (Latack, 1984). Based on Shirom and Mazeh's data, the option of periodic changes in job structure would probably benefit other occupations as well.

---

several alienated workers and found that all of them expressed feeling that they were merely nameless, faceless cogs in a large machine.

Employees are most likely to feel alienated when they perform routine, repetitive actions such as those on an assembly line (Terkel, 1974). Interestingly, many of these functions are being automated and performed by robots. But other workers can become alienated, too. Especially since the beginning of corporate downsizing in the 1980s, many middle-level managers do not feel that they have the same level of job security that they once had (Maslach, 2003) and feel that they have less control (Spector, 2002). Consequently, their feelings toward their employers have become more negative in many cases (Roth, 1991).

How can employers avoid creating alienated workers? Research indicates that it is helpful to involve changing the organizational structure to, for example, include employees in the decision-making process, create flexible work schedules, and institute employee development and enhancement programs (Maslach, 2003; Roth, 1991). Indeed, many organizations have instituted new practices such as total quality management (TQM), partly as a way to address worker alienation. TQM and related approaches make a concerted effort to get employees involved in the operation and administration of their plant or office. Such programs work; absenteeism drops and the quality of work improves in organizations that implement them (Offerman & Growing, 1990).

Sometimes the pace and pressure of one's occupation becomes more than a person can bear, resulting in **burnout**, *a depletion of a person's energy and motivation, the loss of occupational idealism, and the feeling that one is being exploited.* Burnout is a unique type of stress syndrome, characterized by emotional exhaustion, depersonalization, and diminished personal accomplishment (Cordes & Dougherty, 1993; Posig & Kickul, 2003; Schaufeli & Bakker, 2004). Burnout is most common among people in the helping professions, such as teaching, social work, and health care (Cordes & Dougherty, 1993; Posig & Kickul, 2003). For example, nurses in intensive care units have high levels of burnout from stress (Iskra et al., 1996). People in these professions must constantly deal with other people's complex problems, usually under difficult time constraints. Dealing with these pressures every day, along with bureaucratic paperwork, may become too much for the worker to bear. Ideals are abandoned, frustration builds, and disillusionment and exhaustion set in. In short, the worker is burned out. The situation is exacerbated when people must work long shifts in stressful jobs (Iskra et al., 1996; Schaufeli & Bakker, 2004). Finally, burnout tends to increase with increasing age and years on the job (Stanton-Rich, Iso-Ahola, & Seppo, 1998).

The best defenses against burnout appear to be practicing stress-reduction techniques, lowering workers' expectations of themselves, and enhancing communication within organizations. Providing longer rest periods between shifts in highly stressful jobs may help (Iskra et al., 1996), as well as an appropriate vacation schedule (Etzion, 2003). No one in the helping professions can resolve all problems perfectly; lowering expectations of what workers can realistically accomplish will help them deal with real-world constraints. Similarly, improving communication among different sections of organizations to keep workers informed of the outcome of their efforts and creating a positive social atmosphere give workers a sense that what they do matters in the long run (Kalimo et al., 2003). Finally, research also suggests that lack of support from one's co-workers may cause depersonalization; improving such support through teamwork and/or co-worker support can be an effective intervention (Corrigan et al., 1994; Greenglass, Burke, & Konarski, 1998; Kalimo et al., 2003).

In short, making sure that workers feel they are important to the organization by involving them in decisions, keeping expectations realistic, ensuring good communication, and promoting teamwork and co-worker support may help employees avoid alienation and burnout. As organizations adopt different management styles, perhaps these goals can be achieved.

Concept Checks

1. What is Holland's theory?
2. Describe Super's stages of occupational development.
3. What is reality shock?
4. What are the stages in the development of the mentor–protégé relationship?
5. What factors are associated with job satisfaction in older workers?

12.2 Gender, Ethnicity, Bias, and Discrimination

LEARNING OBJECTIVES

- How do women and men's occupational expectations differ? How are people viewed when they enter occupations that are not traditional for their gender?

- What factors are related to women's occupational development?
- What factors affect ethnic minority workers' occupational experiences and occupational development?
- What types of bias and discrimination hinder the occupational development of women and ethnic minority workers?
- What types of bias and discrimination hinder the occupational development of older workers?

Janice, a 35-year-old African American manager at a business consulting firm, is concerned because her career is not progressing as rapidly as she had hoped. Janice works hard and has received excellent performance ratings every year. But she has noticed that there are very few women in upper management positions in her company. Janice wonders whether she will ever be promoted.

Occupational choice and development are not equally available to all, as Janice is experiencing. Although they're in similar occupations, the men and women depicted in the photograph come from different backgrounds. Gender, ethnicity, and age may create barriers to achieving one's occupational goals. Each received somewhat different socialization as children and adolescents, which made it easier or harder for them to set their sights on a career. Bias and discrimination also create barriers to occupational success. In this section, we'll get a better appreciation of the personal and structural barriers that exist for many people.

There has been an increase in ethnically diverse people into various professional careers.

Gender Differences in Occupational Choice

Traditionally, men have been groomed from childbirth for future employment. Boys learn at an early age that men are known by the work they do, and they are strongly encouraged to think about what occupation they would like to have. Occupational achievement is stressed as a core element of masculinity. Important social skills are taught through team games, in which they learn how to play by the rules, to accept setbacks without taking defeat personally, to follow the guidance of a leader, and to move up the leadership hierarchy by demonstrating qualities that are valued by others.

Traditionally, women have not been trained in this manner. The skills that they have learned have been quite different: how to be accommodating, deferential, quiet, and supportive (Shainess, 1984). However, an increasing emphasis has been placed on the importance of providing girls with the necessary skills for occupations outside the home. The growth of women's athletic programs is giving more women the opportunity to learn key skills as well.

Given that over 71% of women are employed outside the home (U.S. Department of Labor, 2006), and that this number will probably continue to increase, it is especially important that women be exposed to the same occupational socialization opportunities as men. However, major structural barriers to women's occupational selection exist (Schwartz, 1992; Shaiko, 1996; Yamagata et al., 1997). Many occupational opportunities are still more available to men than to women (Lyness & Thompson, 1997; Welle & Heilman, 2007).

Traditional and Nontraditional Occupations. In the past, women who were employed tended to enter traditionally, female-dominated occupations such as secretarial, teaching, and social work jobs. This was due mainly to their socialization into these occupational tracks. However, as more women enter the workforce and as new opportunities are opened for women, a growing number of them work in traditionally male-dominated occupations, such as construction and engineering. Research in this area has focused on three issues (Swanson, 1992): selection of nontraditional occupations, characteristics of women in nontraditional occupations, and perceptions of nontraditional occupations.

Why some women end up in nontraditional occupations appears to be related to personal feelings and experiences as well as expectations about the occupation; in other words, women in these occupations are work-centered (Blackburn et al., 2002; Brooks & Betz, 1990; Hakim, 2002). Concerning personal experiences, women who attend single-sex high schools and who have both brothers and sisters end up in the least traditional occupations, apparently because they have been exposed to more options and fewer gender-role stereotypes (Rubenfeld & Gilroy, 1991). Personal feelings are important; a study of Japanese students found that women had significantly lower confidence in their ability to perform in male-dominated occupations than in their ability in female-dominated occupations (Matsui, Ikeda, & Ohnishi, 1989).

The characteristics of women in nontraditional occupations have been studied as well. Betz, Heesacker, and Shuttleworth (1990) found that women who scored high on femininity, as defined by endorsing traditional feminine gender roles, and those in female-dominated occupations had the poorest match between their abilities and their occupational choices. These findings mean that women who score high on traditional measures of femininity have difficulty finding occupations that allow them to take advantage of their abilities. In addition, women in female-dominated occupations generally find that their jobs do not allow them to use their abilities to the fullest. In sum, many women have difficulty finding occupations that match their skills.

Despite the efforts to counteract gender stereotyping of occupations, less than 25% of women obtain nontraditional occupations (U.S. Department of Labor, 2008) and they are still viewed with disapproval by their peers of either sex, even though they have high job satisfaction themselves (Brabeck & Weisgerber, 1989; Pfost & Fiore, 1990). This finding holds up in cross-cultural research as well. In a study conducted in

India, both women and men gave higher "respectability" ratings to males than to females in the same occupation (Kanekar, Koswalla, & Nazareth, 1989). People even make inferences about working conditions based on their perception of an occupation as traditionally masculine or feminine. Scozzaro and Subich (1990) report that occupations such as a secretarial job are not perceived as offering good pay and promotion potential. Worst of all, people are less likely to perceive incidents of sexual coercion as harassing when a woman is in a nontraditional occupation (Burgess & Borgida, 1997).

Taken together, these studies show we still have a long way to go before people can choose any occupation they want without having to contend with gender-related stereotypes. Although differences in opportunities for women in traditional and nontraditional occupations are narrowing, key differences remain. Finally, relatively little research has examined differences between males in traditional and nontraditional occupations (Swanson, 1992). It is important to understand why men choose traditional or nontraditional occupations, and why some men still perpetuate gender stereotypes about particular occupations. Current research is only beginning to address this issue. In a recent study, Lease (2003) found that men's nontraditional occupational choices were related to liberal social attitudes and that higher educational aspirations were related to traditional career choice.

Women and Occupational Development

If you were to guess what the young woman in the photograph who has just graduated from college will be doing occupationally 10 years from now, what would you say? Would you guess that she will be strongly committed to her occupation? Would she have abandoned it for other things? Betz (1984) wanted to know the answers, so she examined the occupational histories of 500 college women 10 years after graduation. Two-thirds of these women were highly committed to their occupations, which for 70% were traditionally female ones. Most had worked continuously since graduation.

Researchers want to know what these women will be doing occupationally.

Only 1% had been full-time homemakers during the entire 10-year period; 79% reported that they had successfully combined occupations with homemaking. Women in traditional female occupations changed jobs less often. If they did change, the move was more likely to be to a job with a lower rank and pay compared to the changes made by women in nontraditional occupations.

An intriguing question is why highly educated women leave what appear to be well-paid occupations. Studies of formerly working women with master of business administration degrees (MBAs) with children have identified a number of family and workplace issues (Gutek & Gilliland, 2007; Rosin & Korabik, 1990, 1991). Family obligations, such as child care, appear to be most important for mothers working part time. For these women,

adequate child-care arrangements or having the flexibility to be at home when children get out of school often make the difference between being able to accept a job or remaining at home. In contrast, mothers who have made the decision to work full time have resolved the problem of child care. The most important workplace issues for these women are gender-related. Unsupportive or insensitive work environments, organizational politics, and the lack of occupational development opportunities appear most important for women working full time (Schwartz, 1992; Welle & Heilman, 2007). In this case, women are focusing on issues that could create barriers to their occupational development and are looking for ways around the barriers.

Such barriers are a major reason why women's workforce participation does not show the developmental upward climb that is evident in men's career development. Because they cannot find affordable and dependable child care, or freely choose to take on this responsibility, many women stay home while their children are young. The lack of continuity in job participation makes it difficult to maintain an upward trajectory in one's career through promotion, and in terms of maintaining skills. Some women make this choice willingly; however, many find they are forced into it.

Ethnicity and Occupational Development

What factors are related to occupational selection and development of people from ethnic minorities? Unfortunately, not much research has been conducted from a developmental perspective. Rather, most researchers have focused on the limited opportunities ethnic minorities have and structural barriers, such as discrimination, that they face. Three topics have received the most focus: nontraditional occupations, vocational identity, and issues pertaining to occupational aspirations.

African American women and European American women do not differ in terms of plans to enter nontraditional occupations (Murrell, Frieze, & Frost, 1991). However, African American women who choose nontraditional occupations tend to plan for more formal education than necessary to achieve

Robert Nicholas / OJO Images / Getty Images

their goal. This may actually make them overqualified for the jobs they get; for example, a woman with a college degree may be working in a job that does not require that level of education. Finally, the degree to which ethnic minorities acculturate to the predominant culture affects career choice. For example, Mexican American women who are more oriented toward Anglo culture tended to choose less prestigious and more traditional careers (Flores & O'Brien, 2002).

Vocational identity *is the degree to which one views one's occupation as a key element of identity.* Research shows that vocational identity varies with both ethnicity and gender. Compared to European American women and Hispanic men, African American and European American men have higher vocational identity when they graduate from college (Steward & Krieshok, 1991). Lower vocational identity means that people define themselves primarily in terms of things in life other than work.

A person's occupational aspiration is the kind of occupation he or she would like to have. In contrast, occupational expectation is the occupation the person believes he or she will actually get. Hispanics differ from European Americans in several ways with regard to these variables. They have high occupational aspirations but low expectations, and they differ in their educational attainment as a function of national origin, generational status, and social class (Arbona, 1990). However, Hispanics are similar to European Americans in occupational development and work values.

Research on occupational development of ethnic minority workers is clear on one point: Whether an organization is responsive to the needs of ethnic minorities like the African American woman in the photograph makes a big difference for employees. For example, greater occupational gender segregation has a greater negative impact on African American women's earnings than on European American women's earnings (Cotter et al., 2003). Both European American and ethnic minority managers who perceive their organizations as responsive and positive for ethnic minority employees are more satisfied with and committed to the organizations (Burke, 1991a, 1991b). But much still remains to be

More and more ethnically diverse individuals are going into managerial positions.

accomplished. African American managers report less choice of jobs, less acceptance, more career dissatisfaction, lower performance evaluations and promotability ratings, and more rapid attainment of plateaus in their careers than European American managers (Greenhaus, Parasuraman, & Wormley, 1990). Over 60% of African American protégés have European American mentors, which is problematic because same-ethnicity mentors provide more psychosocial support than cross-ethnicity mentors (Thomas, 1990). Nevertheless, having any mentor is more beneficial than having none (Bridges, 1996).

Finally, ethnically diverse employees' access to managerial and authority positions is influenced by what is called the "sticky floor" (Smith & Elliott, 2002). In other words, when one's ethnic group dominates only entry-level positions, then leadership

Comstock Images / Getty Images

opportunities are restricted to supervising entry-level workers. However, if one's ethnic group is predominant at higher-level positions, then leadership opportunities increase correspondingly.

Bias and Discrimination

Since the 1960s, organizations in the United States have been sensitized to the issues of bias and discrimination in the workplace. Hiring, promotion, and termination procedures have come under close scrutiny in numerous court cases, resulting in a host of laws to govern these processes.

Gender Bias and the Glass Ceiling. Even though the majority of women work outside the home, women in high-status jobs are unusual (Gutek & Gilliland, 2007; Morrison et al., 1992). Not until 1981 was a woman, Sandra Day O'Connor, appointed to the U.S. Supreme Court; it took another 12 years before a second woman, Ruth Bader Ginsburg, was appointed associate justice; and it was not until 2009 that a third woman was appointed, Sonia Sotomayor. As Janice noticed in the vignette, few women serve in the highest ranks of major corporations, and women are substantially outnumbered at the senior faculty level of most universities and colleges.

Why are there so few women in high-status jobs? The explanation that has received much attention is **sex discrimination**, *which means denying a job to someone solely on the basis of whether the person is a man or a woman.* Baron and Bielby (1985) pull no punches in discussing sex discrimination. "Our analyses portray [sex] discrimination as pervasive, almost omnipresent, sustained by diverse organizational structures and processes. Moreover, this segregation drastically restricts women's career opportunities, by blocking access to internal labor markets and their benefits" (Baron & Bielby, 1985, p. 245). Despite some progress over the past two decades, sex discrimination is still common; many recent high-profile allegations of sex discrimination have been leveled against organizations (Morris, Bonamici, Kaufman, & Neering, 2005; Welle & Heilman, 2007).

Although women are kept out of high-status jobs by the men at the top (Lyness & Thompson, 1997; Shaiko, 1996; Yamagata et al., 1997), we should also note that in the past there have been fewer women vying for these jobs. More recently we are seeing more and more competent women moving into academia and the business world and competing for positions.

Women themselves refer to a **glass ceiling**, *or the level to which they may rise in a company but beyond which they may not go.* This problem is most obvious in companies that classify jobs at various levels (as does the U.S. Civil Service). The greatest barrier facing women is at the boundary between lower-tier and upper-tier job grades (Cotter et al., 2001; Morrison et al., 1992). Women like Janice tend to move to the top of the lower tier and remain there, whereas men are more readily promoted to the upper tier, even when other factors, such as personal attributes and qualifications, are controlled for (Diprete & Soule, 1988). Indeed, a longitudinal study of women in the high school class of 1972 showed that despite better academic records, women's achievement in the workplace is limited by structural barriers (Adelman, 1991). The U.S. Department of Labor (1991) admitted that the glass ceiling pervades the workplace. Some surveys indicate that over 90% of women believe that there is a glass ceiling in the workplace. Clear evidence of the glass ceiling has been found in private corporations (Lyness & Thompson, 1997), government agencies (Yamagata et al., 1997), and nonprofit organizations (Shaiko, 1996). Indeed, estimates are that if the present rate of advancement continues, it will take until the late 25th century for women to achieve equality with men in the executive suite (Feminist Majority Foundation, 1991). To add insult to injury, certain occupations show a **glass elevator** *in which men in traditionally female occupations such as nursing seem to rise at a quicker rate than their female counterparts.*

Besides discrimination in hiring and promotion, women are also subject to pay discrimination. According to the U.S. Department of Labor, in many occupations men are paid substantially more than women in the same positions; indeed, on the average, women are paid about 80% of what men are paid on an annual basis and this earning differential is highest after 45 years of age (U.S. Department of Labor, 2008). The situation is much worse for women of color; African American women only earn roughly 67% and Hispanic women earn roughly 61% as much as white men (U.S. Department of Labor, 2008). Even more distressing, the gender wage gap remains substantial even when educational backgrounds are equivalent (Castro, 1997).

Such averages conceal important developmental aspects of the gender difference: the wage gap widens over women's working years (Institute for Women's Policy Research, 2009). As you can see in the graph in Figure 12.2, the wage gap begins widening rapidly in the 30s, and remains substantial through age 65. These broadening differences reflect several factors: sex discrimination, the discontinuous participation of women in the workforce, and the disproportionate number of women in low-paying jobs (Institute for Women's Policy Research, 2009).

Several solutions to this problem have been promoted. One of these is **comparable worth:** *equalizing*

pay in occupations that are determined to be equivalent in importance but differ in the gender distribution of the people doing the jobs. Determining which male-dominated occupations should be considered equivalent to which female-dominated occupations for pay purposes can be difficult and controversial. One way to do this is with gender-neutral job evaluations, which examine all positions within an organization in order to establish fair-pay policies (Castro, 1997).

Sexual Harassment. Although the sexual harassment of women in the workplace has been documented for centuries, only recently has it received much attention from researchers (Fitzgerald & Shullman, 1993). Interest among U.S. researchers increased dramatically after the 1991 Senate hearings involving U.S. Supreme Court nominee Clarence Thomas and Anita Hill, who accused him of sexual harassment, the scandals involving military personnel, and the impeachment trial of President Bill Clinton.

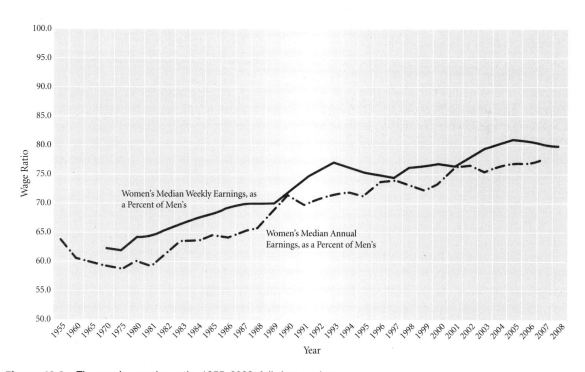

Figure 12.2 The gender earning ratio, 1955–2008, full-time workers.

Source: Institute for Women's Policy Research Fact Sheet: The Gender Wage Gap: 2008.

By no means is sexual harassment a U.S.-only phenomenon; sad to say, it occurs around the world (Luo, 1996; Wasti & Cortina, 2002).

Research on sexual harassment focuses on situations in which there is a power differential between two people, most often involving men with more power over women (Berdahl, Magley, & Waldo, 1996). Such situations exist in the workplace and in academic settings (Zappert, 1996). However, peer-to-peer harassment also occurs, such as among classmates in academic settings (Ivy & Hamlet, 1996). Studies show that authoritarianism is a strong predictor of men's likelihood of engaging in sexual harassment (Begany & Milburn, 2002).

How many people have been sexually harassed? Evidence suggests that about 70% of women report that they have "experienced or heard offensive slurs or jokes or remarks about women" (Piotrkowski, 1998). Interestingly, men report a similar level of such behavior. Reliable statistics on more serious forms of harassment, such as touching and sexual activity, are more difficult to obtain, in part because of the unwillingness of many victims to report harassment and because of differences in reporting procedures. Indeed, estimates are that less than 5% of victims ever report their experiences to anyone in authority (Fitzgerald et al., 1988). Even given these difficulties, several studies document that over 40% of women report having been sexually harassed in the workplace at least once (Fitzgerald & Shullman, 1993). Victims are most often single or divorced women under age 35 (Tang & McCollum, 1996).

What effects does being sexually harassed have? Research evidence shows clear, negative emotional, mental health, and job-related outcomes (Schneider, Swan, & Fitzgerald, 1997). Establishing the degree of problems is difficult, though, because many women try to minimize or hide their reactions or feelings (Tang & McCollum, 1996). It is becoming evident, though, that one does not have to experience the worst kinds of sexual harassment to be affected. Even low-level but frequent experience of sexual harassment can have significant negative consequences for women (Schneider et al., 1997). Finally, although women in general are less tolerant of sexual harassment than are men, both women and men who demonstrate ambivalent sexism and hostility toward women were more tolerant of sexual harassment (Russell & Trigg, 2004).

Sexual harassment also has numerous ripple effects throughout a company (Piotrkowski, in progress, cited in Murray, 1998). For example, men of all ethnic backgrounds who work in companies that have cases of sexual harassment, but who are not harassers themselves, report less satisfaction with their jobs. Productivity at such companies also declines, as does general worker morale.

Of course, the crux of the matter is what constitutes harassment. What would have to be going on in the situation depicted in the photograph for you to say that it was harassment? Using ambiguous situations like this is a technique that many researchers use. In fact, research on perceptions of what constitutes harassing behavior usually requires people to read vignettes of hypothetical incidents involving sexually suggestive touching, sexual remarks, and the like, and then decide whether it was harassment. In general, women are more likely to view such behaviors as offensive than are men (Berdahl, Magley, & Waldo, 1996; Fitzgerald & Ormerod, 1991). Because of this gender gap in perceptions, a federal court, in the case of *Ellison v. Brady*, instituted the **reasonable woman standard** as *the appropriate legal criterion for determining whether sexual harassment has occurred*. If a reasonable woman would view a behavior as offensive, the court held, then it is offensive even if the man did not consider it to be so. Even this standard, though, is more likely to be understood by women than by men (Wiener et al., 1997).

Besides the gender of the perceiver, several other factors influence whether a behavior is considered offensive (Fitzgerald & Ormerod, 1991). These include the degree to which the behavior is explicit or extreme (e.g., rape as against a friendly kiss), victim behavior (whether the victim was at all responsible for what happened), supervisory status (whether the perpetrator was a direct supervisor of the victim), harasser's intentions (whether the perpetrator knew that the victim found the behavior offensive), and frequency of occurrence (e.g., a one-time occurrence as opposed to a regular event). Cultural differences are also important. For example, one study found that U.S. women judged specific interactions as more harassing than U.S. men; women and men from Australia, Brazil, and Germany did not differ (Pryor et al., 1997). Unfortunately, little research has been done to identify what aspects of organizations foster harassment or to determine the impact of educational programs aimed at addressing the problem.

In 1998, the U.S. Supreme Court (in *Oncale v. Sundowner Offshore Services*) ruled that sexual harassment is not limited to female victims and that the relevant laws also protect men. This case is also important for establishing that same-sex harassment is barred by the same laws that ban heterosexual harassment. Thus, the standard by which sexual harassment is judged could now be said to be a "reasonable person" standard.

What can be done to provide people with safe work and learning environments, free from sexual harassment? Training in gender awareness is a common approach that often works (Tang & McCollum, 1996). Clearly providing precise definitions that differentiate between what can be considered a workplace romance and what can be considered sexual harassment is another essential element (Pierce & Aguinis, 1997).

Age Discrimination. Another structural barrier to occupational development is **age discrimination**, *which involves denying a job or promotion to someone solely on the basis of age.* In contrast to older adult bias and discrimination, older worker biases encompass relatively younger ages and specifically relate to the work context (McVittie, McKinlay & Widdicombe, 2003). The U.S. Age Discrimination in Employment Act of 1986 protects workers over age 40. This law stipulates that people must be hired based on their ability, not their age. Under this law, employers are banned from refusing to hire and from discharging workers like the man in the photograph solely on the basis of age. In addition, employers cannot segregate or classify workers or otherwise denote their status on the basis of age.

Employment prospects for middle-aged and older people around the world are lower than for their younger counterparts. The workplace is replete with negative stereotypes of older workers and this prejudice is seen as more acceptable than

© Richard Lord / The Image Works

Employers are banned from firing workers like this man solely on the basis of age.

other prejudices (Blanchard-Fields & Stanley, 2007). Furthermore, age discrimination toward those over age 45 is common in Germany (Frerichs & Naegele, 1997) and Britain (Ginn & Arber, 1996), resulting in long periods of unemployment and early retirement. Such practices may save companies money in the short run, but the loss of expertise and knowledge comes at a high price. Indeed, global corporations are beginning to realize that retraining and integrating middle-aged workers is a better strategy (Frerichs & Naegele, 1997).

Age discrimination occurs in several ways (Avolio & Sosik, 1999). For example, employers can make certain types of physical or mental performance a job requirement and argue that older workers cannot meet the standard. Or they can attempt to get rid of older workers by using retirement. Supervisors sometimes use age as a factor in performance evaluations for raises or promotions or in decisions about which employees are eligible for additional training.

Perceptions of age discrimination are widespread; nearly 1,600 suits were filed in 1993 alone, up from roughly 1,100 in 1990 (Cornish, 1994). Many of these cases stem from the corporate downsizing that began in the late 1980s. Winning an age discrimination case is difficult (Snyder & Barrett, 1988). Job performance information is crucial. However, most companies tend to report this information in terms of general differences between younger and older adults (such as differences in recent memory ability) rather than in specific terms of older and younger workers in a particular occupation (which rarely show any differences in productivity or performance). Surprisingly, many courts do not question inaccurate information or stereotypic views of aging presented by employers, despite the lack of scientific data documenting age differences in actual job performance. In fact, the court system may be taking a more relaxed view of age discrimination. In a ruling by the U.S. Supreme Court, January 11, 2000, the majority opinion held that people do not have a blanket protection from age discrimination under the Fourteenth Amendment's rights to equal protection under the laws. In that case, the majority suggested that age may serve as a useful proxy to determine qualifications for a job if age is related to a legitimate issue. The issue of age discrimination is still an ambiguous issue and should witness an interesting evolution in this new millennium.

Concept Checks

1. What factors lead some women to choose nontraditional occupations?

2. What is the primary reason women in full-time high-status jobs quit after having children?

3. How do ethnic groups differ in terms of choosing nontraditional occupations, vocational identity, occupational aspirations, and occupational development?

4. Define *glass ceiling, comparable worth, sexual harassment,* and *age discrimination.*

12.3 Occupational Transitions

LEARNING OBJECTIVES

- Why do people change occupations?
- Why is worker retraining necessary and important?
- How does the timing of job loss affect the amount of stress one experiences?

Dirk has 32 years of service for an automobile manufacturer. Over the years, more and more assembly-line jobs have been eliminated by robots and other technology, and the export of manufacturing jobs to other countries. Although Dirk has been assured by his boss that his job is safe, he isn't so sure. He worries that he could be laid off at any time.

In the past, people commonly chose an occupation during young adulthood and stayed in it throughout their working years. Today, however, not many people take a job with the expectation that it will last a lifetime. Changing jobs is almost taken for granted; the average North American will change jobs multiple times during adulthood (Cascio, 1995; U.S. Department of Labor, 2006). Some authors view occupational changes as positive; Havighurst (1982), for example, strongly advocates such flexibility. According to his view, building change into the occupational life cycle may help to avoid disillusionment with one's initial choice. Changing occupations may be one way to guarantee challenging and satisfying work, and it may be the best option for those in a position to exercise it (Shirom & Mazeh, 1988).

Several factors have been identified as important in determining who will remain in an occupation and who will change. Some factors—such as whether the person likes the occupation—lead to self-initiated occupation changes. For example, people who really like their occupation may seek additional training like those in the photograph or accept overtime assignments in hopes of acquiring new skills that will enable them to get better jobs. Middle-aged workers are one group that often takes advantage of these opportunities. However, other factors, such as obsolete skills and economic trends, cause forced occupational changes. For example, continued improvement of robots caused some auto industry workers to lose their jobs, corporations

Older workers are encouraged to engage in retraining, especially given that retirement is being pushed further back in time.

send jobs overseas in order to increase profits, and economic recessions usually result in large-scale layoffs. But even forced occupational changes can have benefits. For instance, many adults go to college. Some are taking advantage of educational benefits offered as part of a separation package. Others are pursuing educational opportunities in order to obtain new skills; still others are looking to advance in their careers.

In this section, we will explore the positive and negative aspects of occupational transitions. First we will examine the retraining of mid-career and older workers. The increased use of technology, corporate downsizing, and an aging workforce have focused attention on the need to keep older workers' skills current. Later, we will examine occupational insecurity and the effects of job loss.

Retraining Workers

When you are hired into a specific job, you are selected because your employer believes that you offer the best fit between abilities you already have and those needed to perform the job. However, as noted earlier, the skills needed to perform a job typically change over time. Such changes may be due to the introduction of new technology, to additional responsibilities, or to promotion.

Such rapid changes in the nature of work as we have discussed earlier tend to result in the displacement of older workers in the workforce. According

to the U.S. Census Bureau (1993), 51.4% of displaced workers 55 to 64 years old do not find other employment, whereas 65% to 70% of workers under the age of 55 years are reemployed. One approach to this problem is that mid- and late-career workers need to be involved in continued development and retraining at work. If not, older workers are in jeopardy of cutting their careers short (Greller & Stroh, 1995). We will discuss the implications of job loss further later. Another outcome is career plateauing (Froman, 1994; Kooij et al., 2008). **Career plateauing** *occurs when there is a lack of promotional opportunity in the organization or when a person decides not to seek advancement.*

What is critical here is that unless a person's skills are kept up-to-date, it may be very difficult for older workers to maintain their job or land new jobs when they are forced into retirement, displaced, or victims of downsizing (Froman, 1994; Simon, 1996). In cases of job loss or career plateauing, retraining may be an appropriate response. Nearly one-third of the U.S. workforce participates each year in courses aimed at improving job skills (American Council on Education, 1997). One objective of these courses is to improve technical skills, such as new computer skills. For mid-career or older employees, who make up the largest percentage of those who take courses (American Council on Education, 1997), retraining may focus on how to advance in one's occupation or how to find new career opportunities—for example, through résumé preparation and career counseling.

Many corporations as well as community and technical colleges offer retraining programs in a variety of fields. Organizations that promote employee development typically promote in-house courses to improve one's skills or may offer tuition reimbursement programs for people who successfully complete courses at colleges or universities.

The retraining of mid-career and older workers points to the need for lifelong learning (Sinnott, 1994). To meet the challenges of a global economy, corporations must include retraining in their employee development programs. Such programs will help improve people's chances of advancement in their chosen occupations, and they will help people make successful transitions from one occupation to another.

Despite the benefits and opportunities for retraining workers, some older workers may perceive fewer benefits in participating in such activities, and may have lower self-efficacy for skill development (Maurer, Weiss, & Barbeite, 2003). Self-efficacy in this case is the belief that you possess the capability to successfully learn, develop, and improve yourself at work. These beliefs have been found to be important predictors of effective training and development (Maurer & Tarulli, 1994; Stajkovic & Luthans, 1998). Older adults may tend to have less self-confidence for the development of career-relevant skills. Given the importance of training and development in the older worker's career, it is important to specify the ways in which organizations can be more sensitive to enhancing career development and self-efficacy of older workers.

Occupational Insecurity and Job Loss

Changing economic conditions in the United States over the past few decades (such as the move toward a global economy and most recently the economic recession), as well as changing demographics, have forced many people out of their jobs. Heavy manufacturing and support businesses (such as the steel, oil, and automotive industries) and farming were the hardest hit during the 1970s and 1980s. But no one is immune. Take the banking industry today. Indeed, the corporate takeover frenzy of the 1980s and the recession of the late 2000s put many middle- and upper-level corporate executives out of work in all kinds of businesses.

As a result of these trends, many people feel insecure about their jobs. Like Dirk, the auto worker in the vignette at the beginning of this section, many worried workers have numerous years of dedicated service to a corporation. Unfortunately, people who worry about their jobs and those who experience job loss tend to have poorer mental health as discussed in Chapters 3 and 5 (McKee-Ryan, Song, Wanberg, & Kinicki, 2005; Price et al., 2002; Roskies & Louis-Guerin, 1990). For example, anxiety about one's job may result in negative attitudes about one's

employer or even work in general, which in turn may diminish the desire to be successful. Whether there is any actual basis for people's feelings of job insecurity may not matter; what people think is true about their work situation is sometimes more important than what is actually the case. If people believe that they are at risk of losing their jobs, their mental health and behavior are often affected negatively even when the actual risk of losing their jobs is very low (Roskies & Louis-Guerin, 1990). These effects do vary with age. For example, whereas some middle-aged men are more susceptible to negative effects of losing one's job, others do not always report negative outcomes (Leana & Feldman, 1992). Some may have been planning to retire in the near future and see this as an opportunity to do so, others are hired back as consultants, and still others use their situation to try doing something new. Finally, downsizing in a company creates insecurity and this greatly damages the organizational trust and morale of employees aged 45 and older (Armstrong-Stassen, 2001).

What happens to the mental health of people who remain unemployed for relatively long periods of time? Wanberg (1995) assessed 129 people over a period of 9 months following the loss of a job. Only those people who were satisfied with their new jobs showed significant improvements in mental health; people who were unhappy in their new jobs and people who were still unemployed showed no change. Furthermore, husbands' job loss can have a negative effect on wives' mental health (Siegel et al., 2003).

People who are unemployed show considerable variability. For example, Wanberg and Marchese (1994) showed that four clusters of unemployed people could be identified, varying along the dimensions of financial concerns, employment commitment, job-seeking confidence level, degree of time structure, and adaptation to unemployment. These clusters can be identified as follows: confident, but concerned about getting another job; distressed about being unemployed; unconcerned and indifferent about being unemployed; and optimistic about the future and coping with unemployment. The differing characteristics of these clusters mean that interventions with unemployed individuals must take these differences into account.

The effects of losing one's job emphasize the central role that occupations play in forming a sense of identity in adulthood. How one perceives the loss of a job plays a major role in determining what the long-term effects will be.

Concept Checks

1. What are the major factors that predict occupational transition?
2. What is career plateauing? How can it be avoided?
3. What effects do people experience when they lose their jobs?

12.4 Dual-Earner Couples

LEARNING OBJECTIVES

- What are the issues faced by employed people who care for dependents?
- How do partners view the division of household chores?
- What is work-family conflict? How does it affect couples' lives?

Jennifer, a 38-year-old sales clerk at a department store, feels that her husband doesn't do his share of the housework or child care. Her husband says that real men don't do housework, and that he's really tired when he comes home from work. Jennifer thinks that this isn't fair, especially because she works as many hours as her husband.

One of the most difficult challenges facing adults such as Jennifer is trying to balance the demands of occupation with the demands of family. Over the past few decades, the rapid increase in the number of families in which both parents are employed has fundamentally changed how we view the relation between work and family. As the photograph shows, this can even mean taking a young child to work as a way to deal with the pushes and pulls of being an employed parent. In over half of two-parent households today, both adults work outside the home (U.S. Department of Labor, 2009). The main reason? Families need the dual income in order to pay the bills and maintain a moderate standard of living.

Work-family conflicts may result in mothers taking their very young children to work with them as a way to deal with being an employed parent.

As you will see, dual-earner couples with children experience both benefits and costs from this arrangement. The stresses of living in this arrangement are substantial—and gender differences are clear, especially in the division of household chores.

The Dependent Care Dilemma

Many employed adults must also provide care for dependent children or parents. As we will show, the issues they face are complex.

Employed Caregivers. Many mothers have no option but to return to work after the birth of a child. In fact, 64% of American women with children under the age of six years are in the workforce (U.S. Department of Labor, 2006). The number of mothers in the workforce with children of any age is even higher. As you can see in the graph in Figure 12.3, the overall number of women in the workforce with children under age 18 has increased dramatically since the mid-1970s (U.S. Department of Labor, 2006).

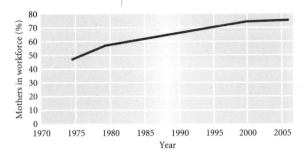

Figure 12.3 Percentage of mothers in the workforce with own children under age 18.

Source: U.S. Department of Labor. (2006). *Current population survey.* Washington, D.C.: U.S. Department of Labor.

Some women, though, grapple with the decision of whether they want to return to work. Surveys of mothers with preschool children reveal that the motivation for returning to work tends to be related to how attached mothers are to their work. For example, in one survey of Australian mothers, those with high work attachment were more likely to cite intrinsic personal achievement reasons for returning. Those with low work attachment cited pressing financial needs. Those with moderate work attachment were divided between intrinsic and financial reasons (Cotton, Anthill, & Cunningham, 1989). Those who can afford to give up careers and stay home also must deal with changes in identity (Milford, 1997). Giving up a career means that those aspects of one's identity that came from work must be redefined to accommodate being a stay-at-home mother. Finally, women in male-dominated occupations make more family trade-offs to maintain their occupational identity (Mennino & Brayfield, 2002).

As discussed in Chapter 11, an increasing and often overlooked group of employed caregivers consists of those caring for a parent or partner and children. Of women in this situation, 60% work at least 35 hours per week (Jenkins, 1997). Consequently, these women show a higher level of inter-role conflict, stress, and depression (Hammer & Neal, 2008; Norton et al., 2002; Stephens, Franks, & Atienza, 1997; Stephens et al., 2001). **Inter-role conflict**

results in a clash between competing sets of roles, in this case between work and family responsibilities.

Whether care is needed for one's children or parent, key factors in selecting an appropriate care site are quality of care, price, and hours of availability (Metropolitan Area Agency on Aging, 1998; Vandell, Pierce, & Stright, 1997). Depending on one's economic situation, it may not be possible to find affordable and quality care that is available when needed. In such cases, there may be no option but to drop out of the workforce or enlist the help of friends and family.

Dependent Care and Effects on Workers. Workers who care for dependents face tough choices. Especially when both partners are employed, dependent care is the central organizing aspect of the couple's lives (Hertz, 1997).

Being responsible for dependent care has significant negative effects, especially for women. For example, when they are responsible for caring for an older parent, women report missing more meetings and being absent from work more often (Gignac, Kelloway, & Gottlieb, 1996; Hammer & Neal, 2008). Such women also report higher levels of stress (Jenkins, 1997). Likewise, parents often experience poor quality of life, and report higher stress and trouble coping with it (Galinsky, Bond, & Friedman, 1996; Scharlach, 2001).

How can these negative effects be lessened? For example, when women's partners provide good support and women have average or high control over their jobs, employed mothers are significantly less distressed than are employed women who are not mothers (Roxburgh, 1997). When support and job controls are lacking, though, employed mothers are significantly more distressed than employed non-mothers. Clearly, having partner support and being in a job that allows one to have control over such things as one's schedule are key. What employers provide is also important, as we will show next.

Dependent Care and Employer Response. Employed parents with small children are confronted with the difficult act of leaving their children in the care of others. In response to pressure from parents, most industrialized countries (but not the United States) provide government-supported child-care centers for employees as one way to help ease this burden. Does providing a center make a difference in terms of an employee's feelings about work, absenteeism, or productivity?

The answer is that it's not as simple as opening a center like the one in the photograph. Just making a child-care center available to employees does not necessarily reduce parents' work-family conflict or their absenteeism (Goff, Mount, & Jamison, 1990; Schmidt & Duenas, 2002). A "family-friendly" company must also pay attention to attitudes of their employees, introduce flexible working conditions, and make sure the company provides broad-based support. The key is how the supervisor acts. Irrespective of where the child-care center is located, when supervisors are sympathetic and supportive regarding family issues and child care, parents report less work-family conflict and have lower absenteeism. Interestingly, university employees seem to be more negative toward their workplace's work-family climate than are corporate employees (Anderson et al., 2002).

Research on specific working conditions and benefits that help caregivers perform optimally on the job points to several consistent conclusions. To the extent that employers provide better job security, autonomy, lower productivity demands, supervisor support, and flexible schedules, caregivers fare better (Aryee & Luk, 1996; Frone & Yardley, 1996; Galinsky et al., 1996; Schmidt & Duenas, 2002).

It will be interesting to watch how these issues, especially flexible schedules, play out in the United States over the next several years. With the passage of the Family and Medical Leave Act in 1993, for the first time people will be able to take unpaid time off to care for their dependents, having the right to return to their jobs. Experience from other countries indicates that parental leave has different effects on each parent. For example, a large-scale study in Sweden showed that fathers who took parental leave were more likely to continue their involvement in child care and to reduce their work involvement. Regardless of fathers' participation, mothers still retained primary responsibility for child care and stayed less involved in and received fewer rewards in the labor market (Haas, 1990; Schwartz, 1992).

Juggling Multiple Roles

When both members of a couple with dependents are employed, who cleans the house, cooks the meals, and takes care of the children when they are ill? This question gets to the heart of the core dilemma of modern, dual-earner couples: How are household chores divided? How are work and family role conflicts handled?

Dividing Household Chores. Despite much media attention and claims of increased sharing in the duties, women still assume the lion's share of housework regardless of employment status. Working mothers spend about twice as many hours per week as their husbands in family work and bear the greatest responsibility for household and child-care tasks (Etzion & Bailyn, 1994; Goldberg & Perry-Jenkins, 2004; Wood & Repetti, 2004). This unequal division of labor creates the most arguments and causes the most unhappiness for dual-earner couples. This is the case with Jennifer and Bill, the couple in the section-opening vignette; Jennifer does most of the housework.

A great deal of evidence indicates that women have decreased the amount of time they spend on housework since the 1970s, especially when they

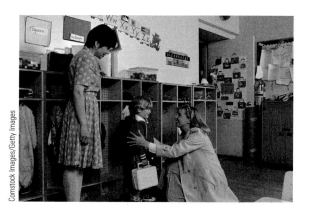

Child care has witnessed a considerable increase with more women entering careers and jobs.

With the increase in dual-career families, effective strategies are needed to juggle many roles.

are employed, and that men have increased the amount of time they spend on such tasks (Swanson, 1992; Wood & Repetti, 2004). The increased participation of men in these tasks is not all it may seem, however. Most of the increase is on weekends, with specific tasks that they agree to perform, and is related to the number of hours the mothers have worked (Wood & Repetti, 2004; Zick & McCullough, 1991). In short, this increase in men's participation has not done much to lower women's burdens around the house as the photograph shows.

Women and men view the division of labor in very different terms. Men were often most satisfied with an equitable division of labor based on the number of hours spent, especially if the amount of time needed to perform household tasks was relatively small. Women perceived greater fairness in the lopsided division of family labor when they enjoyed family work and when the women and their spouses believed the women were competent at it (Grote et al., 2002). When ethnic minorities are studied, much the same is true concerning satisfaction. For example, in African American dual-earner couples, women were twice as likely as men to feel overburdened with housework and to be dissatisfied with their family life (Broman, 1988).

Ethnic differences in the division of household labor are also apparent. In a study of European

American, African American, and Hispanic men, several interesting patterns emerged (Shelton & John, 1993). African American and Hispanic men tend to spend more time doing household tasks than do European American men. In the case of African American men, this finding supports the view that such households are more egalitarian than European American households. Moreover, the increased participation of African American men was primarily true of employed (as opposed to unemployed) men. There was greater participation in traditionally female tasks, such as washing dishes and cooking. Similarly, Hispanic men's participation also tended to reflect increased participation in these tasks. Overall, European American men spent the least time helping with traditionally female tasks. These data clearly indicate that the degree to which men and women divide household tasks varies not only with gender, but with ethnicity as well.

In sum, the available evidence from dual-earner couples indicates that women still perform more household tasks than men, but that the difference varies with ethnic groups. The discrepancy is greatest when the male endorses traditional masculine gender roles and is less when the male endorses more feminine or androgynous gender roles (Gunter & Gunter, 1990; Napholz, 1995).

Work-Family Conflict. When people have both occupations and children, they must figure out how to balance the demands of each. For example, parents may agonize over how to be at their daughter's ballgame at the same time they have to be at an important business meeting. These competing demands cause **work-family conflict**, which is the feeling of being pulled in multiple directions by incompatible demands from one's job and one's family.

Research provides some evidence of how to deal with work-family conflict successfully. When women were clear in their commitment to their careers, marriage, and children, and couples equally shared housework and emotional work, they successfully combined them without high levels of distress (Zimmerman et al., 2003). How did they do it?

Division of Labor and Role Conflict
in Dual-Earner Couples

One of the largest issues still facing American society in the new millennium is how dual-earner couples can balance their occupational and family roles. With the majority of couples now consisting of two wage earners, issues such as who does the household chores and how child care is arranged will become increasingly important.

Many people believe that work and family roles mutually influence each other. That is, when things go bad at work, family suffers, and when problems occur at home, work suffers. As noted in the text, such role conflicts and mutual interaction appear not to be the case. It is more of a one-way street. For the most part, problems at home have little effect on job performance, whereas trouble at work can spill over to home life (Gutek & Gilliland, 2007; Streich, Casper, & Salvaggio, 2008).

Negotiating agreeable arrangements of household

and child-care tasks are critical. But as noted in the text, truly equitable divisions of labor are clearly the exception. Most American households with dual-earner couples still operate under a gender-segregated system: There are wives' chores and husbands' chores. Without question, all these tasks are important and must be performed to ensure domestic sanitation. However, these tasks take time. The important point for women is that it is not how much time is spent in performing household chores that matters but which tasks are performed. The research cited in the text indicates that what bothers wives the most is not that their husbands are lazy but that their husbands will not perform some "women's work." Men may mow the lawn, wash the car, and even cook, but they rarely run the vacuum, scrub the toilet, or change the baby's diaper.

Husbands would be viewed much more positively by their wives if they performed more of the traditionally female tasks. Marital satisfaction would be likely to improve as a result. Moreover, the role modeling provided to children in these households would be a major step in breaking the transmission of age-old stereotypes.

There are benefits of multiple roles: they have a buffering effect by mitigating the stress in one of the roles, and they provide added income, flexible gender ideology, and social support, among others (Frone, 2003; Gutek & Gilliland, 2007). Finally, what role can organizational policies play in reducing work-family conflict? One study suggests that more flexible scheduling can mitigate work-family issues. However, as soon as the organizations' profits are down, such work-family programs typically are eliminated (Hochschild, 1997). It's something to think about.

Contrary to popular belief, the age of the children was not a factor in stress level. However, the number of children was important, as stress increases greatly with each additional child, irrespective of their ages. Guilt was also not an issue for these women. In the same study, men reported sharing more of the child-care tasks as a way of dealing with multiple role pressures. In addition, stress is lower for men who have a flexible work schedule that allows them to care for sick children and other family

matters. Together, these findings are encouraging; they indicate that more heterosexual dual-earner couples are learning how to balance work and family adaptively.

The study just reviewed also indicates the importance of taking a life-stage approach to work-family conflict. For example, a number of studies find that the highest conflict between the competing demands of work and family are at the peak parenting years (the period in which there are two or more preschool children) (Blanchard-Fields, Chen, & Hebert, 1997; Cournoyer & Mahalik, 1995; Shaw & Burns, 1993). By contrast, inter-role conflict is reduced when people experience a high degree of quality in their marriage (Gutek & Gilliland, 2007). Overall, it is important to note that perception of the quality of a person's roles is an important indicator of whether or not the person will experience stress.

Dual-earner couples often have difficulty finding time for each other, especially if both work long hours. The amount of time together is not necessarily the most important issue; as long as the time is spent in shared activities such as eating, playing, conversing, and sharing emotions, couples tend to be happy (Kingston & Nock, 1987; Zimmerman et al., 2003). Unfortunately, many couples find that by the time they have an opportunity to be alone together, they are too tired to make the most of it.

A number of studies suggest that stressors associated with work-family conflict may hold different meanings for women and men (Simon, 1995). Cross-cultural data show that burnout from work and parenting is more likely to affect women. A study of dual-earner married couples in Singapore showed that wives are more likely to suffer from burnout than husbands; wives' burnout resulted from both work and nonwork stress, whereas husbands' burnout resulted only from work stress (Aryee, 1993). This finding was also supported in American men (Greenglass, 1991). Other studies find that women tend to experience more family demands than men do and spend more time on family work (Costigan et al., 2003; Joshi & Sastry, 1995). In contrast, men are more vulnerable to work stress than family stress (Costigan et al., 2003; Izraeli, 1993; Lai, 1995). These findings suggest that the source of men's role stress involves conflict with work roles and the source of women's role stress lies more in the conflict involving family roles.

Issues concerning balancing work and family are extremely important in couples' everyday lives. Learning how to deal with multiple roles is an important process in current industrial societies. We are creating patterns that will provide the anticipatory socialization for our children. Even now, most dual-earner couples feel that the benefits, especially the extra income, are worth the costs. Many dual-earner couples, however, have no choice but to try to deal with the situation as best they can: Both partners must work simply to pay the bills. As discussed in the Current Controversies feature, this means that couples need to take seriously the job of deciding how to divide up tasks.

Concept Checks

1. What differences are there in how husbands and wives divide household tasks?
2. What is the most important thing an organization can do for employees with children?
3. What helps both working fathers and mothers balance work and family obligations?

12.5 Leisure Activities

LEARNING OBJECTIVES

- What types of leisure activities do adults exhibit?
- What developmental differences are there in leisure activities?
- What do people derive from leisure activities?

Anthony is a 55-year-old electrician who has enjoyed outdoor activities his whole life. From the time he was a boy, he has fished and water-skied in the calm inlets of coastal Florida. Although he doesn't compete in slalom races any more, Anthony still skis regularly. He still participates in fishing competitions every chance he gets.

Adults do not work every waking moment of their lives. As each of us knows, we need to relax sometimes and engage in leisure activities. Intuitively, leisure consists of activities not associated with work. More formally, researchers define *leisure* as discretionary activity, which includes simple relaxation, activities for enjoyment, creative pursuits, and sensual transcendence (Gordon, Gaitz, & Scott, 1976). However, men and women differ in their views of leisure, as do people in different ethnic groups (Henderson, 1990). For example, one study of African American women revealed that they view leisure as both freedom from the constraint of needing to work and as a form of self-expression (Allen & Chin-Sang, 1990).

Types of Leisure Activities

Leisure can include virtually any activity. To help organize the options, researchers have classified leisure activities into four categories: cultural—such as attending sporting events, concerts, church services, and meetings; physical—such as basketball, hiking, aerobics, and gardening; social—such as visiting friends and going to parties; and solitary—including reading, listening to music, and watching television (Bossé & Ekerdt, 1981; Glamser & Hayslip, 1985). Leisure activities can also be considered in terms of the degree of cognitive, emotional, or physical involvement; skydivers would have high activity in all three areas. Examples of leisure activities organized along this dimension are listed in Table 12.2.

Table 12.2

Forms of Leisure Activity and How They Vary in Intensity of Cognitive, Emotional, or Physical Involvement

Very high intensity	Sexual activity
	Highly competitive games or sports
	Dancing
Moderately high intensity	Creative activities (art, literature, music)
	Nurturance or teaching (children's arts and crafts)
	Serious discussion and analysis
Medium intensity	Attending cultural events
	Participating in clubs
	Sightseeing or travel
Moderately low intensity	Socializing
	Reading for pleasure
	Light conversation
Low intensity	Solitude
	Quiet resting
	Taking a nap

An alternative approach to classifying leisure activities involves the distinction between preoccupations and interests (Rapoport & Rapoport, 1975). Preoccupations are much like daydreaming. Sometimes preoccupations become more focused and are converted to interests. Interests are ideas and feelings about things one would like to do, is curious about, or is attracted to. Jogging, surfing the Web, fishing, and painting are some examples of interests.

Rapoport and Rapoport's distinction draws attention to a key truth about leisure: Any specific activity has different meaning and value, depending on the individual involved. For example, cooking a gourmet meal is an interest, or a leisure activity, for many people. For professional chefs, however, it is work and thus is not leisure at all.

Given the wide range of options, how do people pick their leisure activities? Apparently, each of us has a leisure repertoire, a personal library of intrinsically motivated activities that we do regularly (Mobily, Lemke, & Gisin, 1991). The activities in our repertoire are determined by two things: perceived competence (how good we think we are at the activity compared to other people our age) and psychological comfort (how well we meet our personal goals for performance). Other factors are important as well: income, interest, health, abilities, transportation, education, and social characteristics (Lawton et al., 2002; Wilcox et al., 2003). For example, some leisure activities, such as downhill skiing, are relatively expensive and require transportation and reasonably good health and physical coordination for maximum enjoyment. In contrast, reading requires minimal finances (if one uses a public library) and is far less physically demanding. It is probable that how these factors influence leisure activities changes through adulthood (e.g., physical prowess typically declines somewhat).

Developmental Changes in Leisure

Cross-sectional studies report age differences in leisure activities (Bray & Howard, 1983). Young adults participate in a greater range of activities than middle-aged adults do. Furthermore, young adults tend to prefer intense leisure activities, such as scuba diving and hang gliding. In contrast, middle-aged adults focus more on home- and family-oriented activities. In later middle age, they spend less of their leisure time in strenuous physical activities and more in sedentary activities such as reading and watching television. Older adults narrow the range of activities and lower their intensity even further (Gordon et al., 1976). People of all ages report feelings of freedom during leisure activities (Larson, Gillman, & Richards, 1997). Most importantly, however, it is not aging per se that is the most influential in limiting leisure activities of older adults. Health problems have the greatest effect (Duke et al., 2002; Fukukawa et al., 2004; Strain et al., 2002).

Longitudinal studies of changes in individuals' leisure activities over time show considerable stability over reasonably long periods (Cutler & Hendricks, 1990; Strain et al., 2002). Anthony, the 55-year-old in the last section-opening vignette who likes to fish and ski, is a good example of this overall trend. As Anthony demonstrates, frequent participation in leisure activities during childhood tends to continue into adulthood. Similar findings hold for the pre- and post-retirement years. Apparently, one's preferences for certain types of leisure activities are established early in life; they tend to change over the life span primarily in terms of how physically intense they are.

Consequences of Leisure Activities

What do people like the woman in the photograph gain from participating in leisure activities? Researchers agree that involvement in leisure activities is related to well-being (Guinn, 1999; Kelly, 1996; McGuire et al., 1996; Warr et al., 2004) and may even be related to reduced risk for Alzheimer's disease (Crowe et al., 2003). The key aspect of this relation is not the level of participation. Instead, how much satisfaction you derive from your leisure activities is the important element in promoting well-being (Lawton, Moss, & Fulcomer, 1986–1987). Whether leisure enhances one's well-being appears to depend on whether you like what you do for

Leisure activities such as this one promote satisfaction and well-being as the stress of work decreases in prominence.

fun. For example, nonsocial aspects of activities (e.g., solitary activities) promote health and longevity in late older age (Lennartsson & Silverstein, 2001; Menec, 2003).

But what if leisure activities are pursued very seriously? In some cases, people create leisure-family conflict by engaging in leisure activities to extremes (Goff, Fick, & Opplinger, 1997). Only when there is support from others for such extreme involvement are problems avoided (Goff et al., 1997). As in most things, moderation in leisure activities is probably best.

Concept Checks

1. How can leisure activities be classified?
2. What age differences have been noted in leisure activities?
3. What benefits do people derive from leisure activities?

12.6 Retirement

LEARNING OBJECTIVES
- What does being retired mean?
- Why do people retire?
- How should people prepare for retirement?
- How satisfied are retired people?
- What specific effects does retirement have on maintaining family and community ties?

Matt is a 77-year-old retired construction worker who labored hard all his life. He managed to save a little money, but he and his wife live primarily on his monthly Social Security checks. Although not rich, they have enough to pay the bills. Matt is largely happy with retirement, and he stays in touch with his friends. He thinks maybe he's a little strange, though—he has heard that retirees are supposed to be isolated and lonely.

You probably take it for granted that someday, after working for many productive years, you will retire. But did you know that until 1934, when a railroad union sponsored a bill promoting mandatory retirement, and 1935, when Social Security was inaugurated, retirement was rarely even considered by most Americans like Matt (Sterns & Gray, 1999). Only since World War II have there been a substantial number of retired people in the United States. Today the number is increasing rapidly, and the notion that people work a specified time and then retire is built into our expectations about work.

In this section, we consider what retirement is like for older adults. We consider people like Matt as we examine how retirement is defined, why people retire, how people adjust to being retired, and how retirement affects interpersonal relationships.

What Does Being Retired Mean?

Like leisure, retirement is difficult to define. Retirement is more difficult to define than just guessing from someone's age (Henretta, 1997; Szinovacz & DeViney, 1999). One way to look at retirement is to equate it with complete withdrawal from the workforce. But this definition is inadequate; many retired people continue to work part time (Mutchler et al., 1997; Ruhm, 1990). Another possibility would be to define retirement as a self-described state. However, this definition does not work either, because some African Americans define themselves with labels other than "retired'" in order to qualify for certain social service programs (Gibson, 1991).

Part of the reason it is difficult to define retirement precisely is that the decision to retire involves

the loss of occupational identity (discussed earlier). What people do for a living is a major part of their identity. Not doing those jobs anymore means we either put that aspect of our lives in the past tense—"I used to work as a manager at the Hilton"—or say nothing at all. Loss of this aspect of identity can be difficult to face, so some people look for a label other than "retired" to describe themselves.

A useful way to view retirement is as a complex process by which people withdraw from full-time participation in an occupation (Henretta et al., 1997; Mutchler et al., 1997; Sterns & Gray, 1999). This withdrawal process can be described as either "crisp" (making a clean break from employment by stopping work entirely) or "blurred" (repeatedly leaving and returning to work, with some unemployment periods) (Mutchler et al., 1997). Bob is a good example of a "crisp" retirement. He retired from TWA at age 65; now in his late 80s, he has done nothing work-related in the interim.

Whereas many people think of retirement as a crisp transition, the evidence shows that less than half of older men who retire fit this pattern (Mutchler et al., 1997). Most men adopt a more gradual or "blurred" process involving part-time work in an effort to maintain economic status. Jack is one of these men. When he retired from DuPont at age 62, he and a friend began a small consulting company. For about five years, Jack worked when he wanted, gradually cutting back over time.

The lack of crisp retirement creates another complicating factor—the idea of a "normal" retirement age such as age 65 may no longer be appropriate (Cornman & Kingston, 1996; Mutchler et al., 1997). Instead, the notion of a typical retirement age changes to a range of ages, further blurring the meaning of "early" or "late" retirement (Cornman & Kingston, 1996).

The complexity of the retirement process must be acknowledged for us to understand what retirement means to people in different ethnic groups. For example, whereas middle-class European Americans often use a criterion of full-time employment to define themselves as retired or not, Mexican Americans use any of several different criteria depending on how the question is asked (Zsembik & Singer, 1990). For example, Mexican Americans are most likely to claim that they are retired when asked directly ("Are you retired?") than when asked indirectly ("What are you doing these days?"). It may be that people want to appear active, so they choose some other descriptor. In contrast, European Americans are just as likely to call themselves retired no matter how they are asked.

The Changing Nature of Retirement. Contributing to the complexity of the retirement process is that issues concerning retirement are changing rapidly. Just as fundamental change is occurring in the definition of work, so too are similar changes occurring in the definition of retirement. More individuals in their post-retirement years are working in part-time jobs, primarily to supplement their incomes but also to maintain adequate levels of activity. Many older adults also volunteer their time to many different organizations.

The need for some older adults to continue working is becoming more formally recognized. For example, one senior center in Wilmington, Delaware, offers job-training programs for older workers. These programs prepare workers for a variety of jobs that provide a way for them to earn a living. Some corporations, such as McDonald's, actively recruit older workers because of their reputation for reliability and responsibility. Indeed, roughly a third of recent retirees report being partially retired (or partially employed) at some point, but their employment is usually in low-paying jobs taken out of economic necessity (Moen & Wethington, 1999). More recently, at DuPont older workers have the opportunity of work-life programs such as part-time jobs that were originally developed for young employees with families (Market, 2008; McCune, 1998).

As more people anticipate longer periods of retirement, and with the virtual removal of all mandatory retirement, one interesting research question will be whether more individuals will choose to continue working if possible, especially with the recent economic downturn. In the latter case, the numbers of employed older adults may also increase if people's financial status is insufficient to support them if they retire. First, there have been many debates in the mid-1990s about the long-term viability of the Social Security system; if this system changes dramatically, it will have a major effect on decisions to retire. Second, a growing number of Americans even at 67 are not retiring because of the failure of Americans to financially bear the burden of retirement, changes in society with respect to the need to work, and the recent economic recession (Market, 2008).

As the baby-boom generation approaches retirement age, examination of retirement programs increases, as do debates about the proper time to retire. As you consider the issues in the following sections, you should recognize that new views on the role and nature of retirement are emerging that may force us to reconsider issues we thought were settled. You can see this for yourself by doing the Discovering Development exercise.

Why Do People Retire?

The decision to retire is an intensely personal one that involves carefully weighing several factors. Overall, more workers retire by choice than for any other reason (Hayward, Friedman, & Chen, 1998; Henretta, Chan, & O'Rand, 1992). People usually retire when they feel financially secure, considering projected income from Social Security, pension plans, and personal savings. Of course, some people are forced to retire because they lose their jobs (Henretta et al., 1992; Stetz & Beehr, 2000). As corporations have downsized in the early and mid-1990s as well as in the more recent economic recession, some older workers have been offered buyout packages involving supplemental payments if they retire. Others have been permanently furloughed, laid off, or dismissed.

The complexity of the retirement decision is also influenced by one's occupational history (Hayward et al., 1998). The longest occupation held in the middle of one's career combines with occupational roles held in the last stages of the career to influence the decision to retire and the connection with health and disability (discussed later). Feeling that retirement is a choice rather than a requirement is associated with an earlier planned retirement age, as well as adjustment to retirement (Quine, Wells, De Vaus, & Kendig, 2007; Sterns & Gray, 1999). Let's examine these factors more closely.

Health. One of the most important influences on retirement decisions is health, regardless of whether someone is approaching mandatory retirement. Poor health is one of the predominant reasons that people retire early (Hansson, DeKoekkoek, Neece, & Patterson, 1997; Mutchler, Burr, Massagli, & Pienta, 1999; Schults & Wang, 2007). The importance of health cuts across ethnic group lines, especially in terms of early retirement. For example, health problems causing functional impairment are the main reason European Americans, African Americans, and Mexican Americans retire early (Burr et al., 1996; Stanford, Happersett, Morton, Molgaard, & Peddecord, 1991). However, it is not a simple relationship. For example, health has its greatest influence on the decision to retire early for individuals who find the idea of work unattractive because of family or economic factors (Mutchler et al., 1999). In other words, it appears that the impact of health on retirement is apparently determined by trends in other work-related characteristics such as marital status. In addition, the specific health problem matters. Persons are most likely to retire when they contract major health conditions such as lung disease and cancer, whereas if they contract minor health conditions such as diabetes and arthritis, they are likely to do either: retire or change jobs (Schultz & Wang, 2007).

Gender Differences. Most of what we know about retirement decisions is based on research on men (Sterns & Gray, 1999). However, women may enter the workforce later, have more discontinuous work histories, spend less time in the workforce, and their financial resources may differ from men's, which may affect women's decisions to retire (Calasanti, 1996; Sterns & Gray, 1999; Stetz & Beehr, 2000). In fact, research indicates that men's and women's decisions to retire may be based on different factors. Talaga and Beehr (1995) found that women whose husbands were in poor health or who had more dependents were more likely to retire; the opposite was true for men. However, there were some similarities; having a retired spouse increased the likelihood that spouses would also retire.

As more women remain in the workforce for much of their adult lives, more research will be necessary to understand the extent to which gender differences matter in the decision to retire. At this point, though, it appears that the male model of retirement is insufficient to account for women's

Few studies have investigated the characteristics of retired African Americans.

experiences (Sterns & Gray, 1999; Szinovacz & DeViney, 1999).

Ethnic Differences. Very little research has been conducted on retirement decisions as a function of ethnicity. A few investigators have examined the characteristics of retired African Americans like the couple in the photograph (e.g., Flippen & Tienda, 2000; Gibson, 1986, 1987; Jackson & Gibson, 1985). These studies show that African Americans tend to label themselves as retired or not based on subjective disability, work history, and source of income, rather than simply on whether or not they are currently employed. An important finding is that gender differences appear to be absent among African Americans; men and women base their self-labels on the same variables. Thus, findings based on European American samples must not be generalized to African Americans, and separate theoretical models for African Americans may be needed (Gibson, 1987). The same may be true for other ethnic groups as well.

Planning for Retirement

What do people need to do to plan for retirement? Is it just a matter of saving money? Or do people need to take psychological factors into account as well? Can prospective retirees anticipate and avoid some of the difficulties? For example, one common problem in adjusting to the retirement role is the abruptness of the transition from employment to unemployment. What processes may minimize the difficulties of this change?

One key element to successful retirement is preparation. People who plan for retirement tend to be more successful in adapting to this major life change (Lo & Brown, 1999; Sterns & Gray, 1999). Getting ready can take several forms: conscious or unconscious planning, informal or formal steps, and so on. *One formal way to prepare for retirement is to participate in a* **preretirement education program.** *Such programs cover a wide variety of topics, from financial planning to adjustment.* A typical content list is contained in Table 12.3. Potential

Table 12.3
Topics in a Typical Preretirement Education Program

  I. Deciding to retire: when is the right time?

 II. Psychological aspects of aging
    A. Work roles and retirement
    B. Personal identity issues
    C. Retirement as a process, paradox, and change
    D. Effects on relationships with family and friends

 III. Finances
    A. Social Security
    B. Pension
    C. Insurance
    D. Employment

 IV. Legal aspects
    A. Wills
    B. Personal rights as senior citizens

  V. Health
    A. Normal aging
    B. Medicare and Medicaid
    C. Health insurance issues

 VI. Where to live: the pros and cons of moving

 VII. Leisure activities
    A. Travel
    B. Hobbies
    C. Clubs and organizations
    D. Educational opportunities
    E. Volunteering

benefits of such planning are more financial equity, the increased possibility of a healthier lifestyle, more positive attitudes toward retirement, exposure to new leisure activities, and ways to explore alternative housing (Atchley, 1996; Hershey, Mowen, & Jacobs-Lawson, 2003; Richardson, 1993; Sterns, Laier, & Dorsett, 1994).

Every comprehensive planning program for retirement focuses on a major obstacle to retirement: finances. Retirement, on average, involves a reduction in income. Obviously, if one is not prepared for this degree of income loss, financial pressures will be severe. Research shows that financial issues are strongly related to the decision to retire and adjustment to retirement (Davies et al., 1991; Feldman, 1994; Hansson et al., 1997). Surprisingly, a large number of people do not adequately plan for the financial changes that accompany retirement (Ferraro & Su, 1999). Overall, older adults who are satisfied with their financial resources tend to make the decision to retire and adjust well to that decision. However, findings also indicate that financial issues influence retirement decisions and adjustment differently depending on the major reason for retirement (Henretta, Chan, & O'Rand, 1996). When retirement is compulsory or forced, financial security tends to increase the rate of retirement. However, when retirement is mainly due to health limitations, financial security tends to decrease the rate of retirement. Finally, when job loss is the main reason for retirement, financial security does not influence retirement rate. However, despite any reason to retire, higher salaries, overall, tend to reduce the decision to retire.

Adjustment to Retirement

Researchers agree on one point about retirement: It is an important life transition. New patterns of involvement must be developed in the context of changing roles and lifestyles (Antonovsky & Sagy, 1990; Wang, 2007). Until the early 1990s, research focused on what was thought to be a sequence of predictable phases of retirement, such as honeymoon, disenchantment, reorientation, acceptance, and termination (Atchley, 1982). Because retirement is now

viewed as a process, the "typical" age of retirement has lost its meaning, and gender differences are evident in the decision to retire, the idea that retirement proceeds in an orderly stage-like sequence has been abandoned (Sterns & Gray, 1999). Instead, researchers support the idea that people's adjustment to retirement evolves over time as a result of complex interrelation with physical health, financial status, voluntary retirement status, and feelings of personal control (Gall, Evans, & Howard, 1997).

How do most people fare? As long as people have financial security, health, and a supportive network of relatives and friends, they report feeling very good about being retired (Gall et al., 1997; Matthews & Brown, 1987). For men, being in good health, having enough income, and having retired voluntarily is associated with relatively high satisfaction early in retirement; having an internal sense of personal control is correlated with well-being over the long run (Gall et al., 1997, 1998). Wives' retirement expectations were more influenced by husbands' resources than vice versa (Pienta & Hayward, 2002). For both men and women, high personal competence is associated with higher retirement satisfaction, probably because competent people are able to optimize their level of environmental press (as described in Chapter 5).

It is important to consider individual differences in adjustment to retirement. Wang (2007) finds three major patterns. Retirees who held a transitional job, actively engaged in retirement planning, and who were married tended to maintain their familiar patterns. Retirees who retired from highly physically demanding or stressful jobs, and had low job satisfaction to begin with, were more likely to exhibit a recovering pattern where they felt that they were escaping an unpleasant work role. Finally, retirees who experienced health declines during retirement, who were in an unhappy marriage, or who retired prematurely demonstrated a pattern of negative changes in psychological well-being during the retirement transition, although later well-being did rebound.

One stereotype of retirement is that health begins to decline as soon as people stop working. Research findings do not support this belief; in

Retirees tend to maintain a network of friends and are engaged in activities.

fact, well-being typically increases for men during the first year of retirement, especially if they had a choice (Gall et al., 1997; Kim & Moen, 2002; Quine et al., 2007).

A second stereotype is that retirement dramatically reduces the number and quality of personal friendships. Again, there is no research support for this belief. In fact several studies have shown that men like Matt, from the section-opening vignette, are typical; neither the number nor the quality of friendships declines as a result of retiring (Bossé, Aldwin, Levenson, Spiro, & Mroczek, 1993).

Finally, some people believe that retired people become much less active overall. This stereotype is also not supported by research. Although the number of hours in paid work decreases on average with age, older adults are still engaged for hundreds of hours per year in productive activities such as unpaid volunteer work and helping others (Herzog, Kahn, et al., 1989; Kim & Moen, 2001). We will specifically consider volunteer activities in the next section.

Interpersonal Ties

Retirement rarely affects only a single individual. No matter how personal the joys and sorrows of retirement may be, the interpersonal relations they have shape retirees' reactions. Social ties help people deal with the stresses of retirement, as they do in other life transitions. In many cases, these ties involve friendships and other relationships formed earlier in adulthood.

Social relationships help cushion the effects of any life stress throughout adulthood. This support takes many forms: letting people know they are loved; offering help if needed; providing advice; taking care of others' needs; just being there to listen. Retirees who have close and strong social ties have an advantage in adjusting to the life changes that retirement brings (Henkens, 1999; Pinquart & Schindler, 2007; van Solinge, & Henkens, 2007).

Intimate Relationships. In the past, much attention was focused on the role of intimate relationships in adjusting to retirement. Marriage has provided the framework for almost all this research. Ideally, marital partners provide mutual support during the transition to retirement (Moen et al., 2001). Whether marriage actually serves this function is unclear. Marital status by itself has little effect on older women's satisfaction with retirement (Szinovacz, 1996). Never-married men are as satisfied as married retirees, whereas divorced, separated, or widowed retired men are much less happy (Barfield & Morgan, 1978). Perhaps never-married men prefer singlehood and become accustomed to it long before retirement. All in all, these findings point to the stabilizing effects of marriage for men.

Possible benefits aside, retirement undoubtedly has profound effects on intimate relationships such as marriage. It often disrupts long-established patterns of family interaction, forcing both partners (and others living in the house) to adjust (Pearson, 1996). Simply being together more may put strain on the relationship. Daily routines of couples may need rearrangement, which may be stressful. However, because marital satisfaction among older couples tends to be quite high, most couples can resolve these stresses.

One common change that confronts most retired married couples (in traditional households in which only the husband was employed) is the division of household chores. Although retired men tend to do more work around the home than they did before retirement, this situation does not always lead to desirable outcomes (Szinovacz, 1992, 1996). For example, an employed husband may compliment his wife on her domestic skills; after retirement, however, he may suddenly want to teach her to do things "correctly." Part of the problem may be that such men are not used to taking orders. One retired executive remarked that before he retired, when he said "Jump!" highly paid employees wanted to know how high. "Now, I go home, I walk in the door, and my wife says, 'Milton, take out the garbage.' I never saw so much garbage" (Quigley, 1979, p. 9). Finally, part of the problem may be in the perception of one's turf; after retirement men feel that they are thrust into doing things that they, and their partners, may have traditionally thought of as "women's work" (Troll, 1971). As more dual-earner couples retire, it will be interesting to see how these issues are handled.

Intimate family relationships are clearly important sources of support for retirees. However, they are not the only ones; friendship networks also provide support that often complements family networks. Friends sometimes provide types of support that, because of the strong emotional ties, families may be less able to offer: a compassionate, but objective listener; a companion for social and leisure activities; or a source of advice, transportation, and other assistance.

As mentioned earlier, in general, neither the number nor the quality of friendships declines as a result of retirement (Bossé et al., 1993). When friendships change during retirement, it is usually due to some other reason, such as very serious health problems, that interferes with people's ability to maintain friendships. We do need to bear in mind the gender differences in friendships we discussed in Chapter 11, though. Older men have fewer close personal friends for support than do older women. This difference may help explain the gender difference between marital status and satisfaction discussed earlier. Men, because of their fewer close relationships, may be forced to rely more on their wives for support.

Community Ties. Throughout adulthood, most people become and remain connected with their communities. Thus an important consideration is whether the social environment aids retirees' ability to continue old ties and form new ones. The past few decades have witnessed the rapid growth of organizations devoted to providing such opportunities to retirees. National groups such as the American Association of Retired Persons (AARP) provide the chance to learn, through magazines, pamphlets, and websites, about what other retirees are doing and about services such as insurance and discounts. Numerous smaller groups exist at the community level; these include senior centers and clubs. Several trade unions also have programs for their retired members. These activities promote the notion of lifelong learning and help keep older adults cognitively fit.

A common way for retired adults to maintain community ties is by volunteering. Older adults report that they volunteer to help themselves deal with life transitions (Adlersberg & Thorne, 1990), to provide service to others (Hudson, 1996; Okun & Schultz, 2003), and to maintain social interactions and learn more about the world (Okun & Schultz, 2003). There are many opportunities for retirees to help others. One federal agency, ACTION, administers four programs that have hundreds of local chapters: Foster Grandparents, Senior Companions, the Retired Senior Volunteer Program (RSVP), and the Service Corps of Retired Executives (SCORE). Nearly half of older adults aged 65 to 74 volunteer their services in some way, with substantial participation rates even among people over age 80 (Chambré, 1993). These rates represent more than a 400% increase since the mid-1960s, when only about 1 in 10 older adults did volunteer work. What accounts for this tremendous increase?

Several factors are responsible (Chambré, 1993; Morrow-Howell et al., 2003): improved public perception of the skills, increased psychological well-being and functioning, and wisdom older adults have to offer; a redefinition of the nature and merits of volunteer work; a more highly educated population of older adults; and greatly expanded opportunities for people to become involved in volunteer work that they enjoy. In particular, current research indicates that volunteers experience greater increases in psychological well-being and health (Morrow-Howell et al., 2003; Shmotkin, Blumstein, & Modan, 2003). Given the demographic trends of increased numbers and educational levels of older adults discussed in Chapter 1, even higher rates of voluntarism are expected during the next few decades (Chambré, 1993). These opportunities may be a way for society to tap into the vast resources that older adults offer as well as provide additional meaningful roles for older adults.

Concept Checks

1. What is the best way to conceptualize retirement?
2. What are the major predictors of the decision to retire?
3. What is included in a preretirement education program?
4. What factors contribute to adjustment to retirement?
5. How do retirees interact with their communities?

Research reviewed in this chapter has identified a number of factors that promote job satisfaction, help ameliorate the difficulties encountered by dual-career couples, and reduce sexual harassment, among other issues. All of these findings have important implications for public policy. For example, providing flexible work schedules increases job satisfaction and improves the conflict experienced by dual-career couples. However, statistics indicate that although more than 27% of the U.S. workforce reports having the ability to use flex-time, the opportunity of flexibility in the timing of work is not keeping pace with the demand (Golden, 2001; Ronen, Friedman, & Ben-Asher, 2007).

This is an area for public policy to focus on: providing the opportunity for flexible schedules to the 73% of the population without it. As we have learned, combining one's occupation with caregiving responsibilities is stressful and taxes one's ability to make a living. Public policy can help influence employers to develop plans to assist workers in balancing occupation and family responsibilities in order to facilitate more caregivers remaining in the labor market (Evandrou & Glaser, 2002).

Finally, findings indicate that a woman's response to sexual harassment is typically nonconfrontive and intent on maintaining a satisfactory relationship with the perpetrator (Magley, 2002). However, the courts are out of touch with the realities of women's reactions and need to be educated that women's responses to sexual harassment are multifaceted and more complex than what is indicated by their simply reporting or not reporting the event (Magley, 2002).

Summary

12.1 Occupational Choice and Development

How do people view work? How do occupational priorities vary with age?

- Although most people work for money, other reasons are highly variable. Occupational priorities have changed over time; younger workers' expectations from their occupations are now lower, and their emphasis on personal growth potential is higher.

How do people choose their occupations?

- Holland's theory is based on the idea that people choose occupations to optimize the fit between their individual traits and their occupational interests. Six personality types that represent different combinations of these have been identified. They include investigative, social, realistic, artistic, conventional, and enterprising. Research supports the validity of this approach, although some gender differences have been found.

What factors influence occupational development? What roles do mentors play?

- Super's developmental view of occupations is based on self-concept and adaptation to an occupational role. Super describes five stages in adulthood: implementation, establishment, maintenance, deceleration, and retirement.

- Reality shock is the realization that one's expectations about an occupation are different from the reality one experiences. Reality shock is common among young workers.

- A mentor is a co-worker who teaches a new employee the unwritten rules and fosters occupational development. Mentor–protégé relationships develop over time, through stages, as do other relationships.

What factors influence job satisfaction? What causes alienation and burnout?

- Older workers report higher job satisfaction than younger workers, but this may be partly due to self-selection; unhappy workers may quit. Other reasons include intrinsic satisfaction, good fit, lower importance of work, finding nonwork diversions, and life-cycle factors.

- Alienation and burnout are important considerations in understanding job satisfaction. Both involve significant stress for workers.

12.2 Gender, Ethnicity, Bias, and Discrimination

How do women and men's occupational expectations differ and how are they viewed when entering a nontraditional occupation?

- Men and women are socialized differently into occupational roles, and their occupational choices are affected as a result. Women choose nontraditional occupations for many reasons, including expectations and personal feelings. Women in such occupations are still viewed more negatively than men in the same occupations.

What factors are related to women's occupational development?

- Women leave well-paid occupations for many reasons, including family obligations and workplace environment. Women who continue to work full time have adequate child care and look for ways to further their occupational development.

What factors affect ethnic minority workers' occupational experiences and development?

- Vocational identity and vocational goals vary in different ethnic groups. Whether an organization is sensitive to ethnicity issues is a strong predictor of satisfaction among ethnic minority employees.

What types of bias and discrimination hinder the occupational development of women and ethnic minority workers?

- Sex discrimination remains the chief barrier to women's occupational development. In many cases, this operates as a glass ceiling. Pay inequity is also a problem; women are often paid a fraction of what men in similar jobs earn.

- Sexual harassment is a problem in the workplace. Current criteria for judging harassment are based on the reasonable woman standard. Denying employment to anyone over 40 because of age is age discrimination.

- Age discrimination comes into play if a worker is denied promotion or employment because of her or his age. Age discrimination occurs in many ways including differential layoff patterns and stereotypic views of the older worker. Several other labor market barriers also exist for older workers.

12.3 Occupational Transitions

Why is worker retraining necessary?

- To adapt to the effects of a global economy and an aging workforce, many corporations are providing retraining opportunities for workers. Retraining is especially important in cases of outdated skills and career plateauing.

- The belief that one has the ability to learn and develop (a case of self-efficacy) influences whether retraining will be effective.

How does the timing of job loss affect the amount of stress one experiences?

- Important reasons why people change occupations include personality, obsolescence, and economic trends. Occupational insecurity is a growing problem. Fear that one may lose one's job is a better predictor of anxiety than the actual likelihood of job loss.

- Job loss is a traumatic event that can affect every aspect of a person's life. Degree of financial distress and the extent of attachment to the job are the best predictors of distress.

12.4 Dual-Earner Couples

What are the issues faced by employed people who care for dependents?

- Whether a woman returns to work after having a child depends largely on how attached she is to her work. Simply providing on-site child care does not always result in higher job satisfaction. The more important factor is the degree to which supervisors are sympathetic.

How do the partners view the division of household chores?

- Although women have reduced the amount of time they spend on household tasks over the past two decades, they still do most of the work. European American men are less likely than either African American or Hispanic American men to help with traditionally female household tasks.

What is work-family conflict and how does it affect couples' lives?

- Flexible work schedules and number of children are important factors in role conflict. Recent evidence shows that work stress has a much bigger impact on family life than family stress has on work performance. Some women pay a high personal price for having careers.

- Work-family conflicts are influenced by the life stage the individual is in and gender differences in the meaning attributed to the nature of the conflict.

12.5 Leisure Activities

What types of leisure activities do adults engage in?

- Preoccupations can become more focused as interests, which can lead to the selection of particular leisure activities. People develop a repertoire of preferred leisure activities.

What developmental differences are there in leisure activities?

- As people grow older, they tend to engage in leisure activities that are less strenuous and more family-oriented. Leisure preferences in adulthood reflect those earlier in life.

What do people derive from leisure activities?

- Leisure activities enhance well-being and can benefit all aspects of people's lives.

12.6 Retirement

What does being retired mean?

- Retirement is a complex process by which people withdraw from full-time employment. No single definition is adequate for all ethnic groups; self-definition involves several factors, including eligibility for certain social programs.

Why do people retire?

- Most people retire because they choose to, although some people are forced to retire or do so because of financial status or serious health problems, such as cardiovascular disease or cancer. However, there are important gender and ethnic differences in why people retire and how they label themselves after retirement. Most of the research is based on European American men from traditional marriages.

How should people prepare for retirement?

- Preretirement education programs cover a variety of topics, including finances, attitudes, health, and expectations. Financial planning for retirement is essential. Realistic expectations toward retirement are important predictors of future satisfaction.

How satisfied are retired people?

- Retirement is an important life transition. Most people are satisfied with retirement. Most retired people maintain their health, friendship networks, and activity levels, at least in the years immediately following retirement. For men, personal life priorities are all-important; little is know about women's retirement satisfaction. Most retired people stay busy in activities such as volunteer work and helping others.

What specific effects does retirement have on maintaining family and communities?

- Retiring can disrupt long-held behavior patterns in marriages. Social relationships help buffer the stress of retirement. Readjusting to being home rather than at work is difficult for men in traditional marriages. Marriages are sometimes disrupted, but married men are generally happier in retirement than men who are not married. Participation in community organizations helps raise satisfaction. In particular, volunteer work can fill the void. Improved attitudes toward adults in society also help.

Review Questions

12.1 Occupational Choice and Development

- What are occupational priorities and how do they change over time?

- How is work changing as a result of the global economy?

- Briefly describe Holland's theory linking personality and occupational choice. What personality types did Holland identify? How are they related to occupational fit?

- Briefly describe Super's theory of occupational development.

- What is a mentor? What role does a mentor play in occupational development?

- How does the mentor–protégé relationship change over time?

- What is the developmental course of job satisfaction? What factors influence job satisfaction?

- What are alienation and burnout? How are they related to job satisfaction?

12.2 Gender, Ethnicity, Bias, and Discrimination

- What gender differences have been identified that relate to occupational choice?
  How are men and women socialized differently in ways that influence occupational opportunities?

- How are women in nontraditional occupations perceived?

- What are the major barriers to women's occupational development?

- What major barriers to occupational development are related to ethnicity?

- How are sex discrimination and the glass ceiling related?

- What are the structural barriers ethnic minorities face in occupational settings?

- How is sexual harassment defined?

- What is age discrimination and how does it operate?

- What are the main labor market barriers to older workers?

12.3 Occupational Transitions

- What are the major reasons why people change occupations?

- Why is retraining workers important?

- What effects do people report after losing their jobs?

12.4 Dual-Earner Couples

- What factors are important in dependent care for employees?

- How do dual-earner couples balance multiple roles and deal with role conflict?

- What important factors contribute to work-family conflict? What other occupational development effects occur?

12.5 Leisure Activities

- What are the major reasons people engage in leisure activities? What benefits occur?

- What kinds of leisure activities do people perform?

- How do leisure activities change over the life span?

- What gender differences appear in leisure activities?

12.6 Retirement

- In what ways can retirement be viewed? How may the definition of retirement change in the next several years?

- What are the main predictors of the decision to retire?

- What steps should people take to prepare for retirement?

- How do people adjust to being retired?

- What effects does retirement have on relationships with family, friends, and community?

Integrating Concepts in Development

1. What role do personal relationships play in one's work, leisure, and retirement?

2. How does cognitive development and personality influence work roles?

3. What implications are there for the removal of mandatory retirement in terms of normal cognitive changes with age?

Key Terms

age discrimination Denying employment or promotion to someone on the basis of age. Age discrimination is illegal in the United States.

alienation The feeling that results when workers feel that what they are doing is worthless and that their efforts are devalued, or when they do not see the connection between what they do and the final product.

burnout The feeling that results when the pace and the pressure of one's occupation becomes more than one can bear, depleting one's energy and motivation.

career plateauing The lack of promotional opportunity from the organization or the person's decision not to seek advancement.

comparable worth The notion that people should be paid equally for similar work regardless of gender.

glass ceiling An invisible but real barrier to the occupational development of women and minorities that allows them to advance to a certain level in an organization and no higher.

glass elevator The situation where men in traditionally female occupations seem to rise at a quicker rate than their female counterparts.

inter-role conflict A clash between competing or incompatible sets of roles, most often seen in work versus family settings.

job satisfaction How happy one is with one's job.

mentor A person who teaches the informal rules of an organization.

occupational priorities The reasons why one works, and how one views them.

preretirement education program A program aimed at educating workers about the broad range of issues they will face in retirement, including health, adjustment, and finances.

reality shock The realization that the real world does not work like a textbook.

reasonable woman standard The appropriate basis for defining sexual harassment; defined as the standard by which a reasonable woman would consider a behavior as offensive.

sex discrimination Denying a person, a position, or a promotion solely on the basis of gender.

vocational identity The degree to which one views one's occupation as a key element of identity.

vocational maturity The degree to which one's occupational behaviors are congruent with what is expected of one at different ages.

work-family conflict The feeling of being pulled in multiple directions by incompatible demands from one's job and one's family.

Resources

www.cengage.com/psychology/cavanaugh

Visit the companion website, where you will find tutorial quizzes, glossary, flashcards, and more. You can also access the following websites from the companion website.

The U.S. Department of Labor provides many reports on various aspects of workforce participation. Check out the many agencies within the Department by clicking on the "DOL Agencies" button. The Women's Bureau on that list is especially good for statistics on women's employment status. Connect to address above for an up-to-date link to this the site.

A well-organized set of links to all aspects of employment, including career planning, law, unemployment, and women's issues, Connect to the book companion site listed above to see up-to-date link to this site.

Many Websites are devoted to the issue of sexual harassment. An excellent and brief summary about myths and realities concerning sexual harassment, and much additional information.

The AARP provides a web page that reports on major issues related to older adults including community and volunteer programs, legislative issues on retirement benefits, financial and work issues in general, and leisure and fun .

Readings

Bolles, R. N. (1997). *The 1998 what color is your parachute: A practical manual for job-hunters and career changers*. Berkeley, CA: Ten Speed Press. This popular reference is a valuable resource for people in search of careers. It is regularly updated.

Crosby, F. (1991). *Juggling: If you'd like to learn more: The unexpected advantages of balancing career and home for women, their families and society*. New York: Free Press. Intriguing discussion of balancing multiple roles of work and family. Moderately difficult.

Feather, N. T. (1990). *The psychological impact of unemployment*. New York: Springer-Verlag. One of the best scholarly discussions of unemployment. Moderately difficult.

Gerson, K. (1993). *No man's land: Men's changing commitments to family and work*. New York: Basic Books. Based on a series of life history interviews, this book gives a male perspective on balancing work and family. Easy reading.

Keita, G. P., & Hurrell, J. J., Jr. (Eds.). (1994). *Job stress in a changing workforce*. Washington, DC: American Psychological Association. A wide-ranging discussion of issues including diversity, culture, ethnicity, age, and role conflict. Easy to moderately difficult depending on the chapter.

Schaie, K. W., & Schooler, C. (Eds.) (1998). *Impact of work on older adults*. New York: Springer. Edited book discussing work and nonwork factors influencing older adults' work performance and satisfaction. Moderate difficulty.

13

Dying and Bereavement

HEATH LEDGER starred as The Joker in the action drama film The Dark Knight.

WHEN FAMOUS PEOPLE DIE TRAGICALLY, PEOPLE ARE CONFRONTED WITH THE REALITY

that death happens to everyone. Actor Heath Ledger, who died in 2008 at age 28 of an accidental overdose of prescription medication, is only one example, Best known for his roles in the movies *Brokeback Mountain* and *The Dark Knight*, Ledger had established himself as a critically acclaimed actor. Just as the rich and famous die, though, so do we.

People have a paradoxical relationship with death. On one hand, we are fascinated by it, as evidenced by the popularity of news stories about murders or wars and by the crowds of onlookers at accidents. Tourists often visit the places where famous people died or are buried. People around the world watch news broadcasts that show the horrors of war and genocide in which tens of thousands of people are killed. But on the other hand, when pondering our own death or that of people close to us, we face problems, as La Rochefoucauld wrote more than 300 years ago when he said that it is easier to look into the sun than to contemplate death. When death is personal, we become uneasy. We might not be as willing to watch the news if we knew the coverage would concern our own death. It is hard indeed to look at the sun.

For most people in the United States, death does not become a really personal experience until middle age when our parents die. We typically do not experience death up close as children; indeed, many Americans believe it is important to shield children from death. But just a few generations ago in America, death was part of people's everyday life experience, and it still is in most of the world. Children are present when family members die. Viewings and wakes are held in the home, and children actively participate in funeral services. Perhaps we should consider what these changes in personal experience with death mean for life-span development in America today.

In this chapter, we consider death from many perspectives. We examine some of the issues surrounding how it is defined legally and medically. We address several questions: Why do most of us avoid thinking about death? What is it like to die? How are dying people cared for? How do survivors grieve and cope with the loss of a loved one?

13.1 Definitions and Ethical Issues

LEARNING OBJECTIVES
- How is death defined?
- What legal and medical criteria are used to determine when death occurs?
- What are the ethical dilemmas surrounding euthanasia?
- What issues surround the costs of life-sustaining interventions?

Ernesto and Paulina had been married 48 years when Ernesto developed terminal pancreatic cancer. Ernesto was suffering terrible pain and begged Paulina to make it stop. Paulina had heard about "mercy killing" that involved administering high dosages of barbiturates, but she believed this was the same as murder. Yet she could hardly bear to watch her beloved husband suffer. Paulina wondered what she should do.

When one first thinks about it, death seems a very simple concept to define: It is the point at which a person is no longer alive. Similarly, dying is simply the process of making the transition from being alive to being dead. It all seems clear enough, doesn't it? But death and dying are actually far more complicated concepts.

Cultural and religious differences in the definition of death and the customs surrounding it make for rich experiences. The meaning of death depends on the observer's perspective, as well as on the specific medical and biological criteria one uses.

Sociocultural Definitions of Death

What comes to mind when you hear the word *death*? A driver killed in a traffic accident? A transition to an eternal reward? Flags at half-staff? A cemetery? A car battery that doesn't work anymore? Each of these possibilities represents a way in which death can be considered in Western culture, which has its own set of specific rituals (Bustos, 2007; Penson, 2004). All cultures have their own views. Among Melanesians, the term *mate* includes the very sick, the very old, and the dead; the term *toa* refers to all other living people (Counts & Counts, 1985). Other South Pacific cultures believe that the life force leaves the body during sleep or illness; sleep, illness, and death are considered together. Thus people "die" several times before experiencing "final death" (Counts & Counts, 1985). The Kwanga of Papua New Guinea believe that most deaths are caused by sorcery (Brison, 1995).

In Ghana people are said to have a "peaceful" or "good" death if the dying person has finished all business and has made peace with others before death, which implies being at peace with his or her own death (van der Geest, 2004). A good and peaceful death comes "naturally" after a long and well-spent life. Such a death preferably takes place at home, which is the epitome of peacefulness, surrounded by children and grandchildren. Finally, a good death is a death that is accepted by the relatives.

Mourning rituals and states of bereavement also vary in different cultures (Rosenblatt, 2001). There is great variability across cultures in the meaning of death and whether there are rituals or other behaviors to express grief. Some cultures have formalized periods of time during which certain prayers or rituals are performed. For example, after the death of a close relative, Orthodox Jews recite ritual prayers and cover all the mirrors in the house. The men slash their ties as a symbol of loss. The Muscogee Creek tribe's rituals include digging the grave by hand and giving a "farewell handshake" by throwing a handful of dirt into the grave before covering it (Walker & Balk, 2007). Ancestor worship, a deep respectful feeling toward individuals from whom a family is descended or who are important to them, is an integral part of customs surrounding death in Japanese culture and of Buddhism in Japan (Klass, 1996b). Some cultures, such as the Toraja of Indonesia, do not encourage people to dwell on the dead or memories of them; nevertheless, they still maintain contact with the deceased through dreams (Hollan, 1995). We must keep in mind that the experiences of our culture or particular group may not generalize to other cultures or groups.

How people experience loss through death varies a great deal among different cultures.

Death can be a truly cross-cultural experience. The international outpouring of grief over the death of world leaders such as Pope John Paul II in 2005, after terrorist attacks such as the one that killed thousands in the United States in September 2001, or during natural disasters that kill tens of thousands of people such as the cyclone in Burma and the earthquake in China in 2008, draws much attention to the ways in which the deaths of people we do not know personally can still affect us. It is at these times we realize that death happens to us all and that death can be simultaneously personal and public.

Altogether, death can be viewed in at least 10 ways (Kalish, 1987; Kastenbaum, 1985). Look at the list that follows and consider the examples given for these definitions. Then take another moment to think up additional examples of your own.

Death as an image or object

A flag at half-staff

Sympathy cards

Tombstone

Black crepe paper

Monument or memorial

Death as a statistic

Mortality rates

Number of AIDS patients who die

Murder and suicide rates

Life expectancy tables

Death as an event

Funeral

Family gathering

Memorial service

Viewing or wake

Death as a state of being

Time of waiting

Nothingness

Being happy with God all the time

State of being; pure energy

Death as an analogy

Dead as a doornail

Dead-letter box

Dead-end street

You're dead meat

In the dead of winter

Death as a mystery

What is it like to die?

Will we meet family?

What happens after death?

Will I learn everything when I die?

Death as a boundary

How many years do I have left?

What happens to my family?

What do I do now?

You can't come back.

Death as a thief of meaning

I feel so cheated.

Why should I go on living?

Life doesn't mean much anymore.

I have much left to do.

Death as fear and anxiety

Will dying be painful?

I worry about my family.

I'm afraid to die.

Who will care for the kids?

Death as reward or punishment

Live long and prosper

The wicked go to hell

Heaven awaits the just

Purgatory prepares you for heaven

The many ways of viewing death can be seen in various customs involving funerals. You may have experienced a range of different types of funeral customs, from very small, private services to very elaborate rituals. Variations in the customs surrounding death are reflected in some of the oldest monuments on earth, such as the pyramids in Egypt, and some of the most beautiful, such as the Taj Mahal in India.

Legal and Medical Definitions

Sociocultural approaches help us understand the different ways in which people conceptualize and comprehend death. But they do not address a very fundamental question: How do we determine that someone has died? The medical and legal communities have grappled with this question for centuries and continue to do so today. Let's see what the current answers are.

Determining when death occurs has always been subjective. *For hundreds of years, people accepted and applied the criteria that now define* clinical death: *lack of heartbeat and respiration. Today, however, the most widely accepted criteria are those that characterize* whole-brain death. In 1981 the President's Commission for the Ethical Study of Problems in Medicine and Biomedical and Behavioral Research established several criteria still used today that must be met for the determination of whole-brain death:

- No spontaneous movement in response to any stimuli
- No spontaneous respirations for at least one hour
- Total lack of responsiveness to even the most painful stimuli
- No eye movements, blinking, or pupil responses
- No postural activity, swallowing, yawning, or vocalizing

- No motor reflexes
- A flat electroencephalogram (EEG) for at least 10 minutes
- No change in any of these criteria when they are tested again 24 hours later

For a person to be declared dead, all eight criteria must be met. Moreover, other conditions that might mimic death—such as deep coma, hypothermia, or drug overdose—must be ruled out. Finally, according to most hospitals, the lack of brain activity must occur both in the brainstem, which involves vegetative functions such as heartbeat and respiration, and in the cortex, which involves higher processes such as thinking. In the United States all 50 states and the District of Columbia use the whole-brain standard to define death.

It is possible for a person's cortical functioning to cease while brainstem activity continues; this is a persistent vegetative state, *from which the person does not recover.* This condition can occur following disruption of the blood flow to the brain, a severe head injury, or a drug overdose. Persistent vegetative state allows for spontaneous heartbeat and respiration, but not for consciousness. The whole-brain standard does not permit a declaration of death for someone who is in a persistent vegetative state. Because of conditions like persistent vegetative state, family members sometimes face difficult ethical decisions concerning care for the individual. These issues are the focus of the next section.

Some philosophers and scientists argue that the whole-brain standard does not reflect current research on brain functioning, especially with regard to those functions of the cortex that make us "human," as opposed to those in the brainstem that control basic functions in us and in other living beings (e.g., Capron, 2001; Steen, 2007; Truog, 2004). Advocates of this view argue for using a *higher-brain* standard, according to which death is the irreversible cessation of the capacity for consciousness. This standard is often met prior to whole-brain death. Thus, a patient in a permanent coma or persistent vegetative state meets the higher-brain, but not the whole-brain, standard of death.

Ethical Issues

An ambulance screeches to a halt, and emergency personnel rush a woman into the emergency room. As a result of an accident at a swimming pool, she has no pulse and no respiration. Working rapidly, the trauma team reestablishes a heartbeat through electric shock. A respirator is connected. An EEG and other tests reveal extensive and irreversible brain damage. What should be done?

This is an example of the kinds of problems faced in the field of bioethics, *the study of the interface between human values and technological advances in health and life sciences.* Bioethics grew from two bases: respect for individual freedom and the impossibility of establishing any single version of morality by rational argument or common sense. Both of these bases rely increasingly on empirical evidence (Borry, Schotsmans, & Dierickx, 2005). In practice, bioethics emphasizes the minimization of harm over the maximization of good, and the importance of individual choice. That is, bioethics requires people to weigh how much the patient will benefit from a treatment relative to the amount of suffering he or she will endure as a result of the treatment. Examples of the tough choices required are those facing cancer patients with respect to whether they agree to aggressive treatment for cancer that is likely to be fatal, or those facing family members who are asked whether to turn off a life-support machine that is attached to their loved one.

In the arena of death and dying, the most important bioethical issue is euthanasia—*the practice of ending life for reasons of mercy.* The moral dilemma posed by euthanasia becomes apparent when we try to decide the circumstances under which a person's life should be ended, which implicitly forces us to put a value on the life of another (Elliott & Oliver, 2008). It also makes us think about the difference between "killing" and "letting die" at the end of life (Dickens, Boyle, & Ganzini, 2008). In our society this dilemma occurs most often when a person is being kept alive by machines or when someone is suffering from a terminal illness. These are the issues Ernesto and Paulina face in the opening vignette.

Active Euthanasia. Euthanasia can be carried out in two different ways: active and passive. *Active euthanasia involves the deliberate ending of someone's life, which may be based on a clear statement of the person's wishes or be a decision made by someone else who has the legal authority to do so.* Usually, this involves situations in which people are in a persistent vegetative state or suffer from the end stages of a terminal disease. Examples of active euthanasia would be administering a drug overdose, disconnecting a life-support system, or ending a person's life through so-called mercy killing.

Most Americans favor such actions as disconnecting life support in situations involving patients in a persistent vegetative state, and even for the concept of assisted death, but feelings also run strongly against it for religious or other reasons (Dickens et al., 2008). Similarly, Israelis hold a range of opinions (Leichtentritt & Rettig, 2000), as do Germans (Oehmichen & Meissner, 2000). A Swedish study showed that better education about palliative care (care aimed at pain management) options reduced the number of requests for active euthanasia (Valverius, Nilstun, & Nilsson, 2000). A systematic survey of laypersons and health care professionals in The Netherlands and Belgium found that most laypeople and health care professionals said they would support euthanasia under certain specific conditions (Teisseyre, Mullet, & Sorum, 2005). Respondents assigned most importance to patients' specific requests for it and supported these requests; they did not view patients' willingness to donate organs, without another compelling reason, as an acceptable reason to request euthanasia.

Taking one's own life through ritual suicide has never been popular in the United States due to religious and other prohibitions. In other cultures, such as Japan, suicide is viewed as an honorable way to die under certain circumstances. Asian Americans have the highest suicide rate in the United States, and their suicide notes are more likely to reveal that they felt they were a burden on their families (Pascual, 2000). Nationwide, less than one-third of Americans in most ethnic groups oppose physician-assisted suicide or the Oregon Death With Dignity law (Braun, Tanji, & Heck, 2001; Harris Interactive, 2007), and there is even less support among Americans of Filipino and Hawaiian ancestry (Braun et al., 2001).

Several countries—including Switzerland, Belgium, and Colombia—tolerate physician-assisted suicide. In 1984, the Dutch Supreme Court eliminated prosecution of physicians who assist in suicide if five criteria are met:

1. The patient's condition is intolerable with no hope for improvement.
2. No relief is available.
3. The patient is competent.
4. The patient makes a request repeatedly over time.
5. Two physicians must review the case and agree with the patient's request.

The Dutch Parliament approved the policy in April 2001, making The Netherlands the first country to have an official policy legalizing physician-assisted suicide (Deutsch, 2001).

Voters in Oregon passed the Death With Dignity Act in 1994, the first physician-assisted suicide law in the United States. In 2008, voters in Washington state passed a law essentially identical to the Oregon law.

The Death With Dignity law makes it legal for people to request a lethal dose of medication if they have a terminal disease and make the request voluntarily. Although the U.S. Supreme Court ruled in two cases in 1997 (*Vacco v. Quill* and *Washington v. Glucksberg*) that there is no right to assisted suicide, the court decided in 1998 not to overturn the Oregon law.

The Oregon law is more restrictive than the law in The Netherlands (Deutsch, 2001). The Oregon law provides for people to obtain and use prescriptions for self-administered lethal doses of medication. The law requires that a physician inform the person that he or she is terminally ill and describe alternative options (e.g., hospice care, pain control), and the person must be mentally competent and make two oral requests and a written one, with at least 15 days between each oral request. Such provisions are included to ensure that people making the request fully understand the issues and that the request is not made hastily.

Several studies have examined the impact of the Oregon law. The numbers of patients who received prescriptions and who died in the first 10 years in which the law was in effect (1998–2007) are shown in Figure 13.1. Over the 10-year period, a total

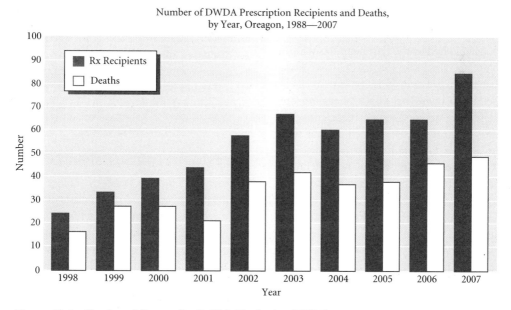

Number of DWDA Prescription Recipients and Deaths, by Year, Oreagon, 1988—2007

Figure 13.1 Number of Oregon Death With Dignity Act (DWDA) prescription recipients and deaths, 1998–2007.

Oregon Department of Human Services (2008).

of 341 patients died under the terms of the law (Oregon Department of Human Services, 2008). Comprehensive reviews of the implementation of the Oregon law soon after its passage concluded that all safeguards worked and that such things as depression, coercion, and misunderstanding of the law were carefully screened (Orentlicher, 2000). Available data also indicate that Oregon's law has psychological benefits for patients, who are comforted by knowing they have this option (Cerminara & Perez, 2000).

There is no question that the debate over physician-assisted suicide has only begun. As the technology to keep people alive continues to improve, the ethical issues about active euthanasia in general and physician-assisted suicide in particular will continue to get more complex.

Passive Euthanasia. *A second form of euthanasia, passive euthanasia, involves allowing a person to die by withholding available treatment.* For example, chemotherapy might be withheld from a cancer patient, a surgical procedure might not be performed, or food may be withdrawn. Again, these approaches are controversial. For example, Garrard and Wilkinson (2005) point out that the idea of passive euthanasia was attacked in February 2001 in a particularly clear and explicit way by an "Ethics Task Force" established by the European Association of Palliative Care (EAPC). The EAPC Task Force claimed that the expression "passive euthanasia" is a contradiction in terms because any ending of a life is by definition active. Despite these concerns, Garrard and Wilkinson (2005) conclude that there is really no reason to abandon the category provided that it is properly and narrowly understood and provided that "euthanasia reasons" for withdrawing or withholding life-prolonging treatment are carefully distinguished from other reasons, such as family members not wanting to wait to divide the patient's estate.

At a practical level, passive euthanasia can be viewed in at least two ways. On the one hand, few would argue with a decision not to treat a newly discovered cancer in a person in the late stages of Alzheimer's disease if treatment would do nothing but prolong and make even more agonizing an already certain death. Indeed, a survey in England revealed that caregivers agreed that treatments could and should be withheld from dementia patients in the case of critical physical conditions (Tadros & Salib, 2001). On the other hand, many people argue against withholding nourishment from a terminally ill person; indeed, such cases often end up in court.

The first high-profile legal case involving passive euthanasia in the United States was brought to the courts in 1990; the U.S. Supreme Court took up the case of Nancy Cruzan, whose family wanted to end her forced feeding. The court ruled that unless clear and incontrovertible evidence is presented that an individual desires to have nourishment stopped, such as through a durable health care power of attorney or living will, a third party, such as a parent or partner, cannot decide to end it.

The most widely publicized and politicized case of passive euthanasia in the United States involved Terri Schiavo, who died in Florida in 2005. This extremely controversial case involving the withdrawal of forced feeding had its origins in a disagreement between Terri's husband Michael, who said that Terri would have wanted to die with dignity and therefore the feeding tube should be removed, and her parents, who argued the opposite. The debate resulted in government officials, state and federal legislators, and courts getting involved. As discussed in the Current Controversies feature, such cases reveal the difficult legal, medical, and ethical issues as well as the high degree of emotion surrounding the topic of euthanasia and death with dignity.

The Price of Life-Sustaining Care

A growing debate in Western society concerns the financial, personal, and moral costs of keeping people alive on life-support machines. For example, many people argue that treating secondary diseases in terminally ill older adults or keeping them alive on life support makes little sense. They argue that such treatment is extremely expensive, that these people will soon die anyway, and that needlessly prolonging their lives is a burden on society. In these cases, it is argued, both the person and society would be better off if the person were allowed to die.

On February 25, 1990, 26-year-old Terri Schiavo collapsed in her home from a possible potassium imbalance caused by an eating disorder, temporarily stopping her heart and cutting off oxygen to her brain. On March 31, 2005, Terri Schiavo died after her feeding tube had been removed 13 days earlier. On these two points everyone connected with Terri's case agreed. But on all other essential aspects of it, Terri's husband Michael and Terri's parents deeply disagreed.

The central point of disagreement was Terri's medical condition. Terri's husband and numerous physicians argued that she was in a persistent vegetative state. Based on this diagnosis, Michael Schiavo requested that Terri's feeding tube be withdrawn and that she be allowed to die with dignity in the way he asserted she would have wanted to.

Terri's parents and some other physicians said she was not in a persistent vegetative state, and that she was capable of recognizing them and others. Based on this diagnosis, their belief that Terri would not want the intervention stopped, and their contention that passive euthanasia is morally wrong, they fought Michael's attempts to remove the feeding tube.

What made this case especially difficult was that Terri left no written instructions that would have clearly stated her thoughts and intentions on the issue. So the ensuing legal and political debates became based on what various people thought Terri would have wanted, as well as reflecting various aspects of people's positions on personal rights regarding life and death.

The legal and political battles began in 1993, when Terri's parents tried unsuccessfully to have Michael removed as Terri's guardian. But the most heated aspects of the case began in 2000, when a circuit court judge ruled that Terri's feeding tube could be removed based on his belief that she had told Michael that she would not have wanted it. In April 2001, the feeding tube was removed after state courts and the U.S. Supreme Court refused to hear the case. However, the tube was reinserted 2 days later when another judge ordered it. In November 2002, the original circuit court judge ruled that Terri had no hope of recovery and again ordered the tube removed, an order eventually carried out in October 2003. Within a week, however, Florida Governor Jeb Bush signed a bill passed by the Florida legislature requiring that the tube be reinserted. This law was ruled unconstitutional by the Florida Supreme Court in September 2004. In February 2005, the original circuit court judge again ordered the tube removed. On March 16 to 27, the Florida House introduced and passed a bill that would have required the tube be reinserted, but the Florida Senate defeated

GULFPORT, FL: A handout photo shows Terri Schiavo and her mother taken at Terri's hospital bed in 2003 in Gulfport, Florida. Terri's Law, enacted earlier this year by Florida Governor Jeb Bush, was enacted for the purpose of keeping Terri alive but the state Supreme Court ruled the law unconstitutional.

(Continued)

a somewhat different version of the bill. On March 19 to 21, bills that would have allowed a federal court to review the case passed in the U.S. House of Representatives and the U.S. Senate, but the two versions could not be reconciled. Over the next 10 days, the Florida Supreme Court, the U.S. district court, and a U.S. circuit court refused to hear the case, as did the U.S. Supreme Court. The original circuit court judge rejected a final attempt by Terri's parents to get the tube reinserted.

The public debate on the case was as long and complex as the legal and political arguments. The debate has had several positive outcomes. The legal and political complexities dramatically illustrated the need for people to reflect on end-of-life issues and to make their wishes known to family members and others (e.g., health care providers) in writing. The case also brought to light the high cost of long-term care, the difficulties in actually determining whether someone is in a persistent vegetative state and in turn what that implies about life, the tough moral and ethical issues surrounding the withdrawal of nutrition, and the individual's personal feelings about death. The legal community has proposed reforms concerning how these types of cases are heard in the courts and the processes used to resolve them (Moran, 2008).

Should Terri Schiavo's feeding tube have been removed? Every answer to this question stirs strong personal emotions, and this case will remain a watershed event for people on all sides of the debate about dying with dignity. That a state governor, state legislators, national legislators, the U.S. president, other elected and government officials, and numerous judges all became directly involved in the case demonstrates that passive euthanasia generates intense feelings and will remain an extremely controversial issue for years to come. The best course of action is to make your end-of-life intentions clearly known to others, a topic we will discuss later in this chapter.

In contrast, many people—including many physicians—go to extraordinary lengths to keep very premature infants alive, despite high risks of permanent brain damage or physical disability from the intervention. Some people point out that not only is the medical care at the time often more expensive for infants (an average of several thousand dollars per day for neonatal intensive care), but the potential cost to families and society if the person needs constant care could be enormous. In addition, the emotional costs can be devastating to many families. But many such children are not affected negatively by the intervention and grow up to be normal in all respects.

Health care costs typically soar during the last year of a person's life. For example, 30% of Medicare's annual budget is spent treating people in the last year of their life. These costs vary a great deal depending on where you live. Appleby (2006) notes that the number of physician visits and medical tests one undergoes differs across the United States for many reasons, including the number of physicians and hospital beds available, patient and family expectations, and the willingness of health care professionals to discuss the end of life.

The biggest challenge in confronting these differences in approach and cost is the difficulty in deciding when to treat or not treat a patient. There are no easy solutions to these dilemmas.

Concept Checks

1. What are the 10 ways in which death can be viewed socioculturally?

2. What are the criteria for determining brain death and clinical death?

3. What is the difference between active and passive euthanasia?

4. What are the issues regarding costs of life-sustaining interventions?

13.2 Thinking about Death: Personal Aspects

LEARNING OBJECTIVES
- How do feelings about death change over adulthood?
- How do people deal with their own death?
- What is death anxiety, and how do people show and cope with it?

Ricardo recently learned that he has amyotrophic lateral sclerosis, better known as Lou Gehrig's disease. He knows the disease is fatal, and he is afraid of dying. He cannot understand why this has happened to him, and he is very angry at God for "doing this to him." Formerly a very religious person, he now refuses to go to church or to talk with his friend, a parish priest.

Being afraid to die is considered normal by most people. Certainly, Ricardo could relate to this. As one research participant put it, "You are nuts if you aren't afraid of death" (Kalish & Reynolds, 1976). Still, death is a paradox, as we noted at the beginning of the chapter. That is, we are afraid of or anxious about death, but we are drawn to it, sometimes in very public ways. We examine this paradox at the personal level in this section. Specifically, we focus on two questions: How do people's feelings about death differ with age? What is it about death that we fear or that makes us anxious?

Before proceeding, however, take a few minutes to complete the exercise in the Discovering Development feature. Although it may be daunting and difficult at first, writing your own obituary is a way to gain insight into what you think are your most important accomplishments and relationships. In a way, it serves as a process for conducting a life review.

A Life Course Approach to Dying

How do you feel about dying? Do you think people of different ages feel the same way? It probably doesn't surprise you to learn that feelings about dying vary across adulthood. Because young adults are just beginning to pursue the family, career, and personal goals they have set, they tend to be more intense in their feelings toward death. If you were to ask young adults who are at a funeral how they feel about death, they would be likely to report a strong sense that those who die at this point in their lives would be cheated out of their future (Attig, 1996).

Although not specifically addressed in research, the shift from formal operational thinking to post-formal thinking could be important in young adults' contemplation of death. Presumably, this shift in cognitive development is accompanied by a lessening of the feeling of immortality as young adults begin to integrate personal feelings and emotions with their thinking.

Midlife is the time when most people confront the death of their parents. Up to that point, people tend not to think much about their own death; the fact that their parents are still alive buffers them from reality. After all, in the normal course of events, our parents are supposed to die before we do.

Once their parents have died, people realize that they are now the oldest generation of their family—the next in line to die. Reading the obituary pages, they are reminded of this, as the ages of many of the people who have died get closer and closer to their own.

Probably as a result of this growing realization of their own mortality, middle-aged adults' sense of time undergoes a subtle yet profound change. It changes from an emphasis on how long they have already lived to how long they have left to live, a shift that increases into late life (Attig, 1996; Cicirelli, 2006; Neugarten, 1969; Tomer & Eliason, 2000). This may lead to occupational change or other redirection such as improving relationships that have deteriorated over the years.

In general, older adults are less anxious about death and more accepting of it than any other age group. Still, because the discrepancy between desired and expected number of years left to live is greater for young-old than for mid-old adults, anxiety is higher for young-old adults (Cicirelli, 2006). In part, this greater overall acceptance of

If you have ever looked carefully at a newspaper, you know that everyone who dies has a brief summary of his or her life published in an obituary. Obituaries serve several purposes, including telling the world the important aspects of one's life and listing one's surviving family members. If you have ever read an obituary, you also realize that they tend to be fairly short, usually less than 200 words in most cases.

Imagine that, unlike most people, you have the opportunity to write your own obituary. Imagine further that you can create the obituary based on the life you hope to have. Take a moment to reflect on this, and then compose a 150- to 200-word obituary that includes your age at the time of your death, the cause of death, your major life accomplishments, and your family survivors. When finished, read it over carefully. What stands out? What would you like to change? You may want to keep it for future reference to see how closely your life turns out in relation to your dreams.

death results from the achievement of ego integrity, as described in Chapter 15. For many older adults, the joy of living is diminishing (Kalish, 1987). More than any other group, they have experienced loss of family and friends and have come to terms with their own mortality. Older adults have more chronic diseases, which are not likely to go away. They may feel that their most important life tasks have been completed (Kastenbaum, 1999).

Understanding how adults deal with death and their consequent feelings of grief is best approached from the perspective of attachment theory (Field, Gao, & Paderna, 2005; Stroebe, Schut, & Stroebe, 2005). In this view, a person's reactions are a natural consequence of forming attachments and then losing them. We consider adult grief a bit later in the chapter.

Dealing with One's Own Death

Thinking about death from an observer's perspective is one thing. Thinking about one's own death, like Ricardo is doing, is quite another. The reactions people have to their own impending death, long thought to be the purview of religion and philosophy, were not researched until well into the 20th century.

Many authors have tried to describe the dying process, often using the metaphor of a trajectory that captures both the duration of time between the onset of dying (e.g., from the diagnosis of a fatal disease) and death and the course of the dying process (Wilkinson & Lynn, 2001). These dying trajectories vary a great deal across diseases, as illustrated in Figure 13.2. Some diseases, such as lung cancer, have a clear and rapid period of decline; this "terminal phase" is often used to determine eligibility for certain services (e.g., hospice, discussed later). Other diseases, such as congestive heart failure, have no clear terminal phase; any significant health event could cause death. The two approaches of describing the dying process that we will consider try to account for both types of trajectories.

Kübler-Ross's Theory. Elisabeth Kübler-Ross became interested in the experience of dying when she was an instructor in psychiatry at the University of Chicago in the early 1960s. When she began her investigations into the dying process, such research was controversial; her physician colleagues initially were outraged, and some even denied that their patients were terminally ill. Still, she persisted. More than 200 interviews with terminally ill people convinced her that most people experienced several emotional reactions. Using her experiences, she

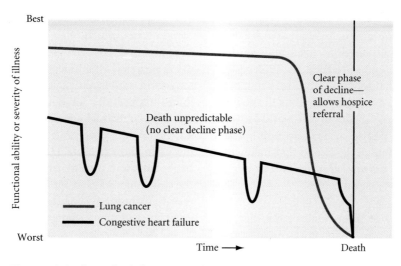

Figure 13.2 Some fatal diseases, such as lung cancer, have a clear decline phase, whereas others, such as congestive heart failure, do not.

Source: From Skolnick, A. A. (1998). MediCaring project to demonstrate and evaluate innovative end-of-life program for chronically ill. *Journal of the American Medical Association, 279,* 1511–1512. Reprinted with permission of the American Medical Association.

described five reactions that represented the ways in which people dealt with death: denial, anger, bargaining, depression, and acceptance (Kübler-Ross, 1969). Although they were first presented as a sequence, it was subsequently realized that the emotions can overlap and can be experienced in different order.

When people are told that they have a terminal illness, their first reaction is likely to be shock and disbelief. Denial is a normal part of getting ready to die. Some want to shop around for a more favorable diagnosis, and most feel that a mistake has been made. Others try to find reassurance in religion. Eventually, though, reality sets in for most people.

At some point, people express anger as hostility, resentment, and envy toward health care workers, family, and friends. People ask, "Why me?" and express a great deal of frustration. The fact that they are going to die when so many others will live seems so unfair. With time and work, most people confront their anger and resolve it.

In the bargaining phase, people look for a way out. Maybe a deal can be struck with someone, perhaps God, that would allow survival. For example,

a woman might promise to be a better mother if only she can live. Or a person sets a timetable: "Just let me live until my daughter graduates from college." Eventually, the person becomes aware that these deals will not work.

When one can no longer deny the illness, perhaps because of surgery or pain, feelings of depression are very common. People report feeling deep loss, sorrow, guilt, and shame over their illness and its consequences. Kübler-Ross believes that allowing people to discuss their feelings with others helps move them to an acceptance of death.

In the acceptance stage, the person accepts the inevitability of death and often seems detached from the world and at peace. "It is as if the pain is gone, the struggle is over, and there comes a time for the 'final rest before the journey' as one patient phrased it" (Kübler-Ross, 1969, p. 100).

Although she believes that these five stages represent the typical range of emotional development in the dying, Kübler-Ross (1974) cautions that not everyone experiences all of them or progresses through them at the same rate or in the same order. Research supports the view that her "stages" should not be viewed as a sequence (Neimeyer, 1997). In fact, we could actually harm dying people by considering these stages as fixed and universal. Individual differences are great, as Kübler-Ross points out. Emotional responses may vary in intensity throughout the dying process. Thus the goal in applying Kübler-Ross's theory to real-world settings would be to help people achieve an appropriate death. An appropriate death is one that meets the needs of the dying person, allowing him or her to work out each problem as it comes.

A Contextual Theory of Dying. One of the difficulties with most theories of dying is a general lack of research evaluating them in a wide variety of contexts (Kastenbaum & Thuell, 1995). By their very nature, stages or sequences imply a particular directionality. Stage theories, in particular, emphasize qualitative differences between the various stages. However, the duration of a particular stage, or a specific phase, varies widely from person to person. Such theories assume some sort of underlying process for moving through the stages or phases but do not clearly state what causes a person to move from one to another.

One reason for these problems is the realization that there is no one right way to die, although there may be better or worse ways of coping (Corr, 1991–1992; Corr, Corr, & Nabe, 2008). A perspective that recognizes this would approach the issue from the mind-set of the dying person and the issues or tasks he or she must face. Corr identified four dimensions of such tasks: bodily needs, psychological security, interpersonal attachments, and spiritual energy and hope. This holistic approach acknowledges individual differences and rejects broad generalizations. Corr's task work approach also recognizes the importance of the coping efforts of family members, friends, and caregivers as well as those of the dying person.

Kastenbaum and Thuell (1995) argue that what is needed is an even broader, contextual approach that provides a more inclusive view of the dying process. They point out that theories must be able to handle people who have a wide variety of terminal illnesses and be sensitive to dying people's own perspectives and values related to death.

The socio-environmental context within which dying occurs, which often changes over time, must be recognized. For example, a person may begin the dying process living independently but end up in a long-term care facility. Such moves may have profound implications for how the person copes with dying. A contextual approach would provide guidance for health care professionals and families for discussing how to protect the quality of life, provide better care, and prepare caregivers for dealing with the end of life. Such an approach would also provide research questions. For example, how does one's acceptance of dying change across various stages?

We do not yet have such a comprehensive theory of dying. But as Kastenbaum and Thuell point out, we can move in that direction by rejecting a reductionistic approach that focuses on set stages for a truly holistic one. One way to accomplish this is to examine people's experiences as a narrative that can be written from many points of view (e.g., the patient, family members, caregivers). What would emerge would be a rich description of a dynamically changing process.

Death Anxiety

We have seen that how people view death varies with age. In the process, we encountered the notion of feeling anxious about death. Death anxiety is tough to pin down; indeed, it is the ethereal nature of death, rather than something about it in particular, that usually makes us feel so uncomfortable. We cannot put our finger on something specific about death that is causing us to feel uneasy. Because of this, we must look for indirect behavioral evidence to document death anxiety. Research findings suggest that death anxiety is a complex, multidimensional construct.

Researchers apply terror management theory (Pyszczynski, Greenbert, & Solomon, 1997, 1999; Strachan et al., 2001) as a framework to study death anxiety. Terror management theory *addresses the issue of why people engage in certain behaviors to achieve particular psychological states based on their deeply rooted concerns about mortality* (Arndt & Vess, 2008). The theory proposes that ensuring that one's life continues is the primary motive underlying behavior; all other motives can be traced to this basic one. Additionally, some suggest that older adults present an existential threat for younger and middle-aged adults because they remind us all that death is inescapable, the body is fallible, and the bases by which we may secure self-esteem (and manage death anxiety) are transitory (Martens, Goldenberg, & Greenberg, 2005). Thus, death anxiety is a reflection of one's concern over dying, an outcome that would violate the prime motive.

On the basis of several diverse studies using many different measures, researchers conclude that death anxiety consists of several components. Each of these components is most easily described with terms that resemble examples of great concern (anxiety) but cannot be tied to any one specific focus. Some research on U.S. and Atlantic Canadian adults indicated that components of death anxiety included pain, body malfunction, humiliation, rejection, nonbeing, punishment, interruption of goals, being destroyed, and negative impact on survivors (Fortner & Neimeyer, 1999; Power & Smith, 2008). To complicate matters further, any of these components can be assessed at any of three levels: public, private, and nonconscious. That is, what we admit feeling about death in public may differ greatly from what we feel when we are alone with our own thoughts. In short, the measurement of death anxiety is complex, and researchers need to specify which aspects they are assessing.

Much research has been conducted to learn what demographic and personality variables are related to death anxiety. Although the results often are ambiguous, some patterns have emerged. For example, older adults tend to have lower death anxiety than younger adults, perhaps because of their tendency to engage in life review and their higher level of religious motivation (Thorson & Powell, 2000a, 2000b). Lower ego integrity, more physical problems, and more psychological problems are predictive of higher levels of death anxiety in older adults (Fortner & Neimeyer, 1999). Men show greater fear of the unknown than women, but women report more specific fear of the dying process (Cicirelli, 2001). And few differences have been reported in death anxiety levels across ethnic groups (Cicirelli, 2000).

Strange as it may seem, death anxiety may have a beneficial side. For one thing, being afraid to die means that we often go to great lengths to make sure we stay alive, as argued by terror management theory (Pyszczynski et al., 1997, 1999). Because staying alive helps to ensure the continuation and socialization of the species, fear of death serves as a motivation to have children and raise them properly.

Learning to Deal with Death Anxiety. Although some degree of death anxiety may be appropriate, we must guard against letting it become powerful enough to interfere with our normal daily routines. Several ways exist to help us in this endeavor. Perhaps the one most often used is to live life to the fullest. Kalish (1984, 1987) argues that people who do this enjoy what they have; although they may still fear death and feel cheated, they have few regrets. Adolescents are particularly likely to do this; research shows that teenagers, especially males, engage in risky behavior that is correlated with low death anxiety (Cotter, 2001).

Koestenbaum (1976) proposes several exercises and questions to increase one's death awareness. Some of these are to write your own obituary (like you did earlier in this chapter) and plan your own death and funeral services. You can also ask yourself, "What circumstances would help make my death acceptable?" "Is death the sort of thing that could happen to me right now?"

These questions serve as a basis for an increasingly popular way to reduce anxiety: death education. Most death education programs combine factual information about death with issues aimed at reducing anxiety and fear to increase sensitivity to others' feelings. These programs vary widely in orientation; they can include such topics as philosophy, ethics, psychology, drama, religion, medicine, art, and many others. Additionally, they can focus on death, the process of dying, grief and bereavement, or any combination of them. In general, death education programs help primarily by increasing our awareness of the complex emotions felt and expressed by dying people and their families. It is important to make education programs reflect the diverse backgrounds of the participants (Fowler, 2008). Research shows that participating in experiential workshops about death significantly lowers death anxiety in younger, middle-aged, and older adults (Abengozar, Bueno, & Vega, 1999).

Concept Checks

1. How do people of different ages deal with the thought of dying?
2. How do people conceptualize their own death?
3. What is death anxiety, and how is it shown and confronted?

13.3 End-of-Life Issues

LEARNING OBJECTIVES

- What is a personal final scenario?
- What are hospices, and what options do they provide?
- How do people make their end-of-life intentions known?

Jean is a 72-year-old woman who was recently diagnosed with advanced colon cancer. She has vivid memories of her father dying a long, protracted death in great pain. Jean is very afraid that she will suffer the same fate. She has heard that the hospice in town emphasizes pain management and provides a lot of support for families. Jean wonders whether that is something she should explore in the time she has left.

Where and how do most of us want to die? Ideally, most people would not like to die alone; indeed, this is one aspect of death anxiety (Kastenbaum, 1999). Whether death occurs in a hospital, hospice, or at home seems less important than having friends and family around. However, most of us do not get our wish. We are most likely to die surrounded by health care workers rather than family. The increasing institutionalization of death has two major consequences (Kastenbaum, 1999). First, health care professionals are playing a more important role in dying people's lives. Thus the medical staff is being forced to provide emotional support in situations largely antithetical to the main mission of healing and curing. This dilemma presents health care workers with problems that we consider later.

A second important result of the institutionalization of death is that dying is being removed from our everyday experience. Not long ago, each of us would have known what it was like to interact with a dying person and to be present when someone died. Institutions isolate us from death, and some argue that the institutions are largely to blame for our increasing avoidance of death and dying people. Unfortunately, researchers cannot evaluate this opinion, because we cannot randomly have some people die at home and others die at hospitals, just to compare the effects of each in an experiment.

What we can do, though, is consider how we may be able to create a final scenario about our own deaths and explore options for end-of-life care. Let's see what is involved in each.

Creating a Final Scenario

When given the chance, many adults would like to discuss a variety of issues, collectively called **end-of-life issues**: management of the final phase of life, after-death disposition of their body and memorial services, and distribution of assets (Green, 2008; Kleespies, 2004). How these issues are confronted represents a significant generational shift (Green, 2008). Parents and grandparents of the baby-boom generation spoke respectfully about those who had "passed away." Baby boomers are far more likely to plan and be more matter-of-fact. People want to manage the final part of their lives by thinking through the choices between traditional care (e.g., provided by hospitals and nursing homes) and alternatives (such as hospices, which we discuss in the next section), completing advance directives (e.g., durable power of attorney, living will), resolving key personal relationships, and perhaps choosing the alternative of ending one's life prematurely through euthanasia.

What happens to one's body and how one is memorialized is very important to most people. Is a traditional burial preferred over cremation? A traditional funeral over a memorial service? Such choices often are based in people's religious beliefs and their desire for privacy for their families after they have died.

Making sure that one's estate and personal effects are passed on appropriately often is overlooked. Making a will is especially important in ensuring that one's wishes are carried out. Providing for the informal distribution of personal effects also helps prevent disputes between family members.

Whether people choose to address these issues formally or informally, it is important that they be given the opportunity to do so. In many cases, family members are reluctant to discuss these matters with the dying relative because of their own anxiety about death. *Making such choices known about how they do and do not want their lives to end constitutes a* final scenario.

One of the most difficult and important parts of a final scenario for most people is the process of separation from family and friends (Corr et al., 2008; Wanzer & Glenmullen, 2007). The final days, weeks, and months of life provide opportunities to affirm love, resolve conflicts, and provide peace to dying people. The failure to complete this process often leaves survivors feeling that they did not achieve closure in the relationship, which can result in bitterness toward the deceased.

Health care workers realize the importance of giving dying patients the chance to create a final scenario and recognize the uniqueness of each person's final passage. A key part of their role is to ease this process (Wanzer & Glenmullen, 2007). Any given final scenario reflects the person's personal past, which is the unique combination of the development forces the person experienced. Primary attention is paid to how people's total life experiences have prepared them to face end-of-life issues (Neimeyer, 1997).

One's final scenario helps family and friends interpret one's death, especially when the scenario is constructed jointly, such as between spouses, and communication is open and honest (Byock, 1997; Green, 2008). The different perspectives of everyone involved are unlikely to converge without clear communication and discussion. Respecting each person's perspective is key and greatly helps in creating a good final scenario.

Encouraging people to decide for themselves how the end of their lives should be handled has helped people take control of their dying (Wass, 2001). Taking personal control over one's dying process is a trend that is occurring even in cultures like Japan that traditionally defer to physician's opinions (Hayashi et al., 2000). The emergence of final scenarios as an important consideration fits well with the emphasis on addressing pain through palliative care, an approach underlying hospice.

The Hospice Option

As we have seen, most people would like to die at home among family and friends. An important barrier to this choice is the availability of support systems when the person has a terminal disease. Most people believe that they have no choice but to go to a hospital or nursing home. However, another alternative exists. Hospice *is an approach to assisting dying people that emphasizes pain management, or palliative care, and death with dignity* (Knee, in press; Russo, 2008). The emphasis in a hospice is on the dying person's quality of life. This approach grows out of an important distinction between the prolongation of life and the prolongation of death, a distinction that is important to Jean, the woman we met in the vignette. In a hospice the concern is to make the person as peaceful and comfortable as possible, not to delay an inevitable death. Although medical care is available at a hospice, it

Hospice nurse talking to couple.

is aimed primarily at controlling pain and restoring normal functioning. This orientation places hospices between hospitals and one's own home in terms of contexts for dying.

Modern hospices are modeled after St. Christopher's Hospice in England, founded in 1967 by Dr. Cicely Saunders. Hospice services are requested only after the person or physician believes that no treatment or cure is possible, making the hospice program markedly different from hospital or home care. The differences are evident in the principles that underlie hospice care: Clients and their families are viewed as a unit, clients should be kept free of pain, emotional and social impoverishment must be minimal, clients must be encouraged to maintain competencies, conflict resolution and fulfillment of realistic desires must be assisted, clients must be free to begin or end relationships, and staff members must seek to alleviate pain and fear (Saunders, 1997).

Two types of hospices exist: inpatient and outpatient. Inpatient hospices provide all care for clients; outpatient hospices provide services to clients who remain in their own homes. The outpatient variation, in which a hospice nurse visits clients in their home, is becoming increasingly popular, largely because more clients can be served at a lower cost. Having hospice services available to people at home is a viable option for many more people, especially in helping home-based caregivers cope with loss (Grande et al., 2004).

Hospices do not follow a hospital model of care (Knee, in press). The role of the staff in a hospice is not so much to treat the client as it is just to be with the client. A client's dignity is always maintained; often more attention is paid to appearance and personal grooming than to medical tests. Hospice staff members also provide a great deal of support to the client's family.

Researchers have documented important differences between inpatient hospices and hospitals (Kastenbaum, 1999). Hospice clients are more mobile, less anxious, and less depressed; spouses visit hospice clients more often and participate more in their care; and hospice staff members are perceived as more accessible. Significant improvements in clients' quality of life have been documented after hospice placement (Cohen et al., 2001).

Although the hospice is a valuable alternative for many people, it may not be appropriate for everyone. Those who trust their physician regarding medical care options are more likely to select hospice than those who do not trust their physician, especially among African Americans (Ludke & Smucker, 2007). Most people who select hospice are suffering from cancer, AIDS, or a progressive neurological condition (most often amyotrophic lateral sclerosis, also known as Lou Gehrig's disease; Kastenbaum, 1999). Other disorders may necessitate treatments or equipment not available at hospices, and some people may find that a hospice does not meet their needs or fit with their personal beliefs.

Research indicates that the perceived needs of hospice clients, their families, and the staff have not always coincided, but getting input from various stakeholders can help improve service (Hiatt et al., 2007). Staff and family members tend to emphasize pain management, whereas many clients want more attention paid to personal issues, such as spirituality and the process of dying. The important point from this study is that the staff and family members may need to ask clients what they need more often rather than making assumptions about what they need.

How do people decide to explore the hospice option? Kastenbaum (1999) lists six key considerations (see also http://www.hospicefoundation.org; Knee, (2009)):

- *Is the person completely informed about the nature and prognosis of his or her condition?* Full knowledge and the ability to communicate with health care personnel are essential to understand what hospice has to offer.

- *What options are available at this point in the progress of the person's disease?* Knowing about all available treatment options is critical. Exploring treatment options also requires health care professionals to be aware of the latest approaches and be willing to disclose them.

- *What are the person's expectations, fears, and hopes?* Some older adults, like Jean, remember or have heard stories about people who suffered greatly at the end of their lives. This can produce anxiety about one's own death. Similarly, fears of becoming dependent play an important role in a person's decision making. Discovering and discussing these anxieties helps clarify options.

- *How well do the people in the person's social network communicate with each other?* Talking about death in many families is taboo (Book, 1996). In others, intergenerational communication is difficult or impossible. Even in families with good communication, the pending death of a loved relative is difficult. As a result, the dying person may have difficulty expressing his or her wishes. The decision to explore the hospice option is best made when it is discussed openly.

- *Are family members available to participate actively in terminal care?* Hospice relies on family members to provide much of the care, which is supplemented by professionals and volunteers. We saw in Chapter 13 that being a primary caregiver can be highly stressful. Having a family member who is willing to accept this responsibility is essential for the hospice option to work.

- *Is a high-quality hospice care program available?* Hospice programs are not uniformly good. As with any health care provider, patients and family members must investigate the quality of local hospice programs before making a choice. The Hospice Foundation of America provides excellent material for evaluating a hospice.

Hospice provides an important end-of-life option for many terminally ill people and their families. Moreover, the supportive follow-up services they provide are often used by surviving family and friends. Most important, the success of the hospice option has had important influences on traditional health care. For example, the American Medical Association (2007) officially endorses the use of prescription medications, including controlled substances, to provide pain management.

Despite the importance of the hospice option for end-of-life decisions, terminally ill older adults cannot benefit from it unless two barriers are overcome (Kastenbaum, 1999): family reluctance to face the reality of terminal illness and participate in the decision-making process; and physician reluctance to approve hospice care for patients until very late in the

terminal process, thereby depriving them of the supportive benefits they may have otherwise received.

As the end-of-life approaches, the most important thing to keep in mind is that the dying person has the right to state-of-the-art approaches to treatment and pain management. Irrespective of the choice of traditional health care or hospice, the wishes of the dying person should be honored, and family members must participate.

Making Your End-of-Life Intentions Known

As has been clearly shown in this section and earlier in the chapter, decisions relating to the end of life raise complex legal, political, and ethical issues. In most jurisdictions, for example, euthanasia is legal only when a person has made known his or her wishes concerning medical intervention. Even a person's preference for hospice might not be honored unless others know about it. Unfortunately, many people fail to take this step, perhaps because it is difficult to think about such situations or because they do not know the options available to them. But without clear directions, medical personnel may be unable to take a patient's preferences into account.

There are two ways to make one's intentions known: a living will, in which a person simply states his or her wishes about life support and other treatments, and durable power of attorney for health care (Figure 13.3), in which an individual appoints someone to act as his or her agent. A major purpose of both is to make one's wishes known about the use of life-support interventions in the event that the person is unconscious or otherwise incapable of expressing them, along with other related end-of-life issues such as organ transplantation and other health care options (Rosenfeld, 2004). A durable power of attorney for health care has an additional advantage: It names an individual who has the legal authority to speak for the person if necessary. Although there is considerable support for both mechanisms, there are several problems as well. Many people fail to inform their relatives and physicians about their health care decisions. Others do not tell the person named in a durable power of attorney where the document

DURABLE POWER OF ATTORNEY FOR HEALTH CARE

I, _____ (name), living in the city of _____ ,
in the county of _____ , in the state of Washington,
designate _____ (name) as my attorney in fact, to act for me in making health care decisions if I become incapacitated. I hereby revoke any and all
health care powers of attorney previously granted by me.

1. **Alternate Attorney in Fact.** If for any reason _____ (name) fails to act, or is not able to act, I designate _____
   (name), then _____ (name) as alternate attorneys in fact, to serve in the order named. An attorney in fact may resign by delivering written notice to that
   effect, in recordable form, to an alternate, successor, or co-attorney in fact. In this Durable Power of Attorney for Health Care, the "attorney in fact" means the then acting attorney in fact.

2. **Power to Make Health Care Decisions.** My attorney in fact shall have the right to make decisions, and to give informed consent on my behalf, as to my health care, to the extent permitted by law. This authority
   shall include, but not be limited to, the right to consent to the withholding or withdrawal of life-sustaining treatment which would only prolong artificially the moment of my death and prevent me from dying
   naturally, in those circumstances in which a physician(s) has/have determined (a) that I am in a permanent unconscious condition, meaning an incurable and irreversible condition in which I am medically assessed
   within reasonable medical judgment as having no reasonable probability of recovery from an irreversible coma or a persistent vegetative state, or (b) that I have a terminal condition, meaning an incurable and
   irreversible condition caused, by injury, disease or illness, that would within reasonable medical judgment cause death within a reasonable period of time in accordance with accepted medical standards. I also
   authorize my attorney in fact to make decisions regarding the artificial administration of food and fluids, consistent with any Health Care Directive (living will) I have executed.

3. **Effectiveness.** This Durable Power of Attorney for Health Care shall become effective upon my incapacity. Incapacity shall include the inability to make health care decisions effectively for reasons such as
   mental illness, mental deficiency, incompetency, physical illness or disability, advanced age, chronic use of drugs or chronic intoxication. Incapacity may be determined by (a) a court order or (b) a written
   qualified attending physician.

4. **Duration.** This Durable Power of Attorney for Health Care becomes effective as provided in Section 3 above and shall remain in effect to the fullest extent permitted by Chapter 11.94 of the Revised Code of
   Washington, or until revoked or terminated as provided in Section 5 or 6 below.

5. **Revocation.** This Durable Power of Attorney for Health Care may be revoked, suspended, or terminated by written notice from me to the designated attorney in fact and, if this power has been recorded, by
   recording this notice in the office where deeds are recorded for real estate located in the _____ County, Washington.

6. **Termination.** If appointed, my guardian may, with court approval, revoke, suspend, or terminate this Durable Power of Attorney for Health Care.

7. **Reliance.** Any person dealing with the assigned attorney in fact shall be entitled to rely upon this Durable Power of Attorney for Health Care to carry out my wishes for health care. No one shall deal with this
   attorney in fact if they know or have written notice of any cancellation, revocation, suspension, or termination of this Durable Power of Attorney for Health Care. Any action so taken, unless otherwise invalid or
   unenforceable, shall be binding on my relatives or inheritors of my estate.

8. **Indemnity.** My estate shall hold harmless and indemnify the attorney in fact from all liability for acts or omissions done in good faith.

9. **Applicable.** The laws of the State of Washington shall govern this Durable Power of Attorney for Health Care.

10. **Execution.** This Durable Power of Attorney for Health Care is signed on the _____ day of _____ , 20 _____ , to be effective as provided in Section 3 above.

Signature of Declarer _____

NOTE: Washington state law does not require a Durable Power of Attorney for Health Care be witnessed or notarized. However, it is recommended that there always be two witnesses and that these witnesses be
persons qualified to witness the signing of a Health Care Directive. Such persons are individuals who are not related to the declarer by blood or marriage and who will not be entitled, under any existing will, to any
portion of the estate of the declarer. Witnessing and/or notarization is also important as evidence to help confirm the declarer's competence and help assure that the declarer's wishes are carried out should family
members of others oppose on the grounds the declarer did not understand what he/she was doing when signing the document.

_____   _____   _____
Date   Witness (print name)   Witness (signature)

_____   _____   _____
Date   Witness (print name)   Witness (signature)

Notarization, If Needed:

STATE OF WASHINGTON

COUNTY OF _____

I certify that I know or have satisfactory evidence that the GRANTOR, _____ signed this instrument and acknowledged it to be his/her free and voluntary act for the uses and purposes mentioned
in this instrument.

Dated this _____ day of _____ , 20 _____ .

NOTARY PUBLIC in and for the State of Washington

Residing at _____

My commission expires _____

Courtesy of the State of Washington, Department of Health

Figure 13.3 Example of a durable power of attorney for health care decisions document.

Source: © California Medical Association, 1996 (revised).

---

is kept. Obviously, this puts relatives at a serious disadvantage if decisions concerning the use of life-support systems need to be made.

A living will or a durable power of attorney for health care can be the basis for a "Do Not Resuscitate" (DNR) medical order. A DNR order applies only to cardiopulmonary resuscitation should one's heart and breathing stop. In the normal course of events, a medical team will immediately try to restore normal heartbeat and respiration. With a DNR order, this treatment is not done. As with living wills and durable powers of attorney, it is very important to let all appropriate medical personnel know that a DNR order is desired.

Concept Checks

1. What is a final scenario?
2. What are the primary characteristics of a hospice?
3. How do people make their end-of-life intentions known?

13.4 Survivors: The Grieving Process

LEARNING OBJECTIVES
- How do people experience the grief process?
- What feelings do grieving people have?
- What is the difference between normal and prolonged grief?
- How do adults of different ages deal with loss?

After 67 years of marriage, Bertha recently lost her husband. At 90, Bertha knew that neither she nor her husband was likely to live much longer, but the death was a shock just the same. Bertha thinks about him much of the time and often finds herself making decisions on the basis of "what John would have done" in the same situation.

Each of us suffers many losses over a lifetime. Whenever we lose someone close to us through death or other separation, like Bertha we experience bereavement, grief, and mourning. Bereavement *is the state or condition caused by loss through death.* Grief *is the sorrow, hurt, anger, guilt, confusion, and other feelings that arise after suffering a loss.* Mourning *concerns the ways in which we express our grief.* For example, you can tell that people in some cultures are bereaved and in mourning because of the clothing they wear. Mourning is highly influenced by culture. For some, mourning may involve wearing black, attending funerals, and observing an official period of grief; for others, it means drinking, wearing white, and marrying the deceased spouse's sibling. Grief corresponds to the emotional reactions following loss, whereas mourning is the culturally approved behavioral manifestations of those feelings. Even though mourning rituals may be fairly standard within a culture, how people grieve varies, as we see next. We will also see how Bertha's reactions are fairly typical of most people.

The Grief Process

How do people grieve? What do they experience? Perhaps you already have a good idea about the answers to these questions from your own experience. If so, you already know that the process of

© Noboru Hashimoto / CORBIS

Customs regarding what bereaved persons should do vary around the world and include wearing certain types and colors of clothing.

grieving is a complicated and personal one. Just as there is no right way to die, there is no right way to grieve. Recognizing that there are plenty of individual differences, we consider some patterns in this section.

The grieving process is often described as reflecting many themes and issues that people confront (Kübler-Ross & Kessler, 2005). Like the process of dying, grieving does not have clearly demarcated stages through which we pass in a neat sequence, although there are certain issues people must face that are similar to those faced by dying people. When someone close to us dies, we must reorganize our lives, establish new patterns of behavior, and redefine relationships with family and friends. Indeed, Attig (1996) considers grief to be the process by which we relearn the world.

Unlike bereavement, over which we have no control, grief is a process that involves choices in coping, from confronting the reality and emotions to using religion to ease one's pain (Ivancovich & Wong, 2008). From this perspective, grief is an active process in which a person must do several things (Worden, 1991):

- *Acknowledge the reality of the loss.* We must overcome the temptation to deny the reality of our loss, fully and openly acknowledge it, and realize that it affects every aspect of our life.

- *Work through the emotional turmoil.* We must find effective ways to confront and express the complete range of emotions we feel after the loss and must not avoid or repress them.

- *Adjust to the environment where the deceased is absent.* We must define new patterns of living that adjust appropriately and meaningfully to the fact that the deceased is not present.

- *Loosen ties to the deceased.* We must free ourselves from the bonds of the deceased in order to reengage with our social network. This means finding effective ways to say good-bye.

The notion that grief is an active coping process emphasizes that survivors must come to terms with the physical world of things, places, and events, as well as our spiritual place in the world; the interpersonal world of interactions with family and friends, the dead, and, in some cases, God; and aspects of our inner selves and our personal experiences (Ivancovich & Wong, 2008). Bertha, the woman in the vignette, is in the middle of this process. Even the matter of deciding what to do with the deceased's personal effects can be part of this active coping process (Attig, 1996).

In considering the grief process, we must avoid making several mistakes. First, grieving is a highly individual experience (Mallon, 2008). The process that works well for one person may not be the best for someone else. Second, we must not underestimate the amount of time people need to deal with the various issues. To a casual observer, it may appear that a survivor is "back to normal" after a few weeks. Actually, it takes much longer to resolve the complex emotional issues that are faced during bereavement (Mallon, 2008). Researchers and therapists alike agree that a person needs at least 1 year following the loss to begin recovery, and 2 years is not uncommon. Finally, "recovery" may be a misleading term. It is probably more accurate to say that we learn to live with our loss rather than that

we recover from it (Attig, 1996). The impact of the loss of a loved one lasts a very long time, perhaps for the rest of one's life. Recognizing these aspects of grief makes it easier to know what to say and do for bereaved people. Among the most useful things are to simply let the person know that you are sorry for his or her loss, that you are there for support, and mean what you say.

Risk Factors in Grief. Bereavement is a life experience that most people have many times, and most people eventually handle it. However, there are some risk factors that may make bereavement much more difficult. Several of the more important are the mode of death, personal factors (e.g., personality, religiosity, age, gender), and interpersonal context (social support, kinship relationship; W. Stroebe & Schut, 2001).

Most people believe that the circumstances or mode of death affects the grief process. A person whose family member was killed in an automobile accident has a different situation to deal with than a person whose family member died after a long period with Alzheimer's disease. It is believed that when death is anticipated, people go through a period of anticipatory grief before the death, which supposedly serves to buffer the impact of the loss when it does come as well as to facilitate recovery (Lane, 2007). However, the research evidence for this is mixed. What does appear to be the case is that people who experience anticipatory grief tend to disengage from the dying person (Lane, 2007).

The strength of attachment to the deceased person makes a difference in dealing with a sudden as opposed to an unexpected death. When the deceased person was one with whom the survivor had a strong and close attachment, and the loss was sudden, greater grief is experienced (Wayment & Vierthaler, 2002). However, such secure attachment styles tend to result in less depression after the loss due to less guilt over unresolved issues (because there are fewer of them), things not provided (because more were likely provided), and so on.

Few studies of personal risk factors have been done, and few firm conclusions can be drawn. To date there are no consistent findings regarding personality traits that either help buffer people from the effects of bereavement or exacerbate them (Lane, 2007; W. Stroebe & Schut, 2001). There is some evidence to suggest that church attendance or spirituality in general helps people deal with bereavement (Ivancovich & Wong, 2008; Nolen-Hoeksema & Larson, 1999), but this effect may be due more to the social support such people receive than to religion per se (W. Stroebe & Schut, 2001). There are, however, consistent findings regarding gender. Men have higher mortality rates following bereavement than women, who have higher rates of depression than men, but the reasons for these differences are unclear (W. Stroebe & Schut, 2001). Research also consistently shows that older adults suffer the least health consequences following bereavement, with the impact perhaps being strongest for middle-aged adults (Nolen-Hoeksema & Larson, 1999; W. Stroebe & Schut, 2001).

Two interpersonal risk factors have been examined: lack of social support and kinship. Studies indicate that social support and mastery help buffer the effects of bereavement more for older adults than for middle-aged adults (Onrust et al., 2007; W. Stroebe & Schut, 2001). The type of kinship relationship involved in the loss matters a great deal. Research consistently shows that the loss of a child is the most difficult, followed by loss of a spouse or partner and parent (Leahy, 1993; Nolen-Hoeksema & Larson, 1999).

Normal Grief Reactions

The feelings experienced during grieving are intense, which not only makes it difficult to cope but can also make a person question her or his own reactions. The feelings involved usually include sadness, denial, anger, loneliness, and guilt. A summary of these feelings is presented in the following list (Vickio, Cavanaugh, & Attig, 1990). Take a minute to read through them to see whether they are what you would expect.

Disbelief

Denial

Shock

Sadness

Anger

Hatred

Guilt

Fear

Anxiety

Confusion

Helplessness

Emptiness

Loneliness

Acceptance

Relief

Happiness

Lack of enthusiasm

Absence of emotion

Many authors refer to the psychological side of coming to terms with bereavement as grief work. Whether the loss is ambiguous and lacking closure (e.g., waiting to learn the fate of a missing loved one) or certain (e.g., verification of death through a dead body), people need space and time in which to grieve (Boss, 2006). Even without personal experience of the death of close family members, people recognize the need to give survivors time to deal with their many feelings. One study asked college students to describe the feelings they thought were typically experienced by a person who had lost particular loved ones (such as a parent, child, sibling, or friend). The students were well aware of the need for grief work, recognized the need for at least a year to do it, and were very sensitive to the range of emotions and behaviors demonstrated by the bereaved (Vickio et al., 1990).

Muller and Thompson (2003) examined people's experience of grief in a detailed interview study and found five themes. *Coping* relates to what people do to deal with their loss in terms of what helps them. *Affect* refers to people's emotional reactions to the death of their loved one; for example, most people have certain topics that serve as emotional triggers for memories of their loved one. *Change* involves the ways in which survivors' lives change as a result of the loss; personal growth (e.g., "I didn't think I could deal with something that painful, but I did") is a common experience. *Narrative* relates to the stories survivors tell about their deceased loved one, which sometimes includes details about the process of the death. Finally, *relationship* reflects who the deceased person was and the nature of the ties between that person and the survivor. Collectively, these themes indicate that the experience of grief is complex and involves dealing with one's feelings as a survivor as well as memories of the deceased person.

How people show their feelings of grief varies across ethnic groups. For example, Latino American men show more of their grief behaviorally than do European American men (Sera, 2001). Such differences also are found across cultures. For example, families in KwaZulu-Natal, South Africa, have a strong desire for closure and need for dealing with the "loneliness of grief" (Brysiewicz, 2008). In many cultures the bereaved construct a relationship with the person who died, but how this happens differs widely, from "ghosts" to appearances in dreams to connection through prayer (Rosenblatt, 2001).

In addition to psychological grief reactions, there are physiological ones, too. Widows report sleep disturbances as well as neurological and circulatory problems (Kowalski & Bondmass, 2008). Physical health may decline, illness may result, and use of health care services may increase (Stroebe, Schut, & Stroebe, 2007). In some cases it is necessary to treat severe depression following bereavement; research indicates that using SSRIs (see Chapter 10) is one effective medical intervention (Simon et al., 2007).

In the time following the death of a loved one, dates that have personal significance may reintroduce feelings of grief. For example, holidays such as Thanksgiving or birthdays that were spent with the deceased person may be difficult times. The actual anniversary of the death can be especially troublesome. *The term* anniversary reaction *refers to changes in behavior related to feelings of sadness on this date.* Personal experience and research show that recurring feelings of sadness or other examples of the anniversary reaction are very common in normal grief (Attig, 1996; Rosenblatt, 1996). Such feelings also accompany remembrances of major catastrophes across cultures, such as Thais remembering the victims of a major flood (Assanangkornchai et al., 2007).

Grief over Time. Most research on how people react to the death of a loved one is cross-sectional. This work shows that grief tends to peak within the first 6 months following the death of a loved one (Maciejewski et al., 2007). However, some work has been done to examine how people continue grieving many years after the loss. Some widows show no sign of lessening of grief after five years (Kowlaski & Bondmass, 2008). Rosenblatt (1996) reported that people still felt the effects of the deaths of family members 50 years after the event. The depth of the emotions over the loss of loved ones never totally went away, as people still cried and felt sad when discussing the loss despite the length of time that had passed.

Norris and Murrell (1987) conducted one of the best longitudinal studies of older adults' grief work; three interviews were conducted before the death and one after. Among bereaved families, overall family stress increased before the death and then decreased. The level of stress experienced by these families was highest in the period right around the death. Moreover, bereavement was the only significant predictor of family stress, meaning that the anticipation and experience of bereavement caused stress.

Even more interesting were the findings concerning the relationship between health and stress. As shown in Figure 13.4, bereaved individuals who reported stress before the death were in poorer health before the death than were bereaved persons who were not experiencing stress. However, as shown in Figure 13.5, bereaved individuals reporting prior stress showed a significant drop in physical symptoms 6 months after the death; bereaved persons reporting no prior stress reported a slight increase. The net result was that both groups ended up with about the same level of physical symptoms 6 months after bereavement. These findings also have important implications for interventions. That is, interventions aimed at reducing stress or promoting health may be more effective if performed before the death. In addition, because health problems increased only among those in the bereaved group who felt no stress before the death, it may be that the stress felt before the death is a product of anticipating it. Lundin (1984) also found it to be the

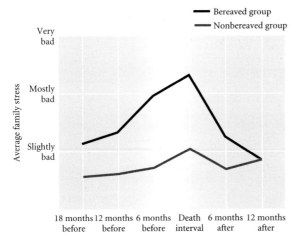

Figure 13.4 Average level of family stress of bereaved and nonbereaved older adults.

Source: Norris, F. N., & Murrell, S. A. (1987). Older adult family stress and adaptation before and after bereavement. *Journal of Gerontology, 42,* 609. Reprinted by permission.

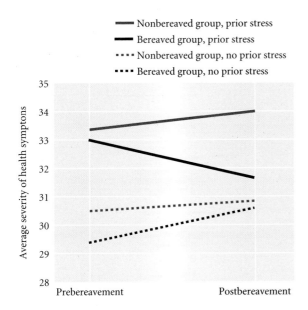

Figure 13.5 Number of health symptoms reported 6 months after a loss as a function of stress level before the loss.

Source: Norris, F. N., & Murrell, S. A. (1987). Older adult family stress and adaptation before and after bereavement. *Journal of Gerontology, 42,* 610. Reprinted by permission.

case that health problems increased only for those bereaved individuals experiencing sudden death.

Religiosity is thought to provide a support mechanism for people following the loss of a loved one. Research evidence for this belief is mixed. Some studies (e.g., Nelson, 2001) show that religiosity has no effect on the duration of grief. Other research points to a different conclusion. For example, Latino men who practice their religion openly show lower levels of grief than do Latino men who are not openly religious or European American men (Sera, 2001). Varying religious practices among the Caribbean island cultures strongly influence demonstrations of grief (Marshall & Southerland, 2008). Bereavement counselors also report better outcomes when religious or spiritual issues are included in the therapeutic process (Golsworthy & Coyle, 2001). Clearly, more and more carefully designed research is needed in order to understand the role that survivors' religious beliefs play in grief.

Coping with Grief

Thus far, we have considered the behaviors people show when they are dealing with grief. We have also seen that these behaviors change over time. How does this happen? How can we explain the grieving process?

Numerous theories have been proposed to account for the grieving process, such as general life event theories, psychodynamic theories, attachment theories, and cognitive process theories (M. Stroebe & Schut, 2001). All of these approaches to grief are based on more general theories, which results in none of them providing an adequate explanation of the grieving process. Two integrative approaches have been proposed that are specific to the grief process: the four component model and the dual process model of coping with bereavement.

The Four Component Model. The four component model proposes that understanding grief is based on four things: (1) *the context of the loss,* referring to the risk factors such as whether the death was expected; (2) *continuation of subjective meaning associated with loss,* ranging from evaluations of everyday concerns to major questions about the meaning of life; (3) *changing representations of the*

Grief Processing and Avoidance in the United States and China

Who were the investigators and what was the aim of the study? Bonanno and colleagues (2005) noted that grief following the loss of a loved one often tends to be denied. However, research evidence related to positive benefits of resolving grief is largely lacking. Thus, whether unresolved grief is "bad" remains an open issue. Likewise, cross-cultural evidence is also lacking.

How did the investigators measure the topic of interest? Collaborative meetings between U.S. and Chinese researchers resulted in a 13-item grief processing scale and a 7-item

grief avoidance scale, with both English and Mandarin Chinese versions. Self-reported symptoms of psychological and physical health were also collected.

Who were the participants in the study? Adults under age 66 who had experienced the loss of either a spouse or child approximately 4 months prior to the start of data collection were asked to participate through solicitation letters. Participants were from either the metropolitan areas of Washington, D.C., or Nanjing, Jiangsu province, in China.

What was the design of the study? Two sets of measures

were collected at approximately 4 months and 18 months after the loss.

Were there ethical concerns in the study? Because participation was voluntary, there were no ethical concerns.

What were the results? Consistent with the grief work as rumination view, scores on the two grief measures were uncorrelated. Overall, women tended to show more grief processing than men, and grief processing decreased over time. As you can see in Figure 13.6, Chinese participants reported more grief processing and grief avoidance than U.S. participants at the first time of

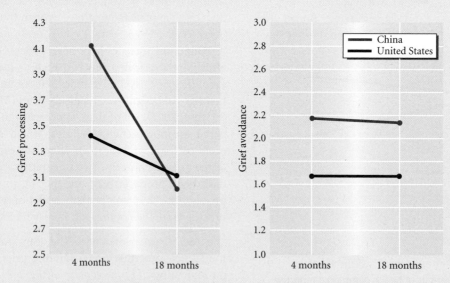

Figure 13.6 Grief processing and deliberate grief avoidance across time in the People's Republic of China and the United States.

Source: From Bonanno et al. (2005), p. 92.

lost relationship over time; and (4) *the role of coping and emotion-regulation processes* that cover all coping strategies used to deal with grief (Bonanno & Kaltman, 1999). The four component model relies heavily on emotion theory, has much in common with the transactional model of stress, and has some empirical support. According to the four component model, dealing with grief is a complex process that can only be understood as a complex outcome that unfolds over time.

There are several important implications of this integrative approach. One of the most important is that helping a grieving person involves helping them make meaning from the loss (Wong, 2008). Second, this model implies that encouraging people to express their grief may actually not be helpful. *An alternative view, called the* grief work as rumination hypothesis, *not only rejects the necessity of grief processing for recovery from loss but views extensive grief processing as a form of rumination that may actually increase distress* (Bonanno, Papa, & O'Neill, 2001). Although it may seem that people who think obsessively about their loss, or ruminate about it, are confronting the loss, rumination is actually considered a way to avoid it because the person is not dealing with his or her real feelings and moving on (Stroebe et al., 2007).

One prospective study has shown, for instance, that bereaved individuals who were not depressed prior to their spouse's death but then evidenced chronically elevated depression through the first year and a half of bereavement (i.e., a chronic grief pattern) had also tended to report more frequently thinking about and talking about their recent loss at the 6-month point in bereavement (Bonanno, Wortman, & Neese, 2004). Thus, some bereaved individuals engage in minimal grief processing, whereas others are predisposed toward more extensive grief processing. Furthermore, the individuals who engage in minimal grief processing will show a relatively favorable grief outcome, whereas those who are predisposed toward more extensive grief processing will tend toward ruminative preoccupation and, consequently, toward a more prolonged grief course (Bonanno et al., 2001; Nolen-Hoeksema, 2001).

As noted earlier, the grief work as rumination hypothesis also views grief avoidance as an independent but maladaptive form of coping with loss (Stroebe et al., 2007). In contrast to the traditional perspective, which equates the absence of grief processing with grief avoidance, the grief work as rumination framework assumes that resilient individuals are able to minimize processing of a loss through relatively automated processes, such as distraction or shifting attention toward more positive emotional experiences (Bonanno et al., 1995). The grief work as rumination framework argues that the deliberate avoidance or suppression of grief represents a less effective form of coping (Wegner & Gold, 1995) that tends to exacerbate rather than minimize the experience of grief (Bonanno et al., 1995; Nolen-Hoeksema, 1998).

The How Do We Know? feature explores grief work regarding the loss of a spouse and the loss of a child in two cultures, the United States and China. As you read it, pay special attention to the question of whether encouraging people to express and deal with their grief is necessarily a good idea.

The Dual Process Model. The dual process model (DPM) of coping with bereavement integrates existing ideas (M. Stroebe & Schut, 2001). As shown in Figure 13.7, the DPM defines two broad types of

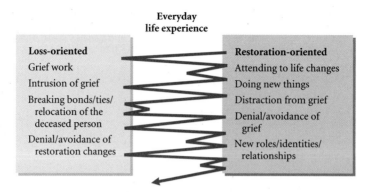

Figure 13.7 The dual process model of coping with bereavement shows the relation between dealing with the stresses of the loss itself (loss-oriented) and moving on with one's life (restoration-oriented).

Source: M. Stroebe & Schut (2001).

stressors. *Loss-oriented stressors* are those having to do with the loss itself, such as the grief work that needs to be done. *Restoration-oriented stressors* are those relating to adapting to the survivor's new life situation, such as building new relationships and finding new activities. The DPM proposes that dealing with these stressors is a dynamic process, as indicated by the lines connecting them in the figure. This is a distinguishing feature of DPM. It shows how bereaved people cycle back and forth between dealing mostly with grief and trying to move on with life. At times the emphasis will be on grief, and at other times on moving forward.

The DPM captures well the process that bereaved people themselves report—at times they are nearly overcome with grief, while at other times they handle life well. The DPM also helps us understand how, over time, people come to a balance between the long-term effects of bereavement and the need to live life. Understanding how people handle grief requires understanding of the various contexts in which people live and interact with others (Sandler, Wolchik, & Ayers, 2008).

Prolonged Grief Reactions

Not everyone is able to cope with grief well and begin rebuilding a life. Sometimes the feelings of hurt, loneliness, and guilt are so overwhelming that they become the focus of the survivor's life to such

an extent that there is never any closure and the grief continues to interfere indefinitely with one's ability to function. When this occurs, individuals are viewed as having prolonged grief disorder, which is distinguished from depression and from normal grief (Boelen & Prigerson, 2007). What distinguishes prolonged grief is (a) symptoms of *separation distress* such as preoccupation with the deceased to the point that it interferes with everyday functioning, upsetting memories of the deceased, longing and searching for the deceased, and isolation following the loss; and (b) symptoms of *traumatic distress* such as feeling disbelief about the death, mistrust, anger, and detachment from others as a result of the death, feeling shocked by the death, and the experience of physical presence of the deceased (Boelen & Prigerson, 2007; Prigerson & Jacobs, 2001).

Two common manifestations of prolonged grief are excessive guilt and self-blame (Anderson, 1997). In some people, guilt results in a disruption of everyday routines and a diminished ability to function. People begin to make judgment errors, may reach a state of agitated depression, may experience problems sleeping or eating, and may have intense recurring thoughts about the deceased person. Many of these individuals either seek professional help voluntarily or are referred by concerned family members or friends.

Identifying traumatic grief is not always easy because cultural variations in the process of grief must be respected (Anderson, 1997). Nevertheless, there is some evidence that compared to European Americans, African Americans have a higher rate of prolonged grief (Goldsmith et al., 2008). Length of time after the loss is not a good indicator, as grief can still be quite strong 10 years after a loss (Derman, 2000). Prigerson and Jacobs (2001) report that the criteria listed earlier for prolonged grief can be used successfully to differentiate the typical grief of bereaved people, even when they are depressed, from prolonged grief.

Adult Developmental Aspects of Grief

The losses that confront us in adulthood are many. For most of us, the loss of parents and partners becomes more likely the older we get. For some, the loss of a child can be extremely hard to deal with. How we handle the grief related to each loss depends in part on how old we are at the time.

Loss of One's Partner in Young Adulthood. Because young adults are just beginning to pursue the family, career, and personal goals they have set, they tend to be more intense in their feelings toward death. When asked how they feel about death, young adults report a strong sense that those who die at this point in their lives would be cheated out of their future (Attig, 1996).

Experiencing the loss of one's partner in young adulthood can be very traumatic, not only because of the loss itself but also because such loss is unexpected. As Trish Straine, a 32-year-old widow whose husband was killed in the World Trade Center attack, put it, "I suddenly thought, 'I'm a widow.' Then I said to myself, 'A widow? That's an older woman, who's dressed in black. It's certainly not a 32-year-old like me'" (Lieber, 2001). One of the most difficult aspects for young widows and widowers is that they must deal with both their own and their young children's grief and provide the support their children need. But that can be very hard. "Every time I look at my children, I'm reminded of Mark," said Stacey, a 35-year-old widow whose husband died of bone cancer. "And people don't want

ARLINGTON, VA—JUNE 15: US Army Brigadier General Bennett Sacolick (L) presents a folded American flag to Sgt. Charles Wyckoff's widow Erika Wyckoff during his funeral at Arlington National Cemetery June 15, 2007 in Arlington, Virginia. Sgt. Wyckoff, 28, of Chula Vista, California, died after being shot by small-arms fire in the Afghanistan's Helmand province. Sgt. Wyckoff is the 52nd member of the military killed in Afghanistan to be buried at Arlington National Cemetery.

to hear you say that you don't feel like moving on, even though there is great pressure from them to do that." Stacey is a good example of what research shows: Young adult widows report that their level of grief does not typically diminish significantly until 5 to 10 years after the loss, and they maintain strong attachments to their deceased husbands for at least that long (Derman, 2000).

Losing one's spouse in midlife often results in the survivor challenging basic assumptions about self, relationships, and life options (Danforth & Glass, 2001). By the first year anniversary of the loss, the surviving spouse has usually begun transforming his or her perspectives on these issues. The important part of this process is making meaning of the death, and continuing to work on and revise it over time (Gillies & Neimeyer, 2006).

Death of One's Child in Young and Middle Adulthood. Many people believe that the death of one's child is the one of, if not the worst, type of loss (Woodgate, 2006). Because children are not supposed to die before their parents, it is as if the natural order of things has been violated, shaking parents to their core (Rubin & Malkinson, 2001). Mourning is always intense, and some parents never recover or reconcile themselves to the death of their child (Klass, 1996a). The intensity of feelings is due to the strong parent-child bond that begins before birth and that lasts a lifetime (Bornstein, 1995).

Young parents who lose a child due to Sudden Infant Death Syndrome (SIDS) report high anxiety, a more negative view of the world, and much guilt, resulting in a devastating experience (Rubin & Malkinson, 2001). The most overlooked losses of a child are those that happen through stillbirth, miscarriage, abortion, or neonatal death (Klass, 1996a; McCarthy, 2002; Rubin & Malkinson, 2001). Attachment to the child begins before birth, especially for mothers, so the loss hurts very deeply. For this reason, ritual is extremely important to acknowledge the death and validate parents' feelings of grief (Kobler, Limbo, & Kavanaugh, 2007). Yet parents who experience this type of loss are expected to recover very quickly. The experience of parents in support groups, such as Compassionate Friends, tells a very different story (Klass, 1996a). These parents report a deep sense of loss and hurt, especially when others do not understand their feelings. Worst of all, if societal expectations for quick recovery are not met, the parents may be subjected to unfeeling comments. As one mother notes, parents often just wish somebody would acknowledge the loss (Okonski, 1996).

The loss of a young adult child for a middle-aged parent is experienced differently but is equally devastating (Rubin & Malkinson, 2001). For example, parents who lost sons in wars (Rubin, 1996) and in traffic accidents (Shalev, 1999) still report strong feelings of anxiety, problems in functioning, and difficulties in relationships with both surviving siblings and the deceased as long as 13 years after the loss.

Death of One's Parent. Most parents die after their children are grown. But whenever parental death occurs, it hurts. Losing a parent in adulthood is a rite of passage as one passes from being a "son" or "daughter" to being "without parents" (Edwards, 2006). We, the children, are now next in line. Indeed, the death of a parent often leads the surviving

children to redefine the meaning of their relationships with their siblings, children, and other family members (Moss, Moss, & Hansson, 2001).

The death of a parent deprives people of many important things: a source of guidance and advice, a source of love, and a model for their own parenting style (Buchsbaum, 1996). It also cuts off the opportunity to improve aspects of their relationship with the parent. Expressing feelings toward a parent before he or she dies is important. In some cases, the death of a parent has a negative effect on the adult child's own marital relationship (Henry, 2006).

The loss of a parent is perceived as very significant; no matter how old we are, society allows us to grieve for a reasonable length of time. For young adult women transitioning to motherhood, losing their own mother during adolescence raises many feelings, such as deep loss at not being able to share their pregnancies with their mothers and fear of dying young themselves (Franceschi, 2005). Middle-aged women who lose a parent report feeling a complex set of emotions (Westbrook, 2002); they have intense emotional feelings of both loss and freedom, they remember both positive and negative aspects of their parent, and they experience shifts in their own sense of self.

The feelings accompanying the loss of an older parent reflect a sense of letting go, loss of a buffer against death, better acceptance of one's own eventual death, and a sense of relief that the parent's suffering is over (Moss et al., 2001). Yet, if the parent died from a disease such as Alzheimer's that involves the loss of the parent-child relationship along the way, bodily death can feel like the second time the parent died (Shaw, 2007). Whether the adult child now tries to separate from the deceased parent's expectations or finds comfort in the memories, the impact of the loss is great.

Death of One's Child or Grandchild in Late Life. The loss of an adult child in late life is something that many older adults experience, and others continue to feel the loss of a child from many years before (Rubin & Malkinson, 2001). Older bereaved parents tend to re-evaluate their grief as experienced shortly after the loss and years and decades later. Even more than 30 years after the death of a child, older adults still feel a keen sense of loss and have continued difficulty coming to terms with it (Malkinson & Bar-Tur, 2004–2005). The long-lasting effects of the loss of a child are often accompanied by a sense of guilt that the pain affected the parents' relationships with the surviving children.

Clearly, the loss of a child has profound, lifelong effects. The meaning of the loss changes somewhat over time (Neimeyer, Keese, & Fortner, 2000), but the feelings of distress may never go away. Indeed, many parents view the relationship to the deceased child as either the closest or one of the closest relationships they ever had (Ben-Israel Reuveni, 1999).

The loss of a grandchild results in similar feelings: intense emotional upset, survivor guilt, regrets about the relationship with the deceased grandchild, and a need to restructure relationships with the surviving family. However, bereaved grandparents tend to control and hide their grief behavior in an attempt to shield their child (the bereaved parent) from the level of pain being felt.

Death of One's Partner in Late Life. Experiencing the loss of one's partner is the type of loss in late life we know most about. The death of a partner differs from other losses. It clearly represents a deep personal loss, especially when the couple has had a long and close relationship (Moss et al., 2001). In a very real way, when one's partner dies, a part of oneself dies too.

There is pressure from society to mourn the loss of one's partner for a period of time, and then to "move on" (Jenkins, 2003). Typically, this pressure is manifested if the survivor begins to show interest in finding another partner before an "acceptable" period of mourning has passed. Although Americans no longer specify the length of the period, many feel that about a year is appropriate. The fact that such pressure and negative commentary usually do not accompany other losses is another indication of the seriousness with which most people take the death of a partner.

Older bereaved spouses may grieve a great deal for a long time (Hansson & Stroebe, 2007); in one study grief lasted for at least 30 months (Thompson et al., 1991). Given that, you might wonder whether having a supportive social network might help people cope. Research findings on this topic are mixed, however. Some studies find that social support plays a significant role in the outcome of the grieving process. For example, during the first 2 years after the death of a partner, some data show that the quality of the support system rather than simply the number of friends is especially important for the grieving partner. Survivors who have confidants are better off than survivors who have many acquaintances (Hansson & Stroebe, 2007). In contrast, other studies find that having a supportive social network plays little role in helping people cope. For example, Miller, Smerglia, and Bouchet (2004) reported that the type of social support available to a widow had no relation to her adjustment to widowhood. It may be that there is a complex relationship between the bereaved person and social supports, depending on whether he or she wants to have contact with others, who in the social network is wanting to provide support, and whether that support is of high quality.

When one's partner dies, how he or she felt about the relationship could play a role in coping with bereavement. One study of spousal bereavement measured how the surviving spouse rated the marriage. Bereaved older widows/widowers rated their relationships at 2, 12, and 30 months after the death of their spouses. Nonbereaved older adults served as a comparison group. The results are summarized in Figure 13.8. Bereaved widows and widowers gave their marriages more positive ratings than nonbereaved older adults. A marriage lost through death left a positive bias in memory. However, bereaved spouses' ratings were related to depression in an interesting way. The more depressed the bereaved spouse, the more positive the marriage's rating. In contrast, depressed nonbereaved spouses gave their marriages negative ratings. This result suggests that depression following bereavement signifies positive aspects of a relationship, whereas depression not connected with bereavement indicates a troubled relationship (Futterman et al., 1990).

Several studies of widows document a tendency for some older women to "sanctify" their husbands (Lopata, 1996). Sanctification involves describing

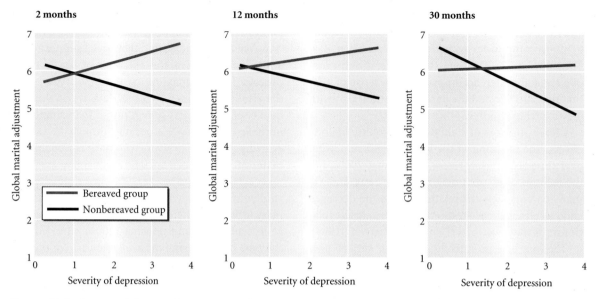

Figure 13.8 In general, bereaved spouses rate their marriages more positively than nonbereaved spouses, and they tend to be more positive the more depressed they are after the loss.

Source: From Futterman, A., Gallagher, D., Thompson, L. W., Lovett, S., & Gilewski, M. (1990). Retrospective assessment of marital adjustment and depression during the first two years of spousal bereavement. *Psychology and Aging, 5,* 277–283. Copyright © 1990 American Psychological Association.

deceased husbands in idealized terms, and serves several functions: validating that the widow had a strong marriage, is a good and worthy person, and is capable of rebuilding her life. European American women who view being a wife as above all other roles a woman can perform are somewhat more likely to sanctify their husbands (Lopata, 1996).

Getting older bereaved spouses to talk about their feelings concerning their loss reduces feelings of hopelessness, intrusive thoughts, and obsessive-compulsive behaviors (Segal et al., 1999). Cognitive-behavioral therapy is one especially effective intervention to help bereaved people make sense of the loss and deal with their other feelings and thoughts (Fleming & Robinson, 2001). A key to this process is helping people make meaning from the death (Neimeyer & Wogrin, 2008).

Unmarried heterosexual couples and gay and lesbian couples may experience other feelings and reactions in addition to typical feelings of grief. For example, family members of the deceased may not make the partner feel welcome at the funeral, making it hard for the partner to bring closure

to the relationship. Gays whose partners died of AIDS may experience increased personal concern, such as contracting AIDS themselves, and have difficulty dealing with their feelings (Goodkin et al., 1997). For gay partners who were also caregivers, the loss impacts one's sense of identity in much the same way as the death of a spouse; making sense of the death becomes the primary issue (Cadell & Marshall, 2007). Lesbian widows also report similar feelings (Bent & Magilvy, 2006).

Death is not as pleasant a topic as children's play or occupational development. It's not something we can go to college to master. What it represents to many people is the end of their existence, and that is a very scary prospect. But because we all share in this fear at some level, each of us is equipped to provide support and comfort for grieving survivors.

Death is the last life-cycle force we encounter, the ultimate triumph of biological forces that limit the length of life. Yet the same psychological and social forces that are so influential throughout life help us deal with death, either our own or someone else's. As we come to the end of our life journey, we understand death through an interaction of psychological forces, such as coping skills and intellectual and emotional understanding of death, and the sociocultural forces expressed in a particular society's traditions and rituals.

Learning about and dealing with death is clearly a developmental process across the life span that fits well in the biopsychosocial framework. Most apparent is that biological forces are essential to understanding death. The very definition of death is based on whether certain biological functions are present; these same definitions create numerous ethical dilemmas that must be dealt with psychologically and socioculturally. Life-cycle forces also play a key role. We have seen that the same concept—death—has varied meanings beyond the mere cessation of life depending on people's age.

How a person's understanding of death develops is also the result of psychological forces. As the ability to think and reflect undergoes fundamental change, the view of death changes from a mostly magical approach to one that can be transcendent and transforming. As we have seen, people who are facing their own imminent death experience certain feelings. Having gained experience through the deaths of friends and relatives, a person's level of comfort with his or her own death may increase.

Such personal experience may also come about by sharing rituals, defined through sociocultural forces. People observe how others deal with death and how the culture sets the tone and prescribes behavior for survivors. The combined action of forces also determines how they cope with the grief that accompanies the loss of someone close. Psychologically, confronting grief depends on many things, including the quality of the support system we have.

Thus, just as the beginning of life represents a complex interaction of biological, psychological, sociocultural, and life-cycle factors, so does death. What people believe about what happens after death is also an interaction of these factors. So, as we bring the study of human development to a close, we end where we began—what we experience in our lives cannot be understood if one uses only a single perspective.

Concept Checks

1. What are the major components of a life-span view of loss through death?
2. What are grief and bereavement, and how do people experience them?
3. What is abnormal grief?
4. How do people cope with different types of loss?

SOCIAL POLICY IMPLICATIONS

As you may have surmised from the text, the topic of euthanasia can be extremely controversial. Although the concept of disconnecting someone from life support, a form of active euthanasia, has gained fairly wide acceptance since the mid-1970s when it was first made legal, other types of euthanasia have not. For example, discontinuing food and hydration for someone, a form of passive euthanasia, can be highly controversial. Despite the U.S. Supreme Court ruling that such action is legal when brain death can be certified, removing food and hydration tends to be much more emotional than disconnecting life support. Coupled with the complications of certifying that a person is actually brain dead, the argument for passive euthanasia is typically complex. This was clearly the case in 2005 regarding the case of Terri Schiavo in Florida that was highlighted earlier in this chapter.

The important social policy issues facing the country include the extent to which the government can and should intervene in a private family decision, and the certainty with which physicians can make a declaration of brain death. The latter issue is key, for without it there may never be enough information for families to make an informed choice, irrespective of the government's position on whether it will allow that choice to be made. It is likely that these issues will become more important as medical technology continues to advance and the line between life and death blurs even more.

Such certifications have much riding on them. Organ transplants usually depend on the death of the donor, so the correctness and timing of the death declaration is crucial (kidney transplants are a notable exception, as many living donors give one of their kidneys to a person in need). Some people criticize the use of life support in these cases to keep donors "alive." Some religions advocate for "natural death," but nevertheless permit some forms of intervention.

Clearly, more serious discussion and debate is needed in order for society to come to grips with the interface between life and death. Beliefs about what death represents vary a great deal from culture to culture and person to person. But one thing is certain: the moral and ethical issues surrounding death must be confronted. Only by doing so will each person be in a position to make better decisions about what is best for him or her.

Summary

13.1 Definitions and Ethical Issues

How is death defined?

- Death is a difficult concept to define precisely. Different cultures have different meanings for death. Among the meanings in Western culture are images, statistics, events, state of being, analogy, mystery, boundary, thief of meaning, basis for anxiety, and reward or punishment.

What legal and medical criteria are used to determine when death occurs?

- For many centuries, a clinical definition of death was used: the absence of a heartbeat and respiration. Currently, whole-brain death is the most widely used definition. It is based on several highly specific criteria, including brain activity and responses to specific stimuli.

What are the ethical dilemmas surrounding euthanasia?

- Two types of euthanasia are distinguished. Active euthanasia consists of deliberately ending someone's life, such as turning off a life-support system. Physician-assisted suicide is a controversial issue and a form of active euthanasia. Passive euthanasia is ending someone's life by withholding some type of intervention or treatment (e.g., by stopping nutrition).

13.2 Thinking about Death: Personal Aspects

How do feelings about death change over adulthood?

- Young adults report a sense of being cheated by death. Cognitive developmental level is important for understanding how young adults view death.
- Middle-aged adults begin to confront their own mortality and undergo a change in their sense of time lived and time until death.
- Older adults are more accepting of death.

How do people deal with their own death?

- Kübler-Ross's theory includes five stages: denial, anger, bargaining, depression, and acceptance. Some people do not progress through all these stages, and some people move through them at different rates. People may be in more than one stage at a time and do not necessarily go through them in order.
- A contextual theory of dying emphasizes the tasks a dying person must face. Four dimensions of these tasks have been identified: bodily needs, psychological security, interpersonal attachments, and spiritual energy and hope. A contextual theory would be able to incorporate differences in reasons people die and the places people die.

What is death anxiety, and how do people show it?

- Most people exhibit some degree of anxiety about death, even though it is difficult to define and measure. Individual difference variables include gender, religiosity, age, ethnicity, and occupation. Death anxiety may have some benefits.

- The main ways death anxiety is shown are by avoiding death (e.g., refusing to go to funerals) and deliberately challenging it (e.g., engaging in dangerous sports). Other ways of showing it include changing lifestyles, dreaming and fantasizing, using humor, displacing fears, and becoming a death professional.
- Several ways to deal with anxiety exist: living life to the fullest, personal reflection, and education. Death education has been shown to be extremely effective.

13.3 End-of-Life Issues

How do people deal with end-of-life issues and create a final scenario?

- Managing the final aspects of life, after-death disposition of the body and memorial services, and distribution of assets are important end-of-life issues. Making choices about what people do and do not want done constitutes making a final scenario.

What is hospice?

- The goal of a hospice is to maintain the quality of life and to manage the pain of terminally ill patients. Hospice clients typically have cancer, AIDS, or a progressive neurological disorder. Family members tend to stay involved in the care of hospice clients.

How do people make their end-of-life intentions known?

- It is essential that people make their wishes known, through either a durable power of attorney or a living will.

13.4 Survivors: The Grieving Process

How do people experience the grief process?

- Grief is an active process of coping with loss. Four aspects of grieving must be confronted: the reality of the loss, the emotional turmoil, adjusting to the environment, and loosening the ties with the deceased. When death is expected, survivors go through anticipatory grief; unexpected death is usually more difficult for people to handle.

What feelings do grieving people have?

- Dealing with grief, called *grief work*, usually takes at least 1 to 2 years. Grief is equally intense for both expected and unexpected death, but it may begin before the actual death when the patient has a terminal illness. Normal grief reactions include sorrow, sadness, denial, disbelief, guilt, and anniversary reactions.

- In terms of dealing with normal grief, middle-aged adults have the most difficult time. Poor copers tend to have low self-esteem before losing a loved one.

What is the difference between normal and prolonged grief?

- The four component model proposes that the context of the loss, continuation of subjective meaning associated with the loss, changing representations of the lost relationship over time, and the role of coping and emotion-regulation processes describe the grief process.

- The dual process model of coping with bereavement focuses on loss-oriented stressors and restoration-oriented stressors.

- Prolonged grief involves symptoms of separation distress and symptoms of traumatic distress. Excessive guilt and self-blame are common manifestations of traumatic grief.

How do adults of different ages deal with loss?

- Young and middle-aged adults usually have intense feelings about death. Attachment theory provides a useful framework to understand these feelings.

- Midlife is a time when people usually deal with the death of their parents and confront their own mortality.

- The death of one's child is especially difficult to cope with.

- The death of one's parent deprives an adult of many important things, and the feelings accompanying it are often complex.

- Older adults are usually less anxious about death and deal with it better than any other age group.

- The death of a grandchild can be very traumatic for older adults, and the feelings of loss may never go away.

- The death of one's partner represents a deep personal loss, especially when the couple had a long and close relationship. Older widowers often have a difficult time coping, whereas older widows often have a difficult time financially.

Review Questions

13.1 Definitions and Ethical Issues

- What are the various sociocultural meanings of death?
- What are the three legal criteria for death?
- What are the criteria necessary for brain death?
- What is bioethics, and what kinds of issues does it deal with?
- What are the two types of euthanasia? How do they differ?
- How does the cost of medical care in the last year of life relate to euthanasia?

13.2 Thinking about Death: Personal Aspects

- How do cognitive development and issues at midlife influence feelings about death?
- Describe Kübler-Ross's theory of dying. How do people progress through the different feelings?
- What is necessary for creating a contextual theory of dying?
- What is death anxiety? What factors influence death anxiety? How does it relate to terror management theory?
- How do people demonstrate death anxiety?
- How do people learn to deal with death anxiety?

13.3 End-of-Life Issues

- What are end-of-life issues?
- How do people create a final scenario?
- What is a hospice? How does hospice care differ from hospital care?
- What are the major ways in which people inform others of their end-of-life decisions?

13.4 Survivors: The Grieving Process

- What is meant by grief, bereavement, and mourning?
- What is the process of grief? What are the risk factors associated with grief?
- What are normal grief reactions and grief work?
- How does grief change over time?
- What is the four component model of grief?
- What is the dual process model of grief?
- What are prolonged grief reactions?
- How do adults of different ages deal with different types of loss?

Integrating Concepts in Development

- What effect do you think being at different levels of cognitive development has on people's thinking about death?
- What parallels are there between the stages of dying and the experience of grief? Why do you think they may be similar?
- How can we use the study of death, dying, bereavement, and grief to provide insights into the psychological development of people across adulthood?

Key Terms

active euthanasia Involves the deliberate ending of a person's life through an intervention or action, which may be based on a clear statement of the person's wishes or a decision made by someone else who has the legal authority to do so.

anniversary reaction Feelings of sadness and loneliness on holidays, birthdays, and the anniversary of a loved one's death.

bereavement The state or condition caused by loss through death.

bioethics The study of the interaction between human values and technological advances in the health and life sciences.

clinical death Definition of death based on lack of heartbeat and respiration.

end-of-life issues Management issues of the final phase of life, after-death disposition of the body and memorial services, and distribution of assets.

euthanasia Meaning "good death," the practice of allowing people who have a terminal illness to die.

final scenario One's choices about end-of-life issues, which can be made known to others.

grief The feelings that arise after one suffers a loss.

grief work The psychological process of coming to terms with bereavement.

grief work as rumination hypothesis Views extensive grief processing as a form of rumination that may actually increase distress.

hospice An approach to assisting dying people that emphasizes pain management and death with dignity.

mourning The ways in which we express grief.

passive euthanasia Allowing a person to die by withholding an available treatment.

persistent vegetative state A state in which a person's brainstem is the only part of the brain that is functioning, a state from which the person does not recover.

terror management theory A theory that addresses the issue of why people engage in certain behaviors to achieve particular psychological states based on their deeply rooted concerns about mortality.

whole-brain death Most widely accepted criteria for death involving eight criteria.

Resources

www.cengage.com/psychology/cavanaugh

Visit the companion website, where you will find tutorial quizzes, glossary, flashcards, and more. You can also access the following websites from the companion website. The Hospice Foundation of America provides leadership in the development of hospices and the hospice philosophy. Its website has a variety of information about hospices and related resources.

AARP provides information and advocacy about complex end-of-life issues. Its site contains information and resources on a variety of topics related to powers of attorney, living wills, and related topics.

The Compassionate Friends is a national organization dedicated to helping parents deal with the loss of a child. In addition to providing information and resources, the home page has a link to help you find a chapter in your area.

Readings

Albom, M. (1997). *Tuesdays with Morrie*. New York: Doubleday. A moving account of the reconnection between a middle-aged man and his former teacher that includes both an excellent example of a final scenario and intergenerational transmission of wisdom. Easy reading.

Kastenbaum, R. (2009). *Death, society, and human experience*. Boston: Allyn & Bacon. General overview of key issues related to dying, bereavement, grief, and how they fit into society. Moderate difficulty.

Kushner, H. S. (1981). *When bad things happen to good people*. New York: Schocken. A classic book that is very thought provoking. This book was written by a rabbi after the death of his son. Easy reading, but take it slowly.

Nuland, S. B. (1994). *How we die: Reflections on life's final chapter*. New York: Knopf. A very important and informative book that provides an excellent discussion of what happens when people die. Great for dispelling myths about dying. Easy reading.

Young, W. P. (2008). *The shack*. Newbury Park, CA: Windblown Media. A *New York Times* best-selling novel about coming to terms with the murder of a man's young daughter and the process of forgiveness. Easy reading.

14

Successful Aging

Crossroads in the Karelian forest.

WELCOME TO THE LOOK DOWN THE ROAD. IN THIS EPILOGUE, WE TAKE A different perspective on aging. Based on what we know now about older adults and the process of aging, we look to our own future. We consider what society must do to keep the social programs we have come to rely on. We consider what each of us can do to keep ourselves in the best health possible in order to delay or even prevent some of the negative aspects of aging. And we also look around the corner and ahead a few decades. Technical advances will make commonplace what is only science fiction today. For example, it is likely that we will be able to get our annual physical examination remotely, be in classes or meetings led by someone's holographic projection because they are actually in another place, and remember fondly those days when you had to spend lots of time downloading movies because the connection speeds were so slow. Our daily lives will likely have vastly different elements from those they have right now. Life undoubtedly will be more complicated. But people are still likely to experience firsthand many of the things discussed in this book: marriage, children, career changes, relocation, personal development, physical and cognitive changes, the loss of friends and loved ones, and so on.

For now, though, we must be content with working with what we do and do not know. Throughout this book we have made predictions about this future and guessed how older people may fare. Some of these predictions are not so happy; for example, as many people live to a very old age, there will be more need for long-term care. Whether we will be able to provide the care for them is very much in doubt. Other aspects of the future may be more positive; for instance, as many people live to very old age there will be a much larger pool of older workers to balance the labor force. These predictions represent our best guess about what life will be like in the next few decades, based on what we know now and what is likely to happen if we continue the way we are going.

The purpose of this epilogue is to pull together several crucial issues facing gerontologists as we move through the 21st century and to illustrate how we can set the best stage for our own aging. This survey will not be exhaustive; rather, we will focus on two things: points that have been singled out for special concern, and areas where major advances may have a dramatic impact on our own development.

14.1 Demographic Trends and Social Policy

LEARNING OBJECTIVES
- What key demographic changes will occur by 2030?
- What are the challenges facing Social Security and Medicare?

N*ancy, a 35-year-old new employee at a marketing and public relations firm, was flipping through the company's benefits package. When it came to the retirement plan, she commented to the human resources person, "I guess I better pay attention. I don't think Social Security will be there for me when the time comes."*

Nancy isn't alone. Many younger adults in the United States do not believe that Social Security or other government programs will be in existence by the time they get old enough to qualify for them. Demographic and financial trends support this pessimistic view. As we will see, the baby-boom generation, coupled with structural problems in Social Security and Medicare, give young adults good reasons to be concerned.

Demographic Trends: 2030

In Chapter 1, we noted several trends in the population of the United States and the rest of the world during the upcoming century. These trends are not likely to change in the foreseeable future. Changes in the composition of the older adult population contribute to potentially critical issues that will emerge over the next few decades. One especially important area concerns the potential for intergenerational conflict.

Because the resources and roles in a society are never divided equally among different age groups, the potential for conflict always exists. One well-known intergenerational conflict is that between adolescents and their parents. Less well known is the potential for conflict between middle-aged and older adults. This type of conflict has not traditionally been a source of serious problems in society, for several reasons: Older adults made up a small proportion of the population, family ties

between adult children and their parents worked against conflict, and middle-aged people were hesitant to withdraw support from programs for older adults. Despite these potent forces protecting against conflict, the situation is changing. For example, the controversy over the rate of growth of Medicare and Social Security that has created heated political debates about social support programs and health care in the late 1990s and 2000s would have been unthinkable just a few years earlier.

To see more clearly how these changing demographics will have an enormous effect on society at large and on the programs that target older adults, let us project forward to the year 2030, when the last of the baby boomers will have reached age 65. Between now and 2030, the following changes will have set in:

- The proportion of older adults in the United States will have nearly doubled.

- Older adults will be much more politically sophisticated and organized. They will be better educated and will be familiar with life in a highly complex society in which one must learn to deal with bureaucracies. And they will be proficient users of the Internet and technology in general.

- Older adults will expect to keep their more affluent lifestyle, Social Security benefits, health care benefits, and other benefits accrued throughout their adult life. A comfortable retirement will be viewed as a right, not a privilege.

- The ratio of workers to retirees will fall from its current level of roughly over 3:1 to 2:1. This means that to maintain the level of benefits in programs such as Social Security, the working members of society will have to pay significantly higher taxes than workers do now. This is because Social Security is a pay-as-you-go system in which the money collected from workers today is used to pay current retirees. Contrary to popular belief, Social Security is not a savings plan. Whether policymakers will make the necessary changes to maintain benefits that citizens came to view as entitlements remains to be seen.

- The increase in divorce that has occurred over the past few decades may result in a lowered sense of obligation on the part of middle-aged adults toward parents who were not involved in their upbringing or who the adult child feels disrespected the other parent. Should this lowered sense of obligation result, it is likely that fewer older adults will have family members available to care for them, placing a significantly greater burden on society for care.

- The rapid increase in the number of ethnic minority older adults compared to white older adults will force a reconsideration of issues such as discrimination and access to health care, goods, and services, as well as provide a much richer and broader understanding of the aging process.

No one knows for certain what society will be like by 2030. However, the changes we have noted in demographic trends suggest a need for taking action now. Two areas facing the most challenge are Social Security and Medicare. Let's take a look at these to understand why they face trouble.

Social Security and Medicare

Without doubt, the 20th and the beginning of the 21st centuries saw a dramatic improvement in the everyday lives of older adults in industrialized countries. The increase in the number of older adults and their gain in political power, coupled with increased numbers of social programs addressing issues specifically involving older adults, created unprecedented gains for the average older person (Crown, 2001). As you can see in Figure 14.1, the economic well-being of the majority of older adults has never been better than it is currently. In 1959, roughly 35% of older adults were below the federal poverty line compared to only about 9.4% in 2006 (AgingStats.gov, 2008a).

Whether this downward trend in poverty rates will continue remains to be seen. The baby boomers, the largest generation in American history to become eligible for such government programs as Social Security and Medicare, will also be extraordinarily expensive due to two factors: their low personal savings rate and the projected costs of chronic disease (Samuelson, 2007).

The Political Landscape. Beginning in the 1970s, older adults began to be portrayed as scapegoats in the political debates concerning government resources.

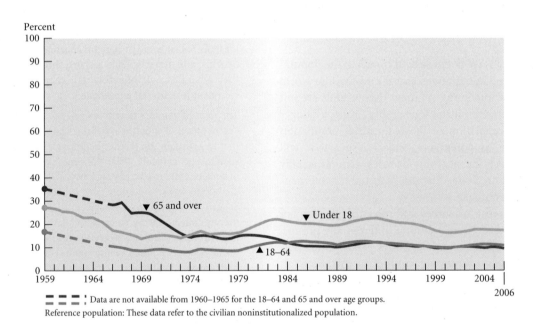

Figure 14.1 Poverty rates in the United States by age group, 1959–2006.

Source: U.S. Census Bureau, Current Population Survey, Annual Society and Economic Supplement, 1960–2007.

Part of the reason was due to the tremendous growth in the amount and proportion of federal dollars expended on benefits to them, such as through the increase of benefits paid from Social Security during the 1970s (Crown, 2001). At that time, older adults were also portrayed as highly politically active, fiscally conservative, and selfish (Fairlie, 1988; Gibbs, 1988; Smith, 1992). The health care reform debate of the early 1990s focused attention on the spiraling costs of care for older adults that were projected to bankrupt the federal budget if left uncontrolled (Binstock, 1999). Consequently, older adults emerged as the source of most of the United States' fiscal problems.

It was in this context that the U.S. Congress began making substantive changes in the benefits for older adults on the grounds of intergenerational fairness. The argument was that the United States must treat all generations fairly and cannot provide differential benefits to any one generation (Binstock, 1994). Beginning in 1983, Congress has made several changes in Social Security, Medicare, the Older Americans Act, and other programs and policies. Some of these changes reduced benefits to wealthy older adults, whereas others provided targeted benefits for poor older adults (Binstock, 1999).

The aging of the baby-boom generation presents very difficult and expensive problems (Congressional Budget Office, 2008). In fiscal year 2009, federal spending on Social Security and Medicare alone was expected to top $1.1 trillion. As you can see in Figure 14.2, if spending patterns do not change, by 2030 (when most of the baby boomers will have reached old age) expenditures for Social Security and Medicare alone are projected to consume roughly 13% of the gross domestic product (GDP) of the United States. Without major reforms in these programs, such growth will force extremely difficult choices regarding how to pay for them.

Clearly, the political and social issues concerning benefits to older adults are quite complex. Driven by the eligibility of the first baby boomers for reduced Social Security benefits in 2008 and their eligibility for Medicare in 2011, the next decade will see increased urgency for action in confronting the issues. There are no easy solutions, and it will be essential to discuss all aspects of the problem. Let's look more closely at Social Security and Medicare.

Social Security. Social Security had its beginnings in 1935 as an initiative by President Franklin Roosevelt to "frame a law which will give some measure of

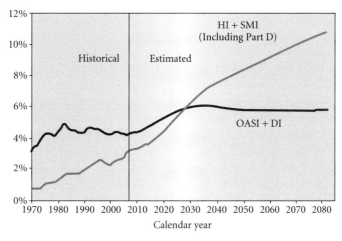

Figure 14.2 Social Security (blue line) and Medicare (red line) as a percentage of the U.S. gross domestic product.

Source: Congressional Budget Office (2008).

protection to the average citizen and to his family against the loss of a job and against poverty-ridden old age." Thus Social Security was originally intended to provide a supplement to savings and other means of financial support.

Over the years, revisions to the original law have changed Social Security so that it now represents the primary source of financial support after retirement for most U.S. citizens, and the only source for many (Henrikson, 2007; Kingson & Williamson, 2001). Since the 1970s, however, increasing numbers of workers have been included in employer-sponsored pension plans such as 401(k), 403(b), and 457 plans, mutual funds, as well as various types of individual retirement accounts (IRAs) (U.S. Department of Labor, 2005). This inclusion of various retirement plans, especially savings options, may permit more future retirees to use Social Security as the supplemental financial source it was intended to be, thereby shifting retirement financial planning responsibility to the individual (Henrikson, 2007).

The primary challenge facing Social Security is the aging of the very large baby-boom generation and the much smaller generation that follows. That's why Nancy, the woman we met in the vignette, and other young adults are concerned. Because Social Security is funded by payroll taxes, the amount of money each worker must pay depends to a large extent on the ratio of the number of people paying Social Security taxes to the number of people collecting benefits. By 2030, this ratio will drop nearly in half; that is, by the time baby boomers have largely retired, there will be nearly twice as many people collecting Social Security per worker paying into the system as there is today (Social Security Administration, 2008). Various plans have been proposed since the early 1970s to address this issue, and several U.S. presidents have made it a major agenda item (including President George W. Bush in 2005), but Congress has not yet taken the actions necessary to ensure the long-term financial stability of Social Security (Social Security Administration, 2008). As discussed in the Current Controversies feature, the suggestions for doing this present difficult choices for politicians.

Medicare.   Roughly 40 million U.S. citizens depend on Medicare for their medical insurance. To be eligible, a person must meet one of the following criteria: be over age 65, be disabled, or have permanent kidney failure. Medicare consists of three parts (Medicare.gov, 2008a): Part A, which covers inpatient hospital services, skilled nursing facilities, home health services, and hospice care; Part B, which covers the cost of physician services, outpatient hospital services, medical equipment and supplies, and other health services and supplies; and Part D, which provides some coverage for prescription medications. Expenses relating to most long-term care needs are funded by Medicaid, another major health care program funded by the U.S. government and aimed at people who are poor. Out-of-pocket expenses associated with co-payments and other charges are often paid by supplemental insurance policies, sometimes referred to as "Medigap" policies (Medicare.gov, 2008b).

Like Social Security, Medicare is funded by a payroll tax. So the funding problems facing Medicare are very similar to those facing Social Security and are grounded in the aging of the baby-boom generation. In addition, Medicare costs have increased dramatically due to more general rapid cost increases in health care.

Due to these rapid increases and the specter of the baby-boom generation, cost containment remains a major concern. In 2008, President Bush and the contenders to replace him all cited rapidly rising health care costs as a major economic problem facing the United States. But unlike Social Security, Medicare is a government program that has been subjected to significant cuts in expenditures, typically through reduced payouts to health care providers. Whether this practice will continue is unclear, especially when baby boomers find out that their health care coverage could be significantly reduced.

Taken together, the challenges facing society concerning older adults' financial security and health will continue to be major political issues throughout the first few decades of the 21st century. There are no easy answers, but open discussion of the various arguments will be essential for creating the optimal solution.

Saving Social Security

Few political issues have been around as long and are as politically sensitive as the issues relating to making Social Security fiscally sound for the long term. The basic issues have been well known for decades: the baby-boom generation and the following smaller workforce will greatly stretch the current system, and the present method for raising and distributing revenues cannot be sustained (Social Security Administration, 2008).

Because Social Security is based on current workers paying a tax to support current retirees, the looming funding problems depend critically on the worker-to-retiree ratio. As you can see in Figure 14.3, this ratio has declined precipitously since Social Security began and will continue to do so, placing an increasing financial burden on workers to provide the level of benefits that people have come to expect. Due

to this declining ratio, if the current tax rate of 12.4% each on workers and employers is maintained, payments will exceed income from payroll taxes by 2017, will exceed all sources of revenue including interest on the available surplus (the trust fund) by 2027, and will be bankrupt by 2041 (Social Security Administration, 2008). So it's little wonder that young adults have little faith that Social Security will be there for them.

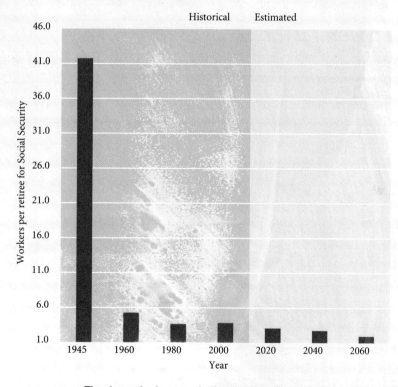

Figure 14.3 The dramatic decrease in the number of workers paying into the Social Security system per retiree is the main reason Social Security taxes have steadily increased.

Source: Data from SSA, 2008.

(Continued)

What steps can be taken to keep Social Security sound in the long term? In 2005, President Bush made a concerted effort to incorporate reports from many special commissions established to study the problem (including one he set up in 2001), economists, and researchers who have all proposed changes in the current operation of Social Security. Among the changes proposed over the years are these:

- *Privatization:* Various proposals have been made for allowing or requiring workers to invest at least part of their money in personal retirement accounts managed by either the federal government or private investment companies. A variation would take trust funds and invest them in private-sector equity markets. Another option would be for people to be allowed to create personal accounts with a portion of the funds paid in payroll taxes.
- *Means-test benefits:* This proposal would reduce or eliminate benefits to people with high incomes.
- *Increase the number of years used to compute the benefit:* Currently, benefits are based on one's history of contributions over a 35-year period. This proposal would increase that to 38 or 40 years.
- *Increase the retirement age:* The age of eligibility for full Social Security benefits is increasing slowly from age 65 in 2000 to age 67 in 2027. Various proposals to speed up the increase, to increase the age to 70, or to connect age at which a person becomes fully eligible to average longevity statistics have been made.
- *Adjust cost-of-living increases downward:* Some proposals have been made to lower the increases given to beneficiaries as a result of increases in cost of living.
- *Increase the payroll tax rate:* One direct way to address the coming funding shortfall is to increase revenues through a higher tax rate.
- *Increase the earnings cap for payroll tax purposes:* This proposal would either raise or remove the cap on income subject to the Social Security payroll tax ($102,000 in 2008).
- *Make across-the-board reductions in Social Security pension benefits:* A reduction in benefits of 3% to 5% would resolve most of the funding problem.

None of these proposals has universal support, and many would significantly disadvantage people, especially minorities and older widows, who depend almost entirely on Social Security for their retirement income (Gonyea & Hooyman, 2005; Syihula & Estes, 2007).

Solving the funding problems facing Social Security will be increasingly important in the next few years. Remember, the first baby boomers became eligible for reduced retirement benefits in 2008. Will it be there for you?

Given the political difficulties inherent in tackling the issue, and the lack of perfect solutions, it is likely that Social Security will remain a major controversy over the next several years.

Concept Checks

1. What major demographic and social policy changes will likely occur by 2030?
2. What are the major issues that confront Social Security?
3. What is Medicare?

- What are the major strategies for maintaining and enhancing competence?
- What are the primary considerations in designing health promotion and disease prevention programs?
- What are the principal lifestyle factors that influence competence?

14.2 Health Issues and Quality of Life

LEARNING OBJECTIVES

- What are the key issues in health promotion and quality of life?

Jack had heard about the many things that were available on the Web, but like many older adults he was a little reluctant to use a computer. He thought that was best left to the grandchildren. But after he purchased his first home computer at age 68, he began surfing. He never stopped. Now at age 73, he's a veteran with a wide array of bookmarked sites, especially those relating to health issues. He also communicates by e-mail, and he designed the community newsletter using his word-processing program.

Jack is like many older adults—better educated and more technologically sophisticated than their predecessors. The coming demographic changes in the United States and the rest of the world in the aging population present a challenge for improving the kind of lives older adults live. For this reason, promoting healthy lifestyles is seen as one of the top health care priorities of the 21st century (Lunenfeld, 2008). Remaining healthy is important for decelerating the rate of aging (Aldwin & Gilmer, 2004). Promoting healthy lifestyles is important in all settings, including nursing homes (Thompson & Oliver, 2008).

Health Promotion and Quality of Life

Even though changing unhealthy habits such as smoking and poor diet are difficult, chronic diseases such as arthritis make exercise challenging, and terminal disease makes it tough to see the benefits of changing one's habits, the fact remains that such changes typically increase functional capability. Current models of behavioral change are complex and include not only behavioral, but also motivational, cognitive, and social components (Aldwin & Gilmer, 2004). Two that are the focus of most research are the self-efficacy model, which emphasizes the role of goal setting and personal beliefs in the degree to which one influences the outcome, and the self-regulation model, which focuses on the person's motivation for change.

There is surprisingly little research on health promotion programs designed specifically for older adults (Aldwin & Gilmer, 2004). However, a few trends are apparent. First, although exercise is key to health, because older adults are more prone to injury, exercise programs for older adults need to take such issues into account. Second, health education programs are effective in minimizing the effects of emotional stress. Third, health screening programs are effective in identifying serious

chronic disease that can limit the quality of life. Each of these areas within health promotion is successful only if ethnic differences are taken into account in designing the programs (Landrine & Klonoff, 2001).

One's state of health influences one's quality of life, that is, one's well-being and life satisfaction. Quality of life includes interpersonal relationships and social support, physical and mental health, environmental comfort, and many psychological constructs such as locus of control, emotions, usefulness, personality, and meaning in life (Kaplan & Erickson, 2000). It is usually divided into environmental, physical, social, and psychological domains of well-being. Personal evaluation of these dimensions is critical to understanding how people view their situations. For example, although half of the people in Strawbridge, Wallhagen, and Cohen's (2002) study did not meet certain objective criteria for successful aging, they nevertheless defined themselves as successful and as having a good quality of life.

In short, quality of life is a person's subjective assessment or value judgment of his or her own life (Aldwin & Gilmer, 2004). This subjective judgment may or may not correspond to the evaluation of others. And even though self- and other-perceived quality of life may diminish in late life, it may not seem like a loss for the older person. For example, an older woman who has difficulty walking may feel happy to simply be alive, whereas another who is in objective good health may feel useless. Quality of

For most people, doing what you enjoy enhances quality of life.

life is best studied from the point of view of the person.

Still, when the level of medical intervention increases as people grow more frail, medical professionals must be concerned about the trade-off between extending life at all costs and the quality of that life (Michel, Newton, & Kirkwood, 2008). This debate will continue, and will benefit from informed discussions of various options at the end of life, as described in Chapter 13.

A Framework for Maintaining and Enhancing Competence

Although most older adults are not as computer literate as Jack, the man introduced in the vignette, increasing numbers of older adults are discovering that computers can be a major asset. Many take advantage of the growing resources available on the Web, including sites dedicated specifically to older adults. E-mail enables people of all ages to stay in touch with friends and family, and the growing success of e-commerce makes it easier for people with limited time or mobility to purchase goods and services. Computers are already used in many health devices and are likely to become ubiquitous in the home environment of older adults in the relatively near future (Lesnoff-Caravaglia, (2009)).

The use of computers is one way in which technology can be used to enhance the competence of older adults. In this section, we consider the general topic of how to maintain and enhance competence through a variety of interventions. How to grow old successfully is a topic of increasing concern in view of the demographic changes we considered earlier.

The life-span perspective we considered in Chapter 1 is an excellent starting point for understanding how to maintain and enhance people's competence. In this perspective, the changes that occur with age result from multiple biological, psychological, sociocultural, and life-cycle forces. Mastering tasks of daily living and more complex tasks (such as personal finances) contributes to a person's overall sense of competence even if the person has dementia (Mayo, 2008). How can this sense be optimized for successful aging?

The answer lies in applying three key adaptive mechanisms for aging: selection, optimization, and compensation (SOC) (Baltes et al., 2006). This framework helps address what Bieman-Copland, Ryan, and Cassano (1998) call the "social facilitation of the nonuse of competence": the phenomenon of older people intentionally or unintentionally failing to perform up to their true level of ability because of social stereotypes that operate to limit what older adults are expected to do. Instead of behaving at their true ability level, older adults behave in ways they believe typical or characteristic of their age group (Heckhausen & Lang, 1996). This phenomenon is the basis for the communication patterns we considered earlier in this chapter.

A key issue in the powerful role of stereotypes is to differentiate usual or typical aging from successful aging (Guralnik, 2008). Successful aging involves avoiding disease, being engaged with life, and maintaining high cognitive and physical functioning. Successful aging is subjective. It is reached when a person achieves his or her desired goals with dignity and as independently as possible (Bieman-Copland et al., 1998; Guralnik, 2008; Mayo, 2008; Schulz & Heckhausen, 1996).

The life-span perspective can be used to create a formal model for successful aging. Heckhausen (Heckhausen & Lang, 1996; Schulz & Heckhausen, 1996) developed a life-span theory of control by applying core assumptions that recognize aging as a complex process that involves increasing specialization and is influenced by factors unrelated to age. The basic premises of successful aging include keeping a balance between the various gains and losses that occur over time and minimizing the influence of factors unrelated to aging. In short, these premises involve paying attention to both internal and external factors impinging on the person. The antecedents include all the changes that happen to a person. The mechanisms in the model are the selection, optimization, and compensation processes that shape the course of development. Finally, the outcomes of the model denote that enhanced competence, quality of life, and future adaptation are the visible signs of successful aging.

Using the SOC model, various types of interventions can be created to help people age successfully. In general, such interventions focus on the individual or aspects of tasks and the physical and social environment that emphasize competence (Allaire & Willis, 2006; Bieman-Copland et al., 1998). When designing interventions aimed primarily at the person, it is important to understand the target person's goals (rather than the goals of the researcher). For example, in teaching older adults how to use automatic teller machines (ATMs), it is essential to understand the kinds of concerns and fears older adults have and to ensure that the training program addresses them (Rogers et al., 1997).

Performance on tests of everyday competence predicts longer term outcomes (Allaire & Willis, 2006). Careful monitoring of competence can be an early indicator of problems, and appropriate interventions should be undertaken as soon as possible.

Health Promotion and Disease Prevention

By now you're probably wondering how to promote successful aging. You may not be surprised to learn that there is no set of steps or magic potion you can take to guarantee that you will age optimally. But research is showing that there are some steps you can take to maximize your chances (Guralnik,

---

Table 14.1

Preventive Strategies for Maximizing
Successful Aging

Adopt a healthy lifestyle. Make it part of your daily routine.

Stay active cognitively. Keep an optimistic outlook and maintain your interest in things.

Maintain a social network and stay engaged with others.

Maintain good economic habits to avoid financial dependency.

2008). As you can see in Table 14.1, most of them are not complex. But they do capture the results of applying the model for maintaining and enhancing competence we examined at the beginning of the section. The key strategies are sound health habits; good habits of thought, including an optimistic outlook and interest in things; a social network; and sound economic habits.

These simple steps are difficult in practice, of course. Nevertheless, they will help maximize the chances of aging successfully. Setting up this favorable outcome is important. Because of the demographic shifts in the population, health care costs for older adults in most developed countries are expected to skyrocket during the first half of the 21st century. Minimizing this increase is key.

To support these changes, the U.S. Department of Health and Human Services created a national initiative to improve the health of all Americans through a coordinated and comprehensive emphasis on prevention. Updated every 10 years, the current version of this effort, the *Healthy People* initiative, sets targets for a healthier population based on three broad goals: increase the length of healthy life, reduce health disparities among Americans, and achieve access to preventive services for all. (You can find the latest version of the initiative at http://www.healthypeople.gov.)

Although significant gains have been made in earlier versions of the initiative, they were not universal. Many members of ethnic minority groups and the poor still have not seen significant improvements in their lives. With this in mind, there has been a shift from a focus that included only prevention to one that also includes optimum health practices.

The U.S. government allocates funds appropriated by the Older Americans Act through the Administration on Aging (AoA) to help support programs specifically aimed at improving the health of older adults. These funds support a wide variety of programs, including health risk assessments and screenings, nutrition screening and education, physical fitness, health promotion programs on chronic disabling conditions, home injury control services, counseling regarding social services, and follow-up health services.

One goal of these low-cost programs is to address the lack of awareness many people have about their own chronic health problems; for example, the AoA estimates that half of those with diabetes mellitus, more than half with hypertension, and 70% of those with high cholesterol levels are unaware that they have serious conditions. Health promotion and disease prevention programs such as those sponsored by the AoA could reduce the cost of treating the diseases through earlier diagnosis and better prevention education.

Issues in Prevention. In Chapter 4, we saw that Verbrugge and Jette's (1994) theoretical model offers a comprehensive account of disability resulting from chronic conditions and provides much guidance for research. Another benefit of the model is that it also provides insight into ways to intervene so that disability can be prevented or its progress slowed. Prevention efforts can be implemented in many ways, from providing flu vaccines to providing transportation to cultural events so that otherwise homebound people can enjoy these activities.

Traditionally, three types of prevention have been discussed: primary, secondary, and tertiary; more recently, the concept of quaternary prevention has

been added (Verbrugge, 1994). A brief summary is presented in Table 14.2. Primary prevention *is any intervention that prevents a disease or condition from occurring.* Examples of primary prevention include immunizing against illnesses such as polio and influenza or controlling risk factors such as serum cholesterol levels and cigarette smoking in healthy people.

Secondary prevention *is instituted early after a condition has begun (but may not yet have been diagnosed) and before significant impairments have occurred.* Examples of secondary intervention include cancer and cardiovascular disease screening and routine medical testing for other conditions. These steps help reduce the severity of the condition and may even reduce mortality from it. In terms of the main pathway in Verbrugge and Jette's (1994) model, secondary prevention occurs between pathology and impairments.

Tertiary prevention *involves efforts to avoid the development of complications or secondary chronic conditions, manage the pain associated with the primary chronic condition, and sustain life through medical intervention.* Some chronic conditions have a high risk of creating additional medical problems; for example, being bedridden as a result of a chronic

---

Table 14.2

Types of Prevention Interventions

Type of Prevention	Description	Examples
Primary	Any intervention that prevents a disease or condition from occurring	Immunizations against diseases, healthy diet
Secondary	Program instituted early after a condition has begun (but may not have been diagnosed) and before significant impairment has occurred	Cancer screening, other medical tests
Tertiary	Efforts to avoid the development of complications or secondary chronic conditions, manage the panic associated with the primary chronic condition, and sustain life	Moving a bedridden person to avoid sores, getting medical intervention, getting a patient out of bed to improve mobility after surgery
Quaternary	Effort specifically aimed at improving the functional capacities of people who have chronic conditions	Cognitive interventions for people with Alzheimer's disease, rehabilitation programs after surgery

disease often is associated with getting pneumonia. Tertiary prevention involves taking steps such as sitting the person up in bed to lower the risk of contracting additional diseases. In terms of the model, tertiary interventions are aimed at minimizing functional limitations and disability.

Historically, tertiary prevention efforts have not focused on functioning but rather on avoiding additional medical problems and sustaining life (Verbrugge, 1994). Consequently, the notion of quaternary prevention has been developed to address functional issues. Quaternary prevention *is efforts specifically aimed at improving the functional capacities of people who have chronic conditions.* Like tertiary prevention, quaternary prevention focuses on the functional limitations and disability components of the model. Some examples of quaternary prevention are cognitive interventions to help people with Alzheimer's disease remember things and occupational therapy to help people maintain their independence.

Although most efforts with older adults to date have focused on primary prevention, increasing attention is being paid to secondary prevention through screening for early diagnosis of diseases such as cancer and cardiovascular disease (see Chapters 2 and 3). Few systematic studies of the benefits and outcomes of tertiary and quaternary prevention efforts have been done with older adult participants. However, the number of such programs being conducted in local senior centers and other settings attractive to older adults is increasing steadily, with the focus of many of them on nutrition and exercise (Coulston & Boushey, 2008). The stakes are high. Because tertiary and quaternary prevention programs are aimed at maintaining functional abilities and minimizing disability, they can be effective, lower-cost alternatives for addressing the needs of older adults with chronic conditions. They can also address concerns about quality of life (Michel et al., 2008).

Lifestyle Factors

Most attention in health promotion and disease prevention programs is on tackling a handful of behaviors that have tremendous payoff, such as keeping fit and eating properly. In turn, these programs educate adults about good health care practices and help identify conditions such as hypertension, high cholesterol levels, and elevated blood sugar levels, which, if left untreated, can cause atherosclerosis, heart disease, strokes, diabetes mellitus, and other serious conditions.

Exercise. Ever since the ancient Greeks, physicians and researchers have known that exercise significantly slows the aging process. Indeed, evidence suggests that a program of regular exercise, in conjunction with a healthy lifestyle, can slow the physiological aging process (Aldwin & Gilmer, 2004). Being sedentary is hazardous to your health.

Adults benefit from aerobic exercise*, which places moderate stress on the heart by maintaining a pulse rate between 60% and 90% of the person's maximum heart rate.* You can calculate your maximum heart rate by subtracting your age from 220. Thus, if you are 40 years old, your target range would be 108–162 beats per minute. The minimum time necessary for aerobic exercise to be of benefit depends on its intensity; at low heart rates, sessions may need to last an hour, whereas at high heart rates, 15 minutes may suffice. Examples of aerobic exercise include jogging, step aerobics, swimming, and cross-country skiing.

What happens when a person exercises aerobically (besides becoming tired and sweaty)? Physiologically, adults of all ages show improved cardiovascular functioning and maximum oxygen consumption; lower blood pressure; and better strength, endurance, flexibility, and coordination (Mayo Clinic, 2008c). Psychologically, people who exercise aerobically report lower levels of stress, better moods, and better cognitive functioning (Mayo Clinic, 2008c).

The best way to gain the benefits of aerobic exercise is to maintain physical fitness throughout the life span, beginning at least in middle age. The benefits of various forms of exercise are numerous, and include lowering the risk of cardiovascular disease, osteoporosis (if the exercise is weight bearing), and a host of other conditions. The Mayo Clinic's Fitness

Exercise is a major way to help delay or prevent health problems.

Center provides an excellent place to start. In planning an exercise program, three points should be remembered. First, check with a physician before beginning an aerobic exercise program. Second, bear in mind that moderation is important. Third, just because you intend to exercise doesn't mean you will; you must take the necessary steps to turn your intention into action (Schwarzer, 2008).

Nutrition. How many times did your parents tell you to eat your vegetables? Or perhaps they said, "You are what you eat." Most people have disagreements with parents about food while growing up, but as adults they realize that those lima beans and other despised foods their parents urged them to eat really are healthy. Experts agree that nutrition directly affects one's mental, emotional, and physical functioning (Mayo Clinic, 2008c). For example, diet has been linked to cancer, cardiovascular disease, diabetes, anemia, and digestive disorders. Nutritional requirements and eating habits change across the life span. *This change is due mainly to differences in* metabolism, *or how much energy the body needs.* Body metabolism and the digestive process slow down with age (Janssen, 2005).

Every five years the U.S. Department of Agriculture publishes dietary guidelines based on current research. In its *Dietary Guidelines for Americans 2005* (U.S. Department of Agriculture, 2005), the USDA recommends that we eat a variety of nutrient-dense foods and beverages across the basic food groups. Most important, we should choose foods that limit the intake of saturated and *trans* fats, cholesterol, added sugars, salt, and alcohol. The USDA recommends that women of child-bearing age consume more iron-rich foods. For a more personal guide to good nutrition, check out the USDA MyPyramid website at http://www.mypyramid.gov/.

Did you ever worry as you were eating a triple-dip cone of premium ice cream that you really should be eating fat-free frozen yogurt instead? If so, you are among the people who have taken to heart (literally) the link between diet and cardiovascular disease. The American Heart Association (2007b) makes it clear that foods high in saturated fat (such as our beloved ice cream) should be replaced with foods low in fat (such as fat-free frozen yogurt). (The American Heart Association provides a website at http://www.deliciousdecisions.org with recipes and alternatives for a heart-healthy diet.)

The main goal of these recommendations is to lower your level of cholesterol because high cholesterol is one risk factor for cardiovascular disease. There is an important difference between two different types of cholesterol, which are defined by their effect on blood flow. Lipoproteins are fatty chemicals attached to proteins carried in the blood. Low-density lipoproteins (LDLs) *cause fatty deposits to accumulate in arteries, impeding blood flow,* whereas high-density lipoproteins (HDLs) *help keep arteries clear and break down LDLs.* It is not so much the overall cholesterol number but the ratio of LDLs to HDLs that matters most in cholesterol screening. High levels of LDLs are a risk factor in cardiovascular disease, and high levels of HDLs are considered a protective factor. Reducing LDL levels is effective in diminishing the risk of cardiovascular disease in adults of all ages; in healthy adults, a high level of LDL (over 160 mg/dL) indicates a higher risk for cardiovascular disease (American Heart Association, 2007b). In contrast, higher levels of HDL are good (in healthy adults, levels at least above 40 mg/dL for men and 50 mg/dL for women). LDL levels can be lowered and HDL levels can be raised through various interventions such as exercise and a high-fiber diet. Weight control is also an important component.

Numerous medications exist for treating cholesterol problems. The most popular of these drugs are from a family of medications called *statins* (e.g., Lipitor, Crestor). These medications lower LDL and moderately increase HDL. Because of potential side effects on liver functioning, patients taking cholesterol-lowering medications should be monitored on a regular basis.

Obesity is a growing health problem related to diet. One good way to assess your own status is to compute your body mass index. Body mass index (BMI) *is a ratio of body weight and height and is related to total body fat.* You can compute BMI as follows:

$$BMI = w/h^2$$

where w = weight in kilograms (or weight in pounds divided by 2.2), and h = height in meters (or inches divided by 39.37).

The National Institutes of Health and the American Heart Association (see http://www.americanheart.org/presenter.jhtml?identifier=3048134 for a convenient calculator) define healthy weight as having a BMI of less than 25. However, this calculation may overestimate body fat in very muscular people and underestimate body fat in those who appear of normal weight but have little muscle mass.

BMI is related to the risk of serious medical conditions and mortality: the higher one's BMI, the higher one's risk (Centers for Disease Control and Prevention, 2007b). Figure 14.4 shows the increased risk for several diseases and mortality associated with increased BMI. Based on these estimates, you may want to lower your BMI if it's above 25. But be careful—lowering your BMI too much may not be healthy either. Very low BMIs may indicate malnutrition, which is also related to increased mortality.

	BMI (Kg/m²⁾)	Obesity Class	Disease Risk * Relative to Normal weight and waist Circumference	
			Men 102 cm (40 in) or less Women 88 cm (35 in) or less	Men > 102 cm (40 in) Women > 88 cm (35 in)
Underweight	< 18.5		-	—
Normal	18.5–24.9		-	—
Overweight	25.0–29.9		Increased	High
Obesity	30.0–34.9	I	High	High
	35.9–39.9	II	Very High	Very High
Extreme obesity	40.0+	III	Extremely High	Extremely High

Figure 14.4 Classification of overweight and obesity by BMI, waist circumference, and associated disease risks.

Source: Centers for Disease Control and Prevention (2007b)

What does it mean to age successfully? Take some time to think about this question for yourself. Develop a thorough list of everything it would take for you to say that you will have aged successfully when the time comes. Then ask this question to several people of different ages and backgrounds. Compare their answers. Do the criteria differ as a function of age or background characteristics? Discuss your findings with others in your class to see whether your results were typical.

Concept Checks

1. What are the most important issues to consider in health promotion and quality of life for older adults?

2. What are the key aspects of a life-span model for maintaining and enhancing competence?

3. What are the major elements in health promotion and disease prevention programs? What are the four types of prevention?

4. What are the key aspects of staying fit and eating right in late life?

14.3 Successful Aging

LEARNING OBJECTIVES

- What is successful aging?

Marie Chen just celebrated her 100th birthday. During the daylong festivities, many people asked her whether she believed she had a good life and had, in a sense, aged successfully. She answered everyone the same way, telling them that she had her health, enough money to live on, and her family. What more could she want?

Marie gives every sign of having aged very well. She's 100 years old, with a loving family, good enough health to live in the community, and enough income to pay her bills. But is there more to it than that? Before you read what researchers have to say about aging successfully, complete the exercise in the Discovering Development feature.

Everyone hopes that his or her later years are ones filled with good health, continued high cognitive and physical competence, and engagement with life. So important and universal are these beliefs that Rowe and Kahn (1998) considered them to be the foundation on which successful aging is built:

> The absence of disease and disability makes it easier to maintain mental and physical function. And maintenance of mental and physical function in turn enables (but does not guarantee) active engagement with life. It is the *combination of all three*—avoidance of disease and disability, maintenance of cognitive and physical function, and sustained engagement with life—that represents the concept of successful aging most fully. (p. 39)

Research participants agree. An extensive study of people's own definitions of successful aging conducted in Canada showed substantial agreement between participants' definitions and Rowe and Kahn's three dimensions (Tate et al., 2003). This three-part view of successful aging has become the central theoretical paradigm in gerontology and geriatrics. Rowe and Kahn's work was grounded in the 10-year, $10-million MacArthur Foundation Study of Successful Aging. On this point, Scheidt, Humphreys, and Yorgason (1999) noted that "at least a hundred studies have shown the efficacy of modifications to environmental and lifestyle factors for increasing the likelihood that older individuals might achieve success under this triarchic definition. So what's not to like?" (p. 277).

Vaillant (2002) proposed a similar model of successful aging which has six criteria rather than three. He proposes three criteria related to health:

- No physical disability at age 75 as rated by a physician
- Good subjective physical health (i.e., no problems with instrumental activities of daily living)
- Length of undisabled life

Vaillant's other three criteria relate to social engagement and productive activity:

- Good mental health
- Objective social support
- Self-rated life satisfaction in eight domains: marriage, income-producing work, children, friendships and social contacts, hobbies, community service activities, religion, and recreation/sports

What is important in Vaillant's model is not only what predicts long life but also what does not. Interestingly, having had long-lived ancestors was important only up to age 60 but not beyond. Stress-related diseases before age 50 were not predictive. Childhood factors that were important predictors of health at midlife did not predict health in late life. Thus Vaillant's research emphasizes that late life has many unique aspects and may not relate to variables that predict health at earlier points in life.

A related view of successful aging is one we encountered several times throughout the book: the selection, optimization, and compensation (SOC) model (Baltes et al., 2006). Recall that in this model *selection* refers to developing and choosing goals, *optimization* to the application and refinement of goal-relevant means or actions, and *compensation* to substitution of means when previous ones are no longer available. The SOC model can be applied to the proactive strategies of life management. From this perspective, it is adaptive (i.e., a sign of successful aging) to set clear goals, to acquire and invest means into pursuing these goals, and to persist despite setbacks or losses. So the point here, in contrast to a coping strategy, which would emphasize a more passive approach, is that taking positive action

to find substitute ways of doing things is adaptive (Freund & Baltes, 2002).

Taking a broad view to defining successful aging permits researchers to establish what is associated with it. Studies indicate that aging successfully is more likely when people have higher levels of education, household income, and personal income (Soong-Nang, Choi, & Kim, 2008).

The increased emphasis on successful aging raises important questions about the quality of life for older adults. For example, researchers have not focused much attention on the issue of whether one can outlive one's *expected* longevity, that is, how long you *think* you will live. For example, if you think you will not live past age 75, perhaps because no one in your family ever has, you may map out your life based on this assumption. But what do you do when you celebrate your 76th birthday? The birthday wasn't planned, and you may feel confused as to what you should be doing with yourself.

Rowe and Kahn's view of successful aging also assumes certain things to be true: that people have the resources to live a healthy life, have access to health care, live in a safe environment, have had life experiences that support individual decision making, and so forth (Holstein & Minkler, 2003). Not all older adults' lives meet these assumptions (Soong-Nang et al., 2008). For example, poverty, widowhood, and differential social expectations based on gender influence whether a person will be able to exert individual control and decisions over health.

© Marcia Keegan

Successful aging is a subjective experience that each person decides individually.

There is another, more serious concern with Rowe and Kahn's model. By equating health and successful aging, they imply that older people who have health problems have not aged successfully (Holstein & Minkler, 2003). By suggesting that people who have disabilities or health limitations signify failure, or at best "usual" aging, the message that only the fit and vigorous are successful is a negative one. It can also inadvertently reinforce the antiaging stereotype for physical beauty as well as a stereotype for the "active older adult."

Holstein and Minkler (2003) point out that we should return to an ancient question: What is the good life—for the whole of life—and what does it take to live a good old age? When she was in her late 60s, the late poet May Sarton (1997) wrote this about the imminence of death: "[P]reparing to die we shed our leaves, without regret, so that the essential person may be alive and well at the end" (p. 230).

Sarton's view may remind you of another, related perspective. Erikson (1982) talked about successful aging as ego integrity, a point made by some researchers as well (Chang et al., 2008). Successful aging may be the ability to pull one's life together from many perspectives into a coherent whole and to be satisfied with it. From this perspective, successful aging is assessed more from the older adult's vantage point than from any other (Bowling, 2007). In this sense, older adults may say that they are aging successfully while others, especially those who adopt a medical model, would not say that about them. But who is to say which perspective is "correct"?

In this book, you have seen a snapshot of what adult development and aging are like today. You have learned about their complexities, myths, and realities. But more than anything else, you have seen what we really know about the pioneers who have blazed the trail ahead of us.

In a short time, it will be your turn to lead the journey. The decisions you make will have an enormous impact on those who will be old: your parents, grandparents, and the people who taught you. The decisions will not be easy ones. But you have an advantage that the pioneers did not. You have the collected knowledge of gerontologists to help. With a continued concerted effort, you will be able to address the problems and meet the challenges that lie ahead. Then, when you yourself are old, you will be able to look back on your life and say, "I lived long—and I prospered."

Summary

14.1 Demographic Trends and Social Policy

What key demographic changes will occur by 2030?

The rapid increase in the number of older adults between now and 2030 means that social policy must take the aging of the population into account. Changing demographics will affect every aspect of life in the United States and in most other countries, including health care and all social service programs.

What are the challenges facing Social Security and Medicare?

Although designed as an income supplement, Social Security has become the primary source of retirement income for most U.S. citizens. The aging of the baby-boom generation will place considerable stress on the financing of the system.

Medicare is the principal health insurance program for adults in the United States over age 65. Cost containment is a major concern, resulting in emphases on health maintenance organizations and home health care.

14.2 Health Issues and Quality of Life

What are the key issues in health promotion and quality of life?

Health promotion will become an increasingly important aspect of health care for older adults. Two models of behavioral change currently drive research: the self-efficacy model and the self-regulation model.

Quality of life, a person's well-being and life satisfaction, is best studied from the perspective of the individual.

What are the major strategies for maintaining and enhancing competence?

A useful framework for enhancing and maintaining competence is the selection, optimization, and compensation (SOC) model.

The life-span approach provides a guide for designing competency-enhancing interventions.

What are the primary considerations in designing health promotion and disease prevention programs?

Effective strategies for health promotion and disease prevention are adopting a healthy lifestyle, staying active cognitively, maintaining a social network, and maintaining good economic habits.

Four levels of prevention are: primary (preventing a disease or condition from occurring), secondary (intervening after a condition has occurred but before it causes impairment), tertiary (avoiding the development of complications), and quaternary (improving functional capacities in people with chronic conditions).

What are the principal lifestyle factors that influence competence?

Maintaining a good exercise program and getting good nutrition are essential for delaying or preventing many negative aspects of physiological aging.

14.3 Successful Aging

What is successful aging?

Successful aging has recently become linked with good health, which is problematic. Two models of successful aging include this notion: Rowe and Kahn's, and Vaillant's. The selection, optimization, and compensation (SOC) model does not have this problem.

Review Questions

14.1 Demographic Trends and Social Policy

What will the population of the United States look like in 2030?

What social policy impact will these changes have?

What pressures are there on Social Security and Medicare?

14.2 Health Issues and Quality of Life

- Why is health promotion likely to become increasingly important?
- What is meant by the term *quality of life?*
- What theoretical framework provides the best approach for enhancing competency?
- What are four effective strategies for health promotion and disease prevention?
- What are the four types of prevention strategies?
- Why are exercise and nutrition important for health promotion and disease prevention?

14.3 Successful Aging

- What is successful aging, and how is it best studied?
- What are the similarities and differences among the Rowe and Kahn, Vaillant, and SOC models?

Integrating Concepts In Development

- Suppose you were brought in as a consultant on aging policy issues to your national government. Based on the demographic information in Chapter 1 and this chapter, what recommendations would you make?
- What trends in health care do you think will emerge based on information in this chapter and in Chapters 3, 4, and 10?
- How do you think older adults will define successful aging in the future?

Key Terms

aerobic exercise Exercise that places moderate stress on the heart by maintaining a pulse rate between 60% and 90% of the person's maximum heart rate.

body mass index (BMI) A ratio of body weight and height that is related to total body fat.

high-density lipoproteins (HDLs) Help keep arteries clear and break down LDLs.

low-density lipoproteins (LDLs) Cause fatty deposits to accumulate in arteries, impeding blood flow.

metabolism How much energy the body needs.

primary prevention Any intervention that prevents a disease or condition from occurring.

quality of life A person's well-being and life satisfaction.

quaternary prevention Efforts specifically aimed at improving the functional capacities of people who have chronic conditions.

secondary prevention Instituted early after a condition has begun (but may not yet have been diagnosed) and before significant impairments have occurred.

tertiary prevention Involves efforts to avoid the development of complications or secondary chronic conditions, manage the pain associated with the primary chronic condition, and sustain life through medical intervention.

Resources

www.cengage.com/psychology/cavanaugh

Visit the companion website, where you will find tutorial quizzes, glossary, flashcards, and more. You can also access the following websites from the companion website.

The Center for Successful Aging, through its educational, research, and service activities, has as its mission the promotion of health and vitality, and the reduction of frailty and disability in later years.

The Centers for Medicare and Medicaid Services site contains much information both for the general public and for professionals interested in more technical background and data. The consumer information section provides a wealth of basic information about how Medicare and Medicaid work and their basic guidelines. In addition, the website provides a superb publication describing in detail the key factors one should use in choosing a nursing home. The booklet gives step-by-step guidelines for what type of facility to consider, important selection factors, nursing home residents' rights, information to collect, and sources of help and other information.

The official website of the Social Security

Administration provides information about Social Security including its history, funding sources, statistics on recipients, and plans for the future.

Readings

Pruchno, R. A., & Smyer, M. A. (2007). *Challenges of an aging society: Ethical dilemmas, policy issues.* Baltimore: Johns Hopkins University Press. A good overview of ethical, social, and political challenges facing the United States as a result of the large number of aging individuals.

Schwalbe, R. (2008). *Sixty, sexy, and successful: A guide for aging male baby boomers.* Westport, CT: Greenwood. An overview of major topics in aging with an eye toward mythbusting. Easy reading.

The Transition Network & Rentsch, G. (2008). *Smart women don't retire—They break free: From working full-time to living full-time.* New York: Grand Central Publishing. A good overview of retirement preparation and setting the stage for successful aging. Easy reading.

References

AARP. (1999). *AARP/Modern Maturity sexuality survey: Summary of findings*. Online document available at http://www.aarp.org/mmaturity/sept_oct99/greatsex.html. Accessed 2005.

Aartsen, M. J., Smits, C. H. M., van Tilburg, T., Knipscheer, K. C. P. M., & Deeg, D. J. H. (2002). Activity in older adults: Cause or consequence of cognitive functioning? A longitudinal study on everyday activities and cognitive performance in older adults. *Journals of Gerontology: Psychological Sciences, 57B,* P153–P162.

Abengozar, M. C., Bueno, B., & Vega, J. L. (1999). Intervention on attitudes toward death along the life span. *Educational Gerontology, 25,* 435–447.

Aberson, C. L., Shoemaker, C., & Tomolillo, C. (2004). The role of interethnic friendships. *Journal of Social Psychology, 144,* 335–347.

Abraham, M. (2000). Isolation as a form of marital violence: The South Asian immigrant experience. *Journal of Social Distress and the Homeless, 9,* 221–236.

Ackerman, S., Zuroff, D. C., & Moskowitz, D. S. (2000). Generativity in midlife and young adults: Links to agency, communion, and subjective well-being. *International Journal of Aging and Human Development, 50,* 17–41.

Adams, C., Labouvie-Vief, G., Hakim-Larson, J., DeVoe, M., & Hayden, M. (1988). *Modes of thinking and problem solving: Developmental transitions from pre-adolescence to middle-adulthood.* Unpublished manuscript, Lane Community College, Eugene, OR.

Adams, C., Labouvie-Vief, G., Hobart, C. J., & Dorosz, M. (1990). Adult age group differences in story recall style. *Journals of Gerontology: Psychological Sciences, 45,* P17–P27.

Adams, C., Smith, M. C., Gaden, C. P., & Perlmutter, M. (1994). Memory in a storytelling context: A story recalled by young and old adults. Unpublished manuscript, Lane Community College, Eugene, OR.

Adams, C., Smith, M. C., Pasupathi, M., & Vitolo, L. (2002). Social context effects on story recall in older and younger women: Does the listener make a difference? *Journals of Gerontology: Psychological Sciences, 57B,* P28–P40.

Adams, R. D. (1980). Morphological aspects of aging in the human nervous system. In J. E. Birren & R. B. Sloane (Eds.), *Handbook of mental health and aging* (pp. 149–160). Englewood Cliffs, NJ: Prentice Hall.

Adams, R. G., Blieszner, R., & de Vries, B. (2000). Definitions of friendship in the third age: Age, gender, and study location effects. *Journal of Aging Studies, 14,* 117–133.

Adams, R. G., & Ueno, K. (2006). Middle-aged and older adult men's friendships. In V. H. Bedford, & B. Formaniak Turner (Eds.), *Men in relationships: A new look from a life course perspective* (pp. 103–124). New York: Springer Publishing.

Adams, V. H., & Hummert, M. L. (2004). African American stereotypes of older adults. Manuscript in preparation. University of Kansas, Lawrence, KS.

Adelman, C. (1991). *Women at thirtysomething: Paradoxes of attainment.* Washington, DC: U.S. Department of Education, Office of Educational Research, Office of Research.

Adler, L. L. (2001). Women and gender roles. In L. L. Adler & U. P. Gielen (Eds.), *Cross-cultural topics on psychology* (2nd ed., pp. 103–114). Westport, CT: Praeger/Greenwood.

Adler, S., & Aranya, N. (1984). A comparison of the work needs, attitudes, and preferences of professional accounts at different career stages. *Journal of Vocational Behavior, 25,* 574–580.

Adler, W. H., & Nagel, J. E. (1994). Clinical immunology and aging. In W. R. Hazzard, E. L. Bierman, J. P. Blass, W. H. Ettinger, & J. B. Halter (Eds.), *Principles of geriatric medicine and gerontology* (3rd ed., pp. 67–75). New York: McGraw-Hill.

Adlersberg, M., & Thorne, S. (1990). Emerging from the chrysalis: Older women in transition. *Journal of Gerontological Social Work, 16,* 4–8.

Administration on Aging. (1999). Number and percent of persons reporting problems with two or more activities of daily living (ADLs), by age, race, gender, poverty, living arrangements, region, and area of residence, 1994–1995. Online document available at http://www.aoa.dhhs.gov/aoa/stats/Disabilities/2plusadls.html. Accessed 2004.

Administration on Aging. (2001). *Americans with disabilities: 1997.* Retrieved March 15, 2009, from http://www.aoa.gov/prof/Statistics/disabilities_data/97sipp-disabiliestable.pdf.

Administration on Aging. (2003a). *Facts and figures: Statistics on minority aging in the U.S.* Online document available at http://www.aoa.gov/prof/Statistics/minority_aging/facts_minority_aging.asp#PopulationbyRace. Accessed September 1, 2003.

Administration on Aging. (2003b). *Older population by age: 1900–2050.* Online document available at http://www.aoa.gov/prof/Statistics/online_stat_data/AgePop2050.asp. Accessed September 1, 2003.

Administration on Aging. (2003c). *A profile of older Americans: 2002.* Online document available at http://www.aoa.gov/prof/Statistics/profile/11.asp. Accessed September 1, 2003.

Adolphs, R. (1999). The human amygdala and emotion. *The Neuroscientist, 5,* 125–137.

AgingStats.gov. (2008a). *Economics.* Retrieved December 27, 2008, from http://agingstats.gov/agingstatsdotnet/Main_Site/Data/2008_Documents/Economics.aspx.

AgingStats.gov. (2008b). *Older Americans 2008: Key indicators of well-being.* Retrieved March 15, 2009, from http://agingstats.gov/agingstatsdotnet/Main_Site/Data/2008_Documents/tables/Tables.aspx.

Agrawal, Y., Platz, E. A., & Niparko, J. K. (2008). Prevalence of hearing loss and differences by demographic characteristics among US adults. *Archives of Internal Medicine, 168,* 1522–1530.

AGS Foundation for Health in Aging. (2007). *Tips for avoiding caregiver burnout.* Retrieved March 15, 2009, from http://www.healthinaging.org/public_education/tipsheet_caregiver.pdf.

Ajrouch, K. (2008). Introduction to a special issue of *Research in Human Development:* Aging families in global context. *Research in Human Development, 5,* 1–5.

Akamigbo, A. B., & Wolinsky, F. D. (2007). New evidence of racial differences in access and their effects on the use of nursing homes among older adults. *Medical Care, 45,* 672–679.

Alain, C., McDonald, K. L., Ostroff, J. M., & Schneider, B. (2004). Aging: A switch from automatic to controlled processing of sounds? *Psychology and Aging, 19,* 125–133.

Albeck, S., & Kaydar, D. (2002). Divorced mothers: Their network of friends pre- and post-divorce. *Journal of Divorce and Remarriage, 36,* 111–118.

Albert, S. M. (1997). Assessing health-related quality of life in chronic care populations. *Journal of Mental Health and Aging, 3,* 101–118.

Aldwin, C. M. (1999). *Stress, coping, and development: An integrative approach.* New York: Guilford.

Aldwin, C. M., & Gilmer, D. F. (2004). *Health, illness, and optimal aging: Biological and psychosocial perspectives.* Thousand Oaks, CA: Sage.

Aldwin, C. M., Sutton, K. J., Chiara, G., & Spiro, A., III. (1996). Age differences in stress, coping, and appraisal: Findings from the Normative Aging Study. *Journals of Gerontology: Psychological Sciences, 51B,* P179–P188.

Aldwin, C. M., & Yancura, L. A. (2004). Coping and health: A comparison of the stress and trauma literatures. In P. P. Schnurr & B. L. Green (Eds.), *Trauma and health: Physical health consequences of exposure to extreme stress.* Washington, DC: American Psychological Association.

Alegría, M., Chatterji, P., Wells, K., Cao, Z., Chen, C.-N., Takeuchi, D., Jackson, J., & Meng, X.-L. (2008). Disparity in depression treatment among racial and ethnic minority populations in the United States. *Psychiatric Services, 59,* 1264–1272.

Allaire, J. C., & Marsiske, M. (1999). Everyday cognition: Age and intellectual ability correlates. *Psychology and Aging, 14,* 627–644.

Allaire, J. C., & Marsiske, M. (2002). Well- and ill-defined measures of everyday cognition: Relationship to older adults' intellectual ability and functional status. *Psychology and Aging, 17,* 101–115.

Allaire, J. C., & Willis, S. L. (2006). Competence in everyday activities as a predictor of cognitive risk and morbidity. *Aging, Neuropsychology, and Cognition, 13,* 207–224.

Allemand, M., Zimprich, D., & Hendriks, A. A. J. (2008). Age differences in five personality domains across the life span. *Developmental Psychology, 44*(3), 758–770.

Allen, C. (2003). Death and ethnicity: A psychocultural study twenty-five years later. *Dissertation Abstracts International: Section B: The Sciences and Engineering, 63*(12-B), 6145.

Allen, K. R., & Chin-Sang, V. (1990). A lifetime of work: The context and meanings of leisure for aging black women. *The Gerontologist, 30,* 734–740.

Allen, P. A., Madden, D. J., & Slane, S. (1995). Visual world encoding and the effect of adult age and word frequency. In P. A. Allen & T. R. Bashore (Eds.), *Age differences in word and language processes* (pp. 30–71). Amsterdam: North-Holland.

Allen, P. A., Sliwinski, M., Bowie, T., & Madden, D. J. (2002). Differential age effects in semantic and episodic memory. *Journals of Gerontology: Psychological Sciences, 57B,* P173–P186.

Allen, R. S., DeLaine, S. R., Chaplin, W. F., Marson, D. C., Bourgeois, M. S., Kijkstra, K., & Burgio, L. D. (2003). Advance care planning in nursing homes: Correlates of capacity and possession of advance directives. *The Gerontologist, 43,* 309–317.

Allen, R. S., & Shuster, J. L. (2002). The role of proxies in treatment decisions: Evaluating functional capacity to consent to end-of-life treatments within a family context. *Behavioral Sciences and the Law, 20,* 235–252.

Allen, T. D., & Eby, L. T. (2004). Factors related to mentor reports of mentoring functions provided: Gender and relational characteristics. *Sex Roles, 50,* 129–139.

Allen, T. D., Eby, L. T., Poteet, M. L., Lentz, E., & Lima, L. (2004). Career benefits associated with mentoring for proteges: A meta-analysis. *Journal of Applied Psychology, 89,* 127–136.

Allen-Burge, R., & Haley, W. E. (1997). Individual differences and surrogate medical decisions: Differing preferences for life-sustaining treatments. *Aging and Mental Health, 1,* 121–131.

Allen-Burge, R., Storandt, M., Kincherf, D. A., & Rubin, E. H. (1994). Sex differences in the sensitivity of two self-report depression scales in older depressed inpatients. *Psychology and Aging, 9,* 443–445.

Alley, J. L. (2004). The potential meaning of the grandparent-grandchild relationship as perceived by young adults: An exploratory study. *Dissertation Abstracts International: Section B: The Sciences & Engineering, 65*(3-B), 1536.

Almendarez, B. L. (2008). Mexican American elders and nursing home transition. *Dissertation Abstracts International: Section B: The Sciences and Engineering, 68*(7-B), 4384.

Alspaugh, M. E. L., Stephens, M. A. P., Townsend, A. L., Zarit, S. H., & Greene, R. (1999). Longitudinal patterns of risk for depression in dementia caregivers: Objective and subjective primary stress as predictors. *Psychology and Aging, 14,* 34–43.

Alzheimer's Association. (1999). *Statistics/prevalence.* Online document available at http://www.alz.org/facts/rstats.htm. Accessed 2005.

Alzheimer's Association. (2008a). 2008 Alzheimer's disease facts and figures. Retrieved October 26, 2008, from http://www.alz.org/national/documents/report_alzfactsfigures 2008.pdf.

Amato, P. R., & Cheadle, J. (2005). The long reach of divorce: Divorce and child well-being across three generations. *Journal of Marriage & Family, 67,* 191–206.

Amato, P. R., & Previti, D. (2003). People's reasons for divorcing: Gender, social class, the life course, and adjustment. *Journal of Family Issues, 24,* 602–626.

American Association of Retired Persons [AARP]. (1999a). *AARP/Modern Maturity sexuality survey: Summary of findings.* Online document available at http://www.aarp.org/mmaturity/sept_oct99/greatsex.html. Accessed 2005.

American Association of Retired Persons [AARP]. (1999b). *Surfing in cyberspace.* Online document available at http://www.aarp.org/ampie/res0799.html. Accessed 2005.

American Bar Association/American Psychological Association. (2005). *Assessment of older adults with diminished capacity: A handbook for lawyers.* Retrieved October 23, 2008, from http://apa.org/pi/aging/capacity_lawyers_handbook.pdf.

American Bar Association/American Psychological Association. (2006). *Judicial determination of capacity of older adults in guardianship proceedings.* Retrieved October 23, 2008, from http://www.apa.org/pi/aging/capacity_judges_handbook.pdf.

American Bar Association/American Psychological Association. (2008). *Assessment of older adults with diminished capacity: A handbook for psychologists.* Retrieved October 23, 2008, from http://www.apa.org/pi/aging/capacity_psychologist_handbook.pdf.

American Cancer Society. (1999). *The prostate cancer resource center.* Online document available at http://www3.cancer.org/cancerinfo/res_home.asp?ct36. Accessed 2005.

American Cancer Society. (2003). *Statistics for 2003.* Online document available at http://www.cancer.org/docroot/STT/stt_0.asp. Accessed November 16, 2003.

American Cancer Society. (2008a). *Statistics 2008.* Retrieved February 24, 2009, from http://www.cancer.org/docroot/stt/stt_0.asp?from=fast.

American Cancer Society. (2008b). *Cancer facts and figures 2008.* Retrieved September 28, 2008, from http://www.cancer.org/downloads/STT/2008CAFFfinalsecured.pdf.

American Cancer Society. (2008b). *Cancer prevention.* Retrieved February 24, 2009, from http://www.cancer.org/docroot/PED/ped_1.asp.

American Cancer Society. (2008c). *Cigarette smoking.* Retrieved September 28, 2008, from http://www.cancer.org/docroot/PED/content/PED_10_2X_Cigarette_Smoking.asp.

American Cancer Society. (2008d). *American Cancer Society guidelines for the early detection of cancer.* Retrieved September 28, 2008, from http://www.cancer.org/docroot/PED/content/PED_2_3X_ACS_Cancer_Detection_Guidelines_36.asp?sitearea=PED.

American Cancer Society. (2008e). *Detailed guide: Prostate cancer.* Retrieved September 28, 2008, from http://www.cancer.org/docroot/CRI/CRI_2_3x.asp?dt=36.

American Cancer Society and National Comprehensive Cancer Network. (1999). *Prostate cancer: Treatment guidelines for patients* (Version 1, 1999). Online document available at http://www.cancer.org. Accessed 2005.

American Cancer Society and National Comprehensive Cancer Network. (2007). *Prostate cancer: Treatment guidelines for patients.* Retrieved September 28, 2008, from http://www.nccn.org/patients/patient_gls/_english/pdf/NCCN%20Prostate%20Guidelines.pdf.

American Council on Education. (1997). Many college graduates participate in training courses to improve their job skills. *Higher Education and National Affairs, 46*(19), 3.

American Geriatrics Society. (2007). *Position statement: Informed consent for research on human subjects with dementia.* Retrieved August 17, 2008, from http://www.americangeriatrics.org/products/positionpapers/infconsent.shtml.

American Geriatrics Society Ethics Committee. (1996). Making treatment decisions for incapacitated older adults without advance directives. *Journal of the American Geriatrics Society, 44,* 986–987.

American Heart Association. (1999). *Heart and stroke A–Z guide.* Online document available at http://www.americanheart.org. Accessed 2004.

American Heart Association. (2004). *Heart disease and stroke statistics—2004 update.* Online document available at http://www.americanheart.org/downloadable/heart/1079736729696HDSStats2004UpdateREV3-19-04.pdf. Accessed April 3, 2004.

American Heart Association. (2007). *Heart disease and stroke statistics—2008 update.* Retrieved September 3, 2008, from http://www.americanheart.org/presenter.jhtml?identifier=3054076.

American Heart Association. (2007b). *What do my cholesterol levels mean?* Retrieved March 15, 2009, from http://www.americanheart.org/downloadable/heart/119618151049911%20CholLevels%209_07.pdf.

American Heart Association. (2008a). *Bridging the gap: CVD health disparities.* Retrieved September 3, 2008, from http://www.americanheart.org/downloadable/heart/1190403824758Disparities%20Fact%20Sheet%209-07%20final.pdf.

American Heart Association. (2008b). *Tissue plasminogen activator.* Retrieved September 7, 2008, from http://www.americanheart.org/presenter.jhtml?identifier=4751.

American Heart Association. (2008c). *Blood pressure.* Retrieved September 7, 2008, from http://www.americanheart.org/presenter.jhtml?identifier=4473.

American Heart Association. (2008d). *Sodium.* Retrieved September 7, 2008, from http://www.americanheart.org/presenter.jhtml?identifier=4708.

American Lung Association. (1998). *Trends in chronic bronchitis and emphysema: Morbidity and mortality.* Online document available at http://www.lungusa.org/data/index.html. Accessed 2004.

American Lung Association. (2008a). *Chronic obstructive pulmonary disease (COPD) fact sheet.* Retrieved September 7, 2008, from http://www.lungusa.org/site/apps/nlnet/content3.aspx?c=dvLUK9O0E&b=2058829&content_id={EE451F66-996B-4C23-874D-BF66586196FF}&notoc=1.

American Medical Association. (2007). *About the AMA and pain management.* Retrieved May 31, 2008, from http://www.ama-assn.org/ama/pub/category/11541.html.

American Medical Association. (2009). *Clinical practice improvement.* Retrieved November 1, 2009 form http://www.ama-assn.org/ama/pub/physician-resources/clinical-practice-improvement.shtml.

American Psychiatric Association. (1994). *Diagnostic and statistical manual of mental disorders* (4th ed. [DSM-IV]). Washington, DC: Author.

American Psychiatric Association. (2000). *Diagnostic and statistical manual-IV-TR*. Washington, DC: Author.

Amodio, D. M., & Frith, C. D. (2006). Meeting of minds: The medial frontal cortex and social cognition. *Nature Reviews Neuroscience, 7*, 268–277.

Andel, R., Crowe, M., Pedersen, N. L., Fratiglioni, L., Johansson, B., & Gatz, M. (2008). Physical exercise at midlife and risk of dementia three decades later: A population-based study of Swedish twins. *Journals of Gerontology: Biological Sciences and Medical Sciences, 63A*, 62–66.

Andersen, G. J., Cisneros, J., Saidpour, A., & Atchley, P. (2000). Age-related differences in collision detection during deceleration. *Psychology and Aging, 15*, 241–252.

Anderson, A. K., Christoff, K., Panitz, D. A., De Rosa, E., & Gabrieli, J. D. E. (2003). Neural correlates of the automatic processing of threat facial signals. *Journal of Neuroscience, 23*,5627–5633.

Anderson, D. M., Morgan, B. L., & Wilson, J. B. (2002). Perceptions of family-friendly policies: University versus corporate employees. *Journal of Family and Economic Issues, 23*, 73–92.

Anderson, E. R., Greene, S. M., Walker, L., Malerba, C., Forgatch, M. S., & DeGarmo, D. S. (2004). Ready to take a chance again: Transitions into dating among divorced parents. *Journal of Divorce & Remarriage, 40*, 61–75.

Anderson, N. D., Craik, F. I. M., & Naveh-Benjamin, M. (1998). The attentional demands of encoding and retrieval in younger and older adults: I. Evidence from divided attention costs. *Psychology and Aging, 13*, 405–423.

Anderson, N. D., Iidaka, T., Cabeza, R., Kapur, S., McIntosh, A. R., & Craik, F. I. M. (2000). The effects of divided attention on encoding- and retrieval-related brain activity: A PET study of younger and older adults. *Journal of Cognitive Neuroscience, 12*, 775–792.

Anderson, V. D. (2007). Religiosity as it shapes parenting processes in preadolescence: A contextualized process model. *Dissertation Abstracts International: Section B: The Sciences and Engineering, 67(9-B)*, 5439.

Anderson, W. T. (1997). Dying and death in aging intergenerational families. In T. D. Hargrave & S. M. Hanna (Eds.), *The aging family* (pp. 270–291). New York: Brunner/Mazel.

Andreoletti, C., & Lachman, M. E. (2004). Susceptibility and resilience to memory aging stereotypes: Education matters more than age. *Experimental Aging Research, 30*,129–148.

Aneshensel, C. S., Pearlin, L. I., Mullan, J. T., Zarit, S. H., & Whitlach, C. J. (1995). *Profiles in caregiving: The unexpected career*. San Diego: Academic Press.

Anstey, K. J., Hofer, S. M., & Luszcz, M. A. (2003). A latent growth curve analysis of late-life sensory and cognitive function over 8 years: Evidence for specific and common factors underlying change. *Psychology and Aging, 18*, 714–726.

Anstey, K. J., & Luszcz, M. A. (2002). Mortality risk varies according to gender and change in depressive status in very old adults. *Psychosomatic Medicine, 64*, 880–888.

Antonovsky, A., & Sagy, S. (1990). Confronting developmental tasks in the retirement transition. *The Gerontologist, 30*, 362–368.

Antonucci, T. C. (1985). Personal characteristics, social support, and social behavior. In R. H. Binstock & E. Shanas (Eds.), *Handbook of aging and the social sciences* (2nd ed., pp. 94–128). New York: Van Nostrand Reinhold.

Antonucci, T. C., Akiyama, H., & Lansford, J. E. (1998). Negative effects of close social relations. *Family Relations, 47*, 379–384.

Appleby, J. (2006). Debate surrounds end of life health care costs. *USA Today*. Retrieved December 21, 2008, from http://www.usatoday.com/money/industries/health/2006-10-18-end-of-life-costs_x.htm.

Appleton, M., & Henschell, T. (1995). *At home with terminal illness: A family guide to hospice in the home*. Englewood Cliffs, NJ: Prentice Hall.

Aranda, M. P., & Knight, B. G. (1997). The influence of ethnicity and culture on the caregiver stress and coping process: A sociocultural review and analysis. *The Gerontologist, 37*, 342–354.

Araujo, A. B., Mohr, B. A., & McKinlay, J. B. (2004). Changes in sexual function in middle-aged and older men: Longitudinal data from the Massachusetts Aging Study. *Journal of the American Geriatrics Society, 52*, 1502–1509.

Arbona, C. (1990). Career counseling research and Hispanics: A review of the literature. *Counseling Psychologist, 18*, 300–323.

Arbuckle, T. Y., Maag, U., Pushkar, D., & Chaikleson, J. S. (1998). Individual differences in trajectory of intellect development over 45 years of adulthood. *Psychology and Aging, 13*, 663–675.

Arias, E. (2006). *United States life tables 2003*. Retrieved March 15, 2009, from http://www.cdc.gov/nchs/data/nvsr/nvsr54/nvsr54_14.pdf.

Armstrong-Stassen, M. (2001). Reactions of older employees to organizational downsizing: The role of gender, job level, and time. *Journals of Gerontology: Psychological Sciences, 56B*, P234–P243.

Arndt, J., & Vess, M. (2008). Tales from existential oceans: Terror management theory and how the awareness of our mortality affects us all. *Social and Personality Psychology Compass, 2*, 909–928.

Arnett, J. J. (2007). Socialization in emerging adulthood: From the family to the wider world, from socialization to self-socialization. In Grusec, J. E., & Hastings, P. D. (Eds.), *Handbook of socialization: Theory and research* (pp. 208–231). New York: Guilford Press.

Arnold, M. (2008). Polypharmacy and older adults: A role for psychology and psychologists. *Professional Psychology: Research and Practice, 38*, 283–289.

Artistico, D., Cervone, D., & Pezzuti, L. (2003). Perceived self-efficacy and everyday problem solving among young and older adults. *Psychology and Aging, 18*, 68–79.

Aryee, S. (1993). Dual-earner couples in Singapore: An examination of work and nonwork sources of their experienced burnout. *Human Relations, 46*, 1441–1468.

Aryee, S., & Luk, V. (1996). Work and nonwork influences on the career satisfaction of dual-earner couples. *Journal of Vocational Behavior, 49*, 38–52.

Ashman, R. D., Bishu, R. R., Foster, B. G., & McCoy, P. T. (1994). Counter measures to improve the driving performance of older drivers. *Educational Gerontology, 20*, 567–577.

Assanangkornchai, S., Tangboonngam, S., Samangsri, N., & Edwards, J. G. (2007). A Thai community's anniversary reaction to a major catastrophe. *Stress and Health: Journal of the International Society for the Investigation of Stress, 23*, 43–50.

Atchley, R. C. (1982). Retirement as a social institution. *American Review of Sociology, 8*, 263–287.

Atchley, R. C. (1996). Retirement. In J. E. Birren (Ed.), *Encyclopedia of gerontology: Age, aging, and the aged* (Vol. 2, pp. 437–449). San Diego: Academic Press.

Attig, T. (1996). *How we grieve: Relearning the world*. New York: Oxford University Press.

Aubert, G., & Lansdorp, P. M. (2008). Telomeres and aging. *Physiological Reviews, 88*, 557–579.

Avis, N. E. (1999). Women's health at midlife. In S. L. Willis & J. D. Reid (Eds.), *Life in the middle: Psychological and social development in middle age* (pp. 105–146). San Diego: Academic Press.

Avolio B. J., & Sosik J. J. (1999). A life-span memory framework for assessing the impact of work on white-collar workers. In S. L. Willis & J. D. Reid (Eds.), *Life in the middle: Psychological and social development in middle age* (pp. 249–274). San Diego: Academic Press.

Ayers, M. S., & Reder, L. M. (1988). A theoretical review of the misinformation effect: Predictions from an activation-based memory model. *Psychonomic Bulletin and Review, 5*, 1–21.

Bäckman, L., & Forsell, Y. (1994). Episodic memory functioning in a common-based sample of older adults with major depression: Utilization of cognitive support. *Journal of Abnormal Psychology, 103*, 361–370.

Bäckman, L., Ginovart, N., Dixon, R. A., Wahlin, T. B., Wahlin, Å ., Halldin, C., et al. (2000). Age-related cognitive deficits mediated by changes in striatal dopamine system. *American Journal of Psychiatry, 157*, 635–637.

Bäckman, L., Hassing, L., Forsell, Y., & Viitanen, M. (1996). Episodic remembering in a population-based sample of nonagenarians: Does major depression exacerbate the memory deficits seen in Alzheimer's disease? *Psychology and Aging, 11*, 649–657.

Bäckman, L., & Larsson, M. (1992). Recall of organizable words and objects in adulthood: Influences of instructions, retention interval, and retrieval cues. *Journals of Gerontology: Psychological Sciences, 47*, P273–P278.

Bäckman, L. Nybert, L., Lindenberger, U., Li, S-C., & Farde, L. (2006). The correlative triad among aging, dopamine, and cognition: Current status and future prospects. *Neuroscience and Behavioral Reviews, 30*, 791–807.

Bäckman, L., Small, B. J., & Wahlin, A. (2000). Aging and memory: Cognitive and biological perspectives. In J. E. Birren & K. W. Schaie (Eds.), *Handbook of the psychology of aging* (5th ed., pp. 349–377). San Diego: Academic Press.

Baek, J. (2005). Individual variations in family caregiving over the caregiving period. *Dissertation Abstracts International: Section B: The Sciences and Engineering, 65(B)*, 3769.

Bagwell, C. L., Bender, S. E., Andreassi, C. L., Kinoshita, T. L., Montarello, S. A., & Muller, J. G. (2005). Friendship quality and perceived relationship changes predict psychosocial adjustment in early adulthood. *Journal of Social & Personal Relationships, 22*, 235–254.

Bailey, D., & Kurland, N. (2002). A review of telework research: Findings, new directions, and lessons for study of modern work. *Journal of Organizational Behavior, 23*, 383–400.

Bakchine, S., & Loft, H. (2008). Memantine treatment in patients with mild to moderate Alzheimer's disease: Results of a randomised, double-blind, placebo-controlled 6-month study. *Journal of Alzheimer's Disease, 13*, 97–107.

Baldassar, L., Baldock, C. V., & Wilding, R. (2007). *Families caring across borders: Migration, ageing and transnational caregiving*. New York: Palgrave Macmillan.

Balk, D. E. (1996). Attachment and the reactions of bereaved college students: A longitudinal study. In D. Klass, P. R. Silverman, & S. L. Nickman (Eds.), *Continuing bonds: New understandings of grief* (pp. 311–328). Washington, DC: Taylor & Francis.

Ball, J. F. (1976–1977). Widow's grief: The impact of age and mode of death. *Omega: Journal of Death and Dying, 7,* 307–333.

Ball, K. (1997). Enhancing mobility in the elderly: Attentional interventions for driving. Assessment and intervention issues across the lifespan. Mahwah, NJ: Erlbaum.

Ball, K., Beard, B. L., Roenker, D. L., Miller, R. L., & Griggs, D. S. (1988). Age and visual search: Expanding the useful field of view. *Journal of the Optical Society of America, A, 5,* 2210–2219.

Ball, K., Berch, D. B., Helmers, K. F., Jobe, J. B., Leveck, M. D., Marsiske, M., et al. (2002). Effects of cognitive training interventions with older adults: A randomized controlled trial. *JAMA [Journal of the American Medical Association], 288,* 2271–2281.

Ball, K., & Owsley, C. (1991). Identifying correlates of accident involvement for the older driver. *Human Factors, 33,* 583–595.

Ball, K., & Owsley, C. (2000). Increasing mobility and reducing accidents of older drivers. In K. W. Schaie & M. Pietrucha (Eds.), *Mobility and transportation in the elderly* (pp. 213–250). New York: Springer.

Ball, K., Owsley, C., Sloane, M. E., Roenker, D. L., & Bruni, J. R. (1993). Visual attention problems as a predictor of vehicle accidents among older drivers. *Investigative Ophthalmology and Visual Science, 34,* 3110–3123.

Ball, K., & Rebok, G. W. (1994). Evaluating the driving ability of older adults. *Journal of Applied Gerontology, 13,* 20–38.

Baltes, M. M. (1994). Aging well and institutional living: A paradox? In R. P. Abeles, H. C. Gift, & M. G. Ory (Eds.), *Aging and quality of life* (pp. 185–201). New York: Springer.

Baltes, M. M., Maas, I., Wihms, H. U., Borchett, M., & Little, T. D. (1999a). Everyday competence in old and very old age: Theoretical considerations and empirical findings. In P. B. Baltes & K. U. Mayer (Eds.), *The Berlin aging study* (pp. 384–402). New York: Cambridge University Press.

Baltes, P. B., Staudinger, U. M., & Lindenberger, U. (1999b). Lifespan psychology: Theory and application to intellectual functioning. *Annual Review of Psychology, 50,* 471–507.

Baltes, P. B. (1987). Theoretical propositions of life-span developmental psychology: On the dynamics between growth and decline. *Developmental Psychology, 23,* 611–626.

Baltes, P. B. (1993). The aging mind: Potential and limits. *The Gerontologist, 33,* 580–594.

Baltes, P. B. (1997). On the incomplete architecture of human ontogeny: Selection, optimization, and compensation as foundations of developmental theory. *American Psychologist, 52,* 366–380.

Baltes, P. B., & Baltes, M. M. (1990). Psychological perspectives on successful aging: The model of selective optimization with compensation. In P. B. Baltes & M. M. Baltes (Eds.), *Successful aging: Perspectives from the behavioral sciences* (pp. 1–27). New York: Cambridge University Press.

Baltes, P. B., & Kliegl, R. (1992). Further testing of limits of cognitive plasticity: Negative age differences in mnemonic skill are robust. *Developmental Psychology, 28,* 121–125.

Baltes, P. B., & Kunzmann, U. (2003). Wisdom. *Psychologist, 16,* 131–133.

Baltes, P. B., & Lindenberger, U. (1997). Emergence of a powerful connection between sensory and cognitive function across the adult life span: A new window to the study. *Psychology and Aging, 12,* 12–21.

Baltes, P. B., Lindenberger, U., & Staudinger, U. M. (1998). Life-span theory in developmental psychology. In R. M. Lerner (Ed.), *Handbook of child psychology: Vol. 1. Theoretical models of human development* (5th ed., pp. 1029–1143). New York: Wiley.

Baltes, P. B., Lindenberger, U., & Staudinger, U. M. (2006). Life span theory in developmental psychology. In R. M. Lerner & W. Damon (Eds.), *Handbook of child psychology: Vol. 1, Theoretical models of human development* (6th ed., pp. 569–664). Hoboken, NJ: Wiley.

Baltes, P. B., & Schaie, K. W. (1974). Aging and IQ: The myth of the twilight years. *Psychology Today, 7,* 35–40.

Baltes, P. B., & Smith, J. (1990). The psychology of wisdom and its ontogenesis. In R. J. Sternberg (Ed.), *Wisdom: Its nature, origins, and development* (pp. 87–120). New York: Cambridge University Press.

Baltes, P. B., & Staudinger, U. M. (2000) Wisdom: A metaheuristic (pragmatic) to orchestrate mind and virtue toward excellence. *American Psychologist, 55,* 122–136.

Baltes, P. B., Staudinger, U. M., Maercker, A., & Smith, J. (1995). People nominated as wise: A comparative study of wisdom-related knowledge. *Psychology and Aging, 10,* 155–166.

Baltes, P. B., & Willis, S. L. (1982). Enhancement (plasticity) of intellectual functioning: Penn State's Adult Development and Enrichment Project (ADEPT). In F. I. M. Craik & S. Trehub (Eds.), *Aging and cognitive processes* (pp. 353–389). New York: Plenum.

Banerjee, A. V., & Duflo, E. (2008). Aging and death under a dollar a day. *National Bureau of Economic Research Working Paper No. 13758.*

Banger, M. (2003). Affective syndrome during perimenopause. *Maturitas, 41*(Suppl. I), S13–S18.

Barfield, R. E., & Morgan, J. N. (1978). Trends in satisfaction with retirement. *The Gerontologist, 18,* 19–23.

Bargh, J. A. (1997). The automaticity of everyday life. In R. S. Wyer, Jr. (Ed.), *Advances in social cognition* (Vol. 10, pp. 1–61). Mahwah, NJ: Erlbaum.

Bargh, J. A., Chen, M., & Burrows, L. (1996). Automaticity of social behavior: Direct effects of trait construct and stereotype activation on action. *Journal of Personality and Social Psychology, 71,* 230–244.

Barja, G. (2008). The gene cluster hypothesis of aging and longevity. *Biogerontology, 9,* 57–66.

Baron, J. N., & Bielby, W. T. (1985). Organizational barriers to gender equality: Sex segregation of jobs and opportunities. In A. S. Rossi (Ed.), *Gender and the life course* (pp. 233–251). New York: Aldine de Gruyter.

Barrett, A. E., & Lynch, S. M. (1999). Caregiving networks of elderly persons: Variation by marital status. *The Gerontologist, 39,* 695–704.

Barrick, M. R., Mount, M. K., & Gupta, R. (2003). Meta-analysis of the relationship between the five-factor model of personality and Holland's occupational types. *Personnel Psychology, 56,* 45–74.

Barry, L. C., Allore, H. G., Guo, Z., Bruce, M. L., & Gill, T. M. (2008). Higher burden of depression among older women: the Effect of onset, persistence and mortality over time. *Archives of General Psychiatry, 65,* 172–178.

Barsalou, L. W. (1998). The content and organization of autobiographical memories. In U. Neisser & E. Winograd (Eds.), *Remembering reconsidered: Ecological and traditional approaches to the study of memory* (pp. 193–243). Cambridge, UK: Cambridge University Press.

Bathum, L., Christiansen, L., Jeune, B., Vaupel, J., McGue, M., & Christensen, K. (2006). Apolipoprotein E genotypes: Relationship to cognitive functioning, cognitive decline, and survival in nonagenarians. *Journal of the American Geriatrics Society, 54,* 654–658.

Baruch, G. (1984). The psychological well-being of women in the middle years. In G. Baruch & J. Brooks-Gunn (Eds.), *Women in midlife* (pp. 317–364). New York: Plenum.

Basak, C., Boot, W. R., Voss, M. W., & Kramer, A. F. (2008). Can training in a real-time strategy videogame attenuate cognitive decline in older adults? *Psychology and Aging, 23*(4), 765–777.

Bashore, T. R., Ridderinkhof, K. R., & Van Der Molen, M. W. (1997). The decline of cognitive processing in old age. *Current Directions in Psychological Science, 6,* 163–169.

Basseches, M. (1984). Dialectical thinking and adult development. Norwood, NJ: Ablex.

Bastida, E., & Gonzalez, G. (1995). Mental health status and needs of the Hispanic elderly: A cross-cultural analysis. In D. K. Padgett (Ed.), *Handbook on ethnicity, aging, and mental health* (pp. 99–112). Westport, CT: Greenwood.

Bastin, C., & Meulemans, T. (2002). Are time-based and event-based prospective memory affected by normal aging in the same way? *Current Psychology Letters: Behaviour, Brain and Cognition, 7,* 105–121.

Baugh, S. G., Lankau, M. J., & Scandura, T. A. (1996). An investment of the effects of protégé gender on responses to mentoring. *Journal of Vocational Behavior, 49,* 309–323.

Baumgartner, R. N., Heymsfield, S. B., & Roche, A. F. (1995). Human body composition and the epidemiology of chronic disease. *Obesity Research, 3,* 73–95.

Bean, F., & Tienda, M. (1987). *The Hispanic population in the United States.* New York: Russell Sage Foundation.

Beck, A. T. (1967). Depression: Clinical, experimental, and theoretical aspects. New York: Harper & Row.

Beck, A. T., Rush, J., Shaw, B., & Emery, G. (1979). *Cognitive therapy of depression.* New York: Guilford.

Beck, J. G., & Averill, P. M. (2004). Older adults. In R. G. Heimberg, C. L. Turk, & D. S. Mennin (Eds.), *Generalized anxiety disorder: Advances in research and practice* (pp. 409–433). New York: Guilford Press.

Becker, B. J. (2003). Introduction to the special section on metric in meta-analysis. *Psychological Methods, 8,* 403–405.

Begany, J. J., & Milburn, M. A. (2002). Psychological predictors of sexual harassment: Authoritarianism, hostile sexism, and rape myths. *Psychology of Men and Masculinity, 3,* 119–126.

Belenky, M. F., Clinchy, B. M., Goldberger, N. R., & Tarule, J. M. (1986). *Women's ways of knowing: The development of self, voice, and mind.* New York: Basic Books.

Bendiksen, M. S., & Bendiksen, I. (1996). Multimodal memory rehabilitation for the toxic solvent injured person. In D. Herman, C. McEvoy, C. Hertzog, P. Herter, & M. K. Johnson (Eds.), *Basic and applied memory research* (Vol. 2, pp. 469–480). Hillsdale, NJ: Erlbaum.

Bengtson, V. L. (1985). Diversity and symbolism in grandparental roles. In V. L. Bengtson & J. F. Robertson (Eds.), *Grandparenthood* (pp. 11–25). Beverly Hills, CA: Sage.

Bengtson, V. L., Mills, T. L., & Parrott, T. M. (1995). Ageing in the United States at the end of the century. *Korea Journal of Population and Development, 24,* 215–244.

Bengtson, V. L., Rosenthal, C., & Burton, L. (1995). Paradoxes of families and aging. In R. H. Binstock & L. K. George (Eds.), *Handbook of aging and the social sciences* (4th ed., pp. 253–282). San Diego: Academic Press.

Ben-Israel Reuveni, O. (1999). *The effects of time on the adjustment of war bereaved parents: Functioning, relationship and marital adjustment.* Unpublished master's thesis, University of Haifa.

Benjamin, A. A. (2001). On the dual effects of repetition on false recognition. *Journal of Experimental Psychology: Learning, Memory, and Cognition, 27,* 941–947.

Bennett, B. (2003). *The lowdown on osteoporosis: What we know and what we don't.* Retrieved February 3, 2008, from http://www.nih.gov/news/WordonHealth/dec2003/osteo.htm.

Bennett, K. M. (2005). Psychological wellbeing in later life: The longitudinal effects of marriage, widowhood and marital status change. *International Journal of Geriatric Psychiatry, 20,* 280–284.

Benokraitis, N. V. (1999). *Marriages and families: Changes, choices, and constraints* (3rd ed.). Upper Saddle River, NJ: Prentice Hall.

Benokraitis, N. V. (2002). *Marriages and families: Changes, choices, and constraints* (6th ed.). Upper Saddle River, NJ: Prentice Hall.

Benokraitis, N. V. (2008). *Marriages and families: Changes, choices, and constraints* (6th ed.). Upper Saddle River, NJ: Prentice Hall.

Bent, K. N., & Magilvy, J. K. (2006). When a partner dies: Lesbian widows. *Issues in Mental Health Nursing, 27,* 447–459.

Berardi, A., Parasuraman, R., & Haxby, J. V. (2001). Overall vigilance and sustained attention decrements in healthy aging. *Experimental Aging Research, 27,* 19–39.

Berdahl, J. L., Magley, V. J., & Waldo, C. R. (1996). The sexual harassment of men? *Psychology of Women Quarterly, 20,* 527–547.

Berg, C. A. (2008). Everyday problem solving in context. In S. M. Hofer & D. F. Alwin (Eds.), *Handbook of cognitive aging: Interdisciplinary perspectives* (pp. 207–223). Greenwich, CT: Sage.

Berg, C. A., Johnson, M. M. S., Meegan, S. P., & Strough, J. (2003). Collaborative problem-solving interactions in young and old married couples. *Discourse Processes, 35*(1), 33–58.

Berg, C. A., & Sternberg, R. J. (1992). Adults' conceptions of intelligence across the adult life span. *Psychology and Aging, 7,* 221–231.

Berg, C. A., Strough, J., Calderone, K. S., Sansone, C., & Weir, C. (1998). The role of problem definitions in understanding age and context effects on strategies for solving every day problems. *Psychology and Aging, 13,* 29–44.

Bergeman, C. S. (1997). *Aging: Genetic and environmental influences.* Thousand Oaks, CA: Sage.

Bergman-Evans, B. (2004). Beyond the basics: Effects of the Eden Alternative model on quality of life issues. *Journal of Gerontological Nursing, 30,* 27–34.

Berlin, L. J., Brady-Smith, C., & Brooks-Gunn, J. (2002). Links between childbearing age and observed maternal behaviors with 14-month-olds in the Early Head Start Research and Evaluation Project. *Infant Mental Health Journal, 23,* 104–129.

Bernal, D., Snyder, D., & McDaniel, M. (1998). The age and job satisfaction relationship: Do its shape and strength still evade us? *Journals of Gerontology: Psychological Sciences, 53B,* P287–P293.

Bernsten, D., & Rubin, D. C. (2002). Emotionally charged autobiographical memories across the life span: The recall of happy, sad, traumatic, and involuntary memories. *Psychology and Aging, 17,* 636–652.

Berry, J. M., West, R. L., & Dennehey, D. M. (1989). Reliability and validity of the Memory Self-Efficacy Questionnaire. *Developmental Psychology, 25,* 701–713.

Berry, M. E. (1999). The development and constructive validation of the revised supervisor work and family support scale. *Dissertation Abstracts International: The Sciences and Engineering, 60,* 1335.

Besdine, R. W. (1995). Hyperthermia and accidental hypothermia. In W. B. Abrams, M. H. Beers, & R. Berkow (Eds.), *The Merck manual of geriatrics* (2nd ed., pp. 47–57). Whitehouse Station, NJ: Merck Research Laboratories.

Best, D. L., & Williams, J. E. (1993). A cross-cultural viewpoint. In A. E. Beall & R. J. Sternberg (Eds.), *The psychology of gender* (pp. 215–250). New York: Guilford.

Betz, E. L. (1984). A study of career patterns of women college graduates. *Journal of Vocational Behavior, 24,* 249–263.

Betz, E. L., Harmon, L. W., & Borgen, F. H. (1996). The relationships of self-efficacy for the Holland themes to gender, occupational group membership, and vocational interests. *Journal of Counseling Psychology, 43,* 90–98.

Betz, N. E., Heesacker, R. S., & Shuttleworth, C. (1990). Moderators of the congruence and realism of major and occupational plans in college students: A replication and extension. *Journal of Counseling Psychology, 37,* 269–276.

Bieman-Copland, S., & Charness, N. (1994). Memory knowledge and memory monitoring in adulthood. *Psychology and Aging, 9,* 287–302.

Bieman-Copland, S., Ryan, E. B., & Cassano, J. (1998). Responding to the challenges of late life. In D. Pushkar, W. M. Bukowski, A. E. Schwartzman, D. M. Stack, & D. R. White (Eds.), *Improving competence across the lifespan: Building interventions based on theory and research* (pp. 141–157). New York: Plenum.

Bigby, C. (2008). Beset by obstacles: A review of Australian policy development to support ageing in place for people with intellectual disability. *Journal of Intellectual and Developmental Disability, 33,* 76–86.

Binet, H. (1903). L'etude experimentale de l'intelligence [The experimental study of intelligence]. Paris: Schleicher.

Binger, C. M., Ablin, A. R., Feuerstein, R. C., Kushner, J. H., Zoger, S., & Mikkelson, C. (1969). Childhood leukemia—Emotional impact on patient and family. *New England Journal of Medicine, 280,* 414.

Binstock, R. H. (1994). Changing criteria in old-age programs: The introduction of economic status and need for services. *The Gerontologist, 34,* 726–730.

Binstock, R. H. (1999). Public policy issues. In J. C. Cavanaugh & S. K. Whitbourne (Eds.), *Gerontology: Interdisciplinary perspectives* (pp. 414–447). New York: Oxford University Press.

Birren, J. E., & Cunningham, W. (1985). Research on the psychology of aging: Principles, concepts, and theory. In J. E. Birren & K. W. Schaie (Eds.), *Handbook of the psychology of aging* (2nd ed., pp. 3–34). New York: Van Nostrand Reinhold.

Birren, J. E., Lubben, J. E., Rowe, J. C., & Deutchman, D. E. (Eds.). (1991). *The concept and measurement of quality of life in the frail elderly.* San Diego: Academic Press.

Birren, J. E., & Renner, V. J. (1980). Concepts and issues of mental health and aging. In J. E. Birren & R. B. Sloane (Eds.), *Handbook of mental health and aging* (pp. 3–33). Englewood Cliffs, NJ: Prentice Hall.

Birren, J. E., Woods, A. M., & Williams, M. V. (1980). Behavioral slowing with age: Causes, organization, & consequences. In L. W. Poon (Ed.), *Aging in the 1980s: Psychological issues* (pp. 293–308). Washington, DC: American Psychological Association.

Bitnes, J., Martens, H., Ueland, Ø., & Martens, M. (2007). Longitudinal study of taste identification of sensory panelists: Effects of ageing, experience and exposure. *Food Quality and Preference, 18,* 230–241.

Black, P. S., & Garbutt, L. D. (2000). Stress, inflammation, and cardiovascular disease. *Journal of Psychosomatic Research, 52,* 1–23.

Blackburn, R. M., Browne, J., Brooks, B., & Jarman, J. (2002). Explaining gender segregation. *British Journal of Sociology, 53,* 513–536.

Blanchard-Fields, F. (1986). Reasoning on social dilemmas varying in emotional saliency: An adult developmental study. *Psychology and Aging, 1,* 325–333.

Blanchard-Fields, F. (1994). Age differences in causal attributions from an adult developmental perspective. *Journals of Gerontology: Psychological Sciences, 49B,* P43–P51.

Blanchard-Fields, F. (1996). Causal attributions across the adult life span: The influence of social schemas, life context, and domain specificity. *Applied Cognitive Psychology, 10* (Special Issue), 5137–5146.

Blanchard-Fields, F. (1999). Social schematicity and causal attributions. In T. M. Hess & F. Blanchard-Fields (Eds.), *Social cognition and aging* (pp. 219–236). San Diego: Academic Press.

Blanchard-Fields, F., & Abeles, R. P. (1996). Social cognition and aging. In J. Birren & K. W. Schaie (Eds.), *Handbook of the psychology of aging* (4th ed., pp. 150–161). New York: Van Nostrand Reinhold.

Blanchard-Fields, F., Baldi, R. A., & Constantin, L. P. (In preparation). *Interrole conflict across the adult life-span: The role of parenting stage, career stages and quality of experiences.* Manuscript in preparation. School of Psychology, Georgia Institute of Technology, GA.

Blanchard-Fields, F., Baldi, R. A., & Stein, R. (1999). Age relevance and context effects on attributions across the adult life span. *International Journal of Behavioral Development, 23,* 665–683.

Blanchard-Fields, F., & Beatty, C. (2005). Age differences in blame attributions: The role of relationship outcome ambiguity and personal identification. *Journals of Gerontology: Psychological Sciences, 60,* P19–P26.

Blanchard-Fields, F., & Camp, C. J. (1990). Affect, individual differences, and real world problem solving across the adult life span. In T. Hess (Ed.), *Aging and cognition: Knowledge organization and utilization* (pp. 461–497). Amsterdam: North-Holland.

Blanchard-Fields, F., Chen, Y., & Herbert, C. E. (1997). Interrole conflict as a function of life stage, gender, and gender-related personality attributes. *Sex Roles, 37,* 155–174.

Blanchard-Fields, F., Chen, Y., & Schrocke, M., & Hertzog, C. (1998). Evidence for content-specificity of causal attributions across the adult life-span. *Aging, Neuropsychology, and Cognition, 5,* 241–263.

Blanchard-Fields, F., & Hertzog, C. (2000). Age differences in schematicity. In U. von Hecker, S. Dutke, & G. Sedek (Eds.), *Processes of generative mental representation and psychological adaptation*. Dordrecht, The Netherlands: Kluwer.

Blanchard-Fields, F., & Horhota, M. (2005). Age differences in the correspondence bias: When a plausible explanation matters, *Journals of Gerontology: Psychological Sciences, 60*, P259–P267.

Blanchard-Fields, F., Horhota, M., & Mienaltowski, A. (2008). Social context and cognition (pp. 614–628). In S. M. Hofer & D. F. Alwin (Eds.), *Handbook of cognitive aging: Interdisciplinary perspectives*. Greenwich, CT: Sage.

Blanchard-Fields, F., & Irion, J. C. (1988). The relation between locus of control and coping in two contexts: Age as a moderator variable. *Psychology and Aging, 3*, 197–203.

Blanchard-Fields, F., Jahnke, H. C., & Camp, C. (1995). Age differences in problem-solving style: The role of emotional salience. *Psychology and Aging, 10*, 173–180.

Blanchard-Fields, F., Mienaltowski, A., & Seay, R. (2007). Age differences in everyday problem-solving effectiveness: Older adults select more effective strategies for interpersonal problems. *Journals of Gerontology: Psychological Sciences, 62*, P61–P64.

Blanchard-Fields, F., & Norris, L. (1994). Casual attributions from adolescence through adulthood: Age differences, ego level, and generalized response style. *Aging and Cognition, 1*, 67–86.

Blanchard-Fields, F., & Stanley, J. T. (2007). Aging at work: Managing perceived and real changes in aging workers (pp. 83–108). In S. Gilliland, D. Steiner, & D. Skarlicki (Eds.), *Research in social issues in management: Vol. 5, Managing social and ethical issues in organizations*. Greenwich, CT: Information Age Publishing.

Blanchard-Fields, F., Stein, R., & Watson, T. L. (2004). Age differences in emotion-regulation strategies in handling everyday problems. *Journals of Gerontology: Psychological Sciences, 59*, P261–P269.

Blasko, I., Jellinger, K., Kemmler, G., Krampla, W., Jungwirth, S., Wichart, I., Tragl, K., & Fischer, P. (2008). Conversion from cognitive health to mild cognitive impairment and Alzheimer's disease: Prediction by plasma amyloid beta 42, medial temporal lobe atrophy and homocysteine. *Neurobiology of Aging, 29*, 1–11.

Blatt-Eisengart, I., & Lachman, M. E. (2004). Attributions for memory performance in adulthood: Age differences and mediation effects. *Aging, Neuropsychology, and Cognition, 11*, 68–79.

Blazer, D. G. (2008). How do you feel about. . . ? Health outcomes in late life and self-perceptions of health and well-being. *The Gerontologist, 48*, 415–422.

Blazer, D., George, L. K., & Hughes, D. C. (1988). Schizophrenic symptoms in an elderly community population. In J. A. Brody & G. L. Maddox (Eds.), *Epidemiology and aging: An international perspective* (pp. 134–149). New York: Springer.

Bleich, S., Wiltfang, J., & Kornhuber, J. (2003). Memantine in moderate-to-severe Alzheimer's disease. *New England Journal of Medicine, 349*, 609–610.

Block, J. (1995). A contrarian view of the five-factor approach to personality description. *Psychological Bulletin, 117*, 187–215.

Block, R., DeVoe, M., Stanley, B., Stanley, M., & Pomara, N. (1985). Memory performance in individuals with primary degenerative dementia: Its similarity to diazepam-induced impairments. *Experimental Aging Research, 11*, 151–155.

Bluck, S. (2003). Autobiographical memory: Exploring its functions in everyday life. *Memory, 11*, 113–123.

Bluck, S., & Habermas, T. (2000). The life story schema. *Motivation and Emotion, 24*, 121–147.

Bobrow, D. G., & Collins, A. (1971). *Representation and understanding: Studies in cognitive science*. New York: Academic Press.

Boelen, P. A., & Prigerson, H. G. (2007). The influence of symptoms of prolonged grief disorder, depression, and anxiety on quality of life among bereaved adults: A prospective study. *European Archives of Psychiatry and Clinical Neuroscience, 257*, 444–452.

Boelen, P. A., & van den Bout, J. (2003). Gender differences in traumatic grief symptom severity after the loss of a spouse. *Omega: Journal of Death and Dying, 46*, 183–198.

Boise, L., Camicioli, R., Morgan, D. L., Rose, J. H., & Congleton, L. (1999). Diagnosing dementia: Perspectives of primary care physicians. *The Gerontologist, 39*, 457–464.

Bojko, A., Kramer, A. F., & Peterson, M. S. (2004). Age equivalence in switch costs for prosaccade and antisaccade tasks. *Psychology and Aging, 19*, 226–234.

Boldy, D., & Grenade, L. (2001). Promoting empowerment in residential aged care: Seeking the consumer view. In L. F. Heumann, M. E. McCall, & D. P. Boldy (Eds.), *Empowering frail elderly people* (pp. 41–52). Westport, CT: Praeger.

Bonanno, G. A., & Kaltman, S. (1999). Toward an integrative perspective on bereavement. *Psychological Bulletin, 125*, 760–776.

Bonanno, G. A., Keltner, D., Holen, A., & Horowitz, M. J. (1995). When avoiding unpleasant emotions might not be such a bad thing: Verbal-autonomic response dissociation and midlife conjugal bereavement. *Journal of Personality and Social Psychology, 69*, 975–989.

Bonanno, G. A., Papa, A., Lalande, K., Zhang, N., & Noll, J. G. (2005). Grief processing and deliberate grief avoidance: A prospective comparison of bereaved spouses and parents in the United States and the People's Republic of China. *Journal of Consulting and Clinical Psychology, 73*, 86–98.

Bonanno, G. A., Papa, A., & O'Neill, K. (2001). Loss and human resilience. *Applied and Preventive Psychology, 10*, 193–206.

Bonanno, G. A., Wortman, C. B., & Neese, R. M. (2004). Prospective patterns of resilience and maladjustment during widowhood. *Psychology and Aging, 19*, 260–271.

Bond, F. W., & Bunce, D. (2003). The role of acceptance and job control in mental health, job satisfaction, and work performance. *Journal of Applied Psychology, 88*, 1057–1067.

Book, P. L. (1996). How does the family narrative influence the individual's ability to communicate about death? *Omega: Journal of Death and Dying, 33*, 323–342.

Booth, A. L., & Carroll, N. (2008). Economic status and the indigenous/non-indigenous health gap. *Economic Letters, 99*, 604–606.

Booth, F. W., Weeden, S. H., & Tseng, B. S. (1994). Effect of aging on human skeletal muscle and motor function. *Medicine and Science in Sports and Exercise, 26*, 556–560.

Bopp, K. L., & Verhaeghen, P. (2005). Aging and verbal memory span: A meta-analysis. *Journals of Gerontology: Psychological Sciences, 60B*, 223–233.

Borg, S., & Lasker, J. (1981). *When pregnancy fails*. Boston: Beacon Press.

Bornstein, M. C. (Ed.). (1995). *Handbook of parenting, Vols. 1–3*. Mahweh, NJ: Erlbaum.

Borry, P., Schotsmans, P., & Dierickx, K. (2005). The birth of the empirical turn in bioethics. *Bioethics, 19*, 49–71.

Bosma, H., van Boxtel, M. P. J., Ponds, R. W. H. M., Houx, P. J. H., & Jolles, J. (2003). Education and age-related cognitive decline: The contribution of mental workload. *Educational Gerontology, 29*, 165–173.

Bosman, E. A., & Charness, N. (1996). Age-related differences in skilled performance and skill acquisition. In F. Blanchard-Fields & T. M. Hess (Eds.), *Perspectives on cognitive change in adulthood and aging* (pp. 428–453). New York: McGraw-Hill.

Boss, P. (2006). *Loss, trauma, and resilience: Therapeutic work with ambiguous loss*. New York: Norton.

Bossé, R., Aldwin, C. M., Levenson, M. R., Spiro, A., & Mroczek, D. K. (1993). Change in social support after retirement: Longitudinal findings from the Normative Aging Study. *Journals of Gerontology: Psychological Sciences, 48B*, P210–P217.

Bossé, R., & Ekerdt, D. J. (1981). Change in self-perception of leisure activities with retirement: Longitudinal findings from the Normative Aging Study. *Journals of Gerontology: Psychological Sciences, 48B*, P210–P217.

Bosworth, H., & Ayotte, B. (2009). The role of cognitive ability in everyday functioning: Medication adherence as an example. In H. B. Bosworth & C. Hertzog (Eds.), *Aging and cognition: Research methodologies and empirical advances*. Washington DC: American Psychological Association.

Bosworth, H., Oddone, E. Z., Weinberger, M. (2005). *Patient treatment adherence concepts, interventions, and measurement*. Philadelphia: Taylor & Francis.

Botwinick, J. (1977). Intellectual abilities. In J. E. Birren & K. W. Schaie (Eds.), *Handbook of the psychology of aging* (pp. 580–605). New York: Van Nostrand Reinhold.

Bouchard, T. J., Jr. (1997). The genetics of personality. In K. Blum & E. P. Noble (Eds.), *Handbook of psychiatric genetics* (pp. 273–296). Boca Raton, FL: CRC Press.

Boult, C., Kane, R. L., Louis, T. A., Boult, L., & McCaffrey, D. (1994). Chronic conditions that lead to functional limitations in the elderly. *Journals of Gerontology: Medical Sciences, 49*, M28–M36.

Bourgeois, M. S., Camp, C., Rose, R., White, B., Malone, M., Carr, J., & Rovine, M. (2003). A comparison of training strategies to enhance use of external aids by persons with dementia. *Journal of Communication Disorders, 36*, 361–378.

Bowling, A. (2007). Aspirations for older age in the 21st century: What is successful aging? *International Journal of Aging and Human Development, 64*, 263–297.

Bozett, F. W. (1988). Gay fatherhood. In P. Bronstein & C. P. Cowan (Eds.), *Fatherhood today: Men's changing role in the family* (pp. 214–235). New York: Wiley.

Brabeck, M. M., & Weisgerber, K. (1989). College students' perception of men and women choosing teaching and management: The effects of gender and sex role egalitarianism. *Sex Roles, 21*, 841.

Brainerd, C. J. (1995). Interference processes in memory development: The case of cognitive triage. In F. N. Dempster & C. J. Brainerd

(Eds.), *Interference and inhibition on cognition* (pp. 108–139). San Diego: Academic Press.

Brandl, B., & Horan, D. L. (2002). Domestic violence in later life: An overview for health care providers. *Women and Health, 35,* 41–54.

Brandt, J., & Rich, J. B. (1995). Memory disorders in the dementias. In A. D. Baddeley, B. A. Wilson, & F. N. Watts (Eds.), *Handbook of memory disorders* (pp. 243–270). Chichester, UK: Wiley.

Brandtstädter, J. (1997). Action culture and development: Points of convergence. *Culture and Psychology, 3,* 335–352.

Brandtstädter, J. (1999). Sources of resilience in the aging self. In T. M. Hess & F. Blanchard-Fields (Eds.), *Social cognition and aging* (pp. 123–141). San Diego: Academic Press.

Brant, L. J., & Fozard, J. L. (1990). Age changes in pure-tone hearing thresholds in a longitudinal study of normal human aging. *Journal of the Acoustical Society of America, 88,* 813–820.

Braun, K. L., Tanji, V. M., & Heck, R. (2001). Support for physician-assisted suicide: Exploring the impact of ethnicity and attitudes toward planning for death. *The Gerontologist, 41,* 51–60.

Braun, S. D. (2007). Gay fathers with children adopted from foster care: Understanding their experiences and predicting adoption outcomes. *Dissertation Abstracts International: Section B: The Sciences and Engineering, 68(2-B),* 1296.

Bray, D. W., & Howard, A. (1983). The AT&T longitudinal study of managers. In K. W. Schaie (Ed.), *Longitudinal studies on adult psychological development* (pp. 266–312). New York: Guilford.

Brehmer, Y., Li, S.-C., Müller, V., von Oertzen, T., & Lindenberger, U. (2007). Memory plasticity across the lifespan: Uncovering children's latent potential. *Developmental Psychology, 43,* 465–478.

Breitner, J. C. S. (1988). Alzheimer's disease: Possible evidence for genetic causes. In M. K. Aronson (Ed.), *Understanding Alzheimer's disease* (pp. 34–49). New York: Scribner.

Brewer, M. B., & Lui, L. (1984). Categorization of the elderly by the elderly. *Personality and Social Psychology Bulletin, 10,* 585–595.

Bridges, C. R. (1996). The characteristics of career achievement perceived by African American college administrators. *Journal of Black Studies, 26,* 748–767.

Brigman, S., & Cherry, K. E. (2002). Age and skilled performance: Contributions of working memory and processing speed. *Brain and Cognition, 50,* 242–256.

Brison, K. J. (1995). You will never forget: Narrative, bereavement, and worldview among Kwanga women. *Ethos, 23,* 474–488.

Brissette, I., Scheier, M. F., & Carver, C. S. (2002). The role of optimism in social network development, coping, and psychological adjustment during a life transition. *Journal of Personality and Social Psychology, 82,* 102–111.

Brissett-Chapman, S., & Isaacs-Shockley, M. (1997). *Children in social peril: A community vision for preserving family care of African American children and youth.* Washington, DC: Child Welfare League of America, Inc.

Brod, M., Stewart, A. L., Sands, L., & Walton, P. (1999). Conceptualization and measurement of quality of life in dementia: The Dementia Quality of Life Instrument (DQoL). *The Gerontologist, 39,* 25–35.

Brodie, D. (1999). *Untying the knot: Ex-husbands, ex-wives, and other experts on the passage of divorce.* New York: St. Martin's Griffin.

Brody, E. M. (1981). Women in the middle and family help to older people. *The Gerontologist, 21,* 471–480.

Broman, C. L. (1988). Household work and family life satisfaction of blacks. *Journal of Marriage and the Family, 50,* 743–748.

Brooks, L., & Betz, N. E. (1990). Utility of expectancy theory in predicting occupational choices in college students. *Journal of Counseling Psychology, 37,* 57–64.

Brown, S. A., Hutchinson, R., Morrisett, J., Boerwinkle, E., Davis, C. E., & Gotto, A. M. (1993). Plasma lipid, lipoprotein cholesterol and apoprotein distributions in selected U.S. communities. *Arteriosclerosis and Thrombosis, 13,* 1139–1158.

Bruce, P. R., Coyne, A. C., & Botwinick, J. (1982). Adult age differences in metamemory. *Journals of Gerontology: Psychological Sciences, 37,* 354–357.

Brush, J. A., & Camp, C. J. (1998). *A therapy technique for improving memory: Spaced retrieval.* Beachwood, OH: Menorah Park Center for Senior Living.

Brysiewicz, P. (2008). The lived experience of losing a loved one to a sudden death in KwaZulu-Natal, South Africa. *Journal of Clinical Nursing, 17,* 224–231.

Buchsbaum, B. C. (1996). Remembering a parent who has died: A developmental perspective. In D. Klass, P. R. Silverman, & S. L. Nickman (Eds.), *Continuing bonds: New understandings of grief* (pp. 113–124). Washington, DC: Taylor & Francis.

Buckle, L., Gallup, C. G., Jr., & Rodd, Z. A. (1996). Marriage as a reproductive contract: Patterns of marriage, divorce, and remarriage. *Ethnology and Sociobiology, 17,* 363–377.

Buckner, R. L. (2004). Memory and executive function in aging and AD: Multiple factors that cause decline and reserve factors that compensate. *Neuron, 44(1),*195–208.

Buffum, M. D., & Buffum, J. C. (1998). Psychotropic drug management. In P. Ebersole & P. Hess (Eds.), *Toward healthy aging: Human needs and nursing response* (5th ed.). St. Louis: Mosby.

Bull, M. J., & McShane, R. E. (2008). Seeking what's best during the transition to adult day health services. *Qualitative Health Research, 18,* 597–605.

Bullock, K. (2004). The changing role of grandparents in rural families: The results of an exploratory study in southeastern North Carolina. *Families in Society 85*(1), 45-54.

Bunce, D. J., Barrowclough, A., & Morris, I. (1996). The moderating influence of physical fitness on age gradients in vigilance and serial choice response tasks. *Psychology and Aging, 11,* 671–682.

Bunce, D. J., Warr, P. B., & Cochrane, T. (1993). Blocks in choice responding as a function of age and physical fitness. *Psychology and Aging, 8,* 26–33.

Burdz, M. P., Eaton, W. D., & Bond, J. B. (1988). Effect of respite care on dementia and nondementia patients and their caregivers. *Psychology and Aging, 3,* 38–42.

Burgess, D., & Borgida, E. (1997). Sexual harassment: An experimental test of sex-role spillover theory. *Personality and Social Psychology and Bulletin, 23,* 63–75.

Burgio, K. L., Locher, J. L., Roth, D. L., & Goode, P. S. (2001). Psychological improvements associated with behavioral and drug treatment of urge incontinence in older women. *Journals of Gerontology: Psychological Sciences, 56B,* P46–P51.

Burgio, L. D. (1996). Interventions for the behavioral complications of Alzheimer's disease: Behavioral approaches. *International Psychogeriatrics, 8*(Suppl. 1), 45–52.

Burgio, L. D., Hardin, M., Sinnott, J., Janosky, J., & Hohman, M. J. (1995). Acceptability of behavioral treatments and pharmacotherapy for behaviorally disturbed older adults: Ratings of caregivers and relatives. *Journal of Clinical Geropsychology, 1,* 19–32.

Burgio, L. D., McCormick, K. A., Scheve, A. S., Engel, B. T., Hawkins, A., & Leahy, E. (1994). The effects of changing prompted voiding schedules in the treatment of incontinence in nursing home residents. *Journal of the American Geriatrics Society, 42,* 315–320.

Burgio, L., Stevens, A. Guy, D., Roth, D. L., & Haley, W. E. (2003). Impact of two psychosocial interventions on white and African American family caregivers of individuals with dementia. *The Gerontologist, 43,* 568–579.

Burke, D. M., & Harold, R. M. (1988). Automatic and effortful semantic processes in old age: Experimental and naturalistic approaches. In L. L. Light & D. M. Burke (Eds.), *Language, memory, and aging* (pp. 100–116). New York: University Press.

Burke, R. J. (1991a). Organizational treatment of minority managers and professionals: Costs to the majority? *Psychological Reports, 68,* 439–449.

Burke, R. J. (1991b). Work experiences of minority managers and professionals: Individual and organizational costs of perceived bias. *Psychological Reports, 69,* 1011–1023.

Burnette, D. (1999). Social relationships of Latino grandparent caregivers: A role theory perspective. *The Gerontologist, 39,* 49–58.

Burns, A. (1992). Mother-headed families: An international perspective and the case of Australia. *Society for Research in Child Development: Social Policy Report, 6,* 1–22.

Burns, E. A. (2002). Commentary: Challenges to using exercise interventions in older adults. In K. W. Schaie, H. Leventhal, & S. Willis (Eds.), *Effective health behavior in older adults* (pp. 179–189). New York: Springer.

Burns, E. A., & Leventhal, E. A. (2000). Aging, immunity, and cancer. *Cancer Control, 7,* 513–522.

Burns, S. T. (2005). The transition to parenthood: The effects of gender role attitudes and level of culture change in Chinese-American couples. *Dissertation Abstracts International: Section B: The Sciences and Engineering, 66(6-B),* 3461.

Burr, D. C., Morrone, M. C., & Frorentini, A. (1996). Spatial and temporal properties of infant color vision. In F. Vital-Dwand & J. Atkinson (Eds.), *Infant vision* (pp. 63–77). Oxford, UK: Oxford University Press.

Burr, J. A. (1990). Race/sex comparisons of elderly living arrangements. *Research on Aging, 12,* 507–530.

Burt, D. B., Zembar, M. J., & Niedereche, G. (1995). Depression and memory impairment. A meta-analysis of the association, its pattern, and specificity. *Psychological Bulletin, 117,* 285–305.

Burton, L. C., Zdaniuk, B., Schulz, R., Jackson, S., & Hirsch, C. (2003). Transitions in spousal caregiving. *The Gerontologist, 43,* 230–241.

Burton, L. M. (1992). Black grandparents rearing children of drug-addicted parents: Stressors, outcomes, and social service needs. *The Gerontologist, 32,* 744–751.

Busch, J. W. (1985). Mentoring in graduate schools of education: Mentors' perceptions. *American Educational Research Journal, 22,* 257–265.

Buschmann, M. T., & Hollinger, L. M. (1994). Influence of social support and control on depression in the elderly. *Clinical Gerontologist, 14,* 13–28.

Buss, D. M., Abbott, M., Angeleitner, A., Asherian, A., Biaggio, A., Blanco Villaseñor, A., Bruchon-Schweitzer, M., Chu'u, H.-Y., Czapinski, J., Deraad, B., Ekehammar, B., El Lohamy, N., Fioravanti, M., Georgas, J., Gjerde, P., Guttman, R., Hazan, F., Iwawaki, S., Janakiramaiah, N., Khosroshani, F., Kreitler, S., Lachenicht, L., Lee, M., Liik, K., Little, B., Mika, S., Moadel-Shahid, M., Moane, G., Montero, M., Mundy-Castle, A. C., Niit, T., Nsenduluka, E., Pienkowski, R., Pirttila-Backman, A.-M., Ponce de Leon, J., Rousseau, J., Runco, M. A., Safir, M. P., Samuels, C., Sanitioso, R., Serpell, R., Smid, N., Spencer, C., Tadinac, M., Todoreva, E. N., Troland, K., Van Den Brande, L., Van Heck, G., Van Langenhove, L., & Yang, K. S. (1990). International preferences in selecting mates: A study of 37 cultures. *Journal of Cross-Cultural Psychology, 21,* 5–47.

Bustos, M. L. C. (2007). La muerte en la cultura occidental: Antropología de la muerte./ Death in Western culture: Anthropology of death. *Revista Colombiana de Psiquiatría, 36,* 332–339.

Byock, I. (1997). *Dying well.* New York: Riverhead.

Cabeza, R. (2002). Hemispheric asymmetry reduction in older adults: The HAROLD model. *Psychology and Aging, 17,* 85–100.

Cabeza, R. (2004). Neuroscience frontiers in cognitive aging. In R. A. Dixon & L. G. Nilsson (Eds.), *New frontiers in cognitive aging* (pp.179–196). Nilsson New York: Oxford University Press.

Cabeza, R., Anderson, N. D., Locantore, J. K., & McIntosh, A. R. (2002). Aging gracefully: Compensatory brain activity in high-performing older adults. *Neuroimage, 17*(3), 1394–1402.

Cabeza, R., Locantore, J. K., & Anderson, N. D. (2003). Lateralization of prefrontal activity during episodic memory retrieval: Evidence for the production-monitoring hypothesis. *Journal of Cognitive Neuroscience, 15,* 249–259.

Cadell, S., & Marshall, S. (2007). The (re)construction of self after the death of a partner to HIV/AIDS. *Death Studies, 31,* 537–548.

Cagney, K. A., & Lauderdale, D. S. (2002). Education, wealth, and cognitive function in later life. *Journals of Gerontology: Psychological Sciences, 57,* P163–P172.

Cairney, J., & Krause, N. (2008). Negative life events and age-related decline in mastery: Are older adults more vulnerable to the control-eroding effect of stress? *The Journals of Gerontology: Psychological Sciences and Social Sciences, 63,* S162–S170.

Calasanti, T. M. (1996). Gender and life satisfaction in retirement: An assessment of the male model. *Journals of Gerontology: Social Sciences, 51,* S18–S29.

Calciano, R., Chodak, G. W., Garnick, M. B., Kuban, D. A., & Resnick, M. I. (1995, April 15). The prostate cancer conundrum. *Patient Care, 29,* 84–88, 91–95, 99–102, 104.

Camp, C. J. (1998). Memory interventions and pathological older adults. In R. Schulz, G. Maddox, & M. P. Lawton (Eds.), *Annotated review of gerontology and geriatrics* (Vol. 18, pp. 155–189). New York: Springer.

Camp, C. J. (Ed.). (1999). *Montessori-based activities for persons with dementia* (Vol. 1). Beachwood, OH: Menorah Park Center for Senior Living.

Camp, C. J. (2001). From efficacy to effectiveness to diffusion: Making transitions in dementia intervention research. *Neuropsychological Rehabilitation, 11,* 495–517.

Camp, C. J., Foss, J. W., Stevens, A. B., Reichard, C. C., McKitrick, L. A., & O'Hanlon, A. M. (1993). Memory training in normal and demented elderly populations: The E-I-E-I-O model. *Experimental Aging Research, 19,* 277–290.

Camp, C. J., Judge, K. S., Bye, C. A., Fox, K. M., Bowden, J., Bell, M., Valencic, K., & Mattern, J. M. (1997). An intergenerational program for persons with dementia using Montessori methods. *The Gerontologist, 37,* 688–692.

Camp, C. J., & McKitrick, L. A. (1991). Memory interventions in Alzheimer-type dementia populations: Methodological and theoretical issues. In R. L. West & J. D. Sinnott (Eds.), *Everyday memory and aging: Current research and methodology* (pp. 155–172). New York: Springer.

Camp, C. J., & Skrajner, M. J. (2005). Early stage dementia client as group leader. *Clinical Gerontologist, 28,* 81–84.

Campbell, A. (2008). Attachment, aggression, and affiliation: The role of oxytocin in female social behavior. *Biological Psychology, 77,* 1–10.

Cannon, C. (1996). Marital stress and coping in alpha 1-antitrypsin deficiency emphysema. Unpublished dissertation, University of Delaware.

Cantor, N. (1990). From thought to behavior: "Having" and "doing" in the study of personality and cognition. *American Psychologist, 45,* 735–750.

Cantor, N., & Harlow, R. E. (1994). Personality, strategic behavior, and daily-life problem solving. *Current Directions in Psychological Science, 3,* 169–172.

Caplan, L. J., & Lipman, P. D. (1995). Age and gender differences in the effectiveness of map-like learning aids in memory for routes. *Journals of Gerontology: Psychological Sciences, 50B,* P126–P133.

Capowski, G. (1994). Ageism and the new diversity issue. *Management Review, 83*(10), 1–15.

Cappelli, P. (2002). Will there really be a labor shortage? *Organizational Dynamics, 32,* 221–233.

Caprara, G. V., Caprara, M., & Steca, P. (2003). Personality's correlates of adult development and aging. *European Psychologist, 8,* 131–147.

Capron A. M. (2001). Brain death: Well settled yet still unresolved. *New England Journal of Medicine, 344,* 1244–1246.

Carlo, G., Koller, S., Raffaelli, M., & de Guzman, M. R. T. (2007). Culture-related strengths among Latin American families: A case study of Brazil. *Marriage & Family Review, 41,* 335–360.

Carlson, M. C., Hasher, L., Connelly, S. L., & Zacks, R. T. (1995). Aging distraction and benefits of predictable location. *Psychology and Aging, 10,* 427–436.

Carlson, N. E., Moore, M. M., Dame, A., Howieson, D., Silbert, L. C., Quinn, J. F., & Kaye, J. A. (2008). Trajectories of brain loss in aging and the development of cognitive impairment. *Neurology, 70,* 828–833.

Caron, C. D., Ducharme, F., & Griffith, J. (2006). Deciding on institutionalization for a relative with dementia: The most difficult decision for caregivers. *Canadian Journal on Aging, 25,* 193–205.

Carr, D. (2004). Gender, preloss marital dependence, and older adults' adjustment to widowhood. *Journal of Marriage and the Family, 66,* 220–235.

Carr, D., House, J. S., Kessler, R. C., Nesse, R. M., Sonnega, J., & Wortman, C. (2000). Marital quality and psychological adjustment to widowhood among older adults: A longitudinal analysis. *Journals of Gerontology: Social Sciences, 55B,* S197–S207.

Carr, D., & Rebok, G. W. (2000). Driving assessment. In J. Gallo, T. Fulmer, G. Paveza, & W. Reichel (Eds.), *Handbook of geriatric assessment* (pp. 149–157). Gaithersburg, MD: Aspen.

Carstensen, L. L. (1993). Motivation for social contact across the lifespan: A theory of socioemotional selectivity. In J. Jacobs (Ed.), *Nebraska Symposium on Motivation* (Vol. 40, pp. 209–254). Lincoln: University of Nebraska Press.

Carstensen, L. L. (1995). Evidence for a life-span theory of socioemotional selectivity. *Current Directions in Psychological Science, 4,* 151–156.

Carstensen, L. L., & Freund, A. M. (1994). The resilience of the aging self. *Developmental Review, 14,* 81–92.

Carstensen, L. L., Fung, H. H., & Charles, S. T. (2003). Socioemotional selectivity theory and the regulation of emotion in the second half of life. *Motivation and Emotion, 27*(2), 103–123.

Carstensen, L. L., Gottman, J. M., & Levenson, R. W. (1995). Emotional behavior in long-term marriage. *Psychology and Aging, 10,* 140–149.

Carstensen, L. L., Graff, J., Levenson, R. W., & Gottmann, J. M. (1996). Affect in intimate relationships: The developmental course of marriage. In C. Magai & S. H. McFadden (Eds.), *Handbook of emotion, adult development, and aging* (pp. 227–247). San Diego, CA: Academic Press.

Carstensen, L. L., Isaacowitz, D. M., & Charles, S. T. (1999). Taking time seriously: A theory of socioemotional selectivity. *American Psychologist, 54,* 165–181.

Carstensen, L. L., & Mikels, J. A. (2005). At the intersection of emotion and cognition: Aging and the positivity effect. *Current Directions in Psychological Science, 14,* 117–121.

Carstensen, L. L., Mikels, J. A., & Mather, M. (2006). Aging and the intersection of cognition, motivation, and emotion. In J. E. Birren & K. W. Schaire (Eds.), *Handbook of the psychology of aging* (6th ed., pp. 343–362). Amsterdam: Elsevier.

Carstensen, L. L., Pasupathi, M., Mayr, U., & Nesselroade, J. R. (2000). Emotional experience in everyday life across the adult lifespan. *Journal of Personality and Social Psychology, 79,* 644–655.

Carstensen, L. L., & Turk-Charles, S. (1994). The salience of emotion across the adult life span. *Psychology and Aging, 9,* 259–264.

Cascio, W. F. (1995). Whither industrial and organizational psychology in a changing world of work? *American Psychologist, 50,* 928–939.

Caserta, M. S., & Gillett, P. A. (1998). Older women's feelings about exercise and their adherence to an aerobic regimen over time. *The Gerontologist, 38,* 602–609.

Caserta, M. S., Lund, D. A., Wright, S. D., & Redburn, D. E. (1987). Caregivers to dementia patients: The utilization of community services. *The Gerontologist, 27,* 209–214.

Caspi, A., Roberts, B. W., & Shiner, R. (2005). Personality development. *Annual Review of Psychology, 56,* 453–484.

Casten, R. J., Rovner, B. W., Edmonds, S. E., DeAngelis, D., & Basford, C. (1999, August). *Personality traits as predictors of vision-specific function among older people experiencing vision loss.* Paper presented at the meeting of the American Psychological Association, Boston.

Castro, I. L. (1997). Worth more than we earn: Fair pay as a step toward gender equity. *National Forum, 77*(2), 17–21.

Cavanaugh, J. C. (1996). Memory self-efficacy as a key to understanding memory change. In F. Blanchard-Fields & T. M. Hess (Eds.), *Perspectives on cognitive changes in adulthood and aging* (pp. 488–507). New York: McGraw-Hill.

Cavanaugh, J. C. (1999a). Caregiving to adults: A life event challenge. In I. H. Nordhus, G. R. VandenBos, S. Berg, & P. Fromholt (Eds.),

Clinical geropsychology (pp. 131–135). Washington, DC: American Psychological Association.

Cavanaugh, J. C. (1999b). Friendships and social networks among older people. In I. H. Nordhus, G. R. VandenBos, S. Berg, & P. Fromholt (Eds.), Clinical geropsychology (pp. 137–140). Washington, DC: American Psychological Association.

Cavanaugh, J. C. (1999c). Theories of aging in the biological, behavioral, and social sciences. In J. C. Cavanaugh & S. K. Whitbourne (Eds.), Gerontology: Interdisciplinary perspectives (pp. 1–32). New York: Oxford University Press.

Cavanaugh, J. C., & Baskind, D. (1996). Relations among basic processes, beliefs, and performance: A lifespan perspective. In D. Herrmann, M. Johnson, C. McEvoy, C. Hertzog, & P. Hertel (Eds.), Basic and applied memory: Research on practical aspects of memory. Hillsdale, NJ: Erlbaum.

Cavanaugh, J. C., Feldman, J., & Hertzog, C. (1998). Memory beliefs as social cognition: A reconceptualization of what memory questionnaires assess. Review of General Psychology, 2, 48–65.

Cavanaugh, J. C., Grady, J. G., & Perlmutter, M. (1983). Forgetting and use of memory aids in 20 to 70 year olds' everyday life. International Journal of Aging and Human Development, 17, 113–122.

Cavanaugh, J. C., & Green, E. E. (1990). I believe, therefore I can: Self-efficacy beliefs in memory aging. In E. A. Lovelace (Ed.), Aging and cognition: Mental processes, self-awareness, and interventions (pp. 189–230). Amsterdam: North-Holland.

Cavanaugh, J. C., & Kinney, J. M. (1994, July). Marital satisfaction as an important contextual factor in spousal caregiving. Paper presented at the 7th International Conference on Personal Relationships, Groningen, The Netherlands.

Cavanaugh, J. C., & Kinney, J. M. (1998). Accuracy of caregivers' recollections of caregiving hassles. Journal of Gerontology: Psychological Sciences, 53B, P40–P42.

Cavanaugh, J. C., Kramer, D. A., Sinnott, J. D., Camp, C. J., & Markley, R. J. (1985). On missing links and such: Interfaces between cognitive research and everyday problem solving. Human Development, 28, 146–168.

Cavanaugh, J. C., & Stafford, H. (1989). Being aware of issues and biases: Directions for research on post-formal thought. In M. L. Commons, J. D. Sinnott, F. A. Richards, & C. Armon (Eds.), Adult development: Vol. 1, Comparisons and applications of adolescent and adult development models (pp. 272–292). New York: Praeger.

Cavanaugh, J. C., & Whitbourne, S. K. (2003). Research methods in adult development. In J. Demick & C. Andreoletti (Eds.), Handbook of adult development (pp. 85–100). New York: Kluwer Academic/Plenum.

Centers for Disease Control and Prevention. (2000). Deaths: Final data for 1998. (National Vital Statistics Reports, Vol. 48, No. 11). Online document available at http://www.cdc.gov/nchs/data/nvs48_11.pdf. Accessed 2004.

Centers for Disease Control and Prevention. (2002). U.S. HIV and AIDS cases reported through June 2001. Online document available at http://www.cdc.gov/hiv/stats/hasr1301.htm. Accessed November 16, 2003.

Centers for Disease Control and Prevention. (2003). Life expectancy. Online document available at http://www.cdc.gov/nchs/fastats/lifexpec.htm. Accessed November 16, 2003.

Centers for Disease Control and Prevention. (2007b). About BMI for adults. Online document retrieved March 15, 2009, from http://www.cdc.gov/nccdphp/dnpa/bmi/adult_BMI/about_adult_BMI.htm.

Centers for Disease Control and Prevention. (2008a). Deaths: Final data for 2005. Retrieved September 7, 2008, from http://www.cdc.gov/nchs/data/nvsr/nvsr56/nvsr56_10.pdf.

Centers for Disease Control and Prevention. (2008b). Heart disease facts and statistics. Retrieved September 7, 2008, from http://www.cdc.gov/heartdisease/facts.htm.

Centers for Disease Control and Prevention. (2008c). Stroke death rates 2000–2004 adults ages 35 years and older by county. Retrieved September 7, 2008, from http://www.cdc.gov/dhdsp/library/fs_stroke.htm.

Centers for Disease Control and Prevention. (2008d). Minority health determines the health of the nation. Retrieved September 7, 2008, from http://www.cdc.gov/omhd/default.htm.

Centers for Disease Control and Prevention. (2008e). HIV/AIDS surveillance report: Cases of HIV infection and AIDS in the United States and dependent areas: 2006. Basic statistics. Retrieved September 28, 2008, from http://www.cdc.gov/hiv/topics/surveillance/basic.htm#aidsage.

Centers for Disease Control and Prevention. (2008f). Adult immunization schedule. Retrieved September 28, 2008, from http://www.cdc.gov/vaccines/recs/schedules/adult-schedule.htm.

Centers for Disease Control and Prevention and National Association of Chronic Disease Directors (2008). The state of mental health and aging in America: Issue Brief 1: What do the data tell us? Retrieved November 16, 2008, from http://www.chronicdisease.org/files/public/IssueBrief_TheStateofMentalHealthandAginginAmerica.pdf.

Centers for Disease Control and Prevention and The Merck Company Foundation. (2007). The state of aging and health in America. Whitehouse Station, NJ: The Merck Company Foundation. Retrieved November 1, 2008, from http://www.agingsociety.org/agingsociety/pdf/SAHA_2007.pdf.

Centers for Medicare and Medicaid Services. (2007). National health expenditure projections. Retrieved October 19, 2008, from http://www.cms.hhs.gov/NationalHealthExpendData/Downloads/proj2007.pdf.

Cerella, J. (1990). Aging and information-processing rate. In J. E. Birren & K. W. Schaie (Eds.), Handbook of the psychology of aging (3rd ed., pp. 201–221). San Diego: Academic Press.

Cerella, J., & Hale, S. (1994). The rise and fall of information processing rates over the life span. Acta Psychologica, 86, 109–197.

Cerminara, K. L., & Perez, A. (2000). Therapeutic death: A look at Oregon's law. Psychology, Public Policy, and Law, 6, 503–525.

Chadiha, L. A., Rafferty, J., & Pickard, J. (2003). The influence of caregiving stressors, social support, and caregiving appraisal on marital functioning among African American wife caregivers. Journal of Marital and Family Therapy, 29, 479–490.

Chambless, D. L., Sanderson, W. C., Shoham, V., Bennett Johnson, S., Pope, K. S., Crits-Christoph, P., Baker, M., Johnson, B., Woody, S. R., Sue, S., Beutler, L., Williams, D. A., & McCurry, S. (1996). An update on empirically validated therapies. Clinical Psychologist, 49, 5–18.

Chambré, S. M. (1993). Voluntarism by elders: Past trends and future prospects. The Gerontologist, 33, 221–228.

Chan, A. Y., & Smith, K. R. (1995). Perceptions of marital stability of black-white intermarriages. In C. K. Jacobson (Ed.), American families: Issues in race and ethnicity (pp. 369–386). New York: Garland.

Chang, S., Kim, J., Kong, E., Kim, C., Ahn, S., & Cho, N. (2008). Exploring ego-integrity in old adults: A Q-methodology study. International Journal of Nursing Studies, 45, 246–256.

Chao, P. (1997). Chinese kinship. London: Kegan Paul.

Charles, S. T. (1998). Genetic and environmental influences on osteoarthritis. Dissertation Abstracts International: Section B: The Sciences and Engineering, 58(11B), 6272.

Charles, S. T., Mather, M., & Carstensen, L. L. (2003). Aging and emotional memory: The forgettable nature of negative images for older adults. Journal of Experimental Psychology: General, 132, 310–324.

Charman, W. N. (2008). The eye in focus: accommodation and presbyopia. Clinical and Experimental Optometry, 91, 207–225.

Charness, N., & Bosman, E. A. (1990). Expertise and aging: Life in the lab. In T. M. Hess (Ed.), Aging and cognition: Knowledge organization and utilization (pp. 343–385). Amsterdam: North-Holland.

Chasseigne, G., Mullett, E., & Stewart, T. R. (1997). Aging and multiple cue probability learning: The case of inverse relationships. Acta Psychologica, 97, 235–252.

Chasteen, A. L. (1994). "The world around me": The environment and single women. Sex Roles, 31, 309–328.

Chasteen, A. L., Schwarz, N., & Park, D. C. (2002). The activation of aging stereotypes in younger and older adults. Journals of Gerontology: Psychological Sciences, 57B, P540–P547.

Chen, J., Hale, S., & Myerson, J. (2003). Effects of domain, retention interval, and information load on young and older adults' visuospatial working memory. Aging, Neuropsychology, and Cognition, 10, 122–133.

Chen, J., & Wu, Z. (2008). Gender differences in the effects of self-rated health status on mortality among the oldest old in China. In Z. Yi, D. L. Poston, Jr., D. Asbaugh Vlosky, & D. Gu (Eds.), Healthy longevity in China (pp. 397–418). New York: Springer.

Chen, T., Han, B., & Wang, J. (2003). A review of the aging of working memory. Psychological Science (China), 26, 127–129.

Chen, Y. (2002). Unwanted beliefs: Age differences in beliefs of false information. Aging, Neuropsychology, and Cognition, 9, 217–228.

Chen, Y., & Blanchard-Fields, F. (1997). Age differences in stages of attributional processing. Psychology and Aging, 12, 694–703.

Chen, Y., & Blanchard-Fields, F. (2000). Unwanted thought: Age differences in the correction of social judgments. Psychology and Aging, 15, 475–482.

Chen, Y., & Sun, Y. (2003). Age differences in financial decision-making: Using simple heuristics. Educational Gerontology, 29, 627–635.

Cheng, S., & Powell, B. (2007). Under and beyond constraints: Resource allocation to young children from biracial families. American Journal of Sociology, 112, 1044–1094.

Cherkas, L. F., Hunkin, J. L., Kato, B. S., Richards, B., Gardner, J. P., Surdulescu, G. L., Kimura, M., Lu, X., Spector, T. D., & Aviv, A. (2008). The association between physical activity in leisure time and leukocyte telomere length. Archives of Internal Medicine, 168, 154–158.

Cherlin, A. J. (1992). *Marriage, divorce, remarriage* (rev. ed.). Cambridge, MA: Harvard University Press.

Cherlin, A. J., & Furstenberg, F. F., Jr. (1986). *The new American grandparent: A place in the family, a life apart.* New York: Basic Books.

Cherlin, A. J., & Furstenberg, F. F., Jr. (1994). Stepfamilies in the United States: A reconsideration. *Annual Review of Sociology, 20,* 359–381(1986).

Cherry, K. E., & Park, D. C. (1993). Individual difference and contextual variables influence spatial memory in younger and older adults. *Psychology and Aging, 8,* 517–526.

Cherry, K. E., Park, D. C., & Donaldson, H. (1993). Adult age differences in spatial memory: Effects of structural context and practice. *Experimental Aging Research, 19,* 333–350.

Chidgey, A. (2008). Effects of growth hormone in enhancing thymic regrowth and T-cell reconstitution. *Expert Review of Clinical Immunology, 4,* 433–439.

Childs, H. W., Hayslip, B., Jr., Radika, L. M., & Reinberg, J. A. (2000). Young and middle-aged adults' perceptions of elder abuse. *The Gerontologist, 40,* 75–85.

Chinen, A. B. (1989). *In the ever after.* Willmette, IL: Chiron.

Chou, K-L., & Chi, I. (2005). Prevalence and correlates of depression in Chinese oldest-old. *International Journal of Geriatric Psychiatry, 20,* 41–50.

Chou, S.-C., Boldy, D. P., & Lee, A. H. (2003). Factors influencing residents' satisfaction in residential aged care. *The Gerontologist, 43,* 459–472.

Christensen, A. (1990). Gender and social structure in the demand/withdrawal pattern of marital conflict. *Journal of Personality and Social Psychology, 59,* 73–81.

Christensen, A. J., & Johnson, J. A. (2002). Patient adherence with medical treatment regimens: An interactive approach. *Current Directions in Psychological Science, 11,* 94–97.

Christensen, H., Mackinnon, A. J., Korten, A., & Jorm, A. F. (2001). The "common cause hypothesis" of cognitive aging: Evidence for a common factor but also specific associations of age with vision and grip strength in a cross-sectional analysis. *Psychology and Aging, 16,* 588–599.

Christensen, H., Mackinnon, A. J., Korten, A. E., Jorm, A. F., Henderson, A. S., Jacomb, P., & Rogers, B. (1999). An analysis of diversity in the cognitive performance of elderly community dwellers: Individual differences in change scores as a function of age. *Psychology and Aging, 14,* 365–379.

Churchill, J. D., Galvez, R., Colcombe, S., Swain, R. A., Kramer, A. F., & Greenough, W. T. (2002). Exercise, experience and the aging brain. *Neurobiology of Aging, 23,* 941–955.

Ciarney, J., & Krause, N. (2008). Negative life events and age-related decline in mastery: Are older adults more vulnerable to the control-eroding effect of stress? *Journal of Gerontology: Social Sciences, 63,* S16–S170.

Cicirelli, V. G. (2000). Older adults' ethnicity, fear of death, and end-of-life decisions. In A. Tomer (Ed.), *Death attitudes and the older adult: Theories, concepts, and applications* (pp. 175–191). Philadelphia: Brunner-Routledge.

Cicirelli, V. G. (2001). Personal meaning of death in older adults and young adults in relation to their fears of death. *Death Studies, 25,* 663–683.

Cicirelli, V. G. (2002). Fear of death in older adults: Predictions from terror management theory. *Journals of Gerontology: Psychological Sciences, 57B,* P358–P366.

Cicirelli, V. G. (2006). Fear of death in mid-old age. *Journals of Gerontology: Psychological Sciences, 61B,* P75–P81.

Cicirelli, V. G., Coward, R. T., & Dwyer, J. W. (1992). Siblings as caregivers for impaired elders. *Research on Aging, 14,* 331–350.

Clancy, S. M., & Hoyer, W. J. (1994). Age and skill in visual search. *Developmental Psychology, 30,* 545–552.

Clare, L., & Giblin, S. (2008). Late onset psychosis. In R. Woods & L. Clare (Eds.), *Handbook of the clinical psychology of ageing* (2nd ed., pp. 133–144). New York: Wiley.

Clarke, L. H., & Griffin, M. (2008). Visible and invisible ageing: Beauty work as a response to ageism. *Ageing and Society, 28,* 653–674.

Clausen, J. A. (1981). Men's occupational careers in the middle years. In D. H. Eichorn, N. Haan, J. Clausen, M. Honzik, & P. Mussen (Eds.), *Present and past in middle life* (pp. 321–351). New York: Academic Press.

Clements, M., & Markman, H. J. (1996). The transition to parenthood: Is having children hazardous to marriage? In N. Vanzetti & S. Duck (Eds.), *A lifetime of relationships* (pp. 290–310). Pacific Grove, CA: Brooks/Cole.

Clemons, A. W., & Axelson, L. J. (1985). The not-so-empty nest: The return of the fledgling adult. *Family Relations, 34,* 259–264.

Coan, J. A., & Gottman, J. M. (2007). Sampling, experimental control, and generalizability in the study of marital process models. *Journal of Marriage and Family, 69,* 73–80.

Cohen, G. (1993). Memory and aging. In G. M. Davies & R. H. Logic (Eds.), *Memory in everyday life* (pp. 419–459). Amsterdam: North-Holland.

Cohen, G. D., Conway, M. A., & Maylor, E. A. (1994). Flashbulb memories in older adults. *Psychology and Aging, 9,* 454–463.

Cohen, R. R., Boston, P., Mount, B. M., & Porterfield, P. (2001). Changes in quality of life following admission to palliative care units. *Palliative Medicine, 15,* 363–371.

Cohen, S., & Herbert, T. B. (1996). Health psychology: Psychological factors and physical disease from the perspective of human psychoneuro-immunology. *Annual Review of Psychology, 47,* 113–142.

Cohen, S., Kessler, R. C., & Gordon, L. U. (1995). Strategies for measuring stress in studies of psychiatric and physical disorders. In S. Cohen & L. U. Gordon (Eds.), *Measuring stress* (pp. 3–26). New York: Oxford University Press.

Cohler, B. J. (1993). Aging, morale, and meaning: The nexus of narrative. In T. R. Cole, W. A. Achenbaum, P. L. Jakobi, & R. Kastenbaum (Eds.), *Voices and visions of aging: Toward a critical gerontology* (pp. 107–133). New York: Springer.

Coke, M. M. (1992). Correlates of life satisfaction among elderly African Americans. *Journals of Gerontology: Psychological Sciences, 47B,* PP. 16–320.

Colcombe, S., & Kramer, A. F. (2003). Fitness effects on the cognitive function of older adults: A meta-analytic study. *Psychological Science, 14,* 125–130.

Cole, M. L. (2000). The experience of never-married women in their thirties who desire marriage and children. *Dissertation Abstracts International Section A: Humanities and Social Sciences, 60(9-A),* 3526.

Cole, T. R., & Holstein, M. (1996). Ethics and aging. In R. H. Binstock & L. K. George (Eds.), *Handbook of aging and the social sciences* (4th ed., pp. 480–497). San Diego: Academic Press.

Coleman, K. A., Casey, V. A., & Dwyer, J. T. (1991, June). Stability of autobiographical memories over four decades. Paper presented at the meeting of the American Psychological Society, Washington, DC.

Coleman, M., & Ganong, L. H. (1990). Remarriage and stepfamily research in the 1980s: Increased interest in an old family form. *Journal of Marriage and the Family, 52,* 925–940.

Coleman, M. T., Looney, S., O'Brien, J., Ziegler, C., Pastorino, C. A., & Turner, C. (2002). The Eden Alternative: Findings after 1 year of implementation. *Journals of Gerontology: Biological Sciences and Medical Sciences, 57,* M422–M427.

Collins, W. A., & van Dulmen, M. (2006). "The course of true love(s). . .": Origins and pathways in the development of romantic relationships. In A. C. Crouter & A. Booth (Eds), *Romance and sex in adolescence and emerging adulthood: Risks and opportunities* (pp. 63–86). Mahwah, NJ: Lawrence Erlbaum.

Collopy, B. J. (1988). Autonomy in long term care: Some crucial distinctions. *The Gerontologist, 28*(Suppl.), 10–17.

Colonia-Willner, R. (1998). Practical intelligence at work: Relationships between aging and cognitive efficiency among managers in a bank environment. *Psychology and Aging, 13,* 45–47.

Comijs, H. C., Deeg, D. J. H., Dik, M. G., Twisk, J. W. R., & Jonker, C. (2002). Memory complaints: The association with psycho-affective and health problems and the role of personality characteristics. A 6-year follow-up study. *Journal of Affective Disorders, 72,* 157–166.

Commons, M. L., Richards, F. A., & Armon, C. (Eds.). (1984). *Beyond formal operations: Late adolescent and adult cognitive development.* New York: Praeger.

Commons, M. L., Richards, F. A., & Kuhn, D. (1982). Systematic and metasystematic reasoning: A case for levels of reasoning beyond Piaget's stage of formal operations. *Child Development, 53,* 1058–1069.

Commons, M. L., Sinnott, J. D., Richards, F. A., & Armon, C. (Eds.). (1989). *Adult development: Vol. 1, Comparisons and applications of adolescent and adult developmental models.* New York: Praeger.

Congressional Budget Office. (2008). *An analysis of the president's budgetary proposals for fiscal year 2009.* Retrieved March 15, 2009, from http://www.cbo.gov/doc.cfm?index=8990.

Connell, C. M., & Gibson, G. D. (1997). Racial, ethnic, and cultural differences in dementia caregiving: Review and analysis. *The Gerontologist, 37,* 355–364.

Connelly, S. L., & Hasher, L. (1993). Aging and the inhibition of spatial location. *Journal of Experimental Psychology: Human Perception and Performance, 19,* 1238–1250.

Connelly, S. L., Hasher, L., & Zacks, R. T. (1991). Age and reading: The impact of distraction. *Psychology and Aging, 6,* 533–541.

Connidis, I. A. (1988, November). *Sibling ties and aging.* Paper presented at the meeting of the Gerontological Society of America, San Francisco.

Connidis, I. A. (1994). Sibling support in older age. *Journals of Gerontology: Social Sciences, 49,* S309–S317.

Connidis, I. A. (2001). *Family ties and aging.* Thousand Oaks, CA: Sage.

Connor, L. T., Dunlowsky, J., & Hertzog, C. (1997). Age-related differences in absolute but not relative meta-memory accuracy. *Psychology and Aging, 12,* 50–71.

Conway, M. A., & Holmes, A. (2004). Psychosocial stages and the accessibility of autobiographical memories across the life cycle. *Journal of Personality, 72,* 461–480.

Cook, I. A., Leuchter, A. F., Morgan, M. L., Dunkin, J. J., Witte, E., David, S., et al. (2004). Longitudinal progression of subclinical structural brain disease in normal aging. *American Journal of Geriatric Psychiatry, 12*(2), 190–200.

Cook-Greuter, S. (1989). Maps for living: Ego development theory from symbiosis to conscious universal embeddedness. In M. L. Commons, J. D. Sinnott, F. A. Richards, & C. Armon (Eds.), *Adult development: Comparisons and application of adolescent and adult developmental models* (Vol. 2, pp. 79–104). New York: Praeger.

Cooney, T. M., Pedersen, F. A., Indelicato, S., & Palkovitz, R. (1993). Timing of fatherhood: Is "on-time" optimal? *Journal of Marriage and the Family, 55*, 205–215.

Cooper, C., Selwood, A., & Livingston, G. (2008). Prevalence of elder abuse and neglect: A systematic review. *Age and Ageing, 37*, 151–160.

Cooper, R. S., Rotimi, C. N., & Ward, R. (1999). The puzzle of hypertension in African-Americans. *Scientific American, 280*, 56–63. Online document available at http://www.sciam.com/1999/0299issue/0299cooper.html. Accessed November, 13, 2004.

Cordes, C. L., & Dougherty, T. W. (1993). A review and integration of research on job burnout. *Academy of Management Review, 18*, 621–656.

Cornelius, S. W. (1990). Aging and everyday cognitive abilities. In T. M. Hess (Ed.), *Aging and cognition: Knowledge organization and utilization* (pp. 411–459). Amsterdam: North-Holland.

Cornelius, S. W., & Caspi, A. (1987). Everyday problem solving in adulthood and old age. *Psychology and Aging, 2*, 144–153.

Cornish, N. (1994). Over the hill? *News Journal* (Wilmington, DE), pp. D10–D11.

Cornman, J. M., & Kingston, E. R. (1996). Trends, issues, perspectives, and values for the aging of the baby boom cohorts. *The Gerontologist, 36*, 15–26.

Corr, C. A. (1991–1992). A task-based approach to coping with dying. *Omega: Journal of Death and Dying, 24*, 81–94.

Corr, C. A., Corr, D. M., & Nabe, C. M. (2008). *Death and dying: Life and living.* Belmont, CA: Wadsworth.

Corrigan, P. W., Holmes, E. P., Luchins, D., Buican, B., Basit, A. J., & Parks, J. (1994). Staff burnout in a psychiatric hospital: A cross-lagged panel design. *Journal of Organizational Behavior, 15*, 65–74.

Cosby, A. (1974). Occupational expectations and the hypothesis of increasing realism of choice. *Journal of Vocational Behavior, 5*, 53–65.

Cosentino, S. A., Jefferson, A. L., Carey, M., Price, C. C., Davis-Garrett, K., Swenson, R., & Libon, D. J. (2004). The clinical diagnosis of vascular dementia: A comparison among four classification systems and a proposal for a new paradigm. *Clinical Neuropsychologist, 18*, 6–21.

Costa, P. T., & McCrae, R. R. (1978). Objective personality assessment. In M. Storandt, I. C. Siegler, & M. F. Elias (Eds.), *The clinical psychology of aging* (pp. 119–143). New York: Plenum.

Costa, P. T., & McCrae, R. R. (1988). Personality in adulthood: A six-year longitudinal study of self-reports and spouse ratings on the NEO Personality Inventory. *Journal of Personality and Social Psychology, 54*, 853–863.

Costa, P. T., & McCrae, R. R. (1994). Set like plaster? Evidence for the stability of adult personality. In T. F. Heatherton & J. L. Weinberger (Eds.), *Can personality change?* (pp. 21–40). Washington, DC: Academic Psychological Association.

Costa, P. T., & McCrae, R. R. (1995). Solid ground in the wetlands of personality: A reply to block. *Psychological Bulletin, 117*, 216–220.

Costa, P. T., & McCrae, R. R. (1997). Longitudinal stability of adult personality. In R. Hogan, J. Johnson, & S. Briggs (Eds.), *Handbook of personality psychology* (pp. 269–292). San Diego: Academic Press.

Costa, P. T., & McCrae, R. R. (1998). Six approaches to the explication of facet-level traits examples from conscientiousness. *European Journal of Personality, 12*, 117–134.

Costa, P. T., McCrae, R. R., & Holland, J. L. (1984). Personality and vocational interests in an adult sample. *Journal of Applied Psychology, 42*, 390–400.

Costigan, C. L., Cox, M. J., & Cauce, A. M. (2003). Work–parenting linkages among dual-earner couples at the transition to parenthood. *Journal of Family Psychology, 17*, 397–408.

Cotman, C. W., & Berchtold, N. C. (2002). Exercise: A behavioral intervention to enhance brain health and plasticity. *Trends in Neurosciences, 25*, 295–301.

Cotter, D. A., Hermsen, J. M., Ovadia, S., & Vanneman, R. (2001). The glass ceiling effect. *Social Forces, 80*, 655–682.

Cotter, D. A., Hermsen, J. M., & Vanneman, R. (2003). The effects of occupational gender segregation across race. *Sociological Quarterly, 44*, 17–36.

Cotton, S., Anthill, J. K., & Cunningham, J. D. (1989). The work motivations of mothers with preschool children. *Journal of Family Issues, 10*, 189–210.

Coughlin, J. F., & Pope, J. (2008). Innovations in health, wellness, and aging-in-place. *Engineering in Medicine and Biology magazine, IEEE, 27*, 47–52.

Coulston, A. M., & Boushey, C. J. (Eds.). (2008). *Nutrition in the prevention and treatment of disease* (2nd ed.). San Diego, CA: Elsevier Academic Press.

Counts, D. A., & Counts, D. R. (1985). I'm not dead yet! Aging and death: Processes and experiences in Kalia. In D. A. Counts & D. R. Counts (Eds.), *Aging and its transformations* (pp. 131–156). Langham, MD: University of America Press.

Cournoyer, R. J., & Mahalik, J. R. (1995). Cross-sectional study of gender role conflict examining college-aged and middle-aged men. *Journal of Counseling Psychology, 42*, 11–19.

Cousins, S. O. (2000). "My heart couldn't take it": Older women's beliefs about exercise benefits and risks. *Journals of Gerontology: Psychological Sciences, 55B*, P283–P294.

Cox, C. B. (2000). Why grandchildren are going to and staying at grandmother's house and what happens when they get there. In C. B. Cox (Ed.), *To grandmother's house we go and stay: Perspectives on custodial grandparents* (pp. 3–19). New York: Springer.

Cox, C. B. (2007). Grandparent-headed families: Needs and implications for social work interventions and advocacy. *Families in Society, 88*, 561–566.

Craik, F. I. M. (1977). Age differences in human memory. In J. E. Birren & K. W. Schaie (Eds.), *Handbook of the psychology of aging* (pp. 384–420). New York: Van Nostrand Reinhold.

Craik, F. I. M. (1986). A functional account of age differences in memory. In F. Klix & H. Hagendorf (Eds.), *Human memory and cognitive capabilities* (pp. 409–422). Amsterdam: Elsevier.

Craik, F. I. M., Anderson, N. D., Kerr, S. A., & Li, K. Z. H. (1995). Memory changes in normal aging. In A. D. Baddeley, B. A. Wilson, & F. N. Watts (Eds.), *Handbook of memory disorders* (pp. 211–241). Chichester, UK: Wiley.

Craik, F. I. M., & Byrd, M. (1982). Aging and cognitive deficits: The role of attentional sources. In F. I. M. Craik & S. Trehub (Eds.), *Aging and cognitive processes* (pp. 191–211). New York: Plenum.

Crimmins, E. M., Saito, Y., & Reynolds, S. L. (1997). Further evidence on recent trends in the prevalence and incidence of disability among older Americans from two sources: The LSOA and the NHIS. *Journals of Gerontology: Social Sciences, 52B*, S59–S71.

Crist, J. D., Garcia-Smith, D., & Phillips, L. R. (2006). Accommodating the stranger en casa: How Mexican American elders and caregivers decide to use formal care. *Research and Theory for Nursing Practice: An International Journal, 20*, 109–126.

Cristofalo, V. J., Tresini, M., Francis, M. K., & Volker, C. (1999). Biological theories of senescence. In V. L. Bengtson & K. W. Schaie (Eds.), *Handbook of theories of aging* (pp. 98–112). New York: Springer.

Crohan, S. E. (1996). Marital quality and conflict across the transition to parenthood in African American and white couples. *Journal of Marriage and the Family, 58*, 933–944.

Crohn, H. M. (2006). Five styles of positive stepmothering from the perspective of young adult stepdaughters. *Journal of Divorce & Remarriage, 46*, 119–134.

Crook, T. H., & Larrabee, G. J. (1992). Normative data on a self-rating scale for evaluating memory in everyday life. *Archives of Clinical Neuropsychology, 7*, 41–51.

Crook, T. H., West, R. L., & Larrabee, G. J. (1993). The driving-reaction time test: Assessing age declines in dual-task performance. *Developmental Neuropsychology, 9*, 31–39.

Cross, S., & Markus, H. (1991). Possible selves across the lifespan. *Human Development, 34*, 230–255.

Crowe, M., Andel, R., Pedersen, N. L., Johansson, B., & Gatz, M. (2003). Does participation in leisure activities lead to a reduced risk of Alzheimer's disease? A prospective study of Swedish twins. *Journals of Gerontology: Psychological Sciences, 56B*, P249–P255.

Crown, W. (2001). Economic status of the elderly. In R. H. Binstock & L. K. George (Eds.), *Handbook of aging and the social sciences* (5th ed., pp. 352–368). San Diego: Academic Press.

Cuddy, A. J. C., & Fiske, S. T. (2002). Doddering but dear: Process, content, and function in stereotyping of older persons. In T. D. Nelson (Ed.), *Ageism: Stereotyping and prejudice against older persons* (pp. 3–26). Cambridge, MA: MIT Press.

Cunningham, M., & Thornton, A. (2007). Direct and indirect influences of parents' marital instability on children's attitudes toward cohabitation in young adulthood. *Journal of Divorce & Remarriage, 46*, 125–143.

Cunningham, W. R. (1987). Intellectual abilities and age. In K. W. Schaie (Ed.), *Annual review of gerontology and geriatrics* (Vol. 7, pp. 117–134). New York: Springer.

Currey, J. D., Brear, K., & Zioupos, P. (1996). The effects of aging and changes in mineral content in degrading the toughness of human femora. *Journal of Biomechanics, 29*, 257–260.

Cusack, B. J. (1995). Clinical pharmacology. In W. B. Abrams, M. H. Beers, & R. Berkow (Eds.), *The Merck manual of geriatrics* (2nd ed., pp. 255–276). Whitehouse Station, NJ: Merck.

Cutler, S. J., & Hendricks, J. (1990). Leisure and time use across the life course. In R. H. Binstock & L. K. George (Eds.), *Handbook of aging and the social sciences* (3rd ed., pp. 169–185). San Diego: Academic Press.

Cutrona, C. E. (1996). *Social support in couples.* Thousand Oaks, CA: Sage.

Cutter, M. A. G. (1991). Euthanasia: Reassessing the boundaries. *Journal of NIH Research, 3*(5), 59–61.

Daatland, S. O. (2007). Marital history and intergenerational solidarity: The impact of divorce and unmarried cohabitation. *Journal of Social Issues, 63,* 809-825.

Dahlin, E., Stigsdotter Neely, A., Larsson, A., Bäckman, L., & Nyberg, L. (2008). Transfer of learning after updating training mediated by the striatum. *Science, 320*(5882), 1510–1512.

Daigneault, G., Joly, P., & Frigon, J. (2002). Executive functions in the evaluation of accident risk of older drivers. *Journal of Clinical and Experimental Neuropsychology, 24,* 221–238.

Dalton, D. S., Cruickshanks, K. J., Klein, B. E. K., Klein, R., Wiley, T. L., & Nondahl, D. M. (2003). The impact of hearing loss on quality of life in older adults. *The Gerontologist, 43,* 661–668.

Dalton, S. T. (1992). Lived experience of never-married women. *Issues in Mental Health Nursing, 13,* 69–80.

Danforth, M. M., & Glass, J. C., Jr. (2001). Listen to my words, give meaning to my sorrow: A study in cognitive constructs in middle-age bereaved widows. *Death Studies, 25,* 513–529.

Das, I., & Agarwai, S. (2000). Effect of aging on memory for spatial locations of objects. *Psycho-Lingua, 30,* 17–20.

Daselaar, S. M., Veltman, D. J., Rombouts, S. A. R. B., Raaijmakers, J. G. W., & Jonker, C. (2003). Neuroanatomical correlates of episodic encoding and retrieval in young and elderly subjects. *Brain, 126*(1), 43–56.

Davies, D. R., Matthews, G., & Wong, C. S. K. (1991). Aging and work. In C. L. Cooper & I. T. Robertson (Eds.), *International review of industrial and organizational psychology* (Vol. 6, pp. 175–199). Chichester, UK: Wiley.

Davies, L. (2000). *Transitions and singlehood: The forgotten life course.* Unpublished manuscript.

Davies, L. (2003). Singlehood: Transitions within a gendered world. *Canadian Journal on Aging, 22,* 343–352.

Davies, P. G. (2007). Between health and illness. *Perspectives in Biology and Medicine, 50,* 444–452.

Davis, E. T., Fujawa, G., & Shikano, T. (2002). Perceptual processing and search efficiency of young and older adults in a simple-feature search task: A staircase approach. *Journals of Gerontology: Psychological Sciences, 57B,* P324–P337.

Davis, J. A., & Lapane, K. L. (2004). Do characteristics associated with nursing home residents vary by race/ethnicity? *Journal of Health Care for the Poor and Underserved, 15,* 251–266.

Davis, M., McKay, M., & Eshelman, E. R. (2000). *The relaxation and stress reduction workbook.* Oakland, CA: New Harbinger.

Dawson Hughes, B. (1996). Calcium and vitamin D nutritional needs of elderly women. *Journal of Nutrition, 126,* 1165s–1167s.

Day, D. V., & Bedeian, A. G. (1995). Personality similarity and work-related outcomes among African-American nursing personnel: A test of the supplementary model of person–environment congruence. *Journal of Vocational Behavior, 46,* 55–70.

Day, S. X., Rounds, J., & Swaney, K. (1998). The structure of vocational interests for diverse racial–ethnic groups. *Psychological Science, 9,* 40–44.

Deeg, D. J. H., Kardaun, J. W. P. F., & Fozard, J. L. (1996). Health, behavior, and aging. In K. W. Schaie & J. E. Birren (Eds.), *Handbook of the psychology of aging* (4th ed., pp. 129–149). San Diego: Academic Press.

de Frias, C. M., Dixon, R. A., & Bäckman, L. (2003). Use of memory compensation strategies is related to psychosocial and health indicators. *Journals of Gerontology: Psychological Sciences, 58B,* P12–P22.

DeFries, E., & Andresen, E. (in press). Caregiving and health. In J. C. Cavanaugh & C. K. Cavanaugh (Eds.), *Aging in America.* Westport, CT: Praeger.

de Groot, C. P., Perdigao, A. L., & Deurenberg, P. (1996). Longitudinal changes in anthropometric characteristics of elderly Europeans. SENECA Investigators. *European Journal of Clinical Nutrition, 50,* 2954–3007.

DeGroot, D. W., & Kenney, W. L. (2007) Impaired defense of core temperature in aged humans during mild cold stress. *American Journal of Physiology—Regulatory, Integrative, and Comparative Physiology, 292,* R103–R108.

de Groot, J.C., de Leeuw, F-E., Oudkerk, M., van Gijn, J., Hofman, A., Jolles, J., et al. (2002). Cerebral white matter lesions and cognitive decline. *The Rotterdam Scan Study. Ann Neuro, 52,* 335–341.

Dehon, H., & Bredart, S. (2004). False memories: Young and older adults think of semantic associates at the same rate, but young adults are more successful at source monitoring. *Psychology and Aging, 19,* 191–197.

de Jong Gierveld, J. (2004). Remarriage, unmarried cohabitation, living apart together: Partner relationships following bereavement or divorce. *Journal of Marriage and Family, 66,* 236–243.

de Magalhães, J. P., Costa, J., & Church, G. M. (2007). An analysis of the relationship between metabolism, developmental schedules, and longevity using phylogenetic independent contrasts. *The Journals of Gerontology Series A: Biological Sciences and Medical Sciences, 62,* 149–160.

del Pinal, J., & Singer, A. (1997). Generations of diversity: Latinos in the United States. *Population Bulletin, 52,* whole issue.

Dellefield, M. E. (2008). Best practices in nursing homes: Clinical supervision, management, and human resources practices. *Research in Gerontological Nursing, 1.*

DeMaris, A., & Rao, K. V. (1992). Premarital cohabitation and subsequent marital stability in the United States: A reassessment. *Journal of Marriage and the Family, 54,* 178–190.

Denney, N. W. (1984). A model of cognitive development across the life span. *Developmental Review, 4,* 171–191.

Denney, N. W. (1990). Adult age differences in traditional and practical problem solving. In E. A. Lovelace (Ed.), *Aging and cognition: Mental processes, self-awareness, and interventions* (pp. 329–349). Amsterdam: North-Holland.

Denney, N. W., Dew, J. R., & Kihlstrom, J. F. (1992). An adult developmental study of the encoding of spatial location. *Experimental Aging Research, 18,* 25–32.

Denney, N. W., Dew, J. R., & Kroupa, S. L. (1995). Perceptions of wisdom: What is it and who has it? *Journal of Adult Development, 2,* 37–47.

Denney, N. W., & Pearce, K. A. (1989). A developmental study of practical problem solving in adults. *Psychology and Aging, 4,* 438–442.

Denney, N. W., Pearce, K. A., & Palmer, A. M. (1982). A developmental study of adults' performance on traditional and practical problem-solving tasks. *Experimental Aging Research, 8,* 115–118.

Dennis, N., Howard, J., & Howard, D. (2003). Age deficits in learning sequences of spoken words. *Journals of Gerontology: Psychological Sciences, 38B,* P224–P227.

Department of Urology, Cornell University. (2008). *Types of urinary incontinence.* Retrieved September 28, 2008, from http://www.cornellurology.com/incontinence/gi/types.shtml.

DePaulo, B. M. (2006). *Singled out: How singles are stereotyped, stigmatized, and ignored, and still live happily ever after.* New York: St Martin's Press.

Derman, D. S. (2000). Grief and attachment in young widowhood. *Dissertation Abstracts International Section A: Humanities and Social Sciences, 60*(7-A), 2383.

de St. Aubin, E., & McAdams, D. P. (1995). The relations of generative concern and generative action to personality traits, satisfaction/happiness with life, and ego development. *Journal of Adult Development, 2,* 99–112.

Deutsch, A. (2001, April 11). Dutch parliament OKs strict euthanasia bill. *Wilmington (NC) Morning Star,* 2A.

Devolder, P. A., Brigham, M. C., & Pressley, M. (1990). Memory performance awareness in younger and older adults. *Psychology and Aging, 5,* 291–303.

de Vries, B. (1996). The understanding of friendship: An adult life course perspective. In C. Magai & S. H. McFadden (Eds.), *Handbook of emotion, adult development, and aging.* San Diego: Academic Press.

Diamond, J. (1986). I want a girl just like the girl. . . . *Discover, 7*(11), 65–68.

Dickens, B. M., Boyle, J. M . , Jr., & Ganzini, L. (2008). Euthanasia and assisted suicide. In P. A. Singer, & A. M. Viens (Eds.), *The Cambridge textbook of bioethics* (pp. 72–77). New York: Cambridge University Press.

Diehl, M. (1998). Everyday competence in later life: Current status and future directions. *The Gerontologist, 4,* 422–433.

Diehl, M., Coyle, N., & Labouvie-Vief, G. (1996). Age and sex differences in strategies of coping and defense across the life span. *Psychology and Aging, 11,* 127–139.

Diehl, M., Hastings, C. T., & Stanton, J. M. (2001). Self-concept differentiation across the adult life span. *Psychology and Aging, 16,* 643–654.

Diehl, M., Marsiske, M., Horgas, A. L., Rosenberg, A., Saczynski, J. S., & Willis, S. L. (2005). The Revised Observed Tasks of Daily Living: A performance-based assessment of everyday problem solving in older adults. *Journal of Applied Gerontology, 24,* 211–230.

Diehl, M., Willis, S. L., & Schaie, K. W. (1995). Everyday problem solving in older adults: Observational assessment and cognitive correlates. *Psychology and Aging, 10,* 478–491.

Diehl, R. L. (1998). Locus equations: A partial solution to the problem of consonant place perception. *Behavioral and Brain Sciences, 21,* 264.

Dijkstra, K., Yazley, R. H., Madden, C. J., & Zwaan, R. A. (2004). The role of age and perceptual symbols in language comprehension. *Psychology and Aging, 19,* 352–356.

Dillaway, H., Byrnes, M., Miller, S., & Rehnan, S. (2008). Talking "among *us*": How women from different racial-ethnic groups define and discuss menopause. *Health Care for Women International, 29,* 766–781.

Dillon, J. J. (2002). The role of the child in adult development. *Journal of Adult Development, 9*, 267–275.

Dimond, M., Lund, D. A., & Caserta, M. S. (1987). The role of social support in the first two years of bereavement in an elderly sample. *The Gerontologist, 27*, 599–604.

Diprete, T. A., & Soule, W. T. (1988). Gender and promotion in segmented job ladder systems. *American Sociological Review, 53*, 26–40.

Ditre, C. M., Griffin, T. D., Murphy, G. F., Sueki, H., Telegan, B., Johnson, W. C., Yu, R. J., & Van Scott, E. J. (1996). Effects of alpha-hydroxy acids on photoaged skin: A pilot clinical, histologic, and ultrastructural study. *Journal of the American Academy of Dermatology, 34*, 187–195.

Dixon, R. A. (1999). Exploring cognition in interactive situations: Aging of N+1 minds. In T. A. Hess & F. Blanchard-Fields (Eds.), *Social cognition and aging* (pp. 267–290). San Diego: Academic Press.

Dixon, R. A., & Bäckman, L. (Eds.). (1995). *Compensating for psychological deficiencies and declines: Managing less and promoting gains.* Mahwah, NJ: Erlbaum.

Dixon, R. A., & Gould, O. N. (1998). Younger and older adults collaborating on retelling everyday stories. *Applied Development Science, 2*, 160–171.

Dixon, R. A., Hultsch, D. F., & Hertzog, C. (1989). The Metamemory in Adulthood questionnaire. *Psychopharmacology Bulletin, 24*, 671–688.

Dobbs, D., Eckert, J. K., Rubinstein, B., Keimig, L., Clark, L., Frankowski, A. C., & Zimmerman, S. (2008). An ethnographic study of stigma and ageism in residential care or assisted living. *The Gerontologist, 48*, 517–526.

Dodge, H. H., Zitzelberger, T., Oken, B. S., Howieson, D., & Kaye, J. (2008). A randomized placebo-controlled trial of Ginkgo biloba for the prevention of cognitive decline. *Neurology, 70*, 1809–1817.

Dodson, C. S., & Schacter, D. L. (2002). Aging and strategic retrieval processes: Reducing false memories with a distinctiveness heuristic. *Psychology and Aging, 17*, 405–415.

Dohanich, G. (2003). Ovarian steroids and cognitive function. *Current Directions in Psychological Science, 12*, 57–61.

Dohm, A. (2000, July). Gauging the labor force effects of retiring baby-boomers. *Monthly Labor Review*, pp. 17–25.

Doka, K. J., & Mertz, M. E. (1988). The meaning and significance of great-grandparenthood. *The Gerontologist, 28*, 192–197.

Donatelle, R. J., & Davis, L. G. (1997). *Health: The basics* (2nd ed.). Englewood Cliffs, NJ: Prentice-Hall.

Donnellan, M. B., & Lucas, R. E. (2008). Age differences in the Big Five across the life span: Evidence from two national samples. *Psychology and Aging, 23*, 558–566.

Doraiswamy, P. M. (2003). Interventions for mild cognitive impairment and Alzheimer's disease: New strategies, new hope. *American Journal of Geriatric Psychiatry, 11*, 120–130.

Doran, G. (2002). Family grief experience at the death of a child in the Mexican American community. *Dissertation Abstracts International: Section B: The Sciences and Engineering, 63*(5-B), 2578.

Dorgan, J. F., Stanczyk, F. A., Longcope, C., Stephenson, H. E., Jr., Chang, L., Miller, R., Franz, C., Falk, R. T., & Kahle, L. (1997). Relationship of serum dehydroepiandrosterone (DHEA), DHEA sulfate, and 5-androstene-3

beta, 17 beta-diol to risk of breast cancer in postmenopausal women. *Cancer Epidemiology, Biomarkers and Prevention, 6*, 177–181.

Doyle, K. O., Jr. (1974). Theory and practice of ability testing in ancient Greece. *Journal of the History of the Behavioral Sciences, 10*, 202–212.

Draganski, B., Gaser, C., Busch, V., Schuierer, G., Bogdahn, U., & May, A. (2004). Neuroplasticity: changes in grey matter induced by training. *Nature, 427*(6972), 311–312.

Draganski, B., Gaser, C., Kempermann, G., Kuhn, H. G., Winkler, J., Büchel, C., May, A. (2006). Temporal and spatial dynamics of brain structure changes during extensive learning. *Journal of Neuroscience: The Official Journal of the Society for Neuroscience, 26*(23), 6314–6317.

Drew, L. M., & Silverstein, M. (2005). Intergenerational role investments of great-grandparents: Consequences for psychological well-being. *Ageing and Society, 24*, 95–111.

Drew, L. M., & Smith, P. (1999, November). The mental health of grandparents in Britain: Regular contact compared to those who have lost contact due to parental separation/divorce. Paper presented at the annual meeting of the Gerontological Society., San Francisco.

DuBois, P. H. (1968). A test-dominated society: China 1115 B.C.–1905 A.D. In J. L. Barnette (Ed.), *Readings in psychological tests and measurements* (pp. 249–255). Homewood, IL: Dorsey Press.

Duke, J., Leventhal, H., Brownlee, S., & Leventhal, E. A. (2002). Giving up and replacing activities in response to illness. *Journals of Gerontology: Psychological Sciences, 57B*, P367–P376.

Duncan, R. E., Gillam, L., Savulescu, J., Williamson, R., Rogers, J. G., & Delatycki, M. B. (2007). "Holding your breath": Interviews with young people who have undergone predictive genetic testing for Huntington's disease. *American Journal of Medical Genetics, Part A, 143A*, 1984–1989.

Duncan, R. E., Gillam, L., Savulescu, J., Williamson, R., Rogers, J. G., & Delatycki, M. B. (2008). "You're one of us now": Young people describe their experiences of predictive genetic testing for Huntington's disease (HD) and familial adenomatous polyposis (FAP). *American Journal of Medical Genetics. Part C, Seminars in Medical Genetics, 148C*, 47–55.

Dunlosky, J., Cavallini, E., Roth, H., McGuire, C. L., Vecchi, T., Hertzog, C. (2007). Do self-monitoring interventions improve older adult learning? *Journals of Gerontology: Series B, Psychological Sciences and Social Sciences, 62*(Spec. No. 1), 70-76.

Dunlosky, J., & Connor, L. (1997). Age difference in the allocation of study time account for age differences in memory performance. *Memory and Cognition, 25*, 691–700.

Dunlosky, J., & Hertzog, C. (1998). Training programs to improve learning in later adulthood: Helping older adults educate themselves. In D. J. Hacker, J. Dunlosky, & A. C. Graessen (Eds.), *Metacognition in educational theory and practice* (pp. 249–275). Hillsdale, NJ: Erlbaum.

Dunlosky, J., Kubat-Silman, A. K., & Hertzog, C. (2003). Training monitoring skills improves older adults' self-paced associative learning. *Psychology and Aging, 18*, 340–345.

Dunn, T. R., & Merriam, S. B. (1995). Levinson's age thirty transition: Does it exist? *Journal of Adult Development, 2*, 113–124.

Dupree, L. W., & Schonfeld, L. (1996). Substance abuse. In M. Hersen & V. B. Van Hasselt (Eds.), *Psychological treatment of older adults* (pp. 281–297). New York: Plenum.

Duvall, E. M. (1977). *Marriage and family development* (5th ed.). Philadelphia: Lippincott.

Dwivedi, Y., Rizavi, H. S., Conley, R. R., Roberts, R. C., Tamminga, C. A., & Pandey, G. N. (2003). Altered gene expression of brain-derived neurotrophic factor and receptor tyrosine kinase b in post-mortem brain of suicide subjects. *Archives of General Psychiatry, 60*, 804–815.

Dwyer, J. W., & Coward, R. T. (1991). A multivariate comparison of the involvement of adult sons versus daughters in the care of impaired parents. *Journals of Gerontology: Social Sciences, 46*, S259–S269.

Dywan, J., & Jacoby, L. L. (1990). Effects of aging on source monitoring: Differences in susceptibility to false fame. *Psychology and Aging, 5*, 379–387.

Earles, J. L., Connor, L. T., Frieske, D., Park, D. C., Smith, A. D., & Zwahr, M. (1997). Age differences in inhibition: Possible causes and consequences. *Aging, Neuropsychology, and Cognition, 4*, 45–57.

Ebersole, P., Hess, P., & Luggen, A. S. (2004). *Toward healthy aging* (6th ed.). St. Louis: Mosby.

Ebner, N. C., Freund, A. M., & Baltes, P. B. (2006). Developmental changes in personal goal orientation from young to late adulthood: From striving for gains to maintenance and prevention of losses. *Psychology and Aging, 21*, 664–678.

Eby, L. T., Butts, M., & Lockwood, A. (2003). Predictors of success in the era of the boundaryless career. *Journal of Organizational Behavior, 24*, 689–708.

Eby, L. T. & McManus, S. E. (2002, April). Protégés' most positive mentoring experience. In R. Day & T. D. Allen (Co-Chairs), *Underlying processes responsible for beneficial mentorships: Implications of emerging research.* Annual meeting of the Society for Industrial and Organizational Psychology, Toronto.

Edelstein, B., & Kalish, K. (1999). Clinical assessment of older adults. In J. C. Cavanaugh & S. K. Whitbourne (Eds.), *Gerontology: An interdisciplinary perspective* (pp. 269–304). New York: Oxford University Press.

Edelstein, B., & Semenchuck, E. M. (1996). Interviewing older adults. In L. L. Carstensen, B. A. Edelstein, & L. Dornbrand (Eds.), *The practical handbook of clinical gerontology* (pp. 153–173). Thousand Oaks, CA: Sage.

Edwards, M. B. (2006). The relationship between the internal working model of attachment and patterns of grief experienced by college students after the death of a parent. *Dissertation Abstracts International Section A: Humanities and Social Sciences, 66*(11-A), 4197.

Einstein, G. O., Earles, J. L., & Collins, H. M. (2002). Gaze aversion: Spared inhibition for visual distraction in older adults. *Journals of Gerontology: Psychological Sciences, 57B*, P65–P73.

Einstein, G. O., & McDaniel, M. A. (1990). Normal aging and prospective memory. *Journal of Experimental Psychology: Learning, Memory, and Cognition, 16*, 717–726.

Einstein, G. O., McDaniel, M. A., Manzi, M., Cochran, B., & Baker, M. (2000). Prospective memory and aging: Forgetting intentions over short delays. *Psychology and Aging, 15*, 671–683.

Eisdorfer, C., Czaja, S. J., Loewenstein, D. A., Rubert, M. P., Argüelles, S., Mitrani, V. B., & Szapocznik, J. (2003). The effect of a family therapy and technology-based intervention on caregiver depression. *The Gerontologist, 43*, 521–531.

Ekerdt, D. J. (1987). Why the notion persists that retirement harms health. *The Gerontologist, 27*, 454–457.

Ekstrom, R. K., French, J. W., & Harman, H. H. (1979). Cognitive factors: Their identification and replication. *Multivariate Behavioral Research Monographs, 79*(2).

ElderCare.gov. (2005). *Fact sheets: Adult day care.* Retrieved November 1, 2008, from http://www.eldercare.gov/eldercare/Public/resources/fact_sheets/adult_day.asp.

El Haber, N., Erbas, B., Hill, K. D., & Wark, J. D. (2008). Relationship between age and measures of balance, strength, and gait: Linear and non-linear analyses. *Clinical Science, 114,* 719–727.

Elias, M. F., Elias, P. K., Cobb, J., D'Agostino, R., White, L. R., & Wolf, P. A. (1995). Blood pressure affects cognitive functioning: The Framingham Studies revisited. In J. E. Dimsdale & A. Braum (Eds.), *Quality of life in behavioral medicine research* (pp. 121–143). Hillsdale, NJ: Erlbaum.

Elliott, J., & Oliver, I. (2008). Choosing between life and death: Patient and family perceptions of the decision not to resuscitate the terminally ill cancer patient. *Bioethics, 22,* 179–189.

Ellison, C. G. (1990). Family ties, friendships, and subjective well-being among black Americans. *Journal of Marriage and the Family, 52,* 298–310.

Emanuel, L. L. (2008). Advance directives. *Annual Review of Medicine, 59,* 187–198.

Emick, M. A., & Hayslip, B., Jr. (1999). Custodial grandparenting: Stresses, coping skills, and relationships with grandchildren. *International Journal of Aging and Human Development, 48,* 35–61.

Emlet, C. A. (1997). HIV/AIDS in the elderly: A hidden population. *Home Care Provider, 2,* 22–28.

Emlet, C. A., & Farkas, K. J. (2002). Correlates of service utilization among midlife and older adults with HIV/AIDS: The role of age in the equation. *Journal of Aging and Health, 14,* 315–335.

Engle, E., Miguel, R., Steelman, L., & McDaniel, M. A. (1994, April). *The relationship between age and work needs: A comprehensive research integration.* Paper presented at the National Meetings of the Society for Industrial and Organizational Psychology, Nashville, TN.

Enright, R. D., Gassin, E. A., & Wu, C. (1992). Forgiveness: A developmental view. *Journal of Moral Education, 21,* 99–114.

Epstein, S., Lipson, A., Holstein, C., & Huh, E. (1992). Irrational reactions to negative outcomes: Evidence for two conceptual systems. *Journal of Personality and Social Psychology, 62,* 328–339.

Erber, J. T., & Prager, I. G. (1997). Age and forgetfulness: Absolute versus comparative decisions about capability. *Experimental Aging Research, 23,* 355–367.

Erber, J. T., & Prager, I. G. (1999). Perceptions of forgetful young and older adults. In T. M. Hess & F. Blanchard-Fields (Eds.), *Social cognition and aging* (pp. 197–217). San Diego: Academic Press.

Erber, J. T., & Szuchman, L. T. (2002). Age and capability: The role of forgetting and personal traits. *International Journal of Aging and Human Development, 54*(3), 173–189.

Erber, J. T., Szuchman, L. T., & Etheart, M. E. (1993). Age and forgetfulness: Young perceivers' impressions of young and older neighbors. *International Journal of Aging and Human Development, 37,* 91–103.

Erber, J. T., Szuchman, L. T., & Rothberg, S. T. (1990). Everyday memory failure: Age differences in appraisal and attribution. *Psychology and Aging, 5,* 236–241.

Ericsson, K. A., & Charness, N. (1994). Expert performance: Its structure and acquisition. *American Psychology, 49,* 725–747.

Erikson, E. H. (1968). *Identity: Youth and crisis.* New York: Norton.

Erikson, E. H. (1982). *The life cycle completed: Review.* New York: Norton.

Erixon-Lindroth, N., Farde, L., Robins Wahlin, T. B., Sovago, J., Halldin, C., et al. (2005). The role of the striatal dopamine transporter in cognitive aging. *Psychiatry Research Neuroimaging, 138,* 1–12.

Espino, D. V., & Maldonado, D. (1990). Hypertension and acculturation in elderly Mexican Americans: Results from 1982–84 Hispanic HANES. *Journals of Gerontology: Medical Sciences, 45,* M209–M213.

Ettinger, W. H. (1995). Bone, joint, and rheumatic disorders. In W. B. Abrams, M. H. Beers, & R. Berkow (Eds.), *The Merck manual of geriatrics* (2nd ed., pp. 925–945). Whitehouse Station, NJ: Merck Research Laboratories.

Etzion, D. (2003). Annual vacation: Duration of relief from job stressors and burnout. *Anxiety, Stress and Coping, 16,* 213–226.

Etzion, D., & Bailyn, L. (1994). Patterns of adjustment to the career/family conflict of technically trained women in U.S. and Israel. *Journal of Applied Social Psychology, 24,* 1520–1549.

Etzioni, A. (1997, August 13). Marriage with no easy outs. *New York Times on the Web.* Online document at http://www.nytimes.com. Accessed November 13, 2004.

Evandrou, M., & Glaser, K. (2004). Changing economic and social roles: The experience of four cohorts of mid-life individuals in Britain, 1985–2000. *Population Trends, 110,* 19–30.

Faber, A. J. (2004). Examining remarried couples through a bowenian family systems lens. *Journal of Divorce & Remarriage, 40,* 121–133.

Fabrigoule, C., Letenneur, L., Dartigues, J. F., Zarrouk, M., Commenges, D., & Barberger-Gateau, P. (1995). Social and leisure activities and risk of dementia: A prospective longitudinal study. *Journal of the American Geriatrics Society, 43,* 485–490.

Fairlie, H. (1988). Talkin' 'bout my generation. *New Republic, 198,* 19–22.

Farrell, M. P., Rosenberg, S., & Rosenberg, H. T. (1993). Changing texts of identity from early to late middle age: On the emergent prominence of fatherhood. In J. Demick & K. Bursik (Eds.), *Parental development* (pp. 203–224). Hillsdale, NJ: Erlbaum.

Faulkner, R. A., Davey, M., & Davey, A. (2005). Gender-related predictors of change in marital satisfaction and marital conflict. *American Journal of Family Therapy, 33,* 61–83.

Fauth, E. B., Zarit, S. H., & Malmberg, B. (2008). Mediating relationships within the Disablement Process model: A cross-sectional study of the oldest-old. *European Journal of Aging, 5,* 161–179.

Feder, J., Komisar, H. L., & Friedland, R. B. (2007). *Long-term care financing: Policy options for the future.* Retrieved October 19, 2008, from http://ltc.georgetown.edu/forum/ltcfinalpaper061107.pdf.

Fehr, B. (1996). *Friendship processes.* Thousand Oaks, CA: Sage.

Felber, M. (2000). *Finding your way after your spouse dies.* Notre Dame, IN: Ave Maria Press.

Feldman, D. C. (1994). The decision to retire early: A review and conceptualization. *Academy of Management Review, 19,* 285–311.

Feldman, H. H., Jacova, C., Robillard, A., Garcia, A., Chow, T., Borrie, M., Schipper, H. M., Blair, M.,

Kertesz, A., & Chertkow, H. (2008). Diagnosis and treatment of dementia: 2. Diagnosis. *Canadian Medical Association Journal, 178,* 825–836. Retrieved October 26, 2008, from http://www.ecmaj.ca/cgi/reprint/178/7/825.

Felton, B. J., & Revenson, T. A. (1987). Age differences in coping with chronic illness. *Psychology and Aging, 2,* 164–170.

Femia, E. E., Zarit, S. H., & Johansson, B. (2001). The disablement process in very late life: A study of the oldest-old in Sweden. *Journals of Gerontology: Psychological Sciences, 56B,* P12–P23.

Feminist Majority Foundation. (1991). *Empowering women in business.* Washington, DC: Author.

Feminist Majority Foundation. (2008). *Domestic violence facts.* Retrieved March 15, 2008, from http://feminist.org/other/dv/dvfact.html.

Fernandes, M. A., & Moscovitch, M. (2003). Interference effects from divided attention during retrieval in younger and older adults. *Psychology and Aging, 18,* 219–230.

Ferraro, K. F., & Su, Y. (1999). Financial strain, social relations, and psychological distinctiveness among older people: A cross-cultural analysis. *Journals of Gerontology: Social Sciences, 54B,* S3–S15.

Fiatarone, M. A., Marks, E. C., Ryan, N. D., Meredith, C. N., Lipsitz, L. A., & Evans, W. J. (1990). High-intensity strength training in nonagenarians: Effects on skeletal muscle. *JAMA [Journal of the American Medical Association], 263,* 3029–3034.

Field, D., & Millsap, R. E. (1991). Personality in advanced old age: Continuity or change? *Journals of Gerontolog: Psychological Sciences, 46B,* P299–P308.

Field, D., & Minkler, M. (1988). Continuity and change in social support between young-old and old-old or very-old age. *Journals of Gerontology: Psychological Sciences, 43,* P100–P106.

Field, N. P., Gal-Oz, E., & Bonanno, G. A. (2003). Continuing bonds and adjustment at 5 years after the death of a spouse. *Journal of Consulting and Clinical Psychology, 71,* 110–117.

Field, N. P., Gao, B., & Paderna, L. (2005). Continuing bonds in bereavement: An attachment theory based perspective. *Death Studies, 29,* 277–299.

Fields, T. M., & Widmayer, S. M. (1982). Motherhood. In B. B. Wolman (Ed.), *Handbook of developmental psychology* (pp. 681–701). Englewood Cliffs, NJ: Prentice Hall.

Fillenbaum, G. G. (1985). Screening the elderly: A brief instrumental activities of daily living measure. *Journal of the American Geriatrics Society, 33,* 698–706.

Fillenbaum, G. G., Blazer, D. G., Burchett, B. M., Saunders, A. M., & Taylor, D. H., Jr. (2002). Apolipoprotein E-4 and risk of mortality in African American and white older community residents. *The Gerontologist, 42,* 381–386.

Finch, C. E., & Seeman, T. E. (1999). Stress theories of aging. In V. L. Bengtson & K. W. Schaie (Eds.), *Handbook of theories of aging* (pp. 81–97). New York: Springer.

Fincham, F. D. (2003). Marital conflict: Correlates, structure, and context. *Current Directions in Psychological Science, 12,* 23–27.

Finckh, U., von der Kammer, H., Velden, J., Michel, T., Andersen, B., Deng, A., Zhang, J., Mueller, T. T., Zuchowski, K., Menzer, G., Mann, U. Papassotiropoulos, A., Jeun, R., Zurdel, J., Holst, F., Benussi, L., Stoppe, G., Reiss, J., Miserez, A. R., Staehelin, H. B., Rebeck, G. W., Hyman, B. T., Binetti, G., Hock, C., Growdon, J. H., & Nitsch, R. M.

(2000). Genetic association of a cystatin C gene polumorphism with late-onset Alzheimer disease. *Archives of Neurology, 57,* 1579–1583.

Finefrock, A. E., Bush, A. I., & Doraiswamy, P. M. (2003). Current status of metals as therapeutic targets in Alzheimer's disease. *Journal of the American Geriatrics Society, 51,* 1143–1148.

Fingerman, K. L. (1996). Sources of tension in the aging mother and adult daughter relationship. *Psychology and Aging, 11,* 591–606.

Finkel, D., Reynolds, C. A., McArdle, J. J., Gatz, M., & Pederson, N. L. (2003). Latent growth curve analyses of accelerating decline in cognitive abilities in late adulthood. *Developmental Psychology, 39,* 535–550.

Finucane, M. L., Slovic, P., Hibbard, J. H., Peters, E., Mertz, C. K., & MacGregor, D. G. (2002). Aging and decision-making competence: An analysis of comprehension and consistency skills in older versus younger adults considering health-plan options. *Journal of Behavioral Decision Making, 15,* 141–164.

Fisher, G., Plassman, B., Heeringa, S., Langa, K. (2008). Assessing the relationship of cognitive aging and processes of dementia. In S. M. Hofer & D. F. Alwin (Eds.), *Handbook of cognitive aging: Interdisciplinary perspectives* (pp. 340–351). Greenwich, CT: Sage.

Fisher, J. E., Drossel, C., Ferguson, K., Cherup, S., & Sylvester, M. (2008). Treating persons with dementia in context. In D. Gallagher-Thompson, A. M. Steffen, & L. W. Thompson (Eds.), *Handbook of behavioral and cognitive therapies with older adults* (pp. 200–218). New York: Springer.

Fisher-Borne, M. (2007). Making the link: Domestic violence in the GLBT community. In L. Messinger & D. F. Morrow (Eds.), *Case studies on sexual orientation and gender expression in social work practice* (pp. 96–98). New York: Columbia University Press.

Fisk, A. D., Cooper, B. P., Hertzog, C., & Anderson-Garlach, M. M. (1995a). Age-related retention of skilled memory search: Examination of associative learning, interference, and task-specific skills. *Journals of Gerontology: Psychological Sciences, 50B,* P150–P161.

Fisk, A. D., Cooper, B. P., Hertzog, C., Anderson-Garlach, M. M., & Lee, M. D. (1995b). Understanding performance and learning in consistent memory search: An age-related perspective. *Psychology and Aging, 10,* 255–268.

Fisk, A. D., & Rogers, W. A. (1991). Toward an understanding of age-related memory and visual search effects. *Journal of Experimental Psychology: General, 120,* 131–149.

Fiske, S. (1993). Social cognition and social perception. *Annual Review of Psychology, 50,* 229–238.

Fitzgerald, J. M. (1999). Autobiographical memory and social cognition: Development of the remembered self in adulthood. In T. M. Hess & F. Blanchard-Fields, *Social cognition in aging* (pp. 147–171). San Diego: Academic Press.

Fitzgerald, J. M. (2000). Younger and older jurors: The influence of environmental supports on memory performance and decision making in complex trials. *Journals of Gerontology: Psychological Sciences, 55B,* P323–P331.

Fitzgerald, J. M., & Lawrence, R. (1984). Autobiographical memory across the life span. *Journals of Gerontology: Psychological Sciences, 39,* 692–698.

Fitzgerald, L. F., & Ormerod, A. J. (1991). Perceptions of sexual harassment: The influence of gender and academic context. *Psychology of Women Quarterly, 15,* 281–294.

Fitzgerald, L. F., & Shullman, S. L. (1993). Sexual harassment: A research analysis and agenda for the 1990s. *Journal of Vocational Behavior, 32,* 5–27.

Fitzgerald, L. F., Shullman, S. L., Bailey, N., Richards, M., Swecker, J., Gold, Y., Ormerod, M., & Weitzman, L. (1988). The incidences and dimensions of sexual harassment in academia and the workplace. *Journal of Vocational Behavior, 32*(2), 152–175.

Fitzsimmons, S. (2002). Alternative therapies. *American Journal of Alzheimer's Disease and Other Dementias, 17,* 200.

Fitzwater, E. L. (2008). *Older adults and mental health: Part 2: Anxiety disorder.* Retrieved April 20, 2008, from http://www.netwellness.org/healthtopics/aging/anxietydisorder.cfm.

Flaks, D. K., Ficher, I., Masterpasqua, F., & Joseph, G. (1995). Lesbians choosing mother-hood: A comparative study of lesbian and heterosexual parents and their children. *Developmental Psychology, 31,* 105–114.

Fleischman, D. A., & Gabrieli, J. D. E. (1998). Repetition priming in normal aging and Alzheimer's disease: A review of findings and theories. *Psychology and Aging, 13,* 88–119.

Fleming, S., & Robinson, P. (2001). Grief and cognitive-behavioral therapy: The reconstruction of meaning. In M. S. Stroebe, R. O. Hansson, W. Stroebe, & H. Schut (Eds.), *Handbook of bereavement research: Consequences, coping, and care* (pp. 647–669). Washington, DC: American Psychological Association.

Flippen, C., & Tienda, M. (2000). Pathways to retirement: Patterns of labor force participation and labor market exit among the pre-retirement population by race, Hispanic origin, and sex. *Journals of Gerontology: Social Sciences, 55,* S14–S27.

Flores, L. Y., & O'Brien, K. M. (2002). The career development of Mexican American adoles-cent women: A test of social cognitive career theory. *Journal of Counseling Psychology, 49,* 14–27.

Flynn, E., Pine, K., & Lewis, C. (2006). The microgenetic method: Time for change? *The Psychologist, 19,*152–155.

Flynn, H. K. (2007). Friendship: A longitudinal study of friendship characteristics, life transitions, and social factors that influence friendship quality. *Dissertation Abstracts International Section A: Humanities and Social Sciences, 67*(9-A), 3608.

Flynn, T. M., & Storandt, M. (1990). Supplemental group discussions in memory training for older adults. *Psychology and Aging, 5,* 178–181.

Foley, D. J., Miles, T. P., Brock, D. B., & Phillips, C. (1995). Recounts of elderly deaths: Endorsements for the Patient Self-Determination Act. *The Gerontologist, 35,* 119–121.

Foley, K. L., Tung, M-J., & Mutran, E. J. (2002). Self-gain and self-loss among African American and White caregivers. *Journals of Gerontology: Social Sciences, 57B,* S14–S22.

Folkman, S., Lazarus, R. S., Pimley, S., & Novacek, J. (1987). Age differences in stress and coping pro-cesses. *Psychology and Aging, 2,* 171–184.

Food and Drug Administration. (2008). *Manufacturers of TNF-blocker drugs must highlight risk of fungal infections.* Retrieved September 28, 2008, from http://www.fda.gov/bbs/topics/NEWS/2008/NEW01879.html.

Fortner, B. V., & Neimeyer, R. A. (1999). Death anxiety in older adults: A quantitative review. *Death Studies, 23,* 387–411.

Fougeyrollas, P., & Beauregard, L. (2001). An interactive person–environment social creation. In G. Albrecht, K. Seelman, & M. Bury (Eds.), *Handbook of disability studies* (pp. 171–194). Thousand Oaks, CA: Sage.

Fowler, K. L. (2008). "The wholeness of things": Infusing diversity and social justice into death education. *Omega: Journal of Death and Dying, 57,* 53–91.

Fozard, J. L. (1981). Speed of mental performance and aging: Costs of age and benefits of wisdom. In F. J. Piorzzolo & G. J. Maletta (Eds.), *Behavioral assessment and psychopharmacology* (pp. 59–94). New York: Praeger.

Fozard, J. L., Vercruyssen, M., Reynolds, S. L., Hancock, P. A., & Quilter, R. E. (1994). Age differences and changes in reaction time: The Baltimore longitudinal study of aging. *Journals of Gerontology: Psychological Sciences, 49,* P179–P189.

Fraas, M., Lockwood, J., Neils-Strunjas, J., Shidler, M., Krikorian, R., & Weiler, E. (2002). "What's his name?" A comparison of elderly participants' and undergraduate students' misnamings. *Archives of Gerontology and Geriatrics, 34,* 155–165.

Franceschi, C., Motta, L., Motta, M., Malaguarnera, M., Capri, M., Vasto, S., Candore, G., Carus, C., & IMUSCE. (2008). The extreme longevity: The state of the art in Italy. *Experimental Gerontology, 43,* 45–52.

Franceschi, K. A. (2005). The experience of the transition to motherhood in women who have suffered maternal loss in adolescence. *Dissertation Abstracts International: Section B: The Sciences and Engineering, 65*(8-B), 4282.

Frank, L., Smyer, M. A., Grisso, T., & Appelbaum, P. (1999). Measurement of advance directive and medical treatment decision-making capacity of older adults. *Journal of Mental Health and Aging, 5,* 257–274.

Franks, M. M., Pierce, L. S., & Dwyer, J. W. (2003). Expected parent-care involvement of adult children. *Journal of Applied Gerontology, 22,* 104–117.

Frazier, L. D., Hooker, K., Johnson, P. M., & Kaus, C. R. (2000). Continuity and change in possible selves in later life: A 5-year longitudinal study. *Basic and Applied Social Psychology, 22,* 237–243.

Frazier, L. D., Johnson, P. M., Gonzalez, G. K., & Kafka, C. L. (2002) Psychosocial influences on possible selves: A comparison of three cohorts of older adults. *International Journal of Behavioral Development, 26,* 308–317.

Frerichs, F., & Naegele, G. (1997). Discrimination of older workers in Germany: Obstacles and options for the integration into employment. *Journal of Aging and Social Policy, 9,* 89–101.

Freund, A. M., & Baltes, P. B. (1998). Selection, optimization, and compensation as strategies of life management: Correlations with subjective indicators of successful aging. *Psychology and Aging, 13,* 531–543.

Freund, A. M., & Baltes, P. B. (2000). The orchestration of selection, optimization, and compensation: An action-theoretical conceptualization of a theory of developmental regulation. In W. J. Perrig & A. Grob (Eds.), *Control of human behavior, mental processes and consciousness* (pp. 35–58). Mahwah, NJ: Erlbaum.

Freund, A. M., & Baltes, P. B. (2002). The adaptiveness of selection, optimization, and compensation as strategies of life management: Evidence from a preference study on proverbs. *Journals of Gerontology: Psychological Sciences, 57B,* P426–P434.

Friedhoff, A. J. (1994). Consensus development conference statement: Diagnosis and treatment of depression in late life. In L. S. Schneider, C. F. Reynolds, B. D. Lebowitz, & A. J. Friedhoff (Eds.), *Diagnosis and treatment of depression in late life: Results of the NIH Consensus Development Conference* (pp. 493–511). Washington, DC: American Psychiatric Press.

Fries, J. F. (2003). Measuring and monitoring success in compressing morbidity. *Annals of Internal Medicine, 139,* 455–459.

Froman, L. (1994). Adult learning in the workplace. In J. D. Sinnott (Ed.), *Interdisciplinary handbook of adult lifespan learning* (pp. 203–217). Westport, CT: Greenwood.

Fromholt, P., & Bruhn, P. (1999). Cognitive dysfunction and dementia. In I. H. Nordhus, G. R. VandenBos, S. Berg, & P. Fromholt (Eds.), *Clinical geropsychology* (pp. 183–188). Washington, DC: American Psychological Association.

Frone, M. R. (2003). Work-family balance. In J. C. Quick & L. E. Tetric (Eds.), *Handbook of occupational health psychology* (pp. 143–162). Washington, DC: American Psychological Association.

Frone, M. R., & Yardley, J. (1996). Workplace family supportive programs: Predictors of employed parents' importance ratings. *Journal of Occupational and Organizational Psychology, 69,* 351–366.

Fruhauf, C. A. (2007). Grandchildren's perceptions of caring for grandparents. *Dissertation Abstracts International Section A: Humanities and Social Sciences. 68(3-A),* 1120.

Fry, P. S. (2003). Perceived self-efficacy domains as predictors of fear of the unknown and fear of dying among older adults. *Psychology and Aging, 18,* 474–486.

Fu, S.-Y., Anderson, D., & Courtney, M. (2003). Cross-cultural menopausal experience: Comparison of Australian and Taiwanese women. *Nursing and Health Sciences, 5,* 77–84.

Fukukawa, Y., Nakashima, C., Tsuboi, S., Niino, N., Ando, F., Kosugi, S., & Shimokata, H. (2004). The impact of health problems on depression and activities in middle-aged and older adults: Age and social interactions as moderators. *Journals of Gerontology: Psychological Sciences, 59B,* P19–P26.

Fuller-Thompson, E., Hayslip, B., Jr., & Patrick, J. H. (2005). Introduction to the special issue: Diversity among grandparent caregivers. *International Journal of Aging and Human Development, 60,* 269–272.

Fuller-Thomson, E., Minkler, M., & Driver, D. (1997). A profile of grandparents raising grandchildren in the United States. *The Gerontologist, 37,* 406–411.

Fulton, G., Madden, C., & Minichiello, V. (1996). The social construction of anticipatory grief. *Social Science and Medicine, 43,* 1349–1358.

Furstenberg, F. F., Jr. (1982). Conjugal succession: Reentering marriage after divorce. In P. B. Baltes & O. G. Brim, Jr. (Eds.), *Life-span development and behavior* (Vol. 5, pp. 108–146). New York: Academic Press.

Futterman, A., Gallagher, D., Thompson, L. W., Lovett, S., & Gilewski, M. (1990). Retrospective assessment of marital adjustment and depression during the first two years of spousal bereavement. *Psychology and Aging, 5,* 277–283.

Gabrieli, J. D. E. (1998). Cognitive neuroscience in human memory. *Annual Review of Psychology, 49,* 87–115.

Gabrieli, J. D. E., Brewer, J. B., Desmond, J. E., & Glover, G. H. (1997). Separate neural bases of two fundamental memory processes in the human medial temporal lobe. *Science, 276,* 264–266.

Gaerta, T. J., Lapolla, C., & Melendez, E. (1996). AIDS in the elderly. *Journal of Emergency Medicine, 14,* 19–23.

Gaeta, H., Friedman, D., & Ritter, W. (2003). Auditory selective attention in young and elderly adults: The selection of single versus conjoint features. *Psychophysiology, 40,* 389–406.

Gage, F. H. (2000). Mammalian neural stem cells. *Science, 287,* 1433–1438.

Gailey, C. W. (1987). Evolutionary perspectives in gender hierarchy. In B. B. Hess & M. M. Feree (Eds.), *Analyzing gender: A handbook of social science research* (pp. 32–67). Thousand Oaks, CA: Sage.

Galinsky, E., Bond, J. T., & Friedman, D. E. (1996). The role of employers in addressing the needs of employed parents. *Journal of Social Issues, 52,* 111–136.

Gall, T. L., Evans, D. R., & Howard, J. (1997). The retirement adjustment process: Changes in the well-being of male retirees across time. *Journals of Gerontology: Psychological Sciences, 52B,* P110–P117.

Gallagher, M. (1996). Re-creating marriage. In D. Popenoe, J. B. Elshtain, & D. Blankenhorn (Eds.), *Promises to keep: Decline and renewal of marriage in America* (pp. 233–246). Lanham, MD: Rowman & Littlefield.

Gallagher-Thompson, D., Coon, D. W., Solano, N., Ambler, C., Rabinowitz, Y., & Thompson, L. W. (2003). Change in indices of distress among Latino and Anglo female caregivers of elderly relatives with dementia: Site-specific results form the REACH national collaborative study. *The Gerontologist, 43,* 580–591.

Gallo, J. J., Anthony, J. C., & Muthen, B. O. (1994). Age differences in the symptoms of depression: A latent trait analysis. *Journals of Gerontology: Psychological Sciences, 49,* P251–P264.

Gallo, J. J., Rebok, G. W., & Lesikar, S. E. (1999). The driving habits of adults aged 60 years and older. *Journal of the American Geriatric Society, 47,* 335–341.

Gamble, W. C., Ramakumar, S., & Diaz A. (2007). Maternal and paternal similarities and differences in parenting: An examination of Mexican-American parents of young children. *Early Childhood Research Quarterly, 22,* 72–88.

Gamboz, N., Russo, R., & Fox, E. (2002). Age differences and the identity negative priming effect: An updated meta-analysis. *Psychology and Aging, 17,* 525–530.

Ganiron, E. E. (2007). Mutuality and relationship satisfaction in the formation of lesbian relationships across the life cycle: Unpacking the u-haul myth. *Dissertation Abstracts International: Section B: The Sciences and Engineering, 68(3-B),* 1924.

Ganong L. H., & Coleman, M. (2004). *Stepfamily relationships: Development, dynamics, and interventions.* New York: Kluwer Academic/Plenum.

Gans, D. (2007). Normative obligations and parental care in social context. *Dissertation Abstracts International Section A: Humanities and Social Sciences, 68(5-A),* 2115.

Gardner, B. K., & O'Connor, D. W. (2008). A review of the cognitive effects of electroconvulsive therapy in older adults. *Journal of ECT, 24,* 68–80.

Garrard, E., & Wilkinson, S. (2005). Passive euthanasia. *Journal of Medical Ethics, 31,* 64–68.

Garrod, A., & Larimore, C. (Eds.). (1997). *First person, first peoples: Native American college graduates tell their life stories.* Ithaca, NY: Cornell University Press.

Gatz, M. (2000). Variations on depression in later life. In S. H. Qualls & N. Abeles (Eds.), *Psychology and the aging revolution* (pp. 239–254). Washington, DC: American Psychological Association.

Gatz, M., Fiske, A., Fox, L. S., Kaskie, B., Kasl-Godley, J. E., McCallum, T. J., & Loebach Wetherell, J. (1998). Empirically validated psychological treatments for older adults. *Journal of Mental Health and Aging, 4,* 9–46.

Gatz, M., Kasl-Godley, J. E., & Karel, M. (1996). Aging and mental disorders. In J. E. Birren & K. W. Schaie (Eds.), *Handbook of the psychology of aging* (4th ed., pp. 365–382). San Diego: Academic Press.

Gatz, M., Pedersen, N. L., Berg, S., Johansson, B., Johansson, K., Mortimer, J. A., Posner, S. F., Viitanen, M., Winblad, B., & Ahlbom, A. (1997). Heritability for Alzheimer's disease: The study of dementia in Swedish twins. *Journals of Gerontology: Medical Sciences, 52A,* M117–M125.

Gatz, M., Pedersen, N. L., Plomin, R., & Nesselroade, J. R. (1992). Importance of shared genes and shared environments for symptoms of depression in older adults. *Journal of Abnormal Psychology, 101,* 701–708.

Gatz, M., & Zarit, S. H. (1999). A good old age: Paradox or possibility. In V. L. Bengtson & K. W. Schaie (Eds.), *Handbook of theories of aging* (pp. 396–416). New York: Springer.

Gaugler, J. E., Kane, R. L., & Newcomer, R. (2007). Resilience and transitions from dementia caregiving. *Journal of Gerontology: Psychological Sciences, 62,* P38–P44.

Gaylord, S. A., & Zung, W. W. K. (1987). Affective disorders among the aging. In L. L. Carstensen & B. A. Edelstein (Eds.), *Handbook of clinical gerontology.* New York: Pergamon.

Gazzaniga, M. S. (1995). *The cognitive neurosciences.* Cambridge, MA: MIT Press.

Gephart, R. P. (2002). Introduction to the brave new workplace: Organizational behavior in the electronic age. *Journal of Organizational Behavior, 23,* 327–344.

Gerhart, T. N. (1995). Fractures. In W. B. Abrams, M. H. Beers, & R. Berkow (Eds.), *The Merck manual of geriatrics* (2nd ed., pp. 79–98). Whitehouse Station, NJ: Merck Research Laboratories.

German, P. S. (1995). Prevention and chronic disease in older individuals. In L. A. Bond, S. J. Cutler, & A. Grams (Eds.), *Promoting successful and productive aging* (pp. 95–108). Thousand Oaks, CA: Sage.

Gewirtz, J. C., Chen, A. C., Terwilliger, R., Duman, R. C., & Marek, G. J. (2002). Modulation of DOI-induced increases in cortical bdnf expression by group ii mglu receptors. *Pharmacology, Biochemistry and Behavior, 73,* 317–326.

Ghisletta, P., & Lindenberger, U. (2003). Age-based structural dynamics between perceptual speed and knowledge in the Berlin Aging Study: Direct evidence for ability dedifferentiation in old age. *Psychology and Aging, 18,* 696–713.

Giacobini, E. (2003). Cholinergic function and Alzheimer's disease. *International Journal of Geriatric Psychiatry, 18*(Suppl. I), S1–S5.

Giambra, L. M. (1993). Sustained attention in older adults: Performance and processes. In J. Cerella, J. Rybash, W. Hoyer, & M. L. Commons (Eds.), *Adult information processing: Limits on loss* (pp. 259–272). San Diego: Academic Press.

Giarusso, R., Feng, D., Silverstein, M., & Marenco, A. (2000). Primary and secondary stressors of grandparents raising grandchildren: Evidence from a national survey. *Journal of Mental Health and Aging, 6,* 291–310.

Gibbs, N. R. (1988). Grays on the go. *Time, 131*(8), 66–75.

Gibran, K. (1923). *The prophet*. New York: Knopf.

Gibson, M. J., & Houser, A. N. (2007). *In brief: Valuing the invaluable: A new look at the economic value of family caregiving*. Retrieved March 22, 2008, from http://www.aarp.org/research/housing-mobility/caregiving/inb142_caregiving.html.

Gibson, R. C. (1986). *Blacks in an aging society*. New York: Carnegie.

Gibson, R. C. (1987). Reconceptualizing retirement for black Americans. *The Gerontologist, 27*, 691–698.

Gibson, R. C. (1991). The subjective retirement of black Americans. *Journals of Gerontology: Social Sciences, 46*, S204–S209.

Gignac, M. A. M., Cott, C., & Badley, M. (2000). Adaptation to chronic illness and disability and its relationship to perceptions of independence and dependence. *Journals of Gerontology: Psychological Sciences, 55B*, P362–P372.

Gignac, M. A. M., Kelloway, E. K., & Gottlieb, B. H. (1996). The impact of caregiving on employment: A meditational model of work–family conflict. *Canadian Journal on Aging, 15*, 525–542.

Gilbert, D. T., & Malone, P. S. (1995). The correspondence bias. *Psychological Bulletin, 117*, 21–38.

Gilchrest, B. A. (1995). Skin changes and disorders. In W. B. Abrams, M. H. Beers, & R. Berkow (Eds.), *The Merck manual of geriatrics* (2nd ed., pp. 1255–1286). Whitehouse Station, NJ: Merck Research Laboratories.

Gilewski, M. J., Zelinski, E. M., & Schaie, K. W. (1990). The Memory Functioning Questionnaire for assessment of memory complaints in adulthood and old age. *Psychology and Aging, 5*, 482–490.

Gillies, J., & Neimeyer, R. A. (2006). Loss, grief, and the search for significance: Toward a model of meaning reconstruction in bereavement. *Journal of Constructivist Psychology, 19*, 31–65.

Ginn, J., & Arber, S. (1996). Gender, age, and attitudes toward retirement in midlife. *Aging and Society, 16*, 27–55.

Gitlin, L. N. (2003). Conducting research on home environments: Lessons learned and new directions. *The Gerontologist, 43*, 628–637.

Glamser, F., & Hayslip, B., Jr. (1985). The impact of retirement on participation in leisure activities. *Therapeutic Recreation Journal, 19*, 28–38.

Glass, T. A. (1998). Conjugating the "tenses" of function: Discordance among hypothetical, experimental, and enacted function in older adults. *The Gerontologist, 38*, 101–112.

Glick, I. O., Weiss, R. S., & Parkes, C. M. (1974). *The first year of bereavement*. New York: Wiley.

Go, C. G., Brustrom, J. E., Lynch, M. F., & Aldwin, C. M. (1995). Ethnic trends in survival curves and mortality. *The Gerontologist, 35*, 318–326.

Goel, V., & Dolan, R. (2000). Anatomical segregation of component processes in an inductive inference task. *Journal of Cognitive Neuroscience, 12*(1), 1–10.

Goff, S. J., Fick, D. S., & Opplinger, R. A. (1997). The moderating effect of spouse support on the relation between serious leisure and spouses' perceived leisure–family conflict. *Journal of Leisure Research, 29*, 47–60.

Goff, S. J., Mount, M. K., & Jamison, R. L. (1990). Employer supported child care, work–family conflict, and absenteeism: A field study. *Personnel Psychology, 43*, 793–809.

Goh, J. O., Chee, M. W., Tan, J. C., Venkatraman, V., Hebrank, A., Leshikar, E. D., Jenkins, L.,

Sutton, B. P., Gutchess, A. H., & Park, D. C. (2007). Age and culture modulate object processing and object-scene binding in the ventral visual area. *Cognitive, Affective, and Behavioral Neuroscience, 7*(1), 44–52.

Golant, S. M. (2008). Affordable clustered housing-care: A category of long-term care options for the elderly poor. *Journal of Housing for the Elderly, 22*, 3–44.

Golant, S. M. (2008). The future of assisted living residences: A response to uncertainty. In S. M. Golant & J. Hyde (Eds.), *The assisted living residence: A vision for the future*. Baltimore: The Johns Hopkins University Press.

Gold, D. T. (1990). Late-life sibling relationships: Does race affect typological distribution? *The Gerontologist, 30*, 741–748.

Gold, D. T., Woodbury, M. A., & George, L. K. (1990). Relationship classification using grade of membership analysis: A typology of sibling relationships in later life. *Journals of Gerontology: Social Sciences, 45*, S43–S51.

Gold, P. E., Cahill, L., & Wenk, G. L. (2002). *Gingko biloba*: A cognitive enhancer? *Psychological Science in the Public Interest, 3*, 2–11.

Goldberg, A. E., & Perry-Jenkins, M. (2004). Division of labor and working-class women's well-being across the transition to parenthood. *Journal of Family Psychology, 18*, 225–236.

Goldberg, L. R., & Saucier, G. (1995). So what do you propose we use instead? A reply to Block. *Psychological Bulletin, 117*, 221–225.

Golden, L. (2001). Flexible work schedules: Which workers get them? *American Behavioral Scientist, 44*, 1157–1178.

Goldfried, M. R., & Wolfe, B. E. (1998). Toward a more clinically valid approach to therapy research. *Journal of Consulting and Clinical Psychology, 66*, 143–150.

Goldsmith, B., Morrison, R. S., Vanderwerker, L. C., & Prigerson, H. G. (2008). Elevated rates of prolonged grief disorder in African Americans. *Death Studies, 32*, 352–365.

Goldstein, E. (1979). Effect of same-sex and cross-sex role models on the subsequent academic productivity of scholars. *American Psychologist, 34*, 407–410.

Golsworthy, R., & Coyle, A. (2001). Practitioners' accounts of religious and spiritual dimension in bereavement therapy. *Counselling Psychology Quarterly, 14*, 183–202.

Gonyea, J. G., & Hooyman, N. R. (2005). Reducing poverty among older women: Social Security reform and gender equity. *Families in Society, 86*, 338–346.

Gonzalez, H. M., Haan, M. N., & Hinton, L. (2001). Acculturation and the prevalence of depression in older Mexican Americans: Baseline results of the Sacramento Area Latino Study on Aging. *Journal of the American Geriatrics Society, 49*, 948–953.

Goode, K. T., Haley, W. E., Roth, D. L., & Ford, G. R. (1998). Predicting longitudinal changes in caregiver physical and mental health: A stress process model. *Health Psychology, 17*, 190–198.

Goodkin, K., Burkhalter, J. E., Blaney, N. T., Leeds, B., Tuttle, R. S., & Feaster, D. J. (1997). A research derived bereavement support group technique for the HIV-1 infected. *Omega: Journal of Death and Dying, 34*, 279–300.

Goodman, C. C. (2003). Intergenerational triads in grandparent-headed families. *Journals of Gerontology: Social Sciences, 58B*, S281–S289.

Goodman, C., & Silverstein, M. (2002). Grandmothers raising grandchildren: Family structure and well-being in culturally diverse families. *The Gerontologist, 42*, 676–689.

Gordon, C., Gaitz, C. M., & Scott, J. (1976). Leisure and lives: Personal expressivity across

the life span. In R. Binstock & E. Shanas (Eds.), *Handbook of aging and the social sciences* (pp. 310–341). New York: Van Nostrand Reinhold.

Gordon-Salant, S., & Fitzgibbons, P. J. (1997). Selected cognitive factors and speech recognition performance among young and elderly listeners. *Journal of Speech, Language, and Hearing Resources, 40*, 423–431.

Gotlib, I. H., Roberts, J. E., & Gilboa, E. (1996). Cognitive interference in depression. In I. G. Sarason, G. R. Pierce, & B. R. Sarason (Eds.), *Cognitive interference: Theories, methods, and findings* (pp. 347–377). Mahwah, NJ: Erlbaum.

Gotthardt, U., Schweiger, U., Fahrenburg, J., Lauer, C. J., Holsboer, F., & Heuser, I. (1995). Cortisol, ACTH, and cardiovascular response to a cognitive challenge paradigm in aging and depression. *American Journal of Physiology, 268*, 865–873.

Gottman, J. M., & Levenson, R. W. (2000). The timing of divorce: Predicting when a couple will divorce over a 14-year period. *Journal of Marriage and the Family, 62*, 737–745.

Gould, O. N., Kurzman, D., & Dixon, R. A. (1994). Communication during prose recall conversations by young and old dyads. *Discourse Processes, 17*, 149–165.

Gould, O. N., Osborn, C., Krein, H., & Mortenson, M. (2002). Collaborative recall in married and unacquainted dyads. *International Journal of Behavioral Development, 26*, 36–44.

Gould, S. J. (1999). A critique of Heckhausen and Schulz's (1995) life-span theory of control from a cross-cultural perspective. *Psychological Review, 106*, 597–604.

Grady, C. L., Bernstein, L., Siegenthaler, A., & Beig, S. (2002). The effects of encoding task on age-related differences in the functional neuroanatomy of face memory. *Psychology and Aging, 17*, 7–23.

Grady, C. L., McIntosh, A. R., Horwitz, B., Maisong, J. M., Ungerleider, L. G., Mentis, M. J., Pietrini, P., Schapiro, M. B., & Haxby, J. V. (1995). Age-related reductions in human recognition memory due to impaired encoding. *Science, 269*, 218–221.

Grady, C. L., & Springer, M.V., Hongwanishkul, D., McIntosh, A.R., & Winocur, G. (2006.) Age-related changes in brain activity across the adult lifespan. *Journal of Cognitive Neuroscience, 18*, 227–241.

Graham-Kevan, N., & Archer, J. (2003). Intimate terrorism and common couple violence: A test of Johnson's predictions in four British Samples. *Journal of Interpersonal Violence, 18*, 1247–1270.

Grande, G. E., Farquhar, M. C., Barclay, S. I. G., & Todd, C. J. (2004). Caregiver bereavement outcome: Relationship with hospice at home, satisfaction with care, and home death. *Journal of Palliative Care, 20*, 69–77.

Grant, B. F., Dawson, D. A., Stinson, F. S., Chou, S. P., Dufour, M. C., & Pickering, R. P. (2004). The 12-month prevalence and trends in DSM-IV alcohol abuse and dependence: United States, 1991–1992 and 2001–2002. *Drug and Alcohol Dependence, 74*, 223–234.

Gratzinger, P., Sheikh, J. I., Friedman, L., & Yesavage, J. A. (1990). Cognitive interventions to improve face-name recall: The role of personality trait differences. *Developmental Psychology, 26*, 889–893.

Green, C. R. (1999). *Total memory workout: 8 steps to maximum memory fitness*. New York: Bantam.

Green, J. S. (2008). *Beyond the good death: An anthropology of modern dying*. Baltimore: University of Pennsylvania Press.

Green, R. L., & Ostrander, R. L. (2008). *Neuroanatomy for students of behavioral disorders.* New York: Norton.

Greenglass, E. R. (1991). Burnout and gender: Theoretical and organizational implications. *Canadian Psychology, 32,* 562–574.

Greenglass, E. R., Burke, R. J., & Konarski, R. (1998). Components of burnout, resources, and gender-related differences. *Journal of Applied Social Psychology, 28,* 1088–1106.

Greenhaus, J. H., Parasuraman, S., & Wormely, W. M. (1990). Effects of race on organizational experiences, job performance evaluations, and career outcomes. *Academy of Management Journal, 33,* 64–86.

Greenwald, A. G., McGhee, D. E., & Schwartz, J. L. K. (1998). Measuring individual differences in implicit cognition: The implicit association test. *Journal of Personality and Social Psychology, 74,* 1464–1480.

Greer, J. (1992). *Adult sibling rivalries.* New York: Crown.

Greller, M., & Stroh, L. (1995). Careers in midlife and beyond: A fallow field in need of sustenance. *Journal of Vocational Behavior, 47,* 232–247.

Greving, K. A. (2007). Examining parents' marital satisfaction trajectories: Relations with children's temperament and family demographics. *Dissertation Abstracts International Section A: Humanities and Social Sciences, 68(4-A),* 1676.

Grey, R. (1756). *Memoria technica* (4th ed.). London: Hinton.

Grinker, J. A., Tucker, K., Vokonas, P. S., & Rush, D. (1995). Body habitus changes among adult males from the normative aging study: Relations to aging, smoking history and alcohol intake. *Obesity Research, 3,* 435–446.

Grob, A., Little, T. D., & Wanner, B. (1999). Control judgements across the lifespan. *International Journal of Behavioral Decisions, 23,* 833–854.

Groger, L. (1995). A nursing home can be a home. *Journal of Aging Studies, 9,* 137–153.

Gross, E. A. (1999). *Telemarketing fraud.* Unpublished doctoral dissertation, Department of Educational Counseling, University of Southern California, Los Angeles.

Grossman, A. H. (1997). The virtual and actual identities of older lesbians and gay men. In M. Duberman (Ed.), *A queer world: The Center for Lesbian and Gay Studies reader* (pp. 615–626). New York: New York University Press.

Grossman, A. H., D'Augelli, A. R., & Hershberger, S. L. (2000). Social support networks of lesbian, gay, and bisexual adults 60 years of age and older. *Journals of Gerontology: Psychological Sciences, 55B,* P171–P179.

Grote, N. K., Naylor, K. E., & Clark, M. S. (2002). Perceiving the division of family work to be unfair: Do social comparisons, enjoyment, and competence matter? *Journal of Family Psychology, 16,* 510–522.

Grover, D. R., & Hertzog, C. (1991). Relationships between intellectual control beliefs and psychometric intelligence in adulthood. *Journals of Gerontology: Psychological Sciences, 46,* 109–115.

Grühn, D., Smith, J., & Baltes, P. B. (2005). No aging bias favoring memory for positive material: Evidence from a heterogeneity-homogeneity list paradigm using emotionally toned words. *Psychology and Aging, 20,* 579–588.

Gruneir, A., Lapane, K. L., Miller, S. C., & Mor, V. (2008a). Is dementia special care really special? A new look at an old question. *Journal of the American Geriatrics Society, 56,* 199–205.

Gruneir, A., Lapane, K. L., Miller, S. C., & Mor, V. (2008b). Does the presence of a dementia special care unit improve nursing home quality? *Journal of Aging and Health, 20,* 837–854.

Guilford, J. P. (1959). *Personality.* New York: McGraw-Hill.

Guillozet, A. L., Weintraub, S., Mash, D. C., & Mesulam, M. M. (2003). Neurofibrillary tangles, amyloid, and memory in aging and mild cognitive impairment. *Archives of Neurology, 60,* 729–736.

Guinn, B. (1999). Leisure behavior motivation and the life satisfaction of retired persons. *Activities, Adapting, and Aging, 23,* 13–20.

Gulya, A. J. (1995). Ear disorders. In W. B. Abrams, M. H. Beers, & R. Berkow (Eds.), *The Merck manual of geriatrics* (2nd ed., pp. 1315–1342). Whitehouse Station, NJ: Merck Research Laboratories.

Gunning-Dixon F. M., & Raz, N. (2003). Neuroanatomical correlates of selected executive functions in middle-aged and older adults: A prospective MRI study. *Neuropsychologia, 41(14),* 1929–1941.

Gunter, N. C., & Gunter, B. G. (1990). Domestic division of labor among working couples: Does androgyny make a difference? *Psycho No–logy of Women Quarterly, 14,* 355–370.

Guralnik, J. M. (2008). Successful aging: Is it in our future? *Archives of Internal Medicine, 168,* 131–132.

Guralnick, J. M., & Simonsick, E. M. (1993). Physical disability in older Americans. *Journals of Gerontology: Psychological Sciences, 48*(Special Issue), 3–10.

Gutchess, A. H., Welsh, R. C., Hedden, T., Bangert, A., Minear, M., et al. (2005). Aging and the neural correlates of successful picture encoding: frontal activations compensate for decreased medial-temporal activity. *Journal of Cognitive Neuroscience, 17(1),* 84–96.

Gutek, B.A., & Gilliland, C. (2007). Work versus the family: Keeping the balance. In S. Gilliland, D. Steiner, & D. Skarlicki (Eds.), *Research in social issues in management: Vol. 5, Managing social and ethical issues in organizations* (pp. 53–82). Greenwich, CT: Information Age Publishing.

Gutmann, D. (1987). Reclaimed powers: Toward a new psychology of men and women in later life. New York: Basic Books.

Gutmann, D. (1994). *Reclaimed powers: Men and women in later life.* Evanston, IL: Northwestern University Press.

Haan, N. (1985). Common personality dimensions or common organization across the life span. In J. M. Munnichs, P. Mussen, E. Olbrich, & P. G. Coleman (Eds.), *Life-span and change in gerontological perspective* (pp. 17–44). New York: Academic Press.

Haan, N., Millsap, R., & Hartka, E. (1986). As time goes by: Change and stability in personality over fifty years. *Psychology and Aging, 1,* 220–232.

Haas, L. (1990). Gender equality and social policy: Implications of a study of parental leave in Sweden. *Journal of Family Issues, 11,* 401–423.

Hacker, M., Messer, W. S., & Bachmann, K. A. (2009). *Pharmacology: Principles and practice.* New York: Elsevier.

Hairston, R. E. (2001). Predicting marital satisfaction among African American couples. *Dissertation Abstracts International Section B: The Sciences and Engineering, 61(10-B),* 5564.

Hakim, C. (2002). Lifestyle preferences as determinants of women's differentiated labor market careers. *Work and Occupations, 29,* 428–459.

Hale, S., Myerson, J., Rhee, S. H., Weiss, C. S., & Abrams, R. A. (1996). Selective interference with the maintenance of location information in working memory. *Neuropsychology, 10,* 228–240.

Haley, W. E., Han, B., & Henderson, J. N. (1998). Aging and ethnicity: Issues for clinical practice. *Journal of Clinical Psychology in Medical Settings, 5,* 393–409.

Hall, D. R., & Zhao, J. Z. (1995). Cohabitation and divorce in Canada: Testing the selectivity hypothesis. *Journal of Marriage and the Family, 57,* 421–427.

Hall, D. T., & Mirvis, P. H. (1995). The new career contract: Developing the whole person at mid-life and beyond. *Journal of Vocational Behavior, 47,* 269–289.

Hamachek, D. (1990). Evaluating self-concept and ego status in Erikson's last three psychosocial stages. *Journal of Counseling and Development, 68,* 677–683.

Hamarat, E., Thompson, D., Zabrucky, K. M., Steele, D., Matheny, K. B., & Aysan, F. (2001). Perceived stress and coping resources availability as predictors of life satisfaction in young, middle-aged, and older adults. *Experimental Aging Research, 27,* 181–196.

Hamilton, J. (1978). Grandparents as grievers. In J. O. Sahler (Ed.), *The child and death.* St. Louis: Mosby.

Hammer, L. B., & Neal, M. B. (2008). Sandwiched generation caregivers: Prevalence, characteristics, and outcomes. *Psychologist-Manager Journal, 11,* 93–112.

Hamon, R. R., & Blieszner, R. (1990). Filial responsibility expectations among adult child–older parent pairs. *Journals of Gerontology: Psychological Sciences, 45,* P110–P112.

Hampel, H., Goernitz, A., & Buerger, K. (2003). Advances in the development of biomarkers for Alzheimer's disease: From CSF total tau and Abeta (1-42) proteins to phosphorylated tau protein. *Brain Research Bulletin, 61,* 243–253.

Hancock, H. E., Rogers, W. A., & Fisk, A. D. (1998). *Product usage and warning symbol comprehension for older adults.* Paper presented at the Human Factors and Ergonomics Society 42nd Annual Meeting, Chicago.

Hannon, D. J., & Hoyer, W. J. (1994). Mechanisms of visual–cognitive aging: A neural network account. *Aging and Cognition, 1,* 105–119.

Hansen, S. R. (2006). Courtship duration as a correlate of marital satisfaction and stability. *Dissertation Abstracts International: Section B: The Sciences and Engineering, 67(4-B),* 2279.

Hansen, T., Moum, T., & Shapiro, A. (2007). Relational and individual well-being among cohabitors and married individuals in midlife: Recent trends from Norway. *Journal of Family Issues, 28,* 910–933.

Hansson, R. O., DeKoekkoek, P. D., Neese, W. M., & Patterson, D. W. (1997). Successful aging at work: Annual review, 1992–1996: The older worker and transitions to retirement. *Journal of Vocational Behavior, 51,* 202–233.

Hansson, R. O. & Stroebe, M. S. (2007). *Bereavement in late life: Coping, adaptation, and developmental influences.* Washington, DC: American Psychological Association.

Harbison, J. (1999). Models of intervention for "elder abuse and neglect": A Canadian perspective on ageism, participation, and empowerment. *Journal of Elder Abuse and Neglect, 10,* 1–17.

Hareven, T. (2001). Historical perspectives on aging and family relations. In R. H. Binstock & L. K. George (Eds), *Handbook of aging and the social sciences* (5th ed., pp. 141–159). San Diego: Academic Press.

Hareven, T. K., & Adams, K. J. (1996). The generation in the middle: Cohort comparisons in assistance to aging parents in an American community. In T. K. Hareven (Ed.), *Aging and generational relations: Life-course and cross-cultural perspectives* (pp. 3–29). New York: Aldine de Gruyter.

Harkins, S. W., & Kwentus, J. (1990). Pain, discomfort, and suffering in the elderly. In J. J. Bonica (Ed.), *Clinical management of pain*. Philadelphia: Lea & Febiger.

Harley, C. B. (2008). Telomerase and cancer therapeutics. *Nature Reviews: Cancer, 8,* 167–179.

Harnett, P. J., & Greaney, A.-M. (2008). Operationalizing autonomy: Solutions for mental health nursing practice. *Journal of Psychiatric and Mental Health Nursing, 15,* 2–9.

Harpaz, I. (2002). Advantages and disadvantages of telecommuting for the individual, organization and society. *Work Study: A Journal of Productivity Science, 51,* 74–80.

Harris, J. E. (1984). Methods of improving memory. In B. Wilson & N. Moffat (Eds.), *Clinical management of memory problems* (pp. 46–62). Rockville, MD: Aspen.

Harris, R. L., Ellicott, A. M., & Holmes, D. S. (1986). The timing of psychosocial transitions and changes in women's lives: An examination of women aged 45 to 60. *Journal of Personality and Social Psychology, 51,* 409–416.

Harris Interactive. (2007). *Views on social issues and their potential impact on the Presidential election*. Retrieved March 15, 2008, from http://www.harrisinteractive.com/harris_poll/index.asp?PID=807.

Hartley, J. T. (1993). Reader and text variables as determinants of discourse memory in adulthood. *Psychology and Aging, 1,* 150–158.

Hartley, J. T., Stojack, C. C., Mushaney, T. J., Annon, T. A. K., & Lee, D. W. (1994). Reading speed and prose memory in older and younger adults. *Psychology and Aging, 9,* 216–223.

Harwood, J., Ryan, E. B., Giles, H., & Tysoski, S. (1997). Evaluations of patronizing speech and three response styles in a non–service-providing context. *Journal of Applied Communication Research, 25,* 170–195.

Hasher, L., Chung, C., May, C. P., & Foong, N. (2002). Age, time of testing, and proactive interference. *Canadian Journal of Experimental Psychology, 56,* 200–207.

Hasher, L., & Zacks, R. T. (1988). Working memory, comprehension, and aging: A review and new view. In G. T. Bower (Ed.), *The psychology of learning and motivation* (Vol. 22, pp. 193–225). New York: Academic Press.

Hasher, L., Zacks, R. T., & May, C. P. (1999). Inhibitory control, circadian arousal, and age. In D. Gopher & A. Koriat (Eds.), *Attention and performance: XVII. Cognitive regulation of performance: Interaction of theory and application*. Cambridge, MA: MIT Press.

Hashtroudi, S., Johnson, M., & Chrosniak, L. (1990). Aging and qualitative characteristics of memories for perceived and imagined complex events. *Psychology and Aging, 5,* 119–126.

Havighurst, R. J. (1982). The world of work. In B. B. Wolman (Ed.), *Handbook of developmental psychology* (pp. 771–787). Englewood Cliffs, NJ: Prentice Hall.

Hawkins, A. J., Nock, S. L., Wilson, J. C., Sanchez, L., & Wright, J. D. (2002). Attitudes about covenant marriage and divorce: Policy implications from a three-state comparison. *Family Relations, 51,* 166–175.

Hawkins, H. L., Kramer, A. F., & Capaldi, D. (1992). Aging, exercise, and attention. *Psychology and Aging, 7,* 643–653.

Hay, J. F., & Jacoby, L. L. (1999). Separation habits in young and older adults: Effects of elaborative processing and distinctiveness. *Psychology and Aging, 14,* 122–124.

Hayashi, M., Hasui, C., Kitamura, F., Murakami, M., Takeuchi, M., Katoh, H., Kitamura, T. (2000). Respecting autonomy in difficult medical settings: A questionnaire study in Japan. *Ethics and Behavior, 10,* 51–63.

Hayflick, L. (1996). *How and why we age* (2nd ed.). New York: Ballantine.

Hayflick, L. (1998). How and why we age. *Experimental Gerontology, 33,* 639–653.

Hayslip, B., Jr., & Goldberg-Glen, R. (2000). *Grandparents raising grandchildren: theoretical, empirical, and clinical perspectives*. New York: Springer.

Hayslip, B., Jr., Henderson, C. E., & Shore, R. J. (2003). The structure of grandparental role meaning. *Journal of Adult Development, 10,* 1–11.

Hayslip, B., Jr., Shore, R. J., Henderson, C. E., & Lambert, P. L. (1998). Custodial grandparenting and the impact of grandchildren with problems on role satisfaction and role meaning. *Journals of Gerontology: Social Sciences, 53B,* S164–S173.

Hayward, M. D., Friedman, S., & Chen, H. (1998). Career trajectories and older men's retirement. *Journals of Gerontology: Social Sciences, 53B,* S91–S103.

Healey, M. K., Campbell, K. L., & Hasher, L. (2008). Cognitive aging and increased distractibility: Costs and potential benefits. In W. S. Sossin, J. C. Lacaille, V. F. Castellucci, & S. Belleville (Eds.), *Progress in brain research* (Vol. 169, pp. 353–363). Amsterdam: Elsevier.

Heckhausen, J., Dixon, R. A., & Baltes, P. B. (1989). Gains and losses in development throughout adulthood as perceived by different adult age groups. *Developmental Psychology, 25,* 109–121.

Heckhausen, J., & Lang, F. R. (1996). Social construction and old age: Normative conceptions and interpersonal processes. In G. R. Semin & K. Fiedler (Eds.), *Applied social psychology* (pp. 374–399). London: Sage.

Heckhausen, J., & Schulz, R. (1995). A life-span theory of control. *Psychological Review, 102,* 284–304.

Heckhausen, J., & Schulz, R. (1998). Developmental regulation in adulthood: Selection and compensation via primary and secondary control. In J. Heckhausen & C. Dweck (Eds.), *Motivation and self-regulation across the lifespan* (pp. 50–77). New York: Cambridge University Press.

Heckhausen, J., & Schulz, R. (1999). Selectivity in lifespan development: Biological and societal canalizations and individuals developmental goals. In J. Brandtstädter, B. M. Lerner, et al. (Eds.), *Action and self development: Theory and research through the lifespan* (pp. 67–130). Thousand Oaks, CA: Sage.

Hedden, T., & Gabrieli, J. D. E. (2004). Insights into the aging mind: A view from cognitive neuroscience. *Nature Reviews, 5,* 87–97.

Heidrich, S. M., & Denney, N. W. (1994). Does social problem solving differ from other types of problem solving during the adult years? *Experimental Aging Research, 20,* 105–126.

Heimann, B., & Pittinger, K. K. S. (1996). The impact of formal mentorship on socialization and commitment of newcomers. *Journal of Managerial Issues, 8,* 108–117.

Helmer, C., Barberger-Gateau, P., Letenneur, L., & Dartigues, J.-F. (1999). Subjective health and mortality in French elderly women and men.

Journals of Gerontology: Social Sciences, 54B, S84–S92.

Helson, R., Kwan, V. S., John, O. P., & Jones, C. (2002). The growing evidence for personality change in adulthood: Findings from research with personality inventories. *Journal of Research in Personality, 36,* 287–306.

Helson, R., & Kwan, V.S.V. (2000). Personality change in adulthood: The big picture and processes in one longitudinal study. In S.E. Hampton (Ed.), *Advances in personality psychology*, (Vol. 1, pp. 77–106). Hove, England: Psychology Press.

Helson, R., & Moane, G. (1987). Personality change in women from college to midlife. *Journal of Personality and Social Psychology, 53,* 176–186.

Helson, R., Stewart, A. J., & Ostrove, J. (1995). Identity in the cohorts of midlife women. *Journal of Personality and Social Psychology, 69,* 544–557.

Henderson, K. A. (1990). The meaning of leisure for women: An integrative review of the research. *Journal of Leisure Research, 22,* 228–243.

Henderson, S., & Gilding, M. (2004). 'I've never clicked this much with anyone in my life': Trust and hyperpersonal communication in online friendships. *New Media & Society, 6,* 487–506.

Henkel, J. (1998). Parkinson's disease: New treatments slow onslaught of symptoms. *FDA Consumer, 32*(4), 13–18. Online document available at http://www.fda.gov/fdac/features/1998/498_pd.html. Accessed November, 13, 2004.

Henkens, K. (1999). Retirement intentions and spousal support: A multi-actor approach. *Journals of Gerontology: Social Sciences, 54B,* S63–S73.

Henkin, R. I. (2008). Taste and appetite loss in the aged. *Perspectives on Psychology, 13,* 20–32.

Henretta, J. C. (1997). Changing perspectives on retirement. *Journals of Gerontology: Social Sciences, 52B,* S1–S3.

Henretta, J. C., Chan, C. G., & O'Rand, A. M. (1992). Retirement reason versus retirement process: Examining the reasons for retirement typology. *Journals of Gerontology: Social Sciences, 47,* S1–S7.

Henrikson, C. R. (2007). Longevity's impact on retirement security. In M. Robinson, W. Novelli, C. Pearson, & L. Norris, (Eds.), *Global health and global aging* (pp. 323–336). San Francisco: Jossey-Bass.

Henry, J. D., MacLeod, M. S., Phillips, L. H., & Crawford, J. R. (2004). A meta-analytic review of prospective memory and aging. *Psychology and Aging, 19,* 27–39.

Henry, N. J. M., Berg, C. A., Smith, T. W., & Florsheim, P. (2007). Positive and negative characteristics of marital interaction and their association with marital satisfaction in middle-aged and older couples. *Psychology and Aging, 22,* 428–441.

Henry, R. G. (2006). Parental death and its impact on the marital relationship of the surviving adult child. *Dissertation Abstracts International: Section B: The Sciences and Engineering,. 67(2-B),* 1181.

Herrera, C. O. (1995). Sleep disorders. In W. B. Abrams, M. H. Beers, & R. Berkow (Eds.), *The Merck manual of geriatrics* (2nd ed., pp. 110–125). Whitehouse Station, NJ: Merck Research Laboratories.

Herrmann, D. J. (1993). *Basic research contributions to the improvement of rehabilitation of memory*. Paper presented at the annual meeting of the American Psychological Association, Washington, DC.

Hershey, D. A., Jacobs-Lawson, J. M., & Walsh, D. A. (2003). Influences of age and training on script development. *Aging, Neuropsychology, and Cognition, 10*, 1–19.

Hershey, D. A., Mowen, J. C., & Jacobs-Lawson, J. M. (2003). An experimental comparison of retirement planning intervention seminars. *Educational Gerontology, 29*, 339–359.

Hertz, R. (1997). A typology of approaches to child care: The centerpiece of organizing family life for dual-earner couples. *Journal of Family Issues, 18*, 355–385.

Hertzog, C. (2008). Theoretical approaches to the study of cognitive aging: An individual differences perspective. In S. M. Hofer & D. F. Alwin (Eds.), *Handbook of cognitive aging: Interdisciplinary perspectives* (pp. 34–49). Greenwich, CT: Sage.

Hertzog, C., & Dixon, R. (1996). Methodological issues in research on cognition and aging. In F. Blanchard-Fields & T. Hess (Eds.), *Perspectives on cognitive change in adulthood and aging* (pp. 66–121). New York: McGraw-Hill.

Hertzog, C., Dixon, R. A., & Hultsch, D. F. (1990). Relationships between metamemory, memory predictions, and memory task performances. *Psychology and Aging, 5*, 215–223.

Hertzog, C., Dixon, R. A., Hultsch, D. F., & MacDonald, S. W. S. (2003). Latent change models of adult cognition: Are changes in processing speed and working memory associated with changes in episodic memory? *Psychology and Aging, 18*, 755–769.

Hertzog, C., & Dunlosky, J. (1996). The aging of practical memory: An overview. In D. Hermann, C. McEvoy, C. Hertzog, P. Hertel, & M. J. Johnson (Eds.), *Basic and applied memory research* (Vol. 1, pp. 337–358). Mahwah, NJ: Erlbaum.

Hertzog, C., Dunlosky, J., & Robinson, A. E. (2007). Intellectual abilities and metacognitive beliefs influence spontaneous use of effective encoding strategies. Unpublished manuscript.

Hertzog, C., Dunlosky, J., Robinson, A. E., & Kidder, D. P. (2003). Encoding fluency is a cue used for judgments about learning. *Journal of Experimental Psychology: Learning, Memory, and Cognition, 29*(1), 22–34.

Hertzog, C., & Hultsch, D. F. (2000). Metacognition in adulthood and aging. In F. I. M. Craik & T. A. Salthouse (Eds.), *Handbook of aging and cognition* (2nd ed., pp. 417–466). Mahwah, NJ: Erlbaum.

Hertzog, C., Hultsch, D. F., & Dixon, R. A. (1989). Evidence for the convergent validity of two self-report metamemory questionnaires. *Developmental Psychology, 25*, 687–700.

Hertzog, C., Hultsch, D. F., & Dixon, R. A. (1999). On the problem of detecting effects of lifestyle on cognitive change in adulthood: Reply to Pushkar et al. (1999). *Psychology and Aging, 14*, 528–534.

Hertzog, C., Kidder, D. P., Powell-Moman, A., & Dunlosky, J. (2002). Aging and monitoring associative learning: Is monitoring accuracy spared or impaired? *Psychology and Aging, 17*, 209–225.

Hertzog, C., McGuire, C. L., & Lineweaver, T. T. (1998). Aging attributions, perceived control, and strategy use in a free recall task. *Aging, Neuropsychology, and Cognition, 5*, 85–106.

Hertzog, C., Park, D. C., Morell, R. G., & Martin, M. (2000). Ask and ye shall receive: Behavioral specificity of accuracy of subjective memory complaints. *Applied Cognitive Psychology, 14*, 257–275.

Hertzog, C., Price, J., Burpee, A., Frentzel, B. J., Feldstein, S., & Dunlosky, J. (2009). Why do people show minimal knowledge updating with task experience: Inferential deficit or experimental artifact? *Quarterly Journal of Experimental Psychology, 62*, 155–173.

Hertzog, C., Touron, D. R., & Hines, J. C. (2007). Does a time monitoring deficit contribute to older adults' delayed shift to retrieval during skill acquisition? *Psychology and Aging, 22*, 607–624.

Hertzog, C., Vernon, M. C., & Rympa, B. (1993). Age differences in mental rotation task performance: The influence of speed/accuracy trade off. *Journals of Gerontology: Psychological Sciences, 48*, P150–P156.

Herzog, A. R., Kahn, R. L., Morgan, J. N., Jackson, J. S., & Antonucci, T. C. (1989). Age differences in productive activities. *Journals of Gerontology: Social Sciences, 44*, S129–S138.

Hess, P., & Lee, S. (1998). Pharmacology and drug use. In P. Ebersole & P. Hess (Eds.), *Toward healthy aging* (5th ed., pp. 352–380). St. Louis: Mosby.

Hess, T. M. (1999). Cognitive and knowledge-based influences on social representations. In T. M. Hess & F. Blanchard-Fields (Eds.), *Social cognition and aging* (pp. 237–263). San Diego: Academic Press.

Hess, T. M. (2005). Memory and aging in context. *Psychological Bulletin,131*, 383–406.

Hess, T. M. (2006). Adaptive aspects of social cognitive functioning in adulthood: Age-related goal and knowledge influences. *Social Cognition, 24*, 279–309.

Hess, T. M., & Auman, C. (2001). Aging and social expertise: The impact of trait-diagnostic information on impressions of others. *Psychology and Aging, 16*, 497–510.

Hess, T. M., Auman, C., Colcombe, S. J., & Rahhal, T. A. (2003). The impact of stereotype threat on age differences in memory. *Journals of Gerontology: Psychological Sciences, 58B*, P3–P11.

Hess, T. M., Bolstad, C. A., & Woodburn, S. M. (1999). Trait diagnosticity versus behavioral consistency as determinants of impression change in adulthood. *Psychology and Aging, 14*, 77–89.

Hess, T., Follet, K., & McGee, K. A. (1998). Aging and impression information: The impact of processing skills and goals. *Journals of Gerontology: Psychological Sciences, 53B*, P175–188.

Hess, T. M., Germain, C. M., & Rosenberg, D. C. (2005). Aging-related selectivity and susceptibility to irrelevant affective information in the construction of attitudes. *Aging, Neuropsychology, and Cognition, 12*, 149–174.

Hess, T. M., Germain, C. M., Rosenberg, D. C., Leclerc, C. M., & Hodges, E. A. (2005). Aging-related selectivity and susceptibility to irrelevant affective information in the construction of attitudes. *Aging, Neuropsychology, and Cognition, 12*, 149–174.

Hess, T. M., Hinson, J. T., & Statham, J. A. (2004). Explicit and implicit stereotype activation effects on memory: Do age and awareness moderate the impact of priming? *Psychology and Aging, 19*, 495–505.

Hess, T. M., McGee, K. A, Woodburn, S. M., & Bolstad, C. S. (1998). Age-related priming effects in social judgments. *Psychology and Aging, 13*, 127–137.

Hess, T. M., Osowski, N. L., & Leclerc, C. M. (2005). Age and experience influences on the complexity of social inferences. *Psychology and Aging, 20*, 447–459.

Hess, T. M., & Pullen, S. M. (1994). Adult age differences in informational biases during impression formation. *Psychology and Aging, 9*, 237–250.

Hess, T. M., & Slaughter, S. J. (1990). Schematic knowledge influences on memory for scene information in young and older adults. *Developmental Psychology, 26*, 855–865.

Hess, T. M., Waters, S. J., & Bolstad, C. A. (2000). Motivational and cognitive influences on affective priming in adulthood. *Journals of Gerontology: Psychological Sciences, 55B*, P193–P204.

Hestad, K., Ellersten, J., & Kløve, H. (1999). Neuropsychological assessment in old age. In I. H. Nordhus, G. R. VandenBos, S. Berg, & P. Fromholt (Eds.), *Clinical geropsychology* (pp. 259–288). Washington, DC: American Psychological Association.

Hiatt, K., Stelle, C., Mulsow, M., & Scott, J. P. (2007). The importance of perspective: Evaluation of hospice care from multiple stakeholders. *American Journal of Hospice & Palliative Medicine, 24*, 376–382.

Higgins, E. T., Rholes, W. S., & Jones, C. R. (1977). Category accessibility and impression formation. *Journal of Experimental Social Psychology, 13*, 141–154.

Higuera, D., Harmon, A., Honeywell, M., & Emanuel, F. (2008). At-home test for Alzheimer's disease. *U.S. Pharmacist, 33*, 49–50.

Hill, C. D., Thompson, L. W., & Gallagher, D. (1988). The role of anticipatory bereavement in older women's adjustment to widowhood. *The Gerontologist, 28*, 792–796.

Hilleras, P. K., Jorm, A. F., Herlitz, A., & Winblad, B. (2001). Life satisfaction among the very old: A survey on a cognitively intact sample aged 90 years or above. *International Journal of Aging and Human Development, 52*, 71–90.

Himsel, A. J., Hart, H., Diamond, A., & McAdams, D. P. (1997). Personality characteristics of highly generative adults as assessed in Q-sort ratings of life stories. *Journal of Adult Development, 4*, 149–161.

Hobart, C. (1988). The family system in remarriage: An exploratory study. *Journal of Marriage and the Family, 50*, 649–661.

Hochschild, A. R. (1997). The time bind: When work becomes home and home becomes work. New York: Henry Holt.

Hock, C., Konietzko, U., Streffer, J. R., Tracy, J., Signorell, A., Muller-Tillmanns, B., Lenke, U., Henke, K., Moritz, E., Garcia, E., Wollmer, M. A., Umbricht, D., de Quervain, D. J., Hoffmann, M., Maddalena, A., Papassotiropoulos, A., & Nitsch, R. M. (2003). Antibodies against beta-amyloid slow cognitive decline in Alzheimer's disease. *Neuron, 38*, 547–554.

Hofer, S. M., Christensen, H., Mackinnon, A. J., Korten, A. E., Jorm, A. F., Henderson, A. S., et al. (2002). Change in cognitive functioning associated with ApoE genotype in a community sample of older adults. *Psychology and Aging, 17*, 194–208.

Hofland, B. F. (1988). Autonomy in long term care: Background issues and a programmatic response. *The Gerontologist, 28*(Suppl.), 3–9.

Holahan, C. K. (2003). Stability and change in positive self-appraisal from midlife to later aging. *International Journal of Aging and Human Development, 56*, 247–267.

Hollan, D. (1995). To the afterworld and back: Mourning and dreams of the dead among the Toranja. *Ethos, 23*, 424–436.

Holland, C. A., & Rabbitt, P. M. A. (1994). The problems of being an older driver: Comparing the perceptions of an expert group and older drivers. *Applied Ergonomics, 25*, 17–27.

Holland, J. L. (1985). *Self-directed search professional manual*. Lutz, FL: Psychological Assessment Resources.

Holland, J. L. (1987). Current status of Holland's theory of careers: Another perspective. *Career Development Quarterly, 36,* 24–30.

Holland, J. L. (1996). Exploring careers with a typology: What we have learned and some new directions. *American Psychologist, 51,* 397–406.

Hollon, S. D., Thase, M. E., & Markowitz, J. C. (2002). Treatment and prevention of depression. *Psychological Science in the Public Interest, 3,* 39–77.

Holstein, M. B., & Minkler, M. (2003). Self, society, and the "new gerontology." *The Gerontologist, 43,* 787–796.

Hood, A. B., & Deopere, D. L. (2002). The relationship of cognitive development to age, when education and intelligence are controlled for. *Journal of Adult Development, 9,* 229–234.

Hooker, K. (1991). Change and stability in self during the transition to retirement: An individual study using P-technique factor analysis. *International Journal of Behavioral Development, 14,* 209–233.

Hooker, K. (1999). Possible selves in adulthood. In T. M. Hess & F. Blanchard-Fields (Eds.), *Social cognition and aging* (pp. 97–122). San Diego: Academic Press.

Hooker, K. (2002). New directions for research in personality and aging: A comprehensive model for linking levels, structures, and processes. *Journal of Research in Personality, 36,* 318–334.

Hooker, K., Fiese, B. H., Jenkins, L., Morfei, M. Z., & Schwagler, J. (1996). Possible selves among parents of infants and pre-schoolers. *Developmental Psychology, 32,* 542–550.

Hooker, K., & Kaus, C. R. (1994). Health-related possible selves in young and mid-adulthood. *Psychology and Aging, 9,* 126–133.

Hooker, K., & McAdams, D. P. (2003). Personality reconsidered: A new agenda for aging research. *Journals of Gerontology: Psychological Sciences, 58B,* P296–P304.

Hooyman, N., & Kiyak, H. A. (2002). *Social gerontology: A multidisciplinary perspective* (6th ed.). Boston: Allyn & Bacon.

Horn, J. L. (1982). The aging of human abilities. In B. B. Wolman (Ed.), *Handbook of developmental psychology* (pp. 847–870). Englewood Cliffs, NJ: Prentice Hall.

Horn, J. L., & Hofer, S. M. (1992). Major abilities and development in the adult period. In R. J. Sternberg & C. A. Berg (Eds.), *Intellectual development* (pp. 44–99). Cambridge, UK: Cambridge University Press.

Howard, A., & Bray, D. W. (1988). Managerial lives in transition: Advancing age and changing times. New York: Guilford.

Howard, R. J., Juszczak, E., Ballard, C. G., Bentham, P., Brown, R. G., Bullock, R., Burns, A. S., Holmes, C., Jacoby, R., Johnson, T., Knapp, M., Lindesay, J., O'Brien, J. T., Wilcock, G., Katona, C., Jones, R. W., DeCesare, J., & Rodger, M. (2007). Donepezil for the treatment of agitation in Alzheimer's disease. *New England Journal of Medicine, 357,* 1382–1392.

Hoyer, W. J., & Rybash, J. M. (1994). Characterizing adult cognitive development. *Journal of Adult Development, 1,* 7–12.

Hoyer, W. J., Stawski, R. S., Wasylyshyn, C., & Verhaeghen, P. (2004). Adult age and digit symbol substitution performance: A meta-analysis. *Psychology and Aging, 19,* 211–214.

Hu, M.-H., & Woollacott, M. H. (1994a). Multisensory training of standing balance in older adults: I. Postural stability and one-leg stance balance. *Journals of Gerontology: Medical Sciences, 49,* M52–M61.

Hu, M.-H., & Woollacott, M. H. (1994b). Multisensory training of standing balance in

older adults: II. Kinetic and electromyographic postural responses. *Journals of Gerontology: Medical Sciences, 49,* M62–M71.

Hubbard, G., Downs, M. G., & Tester, S. (2003). Including older people with dementia in research: Challenges and strategies. *Aging and Mental Health, 7,* 351–362.

Hudson, R. B. (1996). Social protection and services. In R. H. Binstock & L. K. George (Eds.), *Handbook of aging and the social sciences* (4th ed., pp. 446–466). San Diego: Academic Press.

Hultsch, D. F., & Dixon, R. A. (1990). Learning and memory in aging. In J. E. Birren & K. W. Schaie (Eds.), *Handbook of the psychology of aging* (3rd ed., pp. 258–274). San Diego: Academic Press.

Hultsch, D. F., MacDonald, S. W. S., & Dixon, R. A. (2002). Variability in reaction time performance of younger and older adults. *Journals of Gerontology: Psychological Sciences, 57B,* P101–P115.

Hummert, M. L. (1999). A social cognitive perspective on age stereotypes. In T. M. Hess & F. Blanchard-Fields (Eds.), *Social cognition and aging* (pp. 175–196). San Diego: Academic Press.

Hummert, M. L. (2003). When is an age stereotype an aging self-stereotype? A commentary. *Journals of Gerontology: Psychological Sciences, 58B,* P212–P216.

Hummert, M. L., Garstka, T. A., O'Brien, L. T., Greenwald, A. G., & Mellott, D. S. (2002). Using the implicit association test to measure age differences in implicit social cognitions. *Psychology and Aging, 17,* 482–495.

Hummert, M. L., Garstka, T. A., Shaner, J. L., & Strahm, S. (1994). Stereotypes of the elderly held by young, middle-aged, and elderly adults. *Journals of Gerontology: Psychological Sciences, 49B,* P240–P249.

Hummert, M. L., Shaner, J. L., Garstka, T. A., & Henry, C. (1998). Communication with older adults: The influence of age stereotypes, context, and communicator age. *Human Communication Research, 25,* 124–151.

Huston, M., & Schwartz, P. (1995). The relationships of lesbians and of gay men. In J. T. Wood & S. Duck (Eds.), *Understudied relationships: Off the beaten track* (pp. 89–121). Thousand Oaks, CA: Sage.

Huston, T. L., Caughlin, J. P., Houts, R. M., Smith, S. E., & George, L. J. (2001). The connubial crucible: Newlywed years as a predictors of marital delight, distress, and divorce. *Journal of Personality and Social Psychology, 80,* 237–252.

Huyck, M. H. (1996). Continuities and discontinuities in gender roles and gender identity. In V. Bengston (Ed.), *Continuities and discontinuities in the adult life course and aging.* New York: Springer.

Huyck, M. H. (1999). Gender roles and gender identity in midlife. In S. Willis & J. D. Reid (Eds.), *Life in the middle* (pp. 209–233). San Diego: Academic Press.

Hyde, J. S., Krajnik, M., & Skuldt-Niederberger, K. (1991). Androgyny across the life span: A replication and longitudinal follow-up. *Developmental Psychology, 27,* 516–519.

Idler, E. L., & Benyamini, Y. (1997). Self-rated health and mortality: A review of twenty-seven community studies. *Journal of Health and Social Behavior, 38,* 21–37.

Idler, E. L., Kasl, S. V., & Hays, J. C. (2001). Patterns of religious practice and belief in the last year of life. *Journals of Gerontology: Psychological Sciences, 56B,* P326–P334.

Ingersoll-Dayton, B., Neal, M. B., Ha, J. W., & Hammer, L. B. (2003). Redressing inequity in parent care among siblings. *Journal of Marriage and the Family, 65,* 201–212.

Institute for Womens's Policy Research (2009). The genter wage gap. Online document available at http://www.iwpr.org/femstats/wocdata.htm. Accessed 2009.

Irwin, M. R. (2008). Human psychoneuroimmunology: 20 years of discovery. *Brain, Behavior, and Immunity, 22,* 129–139.

Isaacowitz, D. M., Charles, S. T., & Carstensen, L. L. (2000). Emotion and cognition. In F. I. M. Craik & T. A. Salthouse (Eds.), *Handbook of aging and cognition* (2nd ed., pp. 593–631). Mahwah, NJ: Erlbaum.

Ishler, A. L., Johnson, R. T., & Johnson, D. W. (1998). Long term effectiveness of a statewide staff development program on cooperative learning. *Teaching and Teacher Education, 14,* 273–281.

Iskra, G., Folkard, S., Marek, T., & Noworol, C. (1996). Health, well-being and burnout of ICU nurses on 12- and 8-hour shifts. *Work and Stress, 10,* 251–256.

Ivancovich, D. A., & Wong, T. P. (2008). The role of existential and spiritual coping in anticipatory grief. In T. Armer, G. T. Eliason, & P. T. P. Wong (Eds.), *Existential and spiritual issues in death attitudes* (pp. 209–233). Mahwah, NJ: Lawrence Erlbaum.

Ivy, D. K., & Hamlet, S. (1996). College students and sexual dynamics: Two studies of peer sexual harassment. *Communication Education, 45,* 149–166.

Iwarsson, S. (2005). A long-term perspective on person-environment fit and ADL dependence among older Swedish adults. *The Gerontologist, 45,* 327–336.

Izquierdo-Porrera, A. M., & Waldstein, S. R. (2002). Cardiovascular risk factors and cognitive function in African Americans. *Journals of Gerontology: Psychological Sciences, 57B,* P377–P380.

Izraeli, D. N. (1993). Work/family conflict among women and men managers in dual career couples in Israel. *Journal of Social Behavior and Personality, 8,* 371–385.

Jacka, F., & Berk, M. (2007). Food for thought. *Acta Neuropsychiatrica, 19,* 321–323.

Jackson, B., Taylor, J., & Pyngolil, M. (1991). How age conditions the relationship between climacteric status and health symptoms in African American women. *Research in Nursing and Health, 14,* 1–9.

Jackson, J. S. (1993). Racial influences on adult development and aging. In R. Kastenbaum (Ed.), *The encyclopedia of adult development* (pp. 18–26). Phoenix, AZ: Oryx.

Jackson, J. S., Antonucci, T. C., & Gibson, R. C. (1995). Ethnic and cultural factors in research on aging and mental health: A life-course perspective. In D. K. Padgett (Ed.), *Handbook on ethnicity, aging, and mental health* (pp. 22–46). Westport, CT: Greenwood.

Jackson, J. S., & Gibson, R. C. (1985). Work and retirement among the black elderly. In Z. Blau (Ed.), *Current perspectives on aging and the life cycle* (pp. 193–222). Greenwich, CT: JAI.

Jackson, J. S., Jayakody, R., & Antonucci, T. C. (1996). Exchanges within black American three-generation families. In T. K. Hareven (Ed.), *Aging and generational relations: Life-course and cross-cultural perspectives* (pp. 83–114). New York: Aldine de Gruyter.

Jacobs, S. (1993). *Pathologic grief: Maladaptation to loss.* Washington, DC: American Psychological Association.

Jacoby, L. L. (1991). A process dissociation framework: Separating automatic from intentional uses of memory. *Journal of Memory and Language, 30,* 513–541.

Jacoby, L. L. (1999). Ironic effects of repetition: Measuring age-related differences in memory. *Journal of Experimental Psychology: Learning, Memory, and Cognition, 25*, 3–22.

Jacoby, L. L., & Rhodes, M. G. (2006). False remembering in the aged. *Current Directions in Psychological Science, 15*(2), 49–53.

Jacoby, L. L., Yonelinas, A. P., & Jennings, J. M. (1997). The relation between conscious and unconscious (automatic) influences: A declaration of independence. In J. D. Cohen & J. W. Schooler (Eds.), *Scientific approaches to consciousness* (pp. 13–47). Mahwah, NJ: Erlbaum.

Jacoby, S. (2005). *Sex in America*. Retrieved February 26, 2008, from http://www.aarpmagazine.org/lifestyle/relationships/sex_in_america.html.

James, J. W., & Haley, W. E. (1995). Age and health bias in practicing clinical psychologists. *Psychology and Aging, 10*, 610–616.

James, L. E., & Burke, D. M. (2000). Phonological priming effects on word retrieval and tip-of-the-tongue experiences in young and older adults. *Journal of Experimental Psychology: Learning, Memory, and Cognition, 26*, 1378–1391.

James, W. (1890). *The principles of psychology*. New York: Holt.

Jang, Y., Borenstein, A. R., Chiriboga, D. A., & Mortimer, J. A. (2005). Depressive symptoms among African American and white older adults. *Journal of Gerontology: Psychological Sciences, 60*, P313–P319.

Janssen I, R. R. (2005). Linking age-related changes in skeletal muscle mass and composition with metabolism and disease. *Journal of Nutrition, Health and Aging, 9*, 408–419.

Jecker, N. S., & Schneiderman, L. J. (1994). Is dying young worse than dying old? *The Gerontologist, 34*, 66–72.

Jeffko, W. G. (1979, July 6). Redefining death. *Commonweal*, 394–397.

Jenkins, C. L. (1997). Women, work, and caregiving: How do these roles affect women's well-being? *Journal of Women and Aging, 9*, 27–45.

Jenkins, C. L. (Ed.). (2003). *Widows and divorcees in later life: On their own again*. Binghamton, NY: Haworth Press.

Jenkins, J. (2007). An investigation of marital satisfaction: Assortative mating and personality similarity. *Dissertation Abstracts International: Section B: The Sciences and Engineering, 67*(12-B), 7376.

Jennings, J. M., & Jacoby, L. L. (1993). Automatic vs. intentional uses of memory: Aging, attention and control. *Psychology and Aging, 8*, 283–293.

Jensen, C. J., & Ferrari, M., & Cavanaugh, J. C. (2004). Building on the benefits: Assessing satisfaction and well-being in elder care. *Ageing International, 29*, 88–110.

Jepsen, D. A., & Dickson, G. L. (2003). Continuity in life-span career development: Career exploration as a precursor to career establishment. *Career Development Quarterly, 51*, 217–233.

Jessberger, S., & Gage, F. H. (2009). Fate plasticity of adult hippocampal progenitors: Biological relevance and therapeutic use. *Trends in Pharmacological Sciences, 30*, 61–65.

Jeste, D. V., Naimark, D., Halpain, M. C., & Lindamer, L. A. (1995). Strengths and limitations of research on late-life psychoses. In M. Gatz (Ed.), *Emerging issues in mental health and aging* (pp. 72–96). Washington, DC: American Psychological Association.

Johansson, B., Whitfield, K., Pedersen, N. L., Hofer, S. M., Ahern, F., & McClearn, G. E. (1999). Origins of individual differences in episodic memory in the oldest-old: A population-based study of identical and same-sex fraternal twins aged 80 and older. *Journals of Gerontology: Psychological Sciences, 54B*, P173–P179.

Johnson, B. D., Stone, G. L., Altmaier, E. M., & Berdahl, L. D. (1998). The relationship of demographic factors, locus of control and self-efficacy to successful nursing home adjustment. *The Gerontologist, 38*, 209–216.

Johnson, C. L., & Troll, L. E. (1994). Constraints and facilitators to friendships in late late life. *The Gerontologist, 34*, 79–87.

Johnson, M. M., & Rhodes, R. (2007). Institutionalization: A theory of human behavior and the social environment. *Advances in Social Work, 8*, 219–236. Retrieved October 26, 2008, from http://journals.iupui.edu/index.php/advancesinsocialwork/article/view/143/144.

Johnson, M. M. S. (1990). Age differences in decision making: A process methodology for examining strategic information processing. *Journals of Gerontology: Psychological Sciences, 45*, P75–P78.

Johnson, M. P. (1995). Patriarchal terrorism and common couple violence: Two forms of violence against women. *Journal of Marriage and the Family, 57*, 283–294.

Johnson, M. P. (2001). Conflict and control: Symmetry and asymmetry in domestic violence. In A. Booth, A. C. Crouter, & M. Clements (Eds.), *Couples in conflict* (pp. 95–104). Mahwah, NJ: Erlbaum.

Johnson, M. P., & Ferraro, K. J. (2000). Research on domestic violence in the 1990s: Making distinctions. *Journal of Marriage and the Family, 62*, 948–963.

Johnson, N., Barion, A., Rademaker, A., Rehkemper, G., & Weintraub, S. (2004). The Activities of Daily Living Questionnaire: A validation study in patients with dementia. *Alzheimer Disease and Associated Disorders, 18*, 223–230.

Johnson, R. E. (2003). Aging and the remembering of text. *Developmental Review, 23*, 261–346.

Johnson, R. J., & Wolinsky, F. D. (1994). Gender, race, and health: The structure of health status among older adults. *The Gerontologist, 34*, 24–35.

Johnston, K. E., Swim, J. K., Saltsman, B. M., Deater-Deckard, K., & Petrill, S. A. (2007). Mothers' racial, ethnic, and cultural socialization of transracially adopted Asian children. *Family Relations, 56*, 390–402.

Jones, C. J., & Meredith, W. (1996). Patterns of personality change across the life span. *Psychology and Aging, 11*, 57–65.

Jones, F. L. (1996). Convergence and divergence in ethnic divorce patterns: A research note. *Journal of Marriage and the Family, 58*, 213–218.

Jones, L. Y. (1980). *Great expectations: America and the baby boom generation*. New York: Coward, McCann, & Geoghegan.

Jorm, A. F. (1996). Assessment of cognitive impairment and dementia using informant reports. *Clinical Psychological Review, 16*, 51–73.

Joshi, A., & Sastry, N. (1995). Work and family: Conflict and its resolution. *Indian Journal of Gender Studies, 2*, 227–241.

Joynt, R. J. (1995). Normal aging and patterns of neurologic disease. In W. B. Abrams, M. H. Beers, & R. Berkow (Eds.), *The Merck manual of geriatrics* (2nd ed., pp. 1129–1133). Whitehouse Station, NJ: Merck Research Laboratories.

Juengst, E. T., Binstock, R. H., Mehlman, M. J., & Post, S. G. (2003). Antiaging research and the need for public dialogue. *Science, 299*, 1323.

Juffer, F. (2006). Children's awareness of adoption and their problem behavior in families with 7-year-old internationally adopted children. *Adoption Quarterly, 9*, 1–22.

Jung, C. (1933). *Modern man in search of a soul* (W. S. Dell & C. F. Baynes, Trans.). New York: Harcourt, Brace, & World.

Jylhä, M., Guralnik, J. M., Ferrucci, L., Jokela, J., & Heikkinen, E. (1998). Is self-rated health comparable across cultures and genders? *Journals of Gerontology: Social Sciences, 53B*, S144–S152.

Kahana, E. (1982). A congruence model of person–environment interaction. In M. P. Lawton, P. G. Windley, & T. O. Byerts (Eds.), *Aging and the environment: Theoretical approaches* (pp. 97–121). New York: Springer.

Kahana, E., & Kahana, B. (1983). Environmental continuity, futurity, and adaptation of the aged. In G. D. Rowles & R. J. Ohta (Eds.), *Aging and milieu: Environmental perspectives on growing old* (pp. 205–230). New York: Academic Press.

Kahana, M., & Wingfield, A. (2000). A functional relation between learning and organization in free recall. *Psychonomic Bulletin and Review, 7*, 516–521.

Kail, R., & Salthouse, T. A. (1994). Processing speed as a mental capacity. *Acta Psychologica, 86*, 199–225.

Kakar, S. (1998). The search for middle age in India. In R. A. Shweder (Ed.), *Welcome to middle age!: (And other cultural fictions)* (pp. 75–98). Chicago: University of Chicago Press.

Kalimo, R., Pahkim, K., Mutanen, P., & Toppinen-Tanner, S. (2003). Staying well or burning out at work: Work characteristics and personal resources as long-term predictors. *Work and Stress, 17*, 109–122.

Kalish, R. A. (1984). *Death, grief, and caring relationships* (2nd ed.). Pacific Grove, CA: Brooks/Cole.

Kalish, R. A. (1987). Death and dying. In P. Silverman (Ed.), *The elderly as modern pioneers* (pp. 320–334). Bloomington: Indiana University Press.

Kalish, R. A., & Reynolds, D. (1976). *Death and ethnicity: A psychocultural study*. Los Angeles: University of Southern California Press.

Kallman, D. A., Plato, C. C., & Tobin, J. D. (1990). The role of muscle loss in the age-related decline of grip strength: Cross-sectional and longitudinal perspectives. *Journals of Gerontology: Medical Sciences, 45*, M82–M88.

Kalmijn, M., & Flap, H. (2001). Assortative meeting and mating: Unintended consequences of organized settings for partner choices. *Social Forces, 79*, 1289–1312.

Kane, M. J., Hasher, L., Stoltzfus, E. R., Zacks, R. T., & Connelly, S. L. (1994). Inhibitory attentional mechanisms and aging. *Psychology and Aging, 9*, 103–112.

Kane, R. A., & Brown-Wilson, K. (2001). *Assisted living at the crossroad: Principles for its future*. Retrieved October 28, 2008, from http://www.ilru.org/html/training/webcasts/handouts/2002/10-09-JK/crossroads.html.

Kane, R. A., Lum, T. Y., Cutler, L. J., Degenholz, H. B., & Yu, T.-C. (2007). Resident outcomes in small-house nursing homes: A longitudinal evaluation of the initial Green House program. *Journal of the American Geriatrics Society, 55*, 832–839.

Kane, R. A., & Wilson, K. B. (1993). Assisted living in the United States: A new paradigm for residential care for frail older persons? Washington, DC: AARP.

Kanehisa, M., Araki, M., Goto, S., Hattori, M., Hirakawa, M., Itoh, M., Katayama, T., Kawashima, S., Okuda, S., Tokimatsu, T., & Yamanishi, Y. (2008). KEGG for linking genomes to life and the environment. *Nucleic Acids Research, 36,* D480–D484.

Kanekar, S., Koswalla, M. B., & Nazareth, T. (1989). Occupational prestige as a function of occupant's gender. *Journal of Applied Social Psychology, 19,* 681–688.

Kanter, R. M. (1976, May). Why bosses turn bitchy. *Psychology Today,* pp. 56–59.

Kapaki, E. (2006). Alcoholic dementia: Myth or reality? *Annals of General Psychiatry, 5*(Suppl.), S57.

Kaplan, R., & Erickson, J. (2000). Quality adjusted life expectancy for men and women in the United States. In S. B. Manuck (Ed.), *Behavior, health, and aging.* Mahwah, NJ: Erlbaum.

Kaplan, R. M., Patterson, T. L., & Groessl, E. J. (2004). Outcome assessment for resource allocation in primary care. In R. G. Frank, S. H. McDaniel, J. H. Bray, & M. Heldring (Eds.), *Primary care psychology* (pp. 293–315). Washington, DC: American Psychological Association.

Kapp, M. B. (1999). Geriatrics and the law: Patient rights and professional responsibilities (3rd ed.). New York: Springer.

Kapp, M. B. (2008). Legal issues in dementia. *International Journal of Risk and Safety in Medicine, 20,* 91–103.

Karasu, S. R., & Karasu, T. B. (2005). *The art of marriage maintenance.* Lanham, MD: Jason Aronson.

Karim, S. S., Ramanna, G., Petit, T., Doward, L., & Burns, A. (2008). Development of the Dementia Quality of Life questionnaire (D-QOL): UK version. *Aging and Mental Health, 12,* 144–148.

Karmol, K. S. (2008). Pain management in senior patients. *Internet Journal of Health, 7.* Retrieved September 28, 2008, from http://www.ispub.com/ostia/index.php?xmlFilePath=journals/ijh/vol7n1/pain.xml.

Karney, B. R., & Bradbury, T. N. (1995). The longitudinal course of marital quality and stability: A review of theory, method, and research. *Psychological Bulletin, 118,* 3–34.

Karon, B. P., & VandenBos, G. R. (1999). Schizophrenia and psychosis in elderly populations. In I. H. Nordhus, G. R. VandenBos, S. Berg, & P. Fromholt (Eds.), *Clinical geropsychology* (pp. 219–227). Washington, DC: American Psychological Association.

Karp, J. F., Shega, J. W., Morone, N. E., & Weiner, D. K. (2008). Advances in understanding the mechanisms and management of persistent pain in older adults. *British Journal of Anaesthesia, 101,* 111–120.

Karpel, M. E., Hoyer, W. J., & Toglia, M. P. (2001). Accuracy and qualities of real and suggested memories: Nonspecific age differences. *Journals of Gerontology: Psychological Sciences, 56,* P103–P110.

Kasl-Godley, J. E., Gatz, M., & Fiske, A. (1999). Depression and depressive symptoms in old age. In I. H. Nordhus, G. R. VandenBos, S. Berg, & P. Fromholt (Eds.), *Clinical geropsychology* (pp. 211–217). Washington, DC: American Psychological Association.

Kaslow, F. W., Hansson, K., & Lundblad, A. (1994). Long-term marriages in Sweden: And some comparisons with similar couples in the United States. *Contemporary Family Therapy, 16,* 521–537.

Kastenbaum, R. (1985). Dying and death: A life-span approach. In J. E. Birren & K. W. Schaie (Eds.), *Handbook of the psychology of aging* (2nd ed., pp. 619–643). New York: Van Nostrand Reinhold.

Kastenbaum, R. (1992). *The psychology of death* (rev. ed.). New York: Springer.

Kastenbaum, R. (1999). Dying and bereavement. In J. C. Cavanaugh & S. K. Whitbourne (Eds.), *Gerontology: An interdisciplinary perspective* (pp. 155–185). New York: Oxford University Press.

Kastenbaum, R., & Briscoe, L. (1975). The street corner: Laboratory for the study of life-threatening behavior. *Omega: Journal of Death and Dying, 6,* 33–44.

Kastenbaum, R., & Thuell, S. (1995). Cookies baking, coffee brewing: Toward a contextual theory of dying. *Omega: Journal of Death and Dying, 31,* 175–187.

Kasuya, H., Yoshida, H., Mori, H., & Kido, H. (2008, July). *A longitudinal study of vocal aging: Changes in F0, jitter, shimmer, and glottal noise.* Paper presented at Acoustics '08 Paris, Paris.

Katz, S., & Peters, K. R. (in press). Enhancing the mind? Memory, medicine, dementia, and the aging brain. *Journal of Aging Studies.*

Kausler, D. H. (1994). *Learning and memory in normal aging.* San Diego: Academic Press.

Kave, G., Eyal, N., Shorek, A., Cohen-Mansfield, J. (2008). Multilingualism and cognitive state in the oldest old. *Psychology and Aging, 23,* 70–78.

Kawas, C., Resnick, S., Morrison, A., Brookmeyer, R., Corrada, M., Zonderman, A., Bacal, C., Lingle, D. C., & Metter, E. (1997). A prospective study of estrogen replacement therapy and the risk of developing Alzheimer's disease: The Baltimore Longitudinal Study of Aging. *Neurology, 48,* 1517–1521.

Kegan, R. (1982). *The evolving self.* Cambridge, MA: Harvard University Press.

Keller, J. W., Sherry, D., & Piotrowski, C. (1984). Perspectives on death: A developmental study. *Journal of Psychology, 116,* 137–142.

Kelley, C. M. (1986). Depressive mood effects on memory and attention. In L. W. Poon (Ed.), *Handbook for the clinical memory assessment of older adults* (pp. 238–243). Washington, DC: American Psychological Association.

Kelley, H. H. (1967). Attribution theory in social psychology. *Nebraska Symposium on Motivation, 15,* 192–241.

Kelly, J. B. (1982). Divorce: The adult perspective. In B. B. Wolman (Ed.), *Handbook of developmental psychology* (pp. 734–750). Englewood Cliffs, NJ: Prentice Hall.

Kelly, J. R. (1996). Activities. In J. E. Birren (Ed.), *Encyclopedia of gerontology: Age, aging, and the aged* (Vol. 1, pp. 37–49). San Diego: Academic Press.

Kemeny, M. E. (2003). The psychobiology of stress. *Current Directions in Psychological Science, 12,* 124–129.

Kemper, S. (2001). Over-accommodations and under-accommodations to aging. In N. Charness & D. C. Parks (Eds.), *Communication, technology and aging: Opportunities and challenges for the future* (pp. 30–46). New York: Springer.

Kemper, S., Ferrell, P., Harden, T., Finter-Urczyk, A., & Billington, C. (1998). The use of elder-speak by young and older adults to impaired and unimpaired listeners. *Aging, Neuropsychology, and Cognition, 5,* 43–55.

Kemper, S., Herman, R. E., & Lian, C. H. (2003). The costs of doing two things at once for young and older adults: Talking while walking, finger tapping, and ignoring speech of noise. *Psychology and Aging, 18,* 181–192.

Kempermann, G., Gast, D., & Gage, F. H. (2002). Neuroplasticity in old age: Sustained fivefold induction of hippocampal neurogenesis by long-term environmental enrichment. *Annals of Neurology, 52,* 135–143.

Kemtes, K. A., & Kemper, S. (1997). Younger and older adults' on-line processing of syntactic ambiguities. *Psychology and Aging, 12,* 362–371.

Kennedy, G. E. (1991). Grandchildren's reasons for closeness with grandparents. *Journal of Social Behavior and Personality, 6,* 697–712.

Kennedy, Q., Mather, M., & Carstensen, L. L. (2004). The role of motivation in the age-related positivity effect in autobiographical memory. *Psychological Science, 15,* 208–214.

Kennel, K. (2007). *Osteoporosis treatment puts brakes on bone loss.* Retrieved March 15, 2009, from http://www.mayoclinic.com/print/osteoporosis-treatment/WO00127/METHOD=print.

Kenney, W. L., & Munce, T. A. (2003). Invited review: Aging and human temperature regulation. *Journal of Applied Physiology, 95,* 2598–2603.

Kensinger, E. A. (2006). Remembering emotional information: Effects of aging and Alzheimer's disease. *Progress in Alzheimer's disease research.* Hauppauge, NY: Nova Science Publishers, Inc.

Kensinger, E. A. (2008). Age differences in memory for arousing and nonarousing emotional words. *Journals of Gerontology: Psychological Sciences, 63,* P13–18.

Kensinger, E. A., & Corkin, S. (2004). The effects of emotional content and aging on false memories. *Cognitive, Affective and Behavioral Neuroscience, 4,* 1–9.

Kensinger, E. A., Piguet, O., Krendl, A. C., & Corkin, S. (2005). Memory for contextual details: Effects of emotion and aging. *Psychology and Aging, 20,* 241–250.

Kensinger, E. A., & Schacter, D. L. (2008). Neural processes supporting young and older adults' emotional memories. *Journal of Cognitive Neuroscience, 20,* 1161–1173.

Kessler, E.-M., & Staudinger, U. M. (2007). Intergenerational potential: Effects of social interaction between older adults and adolescents. *Psychology and Aging, 22*(4), 690–704.

Keyes, C. L., & Ryff, C. D. (1998). Generativity in adult lives: Social structural contours and quality of life consequences. In D. McAdams & E. de St. Aubin (Eds.), *Generativity and adult development: Perspectives on caring for and contributing to the next generation* (pp. 227–263). Washington, DC: American Psychological Association.

Keyes, C. M., & Ryff, C. D. (1999). Psychological well-being in midlife. In S. Willis & J. D. Reid (Eds.), *Life in the middle* (pp. 161–181). San Diego: Academic Press.

Kier, F. J., & Molinari, V. (2003). "Do-it-yourself" dementia testing: Issues regarding an Alzheimer's home screening test. *The Gerontologist, 43,* 295–301.

Kim, H. K., Capaldi, D. M., & Crosby, L. (2007). Generalizability of Gottman and Colleagues' affective process models of couples' relationship outcomes. *Journal of Marriage and Family, 69,* 55–72.

Kim, J. E., & Moen, P. (2001). Is retirement good or bad for subjective well-being? *Current Directions in Psychological Science, 10,* 83–86.

Kim, J. E., & Moen, P. (2002). Retirement transitions, gender, and psychological well-being: A life-course, ecological model. *Journals of Gerontology: Psychological Sciences, 57B,* P212–P222.

Kim, S., Hasher, L., et al. (2007). Aging and benefit of distractibility. *Psychonomic Bulletin and Review, 14*(2): 301–305.

Kim, S., Healey, M. K., Goldstein, D., Hasher, L., & Wiprzycka, U. J. (2008). Age differences in choice satisfaction: A positivity effect in decision making. *Psychology and Aging, 23*(1), 33–38.

Kimmel, D. C. (1995). Lesbians and gay men grow old. In L. A. Bond, S. J. Cutler, & A. Grams (Eds.), *Promoting successful and productive aging.* Thousand Oaks, CA: Sage.

Kimmel, D. C., & Sang, B. E. (1995). Lesbians and gay men in midlife. In A. R. D'Augelli & C. J. Patterson (Eds.), *Lesbian, gay, and bisexual identities over the lifespan* (pp. 190–214). New York: Oxford University Press.

Kinderman, S. S., & Brown, G. G. (1997). Depression and memory in the elderly: A meta-analysis. *Journal of Clinical and Experimental Neuropsychology, 19,* 625–642.

King, P. M., & Kitchener, K. S. (1994). Developing reflective judgment: Understanding and promoting intellectual growth and critical thinking in adolescents and adults. San Francisco: Jossey-Bass.

King, P. M., Kitchener, K. S., Wood, P. K., & Davison, M. L. (1989). Relationships across developmental domains: A longitudinal study of intellectual, moral, and ego development. In M. L. Commons, J. D. Sinnott, F. A. Richards, & C. Armon (Eds.), *Adult development: Comparisons and applications of adolescent and adult developmental models* (Vol. 1, pp. 57–72). New York: Praeger.

King, S. V., Burgess, E. O., Akinyela, M., Counts-Spriggs, M., & Parker, N. (2006). The religious dimensions of the grandparent role in three-generation African American households. *Journal of Religion, Spirituality and Aging, 19,* 75–96.

King, V., & Scott, M. E. (2005). A comparison of cohabiting relationships among older and younger adults. *Journal of Marriage & Family, 67,* 271–285.

Kingson, E. R., & Williamson, J. B. (2001). Economic security policies. In R. H. Binstock & L. K. George (Eds.), *Handbook of aging and the social sciences* (5th ed., pp. 369–386). San Diego: Academic Press.

Kingston, P. W., & Nock, S. L. (1987). Time together among dual-earner couples. *American Sociological Review, 52,* 391–400.

Kinney, J. M., & Cavanaugh, J. C. (1993, November). *Until death do us part: Striving to find meaning while caring for a spouse with dementia.* Paper presented at the meeting of the Gerontological Society of America, New Orleans.

Kinney, J. M., Ishler, K. J., Pargament, K. I., & Cavanaugh, J. C. (2003). Coping with the uncontrollable: The use of general and religious coping by caregivers to spouses with dementia. *Journal of Religious Gerontology, 14,* 171–188.

Kinsella, G. J., Ong, B., Storey, E., Wallace, J., & Hester, R. (2007). Elaborated spaced-retrieval and prospective memory in mild Alzheimer's disease. *Neuropsychological Rehabilitation, 17,* 688–706.

Kinsella, K., & Phillips, D. R. (2005). Global aging: The challenge of success. *Population Bulletin, 60.* Retrieved September 21, 2008, from http://findarticles.com/p/articles/mi_qa3761/is_/ai_n13453275?tag=artBody;col1.

Kinsella, K., & Velkoff, V. A. (2001). *An aging world: 2001.* U.S. Census Bureau, Series P95/01–1. Washington, DC: U.S. Government Printing Office.

Kirasic, K. C. (1991). Spatial cognition and behavior in young and elderly adults: Implications for learning new environments. *Psychology and Aging, 6,* 10–18.

Kirasic, K. C., & Allen, G. L. (1985). Aging, spatial performance, and spatial competence. In N. Charness (Ed.), *Aging and human performance* (pp. 191–223). Chichester, UK: Wiley.

Kirkwood, T. B. L. (2008). Understanding ageing form an evolutionary perspective. *Journal of Internal Medicine, 263,* 117–127.

Kitchener, K. S., & Fischer, K. W. (1990). A skill approach to the development of reflective thinking. In D. Kuhn (Ed.), *Contributions to human development: Developmental perspectives on teaching and learning* (Vol. 21, pp. 48–62). Basel, Switzerland: Karger.

Kite, M. E., & Wagner, L. S. (2002). Attitudes toward older adults. In T. D. Nelson (Ed.), *Ageism: Stereotyping and prejudice against older persons* (pp. 129–161). Cambridge, MA: MIT Press.

Kitson, G. C. (2000). Adjustment to violent and natural deaths in later and earlier life for black and white widows. *Journals of Gerontology: Social Sciences, 55B,* S341–S351.

Kitson, G. L., & Sussman, M. B. (1982). Marital complaints, demographic characteristics, and symptoms of mental distress in divorce. *Journal of Marriage and the Family, 44,* 87–101.

Kittrell, D. (1998). A comparison of the evolution of men's and women's dreams in Daniel Levinson's theory of adult development. *Journal of Adult Development, 5,* 105–115.

Kivett, V. R. (1991). Centrality of the grandfather role among older rural black and white men. *Journals of Gerontology: Social Sciences, 46,* S250–S258.

Kivnick, H. Q. (1982). *The meaning of grandparenthood.* Ann Arbor, MI: UMI Research.

Kivnick, H. Q. (1985). Grandparenthood and mental health: Meaning, behavior, and satisfaction. In V. L. Bengtson & J. F. Robertson (Eds.), *Grandparenthood* (pp. 151–158). Beverly Hills, CA: Sage.

Klaczynski, P. A., & Robinson, B. (2000). Personal theories, intellectual ability, and epistemological beliefs: Adult age differences in everyday reasoning biases. *Psychology and Aging, 15,* 400–416.

Klass, D. (1996a). Grief in Eastern culture: Japanese ancestor worship. In D. Klass, P. R. Silverman, & S. L. Nickman (Eds.), *Continuing bonds: New understandings of grief* (pp. 59–70). Washington, DC: Taylor & Francis.

Klass, D. (1996b). The deceased child in the psychic and social worlds of bereaved parents during the resolution of grief. In D. Klass, P. R. Silverman, & S. L. Nickman (Eds.), *Continuing bonds: New understandings of grief* (pp. 199–215). Washington, DC: Taylor & Francis.

Klass, D. (1999). Developing a cross-cultural model of grief: The state of the field. *Omega: Journal of Death and Dying, 39,* 153–178.

Klass, D. (2001). Continuing bonds in the resolution of grief in Japan and North America. *American Behavioral Scientist, 44,* 742–763.

Kleespies, P. M. (2004). *Life and death decisions: Psychological and ethical considerations in end-of-life care.* Washington, DC: American Psychological Association.

Kliegl, R., Smith, J., & Baltes, P. B. (1990). On the focus and process of magnification of age differences during mnemonic training. *Developmental Psychology, 26,* 894–904.

Kline, D. W. (1994). Optimizing the visibility of displays for older observers. *Experimental Aging Research, 20,* 11–23.

Kline, D. W., & Schieber, F. (1985). Vision and aging. In J. E. Birren & K. W. Schaie (Eds.), *Handbook of the psychology of aging* (2nd ed., pp. 296–331). New York: Van Nostrand Reinhold.

Kline, T. J., Ghali, L. A., Kline, D. W., & Brown, S. (1990). Visibility distance of highway signs among young, middle-aged, and older observers: Icons are better than text. *Human Factors, 32,* 609–619.

Knapp, M. L., & Taylor, E. H. (1994). Commitment and its communication in romantic relationships. In A. L. Weber & J. H. Harvey (Eds.), *Perspectives on close relationships* (pp. 153–175). Boston: Allyn & Bacon.

Knee, D. (in press). Hospice. In J. C. Cavanaugh & C. K. Cavanaugh (Eds.), *Aging in America.* Westport, CT: Praeger.

Knight, R. G., & Godfrey, H. P. D. (1995). Behavioural and self-report methods. In A. D. Baddeley, B. A. Wilson, & F. N. Watts (Eds.), *Handbook of memory disorders* (pp. 393–410). Chichester, UK: Wiley.

Knodel, J., Chayovan, N., & Siriboon, S. (1996). Familial support and the life course of Thai elderly and their children. In T. K. Hareven (Ed.), *Aging and generational relations: Life-course and cross-cultural perspectives* (pp. 217–240). New York: Aldine de Gruyter.

Knowles, D. R. (2006). *Aging changes in the male reproductive system.* Retrieved February 26, 2008, from http://www.nlm.nih.gov/medlineplus/ency/article/004017.htm.

Knox, D., Custis, L. L., & Zusman, M. E. (2000). Abuse in dating relationships among college students. *College Student Journal, 34,* 505–508.

Knutson, B., Adams, C. S., Fong, G. W., & Hommer, D. (2001). Anticipation of monetary reward selectively recruits nucleus accumbens. *Journal of Neuroscience, 21,* RC159.

Kobler, K., Limbo, R., & Kavanaugh, K. (2007). Meaningful moments: The use of ritual in perinatal and pediatric death. *MCN: The American Journal of Maternal/Child Nursing, 32,* 288–297.

Koenig, B. L., Kirkpatrick, L. A., & Ketelaar, T. (2007). Misperception of sexual and romantic interests in opposite-sex friendships: Four hypotheses. *Personal Relationships, 14,* 411–429.

Koenig, H. G. (2002). A commentary: The role of religion and spirituality at the end of life. *The Gerontologist, 42*(Special Issue III), 20–23.

Koenig, H. G., George, L. K., & Siegler, I. C. (1988). The use of religion and other emotion-regulating coping strategies among older adults. *The Gerontologist, 28,* 303–310.

Koestenbaum, P. (1976). *Is there an answer to death?* Englewood Cliffs, NJ: Prentice Hall.

Kolb, B., Gibb, R., & Robinson, T. E. (2003). Brain plasticity and behavior. *Current Directions in Psychological Science, 12,* 1–5.

Kooij, D., De Lange, A., Jansen, P., & Dikkers, J. (2008). Older workers' motivation to continue to work: Five meanings of age. *Journal of Managerial Psychology, 23*(4), 364–394.

Kornhaber, A. (1985). Grandparenthood and the "new social contract." In V. L. Bengtson & J. F. Robertson (Eds.), *Grandparenthood* (pp. 159–172). Beverly Hills, CA: Sage.

Kosberg, J. I., Lowenstein, A., Garcia, J. L., & Biggs, S. (2002). Challenges to the cross-cultural and cross-national study of elder abuse. *Journal of Social Work Research and Evaluation, 3,* 19–31.

Kosik, K. S. (1992). Alzheimer's disease: A cell biological perspective. *Science, 256,* 780–783.

Kosnik, W., Winslow, L., Kline, D. W., Rasinski, K., & Sekuler, R. (1988). Visual changes in everyday life throughout adulthood. *Journals of Gerontology: Psychological Sciences, 43,* P63–P70.

Kotre, J. N. (1984). Outliving the self: How we live on in future generations. New York: Norton.

Kotre, J. N. (1999). Make it count: How to generate a legacy that gives meaning to your life. New York: Free Press.

Koutstaal, W. (2003). Older adults encode—but do not always use—perceptual details: Intentional versus unintentional effects of detail on memory judgments. *Psychological Science, 14,* 189–193.

Kowalski, S. D., & Bondmass, M. D. (2008). Physiological and psychological symptoms of grief in widows. *Research in Nursing & Health, 31,* 23–30.

Krahn, L. E. (2005). Psychiatric disorders associated with disturbed sleep. *Seminars in Neurology, 25,* 90–96.

Kram, K. E. (1980). *Mentoring processes at work: Developmental relationships in managerial careers.* Unpublished doctoral dissertation, Yale University, New Haven, CT.

Kram, K. E. (1985). Mentoring at work: Developmental relationships in organizational life. Glenview, IL: Scott, Foresman.

Kramer, A. F., Fabiani, M., & Colcombe, S. J. (2006). Contributions of cognitive neuroscience to the understanding of behavior and aging. In J. E. Birren & K. W. Schaire (Eds.), *Handbook of the psychology of aging* (6th ed., pp. 57–83). Amsterdam: Elsevier.

Kramer, A. F., & Larish, J. F. (1996). Aging and dual-task performance. In W. R. Rogers, A. D. Fisk, & N. Walker (Eds.), *Aging and skilled performance* (pp. 83–112). Hillsdale, NJ: Erlbaum.

Kramer, A. F., Larish, J. F., & Strayer, D. L. (1995). Training for attentional control in dual task settings: A comparison of young and old adults. *Journal of Experimental Psychology: Applied, 1,* 50–76.

Kramer, A. F., Larish, J. F., Weber, T. A., & Bardell, L. (1999). Training for executive control: Task coordination strategies and aging. In D. Gopher & A. Koriat (Eds.), *Attention and performance: XVIII.* San Diego: Academic Press.

Kramer, A. F., & Willis, S. L. (2002). Enhancing the cognitive vitality of older adults. *Current Directions in Psychological Science, 11,* 173–177.

Kramer, D. A. (1989). A developmental framework for understanding conflict resolution processes. In J. D. Sinnott (Ed.), *Everyday problem solving: Theory and applications* (pp. 138–152). New York: Praeger.

Kramer, D. A. (1990). Conceptualizing wisdom: The primacy of affect–cognition relations. In R. J. Sternberg (Ed.), *Wisdom: Its nature, origins, and development* (pp. 279–313). New York: Cambridge University Press.

Kramer, D. A., Kahlbaugh, P. E., & Goldston, R. B. (1992). A measure of paradigm beliefs about the social world. *Journals of Gerontology: Psychological Sciences, 47,* P180–P189.

Kramer, D. A., & Woodruff, D. S. (1986). Relativistic and dialectical thought in three adult age-groups. *Human Development, 29,* 280–290.

Krause, N. (1995). Religiosity and self-esteem among older adults. *Journals of Gerontology: Psychological Sciences, 50B,* P236–P246.

Krause, N. (1999). Stress and devaluation of highly salient roles in late life. *Journals of Gerontology: Social Sciences, 54B,* S99–S108.

Krause, N. (2002). Church-based social support and health in old age: Exploring variations by race. *Journals of Gerontology: Psychological Sciences, 57B,* P332–P347.

Krause, N. (2003). Religious meaning and subjective well-being in late life. *Journals of Gerontology: Psychological Sciences, 58B,* P160–P170.

Kriseman, N. L., & Claes, J. A. (1997). Gender issues and elder care. In T. D. Hargrave & S. M. Hanna (Eds.), *The aging family: New visions in theory, practice, and reality* (pp. 199–208). New York: Brunner/Mazel.

Krueger, D., & Ludwig, A. (2007). On the consequences of demographic change for rates of return on capital, and the distribution of wealth and welfare. *Journal of Monetary Economics, 54,* 49–87.

Kruger, D. J. (2006). Male facial masculinity influences attributions of personality and reproductive strategy. *Personal Relationships, 13,* 451–463.

Kruglanski, A. W., Atash, M. N., DeGrada, E., Mannetti, L., Pierro, A., & Webster, D. M. (1997). Psychological theory testing vs. psychometric nay-saying: Comment on Neuberg et al.'s (1997) critique of the Need for Closure Scale. *Journal of Personality and Social Psychology, 76,* 1005–1016.

Kruglanski, A. W., & Webster, D. W. (1996). Motivated closing of the mind, "seizing" and "freezing." *Psychological Review, 103,* 263–283.

Kübler-Ross, E. (1969). *On death and dying.* New York: Macmillan.

Kübler-Ross, E. (1974). *Questions and answers on death and dying.* New York: Macmillan.

Kübler-Ross, E., & Kessler, D. (2005). *On grief and grieving: On finding meaning of grief through the five stages of loss.* New York: Scribner.

Kuhn, D. (1992). Cognitive development. In M. Bornstein & M. Lamb (Eds.), *Developmental psychology: An advanced textbook* (pp. 211–272). Hillsdale, NJ: Erlbaum.

Kukutai, T. H. (2007). White mothers, brown children: Ethnic identification of Maori-European children in New Zealand. *Journal of Marriage and Family, 69,* 1150–1161.

Kulik, L. (2001a). The impact of men's and women's retirement on marital relations: A comparative analysis. *Journal of Women and Aging, 13,* 21–37.

Kulik, L. (2001b). Marital relationships in late adulthood: Synchronous versus asynchronous couples. *International Journal of Aging and Human Development, 52,* 323–339.

Kulwicki, A. D. (2002). The practice of honor crimes: A glimpse of domestic violence in the Arab world. *Issues in Mental Health Nursing, 23,* 77–87.

Kunda, Z., Davies, P. G., Adams, B. D., & Spencer, S. J. (2002). The dynamic time course of stereotype activation: Activation, dissipation, and resurrection. *Journal of Personality and Social Psychology, 82,* 283–299.

Kunda, Z., & Spencer, S. J. (2003). When do stereotypes come to mind and when do they color judgment? A goal-based theoretical framework for stereotype activation and application. *Psychological Bulletin, 129,* 522–544.

Kuniyoshi, S. M., & Jankovic, J. (2003). MDMA and Parkinsonism. *New England Journal of Medicine, 349,* 96–97.

Kunzmann, U., & Baltes, P. B. (2003). Wisdom-related knowledge: Affective, motivational, and interpersonal correlates. *Personality and Social Psychology Bulletin, 29,* 1104–1119.

Kunzmann, U., Little, T., & Smith, J. (2002). Perceiving control: A double-edged sword in old age. *Journals of Gerontology: Psychological Sciences, 57B,* P484–P491.

Kupfer, C. (1995). Ophthalmologic disorders. In W. B. Abrams, M. H. Beers, & R. Berkow (Eds.), *The Merck manual of geriatrics* (2nd ed., pp. 1289–1314). Whitehouse Station, NJ: Merck Research Laboratories.

Kurdek, L. A. (1991b). The relations between reported well-being and divorce history, availability of a proximate adult, and gender. *Journal of Marriage and the Family, 53,* 71–78.

Kurdek, L. A. (1995a). Developmental changes in relationship quality in gay male and lesbian cohabiting couples. *Developmental Psychology, 31,* 86–94.

Kurdek, L. A. (1995b). Lesbian and gay couples. In A. R. D'Augelli & C. J. Patterson (Eds.), *Lesbian, gay, and bisexual identities over the lifespan* (pp. 243–261). New York: Oxford University Press.

Kurdek, L. A. (2004). Are gay and lesbian cohabiting couples really different from heterosexual married couples? *Journal of Marriage and Family, 66,* 880–900.

Kurz, D. (1995). *For richer, for poorer: Mothers confront divorce.* Philadelphia: Women's Studies Program, University of Pennsylvania.

Kwong See, S. T., & Ryan, E. B. (1999). Intergenerational communication: The survey interview as a social exchange. In N. Schwarz & D. C. Park (Eds.), *Cognition, aging, and self-reports* (pp. 245–262). Hove, UK: Psychology Press/Erlbaum (UK).

L'Abate, L. (2006). You can go home again, but should you stay? *PsycCRITIQUES, 51,* 25.

LaBar, K.S., & Cabeza, R. (2006). Cognitive neuroscience of emotional memory. *Nature Reviews Neuroscience, 7,* 54–64.

Labouvie-Vief, G. (1980). Beyond formal operations: Uses and limits of pure logic in life-span development. *Human Development, 23,* 141–161.

Labouvie-Vief, G. (1981). Proactive and reactive aspects of constructivism: Growth and aging in life-span perspective. In R. M. Lerner & N. A. Busch-Rossnagel (Eds.), *Individuals as producers of their development* (pp. 197–230). New York: Academic Press.

Labouvie-Vief, G. (1984). Logic and self-regulation from youth to maturity: A model. In M. L. Commons, F. A. Richards, & C. Armon (Eds.), *Beyond formal operations: Late adolescent and adult cognitive development* (pp. 158–179). New York: Praeger.

Labouvie-Vief, G. (1990). Modes of knowledge and the organization of development. In M. L. Commons & C. Armon (Eds.), *Adult development: Vol. 2, Models and methods in the study of adolescent and adult thought* (pp. 43–62). New York: Praeger.

Labouvie-Vief, G. (1992). Neo-Piagetian perspective on adult cognitive development. In R. J. Sternberg & C. A. Berg (Eds.), *Intellectual development* (pp. 197–229). New York: Cambridge University Press.

Labouvie-Vief, G. (1997). Cognitive–emotional integration in adulthood. In K. W. Schaie & M. P. Lawton (Eds.), *Annual review of gerontology and geriatrics* (Vol. 17, pp. 206–237). New York: Springer.

Labouvie-Vief, G. (2003). Dynamic integration: Affect, cognition, and the self in adulthood. *Current Direction in Psychological Science, 12,* 201–206.

Labouvie-Vief, G., Chiodo, L. M., Goguen, L. A., Diehl, M., & Orwoll, L. (1995). Representations of self across the life span. *Psychology and Aging, 10,* 404–415.

Labouvie-Vief, G., & Diehl, M. (1999). Self and personality development. In J. C. Cavanaugh & S. K. Whitbourne (Eds.), *Gerontology: An interdisciplinary perspective* (pp. 238–268). New York: Oxford University Press.

Labouvie-Vief, G., Diehl, M., Tarnowski, A., & Shen, J. (2000). Age differences in adult personality: Findings from the United States and China. *Journals of Gerontology: Psychological Sciences, 55B*, P4–P17.

Labouvie-Vief, G., Hakim-Larson, J., & Hobart, C. J. (1987). Age, ego level, and the life-span development of coping and defense processes. *Psychology and Aging, 2*, 286–293.

Labouvie-Vief, G., & Marquez, M. G. (2004). Dynamic integration: Affect optimization and differentiation in development. In D. Y. Dai & R. J. Sternberg (Eds.), *Motivation, emotion, and cognition: Integrative perspectives on intellectual functioning and development* (pp. 237–272). Mahwah, NJ: Erlbaum.

Labouvie-Vief, G., & Medler, M. (2002). Emotions optimization and emotions complexity: Modes and styles of regulation in adulthood. *Psychology and Aging, 17*, 571–588.

Lachman, M. E. (Ed.). (2001). *Handbook of midlife development*. New York: Wiley.

Lachman, M. E. (2004). Development in midlife. *Annual Review of Psychology, 55*, 305–331.

Lachman, M. E. (2006). Perceived control over aging-related declines: Adaptive beliefs and behaviors. *Current Directions in Psychological Science, 15*(6) 282–286.

Lachman, M. E., & Andreoletti, C. (2006). Strategy use mediates the relationship between control beliefs and memory performance for middle-aged and older adults. *Journals of Gerontology: Psychological Sciences, 61 (2-B)*, P88–P94.

Lachman, M. E., Bandura, M., Weaver, S. L., & Elliott, E. (1995). Assessing memory control beliefs: The Memory Controllability Inventory. *Aging and Cognition, 2*, 67–84.

Lachman, M. E., Lewkowicz, C., Marcus, A., & Peng, Y. (1994). Images of midlife development among young, middle-aged, and older adults. *Journal of Adult Development, 1*, 201–211.

Lachman, M. E., Rosnick, C., & Rocke, C. (2009) The rise and fall of control beliefs in adulthood: Cognitive and biopsychosocial antecedents of stability and change over nine years. In H. Bosworth & C. Hertzog (Eds.), *Cognition in aging: Methodologies and applications*. Washington, DC: American Psychological Association.

Lachs, M. S., Williams, C., O'Brien, S., Hurst, L., & Horwotz, R. (1997). Risk factors for reported elder abuse and neglect: A nine-year observational cohort study. *The Gerontologist, 37*, 469–474.

Lai, G. (1995). Work and family roles and psychological well-being in urban China. *Journal of Health and Social Behavior, 36*, 11–37.

Lakatta, E. G. (1995). Normal changes of aging. In W. B. Abrams, M. H. Beers, & R. Berkow (Eds.), *The Merck manual of geriatrics* (2nd ed., pp. 425–441). Whitehouse Station, NJ: Merck Research Laboratories.

Lakshmanan, I. A. R. (1997, September 22). Marriage? Think logic, not love. *Baltimore Sun*, p. A2.

Lam, R. E., Pacala, J. T., & Smith, S. L. (1997). Factors related to depressive symptoms in an elderly Chinese American sample. *Clinical Gerontologist, 17*, 57–70.

Lamanna, M. A., & Riedmann, A. (2003). *Marriages and families: Making choices in a diverse society* (8th ed.). Belmont, CA: Wadsworth.

Lambert, L. D., & Fleury, M. (1994). Age, cognitive style, and traffic signs. *Perceptual and Motor Skills, 78*, 611–624.

Lambert-Pandraud, E., Laurent, G., & Lapersonne (2005). Repeat purchasing of new automobiles by older consumers: Empirical evidence and inter-pretations. *Journal of Marketing, 69*(2), 97–113.

Lampman, C., & Dowling-Guyer, S. (1995). Attitudes toward voluntary and involuntary childlessness. *Basic and Applied Social Psychology, 17*, 213–222.

Landi, F., Zuccalà, G., Gambassi, G., Incalzi, R. A., Manigrasso, L., Pagano, F., Carbonin, P., & Bernabei, R. (1999). Body mass index and mortality among older people living in the community. *Journal of the American Geriatrics Society, 47*, 1072–1076.

Landrine, H., & Klonoff, E. A. (2001). Cultural diversity and health psychology. In A. Baum, T. A Revenson, & J. E. Singer (Eds.), *Handbook of health psychology* (pp. 851–891). Mahwah, NJ: Erlbaum.

Lane, B. N. (2007). Understanding anticipatory grief: Relationship to coping style, attachment style, caregiver strain, gender role identification, and spirituality. *Dissertation Abstracts International: Section B: The Sciences and Engineering, 67(8-B)*, 4714.

Lane, C. J., & Zelinski, E. M. (2003). Longitudinal hierarchical linear models of the Memory Functioning Questionnaire. *Psychology and Aging, 18*, 38–53.

Lane, R. D., & Nadel, L. (Eds.). (2000). *Cognitive neuroscience of emotion*. New York: Oxford University Press.

Lang, F. R., & Heckhausen, J. (2001). Perceived control over development and subjective well-being: Differential benefits across adulthood. *Journal of Personality and Social Psychology, 81*, 509–523.

Langer, E. J. (1985). Playing the middle against both ends: The usefulness of older adult cognitive activity as a model for cognitive activity in childhood and old age. In S. Yussen (Ed.), *The growth of reflection in children* (pp. 267–285). New York: Academic Press.

Langer, E. J. (1989). *Mindfulness*. Reading, MA: Addison-Wesley.

Langer, E. J., & Rodin, J. (1976). The effects of choice and enhanced personal responsibility for the aged: A field experiment in an institutional setting. *Journal of Personality and Social Psychology, 34*, 191–198.

Langlieb, A. M., & DePaulo, J. R., Jr. (2008). Etiology of depression and implications on work environment. *Journal of Occupational and Environmental Medicine, 50*, 391–395.

Lankau, M. J., & Scandura, T. A. (2002). An investigation of personal learning in mentoring relationships: Content, antecedents, and consequences. *Academy of Management Journal, 45*, 779–790.

Larson, R. W., Gillman, S. A., & Richards, M. H. (1997). Divergent experiences of family leisure: Fathers, mothers, and young adolescents. *Journal of Leisure Research, 29*, 78–97.

Larsson, M., Nyberg, L., Baeckman, L., & Nilsson, L. (2003). Effects on episodic memory of stimulus richness, intention to learn, and extra-study repetition: Similar profiles across the adult life span. *Journal of Adult Development, 10*(2), 67–73.

LaRue, A., Swan, G. E., & Carmelli, D. (1995). Cognition and depression in a cohort of aging men: Results from the Western Collaborative Group Study. *Psychology and Aging, 10*, 30–33.

Latack, J. C. (1984). Career transitions within organizations: An exploratory study of work,

nonwork, and coping. *Organizational Behavior and Human Decision Processes, 34*, 296–322.

Laver, G. D., & Burke, D. M. (1993). Why do semantic priming effects increase with age? A meta-analysis. *Psychology and Aging, 8*, 34–43.

LaVoie, D., & Light, L. L. (1994). Adult age differences in repetition priming: A meta-analysis. *Psychology and Aging, 9*, 539–555.

Lawlor, D., & York, M. (2007). Assessing goal attainment for quality improvement. *Journal of Intellectual Disabilities, 11*, 241–255.

Lawton, M. P. (1980). *Environment and aging*. Pacific Grove, CA: Brooks/Cole.

Lawton, M. P. (1982). Competence, environmental press, and the adaptation of old people. In M. P. Lawton, P. G. Windley, & T. O. Byerts (Eds.), *Aging and the environment: Theoretical approaches* (pp. 33–59). New York: Springer.

Lawton, M. P. (1989). Environmental proactivity in older people. In V. L. Bengtson & K. W. Schaie (Eds.), *The course of later life: Research and reflections* (pp. 15–23). New York: Springer.

Lawton, M. P. (1996). *Assessing quality of life*. Unpublished manuscript, Philadelphia Geriatric Center.

Lawton, M. P. (1999). Environmental design features and the well-being of older persons. In M. Duffy (Ed.), *Handbook of counseling and psychotherapy with older adults* (pp. 350–363). New York: Wiley.

Lawton, M. P., Moss, M. S., & Fulcomer, M. (1986–1987). Objective and subjective uses of time by older people. *International Journal of Aging and Human Development, 24*, 171–188.

Lawton, M. P., Moss, M., Hoffman, C., Grant, R., Have, T. T., & Kleban, M. H. (1999). Health, valuation of life, and the wish to live. *The Gerontologist, 39*, 406–416.

Lawton, M. P., Moss, M., Hoffman, C., & Perkinson, M. (2000). Two transitions in daughters' caregiving careers. *The Gerontologist, 40*, 437–448.

Lawton, M. P., Moss, M. S., Winter, L., & Hoffman, C. (2002). Motivation in later life: Personal projects and well-being. *Psychology and Aging, 17*, 539–547.

Lawton, M. P., & Nahemow, L. (1973). Ecology of the aging process. In C. Eisdorfer & M. P. Lawton (Eds.), *The psychology of adult development and aging* (pp. 619–674). Washington, DC: American Psychological Association.

Lazarus, R. S. (1984). Puzzles in the study of daily hassles. *Journal of Behavioral Medicine, 7*, 375–389.

Lazarus, R. S., DeLongis, A., Folkman, S., & Gruen, R. (1985). Stress and adaptational outcomes. *American Psychologist, 40*, 770–779.

Lazarus, R. S., & Folkman, S. (1984). *Stress, appraisal, and coping*. New York: Springer.

Lazzara, M., Yonelinas, A., & Ober, B. (2002). Implicit memory in aging: Normal transfer across semantic decisions and stimulus format. *Aging Neuropsychology and Cognition, 9*, 145–156.

Leahy, J. M. (1993). A comparison of depression in women bereaved of a spouse, a child, or a parent. *Omega: Journal of Death and Dying, 26*, 207–217.

Leana, C. R., & Feldman, D. C. (1992). *Coping with job loss*. New York: Lexington.

Lease, S. H. (2003). Testing a model of men's nontraditional occupational choices. *Career Development Quarterly, 51*, 244–258.

Leclerc, C. M., & Kensinger, E. A. (2008). Age-related changes in the neural mechanisms supporting emotion processing and emotional memory. *European Journal of Cognitive Psychology, 21*(2–3), 192–215.

Leclerc, C. M., & Kensinger, E. A. (2008). Age-related differences in medial prefrontal activation in response to emotional images. *Cognitive, Affective, and Behavioral Neuroscience, 8*, 153–164.

Lee, G. R., DeMaris, A., Bavin, S., & Sullivan, R. (2001). Gender differences in the depressive effect of widowhood in later life. *Journals of Gerontology: Social Sciences, 56B*, S56–S61.

Lee, G. R., Seccombe, K., & Shehan, C. L. (1991). Marital status and personal happiness: An analysis of trend data. *Journal of Marriage and the Family, 53*, 839–844.

Lee, G. R., Willetts, M. C., & Seccombe, K. (1998). Widowhood and depression: Gender differences. *Research on Aging, 20*, 611–630.

Lee, H. C., Drake, V., & Cameron, D. (2002). Identification of appropriate assessment criteria to measure older adults' driving performance in simulated driving. *Australian Occupational Therapy Journal, 49*(3), 138–145.

Lee, M-D. (2007). Correlates of consequences of intergenerational caregiving in Taiwan. *Journal of Advanced Nursing, 59*, 47–56.

Lee, R. E., Hitchcock, R., & Biesele, M. (2002). Foragers to first peoples: The Kalahari San today. *Cultural Survival Quarterly, 26*, 8.

Lee, T. R., Mancini, J. A., & Maxwell, J. W. (1990). Sibling relationships in adulthood: Contact patterns and motivation. *Journal of Marriage and the Family, 52*, 431–440.

Leentjens, A. F., Schieveld, J. N., Leonard, M., Lousberg, R., Verhey, F. R., & Meagher, D. J. (2008). A comparison of the phenomenology of pediatric, adult, and geriatric delirium. *Psychosomatic Research, 64*, 219–223.

Leichtentritt, R. D., & Rettig, K. D. (2000). Elderly Israelis and their family members' meanings towards euthanasia. *Families, Systems, and Health, 18*, 61–78.

Leirer, V. O., Morrow, D. G., Sheikh, J. I., & Pariante, G. M. (1990). Memory skills elders want to improve. *Experimental Aging Research, 16*, 155–158.

Lemieux, R., & Hale, J. L. (2002). Cross-sectional analysis of intimacy, passion, and commitment: Testing the assumptions of the triangular theory of love. *Psychological Reports, 90*, 1009–1014.

Lennartsson, C., & Silverstein, M. (2001). Does engagement with life enhance survival of elderly people in Sweden? The role of social and leisure activities. *Journals of Gerontology: Social Sciences, 56*, S335–S342.

Lentzner, H. R., Pamuk, E. R., Rhodenhiser, R. R., & Powell-Griner, E. (1992). The quality of life in the year before death. *American Journal of Public Health, 82*, 1093–1098.

Leon, G. R., Gillum, B., Gillum, R., & Gouze, M. (1979). Personality stability and change over a 30-year period: Middle to old age. *Journal of Consulting and Clinical Psychology, 47*, 517–524.

Lepp, I. (1968). *Death and its mysteries.* New York: Macmillan.

Lerner, R. M. (1986). *Concepts and theories of human development* (2nd ed.). New York: Random House.

Lerner, R. M. (2001). *Concepts and theories of human development* (3rd ed.). Mahwah, NJ: Lawrence Erlbaum.

Lerner, W. (1994). Giving the older driver enough perception-reaction time. *Experimental Aging Research, 20*, 25–33.

LeRoux, H., & Fisher, J. E. (2006). Strategies for enhancing medication adherence in the elderly. In W. T. O'Donohue & E. R. Levensky (Eds). *Promoting treatment adherence: A practical handbook for health care providers* (pp. 353–362). Thousand Oaks, CA: Sage.

Lesnoff-Caravaglia, G. (in press). Technology and aging: The herald of a new age. In J. C. Cavanaugh & C. K. Cavanaugh (Eds.), *Aging in America* (Vol. 3). Westport, CT: Praeger.

Lester, D. (1996). Trends in divorce and marriage around the world. *Journal of Divorce and Remarriage, 25*, 169–171.

Levenson, R. W., Carstensen, L. L., & Gottman, J. M. (1993). Long-term marriage: Age, gender, and satisfaction. *Psychology and Aging, 8*, 301–313.

Levenson, R. W., Carstensen, L. L., & Gottman, J. M. (1994). The influence of age and gender on affect, physiology, and their interrelations: A study of long-term marriages. *Journal of Personality and Social Psychology, 67*, 56–68.

Leveroni, C. L., Seidenberg, M., Mayer, A. R., Mead, L. A., Binder, J. R., and Rao, S. M. (2000). Neural systems underlying the recognition of familiar and newly learned faces. *Journal of Neuroscience, 20*, 878–886.

Levin, J. S., Taylor, R. J., & Chatters, L. M. (1994). Race and gender differences in religiosity among older adults: Findings from four national surveys. *Journals of Gerontology: Social Sciences, 49*, S137–S145.

Levine, B. (2004). Autobiographical memory and the self in time: Brain lesion effects, functional neuroanatomy, and lifespan development. *Brain and Cognition, 55*, 54–68.

Levine, B., Svoboda, E., Hay, J. F., Winocur, G., & Moscovitch, M. (2002). Aging and autobiographical memory: Dissociating episodic from semantic retrieval. *Psychology and Aging, 17*, 677–689.

Levinger, G. (1980). Toward the analysis of close relationships. *Journal of Experimental Social Psychology, 16*, 510–544.

Levinger, G. (1983). Development and change. In H. H. Kelley, E. Berscheid, A. Christensen, J. H. Harvey, T. L. Hutson, G. Levinger, E. McClintock, L. A. Peplau, & D. R. Peterson (Eds.), *Close relationships* (pp. 315–359). New York: Freeman.

Levinson, D. J., Darrow, C., Kline, E., Levinson, M., & McKee, B. (1978). *The seasons of a man's life.* New York: Knopf.

Levinson, D., & Levinson, J. D. (1996). *The seasons of a woman's life.* New York: Knopf.

Levy, B. (1996). Improving memory in old age through implicit stereotyping. *Journal of Personality and Social Psychology, 71*, 1092–1107.

Levy, B., & Langer, E. (1994). Aging free from negative stereotypes: Successful memory in China and among the American deaf. *Journal of Personality and Social Psychology, 66*, 989–997.

Levy, B. R. (2003). Mind matters: Cognitive and physical effects of aging self-stereotypes. *Journals of Gerontology: Psychological Sciences, 58B*, P103–P211.

Levy, B. R., Hausdorff, J. M., Hencke, R., & Wei, J. Y. (2000). Reducing cardiovascular stress with positive self-stereotypes of aging. *Journals of Gerontology: Psychological Sciences, 55B*, P20–P213.

Levy, B. R., & Leifheit-Limson, E. (2009). The stereotype-matching effect: Greater influence on functioning when age stereotypes correspond to outcomes. *Psychology and Aging, 24*(1), 230–233.

Levy, B. R., Slade, M. D., & Kasl, S. V. (2002). Longitudinal benefit of positive self-perceptions of aging on functional health. *Journals of Gerontology: Psychological Sciences, 57B*, P409–P417.

Lewin, K. (1936). *Principles of topological psychology.* New York: McGraw-Hill.

Lewinsohn, P. M. (1975). The behavioral study and treatment of depression. In M. Hersen, R. M. Eisler, & P. M. Miller (Eds.), *Progress in behavior modification* (Vol. 1, pp. 19–64). New York: Academic Press.

Lewis, K. G., & Moon, S. (1997). Always single and single again women: A qualitative study. *Journal of Marital and Family Therapy, 23*, 115–134.

Lewis, M. I. (1995). Sexuality. In W. B. Abrams, M. H. Beers, & R. Berkow (Eds.), *The Merck manual of geriatrics* (2nd ed., pp. 827–838). Whitehouse Station, NJ: Merck Research Laboratories.

Lewis, R. A., & Lin, L.-W. (1996). Adults and their midlife parents. In N. Vanzetti & S. Duck (Eds.), *A lifetime of relationships* (pp. 364–382). Pacific Grove, CA: Brooks/Cole.

Lezak, M. D. (1995). *Neuropsychological assessment* (3rd ed.). New York: Oxford University Press.

Li, F., Harmer, P., Glasgow, R., Mack, K. A., Sleet, D., Fisher, K. J., Kohn, M. A., Millet, L. M., Mead, J., Xu, J., Lin, M.-L., Yang, T., Sutton, B., & Tompkins, Y. (2008). Translation of an effective tai chi intervention into a community-based falls-prevention program. *American Journal of Public Health, 98*, 1195–1198.

Li, K. Z. H., Lindenberger, U., Freund, A. M., & Baltes, P. B. (2001). Walking while memorizing: Age-related differences in compensatory behavior. *Psychological Science, 12*, 230–237.

Li, S., Lindenberer, U., Hommel, B., Aschersleben, G., Prinz, W., & Baltes, P. B. (2004). Transformations in the couplings among intellectual abilities and constituent cognitive processes across the life span. *Psychological Science, 15*, 155–163.

Lichtenberg, P. A., MacNeill, S. E., & Mast, B. T. (2000). Environmental press and adaptation to disability in hospitalized live-alone older adults. *The Gerontologist, 40*, 549–556.

Lidz, C. W., Appelbaum, P. S., & Meisel, A. (1988). Two models of implementing informed consent. *Archives of Internal Medicine, 148*, 1385–1389.

Lieber, J. (2001, October 10). Widows of tower disaster cope, but with quiet fury. *USA Today*, A1–A2.

Lieberman, A. (1974). Parkinson's disease: A clinical review. *American Journal of Medical Science, 267*, 66–80.

Lieberman, M. D., Gaunt, R., Gilbert, D. T., & Trope, Y. (2002). Reflection and reflexion: A social cognitive neuroscience approach to attributional inference. *Advances in Experimental Social Psychology, 34*, 199–249.

Liebold, M., & Voelpel, S. (2006). *Managing the aging workforce.* Germany: Wiley.

Light, L. L. (1990). Interactions between memory and language in old age. In J. E. Birren & K. W. Schaie (Eds.), *Handbook of the psychology of aging* (3rd ed., pp. 275–290). San Diego: Academic Press.

Light, L. L. (1996). Memory and aging. In E. C. Carterette & M. P. Friedman (Eds.), *Handbook of perception and cognition* (2nd ed., pp. 443–490). San Diego: Academic Press.

Light, L. L., Capps, J. L., Singh, A., & Albertson-Owens, S. A. (1994). Comprehension of metaphors by young and older adults. In J. Cerella, J. Rybash, W. Hoyer, & M. L. Commons (Eds.), *Adult information processing: Limits on loss* (pp. 459–488). San Diego: Academic Press.

Lindenberger, U., & Baltes, P. B. (1995). Testing-the-limits and experimental simulation: Two methods to explicate the role of learning development. *Human Development, 38,* 349–360.

Lindenberger, U., & Baltes, P. B. (1997). Intellectual functioning in old and very old age: Cross sectional results from the Berlin Aging Study. *Psychology and Aging, 12,* 410–432.

Lindenberger, U., & Reischies, F. M. (1999). Limits and potentials of intellectual functioning in old age. In P. B. Baltes & K. U. Mayer (Eds.), *The Berlin ageing study: Ageing from 70 to 100.* New York: Cambridge University Press.

Lindenberger, U., Scherer, H., & Baltes, P. B. (2001). The strong connection between sensory and cognitive performance in old age: Not due to sensory acuity reductions operating during cognitive assessment. *Psychology and Aging, 16,* 196–205.

Lindsay, D. S., & Johnson, M. K. (1989). The eyewitness suggestibility effect and memory for source. *Memory and Cognition, 17,* 349–358.

Lineweaver, T. T., & Hertzog, C. (1998). Adults' efficacy and control beliefs regarding memory and ageing: Separating general from personal beliefs. *Aging, Neuropsychology, and Cognition, 5,* 264–296.

Linnehan, F. (2001). A longitudinal study of work-based, adult-youth mentoring. *Journal of Vocational Behavior, 63,* 40–54.

Lipman, P. D. (1991). Age and exposure differences in acquisition of route information. *Psychology and Aging, 6,* 128–133.

Lisansky Gomberg, E. S., & Zucker, R. A. (1999). Substance use and abuse in old age. In I. H. Nordhus, G. R. VandenBos, S. Berg, & P. Fromholt (Eds.), *Clinical geropsychology* (pp. 189–204). Washington, DC: American Psychological Association.

Litiecq, B. L., Bailey, S. J., & Kurtz, M. A. (2008). Depression among rural Native American and European American grandparents rearing their grandchildren. *Journal of Family Issues, 29,* 334–356.

Livson, F. B. (1981). Paths to psychological health in the middle years: Sex differences. In D. Eichorn, N. Haan, J. Clausen, M. Honzik, & P. Mussen (Eds.), *Past and present in middle life* (pp. 183–194). New York: Academic Press.

Lo, R., & Brown, R. (1999). Stress and adaptation: Preparation for successful retirement. *Australian and New Zealand Journal of Mental Health Nursing, 8,* 30–38.

Lock, M. (1991). Contested meanings of the menopause. *The Lancet, 337,* 1270–1272.

Löckenhoff, C. E., & Carstensen, L. L. (2004). Socioemotional selectivity theory, aging, and health: The increasingly delicate balance between regulating emotions and making tough choices. *Journal of Personality, 72,* 1395–1424.

Löckenhoff, C. E., & Carstensen, L. L. (2007). Aging, emotion, and health-related decision strategies: Motivational manipulations can reduce age differences. *Psychology and Aging, 22*(1), 134–146.

Lockwood, K. A., Alexopoulos, G. S., Kakuma, T., & Van Gorp, W. G. (2000). Subtypes of cognitive impairment in depressed older adults. *American Journal of Geriatric Psychiatry, 8,* 201–208.

Lockwood, K. A., Alexopoulos, G. S., & van Gorp, W. G. (2002). Executive dysfunction in geriatric depression. *American Journal of Psychiatry, 159,* 1119–1126.

Loevinger, J. (1976). *Ego development.* San Francisco: Jossey-Bass.

Loevinger, J. (1997). Stages of personality development. In R. Hogan & J. A. Johnson (Eds.), *Handbook of personality psychology.* St Louis: Washington University, Department of Psychology.

Loevinger, J. (Ed.). (1998). Technical foundations for measuring ego development: The Washington University Sentence Completion Test. Mahwah, NJ: Erlbaum.

Loftus, E. F. (1975). Spreading activation within semantic categories: Commenting on Rosch's "Cognitive representation of semantic categories." *Journal of Experimental Psychology: General, 104,* 234–240.

Logan, J. M., Sanders, A. L., Snyder, A. Z., Morris, J. C., & Buckner, R. L. (2002). Under-recruitment and nonselective recruitment: Dissociable neural mechanisms associated with aging. *Neuron, 33,* 827–840.

Logan, R. D. (1986). A reconceptualization of Erikson's theory: The repetition of existential and instrumental themes. *Human Development, 29,* 125–136.

Logie, R. H. (1995). *Visuo-spatial working memory.* Hove, England: Erlbaum.

Lombardi, W. J., & Weingartner, H. (1995). Pharmacological treatment of impaired memory function. In A. D. Baddeley, B. A. Wilson, & F. N. Watts (Eds.), *Handbook of memory disorders* (pp. 577–601). Chichester, UK: Wiley.

Londoño-Vallejo, J. A. (2008). Telomere instability and cancer. *Biochimie, 90,* 73–82.

Longo, B., Camoni, L., Boros, S., & Suligoi, B. (2008). AIDS patient care and STDs. *ADIS Patient Care and STDs, 22,* 365–371.

Lopata, H. Z. (1993). The interweave of public and private: Women's challenge to American society. *Journal of Marriage and the Family, 55,* 176–190.

Lopata, H. Z. (1996). Widowhood and husband sanctification. In D. Klass, P. R. Silverman, & S. L. Nickman (Eds.), *Continuing bonds: New understandings of grief* (pp. 149–162). Washington, DC: Taylor & Francis.

Lorayne, H., & Lucas, J. (1996). *The memory book.* New York: Ballantine.

Lorist, M. M., Snel, J., Mulder, G., & Kok, A. (1995). Aging, caffeine, and information processing: An event-related potential analysis. *Electroencephalography and Clinical Neuropsychology: Evoked Potential, 96,* 453–467.

Lövdén, M., Rönnlund, M., Wahlin, Å., Bäckman, L., Nyberg, L., & Nilsson, L. (2004). The extent of stability and change in episodic and semantic memory in old age: Demographic predictors of level and change. *Journals of Gerontology: Psychological Sciences, 59B,* P130–P134.

Lu, B. (2003). BDNF and activity-dependent synaptic modulation. *Learning and Memory, 10,* 86–98.

Lu, T., & Finkel, T. (2008). Free radicals and senescence. *Experimental Cell Research, 314,* 1918–1922.

Luborsky, M. R., & McMullen, C. K. (1999). Culture and aging. In J. C. Cavanaugh & S. K. Whitbourne (Eds.), *Gerontology: An interdisciplinary perspective* (pp. 65–90). New York: Oxford University Press.

Luborsky, M. R., & Rubinstein, R. (1997). The dynamics of ethnic identity in elderly widowers' reactions to bereavement. In J. Sokolovsky (Ed.), *The cultural context of aging: Worldwide perspectives* (pp. 304–315). New York: Bergin & Garvey.

Lucero-Liu, A. A. (2007). Exploring intersections in the intimate lives of Mexican origin women. *Dissertation Abstracts International Section A: Humanities and Social Sciences, 68*(3-A), 1175.

Ludke, R. L., & Smucker, D. R. (2007). Racial differences in the willingness to use hospice services. *Journal of Palliative Medicine, 10,* 1329–1337.

Lundin, T. (1984). Morbidity following sudden and unexpected bereavement. *British Journal of Psychiatry, 144,* 84–88.

Lunenfeld, B. (2008). An aging world—demographics and challenges. *Gynecological Endocrinology, 24,* 1–3.

Luo, T. Y. (1996). Sexual harassment in the Chinese workplace: Attitudes toward and experiences of sexual harassment among workers in Taiwan. *Violence Against Women, 2,* 284–301.

Lustig, C., Hasher, L., & Tonev, S. T. (in press). Inhibitory function influences tests of processing speed. *Journal of Experimental Psychology: General.*

Luszcz, M. A., & Lane, A. (2008). Executive function in cognitive ageing. In S. M. Hofer & D. F. Alwin (Eds.), *Handbook of cognitive aging: Interdisciplinary perspectives.* Greenwich, CT: Sage.

Lyness, K. S., & Thompson, D. E. (1997). Above the glass ceiling? A comparison of matched samples of female and male executives. *Journal of Applied Psychology, 82,* 359–375.

Maas, H. S. (1985). The development of adult development: Recollections and reflections. In J. M. A. Munnichs, P. Mussen, E. Olbrich, & P. G. Coleman (Eds.), *Life-span and change in a gerontological perspective* (pp. 161–175). New York: Academic Press.

Maas, H. S., & Kuypers, J. A. (1974). *From thirty to seventy.* San Francisco: Jossey-Bass.

Macatee, T. C. (2007). Psychological adjustment of adult children raised by a gay or lesbian parent. *Dissertation Abstracts International: Section B: The Sciences and Engineering, 68*(3-B), 1983.

MacDermid, S. M., De Haan, L. G., & Heilburn, G. (1996). Generativity in multiple roles. *Journal of Adult Development, 3,* 145–158.

MacDonald, S. W. S., Dixon, R. A., Cohen, A., & Hazlitt, J. E. (2004). Biological age and 12-year cognitive change in older adults: Findings from the Victoria Longitudinal Study. *Gerontology, 50,* 64–81.

MacDonald, S. W. S., Hultsch, D. F., & Dixon, R. A. (2003). Performance variability is related to change in cognition: Evidence from the Victoria Longitudinal Study. *Psychology and Aging, 18,* 510–523.

MacDonald, S. W. S., Hultsch, D. F., Strauss, E., & Dixon, R. A. (2003). Age-related slowing of digit symbol substitution revisited: What do longitudinal age changes reflect? *Journals of Gerontology: Psychological Sciences, 58B,* P187–P194.

Maciejewski, P. K., Zhang, B, Block, S. D., & Prigerson, H. G. (2007). An empirical examination of the stage theory of grief. *JAMA: Journal of the American Medical Association, 297,* 716–723.

MacKay, D. G., & Abrams, L. (1996). Language, memory, and aging. Distributed deficiencies and the structure of new-vs-old connect. In J. E. Birren & K. W. Schaie (Eds.), *Handbook of the psychology of aging* (4th ed., pp. 251–265). San Diego: Academic Press.

Mackey, R. A., Diemer, M. A., & O'Brien, B. A. (2004). Relational factors in understanding satisfaction in the lasting relationships of same-sex and heterosexual couples. *Journal of Homosexuality, 47,* 111–136.

Mackinnon, A., Christensen, H., Hofer, S. M., Korten, A. E., & Jorm, A. F. (2003). Use it and still lose it? The association between activity and cognitive performance established using latent growth techniques in a community sample. *Aging, Neuropsychology, and Cognition, 10*, 215–229.

Madden, D. J., & Gottlob, L. R. (1997). Adult age differences in strategic and dynamic components of focusing visual attention. *Aging, Neuropsychology, and Cognition, 4*, 185–210.

Madden, D. J., Whiting, W. L., Huettel, S. A., White, L. E., MacFall, J. R., & Provenzale, J. M. (2004). Diffusion tensor imaging of adult age differences in cerebral white matter: Relation to response time. *NeuroImage, 21*(3), 1174–1181.

Madeo, A., Feld, S., & Spencer, B. (2008). Ethical and practical challenges raised by an adult day care program's caregiver satisfaction survey. *American Journal of Alzheimer's Disease and Other Dementias, 23*, 423–429.

Magai, C. (2008). Long-lived emotions: A life course perspective on emotional development. In M. Lewis, J. M. Haviland-Jones, & L. F. Barrett (Eds.), *Handbook of emotions* (3rd ed., pp. 376–392). New York: Guilford.

Magalhães, J. P. de, Costa, J., & Church, G. M. (2007). An analysis of the relationship between metabolism, developmental schedules, and longevity using phylogenetic independent contrasts. *Journal of Gerontology: Biological Sciences and Medical Sciences, 62A*, 149–160.

Magley, V. J. (2002). Coping with sexual harassment: Reconceptualizing women's resistance. *Journal of Personality and Social Psychology, 83*, 930–946.

Mahady, G. B., Locklear, T. D., Doyle, B. J., Huang, Y., Perez, A. L. & Caceres, A. (2008). Menopause, a universal female experience: Lessons from Mexico and Central America. *Current Women's Health Reviews, 4*, 3–8.

Maiden, R. J., Peterson, S. A., Caya, M., & Hayslip, B. (2003). Personality changes in the old-old: A longitudinal study. *Journal of Adult Development, 10*, 31–39.

Malinak, D. P., Hoyt, M. F., & Patterson, V. (1979). Adults' reaction to the death of a parent: A preliminary study. *American Journal of Psychiatry, 136*, 1152–1156.

Malkinson, R., & Bar-Tur, I. (1999). The aging of grief in Israel: A perspective of bereaved parents. *Death Studies, 23*, 413–431.

Malkinson, R., & Bar-Tur, L. (2004–2005). Long term bereavement processes of older parents: The three phases of grief. *Omega: Journal of Death and Dying, 50*(2), 103–129.

Mallon, B. (2008). *Dying, death, and grief: Working with adult bereavement.* Thousand Oaks, CA: Sage.

Malone, M. L., & Camp, C. J. (2007). Montessori-Based Dementia Programming*: Providing tools for engagement. *Dementia: The International Journal of Social Research and Practice, 6*, 150–157.

Mancil, G. L., & Owsley, C. (1988). "Vision through my aging eyes" revisited. *Journal of the American Optometric Association, 59*, 288–294.

Manson, J. E., Hu, F. B., Rich-Edwards, J. W., Colditz, G. A., Stampfer, M. J., Willett, W. C., Speizer, F. E., & Hennekens, C. H. (1999). A prospective study of walking as compared with vigorous exercise in the prevention of coronary heart disease in women. *New England Journal of Medicine, 341*, 650–658.

Manton, K. G., & Vaupel, J. (1995). Survival after age 80 in the United States, Sweden, France, England, and Japan. *New England Journal of Medicine, 333*, 1232–1235.

Manton, K. G., Wrigley, J. M., Cohen, H. J., & Woodbury, M. A. (1991). Cancer mortality, aging, and patterns of comorbidity in the United States: 1968–1986. *Journals of Gerontology: Social Sciences, 46*, S225–S234.

Mäntylä, T. (1994). Remembering to remember: Adult age differences in prospective memory. *Journals of Gerontology: Psychological Sciences, 49*, P276–P282.

Marcussen, K. A. (2001). Marital status and psychological well-being: A comparison of married and cohabiting individuals. *Dissertation Abstracts International: Section A: Humanities and Social Sciences, 61*(8-A), 3372.

Margrett, J. A., & Marsiske, M. (2002). Gender differences in older adults' everyday cognitive collaboration. *International Journal of Behavioral Development, 2*, 45–59.

Market, J. (2008). The fading dream of retirement: Social and financial considerations affecting the retirement decision. *Sociological Spectrum, 28*, 213–134.

Markson, L. J., Fanale, J., Steel, K., Kern, D., & Annas, G. (1995). Implementing advance directives in the primary care setting. *Archives of Internal Medicine, 154*, 2321–2327.

Markus, H., & Nurius, P. (1986). Possible selves. *American Psychologist, 41*, 954–969.

Marquis, K. S., & Detweiler, R. A. (1985). Does adopted mean different? An attributional analysis. *Journal of Personality and Social Psychology, 48*, 1054–1066.

Mars, G. M. J., Kempen, G. I. J. M., Widdershoven, G. A. M., Janssen, P. P. M., & van Eijk, J. T. M. (2008). Conceptualizing autonomy in the context of chronic physical illness: Relating philosophical theories to social scientific perspectives. *Health, 12*, 333–348.

Marshall, R., & Southerland, P. (2008). The social relations of bereavement in the Caribbean. *Omega: Journal of Death and Dying, 57*, 21–34.

Marshall, V., Matthews, S., & Rosenthal, C. (1993). Elusiveness of family life: A challenge for the sociology of aging. In G. Maddox & M. P. Lawton (Eds.), *Annual review of gerontology and geriatrics: Vol. 13, Kinship, aging, and social change* (pp. 39–72). New York: Springer.

Marsiske, M., Lang, F. R., Baltes, P. B., & Baltes, M. M. (1996). Selective optimization with compensation: Life-span perspectives on successful human development. In R. A. Dixon & L. Bäckman (Eds.), *Compensating for psychological deficits and declines: Managing losses and promoting gains* (pp. 35–79). Mahwah, NJ: Erlbaum.

Marsiske, M., & Willis, S. L. (1995). Dimensionality of everyday problem solving in older adults. *Psychology and Aging, 10*, 269–283.

Marsiske, M., & Willis, S. L. (1998). Practical creativity in older adults' everyday problem solving: Life-span perspectives. In C. E. Adams-Price (Ed.), *Creativity and aging: Theoretical and empirical approaches* (pp. 73–113). New York: Springer.

Marson, D. C., Chatterjee, A., Ingram, K. K., & Harrell, L. E. (1996). Towards a neurologic model of competency: Cognitive predictors of capacity to consent in Alzheimer's disease using three different legal standards. *Neurology, 46*, 666–672.

Marteau, T. M., Roberts, S., LaRusse, S., & Green, R. C. (2005). Predictive genetic testing for Alzheimer's disease: Impact upon risk perception. *Risk Analysis, 25*, 397–404.

Martens, A., Goldenberg, J. L., & Greenberg, J. (2005). A terror management perspective on ageism. *Journal of Social Issues, 61*, 223–239.

Martin, G. M. (1998). Toward a genetic analysis of unusually successful neural aging. In E. Wang & D. Snyder (Eds.), *Handbook of the aging brain* (pp. 125–142). San Diego: Academic Press.

Martin, M., Long, M. V., & Poon, L. W. (2003). Age changes and differences in personality traits and states of the old and very old. *Journals of Gerontology: Psychological Sciences, 57B*, 144–152.

Martin, P., Kliegel, M., Rott, C., Poon, L. W., & Johnson, M. A. (2008). Age differences and changes of coping behavior in three age groups: Findings from the Georgia Centenarian Study. *International Journal of Aging and Human Development, 66*, 97–114.

Martin-Matthews, A. (1999). Widowhood: Dominant renditions, changing demographics, and variable meaning. In S. M. Neysmith (Ed.), *Critical issues for future social work practice with aging persons* (pp. 27–46). New York: Columbia University Press.

Martinson, I. M., Lee, H.-O., Kim, S. (2000). Culturally based interventions for families whose child dies. *Illness, Crisis and Loss, 8*, 17–31.

Masheter, C. (1997). Healthy and unhealthy friendship and hostility between ex-spouses. *Journal of Marriage and the Family, 59*, 463–475.

Maslach, C. (2003). Job burnout: New directions in research and intervention. *Current Directions in Psychological Science, 12*, 189–192.

Maslow, A. H. (1968). *Toward a psychology of being* (2nd ed.). New York: Van Nostrand Reinhold.

Mason, S. E. (1986). Age and gender as factors in facial recognition. *Experimental Aging Research, 12*, 151–154.

Masunaga, H., & Horn, J. (2001). Expertise and age-related changes in components of intelligence. *Psychology and Aging, 16*, 293–311.

Mata, R., Schooler, L. J., & Rieskamp, J. (2007). The aging decision maker: Cognitive aging and the adaptive selection of decision strategies. *Psychology and Aging, 22*(4), 796–810.

Mather, M., Canli, T., English, T., Whitfield, S., Wais, P., Ochsner, K., et al. (2004). Amygdala responses to emotionally valenced stimuli in older and younger adults. *Psychological Science, 15*, 259–263.

Mather, M., Canli, T., English, T., Whitfield, S., Wais, P., Ochsner, K., Gabrieli, J. D. E., & Carstensen, L. L. (2004). Amygdala responses to emotionally valenced stimuli in older and younger adults. *Psychological Science, 15*, 259–263.

Mather, M., & Carstensen, L. L. (2003). Aging and attentional biases for emotional faces. *Psychological Science, 14*, 409–415.

Mather, M., & Johnson, M. K. (2000). Choice-supportive source monitoring: Do our decisions seem better to us as we age? *Psychology and Aging, 15*, 596–606.

Mather, M., & Johnson, M. K. (2003). Affective review and schema reliance in memory in older and younger adults. *American Journal of Psychology, 116*, 169–189.

Mather, M., Johnson, M. K., & DeLeonardis, D. M. (1999). Stereotype reliance in source monitoring: Age differences and neuropsychological test correlates. *Cognitive Neuropsychology, 16*, 437–458.

Mather, M., & Knight, M. (2005). Goal-directed memory: The role of cognitive control in older adults' emotional memory. *Psychology and Aging, 20*, 554–570.

Mather, M., Knight, M., & McCaffrey, M. (2005). The allure of the allignable: Younger and older adults' false memories of choice features. *Journal of Experimental Psychology: General, 134,* 38–51.

Matheson, D. H., Collins, C. L., & Kuehne, V. S. (2000). Older adults' multiple stereotypes of young adults. *International Journal of Aging and Human Development, 51,* 245–257.

Matsui, T., Ikeda, H., & Ohnishi, M. (1989). Relation of sex-typed socializations to career self-efficacy expectations of college students. *Journal of Vocational Behavior, 35,* 1–16.

Matthews, A. M., & Brown, K. H. (1987). Retirement as a critical life event: The differential experiences of men and women. *Research on Aging, 9,* 548–571.

Matthews, S. H. (1996). Friendships in old age. In N. Vanzetti & S. Duck (Eds.), *A lifetime of relationships* (pp. 406–430). Pacific Grove: Brooks/Cole.

Mattson, M. P. (2004). Pathways towards and away from Alzheimer's disease. *Nature, 430*(7000), 631–639.

Matus, A. (2005). Growth of dendritic spines: A continuing story. *Current Opinion in Neurobiology, 15,* 67–72.

Maurer, T. J., & Tarulli, B. (1994). Acceptance of peer/upward performance appraisal systems: Role of work context factors and beliefs about managers' development capability. *Human Resource Management Journal, 35,* 217–241.

Maurer, T. J., Weiss, E. M., & Barbeite, F. G. (2003). A model of involvement in work-related learning and development activity: The effects of individual, situational, motivational, and age variables. *Journal of Applied Psychology, 88,* 707–724.

May, C. P., Rahhal, T., Berry, E. M., & Leighton, E. A. (2005). Aging, source memory, and emotion. *Psychology and Aging, 20,* 571–578.

Mayes, A. R. (1995). The assessment of memory disorders. In A. D. Baddeley, B. A. Wilson, & F. N. Watts (Eds.), *Handbook of memory disorders* (pp. 367–391). Chichester, UK: Wiley.

Maylor, E. A. (1990). Recognizing and naming faces: Ageing memory and retrieval and the tip of the tongue state. *Journals of Gerontology: Psychological Sciences, 45,* P215–P226.

Maylor, E. A., Carter, S. M., & Hallett, E. L. (2002). Olfactory cuing of autobiographical memories in old age. *Journals of Gerontology: Psychological Sciences, 57,* P41–P46.

Mayo, A. M. (2008). Measuring functional status in older adults with dementia. *Clinical Nurse Specialist, 22,* 212–213.

Mayo Clinic. (2002a). *Perimenopause: A period before your period ends.* Online document available at http://www.mayoclinic.com/invoke.cfm?objectid5164C0EE1-3E6A-41D9-897CFA-D83AC7A65B. Accessed November 24, 2003.

Mayo Clinic. (2002b). *Rheumatoid arthritis.* Online document available at http://www.mayoclinic.com/invoke.cfm?id5DS00020. Accessed November 16, 2003.

Mayo Clinic. (2003a). *Alzheimer's drugs: Real benefits despite limitations.* Online document available at http://www.mayoclinic.com/invoke.cfm?objectid5E5A1ECDC-0403-48A2-8C8C7D5F789C336B. Accessed December 14, 2003.

Mayo Clinic. (2003b). *Arthritis treatment trends.* Online document available at http://www.mayoclinic.com/invoke.cfm?objectid55FA6323C-E555-4519-A9BD99E3D9EB80BE. Accessed November 2, 2003.

Mayo Clinic. (2003c). *Parkinson's disease.* Online document available at http://www.mayoclinic.com/invoke.cfm?objectid567352253-4C13-41-A1-A6F790554DDA8474. Accessed November 24, 2003.

Mayo Clinic. (2007a). *Wrinkles.* Retrieved September 1, 2008, from http://www.mayoclinic.com/health/wrinkles/DS00890.

Mayo Clinic. (2007b). *Angina.* Retrieved September 7, 2008, from http://www.mayoclinic.com/health/angina/DS00994.

Mayo Clinic. (2007c). *Alzheimer's disease.* Retrieved October 26, 2008, from http://www.mayoclinic.com/health/alzheimers-disease/DS00161/DSECTION=treatments-and-drugs.

Mayo Clinic. (2008a). *Rheumatoid arthritis.* Retrieved September 1, 2008, from http://www.mayoclinic.com/health/rheumatoid-arthritis/RA99999.

Mayo Clinic. (2008b). *Arteriosclerosis/atherosclerosis.* Retrieved September 7, 2008, from http://www.mayoclinic.com/health/arteriosclerosis-atherosclerosis/DS00525.

Mayr, U., & Kliegl, R. (2003). Differential effects of cue changes and task changes on task-set selection costs. *Journal of Experimental Psychology: Learning, Memory, and Cognition, 29,* 362–372.

Mazzarella, S. R. (2007). Cyberdating success stories and the mythic narrative of living "Happily-Ever-After with the One." In M.-L. Galician & D. L. Merskin, (Eds.), *Critical thinking about sex, love, and romance in the mass media* (pp. 23–37). Mahwah, NJ: Lawrence Erlbaum.

McAdams, D. P. (1994). Can personality change? Levels of stability and growth in personality across the life span. In T. F. Heatherton & J. L. Weinberger (Eds.), *Can personality change?* (pp. 299–313). Washington, DC: American Psychological Association.

McAdams, D. P. (1995). What do we know when we know a person? *Journal of Personality, 63,* 365–396.

McAdams, D. P. (1996). Personality, modernity and the storied self: A contemporary framework for studying persons. *Psychological Inquiry, 4,* 295–321.

McAdams, D. P. (1999). Personal narratives and the life story. In L. Pervin & O. John (Eds.), *Handbook of personality: Theory and research* (2nd ed., pp. 478–500). New York: Guilford.

McAdams, D. P. (2001). The psychology of life stories. *Review of General Psychology, 5,* 100–122.

McAdams, D. P., de St. Aubin, E., & Logan, R. (1993). Generativity in young, midlife, and older adults. *Psychology and Aging, 8,* 221–230.

McAdams, D. P., Hart, H. M., & Maruna, S. (1998). The anatomy of generativity. In D. P. McAdams & E. de St. Aubin (Eds.), *Generativity and adult development: How and why we care for the next generation.* Washington, DC: American Psychological Association.

McAllister, T. W. (1981). Cognitive functioning in the affective disorders. *Comprehensive Psychiatry, 22,* 572–586.

McAuley, E., Katula, J., Mihalko, S. L., Blissmer, B., Duncan, T. E., Pena, M., & Dunn, E. (1999). Mode of physical activity and self-efficacy in older adults: A latent growth curve analysis. *Journals of Gerontology: Psychological Sciences, 54B,* P283–P292.

McAvay, G. J., Seeman, T. E., & Rodin, J. (1996). A longitudinal study of change in domain-specific self-efficacy among older adults. *Journals of Gerontology: Psychological Sciences, 51B,* P243–P253.

McCabe, D. P., & Smith, A. D. (2002). The effect of warnings on false memories in young and older adults. *Memory and Cognition, 30,* 1065–1077.

McCabe, J., & Hartman, M. (2003). Examining the locus of age effects on complex span tasks. *Psychology and Aging, 18,* 562–572.

McCarley, J. S., Kramer, A. F., Colcombe, A. M., & Scialfa, C. T. (2004). Priming of pop-out in visual search: A comparison of young and old adults. *Aging, Neuropsychology, and Cognition, 11,* 80–88.

McCarthy, M. R. (2002). Gender differences in reactions to perinatal loss: A qualitative study of couples. *Dissertation Abstracts International Section B: The Sciences and Engineering, 62(8B),* 3809.

McClelland, J. L., Rumelhart, D. E., & the PDP Research Group. (1986). *Parallel distributed processing: Explorations in the microstructure of cognition.* Cambridge, MA: MIT Press.

McCrae, R. R. (2002). The maturation of personality psychology: Adult personality development and psychological well-being. *Journal of Research in Personality, 36,* 307–317.

McCrae, R. R., & Costa, P. T. (1990). *Personality in adulthood.* New York: Guilford.

McCrae, R. R., & Costa, P. T. (1994). The stability of personality: Observation and evaluations. *Current Directions in Psychological Sciences, 3,* 173–175.

McCrae, S. (1997). Cohabitation: A trial run for marriage? *Sexual and Marital Therapy, 12,* 259–273.

McCune, J. 1998. The future of retirement. *Management Review, 87,* 10–17.

McDaniel, A. K., & Coleman, M. (2003). Women's experiences of midlife divorce after long-term marriages. *Journal of Divorce and Remarriage, 38,* 103–128.

McDaniel, M. A., & Einstein, G. O. (2007). *Prospective memory: An overview and synthesis of an emerging field.* Thousand Oaks, CA: Sage.

McDaniel, M. A., Einstein, G. O., Stout, A. C., & Morgan, Z. (2003). Aging and maintaining intentions over delays: Do it or lose it. *Psychology and Aging, 18,* 823–835.

McDaniel, M. A., Maier, S. F., & Einstein, G. O. (2002). "Brain-specific" nutrients: A memory cure? *Psychological Science in the Public Interest, 3,* 12–38.

McDill, T., Hall, S. K., & Turell, S. C. (2006). Aging and creating families: Never-married heterosexual women over forty. *Journal of Women & Aging, 18,* 37–50.

McDonald, R. S. (1986). Assessing treatment effects: Behavior rating scales. In L. W. Poon (Ed.), *Handbook for the clinical memory assessment of older adults* (pp. 129–138). Washington, DC: American Psychological Association.

McDonald-Miszczak, L., Hertzog, C., & Hultsch, D. F. (1995). Stability and accuracy of metamemory in adulthood and aging: A longitudinal analysis. *Psychology and Aging, 10,* 553–564.

McDowd, J. M., & Birren, J. E. (1990). Aging and attentional processes. In J. E. Birren & K. W. Schaie (Eds.), *Handbook of the psychology of aging* (3rd ed., pp. 222–233). San Diego: Academic Press.

McDowd, J. M., Filion, D. L., & Oseas-Kreger, D. M. (1991, June). *Inhibitory deficits in selective attention and aging.* Paper presented at the annual meeting of the American Psychological Society, Washington, DC.

McDowd, J. M., & Shaw, R. J. (2000). Attention and aging: A functional perspective. In F. I. M. Craik & T. A. Salthouse (Eds.), *Handbook of aging and cognition* (2nd ed., pp. 221–292). Mahwah, NJ: Erlbaum.

McEvoy, C. L., & Moon, J. R. (1988). Assessment and treatment of everyday memory problems in the elderly. In M. M. Gruneberg, P. E. Morris, & R. N. Sykes (Eds.), *Practical aspects of memory: Current research and issues* (Vol. 2, pp. 155–160). Chichester, UK: Wiley.

McFadden, J. (1996). A transcultural perspective and reaction to C. A. Patterson's "Multi-cultural counseling: From diversity to univer-sality." *Journal of Counseling and Development, 74,* 232–235.

McGarry, K., & Schoeni, R. F. (2005). Widow(er) poverty and out-of-pocket medical expen-ditures near the end of life. *Journal of Gerontology: Social Sciences, 60,* S160–S168.

McGee, W. (2007). *Sodium in diet.* Retrieved September 7, 2008, from http://www.nlm.nih.gov/medlineplus/ency/article/002415.htm.

McGraw, L. A. & Walker, A. J. (2004). Negotiating care: Ties between aging mothers and their caregiving daughters. *Journals of Gerontology: Social Sciences, 59B,* S324–S332.

McGuire, F. A., Boyd, R. K., & Tedrick, R. K. (1996). *Leisure and aging: Ulyssean living in later life.* Champaign, IL: Sagamore.

McGuire, L. C., & Codding, R. (1998, August). *Improving older adults' memory for medical information: The efficacy of note taking and elder speak.* Paper presented at the annual meeting of the American Psychological Association, San Francisco, CA.

McGuire, L. C., Morian, A., Codding, R., & Smyer, M. A. (2000). Older adults' memory for medical information: Influence of elderspeak and note taking. *International Journal of Rehabilitation and Health, 5,* 117–128.

McGwin, G., Jr., Chapman, V., & Owsley, C. (2000). Visual risk factors for driving difficulty among older drivers. *Accident Analysis and Prevention, 32,* 735–744.

McKee-Ryan, F., Song, Z., Wanberg, C. R., & Kinicki, A. J. (2005). Psychological and physical well-being during unemployment: A meta-analytic study. *Journal of Applied Psychology, 90*(1), 53–76.

McLeod, J. D. (1996). Life events. In J. E. Birren (Ed.), *Encyclopedia of gerontology* (Vol. 2, pp. 41–51). San Diego: Academic Press.

McMahon, P., & Koch, W. (1999, November 22). Assisted suicide: Aright or a surrender? *USA Today,* pp. 21A–22A.

McQueen, M. B., & Blacker, D. (2008). Genetics of Alzheimer's disease. In J. W. Smoller, B. R. Sheidley, & M. T. Tsuang (Eds.), *Psychiatric genetics: Applications in clini-cal practice* (pp. 177–193). Arlington, VA: American Psychiatric Publishing.

McVittie, C., McKinlay, A., & Widdicombe, S. (2003). Committed to (un)equal opportunities?: "New ageism" and the older worker. *British Journal of Social Psychology, 42,* 595–612.

Medicare.gov. (2008a). *Am I eligible?* Retrieved March 15, 2009, from http://www.medicare.gov/MedicareEligibility/home.asp?version=default&browser=Firefox%7C2%7CWinXP&language=English.

Medicare.gov. (2008b). *Medigap (supplemental insurance) policies.* Retrieved March 15, 2009, from http://www.medicare.gov/medigap/default.asp.

MedlinePlus. (2008). *Arthritis.* Retrieved September 28, 2008, from http://www.nlm.nih.gov/medlineplus/ency/article/001243.htm#Treatment.

Meegan, S. P., & Berg, C. A. (2002). Contexts, functions, forms, and processes of collaborative everyday problem solving in older adulthood.

International Journal of Behavioral Development, 26, 6–15.

Mehta, K. K. (1997). The impact of religious beliefs and practices on ageing: A cross-cultural comprehension. *Journal of Aging Studies, 11,* 101–114.

Meijer A. M., & van den Wittenboer, G. L. H. (2007). Contribution of infants' sleep and crying to marital relationship of first-time parent couples in the 1st year after childbirth. *Journal of Family Psychology, 21,* 49–57.

Meiran, N., Gotler, A., & Perlman, A. (2001). Old age is associated with a pattern of rela-tively intact and relatively impaired task-set switching abilities. *Journals of Gerontology: Psychological Sciences, 56B,* P88–P102.

Meisami, E. (1994). Aging of the sensory systems. In P. Timiras (Ed.), *Physiological basis of aging and geriatrics* (2nd ed., pp. 115–131). Boca Raton, FL: CRC Press.

Melikterminas, E., Ranganath, V., & Furst, D. E. (2008). Treatment of the elderly rheumatoid arthritis patient. *Future Rheumatology, 3,* 235–238.

Memon, A., Bartlett, J., Rose, R., & Gray, C. (2003). The aging eyewitness: Effects of age on face, delay, and source-memory ability. *Journals of Gerontology: Psychological Sciences, 58,* P338–P345.

Mendes de Leon, C. F., Seeman, T. E., Baker, D. I., Richardson, E. D., & Tinetti, M. E. (1996). Self-efficacy, physical decline, and change in functioning in community-living elders: A prospective study. *Journals of Gerontology: Social Sciences, 51B,* S183–S190.

Menec, V. H. (2003). The relation between everyday activities and successful aging: A 6-year longitudinal study. *Journals of Gerontology: Social Sciences, 58,* S74–S82.

Mennino, S. F., & Brayfield, A. (2002). Job–family trade-offs: The multidimensional effects of gender. *Work and Occupations, 29,* 226–256.

Menon, U. (2001). Middle adulthood in cultural perspective: The imagined and the experienced in three cultures. In M. E. Lachman (Ed.), *Handbook of midlife development* (pp. 40–74). New York: Wiley.

Menon, U., & Shweder, R. A. (1998). The return of the "White man's burden": The moral discourse of anthropology and the domestic life of Hindu women. In R. A. Shweder (Ed.), *Welcome to the middle age!: (And other cultural fictions)* (pp. 139–188). Chicago: University of Chicago Press.

Mera, S. L. (1998). The role of telomeres in ageing and cancer. *British Journal of Biomedical Science, 55,* 221–225.

Mercado-Crespo, M. C., Arroyo, L. E., Rios-Ellis, B., D'Anna, L. H., Londoño, C., Núñez, L., Salazar, J., D'Oliveira, V., & Millar, C. (2008, October). *Latinos and depression: Findings from a community-based mental health promotion effort.* Paper presented at the annual meeting of the American Public Health Association, San Diego, CA.

MetLife. (2006). *Adult day care centers.* Retrieved December 22, 2008, from http://www.metlife.com/FileAssets/MMI/MMICPAdultdayhint.pdf.

MetLife Mature Market Institute and National Alliance for Caregiving. (2006). *Resources for caregivers, 2007.* Retrieved November 1, 2008, from http://www.metlife.com/WPSAssets/6778165140117258575 8V1FResourcesforCaregivers2007.pdf.

Metropolitan Area Agency on Aging. (1998). *Checklist on adult day care.* Online document available at http://www.tcaging.org/com_adck.htm. Accessed October 20, 2004.

Meyer, B. J. F., Russo, C., & Talbot, A. (1994). Discourse comprehension and problem solving: Decisions about the treatment of breast cancer by women across the lifespan. *Psychology and Aging, 10,* 84–103.

Meyer, B. J. F., Talbot, A. P., & Ranalli, C. (2007). Why older adults make more immediate treatment decisions about cancer than younger adults. *Psychology and Aging, 22*(3), 505–524.

Meyer, J. F. (2007). Confucian "familism" in America. In D. S. Browning & D. A. Clairmont (Eds.), *American religions and the family: How faith traditions cope with modernization and democracy* (pp. 168–184). New York: Columbia University Press.

Michel, J. P., Newton, J. L., & Kirkwood, T. B. (2008). Medical challenges of improving the quality of a longer life. *JAMA: Journal of the American Medical Association, 299,* 688–690.

Mickler, C., & Staudinger, U. M. (2008). Personal wisdom: Validation and age-related differences of a performance measure. *Psychology and Aging, 23*(4), 787–799.

Mickley, K. R., & Kensinger, E. A. (2008). Neural processes supporting subsequent recollection and familiarity of emotional items. *Cognitive, Affective, and Behavioral Neuroscience, 8,* 143–152.

Mietkiewicz, M.-C., & Venditti, L. (2004). Les arrière-grands-pères le point de vue de leurs arrière-petits-enfants./Great-grandfathers from their great-grandchildren's point of view. *Psychologie & NeuroPsychiatrie Du Vieillissement, 2,* 275–283.

Milford, M. (1997, November 9). Making a tough transition. *News Journal* (Wilmington, DE), pp. G1, G6.

Miller, G. A. (1956). The magical seven plus or minus two. Some limits on our capacity for processing information. *Psychological Review, 63,* 81–97.

Miller, K. I., Shoemaker, M. M., Willyard, J., & Addison, P. (2008). Providing care for elderly parents: A structurational approach to family caregiver identity. *Journal of Family Communication, 8,* 19–43.

Miller, L. M. S. (2003). The effects of age and domain knowledge on text processing. *Journals of Gerontology: Psychological Sciences, 58,* P217–P223.

Miller, N. B., Smerglia, V. L., & Bouchet, N. (2004). Women's adjustment to widowhood: Does social support matter? *Journal of Women and Aging, 16,* 149–167.

Miller, R. A. (1996a). Aging and the immune response. In E. L. Schneider & J. W. Rowe (Eds.), *Handbook of the biology of aging* (4th ed., pp. 355–392). San Diego: Academic Press.

Miller, R. A. (1996b). The aging immune system: Primer and prospectus. *Science, 273,* 70–74.

Miller, R. B., Hemesath, K., & Nelson, B. (1997). Marriage in middle and later life. In T. D. Hargrave & S. M. Hanna (Eds.), *The aging family: New visions in theory, practice, and reality* (pp. 178–198). New York: Brunner/Mazel.

Miller, S. S., & Cavanaugh, J. C. (1990). The meaning of grandparenthood and its relationship to demographic, relationship, and social participation variables. *Journals of Gerontology: Psychological Sciences, 45,* P244–P246.

Ministry of Internal Affairs and Communications. (2005). *Statistical handbook of Japan 2004.* Retrieved August 15, 2008, from http://www.stat.go.jp/english/data/handbook/c02cont.htm#cha2_2.

Miranda, J., McGuire, T. G., Williams, D. R., & Wang, P. (2008). Mental health in the context of health disparities. *American Journal of Psychiatry, 165,* 1102–1108.

Mischel, W., & Shoda, Y. (1995). A cognitive–affective system theory of personality: Reconceptualizing situations, dispositions, dynamics, and invariance in personality structure. *Psychological Review, 102,* 246–268.

Missildine, W., Feldstein, G., Punzalan, J. C., & Parsons, J. T. (2005). S/he loves me, s/he loves me not: Questioning heterosexist assumptions of gender differences for romantic and sexually motivated behaviors. *Sexual Addiction & Compulsivity, 12,* 65–74.

Mitchell, B. A. (2006). *The boomerang age: Transitions to adulthood in families.* New Brunswick, NJ: AldineTransaction.

Mitchell, D. B., & Bruss, P. J. (2003). Age differences in implicit memory: Conceptual, perceptual, or methodological? *Psychology and Aging, 18,* 807–822.

Mitchell, K. J., & Johnson, M. K. (2000). Source monitoring: Attributing mental experiences. In E. Tulving & F. I. M. Craik (Eds.), *The Oxford handbook of memory* (pp. 179–196). New York: Oxford University Press.

Miwa, S., Beckman, K. B., & Muller, F. L. (2008). *Oxidative stress in aging.* New York: Humana Press.

Mobily, K. E., Lemke, J. H., & Gisin, G. J. (1991). The idea of leisure repertoire. *Journal of Applied Gerontology, 10,* 208–223.

Moen, P., Kim, J. E., & Hofmeister, H. (2001). Couples' work/retirement transitions, gender, and marital quality. *Social Psychology Quarterly, 64,* 55–71.

Moen, P. (2001). The gendered life course. In R. H. Binstock & L. K. George (Eds.), *Handbook of aging and the social sciences* (5th ed., pp. 179–196). San Diego: Academic Press.

Moen, P., & Wethington, E. (1999). Midlife development in a life course context. In S. L. Willis & J. D. Reid (Eds.), *Life in the middle: Psychological and social development in middle age* (pp. 2–23). San Diego: Academic Press.

Mohlman, J., de Jesus, M., Gorenstein, E. E., Kleber, M., Gorman, J. M., & Papp, L. A. (2004). Distinguishing generalized anxiety disorder, panic disorder, and mixed anxiety states in older treatment-seeking adults. *Journal of Anxiety Disorders, 18,* 275–290.

Mojon-Azzi, S. M., Sousa-Poza, A., & Mojon, D. S. (2008). Impact of low vision on well-being in 10 European countries. *Ophthalmologica, 222,* 205–212.

Molinari, V. (2003). Nursing homes as primary care sites for psychological practice. *Clinical Psychology: Science and Practice, 10,* 112–114.

Mollica, R. (2008). Forward. In S. M. Golant & J. Hyde (Eds.), *The assisted living residence: A vision for the future.* Baltimore: The Johns Hopkins University Press.

Molony, S. L., McDonald, D. D., & Palmisano-Mills, C. (2008). Psychometric testing of an instrument to measure the experience of home. *Research in Nursing and Health, 30,* 518–530.

Monane, M., Gurwitz, J. H., & Avorn, J. (1993). Pharmacotherapy with psychoactive medications in the long-term care setting: Challenges, management, and future directions. *Generations, 17,* 57–60.

Monczunski, J. (1991). That incurable disease. *Notre Dame Magazine, 20*(1), 37.

Monden, C. (2007). Partners in health? Exploring resemblance in health between partners in married and cohabiting couples. *Sociology of Health & Illness, 29,* 391–411.

Moon, A., & Williams, O. (1993). Perceptions of elder abuse and help-seeking patterns among African-American, Caucasian American, and Korean-American elderly women. *The Gerontologist, 33,* 386–395.

Moore, K. D. (2005). Using place rules and affect to understand environmental fit: A theoretical exploration. *Environment and Behavior, 37,* 330–363.

Moore, K. D., Van Haitsma, K., Curyto, K., & Saperstein, A. (2003). A pragmatic environmental psychology: A metatheoretical inquiry into the work of M. Powell Lawton. *Journal of Environmental Psychology, 23,* 471–482.

Moos, R. H., Brennan, P. L., Schutte, K. C., & Moos, B. S. (2006). Older adults' coping with negative life events: Common processes of managing health, interpersonal, and financial/work stressors. *International journal of Aging and Human Development, 62,* 39–59.

Moos, R. H., & Lemke, S. (1984). *Multiphasic environmental assessment procedure: Manual.* Palo Alto, CA: Social Ecology Laboratory, Stanford University Press.

Moos, R. H., & Lemke, S. (1985). Specialized living environments for older people. In J. E. Birren & K. W. Schaie (Eds.), *Handbook of the psychology of aging* (2nd ed., pp. 864–889). New York: Van Nostrand Reinhold.

Morahan-Martin, J., & Schumacher, P. (2003). Loneliness and social uses of the Internet. *Computers in Human Behavior, 19,* 659–671.

Moran, J. D. (2008). Families, courts, and the end of life: *Schiavo* and its implications for the family justice system. *Family Court Review, 46,* 297–330.

Morfei, M. Z., Hooker, K., Fiese, B. H., & Cordeiro, A. M. (2001). Continuity and change in parenting possible selves: A longitudinal follow-up. *Basic and Applied Social Psychology, 23,* 217–223.

Morganti, C. M., Nelson, M. E., Fiatarone, M. A., Dallal, G. E., Economos, C. D., Crawford, B. M., & Evans, W. J. (1995). Strength improvements with 1 yr of progressive resistance training in older women. *Medicine and Science in Sports and Exercise, 27,* 906–912.

Morioka, K. (1996). Generational relations and their changes as they affect the status of older people in Japan. In T. K. Hareven (Ed.), *Aging and generational relations: Life-course and cross-cultural perspectives* (pp. 263–280). New York: Aldine de Gruyter.

Morioka, K. (1998). Comment 1: Toward a paradigm shift in family sociology. *Japanese Journal of Family Sociology, 10,* 139–144.

Morris, B., Bonamici, K., Kaufman, S. M. & Neering, P. (2005, January 10). How corporate America is betraying women. *Fortune.*

Morris, W. L., Sinclair, S., & DePaulo, B. M. (2007). No shelter for singles: The perceived legitimacy of marital status discrimination. *Group Processes & Intergroup Relation, 10,* 457–470.

Morrison, A. M., White, R. P., Van Vesor, E., & The Center for Creative Leadership. (1992). *Breaking the glass ceiling: Can women reach the top of America's largest corporations?* Reading, MA: Addison-Wesley.

Morrow, D. G., Hier, C. M., Menard, W. E., & Von Leirer, O. (1998). Icons improve older and younger adults' comprehension of medication information. *Journals of Gerontology: Psychological Sciences, 53B,* P240–P254.

Morrow, D. G., Menard, W. E., Stine-Morrow, E. A. L., Teller, T., & Bryant, D. (2001). The influence of expertise and task factors on age differences in pilot communication. *Psychology and Aging, 16,* 31–46.

Morrow, D. G., Ridolfo, H. E., Menard, W. E., Sanborn, A., Stine-Morrow, E. A. L., Magnor, C., et al. (2003). Environmental support promotes expertise-based mitigation of age differences on pilot communication tasks. *Psychology and Aging, 18,* 268–284.

Morrow, D. G., Stine-Morrow, E. A. L., Von Leirer, O., Andrassy, J. M., & Kahn, J. (1997). The role of reader age and focus of attention in creating situation models from narratives. *Journals of Gerontology: Psychological and Social Sciences, 52B,* 73–80.

Morrow, P. C., & McElroy, J. C. (1987). Work commitment and job satisfaction over three career stages. *Journal of Vocational Behavior, 30,* 330–346.

Morrow-Howell, N., Hinterlong, J., Rozario, P. A., & Tang, F. (2003). Effects of volunteering on the well-being of older adults. *Journals of Gerontology: Social Sciences, 58,* S137–S145.

Morse, C., & Wisocki, P. (1991). Residential factors in programming for elderly. In P. A. Wisocki (Ed.), *Handbook of clinical behavior therapy with the elderly client* (pp. 97–120). New York: Plenum.

Mortimer, J. T., Finch, M. D., & Kumka, D. (1982). Persistence and change in development: The multidimensional self-concept. In P. B. Baltes & O. G. Brim, Jr. (Eds.), *Life-span development and behavior* (Vol. 4, pp. 263–313). New York: Academic Press.

Mosello, E., Caleri, V., Razzi, E., Di Bari, M., Cantini, C., Tonon, E., Lopilato, E., Marini, M., Simoni, D., Cavallini, D. C., Marchionni, N., Biagini, C. A., & Masotti, G. (2008). Day care for older dementia patients: Favorable effects on behavioral and psychological symptoms and caregiver stress. *International Journal of Geriatric Psychiatry, 23,* 1066–1072.

Moss, M. S., Moss, S. Z., & Hansson, R. O. (2001). Bereavement and old age. In M. S. Stroebe, R. O. Hansson, W. Stroebe, & H. Schut (Eds.), *Handbook of bereavement research: Consequences, coping, and care* (pp. 241–260). Washington, DC: American Psychological Association.

Mouloua, M., & Parasuraman, R. (1995). Aging and cognitive vigilance: Effects of spatial uncertainty and event rate. *Experimental Aging Research, 21,* 17–32.

Moulton, C. P. (1997). Special health considerations in African-American elders. *American Family Physicians, 55,* 1243–1253.

Moynehan, J., & Adams, J. (2007). What's the problem? A look at men in marital therapy. *American Journal of Family Therapy, 35,* 41–51.

Mroczek, D. K., & Spiro, A. (2003). Modeling intraindividual change in personality traits: Findings from the normative aging study. *Journals of Gerontology: Psychological Sciences, 58B,* P153–P165.

Mui, A. C. (1995). Caring for frail elderly parents: A comparison of adult sons and daughters. *The Gerontologist, 35,* 86–93.

Muller, E. D., & Thompson, C. L. (2003). The experience of grief after bereavement: A phenomenological study with implications for mental health counseling. *Journal of Mental Health Counseling, 25,* 183–203.

Mulley, G. (2008). Depression in physically ill older patients. In S. Curran & J. P. Wattis (Eds.), *Practical management of affective disorders in older people* (pp. 126–145). Abingdon, UK: Radcliffe.

Multhaup, K. S., Hersher, L., & Zacks, R. T. (1998). *Age and memory for distracting information: A double dissociation.* Manuscript submitted for publication. Department of Psychology, Davidson College, North Carolina.

Murphy, S. (1988). Mental distress and recovery in a high-risk bereavement sample three years after untimely death. *Nursing Research, 37,* 30–35.

Murray, B. (1998). Workplace harassment hurts everyone on the job. *APA Monitor, 29,* 36.

Murray, C. J. L., & Evans, D. (2003). *Health systems performance assessment.* Geneva, Switzerland: World Health Organization.

Murray, H. A. (1938). *Explorations in personality.* New York: Oxford University Press.

Murrell, A. J., Freize, I. H., & Frost, J. L. (1991). Aspiring to careers in male- and female-dominated professions: A study of black and white college women. *Psychology of Women Quarterly, 15,* 103–126.

Murstein, B. I. (1987). A clarification and extension of the SVR theory of dyadic pairing. *Journal of Marriage and the Family, 49,* 929–933.

Musil, C. M., & Standing, T. (2005). Grandmothers' diaries: A glimpse at daily lives. *International Journal of Aging and Human Development, 60,* 317–329.

Mussen, P. (1985). Early adult antecedents of life satisfaction at age 70. In J. M. A. Munnichs, P. Mussen, E. Olbrich, & P. G. Coleman (Eds.), *Life-span and change in a gerontological perspective* (pp. 45–61). New York: Academic Press.

Mutchler, J. E., Baker, L. A., & Lee, SA. (2007). Grandparents responsible for grandchildren in Native-American families. *Social Science Quarterly, 88,* 990–1009.

Mutchler, J. E., Burr, J. A., Massagli, M. P., & Pienta, A. (1999). Work transitions and health in later life. *Journals of Gerontology: Social Sciences, 54B,* S252–S261.

Mutchler, J. E., Burr, J. A., Pienta, A. M., & Massagli, M. P. (1997). Pathways to labor force exit: Work transitions and work instability. *Journals of Gerontology: Social Sciences, 52B,* S4–S12.

Mutter, S. A. (2000). Illusory correlation and group impression formation in young and older adults. *Journals of Gerontology: Psychological Sciences, 55B,* P224– P227.

Mutter, S. A., & Pliske, R. M. (1994). Aging and illusory correlation in judgments of co-occurrence. *Psychology and Aging, 9,* 53–63.

Mutter, S. A., & Pliske, R. M. (1994). Judging event covariation: Effects of age and memory demand. *Journals of Gerontology: Psychological Sciences, 51B,* P70–P80.

Myers, R. S., Ball, K. K., Kalina, T. D., Roth, D. L., & Goode, K. T. (2000). Relation of useful field of view and other screening tests to on-road driving performance. *Perceptual and Motor Skills, 91,* 279–290.

Myerson, J., Hale, S., Wagstaff, D., Poon, L. W., & Smith, G. A. (1990). The information-loss model: A mathematical theory of age-related cognitive slowing. *Psychological Review, 97,* 475–487.

Myskow, L. (2002). Perimenopausal issues in sexuality. *Sexual and Relationship Therapy, 17,* 253–260.

Nagi, S. Z. (1965). Some conceptual issues in disability and rehabilitation. In M. B. Sussman (Ed.), *Sociology and rehabilitation* (pp. 100–113). Washington, DC: American Sociological Association.

Nagi, S. Z. (1991). Disability concepts revisited: Implications for prevention. In A. M. Pope & A. R. Tarlov (Eds.), *Disability in America: Toward a national agenda for prevention* (pp. 309–327). Washington, DC: National Academy Press.

Nahemow, L. (2000). The ecological theory of aging: Powell Lawton's legacy. In R. L. Rubinstein & M. Moss (Eds.), *The many dimensions of aging* (pp. 22–40). New York: Springer.

Napholz, L. (1995). Mental health and American Indian women's multiple roles. *American Indian and Alaska Native Mental Health Resource, 6,* 57–75.

National Academy on an Aging Society. (2000a). *Caregiving: Helping the elderly with activity limitations.* Washington, DC: Author.

National Academy on an Aging Society. (2000b). *Depression: A treatable disease.* Washington, DC: Author.

National Academy on an Aging Society. (2000c). *Diabetes: A drain on U.S. resources.* Washington, DC: Author.

National Academy on an Aging Society. (2003). *The state of aging and health in America.* Retrieved March 16, 2009, from http://www.agingsociety.org/agingsociety/pdf/state_of_aging_report.pdf.

National Adult Day Services Association. (2008). *Adult day services: Overview and facts.* Retrieved December 22, 2008, from http://www.nadsa.org/adsfacts/default.asp.

National Cancer Institute. (2002a). *Surveillance, epidemiology, and end results program, 1973–1999.* Bethesda, MD: Author.

National Cancer Institute. (2002b). *Tamoxifen: Questions and answers.* Online document available at http://cis.nci.nih.gov/fact/7_16.htm. Accessed November 16, 2003.

National Cancer Institute. (2003a). *Incidence: All cancer sites.* Online document available at http://seer.cancer.gov/faststats/html/inc_all.html. Accessed November 16, 2003.

National Cancer Institute. (2003b). *Treatment.* Online document available at http://www.nci.nih.gov/cancerinfo/treatment/. Accessed November 16, 2003.

National Cancer Institute. (2007). FDA approves raloxifene for breast cancer prevention. *NCI Cancer Bulletin, 4.* Retrieved February 24, 2009, from http://www.cancer.gov/ncicancerbulletin/NCI_Cancer_Bulletin_092507/page5.

National Cancer Institute. (2008). *Types of treatment.* Retrieved September 28, 2008, from http://www.cancer.gov/cancertopics/treatment/types-of-treatment.

National Center for Health Statistics. (1999). *Health, United States, 1998, with socioeconomic status and chartbook.* Online document available at http://www.cdc.gov/nchswww/data/hus98ncb.pdf. Accessed 2004.

National Center for Health Statistics. (2002). *The national nursing home survey: 1999 summary.* Online document available at http://www.cdc.gov/nchs/data/series/sr_13/sr13_152.pdf. Accessed January 18, 2004.

National Center for Health Statistics. (2003). *Nursing home care.* Online document available at http://www.cdc.gov/nchs/fastats/nursingh.htm. Accessed January 18, 2004.

National Center for Health Statistics. (2008a). *Births, marriages, divorces, and deaths: Provisional data for 2007.* Retrieved September 21, 2008, from http://www.cdc.gov/nchs/data/nvsr/nvsr56/nvsr56_21.htm.

National Center for Health Statistics. (2008b). *January–March 2008 National Health Interview Survey.* Retrieved September 28, 2008, from http://www.cdc.gov/nchs/about/major/nhis/released200809.htm.

National Center on Elder Abuse. (1998). *The national elder abuse incidence study: Final report September 1998.* Online document available at http://www.aoa.gov/abuse/report/default.htm. Accessed 2004.

National Center on Elder Abuse. (1999). *The basics: What is elder abuse?* Online document available at http://www.gwjapan.com/NCEA/basic/index.html. Accessed 2004.

National Center on Elder Abuse. (2003). *Frequently asked questions.* Online document available at http://www.elderabusecenter.org/default.cfm?p5faqs.cfm#seven. Accessed January 30, 2003.

National Center on Elder Abuse. (2007a). *Major types of elder abuse.* Retrieved December 6, 2008, from http://www.ncea.aoa.gov/NCEAroot/Main_Site/FAQ/Basics/Types_Of_Abuse.aspx.

National Center on Elder Abuse. (2007b). *Risk factors for elder abuse.* Retrieved December 6, 2008, from http://www.ncea.aoa.gov/NCEAroot/Main_Site/FAQ/Basics/Risk_Factors.aspx.

National Comprehensive Cancer Network. (2007). *NCCN updates prostate cancer guidelines.* Retrieved November 1, 2009 from http://www.nccn.org/about/news/newsinfo.asp?NewsID=90.

National Heart, Lung, and Blood Institute. (2003). *Facts about postmenopausal hormone therapy.* Online document available at http://www.nhlbi.nih.gov/health/women/pht_facts.htm. Accessed November 16, 2003.

National Highway Traffic Safety Administration. (1998). *Traffic safety plan for older drivers.* Washington, DC: U.S. Department of Transportation.

National Institute of Arthritis and Musculoskeletal and Skin Diseases. (2004). *Handout on health: Rheumatoid arthritis.* Retrieved June 9, 2008, from http://www.niams.nih.gov/Health_Info/Rheumatic_Disease/default.asp.

National Institute of Arthritis and Musculoskeletal and Skin Diseases. (2004). *Rheumatoid arthritis.* Retrieved February 24, 2009, from http://www.niams.nih.gov/Health_Info/Rheumatic_Disease/default.asp.

National Institute of Arthritis and Musculoskeletal and Skin Diseases. (2005). *Bone health overview.* Retrieved February 24, 2009, from http://www.niams.nih.gov/Health_Info/Bone/Bone_Health/default.asp.

National Institute of Arthritis and Musculoskeletal and Skin Diseases. (2006). *What is osteoarthritis?* Retrieved February 24, 2009, from http://www.niams.nih.gov/Health_Info/Osteoarthritis/osteoarthritis_ff.asp.

National Institute of Arthritis and Musculoskeletal and Skin Diseases. (2008a). *Osteoporosis.* Retrieved February 3, 2008, from http://nihseniorhealth.gov/osteoporosis/toc.html.

National Institute of Arthritis and Musculoskeletal and Skin Diseases. (2008b). *Nutrition and bone health.* Retrieved February 3, 2008, from http://www.niams.nih.gov/Health_Info/Bone/Bone_Health/Nutrition/default.asp.

National Institute of Neurological Disorders and Stroke. (2007). *Deep brain stimulation for Parkinson's disease.* Retrieved March 16, 2009, from http://www.ninds.nih.gov/disorders/deep_brain_stimulation/deep_brain_stimulation.htm.

National Institute of Neurological Disorders and Stroke. (2008a). *NINDS Parkinson's disease information page.* Retrieved September 13, 2008, from http://www.ninds.nih.gov/disorders/parkinsons_disease/parkinsons_disease.htm.

National Institute of Neurological Disorders and Stroke. (2008b). *Neurological complications of AIDS fact sheet.* Retrieved November 1, 2008, from http://www.ninds.nih.gov/disorders/aids/detail_aids.htm.

National Institute on Aging. (2007). *Alzheimer's disease: General information.* Retrieved

March 16, 2009, from http://www.nia.nih. gov/Alzheimers/AlzheimersInformation/ GeneralInfo/#howmany.

National Institute on Aging. (2008). *Aging hearts and arteries: A scientific quest.* Retrieved September 3, 2008, from http://www.nia. nih.gov/HealthInformation/Publications/ AgingHeartsandArteries/default.htm.

National Institute on Alcohol Abuse and Alcoholism. (1995). *Prevalence and population estimates of DSM–IV alcohol abuse and dependence by age, sex, and ethnicity, United States, 1992.* Online document available at http://www.niaaa.nih.gov. Accessed 2004.

National Institute on Alcohol Abuse and Alcoholism. (2008). *Alcohol research: A lifespan perspective.* Retrieved November 15, 2008, from http://pubs.niaaa.nih.gov/publications/AA74/ AA74.pdf.

National Institute on Mental Health. (2008). *Older adults: Depression and suicide facts.* Retrieved March 16, 2009, from http://www.nimh. nih.gov/health/publications/older-adults-depression-and-suicide-facts.shtml.

National Institutes of Health. (2008). *Osteoporosis.* Retrieved March 16, 2009, from http://www. nlm.nih.gov/medlineplus/osteoporosis.html.

National Parkinson's Foundation. (2007). *A primer on Parkinson's disease.* Retrieved March 16, 2009, from http://www. parkinson.org/NETCOMMUNITY/Page. aspx?pid=226&srcid=201.

National Women's Health Information Center. (2008a). *Understanding menopause.* Retrieved September 7, 2008, from http://womenshealth. gov/menopause/.

National Women's Health Information Center. (2008b). *Understanding menopause.* Retrieved September 11, 2008, from http://www.womenshealth.gov/ menopause/stages/perimenopause.cfm.

Naveh-Benjamin, M. (2000). Adult-age differences in memory performance: Tests of an associative deficit hypothesis. *Journal of Experimental Psychology: Learning, Memory and Cognition, 26,* 1170–1187.

Naveh-Benjamin, M., Craik, F. I. M., Guez, J., & Kreuger, S. (2005). Divided attention in younger and older adults: Effects of strategy and relatedness on memory performance and secondary task costs. *Journal of Experimental Psychology: Learning, Memory and Cognition, 32,* 520–537.

Neal, M. B., & Hammer, L. B. (2006). *Working couples caring for children and aging parents: Effects on work and well-being.* Mahwah, NJ: Lawrence Erlbaum.

Neff, L. A., & Karney, B. R. (2005). To know you is to love you: The implications of global adoration and specific accuracy for marital relationships. *Journal of Personality & Social Psychology, 88,* 480–497.

Neft, N., & Levine, A. D. (1997). *Where women stand: An international report on the status of women in over 140 countries, 1997–1998.* New York: Random House.

Neimark, E. D. (1975). Longitudinal development of formal operational thought. *Genetic Psychology Monographs, 91,* 171–225.

Neimeyer, R. (1997). Knowledge at the margins. *The Forum Newsletter* (Association for Death Education and Counseling), *23*(2), 2, 10.

Neimeyer, R., Keese, B. V., & Fortner, M. (2000). Commemoration and bereavement: Cultural aspects of collective myth and the creation of national identity. In R. Malkinson, S. Rubin, & E. Witztum (Eds.), *Traumatic and non-traumatic loss and bereavement: Clinical theory and practice* (pp. 295–320). Madison, CT: Psychosocial Press/ International Universities Press.

Neimeyer, R. A., & Wogrin, C. (2008). Psychotherapy for complicated bereavement: A meaning-oriented approach. *Illness, Crisis, & Loss, 16,* 1–20.

Neisser, U. (1976). *Cognition and reality.* San Francisco: W. H. Freeman.

Nelson, C. H. (2001). Determinants of grief duration: An exploratory model and multivariate analysis. *Dissertation Abstracts International Section A: Humanities and Social Sciences, 61*(12A), 4963.

Neuberg, A. B., Newberg, S. K., & d'Aquili, E. G. (1997). The philosophy and psychology of consciousness. *American Psychologist, 52,* 177–178.

Neugarten, B. L. (1969). Continuities and discontinuities of psychological issues into adult life. *Human Development, 12,* 121–130.

Neugarten, B. L. (1977). Personality and aging. In J. E. Birren & K. W. Schaie (Eds.), *Handbook of the psychology of aging* (pp. 626–649). New York: Van Nostrand Reinhold.

Neugarten, B. L., & Weinstein, K. K. (1964). The changing American grandparent. *Journal of Marriage and the Family, 26,* 299–304.

Neumann, O. (1996). Theories of attention. In O. Neumann & A. F. Sanders (Eds.), *Handbook of perception and action: Vol. 3, Attention* (pp. 389–446). London: Academic Press.

Newhouse, P. A. (1996). Use of serotonin selective reuptake inhibitors in geriatric depression. *Journal of Clinical Psychiatry, 57*(Suppl. 5), 12–22.

Newman, M. C., & Kaszniak, A. W. (2000). Spatial memory and aging: Performance on a human analog of the Morris water maze. *Aging, Neuropsychology, and Cognition, 7,* 86–93.

Newman, J. P., Engel, R. J., & Jensen, J. E. (1990). Depressive symptom patterns among older women. *Psychology and Aging, 5,* 101–118.

Newman, J. P., Engel, R. J., & Jensen, J. E. (1991). Changes in depressive-symptom experiences among older women. *Psychology and Aging, 6,* 212–222.

Newsom, J. T. (1999). Another side to caregiving: Negative reactions to being helped. *Current Directions in Psychological Science, 8,* 183–187.

New York Life. (2007). *Long term care costs on the rise according to New York Life study.* Retrieved October 19, 2008, from http://www. newyorklife.com/cda/0,3254,16492,00.html.

Nichols, L. O., Chang, C., Lummus, A., Burns, R., Martindale-Adams, J., Graney, M. J., Coon, D. W., & Czaja, S. (2008). The cost-effectiveness of a behavioral intervention with caregivers of patients with Alzheimer's disease. *Journal of the American Geriatrics Society, 56,* 413–420.

Nickerson, C., Schwarz, N., Diener, E., & Kahneman, D. (2003). Zeroing in on the dark side of the American dream: A closer look at the negative consequences of the goal for financial success. *Psychological Science, 14,* 531–536.

Nicolson, N., Storms, C., Ponds, R., & Sulon, J. (1997). Salivary cortisol levels and stress reactivity in human aging. *Journals of Gerontology: Medical Sciences, 53A,* M68–M75.

Niederehe, G., & Schneider, L. S. (1998). Treatment of depression and anxiety in the aged. In P. E. Nathan & J. M. Gorman (Eds.), *Treatments that work.* New York: Oxford University Press.

Nobili, A., Piana, I., Balossi, L., Pasina, L., Matucci, M., Tarantola, M., Trevisan, S., Riva, E., Lucca, U., & Tettamanti, M. (2008). Alzheimer's special care units compared with traditional nursing home for dementia care: Are there differences in admission and in clinical outcomes? *Alzheimer's Disease and Related Disorders, 22,* 352–361.

Noe, R. A. (1987). *An exploratory investigation of the antecedents and consequences of mentoring.* Unpublished manuscript, University of Minnesota, Minneapolis, MN.

Nolen-Hoeksema, S. (1998). The other end of the continuum: The costs of rumination. *Psychological Inquiry, 9,* 216–219.

Nolen-Hoeksema, S. (2001). Ruminative coping and adjustment to bereavement. In M. S. Stroebe, R. O. Hansson, W. Stroebe, & H. Schut (Eds.), *Handbook of bereavement research* (pp. 545–562). Washington, DC: American Psychological Association.

Nolen-Hoeksema, S., & Larson, J. (1999). *Coping with loss.* Mahwah, NJ: Erlbaum.

Noonan, D. (2005, June 6). *A little bit louder, please.* Retrieved June 9, 2008, from http:// services.newsweek.com/search.aspx?offset=0 &pageSize=10&sortField=pubdatetime&sortD irection=descending&mode=summary&q=a+ little+bit+louder+please&site-search-submit. x=0&site-search-submit.y=0&site-search-submit=0.

Nordahl, C. W., Ranganath, C., Yonelinas, A. P., Decarli, C., Fletcher, E., & Jagust, W. J. (2006). White matter changes compromise prefrontal cortex function in healthy elderly individuals. *Journal of Cognitive Neuroscience, 18*(3), 418–429.

Nordberg, A. (2008). Amyloid imaging in Alzheimer's disease. *Neuropsychologia, 46,* 1636–1641.

Norlander, B., & Eckhardt, C. (2005). Anger, hostility, and male perpetrators of intimate partner violence: A meta-analytic review. *Clinical Psychology Review, 25,* 119–152.

Norman, S. M., McCluskey-Fawcett, K., & Ashcraft, L. (2002). Older women's development: A comparison of women in their 60s and 80s on a measure of Erikson's developmental tasks. *International Journal of Aging and Human Development, 54,* 31–42.

Norris, F. N., & Murrell, S. A. (1987). Older adult family stress and adaptation before and after bereavement. *Journals of Gerontology: Psychological Sciences, 42,* 606–612.

Norton, T., Stephens, M., Martire, L., Townsend, A., & Gupta, A. (2002). Change in the centrality of women's multiple roles: Effects of role stress and rewards. *Journals of Gerontology: Social Sciences, 57B,* S52–S62.

Notarius, C. I. (1996). Marriage: Will I be happy or will I be sad? In N. Vanzetti & S. Duck (Eds.), *A lifetime of relationships* (pp. 265–289). Pacific Grove, CA: Brooks/Cole.

Nuland, S. B. (1994). How we die: Reflections on life's final chapter. New York: Knopf.

Nyberg, L., Lars-Goeran, N., Olofsson, U., & Backman, L. (1997). Effects of division of attention during encoding and retrieval on age differences in episodic memory. *Experimental Aging Research, 23,* 137–143.

Nyberg, L., Maitland, S. B., Rönnlund, M., Bäckman, L., Dixon, R. A., Wahlin, Å., & Nilsson, L. (2003). Selective adult age differences in an age-invariant multifactor model of declarative memory. *Psychology and Aging, 18,* 149–160.

Nydegger, C. N. (1986). Asymmetrical kin and the problematic son-in-law. In N. Datan, A. L. Greene, & H. W. Reese (Eds.), *Life-span developmental psychology: Intergenerational relations* (pp. 99–124). Hillsdale, NJ: Erlbaum.

Nygren, C., Oswald, F., Iwarsson, S., Fänge, A., Sixsmith, J., Schilling, O., Sixsmith, A., Széman, Z., Tomsone, S., & Wahl, H-W. (2007). Relationships between objective and perceived housing in very old age. *The Gerontologist, 47,* 85–95.

O'Brien, C.-A., & Goldberg, A. (2000). Lesbians and gay men inside and outside families. In N. Mandell & A. Duffy (Eds.), *Canadian families: Diversity, conflict, and change* (2nd ed., pp. 115–145). Toronto: Harcourt Brace.

O'Brien, L. T., & Hummert, M. L. (2006). Memory performance of late middle-aged adults: Contrasting self-stereotyping and stereotype threat accounts of assimilation to age stereotypes. *Social Cognition, 24,* 338–358.

O'Connor, M., Verfaellie, M., & Cermak, L. S. (1995). Clinical differentiation of amnesic subtypes. In A. D. Baddeley, B. A. Wilson, & F. N. Watts (Eds.), *Handbook of memory disorders* (pp. 53–80). Chichester, UK: Wiley.

O'Dell, C. D. (2007). *Mothering mother: A daughter's humorous and heartbreaking memoir.* Largo, FL: Kunati, Inc.

O'Donoghue, M. (2005). White mothers negotiating race and ethnicity in the mothering of biracial, Black-White adolescents. *Journal of Ethnic & Cultural Diversity in Social Work, 14,* 125–156.

O'Hanlon, A. M. (1993). *Inter-individual patterns of intellectual change: The influence of environmental factors.* Unpublished doctoral dissertation, Department of Family and Human Development, Pennsylvania State University.

O'Leary, K. D. (1993). Through a psychological lens: Personality traits, personality disorders, and levels of violence. In R. J. Gelles & D. R. Loseke (Eds.), *Current controversies on family violence* (pp. 7–30). Newbury Park, CA: Sage.

O'Reilly, R. C., & Frank, M. J. (2006). Making working memory work: A computational model of learning in the frontal cortex and basal ganglia. *Neural Computation, 18,* 283–328.

O'Rourke, N., & Cappeliez, P. (2005). Marital satisfaction and self-deception: Reconstruction of relationship histories among older adults. *Social Behavior and Personality, 33,* 273–282.

Oberauer, K., Wendland, M., & Kliegl, R. (2003). Age differences in working memory—The roles of storage and selective access. *Memory and Cognition, 31,* 563–569.

Oburu, P. O., & Palmérus, K. (2005). Stress related factors among primary and part-time caregiving grandmothers of Kenyan grandchildren. *International Journal of Aging and Human Development, 60,* 273–282.

Ochsner, K. N., & Lieberman, M. D. (2001). The emergence of social cognitive neuroscience. *American Psychologist, 56,* 717–734.

Oehmichen, M, & Meissner, C. (2000). Life shortening and physician assistance in dying: Euthanasia from the viewpoint of German legal medicine. *Gerontology, 46,* 212–218.

Offerman, L. R., & Growing, M. K. (1990). Organizations of the future: Changes and challenges. *American Psychologist, 45,* 95–108.

Office of Minority Health and Health Disparities. (2008). *Eliminate disparities in diabetes.* Retrieved September 28, 2008, from http://www.cdc.gov/omhd/AMH/factsheets/diabetes.htm.

Okonski, B. (1996, May 6). Just say something. *Newsweek,* 14.

Okun, M. A., & Schultz, A. (2003). Age and motives for volunteering: Testing hypotheses derived from socioemotional selectivity theory. *Psychology and Aging, 18,* 231–239.

Old, S., & Naveh-Benjamin, M. (2008). Memory for people and their actions: Further evidence for an age-related associative deficit. *Psychology and Aging, 23,* 467–472.

Olian, J. D., Carroll, S. J., Giannantonia, C. M., & Feren, D. B. (1988). What do protégés look for in a mentor? Results from three experimental studies. *Journal of Vocational Behavior, 33,* 15–37.

Olson, D. H., & McCubbin, H. (1983). *Families: What makes them work.* Newbury Park, CA: Sage.

Olson, L. N. (2000). Power, control, and communication: An analysis of aggressive, violent, and abusive couples. *Dissertation Abstracts International: Section A: Humanities and Social Sciences, 61(2-A),* 427.

Onrust, S., Cuijpers, P., Smit, F., & Bohlmeijer, E. (2007). Predictors of psychological adjustment after bereavement. *International Psychogeriatrics, 19,* 921–934.

Opfer, J. E., & Siegler, R. S. (2004). Revisiting preschoolers *living things* concept: A micro-genetic analysis of conceptual change in basic biology. *Cognitive Psychology, 49,* 301–332.

Oregon Department of Human Services. (2008). *Summary of Oregon's Death with Dignity Act—2007.* Retrieved May 30, 2008, from http://www.oregon.gov/DHS/ph/pas/docs/year10.pdf.

Orentlicher, D. (2000). The implementation of Oregon's Death with Dignity Act: Reassuring, but more data are needed. *Psychology, Public Policy, and Law, 6,* 489–502.

Orr, R., & Luszcz, M. (1994). Rethinking women's ways of knowing: Gender commonalities and intersections with postformal thought. *Journal of Adult Development, 1,* 225–233.

Orwoll, L., & Perlmutter, M. (1990). The study of wise persons: Integrating a personality perspective. In R. J. Sternberg (Ed.), *Wisdom: Its nature, origins, and development* (pp. 160–177). Cambridge, UK: Cambridge University Press.

Osgood, D. W., Ruth, G., Eccles, J. S., Jacobs, J. E., & Barber, B. L. (2005). Six paths to adulthood: Fast starters, parents without careers, educated partners, educated singles, working singles, and slow starters. In R. A. Settersten, Jr., F. F. Furstenberg, Jr., & R. G. Rumbaut (Eds.), *On the frontier of adulthood: Theory, research, and public policy* (pp. 320–355). Chicago: University of Chicago Press.

Osgood, N. J. (1992). *Suicide in later life.* Lexington, MA: Lexington Books.

Otsuka, Y., Osaka, N., Morishita, M., Kondo, H., & Osaka, M. (2006) Decreased activation of anterior cingulate cortex in the working memory of the elderly. *Neuroreport, 17(14),* 1479–1482.

Owen, C. J. (2005). The empty nest transition: The relationship between attachment style and women's use of this period as a time for growth and change. *Dissertation Abstracts International: Section B: The Sciences and Engineering, 65(7-B),* 3747.

Owen, G., Fulton, R., & Markusen, E. (1982). Death at a distance: A study of family survivors. *Omega: Journal of Death and Dying, 13,* 191–225.

Oygard, L., & Hardeng, S. (2001). Divorce support groups: How do group characteristics influence adjustment to divorce? *Social Work with Groups, 24,* 69–87.

Ozawa, M. N., & Yoon, H. S. (2002). The economic benefit of remarriage: Gender and class income. *Journal of Divorce and Remarriage, 36,* 21–39.

Palfai, T., Halperin, S., & Hoyer, W. J. (2003). Age inequalities in recognition memory: Effects of stimulus presentation time and list repetitions. *Aging, Neuropsychology, and Cognition, 10,* 134–140.

Palmore, E. B. (2007). Healthy behaviors or age denials? *Educational Gerontology, 33,* 1087–1097.

Panek, P. E., & Reardon, J. R. (1986). *Age and gender effects on accident types for rural drivers.* Paper presented at the meeting of the Gerontological Society of America, Chicago.

Pankow, L. J., & Solotoroff, J. M. (2007). Biological aspects and theories of aging. In J. A. Blackburn & C. N. Dulmus (Eds), *Handbook of gerontology: Evidence-based approaches to theory, practice, and policy* (pp. 19–56). Hoboken, NJ: John Wiley.

Papalia & Olds (1995). Adapted from Davis, 1985.

Parasuraman, R., & Giambra, L. (1991). Skill development in vigilance: Effects of event rate and age. *Psychology and Aging, 6,* 155–169.

Pargament, K. I., Sullivan, M. S., Balzer, W. K., VanHatsma, K. S., & Raymark, P. H. (1995). The many meanings of religiousness: A policy-capturing approach. *Journal of Personality, 63,* 953–983.

Paris, D. L. (2008). *Alzheimer's disease special care units.* Retrieved December 22, 2008, from http://www.caregiver.com/channels/alz/articles/alz_special_care_unit.htm.

Park, C. D., & Reuter-Lorenz, P. (2008). The adaptive brain: Aging and neurocognitive scaffolding. *Annual Review of Psychology, 60,* 21.1–21.24.

Park, D. C., & Brown, S. C. (2001). Everyday memory and aging. In G. L. Maddox, R. C. Atchley, J. G. Evans, et al. (Eds.), *The encyclopedia of aging* (3rd ed., pp. 363–365). New York: Springer.

Park, D. C., Cherry, K. E., Smith, A. D., & Lafronza, V. N. (1990). Effects of distinctive context on memory for objects and their locations in young and elderly adults. *Psychology and Aging, 5,* 250–255.

Park, D. C., & Hall-Gutchess, A. (2000). Cognitive aging and everyday life. In D. C. Park & N. Schwarz (Eds.), *Cognitive aging: A primer* (pp. 217–232). Philadelphia: Psychology Press.

Park, D., Hertzog, C., Leventhal, H., Morrell, R. W., Leventhal, E., Birchmore, D., Martin, M., & Bennett, J. (1999). Medication adherence in rheumatoid arthritis patients: Older is wiser. *Journal of the American Geriatric Society, 47,* 172–183.

Park, D. C., Lautenschlager, G., Hedden, T., Davidson, N. S., Smith, A. D., & Smith, P. K. (2002). Models of visuospatial and verbal memory across the adult life span. *Psychology and Aging, 17(2),* 299–320.

Park, D. C., Morrell, R. W., Frieske, D. A., Blackburn, A. B., & Birchmore, D. (1991). Cognitive function and the use of over-the-counter medication organizers by arthritis patients. *Human Factors, 33,* 57–67.

Park, D. C., Morrell, R. W., Frieske, D., & Kincaid, D. (1992). Medication adherence behaviors in older adults: Effects of external cognitive supports. *Psychology and Aging, 7,* 252–256.

Park, D. C., Morrell, R. W., & Shifrin, K. (Eds.). (1999). Processing of medical information in aging patients: Cognitive and human factors perspectives. Mahwah, NJ: Erlbaum.

Park, D. C., Puglisi, J. T., & Smith, A. D. (1986). Memory for pictures: Does an age-related decline exist? *Psychology and Aging, 1,* 11–17.

Park, Y.-H. (2008). Day healthcare services for family caregivers of older people with stroke: Needs and satisfaction. *Journal of Advanced Nursing, 61,* 619–630.

Parker, L. D. (2008). A study about older African American spousal caregivers of persons with Alzheimer's disease. *Dissertation Abstracts International: Section B: The Sciences and Engineering, 68(10-B),* 6589.

Parker, R. A., & Aldwin, C. M. (1997). Do aspects of gender identity change from early to middle adulthood? Disentangling age, cohort, and period effects. In M. E. Lachman & J. B. James

(Eds.), *Multiple paths of midlife development* (pp. 67–107). Chicago: University of Chicago Press.

Parkinson's Disease Foundation. (2005). *Treatments.* Retrieved March 17, 2009, from http://www.pdf.org/AboutPD/med_treatment.cfm.

Parkman, A. M. (2007). *Smart marriage: Using your (business) head as well as your heart to find wedded bliss.* Westport, CT: Praeger.

Parrot, A., & Cummings, N. (2006). *Forsaken females: The global brutalization of women.* Lanham, MD: Rowman & Littlefield.

Paschal, A. M., Lewis, R. K., & Sly, J. (2007). African American parents' behaviors and attitudes about substance use and abuse. *Journal of Ethnicity in Substance Abuse, 6,* 67–79.

Pascual, C. (2000, October 3). Asians have highest elderly suicide rate. *Wilmington (NC) Morning Star,* 5D.

Pascual-Leone, J. (2000). Mental attention, consciousness, and the progressive emergence of wisdom. *Journal of Adult Development, 7,* 241–253.

Pasley, K., & Ihinger-Tallman, M. (1987). *Remarriage and stepparenting.* New York: Guilford.

Passarella, S., & Duong, M-T. (2008). Diagnosis and treatment of insomnia. American *Journal of Health-System Pharmacy, 65,* 927–934.

Pastalan, L. A. (1982). Research in environment and aging: An alternative to theory. In M. P. Lawton, P. G. Windley, & T. O. Byerts (Eds.), *Aging and the environment: Theoretical approaches* (pp. 122–131). New York: Springer.

Pasupathi, M. (2001). The social construction of the personal past and its implications for adult development. *Psychological Bulletin, 127,* 651–672.

Pasupathi, M., & Carstensen, L. L. (2003). Age and emotional experience during mutual reminiscing. *Psychology and Aging, 18,* 430–442.

Patel, V. L., & Groen, G. J. (1986). Knowledge-based solution strategies in medical reasoning. *Cognitive Science, 10,* 91–116.

Patrick, S., Sells, J. N., Giordano, F. G., & Tollerud, T. R. (2007). Intimacy, differentiation, and personality variables as predictors of marital satisfaction. *The Family Journal, 15,* 359–367.

Patterson, C. J. (1995). Lesbian mothers, gay fathers, and their children. In A. R. D'Augelli & C. J. Patterson (Eds.), *Lesbian, gay, and bisexual identities over the lifespan* (pp. 262–290). New York: Oxford University Press.

Pauls, J. (1985). Review of stair safety research with an emphasis on Canadian studies. *Ergonomics, 28,* 999–1010.

Pavalko, E. K., & Artis, J. E. (1997). Women's caregiving and paid work: Causal relationships in late midlife. *Journal of Gerontology: Social Sciences, 52,* S170–S179.

Pearlin, L. I., Mullan, J. T., Semple, S. J., & Skaff, M. M. (1990). Caregiving and the stress process: An overview of concepts and their measures. *The Gerontologist, 30,* 583–594.

Pearman, A., & Storandt, M. (2004). Predictors of subjective memory in older adults. *Journals of Gerontology: Psychological Sciences, 59B,* P4–P6.

Pearson, J. C. (1996). Forty-forever years? Primary relationships and senior citizens. In N. Vanzetti & S. Duck (Eds.), *A lifetime of relationships* (pp. 383–405). Pacific Grove, CA: Brooks/Cole.

Pender, N. (1996). *Health promotion in nursing practice* (3rd ed.). Stamford, CT: Appleton & Lange.

Penha-Lopes, V. (1995). "Make room for daddy": Patterns of family involvement among contemporary African American men. In C. K. Jacobson (Ed.), *American families: Issues in race and ethnicity* (pp. 179–199). New York: Garland.

Penninx, B. W. J. H., Geerlings, S. W., Deeg, D. J. H., van Eijk, J. T. M., van Tilburg, W., & Beekman,

A. T. F. (1999). Minor and major depression and the risk of death in older persons. *Archives of General Psychiatry, 56,* 889–895.

Penninx, B. W. J. H., Geerlings, S. W., Deeg, D. J. H., van Eijk, J. T. M., van Tilburg, W., & Beekman, A. T. F. (2008). Minor and major depression and the risk of death in older persons. *Archives of General Psychiatry, 56,* 889–895.

Penson, R. T. (2004). Bereavement across cultures. In R. J. Moore & D. Spiegel (Eds.), *Cancer, culture, and communication* (pp. 241–279). New York: Kluwer Academic/Plenum.

Peplau, L. A. (1991). Lesbian and gay relationships. In J. C. Gonsiorek & J. D. Weinrich (Eds.), *Homosexuality: Research implications for public policy* (pp. 177–196). Thousand Oaks, CA: Sage.

Perfect, T. J., & Harris, L. J. (2003). Adult age differences in unconscious transference: Source confusion or identity blending? *Memory and Cognition, 31,* 570–580.

Perkins, H. W., & Harris, L. B. (1990). Familial bereavement and health in adult life course perspective. *Journal of Marriage and the Family, 52,* 233–241.

Perlmutter, M., Adams, C., Berry, J., Kaplan, M., Person, D., & Verdonik, F. (1987). Aging and memory. In K. W. Schaie (Ed.), *Annual review of gerontology and geriatrics* (Vol. 7, pp. 57–92). New York: Springer.

Perls, T. T. (1995). The oldest old. *Scientific American, 274,* 70–75.

Perls, T., & Terry, D. (2003). Genetics of exceptional longevity. *Experimental Gerontology, 38,* 725–730.

Perry, W. I. (1970). Forms of intellectual and ethical development in the college years. New York: Holt, Rinehart & Winston.

Persad, C. C., Abeles, N., Zacks, R. T., & Denburg, N. L. (2002). Inhibitory changes after age 60 and the relationship to measures of attention and memory. *Journals of Gerontology: Psychological Sciences, 57B,* P223–P232.

Persson, J., Lustig, C., Nelson, J. K., & Reuter-Lorenz, P. A. 2007. Age differences in deactivation: A link to cognitive control? *Journal of Cognitive Neuroscience, 19*(6), 1021–1032.

Peters, E., Hess, T. M., Vastfjall, D., & Auman, C. (2007). Adult age differences in dual information processes. *Perspectives on Psychological Science, 2*(1), 1–23.

Peterson, B. E., & Klohnen, E. C. (1995). Realization of generativity in two samples of women at midlife. *Psychology and Aging, 10,* 20–29.

Pfost, K. S., & Fiore, M. (1990). Pursuit of nontraditional occupations: Fear of success or fear of not being chosen? *Sex Roles, 23,* 15–24.

Phillips, P. A., Bretherton, M., Johnston, C. I., & Gray, L. (1991). Reduced osmotic thirst in healthy elderly men. *American Journal of Physiology, 261,* R166–R171.

Piaget, J. (1970). Piaget's theory. In P. H. Mussen (Ed.), *Carmichael's manual of child psychology* (3rd ed., Vol. 1, pp. 703–732). New York: Wiley.

Piaget, J. (1972). Intellectual evolution from adolescence to adulthood. *Human Development, 15,* 1–12.

Piaget, J. (1980). Les formes et les mentaires de la dialectique. Paris: Gallimard.

Pichora-Fuller, M. K. (2003). Cognitive aging and auditory information processing. *International Journal of Audiology, 42,* S26–S32.

Pichora-Fuller, M. K., Schneider, B. A., & Daneman, M. (1995). How young and old adults listen to and remember speech in noise. *Journal of the Acoustical Society of America, 89,* 382–398.

Picot, S. J., Debanne, S. M., Namazi, K. H., & Wykle, M. L. (1997). Religiosity and perceived

rewards of black and white caregivers. *The Gerontologist, 37,* 89–101.

Pienta, A. M., & Hayward, M. D. (2002). Who expects to continue working after age 62? The retirement plans of couples. *Journals of Gerontology: Social Sciences, 57,* S199–S208.

Pienta, A. M., Hayward, M. D., & Jenkins, K. R. (2000). Health consequences of marriage for the retirement years. *Journal of Family Issues, 21,* 559–586.

Pierce, C. A., & Aguinis, H. (1997). Bridging the gap between romantic relationships and sexual harassment in organizations. *Journal of Organizational Behavior, 18,* 197–200.

Pillemer, K. (1993). The abused offspring are dependent. In R. J. Gelles & D. R. Loseke (Eds.), *Current controversies on family violence* (pp. 237–249). Newbury Park, CA: Sage.

Pillemer, K, Suitor, J. J., & Wethington, E. (2003). Integrating theory, basic research, and intervention: Two case studies from caregiving research. *The Gerontologist, 43*(Special Issue I), 19–28.

Pinquart, M., & Schindler, I. (2007). Changes of life satisfaction in the transition to retirement: A latent-class approach. *Psychology and Aging, 22,* 442–455.

Pioneer Network. (2008). *Creating home in the nursing home: A national symposium on culture change and the environment requirements.* Retrieved October 26, 2008, from http://www.pioneernetwork.net/news-and-events/creating-home.html.

Piotrkowski, C. (1998). Gender harassment, job satisfaction, and distress among employed white and minority women. *Journal of Occupational Health Psychology, 3,* 33–43.

Piquet, B. J. (2007). That's what friends are for. *Dissertation Abstracts International: Section B: The Sciences and Engineering, 67*(7-B), 4114.

Pirttilae-Backman, A. M., & Kajanne, A. (2001). The development of implicit epistemologies during early and middle adulthood. *Journal of Adult Development, 8,* 81–97.

Planned Parenthood. (1998). *Menopause: Another change in life.* Online document available at http://www.plannedparenthood.org/WOMENS HEALTH/menopause.htm. Accessed 2004.

Plosker, G. L., & McTavish, D. (1996). Intranasal salcatonin (salmon calcitonin). A review of its pharmacological properties and role in the management of postmenopausal osteoporosis. *Drugs and Aging, 8,* 378–400.

Plude, D. J., & Doussard-Roosevelt, J. A. (1990). Aging and attention: Selectivity, capacity, and arousal. In E. A. Lovelace (Ed.), *Aging and cognition: Mental processes, self-awareness, and interventions* (pp. 97–133). Amsterdam: North-Holland.

Plude, D. J., & Hoyer, W. J. (1985). Attention and performance: Identifying and localizing age deficits. In N. Charness (Ed.), *Aging and human performance* (pp. 47–99). Chichester, UK: Wiley.

Plude, D. J., Schwartz, L. K., & Murphy, L. J. (1996). Active selection and inhibition in the aging of attention. In F. Blanchard-Fields & T. M. Hess (Eds.), *Perspectives on cognitive change in adulthood and aging* (pp. 165–189). New York: McGraw-Hill.

Polivka, L. & Salmon, J. R. (2008). Assisted living: What it should be and why? In S. M. Golant & J. Hyde (Eds.), *The assisted living residence: A vision for the future.* Baltimore: The Johns Hopkins University Press.

Ponder, R. J., & Pomeroy, E. C. (1996). The grief of caregivers: How pervasive is it? *Journal of Gerontological Social Work, 27,* 3–21.

Poon, L. W. (1985). Differences in human memory with aging: Nature, causes, and clinical implications. In J. E. Birren & K. W. Schaie (Eds.), *Handbook of the psychology of aging* (2nd ed., pp. 427–462). New York: Academic Press.

Poon, L. W., & Fozard, J. L. (1980). Age and word frequency effects in continuous recognition memory. *Journals of Gerontology: Psychological Sciences, 35,* 77–86.

Pope, A. M., & Tarlov, A. R. (Eds.). (1991). *Disability in America: Toward a national agenda for prevention.* Washington, DC: National Academy Press.

Portenoy, R. K. (1995). Pain. In W. B. Abrams, M. H. Beers, & R. Berkow (Eds.), *The Merck manual of geriatrics* (2nd ed., pp. 125–152). Whitehouse Station, NJ: Merck Research Laboratories.

Posig, M., & Kickul, J. (2003). Extending our understanding of burnout: Test of an integrated model in nonservice occupations. *Journal of Occupational Health Psychology, 8,* 3–19.

Power, T. L., & Smith, S. M. (2008). Predictors of fear of death and self-mortality: An Atlantic Canadian perspective. *Death Studies, 32,* 252–272.

Pratt, S. I., Bartels, S. J., Mueser, K. T., & Forester, B. (2008). Helping older people experience success: An integrated model of psychosocial rehabilitation and health care management for older adults with serious mental illness. *American Journal of Psychiatric Rehabilitation, 11,* 41–60.

Prenda, K., & Lachman, M. E. (2001). Planning for the future: A life management strategy for increasing control and life satisfaction in adulthood. *Psychology and Aging, 16,* 206–216.

Price, R. H., Choi, J. N., & Vinokur, A. D. (2002). Links in the chain of adversity following job loss: How financial strain and loss of personal control lead to depression, impaired functioning, and poor health. *Journal of Occupational Health Psychology, 7,* 302–312.

Pride, N. B. (2005). Ageing and changes in lung mechanics. *European Research Journal, 26,* 563–565.

Prigerson, H. G., & Jacobs, S. C. (2001). Traumatic grief as a distinct disorder: A rationale, consensus criteria, and a preliminary empirical test. In M. S. Stroebe, R. O. Hansson, W. Stroebe, & H. Schut (Eds.), *Handbook of bereavement research: Consequences, coping, and care* (pp. 613–637). Washington, DC: American Psychological Association.

Pruchno, R. (1999). Raising grandchildren: The experiences of black and white grandmothers. *The Gerontologist, 39,* 209–221.

Pruchno, R. A., & McKenney, D. (2002). Psychological well-being of black and white grandmothers raising grandchildren: Examination of a two-factor model. *Journals of Gerontology: Psychological Sciences, 57B,* P444–P452.

Pruchno, R. A., Smyer, M. A., Rose, M. S., Hartman-Stein, P. E., & Henderson-Laribee, D. L. (1995). Competence of long-term care residents to participate in decisions about their medical care: A brief, objective assessment. *The Gerontologist, 35,* 622–629.

Prull, M. W., Gabreili, J. D. E., & Bunge, S. A. (2000). Age-related changes in memory: A cognitive neuroscience perspective. In F. I. M. Craik & T. A. Salthouse (Eds.), *Handbook of aging and cognition* (2nd ed., pp. 91–153). Mahwah, NJ: Erlbaum.

Pryor, J. B., Desouza, E. R., Fitness, J., & Hutz, C. (1997). Gender differences in the interpretation of social-sexual behavior: A cross-cultural per-spective on sexual harassment. *Journal of Cross-Cultural Psychology, 28,* 509–534.

Puglisi, J. T., & Park, D. C. (1987). Perceptual elaboration and memory in older adults. *Journals of Gerontology: Psychological Sciences, 42,* 160–162.

Pushkar, D., Etezadi, J., Andres, D., Arbuckle, T., Schwartzman, A. E., & Chaikelson, J. (1999). Models of intelligence in late life: Comment on Hultsch et al. (1999). *Psychology and Aging, 14,* 520–527.

Putnam, M. (2002). Linking aging theory and disability models: Increasing the potential to explore aging with physical impairment. *The Gerontologist, 42,* 799–806.

Pynoos, J. (in press). Housing and aging. In J. C. Cavanaugh & C. K. Cavanaugh (Eds.), *Aging in America.* Westport, CT: Praeger.

Pyszczynski, T., Greenberg, J., & Solomon, S. (1997). Why do we need what we need? A ter-ror management perspective on the roots of human social motivation. *Psychological Inquiry, 8,* 1–20.

Pyszczynski, T., Greenberg, J., & Solomon, S. (1999). A dual-process model of defense against conscious and unconscious death-related thoughts: An extension of terror management theory. *Psychological Review, 106,* 835–845.

Qualls, S. H. (1999). Mental health and mental disorders in older adults. In J. C. Cavanaugh & S. K. Whitbourne (Eds.), *Gerontology: An interdisciplinary perspective* (pp. 305–328). New York: Oxford University Press.

Qualls, S. H. (in press). Mental health. In J. C. Cavanaugh & C. K. Cavanaugh (Eds.), *Aging in America.* Westport, CT: Praeger.

Qualls, S. H., & Benight, C. C. (2007). The role of clinical health geropsychology in the health care of older adults. In C. M. Aldwin, C. L. Park, & A. Spiro (Eds.), *Handbook of health psychology and aging* (pp. 367–389). New York: Guilford.

Query, J. L., Jr., & Flint, L. J. (1996). The caregiving relationship. In N. Vanzetti & S. Duck (Eds.), *A lifetime of relationships* (pp. 455–483). Pacific Grove, CA: Brooks/Cole.

Quigley, M. W. (1979, June 19). Executive corps: Free advice pays off for both sides. *Newsday,* p. 9.

Quine, S., Wells, Y., De Vaus, D., and Kendig, H. (2007). When choice in retirement decisions is missing: Qualitative and quantitative findings of impact on well-being. *Australasian Journal on Ageing, 26*(4), 173–179.

Quinn, M. J. (1998). Undue influence: An emotional con game. *Aging Today, 9,* 11.

Quinn, M. J., & Tomita, S. K. (1997). Elder abuse and neglect: Causes, diagnosis, and intervention strategies (2nd ed.). New York: Springer.

Quist, D. (2003). The role of religion in adapta-tion to bereavement: Section B: The sciences and Engineering, *64(1-B),* 430.

Raabe, B., & Beehr, T. A. (2003). Formal men-toring, versus supervisor and coworker relationships: Differences in perceptions and impact. *Journal of Organizational Behavior, 24,* 271–293.

Rabig, J., Thomas, W., Kane, R. A., Cutler, L. J., & McAlilly, S. (2006). Radical redesign of nursing homes: Applying the green house concept in Tupelo, MS. *The Gerontologist, 46,* 533–539.

Rabinowitz, J. C., Craik, F. I. M., & Ackerman, B. P. (1982). A processing resource account of age differences in recall. *Canadian Journal of Psychology, 36,* 325–344.

Rabins, P. V. (1992). Schizophrenia and psychotic states. In J. E. Birren, R. B. Sloane, & G. D. Cohen (Eds.), *Handbook of mental health and aging* (2nd ed., pp. 463–475). San Diego: Academic Press.

Radloff, L.S. (1977). The CES-D scale: A self report depression scale for research in the general population. *Applied Psychological Measurement, 1,* 385–401.

Radvansky, G. A., Copeland, D. E., Berish, D., & Dijkstra, K. (2003). Aging and situation model updating. *Aging, Neuropsychology, and Cognition, 10,* 158–166.

Raeburn, P. (1995, November 7). Genetic trait may delay Alzheimer's. *News Journal* (Wilmington, DE), p. A3.

Ragozin, A. S., Basham, R. B., Crnic, K. A., Greenberg, M. T., & Robinson, N. M. (1982). Effects of maternal age on parenting role. *Developmental Psychology, 18,* 627–634.

Rahhal, T. A., Hasher, L., & Colcombe, S. J. (2001). Instructional manipulations and age differences in memory: Now you see them, now you don't. *Psychology and Aging, 16,* 697–706.

Rahhal, T. A., May, C. P., & Hasher, L. (2002). Truth and character: Sources that older adults can remember. *Psychological Science, 13,* 101–105.

Rahman, A. N., & Schnelle, J. F. (2008). The nursing home culture-change movement: Recent past, present, and future directions for research. *The Gerontologist, 48,* 142–148.

Rahman, O., Strauss, J., Gertler, P., Ashley, D., & Fox, K. (1994). Gender differences in adult health: An international comparison. *The Gerontologist, 34,* 463–469.

Raichle, M. E., MacLeod, A. M., Snyder, A. Z., Powers, W. J., Gusnard, D. A., & Shulman, G. L. (2001). A default mode of brain function. *Proceedings of the National Academy of Sciences U.S.A., 98*(2), 676–682.

Raley, G. (1999). No good choices: Teenage childbearing, concentrated poverty, and welfare reform. In S. Coontz (Ed.), *American families: A multicultural reader* (pp. 258–272). New York: Routledge.

Ramirez, R., & Schneider, J. (2003). Practical guide to sun protection. *Surgical Clinics of North America, 83,* 97–107.

Rape, Abuse, and Incest National Network (RAINN). (2005). *The facts about rape.* Retrieved March 17, 2009, from http://www.rainn.org/statistics.

Raphael, B. (1983). *The anatomy of bereavement.* New York: Basic Books.

Rapoport, J. L., & Rapoport, R. N. (1975). *Leisure and the family life cycle.* London, UK: Routledge & Kegan Paul.

Raschick, M., & Ingersoll-Dayton, B. (2004). The costs and rewards of caregiving among aging spouses and adult children. *Family Relations, 53,* 317–325.

Raskind, M. A., & Peskind, E. R. (1992). Alzheimer's disease and other dementing disorders. In J. E. Birren, R. B. Sloane, & G. D. Cohen (Eds.), *Handbook of mental health and aging* (2nd ed., pp. 477–513). San Diego: Academic Press.

Ratcliff, R., Spieler, D., & McKoon, G. (2000). Explicitly modeling the effects of aging on response time. *Psychonomic Bulletin and Review, 7,* 1–25.

Rawlins, W. K. (1992). *Friendship matters.* Hawthorne, NY: Aldine de Gruyter.

Rawlins, W. K. (2004). Friendships in later life. In J. F. Nussbaum & J. Coupland (Eds.), *Handbook of communication and aging research* (2nd ed., pp. 273–299). Mahwah, NJ: Erlbaum.

Raz, N. (1996). Neuroanatomy of aging brain: Evidence from structural MRI. In: Bigler,

E.D. (Ed.) *Neuroimaging II: Clinical applications,* (pp. 153–182) New York : Academic Press.

Raz, N. (2000). Aging of the brain and its impact on cognitive performance: An integration of structural and functional findings. In F. I. M. Craik & T. A. Salthouse (Eds.), *Handbook of aging and cognition* (2nd ed., pp. 1–90). Mahwah, NJ: Erlbaum.

Raz N., & Rodrigue, K. M. (2006). Differential aging of the brain: Patterns, cognitive correlates and modifiers. *Neuroscience and Biobehavioral Reviews, 30,* 730–748.

Redmore, C. D., & Loevinger, J. (1979). Ego development in adolescence: Longitudinal studies. *Journal of Youth and Adolescence, 8,* 129–134.

Reed, A. E., Mikels, J. A. & Simon, K. I. (2008). Older adults prefer less choice than young adults. *Psychology and Aging, 23*(3), 671–675.

Reed, D., Satariano, W. A., Gildengorin, G., McMahon, K., Fleshman, R., & Schneider, E. (1995). Health and functioning among the elderly of Marin County, California: A glimpse of the future. *Journals of Gerontology: Medical Sciences, 50A,* M61–M69.

Reese, C. M., & Cherry, K. E. (2002). The effects of age, ability, and memory monitoring on prospective memory task performance. *Aging, Neuropsychology, and Cognition, 9,* 98–113.

Reese, D. (2001, May). Putting the resident first. *Contemporary Long Term Care,* 24–28.

Regnier, V. (1983). Urban neighborhood cognition: Relationships between functional and symbolic community elements. In G. D. Rowles & R. J. Ohta (Eds.), *Aging and milieu: Environmental perspectives on growing old* (pp. 63–82). New York: Academic Press.

Reid, J., & Hardy, M. (1999). Multiple roles and well being among midlife women: Testing role strain and role enhancement theories. *Journals of Gerontology: Social Sciences, 54B,* S329–S338.

Reid, R. C. (2008). Quality of care and mortality among long-term care residents with dementia. *Canadian Studies in Population, 35,* 49–71.

Reifler, B. V. (1994). Depression: Diagnosis and comorbidity. In L. S. Schneider, C. F. Reynolds III, B. D. Lebowitz, & A. J. Friedhoff (Eds.), *Diagnosis and treatment of depression in late life* (pp. 55–59). Washington, DC: American Psychiatric Press.

Reinke, B. J., Holmes, D. S., & Harris, R. L. (1985). The timing of psychosocial change in women's lives: The years 25 to 45. *Journal of Personality and Social Psychology, 48,* 1353–1364.

Reis, M., & Nahmiash, D. (1998). Validation of the Indicators of Abuse (IOA) screen. *The Gerontologist, 38,* 471–480.

Reisberg, B., Doody, R., & Moebius, H. J. (2003). Memantine in moderate-to-severe Alzheimer's disease: Reply. *New England Journal of Medicine, 349,* 609–610.

Reisberg, B., Ferris, S. H., Anand, R., de Leon, M. J., Schneck, M. K., & Crook, T. H. (1985). Clinical assessment of cognitive decline in normal aging and primary degenerative dementia: Concordant ordinal measures. In P. Pinchot, P. Berner, R. Wolf, & K. Thau (Eds.), *Psychiatry* (Vol. 5, pp. 333–338). New York: Plenum.

Reisberg, B., Ferris, S. H., Borenstein, J., Sinaiko, E., de Leon, M. J., & Buttinger, C. (1986). Assessment of presenting symptoms. In L. W. Poon (Ed.), *Handbook for clinical memory assessment of older adults* (pp. 108–128). Washington, DC: American Psychological Association.

Reisberg, B., Ferris, S. H., de Leon, M. J., & Crook, T. H. (1982). The global deterioration scale for assessment of primary degenerative

dementia. *American Journal of Psychiatry, 139,* 1136–1139.

Reitzes, D. C., & Mutran, E. J. (2004). Grandparenthood: Factors influencing frequency of grandparent–grandchildren contact and grandparent role satisfaction. *Journals of Gerontology: Social Sciences, 59B,* S9–S16.

Rentz, D. M., Huh, T. J., Faust, R. R., Budson, A. E., Scinto, L. F. M., Sperling, R. A., & Daffner, K. R. (2004). Use of IQ-adjusted norms to predict progressive cognitive decline in highly intelligent older individuals. *Neuropsychology, 18,* 38–49.

Reuter-Lorenz, P. A. (2002). New visions of the aging mind and brain. *Trends in Cognitive Sciences, 6*(9), 394–400.

Reuter-Lorenz, P. A., & Cappell, K. A. (2008). Neurocognitive aging and the compensation hypothesis. *Current Directions in Psychological Science, 17*(3), 177–182.

Reuter-Lorenz, P. A., & Lustig, C. (2005). Brain aging: Reorganizing discoveries about the aging mind. *Current Opinion in Neurobiology, 15*(4), 245–251.

Reuter-Lorenz, P. A., Marshuetz, C., Jonides, J., Smith, E. E., Hartley, A., & Koeppe, R. (2001). Neurocognitive ageing of storage and executive processes. *European Journal of Cognitive Psychology, 12,* 257–278.

Reuter-Lorenz, P. A., & Mikels, J. A. (2006). The aging mind and brain: Implications of enduring plasticity for behavioral and cultural change. In P. B. Baltes, P. A. Reuter-Lorenz, & F. Rösler (Eds.), *Lifespan development and the brain: The perspective of biocultural co-constructivism* (pp. 255–276). New York: Cambridge University Press.

Reynolds, S. L., Crimmins, E. M., & Saito, Y. (1998). Cohort differences in disability and disease presence. *The Gerontologist, 38,* 578–590.

Riancho, J. A., Zarrabeitia, M. T., & Macías, J. G. (2008). Genetics of osteoporosis. *Aging Health, 4,* 365–376.

Rice, E. H., Sombrotto, L. B., Markowitz, J. C., & Leon, A. C. (1994). Cardiovascular morbidity in high-risk patients during ECT. *American Journal of Psychiatry, 151,* 1637–1641.

Rice, G. E., & Okun, M. A. (1994). Older readers' processing of medical information that contradicts their beliefs. *Journals of Gerontology: Psychological Sciences, 49,* P119–P128.

Richardson, V. E. (1993). *Retirement counseling.* New York: Springer.

Rico, H., Revilla, M., Hernandez, E. R., Gonzalez-Riola, J. M., & Villa, L. F. (1993). Four-compartment model of body composition of normal elderly women. *Age and Ageing, 22,* 265–268.

Ridings, C., & Gefen, D. (2004). Virtual community attraction: Why people hang out online. *Journal of Computer-Mediated Communication, 10,* http://jcmc.indiana.edu/vol10/issue1/ridings_gefen.html.

Riediger, M., Freund, A. M., & Baltes, P. B. (2005). Managing life through personal goals: Intergoal facilitation and intensity of goal pursuit in younger and older adulthood. *Journals of Gerontology: Psychological Sciences and Social Sciences, 60B,* P84–P91.

Riegel, K. F. (1973). Dialectic operations: The final period of cognitive development. *Human Development, 16,* 371–381.

Riegel, K. F. (1976). The dialectic of human development. *American Psychologist, 31,* 689–700.

Riley, K. P., Snowden, D. A., Saunders, A. M., Roses, A. D., Mortimer, J. A., & Nanayakkara, N. (2000). Cognitive function and apolipoprotein E in very old adults:

Findings from the nun study. *Journals of Gerontology: Social Sciences, 55B,* S69–S75.

Riley, L. D., & Bowen, C. (2005). The sandwich generation: Challenges and coping strategies of multigenerational family. *Counseling & Therapy for Couples & Families, 13,* 52–58.

Riley, M. W., & Riley, J. W., Jr. (1996). Generational relations: A future perspective. In T. K. Hareven (Ed.), *Aging and generational relations: Life-course and cross-cultural perspectives* (pp. 283–291). New York: Aldine de Gruyter.

Roberto, K. A., & Jarrott, S. E. (2008). Family caregivers of older adults: A life span perspective. *Family Relations, 57,* 100–111.

Roberto, K. A., & Scott, J. P. (1986). Equity considerations in the friendships of older adults. *Journals of Gerontology: Psychological Sciences, 41,* 241–247.

Roberto, K. A., & Skoglund, R. R. (1996). Interactions with grandparents and great-grandparents: A comparison of activities, influences, and relationships. *International Journal of Aging and Human Development, 43,* 107–117.

Roberts, B. W., Bogg, T., Walton, K., & Caspi, A. (2006). De-investment in work and non-normative personality trait change in young adulthood. *European Journal of Personality, 20,* 461–474.

Roberts, B. W., & DelVecchio, W. F. (2000). The rank-order consistency of personality traits from childhood to old age: A quantitative review of longitudinal studies. *Psychological Bulletin, 126,* 3–25.

Roberts, B. W., Helson, R., & Klohnen, E. C. (2002). Personality development and growth in women across 30 years: Three perspectives. *Journal of Personality, 70,* 79–102.

Roberts, G. (1999). Age effects and health appraisal: A meta-analysis. *Journals of Gerontology: Social Sciences, 54B,* S24–S30.

Roberts, J. A. (2007). Developing an explanatory model of the chronicity of psychologically aggressive behavior among coupled gay and bisexual men. *Dissertation Abstracts International Section A: Humanities and Social Sciences, 68(2-A),* 739.

Roberts, J. D. (1980). *Roots of a black future: Family and church.* Philadelphia: Westminster.

Roberts, P., & Newton, P. M. (1987). Levinsonian studies of women's adult development. *Psychology and Aging, 2,* 154–163.

Robertson, K., & Murachver, T. (2007). It takes two to tangle: Gender symmetry in intimate partner violence. *Basic and Applied Social Psychology, 29,* 109–118.

Robin, D. W. (1995). Falls and gait disorders. In W. B. Abrams, M. H. Beers, & R. Berkow (Eds.), *The Merck manual of geriatrics* (2nd ed., pp. 65–78). Whitehouse Station, NJ: Merck Research Laboratories.

Robinson, G. E., & Gallagher, A. (2008). Culture change impacts quality of life for nursing home residents. *Topics in Clinical Nutrition, 23,* 120–130.

Robinson, J. M., Johnson, A. L., Benton, S. L., Janey, B. A., Cabral, J., & Woodford, J. A. (2002). What's in a picture? Comparing gender constructs of younger and older adults. *Journal of Men's Studies, 11,* 1–27.

Rockwood, K., Howlett, S. E., MacKnight, C., Beattie, B. L., Bergman, H., Hébert, R., et al. (2004). Prevalence, attributes, and outcomes of fitness and frailty in community-dwelling older adults: Report from the Canadian study of health and aging. *Journal of Gerontology: Biological Sciences and Medical Sciences, 59,* 1310–1317.

Röder, B., & Rösler, F. (2003). The principle of brain plasticity, In R. H. Kluwe, G. Lüer, & F. Rösler (Eds.), *Principles of learning and* memory (pp. 27–49). Cambridge, MA: Birkheuser.

Rodin, J., & Langer, E. J. (1977). Long-term effects of a control-relevant intervention with the institutionalized aged. *Journal of Personality and Social Psychology, 35,* 897–902.

Rodin, J., McAvay, G., & Timko, C. (1988). A longitudinal study of depressed mood and sleep disturbances in elderly adults. *Journals of Gerontology, 43,* P45–P53.

Rodrigue, K. M., & Raz, N. (2004). Shrinkage of the entorhinal cortex over five years predicts memory performance in healthy adults. *Journal of Neuroscience, 24*(4), 956–963.

Rodriguez-Aranda, C. (2003). Reduced writing and reading speed and age-related changes in verbal fluency tasks. *Clinical Neuropsychologist, 17,* 203–215.

Roediger, H. L., & McDermott, K. B. (1993). Implicit memory in normal human subjects. In F. Boller & J. Grafman (Eds.), *Handbook of neuropsychology* (Vol. 8, pp. 63–131). New York: Elsevier.

Roediger, H. L., & McDermott, K. B. (2000). Tricks of memory. *Current Directions in Psychological Science, 9,* 123–127.

Rogers, S. J., & Amato, P. R. (1997). Is marital quality declining? The evidence from two generations. *Social Forces, 75,* 1089–1100.

Rogers, W. A., Bertus, E. L., & Gilbert, D. K. (1994). Dual-task assessment of age differences in automatic process development. *Psychology and Aging, 9,* 398–413.

Rogers, W. A., & Fisk, A. D. (1997, January). ATM design and training issues. *Ergonomics in Design,* pp. 4–9.

Rogers, W. A., & Fisk, A. D. (2000). Human factors, applied cognition, and aging. In F. I. M. Craik & T. A. Salthouse (Eds.), *Handbook of aging and cognition* (2nd ed., pp. 559–591). Mahwah, NJ: Erlbaum.

Rogers, W. A., Fisk, A. D., Mead, S. E., Walker, N., & Cabrera, E. F. (1996). Training older adults to use automatic teller machines. *Human Factors, 38,* 425–433.

Rogers, W. A., Gilbert, D. K., & Cabrera, E. F. (1997). An analysis of automatic teller machine usage by older adults: A structured interview approach. *Applied Ergonomics, 28,* 173–180.

Rogers, W. A., Hertzog, C., & Fisk, A. D. (2000). An individual differences analysis of ability and strategy influences: Age-related differences in associative learning. *Journal of Experimental Psychology: Learning, Memory, and Cognition, 26,* 359–394.

Rokach, R., Cohen, O., & Dreman, S. (2004). Triggers and fuses in late divorce: The role of short term crises vs. ongoing frustration on marital break-up. *Journal of Divorce & Remarriage, 40,* 41–60.

Ronen, S., Friedman, S., & Ben-Asher, H. (2007). Flexible working arrangements: Societal forces and implementation. In D. Steiner, S. Gilliland, & D. Skarlicki (Eds.), *Managing social and ethical issues in organizations.* Charlotte, NC: Information Age Publishing.

Rönnlund, M., Nyberg, L., Bäckman, L., & Nilsson, L.G. (2005). Stability, growth, and decline in adult life span development of declarative memory: cross-sectional and longitudinal data from a population-based study. *Psychology and Aging, 20*(1), 3–18.

Rook, K. S. (1994). Assessing the health-related dimensions of older adults' social relationships. In M. P. Lawton & J. A. Teresi (Eds.), *Annual review of gerontology and geriatrics: Focus on assessment techniques* (Vol. 14, pp. 142–181). New York: Springer.

Rook, K. S. (2000). The evolution of social relationships in later adulthood. In S. H. Qualls & N. Abeles (Eds.), *Psychology and the aging revolution* (pp. 173–191). Washington, DC: American Psychological Association.

Rook, K. S., Mavandadi, S., Sorkin, D. H., & Zettel, L. A. (2007). Optimizing social relationships as a resource for health and well-being in later life. In C. M. Aldwin, C. L. Park, & A. Spiro (Eds.), *Handbook of health psychology and aging* (pp. 267–285). New York: Guilford.

Roper, L. L. (2007). Air force single parent mothers and maternal separation anxiety. *Dissertation Abstracts International Section A: Humanities and Social Sciences, 67*(11-A), 4349.

Rose, S., & Zand, D. (2000). Lesbian dating and courtship from young adulthood to midlife. *Journal of Gay and Lesbian Social Services, 11,* 77–104.

Rosen, A. C., Prull, M. W., Gabrieli, J. D., Stoub, T., O'Hara, R., et al. (2003). Differential associations between entorhinal and hippocampal volumes and memory performance in older adults. *Behavioral Neuroscience, 117*(6), 1150–1160.

Rosenberg, E. B. (1992). *The adoption life cycle.* Lexington, MA: Lexington Books.

Rosenberg, R. N. (Ed.). (1991). *Comprehensive neurology.* New York: Raven.

Rosenberg, S. D., Rosenberg, H. J., & Farrell, M. P. (1992). In the name of the father. In G. Rosenwald & R. Ochberg (Eds.), *Telling lives* (pp. 41–59). New Haven, CT: Yale University Press.

Rosenberg, S. D., Rosenberg, H. J., & Farrell, M. P. (1999). Midlife crisis revisited. In S. L. Willis & J. D. Reid (Eds.), *Life in the middle: Psychological and social development in middle age* (pp. 47–70). San Diego: Academic Press.

Rosenblatt, P. C. (1996). Grief that does not end. In D. Klass, P. R. Silverman, & S. L. Nickman (Eds.), *Continuing bonds: New understandings of grief* (pp. 45–58). Washington, DC: Taylor & Francis.

Rosenblatt, P. C. (2001). A social constructivist perspective on cultural differences in grief. In M. S. Stroebe, R. O. Hansson, W. Stroebe, & H. Schut (Eds.), *Handbook of bereavement research: Consequences, coping, and care* (pp. 285–300). Washington, DC: American Psychological Association.

Rosenfeld, B. (2004). Do not resuscitate orders, living wills, and surrogate decision making. In B. Rosenfeld (Ed.), *Assisted suicide and the right to die: The interface of social science, public policy, and medical ethics* (pp. 41–59). Washington, DC: American Psychological Association.

Rosin, H. M., & Korabik, K. (1990). Marital and family correlates of women managers' attrition from organizations. *Journal of Vocational Behavior, 37,* 104–120.

Rosin, H. M., & Korabik, K. (1991). Workplace variables, affective responses, and intention to leave among women managers. *Journal of Occupational Psychology, 64,* 317–330.

Roskies, E., & Louis-Guerin, C. (1990). Job insecurity in managers: Antecedents and consequences. *Journal of Organizational Behavior, 11,* 345–359.

Rosnick, C. B., Small, B. J., Graves, A. B., & Mortimer, J. A. (2004). The association between health and cognitive performance in a population-based study of older adults: The Charlotte county healthy aging study (CCHAS). *Aging Neuropsychology and Cognition, 11,* 89–99.

Roth, G. S., Ingram, D. K., & Lane, M. A. (1995). Slowing ageing by caloric restriction. *Nature Medicine, 1,* 414–415.

Roth, W. F. (1991). Work and rewards: Redefining our work-life reality. New York: Praeger.

Rothermund, K., & Brandtstädter, J. (2003). Depression in later life: Cross-sequential patterns and possible determinants. *Psychology and Aging, 18,* 80–90.

Rousseau, G. K., Lamson, N., & Rogers, W. A. (1998). Designing warnings to compensate for age-related changes in perceptual and cognitive abilities. *Psychology and Marketing, 15,* 643–662.

Rousseau, G. K., & Rogers, W. A. (1998). Computer usage patterns of university faculty members across the life span. *Computers in Human Behavior, 14,* 417–428.

Rowe, J. W., & Kahn, R. L. (1997). Successful aging. *The Gerontologist, 37,* 433–440.

Rowe, J. W., & Kahn, R. L. (1998). *Successful aging.* New York: Pantheon.

Rowles, G. D. (2006). Commentary: A house is not a home: But can it become one? In H. W. Wahl et al. (Eds.), *The many faces of health, competence and well-being in old age.* The Netherlands: Springer.

Rowles, G. D., & Ohta, R. J. (1983). Emergent themes and new directions: Reflections on aging and milieu research. In G. D. Rowles & R. J. Ohta (Eds.), *Aging and milieu: Environmental perspectives on growing old* (pp. 231–240). New York: Academic Press.

Rowles, G. D., & Watkins, J. F. (2003). History, habit, heart, and hearth: On making spaces into places. In K. W. Schaie, H.-W. Wahl, H. Mollenkopf, & F. Oswald (Eds.), *Aging independently: Living arrangements and mobility* (pp. 77–96). New York: Springer.

Rowles, G., Oswald, F., & Hunter, E. (2004). Interior living environments in old age. In K. W. Schaie (Series Ed.), H. W. Wahl, R. J. Scheidt, & P. G. Windley (Vol. Eds.), *Annual review of gerontology and geriatrics: Vol. 23. Aging in context: Socio-physical environments* (pp. 167–194). New York: Springer.

Roxburgh, S. (1997). The effect of children on the mental health of women in the paid labor force. *Journal of Family Issues, 18,* 270–289.

Rozin, P., & Royzman, E. B. (2001). Negativity bias, negativity dominance, and contagion. *Personality and Social Psychology Review, 5,* 296–320.

Rubenfeld, M. I., & Gilroy, F. D. (1991). Relationship between college women's occupational interests and a single-sex environment. *Career Development Quarterly, 40,* 64–70.

Rubin, D. C. (Ed.). (1996). *Remembering our past: Studies in autobiographical memory.* Cambridge, UK: Cambridge University Press.

Rubin, D. C., Rahhal, T. A., & Poon, L. W. (1998). Things learned in early adulthood are remembered best. *Memory and Cognition, 26,* 3–19.

Rubin, D. C., & Schulkind, M. D. (1997). Distribution of important and word-cued auto-biographical memories in 20-, 35-, and 70-year old adults. *Psychology and Aging, 12,* 524–535.

Rubin, S. S., & Malkinson, R. (2001). Parental response to child loss across the life cycle: Clinical and research perspectives. In M. S. Stroebe, R. O. Hansson, W. Stroebe, & H. Schut (Eds.), *Handbook of bereavement research: Consequences, coping, and care* (pp. 169–197). Washington, DC: American Psychological Association.

Ruhm, C. J. (1990). Career jobs, bridge employment, and retirement. In P. Doeringer (Ed.), *Bridges to retirement: Older workers in a changing labor market* (pp. 92–107). Ithaca, NY: ILR Press.

Rush–Presbyterian St. Luke's Medical Center. (1998). Chronic illness. In *The World Book Rush–Presbyterian St. Luke's Medical Center medical encyclopedia*. Online document available at http://my.webmd.com/encyclopedia_article/DMK_ARTICLE_1457076.

Russell, B. L., & Trigg, K. Y. (2004). Tolerance of sexual harassment: An examination of gender differences, ambivalent sexism, social dominance, and gender roles. *Sex Roles, 50,* 565–573.

Russo, R. (Ed.). (2008). *A healing touch: True stories of life, death, and hospice.* Camden, ME: Down East Books.

Ryan, E. B., Giles, H., Bartolucci, G., & Henwood, K. (1986). Psycholinguistic and social psychological components of communication by and with the elderly. *Language and Communication, 6,* 1–24.

Ryan, E. B., Hamilton, J. M., & Kwong See, S. (1993). Patronizing the old: How do younger and older adults respond to baby talk in the nursing home? *International Journal of Aging and Human Development, 41,* 89–107.

Ryan, E. B., Kennaley, D. E., Pratt, M. W., & Shumovich, M. A. (2000). Evaluations by staff, residents, and community seniors of patronizing speech in the nursing home: Impact of passive, assertive, or humorous responses. *Psychology and Aging, 15,* 272–285.

Ryan, E. B., Meredith, S. D., MacLean, M. J., & Orange, J. B. (1995). Changing the way we talk with elders: Promoting health using the communication enhancement model. *International Journal of Aging and Human Development, 41,* 89–107.

Ryan, E. B., Meredith, S. D., & Schantz, G. B. (1994). Evaluative perceptions of patronizing speech addressed to institutionalized elders in contrasting conversational contexts. *Canadian Journal on Aging, 13,* 236–248.

Ryan, J., Carriere, I., Ritchie, K., Stewart, R., Toulemonde, G., Dartigues, J.-F, Tzourio, C., & Ancelin, M.-L. (2008). Late-life depression and mortality: Influence of gender and antidepressant use. *British Journal of Psychiatry, 192,* 12–18.

Ryan, L., Hatfield, C., & Hofstetter, M. (2002). Caffeine reduces time-of-day effects on memory performance in older adults. *Psychological Science, 13,* 68–71.

Rybash, J. M. (1996). Implicit memory and aging: A cognitive neuropsychological perspective. *Developmental Neuropsychology, 12,* 127–179.

Rybash, J. M., Hoyer, W. J., & Roodin, P. A. (1986). *Adult cognition and aging.* New York: Pergamon.

Rye, M. S., Folck, C. D., Heim, T. A., Olszewski, B. T., & Traina, E. (2004). Forgiveness of an ex-spouse: How does it relate to mental health following a divorce? *Journal of Divorce & Remarriage, 41,* 31–51.

Ryff, C. D. (1989). Happiness is everything, or is it? Explorations on the meaning of psychological well-being. *Journal of Personality and Social Psychology, 57,* 1069–1081.

Ryff, C. D. (1991). Possible selves in adulthood and old age: A tale of shifting horizons. *Psychology and Aging, 6,* 286–295.

Ryff, C. D., Lee, Y. H., Essex, M. J., & Schmutte, P. S. (1994). My children and me: Mid-life evaluations of grown children and of self. *Psychology and Aging, 9,* 195–205.

Rypma, B., & D'Esposito, M. (2001). Age-related changes in brain-behaviour relationships: Evidence from event related functional MRI studies. *European Journal of Cognitive Psychology, 13*(1–2), 235–256.

Sackeim, H. A. (1994). Use of electroconvulsive therapy in late-life depression. In L. S.

Schneider, C. F. Reynolds, B. D. Lebowitz, & A. J. Friedhoff (Eds.), *Diagnosis and treatment of depression in late life: Results of the NIH Consensus Development Conference* (pp. 259–273). Washington, DC: American Psychiatric Press.

Saczynski, J. S., Willis, S. L., & Schaie, K. W. (2002). Strategy use in reasoning training with older adults. *Aging, Neuropsychology, and Cognition, 9,* 48–60.

Saito, C. (2003). Bereavement and meaning reconstruction among senior Japanese immigrant women in the San Francisco Bay area: An ethnographic study for spiritual care (California). *Dissertation Abstracts International: Section A: Humanities and Social Sciences, 63*(12-A), 4355.

Sakraida, T. J. (2005). Divorce transition differences of midlife women. *Issues in Mental Health Nursing, 26,* 225–249.

Salat, D. H., Kaye, J. A., & Janowsky, J. S. (2002). Greater orbital prefrontal volume selectively predicts worse working memory performance in older adults. *Cerebral Cortex, 12*(5), 494–505.

Salomone, P. R. (1996). Tracing Super's theory of vocational development: A 40-year retrospective. *Journal of Career Development, 22,* 167–184.

Salthouse, T. A. (1984). Effects of age and skill in typing. *Journal of Experimental Psychology: General, 113,* 345–371.

Salthouse, T. A. (1988). The role of processing resources in cognitive aging. In M. L. Howe & C. J. Brainerd (Eds.), *Cognitive development in adulthood* (pp. 185–239). New York: Springer.

Salthouse, T. A. (1991). *Theoretical perspectives on cognitive aging.* Hillsdale, NJ: Erlbaum.

Salthouse, T. A. (1996). The processing speed theory of adult age differences in cognition. *Psychological Review, 103,* 403–428.

Salthouse, T. A. (1997). Psychological issues related to competence. In S. L. Willis & K. W. Schaie (Eds.), *Societal mechanisms for maintaining competence in old age* (pp. 50–93). New York: Springer.

Salthouse, T. A., Atkinson, R. M., & Berish, D. E. (2003). Executive functioning as a potential mediator of age-related cognitive decline in normal adults. *Journal of Experimental Psychology: General, 132,* 566–594.

Salthouse, T. A., & Babcock, R. L. (1991). Decomposing adult age differences in working memory. *Developmental Psychology, 27,* 763–776.

Salthouse, T. A., Fristoe, N. M., Lineweaver, T. T., & Coon, V. E. (1995). Aging of attention: Does the ability to decide decline? *Memory and Cognition, 23,* 59–71.

Salthouse, T. A., Fristoe, N., McGuthry, K. E., & Hambrick, D. Z. (1998). Relation of task switching to speed, age, and fluid intelligence. *Psychology and Aging, 13,* 445–461.

Salthouse, T. A., Kausler, D. H., & Saults, J. S. (1988). Utilization of path analytic procedures to investigate the role of processing resources in cognitive aging. *Psychology and Aging, 3,* 158–166.

Salthouse, T. A., & Meinz, E. J. (1995). Aging inhibition, working memory and speed. *Journals of Gerontology: Psychological Sciences, 50B,* P297–P306.

Samuelson, R. (2007). *Boomer generation is in a state of denial.* Retrieved March 17, 2009, from http://www.realclearpolitics.com/articles/2007/01/baby_boomers_are_selfishly_sil.html.

Sanders, C. M. (1980–1981). Comparison of younger and older spouses in bereavement outcome. *Omega: Journal of Death and Dying, 11,* 217–232.

Sandler, I. N., Wolchik, S. A., & Ayers, T. S. (2008). Resilience rather than recovery: A contextual framework on adaptation following bereavement. *Death Studies, 32,* 59–73.

Sands, L. P., & Meredith, W. (1992). Blood pressure and intellectual functioning in late midlife. *Journals of Gerontology: Psychological Sciences, 47,* P81–P84.

Sanfey, A. G., & Hastie, R. (2000). Judgment and decision making across the adult life span: A tutorial review of psychological research. In D. Park & N. Schwartz (Eds.), *Cognitive aging: A primer* (pp. 253–273). Philadelphia: Psychology Press.

Sangrador, J. L., & Yela, C. (2000). 'What is beautiful is loved': Physical attractiveness in love relationships in a representative sample. *Social Behavior and Personality, 28,* 207–218.

Saretzki, G., & Zglinicki, T. von. (2002). Replicative aging, telomeres, and oxidative stress. In H. Denham (Ed.), Increasing healthy life span: Conventional measures and slowing the innate aging process (Annals of the New York Academy of Science, 959, 24–29). New York: New York Academy of Sciences.

Sarton, M. (1997). Toward another dimension. In M. Pearsall (Ed.), *The other within us: Feminist explorations of women and aging* (pp. 229–232). Boulder, CO: Westview Press.

Sarvis, C. M. (1995). *Pain management in the elderly.* Sacramento, CA: CMW Resources.

Saunders, S. (1997). Hospices worldwide: A mission statement. In C. Saunders & R. Kastenbaum (Eds.), *Hospice care on the international scene* (pp. 3–12). New York: Springer.

Saxon, S. V., & Etten, M. J. (1994). *Physical changes and aging* (3rd ed.). New York: Tiresias.

Scarmeas, N., & Stern, Y. (2003). Cognitive reserve and lifestyle. *Journal of Clinical and Experimental Neuropsychology, 25*(5), 625–633.

Scarpini, E., Scheltens, P., & Feldman, H. (2003). Treatment of Alzheimer's disease: Current status and new perspectives. *The Lancet: Neurology, 2,* 539–547.

Schacter, D. L. (2000). Understanding implicit memory: A cognitive neuroscience approach. In M. S. Gazzaniga (Ed.), *Cognitive neuroscience: A reader* (pp. 305–324). Oxford, UK: Blackwell.

Schacter, D. L., Alpert, N. M., Savage, C. R., Rauch, S. L., & Albert, M. S. (1996). Conscious recollection and the human hippocampal formation: Evidence from positron emission tomography. *Proceedings of the National Academy of Sciences U.S.A., 93,* 321–325.

Schacter, D. L., Koustaal, W., Johnson, M. K., Gross, M. S., & Angell, K. E. (1997). False recollection induced by photographs: A comparison of older and younger adults. *Psychology and Aging, 12,* 203–215.

Schacter, D. L., Verifaelie, M., Anes, M. D., & Rancine, C. (1998). When true recognition suppresses false recognition: Evidence from amnesic patients. *Journal of Cognitive Neuroscience, 10,* 668–679.

Schaie, K. W. (1977–1978). Toward a stage theory of adult cognitive development. *International Journal of Aging and Human Development, 8,* 129–138.

Schaie, K. W. (1983). The Seattle longitudinal study: A twenty-one year exploration of psychometric intelligence in adulthood. In K. W. Schaie (Ed.), *Longitudinal studies of adult psychological development* (pp. 64–155). New York: Guilford.

Schaie, K. W. (1990). Intellectual development in adulthood. In J. E. Birren & K. W. Schaie (Eds.), *Handbook of the psychology of aging* (3rd ed., pp. 291–309). San Diego: Academic Press.

Schaie, K. W. (1994). The course of adult intellectual development. *American Psychologist, 49,* 304–313.

Schaie, K. W. (1995). Intellectual development in adulthood: The Seattle longitudinal study. New York: Cambridge University Press.

Schaie, K. W. (1996). Intellectual functioning in adulthood. In J. E. Birren & K. W. Schaie (Eds.), *Handbook of the psychology of aging* (4th ed., pp. 266–286). San Diego: Academic Press.

Schaie, K. W. (2005). Developmental influences on adult intelligence: The Seattle longitudinal study. New York: Oxford University Press.

Schaie, K. W. (2008). A lifespan developmental perspective of psychological aging. In K. Laidlaw & B. G. Knight (Eds.), *Handbook of emotional disorders in late life: Assessment and treatment.* Oxford, UK: Oxford University Press.

Schaie, K. W., Maitland, S. B., Willis, S. L., & Intrieri, R. L. (1998). Longitudinal invariance of adult psychometric ability factor structures across seven years. *Psychology and Aging, 13,* 8–20.

Schaie, K. W., Plomin, R., Willis, S. L., Gruber-Baldini, A., & Dutta, R. (1992). Natural cohorts: Family similarity in adult cognition. In T. Sonderegger (Ed.), *Psychology and aging: Nebraska symposium on motivation, 1991* (pp. 205–243). Lincoln: University of Nebraska Press.

Schaie, K. W., Nguyen, H. T., Willis, S. L., Dutta, R., & Yue, G. A. (2001). Environmental factors as a conceptual framework for examining cognitive performance in Chinese adults. *International Journal of Behavioral Development, 25,* 193–202.

Schaie, K. W., & Willis, S. L. (1986). Can decline in adult intellectual functioning be reversed? *Developmental Psychology, 22,* 223–232.

Schaie, K. W., & Willis, S. L. (1995). Perceived family environment across generations. In V. L. Bengston & K. W. Schaie (Eds.), *Adult intergenerational relations: Effects of societal change* (pp. 174–226). New York: Springer.

Schaie, K. W., & Willis, S. L. (1999). Theories of everyday competence and aging. In V. L. Bengtson & K. W. Schaie (Eds.), *Handbook of theories of aging* (pp. 174–195). New York: Springer.

Schaie, K. W., Willis, S. L., & O'Hanlon, A. M. (1994). Perceived intellectual performance change over seven years. *Journals of Gerontology: Psychological Sciences, 49,* P108–P118.

Schaie, K. W., & Zanjani, F. (2006). Intellectual development across adulthood. In C. Hoare (Ed.), *Oxford handbook of adult development and learning* (pp. 99–122). New York: Oxford University Press.

Schaller, M., Boyd, C., Yohannes, J., & O'Brien, M. (1995). The prejudiced personality revisited: Personal need for structure and formation of erroneous group settings. *Journal of Experimental and Social Psychology, 68,* 544–555.

Schapira, A. H. V., & Olanow, C. W. (2004). Neuroprotection in Parkinson disease: Mysteries, myths, and misconceptions. *JAMA, 291,* 358–364.

Scharlach, A. E. (2001). Role strain among working parents: Implications for workplace and community. *Community, Work and Family, 4,* 215–230.

Schaufeli, W. B., & Bakker, A. B. (2004). Job demands, job resources, and their relationship with burnout and engagement: A multi-sample study. *Journal of Organizational Behavior, 25,* 293–315.

Scheibel, A. B. (1996). Structural and functional changes in the aging brain. In J. E. Birren & K. W. Schaie (Eds.), *Handbook of the psychology of aging* (4th ed., pp. 105–128). San Diego: Academic Press.

Scheidt, R. J., Humphreys, D. R., & Yorgason, J. B. (1999). Successful aging: What's not to like? *Journal of Applied Gerontology, 18,* 277–282.

Scheidt, R. J., & Schwarz, B. (in press). Environmental gerontology: A sampler of issues and applications. In J. C. Cavanaugh & C. Cavanaugh (Eds.), *Aging in America* (Vol. 3). Westport, CT: Praeger.

Scheidt, R. J., Humphreys, D. R., & Yorgason, J. B. (1999). Successful aging: What's not to like? *Journal of Applied Gerontology, 18,* 277–282.

Schinka, J. A., Belanger, H., Mortimer, J. A., & Graves, A. B. (2003). Effects of the use of alcohol and cigarettes on cognition in elderly African American adults. *Journal of the International Neuropsychological Society, 9,* 690–697.

Schmeeckle, M., Giarusso, R., & Wang, Q. (1998, November). *When being a brother or sister is important to one's identity: Life stage and gender differences.* Paper presented at the annual meeting of the Gerontological Society, Philadelphia.

Schmidt, D. E., & Duenas, G. (2002). Incentives to encourage worker-friendly organizations. *Public Personnel Management, 31,* 293–308.

Schmiege, C. J., Richards, L. N., & Zvonkovic, A. M. (2001). Remarriage: For love or money? *Journal of Divorce and Remarriage, 36,* 123–140.

Schmitt, D. P., Alcalay, L., Allensworth, M., Allik, J., Ault, L., Austers, I., Bennett, K. L., Bianchi, G., Boholst, F., Cunen, M. A. B., Braeckman, J., Brainerd, E. G., Jr., Caral, L. G. A., Caron, G., Casullo, M. M., Cunningham, M., Daibo, I., De Backer, C., De Souza, E., Diaz-Loving, R., Diniz, G., Durkin, K., Echegaray, M., Eremsoy, E., Euler, H. A., Falzon, R., Fisher, M. L., Foley, D., Fowler, R., Fry, D. P., Fry, S., Ghayur, M. A., Giri, V. N., Golden, D. L., Grammer, K., Grimaldi, L., Halberstadt, J., Haque, S., Herrera, D., Hertel, J., Hitchell, A., Hoffmann, H., Hooper, D., Hradilekova, Z., Hudek-Kene-Evi, J., Huffcutt, A., Jaafar, J., Jankauskaite, M., Kabangu-Stahel, H., Kardum, I., Khoury, B., Kwon, H., Laidra, K., Laireiter, A.-R., Lakerveld, D., Lampert, A., Lauri, M., Lavallée, M., Lee, S.-J., Leung, L. C., Locke, K. D., Locke, V., Luksik, I., Magaisa, I., Marcinkeviciene, D., Mata, A., Mata, R., McCarthy, B., Mills, M. E., Mkhize, N. J., Moreira, J., Moreira, S., Moya, M., Munyae, M., Noller, P., Olimat, H., Opre, A., Panayiotou, A., Petrovic, N., Poels, K., Popper, M., Poulimenou, M., P'Yatokha, V., Raymond, M., Reips, U.-D., Reneau, S. E., Rivera-Aragon, S., Rowatt, W. C., Ruch, W., Rus, V. S., Safir, M. P., Salas, S., Sambataro, F., Sandnabba, K. N., Schleeter, R., Schulmeyer, M. K., Schütz, A., Scrimali, T., Shackelford, T. K., Sharan, M. B., Shaver, P. R., Sichona, F., Simonetti, F., Sineshaw, T., Sookdew, R., Speelman, T., Spyrou, S., Sümer, H. C., Sümer, N., Supekova, M., Szlendak, T., Taylor, R., Timmermans, B., Tooke, W., Tsaousis, I., Tungaraza, F. S. K., Turner, A., Vandermassen, G., Vanhoomissen, T., Van Overwalle, F., Vanwesenbeeck, I., Vasey, P. L., Verissimo, J., Voracek, M., Wan, W. W. N., Wang, T.-W., Weiss, P., Wijaya, A., Woertman, L., Youn, G., & Zupanèiè, A. (2004). Patterns and universals of adult romantic attachment across 62 cultural regions: Are models of self and of other pan-cultural constructs? *Journal of Cross-Cultural Psychology, 35,* 367–402.

Schmitz-Scherzer, R., & Thomae, H. (1983). Constancy and change of behavior in old age: Findings from the Bonn Longitudinal Study on Aging. In K. W. Schaie (Ed.), *Longitudinal studies of adult psychological development* (pp. 191–221). New York: Guilford.

Schneider, B. A., & Pichora-Fuller, M. K. (2000). Implications of perceptual deterioration for cognitive aging research. In F. I. M. Craik (Ed.), *Handbook of aging and cognition* (2nd ed., pp. 155–219). Mahwah, NJ: Erlbaum.

Schneider, E. (1996). *Demographics update: Blind persons who use guide dogs.* New York: American Foundation for the Blind.

Schneider, K. T., Swan, S., & Fitzgerald, L. F. (1997). Job-related and psychological effects on sexual harassment in the workplace: Empirical evidence from two organizations. *Journal of Applied Psychology, 82,* 401–415.

Schneider, L. S. (1995). Efficacy of clinical treatment for mental disorders among older persons. In M. Gatz (Ed.), *Emerging issues in mental health and aging* (pp. 19–71). Washington, DC: American Psychological Association.

Schone, B. S., & Weinick, R. M. (1998). Health-related behaviors and the benefits of marriage for elderly persons. *The Gerontologist, 38,* 618–627.

Schooler, C. & Caplan L. J. (2009) Those who have, get: Social structure, environmental complexity, intellectual functioning and self-directed orientations in the elderly. In R. Abeles & K. W. Schaie (Eds.), *Social structures and aging individuals: Continuing challenges.* New York: Springer.

Schooler, C., Mulatu, M. S., & Oates, G. (1999). The continuing effects of substantively complex workers. *Psychology and Aging, 14,* 483–506.

Schooler, K. K. (1982). Response of the elderly to environment: A stress-theoretical perspective. In M. P. Lawton, P. G. Windley, & T. O. Byerts (Eds.), *Aging and the environment: Theoretical approaches* (pp. 80–96). New York: Springer.

Schuett, A., & Burke, W. J. (2000). *The hazards of participating in sweepstakes games by the elderly.* Unpublished manuscript cited in Wilber & McNeilly (2001).

Schulte, H. A. (2006). Family of origin and sibling influence on the experience of social support in adult friendships. *Dissertation Abstracts International: Section B: The Sciences and Engineering, 67(6-B),* 3510.

Schulz, R. (1985). Emotion and affect. In J. E. Birren & K. W. Schaie (Eds.), *Handbook of the psychology of aging* (2nd ed., pp. 531–543). New York: Van Nostrand Reinhold.

Schulz, R., Bookwala, J., Knapp, J. E., Scheier, M., & Williamson, G. M. (1996). Pessimism, age, and cancer mortality. *Psychology and Aging, 11,* 304–309.

Schulz, R., & Hanusa, B. H. (1979). Environmental influences on the effectiveness of control- and competence-enhancing interventions. In L. C. Perlmuter & R. A. Monty (Eds.), *Choice and perceived control* (pp. 315–337). Hillsdale, NJ: Erlbaum.

Schulz, R., & Heckhausen, J. (1996). A life span model of successful aging. *American Psychologist, 51,* 702-714.

Schulz, R., Martire, L. M., Beach, S. R., & Scheier, M. F. (2000). Depression and mortality in the elderly. *Current Directions in Psychological Science, 9,* 204–208.

Schulz, R., O'Brien, A., Czaja, S., Ory, M., Norris, R., Martire, L. M., Belle, S. H., Burgio, L., Gitlin, L., Coon, D., Burns, R., Gallagher-Thompson, D., & Stevens, A. (2002). Dementia caregiver intervention research: In search of clinical significance. *The Gerontologist, 42,* 589–602.

Schulz, R., Wrosch, C., & Heckhausen, J. (2003). The life span theory of control: Issues and evidence. In S. H. Zarit & L. I. Pearlin (Eds.), *Personal control in social and life course contexts* (pp. 484–491). New York: Springer.

Schwartz, L. S. (1992, April). The older woman worker: The effects of job-type, applicant age, and work hiatus on hiring and pay decisions. *Dissertation Abstracts International, 52,* 5565.

Schwarzer, R. (2008). Modeling health behavior change: How to predict and modify the adoption and maintenance of health behaviors. *Applied Psychology: An International Review, 57,* 1–29.

Scialfa, C. T., Guzy, L. T., Leibowitz, H. W., Garvey, P. M., & Tyrrell, R. A. (1991). Age differences in estimating vehicle velocity. *Psychology and Aging, 6,* 60–66.

Scogin, F. R. (1999). Anxiety in old age. In I. H. Nordhus, G. R. VandenBos, S. Berg, & P. Fromholt (Eds.), *Clinical geropsychology* (pp. 205–209). Washington, DC: American Psychological Association.

Scogin, F. R., & McElreath, L. (1994). Efficacy of psychosocial treatments for geriatric depression. *Journal of Consulting and Clinical Psychology, 62,* 69–74.

Scozzaro, P. P., & Subich, L. M. (1990). Gender and occupational sex-type differences in job outcome factor perceptions. *Journal of Vocational Behavior, 36,* 109–119.

Sears, P. S., & Barbee, A. H. (1978). Career and life satisfaction among Terman's gifted women. In J. C. Stanley, W. C. George, & C. H. Solano (Eds.), *The gifted and the creative: Fifty-year perspective* (pp. 28–66). Baltimore: Johns Hopkins University Press.

Segal, D. L., Coolidge, F. L., & Hersen, M. (1999). Psychological testing of older people. In I. H. Nordhus, G. R. VandenBos, S. Berg, & P. Fromholt (Eds.), *Clinical geropsychology* (pp. 231–257). Washington, DC: American Psychological Association.

Seginer, R., Trommsdorff, G., & Essau, C. (1993). Adolescent control beliefs: Cross-cultural variations of primary and secondary control orientations. *International Journal of Behavioral Development, 16,* 243–260.

Seibert, S. (1999). The effectiveness of facilitated mentoring: A longitudinal quasi-experiment. *Journal of Vocational Behavior, 54,* 483–502.

Seidman, S. M. (2003). The aging male: Androgens, erectile dysfunction, and depression. *Journal of Clinical Psychology, 64,* 31–37.

Sera, E. J. (2001). Men and spousal bereavement: A cross-cultural study of majority-culture and Hispanic men and the role of religiosity and acculturation on grief. *Dissertation Abstracts International Section B: The Sciences and Engineering, 61(11-B),* 6149.

Sergeant, J. F., & Ekerdt, D. J. (2008). Motives for residential mobility in later life: Post-move perspectives of elders and family members. *International Journal of Aging and Human Development, 66,* 131–154.

Seward, R. R., Yeatts, D. E., Amin, I., & DeWitt, A. (2006). Employment leave and fathers' involvement with children: According to mothers and fathers. *Men and Masculinities, 8,* 405–427.

Shaiko, R. G. (1996). Female participation in public interest nonprofit governance: Yet another glass ceiling? *Nonprofit and Voluntary Sector Quarterly, 25,* 302–320.

Shainess, N. (1984). *Sweet suffering: Woman as victim.* Indianapolis: Bobbs-Merrill.

Shalev, R. (1999). *Comparison of war-bereaved and motor vehicle accident-bereaved parents.* Unpublished master's thesis, University of Haifa.

Shapiro, S. (2007). Recent epidemiological evidence relevant to the clinical management of the menopause. *Climacteric, 10* (Suppl. 2), 2–15.

Sharon, I., Ersan, T., & Sharon, R. (2007). *Huntington disease dementia.* Retrieved October 26, 2008, from http://www.emedicine.com/MED/topic3111.htm.

Shaw, E., & Burns, A. (1993). Guilt and the working parent. *Australian Journal of Marriage and Family, 14,* 30–43.

Shaw, S. S. (2007). Losing a parent twice. *American Journal of Alzheimer's Disease and Other Dementias, 21,* 389–390.

Shea, S. C. (2006). *Improving medication adherence: How to talk to patients about their medications.* Philadelphia: Lippincott, Williams & Wilkins.

Sheehy, G. (1976). *Passages.* New York: Dutton.

Sheehy, G. (1981). *Pathfinders.* New York: Morrow.

Sheehy, G. (1995). New passages: Mapping your life across time. New York: Random House.

Sheehy, G. (1998). *Understanding men's passages.* New York: Random House.

Shelly, W., Draper, M. W., Krishnan, V., Wong, M., & Jaffe., R. B. (2008). Selective estrogen receptor modulators: an update on recent clinical findings. *Obstetrical and Gynecological Survey, 63,* 163–181.

Shelton, B. A., & John, D. (1993). Ethnicity, race, and difference: A comparison of white, black, and Hispanic men's household labor time. In J. C. Hood (Ed.), *Men, work, and family* (pp. 131–150). Thousand Oaks, CA: Sage.

Shephard, R. J. (1997). *Aging, physical activity, and health.* Champaign, IL: Human Kinetics.

Sher, T. G. (1996). Courtship and marriage: Choosing a primary relationship. In N. Vanzetti & S. Duck (Eds.), *A lifetime of relationships* (pp. 243–264). Pacific Grove, CA: Brooks/Cole.

Sherman, A. M., de Vries, B., & Lansford, J. E. (2000). Friendship in childhood and adulthood: Lessons across the life span. *International Journal of Aging and Human Development, 51,* 31–51.

Sherrington, R., Rogaev, E. I., Liang, Y., Rogaeva, E. A., Levesque, G., Ikeda, M., et al. (1995). Cloning of a gene bearing missense mutations in early-onset familial Alzheimer's disease. *Nature, 375,* 754–760.

Sherwin, B. B. (1997). Estrogen effects on cognition in menopausal women. *Neurology, 48* (5 Suppl. 7), S21–S26.

Shield, R. R. (1988). *Uneasy endings: Daily life in an American nursing home.* Ithaca, NY: Cornell University Press.

Shirom, A., & Mazeh, T. (1988). Periodicity in seniority–job satisfaction relationship. *Journal of Vocational Behavior, 33,* 38–49.

Shmotkin, D., Blumstein, T., & Modan, B. (2003). Beyond keeping active: Concomitants of being a volunteer in old-old age. *Psychology and Aging, 18,* 602–607.

Shuey, K., & Hardy, M. A. (2003). Assistance to aging parents and parents-in-law: Does lineage affect family allocation decisions? *Journal of Marriage and the Family, 65,* 418–431.

Shultz, K. S., & Wang, M. (2007). The influence of specific physical health conditions on retirement decisions. *International Journal of Aging and Human Development, 65,* 149–161.

Siegel, M., Bradley, E. H., Gallo, W. T., & Kasl, S. V. (2003). Impact of husbands' involuntary job loss on wives' mental health, among older adults. *Journals of Gerontology: Social Sciences, 58B,* S30–S37.

Siegler, I. C., George, L. K., & Okun, M. A. (1979). A cross-sequential analysis of adult personality. *Developmental Psychology, 15,* 350–351.

Silverman, P. (1987). Community settings. In P. Silverman (Ed.), *The elderly as modern pioneers* (pp. 185–210). Bloomington: Indiana University Press.

Simmons, L. W. (1945). *Role of the aged in primitive society.* New Haven, CT: Yale University Press.

Simon, N. M., Thompson, E. H., Pollack, M. H., & Shear, M. K. (2007). Complicated grief: A case series using escitalopram. *American Journal of Psychiatry, 164,* 1760–1761.

Simon, R. (1996). Too damn old. *Money, 25*(7), 118–126.

Simon, R. W. (1995). Gender, multiple roles, role meaning, and mental health. *Journal of Health and Social Behavior, 36,* 182–194.

Simons, J. S., Dodson, C. S., Bell, D., & Schacter, D. L.(2004). Specific- and partial-source memory: Effects of aging. *Psychology and Aging, 19*(4), 689–694.

Simons, L. A., McCallum, J., Friedlander, Y., & Simons, J. (1996). Predictors of mortality in the prospective Dubbo study of Australian elderly. *Australian and New Zealand Journal of Medicine, 26,* 40–48.

Simonton, D. K. (1990). Creativity and wisdom in aging. In J. E. Birren & K. W. Schaie (Eds.), *Handbook of the psychology of aging* (3rd ed., pp. 320–329). San Diego: Academic Press.

Sinaki, M. (1996). Effect of physical activity on bone mass. *Current Opinions in Rheumatology, 8,* 376–383.

Sinnott, J. (1992). The developmental approach: Post-formal thought as adaptive intelligence. In F. Blanchard-Fields & T. H. Hess (Eds.), *Perspectives on cognitive change in adulthood and aging* (pp. 358–383). New York: McGraw-Hill.

Sinnott, J. D. (1984). Postformal reasoning: The relativistic stage. In M. L. Commons, F. A. Richards, & C. Armon (Eds.), *Beyond formal operations: Late adolescent and adult cognitive development* (pp. 298–325). New York: Praeger.

Sinnott, J. D. (1986). Sex roles and aging: Theory and research from a systems perspective. *Contributions to human development* (Vol. 15). New York: Karger.

Sinnott, J. D. (1994a). New science models for teaching adults: Teaching as a dialogue with reality. In J. D. Sinnott (Ed.), *Interdisciplinary handbook of adult lifespan learning* (pp. 90–104). Westport, CT: Greenwood.

Sinnott, J. D. (1994b). Interdisciplinary handbook of adult lifespan learning. Westport, CT: Greenwood.

Sinnott, J. D. (1994c). The relationship of postformal thought, adult learning, and lifespan development. In J. D. Sinnott (Ed.), *Interdisciplinary handbook of adult lifespan learning* (pp. 105–119). Westport, CT: Greenwood.

Sinnott, J. D. (1996). The developmental approach: Postformal thought as adaptive intelligence. In F. Blanchard-Fields & T. M. Hess (Eds.), *Perspectives on cognitive change in adulthood and aging* (pp. 358–383).New York: McGraw-Hill.

Sinnott, J. D., & Shifren, K. (2001). Gender and aging: Gender differences and gender roles. In J. E. Birren & K. W. Schaie (Eds.), *Handbook of the psychology of aging* (5th ed., pp. 454–476). San Diego: Academic Press.

Skelton, D. A., Greig, C. A., Davies, J. M., & Young, A. (1994). Strength, power, and related functional ability of healthy people aged 65–89 years. *Age and Ageing, 23,* 371–377.

Skowronski, J. J., & Carlston, D. E. (1989). Negativity and extremity bias in impression formation: A review of explanations. *Psychological Bulletin, 105,* 131–142.

Skultety, K. M., Whitbourne, S. K., & Collins, K. (1999, August). *Relationship between identity and exercise in middle-aged men and women.* Paper presented at the annual meeting of the American Psychological Association, Boston.

Slater, C. L. (2003). Generativity versus stagnation: An elaboration of Erikson's adult stage of human development. *Journal of Adult Development, 10,* 53–65.

Slivinske, L. R., & Fitch, V. L. (1987). The effect of control enhancing intervention on the well-being of elderly individuals living in retirement communities. *The Gerontologist, 27,* 176–181.

Small, B. (2004). Online personals and narratives of the self: Australia's RSVP. *Convergence: The Journal of Research into New Media Technologies, 10,* 93–107.

Small, B. J., Hertzog, C., Hultsch, D. F., & Dixon, R. A. (2003). Stability and change in adult personality over 6 years: Findings from the Victoria longitudinal study. *Journals of Gerontology: Psychological Sciences, 58B,* P166–P176.

Smith, A. D. (1975). Aging and interference with memory. *Journals of Gerontology: Psychological Sciences, 30,* 319–325.

Smith, A. D. (1996). Memory. In J. E. Birren & K. W. Schaie (Eds.), *Handbook of the psychology of aging* (4th ed., pp. 236–250). San Diego: Academic Press.

Smith, A. D., & Park, D. C. (1990). Adult age differences in memory for pictures and images. In E. A. Lovelace (Ed.), *Aging and cognition: Mental processes, self-awareness, and interventions* (pp. 69–96). Amsterdam: North-Holland.

Smith, C. J., Beltran, A., Butts, D. M., & Kingson, E. R. (2000). Grandparents raising grandchildren: Emerging program and policy issues for the 21st century. *Journal of Gerontological Social Work, 34,* 81–94.

Smith, D. B. D. (1990). Human factors and aging: An overview of research needs and application opportunities. *Human Factors, 32,* 509–526.

Smith, J., & Baltes, P. B. (1990). Wisdom-related knowledge: Age/cohort differences in responses to life-planning problems. *Developmental Psychology, 26,* 494–505.

Smith, J., & Earles, J. L. (1996). Memory. In J. E. Birren & K. W. Schaie (Eds.), *Handbook of the psychology of aging* (4th ed., pp. 236–250). San Diego: Academic Press.

Smith, J., & Freund, A. M. (2002). The dynamics of possible selves in old age. *Journal of Journals of Gerontology: Psychological Sciences, 57B,* P492–P500.

Smith, J., Staudinger, U. M., & Baltes, P. B. (1994). Occupational settings of wisdom-related knowledge: The sample case of clinical psychologists. *Journal of Consulting and Clinical Psychology, 62,* 989–1000.

Smith, K. R., & Zick, C. D. (1996). Risk of mortality following widowhood: Age and sex differences by mode of death. *Social Biology, 43,* 59–71.

Smith, L. (1992). The tyranny of America's old. *Fortune, 125*(1), 68–72.

Smith, R. A., & Elliott, J. R. (2002). Does ethnic concentration influence employees' access to authority? An examination of contemporary urban labor markets. *Social Forces, 81,* 255–279.

Smith, R. E., Lozito, J., & Bayen, U. J. (2005). Adult age differences in distinctive processing: The modality effect in false recall. *Psychology and Aging, 20,* 486–492.

Smyer, M. A., & Allen-Burge, R. (1999). Older adults' decision-making capacity: Institutional settings and individual choices. In J. C. Cavanaugh & S. K. Whitbourne (Eds.), *Gerontology: An interdisciplinary perspective* (pp. 391–413). New York: Oxford University Press.

Smyer, M. A., Gatz, M., Simi, N. L., & Pedersen, N. L. (1998). Childhood adoption: Long-term effects in adulthood. *Psychiatry, 61,* 191–205.

Smyer, M. A., & Qualls, S. H. (1999). *Aging and mental health.* Malden, MA: Blackwell.

Sneed, J. R., & Whitbourne, S. K. (2003). Identity processing and self-consciousness in middle and later adulthood. *Journals of Gerontology: Psychological Sciences, 58B,* P313–P319.

Snyder, C. J., & Barrett, G. V. (1988). The Age Discrimination in Employment Act: A review of court decisions. *Experimental Aging Research, 14,* 3–47.

Social Security Administration. (2008). *The 2008 report of the board of trustees of the old-age and survivors insurance and federal disability insurance trust funds.* Retrieved March 17, 2009, from http://www.ssa.gov/OACT/TR/TR08/trTOC.html.

Soederberg Miller, L. M., & Lachman, M. (1999a). The sense of control and cognitive aging: Toward a model of mediational processes. In T. M. Hess & F. Blanchard-Fields (Eds.), *Social cognition and aging* (pp. 17–41). San Diego: Academic Press.

Soederberg Miller, L. M., & Lachman, M. (1999b, August). *Stress reactivity and cognitive performance in adulthood.* Paper presented at the annual meeting of the American Psychological Association, Boston.

Solano, N. H. (2001). Anxiety, depression, and older veterans: Implications for functional status. *Dissertation Abstract International Section B: The Sciences and Engineering, 61*(7-B), 3862.

Somary, K., & Stricker, G. (1998). Becoming a grandparent: A longitudinal study of expectations and early experiences as a function of sex and lineage. *The Gerontologist, 38,* 53–61.

Somberg, B. L., & Salthouse, T. A. (1982). Divided attention abilities in young and old adults. *Journal of Experimental Psychology: Human Perception and Performance, 8,* 651–663.

Sompayrac, L. M. (2008). *How the immune system works* (3rd ed.). New York: Wiley-Blackwell.

Soong-Nang, J., Choi, Y.-J., & Kim, D.-H. (2008). Association of socioeconomic status with successful ageing: differences in the components of successful ageing. *Journal of Biosocial Science, 41,* 207–219.

Soulsman, G. (1999, March 15). Understanding hearing loss. *News Journal* (Wilmington, DE), pp. E1–E2.

Spaan, P. E. J., Raaijmakers, J. G. W., & Jonker, C. (2003). Alzheimer's disease versus normal ageing: A review of the efficiency of clinical and experimental memory measures. *Journal of Clinical and Experimental Neuropsychology, 25,* 216–230.

Spaniol, J., Madden, D. J., & Voss, A. (2006). A diffusion model analysis of adult age differences in episodic and semantic long-term memory retrieval. *Journal of Experimental Psychology: Learning, Memory, and Cognition, 32,* 101–117.

Spector, A. R. (2004). Psychological issues and interventions with infertile patients. *Women & Therapy, 27,* 91–105.

Spector, P. E. (2002). Employee control and occupational stress. *Current Directions in Psychological Science, 11,* 133–136.

Spencer, W. D., & Raz, N. (1995). Differential effects of aging on memory for content and context: A meta-analysis. *Psychology and Aging, 10,* 527–539.

Spencer, W. D., Steele, C. M., & Quinn, D. M. (1999). Stereotype threat and women's math performance. *Journal of Experimental Social Psychology, 35,* 4–28.

Spirduso, W. W., & MacRae, P. G. (1990). Motor performance and aging. In J. E. Birren & K. W. Schaie (Eds.), *Handbook of the psychology of aging* (3rd ed., pp. 183–200). San Diego: Academic Press.

Spiro, A., III, & Brady, C. B. (2008). Integrating health into cognitive aging research and theory: Quo vadis? In S. M. Hofer & D. F. Alwin (Eds.), *Handbook of cognitive aging: Interdisciplinary perspectives* (pp. 260–283). Greenwich, CT: Sage.

Srinivasan, V., Maestroni, G. J. M., Cardinali, D. P., Esquifino, A. I., Pandi Perumal, S. R., & Miller, S. C. (2005). Melatonin, immune function and aging. *Immunity & Ageing, 2.* Retrieved September 21, 2008, from http://www.immunityageing.com/content/2/1/17.

Srivastava, S., John, O. P., Gosling, S. D., & Potter, J. (2003). Development of personality in early and middle adulthood: Set like plaster or persistent change? *Journal of Personality and Social Psychology, 84,* 1041–1053.

Stajkovic, A., & Luthans, F. (1998). Self-efficacy and work-related task performance. A meta-analysis. *Psychological Bulletin, 124,* 240–261.

Stafford, L., Kline, S. L., & Rankin, C. T. (2004). Married individuals, cohabiters, and cohabiters who marry: A longitudinal study of relational and individual well-being. *Journal of Social & Personal Relationships, 21,* 231–248.

Stanford, E. P., & DuBois, B. C. (1992). Gender and ethnicity patterns. In J. E. Birren, R. B. Sloane, & G. D. Cohen (Eds.), *Handbook of mental health and aging* (2nd ed., pp. 99–117). San Diego: Academic Press.

Stanford, E. P., Happersett, C. J., Morton, D. J., Molgaard, C. A., & Peddecord, K. M. (1991). Early retirement and functional impairment from a multi-ethnic perspective. *Research on Aging, 15,* 5–38.

Stankov, L., & Dunn, S. (1993). Physical substrata of mental energy: Brain capacity and efficiency of cerebral metabolism. *Learning and Individual Differences, 5,* 241–257.

Stanton-Rich, H. M., Iso-Ahola, S. E., & Seppo, E. (1998). Burnout and leisure. *Journal of Applied Social Psychology, 28,* 1931–1950.

Staudinger, U. M. (1999). Social cognition and a psychological approach to the art of life. In T. M. Hess & F. Blanchard-Fields (Eds.), *Social cognition and aging* (pp. 343–375). San Diego: Academic Press.

Staudinger, U. M., & Baltes, P. B. (1994). The psychology of wisdom. In R. J. Sternberg (Ed.), *Encyclopedia of intelligence* (pp. 1143–1152). New York: Macmillan.

Staudinger, U. M., & Baltes, P. B. (1996). Interactive minds: A facilitative setting for wisdom-related performance. *Journal of Personality and Social Psychology, 71,* 746–762.

Staudinger, U. M., & Kessler, E. M. (2009). Adjustment and Growth - Two Trajectories of Positive Personality Development across Adulthood. In M. C. Smith & N. DeFrates-Densch (Eds.), *Handbook of research on adult learning and development,* (PP. 241–268). New York and London: Routledge.

Staudinger, U. M., & Kunzmann, U. (2005). Positive adult personality development: Adjustment and/or growth? *European Psychologist, 10,* 320–329.

Staudinger, U. M., Lopez, D. F., & Baltes, P. B. (1997). The psychometric location of wisdom related performance: Intelligence, personality, and, more? *Personality and Social Psychology Bulletin, 23,* 1200–1214.

Staudinger, U. M., & Pasupathi, M. (2003). Correlates of wisdom-related performance in adolescence and adulthood: Age-graded differences in "paths" toward desirable development. *Journal of Research on Adolescence, 13,* 239–268.

Staudinger, U. M., Smith, J., & Baltes, P. B. (1992). Wisdom-related knowledge in a life review task: Age differences in the role of professional specialization. *Psychology and Aging, 7,* 271–281.

Stauss, J. H. (1995). Reframing and refocusing American Indian family strengths. In C. K. Jacobson (Ed.), *American families: Issues in race and ethnicity* (pp. 105–118). New York: Garland.

Stebbins, G. T., Carrillo, M. C., Dorfman, J., Dirksen, C., Desmond, J. E., Turner, D. A., et al. (2002). Aging effects on memory encoding in the frontal lobes. *Psychology and Aging, 17,* 44–55.

Steele, C. M. (1997). A threat in the air: How stereotypes shape intellectual identity and performance. *American Psychologist, 52,* 613–629.

Steele, C. M., & Aronson, J. (1995). Stereotype threat and the intellectual test performance of African Americans. *Journal of Personality and Social Psychology, 69,* 797–811.

Steen, R. G. (2007). *The evolving brain: The known and the unknown.* Amherst, NY: Prometheus Books.

Steen, T. A., & Peterson, C. (2000, August). *Predicting young adults' return to the nest.* Paper presented at the annual meeting of the American Psychological Association, Washington, DC.

Steffens, D. C., & Potter, G. G. (2008). Geriatric depression and cognitive impairment. *Psychological Medicine, 38,* 163–175.

Stein, R., Blanchard-Fields, F., & Hertzog, C. (2002). The effects of age-stereotype priming on the memory performance of older adults. *Experimental Aging Research, 28,* 169–191.

Steinbart, E. J., Smith, C. O., Poorkaj, P., & Bird, T. D. (2001). Impact of DNA testing for early-onset familial Alzheimer disease and frontotemporal dementia. *Archives of Neurology, 58,* 1828–1831.

Steinmetz, E. (2006). *Americans with disabilities: 2002.* Retrieved March 17, 2009, from http://www.census.gov/prod/2006pubs/p70-107.pdf.

Steinmetz, S. K. (1993). The abused elderly are dependent. In R. J. Gelles & D. R. Loseke (Eds.), *Current controversies on family violence* (pp. 222–236). Newbury Park, CA: Sage.

Stephens, M. A. P., & Clark, S. L. (1996). Interpersonal relationships in multigenerational families. In N. Vanzetti & S. Duck (Eds.), *A lifetime of relationships* (pp. 431–454). Pacific Grove, CA: Brooks/Cole.

Stephens, M. A. P., & Clark, S. L. (1997). Reciprocity in the expression of emotional support among later-life couples coping with stroke. In B. H. Gottlieb (Ed.), *Coping with chronic stress* (pp. 221–242). New York: Plenum.

Stephens, M. A. P., & Franks, M. M. (1999). Intergenerational relationships in later-life families: Adult daughters and sons as caregivers to aging parents. In J. C. Cavanaugh & S. K. Whitbourne (Eds.), *Gerontology: An interdisciplinary perspective* (pp. 329–354). New York: Oxford University Press.

Stephens, M. A. P., Franks, M. M., & Atienza, A. A. (1997). Where two roles intersect: Spillover between parent care and employment. *Psychology and Aging, 12,* 30–37.

Stephens, M. A., Townsend, A. L., Martire, L. M., & Druley, J. A. (2001). Balancing parent care with other roles: Interrole conflict of adult daughter caregivers. *Journals of Gerontology: Series B, Psychological Sciences and Social Sciences, 56*(1), 24–34.

Sternberg, R. J. (1985). *Beyond IQ: A triarchic theory of human intelligence.* New York: Cambridge University Press.

Sternberg, R. J. (1986). A triangular theory of love. *Psychological Review, 93,* 119–135.

Sternberg, R. J. (1998). Metacognition, abilities, and developing expertise: What makes an expert student? *Instructional Science, 26,* 127–140.

Sternberg, R. J., (2004). What is wisdom and how can we develop it? *Annals of the American Academy of Political and Social Science, 591,* 164–174.

Sternberg, R. J. (2006). A duplex theory of love. In R. J. Sternberg & K. Weis (Eds.), *The new psychology of love* (pp. 184–199). New Haven, CT: Yale University Press.

Sternberg, R. J., Conway, B. E., Ketron, J. L., & Bernstein, M. (1981). People's conceptions of intelligence. *Journal of Personality and Social Psychology, 41,* 37–55.

Sternberg, R. J., & Grigorenko, E. L. (2000). Practical intelligence and its development. In R. Bar-On & D. A. Parker (Eds.), *The handbook of emotional intelligence: Theory, development, assessment, and application at home, school, and in the workplace* (pp. 215–243). San Francisco: Jossey-Bass.

Sternberg, R. L., & Grigorenko, E. L. (2004). Intelligence and culture: how culture shapes what intelligence means, and the implications for a science of well-being. *Philosophical Transactions of the royal Society of London B: Biological Sciences, 359,* 1427–1434.

Sterns, A. A., Marsh, B. A., & McDaniel, M. A. (1994). *Age and job satisfaction: A comprehensive review and meta-analysis.* Unpublished manuscript, University of Akron.

Sterns, H. L., & Gray, J. H. (1999). Work, leisure, and retirement. In J. C. Cavanaugh & S. K. Whitbourne (Eds.), *Gerontology: Interdisciplinary perspectives.* New York: Oxford University Press.

Sterns, H. L., & Huyck, M. H. (2001). The role of work in midlife. In M. E. Lachman (Ed.), *Handbook of midlife development* (pp. 447–486). New York: Wiley.

Sterns, H. L., Laier, M. P., & Dorsett, J. G. (1994). Work and retirement. In B. R. Bonder & M. B. Wagner (Eds.), *Functional performance in older adults* (pp. 148–164). Philadelphia: F. A. Davis.

Stetz, T. A., & Beehr, T. A. (2000). Organizations' environment and retirement: The relationship between women's retirement, environmental munificence, dynamism, and local unemployment rate. *Journals of Gerontology: Social Sciences, 55,* S213–S221.

Stevens, J. C. (1992). Aging and spatial acuity of touch. *Journals of Gerontology: Psychological Sciences, 47,* P35–P40.

Stevens, J. C., Cruz, L. A., Hoffman, J. M., & Patterson, M. Q. (1995). Taste sensitivity and aging: High incidence of decline revealed by repeated threshold measures. *Chemical Senses, 20,* 451–459.

Stevens, S. B., & Morris, T. L. (2007). College dating and social anxiety: Using the Internet as a means of connecting to others. *CyberPsychology & Behavior, 10,* 680–688.

Steward, R. J., & Krieshok, T. S. (1991). A cross-cultural study of vocational identity: Does a college education mean the same for all persisters? *Journal of College Student Development, 32,* 562–563.

Stewart, A. J. (1996). *Personality in middle age: Gender, history, and mid-course corrections.* Murray Award Lecture presented at the American Psychological Association, Toronto.

Stewart, A. J., Ostrove, J. M., & Helson, R. (2001). Middle aging in women: Patterns of personality change from the 30s to the 50s. *Journal of Adult Development, 8,* 23–37.

Stigsdotter Neely, A., & Bäckman, L. (1993a). Long-term maintenance of gains from memory training in older adults: Two 3-year follow-up studies. *Journals of Gerontology: Psychological Sciences, 48B,* P233–P237.

Stigsdotter Neely, A., & Bäckman, L. (1993b). Maintenance of gains following multifactorial and unifactorial memory training in late adulthood. *Educational Gerontology, 19,* 105–117.

Stigsdotter Neely, A., & Bäckman, L. (1995). Effects of multifactorial memory training in old age: Generalizability across tasks and individuals. *Journals of Gerontology: Psychological Sciences, 50B,* P134–P140.

Stine-Morrow, E. A. L., Milinder, L., Pullara, O., & Herman, B. (2001). Patterns of resource allocation are reliable among younger and older readers. *Psychology and Aging, 16,* 69–84.

Stoltzfus, E. R., Hasher, L., & Zacks, R. T. (1996). Working memory and aging: Current status of the inhibitory view. In T. J. E. Richardson (Ed.), *Working memory and human cognition.* New York: Oxford University Press.

Stoner, S., O'Riley, A., & Edelstein, B. (in press). Assessment of mental health. In J. C. Cavanaugh & C. K. Cavanaugh (Eds.), *Aging in America.* Westport, CT: Praeger.

Strachan, E., Pyszczynski, T., Greenberg, J., & Solomon, S. (2001). Coping with the inevitability of death: Terror management and mismanagement. In C. R. Snyder (Ed.), *Coping with stress: Effective people and processes* (pp. 114–136). New York: Oxford University Press.

Strain, L. A., Grabusic, C. C., Searle, M. S., & Dunn, N. J. (2002). Continuing and ceasing leisure activities in later life: A longitudinal study. *The Gerontologist, 42,* 217–223.

Strawbridge, W. J., Shema, S. J., Balfour, J. L., Higby, H. R., & Kaplan, G. A. (1998). Antecedents of frailty over three decades in an older cohort. *Journals of Gerontology: Social Sciences, 53B,* S9–S16.

Strawbridge, W. J., Wallhagen, M. I., & Cohen, R. D. (2002). Successful aging and well-being: Self-rated compared with Rowe and Kahn. *The Gerontologist, 42,* 727–733.

Strayer, D. L., & Kramer, A. F. (1994). Aging and skill acquisition: Learning–performance distinctions. *Psychology and Aging, 9,* 589–605.

Streich, M., Casper, W. J., & Salvaggio, A. N. (2008). Examining couples' agreement about work-family conflict. *Journal of Managerial Psychology, 23*(3), 252–272.

Stroebe, M. S., Gergen, M., Gergen, K., & Stroebe, W. (1996). Broken hearts or broken bonds? In D. Klass, P. R. Silverman, & S. L. Nickman (Eds.), *Continuing bonds: New understandings of grief* (pp. 31–44). Washington, DC: Taylor & Francis.

Stroebe, M. S., & Schut, H. (2001). Models of coping with bereavement: A review. In M. S. Stroebe, R. O. Hansson, W. Stroebe, & H. Schut (Eds.), *Handbook of bereavement research: Consequences, coping, and care* (pp. 375–403). Washington, DC: American Psychological Association.

Stroebe, M., Schut, H., & Stroebe, W. (2005). Attachment in coping with bereavement: A theoretical integration. *Review of General Psychology, 9,* 48–66.

Stroebe, M., Schut, H., & Stroebe, W. (2007). Health outcomes of bereavement. *Lancet, 370,* 1960–1973.

Stroebe, M. S., & Stroebe, W. (1983). Who suffers more? Sex differences in health risks of the widowed. *Psychological Bulletin, 93,* 279–301.

Stroebe, M. S., Stroebe, W., Hansson, R. O., & Schut, H. (2001). *Handbook of bereavement research: Consequences, coping, and care.*

Washington, DC: American Psychological Association.

Stroebe, W., & Schut, H. (2001). Risk factors in bereavement outcome: A methodological and empirical review. In M. S. Stroebe, R. O. Hansson, W. Stroebe, & H. Schut (Eds.), *Handbook of bereavement research: Consequences, coping, and care* (pp. 349–371). Washington, DC: American Psychological Association.

Strough, J., Berg, C. A., & Sansone, C. (1996). Goals for solving everyday problems across the interpersonal concerns. *Developmental Psychology, 32*, 1106–1115.

Strough, J., Cheng, S., & Swenson, L. M. (2002). Preferences for collaborative and individual everyday problem solving in later adulthood. *International Journal of Behavioral Development, 26*, 26–35.

Strough, J., Hicks Patrick, J., Swenson, L. M., Cheng, S., & Barnes, K. A. (2003). Collaborative everyday problem solving: Interpersonal relationships and problem dimensions. *International Journal of Aging and Human Development, 56*, 43–66.

Strough, J., & Margrett, J. (2002). Overview of the special section on collaborative cognition in later adulthood. *International Journal of Behavioral Development, 26*, 2–5.

Stuve, O., Youssef, S., Steinman, L., & Zamvil, S. S. (2003). Statins as potential therapeutic agents in neuroinflammatory disorders. *Current Opinion in Neurology, 16*, 393–401.

Sullivan, S. E. (1999). The changing nature of careers: A review and research agenda. *Journal of Management, 25*, 457–484.

Sulmasy, D. P. (2002). A biopsychosocial-spiritual model for the care of patients at the end of life. *The Gerontologist, 42*(Special Issue III), 24–33.

Suls, J., & Wills, T. A. (1991). *Social comparison: Contemporary theory and research*. Hillsdale, NJ: Erlbaum.

Super, D. E. (1957). *The psychology of careers*. New York: Harper & Row.

Super, D. E. (1980). A life span, life space approach to career development. *Journal of Vocational Behavior, 16*, 282–298.

Surgeon General. (1996). *Physical activity and health: A report of the Surgeon General*. Washington, DC: Public Health Service.

Svendsen, C. (2008). Stem cells and Parkinson's disease: Toward a treatment, not a cure. *Cell Stem Cell, 2*, 412–413.

Swanson, J. L. (1992). Vocational behavior, 1989–1991: Life-span career development and reciprocal interaction of work and non-work. *Journal of Vocational Behavior, 41*, 101–161.

Syihula, J., & Estes, C. L. (2007). Social security politics: Ideology and reform. *Journals of Gerontology: Social Sciences, 62B*, S79–S89.

Szinovacz, M. (1992). Social activities and retirement adaptation: Gender and family variations. In M. Szinovacz & D. J. Ekerdt (Eds.), *Families and retirement* (pp. 236–253). Thousand Oaks, CA: Sage.

Szinovacz, M. (1996). Couples' employment/retirement patternsy and perceptions of marital quality. *Research on Aging, 18*, 243–268.

Szinovacz, M. E. (1998). Grandparents today: A demographic profile. *The Gerontologist, 38*, 37–52.

Szinovacz, M. E., & DeViney, S. (1999). The retiree identity: Gender and race differences. *Journals of Gerontology: Social Sciences, 54B*, S207–S218.

Taaffe, D. R., Jin, I. H., Vu, T. H., Hoffman, A. R., & Marcus, R. (1996). Lack of effect of recombinant human growth hormone (GH) on muscle morphology and GH–insulin–like growth factor expression in resistance-trained

elderly men. *Journal of Clinical Endocrinology and Metabolism, 81*, 421–425.

Taconnat, L., & Isingrini, M. (2004). Cognitive operations in the generation effect on a recall test: Role of aging and divided attention. *Journal of Experimental Psychology: Learning, Memory, and Cognition, 30*, 827–837.

Tadros, G., & Salib, E. (2001). Carer's views on passive euthanasia. *International Journal of Geriatric Psychiatry, 16*, 230–231.

Takahashi, M., & Bordia, P. (2000). The concept of wisdom: A cross-cultural comparison. *International Journal of Psychology, 35*, 1–9.

Takahashi, M., & Overton, W. F. (2002). Wisdom: A culturally inclusive developmental perspective. *International Journal of Behavioral Development, 26*, 269–277.

Takema, Y., Yorimoto, Y., Kawai, M., & Imokawa, G. (1994). Age-related changes in the elastic properties and thickness of human facial skin. *British Journal of Dermatology, 131*, 641–648.

Talaga, J. A., & Beehr, T. A. (1995). Are there gender differences in predicting retirement decisions? *Journal of Applied Psychology, 80*, 16–28.

Talbott, M. M. (1998). Older widows' attitudes towards men and remarriage. *Journal of Aging Studies, 12*, 429–449.

Tang, T. L. P., & McCollum, S. L. (1996). Sexual harassment in the workplace. *Public Personnel Management, 25*, 53–58.

Tangredi, L. A., Danvers, K., Molony, S. L., & Williams, A. (2008). New CDEC recommendations for HIV testing in older adults. *Nurse Practitioner, 33*, 37–44.

Tannen, D. (1990). *You just don't understand.* New York: Morrow.

Tatara, T., Thomas, C., & Cyphers, G. (1998). *The national elder abuse incidence study: Final report.* Washington, DC: National Center on Elder Abuse.

Tate, R. B., Lah, L., & Cuddy, T. E. (2003). Definition of successful aging by elderly Canadian males: The Manitoba follow-up study. *The Gerontologist, 43*, 735–744.

Taylor, N. A., Allsopp, N. K., & Parkes, D. G. (1995). Preferred room temperature of young vs aged males: The influence of thermal sensation, thermal comfort, and affect. *Journals of Gerontology: Medical Sciences, 50*, M216–M221.

Taylor, S. E., Klein, L. C., Lewis, B. P., Gruenewald, T. L., Gurung, R. A., & Updegraff, J. A. (2000). Biobehavioral responses to stress in females: Tend-and-befriend, not fight-or-flight. *Psychological Review, 107*, 411–429.

Teisseyre, N., Mullet, E., & Sorum, P. C. (2005). Under what conditions is euthanasia acceptable to lay people and health professionals? *Social Science and Medicine, 60*, 357–368.

Tennstedt, S. L., Crawford, S., & McKinley, J. (1993). Determining the pattern of community care: Is coresidence more important than caregiver relationship? *Journals of Gerontology: Social Sciences, 48*, S74–S83.

Tennstedt, S. L., Link, C. L., Steers, W. D., & McKinlay, J. B. (2008). Prevalence of and risk factors for urinary leakage in a racially and ethnically diverse populations of adults: the Boston Area Community Health (BACH) Survey. *American Journal of Epidemiology, 167*, 390–399.

Tentori, K., Osherson, D., Hasher, L., & May, C. (2001) Wisdom and aging: Irrational preferences in college students but not older adults. *Cognition, 81*(3), B87–B96.

Terkel, S. (1974). *Working.* New York: Pantheon.

Terry, P. (2008). Ageism and projective identification. *Psychodynamic Practice, 14*, 155–168.

Thiele, D. M., & Whelan, T. A. (2006). The nature and dimensions of the grandparent role. *Marriage and Family Review, 40*, 93–108.

Thiele, D. M., & Whelan, T. A. (2008). The relationship between grandparent satisfaction, meaning, and generativity. *International Journal of Aging and Human Development, 66*, 21–48.

Thomas, D. A. (1990). The impact of race on managers' experiences of developmental relationships (mentoring and sponsorship): An intra-organizational study. *Journal of Organizational Behavior, 11*, 479–492.

Thomas, F. (2008). Remarriage after spousal death: Options facing widows and implications for livelihood security. *Gender and Development, 16*, 73–83.

Thomas, J. L. (1986). Age and sex differences in perceptions of grandparenthood. *Journals of Gerontology: Psychological Sciences, 41*, 417–423.

Thomas, J. L., Bence, S. L., & Meyer, S. M. (1988, August). *Grandparenting satisfaction: The roles of relationship meaning and perceived responsibility.* Paper presented at the annual meeting of the American Psychological Association, Atlanta.

Thomas, M. S. C. (2003). Limits on plasticity. *Journal of Cognition and Development, 4*, 99–125.

Thomas, R. C., & Hasher, L. (2006). The influence of emotional valence on age differences in early processing and memory. *Psychology and Aging, 21*, 821–825.

Thomas, V., & Striegel, P. (1994–1995). Stress and grief of a perinatal loss: Integrating qualitative and quantitative methods. *Omega: Journal of Death and Dying, 30*, 299–311.

Thompson, L. W., Gallagher-Thompson, D., Futterman, A., Gilewski, M. J., & Peterson, J. (1991). The effects of late-life spousal bereavement over a 30-month interval. *Psychology and Aging, 6*, 434–441.

Thompson, M. M., Naccarato, M. E., & Parker, K. (1992). Measuring cognitive needs: The development and validation of the Personal Need for Structure and Personal Fear of Invalidity Scales. Unpublished manuscript.

Thompson, S., & Oliver, D. (2008). A new model for long-term care: Balancing palliative and restorative care delivery. *Journal of Housing for the Elderly, 22*, 169–194.

Thomson, E., & Colella, U. (1992). Cohabitation and marital stability: Quality or commitment? *Journal of Marriage and the Family, 54*, 259–267.

Thoresen, C. J., Kaplan, S. A., Barsky, A. P., Warren, C. R., & de Chermont, K. (2003). The affective underpinnings of job perceptions and attitudes: A meta-analytic review and integration. *Psychological Bulletin, 129*, 914–945.

Thorne, A. (2000). Personal memory telling and personality development. *Personality and Social Psychology Review, 4*, 45–56.

Thorne, A., & Klohnen, E. (1993). Interpersonal memories as maps for personality consistency. In D. Funder, R. Parke, C. Tomlinson-Keasey, & K. Widaman (Eds.), *Studying lives through time: Personality and development* (pp. 223–253). Washington, DC: American Psychological Association.

Thornton, J. E. (2002). Myths of aging or ageist stereotypes. *Educational Gerontology, 28*, 301–312.

Thornton, W. J. L., & Dumke, H. A. (2005). Age differences in everyday problem-solving and decision-making effectiveness: A meta-analytic review. *Psychology and Aging, 20*, 85–99.

Thorson, J. A., & Powell, F. C. (2000a). Death anxiety in younger and older adults. In A. Tomer (Ed.), *Death attitudes and the older adult: Theories, concepts, and applications* (pp. 123–136). Philadelphia: Brunner-Routledge.

Thorson, J. A., & Powell, F. C. (2000b). Developmental aspects of death anxiety and religion. In J. A. Thorson (Ed.), *Perspectives on spiritual well-being and aging* (pp. 142–158). Springfield, IL: Charles C. Thomas.

Thurstone, L. L. (1938). *Primary mental abilities.* Chicago: University of Chicago Press.

Tice, C. J., & Perkins, K. (1996). *Mental health issues and aging.* Pacific Grove, CA: Brooks/Cole.

Tilvis, R. S., Kahonen-Vare, M. H., Jolkkonen, J., Valvanne, J., Pitkala, K. H., & Strandberg, T. E. (2004). Predictors of cognitive decline and mortality of aged people over a 10-year period. *Journals of Gerontology: Medical Sciences, 59A,* M268–M274.

Titus, P. A., & Everett, P. B. (1996). Consumer wayfinding tasks, strategies, and errors: An exploratory field study. *Psychology and Marketing, 13,* 265–290.

Tomer, A., & Eliason, G. (2000). Attitudes about life and death: Toward a comprehensive model of death anxiety. In A. Tomer (Ed.), *Death attitudes and the older adult: Theories, concepts, and applications* (pp. 3–22). Philadelphia: Taylor & Francis.

Tomlinson, B. E., Blessed, G., & Roth, M. (1970). Observations on the brains of demented old people. *Journal of the Neurological Sciences, 11,* 205–242.

Toossi, M. (2004, February). Labor force projections to 2012: The graying of the U.S. workforce. *Monthly Labor Review,* pp. 37–57.

Toth, J. P. (2000). Nonconscious forms of human memory. In E. Tulving & F. I. M. Craik (Eds.), *Oxford handbook of memory* (pp. 245–266). Oxford, UK: Oxford University Press.

Tracey, T. J. G., & Hopkins, N. (2001). Correspondence of interests and abilities with occupational choice. *Journal of Counseling Psychology, 48,* 179–189.

Trappe, S. W., Costill, D. L., Vukovich, M. D., Jones, J., & Melham, T. (1996). Aging among elite distance runners: A 22-year longitudinal study. *Journal of Applied Physiology, 80,* 285–290.

Troll, L. E. (1971). The family of later life: A decade review. *Journal of Marriage and the Family, 33,* 263–290.

Troll, L. E., & Bengtson, V. (1982). Intergenerational relations throughout the life span. In B. B. Wolman (Ed.), *Handbook of developmental psychology* (pp. 890–911). Englewood Cliffs, NJ: Prentice Hall.

Troll, L. E., & Fingerman, K. L. (1996). Connections between parents and their adult children. In C. Magai & S. H. McFadden (Eds.), *Handbook of emotion, adult development, and aging* (pp. 185–205). San Diego: Academic Press.

Troyer, A. K., Häfliger, A., et al. (2006). Name and face learning in older adults: Effects of level of processing, self-generation, and intention to learn. *Journals of Gerontology: Series B, Psychological Sciences and Social Sciences, 61*(2), P67–P74.

Truog, R. D. (2004). *Brain death: At once "well settled" and "persistently unresolved."* Retrieved March 17, 2009, from http://virtualmentor.ama-assn.org/2004/08/pfor1-0408.html.

Tsang, P. S., & Shaner, T. L. (1998). Age, attention, expertise, and time-sharing performance. *Psychology and Aging, 13,* 323–347.

Tulving, E., Markowitsch, H. J., Kabur, S., Habib, R., & Houle, S. (1994). Novelty encoding networks in the human brain: Position emission tomography data. *International Journal for the Rapid Communication of Research in Neuropsychology, 5,* 2525–2528.

Tulving, F., & Schacter, D. L. (1990). Priming and human memory systems. *Science, 247,* 301–306.

Tun, P. A., & Wingfield, A. (1993). Is speech special? Perception and recall of spoken language in complex environments. In J. Cerella, W. Hoyer, J. Rybash, & M. L. Commons (Eds.), *Adult information processing: Limits on loss* (pp. 425–457). New York: Academic Press.

Tun, P. A., & Wingfield, A. (1995). Does dividing attention become harder with age? Findings from the Divided Attention Questionnaire. *Aging and Cognition, 2,* 39–66.

Tun, P. A., Wingfield, A., Rosen, M. J., & Blanchard, L. (1998). Response latencies for false memories: Gist-based processes in normal aging. *Psychology and Aging, 13,* 230–241.

Turner, B. F. (1982). Sex-related differences in aging. In B. B. Wolman (Ed.), *Handbook of developmental psychology* (pp. 912–936). Englewood Cliffs, NJ: Prentice Hall.

Turrell, G., Lynch, J. W., Kaplan, G. A., Everson, S. A., Helkala, E., Kauhanen, J., & Salonen, J. T. (2002). Socioeconomic position across the lifecourse and cognitive function in late middle age. *Journals of Gerontology: Social Sciences, 57B,* S43–S51.

Twenge, J. M. (2000). The age of anxiety? Birth cohort change in anxiety and neuroticism, 1952–1993. *Journal of Personality and Social Psychology, 79,* 1007–1021.

Uhlenberg, P., Cooney, T. M., & Boyd, R. (1990). Divorce for women after midlife. *Journals of Gerontology: Social Sciences, 45,* S3–S11.

United Nations. (2005). *Demographic yearbook 2005.* Retrieved December 15, 2008, from http://unstats.un.org/unsd/demographic/products/dyb/dyb2005/Table25.pdf.

University of Virginia Huntington's Disease Program. (2003). *Predictive testing for Huntington's disease.* Retrieved October 26, 2008, from http://www.healthsystem.virginia.edu/internet/huntdisease/geninfo.cfm#deciding.

U.S. Bureau of Labor Statistics. (2003). *Highlights of women's earnings in 2002. Report 972.* Washington, DC: Author.

U.S. Census Bureau. (1993). *Statistical abstracts of the United States* (113th ed.). Washington, DC: U.S. Government Printing Office.

U.S. Census Bureau. (2001). *America's families and living arrangements.* Online document available at http://www.census.gov/prod/2001pubs/p20-537.pdf. Accessed 2004.

U.S. Census Bureau. (2003). *Statistical abstract of the United States.* Washington, DC: Government Printing Office.

U.S. Census Bureau. (2008a). *The 2008 statistical abstract: 2008 edition.* Retrieved March 30, 2008, from http://www.census.gov/compendia/statab/2008edition.html.

U.S. Census Bureau. (2008b). *Median age at first marriage.* Retrieved March 17, 2009, from www.census.gov/population/socdemo/hh-fam/ms2.xls.

U.S. Department of Agriculture. (2005). *Dietary guidelines for Americans, 2005.* Retrieved March 17, 2009, from http://www.health.gov/dietaryguidelines/dga2005/document/.

U.S. Department of Health and Human Services. (1991). *Healthy people 2000: National health promotion and disease prevention.* Publication No. PHS 91-50212. Washington, DC: U.S. Government Printing Office.

U.S. Department of Health and Human Services. (2005). *Assisted living.* Retrieved December 21, 2008, from http://www.eldercare.gov/eldercare/Public/resources/fact_sheets/assisted_living.asp.

U.S. Department of Labor. (1991). *A report on the glass ceiling initiative.* Washington, DC: Author.

U.S. Department of Labor. (2002). *Highlights of women's earnings in 2001.* Washington, DC: Author.

U.S. Department of Labor. (2005). *Retirement plans, benefits, and savings.* Retrieved June 11, 2008, from http://www.dol.gov/dol/topic/retirement/index.htm.

U.S. Department of Labor. (2008). Current population survey: Employment characateristics of families in 2006. Washington, DC: Author.

U.S. Department of Labor. (2009). *Regional and state employment and unemployment summary.* Washington, DC: Author.

U.S. Department of Transportation. (2000). *Traffic safety facts 2000: Older population.* Washington, DC: Author.

Usita, P. M., & Du Bois, B. C. (2005). Conflict sources and responses in mother-daughter relationships: Perspectives of adult daughters of aging immigrant women. *Journal of Women & Aging, 17,* 151–165.

Uttl, B., & Van Alstine, C. L. (2003). Rising verbal intelligence scores: Implications for research and clinical practice. *Psychology and Aging, 18,* 616–621.

Utz, R. L., Carr, D., Nesse, R., & Wortman, C. B. (2002). The effect of widowhood on older adults' social participation: An evaluation of activity, disengagement, and continuity theories. *The Gerontologist, 42,* 522–533.

Vaillant, G. E. (1977). *Adaptation to life.* Boston: Little, Brown.

Vaillant, G. E. (2002). *Aging well: Surprising guideposts to a happier life.* Boston: Little, Brown.

Vaillant, G. E., & Vaillant, C. O. (1990). Natural history of male psychological health: XII. A 45-year study of predictors of successful aging. *American Journal of Psychiatry, 147,* 31–37.

Valentijn, S. A. M., Hill, R. D., et al. (2006). Memory self-efficacy predicts memory performance: Results from a 6-year follow-up study. *Psychology and Aging, 21*(1), 165–172.

Valenzuela, M. J., Jones, M., Wen, W., Rae, S., Graham, R., et al. (2003). Memory training alters hippocampal neurochemistry in healthy elderly. *Neuroreport, 14,* 1333–1337.

Valenzuela, M. J., & Sachdev, P. (2006). Brain reserve and dementia: a systematic review. *Psychological Medicine, 36,* 441–454.

Valverius, E., Nilstun, T., & Nilsson, B. (2000). Palliative care, assisted suicide and euthanasia: Nationwide questionnaire to Swedish physicians. *Palliative Medicine, 14,* 141–148.

van Baarsen, B. (2002). Theories on coping with loss: The impact of social support and self-esteem on adjustment to emotional and social loneliness following a partner's death in later life. *Journals of Gerontology: Social Sciences, 57B,* S33–S42.

Vandell, D. L., Pierce, K., & Stright, A. (1997). Childcare. In G. Bear, K. Minke, & A. Thomas (Eds.), *Children's needs II: Development, problems, and alternatives* (pp. 575–584). Washington, DC: National Association of School Psychologists.

Vandello, J. A. (2000). Domestic violence in cultural context: Male honor, female fidelity, and loyalty. *Dissertation Abstracts International: Section B: The Sciences and Engineering, 61*(5-B), 2821.

VandenBos, G. (1999). Life-span developmental perspectives on aging: An introductory overview. In I. H. Nordhus, G. R. VandenBos, S. Berg, & P. Fromholt (Eds.), *Clinical geropsychology* (pp. 3–14). Washington, DC: American Psychological Association.

VandenBos, G. R., DeLeon, P. H., & Pallack, M. S. (1982). An alternative to traditional medical care for the terminally ill. *American Psychologist, 37,* 1245–1248.

Van Den Wijngaart, M. A. G., Vernooij-Dassen, M. J. F. J., & Felling, A. J. A. The influence of stressors, appraisal and personal conditions on the burden of spousal caregivers of persons with dementia. *Aging & Mental Health, 11*, 626–636.

van der Geest, S. (2004). Dying peacefully: Considering good death and bad death in Kwahu-Tafo, Ghana. *Social Science and Medicine, 58*, 899–911.

Van der Linden, M., Hupet, M., Feyereisen, P., Schelstraete, M., Bestgen, Y., Bruyer, R., et al. (1999). Cognitive mediators of age related differences in language comprehension and verbal memory performance. *Aging, Neuropsychology, and Cognition, 6*, 32–55.

Van Geert, P. (1987). The structure of Erikson's model of eight stages: A generative approach. *Human Development, 30*, 236–254.

Van Maanen, J., & Schein, E. H. (1977). Career development. In R. J. Hackman & J. L. Suttle (Eds.), *Improving life at work* (pp. 30–95). New York: Goodyear.

Van Manen, K., & Whitbourne, S. K. (1997). Psychosocial development and life experience. *Psychology and Aging, 12*, 239–246.

Van Ness, P. H., & Stanislav, V. K. (2003). Religion and cognitive dysfunction in an elderly cohort. *Journals of Gerontology: Psychological Sciences, 58B*, P21–P29.

Van Petten, C. (2004). Relationship between hippocampal volume and memory ability in healthy individuals across the lifespan: Review and meta-analysis. *Neuropsychologia, 42*, 1394–1413.

van Solinge, H., & Henkens, K. (2007). Involuntary retirement: The role of restrictive circumstances, timing, and social embeddedness. *Journals of Gerontology: Social Sciences: Psychological Sciences, 62B*(5), S295–S303.

Van Someren, E. J. W. (2007). Thermoregulation and aging. *American Journal of Physiology—Regulatory, Integrative, and Comparative Physiology, 292*, R99–R102.

Verbrugge, L. M. (1994). Disability in late life. In R. P. Abeles, H. C. Gift, & M. G. Ory (Eds.), *Aging and quality of life* (pp. 79–98). New York: Springer.

Verbrugge, L. M., & Jette, A. M. (1994). The disablement process. *Social Science and Medicine, 38*, 1–14.

Vereeck, L., Wuyts, F., Truijen, S., & Van de Heyning, P. (2008). Clinical assessment of balance: Normative data, and gender and age effects. *International Journal of Audiology, 47*, 67–75.

Verhaeghen, P. (2002). Age differences in efficiency and effectiveness of encoding for visual search and memory search: A time-accuracy study. *Aging Neuropsychology and Cognition, 9*, 114–126.

Verhaeghen, P., Cerella, J., Semenec, S. C., Leo, M. A., Bopp, K. L., & Steitz, D. W. (2002). Cognitive efficiency modes in old age: Performance on sequential and coordinative verbal and visuospatial tasks. *Psychology and Aging, 17*, 558–570.

Verhaeghen, P., Marcoen, A., & Goossens, L. (1993). Facts and fiction about memory aging: A quantitative integration of research findings. *Journals of Gerontology: Psychological Sciences, 48*, P157–P171.

Verhaeghen, P., Palfai, T., Cerella, J., Buchler, N., Johnson, M. P., D'Eredita, M., et al. (2000). Age-related dissociations in time-accuracy functions for recognition memory: Utilizing semantic support versus building. *Aging, Neuropsychology, and Cognition, 7*, 260–272.

Verhaeghen, P., & Salthouse, T. A. (1997). Meta-analysis of age–cognition relations in adulthood: Establishment of linear and non-linear age effects and structural models. *Psychological Bulletin, 122*, 231–249.

Verhaeghen, P., Steitz, D. W., Sliwinski, M. J., & Cerella, J. (2003). Aging and dual-task performance: A meta-analysis. *Psychology and Aging, 18*, 443–460.

Verwoerdt, A. (1981). *Clinical geropsychiatry* (2nd ed.). Baltimore: Williams & Wilkins.

Vickio, C. J., Cavanaugh, J. C., & Attig, T. (1990). Perceptions of grief among university students. *Death Studies, 14*, 231–240.

Villa, R. F., & Jaime, A. (1993). La fe de la gente. [The faith of the people]. In M. Sontomayor & A. Garcia (Eds.), *Elderly Latinos: Issues and solutions for the 21st century*. Washington, DC: National Hispanic Council on Aging.

Viney, L. L. (1987). A sociophenomenological approach to life span development complementing Erikson's sociodynamic approach. *Human Development, 30*, 125–136.

Vinovskis, M. A. (1988). The historian and the life course: Reflections on recent approaches to the study of American family life in the past. In P. B. Baltes, D. L. Featherman, & R. M. Lerner (Eds.), *Life-span development and behavior* (Vol. 8, pp. 33–59). Hillsdale, NJ: Erlbaum.

Vintildea, J. C., & Miguel, J. (2007). Theories of ageing. *IUBMB Life, 59*, 249–254.

Visher, E. B., Visher, J. S., & Pasley, K. (2003). Remarriage families and stepparenting. In F. Walsh (Ed.), *Normal family processes: Growing diversity and complexity* (3rd ed., pp. 153–175). New York: Guilford.

Vitiello, M. V. (1996). Sleep disorders and aging. *Current Opinions in Psychiatry, 9*, 284–289.

Voisin, T., Reynish, E., Portet, F., Feldman, H., & Vellas, B. (2005). What are the treatment options for patients with severe Alzheimer's disease? *CNS Drugs, 18*, 575–583.

Wagenaar, W. A., & Groeneweg, J. (1990). The memory of concentration camp survivors. *Applied Cognitive Psychology, 4*, 77–87.

Wahl, H. W. (1991). Dependence in the elderly from an interactional point of view: Verbal and observational data. *Adult Residential Care Journal, 5*, 113–129.

Wahl, H. W. (2001). Environmental influences on aging and behavior. In J. E. Birren & K. W. Schaie (Eds.), *Handbook of the psychology of aging* (5th ed., pp. 215–237). San Diego, CA: Academic Press.

Wahl, H.W., Fänge, A., Oswald, F., Gitlin, L., & Iwarsson, S. (in press). The home environment and disability-related outcomes in aging individuals: What is the empirical evidence? *The Gerontologist*.

Waite, L. M., Broe, G. A., Casey, B., Bennett, H. P., Jorm, A. F., Creasey, H., et al. (1998). Screening for dementia using an informant interview. *Aging, Neuropsychology and Cognition, 5*, 194–202.

Waldrop, D. P., & Weber, J. A. (2001). From grandparent to caregiver: The stress and satisfaction of raising grandchildren. *Families in Society, 82*, 461–472.

Waldstein, S. (2003). The relation of hypertension to cognitive function. *Current Directions in Psychological Science, 12*, 9–12.

Waldstein, S. R., Brown, J. R. P., Maier, K. J., & Katzel, L. I. (2005). Diagnosis of hypertension and high blood pressure levels negatively affect cognitive function in older adults. *Annals of Behavioral Medicine, 29*, 174–180.

Walker, A. C., & Balk, D. E. (2007). Bereavement rituals in the Muscogee Creek tribe. *Death Studies, 31*, 633–652.

Walker, L. E. A. (1984). *The battered woman syndrome*. New York: Springer.

Walker, N., Fain, W. B., Fisk, A. D., & McGuire, C. L. (1997). Aging and decision making: Driving-related problem solving. *Human Factors, 39*, 439–444.

Wall, S., & Arden, H. (1990). *Wisdomkeepers: Meetings with Native American spiritual elders*. Hillsboro, OR: Beyond Words Publishing.

Wallace, H. M. (2006). A model of gene-gene and gene-environment interactions and its implications for targeting environmental interventions by genotype. *Theoretical Biology and Medical Modelling, 3*. Retrieved September 28, 2008, from http://www.tbiomed.com/content/3/1/35.

Wallace, J. I., Buchner, D. M., Grothaus, L., Leveille, S., Tyll, L., LaCroix, A. Z., & Wagner, E. H. (1998). Implementation and effectiveness of a community-based health promotion program for older adults. *Journals of Gerontology: Medical Sciences, 53A*, M301–M306.

Walsh, B. W., Kuller, L. H., Wild, R. A., Paul, S., Farmer, M., Lawrence, J. B., Shah, A. S., & Anderson, P. W. (1998). Effects of raloxifene on serum lipids and coagulation factors in healthy postmenopausal women. *JAMA [Journal of the American Medical Association], 279*, 1445–1451.

Walsh, D. A., & Hershey, D. A. (1993). Mental models and the maintenance of complex problem-solving skills in old age. In J. Cerella, W. Hoyer, J. Rybash, & M. L. Commons (Eds.), *Adult information processing: Limits on loss* (pp. 553–584). San Diego: Academic Press.

Walsh, E. K., & Cavanaugh, J. C. (1984, November). *Does hospice meet the needs of dying clients?* Paper presented at the annual meeting of the Gerontological Society of America, San Antonio, TX.

Walter, T. (1996). A new model of grief: Bereavement and biography. *Mortality, 1*, 7–25.

Walther, A. N. (1991). *Divorce hangover*. New York: Pocket Books.

Wanberg, C. R. (1995). A longitudinal study of the effects of unemployment and quality of reemployment. *Journal of Vocational Behavior, 46*, 40–54.

Wanberg, C. R., & Marchese, M. C. (1994). Heterogeneity in the unemployment experience: A cluster analytic investigation. *Journal of Applied Social Psychology, 24*, 473–488.

Wang, H. X., Karp, A., Winbald, B., & Fratiglioni, L. (2002). Late-life engagement in social and leisure activities is associated with a decreased risk of dementia: A longitudinal study from the Kungsholmen project. *American Journal of Epidemiology, 155*, 1081–1087.

Wang, M. (2007) Profiling retirees in the retirement transition and adjustment process: Examining the longitudinal change patterns of retirees' psychological well-being. *Journal of Applied Psychology, 92*(2), 455–474.

Wanzer, S. H., & Glenmullen, J. (2007). *To die well: Your right to comfort, calm, and choice in the last days of life*. Cambridge, ME: Da Capo Press.

Ward, R. A., Logan, J., & Spitze, G. (1992). The influence of parent and child needs on coresidence in middle and later life. *Journal of Marriage and the Family, 54*, 209–221.

Ward, R. A., & Spitze, G. D. (2004). Marital implications of parent–adult child coresidence: A longitudinal view. *Journals of Gerontology: Social Sciences, 59B*, S2–S8.

Ward-Griffin, C., & Ploeg, J. (1997). A feminist approach to health promotion for older women. *Canadian Journal on Aging, 16*, 279–296.

Warr, P., Butcher, V., & Robertson, I. (2004). Activity and psychological well-being in older people. *Aging and Mental Health, 8,* 172–183.

Wass, H. (2001). Past, present, and future of dying. *Illness, Crisis, and Loss, 9,* 90–110.

Wasti, S. A., & Cortina, L. M. (2002). Coping in context: Sociocultural determinants of responses to sexual harassment. *Journal of Personality and Social Psychology, 83,* 394–405.

Watanabe, H., Zhao, Q., Matsumoto, K., Tohda, M., Murakami, Y., Zhang, S-H., Kang, T-H., Mahakunakorn, P., Maruyama, Y., Sakakibara, I., Aimi, N., & Takayama, H. (2003). Pharmacological evidence for antidementia effect of Choto-san (Gouteng-san), a traditional Kampo medicine. *Pharmacology, Biochemistry, and Behavior, 75,* 635–643.

Watson, J. A., & Koblinsky, S. A. (1997). Strengths and needs of working-class African-American and Anglo-American grandparents. *International Journal of Aging and Human Development, 44,* 149–165.

Watts, F. N. (1995). Depression and anxiety. In A. D Baddeley, B. A. Wilson, & F. N. Watts (Eds.), *Handbook of memory disorders* (pp. 293–317). Chichester, UK: Wiley.

Wayment, H. A., & Vierthaler, J. (2002). Attachment style and bereavement reactions. *Journal of Loss and Trauma, 7,* 129–149.

Webster, D. M., & Kruglanski, A. W. (1994). Individual differences in need for cognitive closure. *Journal of Personality and Social Psychology, 67,* 1049–1062.

Webster, M. J., Knable, M. B., O'Grady, J., Orthman, J., &Weickert, C. S. (2002). Regional specificity of brain glucocorticoid receptor mRNA alterations in subjects with schizophrenia and mood disorders. *Molecular Psychiatry, 7,* 985–994.

Webster-Marketon, J., & Glaser, R. (2008). Stress hormones and immune function. *Cellular Immunology, 252,* 16–26.

Wechsler, D. (1958). *The measurement and appraisal of adult intelligence* (4th ed.). Baltimore: Williams & Wilkins.

Wegner, D. M., & Gold, D. G. (1995). Fanning old flames: Emotional and cognitive effects of suppressing thoughts of a past relationship. *Journal of Personality and Social Psychology, 68,* 782–792.

Weibel-Orlando, J. (1990). Grandparenting styles: Native American perspectives. In J. Sokolovsky (Ed.), *The cultural context of aging* (pp. 109–125). New York: Bergin & Garvey.

Weinrauch, L. A. (2007). Hypotension. Retrieved September 7, 2008, from http://www.nlm.nih.gov/medlineplus/ency/article/007278.htm.

Weishaus, S., & Field, D. (1988). A half century of marriage: Continuity or change? *Journal of Marriage and the Family, 50,* 763–774.

Weisman, A. D. (1972). *On dying and denying.* New York: Behavioral Publications.

Weiss, A., Bates, T. C., & Luciano, M. (2008). Happiness is a personal(ity) thing: The genetics of personality and well-being in a representative sample. *Psychological Science, 19,* 205–210.

Welch, D. C., & West, R. L. (1995). Self-efficacy and mastery: Its application to issues of environmental control, cognition, and aging. *Developmental Review, 15,* 150–171.

Welle, B. & Heilman, M. E. (2007). Formal and informal discrimination against women at work. In D. Steiner, S. W. Gilliland & D. Skarlicki (Eds.), *Research in social issues in management: Managing social and ethical issues in organizations.* Westport, CT: Information Age Publishing.

Welle, S., Thornton, C., Statt, M., & McHenry, B. (1996). Growth hormone increases muscle mass and strength but does not rejuvenate myofibrillar protein synthesis in healthy subjects over 60 years old. *Journal of Clinical Endocrinology and Metabolism, 81,* 3239–3243.

Wells, Y. D., & Kendig, H. L. (1997). Health and well-being of spouse caregivers and the widowed. *The Gerontologist, 37,* 666–674.

Wentkowski, G. (1985). Older women's perceptions of great-grandparenthood: A research note. *The Gerontologist, 25,* 593–596.

Wentura, D., & Brandtstädter, J. (2003). Age stereotypes in younger and older women: Analyses of accommodative shifts with a sentence-priming task. *Experimental Psychology, 50,* 16–26.

West, R., & Craik, F. I. M. (2001). Influences on the efficiency of prospective memory in younger and older adults. *Psychology and Aging, 16,* 682–696.

West, R., Herdon, R. W., & Covell, E. (2003). Neural correlates of age-related declines in the formation and realization of delayed intentions. *Psychology and Aging, 18,* 461–473.

West, R., Murphy, K. J., Armilio, M. L., Craik, F. I. M., & Stuss, D. T. (2002). Effects of time of day on age differences in working memory. *Journals of Gerontology: Psychological Sciences, 57,* P3–P10.

West, R. L. (1992). Everyday memory and aging: A diversity of tests, tasks, and paradigms. In R. L. West & J. D. Sinnott (Eds.), *Everyday memory and aging: Current research and methodology* (pp. 3–21). New York: Springer.

West, R. L. (1995). Compensatory strategies for age-associated memory impairment. In A. D. Baddeley, B. A. Wilson, & F. Watts (Eds.), *Handbook of memory disorders* (pp. 481–500). London: Wiley.

West, R. L., Thorn, R. M., & Bagwell, D. K. (2003). Memory performance and beliefs as a function of goal setting and aging. *Psychology and Aging, 8,* 111–125.

West, R. L., & Yassuda, M. S. (2004). Aging and memory control beliefs: Performance in relation to goal setting and memory self-evaluation. *Journals of Gerontology: Psychological Sciences, 59B,* P56–P65.

Westbrook, L. A. (2002). The experience of mid-life women in the years after the deaths of their parents. *Dissertation Abstracts International Section A: Humanities and Social Sciences, 62(8A),* 2884.

Wetherell, J. L., Le Roux, H., & Gatz, M. (2003). *DSM-IV* criteria for generalized anxiety disorder in older adults: Distinguishing the worried from the well. *Psychology and Aging, 18,* 622–627.

Wheeler, S. C., & Petty, R. E. (2001). The effects of stereotype activation on behavior: A review of possible mechanisms. *Psychological Bulletin, 127,* 797–826.

Whitbourne, S. K. (1986). The psychological construction of the life span. In J. E. Birren & K. W. Schaie (Eds.), *Handbook of the psychology of aging* (pp. 594–618). New York: Van Nostrand Reinhold.

Whitbourne, S. K. (1987). Personality development in adulthood and old age: Relationships among identity style, health, and well being. In K. W. Schaie (Ed.), *Annual review of gerontology and geriatrics* (Vol. 7, pp. 189–216). New York: Springer.

Whitbourne, S. K. (1996a). *The aging individual: Physical and psychological perspectives.* New York: Springer.

Whitbourne, S. K. (1996b). *Development of a scale to measure identity processes in adults.* Unpublished manuscript, Department of Psychology, University of Massachusetts.

Whitbourne, S. K. (1996c). *Identity and adaptation to the aging process.* Unpublished paper, Department of Psychology, University of Massachusetts.

Whitbourne, S. K. (1999). Physical changes. In J. C. Cavanaugh & S. K. Whitbourne (Eds.), *Gerontology: Interdisciplinary perspectives* (pp. 91–122). New York: Oxford University Press.

Whitbourne, S. K., & Connolly, L. A. (1999). The developing self in midlife. In S. L. Willis & J. D. Reid (Eds.), *Life in the middle* (pp. 25–45). San Diego: Academic Press.

Whitbourne, S. K., Culgin, S., & Cassidy, E. (1995). Evaluation of infantilizing intonation and content of speech directed at the aged. *International Journal of Aging and Human Development, 41,* 109–116.

White, A. T., & Spector, P. E. (1987). An investigation of age-related factors in the age–job satisfaction relationship. *Psychology and Aging, 2,* 261–265.

Whiting, W. L. (2003). Adult age differences in divided attention: Effects of elaboration during memory encoding. *Aging, Neuropsychology, and Cognition, 10,* 141–157.

Whitmer, R. A., Haan, M. N., Miller, J. W., & Yaffe, K. (2003). Hormone replacement therapy and cognitive performance: The role of homocysteine. *Journals of Gerontology: Biological Sciences and Medical Sciences, 58,* M324–M330.

Wickens, C. D., Braune, R., & Stokes, A. (1987). Age differences in the speed and capacity of information processing: A dual task approach. *Psychology and Aging, 2,* 70–78.

Wickrama, K. A. S., Lorenz, F. O., Conger, R. D., & Elder, G. H., Jr. (1997). Marital quality and physical illness: A latent growth curve analysis. *Journal of Marriage and the Family, 59,* 143–155.

Wiener, R. L., Hurt, L., Russell, B., Mannen, K., & Gasper, J. (1997). Perceptions of sexual harassment: The effects of gender, legal standard, and ambivalent sexism. *Law and Human Behavior, 21,* 71–93.

Wilber, K. H., & McNeilly, D. P. (2001). Elder abuse and victimization. In J. E. Birren & K. W. Schaie (Eds.), *Handbook of the psychology of aging* (5th ed., pp. 569–591). San Diego: Academic Press.

Wilcox, S., Bopp, M., Oberrecht, L., Kammermann, S. K., & McElmurray, C. T. (2003). Psychosocial and perceived environmental correlates of physical activity in rural and older African American and White women. *Journals of Gerontology: Psychological Sciences, 58,* P329–P337.

Wilk, C. (1986). Career, women, and childbearing: A psychological analysis of the decision process. New York: Van Nostrand Reinhold.

Wilkinson, A. M., & Lynn, J. (2001). The end of life. In R. H. Binstock & L. K. George (Eds.), *Handbook of aging and the social sciences* (5th ed., pp. 444–461). San Diego: Academic Press.

Wilkniss, S. M., Jones, M. G., Korol, D. L., Gold, P. E., & Manning, C. A. (1997). Age-related differences in an ecologically based study of route learning. *Psychology and Aging, 12,* 372–375.

Williams, A., Giles, H., Ota, H., Pierson, H. D., Gallois, C., Ng, S. H., Lim, T.-S., Ryan, E. B., Somera, L., Maher, J., & Harwood, J. (1997). Young people's beliefs about intergenerational communication: An initial cross-cultural comparison. *Communication Research, 24,* 370–393.

Williams, K. N., Herman, R., Gajewski, B., & Wilson, K. (2008). Elderspeak communication: Impact on dementia care. *America Journal of Alzheimer's Disease and Other Dementias, 23.*

Williams, N. R. (2006). The influence of intimate relationship on the psychological well being of African-American professional women. *Dissertation Abstracts International: Section B: The Sciences and Engineering, 66(8-B),* 4539.

Williams, S. A. (2005). Jealousy in the cross-sex friendship. *Journal of Loss & Trauma, 10,* 471–485.

Williams, S. W., Desai, T., Rurka, J. T., & Mutran, E. J. (2008). Predictors of satisfaction for African-American and white family caregivers of adult home care residents. *Journal of Applied Gerontology, 27,* 568–587.

Williamson, G. M., & Schulz, R. (1990). Relationship orientation, quality of prior relationship, and distress among caregivers of Alzheimer's patients. *Psychology and Aging, 5,* 502–509.

Willander, J., & Larsson, M. (2006). Smell your way back to childhood: Autobiographical odor memory. *Psychonomic Bulletin and Review, 13,* 240–244.

Willis, S. L. (1990). Current issues in cognitive training research. In E. A. Lovelace (Ed.), *Aging and cognition: Mental processes, self-awareness, and interventions* (pp. 263–280). Amsterdam: North-Holland.

Willis, S. L. (1991). Cognition and everyday competence. In K. W. Schaie (Ed.), *Annual review of gerontology and geriatrics* (Vol. 11, pp. 80–109). New York: Springer.

Willis, S. L. (1996a). Everyday competence in elderly persons: Conceptual issues and empirical findings. *The Gerontologist, 36,* 595–601.

Willis, S. L. (1996b). Everyday problem solving. In J. E. Birren & K. W. Schaie (Eds.), *Handbook of the psychology of aging* (4th ed., pp. 287–307). San Diego: Academic Press.

Willis, S. L., Blieszner, R., & Baltes, P. B. (1981). Intellectual training research in aging: Modification of performance on the fluid ability of figural relations. *Journal of Educational Psychology, 73,* 41–50.

Willis, S. L., & Boron, J. B. (2008). Midlife cognition: The association of personality with cognition and risk of cognitive impairment. In S. M. Hofer & D. F. Alwin (Eds.), *Handbook of cognitive aging: Interdisciplinary perspectives* (pp. 647–660). Greenwich, CT: Sage.

Willis, S. L., & Nesselroade, C. S. (1990). Long-term effects of fluid ability training in old-old age. *Developmental Psychology, 26,* 905–910.

Willis, S. L., & Schaie, K. W. (1992, November). *Maintaining and sustaining cognitive training effects in old age.* Paper presented at the annual meeting of the Gerontological Society of America, Washington, DC.

Willis, S. L., & Schaie, K. W. (1993). Everyday cognition: Taxonomic and methodological considerations. In J. M. Puckett & H. W. Reese (Eds.), *Mechanisms of everyday cognition* (pp. 33–53). Hillsdale, NJ: Erlbaum.

Willis, S. L., & Schaie, K. W. (1994). Cognitive training in the normal elderly. In F. Forette, U. Christen, & F. Boller (Eds.), *Cerebral plasticity and cognitive stimulation* (pp. 91–113). Paris: Fondation Nationale de Gerontologie.

Willis, S. L., & Schaie, K. W. (1999). Intellectual functioning in midlife. In S. L. Willis & J. D. Reid (Eds.), *Life in the middle: Psychological and social development in middle age* (pp. 233–247). San Diego: Academic Press.

Wilmot, B., McWeeney, S. K., Nixon, R. R., Montine, T. J., Laut, J., Harrington, C. A., Kaye, J. A., & Kramer, P. L. (2008). Translational gene mapping of cognitive decline. *Neurobiology of Aging, 29,* 524–541.

Wilmoth, J. M., & Chen, P-C. (2003). Immigrant status, living arrangements, and depressive symptoms among middle-aged and older adults. *Journals of Gerontology: Social Sciences, 58B,* S305–S313.

Wilson, R. S., Arnold, S. E., Schneider, J. A., Kelly, J. F., Tang, Y., & Bennett, D. A. (2006). Chronic psychological distress and risk of Alzheimer's disease in old age. *Neuroepidemiology, 27,* 143–153.

Wilson, R. S., Beckett, L. A., Barnes, L. L., Schneider, J. A., Bach, J., Evans, D. A., & Bennett, D. A. (2002). Individual differences in rates of change in cognitive abilities of older persons. *Psychology and Aging, 17,* 179–193.

Wilson, R. S., Bennett, D. A., Mendes de Leon, C. F., Bienias, J. L., Morris, M. C., & Evans, D. A. (2005). Distress proneness and cognitive decline in a population of older persons. *Psychoneuroendocrinology, 30,* 11–17.

Wilson, R. S., Gilley, D. W., Bennett, D. A., Beckett, L. A., & Evans, D. A. (2000). Person-specific paths of cognitive decline in Alzheimer's disease and their relation to age. *Psychology and Aging, 15,* 18–28.

Wilson, R. S., Krueger, K. R., Arnold, S. E., Schneider, J. A., Kelly, J. F., Barnes, L. L., et al. (2007). Loneliness and risk of Alzheimer's disease. *Archives of General Psychiatry, 64,* 234–240.

Wingfield, A. (1996). Cognitive factors in auditory performance: Context, speed of processing and constraints of memory. *Journal of the American Academy of Audiology, 7,* 175–182.

Wingfield, A., & Kahana, M. J. (2002). The dynamics of memory retrieval in older adulthood. *Canadian Journal of Experimental Psychology, 56,* 187–199.

Wingfield, A., & Lindfield, K. C. (1995). Multiple memory systems in the processing of speech: Evidence from aging. *Experimental Aging Research, 21,* 101–121.

Wingfield, A., Lindfield, K. C., & Goodglass, H. (2000). Effects of age and hearing sensitivity on the use of prosodic information in spoken word recognition. *Journal of Speech, Language, and Hearing Research, 43,* 915–925.

Wingfield, A., & Stine-Morrow, E. A. (2000). Language and speech. In F. I. M. Craik & T. A. Salthouse (Eds.), *Handbook of aging and cognition* (2nd ed., pp. 359–416). Mahwah, NJ: Erlbaum.

Wingfield, R. P. (1996). Factors motivating black male students to pass the VA Literacy Passport Test after failing several administrations and being labeled "ungraded." *Dissertation Abstracts International: Section A: Humanities and Social Sciences, 56,* 4332.

Wippold, F. J. (2008). Focal neurological deficit. *American Journal of Neuroradiology, 29,* 1998–2000.

Wippold, F. J., Cairns, N., Vo, K., Holtzman, D. M., & Morris, J. C. (2008). Neuropathology for neuroradiologist: Plaques and tangles. *American Journal of Neuroradiology, 29,* 18–22.

Witko, T. M. (2006). A framework for working with American Indian parents. In Witko, T. M. (Ed.) *Mental health care for urban Indians: Clinical insights from Native practitioners* (pp. 155–171). Washington, DC: American Psychological Association.

Wolf, S. L., Barnhart, H. X., Kutner, N. G., McNeely, E., Coogler, C., Xu, T., & The Atlanta FICSIT Group. (1996). Balance and strength training in older adults: Intervention gains of tai chi and computerized balance training. *Journal of the American Geriatrics Society, 44,* 489–497.

Wolfinger, N. H. (2007). Does the rebound effect exist? Time to remarriage and subsequent union stability. *Journal of Divorce & Remarriage, 46,* 9–20.

Wolfson, L., Whipple, R., Derby, C., Judge, J., King, M., Amerman, P., Schmidt, J., & Smyers, D. (1996). Balance and strength training in older adults: Intervention gains and tai chi maintenance. *Journal of the American Geriatrics Society, 44,* 498–506.

Wolfson, W. (2008). Unraveling the tangled brain of Alzheimer's. *Chemistry and Biology, 15,* 89–90.

Wolinsky, F. D., Miller, T. R., Malmstrom, T. K., Miller, J. P., Schootman, M., Andresen, E. M., & Miller, D. K. (2008). Self-rated health: Changes, trajectories, and their antecedents among African Americans. *Journal of Aging and Health, 20,* 143–158.

Wolinsky, F. D., & Tierney, W. M. (1998). Self-rated health and adverse health outcomes: An exploration and refinement of the trajectory hypothesis. *Journals of Gerontology: Social Sciences, 53B,* S336–S340.

Wolkove, N., Elkholy, O., Baltzan, M., Palayew, M. (2007a). Sleep and aging 1: Sleep disorders commonly found in older people. *Canadian Medical Association Journal, 176,* 1299–1304.

Wolkove, N., Elkholy, O., Baltzan, M., Palayew, M. (2007b). Sleep and aging 2: management of sleep disorders in older people. *Canadian Medical Association Journal, 176,* 1449–1454.

Wong, P. T. P. (2008). Transformation of grief through meaning: Meaning-centered counseling for bereavement. In A. Tomer, G. T. Eliason, & P. T. P. Wong (Eds.), *Existential and spiritual issues in death attitudes* (pp. 375–396). Mahwah, NJ: Lawrence Erlbaum.

Woo, E., & Sharps, M. J. (2003). Cognitive aging and physical exercise. *Educational Gerontology, 29,* 327–337.

Wood, J. J., & Repetti, R. L. (2004). What gets dad involved? A longitudinal study of change in parental child caregiving involvement. *Journal of Family Psychology, 18,* 237–249.

Wood, S., & Kisley, M. A. (2006). The negativity bias is eliminated in older adults: Age-related reduction in event-related brain potentials associated with evaluative categorization. *Psychology and Aging, 21,* 815–820.

Woodgate, R. L. (2006). Living in a world without closure: Reality for parents who have experienced the death of a child. *Journal of Palliative Care, 22,* 75–82.

Woodruff-Pak, D. S. (1988). *Psychology and aging.* Englewood Cliffs, NJ: Prentice Hall.

Woodruff-Pak, D., & Papka, M. (1999). Theories of neuropsychology and aging. In V. L. Bengtson & K. W. Schaie (Eds.), *Handbook of theories of aging* (pp. 113–132). New York: Springer.

Worden, W. (1991). Grief counseling and grief therapy: A handbook for the mental health practitioner (2nd ed.). New York: Springer.

World Health Organization. (1980). *International classification of impairments, disabilities, and handicaps.* Geneva: Author.

World Health Organization. (2007). *Working for health.* Retrieved September 21, 2008, from http://www.who.int/about/brochure_en.pdf.

Wright, L. K. (1991). The impact of Alzheimer's disease on the marital relationship. *The Gerontologist, 31,* 224–237.

WuDunn, S. (1997, September 2). The face of the future in Japan. *New York Times,* pp. D1, D14.

Wurm, L. H., Labouvie-Vief, G., Aycock, J., Rebucal, K. A., & Koch, H. E. (2004). Performance in auditory and visual emotional stroop tasks: A comparison of older and younger adults. *Psychology and Aging, 19,* 523–535.

Xu, X., Ji, J., & Tung, Y. Y. (2000). Social and political assortative mating in urban China. *Journal of Family Issues, 21,* 47–77.

Xu, X., Zhu, F., O'Campo, P., Koenig, M. A., Mock, V., & Campbell, J. (2005). Prevalence of and risk factors for intimate partner violence in China. *American Journal of Public Health, 95,* 78–85.

Yamagata, H., Yeh, K. S., Stewman, S., & Dodge, H. (1997, August). Sex segregation and glass ceilings: A comparative statics model of women's career opportunities in the federal government over a quarter of a century. Paper presented at the annual meeting of the American Sociological Association, Toronto.

Yan, E., Tang, C. S-K., & Yeung, D. (2002). No safe haven: A review on elder abuse in Chinese families. *Trauma, Violence, and Abuse, 3,* 167–180.

Yan, Q., Zhang, J., Liu, H., Babu-Khan, S., Vassar, R., Biere, A. L., Citron, M., & Landreth, G. (2003). Anti-inflammatory drug therapy alters beta-amyloid processing and deposition in an animal model of Alzheimer's disease. *Journal of Neuroscience, 23,* 7504–7509.

Yancura, L., & Aldwin, C. M. (2010). Does psychological stress accelerate the aging process? In J. C. Cavanaugh & C. K. Cavanaugh (Eds.), *Aging in America, Volume 2: Physical and mental health* (pp. 100–118). Santa Barbara, CA: Praeger.

Yang, J. H., Lee, H. C., & Wei, Y. H. (1995). Photoaging-associated mitochondrial DNA length mutations in human skin. *Archives of Dermatological Research, 287,* 641–648.

Yang, Y. K., Chiu, N. T., Chen, C. C., Chen, M., Yeh, T. L., & Lee, I. H. (2003). Correlation between fine motor activity and striatal dopamine D2 receptor density in patients with schizophrenia and healthy controls. *Psychiatry Research, 123*(3), 191–197.

Yang, Z., Bishai, D., & Harman, J. (2008, in press). Convergence of body mass with aging: The longitudinal interrelationship of health, weight, and survival. *Economics & Human Biology.*

Yanik, A. J. (1994). Barriers to the design of vehicles for mature adults. *Experimental Aging Research, 20,* 5–10.

Yankelovich, D. (1981). New rules: Searching for self-fulfillment in a world turned upside down. New York: Random House.

Yates, F. (1966). Developing therapeutic computer programs with a particular reference to a program to teach coping strategies to problem drinkers. *Journal of Mental Health, 5,* 57–63.

Ybarra, O., & Park, D. C. (2002). Disconfirmation of person expectations by older and younger adults: Implications for social vigilance. *Journals of Gerontology: Psychological Sciences, 57B,* P435–P443.

Yeatts, D. E., & Cready, C. M. (2008). Consequences of empowered CAN teams in nursing home settings: A longitudinal assessment. *The Gerontologist, 47,* 323–339.

Yesavage, J. A. (1983). Imagery pre-training and memory training in the elderly. *Gerontology, 29,* 271–275.

Yesavage, J. A., Brink, T. L., Rose, T. L., Lum, O., Huang, V., Adey, M., & Leirer, V. O. (1983). Development and validation of a geriatric depression screening scale: A preliminary report. *Journal of Psychiatric Research, 17,* 37–49.

Yick, A. G. (2000). Domestic violence beliefs and attitudes in the Chinese American community. *Journal of Social Service Research, 27,* 29–51.

Yonelinas, A.P. (2002). The nature of recollection and familiarity: A review of 30 years of research. *Journal of Memory and Language, 46*(3), 441–517.

Yoon, S. (2005). The characteristics and needs of Asian-American grandparent caregivers: A study of Chinese-American and Korean-American grandparents in New York city. *Journal of Gerontological Social Work, 44,* 75–94.

Yu, G., & Yang, Z. (2003). The influence of storage load on implicit memory results. *Psychological Science (China), 26,* 45–48.

Yu, T., & Adler-Baeder, F. (2007). The intergenerational transmission of relationship quality: The effects of parental remarriage quality on young adults' relationships. *Journal of Divorce & Remarriage, 47,* 87–102.

Yu, Y. (1995). Patterns of work and family: An analysis of the Chinese-American family since the 1920s. In C. K. Jacobson (Ed.), *American families: Issues in race and ethnicity* (pp. 131–144). New York: Garland.

Yung, R. L., & Julius, A. (2008). Epigenetics, aging, and autoimmunity. *Autoimmunity, 41,* 329–335.

Zacks, R. T., Hasher, L., & Li, K. Z. H. (2000). Human memory. In F. I. M. Craik & T. A. Salthouse (Eds.), *Handbook of aging and cognition* (2nd ed., pp. 293–357). Mahwah, NJ: Erlbaum.

Zahariou, A. G., Karamouti, M. V., & Papaioannou, P. D. (2008). Pelvic floor muscle training improves sexual function of women with stress urinary incontinence. *International Urogynecology Journal, 19,* 401–406.

Zappert, L. T. (1996). Psychological aspects of sexual harassment in the academic workplace: Considerations for forensic psychologists. *American Journal of Forensic Psychology, 14,* 5–17.

Zarit, S. H., Dolan, M. M., & Leitsch, S. A. (1999). Interventions in nursing homes and other alternative living settings. In I. H. Nordhus, G. R. VandenBos, S. Berg, & P. Fromholt (Eds.), *Clinical geropsychology* (pp. 329–343). Washington, DC: American Psychological Association.

Zarit, S., & Femia, E. (2008). Behavioral and psychosocial interventions for family caregivers. *American Journal of Nursing, 108* (Suppl), 47–53.

Zarit, S. H., & Knight, B. G. (Eds.). (1996). *A guide to psychotherapy and aging: Effective clinical interventions in a life-stage context.* Washington, DC: American Psychological Association.

Zarit, S. H., Stephens, M. A. P., Townsend, A., & Greene, R. (1998). Stress reduction for family caregivers: Effects of adult day care use. *Journals of Gerontology: Social Sciences, 53B,* S267–S277.

Zarit, S. H., & Zarit, J. M. (2006). *Mental disorders in older adults* (2nd ed.). New York: Guilford.

Zebrowitz, L. A. (2003). Aging stereotypes—internalization or inoculation? A commentary. *Journals of Gerontology: Psychological Sciences, 58,* P214–P215.

Zeintl, M., Kliegel, M., et al. (2007). The role of processing resources in age-related prospective and retrospective memory

within old age. *Psychology and Aging, 22*(4), 826–834.

Zelinski, E. M., Burnight, K. P., & Lane, C. J. (2001). The relationship between subjective and objective memory in the oldest old: Comparisons of findings from a representative and a convenience sample. *Journal of Aging and Health, 13,* 248–266.

Zelinski, E. M., & Gilewski, M. J. (2004). A 10-item Rasch modeled memory self-efficacy scale. *Aging and Mental Health, 8,* 293–306.

Zelinski, E. M., Gilewski, M. J., & Anthony-Bergstone, C. R. (1990). Memory functioning questionnaire: concurrent validity with memory performance and self-reported memory failures. *Psychology and Aging, 5,* 388–399.

Zelinski, E. M., & Kennison. R. F., Watts, A., & Lewis, K. L. (2009). Convergence between longitudinal and cross-sectional studies: Cohort matters. In C. Hertzog & H. Bosworth (Eds.), *Cognition in aging methodologies and applications: Festschrift for K. Warner Schaie.* Washington DC: American Psychological Association.

Zhan, H. J. (2006). Joy and sorrow: Explaining Chinese caregivers' reward and stress. *Journal of Aging Studies, 20,* 27–38.

Zick, C. D., & McCullough, J. L. (1991). Trends in married couples' time use: Evidence from 1977/78 and 1987/88. *Sex Roles, 24,* 459–488.

Zimmerman, S., Sloane, P., Eckert, J., Gruber-Baldini, A., Morgan, L., Hebel, J., et al. (2005). How good is assisted living? Findings and implications from an outcome study. *Journal of Gerontology: Social Sciences, 60B,* S195–S204.

Zimmerman, T. S., Haddock, S. A., Current, L. R., & Ziemba, S. (2003). Intimate partnership: Foundation to the successful balance of family and work. *American Journal of Family Therapy, 31,* 107–124.

Zimprich, D., & Martin, M. (2002). Can longitudinal changes in processing speed explain longitudinal age change in fluid intelligence? *Psychology and Aging, 17,* 690–695.

Zisook, S., & Schucter, S. R. (1994). Diagnostic and treatment considerations in depression associated with late life bereavement. In L. S. Schneider, C. F. Reynolds, B. D. Lebowitz, & A. J. Friedhoff (Eds.), *Diagnosis and treatment of depression in late life: Results of the NIH Consensus Development Conference.* Washington, DC: American Psychiatric Press.

Zsembik, B. A., & Singer, A. (1990). The problem of defining retirement among minorities: The Mexican Americans. *The Gerontologist, 30,* 749–757.

Zucker, A. N., Ostrove, J. M., & Stewart, A. J. (2002). College-educated women's personality development in adulthood: Perceptions and age differences. *Psychology and Aging, 17,* 236–244.

Zunzunegui, M., Alvarado, B. E., Del Ser, T., & Otero, A. (2003). Social networks, social integration, and social engagement determine cognitive decline in community-dwelling Spanish older adults. *Journals of Gerontology: Social Sciences, 58B,* S93–S100.

Zwaan, R. A., & Radvansky, G. A. (1998). Situation models in language comprehension and memory. *Psychological Bulletin, 123,* 162–185.

Author Index

Glossary/Subject Index

Note: The terms and locators in **bold** denotes definitions of key terms. Also the 'f', 'illus' and 't' following the locators refers to figures, illustrations and tables cited in the text.

Midlife crisis, 326, 336–337
Mini Mental Status Exam (MMSE),
    364, 365
Monoamine oxidase (MAO), 372
Monocytes, 117
Montessori-based techniques, 169
Mourning The ways in which we express grief.
    513, **529**
MRI (Magnetic resonance imaging), 41–42
Multidimensional The notion that intelligence
    consists of many dimensions. 236, **278**
Multidirectionality The distinct patterns of
    change in abilities over the life span,
    with these patterns being different for
    different abilities. 236, **278**
Multiple causation, 4
Muscles, 72
Myocardial infarction (MI) A heart attack.
    87, **105**

National Institute on Aging (NIA), 275
National Institute on Alcohol Abuse and
    Alcoholism, 393, 394, 395
Natural killer (NK) cells, 117
Nature-nurture controversy A debate over the
    relative influence of genetics and the
    environment on development. 17, **36**
Negativity bias Weighing negative information
    more heavily than positive information in
    a social judgment. 283, **314**
Neglect, 413
Neostriatum Receives input from the cerebral
    cortex and other brain areas and provides
    output to the basal nuclei. 46, **63**
Nervous system, 96–100
Neural presbycusis, 82
Neural stem cells Those that give life to new
    neurons throughout the life span. 53, **63**
Neurofibrillary tangles A normative age-related
    change in the brain involving the
    production of new fibers in the neuron.
    A large number of neurofibrillary tangles
    is a defining characteristic of Alzheimer's
    disease. 97, **105**
Neuropsychological approach Compares brain
    functioning of healthy older adults with
    adults displaying various pathological
    disorders in the brain. 42, **63**
Neurons The basic cells in the brain.
    96, **105**
    diagram, 96f
Neuroscience and Neuropsychology of Aging
    (NNA) Program, 101
Neurostimulator, 389
Neuroticism, 319
Neurotransmitter, 96
New Passages, 335
Nonnormative influences Random events that
    are important to an individual but do not
    happen to most people. 15, **36**
Nonspecific immunity, 83
Normative age-graded influences Experiences
    caused by biological, psychological, and
    sociocultural forces that are closely related
    to a person's age. 14, **36**
Normative aging process, 71 illus
Normative history-graded influences Events
    experienced by most people in a culture at
    the same time.
    14–15, **36**
Numerical facility, 241
Nursing homes
    characteristics, 168–169
    communication with residents, 172–175, 301
        illus
    decision-making capacity, 175–177
    environment of, 164–165

vs home, 169–172
    individual choices, 175–177
    misconceptions, 164
    new directions, 177–178
    residents rate, 164
    special care units, 169–170
    types, 165
    typical residents, 165–168, 167t
Nursing home residents
    benefits, 170 illus
    communication enhancement model, 173
    demographic data, 167f
    satisfaction factors, 171f
    typical, 167t
Nutrition, 225, 544–545

Obama, Barack
    fast tracker, 453 illus
    successful marriage, 403 illus
Obesity, 127, 545
    classification of overweight and obesity by
        BMI, 545f
Occupational choice, 451–453, 460–461
Occupational development, 453–457, 461–464
    mentor/mentee (relationships), 456f
Occupational insecurity, 470–471
Occupational priorities The reasons why one
    works, and how one views them. 449, **491**
Occupational transitions, 468–471
    retraining of senior workers, 469 illus
Older Americans Act, 535, 541
Oncale v. Sundowner Offshore Services, 467
Openness to action, 320
Openness to experience, 220, 319, 320
Optimal level of development In the reflective
    judgment framework, the highest level of
    information-processing capacity that a
    person is capable of. 260, **278**
Optimally exercised ability The ability a normal,
    healthy adult would demonstrate under
    the best conditions of training or practice.
    266, **278**
Osteoarthritis A form of arthritis marked by
    gradual onset and progression of pain and
    swelling, caused primarily by overuse of a
    joint. 75, **105**
Osteoporosis A degenerative bone disease more
    common in women in which bone
    tissue deteriorates severely to produce
    honeycomb-like bone tissue. 73, **105**
    calcium intake recommendations, 75t
    normal bone structures and, 73f
    similarities and differences with,
        arthritis, 77t
    spine curvature, 74f
OTDL, 267
Outpatient hospice, 510
Overflow incontinence, 133
Over-recruitment Occurs when additional
    neurons fire and shore up declining brain
    structures that are inefficient. 50, **63**
Oxytocin, 120

Pain, 133–134
Pap test, 131
Paranoid disorders, 392
Parenthood, 323, 330, 421–422, 441–442
Parkinson's disease A brain disease caused by
    an extreme drop in the neurotransmitter
    dopamine. **63**, 98, **105**
    Michael J. Fox, 98 illus
Part-time cohabitation, 416–417
Partnership for Caring, 160–162
Passages, 335
Passive euthanasia Allowing a person to die by
    withholding an available treatment.
    500, **529**

Patient Self-Determination Act (PSDA), 176
Patriarchal values. 413
Patronizing speech Inappropriate speech to older
    adults that is based on stereotypes of
    incompetence and dependence. 172, **182**
Patronizing talk Using superficial conversation,
    slowed speech, simple vocabulary,
    carefully articulated words, and a
    demeaning emotional tone. 300, **314**
Pay discrimination, 464–465
Perceived age, 17
Perceived competence, 298–299, 424
Perceptual processing, 188
    attention, 188
        See also Attention
    bilateral activation, 50
    cognitive abilities, 237, 253
    concrete operational period, 257
    cultural biases, 48–49
    episodic memory, 199–200
    implicit memory, 196–197
    information-processing model, 241, 248
    intellectual functioning, 248–249
    mechanical abilities, 242
    primary mental abilities, 240
    practical problem solving element, 267
    psychological force, 13
    reflective judgement, 261
Perceptual speed, 241
Perimenopause, 91
Persistent vegetative state A state in which a
    person's brainstem is the only part of the
    brain that is functioning, a state from which
    the person does not recover. 497, **529**
Person–Environment interactions The interface
    between people and the world in
    which they live that forms the basis for
    development, meaning that behavior is
    a function of both the person and the
    environment. 151, **182**
    behavioral and emotional outcomes, 152f
    competence, 151–153
    congruence model, 153–156
    environmental press, 151–153
    everyday competence, 156–157, 157 illus
    everyday devices, 150 illus
    long-term care, 166
        See also Nursing homes
    stress and coping framework, 156
Personal concerns Things that are important
    to people, their goals, and their major
    concerns in life. 317, **355**
    life narrative, 317
    knowing younger generation, 326 illus
    personality research, 317
    solitude, 328 illus
Personal control The belief that what one does
    has an influence on the outcome of an
    event. 304, **314**
    compensatory strategies, 307 illus
    developmental trajectories, 304f
Personality, 315–352
    vs abusive relationships, 412
    ADC (aids dementia complex), 390
    alchohol-related dementia, 389
    Alzheimer's disease, 377, 385
    Berkeley Studies, 322–323
    classmates reunion, 318 illus
    death anxiety, 507
    and delirium, 374
    dispositional traits, 317
    divorce and, 426
    Erikson's stages of psychosocial development,
        328–333
    five-factor model, 319–324
    grief process, 514
    health and, 539